SET-OFF

Set-off

SECOND EDITION

Rory Derham

CLARENDON PRESS · OXFORD
1996

Oxford University Press, Walton Street, Oxford OX2 6DP

Oxford New York

Athens Auckland Bangkok Bombay
Calcutta Cape Town Dar es Salaam Delhi
Florence Hong Kong Istanbul Karachi
Kuala Lumpur Madras Madrid Melbourne
Mexico City Nairobi Paris Singapore
Taipei Tokyo Toronto
and associated companies in
Berlin Ibadan

Oxford is a trade mark of Oxford University Press

Published in the United States
by Oxford University Press Inc., New York

British Library Cataloguing in Publication Data
Data available

Library of Congress Cataloging in Publication Data
Derham, S. R.
Set-off/Rory Derham.—2nd ed.
p. cm.
Includes bibliographical references and index.
1. Set-off and counterclaim—Great Britain. 2. Debtor and
creditor—Great Britain. 3. Bankruptcy–Great Britain. I. Title.
KD7458.D47 1996
346.41'077—dc20
[344.10677] 96–10753
ISBN 0–19–825907–7

1 3 5 7 9 10 8 6 4 2

Typeset by Cambrian Typesetters, Frimley, Surrey
Printed in Great Britain on acid-free paper by
Biddles Ltd., Guildford and Kings Lynn

TO HEATHER AND RYAN

Preface

In the preface to the first edition of this book I commented that set-off for some unknown reason has not proved an attractive subject for academic writers. One reviewer in Canada (Blom, (1989) 5 *Banking and Finance Law Review* 246) thought that the explanation for this was 'fairly simple—set-off is a body of law that offers fearsome technicality but few issues that really stir the blood'. Since then, however, it is apparent that the blood of a number of writers has in fact been stirred. The first edition was followed some two years later by Philip Wood's gargantuan *English and International Set-off* (1989) and, in 1993, by Dr. Sheelagh McCracken's scholarly *The Banker's Remedy of Set-off*. In addition Canadian lawyers now have the benefit of Kelly Palmer's *The Law of Set-off in Canada* (1993). The courts have also been active in the intervening period, with the House of Lords twice being called upon to consider questions of set-off, in *Bank of Boston Connecticut* v. *European Grain and Shipping Ltd.* [1989] 1 AC 1056 in the context of equitable set-off, and in *Stein* v. *Blake* [1995] 2 All ER 961 in relation to insolvency set-off. Similarly, the High Court of Australia made some important observations on insolvency set-off in *Gye* v. *McIntyre* (1991) 171 CLR 609.

One thing that is apparent from the texts and the cases is that disagreement on fundamental issues pervades this area of the law, and it is fair to say that it is this uncertainty, coupled with the importance that set-off rights play in commercial transactions, that has kindled academic interest in the subject in recent years. This in turn has necessitated a re-write of the first edition. In the first place, the growth in the literature and in the case law has resulted in competing theories in some areas which require consideration, for example in relation to combination of bank accounts. Further, issues of practical importance have received more detailed treatment, particularly the growing area of equitable set-off, and set-off in relation to assignments and trusts. Some of the material has its source in articles published in the *Law Quarterly Review*, the *Journal of Business Law* and the *Australian Law Journal*. The articles are listed in the bibliography, and material from them is reproduced with the kind permission of the publishers of those journals.

As in the first edition, the emphasis is on the case and statute law of England and Australia, though relevant authorities from New Zealand and Canada are also referred to. The law is stated on the basis of the reported law available on 1 November 1995. However, I have been able to include at a late stage some discussion of the important judgment of the Court of

Appeal in *Morris* v. *Agrichemicals Ltd.*, which was delivered on 20 December 1995. On a number of occasions I have quoted passages appearing in the transcript of the judgment made available to me. These should be checked against the report of the case when it is published. A report of Jonathan Parker J.'s judgments in *Re ILG Travel Ltd.* [1996] BCC 21, and a copy of Drummond J.'s judgment in the Federal Court of Australia in *Re Kleiss*, 18 January 1996, arrived too late for anything other than reference in the footnotes.

I am grateful to Dr. Wickrema Weerasooria for commenting on a draft of Chapter 11. Of course, the views there expressed should not be taken as necessarily reflecting his own.

RORY DERHAM

Preface to the First Edition

Set-off is an area of the law that, for some unknown reason, has not proved attractive for academic writers. In the early part of the nineteenth century Babington and Montagu each published monographs on the subject, but since then it has received remarkably little attention. This is surprising given the importance that the business community does attach to the right to set cross-demands against each other, particularly in the event of an insolvency. The avowed aim of this book is to provide an exposition of some of the more important principles of the law of set-off. It had its genesis in a thesis for which the author was awarded the degree of Doctor of Philosophy, and subsequently also a Yorke Prize, at the University of Cambridge. The thesis was entitled 'The Law of Set-off in Bankruptcy and Company Liquidation', and more and less constitutes the material set out in Chapters 2 to 12 of the present book. The first chapter, dealing with equitable set-off and the final chapter, on a surety's right of set-off, have been added in order to expand the scope of the work for the purpose of publication.

The emphasis throughout is on the question of when a right of set-off is available. Questions of pleading and procedure are not dealt with. For these, the appropriate rules of court, and commentaries thereon, should be consulted. Moreover the book is concerned with the *principles* of set-off. It does not purport to provide an exhaustive list of the myriad situations in which the courts in the past have allowed a right of set-off. Rather the aim is to indicate the principles upon which the decided case law is based.

During my period of research at Cambridge I was fortunate to have as my supervisors Professor Gareth Jones, of Trinity College, and Michael Prichard, of Gonville and Caius College. I am grateful to these gentlemen for their advice and assistance. The thesis was examined by Dr Len Sealy, of Gonville and Gaius College, and Professor Roy Goode, of Queen Mary College in London. Their comments and criticisms, and the encouragement they gave me to publish this book, are greatly appreciated. Of course none of these people is in any way responsible for any errors of omission or commission that may be contained in the ensuing pages.

The discussion of the various principles of set-off is based primarily upon English case and statute law, though reference is also made to suitable authorities from Australia and New Zealand. There are also extensive cross-references to the relevant Australian statutory provisions. The law is stated on the basis of the available reported law as at 31 December 1986.

However for the second impression of the book cases reported after that date and before 30 September 1988 have been included, but by way of brief reference only in the footnotes. Unfortunately it has not been possible to discuss these cases in any great depth.

R.D.

Contents

Table of Cases

Table of Statutes, Rules and Orders

ENGLAND

AUSTRALIA

US

Introduction

While it is difficult to give a comprehensive definition of set-off without reference to the various forms that it can take, at a general level it can be defined as the setting of cross-claims against each other to produce a balance. It provides a defence to an action although, depending on the form of set-off, the issue need not arise in that context. But the existence of cross-demands is crucial.[1] It is not correct to describe as a set-off a situation in which the damages payable by a defendant to a plaintiff may be reduced because of a benefit incidentally accruing to the plaintiff as a result of the defendant's breach. This is not a case of cross-demands, but rather of calculating the true measure of damages.[2] A similar analysis applies in the case of a running account. A true running account is not within the ambit of the law of set-off[3] because there are not independent cross-demands between the parties requiring to be set off. Rather, there is only one cause of action for the balance.[4]

The existence of a right of set-off may be crucial in the event of an insolvency. If there are cross-demands between a creditor and a debtor who has become insolvent, the creditor, in the absence of a set-off, may be obliged to pay the full amount of his own indebtedness, and yet be confined to receiving a dividend along with the other creditors for the amount for which the insolvent debtor is indebted to him. If however a set-off is available, only the balance remaining after deducting one claim from

---

[1] *Re Dalco; ex parte Dalco and Deputy Commissioner of Taxation (NSW)* (1986) 17 ATR 906, 913; *Buttrose* v. *Versi* unreported, Young J., Supreme Court of NSW, 9 April 1992. Compare *The Ionian Skipper* [1977] 2 Lloyd's Rep. 273, 279.

[2] Compare the discussion in *Nadreph Ltd.* v. *Willmett & Co.* [1978] 1 WLR 1537, *Ocean Glory Compania Naviera SA* v. *A/S PV Christensen (The Ioanna)* [1985] 2 Lloyd's Rep. 164 and *Christianos* v. *Westpac Banking Corporation* (1991) 5 WAR 336. For example, when a defendant who has not been guilty of fraud or negligence has incurred expenses in good faith with respect to goods the subject of an action for detention, and the goods have been delivered up to the plaintiff, who consequently has the benefit of those expenses, the defendant is entitled to have the expenses taken into account in any assessment of damages for detention. See *Peruvian Guano Co. Limited* v. *Dreyfus Brothers & Co.* [1892] AC 166; *Hill* v. *Ziymack* (1908) 7 CLR 352; *Halsbury's Laws of England* (4th edn., 1985) Vol. 45, 677, para. 1458. In *In Re Baldwin (A Bankrupt), and Tasman Fruit-Packers, Limited, ex parte Official Assignee* [1940] NZLR 848, it was held that the value of the interest of a member of a society registered under the Industrial and Provident Societies Act 1908 (NZ) could only be ascertained by deducting the amount of the member's indebtedness to the society. This was independent of any principle of set-off.

[3] Compare Winn L.J. in *Rolls Razor Ltd.* v. *Cox* [1967] 1 QB 552, 575.

[4] *Cottam* v. *Partridge* (1842) 4 Man. & G. 271, 293–4; *Re Armour: ex parte Official Receiver* v. *Commonwealth Trading Bank of Australia* (1956) 18 ABC 69, 75; *Re Convere Pty. Ltd.* [1976] VR 345, 349; *Re Charge Card Services Ltd.* [1987] 1 Ch. 150, 174.

the other would be payable. Therefore, if the debtor's claim against the creditor exceeds in value the creditor's claim against the debtor, the creditor in effect obtains payment in full for his claim in the form of a deduction from his liability, and is only obliged to pay the balance. Alternatively it may be that the creditor's claim is the greater, in which case he receives payment in full to the extent of his liability to the debtor and he need only be confined to a dividend in respect of the balance.

A set-off may also have advantages in the absence of insolvency, although it is important in this regard to understand the distinction between set-off and counterclaim.

A right of counterclaim was introduced by section 24(3) of the Supreme Court of Judicature Act 1873.[5] It differs from set-off in that it does not give rise to a defence, but rather it constitutes a procedural device by which the court may consider independent cross-actions in the same proceedings. These cross-actions are treated as independent actions for all purposes except execution.[6] Since a set-off gives rise to a defence to the plaintiff's claim, there is only one judgment for the balance.[7] In comparison, a successful counterclaim results in two judgments, i.e. judgment for the plaintiff on his claim and judgment for the defendant on the counterclaim, with execution issuing on the balance.[8] In an application by a plaintiff for summary judgment against the defendant, the existence of a counterclaim is not a sufficient justification to prevent judgment being entered, though the court may stay execution on that judgment until the defendant's cross-action has been tried. On the other hand, a defendant with a right of set-off overtopping the plaintiff's claim will be granted leave to defend, so that the defendant is not the subject of an adverse judgment.[9]

---

[5] See now the Supreme Court Act 1981, s. 49, and Ord. 15 r. 2 RSC. The Judicature Acts in introducing a right of counterclaim did not confer any new right of set-off. See *Hanak* v. *Green* [1958] 2 QB 9, 22.

[6] *Stumore* v. *Campbell & Co.* [1892] 1 QB 314, 317 per Lord Esher MR.

[7] If the cross-demand of a defendant asserting a right of set-off is greater in value than the plaintiff's claim against him, he may employ his demand in a set-off to the extent of, and in order to defeat, the plaintiff's claim, and counterclaim for the balance.

[8] *Stooke* v. *Taylor* (1880) 5 QDB 569; *Stumore* v. *Campbell & Co.* [1892] 1 QB 314; *Sovereign Life Assurance Company* v. *Dodd* [1892] 2 QB 573, 578; *Sharpe* v. *Haggith* (1912) 106 LT 13; *McDonnell & East Limited* v. *McGregor* (1936) 56 CLR 50, 59; *Chell Engineering Ltd.* v. *Unit Tool and Engineering Co. Ltd.* [1950] 1 All ER 378; *Hanak* v. *Green* [1958] 2 QB 9. See also *Beddall* v. *Maitland* (1881) 17 Ch. D 174.

[9] See *Morgan & Son Limited* v. *S. Martin Johnson & Company Limited* [1949] 1 KB 107; *James Lamont & Co. Ltd.* v. *Hyland Ltd.* [1950] 1 KB 585; *In re K.L. Tractors Ltd.* [1954] VLR 505, 509; *Edward Ward & Co.* v. *McDougall* [1972] VR 433; *Mottram Consultants Ltd.* v. *Bernard Sunley & Sons Ltd.* [1975] 2 Lloyd's Rep. 197, 212, 214; *Petersville Limited* v. *Rosgrae Distributors Pty. Ltd.* (1975) 11 SASR 433; *General Credits (Finance) Pty. Ltd.* v. *Stoyakovich* [1975] Qd. R 352; *United Dominions Corporation Limited* v. *Jaybe Homes Pty. Ltd.* [1978] Qd. R 111; *Paynter Ltd.* v. *Ben Candy Investments Ltd.* [1987] 1 NZLR 257. Ordinarily the defendant should quantify the value of his set-off to justify leave to defend. Compare *Asco Developments Ltd.* v. *Gordon* (1978) 248 EG 683.

The distinction between set-off and counterclaim is relevant to the question of costs. The general rule is that the plaintiff's costs are awarded on the basis of the amount for which he receives judgment.[10] Since a set-off gives rise to a defence, it follows that, if the debt to be set off is at least as great as that for which the plaintiff sued, the defendant will have successfully defended the action, and accordingly the defendant, rather than the plaintiff, usually will be the recipient of an order for costs. On the other hand, a counterclaim results in two independent judgments. The plaintiff is generally entitled to costs of his claim if successful, while the defendant is awarded costs for his successful counterclaim.[11] There is also the question of assignments. An assignee of a debt as a general rule takes subject to defences available to the debtor against the assignor before the debtor received notice of the assignment. These defences include the defence of set-off. The better view is that an assignee does not take subject to a debtor's right of counterclaim against the assignor if that claim could not have been raised as a set-off.[12]

The importance of a right of set-off has come into prominence in recent years in the context of commercial arbitrations. Arbitration as a means of settling a dispute is generally considered to be quicker and less expensive than proceeding through the courts, and it is common for commercial contracts to stipulate that any 'dispute' arising under the contract should be referred to arbitration.[13] It may be that a person being sued for the price of services performed or goods delivered pursuant to a contract containing an arbitration clause has a cross-claim against the plaintiff for damages for breach of the contract. If this cross-claim can be marshalled as an equitable set-off, the defendant has a substantive defence[14] to the plaintiff's claim, so that the sum claimed by the plaintiff may be regarded as being in dispute. The defendant in such a case may apply for a stay of the action[15] and have

---

[10] It should nevertheless be emphasised that an award of costs is a matter within the discretion of the court. See the Supreme Court Act 1981, s. 51. While this discretion must be exercised with due regard to precedent, rules as to costs are not inflexible. See for example *Box* v. *Midland Bank Ltd.* [1981] 1 Lloyd's Rep. 434.

[11] *Stooke* v. *Taylor* (1880) 5 QBD 569 (overruling *Staples* v. *Young* (1877) 2 Ex. D 324); *Shrapnel* v. *Laing* (1888) 20 QBD 334; *Sharpe* v. *Haggith* (1912) 106 LT 13; *Chell Engineering Ltd.* v. *Unit Tool and Engineering Co. Ltd.* [1950] 1 All ER 378; *E. Reynolds & Sons (Chingford), Ltd.* v. *Hendry Brothers (London) Ltd.* [1955] 1 Lloyd's Rep. 258; *Hanak* v. *Green* [1958] 2 QB 9. [12] See section 13.2.3 below.

[13] For example, Clause 23 of the Baltime form of Charterparty provides that 'Any dispute arising under the Charter to be referred to arbitration in London (or such other place as may be agreed) one Arbitrator to be nominated by the Owners and the other by the Charterers, and in case the Arbitrators shall not agree then to the decision of an Umpire to be appointed by them, the award of the Arbitrators or the Umpire to be final and binding upon both parties'. [14] See section 1.7.4 below.

[15] Under the Arbitration Act 1950, s. 4(1), or, in relation to an arbitration agreement that is not a domestic arbitration agreement, the Arbitration Act 1975, s. 1.

both the claim and the cross-claim referred to arbitration.[16] If on the other hand the cross-claim for damages could not be employed in a set-off, the generally accepted view is that an application by the defendant for a stay of the plaintiff's action will not succeed, so that only the cross-claim may be referred to arbitration.[17]

Essentially there are three 'true' forms of set-off. In the case of parties neither of whom is bankrupt or is a company in liquidation, a set-off may proceed under the right of set-off derived from the Statutes of Set-off enacted in 1729[18] and 1735,[19] or in accordance with the principles of the form of set-off developed independently by courts of equity. These are the subject of discussion in the first chapter. If one of the parties to the cross-demands is a person who is bankrupt or is a company in liquidation, the right of set-off is governed by the set-off section (or, as it is sometimes called, the mutual credit provision) in the insolvency legislation.[20] Insolvency set-off is discussed in the second and succeeding chapters. In addition to these forms of set-off, there are certain rights which are distinct from set-off but which have an analogous effect. Two such rights, combination of bank accounts and the rule in *Cherry* v. *Boultbee*, receive detailed consideration.[21]

---

[16] In order to preserve cash flow, arbitrators may be called upon to make a prompt interim award and to decide that a minimum sum at least is payable by one party to the other. In doing so the arbitrators may decide to award only such sum as proves not to be in dispute after taking into account the extent of a claim for an equitable set-off. Alternatively, it is open to arbitrators, when awarding a minimum sum as due and payable, to reject a claim for an equitable set-off if the party advancing the claim cannot satisfy them that he is seeking to exercise the right in good faith and on reasonable grounds. Of course, if this does occur, it is possible that the cross-claim may be made out later on fuller evidence when the arbitrators proceed to a final award in the case. The fact that arbitrators have rejected a claim for a set-off in an interim award is not inconsistent with a finding that the cross-claim is valid when they have the full evidence before them at a later date. See *The Kostas Melas* [1981] 1 Lloyd's Rep. 18, and *The Bunga Melawis* [1991] 2 Lloyd's Rep. 271.

[17] *The Teno* [1977] 2 Lloyd's Rep. 289; *The Alfa Nord* [1977] 2 Lloyd's Rep. 434; *Nova (Jersey) Knit Ltd.* v. *Kammgarn Spinnerei G.m.b.H.* [1977] 1 WLR 713; *Federal Commerce & Navigation Co. Ltd.* v. *Molena Alpha Inc.* [1978] 1 QB 927, 974; *The Kostas Melas* [1981] 1 Lloyd's Rep. 18, 27; *The Cleon* [1983] 1 Lloyd's Rep. 586. See also *Ellis Mechanical Services Ltd.* v. *Wates Construction Ltd.* [1978] 1 Lloyd's Rep. 33. Compare *Russell* v. *Pellegrini* (1856) 6 El. & Bl. 1020 (which was followed in *Seligmann* v. *Le Boutillier* (1866) LR 1 CP 681), though Lord Wilberforce in the *Nova Knit* case (and see also *The Alfa Nord*) thought that that case should only be regarded as correct, if at all, on the basis of the particularly wide arbitration clause there in issue. On other occasions it has been said that *Russell* v. *Pellegrini* should not be followed. See Bramwell B. in *Daunt* v. *Lazard* (1858) LJ 27 Ex. 399, 400 and Lord Russell of Killowen in the *Nova Knit* case (at 733). *Quaere* whether there was a 'dispute' in *Graham* v. *Seagoe* [1964] 2 Lloyd's Rep. 564, in view of the general principle that an equitable set-off is not available against a claim on a negotiable instrument. See section 1.7.17 below. [18] (1729) 2 Geo. II. c. 22 s. 13.

[19] (1735) 8 Geo. II c. 24. s. 5. [20] Currently the Insolvency Act 1986, s. 323.

[21] See Chapter 11 below for combination of accounts, and Chapter 10 below in relation to *Cherry* v. *Boultbee*.

Set-off is dealt with in the Rules of the Supreme Court[22] made pursuant to the Supreme Court Act 1981. However, it is important to appreciate that the Rules themselves do not determine the availability of a set-off,[23] but merely lay down the procedure for claiming the defence outside bankruptcy or company liquidation. The circumstances in which a set-off is available depend upon the interpretation of the Statutes of Set-off and the set-off section in the insolvency legislation, and, in other cases, upon an examination of the substantive principles developed by the courts independently of the Rules.

---

[22] Ord. 18 r. 17 RSC.
[23] *In re Milan Tramways Company; ex parte Theys* (1882) 22 Ch. D 122, 126; *Stumore* v. *Campbell & Co.* [1892] 1 QB 314, 316–317; *Hanak* v. *Green* [1958] 2 QB 9, 22; *Bank of Boston Connecticut* v. *European Grain and Shipping Ltd.* [1989] 1 AC 1056, 1109. Compare the position in Victoria, discussed in section 1.12 below.

1

Set-off Exclusive of Bankruptcy and Company Liquidation

1.1 EARLY DEVELOPMENTS

Prior to the enactment of the first Statute of Set-off in 1729 there was no general right of set-off available to a defendant in an action at law when he was being sued by a solvent plaintiff, as opposed to the assignees of a bankrupt.[1] This denial of a set-off was consistent with the adoption of strict rules of pleading and of forms of action, which themselves were designed to reduce the question to be decided by the court as far as possible to a single, well-defined issue.[2] There are instances in the late seventeenth and early eighteenth centuries in which equity enforced set-offs of unconnected debts by means of an injunction to restrain the plaintiff in an action at law from proceeding with his claim against the defendant until he had given credit for his own indebtedness to the defendant. However, these cases should not be taken as evidence of a general equitable jurisdiction to set off cross-debts. Equitable relief usually was founded upon a custom that the accounts should be balanced,[3] or alternatively an implied agreement to this effect.[4] There is in fact one early decision which does seem to indicate a general equitable jurisdiction. In 1699, Sir John Trevor M.R. in *Arnold* v. *Richardson*[5] ordered that a plaintiff in an action at law for payment of a debt on a bond should bring into account his own indebtedness to the defendant for food and lodging, even though 'there was no Agreement for that Purpose'. The reporter has attributed to the Master of the Rolls a remark that 'a Discount was natural Justice in all cases'. However, the

---

[1] For a discussion of the early development of set-off in English and Roman law, see Loyd, 'The Development of Set-off' (1916) 64 *University of Pennsylvania Law Review* 541 and Tigar, 'Automatic Extinction of Cross-Demands: *Compensatio* From Rome to California' (1965) 53 *California Law Review* 224.

[2] See Loyd, 'The Development of Set-off' (1916) 64 *University of Pennsylvania Law Review* 541, 544, and also Lord Mansfield in *Green* v. *Farmer* (1768) 4 Burr. 2214, 2220.

[3] See *Curson* v. *African Company* (1682) 1 Vern. 121.

[4] *Downam* v. *Matthews* (1721) Prec. Ch. 580; *Hawkins* v. *Freeman* 2 Eq. Ca. Abr. 10. See also *Sir William Darcy's Case* (1677) 2 Freeman 28; *Jeffs* v. *Wood* (1723) 2 P Wms. 128.

[5] (1699) 1 Eq. Ca. Abr. 8.

judgment of Sir Joseph Jekyll M.R. some 23 years later in *Jeffs* v. *Wood*[6] suggests that, in the absence of an insolvency, equity at that time ordinarily would look for evidence, however slight, of an agreement for a set-off.

There were also certain discrete situations in which rights very much akin to set-off were recognized by the common law courts.[7] By this it is meant that the common law would allow the defendant in an action to plead the existence of certain facts as a means of reducing the amount which otherwise would be awarded to the plaintiff, when those facts could have formed the basis of a separate action by the defendant against the plaintiff. For example, a bailiff who was entitled to receive rent from the manor could obtain payment by recoupment from his obligation to account to his master.[8] Further, if a landlord disseised his tenant and the tenant then brought a writ of assise against him, the landlord was entitled to deduct from the damages payable any rent which the tenant was required to pay for the period of the disseisin.[9] Similarly, if the holder of a rent-charge disseised the owner of the land, the former's right to receive payment under the charge for the period of the disseisin could be recouped from his obligation to pay damages to the landlord.[10] The holder of the rent-charge was given this right in order to avoid circuity of action.[11] This should be compared to the right recognized by Gawdy J. in 1591 in *Taylor* v. *Beal*[12] that, if a landlord under an obligation to repair premises failed to do so, the tenant himself could undertake the repairs and deduct the expenses from his rent.[13] The tenant's right in this situation was not based upon a desire to avoid circuity of action, but rather Gawdy J. said that 'the law giveth this liberty to the lessee to expend the rent in reparations, for he shall be otherwise at great mischief, for the house may fall upon his head before it be repaired; and therefore the law alloweth him to repair it, and recoupe the rent'.

---

[6] (1723) 2 P. Wms. 128.

[7] A number of cases are collected in *Viner's Abridgment* (2nd edn., 1741) Vol. 8, 556–7. See also the discussion in Loyd, 'The Development of Set-off' (1916) 64 *University of Pennsylvania Law Review* 541, 544–6.

[8] See *Viner's Abridgment* (2nd edn., 1741) Vol. 8, 557, and also the note to *Gybson* v. *Searl* (1607) Cro. Jac. 176, 178, citing 20 Hen 7, pl. 5.

[9] *Coulter's Case* 5 Co. Rep. 30a, 30b (discussed in Loyd, 'The Development of Set-off' (1916) 64 *University of Pennsylvania Law Review* 541, 545). Only rent owing for the period of the disseisin could be deducted. Arrears of rent owing from before then could not be recouped in this manner. See *Viner's Abridgment* (2nd edn., 1741) Vol. 8, 556, citing 9 E. 3.8.

[10] See *Viner's Abridgment* (2nd edn., 1741) Vol. 8, 556, and *Coulter's Case* 5 Co. Rep. 30a, 31a.

[11] See *Viner's Abridgment* (2nd edn., 1741) Vol. 8, 556, and *Coulter's Case* 5 Co. Rep. 30a, 31a.   [12] (1591) Cro. Eliz. 222.

[13] The report suggests that Clench J. agreed with this view, though he held against the tenant on a question of pleading. Fenner J. on the other hand said that the tenant had to bring a separate action.

There is an instance in customary law in which unconnected cross-demands apparently could be set against each other. According to the custom of foreign attachment, if a plaint was entered in the court of the mayor or the sheriff of the City of London against a defendant, and the process was returned *nihil*, and thereupon the plaintiff suggested that another person within London was indebted to the defendant, the debtor was warned, and if he did not deny that he was so indebted the debt was attached in his hands as payment to the plaintiff.[14] Apparently the custom contemplated the attachment of a debt owing by the plaintiff himself to the defendant,[15] which in effect would have operated as a set-off of the plaintiff's debt against that of the defendant. It appears nevertheless that this custom has fallen into disuse.[16]

1.2 STATUTES OF SET-OFF

1.2.1 Introduction

The Statutes of Set-off were enacted in 1729 and 1735. The title of the first Statute, 'An Act for the Relief of Debtors with respect to the Imprisonment of their Persons',[17] suggests that their purpose may have been to assist debtors who were liable to be sent to debtors' prison for non-payment of debts, though Willes C.J. not long after their enactment considered that they were designed to avoid circuity of action and multiplicity of suits.[18] The first Statute was a temporary provision intended to last for a period of five years. It provided that:

[W]here there are mutual Debts between the Plaintiff and Defendant, or if either Party sue or be sued as Executor or Administrator, where there are mutual Debts between the Testator or Intestate and either Party, one Debt may be set against the other, and such Matter may be given in Evidence upon the General Issue, or pleaded in Bar, as the Nature of the Case shall require, so as at the Time of his pleading the General Issue, where any such Debt of the Plaintiff, his Testator or Intestate, is intended to be insisted on in Evidence, Notice shall be given of the particular Sum or Debt so intended to be insisted on, and upon what Account it became due, or otherwise such Matter shall not be allowed in Evidence upon such General Issue.

---

[14] See *Comyns' Digest* (5th edn., 1822) Vol. 1, 713–14.

[15] See Brandon, *The Customary Law of Foreign Attachment* (1861), 60–1, 143 n. s, and *Comyns' Digest* (5th edn., 1822) Vol. 1, 716, though compare Bayley J. in *Nonell* v. *Hullett and Widder* (1821) 4 B & Ald. 646.

[16] See *Halsbury's Laws of England* (4th edn., 1975), Vol. 12, 18 para. 428, n. 3.

[17] (1729) 2 Geo. II, c. 22, s. 13.

[18] *Hutchinson* v. *Sturges* (1741) Willes 261, 262; *Pilgrim* v. *Kinder* (1744) 7 Mod. 463, 467. See also *Forster* v. *Wilson* (1843) 12 M & W 191, 203; *ex parte Cleland, in re Davies* (1867) LR 2 Ch. App. 808, 812–13; *In re Unit 2 Windows Ltd.* [1985] 1 WLR 1383, 1387.

Several questions arose upon the construction of this provision, as, for example, whether debts of a different nature (i.e. simple and specialty debts) could be set off against each other, and whether in the case of a bond the penalty was to be considered as the debt.[19] Therefore, when the right of set-off conferred by the first Statute of Set-off was made permanent in 1735 by the second Statute (8 Geo. II, c. 24, s. 4), the Act went on to provide, in section 5, that mutual debts may be set off notwithstanding that in law they are deemed to be of a different nature, and further that, if either of the debts accrued by reason of a penalty in a bond, the amount to be included in the set-off was the amount 'truly and justly due'.

The Statutes themselves were repealed in England in 1879 by section 2 of the Civil Procedure Acts Repeal Act in so far as they applied to the newly founded Supreme Court of Judicature, though it was expressly provided that the repeal was not to affect any 'jurisdiction or principle or rule of law or equity established or confirmed, or right or privilege acquired'.[20] This has been interpreted as preserving the right of set-off originally conferred by the Statutes.[21]

1.2.2 When must the set-off be available?

Prior to the Judicature Acts the courts applied the principle that a set-off under the Statutes could only be pleaded in bar to the plaintiff's action if the set-off was available at the commencement of the action, as opposed to when the defence was delivered. In other words, at the date of the action there had to be a presently existing and payable debt owing by the plaintiff to the defendant.[22] The principle was confirmed in *Richards* v. *James*.[23] The plaintiff in that case became indebted to the defendant after the plaintiff had already commenced proceedings. The defendant pleaded that, because of the cross-debt, the plaintiff ought not further to maintain his

---

[19] See the discussion in *Hutchinson* v. *Sturges* (1741) Willes 261.
[20] Civil Procedure Acts Repeal Act 1879, s. 4(1)(b).
[21] *In re Daintrey* [1900] 1 QB 546, 548; *Hanak* v. *Green* [1958] 2 QB 9, 22. See also *Henriksens Rederi A/S* v. *THZ Rolimpex (The Brede)* [1974] 1 QB 233, 246, 252. See now the Supreme Court Act 1981, s. 49(2) and Ord. 18 r. 17 RSC. There was a similar repeal and saving of the right of set-off in relation to courts other than the Supreme Court of Judicature in the Statute Law Revision and Civil Procedure Act 1883 (which in turn was repealed by the Supreme Court of Judicature (Consolidation) Act 1925). See now s. 3 of the Courts and Legal Services Act 1990 (which is substituted for s. 38 of the County Courts Act 1984).
[22] *Pilgrim* v. *Kinder* (1744) 7 Mod. 462 (plaintiff's debt existing but not payable until after action commenced); *Evans* v. *Prosser* (1789) 3 TR 186; *Richards* v. *James* (1848) 2 Ex. 471. See also *Rogerson* v. *Ladbroke* (1822) 1 Bing. 93; *Leman* v. *Gordon* (1838) 8 Car. & P. 392; *Maw* v. *Ulyatt* (1861) 31 LJ Ch. 33.   [23] (1848) 2 Ex. 471.

action. Pollock C.B. said that, 'The novelty of the plea is supported by no precedent, and there is nothing to warrant us in so construing the statute, so as to enable a defendant to set off a debt which has arisen since the commencement of the action'.[24]

Subsequently in *Bennett* v. *White*[25] Farwell L.J. referred to the form of plea for the right of set-off given in the third edition of Bullen and Leake in 1868, that 'the plaintiff, *at the commencement of this suit*, was and still is indebted to the defendant'.[26] He said that that 'was at that time and always has been the proper form'. However, the Supreme Court Rules in force since the Judicature Acts[27] have allowed a defendant to rely on a ground of defence which arose after the action was commenced, and Mathew J. in *Wood* v. *Goodwin*[28] accepted that this extends to the defence of set-off. Moreover, it is important to appreciate the context in which Farwell L.J. made his remark. In *Bennett* v. *White* the defendant in an action for payment of a debt sought to set off a debt originally due from the plaintiff to a third party, who had assigned it to the defendant. The plaintiff argued that the plea of set-off was bad, since set-off under the Statutes required that the debts originally should have existed between the plaintiff and the defendant. Farwell L.J. did not refer to the form of pleading in order to draw a distinction between debts arising before and after the commencement of the suit, but rather to show that it was not necessary that the plaintiff's debt should have been owing from its inception to the defendant. Of greater concern is *Edmunds* v. *Lloyds Italico SpA*,[29] in which Sir John Donaldson M.R. referred to *Richards* v. *James* in terms suggesting that it was regarded as still representing the law. However, the effect of the Supreme Court Rules after the Judicature Acts was not considered, and as a matter of policy it is difficult to see why a right of set-off arising after the commencement of the plaintiff's action should not be able to be relied on as a defence. There is support for this view in Australia,[30] while Lord Hoffman commented in passing in the House of Lords in *Stein* v. *Blake*[31]

---

[24] (1848) 2 Ex. 471, 473. [25] [1910] 2 KB 643, 648.
[26] Bullen and Leake, *Precedents of Pleadings* (3rd edn., 1868), 682 (emphasis added by Farwell L.J.).
[27] The first such rule was Ord. 21 r. 1 of the Rules of Court set out in the First Schedule to the Supreme Court of Judicature Act 1875. See now Ord. 18 r. 9 RSC.
[28] [1884] WN 17. [29] [1986] 1 WLR 492.
[30] Angas Parsons J. in *Rex* v. *Ray; ex parte Chapman* [1936] SASR 241, 247 noted without adverse comment the views of Farwell L.J. in *Bennett* v. *White*, which seems to suggest that the principle in *Richards* v. *James* was thought to be still applicable. In *Ingleton* v. *Coates* (1896) 2 ALR 154, on the other hand, Madden C.J. in the Victorian Supreme Court held that the Supreme Court Rules permitted the defendant to plead a set-off in respect of an indebtedness of the plaintiff assigned to him after commencement of the plaintiff's action. Powell J. in *McColl's Wholesale Pty. Ltd.* v. *State Bank of NSW* [1984] 3 NSWLR 365, 381 expressed a similar view in relation to the procedure in force at that time in New South Wales.
[31] [1995] 2 All ER 961, 964.

that set-off under the Statutes is confined to debts which are liquidated and due and payable 'at the time when the defence of set-off is filed'.

The view that *Richards* v. *James* should no longer be followed means that a cross-debt which arises after the issue of the plaintiff's writ may be pleaded as a set-off. This is not inconsistent with the notion discussed below, that a cross-debt owing by the plaintiff before the commencement of the action must be enforceable at that date in order to be set off.[32] The most common situation in which this arises is in relation to a debt which is unenforceable because of the expiration of a time bar. The notion that unenforceability in this context is to be determined as at the date of the plaintiff's action has the converse effect to the result in *Richards* v. *James*. *Richards* v. *James* unduly restricts the availability of the defence. On the other hand, the determination of the enforceability of a pre-existing cross-debt under a statute of limitation as at the commencement of the plaintiff's action, rather than the later date when the set-off is pleaded, expands the class of claims which can be set off under the Statutes.

The above discussion relates to a debt of the plaintiff that arises or becomes due and payable after commencement of the suit and before judgment. If, however, the debt arises or becomes payable after judgment, it does not provide a ground for restraining the plaintiff from enforcing the judgment.[33]

1.2.3 Mutuality

For the Statutes of Set-off to apply there must be mutuality. Mutuality is considered later.[34]

1.2.4 Debts

The Statutes only apply when there is a debt on each side of the account. Therefore, a claim for the return of goods,[35] or an entitlement to a statutory benefit which does not create a debt enforceable by action,[36] is not susceptible to a defence of set-off under the Statutes.

The requirement of 'debts' does not refer simply to a claim that could have been the subject of the old action of debt. Rather, Cockburn C.J. in his classic formulation of the principle in *Stooke* v. *Taylor*[37] said that the plea of set-off under the Statutes 'is available only where the claims on

---

[32] See section 1.2.10 below.
[33] *Maw* v. *Ulyatt* (1861) 31 LJ Ch. 33, and see also section 1.4.2 below.
[34] See section 7.4 below.   [35] *Green* v. *Farmer* (1768) 4 Burr. 2214.
[36] *Walker* v. *Department of Social Security* (1995) 129 ALR 198.
[37] (1880) 5 QBD 569, 575.

both sides are in respect of liquidated debts, or money demands which can be readily and without difficulty ascertained'. Each of the demands accordingly must be capable of being liquidated or ascertained with precision at the time of pleading,[38] or, as the House of Lords expressed it in *Stein* v. *Blake*,[39] they must be 'either liquidated or in sums capable of ascertainment without valuation or estimation'. A recent illustration is *Axel Johnson Petroleum AB* v. *MG Mineral Group AG*.[40] The defendant in an action for payment of a sum certain asserted that the plaintiff had agreed to buy all such oil as the defendant itself bought from a third party, the contract price being the same as the price paid by the defendant to the third party together with a sum of US$1.00 per tonne to cover 'local expenses'. The Court of Appeal held that the price payable by the plaintiff under the arrangement as described was liquidated, and accordingly could give rise to a defence under the Statutes so as to entitle the defendant to leave to defend. It was not necessary that the price should be capable of being computed by reference to the contract without investigation.

If the quantum of the claim sought to be set off by the defendant can only be ascertained by litigation or arbitration it will generally be unliquidated, and it makes no difference that an estimate has been made by an expert.[41] On the other hand, a cross-demand may still be regarded as liquidated notwithstanding that the defendant is unable to state at the present time what the precise value of the demand is. It is sufficient that, when full particulars are known, it will merely be a matter of addition and subtraction. In Victoria[42] the defendant in an action on a cheque pleaded that the plaintiffs had been his agents for the sale of tallow, and in breach of their duty as agents themselves purchased the defendant's tallow and sold it on their own account at enhanced prices without accounting for the difference in price. The defendant alleged that the difference in price amounted to more than the value of the cheque sued upon, though he said that he was not at present able to give further particulars. Although the amount was still uncertain, it was held that the demand nevertheless was pleadable as a set-off, because by its nature it was a liquidated demand. The important point is the nature of the claim sought to be set off. If the defendant's claim in its nature is liquidated, it is not fatal to a set-off that it is disputed by the plaintiff as to all or part on grounds that require determination by litigation or arbitration. The defendant in such a case may still plead it as a defence to

---

[38] *Morley* v. *Inglis* (1837) 4 Bing. (NC) 58, 71; *Henriksens Rederi A/S* v. *THZ Rolimpex (The Brede)* [1974] 1 QB 233, 246; *Axel Johnson Petroleum AB* v. *MG Mineral Group AG* [1992] 1 WLR 270, 272.   [39] [1995] 2 All ER 961, 964.
[40] [1992] 1 WLR 270.
[41] *B. Hargreaves Ltd.* v. *Action 2000 Ltd.* [1993] BCLC 1111 (estimate by a surveyor of the amount claimed in respect of faulty workmanship).
[42] *Woodroffe & Co.* v. *J. W. Moss* [1915] VLR 237.

an action brought against him for payment of a debt, and in an application by the plaintiff for summary judgment the defendant may be granted leave to defend.[43]

If the claim of one of the parties has both a liquidated and an unliquidated component, a set-off may proceed against the liquidated part.[44] Further, if the plaintiff's claim in truth is for a liquidated sum, so that prior to the Judicature Acts he could have maintained an action in *indebitatus assumpsit*, he cannot deprive the defendant of a right of set-off by framing his claim instead as an action for damages,[45] though there is admittedly authority to the contrary.[46] *Hutchinson* v. *Reid*,[47] on the other hand, does not support that contrary view. The plaintiff sold goods to the defendant in consideration of the defendant agreeing to accept a bill of exchange for the price, the bill to be payable in two months. The defendant refused to accept the bill whereupon the plaintiff, within the two-month period, commenced this action. As a defence the defendant pleaded a set-off in respect of a debt owing by the plaintiff. The defence failed, because the plaintiff was not suing for the price but rather for damages for failure to accept the bill. However, Lord Ellenborough emphasized in his judgment that the action had been brought within the two-month period. If the plaintiff had sued after the time of payment, the claim in effect would have been for the price, in which case his Lordship indicated that a set-off would have been available.

The test formulated by Cockburn C.J. in *Stooke* v. *Taylor*[48] has two aspects. It encompasses not only liquidated debts but also money demands which can be readily and without difficulty ascertained. The better view, which was favoured by Hirst L.J. in *Aectra Refining and Marketing Inc.* v. *Exmar NV*,[49] is that this second aspect refers to demands that are closely analogous to debts and which can be readily ascertained. Thus, it encompasses the old *indebitatus* counts,[50] including claims in *quantum meruit* and *quantum valebat* where work had been performed or goods sold without a price having been agreed.[51] In an appropriate case it may also

---

[43] *Aectra Refining and Marketing Inc.* v. *Exmar NV* [1994] 1 WLR 1634.

[44] *Crampton* v. *Walker* (1860) 3 El. & El. 321.

[45] *Birch* v. *Depeyester* (1816) 4 Camp. 385; *Crampton* v. *Walker* (1860) 3 El. & El. 321, 331–2. This is also consistent with the approach adopted by the Court of Appeal in a different context in *G.L. Baker Ltd.* v. *Barclays Bank Ltd.* [1956] 1 WLR 1409.

[46] See, e.g., *Colson* v. *Welsh* (1795) 1 Esp. 378; *Cooper* v. *Robinson* (1818) 2 Chit. 161; *Thorpe* v. *Thorpe* (1832) 3 B & Ad. 580, 584, 585; *Hill* v. *Smith* (1844) 12 M & W 618, 631; *Halsbury's Laws of England* (4th edn., 1983) Vol. 42, 246 para. 421.

[47] (1813) 3 Camp. 329.   [48] (1880) 5 QBD 569, 575.

[49] [1994] 1 WLR 1634, 1647, approving of the explanation of counsel (at 1645).

[50] See *Howlet* v. *Strickland* (1774) 1 Cowp. 56, 57.

[51] See the discussion by Farwell L.J. in *Lagos* v. *Grunwaldt* [1910] 1 KB 41, 48 of the meaning of the expression 'debt or liquidated demand', referred to in *Aectra Refining and Marketing Inc.* v. *Exmar NV* [1994] 1 WLR 1634, 1647.

include a demand that strictly sounds in damages if indeed it is ascertainable with precision.[52] The classic example is a liquidated damages clause. It was settled in the eighteenth century that the obligation pursuant to a clause in a contract for the payment of liquidated damages in the event of a breach gives rise to a debt for the purpose of the Statutes,[53] provided, of course, that the clause in truth is not a penalty. Thus, a sum specified in a shipping contract as being payable by way of demurrage constitutes liquidated damages,[54] and in *Axel Johnson* the Court of Appeal had no apparent difficulty in recognizing that it could be the subject of a set-off. This should be compared to *Seeger* v. *Duthie*,[55] in which a claim arising out of a delay in loading a ship was held not to come within the terms of the demurrage clause. Accordingly, it was a claim for unliquidated damages which could not be set off under the Statutes.

It is not intended to go through the catalogue of cases which illustrate whether various forms of claims are regarded as liquidated for the purpose of the Statutes. However, a question of some significance is whether claims on guarantees and indemnities may be set off under the Statutes.

1.2.5 Claims on guarantees

In *Axel Johnson*[56] Leggatt L.J. expressed the view that a claim on a guarantee can be set off under the Statutes if the liability in respect of which the guarantee was given has been established. This would be correct if the liability has been established by judgment or arbitration.[57] The judgment itself gives rise to a debt which comes within the terms of the Statutes. However, apart from this, the traditional view has been that a claim on a guarantee is not susceptible to a set-off.

The difficulty lies in the nature of a guarantor's liability, an issue that was discussed in some detail by Lord Diplock in *Moschi* v. *Lep Air Services Ltd*.[58] His Lordship said that, by the beginning of the nineteenth century, it had become to be accepted in English law that the obligation assumed by a guarantor under the contract of guarantee is to see to it that the debtor performs his obligation to the creditor. Accordingly, even if the subject of the guarantee is the payment of a debt, the creditor's remedy against the

---

[52] In *Axel Johnson Petroleum AB* v. *MG Mineral Group AG* [1992] 1 WLR 270, 272 Leggatt L.J. said that 'For set-off to be available at law the claim and cross-claim must be mutual, but they need not be connected. They need not be debts strictly so called, but may sound in damages'. This was referred to with evident approval by Balcombe L.J. in *B. Hargreaves Ltd.* v. *Action 2000 Ltd.* [1993] BCLC 1111, 1113.
[53] *Fletcher* v. *Dyche* (1787) 2 TR 32.
[54] *President of India* v. *Lips Maritime Corporation* [1988] 1 AC 395.
[55] (1860) 8 CB(NS) 45.   [56] [1992] 1 WLR 270, 272.
[57] See *B. Hargreaves Ltd.* v. *Action 2000 Ltd.* [1993] BCLC 1111, 1115.
[58] [1973] AC 331, 348–9.

guarantor lies in damages for breach of contract. As Lord Diplock pointed out, this is evident from the fact that, prior to the Judicature Acts, the creditor's action against the guarantor in such a case was in special *assumpsit* rather than *indebitatus assumpsit*.[59] Once the nature of a guarantor's liability is characterized in this manner, it is readily apparent why a set-off was denied in *Morley* v. *Inglis*.[60] The Common Pleas held in that case that a claim on a guarantee could not be employed by the defendant in a set-off under the Statutes of Set-off, even though the obligation the subject of the guarantee itself was a debt. Nevertheless, notwithstanding the historical view of the nature of the liability, it is debatable whether *Morley* v. *Inglis* would now be followed, given the broad meaning that has been ascribed to 'debts' in the Statutes.[61] Furthermore, it is unlikely to be applied in Australia following comments by Mason C.J. in the High Court in *Sunbird Plaza Pty. Ltd.* v. *Maloney*.[62] In so far as Lord Diplock's analysis of the nature of the liability of a guarantor of a debt is concerned, his Honour said that, while that analysis may be correct as a matter of history, it does not accord with the modern view, that the guarantor of a debt may be sued for the money sum which the debtor has failed to pay. This should have as a consequence that a set-off should be available in Australia against a guarantor's liability when the subject of the liability is a debt.

There are two cases which support a right of set-off in this situation, though neither is a particularly strong authority. In *National Bank of Australasia* v. *Swan*[63] Stawell C.J. in the Victorian Supreme Court held that a set-off could occur against a guarantor's liability in respect of a debt. However his Honour based his conclusion on the earlier decision in *Brown* v. *Tibbitts*,[64] which in truth was concerned with an indemnity rather than a guarantee. Moreover, the case may be explained on the basis of the particular wording of the guarantee in issue, by which the defendant promised to pay all advances which were made by the plaintiff to a third party in case of default. This arguably was a conditional agreement to pay, in the sense discussed by Lord Reid in *Moschi*[65] and Mason C.J. in *Sunbird Plaza* v. *Maloney*,[66] so that, when the condition occurred (i.e. default), the 'guarantor' himself became liable to pay the advances, as opposed to the usual promise of a guarantor to see to it that the principal debtor performs his payment obligation. The second case is *The Raven*,[67] in

---

[59] See also Lord Simon of Glaisdale (at 357).
[60] (1837) 4 Bing. (NC) 58. See also *Crawford* v. *Stirling* (1802) 4 Esp. 207; *Williams* v. *Flight* (1842) 2 Dowl. NS 11, 16–17.   [61] See section 1.2.4 above.
[62] (1988) 166 CLR 245, 255–6. See also *Hawkins* v. *Bank of China* (1992) 26 NSWLR 562.
[63] (1872) 3 VR (L) 168.   [64] (1862) 11 CB (NS) 855.
[65] [1973] AC 331, 344–5.   [66] (1988) 166 CLR 245, 256–7.
[67] [1980] 2 Lloyd's Rep. 266.

which Parker J. seemed to accept that there could be a set-off against a claim under a guarantee.[68] However, *Morley* v. *Inglis* was not discussed, and moreover it is not entirely clear from the judgment whether his Lordship had in mind set-off under the Statutes or equitable set-off.

The above discussion relates to a guarantee of a debt. If the guarantee is in respect of another obligation, breach of which would give rise to a liability in damages, the claim of the person holding the guarantee against the guarantor similarly would be in damages[69] and accordingly could not be set off under the Statutes.

1.2.6 Indemnities

Whether or not a claim upon an indemnity can be set off under the Statutes depends upon the nature of the indemnity. The basic question is whether the amount of the indemnity has been ascertained with precision at the time of pleading.[70]

An indemnity may be given to a person in respect of a liability owing to that person by a third party. In this sense it is similar to a guarantee, though a guarantee and an indemnity differ in an important respect.[71] A contract of guarantee gives rise to a secondary liability, in that the guarantor promises to answer for the debt, default or miscarriage of another who is to be primarily responsible to the promisee. It is because the promise to answer for the default classically has been regarded as a promise to ensure that the other person performs his obligation that a problem has arisen in the context of set-off. An indemnity, on the other hand, does not create a secondary liability but rather a primary liability, by which the indemnifier agrees to keep the other party harmless against loss. Accordingly, the difficulty apparent from *Morley* v. *Inglis* in relation to guarantees does not apply to an indemnity. When an indemnity is given to a person in respect of the liability of a third party, the characterization of the indemnifier's obligation for the purpose of set-off should be the same as the underlying obligation. If the indemnity is given in respect of a liquidated demand, the liability on the indemnity itself is liquidated, and accordingly may be set off under the statutes.[72] Conversely, a claim on an

---

[68] See the discussion at [1980] 2 Lloyd's Rep. 266, 271–2.

[69] *Sunbird Plaza Pty. Ltd.* v. *Maloney* (1988) 166 CLR 245, 255.

[70] *Axel Johnson* [1992] 1 WLR 270, 274.

[71] See *Argo* v. *Lewis* [1976] 2 Lloyd's Rep. 289, 296, referring to *Yeoman Credit Ltd.* v. *Latter* [1961] 1 WLR 828, 830–1.

[72] *Hutchinson* v. *Sydney* (1854) 10 Ex. 438 (indemnity against expenses incurred); *Brown* v. *Tibbitts* (1862) 11 CB(NS) 855. Compare *Attwooll* v. *Attwooll* (1853) 2 El. & Bl. 23, though that case should be understood as turning on a peculiarity of a claim on a penal bond. See Leggatt L.J. in *Axel Johnson* [1992] 1 WLR 270, 273–4.

indemnity may not be the subject of a set-off if the indemnity is in respect of a damages claim which has not been liquidated by judgment or agreement.[73] If an indemnity on its face extends to both liquidated and unliquidated liabilities, a claim on the indemnity may be included in a set-off if the claim to a set-off is confined to an underlying liability which is liquidated.[74]

An indemnity may be in respect of a loss which arises out of the occurrence of a particular event other than default by a third party. If the indemnity is in respect of any costs and expenses that may be incurred, and these are quantifiable with precision, the claim on the indemnity may be the subject of a set-off.[75] Different considerations apply, however, to claims on policies of indemnity insurance, which for a long time have been regarded as being for unliquidated damages.[76] This is so even after the loss has been adjusted, because the adjustment is said to be merely evidence of the amount due.[77] Accordingly, there may not be set-off under the Statutes in respect of such a claim.[78] The claim is regarded as unliquidated, because the insured must prove the amount of his loss. Nevertheless, it seems unusual to describe the claim as being for damages,[79] and, at least if the loss has been adjusted, it is difficult as a matter of policy to see why a set-off should be denied. The argument that an adjustment is merely evidence of the amount of the loss, so that it may be rebutted, e.g. by proof of a mistake,[80] is not a convincing reason for disallowing a set-off if the adjustment in fact is accepted by both parties. There is no such difficulty, however, when non-indemnity insurance is in issue. The action in this instance undoubtedly is brought to recover a liquidated sum due under the contract, in which case there is no reason for denying a right of set-off under the Statutes against the claim.[81]

---

[73] *Cooper* v. *Robinson* (1818) 2 Chit. 161; *Hardcastle* v. *Netherwood* (1821) 5 B & Ald. 93.

[74] A suggestion to this effect by the judges in *Hardcastle* v. *Netherwood* (1821) 5 B & Ald. 93 was adopted in later cases. See *Crampton* v. *Walker* (1860) 3 El. & El. 321; *Brown* v. *Tibbitts* (1862) 11 CB(NS) 855.

[75] *Hutchinson* v. *Sydney* (1854) 10 Ex. 438; *Brown* v. *Tibbitts* (1862) 11 CB(NS) 855.

[76] *Luckie* v. *Bushby* (1853) 13 CB 864; *Pellas* v. *Neptune Marine Insurance Company* (1879) 5 CPD 34; *William Pickersgill & Sons, Ltd.* v. *London and Provincial Marine and General Insurance Co, Ltd.* [1912] 3 KB 614, 622; *Jabbour* v. *Custodian of Israeli Absentee Property* [1954] 1 WLR 139, 145; *Chandris* v. *Argo Insurance Company, Ltd.* [1963] 2 Lloyd's Rep. 65, 73–4; *Edmunds* v. *Lloyds Italico* [1986] 1 WLR 492, 493.

[77] *Luckie* v. *Bushby* (1853) 13 CB 864; *Jabbour* v. *Custodian of Israeli Absentee Property* [1954] 1 WLR 139, 143.

[78] *Grant* v. *Royal Exchange Assurance Company* (1815) 5 M & S 439; *Castelli* v. *Boddington* (1852) 1 El. & Bl. 66 (affirmed (1853) 1 El. & Bl. 879); *Luckie* v. *Bushby* (1853) 13 CB 864; *Pellas & Co.* v. *Neptune Marine Insurance Company* (1879) 5 CPD 34.

[79] See Pearson J. in *Jabbour* v. *Custodian of Israeli Absentee Property* [1954] 1 WLR 139, 145.

[80] See *Jabbour* v. *Custodian of Israeli Absentee Property* [1954] 1 WLR 139, 145.

[81] *Blackley* v. *National Mutual Life Association (No. 2)* [1973] 1 NZLR 668, 672.

1.2.7 Due and payable

A set-off under the Statutes can only be pleaded in respect of cross-debts that are due and payable.[82] Therefore, a debt which is payable *in futuro*,[83] or which is merely contingent,[84] cannot be employed in a set-off. Where a debt is expressed to be payable on demand, the requirement of a demand is not regarded as creating a contingency if the liability in question is primary rather than secondary,[85] unless, it would seem, if the effect of the demand is to change the nature of the liability.[86] This may arise, for example, where the notice turns a liability to pay by instalments into a liability to pay the whole at once.[87]

The question of when the debt must be due and payable has already been discussed. Prior to the Judicature Acts, the courts applied the principle that a set-off could only be pleaded in bar to the plaintiff's action if the set-off was available at the commencement of the action. The leading case was *Richards* v. *James*.[88] However, it is doubtful whether this still represents the law. The better view is that the Supreme Court Rules now permit a defendant to plead a set-off in respect of matters arising subsequent to the action,[89] so that it should be sufficient that the plaintiff's cross-debt is due and payable when the defence is pleaded.

1.2.8 Freight and negotiable instruments

It has been suggested that a defence of set-off under the Statutes of Set-off is not available in an action against the issuer of a negotiable

---

[82] *Stein* v. *Blake* [1995] 2 All ER 961, 964.

[83] *Pilgrim* v. *Kinder* (1744) 7 Mod. 463; *Smith, Fleming, & Co.'s Case* (1866) LR 1 Ch. App. 538 (which was decided before the bankruptcy set-off section was imported into the law of company liquidation); *Rex* v. *Ray; ex parte Chapman* [1936] SASR 241, 247.

[84] *Fromont* v. *Coupland* (1824) 2 Bing. 170; *Leman* v. *Gordon* (1838) 8 Car. & P 392; Compare *Agra & Masterman's Bank* v. *Hoffman* (1864) 34 LJ Ch. 285, though it would appear that the injunction to restrain the action at law was granted on the basis of an equitable set-off, as opposed to a set-off under the Statutes. This is evident from the references by Stuart V.C. to the question whether the plaintiffs by their bill impeached the title to the defendant's legal demand. But even on this basis it is not easy to explain the decision, given that the demands do not appear to have been sufficiently closely connected to give rise to an equitable set-off. It would appear that the injunction was only interlocutory, and it may be doubted whether a perpetual injunction would have been granted at the final hearing. In fact, the action was settled before this occurred.

[85] See Hoffman L.J. and, in the Court of Appeal, Dillon L.J., in *M. S. Fashions Ltd.* v. *Bank of Credit and Commerce International S.A.* [1993] Ch. 425, 436, 447, and the cases there referred to. The classic example of a secondary liability is a liability under a guarantee.

[86] *Esso Petroleum Co. Ltd.* v. *Alstonbridge Properties Ltd.* [1975] 1 WLR 1474, 1483.

[87] *Esso Petroleum Co. Ltd.* v. *Alstonbridge Properties Ltd.* [1975] 1 WLR 1474, 1483.

[88] (1848) 2 Ex. 471.

[89] See *Wood* v. *Goodwin* [1884] WN 17.

instrument, or against a claim for the payment of freight under a voyage charterparty or a bill of lading, though the better view is that there are no such restrictions.[90]

1.2.9 Procedural defence

Though the right of set-off derived from the Statutes of Set-off operates as a defence to an action at law for payment of a debt, it is only a procedural defence.[91] This is not to suggest that the right is wholly a matter of procedure,[92] a point that has assumed significance in some Australian States where it has been suggested that the Supreme Court Rules themselves can determine the availability of a set-off.[93] Rather, the statement that the defence provided by the Statutes is a procedural defence means that two separate and distinct debts remain in existence until there is judgment for a set-off,[94] and moreover, unlike the substantive defence of equitable set-off,[95] prior to judgment the rights consequent upon being a creditor still attach, as do the obligations and liabilities consequent upon being a debtor. As Lord Hoffman remarked in the House of Lords in *Stein* v. *Blake*,[96] 'Legal set-off does not affect the substantive rights of the parties against each other, at any rate until both causes of action have been merged in a judgment of the court'. For example, the Statute (1605) 3 Jac. 1, c. 15 provided that, if a debt of 40s. or less was owing to the plaintiff, it had to be sued for in a particular court. It was held that the amount owing had to be measured irrespective of any right of set-off available to the defendant under the Statutes,[97] the reason being that the mutual debts were still subsisting at the commencement of the action.[98]

Two lines of authority nevertheless should be distinguished. In some

---

[90] See section 1.7.14 (freight), and section 1.7.17 (negotiable instruments) below.

[91] Compare McCracken, *The Banker's Remedy of Set-off* (1993), 55, 128–30. The judgment of Warner J. in *Smit Tek International* v. *Selco Salvage Ltd*. [1988] 2 Lloyd's Rep. 398, 404–5 is confusing in this regard.

[92] See McCracken, *The Banker's Remedy of Set-off* (1993), 113 et seq.

[93] See section 1.12 below.

[94] *Briscoe* v. *Hill* (1842) 10 M & W 735, 738 per Parke B. *arguendo* ('The meaning of a plea of set-off is, that the plaintiff was and still is indebted to the defendant in a larger amount than his demand against the defendant, and in order to make that defence available, it should be equally true at the time of the trial as at the time of pleading'.); *Lee* v. *Lester* (1849) 7 CB 1008, 1015 per Maule J. *arguendo; Stooke* v. *Taylor* (1880) 5 QBD 569, 575; *In re Hiram Maxim Lamp Company* [1903] 1 Ch. 70, 74; *In re K. L. Tractors Ltd*. [1954] VLR 505, 507; *Stehar Knitting Mills Pty. Ltd*. v. *Southern Textile Converters Pty. Ltd*. [1980] 2 NSWLR 514, 518; *Covino* v. *Bandag Manufacturing Pty. Ltd*. [1983] 1 NSWLR 237, 238. See also *Ciavarella* v. *Balmer* [1983] 2 NSWLR 439, 442. For other authorities in support of this proposition, see Wood, *English and International Set-off* (1989), 43–4.

[95] See section 1.7.4 below.   [96] [1995] 2 All ER 961, 964.

[97] *Pitts* v. *Carpenter* (1743) 1 Wils. KB 19; *Gross* v. *Fisher* (1770) 3 Wils. KB 48.

[98] *Gross* v. *Fisher* (1770) 3 Wils. KB 48, 49.

early cases in which the question concerned arrest for non-payment of a debt, the balance only after setting off any mutual debt owing by the creditor to the debtor was the amount for which the creditor could procure the debtor's arrest.[99] The fact that this was so before judgment for a set-off is indicative of a substantive defence. However, these cases involved the special question of a person's liberty, and on that basis should be regarded as exceptions to the general principle that set-off under the Statutes is a procedural defence. It is also necessary to distinguish another line of cases concerning claims on penal bonds. If a bond provided for payment of a penalty in the event of a default in the payment of a sum of money, and the defendant, having defaulted in payment to the plaintiff, nevertheless was a creditor of the plaintiff for a greater amount, the plaintiff could not obtain judgment for the penalty.[100] This seems to suggest that a set-off was thought to have already occurred against the required payment, so that there was no default and therefore no justification for suing for the penalty, which in turn suggests that the set-off operated substantively. The cases however turned upon a special provision in the second Statute of Set-off ((1735) 8 Geo. II, c. 24, s. 5) that, if one of the debts in a set-off accrued by reason of a penalty contained in a bond or specialty, judgment could be entered 'for no more than shall appear to be truly and justly due to the plaintiff, after one debt being set against the other'. The view was that if the plaintiff himself was indebted to the defendant for an amount which exceeded the amount in respect of which the defendant had defaulted, there was nothing 'truly and justly due to the plaintiff', so that the plaintiff was not entitled to judgment for the amount of the penalty.

There are two concepts inherent in the notion that set-off under the Statutes is a procedural defence. The first is that legal proceedings are required in order to bring about a set-off, so that one of the parties to mutual debts cannot act unilaterally to achieve this result.[101] As Brett L.J. once aptly remarked,[102] 'the right of set-off only arises where there is an action between parties. It is a statutable remedy which only is given in the case of an action'. Indeed, this is evident from the old form of pleading

---

[99] *Dronefield* v. *Archer* (1822) 5 B & Ald. 513; *Austin* v. *Debnam* (1824) 3 B & C 139. Compare the earlier decision in *Brown* v. *Pigeon* (1811) 2 Camp. 594.

[100] *Collins* v. *Collins* (1755) 2 Burr. 820; *Lee* v. *Lester* (1849) 7 CB 1008. See also *Rodgers* v. *Maw* (1846) 15 M & W 444.

[101] See Hoffman L.J. in *Aectra Refining and Marketing Inc.* v. *Exmar NV* [1994] 1 WLR 1634, 1650. In this regard, it is difficult to follow some comments by Kerr L.J. in *BICC Plc* v. *Burndy Corporation* [1985] 1 Ch. 232, 254–5, suggesting that Burndy could have acted unilaterally to bring about a set-off so as to extinguish BICC's claim.

[102] *In re Anglo-French Co-operative Society; ex parte Pelly* (1882) 21 Ch. D 492, 507. While *Pelly* concerned a company in liquidation, it is apparent from Brett L.J.'s reference later in that paragraph to the 'statute of set-off' that he had in mind the Statutes rather than the insolvency set-off section.

applicable to set-off under the Statutes, that 'the plaintiff, before and at the time of the commencement of his suit was and from thence hitherto hath been *and still is* indebted to the defendant'.[103] The plea was bad if it was not stated that the plaintiff 'still is' indebted.[104]

The second concept is that the Statutes only authorized a set-off in legal proceedings where the set-off was being pleaded in those proceedings as a *defence*.[105] The second Statute provided that 'mutual debts may be set against each other, either by being pleaded in bar, or given in evidence on the general issue . . .'. Both the general issue and a special plea in bar were pleas which denied a cause of complaint.[106] The general issue was a plea which imported an absolute and general denial of what was alleged in the plaintiff's declaration, without offering any special matter whereby it was evaded. A special plea in bar, on the other hand, set forth the particular facts which comprised the defence. Rules made in Hilary Term, 4 Will. 4 had the effect that henceforth set-off had to be specially pleaded, and it could not be given in evidence under the general issue.[107] The point remains, though, that these pleas were the only means contemplated in the second Statute for bringing about a set-off. While the pleas themselves are now obsolete, it is apparent that the Statutes only applied where a set-off was pleaded as a defence.

These concepts nevertheless have not always been applied. Two cases are of particular interest in this regard.[108] The first is *Shipton* v. *Casson*,[109] the relevant facts of which may be summarized as follows. The plaintiff and the defendant had agreed that a debt should be payable by instalments, but, in the event of default in the payment of any one instalment, the plaintiff could accelerate the debt so that the full amount was payable. The plaintiff alleged that the first instalment in fact had not been paid in full, and accordingly sued for the full debt. The defendant pleaded that he had sold certain goods to the plaintiff, and that the plaintiff's indebtedness for the price could be set off against the unpaid part of the instalment. On that basis, it was argued that the instalment should be regarded as having

[103] See *Chitty's Precedents in Pleadings* (2nd edn., 1847), 390. If, on the other hand, the defence was that the plaintiff and the defendant had agreed prior to the action that the two debts should be set off, the defendant would plead accord and satisfaction rather than set-off. See Chitty, *op. cit.* 237–8.

[104] *Dendy* v. *Powell* (1838) 3 M & W 442.

[105] See, e.g., Parke B. in *Graham* v. *Partridge* (1836) 1 M & W 395, 401 ('The legislature constituted it a defence . . .'). In *Stein* v. *Blake* [1995] 2 All ER 961, 966 Lord Hoffman said that set-off under the Statutes 'can be invoked only by the filing of a defence in an action'.

[106] See generally *Blackstone's Commentaries* (1768) Vol. 3, 305–6.

[107] *Fidgett* v. *Penny* (1834) 1 C M & R 108; *Graham* v. *Partridge* (1836) 1 M. & W. 395.

[108] Other cases referred to in Wood, *English and International Set-off* (1989), 44–50 may be explained on other grounds. The cases referred to in Wood, *op. cit.* 50–1 should be considered in the context of combination of bank accounts rather than the Statutes of Set-off. See Ch. 11.

[109] (1826) 5 B & C 378.

been paid in full. If the instalment was paid, the plaintiff was not entitled to accelerate the debt. The defendant was successful in the action, though the justification for the result is not readily apparent. The defendant's right of set-off only entitled him to a defence to an action at law. But this should not have helped the defendant, because the point remained that he had not paid the first instalment on time. Payment in full of the instalment would only have occurred at the later date when there was judgment for a set-off. Accordingly, as a matter of principle the plaintiff should have been entitled to accelerate.

The second case is *Parker* v. *Jackson*.[110] The plaintiffs were the trustees of the will of John Parker. Prior to his death Parker had mortgaged some property for £700 to a Mrs. Williams. After Parker's death, his solicitor took a transfer of the mortgage. In addition the solicitor, once again after the death, received a sum of £2,000 constituting the proceeds of an investment made on behalf of the estate. This sum was payable to the plaintiffs as trustees of the estate. The position accordingly was that the solicitor was a creditor of the estate to the extent of £700 on the mortgage, but at the same time was liable to hand over £2,000. Subsequently, the solicitor transferred the mortgage to a client. The client as transferee gave notice of the transfer to the plaintiffs, requesting that all interest henceforth should be paid to her. The plaintiffs then brought this action seeking a declaration that the mortgage debt had been discharged, and an order for the delivery up of the mortgage deed and the documents of title. The impetus for this was that the solicitor was insolvent, so that a claim by the trustees for payment of the £2,000 would not have been satisfied. Equally, if the plaintiffs succeeded in the action so that the mortgage was discharged, the transferee would lose the mortgage and would be left with a worthless claim against the solicitor. As Farwell J. remarked, this was a case in which one of two innocent parties had to suffer. His Lordship held in favour of the plaintiffs. He said that, before the solicitor transferred the mortgage, the plaintiffs as trustees of the estate were entitled to direct the solicitor to apply part of the £2,000 in discharge of the mortgage. This was regarded as a right of set-off.[111] While the plaintiffs in fact did not give a direction to this effect, the transferee nevertheless took subject to the right to do so on the basis of the principle that an assignee takes subject to equities.

It is difficult to support Farwell J.'s view that the trustees of the estate had a right of set-off which entitled them to direct the solicitor to satisfy the mortgage debt out of the money owing to the estate. His Lordship would

---

[110] [1936] 2 All ER 281.
[111] See the judgment at [1936] 2 All ER 281, 289, 291 ('as in this case the mortgagors had an undoubted right of set-off against the assignor . . .').

Set-off

appear to have had in mind a set-off under the Statutes, although this is only a procedural defence. It does not entitle one party to mutual debts to act unilaterally to bring about a set-off by notice to the other party, but rather requires a judgment for a set-off. Indeed, the view expressed by Farwell J. does not sit easily with the principle that interest on a mortgage debt still accrues even though there may be a debt for a greater amount owing by the mortgagee to the mortgagor on another account.[112] It is also inconsistent with a dictum of Megarry J. in *Samuel Keller (Holdings) Ltd.* v. *Martins Bank Ltd.*[113] In *Samuel Keller* mortgaged premises had been sold, and the debts owing to the first and second mortgagees had been satisfied from the proceeds. The third mortgagee said that the remaining proceeds should be paid to it, while the mortgagor argued that the proceeds should be paid into court pending the determination of a damages action which the mortgagor had commenced against the third mortgagee. In holding in favour of the mortgagee Megarry J. said that:

Unless and until the mortgage in this case is discharged in the appropriate way on actual payment and acceptance of the sum due, I think that the mortgage remains a mortgage . . . Even where there is a claim which is both liquidated and admitted, and it exceeds the mortgage debt in amount, it may be to the interest of one party or the other, or both, that the mortgage and the mortgage debt should continue in existence. The rate of interest may be attractively high or seductively low; there may be fiscal advantages in keeping the mortgage alive; there may be new projects to be financed which make liquid cash preferable to the satisfaction of mortgage debts; and so on. Nor have I heard any reason why it should be the mortgagor who is to have a unilateral power to discharge the mortgage debt by appropriation without payment.

While the trustees in *Parker* v. *Jackson* in truth would not have been entitled to act unilaterally to bring about a set-off, it has been suggested that the case was still correctly decided on the ground that they had a *right* of set-off against the solicitor, and the court therefore could give a judgment for a set-off which was binding on the transferees in accordance with the usual principles governing set-off against assignees.[114] There are, however, two potential difficulties with this view.[115]

The first is that the plaintiffs were seeking a declaration that the mortgage had been discharged and an order for redemption. The Statutes

---

[112] *Garforth* v. *Bradley* (1755) 2 Ves. Sen. 675; *Fisher & Lightwood's Law of Mortgage* (10th edn., 1988) 564. See also *Pettat* v. *Ellis* (1804) 9 Ves. Jun. 563, though in any event a set-off under the Statutes was not available in that case.

[113] [1971] 1 WLR 43, 48. This passage in Megarry J.'s judgment was quoted with approval by Russell L.J. on appeal in the Court of Appeal (at 51).

[114] Wood, *English and International Set-off* (1989), 45. See generally Ch. 13.

[115] This is in addition to any difficulty that would have arisen if the solicitor held the proceeds of the investment on trust. See Ch. 6.

of Set-off, on the other hand, only authorized a set-off in legal proceedings where the set-off was pleaded as a defence. Since a set-off was not being raised as a defence in *Parker* v. *Jackson*, the case would not appear to have been within the ambit of the Statutes.[116] If a mortgagee sues for the mortgage debt, he may be met by a set-off. But as Megarry J. remarked in *Samuel Keller*, if he does not do this, and instead relies on the security as a lever in order to obtain the commercial advantages resulting from payment of the mortgage debt in the manner contemplated by the contract, he should be permitted to do so. *Unity Joint Stock Mutual Banking Association* v. *King*[117] may seem to support the contrary view. Sir John Romilly suggested in that case that, where two sons were indebted to their father and at the same time the sons were entitled to an equitable charge or lien on the father's land on the basis of an equitable proprietary estoppel arising from the expenditure of money on improvements, 'the father would be entitled to set off any sum [owing to him by the sons] against any sum due to them upon the security of this land, and that this Court would enforce such right, and cause them to deliver up the land free from any charge upon it'.[118] However, those remarks should be understood in the context of the set-off in issue, which was an equitable set-off permitted in circumstances where the father himself was not indebted to the sons for the expenditure.[119] Since the equitable charge was not security for a debt as such, but rather it was an interest in the land which the court considered that it was appropriate that the sons should have in order to satisfy the equity which arose in their favour as a result of the expenditure of money on improvements, the reasons adduced by Megarry J. for not allowing a mortgagor to appropriate a cross-debt in extinction of the mortgage debt were not applicable.

The second objection to the view that the court in *Parker* v. *Jackson* could have given a judgment for a set-off in the action before it is that, in the particular circumstances of the case, it is difficult to see how the Statutes of Set-off could have applied in any event. The solicitor's liability to the estate arose after the death when the proceeds of sale were received, and equally the solicitor obtained a claim after the death when the mortgage was transferred to him. A set-off would not have been available under the Statutes as between the deceased and the solicitor, because the Statutes required that the debts should originally have existed between two living persons.[120] Nor was there a set-off available as between the solicitor

---

[116] In *P. Rowe Graphics Pty. Ltd.* v. *Scanagraphix Pty. Ltd.* unreported, 6 September 1988, Young J. in the New South Wales Supreme Court doubted that a declaration is available in the case of a procedural defence such as that provided by the Statutes of Set-off.
[117] (1858) 25 Beav. 72.   [118] (1858) 25 Beav. 72, 79–80.
[119] See Sir John Romilly's judgment at (1858) 25 Beav. 72, 78, and also Lord Denning's discussion of the case in *Hussey* v. *Palmer* [1972] 1 WLR 1286, 1290.
[120] See section 9.9.2 below.

and the plaintiffs in their capacity as executors because, while the receipt of the proceeds of sale by the solicitor may be regarded as a debt owing to the plaintiffs in that capacity,[121] the plaintiffs themselves were not liable for payment of the mortgage debt. Consequently, there was no mutuality.[122] If a set-off had been available to the plaintiffs under the Statutes as against the solicitor, they could have waited until the transferee sued for payment, and then defended that action on the ground that the transferee took subject to the right of set-off.[123] This would have provided adequate protection to the plaintiffs. However, in the circumstances that course of action would appear not to have been open in *Parker* v. *Jackson*.

The view that the Statutes only provided a procedural defence to an action, so that separate and distinct debts remain in existence until there is judgment for a set-off, should not be confused with the ability of a court of equity in the exercise of its discretion to take into account the availability of a *right* of set-off, along with other relevant factors, when considering whether to grant an equitable remedy consequent upon the existence of a debt. Prior to judgment for a set-off, when the debts retain their separate identities, the availability of a right pursuant to the Statutes may constitute a ground for refusing the equitable relief sought.[124] An illustration is *BICC Plc* v. *Burndy Corporation*.[125] The plaintiff and the defendant were the joint owners of various patents and other rights. The plaintiff was primarily responsible for paying the costs and fees in relation to the rights, subject to a right of reimbursement of one half by the defendant. If the defendant failed to reimburse, the plaintiff could require the defendant to transfer to it all its interests in the joint rights. The defendant in fact failed to pay an invoice forwarded to it for its share of the costs, but asserted that it was entitled to do so because the plaintiff was also indebted to it, and therefore it had a set-off under the Statutes for an amount which exceeded its own liability. The plaintiff then brought this action seeking specific perform- ance of the assignment. The Court of Appeal held that a right of set-off under the Statutes constituted a defence to an application for specific performance[126] and that, in any event, the set-off provided grounds for relief against forfeiture of the rights. However, this should not be taken as authority for proposition that, because of the availability of the set-off, there had not been default.[127] Rather, given that a claim by the plaintiff for

---

[121] See *Rees* v. *Watts* (1855) 11 Ex. 410, 415 in relation to the plaintiff administrator's claim for money had and received by the defendant for the use of the plaintiff as administrator.

[122] The demands would not have been sufficiently closely connected to give rise to an equitable set-off, for which mutuality is not a strict requirement. See section 1.7.6 below.

[123] See section 13.2 below.

[124] See also *Dodd* v. *Lydall* (1842) 1 Hare 331 (decree of foreclosure), in which the set-off in issue appears to have been an equitable set-off arising by analogy with the Statutes of Set-off, for which see section 1.6 below.   [125] [1985] 1 Ch. 232.

[126] Note however the discussion of *BICC* v. *Burndy* in section 1.8 below.

[127] Compare McCracken, *The Banker's Remedy of Set-off* (1993), 130.

payment would have failed because of the defence of the set-off, it was considered to be inappropriate that a claim for equitable relief which depended upon non-payment instead should be available.[128] Equally, the fact that there was a defence to a claim for payment constituted grounds for equitable intervention in the form of relief against forfeiture.[129]

1.2.10 *Cross-debt must be enforceable*

Because the defence of set-off under the Statutes is merely procedural, the cross-debt sought to be set off must be enforceable by action at the time that the plaintiff commences his suit.[130] In the case of a limitation period applicable to the cross-debt pursuant to the Limitation Act 1980, this principle is reflected in section 35 subsections (1) & (2) of the Act.

In accordance with that principle, the courts have held that a set-off under the Statutes may not be based upon a debt which is unenforceable, not only because of the expiration of a limitation period,[131] but also because of moratorium legislation;[132] because the plaintiff contracted the debt during his infancy;[133] because of the operation of the Statutes of Frauds;[134] or because the plaintiff had obtained a discharge under the former insolvent debtor's legislation.[135] There are, nevertheless, two apparent exceptions. The first arises in relation to the statutory provision that a solicitor must deliver a bill of costs in the proper form before he can bring an action to recover the costs.[136] It has been held that a solicitor may employ the debt for costs in a set-off even though he has not complied with this requirement.[137] In *Rawley* v. *Rawley*[138] Mellish L.J. sought to explain this result on the ground that the statute in question merely postponed the remedy of bringing action until a bill of costs was delivered, and left other remedies untouched,[139] although in Australia and Canada it has been held

---

[128] See the 'crucial question' framed by Dillon L.J. at [1985] 1 Ch. 232, 248.
[129] *Quaere* whether relief against forfeiture indeed was appropriate in this instance. See Note (1985) 101 *Law Quarterly Review* 145, 146.
[130] *Walker* v. *Clements* (1850) 15 QB 1046; *McDonnell & East Ltd.* v. *McGregor* (1936) 56 CLR 50, 57; *Aectra Refining and Marketing Inc.* v. *Exmar NV* [1994] 1 WLR 1634, 1650–1. This principle obviously could not apply in relation to a debt which arises after the commencement of the platintiff's action, assuming that *Richard* v. *James* (1848) 2 Ex. 471 would no longer be followed so that such a debt is capable of being pleaded as a set-off under the Statutes. See section 1.2.2 above. Under that circumstance it may be that enforceability would be determined when the set-off is pleaded.
[131] *Remington* v. *Stevens* (1748) 2 Str. 1271; *Walker* v. *Clements* (1850) 15 QB 1046. See also *Smith* v. *Betty* [1903] 2 KB 317; *In re Morris, Deceased, Coneys* v. *Morris* [1922] 1 I.R. 136.   [132] *Rex* v. *Ray; ex parte Chapman* [1936] SASR 241.
[133] *Rex* v. *Ray; ex parte Chapman* [1936] SASR 241. *Rawley* v. *Rawley* (1876) 1 QBD 460.
[134] *Salisbury Jones* v. *Southwood and Company* (1941), unreported but noted at 193 LT 48.
[135] *Francis* v. *Dodsworth* (1847) 4 CB 202.   [136] Solicitors Act 1974, s. 69.
[137] *Brown* v. *Tibbitts* (1862) 11 CB(NS) 855; *Robinson* v. *Vale* [1905] VLR 405; *Currie* v. *The Law Society* [1977] 1 QB 990, 995.   [138] (1876) 1 QB 160.
[139] (1876) 1 QBD 160, 168.

in other contexts that the principle that the debt sought to be set off must be enforceable by action also applies during any period when the remedy of bringing an action is suspended.[140] The second apparent exception arises in relation to an alien enemy. As a matter of public policy an alien enemy cannot sue as plaintiff in English courts while the state of hostilities subsists,[141] although, when he is being sued as a defendant, he is entitled to appear and be heard in his defence.[142] This includes defending an action by way of set-off.[143] Pleading a cross-demand as a set-off is permitted because it cannot result in an order for payment to the alien enemy.[144] In this regard it should be distinguished from counterclaim. An alien enemy is not permitted to counterclaim because it may result in a larger sum being payable to the alien enemy than would be payable by him to the plaintiff.[145] One commentator has suggested that the right of an alien enemy to plead a set-off should be confined to the substantive form of equitable set-off discussed later in this chapter (see section 1.7 below).[146] However, if the justification for allowing a set-off is that it cannot result in an order for payment to the enemy alien, it is difficult to see why it should be so restricted.

1.2.11 Cross-debt must be able to be determined in the plaintiff's action

Consistent with the notion that set-off under the Statutes of Set-off is merely a procedural defence, any dispute on the cross-debt sought to be set off must be able to be determined by the court in the plaintiff's action. Accordingly, in an application by a plaintiff for summary judgment, leave to defend will not be granted on the basis of a set-off under the Statutes if the court in the plaintiff's action would refuse to try the merits of the case on the cross-debt, because the cross-debt is the subject of an arbitration clause or a foreign jurisdiction clause to which the court would give effect.[147] On the other hand, the court still has a discretion in such a case to stay execution on the judgment given in favour of the plaintiff until the cross-debt is determined by the appropriate tribunal.[148]

---

[140] *Rex* v. *Ray; ex parte Chapman* [1936] SASR 241; *Atlantic Acceptance Corporation Ltd.* v. *Burns & Dutton Construction (1962) Ltd.* (1970) 14 DLR (3d) 175 (though note the criticism of that case in Palmer, *The Law of Set-off in Canada* (1993), 29–30).
[141] *Robinson & Co.* v. *Continental Insurance Company of Mannheim* [1915] 1 KB 155, 159.
[142] *Porter* v. *Freudenberg* [1915] 1 KB 857, 883.
[143] *In re Stahlwerk Becker Aktiengesellschaft's Patent* [1917] 2 Ch. 272, 273, 275–6.
[144] *In re Stahlwerk Becker Aktiengesellschaft's Patent* [1917] 2 Ch. 272, 276.
[145] *In re Stahlwerk Becker Aktiengesellschaft's Patent* [1917] 2 Ch. 272, 276.
[146] See Wood, *English and International Set-off* (1989), 755, who describes this form of set-off as a transaction set-off.
[147] *Aectra Refining and Marketing Inc.* v. *Exmar NV* [1994] 1 WLR 1634.
[148] *Aectra Refining and Marketing Inc.* v. *Exmar NV* [1994] 1 WLR 1634, 1652.

Unlike set-off under the Statutes, equitable set-off and common law abatement are generally regarded as substantive defences.[149] Accordingly, there is no such objection to the court giving effect to the defence in these circumstances.[150]

1.2.12 Trustees

A trustee may hold a debt as trust property, and also may have incurred a debt to the debtor in his capacity as trustee. The question whether these can be set off under the Statutes of Set-off is considered later.[151]

1.3 CONNECTED CROSS-DEMANDS AT COMMON LAW

In *Green* v. *Farmer*[152] Lord Mansfield remarked that:

Where the nature of the employment, transaction, or dealings, necessarily constitutes an account consisting of receipts and payments, debts and credits; it is certain that only the balance can be the debt; and by the proper forms of proceeding in Courts of Law or Equity, the balance only can be recovered.

The third edition of *Halsbury's Laws of England*[153] cited *Green* v. *Farmer* as authority for the proposition that 'Where opposing demands are connected by originating in the same transaction the balance has always been regarded by the common law as the debt so that no question of set-off arises'.

Lord Denning referred to that statement with approval in *The Brede*,[154] and indeed its substance has a long history which can be traced back to similar statements in early books on set-off by Babington in 1827[155] and Montague in 1828.[156] On the other hand, the editors of the fourth edition of *Halsbury* doubted, with some apparent justification, whether it is correct.[157] The better view is that Lord Mansfield had in mind a running

---

[149] See section 1.7.4 below in relation to equitable set-off. While in Australia there is authority for the view that common law abatement is procedural, the English courts regard it as a substantive defence. See section 1.10 below.

[150] *Aectra Refining and Marketing Inc.* v. *Exmar NV* [1994] 1 WLR 1634, 1649, referring to *Gilbert-Ash (Northern) Ltd.* v. *Modern Engineering (Bristol) Ltd.* [1974] AC 689 (esp. at 720, 726).   [151] See section 13.4.1 below.

[152] (1768) 4 Burr. 2214, 2221.

[153] *Halsbury's Laws of England* (3rd edn. 1960) Vol. 34, p. 396 para. 673 n. (*l*).

[154] *Henriksens Rederi A/S* v. *THZ Rolimpex (The Brede)* [1974] 1 QB 233, 246.

[155] Babington, *The Law of Set-off and Mutual Credit* (1827), 4.

[156] Montague, *Summary of the Law of Set-off* (2nd edn., 1828), 1.

[157] *Halsbury's Laws of England* (4th edn., 1983) Vol. 42, p. 246 para. 421 n. 2. See also *P. Rowe Graphics Pty. Ltd.* v. *Scanagraphix Pty. Ltd.* unreported, Young J., Supreme Court of New South Wales, 26 August 1988.

account. A running account is not a case of opposing demands at all. Rather, there is a series of debits and credits which gives rise to a single debt for the balance. It is difficult to find evidence of a general common law principle by which a balance may be struck, without recourse to the principles of set-off, in a case in which there are indeed opposing demands which originated in the same transaction. With the exception of *Dale* v. *Sollett*[158] (discussed below), the cases referred to by Babington and Montague were instances in which there was an agreement between the parties for payment of a liability,[159] or alternatively there was a custom by which payment could be effected by way of a deduction.[160]

There are, nevertheless, certain specific instances in which the common law has recognized that connected cross-demands may produce a balance outside the ambit of the established principles of set-off, though these constitute exceptions rather than the rule. One such case is common law abatement, which is discussed later.[161] Another is to be found in a judgment of Lord Mansfield which was handed down the year before that in *Green* v. *Farmer*. In *Dale* v. *Sollett*[162] it was held that an agent who recovered money on behalf of his principal could deduct from the proceeds an amount sufficient to recompense him for his labour and service in relation to the recovery. This was not by way of set-off as such, but rather was a common law right of deduction.[163] Thus, Lord Mansfield explained the result on the ground that:

The plaintiff can recover no more than he is in conscience and equity entitled to: which can be no more than what remains after deducting all just allowances which the defendant has a right to retain out of the very sum demanded. This is not in the nature of a cross-demand or mutual debt: it is a charge, which makes the sum of money received for the plaintiff's use so much less.[164]

1.4 JUDGMENTS

Usually issues of set-off arise in the situation in which there are two unlitigated cross-claims. It may be, however, that one or both of the claims has proceeded to judgment, and it is sought to rely on that judgment debt as a defence to an action by the judgment debtor to enforce another debt. Alternatively, the judgment debtor may seek to set off that judgment

---

[158] (1767) 4 Burr. 2133.
[159] See *Dobson* v. *Lockhart* (1793) 5 TR 133; *James* v. *Kynnier* (1799) 5 Ves. Jun. 108; *Sturdy* v. *Arnaud* (1790) 3 TR 599; *Roper* v. *Bumford* (1810) 3 Taunt. 76. See also *Le Loir* v. *Bristow* (1815) 4 Camp. 134.   [160] *Bamford* v. *Harris* (1816) 1 Stark. 343.
[161] See section 1.10 below.   [162] (1767) 4 Burr. 2133.
[163] See the discussion in *Re Sutcliffe and Sons Ltd.* [1933] 1 DLR 562, 566.
[164] (1767) 4 Burr. 2133, 2134.

against a judgment that he himself has obtained in separate proceedings against the judgment creditor. A third possibility is that execution on a judgment properly obtained at law is sought to be stayed on the basis of an unlitigated cross-claim. Each of these situations is considered in turn.

1.4.1 Pleading a judgment debt as a defence under the Statutes

A judgment for payment of a sum of money gives rise to a debt,[165] and accordingly it should be able to form the basis of a defence of set-off under the Statutes to an action by the judgment debtor for payment of a separate debt owing to him by the judgment creditor.[166] The case would be one of mutual debts for the purpose of the Statutes. This should apply equally when the judgment arises out of an action for unliquidated damages. Upon the occurrence of the judgment the claim becomes a debt[167] which should be within the ambit of the Statutes.[168]

1.4.2 Stay of execution on the basis of an unlitigated cross-claim

Subject to the discussion below of equitable set-off, a judgment debtor may not extinguish or reduce the amount of the judgment by setting off an unlitigated simple contract debt owing to him by the judgment creditor.[169] The question arises, however, whether an unlitigated cross-claim instead may provide a justification for staying execution on the judgment. In this regard, a distinction must be drawn between a judgment which has been obtained pursuant to the procedure for summary judgment, and a judgment which the plaintiff received after his case went to trial.

Summary judgment is available where it appears that there is no defence to the claim, although a stay of execution may be available on the basis of

---

[165] *Hodsoll* v. *Baxter* (1858) El. Bl. & El. 884.

[166] *Baskerville* v. *Brown* (1761) 2 Burr. 1229; *Watkins* v. *Clark* (1862) 12 CB(NS) 277. See also *Russell* v. *May* (1828) 7 LJOSKB 88; *Cochrane* v. *Green* (1860) 9 CB(NS) 448; *Lawrence* v. *Hayes* [1927] 2 KB 111. Formerly, if a judgment creditor had taken the body of the judgment debtor in execution pursuant to a writ of *capias ad satisfaciendum*, the judgment creditor could not set off the judgment as a defence to an action brought by the debtor on a cross-demand. See *Taylor* v. *Waters* (1816) 5 M & S 103; *Tidd's Practice* (9th edn., 1828) Vol. 2, 1029. See also, and compare, *Thompson* v. *Parish* (1859) 28 LJCP 153 (overruling *Peacock* v. *Jeffrey* (1809) 1 Taunt. 426). However, this principle turned upon a peculiarity of the writ, that the taking of a debtor's body in execution constituted a bar to any other remedy against the debtor during his life, which included employing the judgment debt in a set-off.

[167] See the discussion in *Jones* v. *Thompson* (1858) El. Bl. & Bl. 63.

[168] This seemed to be the view of Balcombe L.J. in *B. Hargreaves Ltd.* v. *Action 2000 Ltd.* [1993] BCLC 1111, 1115.

[169] *Philipson* v. *Caldwell* (1815) 6 Taunt. 176; *Hawkins* v. *Baynes and Ireland* (1823) 1 LJOSKB 167; *Chitty's Practice* (3rd edn., 1837) Vol. 1, 140. See also *Newton* v. *Newton* (1832) 8 Bing. 202, 203.

an alleged cross-claim if the cross-claim appears to be plausible to the extent that it is not unreasonably possible for it to succeed if brought to trial.[170] This is not a particularly rigorous test. It may be justified on the ground that a summary judgment is a judgment obtained at the very outset of proceedings before the defendant has had an opportunity to litigate his cross-claim.[171] Different considerations apply, however, if the action in respect of which judgment was given in fact had proceeded to trial. In such a case, the defendant will not obtain a stay simply by showing that he has an arguable cross-claim.[172] Rather, he must show 'special circumstances', within the meaning of RSC Order 47, rule 1.[173] An illustration is *Schofield* v. *Church Army*.[174] The respondent in that case was summarily dismissed from his employment by the appellant for allegedly stealing money. An industrial tribunal found that the dismissal was unfair, and ordered the appellant to pay him compensation. The respondent obtained an *ex parte* order in the county court to enforce the tribunal's order, and also a garnishee order nisi attaching the appellant's bank account. The amount standing to the credit of the account was paid into court, and the respondent applied for an order that the money be paid to him. Meanwhile the appellant had commenced a civil action against the respondent alleging theft, and opposed the payment to the respondent. The Court of Appeal[175] considered that the question whether the money should be handed over should be determined by the same principles applicable to whether execution on a judgment should be stayed. In the instant case it was held that there were indeed special circumstances sufficient to support a stay. The industrial tribunal had no jurisdiction to entertain the appellant's allegation of theft as a counterclaim to the respondent's claim for unfair dismissal. Nor was there any suggestion that the appellant had been dilatory in prosecuting its claim. Under the circumstances, it was considered to be inappropriate that the money be paid out before the civil action against the respondent came on for trial.

Special considerations apply when the cross-demands are such as to give rise to an equitable set-off, either on the basis of equity acting by analogy with the legal right of set-off conferred by the Statutes of Set-off when the demands are mutual having regard to equitable rights,[176] or alternatively when there is a substantive defence of equitable set-off arising from a sufficiently close connection between the demands.[177] In one case,

---

[170] See Dillon L.J. in *Schofield* v. *Church Army* [1986] 1 WLR 1328, 1334–5, referring to Lord Esher in *Sheppards and Co.* v. *Wilkinson and Jarvis* (1889) 6 TLR 13.
[171] See Dillon L.J. in *Schofield* v. *Church Army* [1986] 1 WLR 1328, 1335.
[172] See Lord Denning M.R. in *Wagner* v. *Laubscher Bros. & Co.* [1970] 2 QB 313, 317.
[173] *Schofield* v. *Church Army* [1986] 1 WLR 1328.
[174] [1986] 1 WLR 1328.   [175] Dillon and Croom-Johnson L.JJ.
[176] See section 1.6 below.   [177] See section 1.7 below.

a judgment had been obtained at law but the assistance of a court of equity was required to enforce the judgment, and an equitable set-off was allowed to be raised in those proceedings. In *Jenner* v. *Morris*[178] the plaintiff had recovered judgment against the defendant, and filed a bill in equity for the purpose of enforcing the judgment against a life interest of the defendant in certain real estate. The defendant argued as a defence that he had made loans to the plaintiff's wife so that she could purchase necessaries, the wife having been deserted by the plaintiff. While a person who actually supplied necessaries to a deserted wife could sue the husband at common law, the common law did not recognize a similar right in a person who merely lent money to the wife for the purpose of acquiring necessaries. However, it was held in *Jenner* v. *Morris* that the lender had a claim in equity against the husband, on the basis that the lender could stand in the shoes of the supplier in respect of the supplier's remedy against the husband, and, further, that the defendant in the instant case could set off against the judgment the plaintiff's liability to him in equity arising from the advances. In allowing a set-off equity acted by analogy with the legal right of set-off in the case of mutual debts, in that there was a debt due at common law from the defendant to the plaintiff and a debt in equity owing by the plaintiff to the defendant.[179]

On a more general ground, prior to the Judicature Acts equitable set-offs could be enforced by means of a common injunction restraining execution obtained on a judgment at law.[180] While a defendant in an action at law may now plead an equitable set-off as a defence in that action, the better view is that he is not obliged to do so, but may still apply separately for equitable relief in accordance with the old practice.[181] Nevertheless, in a particular case the circumstances may be such that it would be inappropriate to grant an injunction (or a stay) on the basis of an unlitigated cross-claim. This may be the case, for example, if the defendant has not diligently pursued his cross-claim.[182] Another instance appears

---

[178] (1860) 1 Dr. & Sm. 218, affirmed (1861) 3 De G F & J 45.

[179] See the comments by Kindersley V.C. in other proceedings between the same parties (*Jenner* v. *Morris* (1860) 1 Dr. & Sm. 334, 336) in relation to his earlier decision in the instant case which was the subject of the appeal to Lord Campbell and Turner L.J. Lord Campbell remarked in his judgment ((1861) 3 De G F & J 45, 53–4) that the cross-demands were wholly unconnected, so that it is clear that a substantive defence of equitable set-off was not in issue.

[180] See *Hamp* v. *Jones* (1840) 9 LJ Ch. 258; *Smith* v. *Parkes* (1852) 16 Beav. 115. Compare *Rawson* v. *Samuel* (1841) Cr. & Ph. 161 and *Hill* v. *Ziymak* (1908) 7 CLR 352, in each of which it was assumed that an equitable set-off could be enforced by means of an injunction to restrain execution on a judgment obtained at law, though it was held that an equitable set-off in any event was not available on other grounds.

[181] Meagher, Gummow & Lehane, *Equity: Doctrines and Remedies* (3rd edn., 1992), 825.

[182] *J. C. Scott Constructions* v. *Mermaid Waters Tavern Pty. Ltd.* [1983] 2 Qd. R 252. Compare *Masterman* v. *Malin* (1831) 7 Bing. 435, in which the hearing of the cross-claim was ready to proceed, so that there would only have been a 'brief suspension' of the plaintiff's right to obtain the benefit of the judgment.

from the leading case of *Rawson* v. *Samuel*.[183] The applicants sought an injunction to restrain execution on a judgment at law for damages for breach of contract until an account could be taken of amounts due under the contract. Lord Cottenham pointed out that the account would be long and complicated,[184] and it could not be assumed that the balance would be in favour of the applicants. If the balance in fact should be found to be in favour of the plaintiff at law, he may not have been adequately compensated for the delay in enforcing the judgment. Accordingly, the applicants did not have a sufficient equitable ground to support an injunction.

Execution on a judgment obtained at law generally will not be stayed on the basis of a cross-claim that accrued *after* the judgment.[185] It is not considered to be reasonable that a cross-demand subsequently acquired should delay the plaintiff from the benefit of his judgment until the validity of the cross-demand can be tested.[186] This should however be subject to an exception in the case of a substantive defence of equitable set-off arising out of a sufficiently close connection, and indeed there is an instance at common law in which cross-demands originated in the same transaction, and execution on a judgment obtained by one party on his demand was stayed until the other party could obtain judgment on the cross-demand,[187] though the facts in issue were exceptional.

1.4.3 Setting off judgments and orders

It has been the practice of the common law courts since the eighteenth century to allow one judgment or order for the payment of a sum of money to be set off against another.[188] This practice extends to a judgment for damages[189] as well as to an order for the costs,[190] including costs in

---

[183] (1841) Cr. & Ph. 161. See also *Preston* v. *Strutton* (1792) 1 Anstr. 50; *Hill* v. *Ziymak* (1908) 7 CLR 352.

[184] This should be compared to Lord Cottenham's judgment a few weeks earlier in *Clark* v. *Cort* (1840) Cr. & Ph. 154 in which an account was also required to be taken, though apparently it was less complicated than that in *Rawson* v. *Samuel* because his Lordship held that it could be the subject of a set-off.

[185] *Whyte* v. *O'Brien* (1824) 1 Sim. & St. 551; *Maw* v. *Ulyatt* (1861) 31 LJ Ch. 33. Compare *Gale* v. *Luttrell* (1826) 1 Y & J 180.

[186] See Sir John Leach in *Whyte* v. *O'Brien* (1824) 1 Sim. & St. 551.

[187] *Alliance Bank of London and Liverpool* v. *Holford* (1864) 16 CB(NS) 460.

[188] See, e.g., *Thrustout* v. *Crafter* (1772) 2 Wm. Bl. 826. Montague, *Summary of the Law of Set-off* (2nd edn., 1828), 4 n. n dates the practice from 23 Geo II (1750), while according to Babington (*The Law of Set-off and Mutual Credit* (1827), 95–6), it became entrenched after 24 Geo II. Prior to these dates, the courts had refused to allow judgments to be set off. See, e.g., *Butler* v. *Inneys* (1731) 2 Stra. 891; *Tito* v. *Duthie* (1744) 2 Stra. 1203.

[189] *Edwards* v. *Hope* (1885) 14 QBD 922, 926.

[190] *Reid* v. *Cupper* [1915] 2 KB 147; *R.* v. *Leeds County Court, ex parte Morris* [1990] 1 QB 523.

bankruptcy proceedings[191] and costs when one of the parties is legally aided.[192] It applies to judgments in the same action or in different actions, or in the same or different courts.[193] Nor is it an objection that one of the judgments had existed at the commencement of the other action, and might have been pleaded as a defence in that action.[194] The set-off in these cases is not pursuant to the Statutes of Set-off, but rather it is allowed in the discretion of the court as part of its inherent jurisdiction.[195] It has been described as a form of 'equitable' jurisdiction possessed by the common law courts for the purpose of preventing absurdity or injustice.[196] In allowing a set-off the court is at liberty to impose such terms as it considers reasonable and just.[197]

Recently the Court of Appeal[198] in *Lockley* v. *National Blood Transfusion Service*[199] suggested that the set-off in question in fact is an equitable set-off arising from a close connection between the claims, though this should not be regarded as correct. Indeed, in many cases it would be difficult to assert that the impeachment test, which is the traditional foundation of equitable set-off,[200] has been satisfied. This is particularly so where judgments and orders in different actions are in issue.[201] The set-off in truth has a common law origin. It is part of the court's inherent jurisdiction.

though between the same parties, nevertheless are in different rights, as where one of the parties is merely a trustee in relation to one judgment but in the other is interested in his own right.[202] Even before the Judicature Acts the common law courts would take notice of a trust and deny a set-off on this ground.[203] Conversely, the common law courts in the exercise of

---

[191] *In re A Debtor, No. 21 of 1950 (No. 2)* [1951] 1 Ch. 612.

[192] *Lockley* v. *National Blood Transfusion Service* [1992] 1 WLR 492.

[193] *Edwards* v. *Hope* (1885) 14 QBD 922, 927. See, e.g., *Hall* v. *Oddy* (1799) 2 Bos. & Pul. 28; *Bridges* v. *Smyth* (1831) 8 Bing. 29; *Bristowe* v. *Needham* (1844) 7 Man. & G 648, 649. The court has a discretion to set off the costs payable by one party in an action against a judgment in that same action for the payment of money to that party. See *Goldsborough Mort & Co. Ltd.* v. *Quin* (1910) 10 CLR 674. In Queensland see in this regard Ord. 91 r. 11 SCR.

[194] *Barker* v. *Braham* (1773) 2 Wm. Bl. 869.

[195] *In re A Debtor, No. 21 of 1950 (No. 2)* [1951] 1 Ch. 612, 617–18. As Lord Campbell C.J. remarked in *Simpson* v. *Lamb* (1857) 7 El. & Bl. 84, 89, 'There is no strict right to such a set-off . . .'.

[196] *Edwards* v. *Hope* (1885) 14 QBD 922, 926; *Reid* v. *Cupper* [1915] 2 KB 147, 149. See also *Simpson* v. *Lamb* (1857) 7 El. & Bl. 84, 89, 90. In *Barker* v. *Braham* (1773) 2 Wm. Bl. 869, 872 Blackstone J. in the Common Pleas described it as an 'equitable remedy'.

[197] *Edwards* v. *Hope* (1885) 14 QBD 922, 927.

[198] Farquharson and Scott L.JJ. and Sir John Megaw.

[199] [1992] 1 WLR 492, 496–7.

[200] See section 1.7 below.   [201] See above.

[202] *David* v. *Rees* [1904] 2 KB 435, 443 (referring to *Lush's Practice* (3rd edn.), 328), 445–6; *Bristowe* v. *Needham* (1844) 7 Man. & G 648.

[203] *Bristowe* v. *Needham* (1844) 7 Man. & G 648.

their 'equitable' jurisdiction would look behind the parties on the record and allow a set-off of judgments if, having regard to the parties truly interested in the judgments, it was considered just that this occur.[204] This applied in particular where A was a judgment creditor of B on one claim, and A had agreed to indemnify C against a judgment obtained against him by B on another claim, so that A was the party who as a matter of substance had the burden of this second judgment.[205]

The principle that the cross-judgments should be held in the same right does not preclude a set-off in the situation in which one of the parties died after obtaining judgment.[206] It does prevent a set-off, however, if one of the judgments was assigned to a third party, and notice of the assignment was given before the cross-judgment was obtained against the assignor.[207] It also applies if one of the parties was bankrupt, and the judgment was obtained in an action brought by the trustee in bankruptcy.[208] In such a case the cross-demands may be such that a set-off would be available in any event under the insolvency legislation. But if a bankruptcy has intervened, and for some reason the set-off section in the insolvency legislation is not applicable to the cross-actions in respect of which the judgments were obtained, Lord Ellenborough warned that the courts have a 'strong disinclination' to allow a set-off of the judgments pursuant to their equitable jurisdiction.[209] Indeed, it is unlikely that a set-off would ever be permitted in that circumstance today.

Where A has a judgment against B and C, and B has a separate judgment against A, the courts have been prepared to set off the judgments,[210] notwithstanding that a joint demand and a several liability

---

[204] See, e.g., *O'Connor* v. *Murphy* (1791) 1 H Bl. 657; *Standeven* v. *Murgatroyd* (1858) 27 LJ Ex. 425. See also, and compare, *Currie & Co.* v. *The Law Society* [1977] 1 QB 990 (assignment of judgment to the debtor on another judgment).

[205] *Schoole* v. *Noble, Lett, and Byrne* (1788) 1 H Bl. 24; *O'Connor* v. *Murphy* (1791) 1 H Bl. 657; *Bourne* v. *Benett* (1827) 4 Bing. 423; *Standeven* v. *Murgatroyd* (1858) 27 LJ Ex. 425.

[206] *Bridges* v. *Smyth* (1831) 8 Bing. 29.

[207] See, and compare, *Simpson* v. *Lamb* (1857) 7 El. & Bl. 84, where the assignment occurred between verdict and judgment, though it seems clear that the court would have reached the same conclusion on this point if the assignment had occurred after the judgment. Compare also *Bank of New South Wales* v. *Preston* (1894) 20 VLR 1, in which the assignment occurred after the cross-judgment had been obtained, and the assignee was aware of all the circumstances. It was held that he took subject to a set-off.

[208] *Doe* v. *Darnton* (1802) 3 East 149.

[209] *Doe* v. *Darnton* (1802) 3 East 149, 150, though compare the special circumstances in *Alliance Bank of London & Liverpool Ltd.* v. *Holford* (1864) 16 CB(NS) 460. Note that, when there have been orders in the same suit for payment of costs by each party to the other, the court subsequently may order that the costs be set off notwithstanding an intervening liquidation of one of the parties. See *J. Earle Hermann Ltd.* v. *North Sydney* (1914) 31 WN (NSW) 166.

[210] *Roberts* v. *Biggs* Barnes 146; *Mitchell* v. *Oldfield* (1791) 4 TR 123; *Dennie* v. *Elliott* (1795) 2 H Bl. 587. Compare *Bourne* v. *Benett* (1827) 4 Bing. 423, 1 Moo. & P 141, in which

are not regarded as mutual.[211] In the cases where this occurred there was no question of a bankruptcy, and the courts in exercising their 'equitable' jurisdiction did not consider that they were limited by the scope of the right of set-off available under the Statutes of Set-off in the case of mutual debts.[212] If, however, B has become bankrupt, so that the separate action against A was brought by his trustee in bankruptcy for the benefit of his general body of creditors, a set-off will not be permitted in respect of judgments upon the cross-actions in circumstances where it is not available under the set-off section in the insolvency legislation.[213]

A solicitor who has conducted a case to trial has a charge (or lien) over the proceeds of a judgment obtained by his client for his costs in relation to the action.[214] Obviously the fund available to satisfy the lien will be reduced if there is a set-off against the judgment. At one time the various common law courts adopted different attitudes to the treatment of a solicitor's lien in an application to set off judgments. The Court of King's Bench held that the set-off was subject to the lien, so that the lien had to be satisfied before the set-off could take effect.[215] The Common Pleas, on the other hand, said that the lien should be disregarded, on the basis that the solicitor should look in the first instance to the personal security of his client for payment.[216] Insofar as the Exchequer was concerned, it would appear that the court exercised its discretion according to the circumstances of the case.[217] The modern view is that a set-off of judgments should not be refused on account of a solicitor's lien, if as between the parties themselves a set-off would be fair and just, and if no fraud or imposition has been practised upon the solicitor by collusion between the parties.[218]

there was the additional element that one of the defendants against whom judgment was given in fact had agreed to indemnify those other parties against the judgment, so that he was principally liable *inter se*. It was held that the judgment should be set off against a separate judgment obtained by that defendant against the plaintiff. In allowing the set-off Park J. emphasized this additional element, though the earlier cases referred to above suggest that a set-off would have been available in any event.

[211] See section 8.2 below.
[212] *Mitchell* v. *Oldfield* (1791) 4 TR 123, 124.
[213] *Doe* v. *Darnton* (1802) 3 East 149.
[214] *In re Wadsworth; Rhodes* v. *Sugden* (1886) 34 Ch. D 155, 158–9.
[215] *Mitchell* v. *Oldfield* (1791) 4 TR 123; *Randle* v. *Fuller* (1795) 6 TR 457.
[216] *Hall* v. *Oddy* (1799) 2 Bos. & Pul. 28; *Bridges* v. *Smyth* (1831) 8 Bing. 29.
[217] See Pickford L.J. in *Reid* v. *Cupper* [1915] 2 KB 147, 156.
[218] *Puddephatt* v. *Leith (No. 2)* [1916] 2 Ch. 168; *Currie* v. *The Law Society* [1977] 1 QB 990, 999. See also *In re A Debtor, No. 21 of 1950 (No. 2)* [1951] 1 Ch. 612, and *Knight* v. *Knight* [1925] 1 Ch. 835. In Australia see *Butcher* v. *Colonial Wholesale Meat Co. Ltd.* (1920) 38 WN(NSW) 24; *Miller & Co. Machinery Pty. Ltd.* v. *Bear* [1934] VLR 85. In Queensland, compare Ord. 91 r. 12 of the Supreme Court Rules, which provides that a set-off of judgments is subject to the solicitor's lien.

1.5 EQUITABLE SET-OFF: INTRODUCTION

Prior to the Judicature Acts, equitable set-offs generally were enforced by means of an injunction to restrain the plaintiff at law from either proceeding with an action or alternatively enforcing a judgment against the defendant until he had given credit to the defendant for the amount of the cross-demand, though since the Judicature Acts the defendant has been permitted to plead the set-off as a defence in the plaintiff's action.[219] An equitable set-off can take a number of forms. There are some early cases in which debts were set off in equity based upon an implied agreement that this should occur,[220] and indeed Sir Joseph Jekyll once said that 'the least evidence of an agreement for a [set-off] will do', and that 'equity will take hold of a very slight thing to do both parties right'.[221] Another instance has arisen in the context of equitable proprietary estoppel. If A as a result of the expenditure of money on B's land is entitled to an equitable charge or lien on the land, but A also happens to be indebted to B, it has been said that A may 'set off' the debt owing to him against the sum secured by the charge.[222] This is not a case of set-off in the strict sense of the word, since B is not indebted to A in respect of the expenditure. Rather, it is an amount that must be paid in order to take the land free of the charge. It is nevertheless analogous to a set-off. Apart from these cases, there are two principal forms of equitable set-off.

1.6 ACTING BY ANALOGY WITH THE STATUTES

In the first place, equity may act by analogy with the legal right of set-off conferred by the Statutes of Set-off when there are mutual liquidated cross-demands having regard to equitable rights. This may arise because one of the demands itself is a matter of equitable jurisdiction[223] (other than for payment of a trust fund, a claim for which generally cannot be met by a set-off under the Statutes[224]), or alternatively because a common law debt is held on trust or has been the subject of an equitable assignment so that the requirement of mutuality is satisfied only by reference to the equitable

---

[219] See now the Supreme Court Act 1981, s. 49, and Ord. 18, r. 17 RSC.

[220] *Downam* v. *Matthews* (1721) Prec. Ch. 580; *Hawkins* v. *Freeman* 2 Eq. Ca. Abr. 10; *Jeffs* v. *Wood* (1723) 2 P Wms. 128; *Wallis* v. *Bastard* (1853) 4 De G M & G 251.

[221] *Jeffs* v. *Wood* (1723) 2 P Wms. 128, 130.

[222] *Unity Joint Stock Mutual Banking Association* v. *King* (1858) 25 Beav. 72, 79–80.

[223] *Kostka* v. *Addison* [1986] 1 Qd. R 416.

[224] See Ch. 6 below.

titles.[225] If special circumstances render it unjust that a set-off should occur, a court of equity in the exercise of its discretion nevertheless may refuse to allow a set-off by analogy with the Statutes.[226] On the other hand, when there are mutual liquidated cross-demands having regard to equitable rights, it is not necessary for the defendant to show some additional equity to support a set-off. Observations to the contrary[227] are difficult to support.[228]

We have already seen that the right of set-off available pursuant to the Statutes is procedural in its operation, so that two separate and distinct debts remain in existence until there is judgment for a set-off.[229] Further, as Lord Eldon once remarked, the construction of the Statutes is the same in equity as at law, unless there is a natural equity going beyond the Statutes.[230] A natural equity would arise if the cross-demands are sufficiently closely connected to give rise to the substantive form of equitable set-off discussed in the next section. Ordinarily, though, the Statutes receive the same construction as at law. This proposition brings into question Street J.'s judgment in the New South Wales Supreme Court in *Stewart* v. *Latec Investments Ltd.*[231] A company had executed a trust deed to regulate the issue of debenture stock. The trust deed was in a common form, by which the trustee appointed under the deed was constituted the creditor of the company in respect of the issued stock, while each individual stockholder was the beneficial owner of his stock. In the event of a transfer of stock, the deed provided that, *upon registration of the transfer*, the transferee should be recognized as entitled to the stock free from any equity, set-off, or counterclaim possessed by the company against the transferor. The court was asked to determine as a question of law, whether the company was bound to register a transferee as the owner of stock when the transferor was indebted to the company on an independent transaction. The perceived difficulty was that the trust deed only stipulated that a transferee should take free from equities after registration had been effected. Accordingly, it was held that the company could assert a set-off against the transferee before this date in order to prevent registration.[232] When the company received the formal transfer, it credited the principal and

[225] See, e.g. *Clark* v. *Cort* (1840) Cr. & Ph. 154; *Cochrane* v. *Green* (1860) 9 CB(NS) 448; *Thornton* v. *Maynard* (1875) LR 10 CP 695; *Manley & Sons Ltd.* v. *Berkett* [1912] 2 KB 329, 333; *High* v. *Bengal Brass Co.* (1921) 21 SR (NSW) 232, 238; *Tony Lee Motors Ltd.* v. *M. S. MacDonald & Son (1974) Ltd.* [1981] 2 NZLR 281.
[226] See Spry, *Equitable Remedies* (4th edn., 1990), 172–3.
[227] *Middleton* v. *Pollock; ex parte Nugee* (1875) LR 20 Eq. 29, 36–7, and see *Welton* v. *Harnett* (1886) 7 NSWR 74.
[228] *Tony Lee Motors Ltd.* v. *M. S. MacDonald (1974) Ltd.* [1981] 2 NZLR 281, 287–8.
[229] See section 1.2.9 above.
[230] *Ex parte Stephens* (1805) 11 Ves. Jun. 24, 27. [231] [1968] 1 NSWR 432.
[232] See e.g. *In re Richard Smith & Co., Ltd.* [1901] 1 IR 73.

interest payable in respect of the debenture stock against the transferor's indebtedness. Street J. said that this book-keeping entry itself amounted to a valid redemption of the debenture.[233] Consistent with that view, *Stewart* v. *Latec Investments* has been referred to as showing a species of equitable set-off having a substantive operation independently of any court order.[234] However, it is difficult to justify this as a matter of principle. Because of the interposition of the trustee there was not mutuality at law as between the company and the transferor. But there was mutuality in equity, so that equity would have acted by analogy with the Statutes. In doing so the Statutes should have received the same construction as at law, given that there does not appear to have been a natural equity taking the case beyond the Statutes. Certainly the demands would not have been sufficiently closely connected so as to give rise to a substantive equitable set-off.[235] Therefore, the right of set-off in issue should have been regarded as merely procedural, in the sense that an order of the court should have been required to give effect to it, and the company should not have been able to bring about a set-off itself by making an entry to this effect in its books. Street J. relied in his judgment on the earlier decision of Buckley J. in *In re Palmer's Decoration & Furniture Company*,[236] which concerned a similar trust deed. However, the cases are distinguishable. In *Palmer* the transferor's title was defective,[237] in that he had obtained the debentures from the company by misrepresentation, and it was held that the transferee took subject to this defect in title. While the question in issue was whether the transferee was entitled to be paid, Buckley J. also said that the defect of title would have provided a ground for the company to refuse to register the transfer. The nature of the equity in that case should be compared to the equity which arises under the Statutes of Set-off. This provides a procedural defence to an action but does not give rise to a defect in the title to the debt in question.

1.7 SUBSTANTIVE EQUITABLE SET-OFF

1.7.1 *The traditional formulation*

There is a second, substantive,[238] defence of equitable set-off which is not

---

[233] His Honour said (at [1968] 1 NSWR 432, 437) that 'when Latec Investments Ltd. purported, on 13 July 1962, to credit the principal and interest payable in respect of the debenture stock against Mr. Stewart's indebtedness to it this amounted to a valid redemption of the debenture'.

[234] See Gummow and von Doussa JJ. in the Federal Court of Australia in *McIntyre* v. *Perkes* (1990) 22 FCR 260, 270.   [235] See section 1.7 below.

[236] [1904] 2 Ch. 743.

[237] Buckley J. expressed it ([1904] 2 Ch. 743, 751) in terms that 'by reason of the company's equity the title is not clear'.   [238] See section 1.7.4 below.

confined to mutual debts,[239] and which has attracted considerable attention in recent years. The seminal authority on this form of equitable set-off is Lord Cottenham's judgment in *Rawson* v. *Samuel*.[240] The Lord Chancellor said in that case that the mere existence of cross-demands is not sufficient to give rise to a set-off. Rather, he said that the applicant for relief must show some good equitable grounds for being protected against the plaintiff's demand, such that the plaintiff's title to his demand is impeached. A number of illustrations of the principle appear from cases referred to by Lord Cottenham in his judgment. In *Beasley* v. *Darcy*[241] a tenant was allowed to set off against his liability for rent a damages claim that he had against the landlord for damage suffered as a result of timber on the demised land being cut down and carried away. Lord Cottenham said that the equity against the landlord was that he should not recover possession of the farm for non-payment of rent while he owed to the tenant a sum for damage to that same farm, though on other occasions it has been suggested that the decision in *Beasley* may be justified on the ground that the produce of the farm may have been lessened as a result of the landlord's conduct which in turn may have affected the tenant's ability to pay the rent.[242] In *Piggott* v. *Williams*[243] a solicitor filed a bill for fore-closure of an estate pledged as security for costs. The relief sought by the solicitor was denied to him because of a set-off held to be available to the client. The cross-claim was based upon an allegation of negligence, and it was argued that the costs claimed would not have been incurred were it not for this negligence. This was a case in which the plaintiff's own breach of duty brought about, or at least contributed to the existence of, the defendant's liability to him.[244] There is also *Lord Cawdor* v. *Lewis*.[245] In

---

[239] In a number of cases in Australia the view was put forward that an unliquidated demand may not be employed in a set-off. See e.g. *McDonnell & East Limited* v. *McGregor* (1936) 56 CLR 50, 62. However, this is incorrect in so far as it relates to equitable set-off. See e.g. *Beasley* v. *Darcy* (1800) 2 Sch. & Lef. 403n. (in which the Lord Chancellor ordered that the defendant's cross-claim for damages be assessed by a jury); *Galambos & Son Pty. Ltd.* v. *McIntyre* (1974) 5 ACTR 10 (in which the cases are discussed); *Knockholt Pty. Ltd.* v. *Graff* [1975] Qd. R 88; *United Dominions Corporation Limited* v. *Jaybe Homes Pty. Ltd.* [1978] Qd. R. 111; *British Anzani (Felixstowe) Ltd.* v. *International Marine Management (U.K.) Ltd.* [1980] 1 QB 137, 145–6.   [240] (1841) Cr. & Ph. 161.

[241] (1800) 2 Sch. & Lef. 403n.

[242] See Lord Redesdale in *O'Mahony* v. *Dickson* (1805) 2 Sch. & Lef. 400, 412, and also Bramwell B. in *Stimson* v. *Hall* (1857) 1 H & N 831, 836.

[243] (1821) 6 Madd. 95.

[244] See also *Popular Homes Ltd.* v. *Circuit Developments Ltd.* [1979] 2 NZLR 642, 659–60. Similarly, in an action by an employer under a building contract against the contractor arising out of a delay in completion, a cross-claim available to the contractor against the employer for hindering or preventing the contractor's performance may give rise to an equitable set-off. See *Hanak* v. *Green* [1958] 2 QB 9; *Rosehaugh Stanhope (Broadgate Phase 6) Plc.* v. *Redpath Dorman Long Ltd.* (1990) 50 Build. LR 75; *Beaufort House Development Ltd.* v. *Zimmcor (International) Inc.* (1990) 50 Build. LR 91.

[245] (1835) 1 Y & C Ex. 427. Compare *Tai Te Whetu* v. *Scandlyn* [1952] NZLR 30.

that case a claim for compensation for improvements effected to another's land was set off against a cross-claim for mesne profits, under circumstances in which the party claiming title to the land had stood by and watched the other spend money on the improvements without giving him notice of his title. On the other hand, Lord Cottenham was critical of the decision in *Williams* v. *Davies*.[246] The plaintiff had obtained judgment at law against the defendant upon a number of promissory notes, and the defendant had obtained judgment at law against the plaintiff for damages for wrongful distress. The plaintiff applied to the Court of King's Bench to set off the judgments pursuant to the Court's inherent jurisdiction.[247] The application was refused, and so the plaintiff then sought an injunction in equity. This succeeded before Sir Lancelot Shadwell, who said that it was right that the judgments should be set off. However, it is not clear why equitable relief should have been available when a remedy had been refused at law, and Lord Cottenham doubted in *Rawson* v. *Samuel* whether there was a sufficient equity to support an equitable set-off.[248]

In *Rawson* v. *Samuel*, the plaintiff at law was suing for damages for breach of contract. The defendant at law (the plaintiff in equity) sought an account of transactions under the contract, and an injunction to restrain the plaintiff at law from executing any judgment obtained at law until he had given credit for any balance that may be found to be due to the defendant on the account. However Lord Cottenham said that 'The object and subject matters are . . . totally distinct' and that 'the fact that the agreement was the origin of both does not form any bond of union for the purpose of supporting an injunction'.[249] The end result was that the absence of a sufficient equity prevented a set-off despite the fact that both demands arose under the same contract.

The basis of this form of equitable set-off is that the title of the plaintiff to his demand is impeached. The concept of impeachment suffers from a sense of vagueness. What it requires, in the absence of some other equitable ground for being protected such as fraud,[250] is that there be a sufficiently close connection between the demands. In its traditional sense this is not a mechanical test such as whether the demands arose out of the same transaction,[251] though it has in fact been expressed in that manner at the

---

[246] (1829) 2 Sim. 461.   [247] See section 1.4.3 above.

[248] (1841) Cr. & Ph. 161, 178. See also *Stimson* v. *Hall* (1857) 1 H & N 831, 836; *Aboussafy* v. *Abacus Cities Ltd.* (1981) 124 DLR (3d) 150, 160; *J.C. Scott Constructions* v. *Mermaid Waters Tavern Pty. Ltd. (No. 1)* [1983] 2 Qd. R 243.

[249] (1841) Cr. & Ph. 161, 178.

[250] See *Ex parte Stephens* (1805) 11 Ves. Jun. 24 and *Vuillamy* v. *Noble* (1817) 3 Mer. 592.

[251] A proper statement of the application of the impeachment principle in this context is that, if cross-demands arise out of the same transaction, equity will *in some cases* interfere. See Bramwell B. in *Stimson* v. *Hall* (1857) 1 H & N 831, 835.

highest level.[252] Rather, it involves a consideration of the circumstances of the particular case, and indeed a close connection may not be sufficient to impeach the title if there are other discretionary factors which militate against equitable relief.[253] The closeness of the connection that prima facie is required in order to result in an impeachment of title has been expressed in various terms, for example that the cross-demand must go to the very root of the plaintiff's claim,[254] or that it must call in question, impugn, disparage or impede the title to the claim,[255] or, as the New Zealand Court of Appeal expressed it, that the link between the demands must be such that the two in effect are interdependent.[256] All of these are correct. It is the nature of the cross-claim relative to the claim, rather than the amount of the damages recoverable or the severity of the breach, that matters.[257] The fact that the plaintiff is insolvent by itself does not give rise to an equity sufficient to support an equitable set-off.[258] Further, *Rawson* v. *Samuel* illustrates that it is not sufficient that the demands arose out of the same contract.[259] Nor indeed is the plaintiff's demand necessarily regarded as impeached merely because the cross-claim is in some way related to the transaction which gave rise to the claim.[260] On the other hand, if cross-demands do arise out of separate transactions, they will generally not be sufficiently closely connected.[261]

However, the rigour with which the impeachment test originally was applied has been weakened over time, so that in some more recent cases it is difficult to see what the basis for the set-off was apart from the fact that both demands arose out of the same contract or transaction. This would appear to be a consequence of the view that has been expressed,[262] that the

---

[252] See *Bank of Boston Connecticut* v. *European Grain and Shipping Ltd.* [1989] 1 AC 1056, discussed in section 1.7.2 below.   [253] See section 1.7.5 below.
[254] *British Anzani (Felixstowe) Ltd.* v. *International Marine Management (U.K.) Ltd.* [1980] 1 QB 137, 145.
[255] See Tadgell J. in the Victorian Supreme Court in *M.E.K. Nominees Pty. Ltd.* v. *Billboard Entertainments Pty. Ltd.* (1993) V Conv. R 54–468.
[256] *Grant* v. *NZMC Ltd.* [1989] 1 NZLR 8, 13.
[257] *Sim* v. *Rotherham Metropolitan Borough Council* [1987] 1 Ch. 216, 262.
[258] *Rawson* v. *Samuel* (1841) Cr. & Ph. 162, 175.
[259] See in particular Lord Cottenham in his judgment (1841) Cr. & Ph. 161, 178, and also *Best* v. *Hill* (1872) LR 8 CP 10; *In re K.L. Tractors Ltd.* [1954] VLR 505, 507–8; *The Raven* [1980] 2 Lloyd's Rep. 266, 272; *Covino* v. *Bandag Manufacturing Pty. Ltd.* [1983] 1 NSWLR 237, 238 (claim for the price of goods supplied and cross-claim for damages for breach of warranty as regards territorial monopoly not set off); *Westwind Air Charter Pty. Ltd.* v. *Hawker De Havilland Ltd.* (1990) 3 WAR 71. Compare *Axel Johnson Petroleum A.B.* v. *M.G. Mineral Group A.G.* [1992] 1 WLR 270, in which Leggatt L.J. said that an equitable set-off was arguable even though the only connection appears to have been that the cross-claims had their origins in the same joint venture agreement.
[260] *Hanak* v. *Green* [1958] 2 QB 9, 23.
[261] *Re Convere Pty. Ltd.* [1976] VR 345, 349.
[262] See Sellers L.J. in *Hanak* v. *Green* [1958] 2 QB 9, 29.

courts should not be astute to restrict the right of set-off, but rather should develop it as a discouragement to litigation. Two Court of Appeal decisions have been the subject of particular criticism by commentators as illustrating a departure from the principles enunciated by Lord Cottenham.[263] The defendant in *Morgan & Son, Limited* v. *S. Martin Johnson & Company, Limited*[264] had delivered a number of vehicles to the plaintiff for the purpose of storage. The plaintiff subsequently claimed a sum for storage charges, and applied for summary judgment. The defendant resisted the application on the basis of an alleged damages claim for non-delivery of one of the vehicles. The Court of Appeal held that the facts set out in the defendant's affidavit did support a claim to an equitable set-off, and that accordingly the defendant should be granted unconditional leave to defend. This conclusion would have had merit if the set-off had been confined to the particular vehicle which was the subject of the cross-action. The equity in favour of a set-off in such a case may be said to have been that the plaintiff should not be permitted to sue for the cost of storing a particular vehicle when he himself had failed to hand over that vehicle.[265] It is not all clear, however, that there was a similar equity in relation to the storage charges for the other vehicles.[266] The second case, *Hanak* v. *Green*,[267] concerned a building contract. The plaintiff sued the defendant builder for breach of contract for failing to complete or properly complete certain items of work. The defendant counterclaimed or claimed by way of set-off (1) on a *quantum meruit* in respect of extra work done outside the contract, (2) on the ground that loss was caused by the plaintiff's refusal to admit the defendant's workmen, and (3) for trespass to the defendant's tools. It may be accepted that the second of these items exhibited a good equitable ground sufficient to impeach the plaintiff's title to his demand. The plaintiff's refusal to admit the defendant's workmen may have been one of the reasons why the defendant had not completed the work, in which case the plaintiff's own breach of duty may have contributed to the existence of the defendant's liability to her.[268] However, it is difficult to see what connection the first and the third items had with the plaintiff's claim (unless, in the latter case, this hindered completion).

---

[263] See Spry, 'Equitable Set-offs' (1969) 43 *Australian Law Journal* 265, 269–70; Meagher Gummow and Lehane, *Equity: Doctrines and Remedies* (3rd edn. 1992), 822.

[264] [1949] 1 KB 107.

[265] In this respect the case would have been analogous to *Beasley* v. *Darcy* (1800) 2 Sch. & Lef. 403n., discussed above.

[266] Nevertheless, the decision was referred to with evident approval by Danckwerts and Winn L.JJ. in *Hale* v. *Victoria Plumbing Co. Ltd.* [1966] 2 QB 746, and by Lord Denning in *Federal Commerce & Navigation Co. Ltd.* v. *Molena Alpha Inc.* [1978] 1 QB 927, 975. See also *Newman* v. *Cook* [1963] VR 659, 674.

[267] [1958] 2 QB 9.

[268] As in *Piggott* v. *Williams* (1821) 6 Madd. 95.

Despite this, the Court of Appeal (Hodson, Morris and Sellers L.JJ.) unanimously held that the first item could be employed in a set-off. The status of the third item was not considered by Hodson and Morris L.JJ., the first and second items when added together being sufficient to overtop the plaintiff's claim, though Sellers L.J. thought that this could also be marshalled as a set-off. *Hanak* v. *Green* nevertheless has become a leading case in the area, and Morris L.J.'s judgment in particular has been described as authoritative[269] and a masterly account of the subject.[270]

In the course of his judgment in *Rawson* v. *Samuel* Lord Cottenham said that,[271]

It was said that the subjects of the suit in this Court, and of the action at law, arise out of the same contract; but the one is for an account of transactions under the contract, and the other for damages for the breach of it. The object and subject-matters are, therefore, totally distinct; and the fact that the agreement was the origin of both does not form any bond of union for the purpose of supporting an injunction.

This should not be taken to mean that a claim for a sum of money expressed to be payable under a contract cannot be met by a set-off in respect of a damages claim arising out of a breach of that contract.[272] Situations of this nature in fact are a prime source of equitable set-offs.[273] Rather, Lord Cottenham's statement should be understood in the context of the case before him. It concerned an agreement by which the defendant was to consign goods to certain mercantile houses in which the plaintiffs had an interest for the purpose of sale. Part of the agreement was that, upon each shipment of goods, the defendant should be at liberty to draw bills of exchange upon the plaintiffs for the amount of his charges and disbursements in respect of the shipments. After the agreement had run for some time the plaintiffs refused to accept bills in accordance with the agreement, whereupon the defendant sued at common law for damages. The plaintiffs sought an injunction restraining execution on any judgment

---

[269] See Dillon L.J. in *BICC Plc.* v. *Burndy Corporation* [1985] 1 Ch. 232, 247.

[270] See Lord Diplock in *Gilbert-Ash (Northern) Ltd.* v. *Modern Engineering (Bristol) Ltd.* [1974] AC 689, 717, and also *The Teno* [1977] 2 Lloyd's Rep. 289, 297; *British Anzani (Felixstowe) Ltd.* v. *International Marine Management (U.K.) Ltd.* [1980] 1 QB 137, 144.

[271] (1841) Cr. & Ph. 161, 178.

[272] *AWA Ltd.* v. *Exicom Australia Pty. Ltd.* (1990) 19 NSWLR 705, 713–4.

[273] For example, in the case of a time charter of a ship there is ample authority for the proposition that a claim for hire may be met by a damages claim for breach of contract which deprives the charterer of the full use of the vessel. See *The Teno* [1977] 2 Lloyd's Rep. 289, 297; *Federal Commerce & Navigation Co. Ltd.* v. *Molena Alpha Inc.* [1978] 1 Q.B. 927, 976. Similarly a damages claim for breach of a building contract may be set off against a claim for money otherwise due under the contract. See e.g. *Young* v. *Kitchin* (1878) 3 Ex. D 127; *Government of Newfoundland* v. *Newfoundland Railway Company* (1888) 13 App. Cas. 199.

that may be obtained at law. Their bill sought an account of the dealings
and transactions between the parties under the agreement, and an order
setting off against their damages liability the amount which, upon taking
the accounts, should be found due from the defendant to the plaintiffs. In
this case the subject-matters of the claims were indeed distinct, and Lord
Cottenham was concerned to emphasize that the fact that they arose out of
the same agreement was not sufficient to give rise to an equitable set-off.
However, this explanation does not appear to have been appreciated in
Best v. *Hill*.[274] The defendant had consigned goods to the plaintiffs for
sale, the agreement between them being that the plaintiffs should make
advances to the defendant against the goods, and that the plaintiffs should
sell the goods and obtain payment from the proceeds for the advances and
their expenses and commission. The plaintiffs sued for money lent and paid
and commission in respect of the goods. The defendant pleaded as a
defence on equitable grounds a cross-claim for damages for negligence in
the care of part of the goods and for negligence in the management of the
sale. The allegation was that the plaintiffs were guilty of such negligence
and improper conduct in the care of the goods and the conduct of the sale
that the goods fetched less than they ought to, such that the amount
recovered was insufficient to satisfy the advances, expenses and commission. The Court of Common Pleas held that the plea was bad. One reason
given was that the proceedings to ascertain the amount of damages would
involve considerable delay. But, in addition, Bovill C.J. held, on the
authority of *Rawson* v. *Samuel*, that an equitable set-off was not available
because, 'although these cross claims in one sense are connected . . . this
does not appear to be sufficient, according to the doctrine of equity in
relation to set-off; one claim arises out of the performance of the contract,
the other out of its breach'.[275] As a general proposition for denying an
equitable set-off, this is difficult to support. One would have thought that,
apart from the discretionary consideration concerning delay in the
assessment of the damages, the cross-claims in fact were such as to give rise
to an equitable set-off. This is so notwithstanding that the Court of
Exchequer in *Atterbury* v. *Jarvie*[276] previously had also held that a set-off
was not available in very similar circumstances. The advances, commission
and expenses the subject of the plaintiffs' claim in *Best* v. *Hill* were
intended to be satisfied out of the proceeds of sale. The substance of the
cross-claim against the plaintiffs was that, as a result of their own
negligence and misconduct, the amount received from the sale was
insufficient to satisfy the debts. This cross-claim would indeed appear to
have impeached the title of the plaintiffs to sue. As counsel unsuccessfully

[274] (1872) LR 8 CP 10.   [275] (1872) LR 8 CP 10, 15.
[276] (1857) 2 H & N 114.

argued in that case, it was similar to *Beasley* v. *Darcy*,[277] where the landlord's claim for rent was impeached by a cross-claim against him for damage done in cutting timber on the demised land, in that this reduced the produce of the farm and therefore affected the tenant's ability to pay the rent.

Equitable set-offs commonly arise when there is a claim for a contract debt on one side of the account, and on the other a claim for damages in either contract or tort which, in the traditional formulation, impeaches the title to the debt. However, the set-off is not confined to this situation, but in an appropriate case may apply when both demands are liquidated.[278] This may apply, for example, where the creditor's claim against the debtor is the source from which the debtor's own cross-claim is to be satisfied. In *Ralston* v. *South Greta Colliery Company*[279] A had leased a coal mine to B, the consideration for which included the payment of a royalty by B in respect of the coal won. In consideration of work and labour done by C, A agreed to pay C a part of the royalty that A received from time to time, and C then assigned this right to B. When A sued B for payment of the royalty, the New South Wales Supreme Court held that B had a set-off to the extent of the portion of the royalty that had been assigned back to him. This was not a case of mutual debts under the Statutes of Set-off, because until A actually received payment there was no debt owing to B. Rather, the set-off in issue was an equitable set-off. Sir William Cullen C.J. said that there was 'a good equity in the defendant to restrain the prosecution of so much of the demand as the plaintiff has parted with and which has come back into the hands of the original debtor'.[280]

1.7.2 New approaches

On a number of occasions in recent years the courts have sought to re-define the basis upon which an equitable set-off is available, the effect of which generally has been to expand the scope of the defence.

In *Henriksens Rederi A/S* v. *THZ. Rolimpex (The Brede)*[281] Lord Denning cited *Morgan* v. *Johnson* and *Hanak* v. *Green* as authorities for the proposition that equitable set-off 'is available whenever the cross-claim arises out of the same transaction as the claim; or out of a transaction that is closely related to the claim'.[282] There was no mention of an additional

---

[277] (1800) 2 Sch. & Lef. 403n.
[278] See e.g. *Telford* v. *Holt* (1987) 41 DLR (4th) 385.
[279] (1912) 13 SR (NSW) 6.   [280] (1912) 13 SR (NSW) 6, 16.
[281] [1974] 1 QB 233.
[282] [1974] 1 QB 233, 248. See also *Box* v. *Midland Bank Ltd.* [1981] 1 Lloyd's Rep. 434, 437, where Lord Denning allowed an equitable set-off on the basis that the 'claim and counterclaim arose out of a whole series of transactions in regard to the obtaining of the loan'.

requirement of some equitable ground sufficient to impeach the plaintiff's title to his demand, and to this extent his statement of the law would appear to represent a broader basis for the defence of equitable set-off than that originally contemplated by Lord Cottenham. Thus Lord Denning accepted that 'with any breach by the plaintiff of the self-same contract, the defendant can in equity set up his loss in diminution or extinction of the contract price',[283] whereas Lord Cottenham had emphasized in *Rawson* v. *Samuel*[284] that the fact that the one contract was the origin of both demands is not sufficient to found an equitable set-off. However, the traditional approach was restored in *Aries Tanker Corporation* v. *Total Transport Ltd.*[285] The House of Lords in that case affirmed the principle that freight owing under a voyage charter must be paid without deduction.[286] Accordingly, the charterers could not deduct a sum for short delivery of cargo. But, even apart from that principle, Lord Simon of Glaisdale said that an equitable set-off would not have been available on the facts. He said that, in order to succeed, the equity of the bill would have had to impeach the title to the legal demand, and the title to a claim for freight is not impeached by short delivery unless it amounts to a repudiation of the contract of carriage. Similarly, Lord Wilberforce referred to *Rawson* v. *Samuel* as setting out the relevant principle, and since then the courts in a number of cases have accepted the impeachment test.[287]

After *Aries Tanker* there were some important observations on equitable set-off in the Court of Appeal in *Federal Commerce & Navigation Co. Ltd.* v. *Molena Alpha Inc.*,[288] particularly by Lord Denning. In contrast with his earlier judgment in *The Brede*, his Lordship acknowledged that there must be some equitable ground sufficient to impeach the plaintiff's demand. However, in doing so he rejected the notion that the categories of equitable grounds should be ascertained by examining the practice of the courts in matters of set-off prior to the Judicature Acts.[289] Rather, he said that the relevant question is: 'what should we do now so as to ensure fair dealing between the parties?'[290] A

---

[283] [1974] 1 QB 233, 249. [284] (1841) Cr. & Ph. 161, 175.
[285] [1977] 1 WLR 185. [286] See section 1.7.14 below.
[287] See also *British Anzani (Felixstowe) Ltd.* v. *International Marine Management (U.K.) Ltd.* [1980] 1 QB 137, 145; *BICC Plc* v. *Burndy Corporation* [1985] Ch. 232, 258, 259; *Sim* v. *Rotherham Council* [1987] 1 Ch. 216, 261; *The Didymi* [1988] 1 Lloyd's Rep. 91 (Canadian Federal Court of Appeal); *Aectra Refining and Marketing Inc.* v. *Exmar NV* [1994] 1 WLR 1634, 1649. [288] [1978] 1 QB 927.
[289] See also *British Anzani (Felixstowe) Ltd.* v. *International Marine Management (U.K.) Ltd.* [1980] 1 QB 137, 155.
[290] [1978] 1 QB 927, 974. In *A. B. Contractors Ltd.* v. *Flaherty Brothers Ltd.* (1978) 16 Build. LR 10, 11 Cumming-Bruce L.J. considered whether the dealings were so connected 'as to make it fair and sensible' that a set-off occur. See also Stephenson L.J. (at 14).

cross-claim should be considered as directly impeaching the plaintiff's demand if it is 'so closely connected with his [demand] that it would be manifestly unjust to allow him to enforce payment without taking into account the cross-claim'.[291] Parker J. earlier had proposed a similar formulation of the principle in *The Teno*,[292] and it has also been adopted by the courts on other occasions.[293]

Fairness, or the prevention of manifest injustice, in truth has always been the concept underlying equitable set-off. The question is what are the circumstances in which equity regards it as unjust or unfair that one claim should be enforced without reference to another, and traditionally this has been expressed in terms that, in the absence of some other equitable ground for being protected,[294] the claims must be so closely connected that the title to sue is impeached. It is apparent that Lord Denning's formulation was not intended to replace the impeachment test as such, but rather to re-define it so that it is based upon a broader concept of fairness.[295] There is one situation in which he was careful not to extend the ambit of the defence. He said that, 'as at present advised', he would limit the right of a time charterer to make deductions from hire to cases where the shipowner has wrongfully deprived the charterer of the use of the vessel or has prejudiced him in the use of it. He said that he would not extend it to other breaches or defaults of the shipowner, such as damage to cargo arising from the negligence of the crew.[296] This is consistent with the traditional approach, because depriving a charterer of the use of the ship or prejudicing the charterer's use is the very type of circumstance that would impeach a claim for hire.[297] It suggests a narrower view than that expressed

---

[291] [1978] 1 QB 927, 975. Similarly, Goff L.J. in *Federal Commerce* said (at 981): 'The circumstances must be such as to make it unfair for the creditor to be paid his claim without allowing that of the debtor if and so far as well founded and thus to raise an equity against the creditor or, as it has been expressed, impeach his title to be paid'.

[292] [1977] 2 Lloyd's Rep. 289, 297.

[293] See, e.g. *British Anzani (Felixstowe) Ltd.* v. *International Marine Management (U.K.) Ltd.* [1980] 1 QB 137, 145; *The Kostas Melas* [1981] 1 Lloyd's Rep. 18, 25; *Dole Dried Fruit and Nut Co.* v. *Trustin Kerwood Ltd.* [1990] 2 Lloyd's Rep. 309, 311. In *National Westminster Bank plc* v. *Skelton* [1993] 1 WLR 72, 76 Slade L.J. said that, in deciding whether to allow a set-off, 'the court will be much influenced by what it regards as the essential requirements of justice'. In *Federal Commerce* v. *Molena* [1978] 1 QB 927, 987 Goff L.J. described Parker J.'s analysis in *The Teno* as 'impeccable'. See also *BICC* v. *Burndy Corporation* [1985] Ch. 232, 250; *Sim* v. *Rotherham Metropolitan Borough Council* [1987] Ch. 216, 261–2.

[294] For example, fraud. See *Vuillamy* v. *Noble* (1817) 3 Mer. 593 and *Ex parte Stephens* (1805) 11 Ves. Jun. 24.

[295] Similarly Parker J. in *The Teno* [1977] 2 Lloyd's Rep. 289, 297 acknowledged that the cross-claim must be such as to impeach the plaintiff's title, but then went on to express the principle in terms whether it was manifestly unjust to allow the claimant to recover without taking into account the cross-claim.

[296] [1978] 1 QB 927, 976. A similar view was expressed by Goff L.J. (at 981). See also *The Aliakmon Progress* [1978] 2 Lloyd's Rep. 499, 501.

[297] See Hobhouse J. in *The Leon* [1985] 2 Lloyd's Rep. 470, 475.

in his earlier judgment in *The Brede*, that an equitable set-off is available whenever cross-claims arise out of the same transaction. But leaving that aside, the re-definition of impeachment in terms of a broader concept of fairness would expand the scope of the defence, a conclusion that may be illustrated by *Dole Dried Fruit & Nut Co.* v. *Trustin Kerwood Ltd*,[298] in which the Court of Appeal allowed an equitable set-off on the basis of Lord Denning's formulation in circumstances that would not appear to have satisfied the traditional test.[299] The difficulty with this approach, however, is that it would introduce greater uncertainty, particularly given that the question of what is fair often depends on from whose point of view the matter is looked at. Indeed, the view that the test is now simply one of fairness was rejected by Hobhouse J. in *The Leon*.[300] He said that, while 'equitable principles derive from a sense of what justice and fairness demand . . . this does not mean that equitable set-off has been reduced to an exercise of discretion. Since the merging of equity and law, equitable set-off gives rise to a legal defence. This defence does not vary according to the length of the Lord Chancellor's, or arbitrator's, foot. The defence has to be granted or refused by an application of legal principle'. He went on to emphasize that Lord Cottenham's judgment should still be regarded as setting out the relevant principle.

After *Federal Commerce* the House of Lords considered the law of equitable set-off in *Bank of Boston Connecticut* v. *European Grain and Shipping Ltd.*,[301] and in doing so made some observations on the availability of the defence which would now appear to set out the position applicable in England. Lord Brandon of Oakbrook in delivering the judgment of the court[302] said that the concept of impeachment is not a familiar one today. Instead, he approved a formulation that had been expressed by the Privy Council in *Government of Newfoundland* v.

---

[298] [1990] 2 Lloyd's Rep. 309.

[299] The plaintiffs had appointed the defendants as their exclusive agent for importing the plaintiffs' goods into and distributing those goods in England. Subsequently the plaintiffs purported to terminate the contract without notice, and proceeded to sue the defendants for the price of goods sold and delivered under a series of sale contracts. The defendants sought to set off their damages claim against the plaintiffs for breach of the agency agreement. Lloyd L.J. (with whom Beldam L.J. concurred) said that the sale contracts were concluded in fulfilment of the agency agreement, and accordingly the claims were sufficiently closely connected to make it unjust to allow the plaintiffs to claim the price of goods sold and delivered without taking into account the cross-claim. It is not easy, though, to see how the cross-claim could be regarded as having impeached the title to the claim, within the traditional meaning of that test. Nor indeed, applying the formulation approved by the House of Lords in the *Bank of Boston* case [1989] 1 AC 1056 (discussed below), is it abundantly clear that the cross-claim for breach of the agency contract was 'inseparably connected' with the sale contracts. [300] [1985] 2 Lloyd's Rep. 470, 474. [301] [1989] 1 AC 1056.

[302] Lord Brandon, Lord Keith of Kinkel, Lord Oliver of Aylmerton, Lord Goff of Chieveley and Lord Jauncey of Tullichettle.

Newfoundland Railway Co.,[303] that an equitable set-off may occur if there is a cross-claim 'flowing out and inseparably connected with the dealings and transactions which also give rise' to the claim.[304] While this has some similarities to the test proposed by Lord Denning in *The Brede*,[305] it is nevertheless slightly narrower. It will be recalled that Lord Denning said in that case that it is sufficient if the cross-claim arises out of a transaction that is 'closely related' to the claim, whereas the Privy Council required that the cross-claim be 'inseparably connected' with the transaction which gives rise to the claim.

A curious aspect of *Bank of Boston* is that their Lordships did not consider that the formulation was a departure from the impeachment test set out in *Rawson* v. *Samuel*. Rather, it was re-affirmed that, in the determination today of whether a particular cross-claim can give rise to an equitable set-off, it is still necessary to see whether it would have provided grounds for a common injunction before the Judicature Acts,[306] which suggests a rejection of Lord Denning's approach in the *Federal Commerce* case. Lord Brandon said that the test approved by the House of Lords was merely a 'different version' of the impeachment test,[307] while Lloyd L.J. later characterized it as 'the same test in different language'.[308] However, this is debatable. The notion that an equitable set-off may arise if the cross-claim is inseparably connected with the transaction suggests a mechanical approach that is not inherent in the concept of impeachment. Thus, it is difficult to see how the *Bank of Boston* approach could ever operate to deny an equitable set-off when the same transaction is the source of both demands,[309] even though it has been emphasized in the context of the traditional impeachment test that it is not sufficient that the cross-demands arose out of the same transaction.[310] As Bramwell B. once expressed the

---

[303] (1888) 13 App. Cas. 199.

[304] See in particular the judgment at [1989] 1 AC 1056, 1102–3, 1110–1.

[305] [1974] 1 QB 233.   [306] [1989] 1 AC 1056, 1101.

[307] [1989] 1 AC 1056, 1102.

[308] *Dole Dried Fruit and Nut Co.* v. *Trustin Kerwood Ltd.* [1990] 2 Lloyd's Rep. 309, 310.

[309] In *A. B. Contractors Ltd.* v. *Flaherty Brothers Ltd.* (1978) 16 Build. LR 10, 12 Cumming-Bruce L.J. seemed to regard it as sufficient if 'the issue on a defence and counterclaim arises out of the same transaction, the same contract, as the issues on the claim'.

[310] See *In re K.L. Tractors Ltd.* [1954] VLR 505, 508; *The Leon* [1985] 2 Lloyd's Rep. 470, 474; *The Aditya Vaibhav* [1991] 1 Lloyd's Rep. 572 (esp. at 574); *Davkot Pty. Ltd.* v. *Custom Credit Corporation Ltd.* unreported, Wood J., New South Wales Supreme Court, 28 March 1991; *Griffiths* v. *Commonwealth Bank of Australia* (1994) 123 ALR 111, 124 (in which Lee J. held that the plaintiff's title was not impeached even though he agreed that the cross-claims arose out of the same transaction); *Walker* v. *Department of Social Security* (1995) 129 ALR 198, 207 (referring to *James* v. *Commonwealth Bank of Australia* (1992) 37 FCR 445). See also Spry, 'Equitable Set-offs' (1969) 43 *Australian Law Journal* 265, 268, referred to in *Popular Homes Ltd.* v. *Circuit Developments Ltd.* [1979] 2 NZLR 642, 659 and *Parry* v. *Grace* [1981] 2 NZLR 273, 276, 277. In the Court of Appeal in *Bank of Boston* [1989] 1 AC 1056, 1075 Mustill L.J. said in relation to equitable set-off that 'the fact that the origin of the demands lay in the same transaction was plainly not enough'.

principle, 'where there is a transaction between two parties, and cross claims originate from it, a court of equity will *in some cases* interfere to prevent the one party from enforcing his claim without allowing the claim of the other'.[311] A recent illustration is *The Aditya Vaibhav*.[312] The owner of a vessel had let the vessel pursuant to a time charter. The charterers alleged that, in breach of the charter, the owner failed to perform its hold-cleaning obligations, which resulted in a delay to the vessel at port of about fourteen days. The charterers suffered consequential loss, which they deducted in part against the hire due during the fourteen-day period, and submitted that they could set off the remainder of the damages against subsequent payments of hire. Saville J. held that the damages claim did not impeach the owner's entitlement to hire for periods during which it had actually provided the services contracted for, and accordingly a set-off in respect of the remainder of the damages was not allowed, even though he agreed that the claims arose out of the same transaction. The case is curious, because it was decided after *Bank of Boston* and yet there was no mention by Saville J. of Lord Brandon's judgment in the House of Lords. However, it does illustrate the application of the impeachment test.

But whatever the position is in this regard, the Court of Appeal[313] undoubtedly reached the correct decision in *Guinness Plc.* v. *Saunders*.[314] The second defendant, through a company controlled by him, received payment from the plaintiff for services performed. The second defendant was also a director of the plaintiff, and it was held that the payment was received in breach of his fiduciary duty to the plaintiff and that he held it as constructive trustee. He said that he nevertheless had a valid defence based upon a cross-claim for *quantum meruit* in respect of these services. But since the cross-demand did not impeach the plaintiff's title to the money claimed, an equitable set-off was held not to be available.

1.7.3 Equitable set-off in Australia

In Australia the courts have tended to be more conservative on questions of equitable set off than their English counterparts, and, with the exception of some recent cases, generally have continued to be faithful to the formulation of the principle enunciated by Lord Cottenham in *Rawson* v. *Samuel*. In *Hill* v. *Ziymack*[315] the plaintiff at law had obtained judgment for damages for conversion against the defendant, and the High Court held

---

[311] *Stimson* v. *Hall* (1857) 1 H & N 831, 835 (emphasis added).
[312] [1991] 1 Lloyd's Rep. 573.
[313] Fox and Glidewell L.JJ. and Sir Frederick Lawton.
[314] [1988] 1 WLR 863, affirmed without reference to the set-off point [1990] 2 AC 703. See also *Zemco Ltd.* v. *Jerrom-Pugh* [1993] BCC 275.
[315] (1908) 7 CLR 352.

that the plaintiff's title to issue execution was not impeached by a cross-claim for an account between the parties of sums paid by the defendant on behalf of the plaintiff in satisfaction of a number of promissory notes given in payment of the property the subject of the conversion claim. A claim for a set-off also failed in *Bayview Quarries Pty. Ltd.* v. *Castley Development Pty. Ltd.*[316] The plaintiff was suing for the price of goods delivered to the defendant pursuant to an arrangement involving a running account between the parties. Sholl J. held that a cross-claim for damages arising out of defects in other earlier deliveries did not constitute a sufficient reason in equity to protect the defendant from the plaintiff's demand, even though, because of payments made pursuant to the running account, the defendant had already paid for the defective goods.[317] Nor, when there are various contracts for the sale of goods, should it be sufficient to justify a different result that the contracts are subject to a supervening master agreement which sets out the terms applicable to all the contracts.[318]

The case law concerning equitable set-off was the subject of an extensive review by Woodward J. in *Galambos & Son Pty. Ltd.* v. *McIntyre.*[319] The case involved an action for payment of the balance due on a building contract. It was held that cross-claims possessed by the defendant against the plaintiff relating to non-performance of the contract or defective work, requiring remedial work or directly reducing the value of the work done, constituted matters of pure defence sufficient to defeat the plaintiff's claim. Further, his Honour said that a claim for damages for loss of enjoyment of the premises was so closely connected with the plaintiff's claim that it would have been appropriate, as a matter of equity, to set it off, had it been so pleaded and had it been necessary to do so.[320] Woodward J. considered generally the situation in which there is a claim for money under a contract and a cross-claim for damages for breach of the same contract. These cross-claims may be set off *provided* that the equity of the case requires that this should be so. This was said to depend upon how closely the respective claims are related, particularly as to time and

---

[316] [1963] VR 445.

[317] See also *W. Pope & Co. Pty. Ltd.* v. *Edward Souery & Co. Pty. Ltd.* [1983] WAR 117. Compare *Edward Ward & Co.* v. *McDougall* [1972] VR 433 (claim by share brokers for the balance due of money paid to the defendant's use as the purchase price of shares or as stamp duty, and for brokerage charged on work done in buying and selling shares, and cross-claim for damages for negligence or breach of contract in respect of the purchase of some of the shares and the sale of others).

[318] Compare *Auspac Trade International Pty. Ltd.* v. *Victorian Dairy Industry Authority* unreported, 30 June 1993, Byrne J., Victorian Supreme Court.

[319] (1974) 5 ACTR 10.

[320] In fact it was not necessary, because the defendant's cross-claims for non-performance of the contract and for defective work in any event were sufficient to overtop the plaintiff's claim.

subject-matter, and also upon the general conduct of the respective parties.[321] Nevertheless, when cross-claims arise out of the same contract and are closely related to each other, a set-off should normally be allowed.[322]

Since *Galambos*, a set-off has been denied in a case in which the plaintiff was suing for money due under a mortgage of land given by the defendant to the plaintiff, and the defendant asserted a cross-claim against the plaintiff for breach of an alleged agreement by the plaintiff to lend other money to the defendant on the security of other lands purchased by the defendant from the plaintiff.[323] On another occasion it was held that a purchaser of land and dwelling-house could not set off against the price a damages claim that he had against the vendor for failure to assign a policy of insurance which indemnified the insured against loss of and damage to the dwelling and its contents.[324] Further, a claim for the price of goods sold was not impeached as a result of a breach by the vendor of a grant of a territorial monopoly in favour of the purchaser.[325] On the other hand, when a plaintiff applied for summary judgment on a claim for payment of his charges for the performance of certain earth-moving works, the Queensland Supreme Court said that there was at least an arguable case that an equitable set-off could arise in relation to a cross-claim for sums incurred by the defendant in repairing the plaintiff's machinery so that the plaintiff could perform the work contracted for.[326] Moreover in *Sidney Raper Pty. Ltd.* v. *Commonwealth Trading Bank of Australia*[327] Moffitt P., as an alternative basis for his judgment, held that a customer of a bank could not sue for the proceeds of a bank cheque issued to him by the bank without giving credit for a dishonoured cheque deposited by him with the bank and which he had used to obtain the issue of the bank cheque.[328]

Nevertheless, there have been instances in which Australian judges have adopted tests similar to Lord Denning's formulation in *Federal Commerce* v. *Molena*.[329] In *Tooth & Co. Ltd.* v. *Smith*[330] Clarke J. said that, 'no general rule can be laid down except by stating that [an equitable] set-off will arise when there exist circumstances which make it unjust or inequitable that a plaintiff should be permitted to proceed with his

[321] (1974) 5 ACTR 10, 26.   [322] (1974) 5 ACTR 10, 22.

[323] *United Dominions Corporation Limited* v. *Jaybe Homes Pty. Ltd.* [1978] Qd. R 111.

[324] *Eagle Star Nominees Limited* v. *Merril* [1982] VR 557.

[325] *Covino* v. *Bandag Manufacturing Pty, Ltd.* [1983] 1 NSWLR 237.

[326] *Phillips* v. *Mineral Resources Developments Pty. Ltd.* [1983] 2 Qd. R 138.

[327] [1975] 2 NSWLR 227.

[328] In fact the customer had paid the bank cheque to a company, and the company was the party suing on the cheque. However, the company held the cheque as trustee for the customer, and so a set-off in equity was still payable to the bank.

[329] [1978] 1 QB 927, 975.

[330] Unreported, New South Wales Supreme Court, 5 September 1984.

claim'.[331] Wood J. later remarked that, as presently advised, he could not see any fault with this.[332] Subsequently Giles J. in *AWA Limited* v. *Exicom Australia Pty. Ltd.*,[333] after referring to these cases, said that the 'ultimate question' is whether it would be 'unjust or inequitable' that the plaintiff should be permitted to proceed with his claim, an approach that Rogers C.J. and McLelland J. referred to with approval in later cases.[334] However, recently there has been a swing back to the traditional formulation.[335] In *M.E.K. Nominees Pty. Ltd.* v. *Billboard Entertainments Pty. Ltd.*[336] Tadgell J. said that a dilution of the requirement of impeachment has not occurred in the Victorian Supreme Court, while, in New South Wales, the Court of Appeal in *Lord* v. *Direct Acceptance Corporation Ltd.*[337] confirmed that the traditional principle still determines the availability of an equitable set-off. This would also appear to be the case in Western Australia.[338] In the Federal Court similar views were expressed by Gummow J. in *James* v. *Commonwealth Bank of Australia*,[339] by Lee J. in *Griffiths* v. *Commonwealth Bank of Australia*,[340] and by Cooper J. (with whom Spender J. agreed) in *Walker* v. *Department of Social Security*,[341] though Gummow J. in *James* nevertheless emphasized that the requirement of impeachment has not been narrowly construed.[342] In *James'* case, a receiver claimed an indemnity from his appointing banks in respect of certain debts and liabilities that he had incurred. The banks in their cross-claim alleged that these debts and liabilities were the result of the personal

---

[331] See also *Sydmar Pty. Ltd.* v. *Statewise Developments Pty. Ltd.* (1987) 73 ALR 289, 295.
[332] *Tooth & Co. Ltd.* v. *Rosier*, unreported, New South Wales Supreme Court, 7 June 1985. His Honour repeated this view in *Davkot* v. *Custom Credit Corporation Ltd.*, unreported, New South Wales Supreme Court, 28 March 1991. See also *Sydmar Pty. Ltd.* v. *Statewise Developments Pty. Ltd.* (1987) 73 ALR 289, 295.
[333] (1990) 19 NSWLR 705, 712.
[334] See Rogers C.J. in *Australian Mutual Provident Society* v. *Specialist Funding Consultants Pty. Ltd.* (1991) 24 NSWLR 326, 328–9, and McLelland J. in *Lambert Pty. Ltd.* v. *Papadatos Pty. Ltd.* (1991) 5 ACSR 468, 470–1 and in *Westmex Operations Pty. Ltd. (in liq)* v. *Westmex Ltd. (in liq)* (1992) 8 ACSR 146, 153. In Victoria Byrne J. indicated support for the approach of Giles J. in *Auspac Trade International Pty. Ltd.* v. *Victorian Dairy Industry Authority*, unreported, 30 June 1993.
[335] In addition to the cases referred to below, see *General Credits (Finance) Pty. Ltd.* v. *Stoyakovich* [1975] Qd. R 352, 355 (Queensland); *W. Pope & Co. Pty. Ltd.* v. *Edward Souery & Co. Pty. Ltd.* [1983] WAR 117, 122.
[336] (1993) V Conv. R 54–468. See also *Eagle Star Nominees Ltd.* v. *Merril* [1982] VR 557, 561; *Indrisie* v. *General Credits Ltd.* [1985] VR 251, 254.
[337] (1993) 32 NSWLR 362. See also *Covino* v. *Bandag Manufacturing Pty. Ltd.* [1983] 1 NSWLR 237, 238.
[338] *Westwind Air Charter Pty. Ltd.* v. *Hawker De Havilland Ltd.* (1990) 3 WAR 71; *Geraldton Building Co. Pty. Ltd.* v. *Christmas Island Resort Pty. Ltd.* (1992) 11 WAR 40.
[339] (1992) 37 FCR 445. See also *Westpac Banking Corporation* v. *Eltran Pty. Ltd.* (1987) 14 FCR 541, 547–8. [340] (1994) 123 ALR 111, 124
[341] (1995) 129 ALR 198, 217. Compare the dissenting judgment of Drummond J. (at 206–13). [342] (1992) 37 FCR 445, 458.

neglect or default of the receiver, and that this gave rise to a cross-claim for damages which could be set off against their indemnity obligation. While for other reasons it was not necessary to decide the point, Gummow J. nevertheless said that the cross-claim would have impeached the receiver's demand, since his demand owed its existence to, or at least it was contributed to by, the receiver's own breach of duty to the banks.

The circumstances in *AWA* v. *Exicom*[343] lent themselves to an equitable set-off on both the traditional and the more recent formulations. The plaintiff as vendor of a business was suing the purchaser for money due under the contract by way of adjustments consequent upon the transfer of the business. These adjustments arose out of orders which had been accepted and contracts which had been undertaken but which were incomplete as at the date of completion. The purchaser claimed damages for breach of warranty which went to the value of the business. Giles J. held that this gave rise to an equitable set-off, on the basis that it would have been unjust or inequitable that AWA should be permitted to proceed with its claim. The same result would have been achieved applying the formulation approved by the House of Lords in *Bank of Boston*, because the cross-claim was inseparably connected with the transaction which gave rise to the claim.[344] Further, the impeachment test would appear to have been satisfied. If the claim had been for the price itself, the cross-claim would certainly have given rise to an equitable set-off under this formulation. Instead, the claim related to adjustments to take into account incomplete contracts. Nevertheless, as Giles J. noted, it affected what the purchaser had to pay, and in such a case it should not make any difference that the adjustments were treated separately in the contract rather than being built into the price.

1.7.4 The substantive nature of equitable set-off

We saw earlier that the right of set-off derived from the Statutes of Set-off takes effect only as a procedural defence.[345] By this it is meant that separate and distinct debts remain in existence until judgment for a set-off, and, moreover, the defence has no effect until judgment. Prior to judgment the rights consequent upon being a creditor still attach, as do the obligations and liabilities consequent upon being a debtor. A similar analysis should apply when equity acts by analogy with the Statutes.[346]

---

[343] (1990) 19 NSWLR 705.
[344] See Giles J. at (1990) 19 NSWLR 705, 707.
[345] See section 1.2.9 above.
[346] Compare *Stewart* v. *Latec Investments Ltd.* [1968] 1 NSWR 432, discussed in section 1.6 above.

However, a characteristic of the form of equitable set-off under discussion which has emerged in recent years is that it operates as a true, or substantive, defence.[347] It may be invoked independently of any order of the court or of arbitrators.[348] It may be set up by a person indebted to another, not merely as a means of preventing that other person from obtaining judgment, but also as an immediate answer to his liability to pay the debt otherwise due.[349] While it is only recently that the substantive nature of this defence has come into prominence,[350] it is consistent with the tenor of Lord Cottenham's judgment in *Rawson* v. *Samuel*.[351] The Lord Chancellor referred to earlier cases in which an equitable set-off had been allowed as cases in which 'the equity of the bill impeached the title to the legal demand'. It was not merely the right to obtain judgment on the demand that was impeached, but the title to the demand itself.

Notwithstanding some judicial statements suggesting the contrary,[352] the view that the defence is substantive does not mean that it operates as an automatic extinction of the cross-demands. A proper statement of the principle is that, if there is an entitlement to an equitable set-off, the creditor *as a matter of equity* is not entitled to treat the debtor as being indebted to him to the extent of the debtor's own claim against him. The cross-demands as a matter of law remain in existence between the parties until extinguished by judgment[353] or agreement, though, as far as equity is concerned, it is unconscionable for the creditor even before then to regard

---

[347] In addition to the cases referred to below, see *Newman* v. *Cook* [1963] VR 659, 674–5; *AWA Ltd.* v. *Exicom Australia Pty. Ltd.* (1990) 19 NSWLR 705, 711. Compare the judgments of Cairns and Roskill L.JJ. in *Henriksens Rederi A/S* v. *THZ Rolimpex (The Brede)* [1974] 1 QB 233, and *In re K.L. Tractors Ltd.* [1954] VLR 505, 507 (though O'Brien J. there relied upon certain observations of Byrne J. in *In re Hiram Maxim Lamp Company* [1903] 1 Ch. 70 which were concerned with the Statutes of Set-off). Since the prevailing view is that the defence is substantive, it has been suggested that it is better described as an equitable defence rather than a set-off. See *The Brede* (at 248); *Sidney Raper Pty. Ltd.* v. *Commonwealth Trading Bank of Australia* [1975] 2 NSWLR 227, 236, 238. See also *Altarama Ltd.* v. *Camp* (1980) 5 ACLR 513, 519.

[348] See Robert Goff J. in the *The Kostas Melas* [1981] 1 Lloyd's Rep. 18, 26.

[349] See Goff L.J. in *Federal Commerce & Navigation Co. Ltd.* v. *Molena Alpha Inc.* [1978] 1 QB 927, 982.

[350] As Cumming-Bruce L.J. remarked in *Federal Commerce* v. *Molena* [1978] 1 QB 927, 997, 'it is probably true to say that it was only Morris L.J.'s judgment in *Hanak* v. *Green* [1958] 2 QB 9 that brought clearly to the attention of the legal profession and the commercial world the possibilities of equitable set-off as a defence'.

[351] (1841) Cr. & Ph. 161, 179.

[352] See, e.g. *Covino* v. *Bandag Manufacturing Pty. Ltd.* [1983] 1 NSWLR 237, 238; *AWA Ltd.* v. *Exicom Australia Pty. Ltd.* (1990) 19 NSWLR 705, 710–11. In *Hanak* v. *Green* [1958] 2 QB 9, 29 Sellers L.J. commented that, 'If there is a set-off at all each claim goes against the other and either extinguishes it or reduces it'. See also *Lockley* v. *National Blood Transfusion Service* [1992] 1 WLR 492, 495.

[353] Even here it will be appreciated that, before the Judicature Acts, the permanency of an equitable set-off was achieved by way of a perpetual injunction.

the debtor as being in default to the extent of the cross-demand if circumstances exist which support an equitable set-off. A court of equity will protect the debtor's position by way of injunction, and it may also be the subject of a declaration.[354] This is an illustration of the maxim that equity acts *in personam*, and it provides an explanation of how equitable set-off operates substantively without working an automatic discharge.[355] The notion that the plaintiff's claim is not extinguished as such prior to judgment for a set-off is apparent from one of the grounds for the decision of the House of Lords in *Aries Tanker Corporation* v. *Total Transport Ltd.*[356] Charterers of a vessel were being sued for payment of freight, and argued as a defence that they had an equitable set-off arising from a damages claim that they had against the owners for short delivery. The defence failed, for two reasons. The first was on the basis of a long-standing principle, that a damages claim in respect of cargo cannot be asserted by way of deduction from freight.[357] But as an alternative ground, which the House of Lords in *Bank of Boston* later described as the primary ground for the decision,[358] the point was made that the time bar set out in Article 3 rule 6 of the Hague Rules for the enforcement of the charterer's damages claim had expired, with the result that the charterer's claim had ceased to exist as distinct from being merely unenforceable. Even apart from the objection relating to deductions from freight, Lord Wilberforce in the leading judgment said that the argument for a set-off failed because the damages claim no longer existed.[359] A claim which had ceased to exist could not be introduced into legal proceedings as a set-off. This was so notwithstanding that the charterers had asserted their claim within the limitation period by deducting the amount of the claim from the freight. Their problem was that they had not taken the extra step of commencing a suit during the period so as to preserve the claim. Because of this, any formerly existing right of equitable set-off that they otherwise may have had was lost. On this basis, it could hardly be argued that any such right of

---

[354] *P. Rowe Graphics Pty. Ltd.* v. *Scanagraphix Pty. Ltd.* unreported, Young J., New South Wales Supreme Court, 6 September 1988.

[355] See in this regard the discussion of *Beasley* v. *Darcy* (1800) 2 Sch. & Lef. 403n in *O'Mahoney* v. *Dickson* (1805) 2 Sch. & Lef. 400, 408, 412, where it was acknowledged that the rent had been due in *Beasley*. In *Westpac Banking Corporation* v. *Eltran Pty. Ltd.* (1987) 14 FCR 541, 549. Fox and Burchett JJ. in their joint judgment in the Federal Court said that, 'Equity permits certain privileged cross-claims to put on the armour of a set-off, but they do not therefore lose the character of cross-claims. They operate to extinguish the debt, not by ceasing to be cross-claims, but by virtue of being cross-claims which possess additional features'. Compare though *Stehar Knitting Mills Pty. Ltd.* v. *Southern Textile Converters Pty. Ltd.* [1980] 2 NSWLR 514, 518.

[356] [1977] 1 WLR 185.   [357] See section 1.7.14 below.

[358] [1989] 1 AC 1056, 1103. See also Mustill L.J. in the Court of Appeal (at 1071).

[359] Compare Lord Denning's reference to the Aries Tanker case in *Federal Commerce & Navigation Co. Ltd.* v. *Molena Alpha Inc.* [1978] 1 QB 927, 973–4, which is difficult to follow.

[360] See generally Wood, *English and International Set-off* (1989), 111–12.

set-off had already taken effect as an automatic extinction of obligations.

Wood has presented a different analysis of the substantive nature of the defence.[360] Essentially, his analysis has two aspects. The first is that an equitable set-off (or, as he terms it, a transaction set-off) is a 'self-help' remedy, by which it is meant that it entitles the debtor himself to 'exercise' or 'declare' the set-off so as to bring about a discharge or payment of the cross-demands.[361] The second is that, if the debtor does not exercise his right in this manner, he may rely on the set-off as a defence in judicial proceedings, in which case the judgment for a set-off has a 'retroactive' effect to the date that the debtor's cross-claim accrued.[362] Taking the second point first, it is not necessary to have recourse to an artificial notion of retroactivity of the judgment. The substantive nature of the defence in the period before the demands have been extinguished by judgment or by agreement is adequately explained on the basis outlined above. Insofar as the concept of 'self-help' is concerned, *Aries Tanker* provides authority for the view that a right of equitable set-off does not entitle the debtor himself to bring about a discharge of the cross-demands by setting them against each other. The charterers in that case had deducted the amount of their claim from the freight payable and tendered the balance before the expiration of the limitation period. Lord Wilberforce (in a judgment with which Viscount Dilhorne, Lord Simon of Glaisdale and Lord Edmund-Davies agreed[363]) rejected the argument that this brought about a set-off. He said that,[364] 'The deduction of $30,000, unaccepted by the respondents, conferred no legal rights, and could not alter the legal position'. This was in the context of the primary ground for the decision in *Aries Tanker*, that a claim that has ceased to exist cannot be relied on by way of set-off. The fact that the charterers had asserted their claim within the limitation period and purported to make a deduction did not affect his view. Even if it were possible to have a set-off against a claim for freight, the unilateral deduction and the assertion of a defence were regarded as insufficient to bring about a cancellation of the cross-demands. This is consistent with a comment made by Megarry J. in an earlier case, in response to an argument that a mortgagor's indebtedness to the mortgagee had been reduced as a result of the appropriation to it by the mortgagor of a damages claim available against the mortgagee. He said that 'the concept that the appropriation of an unliquidated claim to a mortgage debt by the mortgagor will effect a discharge nisi of that debt seems both novel and

---

[361] Wood, *English and International Set-off* (1989), 112 para. 4–25, 663 para. 11–24 (in the context of foreign currency claims), 784 para. 14–56, 894 para. 16–125, and 895 para. 16–128. See also McCracken, *The Banker's Remedy of Set-off* (1993), 123–4, 131.

[362] Wood, *English and International Set-off* (1989), 112, cross-referring to para. 2–192 et seq.   [363] See also Lord Salmon [1977] 1 WLR 185, 196.

[364] [1977] 1 WLR 185, 188.

awkward'.[365] Indeed, it is difficult to find authority for the proposition that one party may act unilaterally to effect a set-off of cross-demands. Admittedly, Robert Goff J. in *The Kostas Melas*[366] described equitable set-off as a self-help remedy, although he appears to have used that term merely in the sense that the debtor was entitled to withhold payment of the debt to the extent of the equitable set-off, which accords with the view that, while the circumstances which support an equitable set-off exist, it is unconscionable for the creditor to regard the debtor as being indebted. It does not require a conclusion that the debtor's equitable right is such as to entitle him to act unilaterally to extinguish the cross-demands at law.

The debtor in most cases will be adequately protected by this principle of unconscionability. For example, the point is made below that he will not be adversely affected by the expiration of the usual form of limitation period, which merely renders the cross-action unenforceable. He will, however, be at risk in a case such as *Aries Tanker*, where the debtor's cross-claim has a shorter limitation period than the plaintiff's claim, and the effect of the expiration of the period is to *extinguish* the cross-claim. In such a case he would be well-advised to commence a suit so as to preserve the position, unless representations by the other party would make it unfair to rely on the time bar in any event. This is in accordance with the view expressed by Lord Wilberforce in that case.[367] A similar difficulty may arise when an equitable set-off is available to a debtor, and the creditor assigns the debt to a third party. The third party assignee should take subject to the set-off in accordance with normal principles.[368] Consider, however, that the assignor becomes bankrupt. Because of the assignment the debt will no longer be an asset of the estate, and accordingly a set-off will not be available under the insolvency set-off section. Normally this would not concern the debtor if he can still assert an equitable set-off against the assignee. But what if the assignee does not proceed against the debtor until *after* the assignor's discharge from bankruptcy? In that circumstance, Wood would appear to be correct in his view that the set-off would be lost.[369] The discharge would release the assignor from liability to the debtor,[370] in which case *Aries Tanker* suggests that the debtor would no

---

[365] *Samuel Keller (Holdings) Limited* v. *Martins Bank Limited* [1971] 1 WLR 43, 47. In the Court of Appeal Russell L.J. (at 51) agreed with this view. While Megarry J. did not mention equitable set-off, the judgment of Russell L.J. suggests that he recognized that the cross-claim in that case may have been available by way of that defence, and his approval of Megarry J.'s comment should be considered with that in mind. See the reference (at 49) to unconditional leave to defend, and also (at 49 and 51) to the earlier Court of Appeal decision in *Morgan & Son Ltd.* v. *S. Martin Johnson & Co. Ltd.* [1949] 1 KB, 107, which was concerned with equitable set-off.   [366] [1981] 1 Lloyd's Rep. 18, 26.
[367] [1977] 1 WLR 185, 189.   [368] See 13.2 below.
[369] Wood, *English and International Set-off* (1989), 894–5.
[370] Insolvency Act 1986, s. 281.

longer have a right of set-off which he could assert against the assignee. The problem is not confined to equitable set-off. It may also apply in relation to the Rule in *Cherry* v. *Boultbee*,[371] as well as set-off under the Statutes of Set-off.[372] It is not, however, a particularly happy result for a debtor. It is justifiable in the case of set-off under the Statutes, which after all is only a procedural defence.[373] On the other hand, when a substantive defence of equitable set-off is in issue, there is much to be said for the view that the title to the assigned debt should remain impeached after the assignor's discharge, notwithstanding the approach adopted in *Aries Tanker*. At least in *Aries Tanker* the charterers could have preserved their position by commencing a suit within the limitation period, though that mechanism would not be available when an assignor has become bankrupt. But even apart from that, the debtor is not necessarily without a remedy. Where, because of an imminent discharge from bankruptcy the substantive defence may be lost, the debtor may be entitled to approach the court for a declaration[374] and for an order giving effect to the set-off by way of an injunction to restrain an action on the assigned debt.

Wood has also expressed a concern in relation to the situation in which a trustee in his capacity as such enters into a transaction pursuant to which he incurs a debt, though a cross-claim for damages is available which is sufficiently closely connected to give rise to an equitable set-off.[375] While the trustee is personally liable for the debt and the damages claim is an asset of the estate, this apparent lack of mutuality would not be a sufficient ground for denying an equitable set-off.[376] The situation posited by Wood is that the set-off is not 'declared' before the bankruptcy of the trustee or the third party. The concern is that the damages claim and the debt in such a case will have retained their separate identities, and accordingly may not be available for a set-off under the insolvency set-off section because of lack of mutuality. In truth, however, there should not be a problem when equitable set-off is analysed in the manner suggested above. If the cross-demands are sufficiently closely connected, the third party's title will be impeached such that it would be unconscionable for him to regard the trustee as a debtor, and this should continue to apply during a

---

[371] See section 10.5 below.   [372] See section 13.2.9 below.

[373] See section 1.2.9 above.

[374] As contemplated by Young J. in the New South Wales Supreme Court in *P. Rowe Graphics Pty. Ltd.* v. *Scanagraphix Pty. Ltd.* unreported, 6 September 1988. On the other hand, Young J. doubted that a similar declaration would be available in the case of a procedural defence such as that conferred by the Statutes of Set-off. For this the defendant would be required to wait until he is sued before the right of set-off can be given effect. See also the discussion of *Parker* v. *Jackson* [1936] 2 All ER 281 in section 1.2.9 above.

[375] Wood, *English and International Set-off* (1989), 784.

[376] *Murphy* v. *Zamonex Pty. Ltd.* (1993) 31 NSWLR 439, discussed in section 13.4.1 below.

bankruptcy or liquidation.[377] While the leave of the court is required for
the commencement of proceedings against a bankrupt or a company after a
winding-up order has been made against it,[378] this should be readily
forthcoming where an injunction is sought in order to prevent any action
being taken which is inconsistent with the substantive nature of the defence
of equitable set-off. A similar result should follow in the converse situation
in which the third party incurs the debt to the trustee but at the same time
has a cross-claim available as an equitable set-off, and the trustee becomes
insolvent. The third party should still retain his equitable set-off.[379]

The characterization of the defence as substantive can have a number of
important consequences. For example, a contract may entitle one party to
take a particular course of action if the other party fails to make a payment
pursuant to the contract. If the other party does indeed fail to pay but
nevertheless has available a substantive defence of equitable set-off
the first party could not treat that other party as being in default, and
accordingly could not take the action which is available upon default.[380]
Consider in this regard *Federal Commerce & Navigation Co. Ltd.* v.
Molena Alpha Inc.[381] The Court of Appeal[382] held in this case that a
charterer of a vessel on a time charter has a right of equitable set-off
entitling it to make a 'deduction'[383] from the hire otherwise stipulated in
the charter if the owner through its neglect or default has deprived the
charterer of the use of the vessel, or has otherwise hindered or prejudiced
the charterer's use, for example through a breach of a speed warranty.[384]
This right arises on the due date for payment, and it does not merely
provide a defence to an action at law for the payment of hire.[385] The
charterer, in paying less than the sum stipulated in the contract, is not

---

[377] See section 2.4 below.
[378] See the Insolvency Act 1986, s. 130(2) for companies and, for bankruptcies, s. 285(3).
[379] Compare Wood, *English and International Set-off* (1989), 1055.
[380] See Lord Denning in *Federal Commerce & Navigation Co. Ltd.* v. *Molena Alpha Inc.*
[1978] 1 QB 927, 974, referred to with approval by Dillon L.J. in *BICC Plc* v. *Burndy
Corporation* [1985] 1 Ch. 232, 248–9. In *Ashley Guarantee Plc* v. *Zacaria* [1993] 1 WLR 62, 68
Nourse L.J. agreed with counsel's argument that if an equitable set-off was available in that
case the company would not have defaulted in any of its obligations.
[381] [1978] 1 QB 927, affirmed on other grounds [1979] AC 757.
[382] Lord Denning M.R. and Goff L.J., Cumming-Bruce L.J. dissenting on the question of
whether there may be a set-off against hire.
[383] While the right in question was described as a right of deduction, the courts have since
shown a marked reluctance to accept that this term encompasses equitable set-off. See for
example *Connaught Restaurants Ltd.* v. *Indoor Leisure Ltd.* [1994] 1 WLR 501, and generally
section 1.13.1 below.
[384] See Lord Denning M.R. and Goff L.J. at [1978] 1 QB 927, 976, 981. Set-off in the
context of charterparties is considered in section 1.7.14 below.
[385] See also *The Teno* [1977] 2 Lloyd's Rep. 289, 294 (explaining *The Agios Giorgis* [1976]
2 Lloyd's Rep. 192); *Santiren Shipping Ltd.* v. *Unimarine S.A. (The Chrysovalandou-Dyo)*
[1981] 1 Lloyd's Rep. 159; *The Kostas Melas* [1981] 1 Lloyd's Rep. 18, 26–7.

considered to be in breach of contract. Therefore, when the time charter contains the usual provision whereby the owner may withdraw the vessel in the event of non-payment of hire, the charterer may tender a reduced amount in consequence of the cross-demand without bringing into existence the right of withdrawal.[386] If the owner does not accept this it acts at its peril. It will be liable in damages if it withdraws the vessel. If, on the other hand, the defence was merely procedural rather than substantive, the owner would have been entitled to withdraw the vessel because, until there had been a judgment for a set-off, the charterer would still have been regarded as being in default. The same analysis applies when a landlord asserts a right to re-take possession of the premises because of the tenant's failure to pay rent. If an equitable set-off is available the tenant is entitled to say that there was no such failure upon which the landlord can rely.[387] Further, a lease may give an option to the tenant to renew the lease for a further term if it has complied with its obligations under the lease, including payment of rent. In a case in Queensland the tenants in question admittedly had not tendered the rent stipulated in the lease, though, since they had an equitable set-off, it was held that they had not breached the payment obligation and accordingly they were entitled to exercise the option.[388] This is the converse of the other instances referred to above, in that 'debtors' had to show that they were not in default before they could exercise a right (i.e. renew the lease), rather than that a right of a creditor to take a particular course of action depended upon whether the debtor had defaulted, although the principle nevertheless is the same.

Since the cross-demand in these cases usually is for an unliquidated sum, a person asserting a right to an equitable set-off may have to make an estimate of the value of his damages claim when the date accrues for payment of the sum stipulated in the contract. For example, a charterer of a vessel may not be in a position to calculate with precision the value of a cross-demand available to it against the owner for breach of a speed warranty when the next payment of hire becomes due. Goff L.J. in the *Federal Commerce* case[389] suggested that the charterer acts at its peril if it pays less than the amount otherwise required by the contract. If it is wrong

---

[386] See Lord Denning and Goff L.J. at [1978] 1 QB 927, 974, 982. A similar analysis may apply when a shipowner claims to exercise a lien in the event of non-payment of hire. See *Santiren Shipping Ltd.* v. *Unimarine S.A. (The Chrysovalandou-Dyo)* [1981] 1 Lloyd's Rep. 159.

[387] *Federal Commerce & Navigation Co. Ltd.* v. *Molena Alpha Inc.* [1978] 1 QB 927, 974; *Televantos* v. *McCulloch* [1991] 1 EGLR 123; *Tomlinson* v. *Cut Price Deli Ltd.* (1992) 38 FCR 490, 494–5; *MEK Nominees Pty. Ltd.* v. *Billboard Entertainments Pty. Ltd.* (1993) V Conv. R 54–468. See also *BICC Plc.* v. *Burndy Corporation* [1985] 1 Ch. 232, 249 (referring to *British Anzani (Felixstowe) Ltd.* v. *International Marine Management (U.K.) Ltd.* [1980] 1 QB 137), and *Connaught Restaurants Ltd.* v. *Indoor Leisure Ltd.* [1994] 1 WLR 501.

[388] *Knockholt Pty. Ltd.* v. *Graff* [1975] Qd. R 88.   [389] [1978] 1 QB 927, 982.

the owner is justified in withdrawing the vessel for non-payment of hire. However the better view was expressed by Lord Denning in that case,[390] that the charterer is not regarded as being in default if in fact it has quantified the loss by a reasonable assessment made in good faith. This approach has since been adopted in other cases.[391]

The substantive nature of the defence of equitable set-off may become important when there is a time bar imposed by a statute of limitation in enforcing a right of action. The usual form of statute of limitation preserves the existence of the right but takes away the remedy of enforcing that right by action at law.[392] Since the Statutes of Set-off merely perform a procedural function, a defence of set-off under the Statutes may only be based upon a debt that is still enforceable by action. Therefore, a debt owing by the plaintiff which is unenforceable as a result of the expiration of a limitation period[393] may not be employed by the defendant in this statutory form of set-off.[394] Equitable set-off on the other hand is a substantive defence which does not require an order of the court for its enforcement.[395] Consequently the better view is that an equitable set-off may be asserted notwithstanding that the cross-demand upon which it is based is no longer enforceable by action because of a time bar.[396] This is so notwithstanding the provisions of sections 35(1) and (2) of the Limitation Act 1980, according to which any claim by way of set-off or counterclaim is

---

[390] [1978] 1 QB 927, 975.

[391] *The Kostas Melas* [1981] 1 Lloyd's Rep. 18, 26–7; *Santiren Shipping Ltd.* v. *Unimarine S.A. (The Chrysovalandou-Dyo)* [1981] 1 Lloyd's Rep. 159. Compare *The Agios Giorgis* [1976] 2 Lloyd's Rep. 192.

[392] For example, the Limitation Act 1980, ss. 2 and 5, which deal respectively with claims in tort and contract, each stipulate that 'An action . . . shall not be brought' after the expiration of six years from the date on which the cause of action accrued.

[393] The relevant date from which the period is calculated is the date of the issue of the plaintiff's writ. See *Walker* v. *Clements* (1850) 15 QB 1046; *McDonnell & East Ltd.* v. *McGregor* (1936) 56 CLR 50, 57.   [394] See section 1.2.10 above.

[395] *The Kostas Melas* [1981] 1 Lloyd's Rep. 18, 26.

[396] See Lord Denning in *Henriksens Rederi A/S* v. *THZ Rolimpex (The Brede)* [1974] 1 QB 233, 245–6, 249 (though compare Cairns and Roskill L.JJ. at 254 and 264), and again in *Federal Commerce* v. *Molena* [1978] 1 QB 927, 973–4. See also *Sidney Raper Pty. Ltd.* v. *Commonwealth Trading Bank of Australia* [1975] 2 NSWLR 227, 236–40 per Moffitt P. (though compare the somewhat confusing passage in the judgment of Glass J.A. at 255–6); *AMP* v. *Specialist Funding Consultants Pty. Ltd.* (1991) 24 NSWLR 326, 331–2; *Westdeutsche Landesbank* v. *Islington BC* [1994] 4 All ER 890, 944–5. There is also support for this view in the judgment of Lord Salmon in *Aries Tanker Corporation* v. *Total Transport Ltd.* [1977] 1 WLR 185, 196–7 (on the assumption that English law permitted deductions from freight by way of equitable set-off). For the contrary view, see *The Tojo Maru* [1970] P 21, 48; *Renner* v. *Racz* (1971) 22 DLR (3d) 443. On this same principle a possessory lien may be exercised in respect of a statute-barred debt, because the right to exercise the lien is not dependent upon an action at law. See for example *Spears* v. *Hartly* (1800) 3 Esp. 81 and *Higgins* v. *Scott* (1831) 2 B & Ad. 413. See also the discussion of unenforceable claims in the context of the rule in *Cherry* v. *Boultbee* (1839) 4 My. & Cr. 442 in section 10.5 below.

deemed to be a separate action and to have been commenced on the same date as the original action. Unlike the procedural defence of set-off available under the Statutes of Set-off, a right of equitable set-off does not require an action at law before it may be invoked. Consequently, section 35 would not appear to be relevant to equitable set-off, but seems to refer only to the right of set-off available under the Statutes of Set-off.[397] When questions of equitable set-off arise in relation to time bars, the conclusion that the defence is still available notwithstanding the expiration of the limitation period assumes that the statute of limitation in question merely takes away the remedy without affecting the existence of the underlying right. If, however, the right itself is abolished, as, for example, pursuant to Article 3, rule 6 of the Hague Rules in relation to a contract for the carriage of goods by sea, the circumstances necessary to support an equitable set-off will no longer exist, and the debtor will not be successful in an application for an equitable set-off as a defence to an action brought against him for payment of the debt. This was held to be the case in *Aries Tanker Corporation* v. *Total Transport Ltd.*,[398] to which reference has already been made.

Consider the case of an interest-bearing debt. If the debtor has a valid claim for an equitable set-off, the principal sum upon which interest is payable is reduced to the extent of the value of the cross-demand during the period while the circumstances exist which support an equitable set-off.[399] This is indicative of a substantive defence, as opposed to the form of procedural defence available under the Statutes of Set-off.

If an equitable set-off is available to the debtor, the creditor will be restrained from presenting a winding-up petition because of failure to pay, given that the set-off provides a substantive defence to the debtor.[400]

---

[397] See Lord Denning M.R. in *Henriksens Rederi A/S* v. *THZ Rolimpex (The Brede)* [1974] 1 QB 233, 246 (though compare Cairns and Roskill L.JJ. at 254 and 264), and Hobhouse J. in *Westdeutsche Landesbank* v. *Islington BC* [1994] 4 All ER 890, 943. Compare Article 32(4) of the Convention on the Contract for the International Carriage of Goods by Road (CMR), which stipulates that 'A right of action which has become barred by lapse of time may not be exercised by way of counter claim or set-off'. While *Impex Transport Aktieselskabet* v. *A.G. Thames Holdings Ltd.* [1981] 2 Lloyd's Rep. 566 supports the view that this encompasses equitable set-off, it was subsequently held in *R H & D International Ltd.* v. *IAS Animal Air Services Ltd.* [1984] 1 WLR 573 that freight payable under a contract for the carriage of goods by road cannot be reduced by equitable set-off in any event. See section 1.7.14 below.

[398] [1977] 1 WLR 185.

[399] See *Connaught Restaurants Ltd.* v. *Indoor Leisure Ltd.* [1994] 1 WLR 501, and also *Newman* v. *Cook* [1963] VR 659 (particularly the judgment of Hudson J. at 676–7). Compare *Axel Johnson Petroleum AB* v. *MG Mineral Group AG* [1992] 1 WLR 270, 275 with respect to a counterclaim. In *Wallis* v. *Bastard* (1853) 4 De G M & G 251, the court found an implied agreement for a set-off so that interest was only payable on the balance.

[400] *McDonald's Restaurants Ltd.* v. *Urbandivide Co. Ltd.* [1994] BCLC 306.

1.7.5 Discretion

While the determination of whether to allow an equitable set-off is not merely an exercise of discretion dependent solely upon notions of fairness,[401] an equitable set-off may still be denied, notwithstanding that the cross-demands are otherwise sufficiently closely connected, if in the circumstances it would be unjust that a set-off occur. Thus, the conduct of the parties may be relevant to the question whether equitable relief by way of set-off should be granted.[402] The courts have given little guidance as to the circumstances in which this concept can apply, though in one case in Australia an equitable set-off was denied, even though it was agreed that the claims were closely connected, because the cross-claimant had failed to investigate, quantify or press his claim.[403]

An equitable set-off may not be allowed if the cross-claim depends upon the outcome of the taking of a long and complicated account,[404] or if the determination of the cross-claim would otherwise involve considerable delay so that the plaintiff may find that he is not adequately compensated for being kept from his money for this period,[405] though interest in some cases may be an adequate remedy if it turns out that some or all of the plaintiff's claim is not reduced by a set-off.[406] There have also been exceptional cases in which the defendant was given leave to defend, or the plaintiff was restrained from exercising a right consequent upon non-payment, only on condition that the defendant pays all or part of the plaintiff's claim into court, or provides some other acceptable form of security pending the determination of the cross-claim.[407] This has arisen

---

[401] See Hobhouse J. in *The Leon* [1985] 2 Lloyd's Rep. 470, 474.

[402] *Galambos & Son Pty. Ltd.* v. *McIntyre* (1974) 5 ACTR 10, 26; *Sydmar Pty. Ltd.* v. *Statewise Developments Pty. Ltd.* (1987) 73 ALR 289, 296; *AMP* v. *Specialist Funding Consultants Pty. Ltd.* (1991) 24 NSWLR 326, 329; *AWA Ltd.* v. *Exicom Australia Pty. Ltd.* (1990) 19 NSWLR 705, 712; *Walker* v. *Department of Social Security* (1995) 129 ALR 198, 208. See also *Televantos* v. *McCulloch* [1991] EGLR 123, in which it was argued that the defendant should be precluded from asserting an equitable set-off because of her conduct, though it was held that the conduct in question was not sufficient to have this effect.

[403] *APM Wood Products Pty. Ltd.* v. *Kimberley Homes Pty. Ltd.*, unreported, Cole J., New South Wales Supreme Court, 17 February 1989, referred to in *AWA Ltd.* v. *Exicom Australia Pty. Ltd.* (1990) 19 NSWLR 705, 712.

[404] *Rawson* v. *Samuel* (1841) Cr. & Ph. 161, and see also *General Credits (Finance) Pty. Ltd.* v. *Stoyakovich* [1975] Qd. R 352.

[405] *Best* v. *Hill* (1872) LR 8 CP 10, 15. Some remarks by Lord Cottenham in *Rawson* v. *Samuel* (1841) Cr. & Ph. 161, 179 may be interpreted as supporting this view, though they should be considered in light of the circumstances there in issue.

[406] *Best* v. *Hill* (1872) LR 8 CP 10, 15.

[407] In addition to the mortgage cases referred to below, see *General Credits (Finance) Pty. Ltd.* v. *Stoyakovich* [1975] Qd. R. 352; *Tomlinson* v. *Cut Price Deli Pty. Ltd.* (1992) 38 FCR 490. See also Bramwell B. in *Atterbury* v. *Jarvie* (1857) 2 H & N 114, and the order made by Alexander C.B. in *Gale* v. *Luttrell* (1826) 1 Y & J 180, 195.

particularly in the context of mortgages, where a mortgagor has sought to restrain the mortgagee from exercising his security rights consequent upon default on the basis of an alleged equitable set-off.[408]

If the claims are otherwise sufficiently closely connected, it is not necessary that the defendant should have commenced proceedings against the plaintiff on the cross-claim.[409] Furthermore, a defendant will not be precluded from raising a cross-claim as a defence by way of equitable set-off merely because the parties had agreed that the cross-claim should be the subject of arbitration, or that it should be determined by the courts of a foreign jurisdiction. Therefore, in an application by the plaintiff for summary judgment the defendant in such a case may be granted leave to defend.[410] Indeed, in the case of the usual arbitration which provides for all disputes to be referred to arbitration, the availability of an equitable set-off would mean that the plaintiff's claim is also in dispute, so that both the claim and the cross-claim must be referred.[411] This is a consequence of the substantive nature of the defence.[412]

1.7.6 Mutuality

In *The Evelpidis Era*[413] Mocatta J. accepted as correct a submission by counsel that an equitable set-off where different parties are involved in the respective claims is 'a creature unknown to the law'. However this is not strictly correct because, unlike set-off under both the Statutes of Set-off and the set-off section in the insolvency legislation, mutuality is not a strict requirement of equitable set-off.[414] There are indeed a number of instances where a court of equity considered that, because of special circumstances, it was appropriate that a set-off should occur despite the absence of mutuality. In *ex parte Hanson*[415] one of two joint debtors on a bond given as security for a debt had only joined in the bond as a surety. It was held that the person who was the principal debtor could employ the joint debt in a set-off against a separate claim that he had against

---

[408] See section 1.7.13 below.

[409] *McDonald's Restaurants Ltd.* v. *Urbandivide Co. Ltd.* [1994] 1 BCLC 306.

[410] *Aectra Refining and Marketing Inc.* v. *Exmar NV* [1994] 1 WLR 1634, 1649, referring to *Gilbert-Ash (Northern) Ltd.* v. *Modern Engineering (Bristol) Ltd.* [1974] AC 689 (esp. at 720, 726). Compare section 1.2.11 above in relation to the Statutes of Set-off.

[411] See e.g. *Federal Commerce & Navigation Co. Ltd.* v. *Molena Alpha Inc.* [1978] 1 QB 927, 974, and generally the discussion in the Introduction.

[412] See section 1.7.4 above.   [413] [1981] 1 Lloyd's Rep. 54, 67.

[414] *Sidney Raper Pty. Ltd.* v. *Commonwealth Bank of Australia* [1975] 2 NSWLR 227, 255; *CIBC* v. *Tuckerr Industries Inc.* (1983) 149 DLR (3d) 172, 175; *Telford* v. *Holt* (1987) 41 DLR (4th) 385, 394 (Canadian Supreme Court); *Westmex Operations Pty. Ltd. (in liq)* v. *Westmex Ltd. (in liq)* (1992) 8 ACSR 146, 153; *Murphy* v. *Zamonex Pty. Ltd.* (1993) 31 NSWLR 439, 464; *Walker* v. *Department of Social Security* (1995) 129 ALR 198, 210.

[415] (1811) 18 Ves. Jun. 232.   [416] (1840) 9 LJ Ch. 258.

the creditor, despite the fact that a joint debt and a separate claim are not mutual. *Hamp* v. *Jones*[416] was a similar case. A judgment had been obtained against both Hamp and his bailiff for damages for wrongful distress. In addition, Hamp had a separate claim against the judgment creditor. Because the demands were not mutual they could not be set off at law. However, Hamp had agreed to indemnify the bailiff on the judgment. Since Hamp was the party who would bear the ultimate burden of the judgment, it was held that he could set it off against his separate claim. Another example is *Vuillamy* v. *Noble*,[417] which concerned bankers who had fraudulently sold a debtor's property and applied the proceeds to their own use. The debtor in this case was jointly indebted to the bank with another person, though Lord Eldon allowed the debtor to set off his separate claim arising from fraud against the joint debt.

Nevertheless, while mutuality is not an absolute prerequisite to an equitable set-off, usually it would not be just or equitable that a set-off occur unless the same parties are beneficially involved in the respective claims. It is not generally just that a claim by A against B be set off against a liability of A to C, because this would involve C's asset being used to satisfy B's debt. If A becomes insolvent, and B and C are related in some way, it may well be advantageous for them that there should be a set-off. However, the fact that one of the parties to a dealing has become insolvent on its own does not give rise to an equity sufficient to support an equitable set-off. Lord Cottenham himself emphasized this in *Rawson* v. *Samuel*.[418] If a set-off is to occur, the facts should support an equitable set-off irrespective of A's insolvency. This is particularly relevant to *Bank of New Zealand* v. *Harry M. Miller & Co. Ltd.*,[419] a decision of Brownie J. in the New South Wales Supreme Court. A lender entered into a loan agreement with the defendant debtor, as security for which a number of guarantees were obtained. Pursuant to the deed of guarantee, the guarantors promised to deposit their surplus funds with the lender on interest-bearing deposits, and the lender was authorized on the happening of an event of default to appropriate the money so deposited in reduction of the debtor's debt arising from the loan. Subsequently the lender assigned both the debt and the benefit of the guarantees to the plaintiff. However, the deposits made by the guarantors remained with the lender. The amount paid by the plaintiff assignee in respect of the assignment of the debt was the sum calculated as the principal debt then outstanding together with accrued interest, and no deduction was made for the deposits. The lender went into liquidation, and, after that, the assignee brought this action

---

[417] (1817) 3 Mer. 593. See also *Ex parte Stephens* (1805) 11 Ves. Jun. 24 (joint and several debt).   [418] (1841) Cr. & Ph. 161, 175.
[419] (1992) 26 NSWLR 48.

against the debtor claiming the amount outstanding and interest. The debtor asserted as a defence an entitlement to an equitable set-off in respect of the amounts deposited with the lender by the guarantors. Brownie J. held that the defence was available. He analysed the situation in two parts. First he considered the position that would have applied if the deposits had been made by the debtor itself rather than by the guarantors. In such a case, if the lender had sued the debtor, his Honour said that there would have been available to the debtor a substantive defence by way of equitable set-off to the extent of the deposits made, since the cross-claim in respect of the deposits raised an equity which impeached, or was essentially bound up with or went to the root of, the lender's title to the claim against the debtor, and it flowed out of and was inseparably connected with the dealing and the transactions which gave rise to the lender's claim. Further, his Honour said that an assignee would have taken subject to this equity available against the lender/assignor.[420] In fact, the guarantors, rather than the debtor, made the deposits, and his Honour then considered whether this made any difference to the result. He concluded that it did not. Admittedly there was a lack of mutuality, since the lender had a claim against the debtor but was subject to a cross-claim from the guarantors in respect of the deposits, although, as his Honour noted, mutuality is not an essential requirement of an equitable set-off. The important point was that the lender had agreed to advance the money to the debtor upon terms which included the taking of the guarantee and the guarantors agreeing to deposit and keep deposited their surplus funds, with a right in the lender upon the happening of an event of default to appropriate those funds towards satisfaction of the debt owing by the debtor. The deposits were said to be inseparably connected with the obligations arising out of the loan agreement. Accordingly, it was held that an equitable set-off was available to the debtor and the guarantors in respect of the deposits,[421] notwithstanding the lack of mutuality,[422] and the assignee took subject to this equity.

Was it appropriate to allow an equitable set-off in *Harry M. Miller* when different parties were involved in the claims, notwithstanding that the claims arose out of and were inseparably connected with the same transaction? In *Lord* v. *Direct Acceptance Corporation Ltd.*[423] the New

---

[420] See section 13.2 below.

[421] Brownie J. acknowledged ((1992) 26 NSWLR 48, 56) that some adjustment may have had to be made as between the debtor and the guarantors, but he said that the question did not arise for decision in the proceedings before him.

[422] Because of the assignment, and the consequent lack of mutuality, the insolvency set-off section did not apply, and for this reason the case is distinguishable from *M. S. Fashions Ltd.* v. *Bank of Credit and Commerce International* [1993] Ch. 425, discussed in section 8.3 below.

[423] (1993) 32 NSWLR 362.

South Wales Court of Appeal expressed considerable doubt as to the correctness of Brownie J.'s decision. The agreement between the parties in *Harry M. Miller* was that the debtor should be primarily liable to discharge the debt, though the lender in its discretion could appropriate the deposits for this purpose if an event of default occurred. On the other hand, the effect of allowing an equitable set-off to the debtor was to make the guarantors primarily liable to the extent of their deposits. As the Court of Appeal noted, there was no equity in that result. As it turned out, because of the insolvency of the lender and the assignment of the loan a set-off would have benefited the guarantors, since the guarantors and the debtor were closely associated, and it was not in their interests that the debtor should be liable to pay the principal debt in full and the guarantors be confined to a dividend in respect of their deposits. Nevertheless, the mere fact of insolvency is not a justification for allowing an equitable set-off.[424] If the intention was that the guarantors should be primarily liable to the extent of their deposits, this should have been made clear in the agreement.

While the facts considered in *Lord* v. *Direct Acceptance* were similar to those in *Harry M. Miller*, they differed in that the person providing the deposit as 'security' for the loan to the borrower had not assumed any personal liability, whether as guarantor or by agreeing to be jointly and severally liable. Rather, the deposit was provided merely by way of collateral security on terms that the lender 'may in its discretion' set off the deposit in satisfaction of the loan. For this reason the New South Wales Court of Appeal considered that *Harry M. Miller* in any event was distinguishable. The view that an equitable set-off is not available in the circumstances that prevailed in *Lord* v. *Direct Acceptance* has now been confirmed in England by the Court of Appeal in *Morris* v. *Agrichemicals Ltd.*[425] A bank lent money to a customer secured by a deposit made by a third party which was 'charged' with repayment of the loan, though without the third party providing a guarantee or other personal covenant as to repayment. The bank subsequently went into liquidation. The liquidator declined to apply the deposit against the loan, preferring to proceed against the customer and to confine the depositor to a proof in the liquidation. It was held that there was a lack of mutuality which prevented a set-off under the insolvency set-off section,[426] and nor was there any basis for the customer and the third party to assert an equitable set-off.

[424] *Rawson* v. *Samuel* (1841) Cr. & Ph. 161, 175.
[425] Rose, Saville and Millett L.JJ., 20 December 1995.
[426] See also *Lord* v. *Direct Acceptance* (1993) 32 NSWLR 362, and generally section 8.4.

1.7.7 *Different contracts*

Lord Cottenham emphasized in *Rawson* v. *Samuel*[426a] that it is not sufficient for an equitable set-off that both demands arose out of the same contract.[427] Equally, though, it is not an essential requirement of an equitable set-off that the claim and the cross-claim should have originated in the same contract,[428] and opinions which seem to indicate the contrary should not be regarded as representing the true position.[429] The crucial question is whether the claims are so closely connected that the title of the plaintiff at law to prosecute his demand is impeached, or, under the formulation approved by the House of Lords in *Bank of Boston*,[430] whether the cross-claim is inseparably connected with the transaction that gave rise to the claim. While the fact that the claim and the cross-claim each arose under different contracts, or indeed that one claim is based on contract and the other is in tort, is a factor to be considered in relation to the question whether there is a sufficient connection, it is not conclusive. An example is *The Angelic Grace*.[431] The owners of a vessel had let the vessel under three consecutive charterparties to the same charterers. When the vessel was re-delivered after the expiration of the third charter it contained a large quantity of bunkers for which the owners were liable to reimburse the charterers. However, the owners had a cross-claim for stevedore damage occurring during the currency of both the second and the third charterparties for which the charterers were liable under the terms of the charterparties. Lord Denning and Waller L.J. considered that the claim and cross-claim under the charters were so closely connected that it would be a case for equitable set-off. The three charterparties in this

---

[426a] (1841) Cr. & Ph. 161, 178.

[427] See also *Government of Newfoundland* v. *Newfoundland Railway Company* (1888) 13 App. Cas. 199, 212; *The Didymi* [1988] 1 Lloyd's Rep. 97; *Bank of Boston* v. *European Grain and Shipping* [1989] 1 AC 1056, 1102; *AWA Ltd.* v. *Exicom Australia Pty. Ltd.* (1990) 19 NSWLR 705, 712; *Lambert Pty. Ltd.* v. *Papadatos Pty. Ltd.* (1991) 5 ACSR 468, 470; *Westwind Air Charter Pty. Ltd.* v. *Hawker De Havilland Ltd.* (1990) 3 WAR 71.

[428] See *Galambos & Son Pty. Ltd.* v. *McIntyre* (1974) 5 ACTR 10, 26; *The Angelic Grace* [1980] 1 Lloyd's Rep. 288; *British Anzani (Felixstowe) Ltd.* v. *International Marine Management (U.K.) Ltd.* [1980] 1 QB 137; *The Raven* [1980] 2 Lloyd's Rep. 266, 272; *Coba Industries Ltd.* v. *Millie's Holdings (Canada) Ltd.* [1985] 6 WWR 14; *Grant* v. *NZMC Ltd.* [1989] 1 NZLR 8; *National Westminster Bank plc* v. *Skelton* [1993] 1 WLR 72, 76. See also *Melville* v. *Grapelodge Developments Ltd.* (1978) 39 P & CR 179. Thus Sellers L.J. evidently assumed in *Hanak* v. *Green* [1958] 2 QB 9, 31 that a set-off may proceed if the cross-claim is 'closely associated with and incidental to the contract'. In *Telford* v. *Holt* (1987) 41 DLR (4th) 385, 401 the Canadian Supreme Court said that the debts in that case could only be set off if they arose out of the same contract or closely related contracts.

[429] See e.g. *Provident Finance Corporation Pty. Ltd.* v. *Hammond* [1978] VR 312, 321, and also the statement of the principle by Parker J. in *The Teno* [1977] 2 Lloyd's Rep. 289, 297.

[430] [1989] 1 AC 1056, discussed in section 1.7.2 above.

[431] [1980] 1 Lloyd's Rep. 288.

case involved the same vessel being chartered to the same charterers over a continuous period. In effect they were all a part of the same transaction. The decision perhaps illustrates the difference between the modern and the traditional approaches to equitable set-off. While the cross-claim for stevedore damage could be said to have been inseparably connected with the same transaction which gave rise to the claim, it is not easy to see how one claim could be said to be impeached by the other within Lord Cottenham's traditional formulation in *Rawson* v. *Samuel*.[432] Nevertheless, the principle that in appropriate circumstances claims under separate contracts can give rise to an equitable set-off is correct.

If on the other hand separate contracts in truth each involve separate transactions, a set-off generally should not be allowed.[433] This brings into question *Bankes* v. *Jarvis*.[434] The plaintiff's son bought a veterinary surgeon's practice from the defendant. The defendant was lessee of a house used in connection with the practice, and at the time of the sale he also assigned the lease to the plaintiff's son, who covenanted to pay the rent and perform the covenants in the lease and also to indemnify the defendant against all claims arising thereunder. Some six years later the plaintiff's son left the country, having given the plaintiff authority to sell the practice. The plaintiff then sold it back to the defendant. When the plaintiff sued for the balance of the purchase price the defendant sought to set-off a cross-claim for damages against the plaintiff's son for breach of the covenant to indemnify against claims arising under the lease. It was held that, if the son instead had been the plaintiff, the defendant would have been entitled to the set-off, and that the plaintiff suing as a trustee accordingly should also be subject to this defence.[435] Although Morris L.J. later commented in *Hanak* v. *Green*[436] that this 'conclusion seems to me to be clearly correct and obviously fair', the transactions appear to have been totally separate and distinct, and it is not at all clear what was the justification for a set-off.[437]

---

[432] Stone J. in the Canadian Federal Court of Appeal in *The Didymi* [1988] 1 Lloyd's Rep. 97, 105 appears not to have been entirely comfortable with the view that *The Angelic Grace* was an appropriate case for an equitable set-off.

[433] See in this regard *Minshull* v. *Oakes* (1858) 2 H & N 793; *Indrisie* v. *General Credits Ltd.* [1985] VR 251, 254. See also the fact situation considered by Isaacs J. in *Tooth* v. *Brisbane City Council* (1928) 41 CLR 212, 223–4. A claim for an indemnity under a policy of insurance and a cross-claim for premiums due on other policies covering other subject-matters are not sufficiently connected for an equitable set-off. See *E. Pellas & Co.* v. *Neptune Marine Insurance Co.* (1979) 5 CPD 34, and also *Baker* v. *Adam* (1910) 15 Com. Cas. 227.

[434] [1903] 1 KB 549.

[435] Wills J. in his judgment ([1903] 1 KB 549, 552) said that he had some difficulty in seeing how the plaintiff even had standing to sue in this case, though he declined to express a decided opinion on the point.   [436] [1958] 2 QB 9, 24.

[437] Channell J. in *Bankes* v. *Jarvis* [1903] 1 KB 549, 553 said that 'the Judicature Act, and more especially the rules, distinctly put an unliquidated claim on the same footing as a

1.7.8 Misrepresentation inducing a contract

A question in respect of which there are conflicting views is whether a claim in tort for damages for fraudulent misrepresentation inducing a contract may be brought into account in an action for payment of a sum of money owing under the contract, as, for example, when the vendor of a business is suing for the price and the purchaser has a cross-claim for damages for fraud inducing the contract. It has been held in the context of assignments that an assignee of the contract debt does not take subject to the cross-claim for fraud, because this is not a claim arising under the contract, or for breach of the contract, but is a claim outside the contract.[438] Since an assignee takes subject to rights of set-off available to the debtor against the assignor, but not mere counterclaims,[439] these cases suggest that the damages claims similarly would not have given rise to an equitable set-off in an action between the original parties. However, there are two difficulties with this view. The first is that it is contrary to the principle applied in bankruptcy, that a claim for damages for misrepresentation inducing a contract is not a mere personal tort but rather is a breach of the obligation arising under the contract, so that, even before the insolvency legislation was amended in 1986 to allow claims in tort to be proved in a bankruptcy, it could be employed in a set-off.[440] The second is that, in any event, it is not a prerequisite to an equitable set-off that both demands should have arisen under the same contract.[441] The better view is that a cross-claim available to a purchaser against the vendor for fraud inducing the purchaser to enter into the contract is capable of being set off in an action brought by the vendor for the price. While this argument has been rejected in New Zealand,[442] there is support for it in Australia.[443] To

---

liquidated claim for the purpose of set-off. This is clearly incorrect (see *McDonnell & East Limited* v. *McGregor* (1936) 56 CLR 50, 61–2; *Galambos & Son Pty. Ltd.* v. *McIntyre* (1974) 5 ACTR 10, 19), and to this extent it detracts from the weight which otherwise would be attached to his Lordship's judgment.

[438] *Stoddart* v. *Union Trust, Limited* [1912] 1 KB 181; *Cummings* v. *Johnson* (1913) 4 WWR 543; *Provident Finance Corporation Pty. Ltd.* v. *Hammond* [1978] VR 312. See also *Birchal* v. *Birch, Crisp & Co.* [1913] 2 Ch. 375, 379.

[439] See section 13.2.3 below.

[440] *Jack* v. *Kipping* (1882) 9 QBD 113; *Tilley* v. *Bowman, Ltd.* [1910] 1 KB 745.

[441] See section 1.7.7 above.

[442] *Wilsons (NZ) Portland Cement Ltd.* v. *Gatx-Fuller Australasia Pty. Ltd. (No. 2)* [1985] 2 NZLR 33 (in particular at 37–8).

[443] *Petersville Ltd.* v. *Rosgrae Distributors Pty. Ltd.* (1975) 11 SASR 433; *Alterama Ltd.* v. *Camp* (1980) 5 ACLR 513, 519–20; *AMP* v. *Specialist Funding Consultants Pty. Ltd.* (1991) 24 NSWLR 326; *Tomlinson* v. *Cut Price Deli Pty. Ltd.* (1992) 38 FCR 490, 494; *Re Kleiss*, Federal Court of Australia, Drummond J., 18 January 1996. See also section 1.7.10 below in relation to s. 52 of the Trade Practices Act. Compare *Provident Finance Corporation Pty. Ltd.* v. *Hammond* [1978] VR 312 (discussed below).

adopt the test approved by the House of Lords in *Bank of Boston*,[444] the cross-claim for damages would be inseparably connected with the transaction which gave rise to the claim,[445] though the traditional impeachment test espoused by Lord Cottenham in *Rawson* v. *Samuel* would also appear to be satisfied. If the fraud induced the purchaser to enter into the contract, in its absence he may not have contracted, in which case he would not have breached any contractual obligation to the vendor to tender a sum of money as payment of a purchase price. On this analysis it can be said that the vendor's own conduct may have contributed (albeit indirectly) to the existence of the purchaser's liability to him, so as to impeach the vendor's title to his demand.[446] The argument for a set-off would be even stronger if the statements which gave rise to the fraud also constituted a term of the contract.[447] Further, it should not make any difference to the set-off if the action for the price is brought upon a bill of sale given by the purchaser to the vendor rather than on the contract of sale itself, given that it is not necessary for an equitable set-off that the demands should have arisen under the same contract.[448] For this reason the decision of Lush J. in the Victorian Supreme Court in *Provident Finance Corporation Pty. Ltd.* v. *Hammond*[449] should be regarded as doubtful. His Honour suggested in that case that one of the objects of the contract of sale in providing for the execution of a bill of sale was to give the debt and security aspects of the contract a separate existence in separate contracts, though this is debatable. In any event, this should not have been sufficient to exclude an equitable set-off, given that the attitude of the courts generally is that clear words are required to have this effect.[450]

A party may have been induced to enter into a contract by a false representation that was not fraudulent, although the same principle should apply as for fraudulent misrepresentation. A resulting damages claim should be able to be employed in a set-off against a claim on a contract, the important point being that the party would not have entered into the contract but for the false representation.[451] This should also apply

---

[444] See section 1.7.2 below.
[445] See *Altarama Ltd.* v. *Camp* (1980) 5 ACLR 513, 519–20.
[446] See in this regard *Piggott* v. *Williams* (1821) 6 Madd. 95.
[447] As in *Sun Candies Pty. Ltd.* v. *Polites* [1939] VLR 132.
[448] See section 1.7.7 below.   [449] [1978] VR 312.
[450] See section 1.13.1 below.
[451] *Aquaflite Ltd.* v. *Jaymar International Freight Consultants Ltd.* [1980] 1 Lloyd's Rep. 36. See also *Box* v. *Midland Bank Ltd.* [1981] 1 Lloyd's Rep. 434 (customer of a bank induced to draw on an overdraft as a result of negligent advice by a manager of the bank that further facilities would be made available).

where the representation was contained in a collateral contract.[452] It should be the fact of the inducement, not the nature of the misrepresentation, that gives rise to the impeachment of title.

1.7.9 Fraudulent claim on a contract

The discussion in the preceding section concerned fraud inducing a contract. This should be compared to *Etablissement Esefka International Anstalt* v. *Central Bank of Nigeria*,[453] in which the question instead related to an alleged fraudulent claim on a contract. The plaintiff made a claim on letters of credit issued by the defendant in respect of demurrage. Prior to the action the plaintiff had been paid various sums of money on the same letters of credit in respect of demurrage when there was evidence to suggest that the shipments in question had never taken place. As a result, the defendant appeared to have a cross-claim to recover this as money paid under a mistake of fact. Lord Denning said that all the claims on the letter of credit should be considered as part of the one transaction, and that the cross-claim was so closely connected with the instant claim that it could well be a case for an equitable set-off. Whether in fact this would have been a suitable case for an equitable set-off is by no means clear,[454] though the question may well have been unnecessary. The cross-claims in any event would appear to have constituted mutual debts giving rise to a defence of set-off under the Statutes of Set-off, in which case it would not have been necessary to show any connection between them.

1.7.10 Misleading or deceptive conduct in Australia

In Australia, section 52 of the Trade Practices Act 1974 (Cth) provides that, 'A corporation shall not, in trade or commerce, engage in conduct that is misleading or deceptive or is likely to mislead or deceive'. A question of interest to Australian lawyers is whether a claim arising as a result of a contravention of section 52 is capable of being employed defensively as an equitable set-off. In New South Wales, Rogers C.J. in *AMP* v. *Specialist Funding Consultants Pty. Ltd.*[455] held that it could, if it was otherwise sufficiently closely connected with the claim. This was also

---

[452] *Grant* v. *NZMC Ltd.* [1989] 1 NZLR 8. See also *British Anzani (Felixstowe) Ltd.* v. *International Marine Management (UK) Ltd.* [1980] 1 QB 137.

[453] [1979] 1 Lloyd's Rep. 445. See also *The Litsion Pride* [1985] 1 Lloyd's Rep. 437, 518–19.

[454] Compare *Attorney-General* v. *McLeod* (1893) 14 NSWLR 121, in which a plea of cross-action, pursuant to the Common Law Procedure Act 1857 (NSW), for breach of contract in an action for damages for fraud was held to be bad, on the ground that the cause of action could not be said to have arisen out of the same subject-matter.

[455] (1991) 24 NSWLR 326.

accepted by Giles J. in the New South Wales Supreme Court,[456] and by Drummond J. in the Federal Court.[457] The difficulty is that neither Giles J. nor Drummond J. considered *Bank of New Zealand* v. *Spedley Securities Ltd.*,[458] a decision of the New South Wales Court of Appeal which occurred after the *AMP* case.

The question in *Spedley Securities* was whether conduct prohibited by section 52 could be relied on as a defence in proceedings to establish a constructive trust. Kirby P. in his judgment endorsed earlier authority to the effect that section 52 of its own does not give rise to a duty which is enforceable at law.[459] Rather, it was regarded as merely describing a 'norm of conduct' which 'should not be interpreted according to established principles of liability under the general law and which, since it may be offended by acts both honest and reasonable . . . is morally neutral'.[460] If the 'norm of conduct' specified in section 52 is not complied with, sanctions are provided elsewhere in the Act. Thus, section 82 provides that a person who suffers loss by the conduct of another person which contravenes section 52 may recover the amount of the loss 'by action against that other person'. Section 82, it has been said, is a provision which creates both right and remedy.[461] The difficulty is that section 82 is drafted only in terms of bringing an action to recover the amount of the loss, and accordingly Kirby P. commented that 'the words of that section are not apt to support a defence'.[462] *Spedley Securities* admittedly was concerned with a question of a constructive trust as opposed to set-off, and indeed Mahoney J.A. in that case expressed his views on the availability of a defence only in that context. Kirby P.'s remarks, on the other hand, were more general in their scope. Moreover, Cole J. at first instance in *Spedley Securities*[463] indicated that *AMP* v. *Specialist Funding* should not be followed. It is doubtful, however, that Kirby P.'s view would be held to extend to equitable set-off, particularly given the subsequent judgments of Giles and Drummond JJ.

In *Spedley Securities* a claim for relief under section 82 had not actually been made.[464] It was merely argued that conduct which contravened

---

[456] *Murphy* v. *Zamonex Pty. Ltd.* (1993) 31 NSWLR 439, 463.

[457] See his dissenting judgment in *Walker* v. *Department of Social Security* (1995) 129 ALR 198, 210, and also *Tomlinson* v. *Cut Price Deli Pty. Ltd.* (1992) 38 FCR 490.

[458] (1992) 27 NSWLR 91.

[459] See, e.g. *Western Australia* v. *Wardley Australia Ltd.* (1991) 30 FCR 245, 256–7, referring to *Tobacco Institute of Australia Ltd.* v. *Australian Federation of Consumer Organisations Inc.* (1988) 19 FCR 469. See also Toohey J. on appeal in the High Court in *Wardley* (1992) CLR 514, 551.

[460] *Commonwealth Bank of Australia* v. *Mehta* (1991) 23 NSWLR 84, 88 per Samuels J.A.

[461] *Western Australia* v. *Wardley Australia Ltd.* (1991) 30 FCR 245, 257.

[462] (1992) 27 NSWLR 91, 99.   [463] (1991) 13 ATPR 41–143 (at 53,066).

[464] This was emphasized by Cole J. at first instance. See *Spedley Securities Ltd.* v. *Bank of New Zealand* (1991) 13 ATPR 41–143 (at 53,066).

section 52 gave rise to a defence. Even if Kirby P.'s view of section 82 is held to be otherwise applicable to set-off, if a cross-claimant has actually taken the step of commencing an action pursuant to section 82, that action, as opposed to merely the bare assertion of a contravention of the 'norm of conduct' described in section 52, should be able to provide a basis for a defence of equitable set-off. This is suggested by the judgment of Hope A-J.A. in the Court of Appeal in *Spedley Securities*, in which he commented that,[465] 's. 52 of the Trade Practices Act cannot be pleaded by way of defence, *absent a claim for relief under s. 82*'. Similarly, in *Westpac Banking Corporation* v. *Eltran Pty. Ltd.*[466] the defendant had commenced proceedings against the plaintiff claiming damages for breach of section 52. The Full Court of the Federal Court,[467] in ordering that the plaintiff's action against the defendant should by stayed, accepted that there was a serious question to be tried as to whether the defendant's cross-claim gave rise to an equitable set-off.[468] It was not suggested that under no circumstances could the claim be employed defensively in a set-off. *Westpac* v. *Eltran* was decided before *Spedley Securities*, though it was not referred to in that case.

1.7.11 Limitation on liability

It may be that the liability of one of the parties is limited by contract or statute to a certain amount. In such a case the principle is that the liability is first limited, and a set-off may then take place against this limited sum, rather than that the two demands are first set against each other at their full face value with the limitation rule then being applied to the balance.[469] This should be compared to the rule applied in admiralty law in the event of a collision at sea, that a balance should be struck before the limit is applied.[470]

---

[465] (1992) 27 NSWLR 91, 109 (emphasis added). See also Cole J. at first instance (1991) 13 ATPR 41–143 (at 53,066).   [466] (1987) 14 FCR 541.

[467] Fox and Burchett JJ., Northrop J. dissenting on another ground.

[468] See also *AWA Ltd.* v. *Exicom Australia Ltd.* (1990) 19 NSWLR 705. The defendant had commenced an action against the plaintiff claiming damages for breach of contract and for contravention of s. 52. The plaintiff subsequently commenced proceedings against the defendant, and the defendant argued that it could set off the amounts due to it pursuant to its earlier claim. An application by the plaintiff to strike out the defence failed, though Giles J. in his judgment admittedly concentrated on the breach of contract claim and gave little attention to the s. 52 claim.

[469] *The Tojo Maru* [1970] P 21, 48, 67–8, 75.

[470] For a discussion on the practice of the courts in these cases, see *Stoomvaart Maatschappij Nederland* v. *Peninsular and Oriental Steam Navigation Company (The Khedive)* (1882) 7 App. Cas. 659. As Lord Selbourne noted (at 806–7), this admiralty rule operates independently of any principle of set-off.

1.7.12 *Periodic payments*

Sometimes a particular transaction imposes an obligation on one party to
make periodic payments to another, as for example a tenant's obligation
to pay rent to his landlord under a periodic tenancy, or a time charterer's
obligation to pay hire to the owner of the vessel. The question arises
whether a damages claim for breach of contract may be employed in a set-
off against payment obligations that accrue in respect of subsequent
periods, or whether the set-off is confined to the payment obligation that
relates to the particular period in which the breach occurred. The answer
will depend on the circumstances of the case. In *Government of
Newfoundland* v. *Newfoundland Railway Company*[471] it was held that a
claim for damages against a contractor for failure to complete a railway line
could be set off against the contractor's entitlement to an annual subsidy
for each five mile section of the track that had been completed. In this case
the failure to complete went to the value of what had in fact been performed.
On the other hand, in the context of time charters the view has been that,
if the operation of the breach was confined to particular periods, and in
subsequent periods the party affected by the breach received all that he was
entitled to receive under the contract during those periods, he cannot set
off his damages claim against the obligation to pay the hire applicable to
those periods.[472] In *The Aditya Vaibhav*[473] charterers alleged that, in
breach of the charter, the owners had failed to perform their hold-cleaning
obligations, which resulted in a delay to the vessel at port of about fourteen
days. The charterers suffered consequential loss and expense as a result of
the vessel not being available for service, which they deducted in part from
the hire due during the fourteen-day period. They then submitted that they
could set off the remainder of the damages claim against subsequent
payments of hire. Saville J. held that the damages claim did not impeach
the owners' entitlement to hire for periods during which they had actually
performed the services contracted for, so that a set-off was not available in
respect of the remainder of the damages. This accords with Parker J.'s
explanation in *The Teno*[474] of the rationale for allowing an equitable set-off
against a claim for hire under a time charter, that 'it would be grossly

---

[471] (1888) 13 App. Cas. 199.
[472] Compare *The Angelic Grace* [1980] 1 Lloyd's Rep. 288, which concerned successive
charters, though it did not involve a periodic payment obligation.
[473] [1991] 1 Lloyd's Rep. 573.
[474] [1977] 2 Lloyd's Rep. 289, 296. See also *The Didymi* [1988] 1 Lloyd's Rep. 97, 110
(Canadian Federal Court of Appeal). This is also consistent with Lord Denning's comments
in *Federal Commerce & Navigation Co. Ltd.* v. *Molena Alpha Inc.* [1978] 1 QB 927, 975, 976
to the effect that the charterer had been deprived of part of the consideration for which hire
had been paid in advance (for which, see below).

unjust to allow an owner to recover hire in respect of a period during which he had, in breach of contract, failed to provide that for which the hire was payable'.

The contract may provide for payment in advance at the commencement of each period. If during the period there is a breach of contract which has the effect of depriving the payer of part of the consideration for which the advance payment was made, obviously it is too late for a set-off against the pre-paid consideration for that period. Instead, a set-off can take place against the amount due in respect of the next period, even though the contract was performed properly during that period.[475]

The Aditya Vaibhav concerned an attempt to obtain a set-off against a payment obligation relating to a subsequent period when the contract in fact was properly performed. It may be that instead it is sought to set off a damages claim that arose out of a breach occurring in one period against a payment obligation relating to a *prior* period. Once again it will depend on the circumstances of the case, though a set-off was allowed in *Melville* v. *Grapelodge Developments Ltd.*[476] A tenant had gone into occupation of the premises, at the outset rent free. Protracted negotiations then occurred concerning the condition of the premises. It was subsequently agreed that, if the tenant signed a lease, the landlord would carry out repairs as soon as possible. The first quarter's rent became due a few days later. It appears that this was in arrears, so that it related to the period during which negotiations were taking place. When the landlord failed to carry out the repairs, it was held that the tenant could set off the resulting damages claim against unpaid rent, including the first quarter's rent, even though the landlord could not be said to be in breach of the repair obligation at the time that this became due. Nevertheless, it is apparent that the agreement to assume the rent payment obligation was inextricably bound up with the landlord's undertaking that it would repair as soon as possible, so that the right to claim the first quarter's rent could be said to have been impeached.

1.7.13 Mortgages

The right to an equitable set-off against a mortgage debt has been recognized in a number of circumstances, including where the mortgagee is liable to the mortgagor for failure to renew the insurance on the mortgaged property,[477] or the mortgagee's title to sue is impeached as a result of a sale of the mortgaged property at a gross undervalue,[478] or the mortgagee is

---

[475] *Federal Commerce & Navigation Co. Ltd.* v. *Molena Alpha Inc.* [1978] 1 QB 927, 975, 976.　　　　　　　　　　　　　　　　　　　[476] (1978) 39 P & CR 179.

[477] *Campbell* v. *Canadian Co-operative Investment Co.* (1906) 16 Man. LR 464.

[478] *General Credits (Finance) Pty. Ltd.* v. *Stoyakovich* [1975] Qd. R 352, 355.

liable in damages to the mortgagor for breach of contract in not providing further finance to the mortgagor, with the result that the mortgagor is unable to complete a development on the mortgaged property and consequently to repay the debt.[479] Usually, however, questions of equitable set-off in this context arise in relation to contracts for the sale of property which stipulate for a mortgage or other form of security to secure payment of the unpaid balance of the purchase price. A purchaser being sued for the price could generally set off in that action a cross-claim for damages for breach of warranty in the contract of sale directly affecting the value of the property,[480] and this right of set-off should also be available when the action for payment is brought instead on a mortgage given as security for the price.[481] It should not be a sufficient objection that the damages claim arises under a different contract to the mortgage,[482] because it is not an essential requirement of an equitable set-off that the same contract should be the source of both demands.[483] The mortgage is part of the same transaction as the contract of sale.[484] Its purpose is to secure payment of the price, and if the purchaser would have had a set-off in any action brought against him on the contract of sale, the amount outstanding secured by the mortgage should be regarded as reduced *pro tanto*.[485] This is consistent with the substantive nature of this form of equitable set-off.[486]

Sometimes a different arrangement is adopted. Instead of the mortgage securing the unpaid price, the price is in fact satisfied by means of a loan, and it is the repayment of this loan which is secured by a mortgage. In such a case, the Privy Council in *Bow, McLachlan & Co., Ltd.* v. *Ship 'Camosun'*[487] held that a damages claim for breach of warranty will not provide the purchaser with a defence to an action to enforce the mortgage debt, since the sale and the loan secured by the mortgage are considered to be separate contracts.[488] It is doubtful, however, whether this would be

---

[479] *Popular Homes Ltd.* v. *Circuit Developments Ltd.* [1979] 2 NZLR 642. Compare *United Dominions Corporation Ltd.* v. *Jaybe Homes Pty. Ltd.* [1978] Qd. R 111, in which the agreement to provide finance was not part of the same transaction as the debt sued upon.

[480] *Altarama Ltd.* v. *Camp* (1980) ACLR 513, 519–20.

[481] This is implicit in the remarks of Russell L.J. in *Samuel Keller (Holdings) Ltd.* v. *Martins Bank Ltd.* [1971] 1 WLR 43, 49 with respect to unconditional leave to defend. See also *Newman* v. *Cook* [1963] VR 659; *Popular Homes Ltd.* v. *Circuit Developments Ltd.* [1979] 2 NZLR 642; *Altarama Ltd.* v. *Camp* (1980) 5 ACLR 513.

[482] Compare *Provident Finance Corporation Pty. Ltd.* v. *Hammond* [1978] VR 312.

[483] See section 1.7.7 above.

[484] *Altarama Ltd.* v. *Camp* (1980) 5 ACLR 513, 520. See also *Popular Homes Ltd.* v. *Circuit Developments Ltd.* [1979] 2 NZLR 642, 658.

[485] See the discussion in *Newman* v. *Cook* [1963] VR 659.

[486] See section 1.7.4 above.   [487] [1909] A.C. 597.

[488] [1909] A.C. 597, 612–13. See also *Newman* v. *Cook* [1963] VR 659, 675–6; *Altarama Ltd.* v. *Camp* (1980) 5 ACLR 513, 520.

followed today in circumstances where the loan and the contract of sale in truth are part of the one transaction,[489] particularly since the House of Lords in *Bank of Boston*[490] approved the formulation of the test for equitable set-off in terms whether the cross-claim flows out of and is inseparably connected with the transaction which gave rise to the claim. Indeed, it is noticeable that the Privy Council in its judgment in *Bow, MacLachlan* concentrated on the availability of a defence on the basis of common law abatement,[491] and did not discuss the principles of equitable set-off.[492]

The position is more complex, however, when the mortgagee is not suing for the debt but rather is seeking to enforce his rights as mortgagee. In this regard, a distinction must be drawn between a claim by a legal mortgagee for possession of the mortgaged premises, and the exercise of other rights by a mortgagee which depend upon default, for example the exercise of a power of sale.

In England the right of a legal mortgagee to possession of the premises ordinarily is independent of any question of default.[493] He 'may go into possession before the ink is dry on the mortgage unless there is something in the contract, express or by implication, whereby he has contracted himself out of that right'.[494] This is a consequence of the mortgagee's legal estate.[495] In *Birmingham Citizens Permanent Building Society* v. *Caunt*[496] Russell J. said that the court has no jurisdiction to decline to order possession in favour of the mortgagee unless the mortgagor pays the full principal, interest, and costs secured by the mortgage,[497] the 'sole exception' to this being that the application may be adjourned for a short time to afford to the mortgagor a chance of paying off the mortgagee in full, though he emphasized that this should not be done if there is no reasonable prospect of this occurring.[498] Consistently with this strict approach, the courts have held that a mortgagee should not be denied

---

[489] See, e.g. *Samuel Keller (Holdings) Ltd.* v. *Martins Bank Ltd.* [1971] 1 WLR 43 (discussed below), in which the price had been paid in full by means of a loan secured by a mortgage. Russell L.J.'s reference (at 49) to unconditional leave to defend suggests that he contemplated the possibility of setting off the damages claim against the mortgage debt.

[490] [1989] 1 AC 1056. [491] See section 1.10 below.

[492] While the Privy Council did mention set-off ([1909] AC 597, 610), it seems to have had in mind only set-off under the Statutes of Set-off.

[493] Compare the various Australian jurisdictions under the Torrens system, where the mortgagor is entitled to possession until default. See Sykes and Walker, *The Law of Securities* (5th edn., 1993), 248.

[494] *Four-Maids Ltd.* v. *Dudley Marshall (Properties) Ltd.* [1957] 1 Ch. 317, 320.

[495] The same principle applies where a legal mortgage of land is created by a charge by deed expressed to be by way of legal mortgage. See the Law of Property Act 1925, s. 87(1), and *Four-Maids Ltd.* v. *Dudley Marshall (Properties) Ltd.* [1957] 1 Ch. 317, 320.

[496] [1962] 1 Ch. 883. [497] [1962] 1 Ch. 883, 891.

[498] [1962] 1 Ch. 883, 912.

possession of the premises on the ground that the mortgagor has a counterclaim against the mortgagee for an amount in excess of the mortgage debt.[499] This has also been held to apply when there is a cross-claim which would give rise to an equitable set-off in an action to enforce the debt.[500] Nor does it make any difference that the mortgagor is willing to pay into court the difference between the amount owing under the mortgage and the estimate of the sum sought to be set off.[501] An equitable set-off admittedly is a substantive defence, in that it is unconscionable for a creditor against whom the defence may be asserted to regard the debtor as being in default to the extent of the set-off while circumstances continue to exist which support an equitable set-off.[502] Nevertheless, until there is judgment for a set-off and the mortgage is redeemed, the principle by which the mortgagee as the party with the legal estate is entitled to possession still applies. When Slade L.J. re-affirmed the general principle in *National Westminster Bank plc* v. *Skelton*,[503] he left open the question whether this would apply where the mortgagor 'establishes that he has a claim to a quantified sum by way of equitable set-off'.[504] When there is a cross-demand which is both liquidated and admitted and which exceeds the mortgage debt, there is indeed some attraction in the view that an application for possession should be able to be adjourned for a 'short time', in accordance with the exception referred to by Russell J. in *Birmingham Building Society* v. *Caunt*, if it appears that the mortgagor is in a position to obtain a summary judgment against the mortgagee on the liquidated and admitted debt, and thereby obtain sufficient money to pay the mortgagee in full. If this suggestion is adopted, there is no apparent reason why indeed it should be confined to the situation in which that debt and the mortgage debt are sufficiently closely connected to give rise to an equitable set-off, given that the right to possession does not depend upon default in any event.

The view that a mortgagee is entitled to possession notwithstanding that an action to enforce the mortgage debt could be met by an equitable set-off also applies when the mortgage was given by a third party as surety for the debt secured by the mortgage,[505] and, *a fortiori*, when the third party had

---

[499] *Mobil Oil Co. Ltd.* v. *Rawlinson* (1981) 43 P & CR 221, 226; *Citibank Trust Ltd.* v. *Ayivor* [1987] 1 WLR 1157.

[500] *Mobil Oil Co. Ltd.* v. *Rawlinson* (1981) 43 P & CR 221; *National Westminster Bank plc* v. *Skelton* [1993] 1 WLR 72; *Ashley Guarantee plc* v. *Zacaria* [1993] 1 WLR 62, 66–7, 70.

[501] *Mobil Oil Co. Ltd.* v. *Rawlinson* (1981) 43 P & CR 221. Indeed Nourse J. said (at 227) that payment of the full amount secured into court will not suffice to prevent the mortgagee obtaining possession. Payment must be made to the mortgagee himself.

[502] See section 1.7.4 above.   [503] [1993] 1 WLR 72.

[504] [1993] 1 WLR 72, 78.

[505] *Ashley Guarantee plc* v. *Zacaria* [1993] 1 WLR 62, 69.

agreed that the mortgage should apply as if the third party was primarily liable for the debt.[506]

The Administration of Justice Act 1970, section 36[507] has provided some relief to mortgagors in the face of applications by mortgagees for possession when the mortgaged property is a dwelling-house. Section 36 provides that where, in an application for possession of a dwelling-house, it appears to the court that the mortgagor is likely to be able within a reasonable period to pay any sums due under the mortgage or to remedy any other default, the court may adjourn the proceedings or postpone the date for delivery of possession for such period as it thinks reasonable. In *Citibank Trust Ltd.* v. *Ayivor*[508] Mervyn Davies J. suggested that, in determining whether the mortgagor is likely to be able to pay the sums due within a reasonable time, it may be an inadmissible consideration to take into account that the mortgagor may succeed on its cross-claim, since this might nullify or circumvent the general rule that the existence of a cross-claim does not prevent the mortgagee from taking possession. Indeed, the Court of Appeal held in *Royal Trust Co. of Canada* v. *Markham*[509] that, for section 36 to apply, the court must be able to fix a period ending with some specified or ascertainable date during which it is likely that payments will be made, and it may be difficult to do this when reliance is placed on the fruits of an unlitigated cross-claim as the source of the repayment. Notwithstanding this, in *Ashley Guarantee plc* v. *Zacaria*[510] Ralph Gibson L.J. noted the possibility that a stay under section 36 pending trial of the cross-claim may in fact be appropriate if the existence and prospects of success of the cross-claim could, in all the circumstances, be regarded as enabling the sums due to be paid within a reasonable period. Woolf L.J. also countenanced that possibility in his judgment.

Consider that the remedy sought to be exercised by the mortgagee depends upon default, as, for example, the exercise of a power of sale, or a claim to possession of the premises in circumstances where either the mortgage limits the mortgagee's right to possession to the occurrence of a default by the mortgagor[511] or, as in Australia in relation to land under the Torrens system, where this is the position that applies in any event.[512] In Australia, the High Court in *Inglis* v. *Commonwealth Trading Bank of Australia*[513] held that a mortgagee will not be restrained from exercising a

---

[506] *National Westminster Bank plc.* v. *Skelton* [1993] 1 WLR 72.
[507] See also the Administration of Justice Act 1973, s. 8.
[508] [1987] 1 WLR 1157, 1163–4.   [509] [1975] 1 WLR 1416.
[510] [1993] 1 WLR 62, 71.
[511] The courts will not readily imply such a restriction in the mortgage. See *National Westminster Bank plc* v. *Skelton* [1993] 1 WLR 72, 77.
[512] Sykes and Walker, *The Law of Securities* (5th edn., 1993), 248.
[513] (1972) 126 CLR 161.

power of sale on the basis of an unlitigated cross-claim which, if established, would give rise to an equitable set-off exceeding the debt secured by the mortgage,[514] unless some other compensatory form of security is provided, for example payment into court of the amount secured or perhaps the provision of a banker's bond for this amount.[515] Walsh J. considered that this was in accordance with the decision of Megarry J., and also that of the Court of Appeal on appeal, in *Samuel Keller* v. *Martins Bank*.[516] In *Samuel Keller* a prior mortgagee had sold the mortgaged property. A third mortgagee sought to have paid to it the balance of the proceeds of sale after satisfying the prior mortgages. However, the mortgagor said that it had a damages claim against the third mortgagee exceeding the mortgage debt, and that, until this could be litigated, the surplus should be paid into court. The judgment of Russell L.J.[517] in the Court of Appeal suggests that he recognized that the cross-claim may have given rise to an equitable set-off,[518] though it was held that, notwithstanding the cross-claim, the proceeds should be paid to the third mortgagee rather than into court. *Inglis* and *Samuel Keller* differed in that, unlike the exercise of the power of sale by the mortgagee in *Inglis*, the third mortgagee's right to the surplus in *Samuel Keller* was not dependent upon default. On the other hand, Russell L.J. in *Samuel Keller* seems to have accepted the proposition that a court would not prevent a mortgagee from exercising a power of sale on the basis of a cross-claim arising out of the same transaction as the mortgage.[519]

Notwithstanding the Court of Appeal's evident view in *Samuel Keller*, the recent judgments of Nourse and Woolf L.JJ. in the Court of Appeal in *Ashley Guarantee plc* v. *Zacaria*[520] suggest that *Inglis* may not be followed

---

[514] See also *Indrisie* v. *General Credits Ltd.* [1985] VR 251, though possession was denied on another perceived ground, that the mortgagor was only a surety for the debt and a surety is not entitled to assert a set-off against the creditor based upon a cross-claim available to the principal debtor. However, as a general principle this is doubtful if the principal debtor is before the court. See Ch. 14.

[515] See also *Booth* v. *Booth* (1742) 2 Atk. 343 (mortgagee restrained from foreclosing upon other security being provided pending the taking of an account of the rents and profits), *Altarama Ltd.* v. *Camp* (1980) 5 ACLR 513, and the order made by Wigram V.C. in *Dodd* v. *Lydall* (1842) 1 Hare 333 (in which the mortgagor sought to establish an equitable set-off based upon equity acting by analogy with the Statutes). In *Parry* v. *Grace* [1981] 2 NZLR 273 Thorp J., without deciding the point, seemed inclined to accept that an unlitigated cross-claim which, if successful, would give rise to an equitable set-off would not be sufficient ground for restraining the mortgagee in the absence of payment into court.

[516] [1971] 1 WLR 43.   [517] Edmund Davies and Cross L.JJ. concurring.

[518] See the reference in Russell L.J.'s judgment ([1971] 1 WLR 43, 49) to unconditional leave to defend, and also (at 49 and 51) to the earlier Court of Appeal decision in *Morgan & Son Ltd.* v. *S. Martin Johnson & Co. Ltd.* [1949] 1 KB 107, which was concerned with equitable set-off.

[519] See his Lordship's judgment at [1971] 1 WLR 43, 50–1.

[520] [1993] 1 WLR 62.

now in England. In *Ashley Guarantee* the plaintiff lent money to a company, repayment of which was secured by a mortgage given by the defendant. The mortgage contained a provision to the effect that the plaintiff could exercise its rights and remedies over the mortgaged property only in the event of default by the company. The plaintiff in this case was seeking possession of the property consequent upon a default in repayment of the loan. The defendant argued that the company had a cross-claim against the plaintiff which gave it a right of equitable set-off, and that, as a result, nothing was owing to the plaintiff. Accordingly, it was argued that the company was not in default, so that the plaintiff was not entitled to enforce any right to possession. The argument failed because, as Nourse L.J. pointed out, the cross-claim did not come anywhere near the amount of the company's debt to the plaintiff. But if it had exceeded the debt, he said that he would have accepted the argument. Similarly Woolf L.J. indicated that possession would have been refused if a set-off had been available for a sum greater than the mortgage debt.

There is early authority which supports this approach in the context of foreclosure.[521] In *Piggott* v. *Williams*[522] a solicitor failed in an application before Sir John Leach V.C. for an order for foreclosure of an estate pledged as security for costs, because of an allegation by the client that the costs claimed would not have been incurred were it not for the solicitor's own negligence. The Vice Chancellor said that the client had a clear case to restrain the solicitor from proceeding to enforce his security and leaving the client's demand for damages unsatisfied. He indicated that he would retain the solicitor's bill until an action for damages could be tried. Walsh J. in *Inglis*[523] sought to distinguish *Piggott* v. *Williams* on the ground that the client's allegation in that case went to the question whether the debt which the security was intended to secure had ever been incurred at all, though Sir John Leach proceeded on the basis that the facts alleged, if true, disclosed 'a clear case of equitable set-off'.[524] Indeed, in *Coba Industries Ltd.* v. *Millie's Holdings (Canada) Ltd.*[525] the British Columbia Court of Appeal refused foreclosure on the basis of an equitable set-off available to the mortgagor.

---

[521] In addition to the cases discussed below, see *Dodd* v. *Lydall* (1841) 1 Hare 333. Wigram V.C. in that case said that he would not suspend a decree of foreclosure because of a cross-claim by the mortgagor for an account of amounts due from the mortgagee in his capacity as trustee of a trust in which the mortgagor was beneficially interested. In doing so he emphasized that the mortgage and the trust accounts had no original or necessary connection with each other, though the tenor of his judgment suggests that, if this had not been the case, he would not have made the decree. In any event, the Vice Chancellor said that he would suspend the decree until the trust account could be taken if the amount of the mortgage debt was paid into court.

[523] (1972) 126 CLR 161, 167.
[525] [1985] 6 WWR 14.
[522] (1821) 6 Madd. 95.
[524] (1821) 6 Madd. 95.

   If an unlitigated cross-claim giving rise to an equitable set-off is to be
regarded as a basis for restraining the mortgagee from exercising rights
dependent upon default, the amount of the cross-claim obviously would
have to exceed the amount payable to the mortgagee as a result of the
default. That much is clear from *Ashley Guarantee*. Further, the mere
allegation of a cross-claim of a type which would give rise to an equitable
set-off should not suffice. The cross-claim may have to be admitted, or at
least be likely to succeed.[526] It follows that a mortgagee would not be
permitted to exercise a power of sale if the cross-claim in fact has been
liquidated and the equitable set-off established by the court. This occurred
in Victoria in *Newman* v. *Cook*,[527] where a vendor's declaration that he
was entitled to exercise a power of sale pursuant to a mortgage given as
security for the unpaid part of the purchase price took the form of a
counterclaim in the purchaser's action for damages for breach of contract.
The court was in a position to declare that the damages claim should be
brought into an account with the price, on the basis of common law
abatement,[528] but also, in the judgment of Hudson J., by way of equitable
set-off, so that to this extent the price was paid.
   A related question is whether the court on the application of the
mortgagor will order that an independent cross-debt owing to
the mortgagor be set off against the mortgage debt, so as to allow the
mortgagor to redeem. This was considered earlier in the context of a
discussion of *Parker* v. *Jackson*.[529]
   The question occasionally arises as to whether a mortgagee in possession
who is entitled to rent payable by a tenant takes subject to an equitable set-
off that otherwise would have been available to the tenant as against the
mortgagor. This issue is considered later.[530]

1.7.14 *Charterparties: set-off against freight and hire*

Questions of set-off in the context of charterparties have been the subject
of particular attention in recent years.[531] In this regard the courts have
drawn a distinction between freight payable under a voyage charter or a
bill of lading, and hire payable under a time charter or a charter by
demise.[532] In the former case it appears that equitable set-off generally is
not available, whereas it may apply in the latter.

---

[526] See Ralph Gibson L.J. in *Ashley Guarantee* [1993] 1 WLR 62, 70.
[527] [1963] VR 659.
[528] See section 1.10 below.
[529] [1936] 2 All ER 281, discussed in section 1.2.9 above.
[530] See section 13.2.19 below.
[531] See Rose, 'Deductions From Freight and Hire under English Law' [1982] *Lloyd's
Maritime and Commercial Law Quarterly* 33.
[532] For the difference between a time charter and a charter by demise, see McKinnon L.J.
in *Sea and Land Securities Ltd.* v. *William Dickinson and Company, Ltd.* [1942] 2 KB 65, 69.

At common law, the defendant in an action for payment of the price of goods sold with a warranty, or of work which was to be performed according to a contract, could deduct the amount of any damages sustained by reason of the plaintiff's breach of contract. This was not by way of set-off, but rather it was a means by which the defendant could defend himself by showing how much less the subject-matter of the action was worth as a result of the plaintiff's breach. This principle, known as common law abatement, or the rule in *Mondel* v. *Steel*,[533] is considered later.[534] Nevertheless, the right to abate did not apply to every contract for work and labour. It was established in *Sheels* v. *Davies*[535] that, in the case of a contract for the carriage of goods by sea, the bill of lading holder or the voyage charterer could not make any deductions from the freight payable[536] except to the extent specifically allowed by the contract.[537] As a consequence of this exception,[538] a claim for a defence of abatement has failed in the case of damage done to the goods,[539] for short delivery,[540] and for delay.[541] It is unclear whether this rule against deductions from freight originally was thought to extend to the equitable defence of set-off as well as the common law defence. In *Stimson* v. *Hall*[542] a lighterman brought an action against a goods owner for freight owing for the conveyance of goods. The goods owner alleged that certain other goods had been lost as a

---

[533] (1841) 8 M & W 858. [534] See section 1.10 below.

[535] (1814) 4 Camp. 119, subsequent proceedings *sub nom. Shields* v. *Davis* (1815) 6 Taunt. 65. See also *Bornmann* v. *Tooke* (1808) 1 Camp. 376.

[536] In addition to the cases cited below, see *Mondel* v. *Steel* (1841) 8 M & W 858, 871; *Kish* v. *Charles Taylor, Sons & Co.* [1912] AC 604, 616; *St. John Shipping Corporation* v. *Joseph Rank Ltd.* [1957] 1 QB 267, 291.

[537] As e.g. in *The Olympic Brilliance* [1982] 2 Lloyd's Rep. 205.

[538] Strictly, the rule prohibiting deductions from freight is an application of the rule which was in force generally before the common law courts developed the defence of abatement. See *Aries Tanker Corporation* v. *Total Transport Ltd.* [1977] 1 WLR 185, 192–3. Nevertheless, to the extent that the allowance of an abatement in a contract for work and labour has now become the general rule, the freight rule may be regarded as the exception.

[539] *Davidson* v. *Gwynne* (1810) 12 East 381; *Sheels* v. *Davies* (1814) 4 Camp. 119; *Garrett* v. *Melhuish* (1858) 33 LTOS 25; *Dakin* v. *Oxley* (1864) 15 CB(NS) 646; *Henriksens Rederi A/S* v. *THZ Rolimpex (The Brede)* [1974] 1 QB 233. Compare *Bellamy* v. *Russell* (1681) 2 Show. KB 167, in which the Court of King's Bench indicated that a merchant could retain the freight otherwise payable under a charterparty as compensation for damage caused to the goods by the fault of the master. This was not based upon a defence of abatement or set-off, but rather upon a custom of merchants which the court said permitted a deduction.

[540] *Aries Tanker Corporation* v. *Total Transport Ltd.* [1977] 1 WLR 185 (in which freight was to be calculated according to the *intaken* quantity of cargo rather than the quantity delivered, for which see *Dakin* v. *Oxley* (1864) 15 CB(NS) 646, 664–5). See also *Blanchet* v. *Powell's Llantivit Collieries Company, Limited* (1874) LR 9 Ex. 74. *A fortiori* there may not be a deduction in respect of the value of missing goods against the freight due upon other goods actually delivered. See *Meyer* v. *Dresser* (1864) 16 CB(NS) 646.

[541] *The Alfa Nord* [1977] 2 Lloyd's Rep. 434. See also *Bornmann* v. *Tooke* (1808) 1 Camp. 376; *R.H. & D. International Ltd.* v. *I.A.S. Animal Air Services Ltd.* [1984] 1 WLR 573.

[542] (1857) 1 H & N 831, 5 WR 367.

result of the negligence of the lighterman,[543] and said that his cross-claim for damages for the loss of those goods gave rise to an equitable defence to the claim. While the Court of Exchequer rejected this contention on the ground that the facts failed to disclose a natural equity sufficient to ground a set-off, there is nothing in the judgments or in the arguments of counsel to suggest that an equitable set-off was considered not to be available in any event against a claim for freight. However, the courts have since accepted that equitable set-off is indeed subject to the same restriction as for common law abatement with respect to the payment of freight.[544] It applies to any damages claim available to the charterer or bill of lading holder. It is not confined to cases of short or damaged delivery of cargo or delay in its delivery,[545] and indeed the House of Lords held in *Bank of Boston Connecticut* v. *European Grain and Shipping Ltd.*[546] that the restriction extends to the situation in which the voyage was never completed as a result of the shipowner's own wrongful repudiation of the charterparty.

The House of Lords in *Bank of Boston*[547] also warned that the rules of procedure should not be used to bring about a result contrary to this principle. Lord Brandon in that case rejected an argument that the court could try both the claim and the counterclaim and then make an order pursuant to Order 15 rule 2(4), which provides that, 'Where a defendant establishes a counterclaim against the claim of a plaintiff and there is a balance in favour of one of the parties, the court may give judgment for the balance . . .'. To utilise the rule for this purpose would constitute a wrong exercise of the court's discretion. Similarly, a cross-claim available to a

---

[543] The plaintiff's claim for freight apparently was not in respect of the goods alleged to have been lost. This appears more clearly from the report of the case at 5 WR 367. Watson B. said (at 368) that he was not certain how equity would have dealt with the matter in a case in which there was a demand for freight and the goods in respect of which the freight was claimed were damaged by the shipowner or carrier.

[544] *The Cleon* [1983] 1 Lloyd's Rep. 586; *The Elena* [1986] 1 Lloyd's Rep. 425; *Bank of Boston Connecticut* v. *European Grain and Shipping Ltd.* [1989] 1 AC 1056. This seemed to be the view of Lord Denning in *Henriksens Rederi A/S* v. *THZ Rolimpex (The Brede)* [1974] 1 QB 233, and of Lord Simon of Glaisdale and Lord Salmon in *Aries Tanker Corporation* v. *Total Transport Ltd.* [1977] 1 WLR 185, 193, 195. See also *The Teno* [1977] 2 Lloyd's Rep. 289, 293; *The Alfa Nord* [1977] 2 Lloyd's Rep. 434; *Nova (Jersey) Knit Ltd.* v. *Kammgarn Spinnerei G.m.b.H.* [1977] 1 WLR 713, 721. However, compare Stephenson L.J. in *James & Co. Scheepvaart en Handelmij B.V.* v. *Chinecrest Ltd.* [1979] 1 Lloyd's Rep. 126, 129 ('unless you can find an equity sufficient to override that long-standing rule of common law').

[545] Thus, Roskill L.J. in *The Alfa Nord* [1977] 2 Lloyd's Rep. 434, 436 referred to 'the well-established principle that there is no right of set-off for claims for damages for breach of charter, whether for loss of or damage to goods or for alleged failure to prosecute a voyage with reasonable dispatch or otherwise, against a claim for freight'.

[546] [1989] 1 AC 1056.

[547] [1989] 1 AC 1056, 1109.

charterer ordinarily does not constitute a ground for staying execution on a judgment obtained against the charterer for payment of freight.[548]

This principle precluding deductions is not confined to the situation in which a shipowner is suing a voyage charterer or bill of lading holder for freight. An agent who collects freight on behalf of the shipowner or charterer entitled to it similarly must account for it without deduction or set-off.[549] The principle is also relevant when the right to freight has been assigned. The assignee is entitled to the freight undiminished by an equitable set-off.[550] Moreover, it applies equally to advance freight and to freight payable on delivery of the goods at the port of discharge.[551] Nor, apparently, is it confined to shipping. It has been held that a contract for the carriage of goods by road pursuant to the Convention on the Contract for the International Carriage of Goods by Road (CMR) is subject to the rule, even though Articles 32 and 36 of the Schedule to the Convention seem to contemplate that set-offs are possible.[552] Further, May J. held, though with reluctance, that the principle is equally applicable to a domestic contract for carriage by land.[553]

Different considerations apply to hire payable under a time charter. Admittedly, in *Russell* v. *Pellegrini*[554] the Court of Queen's Bench assumed, after a concession by counsel to this effect, that a cross-claim for damages for breach of an implied warranty of seaworthiness could not be set off against a claim for hire,[555] while more recently Donaldson J. applied

---

[548] *The Cleon* [1983] 1 Lloyd's Rep. 586; *The Dominique* [1987] 1 Lloyd's Rep. 239, 257–8. See also *Sherborne* v. *Siffkin* (1811) 3 Taunt. 525, in which the court refused to order that the freight be paid into court to be applied towards payment of any damages that may be awarded for damage to cargo. In *James & Co. Scheepvaart en Handelmij B.V.* v. *Chinecrest Ltd.* [1979] 1 Lloyd's Rep. 126 a stay was granted on condition that the amount of the freight be paid into court, though in that case there was an unresolved issue as to the terms of the contract.

[549] *James & Co. Scheepvaart en Handelmij B.V.* v. *Chinecrest Ltd.* [1979] 1 Lloyd's Rep. 126. The decision in *Samuel* v. *West Hartlepool Steam Navigation Co.* (1906) 11 Com Cas. 115, (1907) 12 Com Cas. 203, insofar as it allowed a set-off of the damages claim, seems contrary to this principle and is difficult to support. See *The Dominique* [1987] 1 Lloyd's Rep. 239, 256–7, where Hobhouse J. nevertheless left open the question whether the two decisions can stand together. Compare also *Wehner* v. *Dene Steam Shipping Co.* [1905] 2 KB 92, which is explained later in this section.

[550] *Bank of Boston Connecticut* v. *European Grain and Shipping Ltd.* [1989] 1 AC 1056.

[551] *Bank of Boston Connecticut* v. *European Grain and Shipping Ltd.* [1989] 1 AC 1056, 1100.

[552] *R.H. & D. International Ltd.* v. *I.A.S. Animal Air Services Ltd.* [1984] 1 WLR 573, following six unreported cases to the same effect. Compare *Impex Transport Aktieselskabet* v. *A.G. Thames Holdings Ltd.* [1981] 2 Lloyd's Rep. 566, in which Robert Goff J. seemed to assume that a set-off is possible in contracts for the carriage of goods by road though in the particular case it was denied on other grounds.

[553] *United Carriers Ltd.* v. *Heritage Food Group (UK) Ltd.* [1995] 2 Lloyd's Rep. 269.

[554] (1856) 26 LJQB 75, 6 El. & Bl. 1020.

[555] See also, and compare, *Daunt* v. *Lazard* (1858) 27 LJ Exch. 399. For a discussion of these cases, see *The Teno* [1977] 2 Lloyd's Rep. 289, 295.

the freight rule in this context in two unreported judgments[556] and also in *Seven Seas Transportation Ltd.* v. *Atlantic Shipping Company S.A.*[557] However, subsequently Parker J. in *The Teno*[558] followed an unreported case in which Ackner J. reached the contrary conclusion,[559] and held that the rule by which freight must be paid without deduction in fact does not extend to hire. Parker J.'s judgment received the approval of the Court of Appeal in *Federal Commerce & Navigation Co. Ltd.* v. *Molena Alpha Inc.*,[560] and the principle has since become generally accepted.[561] It applies in the case of a charter by demise (sometimes called a bareboat charter),[562] as well as when a time charter is expressed to be for the period of a particular voyage,[563] so that in substance it resembles a voyage charter.[564]

This right to an equitable set-off against a claim for hire is not confined to cases in which there has been a total withdrawal of the vessel for a specified time.[565] A set-off against hire may take place when the master has wrongfully refused to load a full cargo,[566] and when a speed warranty has been breached.[567] An equitable set-off is also available when the owners have failed to perform their hold-cleaning obligations resulting in a delay to the vessel at port.[568] A time charterparty may contain a clause to the effect that the owner must 'provide and pay for all provisions and

---

[556] These cases are mentioned in the judgment of Parker J. in *The Teno* [1977] 2 Lloyd's Rep. 289, 293.

[557] [1975] 2 Lloyd's Rep. 188. See also *The Agios Giorgis* [1976] 2 Lloyd's Rep. 192, 201.

[558] [1977] 2 Lloyd's Rep. 289.

[559] *Naxos Shipping Corporation* v. *Thegra Shipping Co. N.V. (The Corfu Island)* (1973). Parker J. also referred to a number of statements in other cases as constituting authorities in support of the proposition that there may be a set-off against hire. See *Sea and Land Securities, Limited* v. *William Dickinson and Company, Limited* [1942] 1 KB 286, 298; *Halcyon Steamship Company Ltd.* v. *Continental Grain Supply* (1943) 75 Ll. L Rep. 80, 84; *The Charalambos N. Pateras* [1971] 2 Lloyd's Rep. 42, 48. For a discussion of these cases, see Rose, 'Deductions From Freight and Hire under English Law' [1982] *Lloyd's Maritime and Commercial Law Quarterly* 33, 43–8.

[560] [1978] 1 QB 927, the result of which was affirmed by the House of Lords [1979] AC 757 on other grounds.

[561] In addition to the cases cited below, see *The Kostas Melas* [1981] 1 Lloyd's Rep. 18.

[562] See *The Raven* [1980] 2 Lloyd's Rep. 266 (esp. at 273). For the difference between a time charter and a charter by demise, see McKinnon L.J. in *Sea and Land Securities Ltd.* v. *William Dickinson and Company, Ltd.* [1942] 2 KB 65, 69.

[563] *The Kostas Melas* [1981] 1 Lloyd's Rep. 18; *The Chrysovalandou Dyo* [1981] 1 Lloyd's Rep. 159.

[564] See the discussion in *Carver's Carriage by Sea* (13th edn., 1982) Vol. 1, 472–4.

[565] *The Teno* [1977] 2 Lloyd's Rep. 289, 297.

[566] *The Teno* [1977] 2 Lloyd's Rep. 289, 297.

[567] *The Corfu Island* (1973), unreported decision of Ackner J. See also *The Democritos* [1975] 1 Lloyd's Rep. 386, 402; *Federal Commerce & Navigation Co. Ltd.* v. *Molena Alpha Inc.* [1978] 1 QB 927. See also *Santiren Shipping Ltd.* v. *Unimarine S.A. (The Chrysovalandou-Dyo)* [1981] 1 Lloyd's Rep. 159.

[568] Compare *The Aditya Vaibhav* [1991] 1 Lloyd's Rep. 573, discussed in section 1.7.12 above.

wages . . . for insurance of the vessel, for all deck and engine-room stores including lub, oil, galley oil, and fresh water'. If the owner fails to make these payments and the charterer, in order to ensure the vessel's availability and use, instead expends the money, the charterer's damages claim against the owner for breach of the clause may be employed in a set-off against hire.[569] But it is not every cross-claim that can be set off. In *Federal Commerce* v. *Molena*[570] both Lord Denning and Goff L.J. emphasized that the right of deduction should be limited to cases where the owner through his neglect or default has either deprived the charterer of the use of the vessel or has hindered or prejudiced the charterer's use. For example, their Lordships said that a deduction would not be available when the cross-claim arises merely from damage to cargo. Similarly, a charterer may not set off the estimated value of bunkers remaining on re-delivery of the vessel, unless the charterparty specifically sanctions a deduction.[571] The principle is illustrated by *The Leon*.[572] The charterers alleged three breaches by the owners: (1) that the master had failed to keep full and accurate logs of the fuel consumption, (2) that the master had procured that invoices which did not represent the fuel actually taken on board should be sent to and paid for by the charterers, and (3) that the owners had breached their duty as bailees of the bunkers to use them during the charterparty in accordance with the charterer's orders. It was held that none of these breaches affected the use of the vessel, and that consequently they did not give rise to a set-off against hire. However, Hobhouse J. emphasized that there was nothing to show 'overriding fraud' on the part of the owners. If there had been, he suggested that the result may have been different.[573]

After *Molena*, Lord Denning in *The Aliakmon Progress*[574] seemed to narrow the scope of the set-off. A vessel the subject of a time charter sustained damage while attempting to berth at a port in Iceland. Temporary repairs were effected there, and the vessel then sailed to Antwerp where permanent repairs were undertaken. Owing to the resulting delay the vessel lost an anticipated cargo at Antwerp and had to wait some 39 days for a new cargo. Lord Denning, with whom Geoffrey Lane L.J. agreed, doubted that the loss sustained by the charterers constituted a ground for equitable set-off. His Lordship cited *Federal Commerce* v. *Molena* as authority for the proposition that equitable set-off

---

[569] *The Raven* [1980] 2 Lloyd's Rep. 266, 273.

[570] [1978] 1 QB 927, 976, 981, following Parker J. in *The Teno* [1977] 2 Lloyd's Rep. 289, 297. See also *The Didymi* [1988] 1 Lloyd's Rep. 97, 104 (Canadian Federal Court of Appeal).

[571] *The Tropwind* [1981] 1 Lloyd's Rep. 45, 48. Compare *The Maistros* [1984] 1 Lloyd's Rep. 646, in which there was an agreement for a set-off.

[572] [1985] 2 Lloyd's Rep. 470.   [573] [1985] 2 Lloyd's Rep. 470, 476.

[574] [1978] 2 Lloyd's Rep. 499.

is only available against a claim for hire 'where the charterers have been deprived of the use of the ship by the fault of the owner'.[575] He said that, in the case before him, the charterers in fact did have the use of the ship but could not get a cargo. There was no mention of whether a set-off may arise when the shipowner has merely prejudiced the charterer in the use of the vessel, and there was no discussion of whether in the instant case there had been any such prejudice. Subsequently, though, the courts have reiterated that prejudice in the use of the vessel not amounting to total deprivation may ground a set-off.[576]

Counsel in *The Leon*[577] attacked the proposition that equitable set-off in the context of time charters should be limited to cases in which the charterer has been deprived of or prejudiced in the use of the vessel. Rather, it was suggested that the allowance or otherwise of a set-off should be determined by reference to whether it would be unfair in the particular case to allow the owner to sue for hire without giving credit for the cross-demand. However, Hobhouse J. declined to depart from the statements of the ambit of the set-off by Lord Denning and Goff L.J. in *Federal Commerce* v. *Molena*, and emphasized that the relevant general principle is set out in Lord Cottenham's judgment in *Rawson* v. *Samuel*,[578] that the equity of the bill must impeach the title to the legal demand. In the case of a time charter, hire is paid for the right to use the vessel for a specified period of time, irrespective of whether the charterer chooses to use it for carrying cargo or instead lays it up out of use. The hire is required to be paid in advance, and failure to make punctual payment gives the owner the right to withdraw the vessel. Accordingly, Hobhouse J said that it is not surprising that, for an equitable set-off, the cross-claim should involve something which could be identified as depriving the charterer of the use of the vessel or which prejudices or hinders that use, because, in the context of a time charter contract and a claim for time charter hire, it is that type of cross-claim which has the requisite effect of impeaching the plaintiff's demand.

In a case where hire is payable periodically under a time charter, the charterer may have been prejudiced in the use of the vessel only in certain defined periods. In other periods the vessel in fact may have been made available in accordance with the contract. If the charterer's damages claim in such a case exceeds the amount of hire owing for the periods during which the use of the vessel was prejudiced, the charterer may wish to set off the excess against payments of hire relating to other periods. The question whether this is permissible was considered earlier.[579]

---

[575] [1978] 2 Lloyd's Rep. 499, 501.
[576] *The Raven* [1980] 2 Lloyd's Rep. 266, 273; *The Leon* [1985] 2 Lloyd's Rep. 470, 475.
[577] [1985] 2 Lloyd's Rep. 470.   [578] (1841) Cr. & Ph. 161.
[579] See section 1.7.12 above.

Given that there is this distinction between freight and hire as regards equitable set-off, the question arises whether there is any justification for it. It has been suggested that the original justification for the freight rule may well have been based upon cash flow considerations, in that the master would require the freight to be paid in full at the end of the voyage in order to pay off his crew, and to refit and victual his ship. Communications in those days were slow, and the master could not wait for a long time for funds to be remitted to him.[580] Yet, at least in the context of building contracts the courts have said that cash flow considerations are no longer regarded as a sufficient reason for denying a set-off.[581] On the other hand, Lord Wilberforce has expressed doubts as to whether the freight rule indeed is anything other than an arbitrary rule, 'in the sense that no very clear justification for it has ever been stated and perhaps also in the sense that the law might just, or almost, as well have settled for a rule to the opposite effect'.[582] Despite this he concluded that the rule is too well established to be departed from now.[583] There are, nevertheless, dicta to the effect that it should not be extended,[584] and the attitude of the courts has been that voyage and time charters are sufficiently dissimilar in their operation to justify the application in the case of hire of the general rule permitting deductions, rather than having resort to the exception precluding deductions found in the freight rule. Thus, Lord Denning in justifying the distinction noted that freight is the sum payable for the carriage of goods from one place to another, while hire is paid for the right to use the vessel for a specified period of time irrespective of whether or not the charterer chooses to use it for carrying cargo.[585] But

---

[580] See Goff L.J. in *Federal Commerce & Navigation Co. Ltd.* v. *Molena Alpha Inc.* [1978] 1 QB 927, 983. See also *Henriksens Rederi A/S* v. *THZ Rolimpex (The Brede)* [1974] 1 QB 233, 263. Thus Willes J. said in *Meyer* v. *Dresser* (1864) 16 CB(NS) 646, 663 that it would have been inconvenient for a vessel to be delayed while disputes as to the amount of freight were being settled. See also *Dakin* v. *Oxley* (1864) 15 CB(NS) 646, 667.

[581] *Gilbert-Ash (Northern) Ltd.* v. *Modern Engineering (Bristol) Ltd.* [1974] AC 689, 707, 718; *Mottram Consultants Ltd.* v. *Bernard Sunley & Sons Ltd.* [1975] 2 Lloyd's Rep. 197, 214. See generally the discussion of building contracts in section 1.7.20 below. See also *Federal Commerce & Navigation Co. Ltd.* v. *Molena Alpha Inc.* [1978] 1 QB 927, 983, 986.

[582] *Aries Tanker Corporation* v. *Total Transport Ltd.* [1977] 1 WLR 185, 190. Similarly Lord Simon of Glaisdale said (at 193) that 'there is no question of high legal policy involved at all'. See also *Dole Dried Fruit and Nut Co.* v. *Trustin Kerwood Ltd.* [1990] 2 Lloyd's Rep. 309, 310. Compare Lord Salmon in *Aries Tanker* (at 195), who remarked that the incidence of insurance cover in respect of freight may be based upon the rule. See also with respect to insurance *Henriksens Rederi A/S* v. *THZ Rolimpex (The Brede)* [1974] 1 QB 233, 244, 263.

[583] Similarly, Lord Brandon in the House of Lords in *Bank of Boston* [1989] 1 AC 1056, 1100 said that, whatever its merits or demerits, the rule is not open to challenge.

[584] *Seven Seas Transportation Ltd.* v. *Atlantic Shipping Co. S.A.* [1975] 2 Lloyd's Rep. 188, 191; *Federal Commerce & Navigation Co. Ltd.* v. *Molena Alpha Inc.* [1978] 1 QB 927, 982.

[585] *Federal Commerce & Navigation Co. Ltd.* v. *Molena Alpha Inc.* [1978] 1 QB 927, 973.

even this as a basis for treating them differently becomes blurred when a time charter is for the period of a particular trip.[586]

1.7.15 *The Statutes of Set-off and claims for freight*

A question in respect of which there is conflicting recent authority is whether the principle which precludes a defence of equitable set-off against a claim for freight also extends to the defence provided by the Statutes of Set-off in the case of mutual debts.[587] Hirst J. in *The Khian Captain (No. 2)*[588] held that it does, though Hobhouse J. at first instance in *Bank of Boston*[589] expressed doubts as to whether this is correct. Apart from *The Khian Captain*, it is difficult to find any authority which supports the negative view. Two cases which have been said to support it[590] in fact are explicable on other grounds.

In *Weguellin* v. *Cellier*[591] the consignee of cargo had a claim against the shipowner as a result of accepting six-month bills at the request of the shipowner. The shipowner assigned the freight by way of security to the respondents, who then brought the present action seeking a declaration that they were entitled to be paid the freight. However the consignees, having honoured the bills, had a claim against the shipowner, and argued that this gave rise to a set-off against the liability for freight and that the respondents as assignees took subject to this. It is apparent that any right of set-off would have arisen under the Statutes, based upon mutual debts, given that the demands would not have been sufficiently closely connected to give rise to an equitable set-off. While Lord Chelmsford held that there was no such set-off which would defeat the respondent's right to the freight, this was not because of a general principle that a claim for freight is not susceptible to a defence of set-off under the Statutes. In the first place, as counsel pointed out during argument, the bills did not mature until after the consignees received notice of the consignment, so that at the date of notice any debt owing by the shipowner was merely contingent. An assignee does not take subject to a cross-debt which arises after notice,

---

[586] See e.g. *The Kostas Melas* [1981] 1 Lloyd's Rep. 18 and *Santiren Shipping Ltd.* v. *Unimarine S.A. (The Chrysovalandou-Dyo)* [1981] 1 Lloyd's Rep. 159, and generally the discussion in *Carver's Carriage by Sea* (13th edn., 1982) Vol. 1, 472–4. Note however Steyn J.'s justification of the distinction in *The Cebu (No. 2)* [1990] 2 Lloyd's Rep. 316, 320.

[587] There is no reason, however, why a set-off under the Statutes should not be available against a claim for hire under a time charter, given that it is susceptible to an equitable set-off. This was assumed to be the case in *Aectra Refining and Marketing Inc.* v. *Exmar NV* [1994] 1 WLR 1634.   [588] [1986] 1 Lloyd's Rep. 429.

[589] *Sub nom. The Dominique* [1987] 1 Lloyd's Rep. 239, 251.

[590] Wood, *English and International Set-off* (1989), 707.

[591] (1873) LR 6 HL 286, 42 LJ Ch. 758.

albeit as a result of a prior contract.[592] But even apart from that, the Statutes of Set-off only provided a procedural defence to an action for payment of a debt, and until a judgment for a set-off is obtained separate and distinct debts remain in existence.[593] In *Weguellin* v. *Cellier*, when the goods arrived at the port of discharge the respondents put a stop on them. They had a lien and, as Lord Chelmsford pointed out, the consignees could not have obtained the cargo without payment of the freight, and the master of the ship would have been bound to insist upon payment before delivery.[594] Because of the procedural nature of the defence, the consignees could not have unilaterally brought about a set-off so as to obtain the release of goods the subject of the lien. While the circumstances in *Weguellin* differed from this, in that the consignees after some correspondence had paid the amount of the freight to the dock company holding the goods so as to obtain their release, and the respondents then filed a bill seeking a declaration that the freight in the hands of the dock company should be applied towards payment of what was due to them by the shipowner,[595] it was still not a case of set-off under the Statutes, because it was not an action against the consignees for payment.

The second case, *Tanner* v. *Phillips*,[596] similarly may be explained on other grounds. The plaintiff was mortgagee of a ship, and as further security held a mortgage of freight. The ship was chartered to the defendant. The charterparty provided that the defendant could make advances not exceeding £150 to the master as agent for the mortgagor/owner on account of freight, though other advances in excess of that amount were made. Before the cargo was unloaded, and freight became due, the mortgagee took possession. When he sued the defendant for payment of the freight after it later became payable, it was held that the defendant could not set off the excess advances. This was so notwithstanding that these advances were made before the defendant had notice of the security, whereas ordinarily, if there are mutual debts in existence before notice of an assignment, the assignee takes subject to a right of set-off under the Statutes.[597] However, the important point in *Tanner* v. *Phillips* is that the mortgagee's entitlement to freight was not based upon an assignment of a debt. Rather, it was claimed as mortgagee in possession. The mortgagee became entitled in his own right to freight which

---

[592] *Watson* v. *Mid Wales Railway Company* (1867) LR 2 CP 593, and see generally section 13.2.4 below.   [593] See section 1.2.9 above.

[594] Compare *Campbell* v. *Thompson* (1816) 1 Stark. 490, in which the issue seems to have been whether the assignee of freight was entitled to refuse to allow delivery of the cargo unless freight was paid without deduction, though the authority of that case was doubted by Dr. Lushington in *The Salacia* (1862) Lush. 578.

[595] This appears more clearly from the report at (1873) 42 LJ Ch. 758, 760.

[596] (1872) 42 LJ Ch. 125.   [597] See section 13.2.4 below.

the ship was in the course of earning. As Lord Cairns pointed out in *Keith* v. *Burrows*,[598] the right of a mortgagee in possession to freight in the course of being earned does not arise by virtue of any contract or antecedent right, but rather it is payable to the mortgagee once he goes into possession because the mortgagee is then regarded as the master or owner of the ship.[599] His right depends on property, not on contract.[600] Accordingly, *Tanner* v. *Phillips* was not a case in which there were mutual debts between the mortgagor and the charterer which would have given rise to a set-off available against the mortgagee, were it not for a supposed principle that there may not be a set-off under the Statutes against a claim for freight. Rather, mutuality for the purposes of the Statutes was lacking, in that, on the one hand, the charterer had a claim against the mortgagor for the excess advances and, on the other, the mortgagee in his own right was entitled to the freight from the charterer.[601]

The view that a set-off against freight is permissible under the Statutes is supported by *Wilson* v. *Gabriel*.[602] In that case the Court of Queen's Bench had no apparent doubt as to the right of a defendant in an action for freight to set off a debt due to him from the shipowner, and held that an assignee of the freight took subject to this set-off. Hirst J. in *The Khian Captain* said that *Wilson* v. *Gabriel* was impliedly overruled by the House of Lords in *Aries Tanker Corporation* v. *Total Transport Ltd.*,[603] though the issue there was whether a damages claim in respect of cargo could be applied in reduction of a liability for freight either on the basis of equitable set-off or common law abatement. There was no discussion of the availability of a set-off under the Statutes of Set-off in the case of mutual debts. The better view is that a set-off on this ground can indeed be asserted as a defence in an action for payment of freight. The important point is that the right is statutory in origin. The Statutes of Set-off specifically allowed a set-off in the case of mutual debts. While the Statutes themselves have been repealed, the repealing legislation preserved the right of set-off conferred by the Statutes.[604] The proper approach in the case of a statutory-based defence is to consider the language of the relevant legislation, and there is nothing in the legislation to suggest that there is an exception in the case of

---

[598] (1877) 2 App. Cas. 636, 646. See also *Kerswill* v. *Bishop* (1832) 2 C & J 529; *Japp* v. *Campbell* (1888) 57 LJQB 79; *Wilson* v. *Wilson* (1872) LR 14 Eq. 32 (mortgagee's right to freight has priority over an earlier assignment of freight of which the mortgagee did not have notice).

[599] In the same way, when there is a sale of a ship the right to freight in the course of being earned passes to the purchaser. See e.g., *Morrison* v. *Parsons* (1810) 2 Taunt. 407. As Lord Ellenborough remarked in *Case* v. *Davidson* (1816) 5 M & S 79, 82, 'freight follows, as an incident, the property in the ship'.

[600] *Rusden* v. *Pope* (1868) LR 3 Ex. 269, 276–7.

[601] See section 13.2.20 below.

[602] (1863) 4 B & S 243.

[603] [1977] 1 WLR 185.

[604] See section 1.2.1 above.

an action for freight.[605] Consistently with that view, in *Jones* v. *Moore*[606] it was held that an equitable set-off derived from an analogy with the right of set-off available at law under the Statutes[606a] was available against a claim for freight.

1.7.16 Bill of lading freight when the vessel is chartered

When a ship has been chartered, and the master signs bills of lading with third party shippers for the carriage of goods, the question whether the shipowner or the charterer is entitled to the bill of lading freight depends upon whether the master signed as agent for the shipowner or the charterer. If the charter is by demise the contract will be with the charterer, though in other cases the question will depend upon the documents and circumstances in the particular case.[607] When the contract is with the shipowner, he can sue the shipper for freight. If the charterer nevertheless has appointed as agent to collect the freight, and the shipowner gives notice to the agent before the freight has been received requiring the freight to be paid to him rather than the charterer, the shipowner can sue the agent for the freight as money had and received.[608] Any expenses incurred by the agent in carrying out the charterer's instructions cannot be set off by the agent,[609] since mutuality for the purpose of the Statutes of Set-off is lacking. However, when the owner as the contracting party is paid the bill of lading freight, he is only entitled to retain an amount equal to the hire or freight then unpaid under the charterparty. The surplus must be paid to the charterer. This was held to be the case in *Wehner* v. *Dene Steam Shipping Company*.[610] The reason for this is not that the owner is liable to the charterer for the bill of lading freight received and the charterer is liable for hire or freight under the charterparty, and that these obligations are set off.[611] It is not a case of cross-demands at all. Rather, the owner had contracted by the charterparty that he would be satisfied

---

[605] Compare *Isberg* v. *Bowden* (1853) 8 Ex. 852, though in that case the action for freight was brought by the master rather than the owner of the vessel. It was held that a debt owing by the owner could not be set off, though this was on the basis of a perceived lack of mutuality. There is nothing in the judgments, or indeed in the arguments of counsel, to suggest that it was thought that an action for freight was never susceptible in any event to a defence of set-off under the Statutes.

[606] (1841) 4 Y & C Ex. 351.   [606a] See section 1.6 above.

[607] *Samuel* v. *West Hartlepool Steam Navigation Co.* (1906) 11 Com. Cas. 115, 125–6.

[608] *Molthes Rederi Aktieselskabet* v. *Ellerman's Wilson Line, Ltd.* [1927] 1 KB 710, 715–16. Greer J. left open the question whether the agent similarly could be sued in respect of freight received before notice from the shipowner.

[609] *Molthes Rederi* v. *Ellerman's Wilson Line* [1927] 1 KB 710.

[610] [1905] 2 KB 92.

[611] Compare Wood, *English and International Set-off* (1989), 705, 978–9.

with the payment of the freight or hire specified in the charterparty for the use of the ship, and accordingly if the owner receives the bill of lading freight it is part of their contract that it will account for any surplus to the charterer.[612]

When the contract is with the charterer rather than the shipowner, the shipowner may have reserved a lien on sub-freights, entitling the shipowner to require payment to him of the bill of lading freight that is otherwise due to the charterer.[613] This lien can only be exercised before the freight has been paid to the charterer or his agent.[614] Moreover, it can only be exercised in respect of sums due to the shipowner at the time that the demand for payment is made pursuant to the lien.[615] When there is a valid exercise of the lien, the shipowner presumably would take subject to any equities available to the shipper against the charterer before the shipper had notice of the lien, including any right of set-off under the Statutes in the case of mutual debts.[616]

1.7.17 Negotiable instruments and letters of credit

As between parties to a bill of exchange or other negotiable instrument[617] the attitude of English courts generally has been that an unliquidated cross-demand may not be employed in an equitable set-off in an action to enforce payment of the instrument.[618] This has also been accepted by the

---

[612] *Wehner* v. *Dene Steam Shipping Company* [1905] 2 KB 92, 99, explained in *Molthes Rederi* v. *Ellerman's Wilson Line* [1927] 1 KB 710. See also *Carver's Carriage by Sea* (13th edn., 1982) Vol. 2, 1225–6 para. 1744.

[613] See generally *Carver's Carriage by Sea* (13th edn., 1982) Vol. 2, 1395 para. 2013.

[614] *Tagart, Beaton & Co.* v. *Fisher & Sons* [1903] 1 KB 391.

[615] *Wehner* v. *Dene Steam Shipping Company* [1905] 2 KB 92.

[616] See generally Ch. 13.

[617] This includes a cheque. See *Finch Motors Ltd.* v. *Quin* [1980] 2 NZLR 513, 516.

[618] *Morgan* v. *Richardson* (1806) 7 East 482n.; *Tye* v. *Gwynne* (1810) 2 Camp. 346; *Solomon* v. *Turner* (1815) 1 Stark. 51; *Day* v. *Nix* (1824) 2 LJOSCP 133; *Obbard* v. *Betham* (1830) M & M 483; *Glennie* v. *Imri* (1839) 3 Y & C Ex. 436; *Trickey* v. *Larne* (1840) 6 M & W 278; *Sully* v. *Frean* (1854) 10 Ex. 535; *Warwick* v. *Nairn* (1855) 10 Ex. 762; *Jackson* v. *Murphy* (1886) 4 TLR 92n.; *Bow, McLachlan & Co. Limited* v. *Ship 'Camosun'* [1909] AC 597, 612; *James Lamont & Co. Ld.* v. *Hyland Ld.* [1950] 1 KB 585; *Nova (Jersey) Knit Ltd.* v. *Kammgarn Spinnerei G.m.b.H.* [1977] 1 WLR 713; *Montecchi* v. *Shimco (U.K.) Ltd.* [1979] 1 WLR 1180, 1183; *Montebianco Industrie Tessili S.p.A.* v. *Carlyle Mills (London) Ltd.* [1981] 1 Lloyd's Rep. 509; *Case Poclain Corporation Limited* v. *Jones* [1986] ECC 569. Compare the uncertainty of the Court of Appeal in *Oscar Harris, Son & Co.* v. *Vallarman & Co.* [1940] 1 All ER 185, and the decision in *Court* v. *Sheen* (1891) 7 TLR 556 (the report of which is criticized in *James Lamont* v. *Hyland* (at 592)). Compare also the statement by Thesiger L.J. in *Anglo-Italian Bank* v. *Wells* (1878) 38 LT 197, 201, though note the more cautious approach of Jessel M.R. (at 199). The view of the Master of the Rolls was preferred in *James Lamont* v. *Hyland* (at 592–3).

courts in Australia[619] and New Zealand.[620] The principle applies whether the parties are immediate or remote,[621] and also whether the cross-demand arose out of the particular transaction in respect of which the instrument came into existence, or, *a fortiori*, in any other way.[622] The classic situation is when a bill of exchange is given as payment for the purchase of goods or other property, or for the performance of work. A breach by the vendor of a term in the contract of sale etc. which amounts to a partial failure of consideration[622a] and which gives rise to a claim against him for unliquidated damages does not provide the purchaser with a defence to an action on the bill. This is sometimes explained on the ground that the bill is a separate contract from the contract of sale, though in fact it is not an essential requirement of an equitable set-off that the claim and the cross-claim should

---

[619] *Eversure Textiles Manufacturing Co. Ltd.* v. *Webb* [1978] Qd. R. 347; *K.D. Morris & Sons Ltd.* v. *Bank of Queensland* (1980) 30 ALR 321, 350; *Rigg* v. *Commonwealth Bank of Australia* (1989) 97 FLR 261, 267–8. See also the discussion in, and compare, *John Shearer Ltd.* v. *Gehl Company* (1995) 14 ACLC 147 (application under the Corporations Law, s. 459G to set aside a statutory demand). In *Mobil Oil Australia Ltd.* v. *Caulfield Tyre Service Pty. Ltd.* [1984] VR 440 it was held that the principle under discussion also applies when the claim on the bill is brought pursuant to the summary procedure set out in the Instruments Act 1958 (Vic.). Compare *Graham* v. *Seagoe* [1964] 2 Lloyd's Rep. 564, in which an action on promissory notes given in connection with the sale of a boat was stayed while disputes as to the condition of a boat were referred to arbitration. However, the court concerned itself only with the construction of the particular arbitration clause, and no mention was made of the principle under discussion. Compare also Moffitt P. and Glass J.A. in *Sidney Raper Pty. Ltd.* v. *Commonwealth Trading Bank* [1975] 2 NSWLR 227, 238–9, 255, who seemed to accept that a claim on a bank cheque could be the subject of an equitable set-off. This aspect of their judgment is unlikely to be followed, though a set-off may have been available in any event in that case on the basis of equity acting by analogy with the Statutes of Set-off. See the discussion of the Statutes in section 1.7.18 below. In New South Wales, the Common Law Procedure Act 1899, s. 79 provided that matters which were the subject of a cross-action between the parties could by leave of a judge be pleaded by way of set-off. The courts accepted that s. 79 permitted a damages claim to be pleaded by way of set-off against a claim on a promissory note if the demands arose out of the same transaction. See e.g. *Karbowsky* v. *Radaelli* (1914) 31 WN(NSW) 80; *Richardson* v. *Hill* (1922) 22 SR(NSW) 326. The requirement that the demands should have originated in the same transaction followed from a requirement that the courts held was inherent in s. 79 and applied generally. See e.g. *Assets & General Finance Co.* v. *Crick* (1911) 28 WN(NSW) 91; *Austral Bronze Co. Ltd.* v. *Sleigh* (1916) 34 WN(NSW) 143. For a general discussion of s. 79, see Russell, 'Defences by Way of Set-off, Counterclaim and Cross Action' (1928) 2 *Australian Law Journal* 80. However s. 99 was repealed by the Supreme Court Act 1970, and so these cases would no longer apply.

[620] *Finch Motors Ltd.* v. *Quin* [1980] 2 NZLR 513; *International Ore & Fertilizer Corporation* v. *East Coast Fertilizer Co. Ltd.* [1987] 1 NZLR 9. *Union Bank of Australia* v. *Williams* (1892) 11 NZLR 65 would no longer appear to be good law.

[621] For remote parties see, e.g. *All Trades Distributors Ltd.* v. *Agencies Kaufman Ltd.* (1969) 113 Sol. Jo. 995, 996; *Brown, Shipley & Co., Ltd.* v. *Alicia Hosiery, Ltd.* [1966] 1 Lloyd's Rep. 668.

[622] *Cebora S.N.C.* v. *S.I.P. (Industrial Products) Ltd.* [1976] 1 Lloyd's Rep. 271, 278–9; *Buying Systems (Aust) Pty. Ltd.* v. *Tien Mah Litho Printing Co. Ltd.* (1986) 5 NSWLR 317, 328. [622a] Compare total failure of consideration, discussed below.

have originated in the same contract.[623] It has also been said that the bill constitutes a separate transaction from the sale,[624] though as a general proposition this is debatable.[625] The better explanation is that the rule precluding a defence of equitable set-off is based upon a policy consideration, that a bill of exchange is considered to be equivalent to cash, albeit with payment deferred, and if an unliquidated cross-demand could provide a defence to an action on the bill there would be a substantial inroad upon this commercial principle.[626]

The rule also extends to irrevocable letters of credit. An irrevocable letter of credit is regarded in mercantile practice as being the equivalent of cash in hand.[627] In the absence of fraud it must be paid regardless of any cross-claim against the holder available to the person at whose request the letter was issued, even if the cross-claim arose out of the transaction on which the letter was based.[628] Bank guarantees, when they are given in circumstances such that they are equivalent to letters of credit, are subject to the same principle.[629]

A similar restriction applies to counterclaim. Normally a defendant in an application for summary judgment who asserts a counterclaim not amounting to a set-off will not be granted leave to defend, though the court may order a stay of execution on the judgment until the defendant's cross-action has been tried[630] so that, if the defendant succeeds in the cross-action, execution may only issue for the balance of the two claims. However, this does not apply when the plaintiff's claim is on a bill of exchange. The fact that the defendant in an action to enforce payment of a bill of exchange asserts a counterclaim for unliquidated damages is not regarded as a ground for staying execution.[631] It appears, though, that this

---

[623] See section 1.7.7 above.

[624] *Eversure Textiles Manufacturing Co. Ltd.* v. *Webb* [1978] Qd. R. 347, 348–9.

[625] See e.g. *Montecchi* v. *Shimco (U.K.) Ltd.* [1979] 1 WLR 1180, 1183.

[626] See Lord Wilberforce and Viscount Dilhorne in *Nova (Jersey) Knit Ltd.* v. *Kammgarn Spinnerei G.m.b.H.* [1977] 1 WLR 713, 721, 722.

[627] *Intraco Ltd.* v. *Notis Shipping Corporation* [1981] 2 Lloyd's Rep. 256, 257. *Power Curber International Ltd.* v. *National Bank of Kuwait SAK* [1981] 1 WLR 1233, 1241, 1243.

[628] *Power Curber International Ltd.* v. *National Bank of Kuwait SAK* [1981] 1 WLR 1233, 1241, 1243; *Hongkong and Shanghai Banking Corporation* v. *Kloeckner & Co. AG* [1990] 2 QB 514, 521–2.

[629] *Intraco Ltd.* v. *Notis Shipping Corporation* [1981] 2 Lloyd's Rep. 256. See also *Continental Illinois National Bank* v. *Papanicolaou* [1986] 2 Lloyd's Rep. 441, 445; *Sim* v. *Rotherham Metropolitan Borough Council* [1987] 1 Ch. 216, 259.

[630] See e.g. *Mottram Consultants Ltd.* v. *Bernard Sunley & Sons Ltd.* [1975] 2 Lloyd's Rep. 197, 214.

[631] *Brown, Shipley & Co. Ltd.* v. *Alicia Hosiery Ltd.* [1966] 1 Lloyd's Rep. 668; *Cebora S.N.C.* v. *S.I.P. (Industrial Products) Ltd.* [1976] 1 Lloyd's Rep. 271; *Walek & Co. K.G.* v. *Seafield Gentex Limited* [1978] IR 167; *Montecchi* v. *Shimco (U.K.) Ltd.* [1979] 1 WLR 1180, 1183; *Montebianco Industrie Tessili S.p.A.* v. *Carlyle Mills (London) Ltd.* [1981] 1 Lloyd's Rep. 509.

is only a general rule, because on a number of occasions it has been said that the courts do have a discretion to grant a stay, pursuant to Order 14 rule 3(2) RSC, if there are exceptional circumstances.[632] Nevertheless, while there have been statements to this effect, the truth is that judges have shown a marked reluctance to recognize 'exceptional circumstances' which may detract from the general principle that bills of exchange should be treated as cash.[633] Indeed, in *Nova (Jersey) Knit Ltd.* v. *Kammgarn Spinnerei GmbH*[634] Viscount Dilhorne said that it would 'seldom, *if ever*'[635] be right to allow a cross-claim to operate as a bar to execution, while Lord Russell of Killowen was prepared to state that an unliquidated cross-demand is not available as a counterclaim in an action on a bill without any apparent recognition of an exception of 'exceptional circumstances'.[636]

There is, however, a case in which a stay was granted. In *Barclays Bank Ltd.* v. *Aschaffenburger Zellstoffwerke AG*[637] a German acceptor of bills had a cross-claim against the English drawer that was the subject of an arbitration to be held in Copenhagen. While judgment was given on the

---

[632] *Brown, Shipley & Co., Ltd.* v. *Alicia Hosiery, Ltd.* [1966] 1 Lloyd's Rep. 668, 669; *Mottram Consultants Ltd.* v. *Bernard Sunley & Sons Ltd.* [1975] 2 Lloyd's Rep. 197, 214; *Eversure Textiles Manufacturing Co. Ltd.* v. *Webb* [1978] Qd. R 347, 350–1; *Continental Illinois National Bank* v. *Papanicolaou* [1986] 2 Lloyd's Rep. 441, 445; *Thoni G.m.b.H.* v. *RTP Equipment Ltd.* [1979] 2 Lloyd's Rep. 282, 284, 285; *Case Poclain Corporation Limited* v. *Jones* [1986] ECC 569, 573. See also *Begley Industries Ltd.* v. *Cramp* [1977] 2 NZLR 207, 213, and Lord Salmon in his dissenting judgment in *Nova (Jersey) Knit Ltd.* v. *Kammgarn Spinnerei G.m.b.H.* [1977] 1 WLR 713, 726. Any such discretion presumably would be available whether or not the counterclaim arises directly out of the transaction in respect of which the bills were given. See *Cebora* v. *S.I.P.* [1976] 1 Lloyd's Rep. 271, 275 (referring to *James Lamont* v. *Hyland* [1950] 1 KB 585). Certainly, though, it would not be sufficient for a stay that the claim on the bill and the cross-action for unliquidated damages are a part of the same transaction. See e.g. *Walek & Co. K.G.* v. *Seafield Gentex Limited* [1978] IR 167.

[633] In *Cebora S.N.C.* v. *S.I.P. (Industrial Products) Ltd.* [1976] 1 Lloyd's Rep. 271, 279 Sir Eric Sachs warned that 'the Courts should be really careful not to whittle away the rule of practice by introducing unnecessary exceptions to it under the influence of sympathy-evoking stories, and should have due regard to the maxim that hard cases can make bad law. Indeed, in these days of increasing international interdependence and increasing need to foster liquidity of resources, the rule may be said to be of special import to the business community. Pleas to leave in Court large sums to deteriorate in value while official referee scale proceedings are fought out may well to that community seem rather divorced from business realities, and should perhaps be examined with considerable caution'.

[634] [1977] 1 WLR 713.   [635] [1977] 1 WLR 713, 722 (emphasis added).

[636] [1977] 1 WLR 713, 732. See also Lord Denning M.R. in *Associated Bulk Carriers Ltd.* v. *Koch Shipping Inc.* [1978] 1 Lloyd's Rep. 24, 28.

[637] [1963] 1 Lloyd's Rep. 387. There is a suggestion in an Australian case that if the bill of exchange the subject of the action constituted the consideration for the purchase of goods which were acquired by the defendant for resale to third parties, the defendant 'might at least have an argument' in support of a stay if the plaintiff had acted in some manner which made it difficult for the defendant to sell the goods. However, Connolly J. said that it was still 'extremely doubtful' whether this would lead to a stay. See *Eversure Textiles Manufacturing Co. Ltd.* v. *Webb* [1978] Qd. R. 347, 350–1.

bills, the Court of Appeal stayed execution until the result of
the arbitration was known. The reason for the stay is not altogether clear,
though it appears from the judgment of Harman L.J.[638] that the German
acceptor had argued that there may have been some difficulty in obtaining
payment if it succeeded. However, this case received a mixed reception
when it was considered by the Court of Appeal in *Cebora SNC* v. *SIP
(Industrial Products) Ltd.*[639] Buckley L.J. said that it should be regarded as
turning on its own particular facts. Stephenson L.J. was more positive. He
said that he was 'not surprised'[640] that a stay was granted in the
circumstances of the case. Sir Eric Sachs, on the other hand, was critical of
the decision. He noted that the report of the case, 'perhaps wisely',[641] has
not been included in the Law Reports or the All England Reports, and
suggested that it was out of line with other authorities. Notwithstanding
this, a judge in chambers ordered a stay of execution in similar
circumstances in *Montecchi* v. *Shimco (U.K.) Ltd.*[642] The plaintiff was an
Italian businessman who had sold certain goods to the defendant English
company. Payment for the goods had been by bill of exchange drawn by
the defendant. The defendant alleged that the goods were defective, and
refused to honour the bill. The plaintiff then sought, and obtained,
summary judgment for the amount of the bill. However, the judge stayed
execution until after the hearing of the counterclaim on condition that the
defendant paid the amount of the judgment into a joint account or into
court, and he further granted a Mareva injunction restraining the plaintiff
from dealing in any way with the proceeds of the judgment. The Court of
Appeal subsequently upheld an appeal by the plaintiff against the order,
principally on the ground that in this particular case a Mareva injunction
was not suitable because there was no evidence that the plaintiff would
attempt to avoid enforcement of any judgment obtained against him on the
cross-action. Nevertheless, Bridge L.J. in delivering the judgment of
the Court[643] rightly indicated that the mere fact that the plaintiff suing on
the bill, and against whom there is a cross-claim for damages, is foreign is
not a sufficient ground for a stay,[644] though he emphasized that he should
not be taken as saying that in no circumstances whatever could a Mareva
injunction be granted to restrain a plaintiff from dealing with the fruits of a
judgment in a case such as this.

It is clear, then, that a stay will not be granted merely on the ground that
the plaintiff is foreign. This is particularly so if the plaintiff has a substantial

---

[638] [1963] 1 Lloyd's Rep. 387, 389.   [639] [1976] 1 Lloyd's Rep. 271.
[640] [1976] 1 Lloyd's Rep. 271, 278.   [641] [1976] 1 Lloyd's Rep. 271, 279.
[642] [1979] 1 WLR 1180.   [643] Bridge, Geoffrey Lane and Roskill L.JJ.
[644] See also *Cebora S.N.C.* v. *S.I.P. (Industrial Products) Ltd.* [1976] 1 Lloyd's Rep. 271,
followed and applied in *Walek & Co. K.G.* v. *Seafield Gentex Ltd.* [1978] IR 167.

business in its own country.[645] Moreover, the size of the paid-up capital of the foreign company is regarded as being of little significance,[646] while Sir Eric Sachs in *Cebora SNC v. SIP (Industrial Products) Ltd.*[647] rejected a submission that it is material to inquire into the virtues or defects of legal procedures in the country of the foreign plaintiff to which recourse may be necessary to enforce any judgment obtained on the cross-action. It has been suggested that a stay may be granted if there are 'real grounds' for supposing that the foreign plaintiff would not be likely to meet the counterclaim.[648] In this regard, if Sir Eric Sachs indeed was correct in *Cebora*, that it is not relevant to inquire into the defects of the legal procedures of the plaintiff's country, it is difficult to see what could give rise to 'real grounds' for supposing that the counterclaim would not be met other than issues relating to the solvency of the plaintiff. But one would have thought that this would be just as relevant in the case of an English plaintiff, although it has not been suggested that enforcement of a judgment obtained by an English holder of a bill of exchange may be stayed solely on this ground.

The result is that, while the courts have indicated that execution on a bill may be stayed on the basis of an unliquidated cross-claim in exceptional circumstances, the question of what may constitute exceptional circumstances remains unclear. However, it is debatable whether there should be any such exception at all. An alternative approach is not to concentrate on whether a stay as such should be granted according to the law of bills of exchange, but rather to consider whether it is appropriate to grant a Mareva injunction to prevent the proceeds of the judgment being removed from the jurisdiction or otherwise dissipated, on the basis of the principles applicable to granting injunctions to restrain the removal or dissipation of cash. This is consistent with the tenor of the judgment of Bridge L.J. in *Montecchi v. Shimco*, while the validity of the distinction was recognized by the Court of Appeal in *Intraco Ltd. v. Notis Shipping Corporation*[649] in the context of a bank guarantee. It has the advantage of being consistent with the notion that a bill should be treated as cash.

There is authority for the view that the concept of exceptional circumstances is relevant, not only to the issue of whether execution on a judgment on a bill may be stayed, but also to the primary question whether

---

[645] *Cebora S.N.C. v. S.I.P. (Industrial Products) Ltd.* [1976] 1 Lloyd's Rep. 271, 280.
[646] *Cebora S.N.C. v. S.I.P. (Industrial Products) Ltd.* [1976] 1 Lloyd's Rep. 271, 277.
[647] [1976] 1 Lloyd's Rep. 271, 279.
[648] See Stephenson L.J. in *Montebianco Industrie Tessili S.p.A. v. Carlyle Mills (London) Ltd.* [1981] 1 Lloyd's Rep. 509, 512, referring to *Cebora S.N.C. v. S.I.P. (Industrial Products) Ltd.* [1976] 1 Lloyd's Rep. 271 ('In that case also comment was made on the need to have real grounds for supposing that the Italian company would not be likely to meet any counterclaim that was made').   [649] [1981] 2 Lloyd's Rep. 256, 258.

the holder of the bill is entitled to judgment.[650] In *Barclays Bank Ltd.* v. *Aschaffenburger Zellstoffwerke AG*[651] Lord Denning said that, while the holder of a bill of exchange ordinarily is entitled to judgment notwithstanding a cross-claim for damages available against him, there may be exceptions to the rule,[652] and similarly Salmon L.J. indicated that the rule is not invariable.[653] However, it is noticeable that a stay of execution was granted to the defendant in that case, as opposed to a judgment recognizing that there was a defence to the extent of the cross-claim. Subsequently, in *Brown, Shipley & Co. Ltd.* v. *Alicia Hosiery Ltd.*,[654] Lord Denning once again expressed the principle in terms that 'in the ordinary way' judgment should be given upon a bill notwithstanding a cross-claim, though later in his judgment the discussion concerned instead the possibility that the court in its discretion may grant a stay of execution, and indeed the availability of a stay was the issue in the case. In *Saga of Bond Street Ltd.* v. *Avalon Promotions Ltd.*[655] the defendant against whom judgment had been given on a bill in fact succeeded in an application to set aside the judgment because of a breach of contract by the plaintiff. However, the courts on other occasions have sought to distinguish this case (albeit unsatisfactorily),[656] and it is doubtful whether it would now be followed. Indeed, in view of the tenor of the judgments of the House of Lords in the *Nova (Jersey) Knit* case, it is debatable whether an unliquidated cross-claim arising from a partial failure of consideration would ever give rise to a defence to a claim on a bill.[657]

cross-demand either is unrelated to the transaction for which the bill of exchange constituted consideration, or, if it arose out of the same transaction as the bill, it merely gives rise to a case of partial failure of consideration. Nevertheless, an acceptor of a bill of exchange has a defence to a claim on the bill brought against him by the drawer if his acceptance was procured by fraud, invalidity, or for a consideration which

---

[650] In addition to the cases referred to below, see the remarks of Stephen J. in *Newman* v. *Lever* (1887) 4 TLR 91, 92, although the judgment is inadequately reported. In *Finch Motors Ltd.* v. *Quin* [1980] 2 NZLR 513, 516 it is unclear whether the reference to 'exceptional circumstances' was in the context of a stay of execution or leave to defend on the basis of a set-off.   [651] [1967] 1 Lloyd's Rep. 387.

[652] [1967] 1 Lloyd's Rep. 387, 388.   [653] [1967] 1 Lloyd's Rep. 387, 391.

[654] [1966] 1 Lloyd's Rep. 668, 669.   [655] [1972] 2 QB 325.

[656] See *Cebora S.N.C.* v. *S.I.P. (Industrial Products) Ltd.* [1976] 1 Lloyd's Rep. 271, 279, in which Sir Eric Sachs said that *Saga of Bond Street* 'was a case extremely close to a total failure of consideration', and *Eversure Textiles Manufacturing Ltd.* v. *Webb* [1978] Qd. R. 347, 349.

[657] In *Anglo-Italian Bank* v. *Wells* (1878) 38 LT 197, 199, Jessel M.R. said that he could not imagine the existence of circumstances which would justify allowing an equitable set-off against a claim on promissory notes.

has totally failed.[658] Accordingly, if the cross-claim is such as to indicate that there has been a *total* failure of the consideration for which the bill was given,[659] the acceptor has a defence.[660] Similarly, fraud in relation to the transaction in respect of which the bill constituted payment or security may provide a defence to an action on the bill,[661] while in Australia it has been held that the principle under discussion does not apply where the cross-claim is to have the bill set aside or treated as a nullity pursuant to section 87 of the Trade Practices Act.[662]

The principle precluding an equitable set-off against a claim on a bill should not apply where it is the holder who instead is looking to employ the bill in a set-off. In *Williams* v. *Davies*[663] Sir Lancelot Shadwell permitted a person who had obtained judgment on some promissory notes to set off the judgment against a damages liability to the maker of the notes. While the case has been criticized on the ground that the cross-demands were not sufficiently closely connected to give rise to an equitable set-off,[664] it does nevertheless suggest that a liability on a negotiable instrument may be employed defensively in a set-off. Further, the availability of a cross-demand to the acceptor of a bill against the holder should provide a basis for setting aside a statutory demand served under s. 268 of the Insolvency Act as a prelude to a bankruptcy petition based upon non-payment of the bill.[664a]

---

[658] See *Churchill & Sim* v. *Goddard* [1937] 1 KB 92, 109; *Nova (Jersey) Knit Ltd.* v. *Kammgarn Spinnerei G.m.b.H.* [1977] 1 WLR 713, 721, 722, 726.

[659] Compare *Fielding & Platt Ltd.* v. *Najjar* [1969] 1 WLR 357. *Quaere* if it is sufficient if it is a case 'extremely close to a total failure of consideration'. See Sir Eric Sachs in *Cebora S.N.C.* v. *S.I.P. (Industrial Products) Ltd.* [1976] 1 Lloyd's Rep. 271, 279 (distinguishing the *Saga of Bond Street* case [1972] 2 QB 325).

[660] *Obbard* v. *Betham* (1830) M. & M. 483, 485; *Glennie* v. *Imri* (1839) 3 Y. & C. Ex. 436, 443; *Trickey* v. *Larne* (1840) 6 M. & W. 278, 280; *Bow, McLachlan & Co. Limited* v. *Ship 'Camosun'* [1909] AC 597, 612; *James Lamont & Co. Ltd.* v. *Hyland Ltd.* [1950] 1 KB 585, 592; *Cebora S.N.C.* v. *S.I.P. (Industrial Products) Ltd.* [1976] 1 Lloyd's Rep. 271, 279; *Nova (Jersey) Knit Ltd.* v. *Kammgarn Spinnerei G.m.b.H.* [1977] 1 WLR 713, 732–3; *Finch Motors Ltd.* v. *Quin* [1980] 2 NZLR 513; *Montebianco Industrie Tessili S.p.A.* v. *Carlyle Mills (London) Ltd.* [1981] 1 Lloyds Rep. 509, 511; *International Ore & Fertilizer Corporation* v. *East Coast Fertilizer Co. Ltd.* [1987] 1 NZLR 9. In *All Trades Distributors Ltd.* v. *Agencies Kaufman Ltd.* (1969) 113 Sol. Jo. 995 there was a thin, but at least arguable, case of total failure of consideration. Accordingly, conditional leave to defend was granted, the condition being that the money due on the bill should be brought into court.

[661] *Brown* v. *Trynor* (1980) 109 DLR (3d) 312. See also *Ledger* v. *Ewer* (1794) Peake 283; *Fleming* v. *Simpson* (1806) 1 Camp. 40n.; *Solomon* v. *Turner* (1815) 1 Stark. 51; *Glennie* v. *Imri* (1839) 3 Y. & C. Ex. 436, 443. See also *Ex parte Stephens* (1805) 11 Ves. Jun. 24, in which the set-off was an equitable set-off.

[662] *Ferro Corporation (Aust) Pty. Ltd.* v. *International Pools Aust Pty. Ltd.* (1993) 30 NSWLR 539.   [663] (1829) 2 Sim. 461.

[664] See *Rawson* v. *Samuel* (1841) Cr. & Ph. 161, 178, 179, and also section 1.7.1 above.

[664a] See the Insolvency Rules, r. 6.5(4)(a). In Australia see *John Shearer Ltd.* v. *Gehl* (1995) 14 ACLC 147, distinguishing *Buying Systems* v. *Tien Mah* (1986) 5 NSWLR 317.

1.7.18 The Statutes of Set-off and negotiable instruments

While it is reasonably settled that an equitable set-off based upon a cross-claim for damages is not available as a defence to an action on a bill of exchange or other negotiable instrument, there is an element of confusion in relation to the availability of a set-off under the Statutes of Set-off in the case of mutual debts. It is sometimes suggested that the principle which precludes an equitable set-off in respect of an unliquidated cross-demand also applies to the Statutes, so that generally the acceptor of a bill cannot raise as a defence an independent debt owing by the holder. There is one situation in which it is generally recognized that a set-off may arise under the Statutes, and that is when a bill is given as payment for goods sold or services performed and there is a liquidated cross-demand arising from a partial failure of consideration.[665] If, however, the cross-debt is not connected in this way, it has been said that it cannot be set off.[666] This is said to be supported by a comment by Sir Eric Sachs in *Cebora SNC* v. *SIP (Industrial Products) Ltd.*,[667] which has been referred to by the courts on a number of other occasions with evident approval.[668] His Lordship remarked that the court will refuse to regard as a defence to a claim on a bill of exchange 'any set off, *legal or equitable*, or any counterclaim, whether arising on the particular transaction upon which the bill of exchange came into existence, or, a fortiori, arising in any other way'.[669] There are three points to note in respect of this. The first is that, insofar as it extended to legal set-offs, it was *obiter*. The second is that the reference to 'legal' set-off may have been intended to refer to the common law cases which held that the principle of abatement[670] did not apply when the price had been paid by way of bill of exchange, as opposed to the form of set-off conferred by the Statutes of Set-off in the case of mutual debts.[671] The

---

[665] *Agra & Masterman's Bank* v. *Leighton* (1866) L.R. 2 Ex. 56, 65; *Nova (Jersey) Knit Ltd.* v. *Kammgarn Spinnerei G.m.b.H.* [1977] 1 WLR 713, 720, 732–3. See also *Eversure Textiles Manufacturers Co. Ltd.* v. *Webb* [1978] Qd. R. 347, 349.

[666] See e.g., Wood, *English and International Set-off* (1989), 700–1.

[667] [1976] 1 Lloyd's Rep. 271.

[668] *Begley Industries Ltd.* v. *Cramp* [1977] 2 NZLR 207, 212–13; *Buying Systems (Aust) Pty. Ltd.* v. *Tien Mah Litho Printing Co. Ltd.* (1986) 5 NSWLR 317, 327–8; *Re Julius Harper Ltd.* [1983] NZLR 215, 224; *Finch Motors Ltd.* v. *Quin* [1980] 2 NZLR 513, 516; *Halsbury's Laws of England* (4th edn., 1992) Vol. 4(1), 246 para. 497. In *Power Curber International Ltd.* v. *National Bank of Kuwait* [1981] 1 WLR 1233, 1241 Lord Denning M.R. said that 'No set-off or counterclaim is allowed to detract from' the principle that a bill is equivalent to cash, though this comment was made in the context of a bill given for the price of goods and his Lordship may have only had in mind a damages claim arising out of the underlying contract.

[669] [1976] 1 Lloyd's Rep. 271, 278 (emphasis added).

[670] See section 1.10 below.

[671] In *Bank of Boston Connecticut* v. *European Grain & Shipping Ltd.* [1989] 1 AC 1056, 1105 Lord Brandon would appear to have used the expression 'legal set-off' in the sense of a claim for an abatement (though in the context of freight payable under a charterparty).

third point is that, if his Lordship did intend to refer to the Statutes, it is not an accurate statement of the traditionally accepted position. It should be remembered that, unlike equitable set-off, the right of set-off in the case of mutual debts was not developed as an equitable or a common law doctrine, but rather is statutory in origin. In the case of a defence conferred by statute, the proper approach is to examine the words of the relevant legislation, and the Statutes of Set-off simply stipulated that a set-off could occur in the case of mutual debts. There was nothing in them to suggest that they were not intended to apply when the plaintiff is suing on a bill of exchange.

At least since the latter half of the eighteenth century the courts have recognized that an independent cross-debt may be set off under the Statutes against a claim on a negotiable instrument.[672] In *Baskerville* v. *Brown*[673] Lord Mansfield accepted that Baskerville could have pleaded the debt owing to him as a defence in Brown's action against him on the promissory note, and indeed Lord Kenyon allowed a set-off in a similar situation in *Lechmere* v. *Hawkins.*[674] In *Wake* v. *Tinkler*[675] it seems to have been generally assumed that a set-off under the Statutes was available against a claim on a promissory note, although it was denied on another ground. The availability of a set-off is also supported by the line of cases which developed in the middle of the nineteenth century dealing with overdue bills and promissory notes.[676] These established the principle that, when the indorsee of an overdue bill sues the acceptor, he does not take subject to a right of set-off under the Statutes that the acceptor otherwise would have had in respect of an unconnected cross-debt owing to the acceptor by an earlier holder.[677] However, the interesting point is that there was an apparent acceptance in the judgments that a set-off would have been available if the prior holder himself had sued. For example, in *Burrough* v. *Moss*[678] the defendant gave a promissory note to a married woman. According to the then applicable law, this entitled the husband (one Fearn) to treat it as his own property. Fearn himself was indebted to

---

[672] In addition to the cases cited below, see *L.D. Nathan & Company Ltd.* v. *Vista Travel Ltd.* [1973] 1 NZLR 233, which may have been correctly decided on the basis of a set-off under the Statutes, though compare *Finch Motors Ltd.* v. *Quin* [1980] 2 NZLR 513, 516 and *International Ore & Fertilizer Corporation* v. *East Coast Fertilizer Co. Ltd.* [1987] 1 NZLR 9, 15. This may also explain *Murphy* v. *Glass* (1869) LR 2 PC 408, where the cross-claim had been the subject of an award by an arbitrator. [673] (1761) 2 Burr. 1229.

[674] (1798) 2 Esp. 626. See also *Ord* v. *Ruspini* (1797) 2 Esp. 569.

[675] (1812) 16 East 36.

[676] The relevant cases are *Burrough* v. *Moss* (1830) 10 B. & C. 558; *Stein* v. *Yglesias* (1834) 1 Cr. M. & R. 565; *Whitehead* v. *Walker* (1842) 10 M. & W. 696; *Oulds* v. *Harrison* (1854) 10 Ex. 572; *In re Overend Gurney; ex parte Swan* (1868) LR 6 Eq. 344.

[677] See also section 13.2.18 below. Compare *Holmes* v. *Kidd* (1858) 3 H. & N. 391, in which there was an agreement for a set-off which constituted an equity attaching to the bill, as opposed to merely a personal equity. [678] (1830) 10 B. & C. 558.

the defendant on an unrelated matter. After the note became due, Fearn indorsed it to the plaintiff. When the plaintiff sued the defendant on the note, the defendant sought to set off Fearn's indebtedness to him. It was held that the set-off was not available against the plaintiff as indorsee. On the other hand, Bayley J. recognized that one of the consequences of Fearn treating the note as his own 'would be, to let in by way of set-off to any claim by him, any debts due from him',[679] and that, 'As to the other sum of £28 due from Fearn alone . . . it might have been set off had Fearn sued on the note'.[680] Indeed, counsel for both parties acknowledged during the argument that this would have been the case. Similarly in *Oulds* v. *Harrison*,[681] which concerned an overdue bill, Parke B. commented that,[682]

[W]hat is the effect of an indorsement of an overdue bill under the circumstances mentioned in the plea? These though inaccurately stated, we think, amount to an averment, that both the indorser and indorsee, knowing that *there was a debt due to the defendant, which would be set off if the action should be brought by the indorser against the defendant*, in order to defeat that set-off, and fraudulently, so far as that was a fraud but no further, agreed that the bill should be indorsed, and it was therefore indorsed, without value, to the plaintiff.

It was held that the circumstances referred to did not prevent the application of the principle that an indorsee of an overdue note takes free from rights of set-off available against the indorser. Nevertheless it was recognized that, if the indorser instead had been the party suing on the bill, he could have been met by a set-off under the Statutes in respect of the debt that he owed to the acceptor. These cases were decided after some of the early cases which established that a claim on a bill of exchange given as payment of the price of goods sold and delivered cannot be met by a defence based upon a cross-claim for damages for a defect in the goods,[683] and it may be assumed that the judges were aware of them.

In Victoria there are instances in which the courts have held that an unconnected cross-debt may be set off under the Statutes against a claim on a negotiable instrument. One such case is *Ingleton* v. *Coates*.[684] Recently Young C.J. in *Mobil Oil Australia Ltd.* v. *Caulfield Tyre Service Pty. Ltd.*,[685] having quoted the passage from the judgment of Sir Eric Sachs in *Cebora* referred to above, suggested that the decision in *Ingleton* v. *Coates* may need to be reconsidered,[686] though the better view is that in

---

[679] (1830) 10 B. & C. 558, 562.   [680] (1830) 10 B. & C. 558, 562.
[681] (1854) 10 Ex. 572.   [682] (1854) 10 Ex. 572, 579 (emphasis added).
[683] See, for example, *Morgan* v. *Richardson* 1 Camp. 40n; *Tye* v. *Gwynne* (1810) 2 Camp. 346; *Day* v. *Nix* (1824) 2 LJOSCP 133; *Obbard* v. *Bentham* (1830) M. & M. 483; *Glennie* v. *Imri* (1839) 2 Y. & C. Ex. 436.   [684] (1896) 2 ALR 154.
[685] [1984] VR 440.   [686] [1984] VR 440, 443.

fact it was correct. This is supported by two other Victorian cases. The first is *Nisbet* v. *Cox*,[687] which concerned a set of bills. The report only takes the form of a short note, though it appears to have been accepted that a set-off under the Statutes was available once the last bill became due. The second is *Woodroffe* v. *Moss*.[688] The defendant in an action against him on a cheque pleaded by way of defence that the plaintiffs had been his agents for the sale of some goods, and in breach of their duty as agents themselves purchased the goods and sold them on their own account at enhanced prices without accounting for the difference in price. The Full Court of the Supreme Court held that this could be pleaded as a defence of set-off. It has been suggested that the case turned on the circumstance that it involved delinquency by a fiduciary.[689] However, this point was not emphasized in argument or in any of the judgments. The whole discussion centred on whether the claim against the plaintiff was liquidated. It was held that it was. Therefore, a set-off was allowed under the Statutes.

In *Hongkong and Shanghai Banking Corporation* v. *Kloeckner & Co. AG*[690] Hirst J. accepted as 'well settled' a statement by counsel to the effect that a set-off is permissible against a claim on a bill of exchange when the cross-claim is liquidated though not when it is unliquidated.[691] The case itself concerned a letter of credit. The beneficiary sought summary judgment against the bank on the letter. The bank asserted a set-off in respect of a liquidated sum owing to it by the beneficiary. Hirst J. allowed the set-off, though he emphasized that it was a 'striking feature' that the debt to the bank arose out of the same transaction as the letter. However, he went on to say that this was an *additional* circumstance for allowing a set-off.[692] The Statutes of Set-off themselves do not require that the cross-debts should be connected in any way, and the better view is that the set-off in *Kloeckner* was not dependent upon the connection referred to by Hirst J.

It is evident that the courts for a long time have recognized that the Statutes of Set-off provide a defence when a cross-demand is liquidated. Further, since the Statutes do not require any connection between the debts sought to be set off, there is no reason in principle why a set-off should be confined to the case of a liquidated cross-demand arising out of a partial failure of consideration.

1.7.19 Set-off against a subsequent holder

Given that a set-off under the Statutes of Set-off may be asserted against a claim on a bill of exchange or other negotiable instrument, the question

---

[687] (1873) 4 AJR 115.
[688] [1915] VLR 237.
[689] Wood, *English and International Set-off* (1989), 700.
[690] [1990] 2 QB 514.
[691] [1990] 2 QB 514, 524.
[692] [1990] 2 QB 514, 526.

then arises whether a subsequent holder of a bill takes subject to a right of set-off that would have been available against the prior holder under the Statutes if the prior holder had sued on the bill. Clearly, if the subsequent holder is a holder in due course, he takes free from personal defences between prior parties, which include rights of set-off. This is a long-standing principle which has been codified in section 38(2) of the Bills of Exchange Act 1882. On the other hand, section 38(2) does not state what happens when the subsequent holder is not a holder in due course, and opinions differ amongst text-writers as to whether a subsequent holder in such a case is bound by rights of set-off between prior parties.[693] The issue is dealt with later.[694] The better view is that he is not bound, even if he is a mere holder who has not given value.

1.7.20 Building contracts

As a general principle a cross-claim for damages for delay or for bad workmanship may be employed in a set-off against the price due under a building contract.[695] At one time it was thought that this right of set-off was not available in cases in which the price was to be paid by instalment on the certificate of an architect or some other such person. In a series of cases, commencing in 1971 with the Court of Appeal decision in *Dawnays Ltd.* v. *F. G. Minter Ltd.*,[696] it was held that a certificate issued in respect of the

[693] For the view that a subsequent holder who is not a holder in due course takes subject to rights of set-off available between prior parties, see Wood *English and International Set-off* (1989), 901. See also *Paget's Law of Banking* (10th edn., 1989) 434, where it is said that a mere holder for value takes subject to personal defences available to prior parties among themselves. For the contrary view, see Crawford and Falconbridge, *Banking and Bills of Exchange* (8th edn., 1986) Vol. 2, 1524 et seq. and *Chitty on Contracts* (27th edn., 1994) Vol. 2, 220. See also *Chalmers and Guest on Bills of Exchange* (14th edn., 1991), 249 in relation to a holder for value. Compare *Byles on Bills of Exchange* (26th edn., 1988) 230.

[694] See section 13.2.18 below.

[695] For cases concerned with delay, see *Young* v. *Kitchin* (1878) 3 Ex. D 127; *Mitchell* v. *Purnell Motors Pty. Ltd.* [1961] NSWLR 165; *M.L. Paynter Ltd.* v. *Ben Candy Investments Ltd.* [1987] 1 NZLR 257. See also *Galambos & Sons Pty. Ltd.* v. *McIntyre* (1974) 5 ACTR 10. In an action by an employer arising out of a delay in completion, a cross-claim available to the contractor against the employer for hindering or preventing the contractor's performance of the contract may give rise to an equitable set-off. See *Rosehaugh Stanhope (Broadgate Phase 6) Plc.* v. *Redpath Dorman Long Ltd.* (1990) 50 Build. LR 75; *Beaufort House Development Ltd.* v. *Zimmcor (International) Inc.* (1990) 50 Build. LR 91. See also *Hanak* v. *Green* [1958] 2 QB 9. For cases concerned with bad workmanship, see *Mitchell* v. *Purnell Motors Pty. Ltd.* and *Galambos & Son Pty. Ltd.* v. *McIntyre* (above). See also *Lowe* v. *Holme* (1883) 10 QBD 286; *Hanak* v. *Green* (above).

[696] [1971] 1 WLR 1205. See also *Frederick Mark Ltd.* v. *Schield* [1972] 1 Lloyd's Rep. 9; *G.K.N. Foundations Ltd.* v. *Wandsworth London Borough Council* [1972] 1 Lloyd's Rep. 528; *John Thompson Horseley Bridge Ltd.* v. *Wellingborough Steel & Construction Co. Ltd.* (1972) 1 Build. LR 69; *Token Construction Co. Ltd.* v. *Naviewland Properties Ltd.* (1972) 2 Build. LR 1; *Carter Horseley (Engineers) Ltd. and John Thompson Horseley Bridge Ltd.* v. *Dawnays Ltd.* (1972) 2 Build. LR 8.

work done to date by a contractor or subcontractor under a building contract should be regarded as being equivalent to cash, and that the debt due under the certificate should be paid save only for deductions permitted by the contract. A claim on the certificate by the contractor against the employer, or by a subcontractor against the contractor, could not be met by a set-off or counterclaim in respect of an unliquidated cross-demand. Nor could the existence of the unliquidated cross-demand provide a justification for a stay of the action on the certificate pending arbitration. Provisions in the contract permitting certain deductions or set-offs were interpreted as referring only to liquidated ascertained sums which were established or admitted as being due.[697] Unliquidated cross-demands had to be prosecuted separately. The impetus for these decisions was cash flow. It was said that, if the contractor or subcontractor failed to receive the money stipulated in the certificate, it may not be in a position to complete the contract works. Accordingly, the contracts in question were construed so as to give effect to the presumed intention of the parties that cash flow should be preserved.[698] However, *Dawnays* v. *Minter* and the cases following it were the subject of trenchant criticism by one commentator,[699] and they were effectively overruled some two years later by the House of Lords in *Gilbert-Ash (Northern) Ltd.* v. *Modern Engineering (Bristol) Ltd.*[700] Lord Reid, Lord Morris of Borth-y-Gest, Viscount Dilhorne, Lord Diplock, and Lord Salmon all agreed that there is no presumption in building cases in which the price is to be paid by instalment on certificate that the parties intend that the ordinary rights of equitable set-off and common law abatement should not be applicable. The perceived desirability of facilitating cash flow was not considered to be

[697] See e.g. *Algrey Contractors Ltd.* v. *Tenth Moat Housing Society Ltd.* [1973] 1 Lloyd's Rep. 369 (liquidated damages clause).

[698] Curiously, though, the courts also denied a right of deduction when the claim for payment was on the final certificate or the contract works in any event were completed, despite the fact that the case obviously would not have been one in which the funds were required in order to finance the completion of the contract works. See *G.K.N. Foundations Ltd.* v. *Wandsworth L.B.C.* [1972] 1 Lloyd's Rep. 528; *Token Construction Co. Ltd.* v. *Naviewland Properties Ltd.* (1972) 2 Build. LR 1; *Carter Horseley (Engineers) Ltd.* v. *Dawnays Ltd.* (1972) 2 Build. LR 8. See the discussion of these cases in Wallace, 'Set Back to Set-off' (1973) 89 *Law Quarterly Review* 36, 54–6, 58–9, 59–60.

[699] Wallace, 'Set Back to Set-off' (1973) 89 *Law Quarterly Review* 36.

[700] [1974] AC 689, discussed in Wallace, 'Set Fair for Set-off' (1974) 90 *Law Quarterly Review* 21. See also *Mottram Consultants Ltd.* v. *Bernard Sunley & Sons Ltd.* [1975] 2 Lloyd's Rep. 197 (discussed below) and *M.L. Paynter Ltd.* v. *Ben Candy Investments Ltd.* [1987] 1 NZLR 257. *Gilbert-Ash* has been followed in Scotland. See *Redpath Dorman Long Ltd.* v. *Cummins Engine Co. Ltd.* [1981] SC 370. See also, in Ireland, *P.J. Hegarty & Sons Limited* v. *Royal Liver Friendly Society* [1985] IR 524.

something unique to the building industry, and it was not regarded as a sufficient justification for ousting those rights.[701]

While there is no presumption in building cases in which the price is to be paid by instalment on certificate that the usual rights of set-off or abatement should not be available, it is still possible for the parties to choose to exclude them by agreement. However, when two parties deal with each other, there is a presumption that neither intends to give up any remedy which would arise by operation of law in the event of a breach of contract by the other, and clear express words must be used to rebut this presumption, or at least there must be a clear implication.[702] It is particularly important to bear this in mind in the context of building contracts, where a cross-claim for damages for defective workmanship can give rise to both an equitable set-off and a common law defence of abatement. If it is intended that the contract sum should be paid in full without deduction in respect of a cross-claim, care must be taken to negative both defences. In *Acsim (Southern) Ltd.* v. *Danish Contracting and Development Co. Ltd.*[703] the contract provided that Danish Contracting ('Dancon') could set off against any money otherwise due to Acsim as contractor the amount of any claim for loss only if the claim had been quantified and notified to Acsim within a time limit. The contract went on to provide that this fully set out the rights of the parties in respect of set-off. While the Court of Appeal held that the contract was effective to prevent a cross-claim for damages for bad workmanship that was quantified outside the required period from being employed as an equitable set-off, there were not sufficiently clear and express words to exclude the common law defence of abatement. The subject of the cross-claim was not being raised as a set-off as such. Rather, Dancon was defending itself by showing that, by reason of Acsim's breaches of contract, the value of the work was less than the sum claimed. This defence was not prohibited by the contract.

1.7.21 Contracts of employment

If an employee had refused to work in accordance with his contract of employment for part of a period in respect of which he is claiming wages, the relevant principle is not that the employee has a claim for his wages for that period although subject to a right of set-off in the employer to the

---

[701] See Viscount Dilhorne and Lord Diplock [1974] AC 689, 707, 718. See also *Mottram Consultants Ltd.* v. *Bernard Sunley & Sons Ltd.* [1975] 2 Lloyd's Rep. 197, 214; *The Teno* [1977] 2 Lloyd's Rep. 289, 293–4; *Federal Commerce & Navigation Co. Ltd.* v. *Molena Alpha Inc.* [1978] 1 QB 927, 983, 986.   [702] See section 1.13.1 below.
[703] (1989) 47 Build. LR 59.

extent of a proportion of the wages equal to the proportion which that part of the period bears to the whole period.[704] Rather, the employee fails at the first hurdle, in that he is not entitled to wages to the extent that he was not ready and willing to perform the services required by the contract.[705]

The case instead may be one in which an employer has suffered loss as a result of other actions of the employee which give rise to a damages claim. An equitable set-off may well be available against the employee in this situation,[706] though it has been said that the principles upon which an equitable set-off can be effective in a claim for wages are extremely limited, and that it would depend upon a careful analysis of the nature of the breach relative to the nature of the employee's contractual claim.[707] It is true that section 1 of the Wages Act 1986 prohibits an employer from making a deduction from wages except in certain defined circumstances. However, if a substantive defence of equitable set-off were available, it would not give rise to a deduction as such from an entitlement to wages. Rather, it would be unconscionable for the employee to consider that the employer has a liability for wages to the extent of the cross-claim.[708] Thus, a stipulation in a contract that a payment is to be made 'without any deduction' has been held in other contexts not to be effective to exclude an equitable set-off.[709] It is uncertain, nevertheless, whether 'deduction' would be given this meaning in relation to section 1 of the Wages Act, when to do so may be regarded as inconsistent with the legislative intent in enacting the provision.

1.7.22 Rent

At one time it was thought that special considerations applied to a landlord's claim for rent, so that a tenant could not raise an unliquidated cross-claim against the landlord, for example for breach of an obligation to repair, as a defence to an action instituted by the landlord against the

---

[704] Compare *Sim* v. *Rotherham Metropolitan BC* [1987] 1 Ch. 216.

[705] *Miles* v. *Wakefield Metropolitan DC* [1987] 1 AC 539; *Wiluszynski* v. *Tower Hamlets LBC* [1989] ICR 493. However, as Lord Oliver of Aylmerton noted in *Miles* (at 571), this would be subject to an implied term exonerating the employee from inability to perform in certain circumstances, e.g. illness.

[706] This is consistent with *Sim* v. *Rotherham Metropolitan BC* [1987] 1 Ch. 216, and see also *Sager* v. *H. Ridehalgh and Son, Ltd.* [1931] 1 Ch. 310; *New Centurion Trust* v. *Welch* [1990] ICR 383. In *Miles* v. *Wakefield Metropolitan DC* [1987] 1 AC 539, 570 Lord Oliver of Aylmerton left open the possibility of a set-off in this situation. However, doubts have been expressed as to whether this would be applied in Australia. See Macken, McCarry and Sappideen, *The Law of Employment* (3rd edn., 1990), 294–5.

[707] *New Centurion Trust* v. *Welch* [1990] ICR 383, 386 (EAT).

[708] See section 1.7.4 above.   [709] See section 1.13.1 below.

tenant for payment of arrears of rent.[710] Whether indeed this was ever the view of equity is a matter of debate. Thus, in *Beasley* v. *Darcy*[711] a landlord had served the tenant with an ejectment for non-payment of rent and duly recovered possession, but the tenant obtained an injunction restoring him to possession on the basis of a cross-claim in damages available against the landlord for damage suffered as a result of timber on the demised land being cut down and carried away.[712] But whatever the position formerly was, a tenant's liability to pay rent is no longer regarded as being different in kind to other forms of indebtedness as regards set-off, so that an equitable set-off may proceed if the tenant's cross-demand is sufficiently closely connected with his liability to pay rent.[713] The first modern case in which this was recognized is *British Anzani (Felixstowe) Ltd.* v. *International Marine Management (U.K.) Ltd.*[714] The plaintiff had a leasehold interest in a plot of land. It agreed with the defendant to construct a warehouse on part of the land, and then to grant an underlease to the defendant. Under the terms of the agreement, the plaintiff was to be liable to make good any defects which appeared in the floor of the warehouse. The building was completed and a sub-lease entered into. The defendant subsequently was sued for arrears of rent, but raised as a defence a cross-demand against the plaintiff for breach of the agreement to repair defects in the floor. Forbes J. held that there was a sufficiently close connection between these demands to give rise to an equitable set-off, notwithstanding that the cross-demand did not arise out of the lease itself,

---

[710] *Hart* v. *Rogers* [1916] 1 KB 646; *Fong* v. *Cilli* (1968) 11 FLR 495; *Galambos & Son Pty. Ltd.* v. *McIntyre* (1974) 5 ACTR 10, 24–5; *Chatfield* v. *Elmstone Resthouse Ltd.* [1975] 2 NZLR 269; *Knockholt Proprietary Limited* v. *Graff* [1975] Qd. R 88, 91; *Halsbury's Laws of England* (3rd edn., 1960) Vol. 34, 406–7, para. 705. In *Taylor* v. *Webb* [1937] 2 KB 283, du Parcq J. held that the landlord in that case was not absolved from his obligation to repair because of the tenant's non-payment of rent. Scrutton J. in *Hart* v. *Rogers* was influenced by *Surplice* v. *Farnsworth* (1844) 7 Man. & G 576, though in truth questions of equitable set-off were not considered in that case.
[711] (1800) 2 Sch. & Lef. 403n, explained in *Rawson* v. *Samuel* (1841) Cr. & Ph. 161, 179.
[712] See also *O'Connor* v. *Spaight* (1804) 1 Sch. & Lef. 305 (explained in *Rawson* v. *Samuel* (1841) Cr. & Ph. 161, 179), in which Lord Redesdale granted an injunction to restrain an action for ejectment so that an account could be taken of the various dealings between the landlord and the tenant, the justification for equitable relief being that the account was too complicated to be taken at law. Compare *O'Mahony* v. *Dickson* (1805) 2 Sch. & Lef. 400.
[713] In addition to the cases referred to below, see *Melville* v. *Grapelodge Developments Ltd.* (1978) 39 P & CR 179; *BICC Plc* v. *Burndy Corporation* [1985] 1 Ch. 232, 249; *Lambert Pty. Ltd.* v. *Papadatos Pty. Ltd.* (1991) 5 ACSR 468, 471; *Gibb Australia Pty. Ltd.* v. *Cremor Pty. Ltd.* (1992) 108 FLR 129; *MEK Nominees Pty. Ltd.* v. *Billboard Entertainments Pty. Ltd.* (1993) V Conv. R 54–468; *Televantos* v. *McCulloch* [1991] 1 EGLR 123; *Connaught Restaurants Ltd.* v. *Indoor Leisure Ltd.* [1994] 1 WLR 501. In *Coba Industries Ltd.* v. *Millie's Holdings (Canada) Ltd.* [1985] 6 WWR 14 a cross-claim for damages for repudiating a lease was held to give rise to an equitable set-off.
[714] [1980] 1 QB 137.

but rather pursuant to the original agreement.[715] Equitable set-off against rent is not limited to breach of a covenant to repair or other similar undertaking.[716] For example, it has been held to be available when the landlord has breached a covenant for quiet enjoyment[717] and, in New Zealand, when a tenant was induced to enter into the lease as a result of a collateral contract by the lessor to refer business to the lessee, and the lessor breached that contract.[718]

The above discussion relates to equitable set-off of unliquidated cross-demands. If the tenant's cross-demand is for a liquidated sum, it has been recognized from early times that a set-off against a claim for rent may proceed on the basis of mutual debts under the Statutes of Set-off.[719]

Equitable set-off and the right of set-off conferred by the Statutes of Set-off differ in an important respect. Equitable set-off is a substantive defence which may be set up by a person as an immediate answer to liability.[720] The Statutes, on the other hand, only provided a procedural defence, in the sense that prior to judgment for a set-off the rights and obligations consequent upon being a creditor or a debtor still attach.[721] This distinction may be important in the context of forfeiture for non-payment of rent. Because equitable set-off is a substantive defence, a landlord is not entitled to regard a tenant possessed of this form of set-off as being indebted for rent. As a result there would be no basis for a forfeiture, and the tenant would have a defence to an action for possession.[722] Given, however, that the defence under the Statutes is merely procedural, a landlord would be entitled to assert that a tenant relying on this defence nevertheless still has a liability for unpaid rent, and therefore under the contract the landlord has a ground for forfeiting the lease. It would then be a matter for the court in its discretion to consider whether relief from forfeiture is appropriate.[723]

---

[715] See also *Melville* v. *Grapelodge Developments Ltd.* (1978) 39 P & CR 179 (covenant to repair contained in a separate letter), and *Grant* v. *NZMC Ltd.* [1989] 1 NZLR 8 (damages claim for breach of a collateral contract).

[716] In addition to *British Anzani* see *Melville* v. *Grapelodge Developments Ltd.* (1978) 39 P & CR 179; *Re Partnership Pacific Securities Ltd.* [1994] 1 Qd. R 410; *Mirvac Hotels Pty. Ltd.* v. *333 Collins St. Pty. Ltd.* unreported, Byrne J., Victorian Supreme Court, 20 December 1994.

[717] *Connaught Restaurants Ltd.* v. *Indoor Leisure Ltd.* [1994] 1 WLR 501; *MEK Nominees Pty. Ltd.* v. *Billboard Entertainments Pty. Ltd.* (1993) V Conv. R 54–468.

[718] *Grant* v. *NZMC Ltd.* [1989] 1 NZLR 8.

[719] *Gower* v. *Hunt* (1734) Barnes 290, 291; *Brown* v. *Holyoak* (1734), cited in Willes 263 and reversing Barnes 290; *Cleghorn* v. *Durrant* (1858) 31 LTOS 235. See also *Hamp* v. *Jones* (1840) 9 LJ Ch. 258 (cross-demand for rent set off against judgment obtained by tenant against landlord). Compare *Samways* v. *Eldsley* (1676) 2 Mod. 73, which was decided before the enactment of the Statutes of Set-off.   [720] See section 1.7.4 above.

[721] See section 1.2.9 above.

[722] See e.g. *Televantos* v. *McCulloch* [1991] 1 EGLR 123.

[723] See generally with respect to forfeiture for non-payment of rent the Supreme Court Act 1981, s. 38(1), and *Belgravia Insurance Co. Ltd.* v. *Meah* [1964] 1 QB 436, 443.

Traditionally a right of set-off under the Statutes has not been regarded as a ground sufficient to protect a tenant against a landlord levying distress for rent.[724] The Statutes only provided a procedural defence to an action at law, whereas distress is a form of self-help remedy to which a landlord is entitled without recourse to legal process. Equitable set-off, on the other hand, is a substantive defence which may be set up independently of any order of the court,[725] in the sense that it makes it unconscionable for a creditor to regard the debtor as being in default to the extent of the set-off.[726] This being the case, where a tenant has an equitable set-off available to him the landlord as a matter of principle should not be entitled to distrain for non-payment of rent, and indeed this was confirmed by the Court of Appeal in *Eller* v. *Grovecrest Investments Ltd.*[727] when it granted an injunction to a tenant to restrain the landlord from proceeding with distraint against the tenant's goods because of an equitable set-off. However, an interesting aspect of the judgments of Hoffman and Neill L.JJ. is that neither of them emphasized the substantive nature of the defence, and there are indications that they would have been sympathetic to the view that the availability of a procedural defence of set-off under the Statutes should have the same effect. Thus, Neill L.J. said that he could 'see no reason to distinguish between the position of a landlord who is asserting his rights in respect of arrears of rent . . . by an action in debt, on the one hand, and that of a landlord who is asserting identical rights, but who is availing himself of the remedy of distress'.[728] Similarly Hoffman L.J. said that, 'It is contrary to principle that a landlord should be able to recover more by distress than he can by action'.[729] This reasoning would appear to be equally applicable when a tenant has a defence to an action for payment of rent under the Statutes. Indeed, Hoffman L.J. concluded his judgment by commenting that 'this court is free to hold that set-off is available against a claim to levy distress',[730] without drawing a distinction

---

[724] *Absolon* v. *Knight* (1743) Barnes 450; *Townrow* v. *Benson* (1818) 3 Madd. 203. See also *Sapsford* v. *Fletcher* (1792) 4 TR 511, 512–13, 514; *Andrew* v. *Hancock* (1819) 1 Brod. & B 37, 43, 46, 47; *Willson* v. *Davenport* (1833) 5 Car. & P 531; *Pratt* v. *Keith* (1864) 33 LJ Ch. 528; *British Anzani (Felixstowe) Ltd.* v. *International Marine Management (U.K.) Ltd.* [1980] 1 QB 137, 149.

[725] See *The Kostas Melas* [1981] 1 Lloyd's Rep. 18, 26.

[726] See section 1.7.4 above.

[727] [1995] QB 272. Compare *Halsbury's Laws of England* (4th edn. Reissue, 1993) Vol. 27(1), 224 para. 234, and the earlier comments of Neill L.J. (one of the judges in the Court of Appeal in *Eller*) in *Connaught Restaurants Ltd.* v. *Indoor Leisure Ltd.* [1994] 1 WLR 501, 511. Note also *Townrow* v. *Benson* (1818) 3 Madd. 203, in which Sir John Leach said that a court of equity would follow the law in relation to the principle that a set-off does not defeat an entitlement to levy distress, though that was in the context of whether equity would grant an injunction to restrain the landlord from levying distress on the basis of a set-off under the Statutes, as opposed to whether the substantive form of equitable set-off under discussion would be subject to the same principle.   [728] [1995] QB 272, 280.

[729] [1995] QB 272, 278.   [730] [1995] QB 272, 278.

between the various forms of set-off. Despite the traditional approach of the courts to set-off under the Statutes, and the differences in the nature of the two forms of set-off, this view is not without merit. However, in his later judgment in *Aectra Refining and Marketing Inc.* v. *Exmar NV*[731] Hoffman L.J. appeared to draw a distinction in this regard between equitable set-off and set-off under the Statutes, so that the traditional position in relation to the Statutes may still apply.

Whatever the position now is in relation to a landlord's right to levy distress where the tenant is entitled to a set-off under the Statutes, it is necessary to distinguish the line of cases which have held that, where a sub-tenant has been compelled by the superior landlord to pay a sum owing by his immediate landlord for unpaid rent or other like charges, to the extent of the payment the immediate landlord himself cannot levy distress for unpaid rent.[732] The principle applied in these cases can only be invoked where the tenant's payment was such as to give rise to a right of action against the immediate landlord for money paid to his use.[733] Notwithstanding this, it is not correct to describe the sub-tenant's right as a set-off.[734] When a tenant is compelled to make a payment to the superior landlord which ought to have been made by the immediate landlord, the tenant is considered as having been authorized by the immediate landlord to apply rent which is either due or accruing due to him in this manner.[735] Accordingly, the basis upon which the tenant impugns a subsequent attempt by the immediate landlord to distrain for unpaid rent is that the rent alleged to be outstanding in fact has been paid.[736]

A principle which is analogous to, but which nevertheless is distinct from, set-off may apply where leased premises have fallen into disrepair and responsibility for the repairs is on the landlord. In such a case, the tenant may expend money in executing the repairs and recoup himself from future payments of rent or from arrears of rent.[737] This is not bound up with technical rules of set-off, but rather is an ancient common law right of recoupment which entitles the tenant to treat the amount expended on

---

[731] [1994] 1 WLR 1634, 1650.

[732] See e.g. *Sapsford* v. *Fletcher* (1792) 4 TR 511, and *Carter* v. *Carter* (1829) 5 Bing. 406. A similar principle applies when a tenant pays sums owing by his landlord to a rent chargee with a power to distrain. See *Taylor* v. *Zamira* (1816) 6 Taunt. 524. See generally *Graham* v. *Allsopp* (1848) 3 Ex. 186, 198.

[733] *Graham* v. *Allsopp* (1848) 3 Ex. 186, 198, 199.

[734] Compare Wood, *English and International Set-off* (1989), 130.

[735] *Graham* v. *Allsopp* (1848) 3 Ex. 186, 198; *Jones* v. *Morris* (1849) 3 Ex. 742, 747.

[736] *Sapsford* v. *Fletcher* (1792) 4 TR 511; *Graham* v. *Allsopp* (1848) 3 Ex. 186, 198; *Jones* v. *Morris* (1849) 3 Ex. 742.

[737] See generally Rank, 'Repairs in Lieu of Rent' (1976) 40 *Conv.* (NS) 196; Waite, 'Repairs and Deduction from Rent' [1981] *The Conveyancer* 199.

repairs as payment of rent.[738] As early as 1591 Gawdy J. in *Taylor* v. *Beal*[739] is reported to have said[740] that 'the law giveth this liberty to the lessee to expend the rent in reparations, for he shall be otherwise at great mischief, for the house may fall upon his head before it be repaired; and therefore the law alloweth him to repair it, and recoupe the rent'.[741] There is a remarkable dearth of case law on this right, though its existence seems to have been accepted in 1795 in *Waters* v. *Weigall*.[742] The tenant in that case had covenanted to keep the premises in repair 'accidents by fire and tempest excepted'. The house was damaged by tempest and, being in want of emergency repairs, the tenant repaired it himself in order to prevent further mischief.[743] The landlord refused to allow the tenant to deduct the cost of repairs from the rent, and brought an action for payment of rent. The tenant then filed a bill in the equity side of the Exchequer seeking relief in the form of a right to retain the amount of the repairs out of the rent. It appears from the argument of Toller in support of the bill that the tenant proceeded in equity because there was no express covenant in the lease that the landlord was liable to repair in the case that happened, and it was thought that consequently the tenant did not have a cross-claim at law against the landlord.[744] For this reason MacDonald C.B. held that the tenant similarly was not entitled to relief from equity. Nevertheless, it seems clear that in the opinion of the Chief Baron a right of recoupment would have been available if the landlord had been bound to repair in consequence of the accident that happened.[745] The next reported occasion on which it appears that English courts were called upon to consider this right was in 1971, in *Lee-Parker* v. *Izzet*.[746] Goff J. in

---

[738] See Goff J. in *Lee-Parker* v. *Izzet* [1971] 1 WLR 1688, 1693, and Waite and Neill L.JJ. in *Connaught Restaurants Ltd.* v. *Indoor Leisure Ltd.* [1994] 1 WLR 501, 507, 511.

[739] (1591) Cro. Eliz. 222.

[740] Citing three cases from the Year Books, for which see Waite, 'Repairs and Deduction from Rent' [1981] *The Conveyancer* 199, 200–1.

[741] Clench J. apparently agreed with the proposition that the tenant 'might well expend the rent in reparations', though he found against the tenant on a point of pleading. Fenner J. on the other hand said that the tenant had to bring a separate action.

[742] (1795) 2 Anst. 575.

[743] It appears from the report of the subsequent proceedings at law in *Weigall* v. *Waters* (1795) 6 TR 488 that 'a violent tempest arose and threw down with great force and violence a stack of chimneys belonging to the house on the roof of the house . . . and damaged the house so much that it would soon have become uninhabitable, if he [the tenant] had not immediately repaired it'.

[744] Indeed, see the subsequent proceedings at law in *Weigall* v. *Waters* (1795) 6 TR 488.

[745] MacDonald C.B. referred in his judgment ((1795) 2 Anst. 575, 576) to a right of 'set-off' against the demand for rent. However, the claim of the tenant appears to have been that he should be allowed to recoup or 'retain' his expenses from the rent otherwise payable to the landlord, rather than that a cross-demand constituted a defence to the landlord's demand for rent. The question appears to have been one of recoupment, or payment, rather than of set-off.

[746] [1971] 1 WLR 1688. See also in Australia *Knockholt Pty. Ltd.* v. *Graff* [1975] Qd. R 88.

that case granted a declaration to tenants to the effect that, in so far as repairs carried out by the tenants were within the express or implied repairing covenants of the landlord, including those imported by section 32(1) of the Housing Act 1961,[747] they were entitled to 'deduct'[748] the proper cost from future payments of rent, and moreover to the extent of such proper costs they were not liable to be sued for the rent. As mentioned, this right of recoupment provides a defence of payment to a tenant being sued for rent and, if the rent is regarded as having been paid, the availability of the right should also provide an answer to a claim to distrain.[749] Subsequently Megarry V.C. held in *Asco Developments Ltd.* v. *Gordon*[750] that a right of recoupment is available not only against future rent but also against arrears of rent, while the existence of the right was referred to with evident approval by Forbes J. in *British Anzani (Felixstowe) Ltd.* v. *International Marine Management (U.K.) Ltd.*[751]

A landlord must have information of the existence of a defect in the premises before any obligation on his part to carry out works of repair arises.[752] Both Goff J. in *Lee-Parker*[753] and Forbes J. in *British Anzani*[754] commented on the necessity of notice of want of repair being given to the landlord before the right can be exercised. This may give rise to difficulties in situations in which the damage is such that emergency repairs are necessary in order to prevent the premises sustaining further damage. The better view is that, in these cases of emergency, the tenant may effect repairs himself and recoup his expense from rent despite the absence of prior notice to the landlord.[755]

Forbes J. in *British Anzani*[756] suggested (*obiter*) a limitation on this right of recoupment, and that is that it must not be based upon a sum which may

---

[747] See now the Landlord and Tenant Act 1985, s. 11.

[748] In truth, deduction is an inaccurate description of the right. See section 1.13.1 below.

[749] *Connaught Restaurants Ltd.* v. *Indoor Leisure Ltd.* [1994] 1 WLR 501, 511. See also *Lee-Parker* v. *Izzet* [1971] 1 WLR 1688, 1692–3, doubting an opinion to the contrary expressed in *Foa's General Law of Landlord and Tenant* (8th edn., 1957), 559.

[750] [1978] 248 EG 683.

[751] [1980] 1 QB 137. The tenants in *British Anzani* could not have had recourse to a common law right of recoupment from rent because they had not expended any money on repairs. Nevertheless, it was held that they had a right of equitable set-off against their liability for rent in respect of their cross-demand against the landlords for breach of the obligation to repair. See also *Melville* v. *Grapelodge Developments Ltd.* (1978) 39 P & CR 179.

[752] *O'Brien* v. *Robinson* [1973] AC 912, 928; *Chatfield* v. *Elmstone Resthouse Ltd.* [1975] 2 NZLR 269.   [753] [1971] 1 WLR 1688, 1693.

[754] [1980] 1 QB 137, 147–8.

[755] See the headnote to *Waters* v. *Weigall* (1795) 2 Anst. 575, and also Waite, 'Repairs and Deduction from Rent' [1981] *The Conveyancer* 199, 203–4. Similarly Waite has argued that if the landlord has disappeared so that notice of disrepair is not possible, a tenant effecting repairs himself should not be deprived of a right of recoupment in respect of his expenditure incurred.   [756] [1980] 1 QB 137, 148.

be regarded as unliquidated damages. By this he meant that it must be in respect of a sum certain which has actually been paid, and of which, in addition, the quantum has either been acknowledged by the landlord or in some other way it can no longer be disputed by him. However, the better view is that there is no such limitation, and that, as long as the expenditure was properly incurred by the tenant,[757] it makes no difference that the quantum is disputed by the landlord.[758] Forbes J. based his suggested limitation upon the judgment of Lord Kenyon C.J. in *Weigall* v. *Waters*.[759] *Weigall* v. *Waters* was decided at common law, and was in respect of the same situation considered in the earlier proceedings in equity referred to above in *Waters* v. *Weigall*. The landlord was suing for rent, and the tenant sought to set off his expenditure incurred in effecting the repairs. Lord Kenyon held against a set-off, inter alia on the ground that, if the landlord indeed was liable to repair the premises, the defendant's cross-demand would have had to be assessed by a jury and consequently it was for unliquidated damages. However, it is important to note that the only defence pleaded by the defendant was set-off, and a prerequisite to a set-off in an action at law under the Statutes of Set-off is mutual debts. The defendant had not pleaded the alternative defence that he was entitled to recoup his expenditure from rent, and that this recoupment constituted payment of the rent.

1.8 SPECIFIC PERFORMANCE

The question occasionally arises whether set-off may constitute a defence to a claim for specific performance of a contract. In *Phipps* v. *Child*[760] the plaintiff had agreed to sell, and the defendant had agreed to purchase, the plaintiff's interest in a colliery. When the defendant failed to complete the contract the plaintiff sought an order for specific performance. The defendant argued that, as a result of dealings between the parties, the plaintiff was liable to him for a sum of money which should be set off against the purchase money. Sir Richard Kindersley V.C. rejected this defence, commenting: 'There may be a right in the Defendant to bring an action against the Plaintiff. But, if there is such a right, that is not a reason for non-performance of the contract'.[761] *Phipps* v. *Child* has been cited as authority for the proposition that a claim for a set-off is no ground for

---

[757] *Lee-Parker* v. *Izzet* [1971] 1 WLR 1688, 1693; *Connaught Restaurants Ltd.* v. *Indoor Leisure Ltd.* [1994] 1 WLR 501, 511.

[758] See Waite, 'Repairs and Deduction from Rent' [1981] *The Conveyancer* 199, 205–7, citing *Mason* v. *Kerver* (1387) Y.B. Barr., 11 Ri. 2 f. 242.

[759] (1795) 6 TR 488.   [760] (1857) 3 Drewry 709.

[761] (1857) 3 Drewry 709, 715.

refusing specific performance of a contract for the sale of land,[762] though an alternative explanation is that the defence failed because the monetary cross-demands in issue were not such as would have given rise to a set-off in an action for the price.[763]

This question of the availability of set-off as a defence to a claim for specific performance was considered by the Court of Appeal in *BICC Plc v. Burndy Corporation.*[764] The plaintiff and the defendant had traded together for a number of years in a joint enterprise. They decided to dissolve the relationship, and accordingly entered into a number of agreements. One agreement provided for the continued sale of goods by the defendant to the plaintiff. According to a second agreement the plaintiff was to be responsible for the processing and maintenance of the joint rights, while the defendant was liable to reimburse the plaintiff for half of any expenses thereby incurred. This second agreement further provided that, if either of the parties failed to fulfil its obligations under the agreement, the party not in default could require the party in default to assign to it all the interests possessed by the party in default in the joint rights concerned. The plaintiff incurred expenses in relation to a number of joint rights and duly invoiced the defendant for half of that sum. When the defendant failed to make reimbursement within the time limit the plaintiff claimed that, in accordance with the second agreement, it was entitled to an assignment of the defendant's interests in the joint rights, and brought an action claiming specific performance of the agreement. As a defence the defendant argued that it had a right to set off against the sums owing by it the sums due to it from the plaintiff under the first agreement for the sale of goods. The form of set-off relied on was the right to set off mutual debts under the Statutes of Set-off. It was not considered to be a case of equitable set-off. Dillon L.J., with whom Ackner L.J. concurred, expressed the majority view, that statutory and equitable set-off both constitute a good defence to a claim for specific performance. This view is no doubt correct with respect to equitable set-off. Equitable set-off operates as a substantive defence which may be invoked independently of any order of the court.[765] If a person is possessed of a right to an equitable set-off it is unconscionable for the other party to regard that person as being indebted to the extent of the value of the cross-demand, in which case that other party should hardly be entitled to an order for specific performance when the right to the

---

[762] See *Halsbury's Laws of England* (4th edn., 1983) Vol. 42, p. 254, para. 440.

[763] See Spry, *Equitable Remedies* (4th edn., 1990), 175, and also *BICC Plc v. Burndy Corporation* [1985] 1 Ch. 232, 250, 257. The defendant's cross-demand appears to have been for an unliquidated sum, in which case a set-off would not have been available under the Statutes of Set-off. Moreover, there does not appear to have been a sufficient connection between the cross-demands to support an equitable set-off.

[764] [1985] 1 Ch. 232.   [765] *The Kostas Melas* [1981] 1 Lloyd's Rep. 18, 26.

equitable relief sought depends upon a recognition of the existence of that very debt. However, this analysis does not apply to the Statutes of Set-off, which merely provided a procedural defence to an action at law. Prior to judgment for set-off each of the parties is still regarded as being indebted to the other, so that it is not at all clear why a right of set-off under the Statutes should be regarded as providing a defence to a claim for specific performance in the same way that equitable set-off does.[766] The third member of the Court of Appeal, Kerr L.J., similarly refused to grant specific performance, though he adopted a different approach. In his Lordship's opinion the existence of a right of set-off, whether legal or equitable, does not *per se* provide a defence to a claim for specific performance, though it does constitute a factor relevant to the exercise of the court's discretion in determining whether to grant the relief sought.[767] The difficulty with this view, in so far as it applies to equitable set-off, is that, if indeed the cross-demands are such that an equitable set-off would be available, it is not easy to see how a court could ever grant an order for specific performance without detracting from the substantive nature of the defence. On the other hand, there is much to commend Kerr L.J.'s analysis in relation to the effect of a statutory right of set-off upon an application for an order for specific performance. The better view is that it does constitute a factor which, along with the other relevant circumstances, the court should take into consideration in the exercise of its discretion. In the instant case Kerr L.J. noted that the conduct of the plaintiff throughout the negotiations between the parties had been inconsistent with the applicability of the agreement for an assignment, which it suddenly sought to impose without any warning. This factor, when combined with the defendant's claim for a set-off under the Statutes, led Kerr L.J. to conclude that an order for specific performance was not appropriate.

In *BICC* v. *Burndy* a set-off was raised as a defence to an application for an order for specific performance. However, it may be that instead it is the applicant for the order who is asserting a set-off. This may arise where the applicant's own obligation under the contract is to pay money. In order to obtain specific performance the applicant must show that he is ready and willing to perform his own obligation and, because of an equitable set-off, he may assert that he need only tender a reduced amount, after taking into account the set-off, in order to satisfy that requirement. This issue is considered in the next section.

Consider that a vendor has entered into a contract to sell land to a purchaser, who happens to be separately indebted to the vendor, but that

---

[766] Compare Dillon L.J. at [1985] 1 Ch. 232, 251.
[767] See also *Handley Page Ltd.* v. *Commissioners of Customs and Excise and Rockwell Machine Tool Company Ltd.* [1970] 2 Lloyd's Rep. 459 (in particular at 466).

the vendor becomes bankrupt before conveyance. In *In re Taylor; ex parte Norvell*[768] the Court of Appeal[769] held that the purchaser in such a case is entitled to specific performance of the contract on terms that the purchase price should be reduced to the extent of a right of set-off available to the purchaser against the price pursuant to the mutual credit provision in the insolvency legislation. Buckley L.J. in his judgment[770] noted that title had been accepted before the bankruptcy, so that, when the bankruptcy occurred, there was nothing to be done but for the purchaser to pay the money and the vendor to execute the conveyance. However, the better view was expressed by Cozens Hardy M.R.,[771] that it was not material when title was accepted as long as a good title had in fact been made. A similar principle should apply when the vendor is not bankrupt or in liquidation, so that the insolvency set-off section is not applicable, but the purchaser has a cross-action which is available as an equitable set-off.[772]

1.9 SET-OFF AS A SWORD

It is sometimes said that set-off is a shield, not a sword,[773] an aphorism that Meagher, Gummow and Lehane in Australia have suggested has the same meaning in this context as it has in the case of equitable estoppel. In other words, whether or not it can be used offensively, it is capable of being pleaded as a defence.[774] Certainly, when a substantive defence of equitable set-off is in issue[775] there is no reason why in an appropriate case it could not be used as a sword. For example, an applicant for a decree of specific performance must show that he is ready and willing to perform his own essential obligations under the contract. If this involves the payment of money, he should be entitled to assert that the liability in question may be regarded as reduced because of an equitable set-off available against the defendant. In this regard, in contracts for the sale of land where there is a deficiency in the quantity or quality of the estate agreed to be transferred, for example, because the vendor does not have title to part of the land,[776]

---

[768] [1910] 1 KB 562.
[769] Cozens-Hardy M.R. and Buckley L.J., Fletcher Moulton L.J. dissenting.
[770] [1910] 1 KB 562, 580.　　　　　　　　　　[771] [1910] 1 KB 562, 572.
[772] Compare *King* v. *Poggioli* (1923) 32 CLR 222 (esp. Starke J. at 248), in which equitable set-off was not considered. See *Eagle Star Nominees Ltd.* v. *Merril* [1982] VR 557, 560.
[773] See e.g. *Stooke* v. *Taylor* (1880) 5 QBD 569, 575 and *Galambos & Son Pty. Ltd.* v. *McIntyre* (1974) 5 ACTR 10, 18 in the context of the Statutes of Set-off.
[774] Meagher, Gummow and Lehane, *Equity Doctrines and Remedies* (3rd edn., 1992), 810. See e.g. the discussion of equitable estoppel in Treitel, *The Law of Contract* (9th edn., 1995), 108–9.　　　　　　　　　　[775] See section 1.7.4 above.
[776] See, e.g. *Western* v. *Russell* (1814) 3 V & B 187; *Jones* v. *Evans* (1848) 17 LJ Ch. 469; *Hooper* v. *Smart* (1874) LR 18 Eq. 683.

or because his title is different to that which he represented,[777] or because the property has deteriorated between the date of the contract and the date the purchaser obtains possession as a result of the vendor's neglect,[778] courts of equity for a long time have allowed the purchaser to obtain specific performance of the contract to the extent of the vendor's ability to comply with it, with an abatement in the price by way of compensation for the deficiency. This right was developed independently of the principle of equitable set-off. While it does not apply where there is a breach of contract by the vendor which does not have the effect of lessening the value of the property as such,[779] the better view is that the purchaser in such a case will be in a similar position in an application for specific performance if the cross-claim nevertheless would give rise to a substantive defence of equitable set-off against the liability for the price, in that the purchaser should only be required to show that he is ready and willing to pay the price as reduced by the set-off.[780]

It is rather more difficult, however, to see how the availability of a right of set-off under the Statutes of Set-off could be used offensively. The nature of this defence is such that it is merely procedural,[781] in the sense that the Statutes only authorized a set-off if it was pleaded as a defence to an action for payment of a debt. Until such time as judgment for a set-off is obtained, each of the parties has the rights and obligations of creditor and debtor in relation to the cross-debts. Therefore, if in the example referred to above the applicant seeking specific performance merely tenders the balance after deducting a separate debt owing to him by the defendant, he will not have shown that he is ready and willing to perform his own obligation.

1.10 COMMON LAW ABATEMENT

It used to be the practice of the common law courts in an action for the agreed price of goods sold with a warranty, or of work which was to be performed according to a contract, to allow the plaintiff to recover the stipulated sum while leaving the defendant to a cross-action for damages for any breach of warranty or contract by the plaintiff.[782] Compliance with

---

[777] See, e.g. *Mortlock* v. *Buller* (1804) 10 Ves. Jun. 292, 315–16; *Nelthorpe* v. *Holgate* (1844) 1 Coll. 203; *Barnes* v. *Wood* (1869) LR 8 Eq. 424.

[778] *Phillips* v. *Silvester* (1872) LR 8 Ch. App. 173. See also *Clarke* v. *Ramuz* [1891] 2 QB 456, 461–2. [779] *King* v. *Poggioli* (1923) 32 CLR 222.

[780] See the comments of Tadgell J. in *Eagle Star Nominees Ltd.* v. *Merril* [1982] VR 557, 560 in relation to *King* v. *Poggioli* (1923) 32 CLR 222, in which equitable set-off was not considered. [781] See section 1.2.9 above.

[782] See for example *Broom* v. *Davis* (1794) 7 East 480n.

the warranty, or proper performance of every portion of the work contracted for, was not regarded as a condition precedent to payment of the stipulated price.[783] However, in the latter part of the eighteenth century and the early part of the nineteenth century, the courts began to develop a different practice, by which the defendant in these cases was permitted to show that the chattel by reason of non-compliance with the warranty, or the work in consequence of the non-performance of the contract, was diminished in value or was of no value.[784] This was not in the nature of raising the cross-demand as a set-off,[785] because at common law the only right of set-off available was under the Statutes of Set-off, and the Statutes required liquidated cross-demands in the form of mutual debts. Rather, the defendant was permitted to defend himself[786] by showing how much less the subject-matter of the action was worth by reason of the breach of contract, and to obtain an abatement of the price accordingly.[787] This revised practice received the imprimatur of the Court of Exchequer in the leading case of *Mondel* v. *Steel*,[788] and is now firmly established.[789] Indeed, in the case of a sale of goods the right has been set out in the sale of goods legislation.[790]

---

[783] The ensuing discussion concerns an action for an agreed price. If the plaintiff is suing for a *quantum meruit* rather than for a specific agreed sum, he must be prepared to show what the work was worth, and it is open to the defendant in such a case to show that in fact the work was not worth as much as the plaintiff claims. See *Basten* v. *Butter* (1806) 7 East 479; *Farnsworth* v. *Garrard* (1807) 1 Camp. 38; *Riverside Motors Pty. Ltd.* v. *Abrahams* [1945] VLR 45.

[784] *King* v. *Boston* (1789) 7 East 481n; *Germaine* v. *Burton* (1821) 3 Stark. 32 (sale by sample); *Poulton* v. *Lattimore* (1829) 9 B & C 259; *Street* v. *Blay* (1831) 2 B & Ad. 456; *Thornton* v. *Place* (1832) 1 M & Rob. 218 (plaintiff only entitled to the agreed price of work minus the sum necessary for the defendant to expend to complete the work according to the specifications); *Allen* v. *Cameron* (1833) 1 Cr. & M 832 (breach of obligation to tend trees the subject of a sale); *Cousins* v. *Paddon* (1835) 2 Cr. M & R 547; *Dicken* v. *Neale* (1836) 1 M & W 556.

[785] *Bright* v. *Rogers* [1917] 1 KB 917; *Hanak* v. *Green* [1958] 2 QB 9, 17, 23; *Henriksens Rederi A/S* v. *THZ Rolimpex (The Brede)* [1974] 1 QB 233, 252, 260; *United Dominions Corporation Limited* v. *Jaybe Homes Pty. Ltd.* [1978] Qd. R. 111, 115–16. Compare *BICC Plc* v. *Burndy Corporation* [1985] 1 Ch. 232, 246. It is independent of the doctrine of equitable set-off. See *Gilbert-Ash (Northern) Ltd.* v. *Modern Engineering (Bristol) Ltd.* [1974] AC 689, 717.

[786] The order as to costs should follow accordingly. See for example *Lowe* v. *Holme* (1883) 10 QBD 286, though compare *Chell Engineering Ltd.* v. *Unit Tool and Engineering Co., Ltd.* [1950] 1 All ER 378.

[787] See Parke B. in *Mondel* v. *Steel* (1841) 8 M & W 858, 870–2.

[788] (1841) 8 M & W 858.

[789] In addition to the cases cited below, see *Parson* v. *Sexton* (1847) 4 CB 899; *Dawson* v. *Collis* (1851) 10 CB 523 and *Towerson* v. *The Aspatria Agricultural Co-Operative Society Limited* (1872) 27 LT 276 (sale by sample); *Webber* v. *Aarons* [1972] 2 NSWLR 95. *Quaere* whether the common law right of abatement ever extended to contracts of employment. See the discussion in *Sim* v. *Rotherham Metropolitan BC* [1987] 1 Ch. 216, 255–9.

[790] See the Sale of Goods Act 1979, s. 53(1)(a).

Baron Parke emphasized in *Mondel* v. *Steel* that the defendant in an action for the agreed price of goods is only entitled to an abatement to the extent that, *at the time of delivery*, the value of the goods themselves[791] has been reduced as a result of the breach of warranty.[792] All claims beyond that, for example on account of a subsequent necessity for more extensive repairs,[793] or for damages for delay,[794] will not result in an abatement under the common law principle. However, there are two points to note in relation to this limitation. The first is that, following the expansion in recent times of the defence of equitable set-off, a damages claim which could not form the subject of an abatement in any event may well give rise now to a defence of set-off.[795] The second is that section 53(1)(a) of the Sale of Goods Act 1979 may have taken the matter further than the common law position. Section 53(1)(a) provides that a damages claim for breach of warranty by a seller may be set up in diminution or extinction of the price. One of the warranties in the Act is that the buyer will enjoy quiet possession of the goods.[796] In Australia the High Court has held that this encompasses a subsequent interference with the goods by the seller himself and, further, that this breach could be set up in diminution of the price pursuant to the New South Wales equivalent of section 53(1)(a).[797] Yet, this could hardly be regarded as evidencing a reduction in the value of the goods themselves as they were delivered. The notion that this breach of warranty comes within the ambit of section 53(1)(a) is difficult to reconcile with the view that section 53(1)(a) is merely a codification of the law laid down in *Mondel* v. *Steel*.[798]

---

[791] The defence of abatement is only available when the plaintiff's action is for the price of the same goods in which the defects occurred. See *W. Pope & Co. Pty. Ltd.* v. *Edward Souery & Co. Pty. Ltd.* [1983] WAR 117. See also *Bayview Quarries Pty. Ltd.* v. *Castley Development Pty. Ltd.* [1963] VR 445.

[792] In addition to the cases cited below, see *Bow, McLachlan & Co., Limited* v. *Ship 'Camosun'* [1909] AC 597, 605; *Henriksens Rederi A/S* v. *THZ Rolimpex (The Brede)* [1974] 1 QB 233, 248.

[793] As in *Mondel* v. *Steel* (1841) 8 M & W 858 itself. See also *Davis* v. *Hedges* (1871) LR 6 QB 687, 691.

[794] See *Oastler* v. *Pound* (1863) 7 LT 852; *Henriksens Rederi A/S* v. *THZ Rolimpex (The Brede)* [1974] 1 QB 233, 248. Compare Windeyer J. in *Healing (Sales) Pty. Ltd.* v. *Inglis Electrix Pty. Ltd.* (1968) 121 CLR 584, 618.

[795] See Lord Denning in *Henriksens Rederi A/S* v. *THZ Rolimpex (The Brede)* [1974] 1 QB 233, 248. Certainly it seems that a cross-demand for damages for delay may be employed in a set-off. See e.g. *Young* v. *Kitchin* (1878) 3 Ex. D 127; *Mitchell* v. *Purnell Motors Pty. Ltd.* [1961] NSWR 165; *Galambos & Son Pty. Ltd.* v. *McIntyre* (1974) 5 ACTR 10; *The Brede* (at 248).

[796] Sale of Goods Act 1979, s. 12(2).

[797] *Healing (Sales) Pty. Ltd.* v. *Inglis Electrix Pty. Ltd.* (1968) 121 CLR 584. Indeed, Barwick C.J. and Menzies J. said in their joint judgment (at 595) that s. 53(1)(a) allows a buyer to set up any breach of warranty against the price.

[798] See, e.g. *Benjamin's Sale of Goods* (4th edn., 1992), 871, and also the minority view of Windeyer J. in *Healing* v. *Inglis* (1968) 121 CLR 584, 617–18.

The defendant in an action for the agreed price of goods or of work and labour is not bound to set up the claim for breach of warranty or for failure to perform the work properly as a defence in that action. He may choose to pay the price and bring a separate action of his own for damages.[799] Alternatively, the purchaser of the goods or services may sue for damages *before* paying the price. In such a case there is no principle of abatement to which the vendor may have recourse as a means of reducing the damages award. He is not entitled to an 'abatement' from his liability for damages to the extent of the unpaid price.[800]

A question in respect of which conflicting views have been expressed is whether common law abatement is a procedural or a substantive defence. Historically it seems that the justification for the introduction of the defence was to avoid circuity of action,[801] which is consistent with a procedural defence. This indeed would appear to be the prevailing view in Australia, where it has been described, in that country's highest court, as a 'procedural concession' which 'the law has come to concede for the sake of convenience'.[802] In England on the other hand the defence now seems to be regarded as substantive.[803] However, it is not entirely clear what exactly is meant by 'substantive' in this context. Certainly it would not mean that the debt for the price is extinguished as from the time of the delivery of the defective goods or completion of the work otherwise than in accordance with the contract.[804] If indeed this were correct, it is difficult to see how the damages claim could be regarded as still in existence so as to entitle the purchaser to elect to pay the full price and sue separately for the damages.[805] Presumably the basis of the substantive view is that the availability of the defence is determined as at the date of delivery of the

---

[799] *Davis* v. *Hedges* (1871) LR 6 QB 687 (disapproving of *Fisher* v. *Samuda* (1808) 1 Camp. 190); *Healing (Sales) Pty. Ltd.* v. *Inglis Electrix Pty. Ltd.* (1968) 121 CLR 584; *Henriksens Rederi A/S* v. *THZ Rolimpex (The Brede)* [1974] 1 QB 233, 248; *Sidney Raper Pty. Ltd.* v. *Commonwealth Trading Bank of Australia* [1975] 2 NSWLR 227, 238. See also *Rigge* v. *Burbidge* (1846) 15 M & W 598, and the Sale of Goods Act 1979, s. 53(1)(b).

[800] *Healing (Sales) Pty. Ltd.* v. *Inglis Electrix Pty. Ltd.* (1968) 121 CLR 584.

[801] *Street* v. *Blay* (1831) 2 B & Ad. 456, 462–3; *Allen* v. *Cameron* (1833) 1 Cr. & M 832, 840; *Mondel* v. *Steel* (1841) 8 M & W 858, 869–70; *Davis* v. *Hedges* (1871) LR 6 QB 687, 691; *Bow, McLachlan & Co., Ltd.* v. *Ship 'Camosun'* [1909] AC 597, 611, 613; *Healing (Sales) Pty. Ltd.* v. *Inglis Electrix Pty. Ltd.* (1968) 121 CLR 584, 614–15.

[802] See Kitto J. in *Healing (Sales) Pty. Ltd.* v. *Inglis Electrix Pty. Ltd.* (1968) 121 CLR 584, 601. The tenor of the judgment of Windeyer J. suggests that he agreed with this view. See also *Cellulose Products Pty. Ltd.* v. *Truda* (1970) 92 WN (NSW) 561, 570. Compare *Newman* v. *Cook* [1963] VR 659, discussed below.

[803] See e.g. Lord Diplock in *Gilbert-Ash (Northern) Ltd.* v. *Modern Engineering (Bristol) Ltd.* [1974] AC 689, 717; *Aectra Refining and Marketing Inc.* v. *Exmar NV* [1994] 1 WLR 1634, 1649–50.

[804] Compare *Impex Transport Aktieselskabet* v. *AG Thames Holdings Ltd.* [1981] 2 Lloyd's Rep. 566, 570. In Australia see *Healing (Sales) Pty. Ltd.* v. *Inglis Electrix Pty. Ltd.* (1968) 121 CLR 584, 602–3.

[805] See above.

goods or the completion of the work. The value of the goods delivered or
the work performed as at that date is reduced because of the breach of
contract, and the nature of the defence is such that the purchaser, if he so
chooses, can defend himself in a subsequent action for the price by showing
the true value of what in fact was received at that date. The difficulty with
this explanation is that one would have thought that it would continue to
apply if the damages claim has ceased to exist as a result of the expiration
of a limitation period which has the effect of taking away, not only the
remedy, but also the right itself. This eventuality would not affect
the proposition that the value of the goods at the time of delivery or the
value of the work that was actually performed was of diminished value.
Yet, Lord Wilberforce in *Aries Tanker Corporation* v. *Total Transport
Ltd.*[806] said that a claim which has ceased to exist cannot be introduced into
legal proceedings as a defence, and his Lordship would seem to have had in
mind common law abatement as well as equitable set-off.[807]

Whatever the explanation of the substantive view, one situation in which
the procedural and the substantive theories would seem to produce
different results is where the damages claim itself remains in existence
though nevertheless it is unenforceable, as, for example, where the
expiration of a time bar merely affects the remedy. If abatement is a
procedural defence which is designed to avoid circuity of action, there
would be no reason for allowing a defence in the situation where the claim
for breach of warranty in any event could not be enforced.[808] This may well
be the position in Australia.[809] In England, however, both Lord Denning
and Roskill L.J. in *Henriksens Rederi A/S* v. *THZ Rolimpex (The Brede)*[810]
considered that the defence of abatement is not defeated by the expiration
of a limitation period, a view which was shared by the Canadian Federal
Court of Appeal in *The Didymi.*[811]

The question whether abatement is a procedural or substantive defence

[806] [1977] 1 WLR 185, 188.
[807] See the discussion of *Aries Tanker* by Mustill L.J. in the Court of Appeal in *Bank of Boston* [1989] 1 AC 1056, 1071.
[808] See the discussion of Roskill L.J. in *Henriksens Rederi A/S* v. *THZ Rolimpex (The Brede)* [1974] 1 QB 233, 259, referring to Kitto J. in *Healing (Sales) Pty. Ltd.* v. *Inglis Electrix Pty. Ltd.* (1968) 121 CLR 584, 601.
[809] In *Buttrose* v. *Versi* unreported, 14 May 1992, Young J. in the New South Wales Supreme Court, after noting that the defence was based upon circuity of action, said that if the defendants in that case could not sue for the damages they had suffered they could not abate the loss against the price, though that was in the context of a loss in respect of which there was no cause of action, as opposed to a right to sue which was unenforceable. Admittedly, in *Sidney Raper Pty. Ltd.* v. *Commonwealth Trading Bank of Australia* [1975] 2 NSWLR 227, 238 Moffitt P. said that a defence of abatement can be used outside a time limitation period, though it is difficult to reconcile that with the cases which suggest that in Australia the defence is regarded as procedural.
[810] [1974] 1 QB 233, 248, 260.   [811] [1988] 1 Lloyd's Rep. 97, 102.

nevertheless in most cases would be of little practical consequence. Following the expansion and development of equitable set-off, the equitable defence to a considerable extent now overlaps the common law defence of abatement, and the tendency in recent cases in which the plaintiff is suing for the price of work done or of goods sold and delivered is to consider both equitable set-off and common law abatement when the defendant sets up a defence that the plaintiff himself has breached the contract on which he sues.[812] Indeed, Lord Salmon remarked in *Aries Tanker Corporation* v. *Total Transport Ltd.*[813] that 'Whether [the defence] stems from the development of the common law in the last century or from equitable defences or equitable set-off, as it is sometimes called, or from both, seems to me to be only of academic interest since the passing of the Judicature Act 1873 made equitable defences available in common law courts'.[814] Consequently, if in any particular case the question arises as to whether the defence raised is procedural or substantive, the court may well decide that it is substantive by reference to principles of set-off without the necessity for recourse to abatement.[815] But while in the vast majority of cases Lord Salmon no doubt was correct in his view, there may in fact be circumstances in which abatement is available but not equitable set-off.[816] Thus, the contract between the parties may have excluded the right of the defendant to assert a set-off but not have affected the right to rely on the common law defence of abatement.[817] Further, abatement is a common law defence available as of right.[818] It would not be subject to discretionary factors relevant to equitable set-off.[819] In these circumstances, the characterization of the defence of abatement as procedural or substantive may well become important.

For reasons of public policy the defence of abatement is not available in

---

[812] See e.g. *Gilbert-Ash (Northern) Ltd.* v. *Modern Engineering (Bristol) Ltd.* [1974] AC 689. See also *The Teno* [1977] 2 Lloyd's Rep. 289, 297, and the judgment of Hudson J. in *Newman* v. *Cook* [1963] VR 659 (discussed below).

[813] [1977] 1 WLR 185, 194.

[814] See also Lord Denning in *Federal Commerce* v. *Molena* [1978] 1 QB 927, 974, where he seemed to accept that equitable set-off and common law abatement are now indistinguishable, while Scott J. in *Sim* v. *Rotherham Metropolitan BC* [1987] 1 Ch. 216, 259 said that 'the need to consider the scope of common law abatement disappeared with the Judicature Acts'.

[815] Compare *Newman* v. *Cook* [1963] VR 659, in which Hudson J considered that equitable set-off but not common law abatement provided a substantive defence to which the purchaser could have recourse in order to defeat the claim to exercise a power of sale, though Herring C.J. and Dean J. decided the case by reference to the common law defence.

[816] This is so notwithstanding the view of Scott J. in *Sim* v. *Rotherham Metropolitan BC* [1987] 1 Ch. 216, 259 that, if the circumstances of the case do not warrant equitable set-off, they would not establish an abatement.

[817] See, e.g. *Acsim (Southern) Ltd.* v. *Danish Contracting and Development Co. Ltd.* (1989) 47 Build. LR 59.

[818] *Gilbert-Ash (Northern) Ltd.* v. *Modern Engineering (Bristol) Ltd.* [1974] AC 689, 717.

[819] See section 1.7.5 above.

an action for payment of freight.[820] Moreover, if a bill of exchange is given
as payment for the purchase of goods or for the performance of work, the
bill must be honoured irrespective of any breach of contract by the vendor
which amounts only to a partial failure of consideration.[821] At one time it
was thought that a similar principle applied in building cases in which the
price is to be paid by instalment on certificate,[822] though this view is no
longer current.[823]

1.11 FOREIGN CURRENCIES

It may be that one or both of the claims in a proposed set-off is in a foreign
currency. The question of how a set-off should proceed is considered, first,
in the context of the Statutes of Set-off, and then in relation to equitable
set-off.

1.11.1 Statutes of Set-off

Until comparatively recently it was a settled principle of English law that,
when a foreign currency obligation was enforced in an English court, any
judgment for the plaintiff had to be in sterling measured at the rate of
exchange prevailing at the date when the obligation became due and
payable.[824] However, in 1975 the House of Lords in *Miliangos* v. *George
Frank (Textiles) Ltd.*[825] held that this restriction no longer applies. An
English court may give judgment for a sum of money expressed in a foreign
currency and, if the defendant fails to tender payment in that currency,
execution may issue for the sterling equivalent. Conversion for this
purpose should take place at the rate prevailing at the date of payment.
Theoretically, this should be the date of actual payment though, as Lord
Fraser of Tullybelton pointed out,[826] theory must yield to practical
necessity to the extent that, if the judgment has to be enforced in England,
it must be converted before enforcement. Accordingly, the date of

---

[820] See *Mondel* v. *Steel* (1841) 8 M & W 858, 871. The defence of abatement is not available
to defeat a claim for hire under a time charter (see *The Aditya Vaibhav* [1991] 1 Lloyd's Rep.
573, 575), though equitable set-off may apply in such a case. See generally section 1.7.14
above.
[821] *Nova (Jersey) Knit Ltd.* v. *Kammgarn Spinnerei G.m.b.H.* [1977] 1 WLR 713, and see
generally section 1.7.17 above.
[822] *Dawnays Ltd.* v. *F.G. Minter Ltd.* [1971] 1 WLR 1205.
[823] See *Gilbert-Ash (Northern) Ltd.* v. *Modern Engineering (Bristol) Ltd.* [1974] AC 689,
and generally section 1.7.20 above.
[824] *In re United Railways of Havana and Regla Warehouses Ltd.* [1961] AC 1007.
[825] [1976] AC 443. See also the earlier Court of Appeal decision in *Schorsch Meier GmbH*
v. *Hennin* [1975] 1 QB 416.   [826] [1976] AC 443, 501.

payment was considered to be the date that the court authorizes enforcement of the judgment in sterling.[827] The effect of this development upon the right of set-off has yet to be determined. The Law Commission in its report on *Private International Law Foreign Money Liabilities*[828] suggested that a right of set-off in fact should not be available in an action when different currencies are involved. Each party should obtain judgment for the amount of his claim expressed in the appropriate currency, though, as a form of qualification, it suggested that neither judgment should be enforceable without the other judgment being taken into account. The difficulty with this is that it may have the effect of making the parties to mutual debts vulnerable to an assignment. If one of the claims is assigned, the debtor on that claim would not have a right of set-off available as a defence to an action brought by the assignor which he could assert against the assignee.[829] The recommendation that the judgments themselves should be capable of being set off at the date of enforcement arguably would not be of any assistance in this situation, since an assignee only takes subject to prior equities, or defences. A right of set-off that only accrues upon the enforcement of a judgment could not be classed as a defence. Nor, on one view, would it be a *prior* equity. An alternative, and the preferable, approach is to convert the foreign currency into sterling at the rate prevailing at the date of judgment for a set-off. If both demands are in foreign currencies, the currency of the lesser debt should be converted into the currency of the greater debt at the date of judgment, and a set-off should then be effected.[830] This is not inconsistent with the *Miliangos* principle, since the set-off effectively constitutes payment and, to the extent of the set-off, conversion accordingly takes place at the time of payment. Once the balance is struck in this manner, if the currency of the balance is not sterling and payment is not forthcoming in that currency, it should be converted into sterling at the date that leave is given to enforce the judgment, in accordance with *Miliangos*.

1.11.2 Equitable set-off

Equitable set-off differs from set-off under the Statutes of Set-off in that generally it is a substantive rather than merely a procedural defence.[831] This does not mean that it operates as an automatic extinction of cross-demands prior to judgment for a set-off. Rather, the notion that the

---

[827] [1976] AC 443, 468–9 (Lord Wilberforce).

[828] *Report on Private International Law Foreign Money Liabilities* (Cmnd. 9064, 1983), 32–5.

[829] See section 13.2 below.

[830] See Brandon J. at first instance in *The Despina R* [1978] 1 QB 396, 414–15 in the context of a 'both to blame' collision under Admiralty law, and also *The Transoceanica Francesca* [1987] 2 Lloyd's Rep. 155.

[831] See section 1.7.4 above.

defence is substantive means that, even before the cross-demands have been extinguished by judgment or by agreement between the parties, it is unconscionable for the creditor to regard the debtor as being in default to the extent of the cross-demand. The question of foreign currency claims in the context of equitable set-off has yet to be considered by the courts, though the following is consistent with the true nature of the defence. When an equitable set-off is pleaded as a defence to an action and one or both of the demands is in a foreign currency, the principle should be the same as for the Statutes of Set-off, so that conversion should take place by reference to the rate applicable at the date of judgment for a set-off. However, before extinction of the cross-demands the creditor's conscience is affected, so that to the extent of the availability of the defence he is not permitted to regard the debtor as being in default. In the determination at any particular time prior to judgment of whether the creditor can consider that the debtor has defaulted, regard should be had to the exchange rate at that time.[832]

1.12 SET-OFF IN AUSTRALIA

The approach adopted by Australian courts in relation to equitable set-off was examined earlier.[833] Insofar as the Statutes of Set-off are concerned, they were originally incorporated into the laws of the various Australian jurisdictions,[834] and, with the exception of New South Wales and Queensland, they are still part of the laws of those jurisdictions.[835]

---

[832] Compare Wood, *English and International Set-off* (1989), 663 para. 11–24, 664–5 para. 11–28, and 665 para. 11–29. However, Wood has a different analysis of the substantive nature of equitable set-off (see section 1.7.4 above), and his view of foreign currency conversions must be considered with that in mind.   [833] See section 1.7.3 above.

[834] See, for example, *Day & Dent Constructions Pty. Ltd.* v. *North Australian Properties Pty. Ltd.* (1981) 34 ALR 595, 599, 600 (Northern Territory). For New South Wales and Queensland see, respectively, *Stehar Knitting Mills Pty. Ltd.* v. *Southern Textile Converters Pty. Ltd.* [1980] 2 NSWLR. 514, 522, and *Phillips* v. *Mineral Resources Developments Pty. Ltd.* [1983] 2 Qd. R 138, though note the discussion below of the present position in those states. In the case of South Australia and Western Australia, the incorporation would have resulted from their being 'settled colonies'. For other jurisdictions, see s. 24 of the Australian Courts Act 1828 (9 Geo. 4, c. 83). See generally Castles, 'The Reception and Status of English Law in Australia' (1963) 2 *Adelaide Law Review* 1. In the Australian Capital Territory, the operation of the Statutes has been expressly preserved, by the Imperial Acts Application Ordinance 1986. The Statutes are also in force in New Zealand. See *Grant* v. *NZMC Ltd.* [1989] 1 NZLR 8, 11.

[835] Note that in Victoria the Statutes were repealed by the Imperial Acts Application Act 1922, s. 7 (and see also the Imperial Acts Application Act 1980), though the legislation had a saving provision similar to that in the legislation (the Civil Procedure Acts Repeal Act 1879, s. 2) which repealed the Statutes in England. See section 1.2.1 above. The current position in Victoria in relation to set-off is discussed below.

In New South Wales the Statutes were repealed by the Imperial Acts Application Act 1969 (NSW). While the Statutes have also been repealed in England, by the Civil Procedure Acts Repeal Act 1879, the legislation contained a provision which has been interpreted as preserving the right of set-off originally conferred by the Statutes.[836] However the New South Wales Act does not have a similar saving provision, so that the operation of the Statutes of Set-off has not been preserved in New South Wales. On the other hand, the former Part 15 rule 25 of the Supreme Court Rules (NSW) contemplated that a monetary cross-demand possessed by the defendant against the plaintiff, whether for an ascertained sum or not, could be included in the defence and set off against the plaintiff's claim. In *Stehar Knitting Mills Pty. Ltd.* v. *Southern Textile Converters Pty. Ltd.*[837] Hutley and Glass JJ.A. said that Part 15 rule 25 should take effect according to its literal terms. As a result, it appeared that in New South Wales *any* monetary cross-demand which was due and payable, whether it was liquidated or unliquidated and whether or not it was connected with the plaintiff's claim, could be the subject of a set-off in an action at law.[838] It was not necessary to show mutual debts, or, if one of the demands was unliquidated, that the cross-demands were sufficiently closely connected so as to give rise to an equitable set-off. In 1984, however, Part 15 rule 25 was omitted from the Supreme Court Rules.[839] Accordingly, the position outlined in *Stehar Knitting Mills* would no longer apply. Since the Statutes of Set-off are no longer in force in New South Wales, it would appear that the only right of set-off available in that state prior to bankruptcy or liquidation would be the form of equitable set-off in which there is a sufficiently close connection between the demands.[840]

Notwithstanding that *Stehar Knitting Mills* is no longer relevant to the position in New South Wales, the view that the Supreme Court Rules themselves could determine when a cross-demand may be set up as a defence is of general interest, particularly in Queensland where the Statutes of Set-off have also been abolished.[841] The essence of the argument in *Stehar* was that the Statutes were wholly procedural in their operation, in which case it was said that there was no reason why Supreme Court Rules made pursuant to legislation which contained a rule-making

---

[836] See e.g. *Hanak* v. *Green* [1958] 2 QB 9, 22, and generally section 1.2.1 above.

[837] [1980] 2 NSWLR 514.

[838] See Hutley J.A. at [1980] 2 NSWLR 514, 523.

[839] Supreme Court Rules (Amendment No. 154), 1984.

[840] See the discussion in *Sydmar Pty. Ltd.* v. *Statewise Developments Pty. Ltd.* (1987) 73 ALR 289, 292. See also Cole J. in *APM Wood Products Pty. Ltd.* v. *Kimberley Homes Pty. Ltd.* unreported, 17 February 1989, NSW Supreme Court, and Young J. in *Buttrose* v. *Versi* unreported, 14 May 1992, NSW Supreme Court. Compare Burton, 'Negotiability: Set-offs and Counterclaims,' *Directions in Finance Law* (1990), 70, and *The Laws of Australia* Vol. 15, para. 66.

[841] See below.

power with respect to matters of practice and procedure could not be the source of a similar right. This reasoning is beset with difficulty. In the first place, there is ample authority in England for the proposition that the Judicature Acts, and the Rules of the Supreme Court made pursuant to those Acts and their successors, themselves did not alter the rights of the parties and, in particular, did not confer any new rights of set-off.[842] Hutley J.A. sought to distinguish the position in New South Wales from that in England, though the analysis was not entirely satisfactory.[843] Of greater concern is the conclusion that the right of set-off that the Statutes conferred in the case of mutual debts is wholly procedural in its operation. This form of set-off admittedly is regarded as a procedural defence.[844] By this it is meant that separate and distinct debts remain in existence until judgment for a set-off, and moreover, as between the two parties to the cross-demands, the defence has no effect until judgment. Prior to judgment the rights consequent upon being a creditor still attach, as do the obligations and liabilities consequent upon being a debtor. It should be distinguished from the form of equitable set-off in which there is a sufficiently close connection between the demands. This is properly described as a substantive defence, in the sense that even prior to judgment it is unconscionable for the creditor to regard the debtor as being indebted while circumstances continue to exist which support an equitable set-off.[845] Notwithstanding this distinction, the fundamental point is that the right of set-off derived from the Statutes is still a defence. In this sense it differs from counterclaim, which merely provides a mechanism by which separate actions may be tried in the same proceedings. Counterclaim is not a defence, and is properly described as being wholly procedural. But because the Statutes provided a defence, the right in question is not wholly procedural. It can have a substantive effect upon the rights and interests of third parties. For example, an assignee of a debt takes subject to any defence, including a right of set-off, that the debtor could have asserted in an action brought against him by the assignor.[846] This includes a secured

---

[842] *Halsbury's Laws of England* (4th edn., 1983) Vol. 42, p. 240, para. 404; *In re Milan Tramways Company; ex parte Theys* (1882) 22 Ch. D 122, 126; *Stumore* v. *Campbell & Co.* [1892] 1 QB 314, 316–317; *Hanak* v. *Green* [1958] 2 QB 9, 22 per Morris L.J. ('the Judicature Acts conferred no new rights of set-off'); *Bank of Boston Connecticut* v. *European Grain and Shipping Ltd.* [1989] 1 AC 1056, 1109. See also in Western Australia *Westwind Air Charter Pty. Ltd.* v. *Hawker De Havilland Ltd.* (1990) 3 WAR 71, 84 per Murray J. ('reference to the rules does not aid one to understand a full statement of the law' of set-off). In New South Wales see *West Street Properties Pty. Limited* v. *Jamison* [1974] 2 NSWLR 435, 438 and, in relation to the Federal Court Rules, *Griffiths* v. *Commonwealth Bank of Australia* (1994) 123 ALR 111, 124. Compare *Edward Ward & Co.* v. *McDougall* [1972] VR 433, 436.

[843] It is considered in Derham, 'Recent Issues in Relation to Set-off' (1994) 68 *Australian Law Journal* 331, 338–9.   [844] See section 1.2.9 above.

[845] See section 1.7.4 above.   [846] See section 13.2 below.

creditor who has appointed a receiver to a company pursuant to a crystallized floating charge, because the creditor is regarded as an equitable assignee of any debt owing to the company which comes within the ambit of the charge.[847] Similarly, when an undisclosed principal sues on a contract entered into by his agent, the principal may be met by any right or set-off under the Statutes, or other defence, that would have been available to the defendant against the agent before the defendant had notice of the agency.[848] The same situation could arise in relation to an action by a subrogated insurer.[849]

When it was held, for example in the case of an assignment of a debt, that the assignee took subject to a right of set-off available to the debtor against the assignor pursuant to the Statutes of Set-off, it was not because there was anything inherently special in the concept of mutual debts insofar as the law of assignments was concerned. Rather, it was because the presence of mutual debts gave rise to a *defence*,[850] and if the ambit of a defence is increased or decreased, it should have a corresponding effect upon the rights of an assignee.[851] If indeed the availability of a defence of set-off can affect the interests of third parties in this manner, it is difficult to see how it can ever be described as being wholly procedural. This is irrespective of whether the defence is truly substantive in its operation, such as the form of equitable set-off arising from a sufficiently close connection between the demands, or whether it is of the type conferred by the Statutes of Set-off. Admittedly, for the purpose of private international law set-off has been said to be a matter of procedure, with the result that it is governed by the *lex fori*.[852] However, this principle should be

---

[847] *N.W. Robbie & Co. Ltd.* v. *Witney Warehouse Co. Ltd* [1963] 1 WLR 1324. See generally section 13.3 below.

[848] See section 9.7.3 below.

[849] See *Sydney Turf Club* v. *Crowley* [1971] 1 NSWLR 724, 734 per Mason J.A. ('When an insurer is subrogated to the rights of the insured against a third party . . . [the action] is brought in the name of the insured and it is subject to all the defences which would be available if the action had been brought by the insured for his own benefit'), and also Derham, *Subrogation in Insurance Law* (1985), 122–3.

[850] See, for example, *Roxburghe* v. *Cox* (1881) 17 Ch. D 520, 526 per James L.J. (an assignee 'takes subject to all rights of set-off and other defences which were available against the assignor'); *White & Tudor's Leading Cases in Equity* (9th edn., 1928) Vol. 1, 136; *Edward Nelson & Co. Ltd.* v. *Faber & Co.* [1903] 2 KB. 367, 375 per Joyce J. ('It is a general rule with respect to a chose in action that an assignee takes it subject to all equities—in other words, whatever defence by way of set-off or otherwise the debtor would be entitled to set up against the assignor's claim up to the time of his receiving notice of the assignment . . .').

[851] It has been suggested that in some circumstances an assignee may take subject to a cross-demand that could only have been employed by the debtor as a counterclaim in an action by the assignor, though it is difficult to support this view. See section 13.2.3 above, and also Derham, 'Recent Issues in Relation to Set-off' (1994) 68 *Australian Law Journal* 331, 334–337.

[852] *Meyer* v. *Dresser* (1864) 16 CB(NS) 646, 665, 666; *Maspons y Hermano* v. *Mildred Goyeneche & Co.* (1882) 9 QBD 530.

approached with caution in other contexts, because historically English private international lawyers have tended to give a wide meaning to the term 'procedure' as means of evading unsatisfactory choice of law rules.[853] Merely because something is regarded as a matter of procedure for the purpose of private international law does not mean that it is matter of procedure for all other purposes. For example, *William Cook Pty. Ltd.* v. *Read*[854] concerned the question whether the power conferred on the Governor in Council by section 5 of the Justices Act 1958 (Vic) to make rules as to practice and procedure included a power to make rules as to evidence. O'Bryan J. held that it did not, even though in private international law the rules of evidence are regarded as a matter of procedure.

The better view is that the right of set-off derived from the Statutes of Set-off is not purely procedural. On this basis, the reasoning in *Stehar Knitting Mills* is difficult to support. The ascertainment of the ambit of the right of set-off ordinarily is not a matter solely of interpreting the Supreme Court Rules, and it should not make any difference whether in a particular jurisdiction the operation of the Statutes has been preserved or not. This is relevant to the position in Queensland. Order 22 rule 3 of the Supreme Court Rules of that State provides that a defendant may plead by way of set-off, or set up by way of counterclaim, against the claim of the plaintiff, any right or claim, whether such set-off or counterclaim sounds in damages or not. In a number of cases it has been assumed, no doubt correctly, that the same principle accepted in England also applies in Queensland, that Order 22 rule 3 itself does not determine when there may be a set-off, and that regard must be had instead to the established principles of set-off.[855] However, in 1984 the Statutes of Set-off were repealed in Queensland, by the Imperial Acts Application Act 1984. This legislation was similar to the corresponding repealing Act in New South Wales (the Imperial Acts Application Act 1969), in that it did not expressly preserve the principle of set-off originally conferred by the Statutes. Accordingly, it would appear that in Queensland there is no longer a right of set-off in the case of mutual debts.[856] Nor, following the repeal of the Statutes, should *Stehar Knitting Mills* be regarded as particularly strong authority for the

---

[853] Dicey and Morris, *The Conflict of Laws* (12th edn., 1993) Vol. 1, 169, and see also McCracken, *The Banker's Remedy of Set-off* (1993), 115–16 where this point is made in relation to set-off.   [854] [1940] VLR 214.

[855] *Knockholt Pty. Ltd.* v. *Graff* [1975] Qd. R 88 (esp. at 90); *General Credits (Finance) Pty. Ltd.* v. *Stoyakovich* [1975] Qd. R 352; *Eversure Textiles Co. Ltd.* v. *Webb* [1978] Qd. R 347 (esp. at 348). See also *Phillips* v. *Mineral Resources Developments Pty. Ltd.* [1983] 2 Qd. R 138.

[856] In *Walker* v. *Department of Social Security* (1995) 129 ALR 198, 217 Cooper J. said that there is 'a serious question' whether the 1984 legislation brought about this result.

proposition that Order 22 rule 3 may nevertheless be interpreted as allowing any monetary cross-demand to be employed in a set-off. But even if, contrary to the view expressed above, the analysis in *Stehar* is accepted as correct, the situation considered in *Stehar Knitting Mills* in relation to New South Wales differed in an important respect from that in Queensland. In New South Wales the legislation which repealed the Statutes was enacted before the Supreme Court Rules in question were made.[857] This is not the case in Queensland, however, given that Order 22 rule 3 appeared in the original Rules of the Supreme Court made in 1900. It is difficult to see how the subsequent repeal of the Statutes could effect the interpretation of pre-existing Rules.

The view that the Supreme Court Rules do not alter substantive rights is subject to legislation which provides to the contrary. Consider in this regard the position in Victoria. In 1987 new Supreme Court Rules came into force. Set-off is dealt with in Order 13 rule 14, which allows a defendant to include in the defence and set off against the plaintiff's claim any claim that the defendant in turn has against the plaintiff for the recovery of a debt or damages. On two occasions Tadgell J. in the Victorian Supreme Court[858] appears to have accepted that Order 13 rule 14 would allow a cross-claim that would not have given rise to a set-off according to traditional principles to be included in the defence and be the subject of a set-off. In other words, the scope of the defence of set-off has been expanded so as to abolish to a large extent the distinction between set-off and counterclaim. This view is not without merit. The new Supreme Court Rules were 'ratified, validated and approved' by section 41(1) of the Supreme Court (Rules of Procedure) Act 1986. When the Bill for the Act was introduced into Parliament, the Minister in the second reading speech[859] noted that some of the Rules arguably changed the substantive law, and said that 'It is of particular importance to remove any doubt that this . . . category of rule is within the rule-making power of the judges'. If indeed Order 13 rule 14 is one of the Rules that was intended to change the substantive law, Tadgell J. would appear to have been correct to ascribe a wide meaning to it, given that regard may be had to the second reading speech in interpreting the Supreme Court (Rules of Procedure) Act 1986, and, consequently, the scope of the new Rules.[860] Curiously, though, his Honour also said that Order 13 rule 14 is not intended to be taken wholly

---

[857] The Supreme Court Rules were made in 1970, whereas the Imperial Acts Application Act (NSW) was enacted in 1969.

[858] *Moffat* v. *Pinewood Resources Ltd.* unreported, 7 April 1989; *MEK Nominees Pty. Ltd.* v. *Billboard Entertainments Pty. Ltd.* (1993) V Conv. R 54–468.

[859] This was delivered by Mr. Mathews, the Minister for the Arts, in the Victorian Legislative Assembly on 7 May 1986.

[860] Acts Interpretation Act 1984 (Vic.), s. 35(b).

literally. For example, he said that the Rule should not be interpreted as overturning the principles that a claim for unliquidated damages cannot be pleaded as a defence to a claim upon a bill of exchange[861] or a claim for freight.[862] This conclusion is difficult to follow. The relevant question should be whether Order 13 rule 14 is one of the new Rules which, according to the second reading speech for the Supreme Court (Rules of Procedure) Act 1986, was intended to change the substantive law. If it was not, it could hardly be correct to say that the Rule has affected the distinction between set-off and counterclaim, because set-off in truth is not a matter of pure procedure. If the Rules were only intended to be procedural in their operation, they could not have the effect of expanding the scope of the defence. If, on the other hand, Order 13 rule 14 was intended to alter substantive law (and the second reading speech would seem to favour this view), it is not altogether easy from a plain reading of the Rule to justify an interpretation that the principles by which an unliquidated cross-demand cannot be pleaded as a set-off against a claim on a bill of exchange or a claim for freight remain untouched.[863] On the assumption that the Rule operates substantively, there is nothing in the language to suggest that these principles still apply. In this regard, it is instructive to compare the approach of the courts in New South Wales in interpreting section 79 of the Common Law Procedure Act 1899, which provided that matters which were the subject of a cross-action between the parties could by leave of a judge be pleaded by way of set-off. This provision was repealed in 1970 by the Supreme Court Act, but it was accepted by the courts that it permitted a damages claim to be pleaded by way of set-off against a claim on a promissory note if the demands arose out of the same transaction.[864]

The broad interpretation of Order 13 rule 14 does not mean that the principles of equitable set-off are no longer relevant in Victoria. The defence available pursuant to Order 13 rule 14 is similar to that provided by the Statutes of Set-off, in that it is a procedural defence. By this it is meant that the set-off does not actually occur until there is judgment for a set-off. On the other hand, the form of equitable set-off which arises when the cross-demands are sufficiently closely connected does not require an order for its enforcement. It may be set up by a person indebted to

---

[861] See section 1.7.17 above.   [862] See section 1.7.14 above.

[863] In *L.U. Simon (Builders) Ltd.* v. *Fowles* [1992] 2 VR 189, 195 Smith J. noted the qualifications discussed by Tadgell J., though he declined to express a view on the subject.

[864] *Karbowsky* v. *Redaelli* (1914) 31 WN (NSW) 80; *Richardson* v. *Hill* (1922) 22 SR(NSW) 326. The requirement that the demands should have originated in the same transaction followed from a requirement that the courts held was inherent in s. 79 and applied generally. See *Assets & General Finance Co.* v. *Crick* (1911) 28 WN(NSW) 91; *Austral Bronze Co. Ltd.* v. *Sleigh* (1916) 34 WN(NSW) 143.

another, not merely as a means of preventing that other person from obtaining judgment, but also as an *immediate* answer to an obligation to pay the debt otherwise due. In this sense it is properly described as a substantive defence.[865] When the success of a defence based upon a cross-demand depends upon the defence being substantive in nature, it will still be crucial to establish an equitable set-off. This is illustrated by Tadgell J.'s decision in *MEK Nominees Pty. Ltd.* v. *Billboard Entertainments Pty. Ltd.*[866] The facts of the case are simple. A landlord sought summary judgment on a claim for possession of leased premises because of non-payment of rent. The tenant on the other hand asserted that it had a damages claim against the landlord arising from a breach of the covenant for quiet enjoyment. Tadgell J. had to determine whether, assuming that the landlord was liable to the tenant in damages upon the cross-claim, the tenant could use the cross-claim as a defence to the claim for possession. Counsel for the tenant argued that the cross-claim could be set off pursuant to Order 13 rule 14. However, while Tadgell J. accepted that in Victoria this Rule has abolished the principle that a cross-claim not amounting to a set-off cannot be raised as a defence, he pointed out that the Rule on its face only permits a cross-claim for damages to be raised as a defence to a *pecuniary* claim, whereas the claim of the landlord was for possession. He said that Order 13 rule 14 does not seek to affect the principle that a pecuniary cross-claim cannot be raised as a defence to a non-pecuniary claim unless the defence amounts to an equitable set-off. In the instant case he held that the tenant's unliquidated damages claim was such that it could provide an equity sufficient to defeat the landlord's claim for possession,[867] and so summary judgment was refused. It is suggested, with respect, that the case was correctly decided, though it is better explained on a different ground. His Honour approached the case on the basis that the question was whether the pecuniary cross-claim for damages could be set off against the non-pecuniary claim for possession. In truth, though, the law of set-off, including equitable set-off, is concerned with money demands in respect of which an account can be taken.[868] A preferable analysis is to say that the set-off was not against the claim for possession as such, but rather against the liability for rent. The set-off in issue was a substantive defence which did not require an order of the court for its enforcement, in that, even

---

[865] See section 1.7.4 above.   [866] (1993) V Conv. R 54–468.

[867] See also *Televantos* v. *McCulloch* [1991] 1 EGLR 123; *Tomlinson* v. *Cut Price Deli Pty. Ltd.* (1992) 38 FCR 484; *Knockholt Pty. Ltd.* v. *Graff* [1975] Qd. R 88 (though the headnote in *Knockholt* is incorrect insofar as it suggests that the claim was for possession of the premises consequent upon non-payment of rent, as opposed to whether the tenant was entitled to exercise an option to extend the term of the lease notwithstanding non-payment of rent); *Connaught Restaurants Ltd.* v. *Indoor Leisure Ltd.* [1994] 1 WLR 501.

[868] *Tony Lee Motors Ltd.* v. *M.S. McDonald & Son (1974) Ltd.* [1981] 2 NZLR 281, 288.

before judgment for a set-off, it was unconscionable for the landlord to treat the tenant as being in default of the obligation to pay rent to the extent of the cross-demand. Accordingly, there was no basis for the landlord to claim possession.[869] Moreover, Order 13 rule 14 did not help because, as Tadgell J. pointed out, the plaintiff landlord was not suing for the recovery of a debt or damages.

1.13 CONTRACTING OUT OF SET-OFF

1.13.1 Equitable set-off, common law abatement, and recoupment

It may be important for cash flow reasons that a party should receive payment in full under a contract so that, if the other party to the contract has a cross-claim which otherwise would give rise to a right of equitable set-off or common law abatement, that other party should not be entitled to rely upon it as a justification for tendering a reduced amount, but instead he should be required to seek his remedy in separate proceedings. There is, nevertheless, a presumption that neither party to a contract intends to give up any remedies that may arise by operation of law in the event of a breach by the other.[870] Accordingly, in order to exclude rights of set-off and abatement the courts have emphasized that there must be clear words to this effect,[871] or at least a clear implication.[872] For example, in *Connaught Restaurants Ltd.* v. *Indoor Leisure Ltd.*[873] a lease provided that rent was to

---

[869] See in this regard Tadgell J.'s earlier analysis in *Eagle Star Nominees Ltd.* v. *Merril* [1982] VR 557, 559.

[870] *Gilbert Ash (Northern) Ltd.* v. *Modern Engineering (Bristol) Ltd.* [1974] AC 689, 717; *Connaught Restaurants Ltd.* v. *Indoor Leisure Ltd.* [1994] 1 WLR 501, 505. Compare the view of Lord Cross in *Mottram Consultants Ltd.* v. *Bernard Sunley & Sons Ltd.* [1975] 2 Lloyd's Rep. 197, 205, that 'one should approach each case without any "parti pris" in favour or against the existence of a right of set-off'.

[871] *Gilbert Ash (Northern) Ltd.* v. *Modern Engineering (Bristol) Ltd.* [1974] AC 689, 717. See also *The Teno* [1977] 2 Lloyd's Rep. 289, 293; *Redpath Dorman Long Ltd.* v. *Cummins Engine Co. Ltd.* [1981] SC 370 (Scotland); *BICC Plc* v. *Burndy Corporation* [1985] 1 Ch. 232, 248; *Wilson's (NZ) Portland Cement Ltd.* v. *Gatx-Fuller Australasia Pty. Ltd. (No. 2)* [1985] 2 NZLR 33, 39; *C. M. Pillings & Co. Ltd.* v. *Kent Investments Ltd.* (1985) 30 Build. LR 80, 92–93; *NEI Thompson Ltd.* v. *Wimpey Construction UK Ltd.* (1987) 39 Build. LR 65; *Acsim (Southern) Ltd.* v. *Danish Contracting & Development Co. Ltd.* (1989) 47 Build. LR 59, 69–70; *Rosehaugh Stanhope (Broadgate Phase 6) Plc.* v. *Redpath Dorman Long Ltd.* (1990) 50 Build. LR 75, 84; *Connaught Restaurants Ltd.* v. *Indoor Leisure Ltd.* [1994] 1 WLR 501, 505.

[872] See Lord Salmon in *Gilbert-Ash* [1974] AC 689, 723. See also *Grant* v. *NZMC Ltd.* [1989] 1 NZLR 8, 13; *Connaught Restaurants Ltd.* v. *Indoor Leisure Ltd.* [1994] 1 WLR 501, 505.

[873] [1994] 1 WLR 501, disapproving of *Famous Army Stores* v. *Meehan* [1993] EGLR 73. See also *Grant* v. *NZMC Ltd.* [1989] 1 NZLR 8; *Re Partnership Pacific Securities Ltd.* [1994] 1 Qd. R 410; Waite, 'Disrepair and Set-off of Damages Against Rent' [1983] *The Conveyancer* 373, 389. Compare *Citibank Pty. Ltd.* v. *Simon Fredericks Pty. Ltd.* [1993] 2 VR 168, 175; *Langford Concrete Pty. Ltd.* v. *Finlay* [1978] 1 NSWLR 14, 17.

be paid 'without any deduction'. The Court of Appeal said that in its strict sense 'deduction' does not describe the process of set-off and, unless in the particular context in which the word is used it is clear that it is intended to have a broader meaning, it will not ordinarily be held to exclude a right of equitable set-off arising from the plaintiff's own breach of the contract.[874] This is so notwithstanding that there have been instances in which 'deduction' has been used by the courts as a shorthand and convenient expression to describe the result which follows when a right of set-off is exercised.[875] A similar conclusion has been reached in relation to a stipulation in a time charter that hire is to be paid 'without discount'.[876] When a debtor asserts that he has a damages cross-claim against the creditor which gives rise to an equitable set-off, it is not a question of him deducting the amount of his cross-claim, or discounting that amount, from the amount of the creditor's valid demand, but rather the essence of the right is that, because of the equitable set-off, the creditor is not permitted to treat the debtor as being indebted to the extent of the cross-claim.[877]

If an equitable set-off is not properly described as a 'deduction' in its strict sense, then *a fortiori* a stipulation in a lease that rent is to be paid without deduction would not extend to the right of recoupment considered by Goff J. in *Lee-Parker* v. *Izzet*.[878] This applies where leased premises have fallen into disrepair, and the tenant himself expends money in executing the repairs in circumstances where responsibility for the repairs is on the landlord. While Goff J. admittedly referred in his order to the right of the tenant to 'deduct' the cost of repairs from future payments of rent,[879] this may well have been for the sake of brevity.[880] The right in question is not a case of a deduction from rent otherwise due, but rather the tenant is considered to have already paid the rent to the extent of the amount expended on repairs. Accordingly, the stipulation for payment 'without deduction' would not be relevant.[881]

The necessity for clear words to rebut the presumption that neither party

---

[874] See in particular the judgments of Waite and Neill L.JJ. at [1994] 1 WLR 501, 510, 511.

[875] See e.g. *Hanak* v. *Green* [1958] 2 QB 9, 26; *Gilbert-Ash (Northern) Ltd.* v. *Modern Engineering (Bristol) Ltd.* [1974] AC 689, 726; *Federal Commerce & Navigation Co. Ltd.* v. *Molena Alpha Inc.* [1978] 1 QB 927, 974; *The Kostas Melas* [1981] 1 Lloyd's Rep. 18, 26.

[876] *The Teno* [1977] 2 Lloyd's Rep. 289.

[877] See section 1.7.4 above, and also Waite 'Disrepair and Set-off of Damages Against Rent' [1983] *The Conveyancer* 373, 389.

[878] [1971] 1 WLR 1688, and see generally section 1.7.22 above.

[879] [1971] 1 WLR 1688, 1695.

[880] See Waite L.J. in *Connaught Restaurants Ltd.* v. *Indoor Leisure Ltd.* [1994] 1 WLR 501, 507.

[881] *Connaught Restaurants Ltd.* v. *Indoor Leisure Ltd.* [1994] 1 WLR 501, 507 (disapproving of the contrary opinion expressed by the New Zealand Court of Appeal in *Grant* v. *NZMC Ltd.* [1989] 1 NZLR 8, 13), and see also Waite, 'Repairs and Deduction From Rent' [1981] *The Conveyancer* 199, 210–11.

to a contract intends to give up remedies that may arise by operation of law in the event of a breach by the other is well illustrated by the decision of the Court of Appeal in *Acsim (Southern) Ltd.* v. *Danish Contracting & Development Co. Ltd.*[882] A building contract provided that Danish Contracting ('Dancon') could set off against any money otherwise due to Acsim as contractor the amount of any claim for loss, only if the claim had been quantified and notified to Acsim within a time limit. The contract went on to provide that this fully set out the rights of the parties in respect of set-off. While the Court of Appeal held that the contract was effective to prevent a cross-claim for damages for bad workmanship that was quantified outside the required period from being employed as an equitable set-off, there were not sufficiently clear and express words to exclude the common law defence of abatement.[883] The subject of the cross-claim was not being raised as a set-off as such. Rather, Dancon was defending itself by showing that, by reason of Acsim's breaches of contract, the value of the work was less than the sum claimed. This defence was not prohibited by the contract.

A provision in a contract that certain payments are to be made 'less only' a list of specified items ordinarily should not be interpreted as excluding equitable set-off or abatement, unless circumstances are such as to show clearly that this was the parties' intention. Thus, in *Mottram Consultants Ltd.* v. *Bernard Sunley & Sons Ltd.*[884] a building contract provided that the employer was to pay the amount specified in an architect's certificate less only retention money and any sum previously paid. The printed form which the parties used originally provided for a third item, being any amount which the employer was entitled to deduct from or set off against any money due to the contractor by virtue of any breach of the contract by the contractor. However, this third item had been deleted. Lord Cross said that, 'When the parties use a printed form and delete parts of it one can . . . pay regard to what has been deleted as part of the surrounding circumstances in the light of which one must construe what they have chosen to leave in'.[885] The fact that they had deleted the third item showed that they had turned their minds to defences arising out of the employer's own breach of contract, and decided that they should not apply.

If there is an effective agreement excluding rights of equitable set-off, ordinarily this will not only prevent the defendant from being able to defend a claim for payment on the basis of a cross-claim, but will also have the effect of disentitling him to a stay of execution pending adjudication on the cross-claim. As the Court of Appeal noted in *Continental Illinois*

---

[882] (1989) 47 Build. LR 59.
[884] [1975] 2 Lloyd's Rep. 197.
[883] See section 1.10 above.
[885] [1975] 2 Lloyd's Rep. 197, 209.

National Bank & Trust Company of Chicago v. *Papanicolaou*[886] when it refused a stay in this situation, the contrary conclusion would negate the very purpose of inserting a provision excluding rights of set-off, i.e. to preserve cash flow. Admittedly the contract in that case specifically stated that the debt should be paid without counterclaim as well as set-off, though Parker J.'s analysis suggests that the same result would have followed if the contract had only excluded set-off. The court does of course have a discretion to grant a stay, and his Lordship postulated that a stay may be granted in exceptional circumstances notwithstanding the exclusion. For example, there may be cogent evidence that the plaintiff, if paid, would be unable to meet a judgment on the cross-claim. But in the absence of any such special circumstances, execution on a judgment should not be stayed pending determination of a cross-claim if the contract has excluded defences of set-off and, in appropriate cases, abatement.

The Court of Appeal in *Continental Illinois* also noted that a clause which excludes rights of set-off is not subject to the same rule of construction applicable to exclusion of liability clauses in relation to claims for negligence. In order to be effective to exclude liability the clause should specifically refer to negligence, or use an all-embracing term such as 'whatsoever'. It is not necessary, however, that similar terminology be employed in order to exclude an equitable set-off based upon a cross-claim for negligence. The clauses serve different functions. An exclusion clause purports to exclude liability altogether, whereas a clause precluding set-off does not touch liability. The debtor can still prosecute the cross-claim to judgment, but in a separate action.

It has been suggested[887] that a party to a contract 'might perhaps' have agreed to exclude equitable set-off in relation to a cross-claim if he has agreed to submit disputes (including the cross-claim) to arbitration, and no arbitration has been held.[888] Obviously this will depend upon the terms of the particular provision, though the usual clause providing for disputes to be referred to arbitration should not have the effect of requiring the debtor to pay in full if the cross-demand available to him has not been arbitrated, because the availability of an equitable set-off would mean that the debt is

---

[886] [1986] 2 Lloyd's Rep. 441. See also *Mottram Consultants Ltd.* v. *Bernard Sunley & Sons Ltd.* [1975] 2 Lloyd's Rep. 197, 210 (in which the contract was interpreted as having excluded the defence of abatement). Compare *Hegarty & Sons Ltd.* v. *Royal Liver Friendly Society* [1985] IR 524, 531, in which Murphy J. indicated that, if he had reached the conclusion in that case that the right of set-off had been excluded, he would have stayed execution.

[887] Wood, *English and International Set-off* (1989), 691.

[888] The authority principally relied on by Wood, *Cuddy* v. *Cameron* (1911) 1 WWR 35, in fact was concerned with a contractual right of deduction rather than equitable set-off, and in any event was ultimately reversed on appeal by the Privy Council in *Cameron* v. *Cuddy* [1914] AC 651. As Wood has conceded, the remarks of Lord Salmon in *Gilbert-Ash (Northern) Ltd.* v. *Modern Engineering (Bristol) Ltd.* [1974] AC 689, 726 (and see also *Aectra Refining and Marketing Inc.* v. *Exmar NV* [1994] 1 WLR 1634, 1649) are inconsistent with his suggestion.

also in dispute, so that both the debt and the cross-claim must be referred.[889] This is a consequence of the substantive nature of the defence.[890]

The Unfair Contract Terms Act 1977 prohibits in certain cases contract terms which exclude or restrict liability in relation to a claim for negligence or breach of contract, except, in some instances, in so far as the term satisfies a requirement of reasonableness. The reference to excluding or restricting liability is expressed in section 13 to encompass also excluding or restricting any right in respect of the liability. In *Stewart Gill Ltd.* v. *Horatio Myer & Co. Ltd.*[891] the Court of Appeal held that this would include a term in a contract which excludes any right of set-off in relation to a cross-claim, and moreover that the term to this effect in the contract under consideration was unreasonable. The test for determining reasonableness is laid down in section 11(1) of the Act. The term in question must have been a fair and reasonable one to be included in the contract having regard to the circumstances which were, or ought reasonably to have been, known to or in the contemplation of the parties when the contract was made. Notwithstanding *Stewart Gill* v. *Horatio*, in a particular case a term excluding set-off may well be regarded as reasonable if, to the knowledge of the defendant at the time of the contract, the plaintiff's cash flow position is such that prompt payment without any set-off is of paramount importance.[892]

1.13.2 Statutes of Set-off

The set-off section in the insolvency legislation[893] is considered to be mandatory in its operation, so that it is not possible to contract out of its terms.[894] This has been justified on two grounds. The first is the mandatory language used in the section, which provides that an account 'shall be taken' in the stated circumstances. The second is based upon a perceived policy ground,[895] that the insolvency set-off section relates to a matter in

---

[889] See e.g. *Federal Commerce & Navigation Co. Ltd.* v. *Molena Alpha Inc.* [1978] 1 QB 927, 974, and generally the discussion in the Introduction.

[890] See section 1.7.4 above.

[891] [1992] 1 QB 600. Compare *Electricity Supply Nominees Ltd.* v. *IAF Group Ltd.* [1993] 1 WLR 1059.

[892] See e.g. the comments of Lord Diplock in *Gilbert-Ash (Northern) Ltd.* v. *Modern Engineering (Bristol) Ltd.* [1974] AC 689, 724.

[893] Insolvency Act 1986, s. 323 and, for company liquidations, r. 4.90 of the Insolvency Rules 1986. See Ch. 2.   [894] See section 2.11 below.

[895] See Lord Simon of Glaisdale in *National Westminster Bank Ltd.* v. *Halesowen Presswork & Assemblies Ltd.* [1972] AC 785, 808–9, and Vinelott J. in *Re Maxwell Communications Corp. plc (No. 2)* [1993] 1 WLR 1402, 1411. For a criticism of this view, see section 2.11.1 below.

which the public have an interest. According to this view, the section was not enacted for the benefit of a particular person or persons, but rather is a part of a code of procedure dealing with the administration of the estate of a bankrupt or a company in liquidation. However, neither of these grounds applies to the right of set-off conferred by the Statutes of Set-off. The Statutes provided that mutual debts 'may', as opposed to 'shall', be set off.[896] Moreover, the occurrence of a set-off under the Statutes would not appear to be a matter in which the public have an interest. Rather, the right was introduced by the Statutes for the benefit of defendants,[897] so that, for example, the courts have held that a defendant is not *obliged* to raise the cross-debt as a defence under the Statutes.[898] The defendant is entitled to bring separate proceedings in respect of it, though if he has acted in bad faith he may be penalized in an application for costs.[899] Prima facie, then, the maxim *quilibet potest renunciare juri pro se introducto*[900] should apply, so that it should be possible to renounce the right to invoke this common law defence. Nevertheless, there is early authority to the contrary.[901] In *Lechmere* v. *Hawkins*[902] the defendant had promised to repay the money borrowed from the plaintiff without taking any notice of a debt due to him from the plaintiff, and without setting one demand against the other. Lord Kenyon said that this was an honorary obligation only, and that the defendant could not be compelled to abide by it when the Statutes themselves conferred upon him the right to set one demand against the other. That decision subsequently was followed by Lord Erskine in *Taylor* v. *Okey*.[903] There are also cases in which a purchaser of goods was allowed a set-off in an action for the price even though he had agreed to pay in ready money,[904] an agreement which would appear to be inconsistent with payment by way of set-off.[905] However, this is no longer the prevailing view. In *Hongkong & Shanghai Banking Corporation* v. *Kloeckner & Co.*

---

[896] See (1729) 2 Geo. II, c. 22, s. 13, and (1735) 8 Geo. II, c. 24, s. 5.

[897] *Davis* v. *Hedges* (1871) LR 6 QB 687, 690.

[898] See e.g. *Green* v. *Law* (1805) 2 Smith KB 668; *Laing* v. *Chatham* (1808) 1 Camp. 251; *Jenner* v. *Morris* (1861) 3 De GF & J 45, 54; *Davis* v. *Hedges* (1871) LR 6 QB 687, 690.

[899] This seems to have been contemplated in *Green* v. *Law* (1805) 2 Smith KB 668.

[900] Anyone may, at his pleasure, renounce the benefit of a stipulation or other right introduced entirely in his own favour. See *Broom's Legal Maxims* (10th edn., 1939), 477.

[901] The cases are discussed by Farrar, 'Contracting Out of Set-off' (1970) 120 *New Law Journal* 771. Professor Farrar rightly pointed out that *Skyring* v. *Greenwood* (1825) 4 B & C 281 was a case in which the debt itself, as opposed to a right of set-off, had been waived. *Quaere* whether this would explain *Baker* v. *Langhorn* (1816) 6 Taunt. 519, in which the broker was claiming payment of a loss as agent for the insured rather than for himself, though in any event the case was concerned with bankruptcy set-off as opposed to the Statutes of Set-off. [902] (1798) 2 Esp. 626. [903] (1806) 13 Ves. Jun. 180.

[904] *Eland* v. *Karr* (1801) 1 East 375; *Cornforth* v. *Rivett* (1814) 2 M & S 510. See also *M'Gillivray* v. *Simson* (1826) 5 LJOSKB 53.

[905] See Lord Campbell in *Brandao* v. *Barnett* (1846) 12 Cl. & Fin. 787, 808.

AG[906] Hirst J. held that a person can contract out of the right of set-off, a view which was shared by Dillon L.J. in *BICC Plc* v. *Burndy Corporation*.[907] The New South Wales Supreme Court came to the same conclusion in. *Stephen* v. *Doyle*,[908] and it is also supported by a number of cases that have established that a debtor may contract with his creditor on terms that he will not enforce against an assignee of his indebtedness any right of set-off otherwise available to him against the assignor.[909]

In the context of equitable set-off the courts have said that there is a presumption that neither party to a contract intends to abandon any remedies for its breach arising by operation of law, and that accordingly there must be clear words to exclude rights of equitable set-off, or at least a clear implication.[910] In *BICC Plc* v. *Burndy Corporation*[911] Dillon L.J. said that this applies 'equally, if not *a fortiori*', to set-off under the Statutes. Given that it is possible to contract out of this right of set-off, in an appropriate case the right may also be held to have been waived.[912]

A creditor may have agreed that security given for the debt is to be second ranking after the security given by the debtor to another creditor. Ordinarily this would not be regarded as an agreement by the first creditor not to set off the debt owing to him until the prior ranking secured creditor has been paid. The agreement goes to the ranking of the security, not the payment of the debts.[913] This should be compared to an agreement by a creditor to subordinate his debt in point of payment to another creditor's debt. In such a case the first creditor may not employ the subordinated debt in a set-off.[914] One possible reason for this is that there is an implied agreement to this effect arising from the subordination,[915] though it is also a consequence of the rule that set-off under the Statutes requires that both debts be due and payable,[916] and until the other creditor's debt has been paid the subordinated debt is not payable.

An agreement by a creditor not to assign the debt to a third party ordinarily would not be interpreted as precluding the creditor from

---

[906] [1990] 2 QB 514. [907] [1985] 1 Ch. 232, 248.
[908] (1882) 3 NSWR (Eq.) 1.
[909] See e.g. *In re Blakely Ordnance Company; ex parte New Zealand Banking Corporation* (1867) LR 3 Ch. App. 154 and *In re Goy & Co., Ltd; Farmer* v. *Goy & Co., Ltd.* [1900] 2 Ch. 149, 154, and generally section 13.2.12 below. [910] See section 1.13.1 above.
[911] [1985] 1 Ch. 232, 248.
[912] See *Baker* v. *Langhorn* (1816) 6 Taunt. 519. Compare *Moore* v. *Jervis* (1845) 2 Coll. 60. *Skyring* v. *Greenwood* (1825) 4 B & C 281 was a case in which the debt itself, as opposed to a right of set-off, was waived. See Farrar, 'Contracting Out of Set-off' (1970) 120 *New Law Journal* 771, 772.
[913] *Edward Nelson & Co. Ltd.* v. *Faber & Co.* [1903] 2 KB 367, 377.
[914] *H. Wilkins & Elkington Ltd.* v. *Milton* (1916) 32 TLR 618.
[915] See Wood, *English and International Set-off* (1989), 690.
[916] See section 1.2.7 above.

employing the debt in a set-off. Admittedly, in *Gathercole* v. *Smith*[917] a statute which provided that a pension payable to a retired incumbent of a benefice was not transferable was interpreted as also precluding a set-off against it. However, that case should be regarded as turning on the object of the Act in question, i.e. to provide for the maintenance of retired clergy. This object would have been defeated if the pension could be reduced or extinguished by a set-off.

1.14 CRITICISMS OF THE STATE OF THE LAW OF SET-OFF

The state of the law of set-off has been described as lacking logic and sense.[918] It has been said to be unsatisfactory that, while a set-off may be allowed at law in respect of debts which are both liquidated, even if unconnected, and a set-off may occur in equity in relation to claims which are sufficiently connected, even if they are unliquidated, there may not be a set-off of claims if one or both is unliquidated and they are unconnected.[919] Presumably it is this sentiment which led to the apparent expansion of the law of set-off in Victoria.[920] But, is the current state of the law so unsatisfactory?

A successful set-off constitutes a defence, so that costs follow accordingly. This is a just result in the case of set-off at law under the Statutes of Set-off. Since for this form of set-off both demands must be for liquidated amounts, the net position should have been apparent to the plaintiff, and it should have been taken into account when considering whether to sue.[921] The same cannot always be said when one or both of the demands is unliquidated. While an equitable set-off nevertheless may be available in the case of an unliquidated demand if the cross-claims are sufficiently closely connected, the justification for the set-off in this instance is apparent from Lord Cottenham's formulation of the relevant principle in *Rawson* v. *Samuel*,[922] that the relationship between the cross-claims is such that the plaintiff's title to his demand is impeached. In other words, the cross-demand goes to the very root of the plaintiff's claim, or calls it into question, or the link between the demands is such that they are

---

[917] (1881) 17 Ch. D 1 (and see further proceedings at (1881) 7 QBD 626).

[918] See Staughton L.J. in *Axel Johnson Petroleum AB* v. *MG Mineral Group AG* [1992] 1 WLR 270, 275–6.

[919] See Leggatt and Staughton L.JJ. in their respective judgments in *Axel Johnson Petroleum AB* v. *MG Mineral Group AG* [1992] 1 WLR 270, 274, 276. See also Nolan L.J. in *B. Hargreaves Ltd.* v. *Action 2000 Ltd.* [1993] BCLC 1111, 1116.

[920] See section 1.12 above.

[921] *Stooke* v. *Taylor* (1880) 5 QBD 569, 576; *Hanak* v. *Green* [1958] 2 QB 9, 23; *BICC Plc* v. *Burndy Corporation* [1985] 1 Ch. 232, 249.   [922] (1841) Cr. & Ph. 161.

interdependent.[923] If however one of the demands is unliquidated, and it is not connected with the cross-claim in this manner, it is debatable whether a defence is indeed justified. In this regard it is important to bear in mind that the decision whether or not to admit a cross-demand as a set-off may affect not only the question of costs, but also the rights of third parties. For example, an assignee of a debt takes subject to any defences, including rights of set-off, available to the debtor against the assignor before the debtor had notice of the assignment.[924] An expansion in the scope of the defence of set-off may reduce the value of the assigned debt in the hands of the assignee, even though the assignee may have provided full consideration for the assignment, and may not have been aware at the time of the assignment of the existence of an unrelated damages claim available to the debtor against the assignor.[925] Given this competing consideration, an expansion in the ambit of the defence of set-off may not be appropriate. If the perceived injustice in not allowing a defendant to employ a cross-demand in a set-off is that the defendant should not suffer in relation to costs,[926] an alternative approach is to re-examine the circumstances in which the courts will award costs, which, after all, is a matter within the discretion of the court.[927]

---

[923] See section 1.7.1 above.   [924] See section 13.2 below.

[925] In Australia it has been suggested that an assignee in some circumstances may take subject to a cross-demand that could only have been asserted by the debtor as a counterclaim in an action by the assignor. However, this is contrary to views expressed by the House of Lords in *Bank of Boston* [1989] 1 AC 1056, 1105–6, 1109–11, and it is difficult to support. See section 13.2.3 below, and Derham, 'Recent Issues in Relation to Set-off' (1994) 68 *Australian Law Journal* 331, 334–337.

[926] A defendant in an action who shows that there is a triable issue as to the availability of a set-off will not have judgment given against him on the plaintiff's claim, but rather will be given leave to defend. However, a defendant possessed of a cross-demand which would not give rise to a set-off can still be put into substantially the same position in this regard, notwithstanding that judgment is given against him on the plaintiff's claim, if execution is stayed pending hearing of the counterclaim. Compare *Axel Johnson Petroleum AB & MG Mineral Group AG* [1992] 1 WLR 270, 275.

[927] See the Supreme Court Act 1981, s. 51, and *Box* v. *Midland Bank Ltd.* [1981] 1 Lloyd's Rep. 434.

2

Set-off in Bankruptcy and Company Liquidation

2.1 THE SCOPE OF THE SET-OFF

The principal source of rights of set-off in the event of a bankruptcy is section 323 of the Insolvency Act,[1] which provides that:

(1) This section applies where before the commencement of the bankruptcy there have been mutual credits, mutual debts or other mutual dealings between the bankrupt and any creditor of the bankrupt proving or claiming to prove for a bankruptcy debt.

(2) An account shall be taken of what is due from each party to the other in respect of the mutual dealings and the sums due from one party shall be set off against the sums due from the other.

(3) Sums due from the bankrupt to another party shall not be included in the account taken under subsection (2) if that other party had notice at the time they became due that a bankruptcy petition relating to the bankrupt was pending.

(4) Only the balance (if any) of the account taken under subsection (2) is provable as a bankruptcy debt or, as the case may be, to be paid to the trustee as part of the bankrupt's estate.

The corresponding provision for company liquidation is set out in Rule 4.90 of the Insolvency Rules 1986.[2]

The existence of a right of set-off is crucial whenever a bankrupt and his creditor have had prior mutual dealings giving rise to cross-demands. In the absence of a set-off, the creditor would be obliged to pay the full amount of his debt to the trustee in bankruptcy, and would be confined to proving with the other creditors for the amount for which the bankrupt is indebted to him. If on the other hand the requirements of the set-off section (or, as it is sometimes called, the mutual credit provision) are satisfied, only the balance remaining after deducting one claim from the

---

[1] In Australia the relevant section is the Bankruptcy Act 1966 (Cth), s. 86.

[2] In Australia, see the Corporations Law, s. 553C, which also applies to the winding up of a Part 5.7 body. See s. 583. For the application of the set-off section to company liquidation, see section 2.2 below.

other is payable. Therefore, if the bankrupt's claim against the creditor exceeds in value the creditor's claim against the bankrupt, the creditor in effect obtains payment in full from his claim in the form of a deduction from his liability, and he is only required to pay the balance to the trustee. Alternatively, it may be that the creditor's claim is the greater, in which case he receives payment in full to the extent of his liability to the bankrupt, and he need only prove for the balance.

Notwithstanding the reference in subsection (1) to a 'creditor of the bankrupt proving or claiming to prove for a bankruptcy debt', it is not necessary that the creditor should have lodged, or attempted to lodge, a proof in the bankruptcy as a prerequisite to invoking the section. In *Stein* v. *Blake*[3] the House of Lords held that the insolvency set-off section takes effect automatically upon the occurrence of the bankruptcy.[4] Accordingly, to the extent of the set-off there is nothing that can be proved in any event. They said that these words should be construed to mean a 'creditor of the bankrupt who (apart from section 323) would have been entitled to prove for a bankruptcy debt'.

The mutual credit provision generally only becomes relevant in the event of a bankruptcy or company liquidation, including when an insolvent partnership is wound up in accordance with the Insolvent Partnerships Order 1994.[5] It does not apply to a company voluntary arrangement under Part 1 of the Insolvency Act,[6] an individual voluntary arrangement under Part VIII, or to a company which is subject to an administration order under Part II.[7] Nor is it applicable to an arrangement under the Deeds of Arrangements Act 1914,[8] unless it has been expressly incorporated into the deed itself.[9]

---

[3] [1995] 2 All ER 961. [4] See section 2.12 below.
[5] See section 8.2.2 below. In Australia a partnership of more than 5 members may be wound up under the Corporations Law as a Part 5.7 body, in which case the set-off section (s. 553C) applies. See s. 583.
[6] Compare Australia, where the right of set-off conferred by the Corporations Law in the event of a company liquidation (s. 553C) is made applicable, by clause 8 of Sch. 8A of the Corporations Regulations, to a deed of company arrangement which is entered into pursuant to Div. 10 of Pt 5.3A of the Law.
[7] Similarly in Australia the set-off section applicable in a liquidation (s. 553C of the Corporations Law) is not relevant to a company under administration pursuant to Pt 5.3A of the Corporations Law.
[8] Compare in Australia the Bankruptcy Act 1966 (Cth.), ss. 231, 237 and 243 dealing with deeds of assignment, deeds of arrangement and compositions.
[9] See *In re E.J. Casse; ex parte G.H. Robinson* v. *The Trustee* [1937] 1 Ch. 405; *In re Rissik* [1936] 1 Ch. 68. See also *Baker* v. *Lloyd's Bank, Limited* [1920] 2 KB 322, though compare *Baker* v. *Adam* (1910) 15 Com. Cas. 227. Compare also the concession made by counsel in *In re Fenton; ex parte Fenton Textile Association, Limited* [1931] 1 Ch. 85, 97. The right of set-off in *Fenton* may be explained on the ground that it resulted from the liquidation of the company proving under the deed, rather than from the deed itself. See e.g. Lord Hanworth M.R at 105, and Romer L.J. at 120, though compare Lawrence L.J. at 111.

2.2 COMPANIES

2.2.1 The Set-off Section in Company Liquidation

Prior to the enactment of the Supreme Court of Judicature Act 1875, the insolvency set-off section was not applicable to company liquidation. Set-offs had been enforced in liquidations,[10] though these were founded upon the right of set-off conferred by the Statutes of Set-off in the case of mutual debts as a defence to an action at law,[11] rather than upon the bankruptcy section. In a number of respects, though, the courts appear to have departed from orthodoxy in allowing a set-off. The Statutes only operated as a procedural defence to an action at law to obtain payment of a debt.[12] Prima facie they should not have justified a set-off in the context of a proof lodged in the liquidation.[13] Yet a set-off was allowed in this context.[14] Moreover, the application of the Statutes when the set-off was asserted as a defence to an action brought by the liquidator in a compulsory liquidation is not free from difficulty. The debt sought to be set off should have been recoverable by action[15] at the time when the plaintiff commenced his action.[16] Yet after a winding-up order no action could have been brought against the company without the leave of the court.[17]

The Supreme Court of Judicature Act 1875, section 10, incorporated the rules of bankruptcy 'as to debts and liabilities provable' into the law of company liquidation whenever the assets of the company were insufficient for the payment of its debts and liabilities and the costs of the winding-up, and it was confirmed by the House of Lords in 1884 that the incorporation included the set-off section.[18] Formerly this right of set-off was considered to be applicable to any company in liquidation unless and until it was shown that the company's assets were sufficient to pay all the company's

---

[10] See e.g. *In re Agra and Masterman's Bank; Anderson's Case* (1866) LR 3 Eq. 337; *Smith, Fleming, & Co.'s Case* (1866) LR 1 Ch. App. 538; *In re South Blackpool Hotel Company; ex parte James* (1869) LR 8 Eq. 225; *Re Progress Assurance Company; ex parte Bates* (1870) 22 LT 430; *Sankey Brook Coal Company, Limited* v. *Marsh* (1871) LR 6 Ex. 185.

[11] *Brighton Arcade Company, Limited* v. *Dowling* (1868) LR 3 CP 175, 182, 184; *Ex parte Price; in re Lankester* (1875) LR 10 Ch. App. 648, 650.

[12] See section 1.2.9 above.

[13] *Ex parte Price* (1875) LR 10 Ch. App. 648, 650; *In re Daintrey* [1900] 1 QB 546, 547–8.

[14] *In re South Blackpool Hotel Company; ex parte James* (1869) LR 8 Eq. 225. See also *In re China Steamship Company; ex parte MacKenzie* (1869) LR 7 Eq. 240 (set-off against an assignee).

[15] See section 1.2.10 above.

[16] *Walker* v. *Clements* (1850) 15 QB 1046.

[17] Companies Act 1862, s. 87. See now the Insolvency Act 1986, s. 130(2).

[18] *Mersey Steel and Iron Co.* v. *Naylor, Benzon & Co.* (1884) 9 App. Cas. 434, 437–8.

debts in full, together with costs of the winding-up.[19] However, this is no longer the case in England. Rule 4.90 of the Insolvency Rules 1986, which now sets out the mutual credit provision in the event of a company liquidation in terms similar to the bankruptcy section, applies in the case of every company liquidation, compulsory or voluntary, irrespective of the solvency or otherwise of the company.[20] This should be compared to Australia, where the right of set-off in section 553C of the Corporations Law in relation to company liquidations is still expressed to apply only to insolvent companies.

2.2.2 Administration

The set-off section in the insolvency legislation only applies to a company which is in liquidation. It does not apply to a company which is subject to an administration order.

While an administration order is in force in relation to a company, section 11(3)(d) of the Insolvency Act provides that a creditor may not commence proceedings or issue execution or other legal process against the company or its property except with the consent of the administrator or the leave of the court.[21] However, this should not prevent the creditor from relying on a substantive defence of equitable set-off, or prevent a bank from asserting combination of accounts.[22] Nor should this provision prevent a creditor from exercising a contractual right of set-off. None of these involve commencing proceedings or other legal process.[23] On the

---

[19] *In re Milan Tramways Company; ex parte Theys* (1884) 25 Ch. D 587, 591; *Fryer* v. *Ewart* [1902] AC 187, 192; *In re Pink; Elvin* v. *Nightingale* [1927] 1 Ch. 237, 241; *In re Rolls-Royce Co. Ltd.* [1974] 1 WLR 1584, 1590. See also *In re Fine Industrial Commodities Ltd.* [1956] 1 Ch. 256. It was held in *In re Canada Cycle and Motor Agency (Queensland) Ltd.* [1931] St. R Qd. 281 (and see also *Page* v. *Commonwealth Life Assurance Society Ltd.* (1935) 36 SR(NSW) 85, 89) that this same principle applied to voluntary liquidations, though compare *Gerard* v. *Worth of Paris, Ltd.* [1936] 2 All ER 95 in relation to a members' voluntary winding-up.

[20] This is the effect of r. 4.90, combined with r. 4.1.

[21] See also the Insolvency Act, s. 252(2) in the situation in which an interim order has been made under Pt VIII in relation to an individual voluntary arrangement. A similar principle applies in Australia when a company is the subject of an administration order, and also in the case of a deed of company arrangement. See the Corporations Law, ss. 440D and 440F in relation to administration and, for deeds of company arrangement, s. 444E(3).

[22] See Ch. 11.

[23] See generally the discussion of 'proceedings' in *Re Olympia & York Canary Wharf Ltd.* [1993] BCLC 453. In Australia, the Corporations Law, s. 437D(1)(b) applies where a person enters into, on behalf of a company under administration, a transaction or dealing affecting property of the company. The transaction is void unless it was consented to by the administrator or the court. However, this should not apply to the exercise of a contractual right of set-off by a creditor of the company, since the creditor does not do so on behalf of the company. See in a different context *Osborne Computer Corporation Pty. Ltd.* v. *Airroad Distribution Pty. Ltd.* (1995) 17 ACSR 614.

other hand, section 11(3)(c) also prohibits any steps being taken to enforce a security over the company's property.[24] Whether this would extend to the exercise of a contractual right of set-off is considered in the context of a discussion of set-off agreements.[25]

The position would appear to differ in relation to the procedural defence of set-off available at law under the Statutes of Set-off. It is necessary for this form of set-off that the debt sought to be set off be enforceable by action,[26] and this is not satisfied in relation to a debt owing by a company the subject of an administration order unless the consent of the administrator or the leave of the court has been obtained. Accordingly, the debt should not be able to be employed defensively under the Statutes.[27]

2.3 PUBLIC POLICY AND THE RATIONALE FOR INSOLVENCY SET-OFF

The right of set-off in insolvency has received almost universal approbation in English law. Its operation has been steadily enlarged since 1705,[27a] while the courts have said that it should be supported and given the widest possible scope.[28] It is designed to ameliorate a perceived injustice, that a person should have to pay the full amount of his liability to a bankrupt and at the same time be confined to lodging a proof for what the bankrupt owes him.[29] It should also be borne in mind, though, that the effect of a set-off is to prefer one creditor over the general body of creditors, and that consequently it operates against the policy favouring equal treatment of creditors. This being the case, it is something of a surprise that the rationale for the existence of the right has not really been questioned, and

---

[24] See also s. 10(1)(b) with respect to the period between the presentation of the petition for an administration order and the making of the order or the dismissal of the petition. In Australia there is a similar provision in s. 440B of the Corporations Law, and see also s. 444F(2) in relation to a proposal to enter into a deed of company arrangement. There is an exception for security which is over all or substantially all of the company's assets. See s. 441A. [25] See section 12.4 below.

[26] See section 1.2.10 above.

[27] For the contrary view, see Wood, *English and International Set-off* (1989), 277. [27a] See section 2.6 below.

[28] See *Peat* v. *Jones & Co.* (1881) 8 QBD 147, 150 per Cotton L.J.; *Mersey Steel and Iron Company* v. *Naylor, Benzon, & Co.* (1882) 9 QBD 648, 660–1; *The Eberle's Hotels and Restaurant Company, Limited* v. *E. Jonas & Brothers* (1887) 18 QBD 459, 465; *Day & Dent Constructions Pty. Ltd.* v. *North Australian Properties Pty. Ltd.* (1982) 150 CLR 85, 108; *Gye* v. *McIntyre* (1991) 171 CLR 609, 619. However compare the warning by Chambré J. in *Ouchterlony* v. *Easterby* (1813) 4 Taunt. 888, 893, that 'we ought to be particularly cautious how we admit these things to be mutual credits; for it may lead, if abused, to great mischief'.

[29] *National Westminster Bank Ltd.* v. *Halesowen Presswork & Assemblies Ltd.* [1972] AC 785, 813; *Day & Dent Constructions Pty. Ltd.* v. *North Australian Properties Pty. Ltd.* (1982) 150 CLR 85, 95, 107.

that Lord Mansfield's aphorism, that 'Natural equity says, that cross demands should compensate each other, by deducting the less from the greater',[30] has been accepted almost without reservation. While admittedly it does seem to be rather harsh that a creditor of the bankrupt should only receive a dividend for what the bankrupt owes him and at the same time be required to pay the full value of what he owes to the bankrupt, it is also harsh for other creditors to be confined to a rateable proportion for the debts owing to them. It is debatable whether the justice in favour of setting off cross-demands is always so great that it should allow the assets available for distribution amongst the general body of creditors to be depleted in favour of the single creditor in possession of the right, with the consequent reduction in the dividend payable generally. Consider, for example, that A has accepted a bill of exchange drawn in favour of C. A also happens to be a creditor of B. If B becomes bankrupt, the result would be that A would only be entitled to lodge a proof for the amount owing by B, and would also at the same time be fully liable on the bill to C. By way of comparison assume that, unknown to A, C had negotiated the bill to B before the bankruptcy. There would then be mutual credit between A and B which would be sufficient to confer a right of set-off upon A. As far as A is concerned, the negotiation of the bill to B was entirely fortuitous, and yet it would still have the result of improving his overall position by effectively enabling him to obtain the full value of his claim against B rather than just a dividend. Under these circumstances, it hardly seems just that A should be favoured with a right of set-off at the expense of the other creditors. Parke B. said in *Forster* v. *Wilson*[31] that the object of the mutual credit provision is 'to do substantial justice between the parties'. This statement is unobjectionable if 'the parties' is taken to include the bankrupt's general body of creditors.[32]

There is an alternative justification for the right of set-off, and that is that it enhances the provision of credit facilities and generally acts as a stimulus to trade and commerce. If an enterprise wishes to raise cash, or does not wish to pay for goods or services immediately, but is otherwise reasonably sound, the possibility of a set-off in any bankruptcy or winding-up may encourage other parties to deal with it, or to deal in negotiable

---

[30] *Green* v. *Farmer* (1768) 4 Burr. 2214, 2220. The justice or equity of set-off has been mentioned on other occasions. See for example *Ex parte Flint* (1818) 1 Swans. 30, 34; *Forster* v. *Wilson* (1843) 12 M & W 191, 203–4.

[31] (1843) 12 M & W 191, 203–4. This view has been repeated on numerous occasions by the courts. See e.g. *Ex parte Cleland; in re Davies* (1867) LR 2 Ch. App. 808, 813; *In re City Life Assurance Company, Limited; Stephenson's Case* [1926] 1 Ch. 191, 216; *In re D.H. Curtis (Builders) Ltd.* [1978] 1 Ch. 173; *Re Cushla Ltd.* [1979] 3 All ER 415, 421; *In re Unit 2 Windows Ltd.* [1985] 1 WLR 1383, 1387; *Stein* v. *Blake* [1994] Ch. 16, 22 (C.A.).

[32] See *Lloyds Bank NZA Ltd.* v. *National Safety Council* [1993] 2 VR 506, 513.

securities upon which the enterprise is liable. In other words, the possibility of a set-off may be perceived as a form of security,[33] and while it is not a security in the strict sense of the word, its existence in many cases would give a degree of confidence to parties dealing with each other.[34] Of course it can only be said in any particular case that there may have been reliance on the security offered by a right of set-off if the party claiming the benefit of the set-off was aware, at the time of transacting the later of the two dealings upon which the set-off is sought to be based, that he was under a liability to the bankrupt, or that such a liability was a possible consequence of either of the dealings. Unless this is the case, the possibility of a set-off obviously could not have influenced his decision to deal with the bankrupt, in which case there hardly seems to be any justification for preferring him over the other creditors by means of a right of set-off. It is difficult, then, to see why a right of set-off should be allowed in situations like that posited above, where the bankrupt's right to sue the creditor only came into existence as a result of a transaction with a third party unknown to the creditor after the creditor himself had already entered into the dealing upon which his own claim against the bankrupt is based. The conferral of a set-off effectively constitutes a windfall in comparison to what he would otherwise have expected to be his overall financial position.

2.4 THE STATUTES OF SET-OFF, EQUITABLE SET-OFF, AND COUNTERCLAIM IN BANKRUPTCY

Counterclaim, when used in contra-distinction to set-off, has no application after the occurrence of a bankruptcy or the commencement of a liquidation.[35] A debtor of the bankrupt who has a claim against the bankrupt's estate is remitted to a proof in respect of his claim unless he has a right of set-off. Similarly, the Insolvency Act 1986 and the Insolvency Rules made pursuant to it would provide the sole statutory right of set-off available as a defence to an action brought by a bankrupt's trustee or the liquidator of a company for payment of a sum owing to the bankrupt or the

---

[33] Thus, Vaughan Williams J. in *In re Washington Diamond Mining Company* [1893] 3 Ch. 95, 104 referred to 'the security, by way of set-off'. See also *Stein* v. *Blake* [1995] 2 All ER 961, 964.

[34] Indeed, Lamar J. once warned in the U.S. Supreme Court that in some situations the abolition of set-off could 'interfere with the course of business as to produce evils of serious and far reaching consequence.' See *Studley* v. *Boylston National Bank of Boston* (1913) 229 US 523, 529.

[35] *Peat* v. *Jones & Co.* (1881) 8 QBD 147, 150. See also, in the context of company liquidations, *Government Security Investment Company* v. *Dempsey* (1880) 50 LJQB 199; *Langley Constructions (Brixham) Ltd.* v. *Wells* [1969] 1 WLR 503.

company.[36] The Statutes of Set-off would not have any application. Admittedly this has not always been the prevailing view. In the eighteenth century defendants in actions at law instituted by assignees in bankruptcy for the recovery of a debt would base their argument for a set-off upon the Statutes of Set-off as well as the bankruptcy section.[37] The Statutes of Set-off were said to apply on the ground that 'the assignees are the bankrupt'.[38] According to Professor Christian,[39] it was only after 1786, when Buller J. in *Grove* v. *Dubois*[40] confirmed that the bankruptcy section provided a defence to such an action, that pleaders began to rely solely on the bankruptcy provision. However, the early view as to the relevance of the Statutes would not be followed today. If, for example, a person against whom a bankruptcy petition was pending incurred a debt to someone who was already indebted to him, this second person would not have the benefit of a set-off under section 323 of the Insolvency Act if at the time that sums became due to him he had notice that the petition was pending.[41] Nor could he avoid this result by pleading a set-off instead under the Statutes of Set-off, and arguing that the trustee in bankruptcy took subject to this equity. This is not to suggest that the right to set off mutual debts under the Statutes of Set-off has no application at all to bankruptcies and company liquidations. When it is said that an assignee of a debt takes subject to rights of set-off available to the debtor against the assignor, it is meant rights of set-off which could have provided a defence to an action brought against him by a solvent assignor. If the assignor has become bankrupt the debtor cannot have recourse to the wider right of set-off provided by the bankruptcy legislation.[42] If an equitable assignment is in issue the action would be brought by the assignee in the assignor's name, notwithstanding the bankruptcy, and a defence of set-off that otherwise would have been available to the debtor against the assignor in circumstances where the cross-debt arose before the debtor had notice of the assignment may be asserted against the assignee.[43] The same result would follow where the requirements of section 136(1) of the Law of Property Act 1925 have been

---

[36] See *Day & Dent Constructions Pty. Ltd.* v. *North Australian Properties Pty. Ltd.* (1981) 34 ALR 595, 599, 601 (Federal Court of Australia); *In re Daintrey* [1900] 1 QB 546, 548, 567. See also *McIntyre* v. *Perkes* (1990) 22 FCR 260, 271 (Federal Court of Australia). Compare the comments of Lord Esher M.R. in *Sovereign Life Assurance Company* v. *Dodd* [1892] 2 QB 573, 577–8.   [37] See e.g. *Ridout* v. *Brough* (1774) 1 Cowp. 133.
[38] *Ridout* v. *Brough* (1774) 1 Cowp. 133, 135. See also *Freeman* v. *Lomas* (1851) 9 Hare 109, 115; *McIntyre* v. *Perkes* (1990) 22 FCR 260, 271 (Federal Court of Australia).
[39] Christian, *Bankrupt Law* (2nd edn., 1818) Vol. 1, 504–5.
[40] (1786) 1 TR 112.
[41] See the Insolvency Act, s. 323(3) and generally section 2.7.2 below.
[42] See e.g. *In re Asphaltic Wood Pavement Company; Lee & Chapman's Case* (1885) 30 Ch. D 216, 225, and generally section 13.2.9 below.
[43] See section 13.2.4 below.

satisfied, so that the assignee can sue in his own name, since the legislation specifically provides that the assignee takes subject to equities.

While the Statutes of Set-off would not provide a defence to an action brought by a trustee in bankruptcy or a liquidator for the benefit of the estate, there should not be any such restriction on a substantive equitable set-off. For example, unlike insolvency set-off, mutuality is not a strict requirement for an equitable set-off.[44] If in an exceptional case an equitable set-off is available notwithstanding the absence of mutuality, the right to rely on it should not be lost on the ground that the person against whom it is asserted is bankrupt or is in liquidation.[45] If a debtor's title to sue was impeached before bankruptcy, it should still be impeached after bankruptcy, and so should the title of the trustee in bankruptcy, who steps into the shoes of the debtor and takes the debtor's property subject to all clogs and fetters affecting it in the hands of the debtor.[46] Statements to the effect that the law regulating the adjustment of cross-claims between a bankrupt and his creditor is to be found exclusively in the bankruptcy set-off section[47] should be regarded as having had in contemplation the Statutes of Set-off and contractual set-offs rather than equitable set-off.[48] This is implicit in Lord Eldon's often-quoted statement in *Ex parte Stephens*,[49] that:

As to the doctrine of set-off, it is not necessary to say much. This Court was in possession of it, as grounded upon principles of equity, long before the law interfered . . . It is true, *where the Court does not find a natural equity going beyond the statute* the construction of the law is the same in equity as at law . . . But that does not affect the general doctrine upon natural equity. So, as to mutual debt and credit, equity must make the same construction as the law.

It is apparent that the concluding remark, that as to mutual debt and credit equity adopts the same construction as the law, was qualified by the earlier reference to a natural equity going beyond the statute. Thus, an equitable set-off has been allowed in bankruptcy in cases involving fraud notwithstanding an absence of mutuality,[49a] and also, in one instance, where a surety was made jointly liable with the principal debtor.[50] Since the joint liability in this latter case was no more than a form of security for the debt

---

[44] See section 1.7.6 above.

[45] Compare *Day & Dent Constructions Pty. Ltd.* v. *North Australian Properties Pty. Ltd.* (1981) 34 ALR 595, 636–7 (Federal Court of Australia), and also *McIntyre* v. *Perkes* (1990) 22 FCR 260, 271 where Gummow and von Doussa JJ. in the Federal Court left the question open.   [46] See Jenkins L.J. in *Bradley-Hole* v. *Cusen* [1953] 1 QB 300, 306.

[47] See, e.g. *In re Daintrey* [1900] 1 QB 546, 567.

[48] Compare *Day & Dent Constructions Pty. Ltd.* v. *North Australian Properties Pty. Ltd.* (1981) 34 ALR 595, 599, 601, 636–7 (Federal Court).

[49] (1805) 11 Ves. Jun. 24, 27 (emphasis added). See also *Ex parte Elliott* (1838) 3 Deac. 343.   [49a] *Vuillamy* v. *Noble* (1817) 3 Mer. 593.

[50] *Ex parte Hanson* (1811) 18 Ves. Jun. 232, affirming (1806) 12 Ves. Jun. 346.

owing by the principal debtor, Lord Eldon said that upon equitable considerations the principal debtor should be permitted to set off that debt in the creditor's bankruptcy against a separate debt owing to him by the creditor, even though the demands were not mutual. Further, while the leave of the court is required for the commencement of proceedings against a bankrupt or a company after a winding-up order has been made against it,[51] this should be forthcoming where an injunction is sought in order to prevent any action being taken which is inconsistent with the nature of the defence of equitable set-off.[52]

Recently the Court of Appeal in *Morris* v. *Agrichemicals Ltd.*[52a] rejected an argument that an equitable set-off should be available in that case in circumstances which were outside the operation of the insolvency set-off section, and said that *Ex parte Stephens* did not provide any assistance. *Morris* however should be considered in the context that the facts in issue did not support an equitable set-off.[52b] In light of earlier authority, it should not be regarded as having settled the question of the availability of equitable set-offs in bankruptcy or liquidation.

2.5 EARLY DEVELOPMENT AND THE INFLUENCE OF EQUITY

Section 323 has a long ancestry which can be traced back to the original mutual credit provision enacted in 1705 by the statute 4 & 5 Anne, c. 17. However, even before then accounts between merchants used to be balanced when one became bankrupt, and indeed the judgment of Flemming C.J. in *Powel* v. *Stuff and Timewell*[53] suggests that this practice had been adopted as early as 1612. The case involved an application of section 13 of the statute (1603) 1 Jac., c. 15, which empowered the commissioners appointed in a bankruptcy to assign to a creditor of the bankrupt a debt owing to the bankrupt by a third party. The creditor could then institute proceedings in his own name to recover the debt.[54] The

---

[51] See the Insolvency Act 1986, s. 130(2) for companies and, for bankruptcies, s. 285(3).

[52] See section 1.7.4 above.

[52a] Rose, Saville and Millett L.JJ., 20 December 1995.

[52b] See section 1.7.6 above. [53] (1612) 2 Bulst. 26.

[54] It seems that the commissioners acting pursuant to this provision would sometimes assign the debts to the creditors as payment of their dividends, though the usual practice was to make an assignment to one or more creditors who would then recover the debts as trustees for the creditors as a whole. See Goodinge, *The Law Against Bankrupts* (2nd edn., 1701), 147–8, and also Christian, *Bankrupt Law* (2nd edn., 1818) Vol. 1, 469–70, 499–500. It was not until 1706 that s. 4 of the statute 5 & 6 Anne, c. 22 empowered the creditors of the bankrupt to choose the assignees to whom the commissioners were required to assign all the bankrupt's estate and effects. These assignees were obliged by s. 33 of (1732) 5 Geo. II, c. 30 to make a distribution to the creditors, and to account to the commissioners for their receipts and for

present case concerned such an action. The Chief Justice in the course of his judgment is reported to have commented that 'if the plaintiff had been in debt, in as great a sum as the bankrupt was indebted unto him, and yet his debt assigned, this assignment had not been good'.[55] However, it was in 1675 that the first proper judicial statement of the right to a balanced account was made. North C.J. said in an anonymous case that,[56]

If there are accounts between two merchants, and one of them become bankrupt, the course is not to make the other, who perhaps upon stating the accounts is found indebted to the bankrupt, to pay the whole that originally was entrusted to him, and to put him for the recovery of what the bankrupt owes him, into the same condition with the rest of the creditors; but to make him pay that only which appears due to the bankrupt on the foot of the account; otherwise it will be for accounts betwixt them after the time of the other's becoming bankrupt, if any such were.

Similarly, there was a reference in *Chapman* v. *Derby*[57] to an earlier judgment of Sir Matthew Hale C.J., in which the Chief Justice apparently said that, where there were dealings on account, a man should not be charged with the account on the credit side and be put to come in as a creditor for the debt owing to himself, but should only answer to the bankrupt's estate for the balance of the account.

There are two competing explanations of how the right to a balanced account in bankruptcy developed before the enactment of the first mutual credit provision in 1705. The first is that it may have originated as a principle of equity. This view apparently was held by Lord Eldon,[58] by Fletcher Moulton L.J.,[59] and also possibly by Sir George Turner.[60] However, another explanation for the early recognition of the right was put forward by Professor Christian,[61] who argued that it had a statutory

their payments concerning the bankrupt's estate. A further modification occurred in 1831, when a number of official assignees were appointed from the ranks of merchants, brokers, accountants, and traders. An official assignee had to be one of the assignees of the bankrupt's estates and effects in every bankruptcy. See (1831) 1 & 2 Will. IV, c. 56, s. 22. Eventually the office of assignee was replaced by that of trustee by the Bankruptcy Act 1869.

[55] (1612) 2 Bulst. 26.   [56] (1675) 1 Mod. 215.
[57] (1689) 2 Vern. 117.
[58] *Ex parte Blagden* (1815) 19 Ves. Jun. 465, 467; *Ex parte Stephens* (1805) 11 Ves. Jun. 24, 27. See also *Bacon's Abridgement of the Law* (7th edn., 1832) Vol. 1, 652; Houlden and Morawetz, *Bankruptcy Law of Canada* (1960), 160.
[59] *Lister* v. *Hooson* [1908] 1 KB 174, 178.
[60] See *Freeman* v. *Lomas* (1851) 9 Hare 109, 112–13. However, it is not altogether clear as to whether his Lordship here was referring to bankruptcy set-off.
[61] See Christian, *Bankrupt Law* (2nd edn., 1818) Vol. 1, 499–500. Christian was the first Downing Professor of the Laws of England at Cambridge, though according to Holdsworth he was not well regarded by his contempories. Indeed, Holdworth tells us that it had been said of Christian upon his death that he died in 'the full vigour of his incapacity'. See Holdsworth, *A History of English Law* (1952) Vol. 13, 480–1. Whether Christian deserved this harsh judgment is debatable. For example Maddock, in his *Principles and Practice of the High Court*

basis. The law of bankruptcy in force during the seventeenth century was set out primarily in an Elizabethan statute, (1570) 13 Eliz., c. 7. The commissioners in bankruptcy were required by section 2 of that Act to pay 'to every of the said creditors a portion, rate and rate like, according to the quantity of his or their debts'. The quantity of the creditor's debt, Christian asserted, was taken to mean any balance due to him.[62] The early cases mentioned above support this explanation, and it should be preferred over the view that a right of set-off in bankruptcy was developed by equity.

The important thing to note is that both North and Hale were common law judges. This by itself is not conclusive, because they may have been enunciating a principle that had been adopted by the commissioners as a result of the influence of the Chancellor. However, there are two arguments against this explanation. The first is the apparent lack of Chancery cases reported from this period in which a right of set-off may have been enforced in a bankruptcy.[63] It is true that, towards the end of the seventeenth century, equity was beginning to enforce set-offs in actions at law by restraining the plaintiff at law from proceeding with his claim unless he gave credit to the defendant for his cross-demand.[64] However, these cases were not concerned with bankruptcies, and in fact there is evidence to suggest that equity was encouraged to advance its jurisdiction in this area because of the fact that such a right already existed in bankruptcy.[65]

There is a second reason for doubting that the Chancellor may have originated the early practice of balancing accounts. This arises from an

---

of Chancery (3rd edn., 1837) Vol. 2, 786 n.d described Christian's *Bankrupt Law* as 'a work, profound, original and useful. No book so strikingly exhibits the fallibility of judges'. For a recent discussion of Christian's contribution to the law, see Hoffheimer, 'The Common Law of Edward Christian' [1994] *Cambridge Law Journal* 140.

[62] Therefore when the commissioners, acting pursuant to (1603) 1 Jac. 1, c. 15, s. 13, assigned the debts owing to the bankrupt to one creditor as trustee for the creditors as a whole, the accounts between the bankrupt and his creditors would already have been balanced. See Christian, *Bankrupt Law* (2nd edn., 1818) Vol. 1, 499–500.

[63] Compare *Peters* v. *Soame* (1701) 2 Vern. 428, in which the Lord Keeper, Sir Nathan Wright, said that the assignee of a debt should take subject to a right of set-off that the debtor could have asserted in an action brought against him by the assignor, who had become bankrupt. However, the bankruptcy in that case appears to have been incidental to the main question of the effect of an assignment, which was within the exclusive jurisdiction of equity. Apparently the fact of the assignor's bankruptcy prevented the assignee from bringing an action at law against the debtor in the assignor's name (though compare now *Winch* v. *Keeley* (1787) 1 TR 619), and so the assignee had to bring this bill in equity in order to obtain payment. [64] See section 1.1 above.

[65] In *Arnold* v. *Richardson* (1699) 1 Eq. Ca. Abr. 8 the Master of the Rolls, Sir John Trevor, ordered that the plaintiff in an action at law should reduce his claim to the extent that he was indebted to the defendant, commenting that if the plaintiff at law had been bankrupt, the commissioners would have allowed a discount. Indeed, it is noticeable that when the court in *Chapman* v. *Derby* (1689) 2 Vern. 117 was considering whether to sanction a set-off, it saw fit to refer to a judgment of Hale, a common law judge, for the proposition that accounts may be balanced in bankruptcy.

examination of the development of the Chancellor's jurisdiction in matters of bankruptcy. In particular, this brings into question the assertion made by Fletcher Moulton L.J. in *Lister* v. *Hooson*,[66] that 'the jurisdiction in bankruptcy was from the first an equitable jurisdiction'. What was meant by this statement is not clear. The jurisdiction and power of the commissioners over the person and property of the bankrupt arose by force of an Act of Parliament, and presumably his Lordship meant that the exercise of those powers was controlled and influenced by the Chancellor. In fact this is not an accurate description of what appears to have happened. Section 2 of the statute 13 Eliz., c. 7 empowered the Lord to conduct bankruptcy proceedings. This was the only power conferred on the Chancellor by the statute, and initially it seems to have represented the extent of the Chancellor's involvement in bankruptcy. Cooper explained in 1828[67] that, while the Chancellor would act to prevent unfair dealing or abuse of power by the commissioners he had appointed,[68] he did not exercise an extensive jurisdiction in matters of bankruptcy in the early years of the operation of the legislation. The common law courts from early times had reserved the right to review a finding by the commissioners that a person was bankrupt.[69] Moreover, when the Elizabethan bankruptcy legislation was first enacted, commissioners acting in bankruptcy proceedings often applied to the common law judges, rather than to the Chancellor, for advice as to how they should exercise the extensive powers conferred upon them.[70] It was only in 1676[71] that the Chancellor was prepared for the first

---

[66] [1908] 1 KB 174, 178.

[67] *Cooper's Parliamentary Proceedings* (1828), 242–5. Holdsworth referred extensively to this section of Cooper's book. See Holdsworth, *A History of English Law* (1952) Vol. 1, 470–3. [68] See e.g. *Wood* v. *Hayes* (1606–7) Tothill 62.

[69] See *Dr. Bonham's Case* (1609) 8 Co. Rep. 107a, 121a, where Coke C.J. said that the commissioner's decision was traversable in an action for false imprisonment. It seems from *Bacon's Abridgement of the Law* (7th edn., 1832) Vol. 1, 526–7 that the common law courts continued as the proper forum for determining questions relating to the construction of the bankruptcy legislation, so that if a bankruptcy was denied the Chancellor usually ordered the issue to be tried in a court of law.

[70] See *Cooper's Parliamentary Proceedings* (1828), 246, and also Yale, *Lord Nottingham's Chancery Cases* Vol. 1, 73 *Selden Society* (1957), p. cxv. Neither of these writers have cited any instances in which this happened, though four cases are mentioned in Christian, *Bankrupt Law* (2nd edn., 1818) Vol. 2, 8–10. In *Anon.* (1583) Cro. Eliz. 13, the Common Pleas was asked to determine whether a person who had kept his house in order to avoid arrest had committed an act of bankruptcy. In *Osborne and Bradshaw* v. *Churchman* (1606) Cro. Jac. 127, the King's Bench ruled that a surety who paid the debt was a creditor of the principal debtor within the terms of the bankruptcy legislation. In the first volume of Brownlow and Goldsborough's report of cases in the Common Pleas (at 47) there is a reference to a case decided in 1612, in which 'The Court was moved, to know whether the wife of a bankrupt can be examined by the commissioners upon the Statute of Bankrupt; and they were of the opinion she could not be examined'. Finally, the Common Pleas was asked upon motion in *Ruggles Case* (1619) Hutton 37 to advise on the procedure to be adopted in distributing the estate of the bankrupt. [71] See *Anon* (1676) 1 Chan. Cas. 275.

time to review a decision made by the commissioners, in this case whether a creditor ought to be admitted to proof.[72] It appears from the report of the decision that Lord Nottingham's initial reaction was not to interfere, but to 'leave it to the Course the Statute hath provided'.[73] However, ultimately he changed his mind and ordered that the creditor's debt should be admitted.[74] Thus it was only in the last quarter of the seventeenth century that it can be said that the Chancellor began to exercise any influence over bankruptcy law,[75] and indeed it was not until Lord Hardwicke's time that the jurisdiction flourished.[76] The Chancellor does not appear to have been

---

[72] See Yale, *Lord Nottingham's Chancery Cases* Vol. 1, 73 *Selden Society* (1957), pp. cxv–cxvi. It seems that, as the influence of the Chancellor over bankruptcy law developed, this remained the most extensive part of his jurisdiction, i.e. deciding whether to order the commissioners to admit the proof of a debt which they had rejected, or to expunge the proof of a debt which they had admitted. See Christian, *Bankrupt Law* (2nd edn., 1818) Vol. 2, 11. Yale has pointed out that there were earlier instances in which decrees had been made by the Chancellor in matters concerning bankruptcy. However, the issue of bankruptcy in these cases arose as an incident to a question involving an established area of equitable jurisdiction, for example a bill for an account and for redemption of a mortgage, or a bill for discovery. See Yale, *op. cit.*, pp. cxvi–cxx.   [73] (1676) 1 Chan. Cas. 275.

[74] Indeed there is a passage in the fourth part of Coke's *Institutes* which suggests that little recourse was had to the Chancellor in matters of bankruptcy during the earlier part of the seventeenth century. Coke commented that the commissioners 'are subject to the action of the party grieved, for he hath no other remedy'. Presumably he meant by this an action at law, while the only authority of the Chancellor mentioned was the power to grant the commission. See Coke's *Institutes* (1648), 277.

[75] See Holdsworth, *A History of English Law* (1952) Vol. 8, 241–3. The Chancellor decided a number of issues in the next few decades, particularly in relation to the bankruptcy of partnerships, the distribution of the bankrupt's estate, and the effect of a bankruptcy upon equitable interests.

[76] See Yale, *Lord Nottingham's Chancery Cases* Vol. 1, 73 *Selden Society* (1957), p. cxv. The bankruptcy legislation of the first two decades of the eighteenth century conferred a number of discrete powers upon the Chancellor. Included amongst these was the power to remove the assignees if petitioned by any creditors and to make such order as he thought just and reasonable, for example, that a new assignment be made (see (1718) 5 Geo. 1, c. 24, s. 23), while s. 25 of that Act allowed the Chancellor in some cases to supersede the commission. See generally the statutes (1705) 4 & 5 Anne, c. 17; (1706) 5 & 6 Anne, c. 22, and (1718) 5 Geo. 1, c. 24. However, in no case was general control over bankruptcy vested in the Chancellor. Lord Eldon thought that the bankruptcy legislation was framed with the general authority of the Chancellor in mind, and that, if the legislation was silent as to the means of giving effect to its provisions, the Chancellor had a general jurisdiction to act to attain the objects of the commission. See *Anon.* (1808) 14 Ves. Jun. 449, 451, and also Henley, *A Digest of the Bankrupt Law* (3rd edn., 1832), 451–2. This should be compared to the analysis proposed by Christian. He argued that the Chancellor's authority in matters over which he had not been given express jurisdiction was recommendatory only, but was enforceable by means of his control over the appointment of commissioners. The power and authority of the commissioners was conferred by an Act of Parliament, and for that reason Christian said that they were not bound to obey the Chancellor. They depended upon him, however, for their appointment as commissioners, and failure to follow his directions could have resulted in the Chancellor renewing the commission under (1732) 5 Geo. II, c. 30, s. 45, with other more compliant persons being appointed to act as commissioners. See Christian, *Bankrupt Law* (2nd edn., 1818) Vol. 2, 6–24. In any event, there is probably some truth in Cooper's assertion that equity usurped jurisdiction in this area, possibly because of the immense fees and the control of patronage that went with it. See *Cooper's Parliamentary Proceedings* (1828), 251–2.

active in matters of bankruptcy when North and Hale mentioned the right to a balanced account,[77] and it is unlikely that the Chancellor had any great influence over its development.

2.6 THE DEVELOPMENT OF THE MUTUAL CREDIT PROVISION

A set-off section was first incorporated into the bankruptcy legislation in 1705.[78] Section 11 of the statute (1705) 4 & 5 Anne, c. 17[79] stipulated:

Where there shall appear to the commissioners or the major part of them that there hath been mutual credit given between such person or persons against whom such commission shall issue forth and any person or persons who shall be debtor or debtors to such person or persons and due proof thereof made and that the accounts are open and unbalanced that then it shall be lawful for the commissioners in the said commission named or the major part of them or the assignee or assignees of such commission to adjust the said account and to take the balance due in full discharge thereof and the person debtor to such bankrupt shall not be compelled or obliged to pay more than shall appear to be due on such balance.

This section has formed the basis of the modern right of bankruptcy, though subsequent amendments have considerably enlarged the scope of its operation. The language of the provision was simplified in 1718,[80] while in 1732[81] the ambit of the right was expressed in terms of mutual credit and mutual debts, as opposed to just mutual credit.[82]

It was a feature of this early legislation that there could only be a set-off

---

[77] North C.J. made his statement in 1675, while the judgment of Lord Hale referred to in *Chapman* v. *Derby* could not have been delivered later than 1676, when he retired as Chief Justice of the King's Bench.

[78] Contrary to Jessel M.R.'s assertion in *Peat* v. *Jones & Co.* (1881) 8 QBD 147, 149, that the enactment as to 'mutual credits' appeared in (1732) 5 Geo. II, c. 30.

[79] It was not until 1797 that the mutual credit provision in the bankruptcy legislation was made permanent. Until then, it was to be found in a number of temporary statutes, the operation of each of which was continued, with occasional amendment by a subsequent enactment. The 1705 Act was to remain in force for only 3 years (see s. 17), though it was continued *in toto* by (1708) 7 Anne, c. 25, and then by (1716) 3 Geo. I, c. 12.

[80] See (1718) 5 Geo. 1, c. 24, which was continued by (1724) II Geo. I, c. 29, and by (1726) 13 Geo. I, c. 27. The words 'assignee or assignees' were omitted from the 1718 legislation, so that apparently only the commissioners were empowered to balance the accounts. However these words were later reintroduced in 1732.

[81] See 5 Geo. II, c. 30, s. 28.

[82] Apart from this, there were only minor differences between the language of the 1718 and the 1732 set-off sections, though the latter did bring assignees back within the scope of the right. The Act of 1732 was only to remain in force for a period of 3 years (see s. 49), though its operation was continued by the following statutes: (1736) 9 Geo. II, c. 18; (1743) 16 Geo. II, c. 27; (1751) 24 Geo. II, c. 57; (1758) 31 Geo. II, c. 35; (1763) 4 Geo. III, c. 36; (1772) 12 Geo. III, c. 47; (1776) 16 Geo. III, c. 54; (1781) 21 Geo. III, c. 29; (1786) 26 Geo. III, c. 80; (1788) 28 Geo. III, c. 24, and by (1794) 34 Geo. III, c. 57. It was made perpetual in 1797 by 37 Geo. III, c. 124.

if the mutual debts or mutual credit existed 'at any time such person became bankrupt',[83] by which it was meant when an act of bankruptcy was committed.[84] However in 1806 the legislation was amended so as to offer some protection in the event that the person giving credit to the bankrupt was not aware of the commission of the act.[85] Section 3 of the statute (1806) 46 Geo. III, c. 135 allowed one debt or demand to be set against another notwithstanding that a prior act of bankruptcy had been committed by the bankrupt before the credit was given to him or a debt was contracted by him, though this was made subject to two important provisos. The section only applied when the credit was given to the bankrupt at least two calendar months before the date of the commission,[86] and moreover the person claiming the set-off must not have had, at the time of giving credit, notice of an act of bankruptcy committed by the bankrupt (though the issuing of a commission was deemed notice of an act), or notice that he was insolvent or had stopped payment.

In 1825 the various statutes which up until then had set out the law of bankruptcy were repealed and replaced by a consolidating statute 6 Geo. IV, c. 16.[87] The new mutual credit provision was set out in section 50 of the Act, and contained a number of amendments to the pre-existing law. In particular, there was a further liberalization of the right to a set-off in the event of credit being given to, or a debt contracted by, the bankrupt after the commission of a secret act of bankruptcy. The proviso in (1806) 46 Geo. III, c. 135, section 3, that the credit must have been given at least two calendar months before the date of the commission in bankruptcy, was deleted,[88] while the second proviso was amended so that only notice of a prior act of bankruptcy would invoke the principle that the right of set-off should have existed at the time of the act of the bankruptcy. Notice of the

[83] See s. 28 of (1732) 5 Geo. II, c. 30. This notion first appeared in the statute (1718) 5 Geo. I, c. 24, which required that there should have been 'mutual credit given by the bankrupt and any other person at any time before the person against whom such commission is or shall be awarded became bankrupt'.

[84] See *Bamford* v. *Burrell* (1799) 2 Bos. & Pul. 1. Acts of bankruptcy were a series of defined acts the commission of any one of which constituted a statutory recognition of insolvency. A person must have committed an act of bankruptcy before he could be made bankrupt. The concept of the act of bankruptcy has been abolished in the Insolvency Act 1986, the sole ground for bankruptcy proceedings now being inability to pay debts.

[85] See e.g. Parke J. in *Dickson* v. *Cass* (1830) 1 B & Ad. 343, 358–9.

[86] The date of the commission was the date upon which it was sealed and issued by the Chancellor. See Christian, *Bankrupt Law* (2nd edn., 1818) Vol. 1, 457–9.

[87] In fact an earlier bankruptcy consolidation Act (5 Geo. IV, c. 98) had been enacted the previous year, though it was repealed by 6 Geo. IV, c. 16 the day after it was due to take effect.

[88] Therefore the account could be taken down to the issuing of the commission, rather than 2 months before. See Babington, *The Law of Set-off and Mutual Credit* (1827), 118, and also Henley, *A Digest of the Bankrupt Law* (3rd edn., 1832), 187.

fact that the debtor was insolvent or had stopped payment was no longer sufficient. Further, the issuing of a commission in bankruptcy was no longer deemed to be notice of a prior act of bankruptcy. The legislation also provided that every debt or demand made provable by the Act could be the subject of a set-off against the bankrupt's estate. The idea that all provable debts could be the subject of a set-off was by no means new.[89] However, the insertion of this principle into the 1825 mutual credit provision ensured that contingent debts could be set-off, since it was only as a result of section 56 of (1825) 6 Geo. IV, c. 16 that contingent debts became provable.

The terms of the 1825 set-off section remained virtually unaltered when the law of bankruptcy was once again consolidated in 1849,[90] the only difference being that the creation in 1831 of a separate Court of Bankruptcy with jurisdiction over all matters in bankruptcy[91] meant that the court, rather than the commissioners, was to control the balancing of the accounts.

When another consolidation took place in 1869,[92] the ambit of the right of set-off was extended from mutual credit and mutual debts to cover also mutual dealings. The proviso relating to notice of an act of bankruptcy was also amended. Whereas it had been a prerequisite to the operation of the previous sections that the person claiming the benefit of the set-off should not have given credit to the bankrupt after notice of an act of bankruptcy, the new section stipulated that the notice had to be of an act of bankruptcy that was available against the bankrupt for adjudication. This referred to section 6 of the Act, and required that the act of bankruptcy must have occurred within six months of the presentation of the petition.[93] In addition, the legislation no longer specifically provided that every debt or demand which was provable against the estate of the bankrupt could also be the subject of a set-off, though this omission was of little consequence because the courts in any event continued to emphasize that notion. The 1869 mutual credit provision was, with one exception, virtually identical to the set-off section in the 1914 legislation. The 1869 Act stipulated that the mutual dealings had to be between a 'bankrupt and any other person proving or claiming to prove a debt under his bankruptcy'. However, in the Bankruptcy Act 1883, section 38,[94] which was similar to the Bankruptcy Act 1914, section 31, the language was altered so that the mutual dealings had to be 'between a debtor against whom a receiving order shall be made

---

[89] See e.g. Christian, *Bankrupt Law* (2nd edn., 1818) Vol. 1, 509.
[90] See the Bankrupt Law Consolidation Act 1849, s. 171.
[91] See (1831) 1 & 2 Will. IV, c. 56.   [92] See the Bankruptcy Act 1869, s. 39.
[93] Compare the Bankruptcy Act 1914, s. 4(1)(c), which specified a 3-month period.
[94] The Bankruptcy Act 1883 repealed the Bankruptcy Act 1869, and amended and consolidated the law of bankruptcy.

under this Act, and any other person proving or claiming to prove a debt under such receiving order'. The concept of the receiving order was introduced in the 1883 Act[95] as a step between the presentation of the petition and the adjudication of bankruptcy. It served to stay all actions against the debtor, and also to vest the possession and control of the debtor's property in an official receiver,[96] while the creditors considered whether any proposals for a composition or scheme of arrangement should be accepted, or whether it was expedient for the debtor to be adjudged bankrupt. The receiving order has been discarded in the Insolvency Act 1986, which instead is drafted in terms of sanctioning a set-off in the event of 'mutual dealings between the bankrupt and any creditor of the bankrupt proving or claiming to prove for a bankruptcy debt'.

2.7 THE RELEVANT DATE FOR DETERMINING RIGHTS OF SET-OFF

2.7.1 *The general rule*

The right of set-off essentially is an aspect of the rules regulating the proof of debts,[97] and historically the rule generally has been applied that the date which defines the accounts to be balanced should be the same as that which determines what claims may be proved in the bankruptcy.[98] The

---

[95] Bankruptcy Act 1883, ss. 5–14, and also the Bankruptcy Act 1914, s. 7.

[96] See the Bankruptcy Act 1914, s. 7.

[97] See *Mersey Steel and Iron Co. Limited* v. *Naylor, Benzon, & Co.* (1884) 9 App. Cas. 424, 437–8; *Re Northside Properties Pty. Ltd. and the Companies Act* [1971] 2 NSWLR 320, 323.

[98] Before the amendment of the 1732 Act in 1806, the date of the act of bankruptcy applied to both proof and set-off. See e.g. *Bamford* v. *Burrell* (1799) 2 Bos. & Pul. 1, 7 for the proof of debts, and *Collins* v. *Jones* (1830) 10 B & C 777, 780 for set-off. Under the 1825 consolidation the date of the issuing of the commission, and after 1831 of the fiat, was applied in both instances. See s. 47 of (1825) 6 Geo. IV, c. 16 for the proof of debts, and for set-off *Collins* v. *Jones* (at 780–1). However, the dates did not always coincide when the legislature intervened in 1806 to ameliorate the harsh consequences under the 1732 Act of a secret act of bankruptcy. As a general rule, s. 2 of the statute (1806) 46 Geo. III, c. 135 allowed debts contracted before the issuing of the commission to be proved, while for set-off s. 3 only provided relief when credit was given to the bankrupt at least 2 calendar months before the issuing of the commission. It is difficult to ascertain the state of the law under the 1849 and 1869 Acts. The Bankrupt Law Consolidation Act 1849, s. 165 allowed a creditor to prove any debt or demand contracted before the filing of the petition, and similarly it was accepted in Doria and Macrae *The Law and Practice of Bankruptcy* (1863) Vol. 2, 804–5 that this date applied to set-off, though in *Astley* v. *Gurney* (1869) LR 4 CP 714 the court seems to have applied the date of the adjudication order. The Bankruptcy Act 1869, s. 31 differed from its 1849 predecessor in relation to the proof of debts, in that it allowed claims to which the bankrupt was subject at the date of the adjudication order to be proved, though in 1874 Doria had not changed his opinion that the existence of any right of set-off should be ascertained as at the date of the petition. See Doria, *The Law and Practice of Bankruptcy* (1874), 679. The 1883 and 1914 Acts both conformed with the general rule, since the date of the receiving order in each case determined questions relating to both proof and set-off. See *In re Daintrey* [1900] 1 QB 546.

Insolvency Act 1986 conforms with this approach, since the 'commencement of the bankruptcy' is expressed to constitute the relevant date in both cases.[99] This would seem to refer to the date of the bankruptcy order, as opposed to the date of the petition.[100]

In the case of a company liquidation, both the right of proof and the right of a set-off are determined by reference to when the company goes into liquidation.[101] A company goes into liquidation if it passes a resolution for a voluntary winding-up, or if an order is made for its winding up by the court at a time when it has not already gone into liquidation by passing such a resolution.[102]

In Australia, the date of the bankruptcy determines the availability of rights of proof and also rights of set-off in bankruptcy.[103] In the case of a company liquidation, provable debts are determined by reference to 'the relevant date',[104] which in essence is defined[105] as the day of the winding-up order or the day on which a resolution was passed for a winding-up, though if the company had been under administration, it is the day on which the administration began. However, the concept of 'the relevant date' has not been specifically incorporated into section 553C of the Corporations Law dealing with mutual credit and set-off. Traditionally the question whether there are mutual debts, mutual credits or other mutual dealings between a company in liquidation and a creditor so as to qualify for a set-off has been said to be determined by reference to the date of the liquidation.[106] In a voluntary liquidation this refers to the date of the resolution, while in a court-ordered winding-up the weight of authority

---

[99] See s. 323 for set-off, and, for proof, the definition of 'bankrupt debt' in s. 382. In Australia the date of the sequestration order is the relevant date in bankruptcies. See *Hiley* v. *The Peoples Prudential Assurance Co. Ltd.* (1938) 60 CLR 468, 487.

[100] See e.g. s. 284(4), which draws a distinction between the commencement of the bankruptcy and the presentation of the petition. See also rr. 6.98(1)(b), 6.111–6.114 of the Insolvency Rules with respect to proof.

[101] See the Insolvency Rules 1986, r. 13.12 with respect to proof of debts, and for set-off r. 4.90.

[102] See the Insolvency Act 1986, s. 247(2) which should be distinguished from s. 129 dealing with the commencement of the winding-up. While s. 247(2) is not strictly expressed to apply to the mutual credit provision in r. 4.90 of the Insolvency Rules, it is consistent with the principle which generally has been accepted by the courts. See *In re Fenton* [1931] 1 Ch. 85, 105; *Barclays Bank Ltd.* v. *TOSG Trust Fund Ltd.* [1984] BCLC 1, 25; *Re Charge Card Services Ltd.* [1987] 1 Ch. 150, 177; *M.S. Fashions Ltd.* v. *Bank of Credit and Commerce International SA* [1993] Ch. 425, 446. Compare *In re City Equitable Fire Insurance Co. Ltd.* [1930] 2 Ch. 293, 310 and *In re Dynamics Corporation of America* [1976] 1 WLR 757, 769, which supported the date of the petition rather than the date of the winding-up order.

[103] See, for proof of debts, the Bankruptcy Act 1966 (Cth.), s. 82(1) and, for set-off, *Gye* v. *McIntyre* (1991) 171 CLR 609, 619–20.

[104] See the Corporations Law, s. 553(1).

[105] See the Corporations Law, ss. 9, 513A, 513B and 513C.

[106] *Day & Dent Constructions Pty. Ltd.* v. *North Australian Properties Pty. Ltd.* (1982) 150 CLR 85, 98.

favours the view that it means the date of order.[107] While this produces a result generally similar to that which would have applied if 'the relevant date' had been expressed to extend to the set-off section, it nevertheless differs in that it does not take into account a prior administration. In this regard, three points may be made. In the first place, if a company incurs a debt after the commencement of the administration, so that it is not provable, that debt could not be employed in a set-off in any event since the set-off section requires that the creditor's claim must be provable. Accordingly, any difference between the two concepts would only manifest itself in relation to a claim *acquired by the company* after the commencement of administration and before the commencement of the liquidation. The second point is that the traditional date for determining rights of set-off often will produce the same result in relation to a debt accruing to the company after the commencement of the administration as if the commencement of the administration were instead the determinative date. This is because the qualification to the set-off section, in section 553C(2), provides that a creditor is not entitled to claim a set-off in relation to a debt which becomes owing to the company if at the time the creditor had notice that the company was insolvent. A board of a company may resolve to appoint an administrator if in the opinion of the directors the company is insolvent, or is likely to become insolvent, or if they consider that an administrator in any event should be appointed.[108] If in fact an administrator has been appointed because of actual insolvency, and a creditor has notice of this, any debt subsequently incurred to the company could not be set-off. The third point is that a creditor often will not be disadvantaged by being unable to prove a debt incurred by the company after an administrator has been appointed,[109] and therefore being denied a set-off in respect of it. This is because an administrator is personally liable for debts incurred in the exercise of his functions and powers for services rendered, goods brought or property hired, leased, used or occupied,[110] so that in those circumstances a creditor in any event would have a claim against the administrator, and, moreover, debts incurred by an administrator in preserving, realizing or gathering in property of the company or

---

[107] See Street J. in *Re Northside Properties Pty. Ltd. and the Companies Act* [1971] 2 NSWLR 320, 323 (the result of which was affirmed by the Court of Appeal [1972] 2 NSWLR 573), whose view was accepted by Mason J. in *Day and Dent Constructions Pty. Ltd. v. North Australian Properties Pty. Ltd.* (1982) 150 CLR 85, 98–9. The date of the winding-up order should be preferred over the opinions of Barwick C.J. and Taylor J. in *Motor Inns Co. Pty. Ltd. v. Liberty Insurance Ltd.* (1967) 116 CLR 177, that one should look to the date of the presentation of the petition in order to ascertain the rights of the creditors.

[108] See the Corporations Law, s. 436A(1).

[109] When performing a function or exercising a power as administrator of a company the administrator acts as the company's agent. See the Corporations Law, s. 437B.

[110] See the Corporations Law, s. 443A.

carrying on the company's business have priority of payment in a liquidation.[111]

Once a particular date is fixed for determining the existence of any right of set-off, then the acquisition of a right or a liability after that date, when it is not the result of a prior dealing between the parties or it is not a natural result of a prior transaction so as to come within the concept of giving credit,[112] will not give rise to a set-off.[113] Thus, a sale of goods by a liquidator in the course of winding up the company will not entitle the purchaser to employ his liability for the price in a set-off against a provable debt owing to him by the company.[114] An amount paid by a director of a company after the commencement of the company's liquidation in order to settle an action that had been commenced against both the director and the company similarly has been held not to be available as a set-off in the liquidation,[115] and a set-off cannot be based upon an assignment of the benefit of a proof of debt lodged by someone else.[116] On the same principle, save for the exception relating to a temporary suspension of mutuality,[117] a set-off may not be based upon an assignment of a debt or a dealing with a negotiable instrument that only took place after the relevant date.[118] A debt or a negotiable instrument admittedly may be proved even though it may have been acquired from another party after the cut-off date for determining rights of proof.[119] However, the proof should not be lodged by the subsequent holder, but rather by the holder at the relevant

---

[111] See the Corporations Law, s. 556(1).   [112] See section 3.1 below.

[113] In addition to the cases referred to below, see *Glennie* v. *Edmunds* (1813) 4 Taunt. 775; *Re Henley, Thurgood, & Co.* (1863) 11 WR 1021; *Sankey Brook Coal Company, Limited* v. *Marsh* (1871) LR 6 Ex. 185; *In re The United Ports and General Insurance Company; ex parte The Etna Insurance Company* (1877) 46 LJ Ch. 403; *In re Milan Tramways Company; ex parte Theys* (1884) 24 Ch. D 587; *Re Gunson (A Bankrupt); ex parte Official Receiver* [1966] NZLR 187. See also *Re Buchanan Enterprises Pty. Ltd.* (1982) 7 ACLR 407 (no equitable set-off). Given the inclusion of the mutual dealings head in the set-off section in 1869, *quaere* whether *Graham* v. *Allsopp* (1848) 3 Ex. 186 would now be followed in relation to the claim for a set-off against the rent due before the immediate landlord's bankruptcy, since the payment by the lessee after the bankruptcy to the superior landlord as a result of the distress levied pursuant to the lease not taken up by the assignees in bankruptcy nevertheless arose out of a prior dealing, in the form of that lease.

[114] *Hiley* v. *The Peoples Prudential Assurance Co. Ltd.* (1938) 60 CLR 468, 496; *Re Kidsgrove Steel, Iron, and Coal Co.* (1894) 38 Sol. Jo. 252. See also *Re Henley, Thurgood, & Co.* (1863) 11 WR 1021. However, this may not apply if assets are purchased from a company in liquidation pursuant to a prior option. See section 9.4.4 below.

[115] *Re Buchanan Enterprises Pty. Ltd.* (1982) 7 ACLR 407.

[116] *Re Gill; ex parte Official Receiver* (1964) 6 FLR 273, 276.

[117] See section 2.8 below.

[118] *Marsh* v. *Chambers* (1749) 2 Str. 1234; *Dickson* v. *Evans* (1794) 6 TR 57; *Sempill* v. *The Oriental Bank* (1868) 7 SCR (NSW) 68; *Middelton* v. *Pollock; ex parte Nugee* (1875) LR 20 Eq. 29 (assignment of debt); *In re Gillespie; ex parte Reid & Sons* (1885) 14 QBD 963. See also *McColl's Wholesale Pty. Ltd.* v. *State Bank of NSW* [1984] 3 NSWLR 365, 381.

[119] *Ex parte Deey* (1796) 2 Cox 423; *Ex parte Atkins; in re Atkins* (1820) Buck 479; *Ex parte Rogers; in re Bowles* (1820) Buck 490.

date as trustee for the latter.[120] Indeed, the subsequent holder takes subject to any right of set-off that may have been available to the bankrupt against the holder at the relevant date because, as Lord Loughborough emphasized in *Ex parte Deey*[121] in relation to a bill of exchange, the subsequent indorsement or delivery could not alter the state of the mutual credit between the holder and the bankrupt at that date.

If a person designated as an agent receives the principal's money after the principal has become bankrupt, usually he could not employ his liability to account in a set-off because the bankruptcy will have terminated the agency. Accordingly, a claim of mutual credit or mutual dealings based upon an expectation of the continuance of the agency cannot be supported.[122] This is in addition to any difficulty arising from the possibility that the agent may have received the money impressed with a trust.[123]

It has been suggested that a claim arising after the relevant date, and not related to a dealing entered into before that date, may be employed in a set-off if the fact of the bankruptcy was unknown to the other party.[124] The only instance in which this has actually occurred is *Billon* v. *Hyde*,[125] though the facts in issue were exceptional. The case concerned the old doctrine of relation back, and an attempt by Lord Hardwicke to use set-off as a means of bringing about a result consistent with a statute[126] which had been enacted in order to ameliorate the harshness of the doctrine, but which had not come into force when the dealings before him occurred. In *Kinder* v. *Butterworth*,[127] claims entered into after the relevant date in ignorance of the bankruptcy were not allowed to be set-off,[128] and moreover the contrary conclusion would seem to conflict with judicial opinions to the effect that the question of whether there is a right of set-off cannot be varied by transactions entered into subsequent to the relevant date.[129]

2.7.2 Notice of a pending petition

Although in England the claims which may be brought into an account in a bankruptcy are generally determined by reference to the bankruptcy

---

[120] *Ex parte Dickenson; in re Gibson* (1832) 2 Deac. & Ch. 520.

[121] (1796) 2 Cox 423, 424.

[122] See Collins J. in *Elgood* v. *Harris* [1896] 2 QB 491, 495, though compare in Australia *Re Clune* (1988) 14 ACLR 261, 267–8.   [123] See Ch. 6.

[124] *Re Gill; ex parte Official Receiver* (1964) 6 FLR 273, 276. See also *Re Clements* (1931) 7 ABC 255, 268.   [125] (1749) 1 Ves. Sen. 326.

[126] (1746) 19 Geo. II, c. 32.   [127] (1826) 6 B & C 42.

[128] Compare the headnote to *In re Gillespie; ex parte Reid & Sons* (1885) 14 QBD 963, though Cave J. in his judgment seems to have been referring to notice of an act of bankruptcy.

[129] See *Dickson* v. *Evans* (1794) 6 TR 57, 59; *In re Milan Tramways Company; ex parte Theys* (1884) 25 Ch. D 587, 591; *Savage* v. *Thompson* (1903) 29 VLR 436, 440.

order, this is subject to the qualification in section 323(3), that 'Sums due from the bankrupt to another party shall not be included in the account . . . if that other party had notice at the time they became due that a bankruptcy petition relating to the bankrupt was pending'. A petition is regarding as pending if the petition has been presented though as yet a bankruptcy order has not been made consequent upon it.[130]

The equivalent concept for company liquidations is set out in Rule 4.90 (3) of the Insolvency Rules 1986. Sums due from the company may not be included in the account if the other party had notice at the time they became due that a meeting of creditors had been summoned under section 98 of the Act, or that a petition for the winding-up of the company was pending. A petition is filed in a court-ordered winding-up, and a section 98 meeting takes place in a creditors' voluntary winding-up. A creditors' voluntary winding-up should be distinguished from a members' voluntary winding-up. Briefly, a voluntary winding-up may proceed as a members' voluntary winding-up if the directors made a statutory declaration within the five-week period immediately preceding the date of the passing of the resolution for winding-up to the effect that in their opinion the company would be able to pay its debts in full together with interest.[131] A creditor's voluntary winding-up is a voluntary winding-up in which the directors failed to make such a declaration. The proviso to the mutual credit provision applies in the case of a creditors', but not a members', voluntary winding-up.

The qualification evidently is intended to discourage dealings in debts owing by the bankrupt or the company, as the case may be, in a way that would negate the principle of a *pari passu* distribution of the bankrupt's or the company's property. A person who buys a debt at a discount is entitled to base a claim for a set-off upon the full face value of the debt.[132] Therefore, in the absence of a provision such as section 323(3), a particular creditor who otherwise would only receive a dividend could sell the debt at a discount to a person who himself is indebted to the insolvent party, and who could obtain the full value of the assigned debt by means of a set-off in the ensuing bankruptcy. However, the scope of the qualification is not entirely satisfactory. It only operates as from notice of the date of the presentation of the petition, or, in a creditors' voluntary winding-up, the summoning of a meeting under section 98, and yet it may be evident well before then that bankruptcy or liquidation is likely. In such a case it seems

---

[130] This seems clear from s. 266(4) of the Insolvency Act 1986, and see also s. 285(1).

[131] See the Insolvency Act 1986, ss. 89 and 90.

[132] *Stonehouse* v. *Read* (1825) 3 B & C 669. Similarly, in the absence of fraud in the inception or preparation of a bill of exchange, a discounter is entitled to prove for its face value. See *In re Gomersall* (1875) 1 Ch. D. 137, 146–7.

that a debt assigned before the petition may be able to be employed in a set-off, even though the very purpose of the assignment may have been to ensure that in any subsequent bankruptcy or liquidation the full value of the debt is obtainable rather than just a dividend. This issue is discussed below. The Cork Committee in its report on the reform of insolvency law originally recommended that the qualification should be framed in terms of notice of inability to pay debts,[133] an approach that has been adopted in Australia in relation to company liquidation. The qualification in section 553C(2) of the Australian Corporations Law applies where the creditor had notice of the fact that the company was insolvent. It is not clear why the Cork Committee's suggestion did not appear in the Insolvency Act.

2.7.3 *Assignment of a debt as a preference*

The effect of section 323(3), and of Rule 4.90(3) in a company liquidation, would appear to be that a person who takes an assignment of a debt after notice of the debtor's insolvency but before notice of a pending petition may be able to employ the debt in a set-off, even though in the absence of a right of set-off any repayment of the debt may have been voidable as a preference. While the decision of Lord Langdale in *Watts* v. *Christie*[134] appears to be inconsistent with that view, the judgment is not entirely satisfactory. A partnership consisting of A and B was indebted to a bank, while the bank was separately indebted to A on an account in credit. After the partners became aware of the bank's insolvency they entered into an agreement by which A purported to assign the credit account to the partnership. Any assignment would have been an equitable assignment, since the ability to assign at law only arose later with the enactment of the Judicature Acts. The partners gave notice of the assignment to the bank, and requested that the balance on that account be applied in reduction of the partners' joint indebtedness. However, this direction was not complied with. After the bankruptcy the assignees in bankruptcy sued the partners on their joint debt, whereupon the partners filed a bill for an injunction to restrain the action on the ground that the assigned debt should be set off against their joint debt. In this regard, if A instead had withdrawn the credit balance in order to pay off the partnership debt, the payment to A would have constituted a preference, since A had notice of the bank's insolvency. The purpose of the assignment evidently was to avoid this result, by bringing about a situation in which the partners' joint liability could be set off against a joint asset in the form of the credit account

---

[133] *Cork Committee Report on Insolvency Law and Practice* (Cmnd. 8558, 1982), 127, 307.
[134] (1849) 11 Beav. 546.

assigned to them.[135] Under the bankruptcy legislation then in force the qualification to the set-off section was drafted in terms of notice of an act of bankruptcy,[136] whereas, while the assignment in *Watts* v. *Christie* had occurred after notice of insolvency, an act of bankruptcy had not actually been committed at that date. Therefore, the qualification was not applicable. Despite this, it was held that a set-off was not available. Lord Langdale in his judgment concentrated on the direction to the bank to apply A's credit balance in reduction of the joint debt.[137] Since this occurred after notice of insolvency, he said that an application of the credit balance in accordance with the direction would have constituted a preference. It is not altogether clear, however, why the case was decided only in terms of the direction as opposed to the assignment itself. Certainly it is now recognized that a direction to pay, or indeed notice to the debtor, is not a necessary requirement of an equitable assignment.[138] Notice is desirable for the purpose of preserving the assignee's priority in accordance with the rule in *Dearle* v. *Hall*,[139] and to ensure that the debtor cannot discharge the debt by payment to the assignor.[140] But the failure to give notice does not mean that the assignment itself is ineffective. If in a case such as *Watts* v. *Christie* there has been a valid assignment, whether legal or equitable, it is difficult on the current language of the set-off section to see why the fact that a payment by the debtor at the time of the assignment would have constituted a preference should be fatal to the argument for a set-off.

It has been suggested that the transaction could constitute a preference if the bankrupt or the company was involved in it with a preferential motive as, for example, where consent to the assignment was required.[141] However, this would depend on the circumstances of the case. The preference section is expressed to apply where a person does something or suffers something to be done in favour of a *creditor*,[142] by which is meant someone who, but for the payment or other transaction being impugned, would share in the administration of the estate.[143] Further, the person must

---

[135] In the absence of an effective assignment a set-off would not have been available, since A's separate demand and the partners' joint liability would not have been mutual for the purpose of the set-off section. See section 8.2 below.

[136] See (1825) 6 Geo. IV, c. 16, s. 50.

[137] This accords with the argument of counsel for the partners, which was presented in terms that the direction to transfer operated as an equitable transfer of the separate debt to the partners. See (1849) 11 Beav. 546, 548.

[138] *In re Patrick; Bills* v. *Tatham* [1891] 1 Ch. 82.   [139] (1823) 3 Russ. 1.

[140] Compare *Brice* v. *Bannister* (1878) 3 QBD 569.

[141] Wood, *English and International Set-off* (1989), 358, 371–2.

[142] See the Insolvency Act 1986, ss. 239(4)(a) & 340(3)(a).

[143] *In re Paine; ex parte Read* [1897] 1 QB 122, 123, and see generally the discussion in *In re Blackpool Motor Car Company, Ltd.* [1901] 1 Ch. 77.

have been influenced by a desire to improve the position *of that creditor*. In the assignment under discussion there are two parties to consider, the assignor and the assignee. If the debtor in consenting to the assignment was influenced by a desire to improve the position of the assignor, for example because the consideration for the assignment was greater than what the assignor otherwise would have received in the bankruptcy or liquidation, the giving of the consent could well have been a preference. If, however, the debtor was influenced only by a desire to benefit the assignee, because the consideration payable by the assignee for the debt was less than the benefit accruing to him by being able to set off the full value of the assigned debt against his liability, it is doubtful whether the debtor's consent would be a preference. The assignee is not a person who, apart from the transaction in question, would have shared in the administration of the estate. The assignee before the assignment was a debtor, not a creditor. Nor does *In re Land Development Association: Kent's Case*[144] support the contrary view. A shareholder who held partly paid shares in a company, and who therefore had a contingent liability to contribute the unpaid amount, took an assignment of a debt owing by the company to a third party. The company resolved that the seal of the company be affixed to the assignment,[145] and also, on that same day, that the debt be applied in paying up the shares. This arrangement was struck down as giving the shareholder a preference. Since one of the debts was for an amount unpaid on shares, it could not have been employed in a set-off in a subsequent liquidation.[146] The shareholder would have been obliged to pay the unpaid capital, and only receive a dividend on the assigned debt. It is readily apparent that an agreement involving the company prior to the liquidation to set off the cross-demands did indeed give the shareholder a preference.[147] However the preference was not the assignment, but rather the company's agreement that the debt, having been assigned, should be set off against the liability for unpaid capital. In other words, the event constituting the preference took effect in favour of a person who at that time was a creditor. On the other hand, where the issue is whether the giving of a required consent to an assignment can constitute a preference in relation to the assignee, the giving of the consent does not have the effect of preferring an existing creditor because, if consent is a prerequisite to the validity of the assignment, the assignee was not a creditor before the consent was given.

---

[144] (1888) 39 Ch. D 259, referred to in Wood, *English and International Set-off* (1989), 371–2.
[145] It is not clear what the significance of this in fact was, though it appears from the judgment of Fry L.J. ((1888) 39 Ch. D 259, 267) that it may have been done in order to fix the amount of one of the instalments of the debt.   [146] See section 4.6 below.

While this appears to be the effect of the preference and set-off sections, it is not a felicitous result. The better view is that the proviso to the set-off section should be amended to reflect the Cork Committee's original recommendation, that it be framed in terms of notice of inability to pay debts.

2.7.4 *The meaning of 'due'*

A question of some importance in relation to section 323(3) is the meaning of 'due'. Sums due from the bankrupt cannot be included in a set-off if the creditor had notice at the time they 'became due' that a bankruptcy petition was pending. If 'due' were to be interpreted as meaning 'due and payable', the qualification in many cases would operate to deny a set-off in respect of a debt which was contracted by the debtor well before insolvency but which only became payable after the presentation of the petition. Obviously this conclusion would have little merit, and in order to overcome the problem one imagines that the courts would readily conclude that 'due' in this context means 'owing but not necessarily payable'. If at the time that the debt was incurred the creditor did not have notice of a bankruptcy petition, it should not matter that a petition is presented before the due date for payment. However, this approach would not provide a solution in the situation in which a person incurs a contingent liability while solvent and that liability vests after presentation of a petition. Until the liability vests nothing is owing so that, even if 'due' were interpreted as meaning 'owing' rather than merely 'payable', the liability in question could not be set off. Yet it is difficult to see why a set-off would be objectionable in this situation. If the purpose of section 323(3) is to prevent a creditor buying up liabilities of an insolvent person at a discount with the intention of obtaining payment in full in a subsequent bankruptcy in the form of a set-off against the creditor's own indebtedness, the important point should be whether the creditor had the requisite notice at the time that the parties initially entered into the transaction in question, as opposed to the time that an obligation vested pursuant to it. Accordingly, the better view is that the reference to sums becoming due in section 323(3) contemplates the time that a contract was entered into out of which a liability subsequently arose, rather than the time that the liability actually vested pursuant to it. As long as the creditor did not have notice at the time of entering into the contract, any liability of the debtor which subsequently arises out of the contract should not be precluded from being employed in a set-off merely on the ground that a bankruptcy petition was presented before the liability vested. In essence this appears to have been the position under prior bankruptcy legislation, where the qualification was drafted instead in terms of whether the creditor had notice of an available act of bankruptcy at the time that credit was given to the debtor.[148] For example, when it was held that an accommodation acceptor or indorser of a bill of exchange could employ his claim for an indemnity in a set-off in the drawer's bankruptcy, the pleadings were framed in terms that the acceptor or indorser gave credit for the purpose of the qualification when he accepted or indorsed the bill, as distinct from when his claim for an indemnity subsequently vested by payment.[149]

Admittedly the suggested interpretation of 'due' may be regarded as strained. Moreover, it would mean that 'due' has a different meaning in this context than in section 323(2). Subsection (2) provides that an account shall be taken of what is due from each party to the other. It is apparent that 'due' for this purpose means 'owing'. Unless there is an amount owing, there is nothing that can be set off.[150] While there is a presumption that a word appearing in different parts of the same section of an Act of Parliament has the same meaning,[151] this is not an invariable rule,[152] and the set-off section should be regarded as an exception. If 'due' when it appears in the qualification is not given the wide meaning suggested, it would have the result that a contingent liability of a bankrupt in the vast majority of cases could not be the subject of a set-off if the contingency occurs after the occurrence of the bankruptcy itself, even though in many situations it now appears established that a contingent debt can be set off.[153] In this regard, the bankruptcy Acts of 1825 and 1849 both stipulated that a proof could be lodged in respect of a debt which was still contingent at the time of the bankruptcy,[154] and also specifically provided that all provable

---

[147] See also *In re Washington Diamond Mining Company* [1893] 3 Ch. 95, and generally section 9.3.1 below.

[148] See e.g. the Bankruptcy Act 1914, s. 31. In *Old Style Confections Pty. Ltd.* v. *Microbyte Investments Pty. Ltd.* (1994) 15 ACSR 191 Hayne J. held that, in the case of a licence fee payable periodically, credit was not given (for the purpose of the Australian Corporations Law, s. 553C(2)) each time that an instalment of the licence fee became payable, but rather when the transaction was entered into which gave rise to the fee.

[149] *Hulme* v. *Muggleston* (1837) 3 M & W 30; *Russell* v. *Bell* (1841) 8 M & W 277; *Bittleston* v. *Timmis* (1845) 1 CB 389. The set-off section in issue in these cases was s. 50 of (1825) 6 Geo. IV, c. 16, which provided that the creditor claiming the benefit of a set-off must not have had 'when such credit was given, notice of an act of bankruptcy by such bankrupt committed'.

[150] See generally the discussion of the nature of insolvency set-off in section 2.12 below. In the case of a contingent liability of a bankrupt or a company in liquidation, the trustee in bankruptcy or the liquidator is required to value the liability for the purpose of proof. See the Insolvency Act, s. 322 and Rule 4.86 of the Insolvency Rules. The provable amount resulting from the valuation may be regarded as the sum 'due' for the purpose of the set-off section.

[151] *Black-Clawson International Ltd.* v. *Papierwerke Waldhof-Aschaffenburg A-G* [1975] AC 591, 651.

[152] See e.g. *Doe d Angell* v. *Angell* (1846) 9 QB 328, 355; *In re Smith; Green* v. *Smith* (1883) 24 Ch. D 672, 678; *Clyne* v. *Deputy Commissioner of Taxation* (1982) 150 CLR 1, 10, 15.   [153] See section 4.3 below.

[154] See (1825) 6 Geo. IV, c. 16, s. 56 and the Bankrupt Law Consolidation Act 1849, s. 177.

debts could be set off.[155] As Sir George Jessel M.R. once remarked, the whole tendency of the history of the bankruptcy legislation has been to extend the principle upon which the right of set-off is based,[156] and it would be strange if in this context it has been narrowed. The courts have emphasized that the right of set-off should be given the widest possible scope,[157] which suggests that they would lean towards an interpretation of 'due' in section 323(3) that would not restrict the availability of the right in comparison with the previously accepted position, in the absence of a compelling policy reason for doing so. Nevertheless, the uncertainty surrounding the proper meaning of section 323(3) is unsatisfactory, and it would be appropriate for Parliament to clarify the position.

Consider that a debt is assigned before the bankruptcy or liquidation of the debtor. The qualification to the set-off section provides that a sum due from the bankrupt or the company to another party cannot be included in an account if that other party had the requisite notice at the time that the sums became 'due'. Shea would appear to be correct in his view that this refers to the time that sums became due to the person asserting the right to the set-off, i.e. the assignee.[158] If the assignee did not have notice at the time that sums first became due on the assigned debt to the assignor, but he did at the time of the assignment itself, he should not be entitled to employ the debt in a set-off.

A noticeable feature of section 323(3) is that it only prevents a set-off in relation to sums due *from* the bankrupt after notice of the petition. It does not apply when sums become due to the bankrupt after notice. In Australia, on the other hand, the set-off section[159] covers both sides of the account. Moreover, it is drafted in terms similar to the provision formerly applicable in England,[160] in that it refers to credit being given rather than sums becoming due, so that the above discussion of the difficulty in the meaning of 'due' does not apply. In bankruptcy a creditor is not entitled to claim the benefit of a set-off if at the time of giving credit to the person who

---

[155] See s. 50 of (1825) 6 Geo. IV, c. 16, and the Bankrupt Law Consolidation Act 1849, s. 171.

[156] *Peat* v. *Jones & Co.* (1881) 8 QBD 147, 149. See also Lord Hanworth MR in *In re Fenton; ex parte Fenton Textile Association Ltd.* [1931] 1 Ch. 85, 107.

[157] *Eberle's Hotels and Restaurant Co. Ltd.* v. *E. Jonas & Brothers* (1887) 18 QBD 459, 465; *Day & Dent Constructions Pty. Ltd.* v. *North Australian Properties Pty. Ltd.* (1982) 150 CLR 85, 108; *Gye* v. *McIntyre* (1991) 171 CLR 609, 619; *Central Brake Service (Sydney) Pty. Ltd.* v. *Central Brake Service (Newcastle) Pty. Ltd.* (1992) 27 NSWLR 406, 411. See also *Peat* v. *Jones & Co.* (1881) 8 QBD 147, 150 per Cotton L.J.; *Mersey Steel and Iron Company* v. *Naylor, Benzon, & Co.* (1882) 9 QBD 648, 660–1.

[158] Shea, 'Further Reflections on Statutory Set-off' (1987) 3 *Journal of International Banking Law* 183, 184. See also *Re Citizens Investments Pty. Ltd.* (1994) 14 ACSR 575.

[159] Bankruptcy Act 1966 (Cth.), s. 86(2) and, for companies, the Corporations Law, s. 553C(2).   [160] See the Bankruptcy Act 1914, s. 31.

became bankrupt or at the time of receiving credit from that person he had notice of an available act of bankruptcy. An available act of bankruptcy is an act of bankruptcy committed within 6 months of the presentation of the petition,[161] while notice of the act means such knowledge of the act and its attendant circumstances, conditions and consequences as are necessary to make it an act of bankruptcy.[162] In company liquidation, section 553C(2) of the Corporations Law prohibits a set-off if at the time of receiving or giving credit the person had notice of the fact that the company was insolvent.

2.8 TEMPORARY SUSPENSION OF MUTUAL CREDIT

The insolvency set-off section requires that there be mutual credits, mutual debts or other mutual dealings as at the relevant date for determining rights of set-off. However, a right of set-off may still be available notwithstanding a temporary suspension of mutuality either on or after[163] the relevant date.[164] In *Bolland* v. *Nash*[165] a bill of exchange had been accepted by a creditor of the bankrupts, and having come into the hands of the bankrupts, it was indorsed by them before their bankruptcy to a third person. After the bankruptcy the bill was dishonoured by the creditor, and was then returned to the bankrupts as indorsers. It was held that the creditor could set off his liability on the bill against a separate debt owing to him by the bankrupt, even though at the date of the bankruptcy itself the bill was in the hands of the third party so that at the date there was not mutual credit as between the creditor and the bankrupt. Conversely, in *Collins* v. *Jones*,[166] it was the bankrupt acceptor who dishonoured a bill,

---

[161] See the Bankruptcy Act 1966 (Cth.), ss. 5 and 44(1)(c). In the case of an assignment, the 'time of giving credit' for the purpose of s. 86(2) is the time when the assignment became effective. See *Southern Cross Construction Limited (In Liquidation)* v. *Southern Cross Club Limited* [1973] 1 NZLR 708.

[162] *Central Brake Service (Sydney) Pty. Ltd.* v. *Central Brake Service (Newcastle) Pty. Ltd.* (1992) 27 NSWLR 406, 412, referring to *Re Hardman* (1932) 4 ABC 207, 212.

[163] See in this regard *In re Anglo-Greek Steam Navigation and Trading Company; Carralli & Haggard's Claim* (1869) LR 4 Ch. App. 174.

[164] This is also the case for the proof of debts. See for example *Joseph* v. *Orme* (1806) 2 Bos. & Pul. (NR) 180, where the indorser had been obliged to take up the bill again after the acceptor's bankruptcy, though compare *Ex parte Isbester* (1810) 1 Rose 20.

[165] (1828) 8 B & C 105. *Bolland* v. *Nash* was followed by Selwyn L.J. as an alternative ground for his decision in *In re Anglo-Greek Steam Navigation and Trading Company* (1869) LR 4 Ch. App. 174. See also *Ex parte Banes; re the Royal British Bank* (1857) 28 LTOS 296.

[166] (1830) 10 B & C 777. See also *Ex parte Hastie and Hutchinson, in re Alexander and Co.* (1850) 1 Fonbl. 59, 14 LTOS 402; *McKinnon* v. *Armstrong Brothers & Co.* (1877) 2 App. Cas. 531; *Hiley* v. *The Peoples Prudential Assurance Co. Ltd.* (1938) 60 CLR 468, 501. A similar principle applies in the context of receivership. See *Handley Page Ltd.* v. *Commissioners of Customs and Exercise and Rockwell Machine Tool Company Ltd.* [1970] 2 Lloyd's Rep. 459.

and a debtor of the bankrupt who had indorsed it prior to the bankruptcy was forced to take it up again as indorser after the bankruptcy. Once again, it was held that the creditor could set off the claim on the bill against an indebtedness that he owed to the bankrupt acceptor, despite the absence of mutual credit between the parties when the bankruptcy occurred. This exception can also apply when a creditor assigns the debt owing to him by way of security to a third party. If after the bankruptcy of either the creditor or the debtor the debt is redeemed by the creditor, it can be the subject of a set-off between them.[167] The important point in these cases is that the debt was taken up again as a result of a prior obligation[168] or a prior right of redemption. Unless this limitation is imposed, a debtor of the bankrupt would be able to buy up at a discount any liabilities of the bankrupt that had passed through his hands, and yet be able to obtain the full value of those liabilities by means of a set-off.[169] Obviously this would be unfair to the general body of creditors, and the courts have emphasized that the buying-up of liabilities in order to obtain rights of set-off should not be encouraged.[170]

The essence of a set-off on this ground is that there was merely a temporary suspension of mutual credit. If there never was mutuality prior to the relevant date in relation to the debt in question and the cross-debt sought to be set off, the person upon acquiring the debt will not be entitled to employ it in a set-off. This may apply, for example, when a person has contracted with a creditor to take an assignment of a debt upon the occurrence of an event which occurs after the relevant date for determining rights of set-off in the debtor's bankruptcy. In such a case, even though the debt was acquired pursuant to a pre-existing obligation, there never was

---

[167] See *Hiley* v. *The Peoples Prudential Assurance Co. Ltd.* (1938) 60 CLR 468, where the debt in question was redeemed as part of a compromise rather than by payment to the assignee of the secured amount. *In re City Life Assurance Co. Ltd.; Stephenson's Case* [1926] 1 Ch. 191, 214 was distinguished on the ground that the mortgages in that case had not been redeemed.

[168] See *Collins* v. *Jones* (1830) 10 B & C 777, 782, and also Robson, *Law of Bankruptcy* (7th edn., 1894), 367. Compare *Ex parte Isbester* (1810) 1 Rose 20 in the context of proof of debts.

[169] In the absence of fraud in the inception or preparation of a bill of exchange, a discounter is entitled to prove for its full value. See *In re Gomersall* (1875) 1 Ch. D 137, 146–7 per Baggallay J.A. In *Stonehouse* v. *Read* (1825) 3 B & C 669, an accommodation acceptor on various bills had entered into a composition with the holders of the bills, so that the bills were delivered up to him upon payment of a sum less than their full face value. Since the composition had been effected solely for the relief of the acceptor, and not for the drawer, the acceptor was entitled to a set-off in the drawer's bankruptcy to the extent of the full face value of the bills.

[170] *In re Moseley Green Coal and Coke Co. Ltd.; Barrett's Case (No. 2)* (1865) 4 De G J & S 756, 760; *Day & Dent Constructions Pty. Ltd.* v. *North Australian Properties Pty. Ltd.* (1982) 150 CLR 85, 95.

mutuality prior to the relevant date so as to entitle the person to employ the debt in a set-off as against the bankrupt debtor.

If a bankrupt prior to his bankruptcy had deposited by way of mortgage with a third party a bill of exchange accepted by a person who is a creditor of the bankrupt on another transaction, and furthermore the third party mortgagee is in a position to satisfy the mortgage debt from other securities without recourse to the bill, the case will be treated as one in which the bill has remained in the possession of the bankrupt,[171] and the acceptor will be permitted to employ his liability in a set-off when the bill comes back to the bankrupt. Nor will it be fatal to this result if, after the bankruptcy, the mortgagee, instead of having recourse to the other securities, had called upon the acceptor to pay and the acceptor had paid the amount of the bill. If in fact the mortgage debt was sufficiently secured by other sources, the bankrupt's trustee may be ordered to repay to the acceptor the amount paid to the mortgagee on account of the mortgage debt so that a set-off may proceed.[172] This principle should not be confined to bills of exchange, but should apply in the case of any debt which is assigned by way of security.

2.9 THE NECESSITY FOR CROSS-DEMANDS

As in the case of any set-off, set-off in bankruptcy and company liquidation depends upon the existence of cross-demands between the parties to the proposed set-off. Consider, for example, that a bank has made a loan to a customer on the security of a deposit provided by a third party. If the third party has not assumed a personal liability in respect of the customer's debt, whether on the basis of a joint or a joint and several liability or as a guarantor, the case is not one of mutual cross-demands between the bank and the third party. Nor, if the bank has gone into liquidation, can the bank's claim against the customer be set off against its liability to the third party on the deposit, because the requirement of mutuality is lacking.[173] Rather, the liquidator is entitled to sue the customer on the loan and to confine the third party to a proof in the liquidation in respect of the deposit,[174] subject, however, to any contractual limitation on the right to recover all or part of the deposit until repayment of the loan in full.[175]

---

[171] See also *In re Anglo-Greek Steam Navigation and Trading Company; Carralli & Haggard's Claim* (1869) LR 4 Ch. App. 174, in which bills of exchange were indorsed to an agent solely for the purpose of collection.

[172] *Ex parte Staddon; in re Wise* (1843) 3 Mont. D & De G 256, 12 LJ Bcy. 39.

[173] See Ch. 7.

[174] *Lord* v. *Direct Acceptance Corporation Ltd.* (1993) 32 NSWLR 362; *Morris* v. *Agrichemicals Ltd.* Court of Appeal, 20 December 1995.

[175] See the discussion in *Morris* v. *Agrichemicals Ltd.* 20 December 1995.

2.10 ENFORCEABLE DEMANDS

A creditor may not prove in a bankruptcy or a company liquidation for a debt owing to him which is unenforceable, as, for example, because of the expiration of a limitation period.[176] Further, because the set-off section only applies when the creditor has a provable debt,[177] this unenforceable debt similarly cannot be subject to a set-off.[178] Consider, however, that it is the debt owing to the bankrupt, or the company, which is unenforceable. There is nothing in the language of the set-off section itself to suggest that this may not be set off. While the debt may not be enforceable, it is still an existing debt and, if the person liable on the debt in turn has a provable claim against the bankrupt or the company, it may well be said that there are mutual debts which, according to the set-off section, must be set against each other. The creditor would regard this as unfair. In the absence of a set-off, he would have been entitled to receive a dividend on the provable debt, and at the same time he could not have been sued on his unenforceable liability. The effect of setting off the unenforceable liability against the provable debt would be to deprive him of the dividend that he otherwise would have received. While the set-off section on its face appears to apply, the courts nevertheless may incline against this result on the ground that the purpose of the set-off section is to do substantial justice between the parties,[179] and a set-off in this situation is hardly just.

2.11 CONTRACTING OUT OF INSOLVENCY SET-OFF

2.11.1 The prohibition

The House of Lords in *National Westminster Bank Limited* v. *Halesowen Presswork & Assemblies Ltd.*[180] held that the set-off section in the insolvency legislation is mandatory in its operation, so that the parties to mutual dealings cannot contract out of its terms. This has since been followed in Australia[181] and New Zealand.[182] If it is not possible to contract out of the terms of the set-off section, it should not be possible to waive the operation of the section,[183] and nor could the creditor be

---

[176] *Ex parte Dewdney* (1809) 15 Ves. Jun. 479.
[177] This is apparent from the Insolvency Act, s. 323(1) and the Insolvency Rules, r. 4.90(1).
[178] *Pott* v. *Clegg* (1847) 16 M & W 321.
[179] *Forster* v. *Wilson* (1843) 12 M & W 191, 203–4.
[180] [1972] AC 785. See also *Stein* v. *Blake* [1995] 2 All ER 961.
[181] *Re Paddington Town Hall Centre Ltd.* (1979) 41 FLR 239. In *Gye* v. *McIntyre* (1991) 171 CLR 609, 622 the High Court described this as 'the traditional and better view'.
[182] *Rendell* v. *Doors and Doors Ltd.* [1975] 2 NZLR 191.
[183] *Re Cushla Ltd.* [1979] 3 All ER 415, 423.

estopped by his conduct from asserting a right of set-off otherwise available.[184] However, while Lord Kilbrandon in *Halesowen* agreed with the view that terms of the set-off section are mandatory, he expressed reservations about the desirability of preserving the rule.[185] Subsequently the Cork Committee reiterated his Lordship's call for legislative intervention in this area, and recommended that *Halesowen* be reversed.[186] As a result of the decision in that case, whenever a company which is indebted to a bank attempts to realize its assets for the benefit of its creditors generally, or to arrange a moratorium, if properly advised it should open a new account with a different bank in order to ensure that future credits instead do not solely benefit the first bank in the event of the company's winding up in the form of a set-off against the debt. In the opinion of the Cork Committee this is an unnecessary and undesirable complication. It is difficult to see any convincing reason why a creditor who otherwise would be benefited by a set-off should not be permitted to renounce that benefit, with a consequent increase in the value of the assets available for distribution generally, and it is unfortunate that the Cork proposal has not been included in the Insolvency Act.

In *Halesowen* Lord Simon of Glaisdale [187] justified the House of Lords' view on two grounds. The first is the mandatory language appearing in the set-off section, which provides that an account 'shall' be taken and that the sums due on each side of the account 'shall' be set-off.[188] But, in addition, he supported their Lordships' view on the basis of an issue of policy, that the set-off section appears in a part of the insolvency legislation which lays down a procedure for a proper and orderly administration of a bankrupt's estate, and that this is a matter in which the commercial community has an interest. It is not clear why the setting off of cross-demands should be regarded as necessary for a proper and orderly administration of the estate, though Vinelott J. suggested a reason in *Re Maxwell Communications Corp plc (No 2)*.[189] If a creditor could waive his right of set-off, he might

---

[184] *Re Paddington Town Hall Centre Ltd.* (1979) 41 FLR 239. Compare *Hunter* v. *The Official Assignee of Bispham* (1898) 17 NZLR 175.

[185] His Lordship said that 'such a rule . . . may be expected to form a serious embarrassment to those wishing to adopt the beneficial course of agreeing to moratoria for the assistance of a business in financial difficulties'. [1972] AC 785, 824.

[186] *Cork Committee Report*, 305–6. If this recommendation is ever adopted, then obviously any agreement should be such that it was intended to survive bankruptcy or winding-up proceedings. Compare in this regard *Victoria Products Ltd.* v. *Tosh and Company Ltd.* (1940) 165 LT 78; *Ex parte Fletcher; in re Vaughan* (1877) 6 Ch. D 350; *National Westminster Bank Ltd.* v. *Halesowen Presswork & Assemblies Ltd.* [1972] AC 785.

[187] [1972] AC 785, 808–9. See also Viscount Dilhorne (at 805) and Lord Kilbrandon (at 824).

[188] Compare the New Zealand legislation considered in *Rendell* v. *Doors and Doors Ltd.* [1975] 2 NZLR 191, which provided that a debt 'may' be set off, though Chilwell J. nevertheless followed *Halesowen* and held that the section is mandatory.

[189] [1993] 1 WLR 1402, 1411.

then prove in the bankruptcy and leave it to the trustee to recover the debt due to the estate in proceedings that might be protracted and expensive, and which might not result in the recovery of the full amount of the debt. Vinelott J. said that in the meantime the distribution of the insolvent estate might be held up, and a question might arise whether the creditor would be entitled to a dividend while proceedings to recover the debt due from him were on foot. This last comment is the key to the issue. If it were indeed possible to contract out of the right of set-off, and a creditor had done so, the rule in *Cherry* v. *Boultbee*[190] should apply so that, when the creditor sought to participate in the fund represented by the insolvent's estate by claiming a dividend, he would be told that he already had an asset of the estate, in the form of his own indebtedness, which should be appropriated as satisfaction of the right to the dividend.[191] Vinelott J. was concerned that the trustee in bankruptcy or the liquidator may have to undertake protracted and expensive legislation. If the purpose of the litigation was to *establish* the creditor's liability, in circumstances where the creditor was denying that he was liable and at the same time was claiming a dividend on the bankrupt's or the company's liability to him, presumably this would have to be undertaken in any event before the set-off could be accepted. If, however, his Lordship had in mind proceedings merely to enforce an otherwise admitted liability, the application of *Cherry* v. *Boultbee* should obviate that concern. The adoption of a rule that a creditor can renounce the benefit of any right of set-off that otherwise may be available to him in the insolvency of the debtor would have the effect of increasing the estate available for distribution to the other creditors, and it is difficult to see what policy ground there is which is sufficient to override this benefit.

2.11.2 *Agreement not to prove*

While it appears that the parties to mutual dealings cannot contract out of the right of set-off in insolvency, a creditor may agree not to prove for his debt in the debtor's bankruptcy or liquidation. In such a case there would not be a creditor proving or claiming to prove for a debt, so that the prerequisite to the operation of the set-off section to this effect in section 323(1) of the Insolvency Act and Rule 4.90(1) of the Insolvency Rules would not be satisfied.[192] By this method a creditor can indeed renounce a

---

[190] (1839) 4 My. & Cr. 442, discussed in Ch. 10.

[191] Williams J. in *Fused Electrics Pty. Ltd.* v. *Donald* [1995] 2 Qd. R 7 was not convinced that *Cherry* v. *Boultbee* applies in the context of a company liquidation, though the cases suggest otherwise. See section 10.3 below.

[192] *Kitchen's Trustee* v. *Madders* [1950] 1 Ch. 134.

right of set-off, although it comes at a cost. The creditor gives up not only the set-off but also the right to a dividend on the debt owing to him.

2.11.3 Subordinated debt

While it is a basic principle of insolvency law that the debts of a bankrupt or a company in liquidation (other than preferential and secured debts) must be paid *pari passu*,[193] recent case law suggests that this does not render subordination agreements ineffective. Under a subordination agreement, a creditor agrees that a debt owing to him is to be subordinated, or postponed, to debts owing to other unsubordinated creditors, so that the subordinated creditor is not to be paid anything until the unsubordinated creditors have been paid in full. One method of effectively subordinating a debt is for the creditor to agree to hold the debt or its proceeds on trust for other creditors,[194] or to assign the benefit of the debt to those creditors, so that they obtain the benefit of the debt in question.[195] However, in *Re Maxwell Corporation Corp plc (No 2)*[196] Vinelott J. held that a simple contractual subordination, without a trust or an assignment, similarly is effective in the insolvency of the debtor. The courts have expressed a similar view in Australia.[197] Contractual subordination has been said[198] not to infringe the requirement of a *pari passu* distribution because it does not lessen the rights of creditors who are not a

---

[193] For voluntary liquidations, see the Insolvency Act 1986, s. 107. The same principle applies to compulsory liquidations. See r. 4.181 of the Insolvency Rules, and *Webb* v. *Smith* (1872) LR 5 HL 711, 735. For bankruptcies see s. 328(3) of the Insolvency Act.

[194] The distinction between a trust of a debt and a trust of the proceeds of a debt when received may be important in relation to set-off. In the former case a declaration of trust by the subordinated creditor will mean that mutuality will be lacking between the subordinated debt and a separate debt owing by the subordinated creditor to the debtor. If, however, the trust only attaches to the proceeds of the debt once received, the subordinated creditor will still have the beneficial title to the debt itself, so that the debt and the subordinated creditor's separate indebtedness would be mutual. As Lord Templeman remarked in *Barclays Bank Ltd.* v. *TOSG Trust Fund Ltd.* [1984] 1 AC 626, 674 (though in another context), equity does not overlook the distinction between a debt and a dividend on a debt. Before bankruptcy or liquidation, the question of a set-off under the Statutes of Set-off may depend, not only on whether the subordination agreement has given rise to a trust of the debt, but also whether the debt is enforceable at that time. See *Atlantic Acceptance Corporation Ltd.* v. *Burns & Dutton Construction (1962) Ltd.* (1970) 14 DLR (3d) 175.

[195] See *Re Maxwell Communications Corp plc (No. 2)* [1993] 1 WLR 1402, 1404–5, 1416, referring to *Re British and Commonwealth Holdings plc (No. 3)* [1992] 1 WLR 672.

[196] [1993] 1 WLR 1402. See also *Cheah* v. *Equiticorp Finance Group Ltd.* [1992] 1 AC 472, 477 (Privy Council).

[197] *Horne* v. *Chester and Fein Property Developments Pty. Ltd.* [1987] VR 913; *United States Trust Company of New York* v. *Australia & New Zealand Banking Group Ltd.* (1993) 11 ACLC 707, affirmed (1995) 37 NSWLR 131; *Re NIAA Corporation Ltd.* (1993) 12 ACSR 141. See now s. 563C of the Corporations Law in the context of company liquidation.

[198] See Southwell J. in the Victorian Supreme Court in *Horne* v. *Chester and Fein Property Developments Pty. Ltd.* [1987] VR 913.

party to it, although this explanation has not been universally accepted.[199]

If contractual subordination is recognized as being effective, it is apparent that the effect of the subordination nevertheless would be defeated if the creditor could set off the subordinated debt against a separate debt owing to him by the debtor in the latter's bankruptcy or liquidation. The better view, however, is that the subordinated creditor's debt cannot give rise to a set-off.[200] There are two reasons for this. The first is that an agreement for subordination of a debt has the consequence that, until the debts of the unsubordinated creditors have been paid in full, the subordinated creditor's debt is not provable. If the debt is not provable, it cannot be the subject of a set-off, since it is a prerequisite to the operation of the set-off section that there be a creditor 'proving or claiming to prove' for a debt.[201] But even if contractual subordination does not preclude the creditor from proving, and instead has the effect only of postponing his provable debt to the provable debts of the unsubordinated creditors in the distribution of the estate, the subordinated creditor should still not be able to employ it in a set-off because, until the subordinated creditors have been paid in full, nothing is due to the subordinated creditor, including by way of dividend.[202] The set-off section provides that

---

[199] See Goode, *Legal Problems of Credit and Security* (2nd edn., 1988), 96.

[200] The Partnership Act 1890, s. 3 provides that, if a person lends money in return for a share of profits in a business, and the borrower becomes bankrupt, the lender shall not be entitled to 'recover' anything in respect of the loan until the claims of the other creditors of the borrower have been satisfied. In *Ex parte Sheil; in re Longeran* (1877) 4 Ch. D 789, 791 James L.J. suggested during argument that a similar provision in the Partnership Law Amendment Act 1865 would not have prevented the lender from setting off his claim on the loan against a separate indebtedness to the borrower. However, this conclusion turned on the meaning of 'recover' in the legislation. A set-off was not thought to be prohibited because it does not involve any form of recovery. Accordingly, James L.J.'s comment is not an authority against the view expressed in the text in relation to set-off against subordinated debt generally. In *Atlantic Acceptance Corporation Ltd.* v. *Burns & Dutton Construction (1962) Ltd.* (1970) 14 DLR (3d) 175 it was held that a subordinated debt could not be set off, though that case concerned a claim for a set-off under the Statutes of Set-off where the debtor was not in liquidation. The debt could not be the subject of a set-off under the Statutes because according to its terms it was unenforceable at that time. See section 1.2.10 above.

[201] See the Insolvency Act, s. 323(1) and, for companies, the Insolvency Rules, r. 4.90(1).

[202] Contractual subordination is sometimes explained on the basis that the subordinated debt is subject to a contingency, the contingency being that the unsubordinated debts have been paid in full. Accordingly, if the debtor's assets are insufficient to pay the unsubordinated creditors' claims in full, the value of the subordinated debt will be nil for the purpose of proof. See e.g. in Australia *United States Trust Company of New York* v. *Australia & New Zealand Banking Group Ltd.* (1993) 11 ACLC 707, 711; *Re NIAA Corporation Ltd.* (1993) 12 ACSR 141, 153. However, Vinelott J. in *Re Maxwell Communications Corp plc (No. 2)* [1993] 1 WLR 1402, 1418 doubted that a subordinated debt is accurately described as a contingent liability. Indeed, the contingent theory does not adequately reflect the intended effect of subordination in all cases. Consider that the value of the debtor's assets exceeds the amount of the unsubordinated debts, but is less than the aggregate of the subordinated and the unsubordinated debts. According to the contingent theory, the trustee in bankruptcy or the

'the sums due from one party shall be set off against the sums due from the other'.[203] If there is nothing due, there is nothing that can be set off. It may transpire that the debtor's estate is indeed sufficient to pay something to the subordinated creditor after payment in full of the unsubordinated creditors' debts. In such a case the subordinated debt should be capable of being employed in a set-off, because there is a debt which is then 'due' to the subordinated creditor. But this should only occur if the debtor's estate is sufficient to pay the unsubordinated creditors without taking into account the asset of the estate represented by the claim against the subordinated creditor, because obviously this particular asset would disappear if the subordinated creditor could utilize it in a set-off.

Section 74(2)(f) of the Insolvency Act 1986 provides that a sum due to a member of a company in that capacity is not deemed to be a debt of the company payable to that member in a case of competition between himself and external creditors, though it may be taken into account for the purpose of the final adjustment of rights as between members. The section effects a statutory subordination,[204] so that the sum due could not be employed by the member in a set-off against a separate liability owing to the company where this would operate to the detriment of the external creditors. A similar interpretation would apply in Australia in relation to section 563A of the Corporations Law, which provides that payment of a debt owed by a company to a member in that capacity is to be 'postponed' to other creditors.

2.12 THE NATURE OF INSOLVENCY SET-OFF

2.12.1 *Automatic or procedural?*

A fundamental issue in relation to the set-off section in the insolvency legislation is whether it operates automatically upon the occurrence of a bankruptcy or a winding-up so as to bring about a set-off at that date, or whether the section is procedural in its operation, in the sense that it requires the taking of an account at some stage during the bankruptcy or liquidation and, until this occurs, the demands retain their separate identities. In this regard, there is no doubt that the date of the bankruptcy,

---

liquidator would be required to value the subordinated debt. In the situation posited above, the subordinated debt would have a value, because there are assets available to pay part of it after satisfying the unsubordinated debts. The difficulty is that, once a value is put upon the subordinated debt, that value under normal principles would be provable and would rank *pari passu* with the unsubordinated debts. Obviously, this is not the intended effect of subordination.

[203] See the Insolvency Act, s. 323(2) and, for companies, the Insolvency Rules, r. 4.90(2).
[204] See e.g. the discussion in *Soden* v. *British & Commonwealth Holdings Plc* [1995] BCC 531.

or, as the case may be, of the winding-up is the date for determining what mutual debts, credits, and dealings can be brought into an account.[205] But it does not necessarily follow that this is also the time when the demands are actually set against each other to produce a balance.

The key provision in the insolvency set-off section is the stipulation that, 'An account shall be taken of what is due from each party to the other in respect of the mutual dealings and the sums due from one party shall be set off against the sums due from the other'. On its face this may be thought to support a procedural operation, given that it appears to require the taking of an account of amounts which are due at the date of the account. The account could be taken either by the trustee in bankruptcy or by the court in proceedings before it. In the case of a trustee, the obvious opportunity for taking an account is when a proof is lodged in the bankruptcy, though there is nothing in the language of the set-off section to suggest that the trustee cannot act otherwise than in that context. This does not mean that the trustee would have a discretion as to whether a set-off should occur,[206] and nor is it inconsistent with the view that set-off in insolvency cannot be contracted out of,[207] particularly given that Lord Simon of Glaisdale who, as one of the majority in the *Halesowen* case[208] held that contracting out is not possible, nevertheless regarded the section as prescribing a course of procedure.[209] In other words, it lays down a code of procedure[210] which must be followed regardless of any agreement to the contrary. Similarly, while Hallett J. in *Victoria Products Ltd.* v. *Tosh & Co.*[211] agreed that the set-off section cannot be contracted out of, he nevertheless described it in terms of laying down a process. In *Stein* v. *Blake*[212] the Court of Appeal held that the procedural view is correct, and this was also accepted by Rattee J. in *Re Bank of Credit and Commerce International SA (No. 8)*.[213] In Australia, Gummow and von Doussa JJ. in the Federal Court in *Gye* v. *McIntyre*[214] said that the set-off section 'is directed to a particular

---

[205] *Ellis & Company's Trustee* v. *Dixon-Johnson* [1924] 1 Ch. 342, 356, and see generally section 2.7 above.

[206] A creditor could request the trustee to take an account and, if the trustee refused, or the creditor was otherwise dissatisfied with the result, the creditor could ask the court to review the decision under the Insolvency Act 1986, s. 303. See *Stein* v. *Blake* [1994] Ch. 16, 29. Moreover, if the trustee assigned the bankrupt's claim against the creditor to a third party, the third party would take subject to the right of set-off on the basis of taking subject to equities.

[207] See section 2.11 above. [208] [1972] AC 785.

[209] [1972] AC 785, 808. This is also consistent with his Lordship's reference (at 808) to the imposition of a duty on a public officer. The officer that he had in mind presumably was a trustee in bankruptcy, with the duty being the taking of an account. This comment would hardly have been apt if set-off was regarded as something that occurs automatically. Viscount Dilhorne referred (at 305) to the set-off section as 'prescribing the course to be followed in the administration of the bankrupt's property'. [210] [1972] AC 785, 809.

[211] (1940) 165 LT 78, 80. [212] [1994] Ch. 16.

[213] [1995] Ch. 46, 63–4.

[214] *Sub nom. McIntyre* v. *Perkes* (1990) 22 FCR 260, 270.

procedure, the taking of an account', and that the cross-obligations subsist until the account is taken.[215] This was also accepted by Drummond J. in the Federal Court in *Re Capel*.[216] It is apparent that Lord Esher M.R. in *Sovereign Life Assurance Co.* v. *Dodd*[217] considered that the cross-demands in issue in that case were still subsisting at the date of the liquidator's action,[218] which would not have been the case if they had already been extinguished at the date of the liquidation.[219] In a similar vein, Rich J. in the Australian High Court[220] referred with evident approval to Bigham J.'s description of the operation of the set-off section in *In re Daintrey*[221] in terms that, 'the account which the section of the Act directed should be taken is to be taken when the claim on the one side or the other is presented'. Once again, this suggests that an account is required to be taken in respect of subsisting cross-demands. The other judge in the Divisional Court in *Daintrey* was Wright J., who commented that, while the date of the receiving order was the relevant date for determining whether there were mutual dealings, it was in general immaterial whether the amount of a particular liability could have been ascertained at that date, 'provided it can be ascertained when the account is taken'.[222] Similarly Romer L.J. in the Court of Appeal said that, 'It is sufficient if the account can be taken when the set-off arises'.[223]

On the other hand, it is difficult to find clear evidence of the automatic extinguishment theory before 1984,[224] when it was adopted by Neill J. in

---

[215] This also seems to have been the view of Murphy J. in *Day & Dent Constructions Pty. Ltd.* v. *North Australian Properties Pty. Ltd.* (1982) 150 CLR 85, 109.

[216] *Re Capel; ex parte Marac Finance Australia Ltd.* v. *Capel* (1994) 48 FCR 195.

[217] [1892] 2 QB 573.   [218] [1892] 2 QB 573, 578.

[219] This accords with Lord Esher's earlier *dictum* (as Brett J.) in *New Quebrada Company, Ltd.* v. *Carr* (1869) LR 4 CP 651, 653–4, that the set-off section does not extinguish mutual debts. While the House of Lords in *Stein* v. *Blake* [1995] 2 All ER 961, 969 distinguished that dictum on the ground that the language of the set-off section there in issue differed from the current section, the same could not be said of *Sovereign Life* v. *Dodd*.

[220] *Hiley* v. *The Peoples Prudential Assurance Co. Ltd.* (1938) 60 CLR 468, 487.

[221] [1900] 1 QB 546, 568. See also Romer L.J. at 574.

[222] [1900] 1 QB 546, 556–7. Wright J. also noted (at 552) that Lord Selborne in *Ex parte Barnett; in re Deveze* (1874) LR 9 Ch. App. 293, 295 seemed to have considered that a set-off took effect at the time that the creditor came in to prove. Indeed, Lord Selborne was a member of the House of Lords in *Mersey Steel and Iron Co.* v. *Naylor, Benzon & Co.* (1874) 9 App. Cas. 434 when it affirmed an order made by the Court of Appeal ((1882) 9 QBD 648, 672) in an action brought by a liquidator for payment, to the effect that 'the defendants are entitled to set-off against the £1713 *admitted to be due* to the plaintiffs such damages as they the defendants may have sustained' (emphasis added). This contemplated that there was still an amount due to the plaintiffs at the time of the action, notwithstanding the availability of a set-off, and that it was the order of the court itself which brought about the set-off. See also Lord Selborne in *In re Milan Tramways Company; ex parte Theys* (1884) 25 Ch. D 587, 591.

[223] [1900] 1 QB 546, 574. See also *In re Fenton* [1931] 1 Ch. 85, 113.

[224] Admittedly Wright J. in *Watkins* v. *Lindsay and Co.* (1898) 67 LJQB 362, 364 remarked in passing that set-off in bankruptcy is automatic, though the weight to be attached to that is

Farley v. *Housing and Commercial Developments Ltd.*[225] After that judgment, however, it gained rapid support. Some comments in *Gye* v. *McIntyre*[226] suggest that it was favoured by the High Court of Australia on appeal in that case,[227] and it was also accepted by Hoffman L.J. in the Chancery Division, as well as by the Court of Appeal on appeal, in *M. S. Fashions Ltd.* v. *Bank of Credit and Commerce International S.A.*[228] *M. S. Fashions* concerned a bank which had provided an advance to a customer secured by both a guarantee and a cash deposit by the guarantor. The bank went into liquidation and the liquidator, instead of proceeding against the guarantor, made a demand on the debtor, and said that the guarantor should be confined to a proof in the liquidation in respect of the deposit. The Court of Appeal held that there was a right of set-off as between the guarantor and the bank which had the effect of automatically satisfying the guarantor's liablity to the bank, and since the guarantor had paid the debt by means of this set-off the customer could no longer be sued.[229] Following the conflicting decisions by differently constituted Courts of Appeal in *M. S. Fashions* and *Stein* v. *Blake*, the issue came before the House of Lords by way of an appeal in *Stein* v. *Blake*.[230] Their Lordships[231] were unanimous in their view that the automatic extinction theory indeed provides the correct analysis of the operation of the insolvency set-off section, and rejected the argument that the section has a procedural operation.

The issue in *Stein* v. *Blake* was whether a trustee in bankruptcy could assign a debt owing to the bankrupt when the debtor had a cross-claim available for a set-off. The Court of Appeal held that the debt could be assigned. The set-off section was regarded as being procedural in its operation, so that it did not of itself extinguish the mutual debts. For this to occur an account had to be taken,[232] either by the trustee in bankruptcy or by the court. Since this had not occurred at the date of the assignment, it was held that the separate debts retained their separate identities and therefore they could be assigned. This did not mean that the defendant lost the benefit of the set-off otherwise available in the bankruptcy. Because

diminished as a result of his later comment in *Daintrey*, noted above. Mellish L.J. in *Ex parte Barnett; in re Deveze* (1874) LR 9 Ch. App. 293, 297 commented in relation to the insolvency set-off section that, 'I doubt whether it does not affect it even before either party comes in to prove; but, at any rate, when the party does come in to prove, the statute sets the one debt against the other, and that is equivalent to payment'.

[225] (1984) 26 Build. LR 66.   [226] (1991) 171 CLR 609, 622.
[227] Compare, however, the interpretation of those comments by Drummond J. in *Re Capel* (1994) 48 FCR 195, discussed in section 2.12.2 below.
[228] [1993] Ch. 425.
[229] Why was a set-off available as between the guarantor and the bank? See the discussion of the case in section 8.3 below.   [230] [1995] 2 All ER 961.
[231] Lord Keith of Kinkel, Lord Ackner, Lord Lloyd of Berwick, Lord Nicholls of Birkenhead and Lord Hoffman.   [232] See Staughton L.J. at [1994] Ch. 16, 29.

the assignment occurred after the bankruptcy, the assignee would still have taken subject to an equity in the form of the defendant's right of set-off under the insolvency legisation. Nevertheless, on appeal the House of Lords rejected the Court of Appeal's analysis.[233] The judgment of their Lordships was delivered by Lord Hoffman, who had delivered the judgment in the Chancery Division in the *M. S. Fashions* case and had since been elevated to the House of Lords. His view on the point had not changed. He said that insolvency set-off 'is self-executing and takes effect on the bankruptcy date'.[234] Its operation does not depend upon any procedural step, but rather it 'results, as of the bankruptcy date, in only a net balance being owing',[235] so that at that date the cross-claims cease to exist as separate choses in action. Accordingly, it was not possible for a trustee in bankruptcy to assign the debt owing to the bankrupt to the extent that it had already been extinguished by a set-off.

There is no doubt that in many respects the notion of an automatic cancellation of cross-demands at the date of the bankruptcy is a convenient result (though there may be circumstances where the opposite is the case[236]). For example, when an interest-bearing debt is owing to a bankrupt, it prevents an argument that interest continues to run until the account is taken.[237] Furthermore, when a trustee in bankruptcy assigns a debt owing to the bankrupt, and the debtor has a cross-claim available as a set-off, the set-off will have occurred automatically, and the assignee will be bound by it. It would not be necessary for the debtor to insist that the trustee take an account, so as to prevent a situation arising whereby the assignee could take free of the set-off if the bankrupt is discharged from bankruptcy, and as a result is released from his liability to the debtor, before a set-off has occurred.[238] From this perspective *Stein* v. *Blake* is a welcome development. Having said that, there are a number of difficulties with the judgment.

---

[233] [1995] 2 All ER 961.   [234] [1995] 2 All ER 961, 968.

[235] [1995] 2 All ER 961, 967.

[236] The notion of an automatic cancellation may be inconvenient when a trustee in bankruptcy proposes to assign a debt owing to the bankrupt. Neither the trustee nor the bankrupt may be aware that the debtor has a cross-claim extinguishing the debt, for example where the debtor has acquired a bill of exchange accepted by the bankrupt from a third party. Under the automatic approach the debtor will do nothing. There would not be any incentive for him to notify the trustee of the entitlement to a set-off, or indeed to respond to inquiries, since a set-off will have occurred automatically. It may not be until some time later, when the assigned debt matures and the assignee seeks payment, that the set-off comes to light. If set-off was procedural, it is more likely that the trustee would have been informed of the set-off by the debtor, and he could have tempered his dealings with the assignee accordingly.

[237] See section 2.14 below.

[238] *Farley* v. *Housing and Commercial Developments Ltd.* (1984) 26 Build LR 66, though in Australia see *Re Capel; ex parte Marac Finance Australia Ltd.* v. *Capel* (1994) 48 FCR 195, discussed in section 2.12.2 below.

(1) A trustee in bankruptcy may sue for a debt owing to the estate, and the defendant may plead as a defence a set-off under the insolvency legislation. The House of Lords in *Stein* v. *Blake* said that this does not mean that separate claims exist until the court has decided the issue. Rather, their Lordships considered that the litigation is merely part of a process of retrospective calculation, from which it will appear that from the date of the bankruptcy the only chose in action that continued to exist was a claim for the balance.[239] However, this is not the way that the issue appears to have been regarded historically. From early days, the defendant in an action brought against him by assignees in bankruptcy who wished to defend the action on the basis of a set-off would not deny that he was liable to the bankrupt because of a set-off that had already occurred at the date of the bankruptcy. Rather, he would plead that the bankrupt 'was, *and still is*, indebted to the defendant'.[240] A similar form of pleading has continued to be set out in successive editions of *Bullen and Leake* down to the present day.[241] This suggests that the cross-demands have been regarded as still retaining their separate identities at the date of the action, which of course is after the bankruptcy. Indeed, when the Court of Appeal in *Peat* v. *Jones & Co.*[242] confirmed that insolvency set-off can be relied on as a defence to an action at law brought by a trustee in bankruptcy for payment of a debt owing to the bankrupt, Sir George Jessel explained this on the ground that, while the bankruptcy legislation contemplated a set-off occurring in the bankruptcy court, the common law courts considered that it was within 'the equity of the statute' that it should also provide a defence to a trustee's action.[243] However, if the bankruptcy legislation was regarded as bringing about an automatic extinguishment of cross-demands upon the occurrence of a bankruptcy, it would hardly have been necessary for the common law to have recourse to that concept.

---

[239] [1995] 2 All ER 961, 967–8. Compare Bingham J. in *In re Daintrey* [1900] 1 QB 546, 568, who equated the stipulation in the 1883 bankruptcy set-off section (Bankruptcy Act 1883, s. 38) that there should be a person 'proving or claiming to prove a debt under such receiving order' with the notion that there should be a person 'having a right to prove a debt' in the bankruptcy proceedings initiated by the receiving order.

[240] See e.g. *Hulme* v. *Muggleston* (1837) 3 M & W 30, 31; *Russell* v. *Bell* (1841) 8 M & W 277, 278; *Bittleston* v. *Timmis* (1845) 1 CB 389, 391. See also *West* v. *Baker* (1875) 1 Ex. D 44, 45. In *Gibson* v. *Bell* (1835) 1 Bing. NC 743 the defendant pleaded (at 746) that 'the said sum of money still remained unpaid and unsatisfied to the Defendant'.

[241] In the second edition of Bullen & Leake, *Precedents of Pleading* in 1863 the plea was set out (at 580) in terms that a debt owing by the bankrupt 'at the commencement of this suit was and still is due to the defendant'. The substance of the plea was repeated in subsequent editions, save for the 13th edition in 1990, where the plea was set out instead (at 1420–1) in terms that 'there *is* a debt due from the plaintiff to the defendants' (emphasis added). This revised form of plea also suggests a procedural operation to the set-off section.

[242] (1881) 8 QBD 147.

[243] See also *Mersey Steel and Iron Co.* v. *Naylor, Benzon & Co.* (1882) 9 QBD 648, 664; *McIntyre* v. *Perkes* (1990) 22 FCR 260, 270–1 (Federal Court of Australia).

(2) The set-off section stipulates that 'the sums due from one party shall be set off against the sums due from the other'. It is apparent that there must be a sum due on each side of the account at the date that the set-off occurs, which, according to the House of Lords, is the date of the bankruptcy. This requirement would be satisfied in relation to a claim which has accrued and is presently payable at that date. It would also be satisfied in relation to a debt which is presently existing but which is expressed not to be payable until a future date. In this regard, it would be perfectly proper to interpret 'due' as including 'owing, although not payable until some future date'.[244] It may also be accepted that 'due' would encompass a liability which has accrued but which remains to be quantified.[245] Consider, however, a liability which is still contingent at the date of the bankruptcy. If the liability in question is owing *by* the bankrupt, the fact that the liability is contingent at the date of the bankruptcy is not inconsistent with the automatic extinction theory. Debts must be proved according to their value as at the date of the bankruptcy. If a liability of the bankrupt is contingent, the trustee must estimate its value as at that date, and that value may then be proved.[246] This valuation provable in the bankruptcy is regarded as the amount due for the purpose of the administration of the bankruptcy, including in relation to the set-off section. The situation is more difficult, however, when the bankrupt is possessed of a contingent *claim*. Unlike in the case of a bankrupt's contingent liabilities, there is no power in the Insolvency Act for a trustee or the court to value a contingent claim of the bankrupt. Provided that the contingency occurs after the bankruptcy, it should be capable of being employed in a set-off.[247] But, given that there is no power in the insolvency legislation to put a value on the contingent claim as at the date of the bankruptcy, prima facie it seems difficult to say that anything is due in respect of it at that date. In *Stein* v. *Blake*[248] Lord Hoffman sought to explain the position with respect to contingencies by reference to two 'techniques':

The first is to take into account everything which has actually happened between the bankruptcy date and the moment when it becomes necessary to ascertain what, on that date, was the state of account between the creditor and the bankrupt. If by that time the contingency has occurred and the claim has been quantified, then that is the amount which is treated as having been due at the bankruptcy date . . .

---

[244] *Clyne* v. *Deputy Commissioner of Taxation* (1981) 150 CLR 1, 8.

[245] See e.g. *Gye* v. *McIntyre* (1991) 171 CLR 609. See also Malins V.C. in *Booth* v. *Hutchinson* (1872) LR 15 Eq. 30, 34 in the context of the judgment for damages for £50 given after the deed of assignment in relation to the prior breach.

[246] See the Insolvency Act 1986, s. 322 and, for company liquidations, the Insolvency Rules 1986, r. 4.86.   [247] See section 4.4 below.   [248] [1995] 2 All ER 961, 965.

But the winding up of the estate of a bankrupt or an insolvent company cannot always wait until all possible contingencies have happened and all the actual or potential liabilities which existed at the bankruptcy date have been quantified. Therefore the law adopts a second technique, which is to make an estimation of the value of the claim.

Later he remarked that ' "due" merely means treated as having been owing at the bankruptcy date with the benefit of the hindsight and, if necessary, estimation prescribed by the bankruptcy law'.[249]

While this analysis undoubtedly is correct in the case of a contingent liability of a bankrupt, there would still appear to be a question in relation to a bankrupt's claim that was contingent at the bankruptcy date,[250] given that the power of estimation does not apply.[251] In this regard it is important to appreciate that the first technique of hindsight is not independent of the second technique of estimation. Consider the application of the techniques when a bankrupt's contingent liability is in issue. In such a case, a subsequent occurrence of the contingency may be taken into account for the purpose of proof and of set-off, though this is not because the happening of the contingency is accelerated so as to fix the amount of the claim on the basis of the contingency having occurred at the date of the bankruptcy.[252] It is not a matter of deeming a state of affairs to have existed at the bankruptcy date that in fact did not exist. Rather, the insolvency legislation has provided in the case of a contingent liability that a sum is to be regarded as due for the purpose of the administration of the bankruptcy, in the form of the value which the trustee must put on it.[253] This has been interpreted as requiring a valuation as at the date of the bankruptcy,[254] and in taking into account a subsequent occurrence of the contingency the trustee is merely using all the available evidence to ascertain what, with hindsight, was in fact the true value of the liability as at that date.[255] The position is entirely different, however, when a bankrupt's *claim* was still subject to a

---

[249] [1995] 2 All ER 961, 969.

[250] Similarly Lord Hoffman's earlier discussion of contingent claims in the *M. S. Fashions* case [1993] Ch. 425, 435 with respect did not adequately address the issue.

[251] *Sovereign Life Assurance* v. *Dodd* [1992] 2 QB 573, to which Lord Hoffman referred in his judgment [1995] 2 All ER 961, 965, concerned a contingent liability of a company in liquidation, rather than a contingent claim. The full matured value of the policies was allowed to be set off, because that was the provable value. In other words, this was an aspect of the second technique, which only applies to a contingent liability owing by a bankrupt, and not to a contingent claim.

[252] *Ellis & Company's Trustee* v. *Dixon-Johnson* [1924] 1 Ch. 342, 356–7.

[253] A similar principle applies in a company liquidation. See the Insolvency Rules 1986, r. 4.86.

[254] *In re Northern Counties of England Fire Insurance Company; Macfarlane's Claim* (1880) 17 Ch. D 337, 340.

[255] *Ellis & Company's Trustee* v. *Dixon-Johnson* [1924] 1 Ch. 342, 356–7; *In re Dynamics Corporation of America* [1976] 1 WLR 757, 767–8; *Re Hurren* [1982] 3 All ER 982, 987.

contingency when the bankruptcy occurred. In such a case there is no question of a valuation as at the date of the bankruptcy, because there is no machinery in the insolvency legislation for a trustee or the court to put a value on it as at that date.[256] If there is no basis for valuing it as at the date of the bankruptcy, then, unlike a contingent liability of the bankrupt, there is no apparent justification for saying that there was an amount then due for the purpose of the administration of the bankrupt's estate. The set-off section provides that 'the sums due from one party shall be set off against the sums due from the other'. The fundamental point is that it only contemplates a set-off occurring against a sum which is then due,[257] and it seems difficult to assert that a sum was due to the bankrupt at the date of the bankruptcy for the purpose of an automatic set-off occurring at that date if the claim in question was still contingent. Nor would it be satisfactory to suggest that the set-off itself may not occur until after the bankruptcy but that it is then deemed to have occurred retrospectively at the date of the bankruptcy,[258] particularly if the statutory requirements for an insolvency set-off to occur had not been satisfied at that date, and given also the approach of the courts in relation to contingent liabilities.[259]

For example, there have been cases in which property was deposited with a person with authority to sell, and the sale did not occur until after the depositor's bankruptcy,[260] or a policy of insurance was deposited by an insured with a broker with authority to collect the insurance money in the event of a loss, and the loss occurred and the proceeds were received after the insured had become bankrupt.[261] In each case it was held that the claim brought by the assignees or the trustee in bankruptcy of the depositor could

---

[256] *In re Daintrey* [1900] 1 QB 546, 557, 565, 573.

[257] The question is whether 'there was any sum due . . . when the right to set off was claimed . . .'. See Lawrence L.J. in *In re Fenton* [1931] 1 Ch. 85, 113.

[258] Lord Hoffman in his earlier judgment in the *M. S. Fashions* case [1993] Ch. 425, 432 referred to the 'retroactivity principle'. However, 'retroactivity' was used in a different sense, that the account is taken as at the date of the bankruptcy or liquidation, though taking into consideration events which have occurred since the bankruptcy or liquidation. This gives rise to the same issue, that the account could not always be taken as at that date given the requirement of a sum due on each side of the account.

[259] Nor would this approach have any support from the cases dealing with a contract for value to charge future property. In such a case the charge does not attach to the property until it is acquired, but for priority purposes it is regarded as having arisen when the agreement was entered into. The reason for that, however, is that, even before acquisition of the property by the chargor, the chargee is regarded as having something in the nature of an estate or interest which is more than a mere right in contract. See *In re Lind* [1915] 2 Ch. 345, 364, 373–4 and *Federal Commissioner of Taxation* v. *Everett* (1978) 21 ALR 625, 643–4.

[260] *Palmer* v. *Day & Sons* [1895] 2 QB 618; *French* v. *Fenn* (1783) 3 Dougl. 257. See also *Astley* v. *Gurney* (1869) LR 4 CP 714.

[261] *Olive* v. *Smith* (1813) 5 Taunt. 56. See also *Parker* v. *Carter* (1788), unreported but noted in Cooke, *The Bankrupt Laws* (8th edn., 1823) Vol. 1, 578.

be the subject of a set-off. But until the sale occurred, or the insurance proceeds were received in respect of the loss occurring after the bankruptcy, it could hardly be argued, whether with the benefit of hindsight or not, that there was a sum due to the bankrupt. Until the relevant event occurred, there was nothing due. This suggests that bankruptcy set-off was not regarded by the courts as something that occurred automatically at the date of the bankruptcy.[262] Consider also *Graham* v. *Russell*.[263] An underwriter was allowed to set off his liability on a policy in the insured's bankruptcy, even though the loss occurred after the bankruptcy.[264] If there was no loss at the date of the bankruptcy, on what basis could it be said that there was then a sum due from the underwriter to the bankrupt insured for the purpose of a set-off occurring at that date? In *Lee & Chapman's Case*[265] a company had contracted with the Commissioners of Sewers to pave a street. The company went into liquidation before completion of the works, though the liquidator subsequently completed them and claimed the price. The Court of Appeal held that the Commissioners were entitled to a set-off under the Bankruptcy Act 1869 in respect of a damages claim that they had against the company. But once again it would be difficult to argue that the price was due to the company at the date of the liquidation, given that the works had not then been completed. Indeed, Brett M.R. referred in his judgment to 'a right of set-off as between the company in liquidation and these Commissioners accruing *after* the winding-up'.[266]

Admittedly the set-off section in issue in some of these cases did not specifically provide that the debts to be set off had to be 'due'. The section was not drafted in this manner until the 1869 Act,[267] which was similar to the current provision. It has never been suggested, however, that the 1869 Act had the effect of narrowing the scope of insolvency set-off, which would have been the consequence if those early cases were not good

---

[262] See also *Booth* v. *Hutchinson* (1872) LR 15 Eq. 30, 35 with respect to rent accruing to a bankrupt landlord *after* the bankruptcy.   [263] (1816) 5 M & S 498.
[264] The court declined to follow *Glennie* v. *Edmunds* (1813) 4 Taunt. 775. Compare also *Ex parte Blagden* (1815) 19 Ves. Jun. 465.   [265] (1885) 30 Ch. D 216.
[266] (1885) 30 Ch. D 216, 222 (emphasis added).
[267] Prior to the 1869 Act the set-off section in force was the Bankrupt Law Consolidation Act 1849, s. 171 which provided that, where there was mutual credit between a bankrupt and another person, 'the court shall state the account between them, and one debt or demand may be set against another . . .'. The House of Lords in *Stein* v. *Blake* [1995] 2 All ER 961, 969 noted the reference to 'may', and suggested that, because of this, the self-executing nature of the set-off may not have been as fully apparent then as it is today. On the contrary, the stipulation that the court (i.e. the Court of Bankruptcy) 'shall' state the account indicates a procedural operation. Nor has there been any suggestion that the 1869 Act itself may have been the source of a change to a self-executing provision. Indeed, in Robson, *A Treatise on the Law of Bankruptcy* (3rd edn., 1876), 330 the view was expressed in relation to the 1869 section that the principles and practice relating to set-off did not appear to have been changed, and a similar view was expressed in the first edition of Williams, being Williams and Williams, *The New Law and Practice in Bankruptcy* (1870), 51.

law after that Act. On the contrary, as Sir George Jessel M.R. remarked in the context of a discussion of the 1869 Act, the whole tendency of the history of the insolvency legislation has been to extend the principle upon which the right of set-off is founded.[268]

(3) The problem comes even more sharply into focus if one considers the cases dealing with a temporary suspension of mutual credit,[269] such as *Bolland* v. *Nash*.[270] In *Bolland* v. *Nash* a creditor of a firm of bankers accepted two bills of exchange. The bankers discounted the bills, and indorsed them to a third party. The bankers became bankrupt, after which the creditor dishonoured his acceptances. The bills were then returned to the bankrupts as indorsers. It was held that the creditor could set off a debt owing to him by the bankrupts against his liability to them on the bills, the important point being that the bankrupts were required to take up the bills again as a result of a prior obligation. Yet at the date of the bankruptcy the bills were held by the third party, and so it is difficult to see how it could be said that a set-off occurred at that date.[271] Consider also the decision of the High Court of Australia in *Hiley* v. *The Peoples Prudential Assurance Co. Ltd.*[272] A mortgagee had assigned the mortgage to a bank before the mortgagee went into liquidation. After the liquidation the mortgage was transferred back to the mortgagee. When the mortgagee's liquidator brought proceedings to enforce the mortgage debt, it was held that the mortgagor could set off a cross-demand that he had against the mortgagee. The justification for the set-off was that the mortgage had been assigned by way of security, so that the mortgagee had an equity of redemption, and the mortgagee got back the claim by virtue of this right subsisting at the commencement of the winding-up. However, the equity of redemption by itself was not regarded as sufficient to give rise to a set-off, at least to the extent of the amount of the debt in respect of which the mortgage had been assigned by way of security.[273] If the mortgage had not been transferred back, a set-off would not have occurred to the extent of this amount.[274] But, once again, the view that a set-off occurred at the date of the

---

[268] *Peat* v. *Jones & Co.* (1881) 8 QBD 147, 149. See also Brett L.J. (at 149–50), referring to Malins V.C. in *Booth* v. *Hutchinson* (1872) LR 15 Eq. 30, 35 with respect to the addition of 'mutual dealings' to the set-off section; *Sovereign Life Assurance Co.* v. *Dodd* [1892] 2 QB 573, 582; Williams and Williams, *The New Law and Practice in Bankruptcy* (1870), 51.

[269] See section 2.8 above.   [270] (1828) 8 B & C 105.

[271] *Bolland* v. *Nash* was followed by Selwyn L.J. as an alternative ground for his decision in *In re Anglo-Greek Steam Navigation and Trading Company* (1869) LR 4 Ch. App. 174. See also *Ex parte Banes; re the Royal British Bank* (1857) 28 LTOS 296.

[272] (1938) 60 CLR 468.

[273] Compare *Lee & Chapman's Case* (1885) 30 Ch. D 216, explained by Dixon J. in *Hiley* (1938) 60 CLR 468, 497–9.

[274] See *In re City Life Assurance Co. Stephenson's Case* [1926] 1 Ch. 191, 214, explained by Rich J. and Dixon J. in *Hiley* (1938) 60 CLR 468, 488, 501–5.

liquidation would not be easy to explain in this context, given that the mortgage at that date was held by a third party.

(4) Consider the case of a surety who pays the creditor after the principal debtor's bankruptcy. In Australia the High Court held in *Day & Dent Constructions Pty. Ltd.* v. *North Australian Properties Pty. Ltd.*[275] that the surety is entitled to employ the resulting claim for an indemnity in a set-off. This admittedly is contrary to views expressed in the Court of Appeal in *In re A Debtor (No. 66 of 1955)*,[276] though it is consistent with opinions expressed in other cases[277] and as a matter of policy it should be followed.[278] Nevertheless, while in the period before payment to the creditor the surety would have had a contingent claim for an indemnity, the rule against double proof would have had the effect that that claim would not have been provable, and nor would it have given rise to a set-off.[279] In this regard the surety's position as a contingent creditor differs from that of a contingent creditor who does in fact have a provable debt as at the bankruptcy date, which appears to be the situation that the House of Lords had in mind in *Stein* v. *Blake*[280] in its discussion of contingent debts. In such a case a subsequent occurrence of the contingency may be taken into account for the purpose of both proof and set-off, not on the ground that the contingency is deemed to have occurred retrospectively at the bankruptcy date, but rather because the subsequent occurrence of the contingency is the best evidence of what was the true value of the contingent debt as at that date.[281] This was regarded by the House of Lords as the basis for determining what, on that date, was the state of the account between the bankrupt and the creditor. But if in the context of suretyship the position is that a set-off was not available as a matter of law to the surety at the date of the bankruptcy because of the rule against double proof, it would be artificial to suggest that, when the surety later pays the creditor and obtains a right of set-off, that set-off in fact occurred at the earlier date.[282]

---

[275] (1982) 150 CLR 85.

[276] [1956] 1 WLR 1226. In *re A Debtor* itself was a case in which the surety rather than the principal debtor was bankrupt, though it is apparent that the observations in the judgments were also intended to apply when the principal debtor is the bankrupt party.

[277] See *Jones* v. *Mossop* (1844) 3 Hare 568, 571 and *In re The Moseley Green Coal and Coke Company; Barrett's Case (No. 2)* (1865) 4 De G J & S 756.

[278] See section 4.3.3 below.

[279] *In re Fenton* [1931] 1 Ch. 85. See section 4.3.2 below.

[280] [1995] 2 All ER 961, 965.

[281] See Lawrence J. in *Ellis & Company's Trustee* v. *Dixon-Johnson* [1924] 1 Ch. 342, 356–7. See also *In re Dynamics Corporation of America* [1976] 1 WLR 757, 768; *Re Hurren* [1983] 1 WLR 183, 189.

[282] On the other hand, *Day & Dent Constructions* was referred to in *Stein* v. *Blake* [1995] 2 All ER 961, 968–9 without any suggestion that it was wrongly decided. The same issue would arise in the situation in which the creditor had proved in the bankruptcy before payment by the surety. See section 4.3.4 below.

2.12.2 *Australia*

In Australia the High Court in *Gye* v. *McIntyre*[283] considered the nature of insolvency set-off, and in doing so made some observations by way of *obiter dictum*[284] which appear to support the position adopted by the House of Lords in *Stein* v. *Blake*. This is so notwithstanding that two earlier High Court decisions[285] do not sit comfortably with that position.

Section 86[286] is a statutory directive ('shall be set off') which operates as at the time the bankruptcy takes effect. It produces a balance upon the basis of which the bankruptcy administration can proceed. Only that balance can be claimed in the bankruptcy or recovered by the trustee. If its operation is to produce a nil balance, its effect will be that there is nothing at all which can be claimed in the bankruptcy or recovered in proceedings by the trustee. The section is self-executing in the sense that its operation is automatic and not dependent upon 'the option of either party' . . .

However, in *Re Capel; ex parte Marac Finance Australia Ltd.* v. *Capel*[287] Drummond J. suggested a different interpretation of this passage which constitutes a half-way position between the automatic extinction theory favoured by the House of Lords and the procedural view. *Capel* concerned an assignment of a claim by a trustee in bankruptcy to the bankrupt himself in circumstances where the debtor on the claim had a provable debt against the bankrupt which nevertheless had not been proved. Drummond J. agreed with the approach adopted by the Court of Appeal in *Stein* v. *Blake*,[288] and held that the insolvency set-off section did not prevent the assignment. Insofar as *Gye* v. *McIntyre* was concerned, he expressed the view that the High Court in that case was not saying that the insolvency set-off section operates automatically at the date of the bankruptcy or liquidation to extinguish the cross-demands. Rather, all that the High Court meant was that 'the account, whenever taken, is to be taken by

[283] (1991) 171 CLR 609.
[284] (1991) 171 CLR 609, 622. See also *Lord* v. *Direct Acceptance Corporation Ltd.* (1993) 32 NSWLR 362, 372. Compare Gummow and von Doussa JJ. in the Federal Court in *McIntyre* v. *Perkes* (1990) 22 FCR 260, 270. Compare also *Day & Dent Constructions Pty. Ltd.* v. *North Australian Properties Pty. Ltd.* (1982) 150 CLR 85, 109, in which Murphy J. appeared to distinguish between the date of the winding-up and the time when the account was taken. Similarly some comments by Mason J. in that case (at 107) appear to support the procedural view, though little weight should now be attached to this given that his Honour, as Chief Justice, headed the Court in *Gye* v. *McIntyre*.
[285] *Hiley* v. *The Peoples Prudential Assurance Co. Ltd.* (1938) 60 CLR 468 and *Day & Dent Constructions Pty. Ltd.* v. *North Australian Properties Pty. Ltd.* (1982) 150 CLR 85, discussed in section 2.12.1 above.
[286] Bankruptcy Act 1966 (Cth.), s. 86 is the set-off section applicable to bankruptcies in Australia.
[287] (1994) 48 FCR 195. See also *Re Turner; ex parte Mulley* unreported, Northrop J., Federal Court of Australia, 22 June 1995. [288] [1994] Ch. 16.

reference to the position obtaining at that date', and that, independently of whether an account has ever been taken, the rights of the parties to the cross-claims 'are to be taken to be the right to recover or to prove for the balance (if any) that would exist if the two claims were set-off against each other at the date of the sequestration order. That is not at all the same as saying that the various claims are extinguished by the operation of the section on the day the sequestration order is made'.[289] Whether indeed this is what the High Court had in mind is debatable,[290] although in any event, to the extent that it goes beyond the notion that the date of the bankruptcy is the reference point for determining what claims can be brought into an account, some of the difficulties discussed above in the context of the automatic extinction theory would still be relevant.

While Drummond J.'s view was that the insolvency set-off section did not prevent an assignment of a debt owing to a bankrupt, he agreed that the assignee would still take subject to the equity constituted by the right of set-off otherwise available to the debtor in the bankruptcy. One of the decisions that he considered in this regard was *Martin* v. *Lewis*.[291] A debt which was owing to a bankrupt, and which had become vested in the trustee in bankruptcy, was assigned back to the bankrupt after he had obtained his discharge.[292] The debtor had a cross-claim against the bankrupt, though a proof of debt had not been lodged in the bankruptcy and nor had an account otherwise been taken. A discharge from bankruptcy has the effect of releasing the bankrupt from all bankruptcy debts,[293] although the Queensland Supreme Court[294] held that the assignee took subject to a set-off in respect of the cross-claim even though an account had not actually been taken in the bankruptcy.[295] While the circumstances in issue in *Capel* were similar, the cases differed in one respect. Whereas in *Martin* v. *Lewis* the assignment occurred after the bankrupt's discharge from bankruptcy, in *Capel* it occurred before discharge, though the question of the efficacy of the assignment did not arise until later. Drummond J. expressed doubts as to the correctness of

---

[289] (1994) 48 FCR 195, 206–7.

[290] In subsequent proceedings in the *Gye* v. *McIntyre* litigation (unreported, Federal Court of Australia (NSW District Registry), 8 October 1992), Beaumont J. appeared to accept that the insolvency set-off section operates as an automatic extinction, so that thereafter all that is owing is the balance of the account.

[291] Unreported, Full Court of the Queensland Supreme Court, 7 June 1985.

[292] This was possible because the right of action remained vested in the trustee notwithstanding the discharge. See *Piwinski* v. *Corporate Trustees of the Diocese of Armidale* [1977] 1 NSWLR 266.

[293] See the Insolvency Act 1986, s. 281 and, in Australia, the Bankruptcy Act 1966 (Cth.), s. 153.   [294] Andrews A.C.J., Kelly and Shepherdson JJ.

[295] See also in England *Farley* v. *Housing and Commercial Developments Ltd.* (1984) 26 Build. LR 66.

Martin v. *Lewis*. Since the cause of action in that case was assigned after the bankrupt's discharge, he found it difficult to see how the creditor could retain the right to set off the amount owing to him when the bankrupt had been released from liability.[296] In *Capel*, on the other hand, where the assignment occurred before the discharge, Drummond J. accepted that the creditor could still assert a set-off against the assignee notwithstanding the later discharge. He considered that the essence of the equity to which the assignee took subject was that the account, whenever it was taken, was to be taken by reference to the position obtaining at the date of the bankruptcy, and that this also applied when the account was taken outside the bankruptcy administration in the context of a claim by the assignee.[297] Because the assignment occurred before the discharge, the debt when assigned had the equity 'attached'[298] to it, and in a later accounting reference would have to be made to the position at the time of the bankruptcy when the bankrupt was still liable to the creditor. It remains to be seen, however, whether courts in Australia will follow the analysis in *Capel*,[299] given the views expressed in *Stein* v. *Blake*.

2.13 FOREIGN CURRENCIES

Consider that one or both of the cross-demands between a bankrupt and a creditor is in a foreign currency.[300]

For the purpose of proving a debt in a bankruptcy or a company liquidation a foreign currency claim is converted into sterling at the rate prevailing at the date of the bankruptcy order or, as the case may be, on the date when the company went into liquidation, as opposed to the date of payment of the dividend itself.[301] This accords with the rule applied with respect to the valuation of debts for the purpose of proof. Debts or liabilities which do not have a certain value at the commencement of a

---

[296] See the discussion at (1994) 48 FCR 195, 205.
[297] See the discussion at (1994) 48 FCR 195, 206–7.
[298] (1994) 48 FCR 195, 203.
[299] Northrop J. in *Re Turner; ex parte Mulley* unreported, Federal Court of Australia, 22 June 1995, regarded Drummond J.'s analysis as correct.
[300] The following discussion assumes that the obligation in question is a money obligation, which may not always be the case when foreign money is in issue. See section 5.3.2 below.
[301] *In re Dynamics Corporation of America* [1976] 1 WLR 757; *In re Lines Bros. Ltd.* [1983] 1 Ch. 1; *In re Amalgamated Investment and Property Co. Ltd.* [1985] 1 Ch. 349, 364. This principle is now set out in the Insolvency Rules 1986, rr. 4.91 and 6.111. In Australia, see the Corporations Law, s. 554C. A company goes into liquidation if it passes a resolution for voluntary winding-up, or an order for its winding-up is made by the court at a time when it has not already gone into liquidation by passing such a resolution. See the Insolvency Act 1986, s. 247(2). Compare *Re Pearce* (1933) 6 ABC 126 (conversion at the date when the debt became payable), which was decided before *Miliangos*.

bankruptcy or a liquidation are valued as at that date. Admittedly later events may be looked at, but only in the sense that they may provide *pro tanto* evidence of the true value that the debt did in fact have at the relevant date. In the case of a foreign currency claim there is no need to look at later events. The exchange rate current at the commencement of the bankruptcy or the liquidation provides a clear measure for ascertaining its value at that date.[302] Further, this is consistent with the principle applied in *Miliangos* v. *George Frank (Textiles) Ltd.*[303] The House of Lords held in that case that an English court in an action to enforce a foreign currency debt can give judgment expressed in the foreign currency, with the debt being converted into sterling for the purpose of enforcement of the judgment at the exchange rate applicable on the date that the plaintiff is given leave to enforce. Since bankruptcy and company liquidation provide a process of collective enforcement, the Court of Appeal in *In re Lines Bros. Ltd.*[304] considered that it is in accordance with *Miliangos* to convert currencies for the purpose of proof by reference to the rate prevailing at the commencement of that process.[305]

The House of Lords in *Stein* v. *Blake*[306] held that the set-off section in the insolvency legislation takes effect automatically upon the occurrence of the bankruptcy or liquidation.[307] The extinction of the cross-demands does not depend upon the procedural step of taking an account. Accordingly, conversion of a foreign currency claim should take place as at the date of the bankruptcy or liquidation,[308] since that is regarded as the date of payment. But even if the insolvency set-off section was regarded as procedural, the better view is that the same result would follow.[309] Insofar as a foreign currency debt owing by a bankrupt is concerned, in order to be able to employ it in a set-off the debt must be provable, and we have seen that, for the purpose of proof, foreign currency debts are converted into sterling as at the date of the bankruptcy or liquidation. Similarly, under the procedural view that date probably would apply in relation to a foreign currency debt

---

[302] *In re Dynamics Corporation of America* [1976] 1 WLR 757, 767–8. See also *In re Lines Bros. Ltd.* [1983] 1 Ch. 1, 19–20. [303] [1976] AC 443.

[304] [1983] 1 Ch. 1 (in particular, see Lawton L.J. at 12–13 and Brightman L.J. at 20).

[305] In *Miliangos* [1976] AC 443, 498, Lord Wilberforce and Lord Cross of Chelsea suggested that, in the case of a liquidation, conversion should take place at the date when the creditor's claim is admitted by the liquidator. However, these statements were merely *obiter*, and the Court of Appeal in *In re Lines Bros.* said that the date of the liquidation in fact is more in accordance with the principle actually applied by the House of Lords in *Miliangos*. The approach adopted in *In re Lines Bros.* was also accepted in *In re Amalgamated Investment and Property Co. Ltd.* [1985] 1 Ch. 349, 364, and in Australia in *Re Gresham Corp. Pty. Ltd.* (1989) 15 ACLR 461. [306] [1995] 2 All ER 961.

[307] See section 2.12 above. [308] *Stein* v. *Blake* [1995] 2 All ER 961, 964.

[309] Compare the contrary view expressed by the author in 'Some Recent Issues in Relation to Set-off' (1994) 68 *Australian Law Journal* 331, 360–2.

owing *to* the bankrupt. When set-off is available pursuant to the insolvency legislation, the insolvency proceedings provide a process for the enforcement, not only of the creditors' provable debts, but also of the bankrupt's or the company's cross-claims to the extent that they are satisfied by the set-off. Consistent with *Miliangos*, the better view is that conversion accordingly would take place at the rate applicable at the commencement of that process.

If the bankrupt's or the company's foreign currency cross-claim overtops the creditor's provable debt, the remainder of the cross-claim not extinguished by the set-off may be converted at a different rate. Once judgment is obtained against the creditor for that amount, conversion should take place in accordance with the normal principle at the exchange rate applicable when leave to enforce is given.

2.14 INTEREST

When a bankruptcy occurs, and there are cross-demands the subject of a set-off under the insolvency set-off section, interest should stop running, not only on the creditor's claim against the bankrupt, but also on the bankrupt's claim against the creditor. While in *Ex parte Prescot*[310] interest appears to have been allowed on the bankrupt's claim for the period between the bankruptcy and the taking of the account, that could no longer stand following the decision of the House of Lords in *Stein,* v. *Blake*,[311] that the set-off takes effect automatically upon the occurrence of the bankruptcy.

2.15 SET-OFF AS A VOID DISPOSITION OF PROPERTY

The Insolvency Act 1986, section 127 provides that a disposition of a company's property after the commencement of a court ordered winding-up is void unless the court otherwise orders. In *Barclays Bank Ltd.* v. *TOSG Trust Fund Ltd.*[312] Nourse J. said that, where there is a conflict between the then equivalent of section 127[313] and the insolvency set-off section, section 127 must prevail. This cannot be supported. Section 127 refers to a disposition after the commencement of the winding-up, which is the time of the presentation of the petition. But it would always be the case that a set-off would not occur until later, when the order is made for a

---

[310] (1753) 1 Atk. 230. [311] [1995] 2 All ER 961.
[312] [1984] BCLC 1, 25–6. [313] Section 227 of the Companies Act 1948.

winding-up.[314] In other words, there would always be a conflict between section 127 and the insolvency set-off section. If the set-off section is to have any meaning in a compulsory winding-up, it must prevail over section 127.

2.16 MISTAKE AS TO SET-OFF

It may be that money is paid to a trustee in bankruptcy in satisfaction of a liability owing to the bankrupt, when that liability was the subject of a set-off. If the mistake is a mistake of fact the money should be recoverable. In the case of bankruptcy the assets of the bankrupt vest in the trustee for division amongst the bankrupt's creditors.[315] Unlike the bankrupt, the trustee is not insolvent, and so the mistaken payment should be recoverable in full from the trustee in an action for money had and received.[316] On the other hand the assets of a company in liquidation do not pass to the liquidator[317] who is really only an agent of the company, though he occupies a position which is fiduciary in some respects and is bound by the statutory duties imposed on him by the insolvency legislation.[318] Rather, the money instead will have vested in the insolvent company itself. In order to recover it in full from the insolvent company the payer's right to it ordinarily should be proprietary in nature. It was held by Goulding J. in *Chase Manhattan Bank N.A.* v. *Israel-British Bank (London) Ltd.*[319] that 'a person who pays money to another under a factual mistake retains an equitable property in it and the conscience of that other is subjected to a fiduciary duty to respect his proprietary right'.[320] Assuming that the case is followed[321] it would enable the mistaken payment to be recovered *in toto*,[322] provided that it can be traced.

---

[314] See *Stein* v. *Blake* [1995] 2 All ER 963, discussed in section 2.12.1 above. Rule 4.90 of the Insolvency Rules refers to the time that the company goes into liquidation.

[315] See the Insolvency Act 1986, s. 306, and in Australia the Bankruptcy Act 1966 (Cth), s. 58.

[316] As in *Bize* v. *Dickason* (1786) 1 TR 285. See also *Edmeads* v. *Newman* (1823) 1 B & C 418; *Booth* v. *Hutchinson* (1872) LR 15 Eq. 30.

[317] Note though the Insolvency Act 1986, s. 145, and in Australia the Corporations Law, s. 474(2), each of which enable the court, on the application of the liquidator, to direct that the property of the company is to vest in the liquidator.

[318] *Thomas Franklin & Sons Ltd.* v. *Cameron* (1935) 36 SR(NSW) 286, 296; *Re Timberland Ltd.* (1979) 4 ACLR 259, 285. See also *Ayerst* v. *C. & K. (Constructions) Ltd.* [1976] AC 167, 176–7.   [319] [1981] 1 Ch. 105.   [320] [1981] 1 Ch. 105, 119.

[321] The *Chase Manhattan* case has been both criticized and applauded. See the comments of Tettenborn and Professor Jones in [1980] *Cambridge Law Journal* 272, 275. However, as Professor Jones conceded, it is difficult to see how it could be said that the Israel-British Bank in that case was in a fiduciary relationship with a commercial competitor.

[322] In *Re Cushla Ltd.* [1979] 3 All ER 415 a payment was made to a company in liquidation in circumstances where the payer did not realize that it had a right of set-off. It was held that

However, recovery under this head, whether from a trustee in bankruptcy or a company in liquidation, would be subject to the principle which, at least for the present, is still applicable in England to the law of mistake, that the mistake ordinarily should be one of fact rather than of law.[323] Alternatively, the rule in *Ex parte James*[324] may provide relief. According to this rule, trustees in bankruptcy are officers of the court, and as such may be ordered by the court not to rely on their strict legal rights when to do so would be regarded as dishonourable. The advantage of *Ex parte James* is that it allows recovery of payments made under a mistake of law, as for example the law of set-off[325] (though it is not confined to mistakes of law[326]). A liquidator in a compulsory winding-up certainly is an officer of the court,[327] and indeed on two occasions recently[328] recourse has been had to this rule as a means of ordering the return of a sum of money mistakenly paid to a liquidator in a compulsory winding-up in satisfaction of a liability to the company. Consequently a set-off based upon that liability could proceed against an independent indebtedness of the company to the payer. However, a liquidator in a voluntary winding-up is not an officer of the court, and so he is not amenable to *Ex parte James*.[329]

Another possibility is that a creditor, in ignorance of the availability of a set-off, lodges a proof in the debtor's bankruptcy in respect of the debt. On its own this should not prevent the creditor from subsequently asserting a set-off. But what if, before he asserts the right, he receives payment of a dividend? It may be said in such a case that the debt has been paid, so that there is nothing 'due' to the creditor within the meaning of the set-off section, and that therefore the creditor has lost his right of set-off. There is some

the payer was entitled to recover the money and that a set-off should proceed, though there is no consideration given to the question whether the claim for the recovery of the money was proprietary in nature.

[323] While in *Woolwich Equitable Building Society* v. *Inland Revenue Commissioners* [1993] AC 70 the House of Lords did not go so far as to declare that the principle by which money paid under a mistake of law is not recoverable no longer applies, they did note that the principle has been subjected to strong criticism, and there are indications in some of the judgments that in a future case their Lordships would be sympathetic to the view that the principle should be discarded. This indeed has occurred in Australia. See *David Securities Pty. Ltd.* v. *Commonwealth Bank of Australia* (1992) 175 CLR 353.

[324] *Ex parte James; in re Condon* (1874) LR 9 Ch. App. 609.

[325] See *Re Paddington Town Hall Centre Ltd. (In Liquidation)* (1979) 41 FLR 239.

[326] *In re Tyler; ex parte The Official Receiver* [1907] 1 KB 865.

[327] See for example *Re Associated Dominions Assurance Society Pty. Ltd.* (1962) 109 CLR 516.

[328] *Re Cushla Ltd.* [1979] 2 All ER 415; *Re Paddington Town Hall Centre Ltd.* (1979) 41 FLR 239.

[329] *Re T.H. Knitwear (Wholesale) Ltd.* [1988] 1 All ER 860 (overruling *Re Temple Fire and Accident Assurance Company*, unreported but noted at (1910) 129 LT Jo. 115). See also *In re David A. Hamilton and Co. Ltd.* [1928] NZLR 419.

support for this view in the judgment of Knight Bruce V.C. in *Ex parte Staddon: in re Wise*,[330] where the Vice Chancellor in allowing a set-off said that he would disregard a proof of debt made by the creditor since the creditor had not received a dividend or obtained any benefit from the proof. However, under the automatic extinction theory adopted by the House of Lords in *Stein* v. *Blake*,[331] the analysis now would be that a set-off would have occurred in any event, though the dividend usually would be recoverable by the trustee as a mistaken payment.[332]

2.17 PREFERENTIAL DEBTS

The insolvency legislation accords preferential status to certain classes of debts. In the event of a bankruptcy or a company liquidation, these debts, or, at least in some cases a certain part of them, are paid in priority to other debts of the bankrupt or the company.[333] If the preferred creditor is possessed of a second, separate claim against the bankrupt or the company, or the amount of the claim in question is greater than the amount for which preferential status is accorded, the question may arise whether a set-off should take effect in the first instance against the preferred debt, or the preferred part of the debt, or whether it should operate first against the debt, or the part of it, which is not preferred, or indeed any other way. The creditor obviously would be better off if the set-off occurred first against the non-preferred debt, because the preferred debt still in existence after the set-off would have priority in the bankruptcy or the liquidation, whereas the creditor could not claim priority if the set-off instead has extinguished the debt which otherwise would have been preferred.

An early authority on point is *Ex parte Boyle, re Shepherd*, a decision of Lord Eldon which appears not to have been reported but which nevertheless is noted in Cooke's *Bankrupt Laws*.[334] The case concerned some promissory notes drawn by Lord Cork at the request of the bankrupt, the bankrupt having agreed to indemnify Lord Cork in respect of payments made pursuant to them. Lord Cork paid one of the notes before the bankruptcy and two of these afterwards. In addition, Lord Cork was separately indebted to the bankrupt. Under the bankruptcy legislation then in force, Lord Cork could only have proved in the bankruptcy for the payment made before the bankruptcy, though it was considered that his

---

[330] (1843) 3 Mont. D & De G 256, 12 LJ Bcy. 39.   [331] [1995] 2 All ER 963.
[332] See also Hoffman L.J. (as he then was) in the *M.S. Fashions* case [1993] Ch. 425, 435.
[333] See the Insolvency Act 1986, ss. 175, 328 and 386.
[334] Cooke, *The Bankrupt Laws* (8th edn., 1823) Vol. 1, 571–2.

right to an indemnity for the subsequent payments, though not provable, could still be the subject of a set-off.[335] It would have been better for Lord Cork if his liability to the bankrupt could be set off against the claim for an indemnity which was not provable, because he would still have had a right to receive a dividend on the provable claims, and indeed this was the effect of the order made by Lord Eldon.

Lord Eldon's approach favoured the creditor. Buckley J., however, adopted the opposite approach in *In re E.J. Morel (1934) Ltd.*[336] In his view, the set-off section in the insolvency legislation should be applied on the basis that the debt which would otherwise be preferential in a company liquidation should be the first claim brought into an account. His Lordship said that the result of a set-off is to give a creditor payment in full of his claim to the extent of the set-off, and in that way he is better off than creditors who merely have to rely on their right to prove and receive a dividend. Accordingly, if he obtains payment in full by means of a set-off, it is 'reasonable' that that payment should be treated as being in respect of the debt which would rank first in priority.

The issue subsequently was considered by Walton J. in *In re Unit 2 Windows Ltd.*[337] While there was no discussion of Lord Eldon's decision in *Ex parte Doyle*, Walton J. did consider *Morel*, though he was not persuaded by Buckley J.'s analysis. As his Lordship remarked, 'reasonableness' often depends on the point of view of the person considering it. Instead, he proposed a third approach. He said that the maxim that equality is equity should apply, and accordingly held that the set-off in that case should occur rateably between the preferential and the non-preferential parts of the indebtedness of the company in liquidation.[338] This has since been followed in Australia,[339] and would now appear to represent the law.

The *Unit 2 Windows* approach does not apply when a creditor of a bankrupt has two debts owing to him, one secured and the other unsecured. The creditor is entitled to rely on his security in respect of the secured debt and not have it dealt with in the liquidation, in which case the debt is not susceptible to a set-off under the insolvency legislation. If the bankrupt has a cross-demand, it can only be set off against the unsecured debt.[340]

---

[335] See section 3.5 below.   [336] [1962] 1 Ch. 21.   [337] [1985] 1 WLR 1383.
[338] In Scotland compare *Turner, Petitioner* [1993] BCC 299.
[339] *Central Brakes Service (Newcastle) Pty. Ltd.* v. *Central Brakes Service (Sydney) Pty. Ltd. (in liq)* (1989) 7 ACLC 1199.
[340] *Re Norman Holding Co. Ltd.* [1991] 1 WLR 10.

2.18 SECURED DEBTS

The fact that a creditor of a bankrupt or a company in liquidation has security for a debt (including from a third party[341]) does not mean that he cannot avail himself of a set-off against the debt.[342] A secured creditor has a choice. He can rely entirely on the security and elect not to prove in the bankruptcy or liquidation, in which case, since the creditor is not 'proving or claiming to prove'[343] for the debt, it cannot be the subject of a set-off under the insolvency set-off section.[344] Alternatively, the creditor can surrender the security and prove for the whole debt, or value the security and prove for the difference between the amount of the debt and the value, or enforce the security and prove for the balance remaining of the debt. In any of these instances the provable debt can be the subject of a set-off.[345]

When a negotiable instrument is lodged as security for an advance, the trustee in bankrutcy of the debtor on the instrument is entitled to recover it after tendering the amount of the advance, and the creditor is not entitled to retain it for a set-off against another debt owing to him by the debtor.[246]

It may be that the secured debt is owing to the bankrupt or the company in liquidation, in which case the debtor on that debt may set it off against a separate debt owing to him. To the extent of the set-off the security is then freed.[347]

A creditor may have both a secured and an unsecured debt owing to him. In such a case Mervyn Davies J. held in *Re Norman Holding Co.*

---

[341] *McKinnon* v. *Armstrong Brothers & Co.* (1877) 2 App. Cas. 531.

[342] *M.S. Fashions Ltd.* v. *Bank of Credit and Commerce International* [1993] Ch. 425, 446. This also applies in the case of set-off under the Statutes of Set-off. See *Lechmere* v. *Hawkins* (1798) 2 Esp. 626.

[343] See the Insolvency Act 1986, s. 323(1) and, for company liquidations, the Insolvency Rules, r. 4.90(1).

[344] *Re Norman Holding Co. Ltd.* [1991] 1 WLR 10, 15. In *Morris* v. *Agrichemicals Ltd.*, 20 December 1995, the Court of Appeal said that set-off ought not to prejudice the right of a secured creditor to enforce his securities in any order he chooses and at a time of his choice. Compare *McColl's Wholesale Pty. Ltd* v. *State Bank of NSW* [1984] 3 NSWLR 365, 380 where Powell J. considered that the requirement that debts be set off means that a secured creditor may *only* enforce his rights under the security to the extent of the balance of the cross-debts.

[345] See the discussion in *Re Norman Holding Co. Ltd.* [1991] 1 WLR 10. In *Clark* v. *Cort* (1840) Cr. & Ph. 154 a set-off was allowed to the extent of the difference between the value of the bankrupt's indebtedness and the proceeds of realization of a security for that debt.

[346] *Key* v. *Flint* (1817) 8 Taunt. 21, affirmed in equity *Ex parte Flint* (1818) 1 Swans. 30. See also *Trustee of the Property of Ellis and Company* v. *Dixon-Johnson* [1925] AC 489.

[347] See Dixon J. in *Hiley* v. *The Peoples Prudential Assurance Company Ltd.* (1938) 60 CLR 468, 498, referring to *Ex parte Barnett; in re Deveze* (1874) LR 9 Ch. App. 293 and *Ex parte Law; in re Kennedy* (1846) De Gex 378. See also *Lord Lanesborough* v. *Jones* (1716) 1 P Wms. 325; *M.S. Fashions Ltd.* v. *Bank of Credit and Commerce International* [1993] Ch. 425, 446; *Re ILG Travel Ltd.* [1996] BCC 21. Compare *Clarke* v. *Fell* (1833) 4 B & Ad. 404.

Ltd.[348] he is entitled to rely on the security in respect of the secured debt and to utilize the unsecured debt in a set-off.

After a security is realized the proceeds may be more than sufficient to satisfy the secured money. The question whether the creditor may set off his obligation to account for the surplus proceeds against a separate unsecured debt owing to him by the debtor is considered later in the context of a discussion of *Rose* v. *Hart*.[349]

A debt itself may be property the subject of a security. This is considered later in a context of mutuality.[350]

---

[348] [1991] 1 WLR 10.   [349] (1818) 8 Taunt. 499. See section 6.4 below.
[350] See section 7.6 below.

3

Debts, Credits, and Dealings

3.1 MUTUAL CREDIT

The insolvency set-off section applies when there are mutual credits, mutual debts or other mutual dealings. It was not always in this form. Originally the section only encompassed mutual debts and mutual credits in existence at the date of the bankruptcy, and it was not until 1869 that mutual dealings was added.[1]

The courts have interpreted mutual debts as referring to debts that were both in existence and presently payable before the bankruptcy.[2] Insofar as mutual credits is concerned, this would include mutual debts, in the sense that, in the case of a debt, credit is given to the debtor for payment. However, it is broader than that. An early authority on the meaning of the expression is *Rose* v. *Hart*.[3] The question in issue was whether a fuller with whom cloths had been deposited by a bankrupt prior to the bankruptcy could retain them as a set-off against a debt owing by the bankrupt. Gibbs C.J. said that mutual credit meant 'such credits only as must in their nature terminate in debts, as where a debt is due from one party, and credit given by him on the other for a sum of money payable at a future day, and which will then become a debt, or where there is a debt on one side, and a delivery of property with directions to turn it into money on the other; in such case the credit given by the delivery of the property must in its nature terminate in a debt . . .'.[4] Since the cloths in that case had not been deposited with authority to turn them into money, there was not mutual credit for the purpose of the set-off section.

The essence of mutual credit was said to be that the credit in its nature must be such that it *must* end in a debt. In later cases, however, this was relaxed,[5] so that it came to be regarded as sufficient if the transaction in question was such that it would naturally or in the ordinary course of

---

[1] Bankruptcy Act 1869, s. 39.
[2] *Ex parte Prescot* (1753) 1 Atk. 230, and see also *Young* v. *Bank of Bengal* (1836) 1 Moore 150, 164–5.   [3] (1818) 8 Taunt. 499.
[4] (1818) 8 Taunt. 499, 506.
[5] Compare *Young* v. *Bank of Bengal* (1836) 1 Moore 150, 168–9.

business end in a debt,[6] or if it would probably result in a debt,[7] or if a debt was the likely result.[8] This is consistent with the courts' expressed policy of construing the set-off section liberally.[9]

3.2 DEALINGS

In 1861 the range of provable debts was expanded, the principal change being the inclusion of a right of proof in respect of damages claims for breach of contract.[10] In addition, the Bankruptcy Act 1869 contained a general right of proof in respect of debts and liabilities to which the bankrupt became subject after the bankruptcy by reason of an obligation incurred before the bankruptcy.[11] This was broader than the situation which had applied under the Bankrupt Law Consolidation Act 1849, by which only certain types of contingent liabilities were provable.[12] A set-off section that referred only to mutual debts and mutual credit would not have been adequate to bring about an expansion in the scope of the right of set-off that corresponded to these changes, since mutual debts and mutual credit encompassed only debts which were in existence and presently payable before the bankruptcy, and debts which came into existence subsequent to the bankruptcy but which were a natural result of a prior transaction. A damages claim is not a debt, and therefore would not have come within those concepts.[13] As Lord Russell of Killowen C.J. once

---

[6] See Gibbs C.J. and Mason J. in *Day & Dent Constructions Pty. Ltd.* v. *North Australian Properties Pty. Ltd.* (1982) 150 CLR 85, 95, 103–4, referring to *Naoroji* v. *The Chartered Bank of India* (1868) LR 3 CP 444, 451. See also *Palmer* v. *Day & Sons* [1895] 2 QB 618, 621; *In re Mid-Kent Fruit Factory* [1896] 1 Ch. 567, 569; *Smith's Leading Cases* (12th edn., 1915) Vol. 2, 281.   [7] *Sovereign Life Assurance Co.* v. *Dodd* [1892] 1 QB 405, 411–12.

[8] *Easum* v. *Cato* (1822) 5 B & Ald. 861, 867.

[9] *Eberle's Hotels and Restaurant Company, Ltd.* v. *E. Jonas & Brothers* (1887) 18 QBD 459, 465; *Day & Dent Constructions Pty. Ltd.* v. *North Australian Properties Pty. Ltd.* (1982) 150 CLR 85, 108; *Gye* v. *McIntyre* (1991) 171 CLR 609, 619; *Re Kolb* (1994) 128 ALR 156, 159.

[10] See the Bankruptcy Act 1861, ss. 149–54. Damages claims for breach of contract were dealt with in s. 153.   [11] Bankruptcy Act 1869, s. 31.

[12] See the Bankrupt Law Consolidation Act 1849, ss. 174–8. For example, s. 177 conferred a right of proof in respect of contingent *debts*. While s. 178 conferred a right of proof in respect of contingent *liabilities*, this was confined to traders.

[13] *Rose* v. *Sims* (1830) 1 B & Ad. 521. Compare *Makeham* v. *Crow* (1864) 15 CB(NS) 847, in which an unliquidated damages claim arising out of a contract of sale was set off in an action by the vendor's assignees in bankruptcy for the price. However the purchaser presented alternative arguments for a set-off. It was based not only upon the scope of the proof of debt provision in the 1861 Act, but also equitable set-off. The report is silent as to which of these was regarded as the justification for the decision. Certainly, in cases decided after the 1869 Act, set-off of unliquidated damages was justified on the basis of mutual dealings as opposed to mutual credit. Indeed, in *Booth* v. *Hutchinson* (1872) LR 15 Eq. 30, 32 Malins V.C. said that he would probably have concluded that the damages claim in that case could not have been set off under the old law. He said (at 34) that there was no mutual debt, and there was hardly a mutual credit, but that there was certainly a mutual dealing.

remarked in relation to the giving of credit,[14] 'the credits must be such as either must terminate in debts or have a natural tendency to terminate in debts, and must not be such as terminate in claims differing in nature from debts'. Moreover, a debt which arose after the bankruptcy pursuant to a prior transaction would not have come within the concept of giving credit if for some reason the debt could not be said to be a natural result of that transaction. It would appear that 'mutual dealings' was added to the set-off section in the 1869 Act in order to accommodate these increases in the range of provable debts,[15] a view which is consistent with judicial observations equating the scope of the set-off section in that Act with the ambit of the proof of debt provision.[16] It is also consistent with the opinion expressed by Brett L.J. in *Peat* v. *Jones & Co*,[17] that 'mutual dealings was added to get rid of any questions which might arise whether a transaction would end in a debt or not'. This statement takes in damages claims for breach of contract, which the courts quickly settled were within the scope of the mutual dealings head of the 1869 set-off section.[18] In addition, it would encompass any *debt* which arises after the bankruptcy as a result of a prior transaction, and without the intervention of any new and independent transaction,[19] irrespective of whether the situation is such as to come within the judicially accepted definition of giving credit. In such a case the debt is still the product of a dealing between the parties, and accordingly may be included in a set-off on that ground.

What does mutual dealings encompass? The expression has never been precisely defined, though it is apparent that not every claim can be said to arise out of a dealing. As Lord Esher M.R. once remarked:[20]

There are, no doubt, matters which give rise to claims, but are not dealings within the section. If one man assaults another or injures him through negligence, that gives rise to a claim, but is not a dealing; but I am disposed to think that whatever comes within the description of an ordinary business transaction would be a dealing within the section.

---

[14] *Palmer* v. *Day & Sons* [1895] 2 QB 618, 621.

[15] In *Turner* v. *Thomas* (1871) LR 6 CP 610, 613–14 Willes J. discussed the 'very large extension of the law of set-off' in the 1869 Act by reference to the proof of debt provision.

[16] See e.g. Brett M.R. and Cotton L.J. in *Lee & Chapman's Case* (1885) 30 Ch. D 216, 222, 224. [17] (1881) 8 QBD 147, 149.

[18] See, for example, *Booth* v. *Hutchinson* (1872) LR 15 Eq. 30; *Peat* v. *Jones & Co.* (1881) 8 QBD 147; *Mersey Steel & Iron Co.* v. *Naylor, Benzon, & Co.* (1884) 9 App. Cas. 434; *Lee & Chapman's Case* (1885) 30 Ch. D 216.

[19] See Starke and Dixon JJ. in *Hiley* v. *The Peoples Prudential Assurance Co. Ltd.* (1938) 60 CLR 468, 487, 499.

[20] *Eberle's Hotels and Restaurant Co. Ltd.* v. *E. Jonas & Brothers* (1887) 18 QBD 459, 465, referred to with evident approval by Astbury J. in *In re H E Thorne & Son, Ltd.* [1914] 2 Ch. 438, 451–2.

On the other hand, in Australia the High Court in *Gye* v. *McIntyre*[21] suggested that 'dealings' is used in a non-technical sense in the set-off section, and is a term of very wide scope. Their Honours went on to say in relation to the term that,[22]

It has been construed as referring to matters having a commercial or business flavour . . . Even if it is correct to construe 'dealings' in [the set-off section] as confined to a commercial or business setting, it covers the communings, the negotiations, verbal and by correspondence, and other matters which occur or exist in that setting. Whatever may be the outer limits of the word 'dealings' in [the set-off section], it encompasses, as a matter of ordinary language, commercial transactions and the negotiations leading up to them.

Thus, where a fraudulent misrepresentation is made in the course of negotiations leading up to a contract, but is not a term of the contract itself, the High Court said that the misrepresentation nevertheless is part of a dealing for the purpose of the set-off section.

3.3 THE REQUIREMENT OF A DEALING

On occasions the courts have indicated that the set-off section is limited to claims that arose out of contract,[23] though this was rejected by Brightman J. in *In re D. H. Curtis (Builders) Ltd.*[24] The purpose of set-off in insolvency, he said, is to do substantial justice between a bankrupt and his creditors.[25] On this basis, he concluded that 'one would expect to find that any mutual demands capable of being proved in bankruptcy can be the subject-matter of set-off whether or not arising out of contract'.[26] In *Curtis* the Crown had a claim for unpaid taxes against a company in liquidation, and at the same time the Crown was indebted to the company for the repayment of another tax. It was held that these cross-demands could be set off, even though they were statutory rather than contractual in origin. This view has been accepted and applied in subsequent cases.[27] At first

---

[21] (1991) 171 CLR 609, 625.   [22] (1991) 171 CLR 609, 625.

[23] *Palmer* v. *Day & Sons* [1895] 2 QB 618, 621; *In re Mid-Kent Fruit Factory* [1896] 1 Ch. 567, 571; *In re Canada Cycle & Motor Agency (Queensland) Ltd.* [1931] St. R Qd. 281; *In re Hurburgh* [1959] Tas. SR 25, 46.

[24] [1978] 1 Ch. 162.

[25] As authority for this proposition Brightman J. referred to *Forster* v. *Wilson* (1843) 12 M & W 191, 203–4, *Ex parte Cleland; in re Davies* (1867) LR 2 Ch. App. 808, 812–13, and *Re City Life Assurance Co.* [1926] Ch. 191, 216.

[26] [1978] 1 Ch. 162, 173. Brightman J.'s view that all provable demands are capable of being set off should be considered in the context of the legislation then in force. See section 3.5 below.

[27] *Re Cushla* [1979] 3 All ER 415; *Re Unit 2 Windows Ltd.* [1985] 1 WLR 1383; *Re Kolb* (1994) 128 ALR 156. In Australia the High Court in *Gye* v. *McIntyre* (1991) 171 CLR 609, 630–4 similarly rejected the view that the claims must have arisen out of contract.

sight, however, one could be forgiven for thinking that Brightman J. had strained the language of the section. The set-off section stipulates that there should be 'mutual credits, mutual debts or other mutual dealings' between the creditor and the bankrupt or, as the case may be, between a company in liquidation and a creditor. The concept of a 'dealing' may be thought to connote a contractual relationship between the parties. Further, the insertion of 'other' before 'mutual dealings' appears to qualify both mutual credits and mutual debts, so that they should also have arisen out of a dealing between the parties to the proposed set-off. There are, nevertheless, two difficulties with this analysis.

The first is that 'dealing' would appear to be a broader concept than 'contract', a point emphasized by the High Court of Australia in *Gye* v. *McIntyre*.[28] It would encompass claims which arise out of the negotiations which lead up to a commercial transaction, and not just claims which arise out of an ensuing contract. The second is that, in any event, it has never been a necessary requirement for a set-off that the claims should have arisen out of a dealing between the parties. The current form of set-off section first appeared in the Bankruptcy Act 1869, s. 39. Prior to that enactment, the section only encompassed mutual credit and mutual debts. In determining whether the case was one of mutual credit or mutual debts, it was not necessary that the parties should have dealt directly with each other. This is apparent from the decision in 1789 in *Hankey* v. *Smith*,[29] in which it was held that an indebtedness of a bankrupt acceptor upon a bill of exchange could be brought into an account by the holder, even though the bankrupt was unaware that the bill had been indorsed to the holder.[30] The acceptor and the holder had not dealt with each other, and yet a set-off was allowed. As Buller J. noted in his judgment, in order to constitute mutual credit it is not necessary that the parties should have intended to trust each other in the transaction in question. A similar result occurred in *Forster* v. *Wilson*[31] in the context of bearer promissory notes, while the same point may be made in relation to the situation in which one of the parties to the proposed set-off gained a right to sue the other only as a result of an assignment to him of the other's indebtedness.[32] When the set-off section

---

[28] (1991) 171 CLR 609, 625.   [29] (1789) 3 TR 507n.

[30] See also *Collins* v. *Jones* (1830) 10 B & C 777; *Ex parte Hastie and Hutchinson; re Alexander and Co.* (1850) 14 LTOS 402; *Re Morris and M'Murray* (1874) 5 AJR 157, affd. at 185 (in which it was specifically argued that there was no dealing between the parties, though a set-off nevertheless was allowed).   [31] (1843) 12 M & W 191.

[32] *Clark* v. *Cort* (1840) Cr. & Ph. 154; *Mathieson's Trustee* v. *Burrup, Mathieson and Company* [1927] 1 Ch. 562; *Southern Cross Construction Ltd.* v. *Southern Cross Club Ltd.* [1973] 1 NZLR 708; *Kon Strukt Pty. Ltd.* v. *Storage Developments Pty. Ltd.* (1989) 96 FLR 43. Compare *In re Eros Films Ltd.* [1963] 1 Ch. 565 and *Law* v. *James* [1972] 2 NSWLR 573, in which the assignment occurred after the company law equivalent of notice of an act of bankruptcy.

was recast in 1869 in terms of mutual credits, mutual debts or other mutual dealings, it was never suggested that this had the effect of narrowing the scope of mutual credits and mutual debts, so that henceforth they should be considered as encompassing only debts and credits arising out of dealings between the parties. On the contrary, as Sir George Jessel M.R. remarked in the context of the 1869 Act,[33] the whole tendency of the history of the insolvency legislation has been to extend the principle upon which the right of set-off is founded.

Because traditionally a dealing has never been considered to be a prerequisite to a set-off, the better view is that the word 'other' before 'mutual dealings' should be regarded as otiose. Admittedly there are problems with this. It is difficult to reconcile with Lawrence L.J.'s comment in *In re Fenton; ex parte The Fenton Textile Association, Ltd.*,[34] that 'the account which has to be taken . . . is an account of what is due from the one party to the other in respect of the mutual dealings'. Further, it is contrary to the view of Winn L.J. in the Court of Appeal in *Rolls Razor Ltd.* v. *Cox*,[35] that the proper construction of the set-off section 'involves placing emphasis primarily upon the concept of mutual dealings and consequentially regarding the debts and credits referred to as such mutual debts and mutual credits as arise from mutual dealings'. It also may be regarded as inconsistent with the stipulation in the set-off section that an account is to be taken of what is due from each party to the other 'in respect of the mutual dealings'. Once again, this suggests that the set-off section only applies to claims which arose out of a dealing. However, in order to give an intelligible meaning to the section in the light of its history, this should be interpreted as referring to an account of sums due in respect of cross-demands each of which constitutes a debt, a credit or the product of a prior dealing. Further, the point is made below[36] that, when the only justification for allowing a particular demand to be employed in a set-off is that it does arise out of a dealing, it should not be necessary that the cross-demand similarly should have originated in a dealing, despite the contrary impression that may be gained from the use of the plural in the expression 'mutual dealings'.

If indeed it is not necessary for a set-off that the parties should have dealt with each other, there is no apparent justification for limiting the scope of the section to cross-demands that arose out of contracts. However, this is not to suggest that it would never be necessary to show a dealing. In *Curtis* there were mutual debts, and for that you do not need a dealing. Similarly

---

[33] *Peat* v. *Jones & Co.* (1881) 8 QBD 147, 149.
[34] [1931] 1 Ch. 85, 113.
[35] [1967] 1 QB 552, 574. See also the discussion in *Gye* v. *McIntyre* (1991) 171 CLR 609, 623.   [36] See section 3.4 below.

a dealing is not necessary for mutual credit. If, on the other hand, it is sought to base a set-off upon a claim that is not a presently existing debt at the date of the bankruptcy, or a debt which is a natural result of a prior transaction so as to constitute the giving of credit within the meaning that has been ascribed to that expression by the courts, it would appear that it could not be employed in a set-off unless it does arise out of a dealing between the parties.[37] This is apparent from the plain words of the set-off section. It is particularly relevant to the reform set out in the 1986 insolvency legislation, by which damages claims in tort become provable.[38] The issue of set-off against damages claims, including claims in tort, is considered later.[39]

3.4 DIFFERENT DEALINGS AND CONTRACTS

In *Peat* v. *Jones & Co.*[40] Jessel M.R. said that, 'a contract of sale and purchase is in its nature mutual, imposing reciprocal obligations on the vendor and purchaser. Any claim arising out of the mutual dealings could be set off'.[41] While reciprocal obligations under a contract usually would be mutual,[42] this statement does not mean that, when it is sought to base a set-off upon a damages claim for breach of contract, the principle of mutuality *requires* that the cross-demands should have arisen out of the same contract.[43] Nor would the courts conclude that, when the only justification for allowing a particular claim to be brought into an account is that it arose out of a prior dealing, the cross-claim similarly should be derived from a dealing between the parties. This is so despite the contrary impression that may be gained from the use of the plural in the expression 'mutual dealings'. For example, one of the demands may be for damages for breach of contract, and therefore it may be included in a set-off only because it is derived from a dealing. In addition, the party possessed of the

---

[37] This is consistent with Brightman J.'s explanation in *Curtis* [1978] Ch. 162, 172 of the comment of Lord Russell in *Palmer* v. *Day & Sons* [1895] 2 QB 618, 621 regarding the necessity for the claims to arise out of contract. See also Pincus J. in *McIntyre* v. *Perkes* (1990) 22 FCR 260, 262 (Federal Court), referring to the earlier judgment of Hill J. in that case at (1989) 89 ALR 460, 470–1.

[38] See the Insolvency Act 1986, s. 322, 'bankruptcy debt' being defined in s. 382 as including tortious liabilities. For companies, see the Insolvency Rules, r. 13.12. In Australia see the Corporations Law, s. 553(1) in relation to company liquidation.

[39] See section 4.5 below.   [40] (1881) 8 QBD 147.

[41] (1881) 8 QBD 147, 149. See also *Jack* v. *Kipping* (1882) 9 QBD 113, 116.

[42] Unless, for example, the benefit of the contract is held on trust for someone else.

[43] See Pincus J. in *McIntyre* v. *Perkes* (1990) 22 FCR 260, 263 (referring to *Hiley* v. *The Peoples Prudential Assurance Co. Ltd.* (1938) 60 CLR 468), and also 'Set-off in Case of Mutual Dealings' (1882) 26 *Sol. Jo.* 575.

damages claim may be the acceptor of a bill of exchange, and may be unaware that the bill had been endorsed to the party liable for the damages. In such a case, the acceptor's liability to the holder is not derived from a dealing between them. A set-off nevertheless should be available in respect of the cross-claims, despite the fact that, while one of the demands is based upon a dealing, the other can only be brought into account because it is a debt, or alternatively the product of giving credit. In order for the set-off section to apply, there must be mutual credits, mutual debts or other mutual dealings. Mutuality means that the cross-demands must be between the same parties, and be held in the same capacity or right.[44] The requirements of the set-off section should be satisfied if, on each side of the account, there is either a presently existing and payable debt at the date of the bankruptcy, or a debt arising after the bankruptcy in respect of which credit had been given before the bankruptcy, or a money demand arising either before or after the bankruptcy as a result of a prior dealing, and if in addition mutuality is present. When it is sought to have recourse to the 'mutual dealings' head, it should not be necessary that *both* demands should have arisen out of a dealing. This is consistent with the view that the set-off section should be given the widest possible scope.[45]

3.5 THE INSOLVENT'S LIABILITY

For the insolvency set-off section to apply there must be mutual credits, mutual debts or other mutual dealings between the bankrupt and 'any creditor of the bankrupt proving or claiming to prove for a bankruptcy debt'. A similar principle underlies the right of set-off available pursuant to rule 4.90 of the Insolvency Rules 1986 in the case of a company liquidation. The requirement that there should be a person proving or claiming to prove for a debt in the bankruptcy has as a corollary that the creditor's claim against the bankrupt should be capable of proof. But in addition the courts have often indicated that the converse proposition also applies, that the fact that a claim may be proved means that it should also be capable of being employed in a set-off.[46] No doubt this has been regarded as a

---

[44] See section 7.1 below.

[45] *Eberle's Hotels and Restaurant Company, Ltd.* v. *E. Jonas & Brothers* (1887) 18 QBD 459, 465; *Day & Dent Constructions Pty. Ltd.* v. *North Australian Properties Pty. Ltd.* (1982) 150 CLR 85, 108; *Gye* v. *McIntyre* (1991) 171 CLR 609, 619; *Re Kolb* (1994) 128 ALR 156, 159.

[46] *Graham* v. *Russell* (1816) 5 M & S 498, 501; *In re Asphaltic Wood Pavement Company; Lee & Chapman's Case* (1885) 30 Ch. D 216, 222, 224; *Palmer* v. *Day & Sons* [1895] 2 QB 618, 621; *In re Taylor; ex parte Norvell* [1910] 1 KB 562, 580; *Paddy* v. *Clutton* [1920] 2 Ch.

consequence of the notion that insolvency set-off is an aspect of the rules relating to proof of debts.[47] There is, nevertheless, a difficulty with the view that it constitutes a principle of general application, and that is that there is nothing in the set-off section which expressly supports it. The section merely states that the creditor must be proving or claiming to prove a debt. It does not stipulate that the characteristic of provability is *sufficient* to bring the claim in question within the ambit of the right of set-off. In deciding whether a particular demand may be employed in a set-off, the primary question should always be whether the cross-demands are such as to come within the language of the section. In other words, there must be mutual credits, mutual debts or other mutual dealings. Indeed, the connection between proof and set-off is not something that has always been emphasized by the courts, particularly in the early years of the bankruptcy legislation. For example, in 1791 in *Smith* v. *Hodson*[48] it was held that an accommodation acceptor paying after the bankruptcy of the drawer could employ his claim for an indemnity in a set-off, even though prior to 1809 an acceptor paying under these circumstances did not have a right of proof.[49]

That case arose under the 1732 set-off section, which only applied to mutual debts and mutual credit. A feature of this section was that there was no mention of any connection between set-off and provable debts, so that on its face there was nothing objectionable in the decision in *Smith* v. *Hodson*. In 1825 new legislation (6 Geo. IV, c. 16) came into force. While the set-off section (s. 50) was still confined to mutual credit and mutual debts, it contained an express statutory recognition of the principle that all

554, 567; *Ellis and Company's Trustee* v. *Dixon-Johnson* [1924] 1 Ch. 342, 357; *In re City Life Assurance Co. Ltd.; Grandfield's Case* [1926] 1 Ch. 191, 210–11, 212; *In re Fenton* [1931] 1 Ch. 85, 113; *Hiley* v. *The Peoples Prudential Assurance Co., Ltd.* (1938) 60 CLR 468, 490; *Kitchen's Trustee* v. *Madders* [1950] 1 Ch. 134, 143. See also *Peat* v. *Jones & Co.* (1881) 8 QBD 147, 150; *Sovereign Life Assurance Co.* v. *Dodd* [1892] 1 QB 405, 412; *In re D H Curtis (Builders) Ltd.* [1978] 1 Ch. 162, 173–4; *Re Cushla Ltd.* [1979] 3 All ER 415, 420; *Willment Brothers Ltd.* v. *North West Thames Regional Health Authority* (1984) 26 Build. LR 51, 59; *Re Charge Card Services Ltd.* [1987] 1 Ch. 150, 179, 181, 187.

[47] See the Earl of Selborne in *Mersey Steel and Iron Co.* v. *Naylor, Benzon & Co.* (1884) 9 App. Cas. 434, 437–8.

[48] (1791) 4 TR 211. See also *Ex parte Boyle; re Shepherd* unreported, but noted in Cooke, *The Bankrupt Laws* (8th edn., 1823) Vol. 1, 571, and *Ex parte Wagstaff* (1806) 13 Ves. Jun. 65.

[49] *Chilton* v. *Whiffin* (1768) 3 Wils. KB 13; *Young* v. *Hockley* (1772) 3 Wils. KB 346; *Snaith* v. *Gale* (1797) 7 TR 364. The statute (1809) 49 Geo. III, C. 121, s. 8 introduced a right of proof in favour of a surety who paid after the bankruptcy of the debtor. Though an accomodation acceptor strictly is not a surety (see *Fentum* v. *Pocock* (1813) 5 Taunt. 192), it was considered nevertheless that the statute applied to accomodation acceptors. See Cooke, *The Bankrupt Laws* (8th edn., 1823) Vol. 1, 175, referring to *Ex parte Yonge* (1814) 3 V & B 31, 39–40.

provable debts could be set off.[50] A provision to this effect also appeared in the set-off section in the bankruptcy legislation of 1849.[51] Neither of these sections, however, specifically addressed the question of the susceptibility to a set-off of demands that were *not* in the nature of provable debts. Sometimes, when the courts held that a particular demand could not be employed in a set-off pursuant to the 1825 or the 1849 set-off section, the justification indeed was that the demand was not provable, though this was not always the case. There are instances in which the courts instead had regard to the definition of mutual credit adopted in *Rose* v. *Hart* as a means of rejecting an argument for a set-off. For example, in *Abbott* v. *Hicks*[52] it was held that a contingent liability of the bankrupt could not be the subject of a set-off, the court emphasizing that the liability was not provable.[53] This should be compared to *Rose* v. *Sims*,[54] in which a person indebted to a bankrupt sought to set off a claim that he had against the bankrupt for damages for breach of contract. Prior to 1861 damages claims were not provable in a bankruptcy.[55] It was held that the cross-demand could not be employed in a set-off, not because it was not provable, but on the basis of the principle that mutual credit was confined to transactions that would end in debts, and a damages claim obviously is not a debt.[56]

Whereas the 1825 and 1849 sections provided that all provable debts could be set off, this was omitted from the 1869 and the subsequent sections, though the courts continued to emphasize the principle. However, this should be considered in the context of the changes to the proof of debt and set-off sections that occurred in 1861 and 1869. In 1861 damages claims for breach of contract became provable. A claim for damages is not a case of giving credit[57] so that, if the intention was to allow such claims to be able to be set off, it would hardly have sufficed to rely on a statement to the effect that all provable debts could be set off if at the same time the scope

---

[50] The section provided that, 'every Debt or Demand hereby made proveable against the Estate of the Bankrupt, may also be set off in manner aforesaid'.

[51] Bankrupt Law Consolidation Act 1849, s. 171.   [52] (1839) 5 Bing. (NC) 578.

[53] See in particular the judgments of Coltman and Erskine JJ. Thus *Abbott* v. *Hicks* was cited in *Smith's Leading Cases* (2nd edn., 1842) Vol. 2, 182 as authority for the proposition that a demand that was not provable under the fiat could not be set off. While s. 56 of the statute (1825) 6 Geo. IV, c. 16 allowed a right of proof in respect of contingent debts, the contingent liability in *Abbott* v. *Hicks* was not within the ambit of that section.

[54] (1830) 1 B & Ad. 521.   [55] See the Bankruptcy Act 1861, s. 153.

[56] While *Rose* v. *Hart* was not mentioned in the judgments, it was referred to in a note to the report, and it is evident that the decision in *Rose* v. *Sims* was based upon that case. Note however that, even though a particular claim may have been framed as a claim for damages, if in truth it was liquidated so that the amount could be ascertained without the intervention of a jury, it could be proved in a bankruptcy, and similarly it could be the subject of a set-off. See, as to proof, *Utterson* v. *Vernon* (1790) 3 TR 539 and, as to set-off, *Gibson* v. *Bell* (1835) 1 Bing. (NC) 743 and *Groom* v. *West* (1838) 8 Ad. & E. 758.

[57] See section 3.2 above.

of the set-off section was confined to mutual debts and mutual credit. Accordingly, the reference to provable debts being able to be set off was omitted from the 1869 section, and the scope of the section instead was expanded to include mutual dealings. On this basis, the subsequent and repeated judicial statements to the effect that a provable debt can always be included in a set-off may well have been a correct summary of the position that applied after 1869, and that continued to apply in relation to the 1883 and the 1914 Bankruptcy Acts. However, it should not be regarded as an immutable principle that applies regardless of the language of the set-off section and of any changes to the right of proof. In truth, as Mason J. remarked in the High Court of Australia,[58] the fact that a claim against a bankrupt is provable should only provide indirect assistance in considering whether it can be set off. While the set-off section requires that the claim against the bankrupt must be capable of proof, the language of the section suggests that this is a necessary, rather than a sufficient, condition for being able to employ it in a set-off. The primary question should always be whether there are mutual credits, mutual debts or other mutual dealings.[59] In this regard, the Insolvency Act 1986 has further increased the range of provable debts, by introducing a right of proof in respect of a claim in tort for damages,[60] though without any corresponding change to the language of the set-off section. The position accordingly would appear to be that, if a claim in tort arose out of a prior dealing between the parties, it should be able to be included in a set-off. But if the claim in question did not arise out of a dealing, it is difficult to see what basis there is for including it in a set-off, notwithstanding that it is provable, since it is not a debt and it does not come within the concept of giving credit.[61]

3.6 THE INSOLVENT'S CLAIM

Consider the claim on the other side of the account, being the bankrupt's or the company's claim against the creditor. In *Graham* v. *Russell*[62] Lord

---

[58] *Day & Dent Constructions Pty. Ltd.* v. *North Australian Properties Pty. Ltd.* (1982) 150 CLR 85, 108.

[59] Lord Hoffman correctly stated the principle in *Stein* v. *Blake* [1995] 2 All ER 961, 964 when he said that insolvency set-off 'applies to any claim arising out of mutual credits or other mutual dealings before the bankruptcy for which a creditor would be entitled to prove as a "bankruptcy debt" '.

[60] See the Insolvency Act 1986, s. 322, 'bankruptcy debt' being defined in s. 382 as including liabilities in tort. For company liquidations, see r. 13.12 of the Insolvency Rules 1986. In Australia, a liability in tort is still not provable in a bankruptcy (see the Bankruptcy Act 1966 (Cth.), s. 82(2)), though it may now be proved in a company liquidation. See the Corporations Law, s. 553(1).   [61] See section 4.5.2 below.

Ellenborough said that, 'in taking an account between parties, the question, whether any particular item shall be introduced into it, must depend upon the nature and character of the item itself, and not upon the side of the account at which it is to be placed'. The case concerned a statute[63] which allowed an insured under a policy of insurance to prove a claim on the policy in the bankruptcy of the underwriter, even though the loss may not have occurred until after the bankruptcy.[64] *Graham* v. *Russell* differed from the situation specifically contemplated by the statute in that it was the insured rather than the underwriter who was bankrupt, and the underwriter wanted to set off a liability that had accrued on the policy after the insured's bankruptcy against a prior debt of the insured for premiums. Because the bankrupt's claim against the underwriter would have been provable in the bankruptcy of the underwriter, and could have been the subject of a set-off, if the underwriter instead had been the bankrupt party, it was held that the underwriter could employ his liability on the claim in a set-off when the question arose in the context of the bankruptcy of the insured. The converse of this proposition is that, if the bankrupt's claim against the creditor is *not* such that it could have been proved if the creditor had been bankrupt, it should not be capable of being employed in a set-off, irrespective of whether it arises out of a dealing between the parties. However, recently the High Court of Australia in *Gye* v. *McIntyre*[65] said that this converse proposition in fact does not apply, a view that had also been expressed in the Federal Court by Gummow and von Doussa JJ. before that case went on appeal to the High Court.[66] The High Court reached its conclusion without any discussion of *Graham* v. *Russell*. However, that case was considered by Gummow and von Doussa JJ., their Honours distinguishing it on the basis that it was concerned only with facilitating, not restricting, the right of set-off. Certainly it is true that, in *Graham* v. *Russell*, the Court of Exchequer Chamber looked at whether the bankrupt's claim would have been provable if the creditor had been bankrupt as a means of *allowing* a right of set-off. It is, nevertheless, correct to say that the rationale underlying Lord Ellenborough's judgment in *Graham* v. *Russell* was that the question whether any particular item can be included in a set-off must depend upon the nature and character of the item itself, and not upon the side of the account at which it is to be placed.[67] Recourse was had to this principle in *Graham* v. *Russell* in order to allow a set-off. But given that, since 1869, it has been a requirement of

---

[62] (1816) 5 M & S 498, 502.

[63] (1746) 19 Geo. II, c. 32, s. 2.

[64] Prior to 1825 (see s. 56 of 6 Geo. IV, c. 16) contingent debts as a general rule could be neither proved nor set off in a bankruptcy.   [65] (1991) 171 CLR 609.

[66] (1990) 22 FCR 260, 273–4. Compare the earlier judgment of Hill J. at (1989) 89 ALR 460, 471, 472.   [67] (1816) 5 M & S 498, 502.

the set-off section that the creditor's claim against the bankrupt be provable, the rationale upon which the decision in *Graham* v. *Russell* was based would seem to require that the bankrupt's claim should also now be in the nature of a provable debt. *Graham* v. *Russell* suggests that it is the *nature* of the claim that matters, not the side of the account on which it appears. Indeed, there are other cases which support this view. In *Young* v. *Bank of Bengal*[68] debtors defaulted after the date of their bankruptcy in payment of a secured debt. The creditor realized the security and, after satisfying the secured debt, held a surplus. The creditor then sought to apply the surplus in reduction of a separate unsecured indebtedness of the bankrupts. One of the reasons why the Privy Council held against a set-off was that the creditor's contingent liability to account for any surplus would not have been a provable debt under the then current legislation if the creditor instead had been made bankrupt before selling the security.[69] In other words, provability was used to restrict the right of set-off in the context of the bankrupt's claim. This was also the approach adopted by Maule J., with whom Cresswell and Williams JJ. concurred, in *Bell* v. *Carey*.[70] In that case the bankrupt had a claim in damages against a creditor. Maule J. said that the claim could not be the subject of a set-off because, under the bankruptcy legislation in force at that time, 'you could not say that the damages, great or small, would be a demand provable under a fiat'.[71] Reference also may be made to *Booth* v. *Hutchinson*,[72] in which Malins V.C., in deciding that a claim for rent which accrued to a landlord after the landlord had executed a deed of assignment could be the subject of a set-off,[73] relied on the definition of 'liability' in section 31 of the Bankruptcy Act 1869 in relation to the right of proof.[74] These cases, which suggest that the availability of a set-off in relation to a bankrupt's claim is indeed limited by the scope of the proof of debt provision, were not considered by the High Court. Furthermore, recent remarks by the Court of Appeal in *Morris* v. *Agrichemicals Ltd.*[75] would appear to

---

[68] (1836) 1 Moore 150.

[69] See the discussion at (1836) 1 Moore 150, 166–7. This view is also consistent with Brightman J.'s comment in *In re D H Curtis* [1978] Ch. 162, 173, that a natural assumption would be that the set-off section is intended to cover the same subject-matter as the section dealing with proof of debt.   [70] (1849) 8 CB 887.

[71] (1849) 8 CB 887, 894. See also the comments of Cresswell J. during argument (at 892).

[72] (1872) LR 15 Eq. 30 (esp. at 35).

[73] While the case concerned a deed of assignment rather than a bankruptcy, it was considered that it was subject to the same principle as a bankruptcy.

[74] The decision nevertheless is unsatisfactory, because the Vice Chancellor failed to consider the question of mutuality which arises in lease cases as a result of privity of estate. See section 9.5.1 below.

[75] Rose, Saville and Millett L.JJ., 20 December 1995.

support the approach in those early cases. Nevertheless, notwithstanding that array of authority, the view of the Australian High Court is to be preferred, for the simple reason that there is nothing in the language of the set-off section to suggest that the bankrupt's claim against the creditor should be in the nature of a provable debt. The relevant question should be whether the claim constituted a debt at the date of the bankruptcy, or whether it is a debt which arose later but which was a natural result of a prior transaction so as to come within the concept of giving credit, or whether the claim in any event arose out of a prior dealing.

Gye v. *McIntyre* concerned two debtors who had entered into compositions with their creditors, one of whom was liable to the debtors in tort for damages for fraudulent misrepresentation.[76] The misrepresentations in question arose in the course of negotiations for the purchase of a hotel by the debtors from a company associated with the creditor. It is apparent that the misrepresentations did not arise out of a contract between the debtors and the creditor, the parties to the contract instead being the debtors and the company. However, they did arise in the course of the negotiations between the debtors and the creditor leading up to the contract. The High Court said that the concept of 'dealing' in the set-off section includes contractual negotiations. It is not confined to the resulting contract. Accordingly, the claim in this case did arise out of a dealing and could be set off. The claim in question was a claim in tort. Unlike in England, the proof of debt provision in the Australian Bankruptcy Act does not extend to tortious demands.[77] For this reason, Gummow and von Doussa JJ. in the Federal Court in *Gye* v. *McIntyre* conceded that the debtors' claim would not have been a provable debt if the creditor had been bankrupt, though they said that this was not a valid reason for denying a set-off. Similarly, the High Court said that there was nothing in the language of the set-off section to suggest that the bankrupt's claim (or, as in that case, the claim of the debtors subject to the compositions) should be in the nature of a provable debt.

On the other hand, the High Court in *Gye* v. *McIntyre* indicated that the availability of a set-off in relation to the bankrupt's claim is not unqualified. Clearly, in order to come within the set-off section, the bankrupt's claim must be a presently payable debt at the date of the bankruptcy, or the product of giving credit, or it must arise out of a prior dealing between the parties. In addition, however, the High Court said

---

[76] The Bankruptcy Act 1966 (Cth.), s. 243 provides that the set-off section (s. 86) is to apply to compositions.

[77] See the Bankruptcy Act 1966 (Cth.), s. 82(2). However, this is no longer the case in a company liquidation. See the Corporations Law, s. 553.

that the claim must be such that it would vest in a trustee in bankruptcy,[78] a view also expressed by Wood.[79] The effect of this is to exclude, for example, income earned by the bankrupt,[80] unless an income payments order is made under section 310 of the Insolvency 1986, and claims for damages for personal injury or wrong done to the bankrupt.[81] This requirement follows from the stipulation in the set-off section that the balance of the account is provable in the bankruptcy, or, as the case may be, is payable to the trustee in bankruptcy. If the balance is payable to the trustee, the section could only apply if the bankrupt's claim has vested in the trustee. This limitation should also apply in England, where tortious demands are now provable. The better view is that a damages claim in tort should not be able to be employed in a set-off unless it arose out of a dealing between the parties to the proposed set-off, since the claim obviously does not constitute a debt and nor does it come within the judicially accepted definition of giving credit.[82] Normally, the claims in tort which do not pass to the trustee, as, for example, a damages claim for personal injury, are unlikely to arise out of a dealing. But even if in an exceptional case the claim is derived from a dealing, the fact that it does not vest in the trustee should mean that it cannot be set off.

---

[78] (1991) 171 CLR 609, 626–7. See also *De Mattos* v. *Saunders* (1872) LR 7 CP 570, 582. While the claim in *Gye* v. *McIntyre* had not been included in the composition, the High Court considered that it would be unjust if a statutory majority of creditors could, by excluding a claim of the debtor against a particular creditor from the property vesting in the trustee of the composition, deprive that creditor of the benefit of a set-off to which he would have been entitled if a bankruptcy had occurred. The important point was that the claim would have vested in a trustee in bankruptcy.

[79] Wood, *English and International Set-off* (1989), 315–16.

[80] See the Insolvency Act 1986, s. 307(5).

[81] See, for example, *Beckham* v. *Drake* (1849) 2 HLC 579, 604, 621; *Ex parte Vine; in re Wilson* (1878) 8 Ch. D 364; *Wilson* v. *United Counties Bank, Ltd.* [1920] AC 102. In Australia, see the Bankruptcy Act 1966 (Cth.), s. 116(2)(g).

[82] See the discussion of damages claims in section 4.5 below.

4

Claims Susceptible to Insolvency Set-off

In the preceding chapter some general observations were made on the meaning of mutual credit and mutual dealings. In this chapter, it is proposed to consider particular forms of claims that may be the subject of a set-off in insolvency.

4.1 PRESENTLY EXISTING AND PAYABLE DEBT

A debt which is both presently existing and payable at the relevant date for determining rights of set-off in a bankruptcy or liquidation[1] may be the subject of a set-off. This includes a debt in equity,[2] other than an equitable debt in the form of an obligation to account for a trust fund.[3]

4.2 PRESENTLY EXISTING BUT UNMATURED OR UNQUANTIFIED DEBT

Similarly a debt on either side of the account which is in existence at the relevant date, though not payable until a future date, may be the subject of a set-off.[4] In some early cases doubts were expressed as to whether this was strictly a debt for the purpose of the expression of 'mutual debts', though in any event it was held to constitute the giving of credit so as to be available as a set-off on that account.[5]

A set-off is also available in respect of a debt which, though existing, was unquantified at the relevant date,[6] as, for example, where the amount

---

[1] See section 2.7 above. [2] *Ryall* v. *Rowles* (1750) 1 Ves. Sen. 348, 376.
[3] See Ch. 6.
[4] See e.g. *Ex parte Prescot* (1753) 1 Atk. 230 (debt owing to the bankrupt); *Atkinson* v. *Elliott* (1797) 7 TR 378 (debt owing by the bankrupt); *Rolls Razor Ltd.* v. *Cox* [1967] 1 QB 552, 569, 576.
[5] *Ex parte Prescot* (1753) 1 Atk. 230; *Atkinson* v. *Elliott* (1797) 7 TR 378, 381. See also *Hankey* v. *Smith* (1789) 3 TR 507n; *Re Morris and M'Murray* (1874) 5 AJR 157 (affirmed at 185).
[6] See *In re Daintrey; ex parte Mant* [1900] 1 QB 546, though compare the interpretation put upon that case in *Day & Dent Constructions Pty. Ltd.* v. *North Australian Properties Pty. Ltd.* (1982) 150 CLR 85, 92, 94, 103 and *Re Charge Card Services Ltd.* [1987] 1 Ch. 150, 182–3, 188.

depended upon a valuation by a valuer,[7] or an arithmetical calculation had to be undertaken,[8] or where an award of costs had been made before the relevant date though it was not taxed until after that date.[9] In an Australian case,[10] a shareholder who was indebted to the company became bankrupt. Prior to the bankruptcy the company had gone into voluntary liquidation. Its assets were more than sufficient to pay its liabilities, though the extent to which this was the case had not as yet been ascertained. When a dividend subsequently was declared, it was held that the company could set this off in the bankruptcy against the bankrupt's indebtedness to it, the important point being that, because the company went into voluntary liquidation before the bankruptcy under circumstances where there would be a surplus, the bankrupt at the date of the bankruptcy had a claim for a share of the surplus which could be the subject of a set-off notwithstanding that the amount of the claim had not been ascertained at that date.

When a creditor has proved in a bankruptcy or a liquidation for a debt the due date for payment of which has not yet occurred, rule 11.13 of the Insolvency Rules provides that, for the purpose of dividend 'and for no other purpose', the amount of the creditor's proof is to be discounted according to a formula to take into account that payment is to be received early. This should not apply to the extent that the debt is to be employed in a set-off, because to that extent no dividend is payable. Rule 11.13 should be compared to section 554B of the Corporations Law in Australia, which instead is drafted in terms that the 'amount of a debt that is admissible to proof' is reduced to take into account early payment. Unlike in England, the reduction is not expressed to occur solely for the purpose of payment of a dividend, and the reduction in the proof should have a corresponding effect on the value of the debt for the purpose of set-off. On the other hand, the section only provides for a reduction in the case of the company's debt to the creditor. If the debt instead is payable *to* the company, there is no basis for reducing the amount of that debt to compensate for early payment by means of a set-off.[11]

A presently existing debt payable at a future date should be distinguished from the case of a deposit made on terms that interest is to be capitalized so that, upon maturity, the value of the deposit will have increased. If prior to the maturity the depositor becomes bankrupt, for the purpose of an

[7] *Ex parte Hope; in re Hanson* (1858) 3 De G & J 92. See also *Re Rushforth; ex parte J R Holmes and Sons* (1906) 95 LT 807.

[8] *Greater Britain Insurance Corporation Ltd.* v. *C. T. Bowring & Co. (Insurance), Ltd.* (1926) 24 Ll. L. Rep. 7, 9.

[9] *Shand* v. *M J Atkinson Ltd* [1966] NZLR 551; *Re Collinson; Smith* v. *Sinnathamby* (1977) 33 FLR 39. Compare *Ex parte Rhodes* (1809) 15 Ves. Jun. 539.

[10] *In re The West Australian Lighterage, Stevedoring and Transport Co. Ltd.* (1903) 5 WALR 132. [11] See e.g. *Ex parte Prescot* (1753) 1 Atk. 230.

automatic set-off on the insolvency date the amount of the debt presumably would be the initial deposit together with accrued interest at that date,[12] as opposed to the value that the debt would have had if interest had continued to be capitalized until the agreed maturity date.

4.3 CONTINGENT DEBT OWING BY THE INSOLVENT

4.3.1 *Introduction*

The set-off section requires that there be a creditor proving or claiming to prove for a debt in the bankruptcy or the liquidation, so that it is a necessary requirement of a set-off that the claim against the bankrupt or the company be provable. When a person who becomes bankrupt or goes into liquidation has a contingent liability, the fact of the bankruptcy or liquidation will sometimes constitute a repudiation of the contract in question which, if accepted, will give rise to a vested liability in damages,[13] though this will not always be the case.[14] Where a debt is contingent, and the case is not one involving an accepted repudiation, the insolvency legislation requires the trustee or liquidator to estimate its value,[15] and a proof may be lodged for this amount. If the contingency subsequently occurs the full amount of the debt may be proved notwithstanding an earlier estimation or, if a proof has already been lodged based upon the estimation, the proof may be adjusted, but not so as to disturb prior dividends.[16] The reason that a subsequent occurrence of the contingency is taken into account is not that the bankruptcy or liquidation is deemed to have accelerated the contingency, so as to fix the value of the claim on the basis of the contingency having occurred on the relevant date. Rather, it is because the fact of the occurrence of the contingency is the best evidence of the true value of the claim as at that date.[17]

4.3.2 *Rule against double proof*

While as a general rule contingent debts are provable, this is subject to the rule against double proof, which essentially provides that there can only be

---

[12] See section 2.12 above in relation to the automatic theory. If it is the deposit-taker rather than the depositor which is in liquidation or bankrupt, interest in any event would cease to accrue as from the date of commencement of the liquidation or the bankruptcy. See r. 4.93 of the Insolvency Rules and, for bankruptcies, the Insolvency Act, s. 322(2).

[13] See e.g. *Baker* v. *Lloyd's Bank, Ltd.* [1920] 2 KB 322, 326.

[14] See section 5.2 below.

[15] See the Insolvency Act, s. 322, and the Insolvency Rules, r. 4.86.

[16] *Ellis and Company's Trustee* v. *Dixon-Johnson* [1924] 1 Ch. 342, 357, and see the Insolvency Rules 1986, r. 4.86.

[17] *Ellis and Company's Trustee* v. *Dixon-Johnson* [1924] 1 Ch. 342, 356–7; *In re Dynamics Corporation of America* [1976] 1 WLR 757, 768; *Re Hurren* [1983] 1 WLR 183, 189.

one dividend in respect of what in substance is the same debt, even though the claims for a dividend may be based upon different contracts.[18] The rule can apply in a number of situations,[19] but often finds its expression in the context of guarantees. A guarantor who has guaranteed the whole of the debt owing to a creditor, and who pays the creditor in accordance with the guarantee, is entitled to be indemnified by the debtor. Prior to payment to the creditor the right of indemnity is subject to a contingency. If the debtor is bankrupt, and the guarantor pays the creditor *after* the bankruptcy but before the creditor has lodged a proof in the bankruptcy, the guarantor may prove for his claim for an indemnity notwithstanding that at the date of the bankruptcy it was still contingent.[20] Different considerations apply, however, if the creditor has not been paid in full and has either proved in the debtor's bankruptcy or, if he has not proved, he is entitled to do so.[21] Prior to payment under the guarantee the guarantor still has a contingent claim for an indemnity which prima facie would appear to be provable in the debtor's bankruptcy, on the basis of a valuation of that contingent claim by the trustee in bankruptcy. But, if the creditor has proved or is entitled to prove in the bankruptcy, and in addition the guarantor were allowed to prove for his contingent claim, the debtor's estate could be subjected to two proofs in respect of what essentially is the same debt. The creditor is the party who is out of pocket, and so his right of proof should be preserved. Therefore, in order to prevent the possibility of a double proof the guarantor is not permitted to prove for his contingent claim.[22] The same principle applies if the guarantor makes a payment to the creditor after the creditor has lodged a proof, including in the form of a dividend in the guarantor's own bankruptcy. Indeed, the principle is still applicable if the creditor, having proved in the debtor's bankruptcy and received a dividend, is paid the full amount which remains outstanding by the guarantor. Because the creditor has proved in the debtor's bankruptcy, the debtor's estate cannot be subjected to a second proof from the guarantor for the same debt.[23] On the other hand, if the guarantor's

---

[18] *In re Oriental Commercial Bank* (1871) LR 7 Ch. App. 99, 103–4.
[19] See e.g. *Deering* v. *Bank of Ireland* (1886) 12 App. Cas. 20; *The Liverpool (No. 2)* [1960] 3 WLR 597.   [20] *In re Fenton* [1931] 1 Ch. 85, 118.
[21] See e.g. *In re Fenton* [1931] 1 Ch. 85, in which not all the creditors had proved in the principal debtor's liquidation and the rule against double proof was held to apply.
[22] *In re Fenton* [1931] 1 Ch. 85 (esp. at 107, 114, 118–19), not following *In re Herepath & Delmar* (1890) 7 Morr. 129, 190. It was held in *In re Paine; ex parte Read* [1897] 1 QB 122, and again in *In re Blackpool Motor Car Co., Ltd.* [1901] 1 Ch. 77, that a surety before payment to the creditor is a 'creditor' of the bankrupt for the purposes of the preference provision. In *Fenton* both Lord Hanworth M.R. (at 106) and Romer L.J. (at 118–20) agreed that these two cases were correctly decided, though they said that the issue determined was separate from the question whether the surety should be entitled to prove in the bankruptcy. See also *The Liverpool (No. 2)* [1960] 3 WLR 597, 606; *Re Bruce David Realty Pty. Ltd.* [1969] VR 240, 243.

payment is such that the creditor is paid in full, the guarantor is entitled to be subrogated to the benefit of the creditor's proof in the bankruptcy as regards future dividends to the extent required to indemnify him for his payment to the creditor.[24] It has been suggested that the guarantor is only entitled to be subrogated to the rights of the creditor if the guarantor himself has paid the full amount of the debt,[25] though the better view is that the right or subrogation arises when the creditor is paid in full, whether or not entirely by the guarantor.[26]

The guarantee may be limited to a stated amount. If this is less than the debt owing to the creditor, and the guarantor pays the full amount for which he is liable under the guarantee, the question whether the rule against double proof continues to apply depends upon whether the guarantee is of the whole of the indebtedness, with a limitation of liability to a certain amount, or whether the guarantee is of only part of the debt.[27] In the former case any proof by the guarantor would be in respect of the same debt owing by the debtor to the creditor, so that the rule would still apply.[28] Nor would the guarantor be subrogated to any part of the creditor's proof before the creditor has been paid in full.[29] If, however, the guarantee is merely in respect of part of the debt, and the guarantor has paid the creditor that part in accordance with the guarantee before the creditor has proved, the guarantor may prove in the debtor's bankruptcy for an indemnity relating to that part and the creditor may prove for the unpaid part.[30] If the creditor has already proved for the whole debt, the guarantor upon payment of the part guaranteed becomes subrogated to the proof to the extent of that part.[31] When a guarantee in truth relates only to a part of a debt, that part as between the creditor and the guarantor is treated as a separate debt.[32]

When a guarantee is of the whole indebtedness, the creditor is entitled to prove for the full debt notwithstanding that a payment may have been

---

[23] *In re Oriental Commercial Bank* (1871) LR 7 Ch. App. 99; *In re Fenton* [1931] 1 Ch. 85, 115.

[24] *In re Whitehouse; Whitehouse* v. *Edwards* (1887) 37 Ch. D 683, 694–5; *In re Fenton* [1931] 1 Ch. 85, 118; *Westpac Banking Corporation* v. *Gollin & Co. Ltd.* [1988] VR 397, 403.

[25] See e.g. Lawrence L.J. in *Fenton* [1931] 1 Ch. 85, 115, Mellish L.J. in *Ex parte Brett* (1871) LR 6 Ch. App. 838, 841, and James L.J. in *Ex parte Turquand; in re Fothergill* (1876) 3 Ch. D 445, 450.

[26] See *A. E. Goodwin Ltd.* v. *A. G. Healing Ltd.* (1979) 7 ACLR 481; *McColl's Wholesale Pty. Ltd.* v. *State Bank of NSW* [1984] 3 NSWLR 365, 378; *Westpac Banking Corporation* v. *Gollin & Co. Ltd.* [1988] VR 397, 402.

[27] See generally the discussion in *Barclay's Bank Ltd.* v. *TOSG Trust Fund Ltd.* [1984] 1 AC 626, 643–4.   [28] *In re Fenton* [1931] 1 Ch. 85, 115.

[29] This is consistent with the discussion in *In re Sass* [1896] 2 QB 12, 15, and see also *Westpac Banking Corporation* v. *Gollin & Co. Ltd.* [1988] VR 397, 405–6.

[30] *In re Sass* [1896] 2 QB 12, 15.

[31] *In re Sass* [1896] 2 QB 12, 15; *Westpac Banking Corporation* v. *Gollin & Co. Ltd.* [1988] VR 397, 405.   [32] See *In re Sass* [1896] 2 QB 12, 15.

made to him by the guarantor, if in fact any part of the debt still remains unpaid.[33] However, there is an apparent exception to this principle in the case of bills of exchange. The position of the drawer and a prior indorser of a bill is similar to that of a guarantor, though it is nevertheless accepted that the holder in proving in the bankruptcy of the acceptor must give credit for anything that he received from the drawer or the indorser *before* the proof.[34] In such a case, Wood's view that the rule against double proof would not apply so as to prevent a proof by the drawer or the indorser would appear to be correct.[35]

The rule against double proof is also important in the context of rights of contribution between guarantors. When there is more than one guarantor of the same debt, a guarantor who has paid more than his share is entitled to claim contribution from a co-guarantor.[36] Consider that the co-guarantor has become bankrupt. Prior to payment to the creditor the guarantor has a contingent right to contribution from the co-guarantor though, since the creditor has a provable debt in the co-guarantor's bankruptcy, the co-guarantor cannot prove for his contingent claim. Further, if the guarantor has paid more than his just share, but the creditor nevertheless has not been paid in full so that the creditor remains entitled to prove in the co-guarantor's bankruptcy, the rule against double proof would still operate to prevent a proof by the guarantor. This objection would also apply if the guarantor pays more than his share *after* the creditor has lodged a proof in the co-guarantor's bankruptcy. On the other hand, once the creditor has been paid in full, the guarantor is entitled to be subrogated to the creditor's proof and to receive the dividends until he has received an amount sufficient to satisfy his claim for contribution.[37]

If the rule against double proof operates to deny a contingent creditor a right of proof, it is apparent that the contingent creditor similarly could not employ his claim in a set-off, since the set-off section stipulates that there should be a creditor proving or claiming to prove for a debt. For example, in *In re Fenton; ex parte Fenton Textile Association, Ltd*[38] a debtor had

---

[33] *In re Sass* [1896] 2 QB 12, 14–15; *Ulster Bank Ltd.* v. *Lambe* [1966] NI 161; *Westpac Banking Corporation* v. *Gollin & Co. Ltd.* [1988] VR 388, 401, 403.

[34] However, the acceptor is not obliged to reduce his proof in respect of anything paid to him after lodging the proof. See generally *In re Houlder* [1929] 1 Ch. 205, 212. This principle is confined to negotiable instruments. See *In re Blackburne* (1892) 9 Morr. 249, 252, and also the discussion in *Westpac Banking Corporation* v. *Gollin & Co. Ltd.* [1988] VR 388, 407–8. Note that, when the acceptor is not bankrupt or in liquidation, and the holder is suing the acceptor in an action at law on the bill, the holder need not reduce his claim to the extent of a part payment received from the drawer or a prior indorser, though to the extent of that part payment he sues as trustee for the drawer or prior indorser. See *Thornton* v. *Maynard* (1875) LR 10 CP 695.   [35] Wood, *English and International Set-off* (1989), 611.

[36] See e.g. *Craythorne* v. *Swinburne* (1807) 14 Ves. Jun. 160.

[37] *Ex parte Stokes* (1848) De Gex 618; *In re Parker; Morgan* v. *Hill* [1894] 3 Ch. 400.

[38] [1931] 1 Ch. 85.

gone into liquidation and, while the contingent creditor had lodged a proof in a scheme of arrangement executed by a guarantor, the creditor had not been paid anything by either the debtor or the guarantor. Since the guarantor by reason of the rule against double proof did not have a debt which was provable in the liquidation, the Court of Appeal held that he was not permitted to employ his claim for an indemnity in a set-off.

4.3.3 *Set-off in the absence of a double proof problem*

Consider that in a particular case the rule against double proof does not apply, so that the contingent debt arising out of a prior agreement is provable. A prime example is the case of a guarantor who pays the creditor in full after the debtor's bankruptcy or liquidation but before the creditor has lodged a proof.[39] As a matter of principle the debt should be able to be employed in a set-off, either because the debt is a natural result of a prior transaction so as to come within the concept of giving credit,[40] or alternatively because the debt arose out of a prior dealing between the parties to the proposed set-off. This assumes, however, that the qualification to the set-off section is not a bar to a set-off in respect of contingent debts. According to that qualification,[41] sums due from a bankrupt may not be included in an account if the creditor had notice at the time they became 'due' that a bankruptcy petition was pending. In the case of a contingent debt the better view is that this would be interpreted broadly as referring to the creditor's knowledge at the time that a binding transaction was entered into out of which a debt subsequently arose, as opposed to the time that a liability vested upon the occurrence of the contingency.[42] Assuming that it is otherwise possible for a contingent debt owing by a bankrupt or a company in liquidation to be employed in a set-off, the contrary conclusion would mean that in the vast majority of cases the operation of the qualification in any event would preclude this.

Leaving aside this question of the interpretation of the qualification to the set-off section, there is in any event authority for the proposition that a debt which is contingent at the relevant date cannot be set off. *In re A Debtor (No. 66 of 1955); ex parte The Debtor* v. *The Trustee of the Property of Waite (A Bankrupt)*[43] concerned a bankrupt surety. After the bankruptcy the surety's trustee in bankruptcy paid the creditor in full in order to obtain the release of security given by the surety to the creditor. The trustee then sought to recover this amount from the debtor and, when the debtor failed to pay, issued a bankruptcy notice against him. The

---

[39] *In re Fenton* [1931] 1 Ch. 85, 118. [40] See section 3.1 above.
[41] Insolvency Act, s. 323(3) and, for companies, the Insolvency Rules, r. 4.90(3).
[42] See section 2.7.4 above. [43] [1956] 1 WLR 1226.

debtor argued that, because of a separate debt owing to him by the surety, he had a right of set-off in the surety's bankruptcy against his indemnity obligation, and that after a set-off the amount for which he was indebted would have been less than the amount required for a bankruptcy notice. The Court of Appeal rejected this argument, on the ground that a claim which is merely contingent at the relevant date, and consequently not 'due', may not be employed in a set-off. It is noticeable that in *In re A Debtor* the surety, rather than the principal debtor, was the bankrupt party. The case was not one in which a bankrupt had a contingent liability at the relevant date. Rather, he had a contingent claim, and the case is considered later in that context.[44] However, the Court of Appeal based its decision to deny a set-off on the broader proposition that both demands must be 'due' at the relevant date so that, irrespective of whether the principal debtor or the surety is the bankrupt party, a surety's right to an indemnity will not give rise to a set-off as between those parties if the right was still contingent at the relevant date.[45] In doing so the Court distinguished *In re Daintrey*[46] on the ground that that case was not concerned with a contingent debt, but rather with a debt which was due at the relevant date but which remained to be quantified.[47] In *Daintrey* a business was sold on terms that the price was to be calculated as a proportion of the profits made over a three-year period. The vendor became bankrupt before any profits in fact had been earned. At the end of the three-year period, when the price was calculated in accordance with the agreed formula, it was held that the purchaser could set off his liability against a separate debt owing to him by the vendor. Notwithstanding the Court of Appeal's analysis of the case in *In re A Debtor*, the debt in *Daintrey* would indeed appear to have been contingent. No profits had been earned at the

---

[44] See section 4.4 below.

[45] See Lord Evershed M.R. and Hodson L.J. at [1956] 1 WLR 1226, 1230, 1237. In later cases *In re A Debtor* has been regarded as authority for that proposition. See *Carreras Rothmans Ltd.* v. *Freeman Mathews Treasure Ltd.* [1985] 1 Ch. 207; *In re Hawkins, dec'd* unreported, Walton J., 2 February 1978; *Re Charge Card Services Ltd.* [1987] 1 Ch. 150, 188–90. See also *Re Bruce David Realty Pty. Ltd.* [1969] VR 240, 243, in which Adam J. accepted that a surety must have paid the creditor before the principal debtor's bankruptcy in order to have a set-off in the bankruptcy, and *Brown* v. *Cork* [1985] BCLC 363, 368, 376. In Canada see *Re Mitchell, Houghton Ltd.* (1970) 14 CBR 301.

[46] [1900] 1 QB 546. The Court of Appeal in *In re A Debtor* also relied on dicta in *In re Fenton* [1931] 1 Ch. 85, though, as Gibbs C.J. noted in *Day & Dent Constructions Pty. Ltd.* v. *North Australian Properties Pty. Ltd.* (1982) 150 CLR 85, 94, the dicta in question are ambiguous, if not misleading. Indeed, Mason J. (at 102) said that, according to his reading of the judgments, the surety would have been entitled to a set-off in *Fenton* if he had paid the debt.

[47] This view has been expressed on other occasions. See e.g. Eve J. in *In re National Benefit Assurance Co., Ltd.* [1924] 2 Ch. 339, 343, and Peter Gibson J. in *Carreras Rothmans Ltd.* v. *Freeman Mathews Treasure Ltd.* [1985] 1 Ch. 207, 230.

date of the bankruptcy, so that the debt was contingent at that date upon profits subsequently being earned.[48] *Daintrey* accordingly supports the view that a contingent debt may be the subject of a set-off.

In re A Debtor would appear to be wrong on this point, which is the position that has been adopted in Australia following the criticism of that case by the High Court in *Day & Dent Constructions Pty. Ltd. v. North Australian Properties Pty. Ltd.*[49] It was also assumed by the House of Lords in *Stein v. Blake*[50] that a contingent debt can be set off, and indeed the contrary view is inconsistent with Dixon J.'s often-quoted statement in the High Court in *Hiley v. The People's Prudential Assurance Co. Ltd.*[51] that, 'It is enough that at the commencement of the winding up mutual dealings exist which involve rights and obligations whether absolute or contingent of such a nature that afterwards in the events that happen they mature or develop into pecuniary demands capable of set-off'. There are in fact a number of instances, in addition to *In re Daintrey*, in which English courts have recognized that a debt owing by a bankrupt which was contingent at the relevant date could be the subject of a set-off.[52] For example, the holder of a bill of exchange has been permitted to set off his claim against the drawer or an indorser of the bill in the drawer's or the indorser's bankruptcy, even though dishonour by the acceptor only occurred after the bankruptcy.[53] Similarly, it has been held that an accommodation acceptor or indorser of a bill could set off his claim for an indemnity in the drawer's bankruptcy notwithstanding that the bill was

---

[48] See Millett J. in *Re Charge Card Services Ltd.* [1987] 1 Ch. 150, 182–3, and the cases to which he refers. As Millett J. noted, this was the view of Gibbs C.J. and Mason J. in the High Court of Australia in *Day & Dent Constructions Pty. Ltd. v. North Australian Properties Pty. Ltd.* (1982) 150 CLR 85, 92, 94, 103. Compare, however, Lindley M.R. in the Court of Appeal in *Daintrey* [1900] 1 QB 546, 572.

[49] (1982) 150 CLR 85. Gibbs C.J. (at 94) left open the question whether *In re A Debtor (No. 66 of 1955)* was correctly decided on the ground that the surety, rather than the debtor, was bankrupt, and the payments were made by the trustee to enable him to obtain the bankrupt's property, though the better view is that this does not justify the result. See section 9.4.2 below.

[50] [1995] 2 All ER 961, 965. See also Hoffman L.J. in the Chancery Division in *M.S. Fashions Ltd. v. Bank of Credit and Commerce International SA* [1993] Ch. 425, 435.

[51] (1938) 60 CLR 496–7.

[52] In addition to the cases referred to below, see *Jones v. Mossop* (1844) 3 Hare 568, 571 (on the assumption that Richard Reed was bankrupt); *In re Taylor; ex parte Norvell* [1910] 1 KB 562, 568; *Baker v. Lloyd's Bank, Ltd.* [1920] 2 KB 322; *Hiley v. The Peoples Prudential Assurance Co. Ltd.* (1938) 60 CLR 468, 491, 497; *Re Northside Properties Pty. Ltd.* [1971] 2 NSWLR 320, 324. In *Willment Brothers Ltd. v. North West Thames Regional Health Authority* (1984) 26 Build. LR 51 Ackner and O'Connor L.JJ. said that, even if the creditor's claim against the company in liquidation was indeed merely contingent at the date of the liquidation, it could still be employed in a set-off, though no mention was made of the earlier decision in *Waite*.

[53] *Arbouin v. Tritton* (1816) Holt 408; *Alsager v. Currie* (1844) 12 M & W 751.

paid after the bankruptcy.[54] In *Graham* v. *Russell*[55] the Court of Exchequer Chamber accepted that an insured could set off in the underwriter's bankruptcy the liability of the underwriter on a loss which occurred after the bankruptcy, despite the contingent nature of the liability at the relevant date. It has also been held that the holder of a policy of life insurance who was indebted to the insurance company could set off the value of the policy in the winding-up of the company, even though the policy had not matured at the relevant date for determining rights of set-off in the liquidation either by payment of the requisite number of premiums or by death.[56] In *Lee & Chapman's Case*[57] a damages claim for breach of contract against a company, where the breach occurred after the liquidation, was the subject of a set-off.[58]

Subsequently Millett J. considered the question in detail in *Re Charge Card Services Ltd.*[59] The case concerned a company which operated a charge card scheme. The company assigned its receivables to a factor, the agreement providing that, if the company went into liquidation, the factor could require it to re-purchase the debts at face value. One of the issues in dispute was whether, if a notice of re-purchase was given after the liquidation, the factor could set off the company's resulting liability to pay the price against a debt owing by the factor to the company. It is apparent that any liability of the company to pay the price was contingent at the date of the liquidation, a notice of re-purchase not having then been given, and accordingly it was argued that *In re A Debtor* was authority against a set-off in this situation. However Millett J. held that a contingent claim may be employed in a set-off provided that it is exclusively referable to a prior agreement between the parties to the proposed set-off.[60] In the case of a principal debtor's obligation to indemnify the surety, the obligation is not exclusively referable to a contract between the principal debtor and the surety. Rather, it is referable to the contract of guarantee to which the principal often is not a party. On the other hand, since the particular contingent liability in issue in *Charge Card* was exclusively referable to a

[54] *Smith* v. *Hodson* (1791) 4 TR 211; *Ex parte Boyle, re Shepherd*, unreported but noted in Cooke, *The Bankrupt Laws* (8th edn., 1823) Vol. 1, 571; *Ex parte Wagstaff* (1806) 13 Ves. Jun. 65; *Hulme* v. *Muggleston* (1837) 3 M & W 30; *Russell* v. *Bell* (1841) 8 M & W 277; *Bittleston* v. *Timmis* (1845) 1 CB 389. [55] (1816) 5 M & S 498.

[56] *In re City Life Assurance Co., Ltd; Grandfield's Case* [1926] 1 Ch. 191 (not following *Ex parte Price; in re Lankester* (1875) LR 10 Ch. App. 648 and *Paddy* v. *Clutton* [1920] 2 Ch. 554). See also *Sovereign Life Assurance Company* v. *Dodd* [1892] 2 QB 573, in which the insured paid the final premium after the petition and before the winding-up order, though the date of the petition seems to have been regarded as the relevant date. Compare *In re National Benefit Assurance Company, Ltd.* [1924] 2 Ch. 339 (and see also *Hiley* v. *The Peoples Prudential Assurance Co., Ltd.* (1938) 60 CLR 468, 493), in which the winding-up was treated as a repudiation by the company. [57] (1885) 30 Ch. D 216.

[58] See also section 4.5.1 below. [59] [1987] 1 Ch. 150.

[60] See the discussion at [1987] 1 Ch. 150, 189–90.

contract between the parties to the proposed set-off, he concluded that *In re A Debtor* did not constitute authority against a set-off in the case before him.

The source of Millett J.'s analysis appears to have been a comment by Lord Evershed M.R. in *In re A Debtor*,[61] in which the Master of the Rolls distinguished the case before him from *In re Daintrey*[62] on the ground that in *Daintrey* the amount of the indebtedness in question was exclusively referable to an obligation to pay the price incurred prior to the relevant date. However, that comment was in the context of Lord Evershed's characterization of *Daintrey* as a case in which there was a prior debt which merely remained to be quantified after the relevant date, as opposed to a subsequently arising debt. No doubt a proper quantification of a debt would require that the quantum be exclusively referable to that debt. On the other hand, when a contingent debt is in issue it is not clear why there should be a requirement that it must be exclusively referable to a prior agreement between the parties to the proposed set-off. It may have been the result of a perception that only a claim that arises out of mutual dealings between the parties can be the subject of a set-off.[63] However, while this undoubtedly would be a ground for a set-off, it was earlier pointed out[64] that, if it is sought to base a set-off upon the concept of giving credit, it is not necessary to show that there was a dealing between the parties in question, or, as Buller J. expressed it in *Hankey* v. *Smith*,[65] that the parties meant to trust each other in the transaction in question. For example, an acceptor of a bill of exchange may not have even been aware at the time of his bankruptcy that the bill had been endorsed to the holder. While in such a case it could hardly be said that these two parties had ever dealt with each other in relation to the bill, or indeed that the indebtedness of the acceptor to the holder was 'exclusively referable' to an agreement between them, it was held in *Hankey* v. *Smith* that the holder can employ the claim on the bill in a set-off in the bankruptcy, on the ground that credit nevertheless has been given by the holder.[66] Mutual dealings as a ground

---

[61] [1956] 1 WLR 1226, 1230.   [62] [1900] 1 QB 546.

[63] On other occasions it has been said that a contingent debt may be set off if it arose out of mutual dealings. See e.g. Phillimore J. in the Divisional Court in *In re Taylor; ex parte Norvell* [1910] 1 KB 562, 568, and Buckley L.J. in the Court of Appeal (at 580). See also Romer L.J. in *In re Fenton* [1931] 1 Ch. 85, 117 ('For contingent liabilities are in general debts provable in the bankruptcy, and it is well settled that, provided there are mutuality of dealings, claims provable may be set off'). In *Hiley* v. *The Peoples Prudential Assurance Co. Ltd.* (1938) 60 CLR 468, 496 Dixon J. said that it is 'enough' for a set-off that 'at the commencement of the winding up mutual dealings exist which involve rights and obligations whether absolute or contingent of such a nature that afterwards in the events that happen they mature or develop into pecuniary demands capable of set-off'.   [64] See section 3.3 above.
[65] (1789) 3 TR 507n.   [66] *Hankey* v. *Smith* (1789) 3 TR 507n.

for a set-off first appeared in the set-off section in the 1869 Act,[67] though even before then contingent debts could be the subject of a set-off,[68] which suggests that it is not necessary to base a set-off in such a case on the mutual dealings head. Indeed, the 1825 and 1849 Bankruptcy Acts both specifically provided that all debts provable against the estate could be set off, and the legislation in each case allowed a right of proof to a person who was a surety at the time of the bankruptcy of the principal debtor, if the surety paid the debt.[69] The contingent debt was allowed to be set off on the ground that credit was given at the date of the debtor's bankruptcy. In other words, there was a prior transaction which would naturally, or in the ordinary course of business, end in a debt.[70] Further, when it is sought to base a set-off of a contingent debt upon the mutual credit head, the principle of *Hankey* v. *Smith* applicable to mutual credit should be relevant, so that as a matter of principle it should not be necessary that the parties to the transaction of which the debt was the natural result should be the same as the parties to the set-off.

Consider the particular case of a surety who pays the creditor after the debtor's bankruptcy. If the rule against double proof does not apply, the surety's claim for an indemnity should be able to be employed in a set-off, on the basis that the debt was a natural result of a prior transaction and therefore it constituted the giving of credit. This in fact was the ground upon which the High Court of Australia upheld the surety's claim for a set-off in *Day & Dent Constructions Pty. Ltd.* v. *North Australian Properties Pty. Ltd.*[71] It should not be necessary to show that the parties to the proposed set-off had dealt with each other, or had intended to trust each other, or, in Millett J.'s terminology, that the debt in question is exclusively referable to an agreement between them. But even if, contrary to this view, a dealing is required when it is sought to base a set-off upon a debt in respect of which credit had been given, the surety's claim usually will arise out of a dealing between the principal debtor and the surety,[72] the dealing being the giving of the guarantee at the request (express or

---

[67] Bankruptcy Act 1869, s. 39.

[68] See e.g. *Smith* v. *Hodson* (1791) 4 TR 211 and *Russell* v. *Bell* (1841) 8 M & W 277 (accommodation acceptor paying after the bankruptcy of the drawer permitted to set off his claim for an indemnity in the drawer's bankruptcy); *Arbouin* v. *Tritton* (1816) Holt 408 and *Alsager* v. *Currie* (1844) 12 M & W 751 (holder of a bill of exchange permitted to set off his claim against the drawer or an indorser of the bill in the drawer's or the indorser's bankruptcy, even though dishonour by the acceptor occurred after the bankruptcy). See also *Graham* v. *Russell* (1816) 5 M & S 498. Compare Millett J. in *Re Charge Card Services Ltd.* [1987] 1 Ch. 150, 179.

[69] See ss. 50 and 52 of (1825) 6 Geo. IV, c. 16, and ss. 171 and 173 of the Bankrupt Law Consolidation Act 1849. [70] See section 3.1 above.

[71] (1982) 150 CLR 85.

[72] It is noticeable that Hodson L.J. in *In re A Debtor* [1956] 1 WLR 1226, 1237 agreed that there were mutual dealings in that case. See also *In re Fenton* [1931] 1 Ch. 85, 117.

implied) of the principal debtor.[73] While the surety's claim admittedly may not be *exclusively* referable to that dealing, it is difficult to understand as a matter of principle why indeed there should be a requirement of exclusivity. Millett J. was bound by the decision of the Court of Appeal in *In re A Debtor*, and in order to justify a set-off in *Charge Card* he had to find grounds for distinguishing the earlier case. The better view is that *In re A Debtor* was wrongly decided.

Day & Dent Constructions[74] does not stand alone in this regard.[75] In *Hiley* v. *The Peoples Prudential Assurance Co. Ltd.*[76] Starke J. indicated that that a surety paying the creditor after the debtor's bankruptcy could employ his claim for an indemnity in a set-off, and this is also consistent with a suggestion by Wigram V.C. in *Jones* v. *Mossop*,[77] that if the person who in that case was the principal debtor on some promissory notes in respect of which the plaintiff was surety had been made bankrupt, the plaintiff subsequently paying the notes would have had a right of set-off. It is also supported by *In re The Moseley Green Coal and Coke Company, Ltd; Barrett's Case (No. 2)*.[78] *Barrett's Case* was distinguished in *In re A Debtor* on the ground that the surety's claim against the principal debtor was based on a promissory note given as security to the creditor, although it is difficult to see why this should justify a different result, given that a surety's right to securities held by the creditor is just as much a consequence of the payment to the creditor as is the right to an indemnity.[79] Thus, in *Day & Dent Constructions*[80] both Gibbs C.J. and Mason J. considered that *Barrett's Case* was directly on point.

---

[73] In essence, this is the view expressed by counsel in *Charge Card* but not adopted by Millett J. (see [1987] 1 Ch. 150, 189–90). It was held in *Owen* v. *Tate* [1976] 1 QB 402 that, if a surety had acted officiously in giving the guarantee, he is not entitled to an indemnity from the principal debtor, in which case he would not have a provable debt which could be set off. However, the decision in *Owen* v. *Tate* has been criticized by commentators. See Goff and Jones, *The Law of Restitution* (4th edn., 1993), 597–8, and Birks, *An Introduction to the Law of Restitution* (1989), 311–12.   [74] (1982) 150 CLR 85.

[75] In addition to the cases referred to below see *Re Last; Ex parte Butterell* (1994) 124 ALR 219. Note, however, the discussion in section 2.12.1 above of whether *Day & Dent Constructions* is compatible with the automatic extinction theory of insolvency set-off approved by the House of Lords in *Stein* v. *Blake* [1995] 2 All ER 961. On the other hand, *Day & Dent Constructions* was referred to in *Stein* v. *Blake* at (968–9) without any suggestion that it was wrongly decided.

[76] (1938) 60 CLR 468, 491. See also Latham C.J. (at 483) and Dixon J. (at 500–1), referring to *In re The Moseley Green Coal and Coke Company, Ltd; Barrett's Case (No. 2)* (1865) 4 De G J & S 756, 34 LJ Bcy. 41, discussed below.

[77] (1844) 3 Hare 568, 571.   .

[78] (1865) 4 De G J & S 756, 12 LT 193, 34 LJ Bcy. 41.

[79] There are two points to note in relation to *Barrett*. The set-off was against a liability to the company in liquidation for an unpaid call. While it is now accepted that a set-off is not available in such a case (see section 4.6 below), the applicable legislation when Barrett was decided specifically allowed a set-off to a contributory in respect of any sums due to him from the company on an independent contract or dealing. See the Joint Stock Companies

4.3.4 *Creditor had proved before the surety's payment*

The creditor may in fact have proved for the debt in the debtor's bankruptcy before payment by the surety, in which case the rule against double proof will have the effect of preventing the guarantor himself from lodging a second proof. It has been suggested that, where the guarantor is denied the right to lodge a separate proof in the debtor's bankruptcy after payment in full to the creditor, the guarantor similarly cannot set off his claim for an indemnity against a liability that he has to the debtor.[81] If this indeed were the law, it would be unsatisfactory. The better view, however, is that a set-off is available to the guarantor. The set-off section admittedly stipulates that there should be a person proving or claiming to prove for a bankruptcy debt.[82] The guarantor himself does not have a provable debt. That much is clear.[83] Nevertheless, upon payment in full to the creditor the guarantor is entitled to be subrogated to the creditor's proof in the bankruptcy.[84] The court of bankruptcy is a court of equitable jurisdiction[85] and, though the proof is still nominally the creditor's, it should be possible to go behind it and proceed on the basis that as a matter of equity the proof has become the proof of the guarantor. As far as equity is concerned the position should be regarded in the same way as if the surety had acquired a right to prove in his own name upon payment to the creditor, so that *Day & Dent Constructions* should apply (see section 4.3.3 above). The important point is that the guarantor's entitlement to the benefit of the proof is exclusively referable to an obligation incurred before the bankruptcy. It does not involve any new and independent transaction.[86] This should be the position notwithstanding the judgment of Helsham C.J. in Eq. in the New South Wales Supreme Court in *MPS Constructions Pty. Ltd.* v. *Rural Bank of New South Wales*,[87] which suggests that the acquisition of an interest in a pre-existing claim after bankruptcy or

Amendment Act 1858, s. 17. The second is that the set-off section in the bankruptcy legislation at that time had not been incorporated into the joint stock companies legislation, though it was nevertheless accepted that the right of set-off allowed to a contributory should be governed by the same principles. See the comments of Lord Cranworth in subsequent proceedings at (1865) 4 De G J & S 756, 762.

[80] (1982) 150 CLR 85, 94, 106. As Mason J. noted (at 106), the interposition of the surety's sister in *Barrett's Case* was not relevant, since the surety still paid the debt pursuant to the guarantee, albeit indirectly.

[81] Wood, *English and International Set-off* (1989), 303, 608.
[82] See the Insolvency Act, s. 323(1).   [83] *In re Whitehouse* (1887) 37 Ch. D 683, 694–5.
[84] See section 4.3.2. above, and *In re Whitehouse; Whitehouse* v. *Edwards* (1887) 37 Ch. D 683, 694–5; *In re Fenton* [1931] 1 Ch. 85, 118; *Westpac Banking Corporation* v. *Gollin & Co. Ltd.* [1988] VR 397, 403.
[85] *Mathieson's Trustee* v. *Burrup, Mathieson & Company* [1927] 1 Ch. 562, 569.
[86] See Dixon J. in *Hiley* v. *The Peoples Prudential Assurance Co., Ltd.* (1938) 60 CLR 468, 499.
[87] (1980) 4 ACLR 835.

liquidation is not capable of forming the basis of a set-off. In *MPS Constructions* a building contractor had entered into a contract with a local council for the construction of a building. The contract provided for the establishment of a retention 'fund' by the deposit of a percentage of the progress payments due to the contractor in a bank account. The account was required to be in the joint names of the council and the contractor, and it was to be held by them on trust for the council subject to the discharge by the contractor of its obligations. Before final completion the contractor went into liquidation. The liquidator decided to complete the contract, as a result of which the retention money would be released. The bank then asserted that it was entitled to set off the account against a separate debt owing to it by the contractor. One of the reasons given by Helsham C.J. in Eq. for not allowing the set-off was that at the commencement of the liquidation the account was held on trust for the council, so that there was a lack of mutuality.[88] The contractor's interest in the account at that time was still contingent on completion of construction. But the fact that the contractor was not then the beneficial owner of the debt should not have been sufficient to prevent a set-off.[89] The contractor gave credit to the bank before the liquidation (see section 3.1 above), by entering into a transaction which would naturally or in the ordinary course of business end in a debt owing by the bank to the contractor without the interposition of any new and independent transaction.[90] The case however may still have been correctly decided. It involved a contingent claim possessed by a company in liquidation, as opposed to a contingent liability. Unlike a contingent liability, when a contingent claim is in issue the contingency must have occurred before an account can be taken,[91] whereas it appears from the report that the liquidator had not as yet obtained the final certificate discharging the council's interest in the account.

The creditor may have been paid a dividend in the debtor's bankruptcy before the guarantor paid the balance of the debt. It has been suggested that a guarantor is only entitled to be subrogated to the rights of the creditor if the guarantor himself has paid the full amount of the debt,[92] though the better view is that the right of subrogation arises when the

---

[88] (1980) 4 ACLR 835, 845.

[89] Moreover, the better view is that the decision of Watkin Williams J. in *Ince Hall Rolling Mills, Ltd.* v. *The Douglas Forge Company* (1882) 8 QBD 179 similarly would not prevent a set-off in this situation. See section 9.4.2 below.

[90] See Dixon J. in *Hiley* v. *The Peoples Prudential Assurance Co., Ltd.* (1938) 60 CLR 468, 499.   [91] See section 4.4 below.

[92] *In re Fenton* [1931] 1 Ch. 85, 115 per Lawrence L.J.; *Ex parte Brett; in re Howe* (1871) LR 6 Ch. App. 838, 841 per Mellish L.J.; *Ex parte Turquand; in re Fothergill* (1876) 3 Ch. D 445, 450 per James L.J.

creditor is paid in full whether or not entirely by the guarantor.[93] Assuming that the guarantor does have a right of subrogation in this situation, because of the dividend received by the creditor from the estate it is apparent that he will be subrogated to a debt the face amount of which is greater than the amount that he in fact has paid to the creditor, and in respect of which he has a claim for an indemnity. Nevertheless, he should still be entitled to receive future dividends on the full amount of the debt. A similar issue has arisen in the context of contribution between guarantors. Consider that there are two guarantors of a debt, one of whom has become bankrupt, and the creditor has proved for the full amount of the debt in the bankruptcy. Subsequently the creditor is paid in full, including as a result of a payment from the solvent guarantor which is more than his *pro rata* share. That guarantor is entitled to be subrogated to the creditor's proof in the co-guarantor's bankruptcy, and to be paid dividends until he has received an amount sufficient to satisfy his claim for contribution.[94] The right of subrogation extends in this case to the full amount of the debt for which the creditor proved, and not just to a part equal to the claim for contribution itself, though obviously the guarantor cannot recover by way of dividend more than his contribution entitlement. The same analysis should apply when a guarantor is subrogated to the creditor's proof in the debtor's bankruptcy. But how would this concept work if the guarantor wishes to use the creditor's proof to which he is subrogated in a set-off? In the first place, credit should be given in the set-off for any dividend already paid to the creditor.[95] Unless this occurs, the bankrupt estate will have paid twice in respect of the debt, once in the form of a dividend to the creditor and a second time through a set-off. Further, while the right of subrogation extends to the full amount proved by the creditor, the guarantor would not be entitled to receive by way of dividend more than his actual entitlement. By parity of reasoning, if he wishes to utilize the proof to which he is subrogated in a set-off against a separate debt that he owes to the bankrupt debtor or co-guarantor, he should not be entitled to do so for an amount in excess of that entitlement.

4.3.5 *Must the contingency have occurred?*

Occasionally it has been suggested that a debt which was contingent at the relevant date may only be employed in a set-off if the contingency in fact

---

[93] *A. E. Goodwin Ltd.* v. *A. G. Healing Ltd.* (1979) 7 ACLR 481; *McColl's Wholesale Pty. Ltd.* v. *State Bank of New South Wales* [1984] 3 NSWLR 365, 378; *Westpac Banking Corporation* v. *Gollin & Co. Ltd.* [1988] VR 397, 402.

[94] *Ex parte Stokes* (1848) De Gex 618; *In re Parker; Morgan* v. *Hill* [1894] 3 Ch. 400.

[95] See in a different context Hoffman L.J. in the Chancery Division in *M.S. Fashions Ltd.* v. *Bank of Credit and Commerce International SA* [1993] Ch. 425, 435.

has occurred and the debt has vested.[96] However, since a contingent debt may be proved even if the contingency has not occurred, based upon an estimation of its value made by the trustee in bankruptcy or the liquidator, it should not be necessary that the contingency should have occurred for the purpose of set-off. The test as to whether credit has been given requires a characterization of the nature of the transaction that was entered into. In other words, is the transaction of the kind that would naturally or in the ordinary course of business end in a debt?[97] In the case of a contingent debt, if the contingency has not occurred it should be possible to base a set-off upon an estimate of the value made for the purpose of proof.[98] The estimated value may be regarded as the sum 'due' from the bankrupt for the purpose of the set-off section.

4.4 CONTINGENT DEBT OWING TO THE INSOLVENT

In order for a set-off to occur there must be a sum 'due' on each side of the account. In the case of a contingent debt owing *by* a bankrupt or a company in liquidation, the trustee or the liquidator is empowered to put a value on the debt for the purpose of proof if the contingency has not occurred, and that value may be regarded as the sum due for the purpose of the set-off section. However, there is no corresponding provision empowering the trustee or liquidator to estimate the value of a contingent liability owing by another person *to* the bankrupt or the company. Accordingly, while the debt is still contingent the fact that nothing is due in respect of it should mean that it cannot be brought into an account.[99]

What if the contingency subsequently occurs after the bankruptcy or liquidation? The better view is that there is then a sum 'due' which can be

---

[96] In *Re Charge Card Services Ltd.* [1987] 1 Ch. 150, 183 Millett J. said that, 'In every case the claim to set off requires that any contingency to which the liability was still subject at the date of the receiving order has since occurred'. On other occasions it has been said that 'it is enough' for a set-off of a contingent debt that it has matured into a pecuniary demand. See Dixon J. in *Hiley* v. *The Peoples Prudential Assurance Co., Ltd.* (1938) 60 CLR 468, 497, and Gibbs C.J. in *Day & Dent Constructions Pty. Ltd.* v. *North Australian Properties Pty. Ltd.* (1982) 150 CLR 85, 95. See also Murphy J. in *Day & Dent* (at 109).

[97] See Byles, Keating and Montague Smith JJ. in *Naoroji* v. *Chartered Bank of India* (1868) LR 3 CP 444, 451, 452.

[98] This appeared to be the view of Wright J. in *In re Daintrey* [1900] 1 QB 546, 557, and of Hoffman L.J. in the Chancery Division in *M.S. Fashions Ltd.* v. *Bank of Credit and Commerce International SA* [1993] Ch. 425, 435.

[99] *In re Daintrey* [1900] 1 QB 546, 557, 565, 573; *M.S. Fashions Ltd.* v. *Bank of Credit and Commerce International SA* [1993] 1 Ch. 425, 435 (Chancery Division). See also *MPS Constructions Pty. Ltd.* v. *Bank of New South Wales* (1980) 4 ACLR 835, as explained in section 4.3.4 above. A comment by Phillimore J. in the Divisional Court in *In re Taylor; ex parte Norvell* [1910] 1 KB 562, 568 suggesting the contrary is difficult to follow.

the subject of a set-off, given that it arose out of a prior obligation.[100] An example is *In re Daintrey*.[101] A business was sold on terms that the price was to be calculated as a proportion of the profits earned over a 3-year period, though the vendor became bankrupt before any profits in fact had been made. At the end of the 3-year period, when the price was calculated in accordance with the agreed formula, it was held that the purchaser could set off his liability against a separate debt owing to him by the vendor. While this is sometimes characterized as a case in which there was a presently existing debt at the relevant date for determining rights of set-off which only remained to be quantified,[102] in truth it is an example of a contingent debt.[103] No profits had been earned as at the relevant date, so that any debt to the bankrupt was contingent upon profits subsequently being earned. There are other examples. In *Booth v. Hutchinson*[104] Malins V.C. accepted that rent accruing to a bankrupt landlord[105] after the bankruptcy could be the subject of a set-off. The judgment is not entirely satisfactory, because the Vice Chancellor failed to consider issues of mutuality which arise in lease cases as a result of privity of estate.[106] It does, however, indicate an acceptance of the view that a debt arising in favour of a bankrupt after the bankruptcy but pursuant to a prior contract can be included in an account in a bankruptcy. In *Palmer v. Day & Sons*[107] a person before his bankruptcy had delivered some pictures to auctioneers for the purpose of sale. The sale occurred after the bankruptcy, and it was

---

[100] Compare *MPS Constructions Pty. Ltd.* v. *Rural Bank of NSW* (1980) 4 ACLR 835, discussed in section 4.3.4 above. In addition to the cases discussed below, see *Wreckair Pty. Ltd.* v. *Emerson* [1992] 1 Qd. R 700; *In re Taylor; ex parte Norvell* [1910] 1 KB 562, 568 (Phillimore J.); *M.S. Fashions Ltd.* v. *Bank of Credit and Commerce International SA* [1993] Ch. 425, 435 (Chancery Division); *Stein* v. *Blake* [1995] 2 All ER 961, 965. See also the cases concerned with a temporary suspension of mutuality discussed in section 2.8 above. In *Ex parte Hope; in re Hanson* (1858) 3 De G & J 92 the bankrupts' claim for improvements appears to have been contingent at the date of the bankruptcy on the lease being determined. When this subsequently occurred, a set-off was allowed in respect of the claim. Similarly, in *Thornton* v. *Maynard* (1872) LR 10 CP 695 the bankrupt drawer's estate first obtained the claim against the acceptor after the bankruptcy when the dividend was paid to the plaintiff indorsee, though this arose out of the prior obligation incurred as drawer. See also *Re Inglis; ex parte The Trustee* (1932) 5 ABC 255. A contract for the sale of wheat was on terms that the purchaser could elect to pay cash or deliver wheat of equal quality. The wheat was delivered before the vendor's bankruptcy, though it was not until later that the purchaser elected to pay cash. It was held that the resulting debt could be the subject of a set-off.
[101] [1900] 1 QB 546.
[102] *In re National Benefit Assurance Co., Ltd.* [1924] 2 Ch. 339, 343; *In re A Debtor (No. 66 of 1955)* [1956] 1 WLR 1226, 1230, 1238; *Carreras Rothmans Ltd.* v. *Freeman Mathews Treasure Ltd.* [1985] 1 Ch. 207, 230.
[103] *In re Taylor; ex parte Norvell* [1910] 1 KB 562, 580–1; *In re Fenton* [1931] 1 Ch. 85, 113; *Re Charge Card Services Ltd.* [1987] 1 Ch. 150, 182–3; *Day & Dent Constructions Pty. Ltd.* v. *North Australian Properties Pty. Ltd.* (1982) 150 CLR 85, 92, 94, 103.
[104] (1872) LR 15 Eq. 30, 35.
[105] In fact, the landlord had executed a deed of assignment of his estate upon trust for his creditors, though the deed provided that all questions should be decided according to bankruptcy law. [106] See section 9.5 below. [107] [1895] 2 QB 618.

held that the auctioneers could employ their liability to account for the proceeds of sale in a set-off. *Palmer* v. *Day & Sons* is an example of a set-off based upon the principle enunciated by Gibbs C.J. in *Rose* v. *Hart*.[108] According to that principle, where property has been deposited with a person with directions or authority to turn it into money, the depository may set off the proceeds against a separate debt owing to him by the depositor. In a number of cases this has been held to apply even though the proceeds were received *after* the depositor's bankruptcy.[109] While these *Rose* v. *Hart* cases may also be criticized on the ground that the proceeds of sale may have been impressed with a trust, in which case they should not have been susceptible to a set-off,[110] they were nevertheless instances in which a set-off occurred against a sum that first became due to a bankrupt after the bankruptcy as a result of a prior dealing. Reference also may be made to *Graham* v. *Russell*.[111] The case concerned the statute (1746) 19 Geo. II, c. 32, s. 2, which allowed an insured to prove for his claim on a policy in the underwriter's bankruptcy when the loss occurred after the bankruptcy.[112] Since that claim could have been proved, the court said that it could have grounded a set-off, and if the insured's claim on the policy could have been set off if the underwriter had been bankrupt, the court concluded that the underwriter similarly should be able to set-off his liability on the policy when the insured instead was bankrupt, even though the loss occurred after the insured's bankruptcy.[113] Another illustration is *Lee & Chapman's Case*.[114] A contractor under a construction contract went into liquidation. The liquidator completed the work, whereupon the price became payable to the company. It was held that this could be the subject of a set-off. Further, Dixon J. seems to have had in mind both sides of the account when he said in *Hiley* v. *The Peoples Prudential Assurance Co. Ltd*.[115] that, 'It is enough that at the commencement of the winding up mutual dealings exist which involve rights and obligations whether absolute or contingent of such a nature that afterwards in the events that happen they mature or develop into pecuniary demands capable of set-off'.

The set-off section admittedly provides that an account is to be taken of

---

[108] (1818) 8 Taunt. 499, 506, discussed in section 6.4 below.

[109] In addition to *Palmer* v. *Day & Sons*, see *French* v. *Fenn* (1783) 3 Dougl. 257; *Olive* v. *Smith* (1813) 5 Taunt. 56; *Astley* v. *Gurney* (1869) LR 4 CP 714.

[110] See section 6.4 below.   [111] (1816) 5 M & S 498.

[112] *Graham* v. *Russell* was decided before 1825, when the bankruptcy legislation was amended to allow contingent debts to be set off. The set-off section in the 1825 Act (6 Geo. IV, c. 16, s. 50) stipulated that 'every debt or demand hereby made provable against the estate of the bankrupt, may also be set-off in the manner aforesaid against such estate', and the 1825 bankruptcy legislation was the first to provide for proof in respect of contingent debts. See s. 56.

[113] The court declined to follow *Glennie* v. *Edmunds* (1813) 4 Taunt. 775. Compare also *Ex parte Blagden* (1815) 19 Ves. Jun. 465.   [114] (1885) 30 Ch. D 216.

[115] (1938) 60 CLR 468, 497.

what is due from each party 'to the other' and, in the case of a bankruptcy, a debt arising after the bankruptcy pursuant to a prior contract is a debt due to the trustee rather than the bankrupt, given that the property of the bankrupt is vested in the trustee.[116] Therefore, at no time could it be said that there is, or has been, a sum due to the bankrupt himself. An alternative view is that, when a debt arises in this manner as a result of a prior contract between the bankrupt and a creditor, 'to the other' should be interpreted as including 'to the trustee', on the basis that the trustee takes subject to the prior equity resulting from mutual credits, mutual debts or other mutual dealings. The whole thrust of the set-off section is to look at the position prior to the bankruptcy and, if there have been prior mutual credits or mutual dealings, one would expect that a set-off ordinarily would follow. *In re Daintrey*, *Booth* v. *Hutchinson* and *Palmer* v. *Day & Sons* all suggest this conclusion. In any event, there may not be the same difficulty in this regard in the case of a company liquidation, since the assets of the company after its liquidation ordinarily do not vest in the liquidator,[117] and so any debt arising in favour of the company after the liquidation is still a debt due to the company. While the House of Lords has held that the company in this period is divested of the beneficial title to its assets,[118] which includes debts owing to the company, it is still not possible to identify another person to whom it can be said the debt is owing.[119] In Australia, on the other hand, it has been held that liquidation does not deprive the company of the beneficial title to its assets,[120] so that the point under discussion is even less likely to be regarded as an issue there.

The allowance of a set-off is also inconsistent with *In re A Debtor (No. 66 of 1955)*.[121] The Court of Appeal held that a bankrupt surety's claim for an indemnity from the principal debtor could not be the subject of a set-off, since the payment to the creditor only occurred after the bankruptcy, and therefore at that date there was nothing due for the purpose of the set-off section. In other words, it was regarded as essential that an amount be due at the date of the bankruptcy, even though the resulting debt had its source in a prior obligation. However, the better view is that *In re A Debtor* was wrongly decided.[122]

---

[116] Insolvency Act 1986, s. 306.

[117] *In re Oriental Inland Steam Company* (1874) LR 9 Ch. App. 557, 560. Note that s. 145 of the Insolvency Act 1986 empowers the court on the application of the liquidator to direct that all or part of the company's property shall vest in the liquidator.

[118] *Ayerst* v. *C. & K. Construction Ltd.* [1976] AC 167.

[119] *Ayerst* v. *C. & K. Construction Ltd.* [1976] AC 167, 178–9.

[120] *Franklin's Selfserve Pty. Ltd.* v. *Federal Commissioner of Taxation* (1970) 125 CLR 52.

[121] [1956] 1 WLR 1226.

[122] See section 4.3.3 above. While Gibbs C.J. in *Day & Dent Constructions* (1982) 150 CLR 85, 94 left open the question whether *In re A Debtor* was correct, on the ground that the payment was due to the trustee to enable him to obtain the bankrupt's property, Mason J. (at

It has been suggested[123] that the question whether a contingent debt owing to an insolvent can be the subject of a set-off if the contingency subsequently occurs may depend upon whether it could be said at the insolvency date that the claim was likely to mature into an actual liquidated debt during the course of the insolvency proceedings. This view appears to be based upon the definition of mutual credit[124] though, since the expansion of the set-off section in 1869[125] to include mutual dealings, it should be sufficient if the debt arose out of a prior dealing between the parties without the intervention of any new and independent transaction.[126] It should not be necessary in such a case to show likelihood.

Consider that, before the contingency had occurred, the person contingently liable had proved in the bankruptcy on a debt separately owing to him and had received a dividend. If after the occurrence of the contingency the bankrupt's trustee or the company's liquidator sues him for payment of the resulting debt, the better view was expressed by Hoffman L.J. in the Chancery Division in *M.S. Fashions Ltd.* v. *Bank of Credit and Commerce International SA*,[127] that the person may still rely on his provable debt in a set-off, notwithstanding that he had been paid a dividend, though he must give credit for the dividend in the set-off.

When a trustee in bankruptcy or a liquidator completes a contract for the sale of property or the performance of work so as to earn the price, the purchaser's resulting debt usually will have been contingent at the relevant date. It has been suggested that a lack of mutuality may be an objection to employing the debt in a set-off in these cases, and so the availability of a set-off is considered later in that context.[128]

4.5 DAMAGES CLAIMS

4.5.1 *Breach of contract*

Prior to 1869 the set-off section in the insolvency legislation was confined to mutual credit and mutual debts. The concept of giving credit itself related to debts, in that it encompassed a debt arising out of a transaction

---

106) said that it was anomalous and should not be followed. In *Brown* v. *Cork* [1985] BCLC 363, 367–8 Oliver J. said, on the authority of *In re A Debtor*, that, where a guarantor in liquidation became entitled to a claim for contribution from a co-guarantor after the liquidation, the claim could not be the subject of a set-off even though it arose out of a prior obligation. However, given the criticism that has been levelled at *In re A Debtor*, his Lordship's conclusion in this regard may require reconsideration.

[123] Wood, *English and International Set-off* (1989), 592.
[124] See section 3.1 above. [125] Bankruptcy Act 1869, s. 39.
[126] See Starke and Dixon JJ. in *Hiley* v. *The Peoples Prudential Assurance Co., Ltd.* (1938) 60 CLR 468, 487, 499. [127] [1993] Ch. 425, 435.
[128] See section 9.4.2 below.

entered into before the relevant date for determining rights of set-off, where it could be said that the transaction was of the type that would naturally, or in the ordinary course of business, end in a debt.[129] Accordingly, a claim for damages for breach of contract was regarded as not being within the ambit of the set-off section.[130] Nor on its own would the amendment of the bankruptcy legislation in 1861, by which damages claims for breach of contract became provable,[131] have been sufficient to remedy this. After the amendment the point nevertheless remained that, as long as the set-off section was cast only in terms of mutual debts and mutual credits, it did not contemplate a set-off of damages claims.[132] However, in 1869 the set-off section was expanded to include mutual dealings.[133] This, in conjunction with the 1861 amendment to the proof of debt provision, had the effect of allowing a damages claim for breach of a contract entered into before the bankruptcy to be included in a set-off, since in such a case the claim arose out of a prior dealing between the parties.[134]

In *Carreras Rothmans Ltd.* v. *Freeman Mathews Treasure Ltd.*[135] Peter Gibson J. held that a claim for damages for breach of a prior contract could only be employed in a set-off if the breach occurred on or before the relevant date for determining rights of set-off. This proposition was said to be supported by *In re A Debtor (No. 66 of 1955)*,[136] though the better view is that that case was wrongly decided.[137] *Carreras Rothmans* is contrary to *In re Asphaltic Wood Pavement Company; Lee & Chapman's Case*,[138] in

---

[129] See sections 3.1 and 3.2 above.   [130] *Rose* v. *Sims* (1830) 1 B & Ad. 521.
[131] Bankruptcy Act 1861, s. 153.
[132] Compare *Makeham* v. *Crow* (1864) 15 CB(NS) 847, in which an unliquidated damages claim arising out of a contract of sale was set off in an action by the vendor's assignees in bankruptcy for payment of the price. However, the purchaser presented alternative arguments for a set-off. A set-off was claimed, not only under the bankruptcy legislation based upon the scope of the proof of debt provision in the 1861 Act, but also on equitable set-off. The report is silent as to which of these was regarded as the justification for the decision. Certainly, in cases decided after the Bankruptcy Act 1869, which introduced 'mutual dealings' into the set-off section, set-off of unliquidated damages claims was justified on that ground. Thus, in *Booth* v. *Hutchinson* (1872) LR 15 Eq. 30, 32 Malins V.C. said that he would probably have concluded that the damages claim in that case could not have been set off under the old law. He said (at 34) that there was no mutual debt, and there was hardly a mutual credit, but that there was certainly a mutual dealing.
[133] Bankruptcy Act 1869, s. 39.
[134] See, e.g., *Booth* v. *Hutchinson* (1872) LR 15 Eq. 30; *Peat* v. *Jones & Co.* (1881) 8 QBD 147; *Mersey Steel & Iron Co.* v. *Naylor, Benzon, & Co.* (1884) 9 App. Cas. 434; *In re Asphaltic Wood Pavement Company; Lee & Chapman's Case* (1885) 30 Ch. D 216; *Palmer* v. *Day & Sons* [1895] 2 QB 618, 621. See also *Baker* v. *Lloyd's Bank, Ltd.* [1920] 2 KB 322, in which Roche J. treated the declaration of insolvency as a repudiation, though there is no indication as to whether the repudiation in fact was accepted.
[135] [1985] 1 Ch. 207.   [136] [1956] 1 WLR 1226.
[137] See sections 4.3.3 and 4.4 above.   [138] (1885) 30 Ch. D 216.

which a set-off was allowed notwithstanding that the breach occurred after the winding-up of the company,[139] as well as the decision of Roche J. in *Telsen Electric Co., Ltd.* v. *J. J. Eastick & Sons*,[140] in relation to the alternative finding that the breach occurred when the liquidator refused to accept the return of the goods. This aspect of *Carreras Rothmans* should not be regarded as good law, which indeed was the view of Millett J. in *Re Charge Card Services Ltd.*[141]

4.5.2 *Tort*

Until recently, a claim in tort which remained unliquidated at the date of the bankruptcy or liquidation was not provable,[142] and similarly it could not be employed in a set-off.[143] However the position changed in 1986, when the Insolvency Act introduced a right of proof in respect of an unliquidated claim in tort.[144] This has since been followed in Australia in the context of company liquidations.[145] But this would not appear to have the consequence that a tortious claim which was still unliquidated at the relevant date can always be employed in a set-off.[146] In order for the set-off section to apply there must be mutual debts, mutual credits or other mutual dealings. 'Debts' in this context means a debt which is in existence at the date of the bankruptcy or liquidation.[147] Obviously this does not encompass a damages claim in tort, unless it has been liquidated by

---

[139] See Millett J.'s explanation of *Lee & Chapman's Case* in *Re Charge Card Services Ltd.* [1987] 1 Ch. 150, 180–1.   [140] [1936] 3 All ER 266.

[141] [1987] 1 Ch. 150. 178, 190.

[142] See the Bankruptcy Act 1914, s. 30(1). Compare *In re Berkeley Securities (Property) Ltd.* [1980] 1 WLR 1589 in relation to a claim in tort that had been liquidated by judgment after winding-up but before the claimant lodged a proof in the winding-up, though the development in that case was short-lived. See *Re Islington Metal and Plating Works Ltd.* [1984] 1 WLR 14, and *Re Autolook Pty. Ltd.* (1983) 2 ACLC 30.

[143] *Aliter* if judgment had been obtained and the claim liquidated before the relevant date. See *In re D.H. Curtis (Builders) Ltd.* [1978] 1 Ch. 162, 172, and, with respect to proof, *Page* v. *Commonwealth Life Assurance Society Ltd.* (1935) 36 SR(NSW) 85, 90; *In re Berkeley Securities (Property) Ltd.* [1980] 1 WLR 1589, 1606 and *Re Autolook Pty. Ltd.* (1983) 2 ACLC 30. An award of costs made in the tort action, being a mere addition or appurtenance to the damages, followed the same rule. See *In re Newman; ex parte Brooke* (1876) 3 Ch. D 494, 497.

[144] See s. 322, 'bankruptcy debt' being defined in s. 382 as including tortious liabilities. For company liquidations, see the Insolvency Rules 1986, r. 13.12.

[145] See the Corporations Law, s. 553(1). The old position still applies, however, in bankruptcy. See the Bankruptcy Act 1966 (Cth.), s. 82(2).

[146] Compare the position in New Zealand. Claims in tort are provable if capable of estimation (see the Insolvency Act 1967, ss. 87, 98 and 99), while according to s. 93 it is sufficient for a set-off that a person entitled to prove in respect of any debt or demand is indebted or liable to the bankrupt in respect of any debt or demand.

[147] See e.g. *Ex parte Prescot* (1753) 1 Atk. 230, and *Young* v. *Bank of Bengal* (1836) 1 Moore 150, 164–5.

judgment prior to the relevant date.[148] Nor could it be said that credit is given for the damages ultimately payable,[149] since the concept of giving credit only applies when a transaction would naturally end in a *debt*.[150] It does not extend to damages claims.[151] Not only is a damages claim in tort not a debt, nor the subject of giving credit, but in many cases it will not result from a dealing between the parties, in which case there is no justification in the language of the set-off section for allowing it to be employed in a set-off. As Lord Esher M.R. once remarked,[152] 'There are, no doubt, matters which give rise to claims, but are not dealings within the section. If one man assaults another or injures him through negligence, that gives rise to a claim, but is not a dealing . . .'.

Thus, in New South Wales it was held that a wrongful taking of property giving rise to a liability for damages in conversion is not a dealing for the purpose of the set-off section.[153] This is not to suggest that a tortious claim can never arise out of a dealing. One instance that was recognized even prior to the 1986 legislation is the case of a claim for damages for misrepresentation inducing a contract. The claim, though based upon tort, was considered to be provable[154] on the ground that it is in the nature of a

---

[148] This is implicit in Brightman J.'s comment in *In re D. H. Curtis (Builders) Ltd.* [1978] 1 Ch. 162, 172.

[149] While this argument was contemplated in the first edition of this book (at 94), it is difficult to see how it could succeed consistent with the cases.

[150] *Palmer* v. *Day & Sons* [1895] 2 QB 618, 621, and see generally section 3.2 above.

[151] *Rose* v. *Sims* (1830) 1 B & Ad. 521. Recently in Australia the High Court in *Gye* v. *McIntyre* (1991) 171 CLR 609, 625 suggested, though without deciding the point, that a damages claim for fraudulent misrepresentation may come within the ambit of the expression 'mutual credits'. This suggestion was made in the context of a discussion of a *dictum* of Byles J. in *Naoroji* v. *Chartered Bank of India* (1868) LR 3 CP 444, 451, that mutual credit encompasses reciprocal demands which must (or would) naturally terminate in a debt. In *Gye* v. *McIntyre* the claim had been liquidated by judgment after the relevant date for determining rights of set-off, and, though it is not entirely clear, their Honours may have had in mind that a damages claim would naturally terminate in a *judgment* debt. However, in the context of the question whether credit is given, as distinct from whether a set-off may be based upon a claim arising out of a prior dealing, the relevant inquiry is whether the claim would naturally end in a debt, as opposed to whether it does end in debt, and the courts have never considered that the fact that a damages claim may end in a judgment debt is sufficient to bring it within the concept of giving credit. Indeed, if this view had prevailed, there would not have been any necessity for the courts after 1869 to have recourse to the concept of mutual dealings in order to allow a damages claim for breach of contract to be set off in a bankruptcy. Thus Cotton L.J. in *Peat* v. *Jones & Co.* (1881) 8 QBD 147, 150 said that the damages claim for breach of contract in that case would not have come within the earlier mutual credit clauses, though it did come within the mutual dealing head in the 1869 Act. See also *Booth* v. *Hutchinson* (1872) LR 15 Eq. 30, 33, and the reference to 'mutual dealings' in *Lee & Chapman's Case* (1885) 30 Ch. D 216, 224.

[152] *Eberle's Hotels and Restaurant Company, Limited* v. *E. Jonas & Brothers* (1887) 18 QBD 459, 465. [153] *Re Leeholme Stud Pty. Ltd.* [1965] NSWR 1649.

[154] See *Jack* v. *Kipping* (1882) 9 QBD 113, 117, and also the discussion in *Gye* v. *McIntyre* (1991) 171 CLR 609, 631. Compare *Re Giles; ex parte Stone* (1889) 61 LT 82, in which the damages for misrepresentation were sought from someone who was not a party to the contract.

claim under the contract.[155] Similarly it could be employed in a set-off, the justification being that it arose out of a dealing between the parties.[156] Generally, however, the mere fact that a claim in tort is now in the nature of a provable debt would not appear to be sufficient to bring it within the ambit of the set-off section. Rather, it must be shown that the claim arose out of a dealing between the parties to the proposed set-off. While it is true to say that set-off is an aspect of the rules relating to proof of debts,[157] the better view is that this does not import an absolute principle that all provable debts should always be capable of being set off.[158] The principle was correctly stated by Lord Hoffman in *Stein* v. *Blake*[159] when he said that, 'Bankruptcy set-off . . . applies to any claim *arising out of mutual credits or other mutual dealings* before the bankruptcy for which a creditor would be entitled to prove'.

The set-off section provides that only the balance of the account taken under the section is provable in the bankruptcy or, as the case may be, is to be paid to the trustee in bankruptcy. As a corollary, the High Court of Australia in *Gye v McIntyre*[160] said that the bankrupt's claim against the creditor must be such that it would vest in a trustee in bankruptcy.[161] The effect of this is to exclude claims for damages for personal injury or wrong done to the bankrupt.[162] Normally claims of this nature are unlikely to arise out of a dealing between the parties, so that in any event they could not be employed in a set-off. But even if in an exceptional case the claim is derived from a dealing, the fact that it does not vest in the trustee should mean that it cannot be set off.

In Australia claims in tort for unliquidated damages are still not provable

---

[155] See *Jack* v. *Kipping* (1882) 9 QBD 113, 117; *Palmer* v. *Day & Sons* [1895] 2 QB 618, 622; *Tilley* v. *Bowman, Ltd.* [1910] 1 KB 745, 753.

[156] *Jack* v. *Kipping* (1882) 9 QBD 113; *In re Mid Kent Fruit Factory* [1896] 1 Ch. 567, 571–2; *Tilley* v. *Bowman, Ltd.* [1910] 1 KB 745. Compare *Kitchen's Trustee* v. *Madders* [1950] 1 Ch. 134, in which there was an undertaking not to prove the damages claim in the bankruptcy. Nevertheless, the allowance of a set-off in this situation is not free of difficulty. See *Tilley* v. *Bowman, Ltd.* (at 752), and *Provident Finance Corporation Pty. Ltd.* v. *Hammond* [1978] VR 312, 318. It is not easy to reconcile with the principle applied in the case of an assignment of a debt, that an assignee does not take subject to a cross-claim for damages for fraud inducing the contract out of which the assigned debt arose, on the ground that the damages claim is not a claim arising under the contract itself. See *Stoddart* v. *Union Trust, Ltd.* [1912] 1 KB 181, and generally section 13.2.8 below.

[157] *Mersey Steel and Iron Co.* v. *Naylor, Benzon & Co.* (1884) 9 App. Cas. 434, 437–8.

[158] See section 3.5 above.

[159] [1995] 2 All ER 961, 964 (emphasis added).

[160] (1991) 171 CLR 609, 626–7.

[161] This view previously had been expressed by Wood, *English and International Set-off* (1989), 315–6.

[162] See, e.g., *Beckham* v. *Drake* (1849) 2 HLC 579, 604, 621; *Ex parte Vine; in re Wilson* (1878) 8 Ch. D 364; *Wilson* v. *United Counties Bank, Ltd.* [1920] AC 102. In Australia, see the Bankruptcy Act 1966 (Cth.), s. 116(2)(g).

in bankruptcy.[163] However, while the set-off section requires that the claim against the bankrupt must be provable, the High Court in *Gye* v. *McIntyre*[164] said that there is no such principle that the bankrupt's claim against the creditor should be in the nature of a provable debt, and accordingly an unliquidated damages claim in tort available to the bankrupt against the creditor could be the subject of a set-off if it arose out of a dealing between the parties, even though it would not have been provable in the creditor's bankruptcy if the creditor instead had been the bankrupt party. This aspect of the case is considered elsewhere.[165]

4.5.3 *Breach of trust*

The introduction in 1861 of a right of proof for claims for unliquidated damages only applied to damages arising by reason of a contract or promise.[166] This was extended in the Bankruptcy Act 1883, s. 37 to damages for breach of trust. However, the liability of a trustee who disposed of trust property in breach of trust traditionally has been regarded in equity as being in the nature of an obligation to restore the property or to pay compensation, and as creating an equitable debt, as opposed to being for unliquidated damages.[167] Therefore, even before this amendment to the proof of debt section, the equitable debt could be proved in a bankruptcy.[168]

Insofar as set-off is concerned, there is a question whether a trustee should be permitted to profit from his own breach of trust by employing his resulting liability in a set-off in the beneficiary's bankruptcy. This issue is considered later.[169] Consider, however, that the trustee is the bankrupt party, and it is the beneficiary who is asserting a right of set-off. The beneficiary's claim in such a case is in the nature of an equitable debt. When a set-off is based upon mutual debts or mutual credits, it is not necessary to show that the debt in question had its origin in a dealing between the parties to the proposed set-off.[170] Accordingly, where the liability is in the nature of an equitable debt, and that debt arose before the bankruptcy, it should not be necessary to show a prior dealing between those parties in order that the claim may come within the ambit of the set-off section, though usually in breach of trust cases there would be a dealing

---

[163] Bankruptcy Act 1966 (Cth.), s. 82(2). Compare the Corporations Law, s. 553(1) in relation to company liquidation. [164] (1991) 170 CLR 609.

[165] See section 3.6 above. [166] Bankruptcy Act 1861, s. 153.

[167] *Ex parte Adamson; re Collie* (1878) 8 Ch. D 807, 819; *Target Holdings Ltd.* v. *Redfern* [1995] 3 WLR 352, 360–1.

[168] *Ex parte Westcott; Re White* (1874) LR 9 Ch. App. 626; *Emma Silver Mining Co.* v. *Grant* (1880) 17 Ch. D 122. See also Williams, *The Law and Practice in Bankruptcy* (2nd edn., 1876), 161. [169] See section 4.7.2 below.

[170] See e.g. *Hankey* v. *Smith* (1789) 3 TR 507n, and generally section 3.3 above.

in any event for the purpose of the set-off section. If on the other hand the breach of trust occurred after the bankruptcy, albeit where the trust was subsisting before then, it would not be possible to base a claim on the concept of giving credit, since it could hardly be said that a trust would naturally, or in the ordinary course of business, end in an equitable debt as a result of a breach,[171] in which case the basis of any set-off must be a prior dealing between the trustee and the beneficiary.

4.6 CALLS ON SHARES

Section 17 of the Joint Stock Companies Amendment Act 1858 provided that, in fixing the amount payable by a contributory in the event of a winding-up of a joint stock company, a set-off could occur between the amount of the call made upon him and any sum due to him on an independent contract or dealing with the company. This applied not only to companies in which contributories had unlimited liability, but also to companies where the liability was limited pursuant to the Joint Stock Companies Act 1856.[172] However, in the Companies Act 1862 the right to a set-off was restricted. Section 101 of that Act was drafted in terms similar to the currently applicable section 149 of the Insolvency Act, in that it only provided for a set-off against a call where the company was an unlimited company and, in addition, the call in question had been made before the winding-up. In *Grissell's Case*[173] it was held in the context of the 1862 Act, and it has since become an established principle, that when a limited liability company is being wound up, a shareholder who is also a creditor of the company may not set off the company's debt to him against his liability for unpaid calls.[174] Nor may he set off the dividend payable on that debt against the call. Indeed, given that there is no right of set-off, the rule in

---

[171] See *Day & Dent Constructions Pty. Ltd.* v. *North Australian Properties Pty. Ltd.* (1982) 150 CLR 85, 95, 103–4, *Palmer* v. *Day & Sons* [1895] 2 QB 618, 621 and *In re Mid-Kent Fruit Factory* [1896] 1 Ch. 567, 569.

[172] See e.g. *Garnet and Mosely Gold Mining Company of America Ltd.* v. *Sutton* (1862) 3 B & C 321. This explains Dixon J.'s query in *Hiley* v. *The Peoples Prudential Assurance Co. Ltd.* (1938) 60 CLR 468, 500 in relation to *In re The Moseley Green Coal and Coke Co., Ltd*; *Barrett's Case (No. 2)* (1865) 4 De G J & S 756 (though the application in that case of s. 17 of the 1858 Act emerges more clearly from the reports in 12 LT 193 and 34 LJ Bcy. 41).

[173] *In re Overend, Gurney, and Co.; Grissell's Case* (1866) LR 1 Ch. App. 528. The subsequent introduction of the rules of bankruptcy into the law of company liquidation has not affected the principle enunciated in *Grissell's Case*. See *In re General Works Company; Gill's Case* (1879) 12 Ch. D 755; *In re North Queensland Brick and Pottery Co., Ltd*; *MacBrair's Case* [1902] St. R Qd. 286.

[174] Compare *Re The London and Scottish Bank; Logan's Case* (1870) 21 LT 742. Obviously a counterclaim will not succeed. See *Government Security Investment Company* v. *Dempsey* (1880) 50 LJQB 199.

Cherry v. *Boultbee*[175] dictates that the call, being an obligation to contribute to the fund represented by the company's assets, must be paid in full before the shareholder is entitled to participate in the fund by receiving a dividend along with the other creditors on the debt owing to him.[176] Despite early authority to the contrary,[177] it is now settled that this rule extends to voluntary liquidations.[178] Moreover, it makes no difference that the call may have been made before the winding-up,[179] or that the call is being enforced in an action at law brought by the liquidator in the name of the company rather than in summary proceedings for a balance order,[180] or that the company's unpaid capital has been charged or assigned to a third party.[181] Further, an agreement for a set-off between the company and the shareholder will not be effective to exclude the rule if the set-off has not actually been effected pursuant to the agreement before the liquidation,[182] even though the shareholder may have been induced to take the shares on

---

[175] (1839) 4 My. & Cr. 442, discussed in Ch. 10.

[176] *Grissell's Case* (1866) LR 1 Ch. App. 528, 536; *In re China Steamship Company; ex parte MacKenzie* (1869) LR 7 Eq. 240, 244; *Ramsay* v. *Jacobs* (1987) 12 ACLR 595, 597. In Australia, the Corporations Law, s. 553A specifically provides that a debt owed by a company to a person *in the persons's capacity as a member of the company* is not admissible to proof unless the person has paid all amounts that he is liable to pay as a member of the company.

[177] *Brighton Arcade Company, Ltd.* v. *Dowling* (1868) LR 3 CP 175. See also *Groom* v. *Rathbone* (1879) 41 LT 591.

[178] *Gibbs and West's Case* (1870) LR 10 Eq. 312, 330; *In re Paraguassu Steam Tramroad Company. Black & Co.'s Case* (1872) LR 8 Ch. App. 254, 262–3; *In re Whitehouse & Co.* (1878) 9 Ch. D 595; *Hoby and Co. Limited* v. *Birch* (1890) 62 LT 404; *In re Pyle Works* (1890) 44 Ch. D 534, 585–6; *Ramsay* v. *Jacobs* (1987) 12 ACLR 595.

[179] *In re Breech-Loading Armoury Company; Calisher's Case* (1868) LR 5 Eq. 214; *In re Stranton Iron and Steel Company; Barnett's Case* (1875) LR 19 Eq. 449; *In re Whitehouse and Co.* (1878) 9 Ch. D 595; *In re Auriferous Properties Ltd.* [1898] 1 Ch. 691, 696; *In re Hiram Maxim Lamp Company* [1903] 1 Ch. 70; *Re John Dillon Ltd. (In Liq); ex parte Jefferies* [1960] WAR 30.

[180] *In re Whitehouse & Co.* (1878) 9 Ch. D 595, 604–5; *Alliance Film Corporation, Ltd.* v. *Knoles* (1927) 43 TLR 678.

[181] See *In re International Life Assurance Society; Gibbs and West's Case* (1870) LR 10 Eq. 312, 327 (in which the calls had been charged); *Bank of Australasia* v. *Zohrab* (1891) 10 NZLR 310; *Re John Dillon; ex parte Jefferies* [1960] WAR 30. See also *In re Matheson Bros. & Co. Ltd.; ex parte Matheson* (1884) NZLR 3 SC 323, 324 in the context of an assignment of calls by a liquidator after the commencement of the winding-up. While an assignee of calls takes free from any debt owing by the company to the contributory, the contributory may bring into account an indebtedness of the assignee himself. See Matheson (at 324).

[182] *In re Law Car and General Insurance Corporation* [1912] 1 Ch. 405; *Harding and Co. Ltd.* v. *Hamilton* [1929] NZLR 338. Compare *Re Blakely Ordnance Company; Blakely's Case* (1867) 17 LT 307. *Contra* if the set-off is effected before liquidation. See e.g. *In re Harmony and Montague Tin and Copper Mining Company; Spargo's Case* (1873) LR 8 Ch. App. 407; *In re Jones; Lloyd & Co., Ltd.* (1889) 41 Ch. D 159 (which is explained in *Harding* v. *Hamilton*); *In re The Switchback Railway and Outdoor Amusement Company Ltd.; ex parte Mount* (1890) 16 VLR 339, 341; *In re New Zealand Pine Company Ltd; ex parte The Official Liquidator; Guthrie's Case* (1898) 17 NZLR 257; *Randall* v. *The Liquidator of the Santa Claus Gold Mining Co., Ltd.* (1906) 8 WALR 36. See also *Ramsay* v. *Jacobs* (1987) 12 ACLR 595, 597–8 (payment in advance).

the faith of the agreement.[183] If a set-off against a call has indeed taken place before the company's liquidation, it nevertheless may be avoided by the liquidator if the circumstances were such as to give rise to a voidable preference.[184]

Sir George Jessel sought to explain the denial of a set-off on the basis of lack of mutuality.[185] He said that, once a winding-up has commenced, a liability to contribute unpaid capital no longer takes the form of a debt owing to the company, but rather it constitutes a liability to contribute to the assets of the company enforceable by the liquidator, and there is a lack of mutuality between that liability and an indebtedness of the company.[186] However, this theory has been criticized on the ground that a call in a winding-up in fact does give rise to a debt due to the company.[187] The fact that the call may be made by the liquidator does not mean that it is a liability owed to the liquidator,[188] since the liquidator in making the call would do so as agent for the company.[189] In this regard, the liability to contribute unpaid capital differs from the obligation to repay a preference, against which there similarly cannot be a set-off.[190] In the case of unpaid capital, the shareholder prior to liquidation had a liability to the company itself for unpaid capital, though it was contingent upon a call being made. This is not the position, however, with respect to a preference, since the preferential payment is voidable only by order of the court on the application of the liquidator.[191] Indeed, the lack of mutuality theory is difficult to reconcile with *In re China Steamship Company; ex parte MacKenzie*.[192] *MacKenzie* concerned a shareholder who, after the commencement of the company's liquidation, assigned to a third party a debt owing to him by the company. It was held that the assignee took subject to a right in the *company* to set off a call subsequently made on the assignor's shares against the debt. An assignee takes subject to equities, including rights of set-off, available to the debtor against the assignor.[193] However, if lack of mutuality is indeed the reason that a shareholder after the commencement of the winding-up may not set off a debt against a call,

---

[183] *Black & Co.'s Case* (1872) LR 8 Ch. App. 254.
[184] *In re Land Development Association; Kent's Case* (1888) 39 Ch. D 259; *In re Washington Diamond Mining Company* [1893] 3 Ch. 95.
[185] *In re Whitehouse & Co.* (1878) 9 Ch. D 595.
[186] See also *Ex parte Branwhite* (1879) 40 LT 652; *Monkwearmouth Flour Mill Company Ltd.* v. *Lightfoot* (1897) 13 TLR 327; *In re G.E.B.; A Debtor* [1903] 2 KB 340, 346, 352.
[187] See Cotton and Lindley L.JJ. in *In re Pyle Works* (1890) 44 Ch. D 534, 575, 585–6, and also *In re A Debtor (No. 41 of 1951)* [1952] 1 Ch. 192.
[188] Compare Wood, *English and International Set-off* (1989), 729.
[189] A liquidator has been described generally as an agent of the company. See *Knowles* v. *Scott* [1891] 1 Ch. 717.   [190] See section 9.3.1 below.
[191] Insolvency Act 1986, s. 239. In Australia, see the Corporations Law , s. 588FF(1) in the context of company liquidation.   [192] (1869) LR 7 Eq. 240.
[193] See section 13.2 below.

there should not have been an equity available to the company against the shareholder/assignor in *MacKenzie* to which the assignee would have been subject. An alternative view is that the insolvency legislation itself forbids a set-off. The legislation, when taken as a whole, contemplates that the proceeds of a call are to be used with the other assets of the company in the *pari passu* payment of the company's debts, and it would be contrary to this principle to allow a set-off against the call.[194] But perhaps the simplest explanation is that the change to the legislation which occurred in 1862, by which the right of set-off that was formerly available to a contributory against a call was confined to unlimited companies where the call had been made before the winding-up, gave rise to an implication that in the case of a limited company Parliament intended that the call should be paid without set-off,[195] and this principle has since become entrenched.

While *Grissell's Case* operates to prevent the creditor from asserting a set-off, it is evident from *Ex parte MacKenzie*[196] that there is no objection to the company itself asserting the right. A shareholder after the commencement of the company's liquidation assigned to a third party a debt owing to him by the company, and it was held that the assignee took subject to a right in the company to set off a subsequent call against the debt. The set-off in issue admittedly was based upon the Statutes of Set-off, since at that time the bankruptcy set-off section had not been incorporated into the law of company liquidation.[197] However, as a matter of principle there is no reason why this should produce a different result. There is, nevertheless, a curious aspect to the case. When a debt is assigned after the commencement of a liquidation, any proof in respect of it should still be lodged in the name of the assignor as the creditor at the relevant date for determining the provable debts.[198] The assignee is not considered to be in any better position than the assignor.[199] The liquidator in *MacKenzie* undoubtedly would have been entitled to invoke *Grissell* against the assignor, and similarly he should have been entitled to assert this same equity against the assignee. In fact it was the liquidator in *MacKenzie* who sought the set-off, while it was the assignee who relied on *Grissell* in an attempt to prevent this occurring. It seems to have been assumed that, in the absence of a set-off, the assignee would have been

---

[194] *Grissell's Case* (1866) LR 1 Ch. App. 528, 535–6; *Black & Co.'s Case* (1872) LR 8 Ch. App. 254, 262, 265; *In re Auriferous Properties, Ltd.* [1898] 1 Ch. 691, 696.
[195] See *In re Breech-Loading Armoury Company; Calisher's Case* (1868) LR 5 Eq. 214, 217, though compare *Barnett's Case* (1875) LR 19 Eq. 449, 452.
[196] *In re China Steamship Company; Ex parte MacKenzie* (1869) LR 7 Eq. 240.
[197] This first occurred with the enactment of the Supreme Court of Judicature Act 1875, s. 10. See section 2.2 above.
[198] *Ex parte Dickenson; in re Gibson* (1832) 2 Deac. & Ch. 520.
[199] *In re Wickham* (1917) 34 TLR 158. See also *Ex parte Deey* (1796) 2 Cox 423.

entitled to receive a dividend on the assigned debt, and the liquidator would have had to look to the assignor for payment of the call, and so a set-off was perceived to be a means by which the company in effect could obtain payment to the extent that its liability on the assigned debt was extinguished. Yet it would have been more valuable for the liquidator to assert *Grissell* against the assignee. The liquidator should have been entitled to decline to pay anything at all to the assignee by way of dividend until the call had been satisfied in full.[200] This course of action, for some reason that is not apparent, was not adopted.

An assignee of a debt does *not* take subject to an indebtedness of the assignor that only came into existence after the debtor received notice of the assignment, even if the assignor's indebtedness was the result of a contract entered into before notice.[201] He does, however, take subject to an indebtedness that arose before notice irrespective of whether it was presently payable at that date.[202] The order of events in *Ex parte MacKenzie* was (1) commencement of the winding-up, (2) assignment, and notice of assignment given to the company, and (3) call made in the winding-up. In the normal course of events a shareholder before a call would be regarded as having only a contingent liability to contribute unpaid capital.[203] But this must be considered in the context of section 80 of the Insolvency Act 1986,[204] which stipulates that the liability of a contributory in a winding-up creates a debt accruing due from him at the time when his liability commenced but payable when the call is made. Even though the call in *MacKenzie* was made after notice, the effect of the then equivalent provision of section 80[205] was that the liability to contribute was deemed to have had reference back so as to give rise to an existing debt (payable *in futuro*) before notice.[206] Sir John Romilly said that the debt had reference back to the time when the winding-up began. It was on this ground that Stirling J. held in *Christie* v. *Taunton, Delmard, Lane and Company*[207] that, when the assignment of the company's debt instead had taken place before the winding-up, the assignee did not take subject to a right in the company to set off the assignor's liability for calls made after

---

[200] *Grissell's Case* (1866) LR 1 Ch. App. 528, 536.

[201] *Watson* v. *Mid Wales Railway Co.* (1867) LR 2 CP 593. See section 13.2.4 below.

[202] *In re Pinto Leite and Nephews; ex parte Visconde des Olivaes* [1929] 1 Ch. 221.

[203] Compare *Palmer's Company Law* (looseleaf, 1994), para. 6.202 with respect to public companies.   [204] In Australia see the Corporations Law, s. 527.

[205] Companies Act 1862, s. 75.

[206] For another instance in which a reversion back of a title resulted in a set-off, see *Bailey* v. *Johnson* (1872) LR 7 Ex. 263 (discussed in section 7.3.1 below) in the context of an annulment of a bankruptcy.

[207] [1893] 2 Ch. 175, following a *dictum* of Lord Romilly in *Ex parte MacKenzie* (1869) LR 7 Eq. 240, 244. See also *In re The McKay Harvesting Machinery Company* (1894) 20 VLR 153; *In re Matheson Bros. & Co.* (1884) NZLR 3 SC 323, 325.

the winding-up. The debt for calls in this case was not considered to have had reference back to the time before notice. Nevertheless, while this may be regarded as a sensible conclusion, there is an alternative interpretation of section 80, that the debt is deemed to have been created when the contributory first took out the shares.[208] If this view is applied it is difficult to see why, as a matter of strict principle, the existence or otherwise of a right in the company to set off the calls against the assignee's claim on the assigned debt should depend on whether the assignment took place before or after the commencement of the winding-up. But, whatever the position is in this regard, it is apparent that, if both the call and the assignment had taken place before the winding-up, and notice of the assignment was not given until after the call, the assignee will take subject to the company's pre-existing right of set-off.[209]

The prohibition against setting off a call against a debt only applies in a winding-up. When a company is a going concern, a set-off may take effect under the Statutes of Set-off.[210] It may be that a set-off is pleaded as a defence to an action brought by a company for payment of a call while the company is a going concern, but before judgment the company commences to be wound up. Since a set-off under the Statutes does not take place until a judgment for a set-off is given, the demands will not have been extinguished at the commencement of the winding-up, and so the ordinary rule that a set-off may not proceed in a liquidation will apply.[211]

Grissell does not apply when the contributory is bankrupt. It was held in *In re Duckworth*[212] that, when the liquidator of a company lodges a proof in the bankruptcy of a contributory in respect of a call, the contributory's trustee may bring into account an indebtedness of the company to the contributory.[213] This was considered to be a consequence of the power

---

[208] See *Buckley on the Companies Acts* (14th edn., 1981) Vol. 1, 507 (in relation to the Companies Act 1948, s. 214), referring to *Ex parte Canwell; in re Vaughan* (1864) 4 De G J & S 539, *Williams* v. *Harding* (1866) LR 1 HL 9, and *In re West of England Bank; ex parte Hatcher* (1879) 12 Ch. D 284. In *In re Northern Assam Tea Company; ex parte Universal Life Assurance Company* (1870) LR 10 Eq. 458, 463 Lord Romilly agreed with counsel's argument to this effect. Compare Pennington, *Company Law* (6th edn., 1990), 477.

[209] *Christie* v. *Taunton, Delmard, Lane and Company* [1993] 2 Ch. 175.

[210] *Barnett's Case* (1875) LR 19 Eq. 449, 451. See also *In re White Star Line, Ltd.* [1938] 1 Ch. 458, 470 per Clauson J. *(arguendo).*

[211] *In re Hiram Maxim Lamp Company* [1903] 1 Ch. 70; *In re A. Shadler, Ltd.; McPhillamy's Case* (1904) 4 SR(NSW) 619 (verdict by consent for a set-off obtained after the liquidation held to be ineffective); *Re John Dillon Ltd.; ex parte Jefferies* [1960] WAR 30.

[212] (1867) LR 2 Ch. App. 578. See also *Ex parte Cooper, re A Trust Deed* (1867) 15 LT 637. In Australia see *Re Patrick Corporation Ltd. & the Companies Act* (1980) ACLC 34,268. The estimated amount claimable from a bankrupt in respect of future calls by a solvent company may be brought into an account in the bankruptcy. See *In re Anderson* [1924] NZLR 1163.

[213] However, because the right of set-off only arises after the contributory has become bankrupt, a petition presented by the liquidator of a company for the bankruptcy of a

conferred upon the liquidator by the English Companies Act of 1862 to prove in the bankruptcy of a contributory for any 'balance' against his estate.[214] The current English provision similarly is drafted in terms of a liquidator proving for a 'balance',[215] though this is no longer the case in Australia.[216] However, there is a second justification for the set-off, and that is that, while the insolvency legislation prima facie may purport to prohibit a set-off in the company's liquidation, it does not have the effect of overriding the statutory right of set-off otherwise available in the bankruptcy under the bankruptcy legislation.[217] This explains why a set-off may proceed when the question arises in the context of a proof lodged by the bankrupt's trustee in the winding-up, as opposed to the case of a liquidator proving for the 'balance' in the contributory's bankruptcy.[218] Nevertheless, it should still be necessary to show that a set-off is available in the bankruptcy according to the principles generally applicable to bankruptcy set-off. On this basis, it is difficult to understand the decision of Giffard L.J. in *In re Universal Banking Corporation; ex parte Strang*.[219] A shareholder in a company assigned a debt owing by the company to a third party after an order was made to wind up the company. Subsequently the shareholder executed a deed of composition, which incorporated the principles of bankruptcy. It was held that the shareholder's liability for an unpaid call made in the winding-up could be set off against the assigned debt. However, because the assignment occurred prior to the composition, so that the company's debt henceforth was owing to the assignee while the shareholder was the party liable for the call, lack of mutuality should have prevented a set-off under the bankruptcy set-off section.[220] Nor would a set-off have been available in the company's liquidation on the basis of *Ex parte MacKenzie* (discussed above), since the shareholder, and not the company itself through the liquidator, was the party asserting a right to a set-off. *Strang* should be compared to *In re Matheson Bros. & Co.*,[221] in which Williams J. in the New Zealand Supreme Court correctly held that,

---

contributory based upon the non-payment of calls may not be impugned because of a set-off that will become available in the bankruptcy as a result of an indebtedness of the company. See *In re John Sloss; ex parte Robison Bros., Campbell & Sloss Ltd.* (1893) 19 VLR 710; *In re G.E.B., A Debtor* [1903] 2 KB 340.

[214] Companies Act 1862, s. 95. Compare the explanation offered by Romer L.J. in *In re G.E.B.* [1903] 2 KB 340, 352.

[215] See the Insolvency Act 1986, s. 167, and also s. 165 with respect to voluntary liquidations, in each case referring to Pt. III of Sch. 4.

[216] See the Corporations Law, s. 477(2)(e).

[217] See *In re Duckworth* (1867) LR 2 Ch. App. 578, 580–2.

[218] *In re Anglo-Greek Steam Navigation and Trading Company. Carralli & Haggard's Claim* (1869) LR 4 Ch. App. 174; *In re The Oxford and Canterbury Hall Company Ltd., ex parte Morton* (1869) 38 LJ Ch. 390.   [219] (1870) LR 5 Ch. App. 492.

[220] See e.g. *De Mattos* v. *Saunders* (1872) LR 7 CP 570.

[221] (1884) NZLR 3 SC 323.

when the benefit of a call made by the liquidator, as opposed to the company's indebtedness, was assigned before the contributory's bankruptcy, lack of mutuality prevented a set-off in the bankruptcy. Nor could it be said in a case such as *Matheson* that an assignee of calls takes subject to a prior right of set-off available to the contributory in the liquidation, since the effect of *Grissell's Case* is that there would not have been any such right. But if the assignee himself happens to be indebted to the contributory a set-off should be available in the bankruptcy against the assigned call, since the assignee would be suing personally for the call and there would not be any valid reason in such a case for applying *Grissell*.[222]

The ambit of the right of set-off where the contributory is bankrupt is sometimes framed in terms of a contributory who becomes bankrupt after the commencement of the winding-up.[223] However, if indeed it is correct to say that the debt resulting from a call has relation back to the date of the acquisition of the shares rather than the date of the winding-up,[224] it is not clear that the availability of the set-off would be so limited. Certainly, though, it is apparent from *Duckworth* itself that it is not a sufficient objection to a set-off that the call is made after the commencement of the bankruptcy.

It was held in *In re Auriferous Properties, Limited*[225] that a set-off is not available when the contributory is a company that has gone into liquidation, as opposed to a bankrupt.[226] Rather *Grissell's Case* applied, so that the contributory company had to pay the call in full before receiving a dividend on the debt.[227] It seems difficult to justify this distinction between an incorporated contributory and a contributory who is a natural person, since the statutory right of set-off conferred by the insolvency legislation in a contributor's insolvency is equally applicable to both cases.

The preceding discussion concerned the right to set off a debt incurred by the company before its liquidation. The costs and expenses of the winding-up, including debts or liabilities incurred by the company or the liquidator in the course of carrying on the company's business after the commencement of the winding-up, stand on a different footing. These debts have priority in the liquidation, and are payable in full.[228]

[222] *In re Matheson Bros. & Co.* (1884) NZLR 3 SC 323, 324.
[223] See McPherson, *The Law of Company Liquidation* (3rd edn., 1987), 309.
[224] See above.   [225] [1898] 1 Ch. 691.
[226] Wright J. in *Auriferous Properties* had doubts as to the correctness of *Duckworth*, though he said that it had stood for too long to be interfered with. It was held in *Re West Hartlepool Iron Co. Ltd.; Gunn's Case* (1878) 38 LT 139 that the exception in *Duckworth* does not apply when the estate of a deceased person is being administered in bankruptcy, though compare *Re Bailey, deceased; Duchess Mill Ltd. v. Bailey* (1932) 76 Sol. Jo. 560.
[227] *In re Auriferous Properties, Ltd. (No. 2)* [1898] 2 Ch. 428.
[228] See e.g. *In re International Marine Hydropathic Company* (1884) 28 Ch. D 470.

Alternatively the creditor may employ the debt in a set-off, including against a liability to pay a call on shares.[229]

Section 149 of the Insolvency Act 1986[230] empowers the court, at any time after the making of a winding-up order, to make an order on a contributory to pay any money due from him to the company, exclusive of any sum payable by him by virtue of a call made in pursuance of the Insolvency Act.[231] In this regard, the only sum which could be payable by virtue of a call made in pursuance of the Act is a call made in the winding-up. It does not encompass a call made by the directors *before* the winding-up which remains unpaid. Further, if the company is an unlimited company, the court in making the order may allow[232] the contributory to set off any sum due to him on an independent contract or dealing with the company.[233] Accordingly, the effect of section 149 is to allow a set-off to a contributory in an unlimited company in respect of a prior unpaid call. However, there is competing authority as to whether *Grissell's Case* extends to unlimited companies so as to prevent a set-off against a call made *after* the winding-up. Malins V.C. in *Gibbs and West's Case*,[234] following upon a *dictum* by Lord Chelmsford to this effect in *Grissell's Case*,[235] held in favour of a set-off, though the case is not a satisfactory authority because the Vice Chancellor assumed, mistakenly, that the equivalent provision to section 149[236] in fact extended to this situation. Fry J., on the other hand, held that a set-off was not available in *Ex parte Branwhite*.[237] The appropriate question is whether the legislature, by specifically allowing a set-off in relation to calls made before a winding-up, had intended to indicate that calls made after the winding-up could not be the subject of a set-off. On this basis, Fry J.'s conclusion in *Branwhite* would appear to be correct.

The Insolvency Act 1986, section 149(3)[238] provides that, when all the

---

[229] *In re London and Colonial Company; ex parte Clark* (1869) LR 7 Eq. 550. Compare *In re General Exchange Bank* (1867) LR 4 Eq. 138 with respect to the costs of the petition, though the set-off in that case was sought by the liquidator rather than the contributory.

[230] In Australia see the Corporations Law, s. 483(2).

[231] While s. 149 also excludes a call made pursuant to the Companies Act 1985, this would now have little practical significance.

[232] The court has a discretion in the matter. See *Re Norwich Equitable Fire Assurance Co; Brasnett's Case* (1885) 53 LT 569, in which the shareholder's claim against the company required further investigation.

[233] The section specifically provides that this does not includ any money due to him as a member of the company in respect of any dividend or profit.

[234] *In re International Life Assurance Society; Gibbs and West's Case* (1870) LR 10 Eq. 312.

[235] (1866) LR 1 Ch. App. 528, 536. *Grissell's Case* itself was concerned with a call made after the winding-up. See also *Black & Co.'s Case* (1872) LR 8 Ch. App. 254, 265.

[236] See the Companies Act 1862, s. 101.

[237] *Ex parte Branwhite; re The West of England and South Wales District Bank* (1879) 40 LT 652.   [238] In Australia see the Corporations Law, s. 483(2).

creditors of a company, whether it is limited or unlimited, have been paid in full, any money due on any account whatever to a contributory may be allowed to him by way of set-off against any subsequent call. Lord Romilly once said[239] that it is difficult to put an intelligible construction upon this provision because, if all creditors have been paid in full, prima facie there would not appear to be any scope for a set-off. However, it has been suggested[240] that it may refer to a sum due to a member in his character of member by way of dividend or profit, on the ground that this is not considered to be a debt of the company.[241]

In Australia the courts have held that a debt for equity swap entered into between an insolvent company not in liquidation and creditors of the company, by which the creditors are issued with fully paid shares on terms that the allotment is paid for by setting off debts equal to the nominal value of the shares, does not amount to an issue of shares at a discount, provided that the debts were genuinely created in the course of the company's business and are immediately payable.[242] In such circumstances it is not to the point that the company otherwise had insufficient assets to pay its debts in full, since the value of the debts the subject of the set-off is still considered to be the face value of the legally and immediately enforceable obligations that they represent.

4.7 BASING A CLAIM FOR A SET-OFF UPON A WRONGFUL ACT

It is sometimes said that a person may not rely on his own wrongful act in order to found a set-off,[243] though this should be approached with caution. A principle to this effect has been applied in the case of misfeasance claims against directors and promoters of companies, and it may extend generally to claims based upon fraud or breach of trust in dealing with another's property. But apart from these instances it is doubtful if it has any application.

---

[239] *Calisher's Case* (1868) LR 5 Eq. 214, 217.

[240] *Buckley on the Companies Act* (14th edn., 1981) Vol. 1, 628, cited with approval in *In re Compania de Electricidad de la Provincia de Buenos Aires Ltd.* [1980] 1 Ch. 146, 172.

[241] See the Insolvency Act 1986, s. 74(2)(f). Compare in Australia the Corporations Law, s. 563A which postpones these debts to other debts of the company, and also s. 553A, which restricts the right of proof where the member himself has a liability to the company in his capacity as member.

[242] *Pro-Image Studios* v. *Commonwealth Bank of Australia* (1991) 4 ACSR 586; *Re Keith Bray Pty. Ltd.* (1991) 5 ACSR 450. The courts in each case declined to follow *Re Jarass Pty. Ltd.* (1988) 13 ACLR 728.

[243] See e.g. Shelford, *The Law of Bankruptcy and Insolvency* (3rd edn., 1862), 522; Doria, *The Law and Practice in Bankruptcy* (1874), 685; Williams and Muir Hunter *The Law and Practice in Bankruptcy* (19th edn., 1979), 197.

4.7.1 *Misfeasance claims against directors and promoters*

If in the course of a winding-up it appears that any person who has taken part in the formation, promotion, or management of the company, or any liquidator or officer of the company, has misapplied or become accountable for any of the company's money or other property, or if he has been guilty of any misfeasance or breach of fiduciary duty in relation to the company, then section 212 of the Insolvency Act 1986[244] provides a summary procedure by which the official receiver, or the liquidator or any creditor or contributory, may apply to the court for an order compelling the person to repay or account for the money or other property. The Court of Appeal held in *Ex parte Pelly*,[245] and it has since been confirmed,[246] that a person liable in misfeasance proceedings to repay money may not bring into account a cross-demand that he has against the company. This has been justified on a number of grounds. Brett L.J. in *Pelly*[247] said that a right of set-off arises only when there is an action at law, whereas a provision such as section 212 provides a summary remedy without an action. However, this is not a wholly satisfactory justification for the rule because, while an action at law is a prerequisite to a set-off under the Statutes of Set-off,[248] this is not the case for set-off under the insolvency legislation. A second suggestion is that a set-off is denied on the ground of lack of mutuality, since the summons is brought in the name of the liquidator, or another authorized person, rather than in the name of the company.[249] Once again, this is not satisfactory because, while the liquidator may take out the summons, the debt is a debt owing to the company itself. It is enforced on behalf of the company, and the proceeds collected become part of the company's assets.[250] In this regard it differs from a claim for repayment of a preference, which is voidable only against the liquidator. In such a case lack of mutuality is properly regarded as a ground for denying a set-off.[251] In the event of misfeasance the claim in question is one that the company itself had before the liquidation, whereas this is not so for a preference.

---

[244] In Australia see the Corporations Law, s. 598.

[245] *In re Anglo-French Co-operative Society; ex parte Pelly* (1882) 21 Ch. D 492.

[246] *In re Exchange Banking Company; Flitcroft's Case* (1882) 21 Ch. D 519; *In re Carriage Co-operative Supply Association* (1884) 27 Ch. D 322; *In re Leeds and Hanley Theatres of Varieties, Ltd.* [1904] 2 Ch. 45. Compare *Re Toowoomba Welding Works Pty. Ltd. (No. 2)* [1969] Qd. R 337.   [247] (1882) 21 Ch. D 492, 507.

[248] Indeed, both Sir George Jessel M.R. and Brett L.J. in *Pelly* (1882) 21 Ch. D 492, 502, 507 for some reason seem to have assumed that the Statutes of Set-off provided the only form of set-off that could have applied.

[249] *Re Buena Vista Pty. Ltd.* [1971] 1 NSWLR 72, 74.

[250] *In re Bassett; ex parte Lewis* (1895) 2 Mans. 177, 181.

[251] See section 9.3.1 below.

The denial of a set-off has also been justified as a matter of interpretation of section 212, that the legislature had not intended that a set-off should be available in those proceedings.[252] But there is another explanation, and that is that the set-off is denied on policy considerations.[253] The liability to repay is a liability of a delinquent in breach of a duty in the nature of a breach of trust,[254] and it should not be treated in the delinquent's favour as a debt due from him to the company so as to entitle him to a set-off.[255] Admittedly it is difficult to reconcile this with the view of Vaughan Williams J. in *In re Bassett; ex parte Lewis*[256] that, if an action is brought against the delinquent instead of proceeding by way of summons under section 212, a set-off may occur. On the other hand, it is consistent with Maugham J.'s judgment in *In re Etic, Ltd.*[257] After noting that the misfeasance section applies only to cases where there has been a misapplication or retention of money or property of the company or a positive misfeasance or breach of trust,[258] including a breach of trust by way of negligence, Maugham J. commented that 'the fact that under [the misfeasance section] there is no right of set-off is itself an indication that the Courts have considered that the jurisdiction under [the section] is a special one *and is confined to claims by the company against the officer in which it would not be right for the officer of the company to be entitled to set up a right of set-off*.[259] This suggests that a set-off similarly would be unavailable if the claim is enforced by way of action rather than under section 212,[260] though it remains to be seen if this would be applied in view of Vaughan Williams J.'s opinion expressed in *Bassett*.

If a director's or a promoter's liability for misfeasance is unable to be employed in a set-off, the right of the director or the promoter to receive a dividend on a debt owing to him may be subject to the rule in *Cherry* v. *Boultbee*.[261] This rule is considered later.[262]

4.7.2 *Fraud, and breach of trust in dealing with another's property*

If one accepts Maugham J.'s approach in *In re Etic*, there is no reason why it should not apply generally to cases involving breach of trust in dealing

---

[252] See Sir George Jessel M.R. and Brett L.J. in *Pelly* (1882) 21 Ch. D 492, 503, 507.

[253] In this regard it has been said that, if an innocent contributory liable to pay a call on shares is denied a right of set-off, then a director or other officer of the company who has misapplied company money certainly should not have a right. See Jessel MR and Cotton L.J. in *Pelly* (1882) 21 Ch. D 492, 503, 509–10.

[254] *In re Etic, Ltd.* [1928] 1 Ch. 861.

[255] See Hall V.C. at first instance in *Pelly* (1882) 21 Ch. D 492, 498.

[256] (1895) 2 Mans. 177, 181.   [257] [1928] 1 Ch. 861.

[258] [1928] 1 Ch. 861, 873.   [259] [1928] 1 Ch. 861, 873 (emphasis added).

[260] See also the statement of the principle in *Re Bailey Cobalt Mines Ltd.* (1919) 44 OLR 1.

[261] (1839) 4 My. & Cr. 442.   [262] See Ch. 10.

with another's property. Consider that a trustee ('T') holds property on trust for a beneficiary ('B'), and that T in breach of trust disposes of the property. In such a case B has a claim against T, T's obligation in equity being to restore the property or pay compensation, and constituting an equitable debt.[263] If T becomes bankrupt, B's claim for this equitable debt would be provable in the bankruptcy,[264] and usually it could give rise to a set-off.[265] If on the other hand B is the bankrupt party, T should not be entitled to a set-off in the bankruptcy in his own favour based upon his own breach of trust, given that, if he had retained the trust property, he would have had to account to B's estate without the benefit of a set-off.

Similarly a person should not be entitled to a set-off where his liability is based upon his own fraud. *Ex parte Minton; in re Green*[266] is not inconsistent with that view. In *Minton* an insolvent entered into a composition with her creditors by which each was to receive a rateable dividend, though she agreed with one creditor to pay him in full so as to induce him to sign the composition deed. The payment had been extorted by the creditor, and constituted a fraud upon the other creditors. It was held that the payment was recoverable by the insolvent, and that this claim had passed to her assignees in bankruptcy, but that it could be the subject of a set-off against a separate debt owing to the creditor. The case, however, should be considered in the context that the primary question was as to the liability of the creditor to repay the money, and further that it was the commissioners in the bankruptcy, as opposed to the creditor, who said that the liability should be set off against the separate debt.

4.7.3 *Deliberate breach of contract in order to obtain a set-off*

It is doubtful whether the principle precluding a person from relying on his own wrongful act in order to obtain a set-off extends any further than fraud, or breach of trust, or misfeasance in the nature of breach of trust. Admittedly it has been suggested that a set-off might not arise in favour of a creditor of a bankrupt if the creditor has purposely broken his contract in order to obtain a set-off.[267] However, it should be borne in mind that failure to pay any debt on time constitutes a breach of contract.[268] The

---

[263] *Ex parte Adamson; re Collie* (1878) 8 Ch. D 807, 819. See also *Target Holdings Ltd.* v. *Redferns* [1995] 3 WLR 352, 360–1.   [264] Insolvency Act 1986, ss. 322 and 382.
[265] See section 4.5.3 above.   [266] (1834) 3 Deac. & Ch. 688.
[267] *Turner* v. *Thomas* (1871) LR 6 CP 610, 614. See also *In re Pollitt; ex parte Minor* [1893] 1 QB 175, 179; *Atkinson* v. *Learmouth* (1905) 11 ALR 191, 195; *In re H E Thorne* [1914] 2 Ch. 438, 450. *Williams and Muir Hunter on Bankruptcy* (19th edn., 1979), 197.
[268] See Maugham J. at first instance in *In re City Equitable Fire Insurance Company Ltd.* [1930] 2 Ch. 293, 302.

right of set-off constitutes a form of security in the event of the bankruptcy of a party to mutual dealings, and the very essence of the right would seem to be that one party may breach his contract by refusing to pay a debt when the bankruptcy of his creditor is imminent, relying instead on the security that his indebtedness will constitute for the creditor's own indebtedness to him. A creditor who is aware of his debtor's impending insolvency, and who consequently withholds payment of his own indebtedness to the debtor as a form of security, would not be denied a set-off, and it is difficult to see why a breach of contract in any other form should be treated differently. For example, when a creditor who had purchased goods from an insolvent debtor prior to the latter's bankruptcy immediately refused to pay the price, offering instead to treat that debt as satisfaction for the debtor's indebtedness to him, he was still allowed a set-off in the debtor's subsequent bankruptcy, even though the set-off was based upon his own deliberate breach in not tendering payment.[269] There is also *Bolland* v. *Nash*,[270] in which it was the creditor claiming the benefit of a set-off who had dishonoured his own acceptance and thereby caused the bill to be returned to the bankrupts as indorsers. In other words, the mutuality necessary for the set-off was only revived as a result of the creditor's breach of his own engagement as acceptor to pay the bill according to the tenor of his acceptance.[271] In *Willment Brothers Ltd.* v. *North West Thames Regional Health Authority*[272] an employer under a building contract stopped payment on a cheque that had been forwarded to the contractor so as to obtain a right of set-off in the contractor's liquidation. Despite the employer's conduct a set-off was allowed to proceed.

A contract may stipulate that a sum of money equal in amount to the indebtedness of one of the parties to the other is to be set aside in a separate fund and held on trust. If a trust is set up the trustee would be denied a set-off in the beneficiary's bankruptcy in relation to his obligation to account for the trust fund.[273] However, it may be that, in breach of contract, the person in fact failed to set up the trust, in which case the question may arise whether a set off should be allowed in respect of the resulting damages liability. In some cases the maxim that equity deems as done that which ought to be done may be applicable, so that equity would deem a notional trust to have been created against which there may not be a set-off.[273a] In other cases, though, the bankruptcy of the party having recourse to the maxim may make it difficult for him to obtain an order for

---

[269] *Southwood* v. *Taylor* (1818) 1 B & Ald. 471, and note also in this regard *Holmes* v. *Tutton* (1855) 5 El. & Bl. 65.
[270] (1828) 8 B & C 105.
[271] See the Bills of Exchange Act 1882, s. 54(1).
[272] (1984) 26 Build. LR 51.
[273] See section 6.2 below.
[273a] *Re Arthur Sanders Ltd.* (1981) 17 Build. LR 125.

specific performance, and the application of the maxim depends upon the availability of such an order.[274] One possible objection to a set-off is that the person claiming the benefit of the set-off himself is in breach of contract, in not setting aside a separate fund to which the trust may attach. The contrary argument, however, is that this is no worse than a creditor neglecting to pay, or indeed choosing not to pay, a debt owing by him to his debtor on another transaction on the due date, and if a set-off may arise in the one case then similarly it should be able to arise in the other. A second possible objection is that, by stipulating for a trust, the parties impliedly had agreed to exclude a set-off, though under the current state of the law this argument would not be tenable, since the House of Lords has confirmed that the parties to mutual dealings may not contract out of the operation of the mutual credit provision.[275] If neither of these objections would be valid individually, they should not be valid cumulatively, and so it may be that, unless equity would deem a notional trust fund to have been set up, a set-off could occur.[276]

---

[274] *Re Anstis* (1886) 31 Ch. D 596, 605–6; *Re Plumptre* [1910] 1 Ch. 609, 619. Similarly, the insolvency of the party against whom it is sought to apply the maxim may prevent its application. See *Mac-Jordan Construction Ltd.* v. *Brookmount Erostin Ltd.* [1992] BCLC 350. Compare *Re Arthur Sanders Ltd.* (1981) 17 Build. LR 125. The Greater London Council had failed to pay retention money relating to work performed by a contractor (now in liquidation) and various sub-contractors into a separate trust account, despite a contractual obligation to do so. Nourse J. said that, in the case of a solvent employer such as the GLC, equity would deem as done that which ought to have been done and would find a notional trust. While the availability of an order for specific performance was not considered, it appears that the remaining work under the contract in fact had been completed by another contractor.

[275] *National Westminster Bank Ltd.* v. *Halesowen Presswork & Assemblies Ltd.* [1972] AC 785, discussed in section 2.11.1 above.

[276] See *Mac-Jordan Construction Ltd.* v. *Brookmount Erostin Ltd.* [1992] BCLC 350, 359.

5

Commensurable Demands

5.1 THE REQUIREMENT OF COMMENSURABILITY

The courts have emphasized that the insolvency set-off section only applies when the demands are commensurable, or, in other words, when the claim on each side of the account is a money demand.[1] Set-off under the Statutes of Set-off is subject to the same restriction.[2] A set-off will not occur in relation to a claim which is not monetary in nature, even if its value is measurable with precision in money terms.[3] For example, a set-off has been denied in the context of a claim for the return of specific property in circumstances where the court nevertheless accepted that the property in question had a particular value.[4] In the case of insolvency set-off there are two reasons for the principle. The first, which has been emphasized in the cases, is the perceived difficulty in producing a balance on the account when one of the demands is not a money claim. As Lord Russell of Killowen C.J. once aptly remarked, 'There could not be an "account" as between goods and money, and no balance could be struck.'[5] The second is that the requirement of money demands in any event is inherent in the

---

[1] *Eberle's Hotels and Restaurant Co., Ltd.* v. *E. Jonas & Bros.* (1887) 18 QBD 459; *Palmer* v. *Day & Sons* [1895] 2 QB 618, 622; *In re Taylor; ex parte Norvell* [1910] 1 KB 562, 567; *Hiley* v. *The Peoples' Prudential Assurance Co., Ltd.* (1938) 60 CLR 468, 490, 497; *Gye* v. *McIntyre* (1991) 171 CLR 609, 623; *Lloyds Bank NZA Ltd.* v. *National Safety Council* [1993] 2 VR 506, 510. See also *Rose* v. *Hart* (1818) 8 Taunt. 499; *Ex parte Roy; in re Sillence* (1877) 7 Ch. D 70; *In re Winter; ex parte Bolland* (1878) 8 Ch. D 225, *Peacock* v. *Anderson* (1878) 4 NZ Jur. (NS) SC 67; *Lord (Trustee of)* v. *Great Eastern Railway Company* [1908] 2 KB 54 (reversed on other grounds [1909] AC 109); *Ellis and Co.'s Trustee* v. *Dixon-Johnson* [1925] AC 489; *Re Leeholme Stud Pty. Ltd. (In Liq.)* [1965] NSWR 1649, and the discussion in section 6.4.2 below.
[2] *Tony Lee Motors Ltd.* v. *M.S. MacDonald & Son (1974) Ltd.* [1981] 2 NZLR 281, and see also *Grant* v. *NZMC Ltd.* [1989] 1 NZLR 8, 11.
[3] Compare Balcombe L.J. in the Court of Appeal in *Stein* v. *Blake* [1994] Ch. 16, 22.
[4] See, for example, *Eberle's Hotels and Restaurant Company, Ltd.* v. *E. Jonas & Bros.* (1887) 18 QBD 459; *Ellis and Co.'s Trustee* v. *Dixon-Johnson* [1925] AC 489 (shares readily available on the stock exchange).
[5] *Palmer* v. *Day & Sons* [1895] 2 QB 618, 622. See also the *Eberle's Hotels* case (1887) 18 QBD 457, 465, 467, 468, 469.

stipulation in the set-off section that 'the *sums* due from one party shall be set off against the *sums* due from the other'. Insofar as the Statutes of Set-off are concerned, the requirement of money demands follows from the very basis of the Statutes, that there must be mutual debts.

There is one instance in which a set-off was allowed in respect of a claim to recover property. In *Rolls Razor Ltd.* v. *Cox*[6] a salesman employed by a company had been entrusted with goods for the purpose of sale. The company went into liquidation. When the liquidator of the company brought an action for the return of the goods, the Court of Appeal held that the salesman could retain them as a set-off against the company's indebtedness to him for retained commissions. For the purpose of the set-off the goods were valued at the price at which the salesman had been authorized to sell them. It has been suggested that the right enforced in *Rolls Razor* may be explicable as some sort of lien rather than a set-off,[7] though in fact the question of a lien was specifically argued before and rejected by the Court of Appeal. It is clear from the judgments that the court regarded the right in question as a right of set-off. The better view is that the case was wrongly decided.[8]

Lord Denning M.R. in the leading judgment in *Rolls Razor* relied on a comment by Gibbs C.J. in *Rose* v. *Hart*,[9] to the effect that credit may be given for the purpose of the set-off section where there is a delivery of property with a direction to turn it into money. However, Gibbs C.J. in *Rose* v. *Hart* went on to speak in terms of setting off the 'debt' resulting from the direction to turn the property into money, and while it is true that on another occasion he said that a credit is created when goods are deposited for the purpose of sale and not just when the goods are sold,[10] it is apparent that the set-off itself nonetheless was only intended to relate to the 'debt' constituted by the money received from carrying out those directions. *Rose* v. *Hart* is considered later.[11] For present purposes it is sufficient to say that the concern of the Chief Justice was to limit the perception that Lord Hardwicke's earlier decision in *Ex parte Deeze*[12] stood as authority for the proposition that there could be a set-off against goods. Lord Hardwicke himself later remarked in *Ex parte Ockenden*[13] that in *Ex parte Deeze* there had been evidence of a custom of the trade by which packers could retain goods, not only as security for the price of their work upon the goods, but also for the separate debts of the owner. In

---

[6] [1967] 1 QB 552.   [7] Wood, *English and International Set-off* (1989), 564.

[8] Compare *Rolls Razor* v. *Cox* with *Tony Lee Motors Ltd.* v. *M.S. MacDonald & Son (1974) Ltd.* [1981] 2 NZLR 281 in the context of the Statutes of Set-off.

[9] (1818) 8 Taunt. 499, 506.   [10] *Graham* v. *Russell* (1816) 3 Price 227, 231.

[11] See section 6.4 below.   [12] (1748) 1 Atk. 228.

[13] (1754) 1 Atk. 235, 237.

subsequent cases, however, *Ex parte Deeze* was still referred to as an authority on set-off,[14] and Gibbs C.J. in his judgment in *Rose* v. *Hart* was attempting to rationalize the decisions in those cases with the stipulation in the set-off section in the Bankruptcy Act of 1732[15] that 'one debt may be set against another'. In the cases in question the direction to turn the property into money had been carried out, so that in each case there was indeed a debt in existence when the account was to be taken. On the other hand these debts had not been in existence at the relevant date for determining rights of set-off, a problem that Gibbs C.J. overcame by ascribing a wider meaning to mutual credits than to mutual debts. Therefore a debt which arose after the relevant date could be brought into an account, provided that it was based upon a credit given before that date. Nevertheless, he still required a 'debt' at the taking of the account, so that 'one debt may be set against another' in accordance with the 1732 Act. The true statement of the rule would appear to be that, when goods are deposited for sale, credit is given for any proceeds of sale that *in fact* are received.[16]

5.2 REPUDIATION AND SPECIFIC PERFORMANCE

Consider that a person has entered into a contract for the purchase of goods from someone who is a creditor of the purchaser on another transaction, but prior to delivery the purchaser goes into liquidation.

Insolvency of itself generally does not terminate outstanding contracts to which the insolvent is a party.[17] Nor does it necessarily constitute a repudiation of the contracts so as to entitle the other contracting party to *elect* to treat the contract as terminated.[18] A repudiation may occur if

---

[14] See e.g. *French* v. *Fenn* (1783) 3 Dougl. 257 and *Smith* v. *Hodson* (1791) 4 TR 211. Compare *Olive* v. *Smith* (1813) 5 Taunt. 56.

[15] (1732) 5 Geo. II, c. 30, s. 28.

[16] Thus, the marginal note to the report of *Rose* v. *Hart* in Moore's Reports of Common Pleas Cases (2 Moore CP 547) states that, 'In order to constitute a mutual credit . . . it must be confined to *pecuniary* demands on such credits only as in their nature will terminate in a debt' (emphasis added).

[17] See, for example, *In re Sneezum* (1876) 3 Ch. D 463, 473; *Shipton Anderson & Co. (1927), Ltd. (in liq.)* v. *Micks, Lambert & Co.* [1936] 2 All ER 1032, 1037. *Official Receiver* v. *Henn* (1981) 40 ALR 569, 572; *Re Palmdale Insurance Ltd.* [1982] VR 921, 929.

[18] The ensuing discussion should be distinguished from the situation in which a contract in its terms is such that it is to remain in operation only so long as one of the parties continues in business, so that cessation of business consequent upon insolvency terminates the contract without giving rise to a liability for damages for breach of contract. See for example *Rhodes* v. *Forwood* (1876) 1 App. Cas. 256 and *Re Arawa Dairy Co. Ltd.* [1938] NZLR 411, though compare *Reigate* v. *Union Manufacturing Co. (Ramsbottom) Ltd.* [1918] 1 KB 593.

insolvency is coupled with other circumstances. For example, insolvency may have the effect of putting it beyond the insolvent's power to perform his obligations under the contract.[19] Thus, an order that an insurance company be wound up because of insolvency has been regarded as constituting a repudiation by the company of its contracts of insurance, on the basis that the deficiency in the company's funds makes it impossible to pay claims in full.[20] Similarly, if a bank has discounted bills for a customer prior to the customer's insolvency, the customer has already obtained the benefit of the contract and has only an obligation to reimburse the bank, which he obviously could not do in view of his insolvency.[21] Repudiation may also occur if the conduct of the insolvent or his trustee in bankruptcy shows that the the contract has been abandoned.[22] In this regard the courts have indicated that, if one contracting party notifies the other that he is insolvent, this may be treated as a notice of repudiation if he does not also inform the other that he still intends to complete the contract.[23] Generally though, in the absence of any such circumstances, the courts have shown a marked reluctance to conclude that insolvency of itself constitutes a repudiation of contracts that could return a profit for the insolvent's estate.[24] A striking example is the case of a contract for the sale of goods. The mere fact that the purchaser becomes insolvent before delivery of the goods is not considered to be a sufficient justification to entitle the vendor

[19] See for example the comments of Cotton L.J. in *Lee & Chapman's Case* (1885) 30 Ch. D 216, 223–4 with respect to the obligation of the company in liquidation to maintain the street for a period of 15 years. See also *Ogdens, Limited* v. *Nelson* [1905] AC 109, in which the company had sold its business prior to going into voluntary liquidation.

[20] *In re National Benefit Assurance Company Limited* [1924] 2 Ch. 339, 343; *In re The Federal Building Assurance Co. Ltd.* (1934) 34 SR (NSW) 499, 506; *Hiley* v. *The Peoples Prudential Assurance Co. Ltd.* (1938) 60 CLR 468, 493; *Re Palmdale Insurance Ltd.* [1982] VR 921, 929. See also *In re Northern Counties of England Fire Insurance Company; Macfarlane's Claim* (1880) 17 Ch. D 337, 341, though compare the comments of Lord Cairns in the *Albert Arbitration* (reported as a footnote to *Holdich's Case* LR 14 Eq. 72). *Quaere* whether English courts would reach the same conclusion now in relation to insurance companies carrying on long term business in view of the Insurance Companies Act 1982, s. 56 which requires the liquidator to carry on the long term business with a view to its being transferred to another insurance company. See *MacGillivray and Parkington on Insurance Law* (8th edn., 1988), 400 para. 974.

[21] *Baker* v. *Lloyd's Bank, Ltd.* [1920] 2 KB 322, 326.

[22] As in *Morgan* v. *Bain* (1874) LR 10 CP 15. See also *Lawrence* v. *Knowles* (1839) 5 Bing. (NC) 399, and *In re Tru-Grain Co. Ltd.* [1921] VLR 653.

[23] *Morgan* v. *Bain* (1874) LR 10 CP 15, 25–6, though compare *Mess* v. *Duffus and Co.* (1901) 6 Com. Cas. 165 in which it was held that, in all the circumstances, the notice in that case did not constitute notice of intention not to perform the contract.

[24] In addition to the cases cited in the next footnote, see *Brooke* v. *Hewitt* (1796) 3 Ves. Jun. 253; *In re Tru-Grain Co. Ltd.* [1921] VLR 653, 656; *Lindley on Companies* (6th edn., 1902) Vol. 2, 1014; *Gore-Browne on Companies* (44th edn., 1986: Supplement 2), para. 34.3. See also *Jennings Trustee* v. *King* [1952] 1 Ch. 899; *Shipton, Anderson & Co. (1927), Ltd.* v. *Micks, Lambert & Co.* [1936] 2 All ER 1032, 1037.

to treat the contract as rescinded.[25] In view of his precarious position the vendor is entitled to insist that the whole of the price be tendered to him before delivery, even if the sale was otherwise expressed to be on credit terms.[26] But the insolvency itself, without some additional circumstance, is not regarded as a repudiation of the contract. This is based upon a sound policy consideration, that the insolvent's beneficial contracts should be preserved for the benefit of the creditors.[27] If the contract can be performed at a profit, obviously it makes good sense for the trustee in bankruptcy or liquidator to use the funds of the estate for this purpose and to pay the price.

If the purchaser's trustee accordingly wishes to proceed with the contract and tenders the price, the vendor cannot accept payment and refuse to deliver the goods as a set-off against a separate debt owing to him, since the contractual obligation to deliver is not a money obligation. The vendor nevertheless may adopt a different approach. He may decide that he would be better off if he repudiated the contract, on the premise that he would thereby incur a monetary damages liability to the purchaser which could be set off against the debt owing to him, and at the same time he would then be able to retain the goods for sale elsewhere. In this regard it should not be an objection to a set-off that the damages liability would be incurred to the purchaser after the commencement of the bankruptcy, since the liability would have arisen out of a prior dealing between the parties.[28] Nor should it be a sufficient objection to a set-off that it would be based upon the vendor's own conduct in deliberately breaching the contract for the express purpose of obtaining a right of set-off.[29] Ultimately, however, the vendor's prospect of success would depend upon the purchaser's trustee not being able to obtain specific performance of the contract. If specific performance is available, the vendor would be compelled to perform its obligation under the contract to deliver the goods and, since this obligation is not a money obligation, it could not be the subject of a set-off.

---

[25] *Tolhurst* v. *Associated Portland Cement Manufacturers (1900) Ltd.* [1902] 2 KB 660 (esp. 671, referring to *Ex parte Chalmers* (1873) LR 8 Ch. App. 289 and *Morgan* v. *Bain* (1874) LR 10 CP 15). Similarly the insolvency of a vendor is not a sufficient justification to entitle the purchaser to put an end to the contract. See *Mess* v. *Duffus and Co.* (1901) 6 Com. Cas. 165.

[26] *Ex parte Chalmers* (1873) LR 8 Ch. App. 289. See also *Gunn* v. *Bolckow, Vaughan & Co.* (1875) LR 10 Ch. App. 491, 501; *In re Phoenix Bessemer Steel Company* (1876) 4 Ch. D 108, 112, 114; *In re Sneezum* (1876) 3 Ch. D 463, 473–4; *Grice* v. *Richardson* (1877) 3 App. Cas. 319. This principle has been codified in the sale of goods legislation. See the Sale of Goods Act 1979, s. 41(1)(c).   [27] *Ex parte Chalmers* (1873) 8 Ch. App. 289, 294.

[28] While Peter Gibson J. in *Carreras Rothmans Ltd.* v. *Freeman Mathews Treasure Ltd.* [1985] 1 Ch. 207 held that a claim for damages for breach of contract could only be employed in set-off in a liquidation if the breach occurred before the relevant date for determining rights of set-off, Millett J. in *Re Charge Card Services Ltd.* [1987] 1 Ch. 150, 178, 190 said that this aspect of the case is contrary to principle and should not be followed. See section 4.5.1 above.

[29] See section 4.7.3 above.

If the article the subject of the sale is unique the court, subject to other discretionary considerations, ordinarily would decree specific performance. If on the other hand the contract concerns goods readily available in the market at an ascertainable market price, the courts incline against specific relief. It has been said that in such a case specific performance is not available under any circumstances.[30] However this suggestion is contrary to principle, and should not be regarded as a proper statement of the law.[31] Specific performance is denied, not on an absolute jurisdictional basis, but rather because in the vast majority of cases damages are an adequate remedy,[32] which of course is the original foundation of the decree of specific performance.[33] As a corollary, if in a particular case damages at law would *not* be an adequate remedy, the court in principle should still have a discretion to grant specific relief.[34] There is nevertheless a problem in relation to a contract to sell unascertained goods. The Sale of Goods Act 1979, s. 52 provides for specific performance of a contract to sell specific or ascertained goods, and Lord Atkin in *In re Wait*[35] said that this provision sets out the full extent of equitable remedies in contracts for the sale of goods, so that specific performance is not available where the goods are unascertained. This view however has been condemned by commentators.[36] While Lord Brandon in *The Aliakmon*[37] commented that the Sale of Goods Act provides a complete code of law in contracts for the sale of goods, and he said that there was 'much force' in observations of Lord Atkin in *In re Wait*[38] that included reference to specific performance, he nevertheless emphasized that it was not necessary to decide the point, and that it was only a provisional view.

In determining whether damages are an adequate remedy, it is not a matter of considering merely whether the amount of the loss can be adequately quantified and expressed in a judgment. This is apparent from

---

[30] See Buckley L.J. in *Price* v. *Strange* [1978] 1 Ch. 337, 369.

[31] It is questioned in Jones and Goodhart, *Specific Performance* (1986), 224. See also the more cautious approach of Goff L.J. in *Price* v. *Strange* [1978] 1 Ch. 337, 359.

[32] *Adderley* v. *Dixon* (1824) 1 Sim. & St. 607, 610; *Falcke* v. *Gray* (1859) 4 Drewry 651, 657–8; *In re Clarke* (1887) 36 Ch. D 348, 352; *Thomas Borthwicks & Sons (Australasia) Ltd.* v. *South Otago Freezing Co. Ltd.* [1978] 1 NZLR 538, 548 (PC) ('A contract for the sale of goods obtainable on the market will not *normally* be specifically enforced' (emphasis added)); Spry, *Equitable Remedies* (4th edn., 1990), 54 note 18 and 64–6.

[33] See Lord Redesdale in *Harnet* v. *Yeilding* (1805) 2 Sch. & Lef. 549, 553.

[34] See in this regard *Sky Petroleum Ltd.* v. *V.I.P. Petroleum Ltd.* [1974] 1 WLR 576 (esp. at 578–9).   [35] [1927] 1 Ch. 606, 630.

[36] Treitel, 'Specific Performance in the Sale of Goods' [1966] *Journal of Business Law* 211, 222–4; Jones and Goodhart, *Specific Performance* (1986), 120–1; Spry, *Equitable Remedies* (4th edn., 1990), 54. See also Pollock, 'Re Wait' (1927) 43 *Law Quarterly Review* 293, and Pettit, *Equity and the Law of Trusts* (7th edn., 1993), 617, 618 n. 5.

[37] *Leigh and Sillavan Ltd.* v. *Aliakmon Ltd.* [1986] 1 AC 785, 812.

[38] [1927] 1 Ch. 606, 635–6.

the decision of the House of Lords in *Beswick* v. *Beswick*.[39] The defendant had breached a contract with the plaintiff to make periodic payments to a third party. While a judgment for nominal damages arguably would have constituted an accurate reflection of the plaintiff's own loss, it would not have been adequate to meet the justice of the case. Accordingly, specific performance was allowed. The question is whether a judgment for damages would put the plaintiff in a situation as beneficial to him as if the agreement were specifically enforced,[40] or, in other words, whether damages would provide a 'complete remedy'.[41] Thus the courts have indicated that it is appropriate to consider whether the defendant for any reason is unlikely to satisfy a judgment for damages.[42] In this regard, if the reason that the defendant is unlikely to satisfy the judgment is insolvency, and he has other creditors, the court may refuse to grant relief on the basis that specific performance would have the effect of preferring the plaintiff over the general body of creditors, if in fact there is no other reason apart from inadequacy of damages for granting relief.[43] However, in the absence of this countervailing circumstance, the actual amount that the plaintiff is likely to receive in his hands as a result of a judgment for damages, in comparison to what his position would be if specific performance were granted, is a relevant factor.

In the particular case under discussion an award of damages would not in fact constitute an adequate remedy, even where the goods are readily available in the market at an ascertainable price. If the vendor were to perform his obligation and deliver the goods, the insolvent purchaser's estate would have the full benefit of the contract, and at the same time would only have to pay a dividend on the debt owing to the vendor. If, however, the purchaser is remitted to a judgment for damages against the vendor after the vendor's repudiation, the vendor's liability for damages ordinarily should be capable of set-off against the debt, given that it is not an objection to a set-off that the vendor may have deliberately breached a contract in order to obtain a set-off. The allowance of a set-off where none otherwise would be available may have a considerable effect on the funds available for distribution to the purchaser's creditors, and on this basis an award of damages would not put the purchaser and his creditors in a

---

[39] [1968] AC 58.

[40] *Harnett* v. *Yeilding* (1805) 2 Sch. & Lef. 549, 556; Spry, *Equitable Remedies* (4th edn., 1990), 58. [41] *Adderley* v. *Dixon* (1824) 1 Sim. & St. 607, 610.

[42] See *Hodgson* v. *Duce* (1856) 2 Jur. NS 1014; *Evans Marshall & Co. Ltd.* v. *Bertola S.A.* [1973] 1 WLR 349, 380–1; *The Oakworth* [1975] 1 Lloyd's Rep. 581, 583; Horack, 'Insolvency and Specific Performance' (1918) 31 *Harvard Law Review* 702; Jones and Goodhart, *Specific Performance* (1986), 20–1; Spry, *Equitable Remedies* (4th edn., 1990), 65.

[43] *In re Wait* [1927] 1 Ch. 606. See also *Hewett* v. *Court* (1983) 149 CLR 638, 658; Spry, *Equitable Remedies* (4th edn., 1990), 54 n. 20.

situation as beneficial as if the contract in question were specifically performed. Accordingly, as a matter of principle specific performance may well be available in this situation, subject to other relevant discretionary considerations.

5.3 FOREIGN EXCHANGE CONTRACTS

5.3.1 *Introduction*

The requirement of commensurability has come into prominence in recent years in the context of foreign exchange contracts.

For the sake of simplicity, consider the following situation. A bank has entered into two foreign exchange contracts with a customer or with another bank (referred to as the 'counterparty').[44] In the first contract entered into on, say, 1 September, the bank has agreed to provide an amount expressed in currency A to the counterparty in consideration of the counterparty's agreement to provide an amount expressed in currency B. Performance of the contract is to take place on 31 December. Pursuant to a second contract, entered into on 1 October, the counterparty has agreed to provide an amount expressed in currency C to the bank in consideration of the bank's agreement to provide an amount expressed in currency D. This contract is also to be performed on 31 December. However, on 15 November the counterparty goes into liquidation.

In the event of the liquidation of a counterparty, the liquidator presumably would disclaim any foreign exchange contract which, because of movements in exchange rates, is considered to be unprofitable,[45] and would keep on foot any contract which is profitable to the counterparty. If a contract is disclaimed, any person who sustains consequential loss or damage is deemed by the Insolvency Act[46] to be a creditor of the company to the extent of the loss, and accordingly may prove for the loss in the liquidation. If the liquidator of a counterparty does disclaim one contract as unprofitable but elects to perform another profitable contract, the bank would wish to set off its obligation arising under the continuing contract against its damages claim against the counterparty in liquidation arising as a result of the disclaimer.[47] The question of where the bank would stand in

---

[44] Often there will be a large number of contracts with a particular counterparty involving different currencies and performance dates. The following discussion is adapted from Derham, 'Set-off and Netting of Foreign Exchange Contracts in the Liquidation of a Counterparty' [1991] *Journal of Business Law* 463.

[45] Pursuant to the Insolvency Act 1986, s. 178.

[46] Insolvency Act 1986, s. 178(6).

[47] It is assumed in the following discussion that the reference in the Insolvency Rules, r. 4.90(3) to sums becoming 'due' contemplates the time that the contract was entered into out of which the obligation in question subsequently arose, as opposed to the time that the liability actually vested pursuant to the contract. See section 2.7.4 above.

the event of a liquidation of the counterparty is of paramount concern to banks. It affects dealing limits that banks can impose for their counter-parties. In addition, where the bank requires cash cover or other margin deposit as 'security' in the event of default by the counterparty, it will affect the amount of cover or margin deposit required. It is also important for capital adequacy purposes, that is, in the determination of the amount of capital that the bank is required by the relevant central bank to have to cover its risk assets.

5.3.2 *The nature of the foreign money obligation in a foreign exchange contract*

The question of the nature of the obligation to deliver foreign money pursuant to a foreign exchange contract has yet to be determined authoritatively by the courts. As Dr. Mann explained,[48] foreign money may function either as money or as a commodity, depending on the circumstances. Foreign money should be regarded as money where it serves monetary functions, as, for example, in a foreign currency debt.[49] However, in the particular situation in which foreign money is dealt in and quoted on the foreign exchange market, he considered that it is the object of commercial intercourse and therefore is a commodity.[50] In other words, it is similar to a contract to deliver so many tons of wheat. Nussbaum[51] and Rabel[52] expressed similar views, though in both cases this admittedly was in the context of contracts which require physical delivery of the foreign money, an issue that is discussed below. The concept was justified by Nussbaum in that context in terms of the distinction between acting as a measure and being measured, between *mensura* and *mensuratum*. Money in a general sense is a standard or measure of the value of goods and services.[53] As a corollary, it is correct to say that the value of goods and services is measured by reference to money. Indeed, money has been described as the common denominator of value.[54] But while money is a measure, it is an abstract unit of measurement (in England, the pound

---

[48] Mann, *The Legal Aspect of Money* (5th edn., 1992), 191 *et seq.*
[49] See in this regard the comments of Lord Radcliffe in *In re United Railways of Havana and Regla Warehouses Ltd.* [1961] AC 1007, 1059–60.
[50] See Mann, n. 48 above, 191.
[51] See Nussbaum, *Money in the Law National and International* (1950), 340–4 for a discussion of foreign money in the context of a foreign currency debt, and 24 (and see also 319) in relation to foreign money functioning as a commodity when it is purchased or exchanged on the foreign exchange market.
[52] Rabel, *The Conflict of Laws* (2nd edn., 1964) Vol. 3, 26.
[53] Nussbaum, n. 51 above, 14, referred to with approval in Mann, n. 48 above, 49.
[54] Nussbaum, n. 51 above, 11.

sterling) which cannot be precisely defined.[55] Money as such is not measured by anything else. Money is *mensura*, not *mensuratum*.[56] Yet, when foreign money is sold or exchanged it is being measured. It is measured by its fluctuating exchange value against the fixed unit of account in which domestic money is denominated, the rate of exchange of a foreign currency being the price of that currency in terms of a country's own currency.[57] According to Nussbaum,[58] when foreign money is measured in this manner it has the character of a commodity.[59]

The views of Nussbaum and Rabel were expressed in the context of a physical delivery of foreign money in the form of coins or bank notes, whereas in the foreign exchange contracts under discussion there is not physical delivery in this sense, but rather the contract is performed by arranging a credit to a bank account. However it is suggested below that the absence of physical delivery cannot have the effect of turning a contract the subject of which otherwise would have been characterized as a commodity into a contract in which the obligation is monetary in nature. It

---

[55] Mann, n. 48 above, 49, 86. As Nussbaum, n. 51 above, 14 put it in relation to the U.S. dollar, 'the dollar concept existing at any given time is as little susceptible of definition, as, say, the concept of "blue" '.

[56] Nussbaum, n. 51 above, 28, and see also the discussion in Mann, n. 48 above, 43–9. Under the Bretton Woods Agreement, the 'par value' of the currency of each member was expressed in terms of gold, though in the sense that the par value determined the price for the purchase and sale of gold. See Mann, n. 48 above, 33–6. Accordingly, it is correct to say that the par value constituted a measure. See Mann, *op. cit.* 46. This system effectively had ceased to apply by 1973. See in *Lively Ltd.* v. *City of Munich* [1976] 1 WLR 1004, 1010–13.

[57] See Mann, n. 48 above, 61.

[58] He said (n. 51 above, 24) that, 'in special situations pieces of money are dealt with as commodities. This happens mainly in the market of foreign exchanges. Ever since there has been a theory of money, it has been recognized that money may have a "second use",— namely, to be purchased or exchanged. In the language of Thomas Aquinas, money, if sold or exchanged, is "measured, not a measure;" "*mensuratum*", not "*mensura*". Its intrinsic or exchange value as distinct from the extrinsic or nominal (face) value is controlling in the situation. The latter value is a matter of the law; the former is the result of economic conditions. While the intrinsic value is subject to fluctuations, the extrinsic one is invariable'.

[59] This would not apply, however, in relation to the periodic payment obligations that arise under a currency and interest rate swap. See Derham, 'Set-off and Netting of Foreign Exchange Contracts in the Liquidation of a Counterparty' [1991] *Journal of Business Law* 463, 468–9.
The concept of acting as a measure of the value of goods and services is a general function of money, and Nussbaum's thesis would not require that, if in a particular situation 'money' is not being used specifically for that purpose, it is not money. This would be the case, for example, when money is transferred by way of gift. But where foreign money is being measured, it can be said in that circumstance that it is not functioning as money. Further, the notion that foreign money when sold or exchanged is measured against domestic money should be distinguished from the situation in which parties have agreed that what is admittedly a foreign currency debt should be converted into domestic money at a specified exchange rate for certain purposes, for example because payment is to be made in domestic money, or in order to ascertain whether security top up is required. The measurement as against domestic money is applied to the debt, which in itself is not money. See Mann, n. 48 above, 5 in relation to bank accounts.

may be argued that, unless it is intended that there be physical delivery, the foreign exchange contract cannot be said to be concerned with a commodity. But even accepting this, it would not have as a consequence that the obligation to arrange the credit is a money obligation.

The view that foreign money in the context of a foreign exchange contract is a commodity is not without judicial support.[60] It is consistent with a number of references by the courts to foreign exchange contracts in terms of sale and purchase,[61] though, if the obligation on *both* sides of the contract is a foreign money obligation, the contract would be more appropriately described as one of exchange, similar to a barter. In *Drexel Burnham Lambert International N.V.* v. *El Nasr*[62] Staughton J. had no apparent hesitation in describing Swiss francs the subject of forward contracts of sale and purchase as a commodity, and in New South Wales Lee J. referred to the opinions of Mann and Nussbaum with evident approval when he held that a foreign exchange contract that made provision for physical delivery was a commodity agreement for the purposes of the Futures Industries Code formerly applicable in that jurisdiction.[63] While 'commodity' admittedly had a particular definition in the Code,[64] his Honour said that, 'it is a *natural use of the word* to apply it to foreign currency in circumstances in which it is dealt with in commercial transactions of the kind under consideration'.[65] On another occasion Lord Radcliffe in the House of Lords[66] recognized that there is a distinction between, on the one hand, a contract to pay foreign money abroad in satisfaction of a debt and, on the other, 'a contract to deliver foreign currency in this country or abroad or a true exchange contract', which he defined as a contract to exchange the currency of one country for the currency of another. His Lordship specifically rejected the view that

---

[60] The following authorities are in addition to cases which have dealt with money in a bag, or specific coins. See for example *Taylor* v. *Plumer* (1815) 3 M & S 562 and *Moss* v. *Hancock* [1899] 2 QB 111.

[61] *In re British American Continental Bank Limited; Goldzieher and Penso's Claim* [1922] 2 Ch. 575, 586 per Warrington L.J. ('The subjects of these contracts for sale and purchase were sums of foreign currency'); *Bank of India* v. *Patel* [1982] 1 Lloyd's Rep. 506, 508, 509, and on appeal [1983] 2 Lloyd's Rep. 298, 299, 302; *Isaac Naylor & Sons Ltd.* v. *New Zealand Co-operative Wool Marketing Association Ltd.* [1981] 1 NZLR 361, 366.

[62] [1986] 1 Lloyd's Rep. 356.

[63] *Shoreline Currencies (Aust) Pty. Ltd.* v. *Corporate Affairs Commission (NSW)* (1986) 10 ACLR 847. See also *Carragreen Currency Corporation Pty. Ltd.* v. *Corporate Affairs Commission (NSW)* (1986) 11 ACLR 298, and *Corporate Affairs Commission (NSW)* v. *Lombard Nash International Pty. Ltd.* (1986) 11 ACLR 566, 569 ('there is a bet made on the relative price of a commodity, such *as currency*, gold or platinum' (emphasis added)).

[64] 'Commodity' was defined in s. 4 of the Futures Industries Code as 'a thing that is capable of delivery pursuant to an agreement for its delivery; or . . . an instrument creating or evidencing a thing in action'. See now the definition in the Corporations Law, s. 9.

[65] (1986) 10 ACLR 847, 855 (emphasis added).

[66] *In re United Railways of Havana and Regla Warehouses Ltd.* [1961] AC 1007, 1059–60.

foreign currency debts payable abroad give rise to an obligation to deliver a commodity as opposed to an obligation to pay money. It is tolerably clear, though, that foreign exchange contracts were considered to be contracts for the delivery of a commodity.

In foreign exchange markets where banks and financial institutions deal in foreign currencies, it is debatable nevertheless whether it is technically correct to describe the contract as one of sale and purchase,[67] or, if both obligations are foreign money obligations, a contract of exchange similar to a barter. Invariably the intention is not that there be physical delivery, but rather that the contract be performed by means of a credit to a bank account in the country of the particular currency.[68] Since a contract performed in this manner does not involve a transfer of the beneficial ownership of property, it has been argued that the foreign money the subject of a foreign exchange contract should be treated as money (but not legal tender) rather than as a commodity.[69] In other words, the contract is a bilateral executory contract for the payment of money by both parties.[70] The proponents of this view do not suggest that the obligation to deliver foreign money pursuant to an executory foreign exchange contract constitutes a debt.[71] Rather, it is said that the obligation should be characterized as a money obligation similar to a contract to lend money, in which, if the money is not advanced, the liability is for damages for breach of contract rather than for payment of a debt.[72] However one should not

---

[67] See *Benjamin on Sale* (4th edn., 1992), 67–8.

[68] In the context of a cable transfer of foreign money, the Court of Appeals in New York has characterized the contract in question as a contract to create a credit of the relevant amount of foreign money, as opposed to a sale of foreign money (or a sale of an existing credit). See *Equitable Trust Co. of New York* v. *Keene* (1922) 133 NE 894; *Gravenhorst* v. *Zimmerman* (1923) 139 NE 766. See also *Samuels* v. *E.F. Drew & Co.* (1924) 296 F 882. Compare though *United Equities Co.* v. *First National City Bank* (1976) 383 NYS 2d 6, affirmed (1977) 395 NYS 2d 640, in which the court applied Article 2 of the Uniform Commercial Code (dealing with transactions in goods) in the context of a foreign exchange contract, though the applicability of Article 2 was assumed without being the subject of discussion. See Manire, *Foreign Exchange Sales and the Law of Contracts: A Case for Analogy to the Uniform Commercial Code* (1982) 35 *Vanderbilt Law Review* 1173, 1188.

[69] Wood, *English and International Set-off* (1989), 60. See also Wood and Terray, 'Foreign Exchange Netting in France and England' *International Financial Law Review*, October 1989, 18, 20.   [70] Wood, *English and International Set-off* (1989), 339 para. 7–182.

[71] Compare Shea, 'Foreign Exchange Contracts and Netting in the UK' *International Financial Law Review*, January 1990, 19, referring to a statement by P.O. Lawrence J. in *In re British American Continental Bank, Limited; Credit General Liegeois' Claim* [1922] 2 Ch. 589. However that statement was not made in the context of a foreign exchange contract but rather a foreign money bank overdraft, which, it may be conceded, does give rise to a debt.

[72] See, as regards a contract to make a loan, *Western Wagon and Property Company* v. *West* [1892] 1 Ch. 271. For cases in which the remedy for breach of executory foreign exchange contracts was damages, see *Goldzieher and Penso's Claim* [1922] 2 Ch. 575; *Lisser and Rosenkranz's Claim* [1923] 1 Ch. 276; *Bank of India* v. *Patel* [1982] 1 Lloyd's Rep. 506 (and see also on appeal [1983] 2 Lloyd's Rep. 298).

adopt the 'money' theory as the basis of the obligation merely on the ground that, as a matter of commercial reality, the contract will be performed by arranging a bank credit. In this regard, it is appropriate to consider the nature of the obligation in question.

In *Libyan Arab Foreign Bank* v. *Bankers Trust Co.*[73] Staughton J. analysed the nature of an English bank's payment obligation to its customer in respect of a U.S. dollar bank account. His Lordship said that, at bottom, there are only two methods by which the customer can obtain the fruits of its right against the bank. The first is the delivery of cash, whether dollar bills or any other currency, to or to the order of the customer. The second involves an 'account transfer'. As Staughton J. acknowledged, 'transfer' is a misleading term, since the original obligation is not assigned. Rather, the obligation of the bank to the customer is extinguished and is replaced by a new obligation. The bank may substitute one obligation with another owed by itself, as, for example, if the customer instructs the bank to credit the account of another customer, or if the bank gives the customer a banker's draft, which in effect involves a substitution of one personal obligation owed by the bank to the customer with another obligation similarly owed to the customer. Alternatively, another bank may assume an obligation to the customer in substitution of the first bank's obligation. This method may involve a number of levels of intermediaries, ending, in the case of a U.S. dollar deposit, with two banks that have accounts with the Federal Reserve Bank in the USA, so that the account of one bank is debited, and the obligation of the Federal Reserve to the extent of the debit is extinguished, and the account of the other bank is credited, thereby giving rise to the creation of a liability in the Federal Reserve to the extent of the credit. In the *Libyan Arab Foreign Bank* case the customer, an agency of the Libyan Government, had a Eurodollar account of some U.S.$130,000,000 with the London branch of an American bank. As a result of a United States Presidential Order, the assets of the Government of Libya and its agencies were frozen. The bank argued that the Order had the effect that it could not procure payment by means of an account transfer, since ultimately this would have involved the creation of an obligation in the USA in replacement of the bank's obligation, which would have been illegal under American law. Staughton J. nevertheless held that, despite the size of the deposit, the customer still had a fundamental right to be paid in cash, and there was nothing in English law which rendered this illegal. There was no implied term to the effect that the bank was not required to tender cash. No doubt, as Cairns L.J. once remarked in the context of a clause in charterparty providing for payment of cash in New York,[74] it would have been absurd in modern

---

[73] [1989] 1 QB 728.   [74] *The Brimnes* [1975] 1 QB 929, 968.

conditions to suppose that payment in dollar bills was contemplated. Nevertheless payment in cash was still regarded in *Libyan Arab Foreign Bank* as a fundamental right. In this regard Staughton J. drew an analogy with operations in futures in the commodity markets. Everyone knows that the contracts will be settled by the payment of differences and not by the delivery of the particular commodity. But an obligation to deliver and accept the commodity, in the absence of settlement by some other means, remains the legal basis of the transaction.

The status of *Libyan Arab Foreign Bank* is unclear. In the first place Staughton J.'s decision has been criticized by commentators,[75] and it remains to be seen whether it will be followed. Further, it is uncertain whether it would be applied to foreign currency obligations which are not debts. This should not, however, affect the position. Consider once again the case of a foreign exchange contract in which the bank's obligation is to arrange a credit to the counterparty's bank account in the country of the particular currency. There are two ways of looking at the transaction, neither of which leads to the conclusion that the obligation is an obligation to pay money. The first is that, despite the fact that as a matter of commercial reality it would be contemplated that the obligation would be performed by arranging a bank credit, if all else fails and this method of settlement is not possible an obligation would still remain to arrange for physical delivery direct to the counterparty. In such a case it may be said that an obligation to deliver foreign money remains a fundamental basis of the contract and that, since foreign money delivered pursuant to the contract would be the object of commercial intercourse as far as the parties to the contract are concerned, a fundamental basis of the contract would be to treat foreign money as a commodity. The alternative approach is to concentrate only on the method that as a matter of commercial reality would be used to satisfy the obligation, and that is by arranging a bank credit. In other words, on this view it is assumed either that the *Libyan Arab Foreign Bank* case was wrongly decided, or alternatively that it does not extend to foreign exchange contracts so that, unlike the contract considered in *Libyan Arab Foreign Bank*, the form of foreign exchange contract under discussion is such that this is the *only* required method of performance. But even if this is the correct characterization of the contract, if one considers the meaning of 'money' it is difficult to see how it can be said that foreign money in this instance is being treated as money.

It is trite to say that money is a medium of exchange. But this merely

---

[75] See Kleiner, 'Foreign Exchange Claims Against Banks in Dispute' *International Financial Law Review*, May 1989, 204, and Mann, n. 48 above, 200–1. See also the view earlier expressed by Goode, *Payment Obligations in Commercial and Financial Transactions* (1983), 118–20.

describes the *function* of money. It does not tell us what constitutes money. The legal, as distinct from the economic, view of money is that it is a personal chattel.[76] In order that a particular chattel may be characterized as money, Mann tells us that in addition it should be issued by the authority of law, it should be denominated by reference to a unit of account, and it should be meant to serve as a medium of exchange in the state of issue.[77] But essentially it is a chattel, in modern society a coin or a bank note.[78] A debt is regarded as a money obligation because, if all else fails, payment in money remains a fundamental basis of the contract. As Mann aptly expressed it,[79] 'The debtor of a monetary obligation . . . is under a duty to pay money, i.e. chattels which, among other peculiarities, incorporate a reference to a distinct unit of account'. If, on the other hand, arranging a bank credit as a matter of law is the *only* required method of performance under a foreign exchange contract, it is difficult to see how it can be said that foreign money is being treated as money because, put simply, this method of performance has nothing to do with 'money', in the legal sense of the word.[80] Money is not involved in the transaction. If the subject of a contract is not, and as a matter of law it does not contemplate the possibility of, the payment of a sum of money, there is not a money obligation.[81] The obligation in question is merely to perform an act, i.e. to arrange the credit. As Mann pointed out,[82] this not only may have different consequences in cases such as *Libyan Arab Foreign Bank* where questions of impossibility of performance are in issue, but the methods of enforcement are different. A money obligation is enforced by an action for

---

[76] Mann, n. 48 above, 8. See also Nussbaum, n. 51 above, 13 ('Money, the concrete object . . .').
[77] Mann, n. 48 above, 8.
[78] Thus Darling J. in *Moss* v. *Hancock* [1899] 2 QB 111, 116 defined money as 'that which passes freely from hand to hand throughout the community in final discharge of debts and full payment for commodities'. This definition was taken from Walker, *Money, Trade & Industry* (1882), 4. In *In re Taylor* [1923] 1 Ch. 99, 110 Younger L.J. said that, 'In its strict legal sense the word [money] is confined to ready money actually in hand.'
[79] Mann, n. 48 above, 86. See also at 74 ('Monetary obligations thus appear to be obligations the subject-matter of which is the payment of a sum of money').
[80] However, as matter of construction of a contract and of ascertaining the contractual intent of the parties, a provision to the effect that payment should be made 'in cash' may be interpreted as including payment by means of an account transfer. See for example *The Brimnes* [1975] QB 929, 948, 963, 968–9; *The Chikuma* [1981] 1 WLR 314, 320.
[81] See in this regard Mann's discussion (n. 48 above, 200–1) of Eurodollar accounts. In the fourth edition of his *The Legal Aspect of Money* (1982), 193–4 Mann argued that Eurodollar accounts are subject to an implied term that the obligation on the account can *only* be discharged by way of a bank credit through the CHIPS system. Accordingly, he concluded that the obligation is not a monetary one. Subsequently Staughton J. in the *Libyan Arab Foreign Bank* case [1989] 1 QB 728 specifically rejected Mann's view that the creditor on a Eurodollar account is not entitled to payment in cash. However, the point remains valid that, if the contract does not allow for payment in cash, it can hardly be said that there is a money obligation.
[82] Mann, n. 48 above, 200.

payment, whereas an obligation to arrange a bank credit is enforceable as such[83] only by means of an order for specific performance, which is discretionary.

The result therefore is the same whether or not physical delivery is a permissible method of performance under a foreign exchange contract. In neither case is the obligation monetary in nature. Certainly it would be surprising if foreign money the subject of a foreign exchange contract that requires physical delivery would not be regarded as money, but that the obligation would be a money obligation if the contract stipulates that performance instead is to take place by arranging a bank credit. Nor is there anything in *Miliangos* v. *George Frank (Textiles) Ltd.*,[84] or in the cases that have followed it, which detracts from this view.[85] In *Miliangos* the House of Lords held that, in an action to enforce a foreign currency debt, judgment may be given expressed in the relevant foreign currency. While for the purpose of enforcement the judgment has to be converted into sterling at the exchange rate prevailing at the date that the court authorizes enforcement, there is no reason why judgment itself could not be expressed in the foreign currency. In reaching this conclusion the House of Lords overruled its earlier decision in *In re United Railways of Havana and Regla Warehouses Ltd.*,[86] that an English court could not give judgment for payment of a foreign currency debt in a currency other than sterling. However it is important to note that *Miliangos* was concerned only with a matter of procedure, i.e. whether an English court could give judgment expressed in a foreign currency. The substantive question of the nature of the underlying obligation was not in issue. Indeed, while the view had been expressed in a number of early cases that the obligation of a foreign currency debtor was to deliver a commodity rather than to pay a sum of money,[87] this was rejected by both Lord Radcliffe and Lord Reid in *United Railways of Havana* in the context of a foreign currency debt payable in the country of that currency.[88] In *United Railways of Havana* the action to enforce the foreign currency debt was characterized as an

---

[83] This should be distinguished from an action for damages for failure to perform, the effect of which is considered in section 5.3.4 below in the context of specific performance.

[84] [1976] AC 443.

[85] Compare Wood (*English and International Set-off* (1989), 60) who has suggested that, in view of the rapid development of the attitude of English law to foreign currencies, as exhibited by its acceptance in the *Miliangos* line of cases of the power of the court to give a judgment expressed in a foreign currency, there can hardly be any question that the foreign money obligation under a foreign exchange contract would be treated as a money obligation.

[86] [1961] AC 1007.

[87] See, for example, Vaughan Williams L.J. in *Manners* v. *Pearson & Son* [1898] 1 Ch. 581, 592, and P.O. Lawrence J. in *In re British American Continental Bank, Limited; Credit General Liegeois' Claim* [1922] 2 Ch. 589, 594–5. For a more complete list of the authorities, see Mann, n. 48 above, 192 n. 45.   [88] [1961] AC 1007, 1051, 1059.

action in damages, and accordingly was subject to the 'breach date' rule. This meant that the foreign currency debt had to be converted into sterling for the purpose of judgment at the exchange rate prevailing at the date that the debt became due and payable. The fact that the remedy was in damages does not mean that the debt was considered to be something other than a contract for the payment of money. Lord Radcliffe and Lord Reid were emphatic that a foreign currency debt, at least when it is payable abroad, does give rise to a money obligation. Rather, because it was perceived that an English court could not give a judgment expressed in a foreign currency, it was considered that the claimant could not sue in England to recover a 'debt' in the relevant currency. The claimant's only remedy was for damages in sterling for breach of contract for non-payment of the foreign money.[89] All that occurred subsequently in *Miliangos* was that the procedural obstacle to giving judgment in a foreign currency was removed. As Lord Wilberforce and Lord Edmund Davies emphasized, the decision primarily related to a matter of procedure.[90] *Miliangos*, like *United Railways of Havana*, was concerned with a foreign currency debt payable abroad and, in view of the opinions of Lord Radcliffe and Lord Reid expressed in the earlier case, it is apparent that the decision in *Miliangos* itself did not involve any change in the view of English law as to the nature of the underlying obligation. English law would also now regard a foreign currency debt payable in England as importing a money obligation rather than an obligation to deliver a commodity,[91] despite the contrary view expressed in some cases.[92] However there is nothing in *Miliangos,* or the cases that have followed it, to suggest that under English law a foreign money obligation under a foreign exchange contract is a money obligation.[93]

---

[89] See Lord Denning in *United Railways of Havana* [1961] AC 1007, 1069.

[90] See the judgments of Lord Wilberforce and Lord Edmund Davies at [1976] AC 443, 461, 462, 465, 499–500, referring to Lord Reid in *United Railways of Havana* [1961] AC 1007, 1052. See also *The Teh Hu* [1970] P 106, 126; *Schorsch Meier* v. *Hennin* [1975] 1 QB 416, 424; *Re Dynamics Corporation of America* [1976] 1 WLR 757, 767; *The Despina R* [1979] AC 685, 704; *Australian and New Zealand Banking Group Ltd.* v. *Cawood* [1987] 1 Qd. R 131, 134.

[91] This is implicit in *Choice Investments Ltd.* v. *Jeromninon* [1981] 1 QB 149, and see also *Australian and New Zealand Banking Group Ltd.* v. *Cawood* [1987] 1 Qd. R 131 (esp. at 134).

[92] See, for example, the Privy Council in *Pyrmont, Limited* v. *Schott* [1939] AC 145, 156 and in *Marrache* v. *Ashton* [1943] AC 311, 318, and generally the cases mentioned in Mann, note 48 above, 192 n. 45. Compare, however, *Cohn* v. *Boulken* (1920) 36 TLR 767 and *Syndic in Bankruptcy of Salim Nasrallah Khoury* v. *Khayat* [1943] AC 507 (esp. 511).

[93] The statement by Brandon J. in *The Halcyon the Great* [1975] 1 WLR 515, 520, that 'the word "money", in its ordinary and natural meaning, includes money in a foreign currency as well as money in sterling', should be understood by reference to the facts there being considered. A similar comment applies to the remarks of Mocatta J. in *Barclays Bank International Ltd.* v. *Levin Brothers (Bradford) Ltd.* [1977] 1 QB 270, 282.

5.3.3 *The availability of a set-off*

If it is accepted that the foreign money obligation under a foreign exchange contract is not a money obligation, irrespective of whether the contract would require physical delivery in the event that a bank credit for some reason could not be arranged, the question arises as to how outstanding foreign exchange contracts would be dealt with in the counterparty's liquidation. The situation posited is that a contract has been disclaimed by the counterparty's liquidator because it is considered to be unprofitable. As a result the bank has a damages claim against the counterparty which may be proved in the liquidation. However the liquidator has not disclaimed a second contract, because this contract is considered to be profitable from the counterparty's point of view. In view of the counterparty's insolvency, the bank would not be obliged to perform its obligation under the second contract until the counterparty has first performed its own obligation, despite any term of the contract that may indicate otherwise.[94] If the liquidator accordingly makes available the requisite amount of the currency in question by means of a bank credit, the bank would wish to set off its resulting obligation to perform its side of the contract against the damages claim that it has against the counterparty arising from the disclaimer of the first contract.

Consider first that the counterparty has the foreign money obligation, while the bank's obligation is to pay a sum expressed in sterling. On a first principles analysis the bank should succeed in its argument for a set-off, since the liability is a money obligation[95] that arises out of a contract entered into before the liquidation. This is so notwithstanding the decision of Watkin Williams J. in *Ince Hall Rolling Mills Co. Ltd.* v. *The Douglas Forge Company*.[96] In that case the liquidator of a supplier delivered goods to a purchaser pursuant to a contract that had been entered into before the liquidation, and it was held that the purchaser was not entitled to a set-off in respect of its resulting liability for the price. The better view, however, is that *Ince Hall* was wrongly decided,[97] and that in fact there is no valid reason why a bank with a sterling liability on a foreign exchange contract which becomes due and payable after the counterparty's liquidation should not be able to employ that liability in a set-off in the liquidation.

Alternatively, the bank may have the foreign money obligation. In such a case it would appear that the bank's obligation under the contract (as opposed to a damages liability for failing to perform it, which is considered

---

[94] See *Ex parte Chalmers; in re Edwards* (1873) LR 8 Ch. App. 289, and generally section 5.2 above.

[95] This assumes that the *Libyan Arab Foreign Bank* case [1989] 1 QB 728 applies so that, if all else fails, performance of the obligation could be required by the delivery of cash.

[96] (1882) 8 QBD 179.   [97] See section 9.4.2 below.

below) is not a money obligation. Rather, it is an obligation that relates to a commodity, or alternatively, if the *Libyan Arab Foreign Bank* case either was wrongly decided or does not apply to foreign exchange contracts, the obligation in question may be characterized as an obligation to perform an act in the sense of arranging a bank credit. But whichever of these is the correct characterization, because it is not a money obligation the requirement of commensurability would mean that it could not be employed in a set-off in the counterparty's liquidation. There is not a sum due for the purpose of the set-off section. Nor would the fact that the obligation nevertheless has a readily ascertainable value affect this conclusion. In cases concerned with a claim for the return of specific property, there have been instances in which the courts accepted that the property had a particular value, though it was held nevertheless that that value could not form the basis of a set-off.[98]

The bank would not regard this as satisfactory, and two arguments have been put forward which, it has been suggested, may enable the bank to avoid the result. The first is that the insolvency of the counterparty may be taken as a repudiation by the counterparty of outstanding foreign exchange contracts,[99] though it is suggested that this ordinarily would not be the case in relation to contracts that can be performed profitably by the liquidator.[100] The second is that the bank may convert its non-monetary foreign currency obligation into a monetary liability by refusing to perform the contract, and then seek to employ its resulting monetary damages liability to the counterparty in a set-off. This is considered below.

5.3.4 *Specific performance of foreign exchange contracts*

It has been suggested that the bank may avoid the result outlined above, of having to perform the contracts which are unprofitable from its point of view and being left with a damages claim in the counterparty's liquidation arising from the disclaimer of the contracts that the bank regarded as profitable, by simply refusing to perform the unprofitable contracts.[101]

---

[98] See, for example, *Eberle's Hotels and Restaurant Company, Ltd.* v. *E. Jonas & Bros.* (1887) 18 QBD 459; *Ellis and Co.'s Trustee* v. *Dixon-Johnson* [1925] AC 489 (shares readily available on the stock exchange).

[99] Wood, *English and International Set-off* (1989), 173, 179; Wood and Terray, 'Foreign Exchange Netting in France and England' *International Financial Law Review,* October 1989, 18, 20.

[100] Derham, 'Set-off and Netting of Foreign Exchange Contracts in the Liquidation of a Counterparty' [1991] *Journal of Business Law* 463, 481–4, and see also section 5.2 above.

[101] Wood, *English and International Set-off* (1989), 340; Wood, 'Netting Agreements in Organised and Private Markets' *Current Developments in Banking and Finance* (1989), 11; Wood and Terray 'Foreign Exchange Netting in France and England' *International Financial Law Review,* October 1989, 18, 20.

Presumably it would refuse to accept performance by the liquidator of the counterparty's obligations under the contracts in question. The argument is that the bank would then have a monetary damages liability to the counterparty arising from its breach of the contracts, which it could set off against its damages claim against the counterparty.[102] But if the counterparty's liquidator could obtain an order for specific performance of the contracts against the bank, the bank would be obliged to perform its obligation under each contract to deliver, or to arrange a credit for, the foreign money, and, since this obligation is not a money obligation, it could not employ it in a set-off.

Would a court would order specific performance of the contracts? A foreign exchange contract is said to be analogous to a contract to sell unascertained non-unique property readily available in the market, or alternatively a contract to deliver money, the classic example being a contract of loan. It has been suggested that in neither case will the courts usually order specific performance of the contract in question, and so specific performance similarly should not be available in the case of a foreign exchange contract.[103] It must be remembered, however, that the foundation of the decree of specific performance is the inadequacy of damages at law,[104] and damages would not be an adequate remedy for the insolvent counterparty's estate if it would have the effect of letting in a set-off. Accordingly, it cannot be assumed that a court in the circumstances would not exercise its discretion to grant specific relief to the counterparty.[105] It may be objected nevertheless that the counterparty should not

---

[102] It should not be a sufficient objection to a set-off that the damages liability would be incurred to the counterparty after the commencement of its liquidation, since the liability would arise out of prior dealings between the bank and the counterparty. Nor would a set-off be denied to the bank merely because it would be basing its argument for a set-off upon its own conduct in deliberately breaching the contracts in question for the express purpose of obtaining a right of set-off. See sections 4.5.1, 4.7.3 and 5.2 above.

[103] See Wood and Terray, 'Foreign Exchange Netting in France and England', *International Financial Law Review*, October 1989, 18, 20 with respect to contracts to sell unascertained goods and, for contracts to lend money, Wood, *English and International Set-off* (1989), 58 para. 2–94, 340–1 para. 7–189, and also Wood, 'Netting Agreements in Organised and Private Markets' *Current Developments in Banking and Finance* (1989), 11.

[104] See Lord Redesdale in *Harnet* v. *Yeilding* (1805) 2 Sch. & Lef. 549, 553.

[105] See section 5.2 above, and also Derham, 'Set-off and Netting of Foreign Exchange Contracts' [1991] *Journal of Business Law* 463, 484–93. The Sale of Goods Act 1979, s. 52 provides for specific performance of a contract to sell specific or ascertained goods. In *Re Wait* [1927] 1 Ch. 606, 630 Lord Atkin said that this provision sets out the full extent of equitable remedies in contracts for the sale of goods, so that specific performance is not available for a contract to sell unascertained goods. Insofar as a foreign exchange contract may be performed by a physical delivery of cash, and insofar as cash in this context may be characterized as a commodity, it may be argued that the contract effectively is a contract to sell unascertained goods for which specific performance is not available. There are three answers to this. The first is that 'goods' is defined in s. 61 of the Act as excluding things in action and money. Even

be entitled to specific performance of the contracts profitable to it, given that the liquidator may have disclaimed other contracts which would have been profitable to the bank. The difficulty with this is that each contract usually would be independent of the others, in the sense that, in truth, performance by the counterparty of the disclaimed contracts would not have been a condition upon which performance of the contracts kept on foot depended,[106] in which case the court may incline against refusing specific relief on this ground.[107] The court would consider all the circumstances in determining how to exercise its discretion. The bank presumably would point to the hardship that it would suffer if specific performance were ordered, in the sense that it would be left with a damages claim against an insolvent counterparty on the disclaimed contracts, and it would argue that this constitutes a special consideration which should be taken into account. On the other hand, this would have to be balanced against the hardship that the counterparty's general body of creditors would suffer if specific performance were refused, in that the bank would be breaching the contracts sought to be enforced for the express purpose of obtaining preferential treatment over the other creditors by means of a set-off, and thereby reducing the dividend payable generally.[108] On this basis, the hardship suffered by the bank as a result of the non-performance by the counterparty of other contracts may be considered to be an insufficient reason for the court to refuse specific relief in relation to the contracts sought to be enforced, given that the contracts are independent.

The result is that, in the peculiar circumstances under consideration, the counterparty's liquidator may well be able to obtain specific performance of the bank's foreign currency obligations pursuant to the contracts kept on foot by the liquidator. The effect of an order for specific performance

---

though foreign money in the context of a foreign exchange contract may function as a commodity rather than money, it may be that nevertheless it constitutes 'money' or 'things in action' for the purpose of the Act. See Mann, n. 48 above, 197 n. 42, and *Benjamin on Sale* (4th edn., 1992), 67. The second answer is that the view expressed by Lord Atkin should be regarded as wrong in principle. See in this regard Treitel, 'Specific Performance in the Sale of Goods' [1966] *Journal of Business Law* 211, 222–4; Jones and Goodhart, n. 42 above, 120–1; Spry, n. 42 above, 54 n. 20. See also Pollock, 'Re Wait' (1927) 43 *Law Quarterly Review* 293. The third is that, in any event, this would not preclude an order to the effect that the credit should be arranged by means of an account transfer.

[106] See Dixon J. in *J.C. Williamson Ltd.* v. *Lukey and Mulholland* (1931) 45 CLR 282, 298.

[107] See in this regard *Lewin* v. *Guest* (1826) 1 Russ. 325; *Croome* v. *Lediard* (1834) 2 My. & K 251; *Wilkinson* v. *Clements* (1872) LR 8 Ch. App. 96; Jones and Goodhart n. 42 above, 37; Spry, n. 42 above, 107, 109. *Contra* if the obligations in question are interdependent. See the discussion in *Holliday* v. *Lockwood* [1917] 2 Ch. 47.

[108] This assumes that hardship suffered by the general body of creditors if specific performance were refused would be a relevant consideration. For a general discussion of hardship to third persons, see Spry, n. 42 above, 198–200.

would be that the bank would have to perform the unprofitable contracts the subject of the order, but only receive a dividend on the contracts that would have been profitable for it had they not been disclaimed by the liquidator.[109] The bank would regard this as unsatisfactory, and the question arises whether it can remedy this by means of a properly drafted netting agreement. This is considered later.[110]

---

[109] It is conceded, nevertheless, that this is very much a minority view. On 13 November 1993 the Financial Law Panel issued a Statement of Law in relation to foreign exchange contracts, with which most of the major London law firms expressed their agreement. According to the Statement, where a bank and its corporate customer enter into various transactions, and the customer goes into liquidation before the transactions are closed, the bank will have a claim (or obligation) on a net basis only to receive from (or pay to) the liquidator the net amount in respect of the transactions taken as a whole. As part of the discussion it was stated that 'All obligations in respect of the mutual dealings are required to be brought into account'. This would have been better expressed in terms of money obligations.   [110] See section 12.2 below.

6

Trust Funds

6.1 INTRODUCTION

The ensuing discussion concerns the question whether, and if so under what circumstances, the obligation of a person who holds a fund impressed with a trust to account for the trust fund may be the subject of a set-off against a debt owing to him in his personal capacity. This includes the case of a person who has received trust property and is the subject of an equitable tracing order. It should be distinguished from the situation in which a beneficiary of a trust is obliged to contribute to the trust fund itself. This is not a case of set-off, but rather of the application of a principle known as the rule in *Cherry* v. *Boultbee*,[1] which is considered later.[2]

It is assumed in the following discussion that the trust fund has not been dissipated or, if it has, that the proceeds nevertheless may be traced. If this is not the case there may be a personal claim against the trustee. Whether this personal claim can be set off should be determined according to the general principles applicable to the form of set-off in issue. In this regard, the liability of a trustee for breach of trust is not in damages, but rather it is an obligation to restore the trust property or pay compensation, and as such it constitutes an equitable debt.[3] Accordingly it should be eligible for an equitable set-off on the basis of equity acting by analogy with the Statutes of Set-off,[4] and also under the insolvency set-off section, at least where the trustee is bankrupt or is in liquidation. Where the beneficiary is the insolvent party it may not be appropriate to allow the trustee a set-off in his own favour based upon his own breach of trust.[5]

6.2 INSOLVENCY SET-OFF

If T holds a sum on trust for B, and B becomes bankrupt, T as a general rule must account for the trust fund to B's trustee in bankruptcy without a

---

[1] (1839) 4 My. & Cr. 442.   [2] See Ch. 10.
[3] *Ex parte Adamson; in re Collie* (1878) 8 Ch. D 807, 819, and see generally section 4.5.3 above. Compare *Space Investments Ltd.* v. *CIBC* [1986] 1 WLR 1072, 1074.
[4] See *Taylor* v. *Taylor* (1875) LR 20 Eq. 155, as explained in section 6.3 below.
[5] See section 4.7.2 above.

set-off in respect of an independent debt due to him in his personal capacity.[6] Thus, a sum held on trust by a solicitor for a bankrupt client cannot be the subject of a set-off in bankruptcy,[7] and similarly an insurance broker is not entitled to a set-off in respect of subrogation money held on trust for a bankrupt underwriter.[8] In *Ex parte White*[9] the creditor of a bankrupt was indebted to the bankrupt's assignee in bankruptcy in the assignee's private capacity. When the creditor himself later became bankrupt, the fact of the assignee's trusteeship was held to preclude any right to set off the dividend payable to the creditor against the creditor's own indebtedness to him. The denial of a set-off in these cases may be explained on the ground of lack of mutuality[10] in that, while T has a personal claim against the bankrupt, the bankrupt has a claim *in specie* against a particular trust fund. This is so notwithstanding that a trustee is described as an equitable debtor.[11]

There is nevertheless an exception to the general principle in the situation in which property has been deposited with another with directions or authority to turn it into money. This is considered in the context of a discussion of *Rose* v. *Hart*.[12]

6.3 STATUTES OF SET-OFF

A similar principle applies when the beneficiary of the trust is not bankrupt. If T is a trustee of a sum of money for B, and he is sued by B for

---

[6] In addition to the cases referred to below, see the special purpose payment cases discussed in section 6.6 below. See also *In re The United Ports and General Insurance Company; ex parte The Etna Insurance Company* (1877) 46 LJ Ch. 403; *Elgood* v. *Harris* [1896] 2 QB 491, 494; *Re McMahon and Canada Permanent Trust Co.* (1979) 108 DLR (3d) 71; *Hamilton* v. *Commonwealth Bank of Australia* (1992) 9 ACSR 90, 108; *Lloyds Bank NZA Ltd.* v. *National Safety Council* [1993] 2 VR 506. *Re ILG Travel Ltd.* [1996] BCC 21, 48–9 is difficult to follow, unless there was no traceable trust fund and equity in the circumstances would not deem a fund to have been set aside. See section 4.7.3 above.

[7] *Wright* v. *Watson* (1883) Cab. & El. 171, and see also *Stumore* v. *Campbell* [1892] 1 QB 314 (Statutes of Set-off). Compare *Shand* v. *M. J. Atkinson Ltd.* [1966] NZLR 551, which was concerned with the construction of the Law Practitioners Act 1955 (NZ).

[8] See *Elgood* v. *Harris* [1896] 2 QB 491, though in this case the trust money in any event were received after the bankruptcy.

[9] (1742) 1 Atk. 90, and see also *Ex parte Bailey; in re Howarth* (1840) 1 Mont. D & De G 263. Compare *Ex parte Nockold* (1734), unreported but noted in Cooke, *The Bankrupt Laws* (8th edn., 1823) Vol. 1, 509, which has not been followed. See *Re Henley, Thurgood, & Co.* (1863) 11 WR 1021, 1022.

[10] *National Westminster Bank Ltd.* v. *Halesowen Presswork & Assemblies Ltd.* [1972] AC 785, 821; *Lloyds Bank NZA Ltd.* v. *National Safety Council* [1993] 2 VR 506, 515. Compare *Baillie* v. *Edwards* (1848) 2 HLC 74, in which there was no claim personally against Baillie but merely a right of indemnity from the estate. An equitable set-off nevertheless was allowed on a ground that is somewhat obscure.

[11] *Webb* v. *Stenton* (1883) 11 QBD 518, 526.

[12] (1818) 8 Taunt. 499, discussed in section 6.4 below.

payment of the trust fund, T may not deduct a debt owing to him in his personal capacity by B.[13] Ordinarily equity will act by analogy with the right of set-off available at law under the Statutes of Set-off if the demands are equitably, but not legally, mutual. However, as in the case of insolvency set-off, when the claim is for payment of a trust fund there is a lack of mutuality.[14] On the one hand the trustee has a personal claim against the beneficiary, and on the other the beneficiary has a claim *in specie* against the trust fund itself.

Lack of mutuality should be regarded as the proper basis for the early decision in *Whitaker* v. *Rush*.[15] A testator had bequeathed £400 to a particular legatee, and gave the rest of his estate to the executor. When the legatee brought this bill seeking payment of the legacy the executor said that the legatee was indebted to him on a partnership account, and that the two demands should be set off. However, Sir Thomas Clark held that the demands were in different rights and that consequently a set-off should not be allowed. This seems correct. While the legatee was liable to the executor in the executor's personal capacity, the executor was not personally liable for the legacy, which was payable out of the particular fund constituted by the proceeds of the testator's estate.

Whitaker v. *Rush* should be contrasted with *Taylor* v. *Taylor*,[16] which concerned an intestacy. The deceased left two sons, the plaintiff and the defendant. Letters of administration were granted to the defendant in 1856. In 1860 he submitted an account to the plaintiff, and in accordance with the terms of that account he paid the plaintiff a sum of money. In 1871 the plaintiff filed this bill, alleging that he had recently discovered that he was entitled to more than had actually been paid to him under the intestacy. Sir George Jessel agreed with him on this point, and held that the defendant as administrator was liable to pay the difference. However, he also held that the defendant could set off a debt owing by the plaintiff to him in his personal capacity. The Master of the Rolls said that it was 'clear, on every principle of equity, on every principle of common sense and common justice, and on every principle derived by analogy from the

---

[13] *Talbot* v. *Frere* (1878) 9 Ch. D 568, 573; *Stumore* v. *Campbell & Co.* [1892] 1 QB 314, 316; *Zemco Ltd.* v. *Jerrom-Pugh* [1993] BCC 275 (following *Guinness Plc* v. *Saunders* [1988] 1 WLR 863). See also *Re Jeffrey's Policy* (1872) 20 WR 857 (proceeds of life policy deposited as security). The possibility of a trust was not considered by Malins V.C. when he held in *Thomas* v. *Howell* (1874) LR 18 Eq. 198 that an agent could set off a sum remaining in his hands on account of rent collected for his principal against the principal's liability for unpaid commission. Compare *Smit Tak International Zeesleepen B.V.* v. *Selco Salvage Ltd.* [1988] 2 Lloyd's Rep. 398, 408.

[14] *National Westminster Bank Ltd.* v. *Halesowen Presswork & Assemblies Ltd.* [1972] AC 785, 821.

[15] (1761) Amb. 407. See also *Medlicot* v. *Bowes* (1749) 1 Ves. Sen. 207; *Freeman* v. *Lomas* (1851) 9 Hare 109.

[16] (1875) LR 20 Eq. 155.

Statute of Set-off, or otherwise, that the Defendant . . . is entitled to the set-off claimed, and I intend to allow it'.[17] *Whitaker* v. *Rush* was cited in argument, though it was not referred to at all by Sir George Jessel in his judgment. While the facts of each were similar, they differed in the following respect. In *Whitaker* v. *Rush* the claim of the legatee related to a particular fund. On the other hand, it seems clear that in *Taylor* v. *Taylor* there was no longer any fund in existence into which the proceeds of the testator's estate could traced. The plaintiff only had a personal claim against the administrator for payment of the sum to which he was entitled. Consequently, as Sir George Jessel remarked, this was a case in which the administrator was saying to the plaintiff: 'You have come into equity for a personal equitable debt due from me to you. I ask to set off a personal legal debt due from you to me'.[18] In fact, *Taylor* has been cited as authority for a different proposition. While it is generally conceded that a debt owing to an executor in his own right may not be set off against a legacy, it has been said that a debt due from one of the next of kin to an administrator may indeed be set off against the share of the next of kin in the estate.[19] However, Sir George Jessel himself did not draw any distinction between an executor and an administrator, and indeed it would be difficult to justify as a matter of principle. The case is better explained on the basis suggested above.

Taylor was followed in *In re Jones. Christmas* v. *Jones*.[20] A son had been appointed administrator in his mother's intestacy. In addition he was appointed executor of his father's will. Two people, who were also next of kin of the intestate, brought an action for revocation of the probate of the will. They were unsuccessful, and were ordered to pay the executor's costs. When a demand was made for payment of their shares of the intestate's estate the administrator paid the proceeds of the estate into court, and said that he was entitled to bring into account the next of kin's indebtedness for costs. Kekewich J held that *Taylor* was an authority in favour of a set-off, and that accordingly it should be allowed. No doubt this would have been a correct conclusion if *Taylor* indeed supports a general proposition that an administrator is in a different position to an executor with respect to set-offs. The contrary view is that the distinguishing feature in *Taylor* was the absence of a specific fund in respect of which a claim could have been made. There was merely a personal liability in the administrator. In *Jones*,

---

[17] (1875) LR 20 Eq. 155, 160.   [18] (1875) LR 20 Eq. 155, 160.

[19] *Withers on Reversions* (2nd edn., 1933), 260; *Halsbury's Laws of England* (4th edn., 1983) Vol. 42, 259 para. 457. *In re Cordwell's Estate; White* v. *Cordwell* (1875) LR 20 Eq. 644, which is also referred to in Halsbury, in truth was concerned with the rule in *Cherry* v. *Boultbee* (1839) 4 My & Cr. 644 (discussed in Ch. 10), since the liability in question was to contribute to the fund as opposed to being owed to the administrator personally.

[20] [1897] 2 Ch. 190.

on the other hand, there was still a specific fund, which had been paid into court. The better view is that there was no mutuality for the purpose of a set-off between the next of kin's liability for costs to the administrator, and the next of kin's right to participate in the fund.

6.4 THE DELIVERY OF PROPERTY—*ROSE* V. *HART*

6.4.1 *The general principle*

The right of set-off only applies when the claims are commensurable, or, in other words, when both claims are such that they would result in money demands.[21] This was established authoritatively by Gibbs C.J. in *Rose* v. *Hart*,[22] when he held that a fuller with whom cloths had been deposited by a person who later became bankrupt could not retain the cloths as a set-off against the bankrupt's indebtedness to him. On the other hand, there was a recognition that there may be a set-off where goods were deposited accompanied by a direction to turn them into money:

Something more is certainly meant here by mutual credits than the words mutual debts import; and yet, upon the final settlement, it is enacted merely that one debt shall be set against another. We think this shews that the legislature meant such credits only as must in their nature terminate in debts, as where a debt is due from one party, and credit given by him on the other for a sum of money payable at a future day, and which will then become a debt, or where there is a debt on one side, and a delivery of property with directions to turn it into money on the other; in such case the credit given by the delivery of the property must in its nature terminate in a debt, the balance will be taken on the two debts, and the words of the statute will in all respects be complied with: but where there is a mere deposit of property, without any authority to turn it into money, no debt can ever arise out of it, and, therefore, it is not a credit within the meaning of the statute.[23]

It has been argued[24] that the allowance of a set-off when there is a direction to turn property into money owes its existence to the omission of a relevant fact from the report of the decision in *Ex parte Deeze*.[25] In that case a packer was allowed to retain goods against the assignee in bankruptcy of the owner, not only for the cost of his work upon them, but also for the owner's separate indebtedness to him. In the course of his judgment Lord Hardwicke made a number of references to the law of

---

[21] See Ch. 5. [22] (1818) 8 Taunt. 499. [23] (1818) 8 Taunt. 499, 506.
[24] Bishop, 'Set-off in the Administration of Insolvent and Bankrupt Estates' (1901) 1 *Columbia Law Review* 377. See also *Young* v. *Bank of Bengal* (1836) 1 Moore 150, 169–71.
[25] (1748) 1 Atk. 228.

mutual credit, though later in *Ex parte Ockenden*[26] he remarked that there had been evidence in *Ex parte Deeze* of a specific custom by which packers could retain goods as security for the separate debts of the owner, as well as for the price of their work upon the goods. The case, then, was not one of set-off at all, but rather concerned a lien arising from the custom of the trade.[27] Despite this, *Ex parte Deeze* was still treated in subsequent cases as an authority on set-off.[28] Gibbs C.J. in *Rose* v. *Hart* said that he 'could not persuade [himself] to break in upon a class of cases so long established',[29] and his statement of the law represented an attempt to reconcile the cases decided after *Ex parte Deeze* with the stipulation in the set-off section in the Bankruptcy Act of 1732[30] that 'one debt may be set against another'. One such case was *French* v. *Fenn*.[31] The bankrupt and the defendant together had purchased a string of pearls, the agreement between them being that the defendant would sell the pearls and that they would then share in any resulting profit. The pearls were sold after the bankruptcy, and it was held that the defendant could set off the bankrupt's share of the profit against the bankrupt's indebtedness for his share of the purchase money which had been advanced by the defendant. There were also the cases of *Parker* v. *Carter*[32] and *Olive* v. *Smith*,[33] in each of which an insurance broker had been entrusted with a policy of insurance with authority to collect the insurance money in the event of a loss. It was held that the broker could set off insurance money received after the insured's bankruptcy against the insured's general indebtedness to him.[34] This included debts which were not a part of the insurance account, and consequently were not within the an insurance broker's general lien.

Since *Rose* v. *Hart* the principle has been applied in a number of other situations, as, for example, where goods or their documents of title[35] were

---

[26] (1754) 1 Atk. 235, 237.

[27] This omission from the report of *Ex parte Deeze* inspired Lord Mansfield's condemnation of Atkyn's reports as 'extremely inaccurate'. See *Olive* v. *Smith* (1813) 5 Taunt. 56, 64. An extract from Lord Hardwicke's own notes on *Ex parte Deeze* is set out in a note to *Young* v. *Bank of Bengal* (1836) 1 Moore 150, 170. Lord Henley inclined to the view that Lord Hardwicke in fact had changed his mind in *Ex parte Ockenden* as regards his earlier decision in *Ex parte Deeze*, and that Lord Hardwicke took hold of the circumstance of there being evidence of usage in *Ex parte Deeze* in order to reconcile his two decisions. See Henley, *A Digest of the Bankrupt Law* (3rd edn., 1832), 190.

[28] See e.g. *French* v. *Fenn* (1783) 3 Dougl. 257 and *Smith* v. *Hodson* (1791) 4 TR 211. Compare *Olive* v. *Smith* (1813) 5 Taunt. 56.

[29] (1818) 5 Taunt. 499, 505. See also Lord Mansfield in *Olive* v. *Smith* (1813) 5 Taunt. 56, 67.   [30] (1732) 5 Geo. II, c. 30, s. 28.   [31] (1783) 3 Dougl. 257.

[32] (1788), unreported but noted in Cooke, *The Bankrupt Laws* (8th edn., 1823) Vol. 1, 578.   [33] (1813) 5 Taunt. 56.

[34] See also *Chalmers* v. *Page* (1820) 3 B & Ald. 697.

[35] *M'Gillivray* v. *Simson* (1826) 2 Car. & P 320, affirmed 5 LJOSKB 53 (bills of lading).

delivered to a person for the purpose of sale,[36] and where bills of exchange were deposited with a bank to collect and remit the proceeds.[37]

Gibbs C.J. in *Rose* v. *Hart* said that, for mutual credit, the transaction in question must be such that it 'must' end in a debt, and it was on this basis that the Privy Council in *Young* v. *Bank of Bengal*[38] criticized the decision in *Olive* v. *Smith*. However, the courts have since expanded the concept of giving credit as expounded by Gibbs C.J., so that it is now regarded as sufficient if the transaction would naturally or in the ordinary course of business end in a debt. It is not necessary that the transaction be such that it must of necessity have this result.[39] Moreover, since *Young's* case the scope of the set-off section has been enlarged to include claims arising out of mutual dealings. The decision in *Olive* v. *Smith* may be objectionable on the ground that the insurance proceeds may have been impressed with a trust, depending on whether it was intended that they be kept separate from the broker's own funds or whether they should form an item in the account between the parties, though this is a difficulty with the *Rose* v. *Hart* cases generally. Apart from that possible objection, *Olive* v. *Smith* would appear to be alive and well.[40]

In some cases the allowance of a set-off in the circumstances contemplated by *Rose* v. *Hart* may produce an anomalous result. Often when property is deposited with a person with directions to turn it into money the depository's status is that of a fiduciary, and any money received in respect of the property is impressed with a trust. Accordingly, the allowance of a set-off may conflict with the general principle that a trustee must account for the trust fund without a set-off in respect of an independent debt due to him in his personal capacity. In the *Rose* v. *Hart* cases, on the other hand, the depository's authority to turn the property into money and to receive the proceeds has always been regarded as a sufficient source of credit to found a set-off in the depositor's bankruptcy,

---

[36] *Palmer* v. *Day & Sons* [1895] 2 QB 618 and *Hunter* v. *Official Assignee of Bispham* (1898) 17 NZLR 175 (each concerned with a sale by an auctioneer); *Re Lindsay* (1890) 9 NZLR 192; *In re Rose; ex parte Hasluck & Garrard* (1894) 1 Mans. 218; *Re Clements* (1931) 7 ABC 255; *Rolls Razor Ltd.* v. *Cox* [1967] 1 QB 552 (company salesman). See also *Holmes* v. *Kidd* (1858) 3 H & N 891, in which it was agreed that the proceeds of sale of property were to be applied in reduction of the debt, and *New Zealand and Australian Land Company* v. *Watson* (1881) 7 QBD 374, in which the court rejected the view that the proceeds in that case were impressed with a trust in favour of the owner.

[37] *Naoroji* v. *The Chartered Bank of India* (1868) LR 3 CP 444.

[38] (1836) 1 Moore 150. See also Parke B. in *Alsager* v. *Currie* (1844) 12 M & W 751, 754–5, commenting on *Young* v. *Bank of Bengal*.

[39] See section 3.1 above.

[40] Compare Wood, *English and International Set-off* (1989), 563, who has suggested that *Olive* v. *Smith* was probably overruled by *Rose* v. *Hart*, though Gibbs C.J. in fact seems to have regarded *Olive* v. *Smith* as consistent with his formulation of the relevant principle.

and the courts in reaching this conclusion have not given any consideration to the possibility of a trust.[41]

It is not, however, a universally accepted view that the *Rose* v. *Hart* set-off does produce an anomaly, because it has been argued that the cases in question constitute instances in which the proceeds are not impressed with a trust.[42] The argument is that the depository in these cases extends credit to the depositor in reliance on his prospective receipt of the proceeds of the property, for which the depositor gives credit to him. Accordingly the true basis of *Rose* v. *Hart* is said to be that the depository has implied authority, by virtue of their mutual dealings, to regard himself as a debtor for a sum equal to the proceeds, and not as a trustee of the proceeds themselves. However, it is doubtful whether this explains all the cases. It is, of course, correct to say that, while a depository is *generally* considered to be a trustee in respect of the proceeds of property deposited with him with directions to turn it into money, this is not always the case. For example, if there is an on-going business relationship between the depositor and the depository such that the depository is regularly entrusted with property to be turned into money, the courts may conclude that it was intended that the nature of the relationship in respect of the proceeds should be one of debt rather than trust.[43] The question essentially is whether it was intended that the depository keep the proceeds separate from his own money.[44] But insofar as the *Rose* v. *Hart* set-off is concerned, the turning of property into money has not always been the subject of an on-going commercial arrangement between the parties. Further, in the absence of a relationship of that nature, the argument that the basis of *Rose* v. *Hart* is that the depository extends credit in reliance on his prospective receipt of the proceeds would not apply when the depositor's indebtedness to the depository arose before, rather than after, the deposit. In such a case it could hardly be said that there was reliance by the depository in extending credit.[45]

Consider *Palmer* v. *Day & Sons*.[46] In September 1894 one Langton gave instructions to the defendant auctioneers to sell some furniture, and also to

---

[41] In addition to the cases referred to below, compare *Naoroji* v. *The Chartered Bank of India* (1868) LR 3 CP 444 with *In re Brown; ex parte Plitt* (1889) 6 Morr. 81 in the context of a bill deposited with a bank to collect and remit the proceeds.

[42] Goode, *Principles of Corporate Insolvency Law* (1990), 69.

[43] Finn, *Fiduciary Obligations* (1977), 105. See e.g. the retention of title cases, *Hendy Lennox (Industrial Engines) Ltd.* v. *Grahame Puttick Ltd.* [1984] 1 WLR 485 and *Re Andrabell Ltd.* [1984] 3 All ER 407, referred to in Goode, *Principles of Corporate Insolvency Law* (1990), 69–70.   [44] *Henry* v. *Hammond* [1913] 2 KB 515, 521.

[45] The relationships of debt and trust are not mutually exclusive. See *Barclays Bank Ltd.* v. *Quistclose Investments Ltd.* [1970] AC 567.

[46] [1895] 2 QB 618. See also *Webb* v. *Smith* (1885) 30 Ch. D 192 (Statutes of Set-off) and *Hunter* v. *Official Assignee of Bispham* (1898) 17 NZLR 175.

sell his house. The furniture auction took place on October 15 and 19. The house was put up for auction on 8 November, but no sale was effected. A sum of approximately £31 was due to the auctioneers in respect of their charges for the auctions, of which approximately £24 related to the unsuccessful attempt to sell the house. Between the date of the furniture auction and the attempted auction of the house, some pictures which had been passed in at the furniture auction were sent to the auctioneers for the purpose of sale. This sale took place after the attempt to sell the house, and also after Langton became bankrupt. Lord Russell of Killowen C.J. and Charles J. held that the auctioneers could set off against the bankrupt's indebtedness for £31 in respect of the unpaid charges their obligation to account for the proceeds of sale of the pictures.[47] However, the instructions to sell the house were given *before* the pictures were sent to the auctioneers for sale, in which case it is unlikely that the auctioneers had given credit to Langton for their charges in respect of the auction of the house in reliance on their prospective receipt of the proceeds of sale of the pictures. There was no discussion in the judgment as to whether the proceeds were impressed with a trust, which is curious given that only some 8 years earlier the Court of Appeal had held that auctioneers receive proceeds of sale in a fiduciary capacity for their customers.[48] This suggests that the existence or otherwise of a trust was not considered to be relevant to the question of set-off. Nor is there anything in the judgment to suggest that this was a case in which there was an on-going business relationship such that it may have been intended that the relationship should only be one of debt.

In *Rose* v. *Hart* the proceeds obtained from turning property into money were received after bankruptcy,[49] though the same result presumably would follow when the receipt of the proceeds occurred before then. Furthermore, set-off under the Statutes of Set-off may be subject to the same principle.[50]

The *Rose* v. *Hart* set-off applies in the following circumstances.

---

[47] It was held that there were separate contracts for the sale of the house and the furniture (including the pictures), and so the auctioneers' lien on the proceeds did not extend to their charges in respect of both these sales.

[48] *Crowther* v. *Elgood* (1887) 34 Ch. D 691.

[49] See e.g. *French* v. *Fenn* (1783) 3 Dougl. 257; *Olive* v. *Smith* (1813) 5 Taunt. 56; *Naoroji* v. *The Chartered Bank of India* (1868) LR 3 CP 444 (though it appears more clearly from the report in 37 LJCP 221 that the proceeds in respect of most of the bills were received after the date of the inspectorship deed); *Astley* v. *Gurney* (1869) LR 4 CP 714; *Palmer* v. *Day & Sons* [1895] 2 QB 618.

[50] In *Webb* v. *Smith* (1885) 30 Ch. D 192 the Court of Appeal assumed that an auctioneer would have had a right of set-off under the Statutes of Set-off in respect of proceeds of sale in his hands.

6.4.2 *Authority to turn the property into money*

The courts have consistently held that a person holding chattels *without* authority to turn them into money, and who is sued by the owner's trustee in bankruptcy for their return, may not bring the value of the chattels in as a set-off against the bankrupt's indebtedness to him. The claims are not commensurable.[51] This has been held to be the case when the chattels are in that person's possession wrongfully,[52] or merely for use,[53] or for the performance of work upon them,[54] or, having been lodged as a security, the secured debt has been paid.[55]

Section 2 of the Torts (Interference With Goods) Act 1977 abolished detinue, which was the action formerly used to obtain the return of goods wrongfully detained. Instead, section 3 provides that, in proceedings for wrongful interference against a person who is in possession or control of the goods of another, the relief can take the form of:

(a) an order for delivery of the goods, and for payment of any consequential damages, or
(b) an order for delivery of the goods, but giving the defendant the alternative of paying damages by reference to the value of the goods, together in either alternative with payment of any consequential damages, or
(c) damages.

Relief under (a) is at the discretion of the court, and the claimant may choose between the others.

The better view is that the Act has not changed the position in relation to set-off. If the plaintiff claims the return of the goods under (b), it should not make any difference for the purpose of set-off that the defendant may choose to pay damages. This is consistent with the position formerly applicable in an action in detinue.[56] The form of judgment in a detinue action was for delivery of the chattel or payment of its assessed value together with damages for detention. The defendant in effect had an option, though the Common Law Procedure Act 1854, section 78 gave the court

---

[51] See section 5.1 above.
[52] *Lord (Trustee of)* v. *Great Eastern Railway Company* [1908] 2 KB 54; *Re Leeholme Stud Pty. Ltd.* [1965] NSWR 1649. See also *Peacock* v. *Anderson* (1878) 4 NZ Jur. (NS) SC 67.
[53] *Ex parte Roy; in re Sillence* (1877) 7 Ch. D 70; *In re Winter; ex parte Bolland* (1878) 8 Ch. D 225; *Rolls Razor Ltd.* v. *Cox* [1967] 1 QB 552.
[54] *Rose* v. *Hart* (1818) 8 Taunt. 499.
[55] *Eberle's Hotels and Restaurant Company, Ltd.* v. *E. Jonas & Brothers* (1887) 18 QBD 459. See also *Key* v. *Flint* (1817) 8 Taunt. 21, affirmed in equity *Ex parte Flint* (1818) 1 Swans. 30.
[56] See generally the discussion in *General and Finance Facilities Ltd.* v. *Cooks Cars (Romford) Ltd.* [1963] 1 WLR 644, 650.

the power to order delivery up of the chattel, without giving the defendant the option of paying its assessed value. In *Eberle's Hotels and Restaurant Company, Ltd.* v. *E. Jonas & Brothers*[57] the plaintiff company had deposited some cigars with the defendants as security for a debt. The company was ordered to be wound up and, the debt secured by the cigars having been paid in full, the liquidator brought an action in detinue for the return of the cigars. The defendants claimed that they were entitled to have the value of the cigars assessed and then set off against another unsecured debt owing to them by the plaintiff. The Court of Appeal was not convinced, and held that the plaintiff was entitled to the return of the cigars without being subjected to a set-off. However, an interesting aspect of the case is a comment by counsel during argument, and the responses by Fry L.J. and Lord Esher M.R. Counsel suggested that, if the judge in a detinue action declined to order delivery of the chattels in question, so that the defendant instead could pay their assessed value, the claim would be a money claim which could be set off. Fry L.J. responded that the application or otherwise of the insolvency set-off section depended on the state of things at the time of the winding-up, and at that time there was a right to delivery of the cigars on payment of the secured debt. This was not a right that was susceptible to a set-off.[58] Similary Lord Esher asked,[59] 'Can the applicability of [the set-off section] depend on what the judge may do at the trial? Must it not depend on the nature of the respective rights of the parties antecedently to the action?' This suggests that, even if specific restitution was not ordered, a set-off would have been denied. Similarly, under the regime set out in the Torts (Interference With Goods) Act 1977, if the claimant seeks an order for the delivery of the goods in accordance with section 3(2)(a), the availability of a set-off should not depend upon whether there is a subsequent election by the defendant to pay damages. That conclusion is also suggested by the cases in which the property the subject of an action was sold with the consent of all parties after the bankruptcy. The courts emphasized that the right at the date of the bankruptcy was to the return of the property, and the fact that the dispute subsequently became one over the proceeds of sale did not let in a set-off.[60]

However, what if the goods were destroyed before the bankruptcy, so that at the date of the bankruptcy specific restitution was not possible, and the trustee accordingly is only in a position to claim damages under section

---

[57] (1887) 18 QBD 459.
[58] (1887) 18 QBD 459, 463. See also Fry L.J.'s judgment at 469 and 470.
[59] (1887) 18 QBD 459, 464.
[60] *In re Winter; ex parte Bolland* (1878) 8 Ch. D 225; *Lord (Trustee of)* v. *Great Eastern Railway Company* [1908] 2 KB 54 (reversed on other grounds [1909] AC 109). See also *Ex parte Ockenden* (1754) 1 Atk. 235.

3(2)(c) of the Act?[61] A set-off may be available,[62] though it will depend on the circumstances of the case. A set-off can only proceed where there are mutual debts, mutual credits or other mutual dealings. A damages claim is not a debt. Nor does it come within the concept of giving credit.[63] Moreover, a damages claim for wrongful interference with goods or chattels often will not arise out of a dealing between the parties. In *In re Winter; ex parte Bolland*[64] Bacon V.C. said that a mere authority to possess or use particular chattels unaccompanied by a power to sell is not a dealing, though Lord Esher M.R. adopted a less dogmatic approach in the *Eberle's Hotels* case.[65] In his view, whatever comes within an ordinary business transaction would be a dealing for the purpose of the set-off section,[66] and he suggested that the deposit of the cigars in that case to secure a debt would have constituted a dealing. On the other hand, it would be difficult to categorize a wrongful taking of property as a dealing for the purpose of the set-off section.[67]

6.4.3 *Money claims*

The essence of a *Rose* v. *Hart* set-off is that property was deposited with a person with authority to turn it into money, under circumstances not amounting to a preference.[68] The authority must have been acted upon, so that the claim against the depository is for a sum of money which can be set off against the depositor's own indebtedness to produce a balance on the account. While in *Rolls Razor Ltd.* v. *Cox*[69] a set-off was allowed notwithstanding that the authority had not been acted upon, the better view is that it was wrongly decided.[70]

6.4.4 *Unrevoked authority*

An effective revocation of the authority to turn the property into money should prevent a set-off.[71] However, according to the Court of Appeal in

[61] The question was left open by Cozens Hardy M.R. in *Lord (Trustee of)* v. *Great Eastern Railway Company* [1908] 2 KB 54, 78. If the goods were destroyed after the bankruptcy, so that at the date of the bankruptcy itself the bankrupt's right was to the return of the goods, the fact that the only remedy later available to the trustee is to claim damages should not let in a set-off.

[62] Compare *Peacock* v. *Anderson* (1878) 4 NZ Jur. (NS) SC 67, 70, though the comment by Richmond J. was in the context that a set-off was not available generally against an unliquidated claim. This would not be relevant to the current insolvency set-off section.

[63] *Palmer* v. *Day & Sons* [1895] 2 QB 618, 621, and see section 3.2 above.

[64] (1878) 8 Ch. D 225, 228.   [65] (1887) 18 QBD 459, 465.

[66] See generally section 3.2 above.

[67] *Re Leeholme Stud Pty. Ltd.* [1965] NSWR 1649, 1650.

[68] *Castendyck and Focke* v. *Official Assignee of S. A. McLellan* (1887) 6 NZLR 67, 75.

[69] [1967] 1 QB 552.   [70] See section 5.1 above.

[71] *Palmer* v. *Day & Sons* [1895] 2 QB 618, 623.

Rolls Razor v. *Cox*,[72] a revocation before the bankruptcy or liquidation of the depositor will not always be successful. In that case the authority of the company's salesman to sell the company's goods was revoked after the board of directors publicly announced that the company was insolvent, but before the resolution to wind up the company. The Court of Appeal nonetheless allowed the salesman to set off the value of the goods for sale still in his possession, Lord Denning commenting that 'this right [of set-off] could not be taken away by the insolvent person at the last moment revoking the power of sale'.[73] The courts should reconsider this decision. The state of the bankrupt's solvency before the relevant date may go to the question whether there was notice of a pending petition for the purpose of the qualification to the set-off section in section 323(3) of the Insolvency Act.[74] However, that date merely defines a point beyond which a set-off may not be acquired, rather than a point when the parties may no longer deal with their rights so as to deprive the other of a set-off. There is no justification in the language of the set-off section for the view that a company may not act before the commencement of the liquidation in the interests of the general body of creditors to prevent the depletion of the estate through a set-off. Indeed, Lord Denning's view would appear to conflict with an opinion earlier expressed by Pollock M.R. in *In re City Life Assurance Company, Ltd.; Stephenson's Case*[75] in relation to section 31 of the Bankruptcy Act 1914, which was in similar terms to the current set-off section.

It is suggested that there was an equity between the policy holder and the company that the policy holder should be able to invoke the principle of s. 31 if and when he required to do so, and that the company are not entitled to say that there is no mutuality, because under the dealings between the policy holders and the company the principles of s. 31 ought to have remained available to the policy holder. That argument does not, to my mind, carry weight. There is no equity that the rights which govern the parties, if and when s. 31 applies, should be always available. Sect. 31 appears to me to be applicable if and when there is a bankruptcy or winding up of a company, but until that time has come, the law which governs the rights of the parties is not in force and cannot be held to be an inchoate right which the policy holder had as against the company at the time when the winding up of the company had not been commenced or, indeed, thought of.

---

[72] [1967] 1 QB 552.

[73] [1967] 1 QB 552, 571. The point was not considered by the other member of the majority, Danckwerts L.J., though, since he upheld the salesman's right to a set-off, he presumably agreed with Lord Denning. Winn L.J. in his dissenting judgment said that the revocation of the authority was effective to stop a set-off.

[74] For company liquidations, see the Insolvency Rules, r. 4.90(3). See generally section 2.7.2 above.

[75] [1926] 1 Ch. 191, 217.

While Pollock M.R. referred to the time before the winding-up had even been thought of, his thesis was that there is no equity at any time before the winding-up that the possibility of a set-off should always remain open. Lord Denning noted that the set-off section sanctions the taking of an account where 'there have been mutual credits'. He said that the use of the past tense indicated that 'when the mutual dealings *have been* such as to give rise to mutual credits, there is a right of set-off'.[76] However, if this were a correct interpretation, it is difficult to see why it would be that only a 'last moment' revocation would be ineffective. Moreover, if the insolvent debtor may not act at the last moment to take away a right of set-off by revoking the power of sale, then presumably other methods of destroying the possibility of a set-off would be able to be restrained, for example an assignment by the insolvent debtor to a third party of the benefit of his cross-claim against his creditor.[77] Yet it has never been suggested that a debtor may be restrained at the instance of a creditor from dealing with his own property in this manner before the commencement of bankruptcy or winding-up proceedings. The better view is that the set-off section requires not only that there should 'have been' mutual credits at some stage before the bankruptcy or liquidation, but that these mutual credits should still be subsisting at that date. It introduces uncertainty into the law to say that a debtor facing bankruptcy or a winding-up may not revoke an authority 'at the last moment'.[78] In *Rolls Razor* there was a public declaration of insolvency, but in many cases it would be difficult to say when a debtor became aware that bankruptcy or a winding-up was unavoidable.

In applying *Rose* v. *Hart* it appears not to make any difference that the proceeds in question may have been received after the depositor's bankruptcy or liquidation,[79] provided that the deposit of the property occurred before then under circumstances not giving rise to a preference, and provided also that the authority had not been revoked. While in some cases the authority may be irrevocable because it is coupled with an interest, as for example a deposit of property by way of security with a power of sale,[80] it has been said that any revocation sufficient to prevent a set-off in any event should have occurred before the bankruptcy or

---

[76] [1967] 1 QB 552, 571.

[77] Compare *In re City Life Assurance Company, Ltd; Stephenson's Case* [1926] 1 Ch. 191, 214.

[78] In *Rolls Razor* this meant something like a month before the extraordinary resolution to wind up the company.

[79] See e.g. *French* v. *Fenn* (1783) 3 Dougl. 257; *Olive* v. *Smith* (1813) 5 Taunt. 56; *Naoroji* v. *The Chartered Bank of India* (1868) LR 3 CP 444 (though it appears more clearly from the report in 37 LJCP 221 that the proceeds in respect of most of the bills were received after the date of the inspectorship deed); *Astley* v. *Gurney* (1869) LR 4 CP 714; *Palmer* v. *Day & Sons* [1895] 2 QB 618.

[80] See the security cases discussed in section 6.5 below.

liquidation, on the ground that the rights of the parties are to be determined as at that date.[81] Indeed, this is implicit in *Rolls Razor* v. *Cox*. However, as Dr. Oditah has rightly queried,[82] it is not clear why the fact of bankruptcy itself in some cases would not operate as a revocation of an otherwise revocable authority in accordance with normal principles. In *Elliott* v. *Turquand*[83] the Privy Council said that authorities given in the course of mutual dealings and necessary for the continuance of those dealings are excepted from the rule that authorities are revoked by bankruptcy. Yet, it is not in every case of a *Rose* v. *Hart* set-off that it can be said that the authority to sell was necessary for the continuance of the mutual dealings. One such case is *Palmer* v. *Day & Sons*,[84] to which reference has already been made.[85] There is nothing in the report of the case to suggest that there was an on-going business relationship such that the deposit was necessary for the continuance of mutual dealings, or that the auctioneer gave credit to the depositor on the strength of the prospective receipt of the proceeds of sale. Upon his appointment the trustee in bankruptcy wrote to the auctioneer requesting him to proceed with the sale of the goods previously deposited with him by the bankrupt. The auctioneer did so and, when he received the proceeds, was allowed to utilize them in a set-off under *Rose* v. *Hart* against a separate debt owing to him by the bankrupt. One would have thought, however, that this would have been a case in which the auctioneer's original authority to sell was revoked, but that he was then authorized by the trustee to sell as the *trustee's* agent, the goods in question having vested in the trustee upon his appointment. On this analysis a set-off should have been denied because of lack of mutuality.

Similarly, unless an authority to sell is coupled with an interest,[86] one would have thought that the authority would be revoked when the depositor is a company which is the subject of a court-ordered winding-up. In such a case the Insolvency Act 1986, section 127 provides that a disposition of the company's property made after the commencement of the winding-up is void unless the court otherwise orders.[87] It seems difficult to assert in the face of this that an agent of the depositor, such as

---

[81] See *Naoroji* v. *The Chartered Bank of India* (1868) LR 3 CP 444, 452 (in the context of a deed of inspectorship under the Bankruptcy Act 1861 which, when registered, had an effect equivalent to an adjudication in bankruptcy), and also *Easum* v. *Cato* (1822) 5 B & Ald. 861.

[82] Oditah, 'Assets and the Treatment of Claims in Insolvency' (1992) 108 *Law Quarterly Review* 459, 467 n. 55, and also *Legal Aspects of Receivables Financing* (1991), 248 n. 72.

[83] (1881) 7 App. Cas. 79, 88.   [84] [1895] 2 QB 618.

[85] See section 6.4.1 above.   [86] See below.

[87] Compare s. 284 in relation to bankruptcy, which avoids a disposition in the period beginning with the presentation of the petition and ending with the vesting of the estate in the trustee, at which time the bankrupt would no longer have title to his estate to be able to dispose of it in any event.

an auctioneer, would have continuing authority to sell the company's property.[88]

In *Palmer* v. *Day* the trustee requested the auctioneer to proceed with the sale. However, since the property deposited with the auctioneer had vested in the trustee upon his appointment, why could not the trustee have demanded its return as the legal owner? He could not have done so if the authority to sell was coupled with an interest, and the dictum of the Privy Council in *Elliott* v. *Turquand* may be said to support this characterization of an authority given in the course of mutual dealings. But, does it? If the authority to sell is coupled with an interest, it could not be revoked by the depositor himself before bankruptcy or liquidation, though plainly the fact that authority is given in the course of mutual dealings would not be sufficient to have this effect.[89] The Privy Council's *dictum* in *Elliott* v. *Turquand*, even if it is accepted as correct, should be considered only in the context in which it was made, that is, whether bankruptcy itself terminates an authority to sell given in the course of mutual dealings. With the exception of *Rolls Razor* v. *Cox*, the issue considered in the *Rose* v. *Hart* cases was not whether the property could be retrieved before it was turned into money, but rather whether there could be a set-off against proceeds that were in fact received. Similarly, statements to the effect that the authority must be revoked before the bankruptcy[90] should be understood in that context. While *Rolls Razor* v. *Cox* supports the view that a liquidator cannot demand the return of the property so as to defeat a set-off, there are a number of difficulties with the judgment,[90a] and it should not be followed. In any event, it should not be extended to bankruptcy, given that the property of the bankrupt is vested in the trustee. The trustee's reason for demanding its return may not be based solely on a desire to avoid a set-off. He may regard the method or timing of the sale as not being the most beneficial as far as the estate as a whole is concerned, particulary given that a debtor before his bankruptcy may have delivered goods for sale on a 'fire sale' basis in order to obtain funds to overcome what he thought was a temporary liquidity problem but which culminated in bankruptcy. There may indeed be only a small debt owing to the

---

[88] Compare *Rolls Razor* v. *Cox*, which concerned a voluntary liquidation so that the equivalent provision of s. 127 in force at that time was not applicable.

[89] See *Palmer* v. *Day & Sons* [1895] 2 QB 618, 623. While Lord Russell commented that no action could have been taken by the depositor when the receiving order was made to recover the goods, that was in the context of an argument that the depositor himself could not have maintained an action in detinue for the return of the goods, in which action a set-off admittedly would not have been available, unless he had taken steps to alter the terms on which the goods had been left with the auctioneer. Lord Russell agreed with this view. Since he had not altered the terms, the depositor could not have sued in detinue at the date of the receiving order.   [90] See above.   [90a] See above, and also section 5.1.

depository, and in such a case it hardly seems satisfactory that the trustee should be locked into a sale by the depository solely in order to secure that debt.

6.4.5 *Deposit of the means of completing the transaction*

The essence of a *Rose* v. *Hart* set-off is not merely the conferral of authority to receive the proceeds obtained from turning particular property into money, but rather that authority given under circumstances not amounting to a preference,[91] coupled with a deposit of whatever may be necessary for the depository to complete the transaction and receive the money. For example, in the case of a chattel for sale, usually this will mean a deposit of the chattel itself. Gibbs C.J. in *Rose* v. *Hart* was concerned with cases in which there had been a deposit of property before the relevant date, though the proceeds obtained from turning the property into money were not received by the depository until after that date. The deposit of the property was regarded as the basis of the credit in these cases, presumably because it was thought to confer upon the depository the means by which he could proceed with the transaction himself despite the bankruptcy. He could hand over that property to the third party and receive the money in return. However, possession of the means of completing the transaction does not always require an actual deposit of the property concerned. For example, in the case of goods, it would be sufficient if bills of lading were handed over[92] or, as in *Easum* v. *Cato*,[93] if the conduct of the parties is such that it is 'as if' the goods had been put into the person's hands. Moreover, physical delivery is not feasible when the transaction concerns the sale of immoveable property such as land. In such a case a *Rose* v. *Hart* set-off no doubt would require a deposit of the documentation necessary for the sale. In *Elliott* v. *Turquand*[94] an agent had been authorized to receive the proceeds of sale of land. The Privy Council said that if the agent had been entrusted with the deed of conveyance for the purpose of receiving the purchase money, 'the case would be very like some of the instances referred to in *Rose* v. *Hart'*.[95]

In *Elliott* v. *Turquand* there was insufficient evidence of a deed of conveyance having been handed over to the agent for the purpose of receiving the proceeds of sale. Nevertheless, the agent had actually

---

[91] *Castendyck and Focke* v. *Official Assignee of S. A. McLellan* (1887) 6 NZLR 67, 75.
[92] *M'Gillivray* v. *Simson* (1826) 2 Car. & P 320, affirmed 5 LJOSKB 53.
[93] (1822) 5 B & Ald. 861. [94] (1881) 7 App. Cas. 79.
[95] (1881) 7 App. Cas. 79, 87. See also *Castendyck and Focke* v. *Official Assignee of S.A. McLellan* (1887) 6 NZLR 67, 74. In *Castendyck* the agent was authorized merely to find a purchaser, and not to receive the purchase money, and so he was not allowed to set off the money when it came into his hands.

received the money under an unrevoked authority before the principal's bankruptcy, and he was allowed to bring those proceeds into an account. An agent is often, but not always, a trustee of money received in the course of his agency.[96] While the existence or otherwise of a trust was not canvassed by the Privy Council, it did comment[97] that the agent was authorized to receive the purchase money and to credit it to the mutual account existing between them, a factor militating against a trust. Accordingly, even though the case strictly did not come within the principle discussed in *Rose* v. *Hart*, this did not matter. Because there was no question of a trust there was nothing objectionable in a set-off.

6.5 SURPLUS PROCEEDS AFTER REALIZING A SECURITY

A bankrupt may have given security for a debt and, after default in payment of the debt, the creditor may have turned the property constituting the security into money, either through the exercise of a power of sale or, if the security consists of a life policy or a negotiable instrument, by collecting the money available from the policy or the instrument. If a surplus remains after the secured debt has been satisfied, the creditor may wish to set off his obligation to return the surplus to the bankrupt against a separate unsecured indebtedness of the bankrupt to him.

In this regard, two lines of authority should be distinguished. The first was developed by Lord Romilly who, instead of relying on the law of set-off, attempted to develop a mortgagee's right of retainer. In both *Spalding* v. *Thompson*[98] and *In re Haselfoot's Estate; Chauntler's Claim*[99] a policy of life assurance had been mortgaged to secure a debt, and when the testator died and the insurance money was received, the mortgagee was allowed to retain the surplus against a separate unsecured debt. In *Haselfoot's Estate*[100] Lord Romilly said that the right was not one of set-off at all, but rather it was a right in the mortgagee to retain a part of the testator's estate in his possession in satisfaction of the testator's indebtedness. Subsequently Malins V.C. applied this right of retainer in a case where there was a surplus remaining after the exercise of a power of sale.[101] However in later cases it has been disregarded,[102] and it would appear that it no longer

---

[96] Compare *Palette Shoes Pty. Ltd.* v. *Krohn* (1937) 58 CLR 1, 30 per Dixon J., with *Henry* v. *Hammond* [1913] 2 KB 515.   [97] (1881) 7 App. Cas. 79, 85, 87.

[98] (1858) 26 Beav. 637.   [99] (1872) LR 13 Eq. 327.

[100] (1872) LR 13 Eq. 327, 331.

[101] *In re General Provident Assurance Company; ex parte National Bank* (1872) LR 14 Eq. 507. Compare *Pile* v. *Pile* (1872) 23 WR 440, where the sale of the mortgaged property took place under a court order and the proceeds of sale did not come into the mortgagee's hands.

[102] See *Talbot* v. *Frere* (1878) 9 Ch. D 568 and *In re Gregson; Christison* v. *Bolam* (1887) 36 Ch. D 223.

applies. The second relates to tacking. When a mortgagor died, equity in a number of cases allowed the mortgagee to tack an unsecured debt onto the mortgage as against the successors in title to the equity of redemption, insofar as the mortgaged property was an asset available for payment of the unsecured debt. However, this was only allowed as a means of preventing circuity of action, and it could not be used to obtain priority over other creditors when the mortgagor's estate was insolvent.[103] This right appears to have been abolished in relation to mortgages of land as a result of the general abolition of tacking (save in respect of further advances) by the Law of Property Act 1925, section 94.[104]

With respect to set-off, the fundamental point should be that a mortgagee is a trustee for the mortgagor[105] for any surplus remaining after exercising a power of sale and paying the secured debt.[106] This is not a recent development. Dr. Waters[107] has suggested that it would have been obvious to judicial minds at least since *Cholmondeley* v. *Clinton*[108] in 1820. Accordingly, as a matter of principle the obligation to account for the surplus should not be susceptible to a set-off. *Talbot* v. *Frere*[109] supports this view. In that case Sir George Jessel M.R. said in the context of a deceased mortgagor's insolvent estate that 'the mortgagee cannot plead set-off. He is a trustee of the money for the estate, and his claim is only a simple contract debt against that estate'. Further, it was on this ground that the Victorian Supreme Court in *Lloyds Bank NZA Ltd.* v. *National Safety Council*[110] recently declined to allow a set-off against a surplus obtained through the exercise of a power of sale after the liquidation of the mortgagor. Nor is there any reason for encouraging a set-off. A secured creditor should not be entitled to use the security to obtain priority over other creditors in relation to a debt that otherwise was unsecured.[111] Nevertheless, with the notable exceptions of *Talbot* and *Lloyd's Bank*, the authorities are in an unsatisfactory state.

Consider first cases dealing with a deceased's insolvent estate. In *Talbot*

---

[103] See e.g. *Irby* v. *Irby* (1855) 22 Beav. 217; *Pile* v. *Pile* (1875) 23 WR 440; *Talbot* v. *Frere* (1878) 9 Ch. D 568, 572–573. See generally *Fisher and Lightwood's Law of Mortgage* (10th edn., 1988), 486.

[104] See also the Property Law Act 1958 (Vic.), s. 94 and the Conveyancing and Law of Property Act 1884 (Tas.), s. 38, neither of which applies to mortgages of Torrens title land (see s. 86 of the Victorian Act, and s. 91 of the Tasmanian), and the Property Law Act 1974 (Qld.), ss. 82 and 5(1)(b).

[105] Or a subsequent encumbrancer. See *Tanner* v. *Heard* (1857) 23 Beav. 555.

[106] *Matthison* v. *Clarke* (1854) 3 Drewry 3, 4; *Charles* v. *Jones* (1887) 35 Ch. D 544; Law of Property Act 1925, s. 105. [107] Waters, *The Constructive Trust* (1964), 207.

[108] (1820) 2 Jac. & W 1. [109] (1878) 9 Ch. D 568, 573.

[110] [1993] 2 VR 506.

[111] *Lloyds Bank NZA Ltd.* v. *National Safety Council* [1993] 2 VR 506, 522, referring to Buckley L.J. in *In re Pearce* [1909] 2 Ch. 492, 499–500 and Fry L.J. in *Eberle's Hotels and Restaurant Company, Ltd.* v. *E. Jonas & Brothers* (1887) 18 QBD 459, 470.

v. *Frere*[112] a testator had mortgaged policies of life assurance to a creditor. The testator died insolvent, and the creditor received the policy money which was more than sufficient to pay the mortgage debt. Sir George Jessel held that the creditor could not keep the surplus in payment of another unsecured debt. The creditor was a trustee for the estate, and so his obligation to account for the trust fund was not susceptible to a set-off.[113] The same issue arose on similar facts in *In re Gregson; Christison* v. *Bolam*.[114] A set-off was also denied, though on a different ground. North J. said that the debt was owing by the testator himself, whereas the testator never had a right of action for the surplus which first became payable after his death to the use of the executor. Accordingly, there was a lack of mutuality.[115] If on the other hand surplus proceeds of security had been received in the testator's lifetime, he suggested that there might have been a set-off.[116] It is difficult, however, to reconcile this with *Talbot* v. *Frere*. If there is a trust it should prevent a set-off whether the proceeds are received before or after death. Later in his judgment North J. doubted that the creditor in *Gregson* was a trustee of the surplus,[117] though the basis of this conclusion is not clear.

In other circumstances involving bankruptcy, the cases suggest that the result may differ depending on when the security is realized.

If the security is realized and the proceeds are received *before* the bankruptcy of the debtor, there is authority in favour of a set-off, not on the ground of mutual credit,[118] but rather because there is considered to be a 'debt' subsisting at the date of the bankruptcy.[119] *Young* v. *Bank of Bengal*[120] concerned a security over some promissory notes. While the security was not realized until after the bankruptcy, and a set-off accordingly was denied for the reason explained below, Lord Brougham nevertheless accepted, on the authority of *Atkinson* v. *Elliott*,[121] that a set-off would have been allowed if the bank had realized the security and received the surplus prior to the bankruptcy, 'for then they would have been debtors in that amount to Palmer and Co., and the case would have been one of mutual debts'.[122] This was later applied in *Astley* v.

---

[112] (1878) 9 Ch. D 568.
[113] The set-off in issue in *Talbot* v. *Frere* was pursuant to the Statutes of Set-off, since the deceased had died before the bankruptcy set-off section had been made applicable to deceaseds' insolvent estates by the Supreme Court of Judicature Act 1875, s. 10. See section 9.9.2 below.   [114] (1887) 36 Ch. D 223.
[115] See also *In re Gedney; Smith* v. *Grummitt* [1908] 1 Ch. 804.
[116] (1887) 36 Ch. D 223, 227.   [117] (1887) 36 Ch. D 223, 230.
[118] See e.g. *Astley* v. *Gurney* (1869) LR 4 CP 714, 723.
[119] See also *Samuel, Samuel & Co.* v. *West Hartlepool Steam Navigation Co.* (1907) 12 Com. Cas. 203 (Statutes of Set-off).   [120] (1836) 1 Moore 150.
[121] (1797) 7 TR 378.   [122] (1836) 1 Moore 150, 168.

Gurney[123] in relation to a security over goods which were sold with the assent of the debtor prior to the debtor's insolvency.[124]

In none of these cases was the possibility of a trust canvassed, though it was considered in *In re H. E. Thorne & Son, Ltd.*[125] A company had mortgaged certain machinery, the mortgage agreement containing a covenant by the mortgagor to insure. The machinery was destroyed by fire, and the insurance money was paid to the mortgagee. Some 2 weeks later the company went into liquidation. It was held that the mortgagee could set off the surplus over and above the mortgage debt against a separate unsecured indebtedness of the mortgagor.[126] It was specifically argued that the surplus was held on trust and therefore was not susceptible to a set-off, though Astbury J. was not persuaded. Instead he based his decision upon a statement by Lord Esher in the *Eberle's Hotels* case,[127] that 'wherever in the result the dealings on each side would end in a money claim, [the set-off section] would be applicable'. He said that the liquidator's argument that there may not be a set-off 'where a creditor holds the balance of a realized security in trust for his debtor so that the creditor is not entitled to deal with it in his account . . . would form a serious limitation on the general rule in *Eberle's Hotels Co.* v. *Jonas*'.[128] The difficulty is that this would seem to allow any trust fund to be employed in a set-off, a

---

[123] (1869) LR 4 CP 714.

[124] Marks J. in the Victorian Supreme Court in *Lloyds Bank NZA* v. *National Safety Council* [1993] 2 VR 506, 512 sought to explain the set-off in *Astley* v. *Gurney* on the ground that the creditor had been authorized by the debtor to sell the security prior to default, and that the court in *Astley* v. *Gurney* interpreted this as authority to apply the proceeds in satisfaction of other debts. However, there is nothing in the judgments in *Astley* v. *Gurney* to suggest this. The court emphasized the assent as constituting the basis upon which it could be said that credit was given for the proceeds received in relation to other goods which were not actually sold until after the bankruptcy. It was necessary to find that credit was given, because the fact that the proceeds were received after the bankruptcy precluded the court from relying on the mutual debts head of the set-off section. It was not suggested that the giving of credit also constituted authority to apply any surplus proceeds in reduction of other debts.

[125] [1914] 2 Ch. 438.

[126] The insurance money received under a policy taken out pursuant to a covenant to insure would have taken the place of the property destroyed, and would have been held as security until it was applied in payment of the mortgage debt. See *Edmonds* v. *The Hamilton Provident and Loan Society* (1891) 18 OAR 347.

[127] (1887) 18 QBD 459, 465. Astbury J. found further support for his conclusion in another statement in Lord Esher's judgment in *Eberle's Hotels* (at 466) that, 'These cigars were deposited to secure a debt with power to sell them at once, even before default in payment of the monthly instalments. If the defendants had sold them before the debt was paid, I am disposed to think that the plaintiffs' claim for an account of their proceeds would then have been a mere money claim'. However, this should be understood in the context of a letter written by the plaintiffs to the defendants authorizing them to dispose of the cigars and to 'put the proceeds to their credit'. See the report at 459–60. In other words, it was contemplated that, if the cigars were sold the proceeds were not to be kept separate but rather were to be credited to the general account between them.   [128] [1914] 2 Ch. 438, 453.

conclusion that plainly would not be accepted as a general principle of law.[129]

Different considerations have been held to apply when the security is enforced *after* bankruptcy or liquidation. In *Young* v. *Bank of Bengal*[130] a debtor pledged promissory notes as security for a debt, but became bankrupt prior to default in payment. When default subsequently occurred the bank exercised its security rights and sold the notes, and it was held that the surplus remaining after satisfying the secured debt could not be set off. It has been suggested that a set-off was denied on the ground that the security was deposited only for a particular or special purpose,[131] though this is not the reason that was given. Indeed, it is difficult to reconcile that explanation with Lord Brougham's view that a set-off would have been available if the security had been enforced before the bankruptcy. A set-off in fact was denied because it was thought that credit had not been given[132] within the meaning of Gibbs C.J.'s judgment in *Rose* v. *Hart*. The Privy Council adopted a strict interpretation of *Rose* v. *Hart*, and said that it was necessary to show at the date of the bankruptcy that the transaction *must* end in a debt.[133] However this could not be said with certainty in *Young*, because default had not occurred at that date. As yet there was no authority to sell, and indeed the security could have been redeemed by the assignees in bankruptcy.

Young v. *Bank of Bengal* was applied in *Astley* v. *Gurney*.[134] The security for two debts consisted of bills of lading for cotton and coffee, and also some bills of exchange. Prior to his bankruptcy, and prior to default, the debtor agreed that the creditor should sell the cotton and coffee and receive the proceeds, though there was no such assent in relation to the bills of exchange. Once again, bankruptcy occurred before the due date for

---

[129] In particular, Astbury J.'s analysis fails to account for the denial of a set-off in the special purpose payment cases. These were distinguished, rather unsatisfactorily, by Astbury J. on the ground that the exercise of a right of set-off would have amounted to a breach of a specific contract. See the discussion of these cases in section 6.6 below.

[130] (1836) 1 Moore 150.

[131] *Alsager* v. *Currie* (1844) 12 M & W 751, 757–8; *Naoroji* v. *Chartered Bank of India* (1868) LR 3 CP 444, 448 per Byles J. (*arguendo*); *In re Daintrey* [1900] 1 QB 546, 559. See also *M.S. Fashions Ltd.* v. *Bank of Credit and Commerce International S.A.* [1993] Ch. 425, 451, and *Key* v. *Flint* (1817) 8 Taunt. 21, 23.

[132] Because the security was enforced and the proceeds were obtained after the bankruptcy, there was not a 'debt' in existence at the date of the bankruptcy. Accordingly, if a set-off was to proceed, it was necessary to find that credit was given.

[133] See the discussion at (1836) 1 Moore 150, 168–9. In later cases it was said to be sufficient if the transaction would naturally or in the ordinary course of business end in a debt. See e.g. *Naoroji* v. *Chartered Bank of India* (1868) LR 3 CP 444, 451, 452. Indeed Byles J. in *Naoroji* (at 452) described *Young* as 'a very doubtful authority'.

[134] (1869) LR 4 CP 714. The report of the case suggests that the Exchequer Chamber reversed the decision of the Common Pleas, whereas this is not obvious from a reading of the judgments. The discrepancy is explained in a footnote to the report in 38 LJCP 357, 359.

payment. While the cotton was sold before the bankruptcy, the sale of the coffee was not effected until later. The proceeds of sale of the cotton, together with an amount received on one of the bills that matured before the bankruptcy, were sufficient to pay both debts, leaving a surplus. It was held that this surplus could be set off against a separate unsecured debt, not on the basis that credit had been given for it, but rather because it had been received before the date of the bankruptcy and therefore constituted a 'debt'. In addition, because a sufficient amount had already been received to pay both secured debts, the proceeds of sale of the coffee and of the remaining bills constituted surpluses. It was held, following *Young*, that the surplus in relation to the bills of exchange realized *after* the bankruptcy could not be set off. The coffee was also sold after the bankruptcy, though it was held that this nevertheless could be set off, notwithstanding *Young*, since the creditor had authorized a sale before the bankruptcy and this constituted the giving of credit for the purpose of the set-off section.[135] Presumably the same result would have followed if default had occurred prior to the bankruptcy though the security was not actually sold until later, since after default the creditor would have had authority to act.

The rationale in these cases for denying a set-off when the security was realized after the bankruptcy, in the absence of prior instructions to sell, was that credit had not been given at the date of the bankruptcy. The difficulty with relying on these cases now is that the set-off section has been expanded to include claims arising out of mutual dealings. Accordingly, if the question of a trust is left aside, the ostensible reason given in the cases for denying a set-off would no longer apply.[136] The 'debt' in respect of the surplus is a product of a prior dealing between the parties and therefore is part of their mutual dealings. It is no longer to the point that it may have been uncertain whether the security would be sold because, as Brett L.J. remarked in *Peat* v. *Jones & Co.*,[137] mutual dealings was added to the set-off section in order to get rid of questions which might arise as to whether a transaction would end in a debt or not. In other words, if the courts continue to ignore the trust impressed upon the surplus proceeds, a set-off should be available whether the security is realized before or after bankruptcy. The better approach, however, is to recognize that surplus

---

[135] Oditah, *Legal Aspects of Receivables Financing* (1991), 249–50 has sought to explain the set-off on the ground that the security over the coffee had been released, though this would not appear to have been the case. It was merely agreed that the creditor could sell the coffee and receive the proceeds. Presumably it was intended that the proceeds would then be held as security.

[136] See Derham, 'Some Aspects of Mutual Credit and Mutual Dealings' (1992) 108 *Law Quarterly Review* 99, 109, a point also made recently by Phillips J. in the Victorian Supreme Court in *Lloyds Bank NZA* v. *National Safety Council* [1993] 2 VR 506, 520–2.

[137] (1881) 8 QBD 147, 149.

proceeds from the realization of a security are usually impressed with a trust so that, unless in a particular case it is intended that the surplus be credited to an account between the parties and not be held on trust, a creditor should not be entitled to obtain priority over other creditors in relation to another unsecured debt owing to him by setting off the surplus against that debt.[138] This is the position that has been adopted in Victoria,[139] and on that view the time of realization of the security should not be relevant.[140]

6.6 SPECIAL-PURPOSE PAYMENTS

If a person has paid a sum of money to another to be applied for a special purpose which has failed, or which has not been carried into effect, the depositor is generally entitled to recover it undiminished by a set-off. This applies when the defence of set-off as between solvent parties under the Statutes of Set-off is in issue,[141] and also, if the depositor has become bankrupt or is a company which has gone into liquidation, when it is sought to base a defence on the insolvency set-off section. In *In re Pollitt; ex parte Minor*[142] a client was indebted to his solicitor, who refused to act further unless the client deposited a sum of money to cover future costs. The client became bankrupt, after which the solicitor continued to act on his behalf. The Court of Appeal held that the solicitor was only entitled to his costs for the work performed before notice of the act of bankruptcy, when his authority to act was revoked. Therefore the purpose for which the money had been lodged with him had failed, and he was obliged to return the residue to the bankrupt's trustee without deducting the bankrupt's prior indebtedness to him. The leading judgment in the Court of Appeal was delivered by Lord Esher M.R., who commented:[143] 'If the money was given to the solicitor for a specific purpose, then, as between him and the bankrupt, there could not be a set-off'. It may be that the purpose in

---

[138] Compare *Baker* v. *Lloyd's Bank, Ltd.* [1920] 2 KB 322, though Roche J. seems to have accepted (at 328) that the security in that case was not intended to be confined to the specific advance in respect of which it was given.

[139] *Lloyd's Bank NZA Ltd.* v. *National Safety Council* [1993] 2 VR 506.

[140] An issue for consideration in relation to the surplus produced from the exercise of a power of sale governed by the Law of Property Act 1925 is whether the allowance of a set-off indeed is consistent with s. 105, which provides that any surplus received by a mortgagee, after paying prior claims, 'shall be paid to the person entitled to the mortgaged property'. In Australia see, e.g., the Property Law Act 1958 (Vic.), s. 105. A similar provision is to be found in legislation dealing with pawnbrokers. See the Consumer Credit Act 1974, s. 121(3), and, e.g. in Australia, the Pawnbrokers Act 1958 (Vic.), s. 28.

[141] *Stumore* v. *Campbell & Co.* [1892] 1 QB 314.

[142] [1893] 1 QB 455, affirming [1893] 1 QB 175.

[143] [1893] 1 QB 455, 458.

fact has been carried out, though there is a residue remaining in the hands of the depositor. In *In re Mid-Kent Fruit Factory*[144] a company had handed two cheques to its solicitors for the purpose of discharging the claims of its creditors, the solicitors being instructed to settle for less if possible. The solicitors did manage to settle for less in some cases, though the company was not informed of this. When the company went into liquidation the solicitors sought to set off the balance remaining against the company's liability for costs. Vaughan Williams J. held that, when money is deposited for a special purpose, and after that purpose is fulfilled a balance remains with the depository, the depository may not set off the balance in the bankruptcy of the depositor unless he can show that it was retained by him with the consent of the depositor.[145] In the case before him the company had not known of the surplus, and so obviously it had not consented to the solicitors retaining any surplus. Consequently a set-off was not available.[146]

A similar principle may apply when a negotiable instrument is deposited with a person to collect the proceeds and apply them in a particular way. If the person instead retains the proceeds, and does not apply them as directed, the courts have recognized in a number of cases that the trustee in bankruptcy of the depositor may recover the money undiminished by a set-off.[147]

In some of these special-purpose payment cases the courts, when denying the depository a right of set-off, have emphasized the proprietary nature of the depositor's claim. Sometimes the deposit has been said to give rise to a trust,[148] and in other cases a bailment.[149] However, there is authority suggesting that the rule is based upon something broader, and that the depository may be denied a set-off in the depositor's bankruptcy even though the relationship between the parties is intended to be only one of debt. In *In re City Equitable Fire Insurance Co. Ltd.*[150] a reinsurer under

---

[144] [1896] 1 Ch. 567. See also *In re City Equitable Fire Insurance Company, Ltd.* [1930] 2 Ch. 293, 313–14.

[145] Compare *Buchanan* v. *Findlay* (1829) 9 B & C 738, 749, in which the depository would have been entitled under the agreement to retain the surplus if the proceeds of the bills entrusted with him had been applied as directed.

[146] The depository has the onus of showing the depositor's consent. Note, however, the re-phrasing below of the principles set out in *Pollitt* and *Mid-Kent* in terms of primary and secondary trusts.

[147] *Buchanan* v. *Findlay* (1829) 9 B & C 738; *Atkinson* v. *Learmouth* (1905) 11 ALR 191. See also *Alder* v. *Keighley* (1846) 15 M & W 117, though this was decided by reference to the form of action employed.

[148] See *Wright* v. *Watson* (1883) Cab. & El. 171, and also *Stumore* v. *Campbell & Co.* [1892] 1 QB 314.

[149] See *In re Mid-Kent Fruit Factory* [1896] 1 Ch. 567, 572, and also *Buchanan* v. *Findlay* (1829) 9 B & C 738, 749 (bills of exchange deposited for a specific purpose).

[150] [1930] 2 Ch. 293.

a treaty of reinsurance had agreed to accept a share of all fire insurance policies accepted or renewed by the insurer, and in order to secure the due performance of the reinsurer's obligations under the treaty the insurer was entitled to retain 40 per cent of all premiums credited to the reinsurer in the first year. The reinsurer went into liquidation, and after all its obligations to the insurer under the treaty had been satisfied the insurer still retained a substantial fund. It was held that the deposit constituted money left in the hands of the insurer for a special purpose, and that the balance remaining after that purpose was satisfied had to be returned to the liquidator without the right to set off debts owing to the insurer by the reinsurer under other treaties and policies of insurance and reinsurance. Counsel for the insurer argued that the deposit was not a trust fund but rather was a loan with a conditional right to payment, and that on that basis it should be able to be employed in a set-off. There was no apparent obligation on the insurer to keep the deposit separate from its own funds,[151] and the insurer was required to pay interest to the reinsurer on the deposit,[152] a factor which is usually considered to be a powerful indication of a debt rather than a trust relationship.[153] However, the existence or otherwise of a trust apparently was not considered to be important. Maugham J. commented at first instance:[154] 'It does not seem to me to matter much whether it is or is not regarded as a trust fund. It is, to my mind, moneys "deposited for a specific purpose" . . .'. The Court of Appeal failed to mention the presence or absence of a trust. Lord Hanworth M.R., with whom Lawrence and Romer L. JJ. agreed, was content to find that the accumulated fund was intended to be held for a specific purpose, i.e. as security for the due performance of the reinsurer's obligations under the treaty, and that therefore it should be set aside from any account between the parties.

Winn L.J. in the Court of Appeal in *Halesowen Presswork & Assemblies*

---

[151] See *Henry* v. *Hammond* [1913] 2 KB 515, 521; *In re Nanwa Gold Mines Ld.* [1955] 1 WLR 1080; *In re Bond Worth Ltd.* [1980] 1 Ch. 228, 260–1; Finn, *Fiduciary Obligations* (1977), 103–4.

[152] Since the interest was to be paid to the reinsurer, and not retained by the insurer as part of the retention fund, it was allowed to be set off.

[153] *Pott* v. *Clegg* (1847) 16 M & W 321, 327 per Parke B. (*arguendo*); *Foley* v. *Hill* (1848) 2 HLC 28, 36; *In re Broad; ex parte Neck* (1884) 13 QBD 740; Finn, *Fiduciary Obligations* (1977), 108. The point is made in *Scott on Trusts* (4th edn., 1987) Vol. 1, 135–6 para. 12.2 that an agreement to pay interest is not conclusive evidence of a debt. For example, if the person receiving the money has agreed to invest it for the payer, and to pay the interest that is actually received, a trust is created. However, in cases like the *City Equitable Fire* case, where the agreement is to pay interest at a defined rate, regardless of whether or not the money is invested, Scott says that this almost certainly indicates that the payee is to have the use of the money, and that the transaction gives rise to a debt and not a trust.

[154] [1930] 2 Ch. 293, 303.

Ltd. v. *Westminster Bank Ltd.*[155] suggested that the parties to mutual dealings may 'separate out' a particular debt so that it is not to be regarded as mutual for the purpose of the insolvency set-off section, though Lord Kilbrandon on appeal in the House of Lords regarded this proposition as doubtful.[156] Mutuality in truth is concerned with the status of the parties and their relationship with each other, not with the circumstances in which a debt arose.[157] Alternatively, Willes J. once suggested[158] that 'some difficulty might arise' in allowing a defendant a set-off if he has 'purposely broken his contract in order to create the claim', and Astbury J. had recourse to a similar notion in *In re H.E. Thorne*[159] to explain the special-purpose payment cases. He said that a depository is denied a set-off in these cases 'if it involves a breach of the contract under which he obtained the money'.[160] Other judgments support this view. In *In re Pollitt*[161] Vaughan Williams J. said that, 'The attempt to use the money deposited as security for another purpose than that for which it was deposited is an attempt to do wrong'. In an Australian case[162] a debtor had handed a promissory note to his creditor with instructions to collect the proceeds and pay them (less a discount) into his bank account. The creditor duly collected the proceeds but, instead of applying them as directed, retained them in satisfaction of the debtor's indebtedness to him. While there are statements which suggest that the claim brought by the debtor's assignee in bankruptcy for payment of the proceeds was regarded as proprietary in nature,[163] Hodges and Holroyd JJ. in disallowing a set-off nevertheless commented that[164] 'we should expect that the law would not allow a man by dishonestly breaking his contract, and keeping another man's money, to gain any advantage'. However, the better view is that there is no general principle which precludes a person from basing a set-off upon his own breach of contract, even where the contract is purposely broken in order to bring about this result.[165] For example, failure to pay a debt on time constitutes a breach of contract.[166] A creditor who is aware of his debtor's

---

[155] [1971] 1 QB 1, 43–4, referring to his earlier judgment in *Rolls Razor Ltd.* v. *Cox* [1967] 1 QB 552, 575.

[156] *National Westminster Bank Ltd.* v. *Halesowen Presswork & Assemblies Ltd.* [1972] AC 785, 821.

[157] See section 7.1 below.

[158] *Turner* v. *Thomas* (1871) LR 6 CP 610, 614.

[159] [1914] 2 Ch. 438.

[160] [1914] 2 Ch. 438, 450.

[161] [1893] 1 QB 175, 179.

[162] *Atkinson* v. *Learmouth* (1905) 11 ALR 191.

[163] Hodges and Holroyd JJ. emphasized in their joint judgment ((1905) 11 ALR 191, 195) that the debtor was the owner of the note and the proceeds. They also said (at 196) that the difference between their approach and that of the dissentient, Hood J., was the statement by Hood J. that the dealing in the note was intended to terminate in a debt.

[164] (1905) 11 ALR 191, 195.

[165] See section 4.7.3 above.

[166] See Maugham J. at first instance in *In re City Equitable Fire Insurance Company Ltd.* [1930] 2 Ch. 293, 302.

insolvency and who consequently withholds payment of his own indebtedness to the debtor would not be denied a set-off, and it is difficult to see
why a breach of contract in any other form should be treated differently. In
any event, any supposed principle that a right of set-off may not arise when
a contract has been breached for the very purpose of gaining a set-off
would not be relevant to special-purpose payment cases in which the
purpose has failed for some other reason, or when the purpose has been
carried out leaving a surplus.

Nor is the breach of contract theory supported by the old common law
cases which established that, when either money or a negotiable
instrument was lodged with a depository to be applied by him to a specific
purpose, and the depository instead wilfully retained the money, or the
instrument or its proceeds, in purported satisfaction of the depositor's
indebtedness to him, there could not be a set-off if the depositor brought a
special action for breach of duty, though a set-off was allowed if the
depositor waived the breach and sued instead for money had and
received.[167] These cases are explicable on the basis of the form of action
employed. Actions for damages for breach of duty are unliquidated in
nature, and before 1861[168] claims of this nature could not be proved in a
bankruptcy, and consequently could not be set off.[169] While it was
generally considered in these cases that a set-off was available in an action
for money had and received,[170] they were decided at law where the

---

[167] See generally *Colson* v. *Welsh* (1795) 1 Esp. 378; *Atkinson* v. *Elliott* (1797) 7 TR 378;
Thorpe v. *Thorpe* (1832) 3 B & Ad. 580; *Hill* v. *Smith* (1844) 12 M & W 618; *Alder* v. *Keighley*
(1846) 15 M & W 117; *Bell* v. *Carey* (1849) 8 CB 887. Compare *Buchanan* v. *Findlay* (1829) 9
B & C 738, in which a set-off was disallowed in an action for money had and received in
relation to the proceeds of bills, though in that case the bankrupts prior to their bankruptcy
had demanded the return of the bills, so that the defendants had no right to receive the
proceeds.

[168] Compare the Bankruptcy Act 1861, s. 153.

[169] *Rose* v. *Sims* (1830) 1 B & Ad. 521. An apparent exception to this principle was allowed
in *Gibson* v. *Bell* (1835) 1 Bing. (NC) 743 and *Groom* v. *West* (1838) 8 Ad. & E 758. It was
held in these cases that, when a purchaser of goods who had agreed to pay the price by
accepting a bill of exchange in fact failed to do so, and the vendor's assignees in bankruptcy
brought a special action of assumpsit against him for breach of contract, the purchaser could
set off in that action an independent indebtedness of the bankrupt vendor to him (though
compare *Hutchinson* v. *Reid* (1813) 3 Camp. 329 in the context of the Statutes of Set-off).
However, this was justified on the ground that the claim in reality was for the price of the
goods themselves, so that effectively it was liquidated in nature. Indeed, Lord Denman C.J.
in *Groom* v. *West* distinguished the liquidated nature of the demand before him from the case
of a claim for unliquidated damages for breach of duty in not applying a special purpose
payment in the required manner.

[170] See e.g. *Colson* v. *Welsh* (1795) 1 Esp. 378, 380; *Atkinson* v. *Elliott* (1797) 7 TR 378;
Hill v. *Smith* (1844) 12 M & W 618, 631 (in relation to the Statutes of Set-off). Compare
Buchanan v. *Findlay* (1829) 9 B & C 738, explained in *Thorpe* v. *Thorpe* (1832) 3 B & Ad.
580, 583–4.

presence or absence of a trust arising out of the stated purpose would not have been considered.

The only apparent justification for denying a right of set-off to a depository against his obligation to account for the remains of a fund held for a special purpose, or the proceeds of a negotiable instrument given to him to apply in a particular manner, is that the fund or the proceeds may be impressed with a trust. If in a particular case the amount in question is not intended to be kept separate from the depository's own funds before the purpose is carried out, but rather is to give rise only to a debt, there is no trust, and there is no apparent justification for denying a set-off to the depository in the depositor's bankruptcy. On this view, the *City Equitable Fire* case could only be regarded as correctly decided if, notwithstanding the obligation to pay interest, there was a trust so that the insurer would have been obliged to pay the retention money into a separate account. This seems unlikely. The decision admittedly was referred to without criticism by both Lord Kilbrandon and Lord Simon of Glaisdale in *National Westminster Bank Ltd.* v. *Halesowen Presswork & Assemblies Ltd.*,[171] though their respective explanations for these special-purpose payment cases each seem to countenance a form of trust fund. Lord Kilbrandon said that the funds in these cases were 'impressed with quasi-trust purposes',[172] a concept that has also been used to explain the status of property held under a fiduciary obligation that is similar to a trust, but which nevertheless is not a trust in the technical sense of the word.[173] Indeed, Lord Kilbrandon referred in his judgment to the 'fund' held by way of guarantee against the non-performance of the obligations in *City Equitable Fire*, which suggests that he assumed that there was a trust in that case. The use of the expression 'quasi-trust' was criticized by Lord Simon of Glaisdale as giving 'uncertain guidance in the law'. He preferred to say that 'money is paid for a special (or specific) purpose so as to exclude mutuality of dealing within [the set-off section] if the money is paid in such circumstances that it would be a misappropriation to use it for any other purpose than that for which it is paid'.[174] It is not clear what his Lordship meant by 'misappropriation'. However, it does seem to imply that the parties should have intended that there be a separate fund which is not to be misappropriated, and such a fund may be characterized as a trust fund.

In *National Westminster* v. *Halesowen* a company's current account with its bank was overdrawn. It was agreed between the company and the bank

---

[171] [1972] AC 785. [172] [1972] AC 785, 821.
[173] See *Foley* v. *Hill* (1848) 2 HLC 28, 35–6, and generally Finn, *Fiduciary Obligations* (1977), 89.
[174] [1972] AC 785, 808. See also *Re Arthur Sanders Ltd.* (1981) 17 Build. LR 125, 133, as well as the comments of Vaughan Williams J. in the Divisional Court in *In re Pollitt* [1893] 1 QB 175, 179.

that the account should be frozen, and that a new account should be opened through which the company's current business henceforth should pass. It was held that this new account was not a special-purpose account, and that it could be brought into a set-off. This seems correct. The account was a normal bank account giving rise to a debtor/creditor relationship. Other cases are to a similar effect. In *Pedder* v. *The Mayor, Aldermen, and Burgesses of Preston*[175] the Mayor, etc. of the Corporation of Preston had an account with a bank for the Corporation's general municipal functions. In addition the Mayor, etc. had been constituted the Local Board of Health under the Public Health Act 1848, and for this a separate account was opened with the same bank. The bank entered into an arrangement with its creditors under the Bankrupt Law Consolidation Act 1849, at which time the general account was overdrawn and the Local Board of Health account was in credit. Though section 87 of the 1848 Act provided that the money received by the Local Board of Health 'shall be applied . . . in defraying such of the Expenses incurred or to be incurred by the said Local Board in carrying this Act into execution', it was held that the Corporation could set the credit balance on that account against its indebtedness on the other. A second case is *Ex parte Pearce; in re Langmead*.[176] Commissioners had been appointed for the purposes of improving the harbour of Teignmouth and the navigation of the river Teign. The Commissioners opened two accounts with a bank, headed respectively 'No. 1 Harbour Account' and 'No. 2 River Account'. The Harbour Account was in credit and the River Account in debit. It was held in the bankruptcy of the bank that the two accounts could be set off, notwithstanding that an Act of Parliament provided that the sums standing to the credit of the Harbour Account were to be used in improving Teignmouth Harbour. Admittedly in *Pedder* and *Pearce* it was the debtor on the special purpose account who was bankrupt, whereas in *Halesowen* the creditor on the account was the insolvent party, though the principle should have been the same. In *M. S. Fashions Ltd.* v. *Bank of Credit and Commerce International S.A.*[177] Dillon L.J. held that an account into which money was deposited as security for a debt was not exempt from set-off on the basis of the special-purpose payment cases.

There are, however, two New South Wales cases which suggest that a special purpose bank account cannot be the subject of a set-off. In *National Mutual Royal Bank* v. *Ginges*[178] Brownie J. reached a different conclusion to that of the House of Lords in *Halesowen* on substantially similar facts.

---

[175] (1862) 12 CB(NS) 535.
[176] (1841) 2 Mont. D & De G 142.
[177] [1993] Ch. 425, 448–51.
[178] Unreported, Supreme Court of New South Wales, 15 March 1991.

His Honour accepted that the account in *Ginges* was opened for the purpose of providing creditors participating in a moratorium with a 'fund' to which they could look for payment, this should not have prevented a set-off. The account was still a debt, not a trust.[179] A similar criticism may be made of comments by Helsham C.J. in Eq. in the New South Wales Supreme Court in *MPS Constructions Pty. Ltd.* v. *Rural Bank of New South Wales*[180] regarding a bank account set up for the payment of retention money pursuant to a building contract. Notwithstanding that the deposit was made for a special purpose, it should have been available for a set-off between the bank and the contractor in the contractor's liquidation.

Where the relationship indeed is one of debt, as, for example, where money is paid into a bank account to be applied to a particular purpose which has not been carried out, other factors nevertheless may affect the availability of a set-off. In the first place, there may have been an agreement (express or implied) that the debt is not to be set off, though this will not be effective to exclude a set-off once bankruptcy or liquidation occurs.[181] Secondly, if the money was paid to the bank under circumstances where it was specifically appropriated to meet a liability owing by the depositor to a third party, the circumstances may be such as to give rise to an equitable assignment or, if the bank has communicated its assent to the arrangement to the third party, possibly it may constitute an attornment so as to entitle the third party to sue on the basis of money had and received,[182] though attornment where there is no fund remains a matter of controversy.[183] In either case this would destroy mutuality for the purpose of set-off against the depositor.

If the existence of a trust is recognized as the proper justification for denying a set-off in the event of a special-purpose payment, the statements of law found in *Pollitt* and *Mid-Kent* should be re-phrased. The principle probably is better stated that, if a payment is made on trust for a special purpose, and either that purpose fails, or, having been carried out, a residue remains, the depository may not set off his obligation to return the money if it has been agreed, expressly or by implication, that the fund should be held on a secondary trust in favour of the depositor.[184] This

---

[179] *National Mutual* v. *Ginges* nevertheless was referred to without adverse comment by Clarke J.A. in *Central Brake Service (Sydney) Ltd.* v. *Central Brake Service (Newcastle) Ltd.* (1992) 27 NSWLR 406, 412.

[180] (1980) 4 ACLR 835, 845, discussed in section 4.3.4 above.

[181] *National Westminster Bank Ltd.* v. *Halesowen Presswork & Assemblies Ltd.* [1972] AC 785.

[182] *W.P. Greenhalgh and Sons* v. *Union Bank of Manchester* [1924] 2 KB 153.

[183] See the discussion of *Shamia* v. *Joory* [1958] 2 QB 448 in Goff and Jones, *The Law of Restitution* (4th edn., 1993), 573–4.

[184] See *Barclays Bank Ltd.* v. *Quistclose Investments Ltd.* [1970] AC 567, 581–2. *Semble* the parties need not have realized that they were creating what lawyers call a trust.

should be relevant particularly to the decision in the *Mid-Kent* case that, if there is a residue remaining after the purpose has been carried out, the depository may not bring it into an account unless he can show that it remained in his hands with the depositor's consent. While the depositor's consent to the money remaining with the depository may militate against a trust, this should not be regarded as conclusive.

The distinction between a debt and a trust is important not only for set-off, but also where the depository has become bankrupt before the money was applied to the particular purpose. If the fund deposited was impressed with a trust, and the purpose has failed, a secondary trust in favour of the depositor may have arisen so that the money may be recovered in full from the bankrupt's estate, subject to the rules of tracing.[185] If, however, the relationship between the parties is only one of debtor and creditor, as for example in *In re Barned's Banking Company Limited; Massey's case* where a bank was provided with funds to cover the acceptance of a bill of exchange,[186] the depository is confined to a proof in the depository's bankruptcy.

---

[185] Insolvency Act 1986, s. 283(3). See e.g. *Ex parte Dumas* (1754) 2 Ves. Sen. 582; *In re Rogers; ex parte Holland & Hannen* (1891) 8 Morr. 243; *Barclays Bank Ltd.* v. *Quistclose Investments Ltd.* [1970] AC 567. See also *Tooke* v. *Hollingworth* (1793) 5 TR 215, affirmed (1795) 2 H Bl. 501 for the position at common law.

[186] (1870) 39 LJ Ch. 635. See also *Pott* v. *Clegg* (1847) 16 M & W 321. However, compare *Farley* v. *Turner* (1857) 26 LJ Ch. 710, where the money had been specifically appropriated to the purpose by the bank before its bankruptcy.

7

Mutuality—Introduction

7.1 THE MEANING OF MUTUALITY

For set-off in bankruptcy and company liquidation, as well as under the Statutes of Set-off, there must be mutuality.[1] Mutuality does not require that the claims should arise at the same time,[2] nor that there should be any connection between them.[3] Moreover it is irrelevant that the claims may be of a different nature. Thus, an obligation arising out of an instrument under seal may be set off against a simple contract debt,[4] and a secured debt may be set off against an unsecured debt.[5] Mutuality in fact refers to two characteristics, that the demands must be between the same parties, and that they must be held in the same capacity, or right, or interest.[6] It is concerned with the status of the parties and their relationship to each other. It is not concerned with the nature of the claims themselves. This is covered instead by the requirement of 'debts', or in insolvency set-off 'debts', 'credits' and claims arising out of prior 'dealings'.[7] The requirement of same parties is intended to ensure that A's right to sue B may not be set off against A's indebtedness to C, or that a joint demand may not be set off against a separate demand.[8] The same capacity or right means that each of the parties, who is liable to the other, must be beneficially interested in a cross-claim against that other. In other words, 'there must

---

[1] Lack of mutuality is also a defence to proceedings for specific performance, though it is there used in a different sense, that as a matter of discretion the court will not compel a defendant to perform his obligations specifically if it cannot at the same time ensure that any unperformed obligations of the plaintiff will be specifically performed, unless damages would be an adequate remedy for any default by the plaintiff. See Buckley L.J. in *Price* v. *Strange* [1978] 1 Ch. 337, 367–8.

[2] *Day & Dent Constructions Pty. Ltd.* v. *North Australian Properties Pty. Ltd.* (1981) 34 ALR 595, 600 (Federal Court of Australia).

[3] *Naoroji* v. *Chartered Bank of India* (1868) LR 3 CP 444, 452; *In re Daintrey* [1900] 1 QB 546. [4] See e.g. *Ex parte Law; in re Kennedy* (1864) De Gex 378.

[5] For set-off against a secured debt, see section 2.18 above.

[6] *Ince Hall Rolling Mills Co., Ltd.* v. *The Douglas Forge Company* (1882) 8 QBD 179, 183 ('between the same parties and in the same interest'); *Shand* v. *M. J. Atkinson Ltd.* [1966] NZLR 551, 570 ('by and against a person in the same right'); *Peel* v. *Fitzgerald* [1982] Qd. R 544, 547 ('between the same parties and in the same right').   [7] See Ch. 3.

[8] See section 8.2 below.

be identity between the persons beneficially interested in the claim and the person against whom the cross-claim existed'.[9] In the case of a company, a change of control of the company between the dates that the cross-demands were contracted does not affect mutuality, if in truth the same legal entity was the contracting party in both cases.[10]

The form of the arrangements by which the cross-demands came into existence does not affect mutuality. It is not correct to say, as Lord Denning suggested in the Court of Appeal in *Halesowen Presswork & Assemblies Ltd.* v. *National Westminster Bank Ltd.*,[11] that the nature of the arrangements entered into may be 'so special as to deprive them of mutuality', an approach that Lord Cross of Chelsea on appeal in the House of Lords[12] criticized as being too narrow in the light of the decided cases.[13] Winn L.J. advanced the theory that mutuality is essentially concerned with the intentions of the parties.[14] This theory later led him to conclude that the set-off section in the insolvency legislation 'applies only to cross-claims arising *directly* from dealings between a person who has become a bankrupt and another person all of which are properly called "mutual" '.[15] In essence this appears to be no more than a restatement of the argument that had been rejected in 1798 in *Hankey* v. *Smith*,[16] that for mutual credit the parties should have meant to trust each other in the transaction in question. It was held in that case that an indebtedness of a bankrupt acceptor upon a bill of exchange could be brought into an account by the holder, even though the bankrupt was unaware that the bill had been indorsed to the holder. A similar result has occurred in the context of the Statutes of Set-off.[17] The notion of 'direct' dealings, or of the element of trust, fails to explain the undoubted right of set-off in cases like *Hankey* v. *Smith*, or indeed in any case in which one of the parties to the proposed set-off had gained a right to sue the other only as a result of an assignment to

---

[9] *West Street Properties Pty. Ltd.* v. *Jamison* [1974] 2 NSWLR 435, 441 per Jeffrey J.

[10] *Central Brake Service (Sydney) Pty. Ltd.* v. *Central Brake Service (Newcastle) Pty. Ltd.* (1992) 27 NSWLR 406 (official management). [11] [1971] 1 QB 1, 36.

[12] *National Westminster Bank Ltd.* v. *Halesowen Presswork & Assemblies Ltd.* [1972] AC 785, 812.

[13] However, compare Viscount Dilhorne (at [1972] AC 785, 806) who said that the arrangements before him were not of this special character, without offering any opinion as to the correctness of Lord Denning's approach.

[14] *Rolls Razor Ltd.* v. *Cox* [1967] 1 QB 552, 574.

[15] *Halesowen Presswork & Assemblies Ltd.* v. *Westminster Bank Ltd.* [1971] 1 QB 1, 43 (CA) (emphasis added). However, see Lord Kilbrandon on appeal in the House of Lords [1972] AC 785, 821.

[16] (1789) 3 TR 507n. Nevertheless, there have been other occasions when mutuality has been defined in terms of mutual trust. See Story, *Commentaries on Equity Jurisprudence* (14th edn., 1918) Vol. 3, 471 (and the cases referred to in n. 4), and *Knox* v. *Cockburn* (1862) 1 QSCR 80. See also *Koster* v. *Eason* (1813) 2 M & S 112, 118, where Lord Ellenborough spoke in terms of 'consent'.

[17] See e.g. *Cornforth* v. *Rivett* (1814) 2 M & S 510.

him of the other's indebtedness.[18] Rather, these cases support the view that for mutuality one should look only to the identity of the persons entitled to the benefit and subject to the burden of the cross-demands.

7.2 THE NECESSITY FOR MUTUALITY

It has been said that mutuality must always be present,[19] though the rule is better stated that cross-demands which are not mutual may not be set off 'except under special circumstances'.[20] Reference is made in the ensuing discussion of mutuality to a number of situations in which there may be a set-off despite the absence of strict mutuality.

7.3 EQUITABLE INTERESTS—INSOLVENCY SET-OFF

7.3.1 *The general principle*

A fundamental principle of insolvency law is that mutuality is determined by reference to the equitable interests of the parties, rather than their bare legal rights.[21] Accordingly, the beneficial owner of a debt may set off that debt against an obligation owing by him to the debtor,[22] so that, for example, where an equitable assignee is being sued by the debtor's trustee in bankruptcy in respect of a liability that he has to the debtor, he may bring the assigned debt into an account.[23] Conversely, a set-off will be denied if one of the parties to the proposed set-off only held his right of

---

[18] See e.g. *Clark* v. *Cort* (1840) Cr. & Ph. 154; *Mathieson's Trustee* v. *Burrup, Mathieson and Company* [1927] 1 Ch. 562; *Southern Cross Construction Ltd.* v. *Southern Cross Club Ltd.* [1973] 1 NZLR 708; *Kon Strukt Pty. Ltd.* v. *Storage Developments Pty. Ltd.* (1989) 96 FLR 43. See also, with respect to the Statutes of Set-off, *Bennett* v. *White* [1910] 2 KB 643.

[19] *In re Mid-Kent Fruit Factory* [1896] 1 Ch. 567, 571. See also *Knox* v. *Cockburn* (1862) 1 QSCR 80, 83; *In re City Life Assurance Company, Ltd.* [1926] 1 Ch. 191, 216; *Day & Dent Constructions Pty. Ltd.* v. *North Australian Properties Pty. Ltd.* (1981) 34 ALR 595, 601 (Federal Court of Australia).

[20] See Sir George Turner in *Freeman* v. *Lomas* (1851) 9 Hare 109, 114. See also *West Street Properties Pty. Ltd.* v. *Jamison* [1974] 2 NSWLR 435, 441.

[21] *In re Hett, Maylor, and Co.* (1894) 10 TLR 412; *Hiley* v. *Peoples Prudential Assurance Co., Ltd.* (1938) 60 CLR 468, 488, 497; *Gye* v. *McIntyre* (1991) 171 CLR 609, 623.

[22] *Crosse* v. *Smith* (1813) 1 M & S 545; *Bailey* v. *Johnson* (1872) LR 7 Ex. 263; *Ex parte Morier; in re Willis, Percival, & Co.* (1879) 12 Ch. D 491, 496, 500, 502; *Hiley* v. *Peoples Prudential Assurance Company, Ltd.* (1938) 60 CLR 468, 497. See also *Cochrane* v. *Green* (1860) 9 CB(NS) 448. The observations of Sir George Jessel MR in *Middleton* v. *Pollock; ex parte Nugee* (1875) LR 20 Eq. 29, 36–7 (and see also *Welton* v. *Harnett* (1886) 7 NSWR 74) on the necessity for some 'special jurisdiction' should not be regarded as correct.

[23] *Mathieson's Trustee* v. *Burrup, Mathieson and Company* [1927] 1 Ch. 562.

action as a bare trustee for someone else,[24] or if he had assigned it in favour of a third party,[25] though in such a case there is the possibility of a set-off between the debtor on the assigned debt and the true beneficial owner.[26] This emphasis on equitable rights is a consequence of the influence of equity in matters of bankruptcy. The Chancellor more or less had assumed control over bankruptcy in the nineteenth century, and ever since the creation of a separate Court of Bankruptcy in 1831[27] and its subsequent amalgamation with the Supreme Court of Judicature in 1883,[28] the court administering bankruptcy has been a court of both law and equity.[29] As Clauson J. once aptly remarked:[30]

The Bankruptcy Act . . . is an Act regulating the proceedings of a Court which has always been a Court of equity, proceeding on equitable principles, recognizing equitable debts, subject of course to such infirmities as are sometimes present, but drawing no distinction between equitable and legal rights for purposes of administering the estate of the bankrupt.

When a debt is held on trust, the notion that the debt may be set off against a cross-claim owing by the beneficiary to the debtor on the first-mentioned claim assumes that the debt is held on trust only for that beneficiary. If there are other beneficiaries, a set-off may be denied on the ground that a jointly owned claim may not be set off against a debt owing by one only of the joint claimants.[31]

For a set-off to proceed under the insolvency legislation, the beneficial

---

[24] For example, when a creditor of a bankrupt on a negotiable instrument only holds the instrument as trustee for a third party, he may not employ it in a set-off. See *Fair* v. *M'Iver* (1812) 16 East 130; *Belcher* v. *Lloyd* (1833) 10 Bing. 310; *Lackington* v. *Combes* (1839) 6 Bing. (NC) 71; *Forster* v. *Wilson* (1843) 14 M & W 191; *London, Bombay, and Mediterranean Bank* v. *Narraway* (1872) LR 15 Eq. 93; *Tapper* v. *Matheson* (1884) NZLR 3 SC 312.

[25] *Boyd* v. *Mangles* (1874) 16 M & W 337; *In re Asphaltic Wood Pavement Company; Lee & Chapman's Case* (1885) 30 Ch. D 216; *In re W. Guthrie and Allied Companies* (1901) 4 GLR 155. See also *De Mattos* v. *Saunders* (1872) LR 7 CP 570; *In re City Life Assurance Company, Ltd; Stephenson's Case* [1926] 1 Ch. 191, 214 (as explained by Dixon J. in *Hiley* v. *Peoples Prudential Assurance Company, Ltd.* (1938) 60 CLR 468, 501–505); *Patrick Corporation Ltd. & the Companies Act* (1980) ACLC 34,268.

[26] See e.g. *Thornton* v. *Maynard* (1875) LR 10 CP 695, discussed below.

[27] See (1831) 1 & 2 Will. IV c. 56. The Bankruptcy Act 1869 replaced the Court of Bankruptcy with the London Bankruptcy Court.

[28] The Supreme Court of Judicature Act 1873, ss. 3 and 16 originally contemplated the consolidation of the London Bankruptcy Court with the newly created Supreme Court of Judicature, though the proposal was abandoned with the enactment of s. 9 of the Supreme Court of Judicature Act 1875, and was not carried into effect until the enactment of the Bankruptcy Act 1883, s. 93.

[29] The Lord Chancellor in 1921, pursuant to the power conferred upon him by the Bankruptcy Act 1914, s. 97, assigned the jurisdiction in bankruptcy to the Chancery Division of the High Court. See the Order of the Lord Chancellor, 15 Aug. 1921, No. 1741 (L. 21).

[30] *Mathieson's Trustee* v. *Burrup, Mathieson and Company* [1927] 1 Ch. 562, 569.

[31] See section 8.2 below.

title generally must have been acquired before the relevant date for determining rights of set-off,[32] so that, for example, a set-off may not be based upon an assignment or other acquisition of title that took place after that date.[33] There may, however, be a set-off if a beneficial title, though not actually acquired until after the relevant date, nevertheless reverts back to the time before then. This may occur when a bankruptcy is annulled. In *Bailey* v. *Johnson*[34] the defendant had been adjudicated a bankrupt, so that his property vested in his trustee in bankruptcy on trust for his creditors. The trustee realized the estate, and paid the proceeds into a bank. The bank was also a creditor of the defendant. Subsequently the bank itself was adjudicated bankrupt, and, after this, the defendant's bankruptcy was annulled. The bank's trustee sued the defendant for his debt owing to the bank, and the defendant sought to set off the proceeds of his estate paid into the bank. The annulment took place after the bank's bankruptcy, at which time the defendant's estate was held on trust for his general body of creditors. However, the bankruptcy legislation provides a mechanism by which, upon an annulment, the property of the debtor may 'revert' to him.[35] It was held that this operated retrospectively, and that the money should be considered as having been the defendant's when it was paid into the bank. Therefore, a set-off was allowed.

When the plaintiff is suing only as an assignor or as a trustee, the debtor in certain circumstances may be able to set off a debt owing to him by the assignor or, as the case may be, the trustee, notwithstanding that someone else is the party beneficially interested in the action. The circumstances in which this can occur are considered later.[36] However, if the assignor or the trustee is bankrupt or is a company in liquidation, the debtor's right of set-off is not derived from the insolvency legislation,[37] but rather is based upon the notion that the beneficial owner should take subject to the legal right of set-off available to the debtor against the assignor under the Statutes of Set-off, or alternatively an equitable set-off when the demands are sufficiently closely connected. Therefore, unless an equitable set-off is available, both demands must be liquidated, and also be due and payable, at the date of the action. Since the bankrupt himself is not entitled to the benefit of the claim, it would not have passed to his trustee as property of

---

[32] Compare the discussion of *MPS Constructions Pty. Ltd.* v. *Rural Bank of New South Wales* (1980) 4 ACLR 835 in section 4.3.4 above.

[33] *Middleton* v. *Pollock; ex parte Nugee* (1875) LR 20 Eq. 29.

[34] (1872) LR 7 Ex. 263.

[35] See the Insolvency Act 1986, s. 282(4), and in Australia the Bankruptcy Act 1966 (Cth.), s. 154(2).   [36] See sections 13.2 and 13.4 below.

[37] *Lee & Chapman's Case* (1885) 30 Ch. D 216, 225. See also *De Mattos* v. *Saunders* (1872) LR 7 CP 570 (discussed below) and *Popular Homes Ltd.* v. *Circuit Developments Ltd.* [1979] 2 NZLR 642, 657.

the bankrupt, in which case there is no justification for invoking the insolvency set-off section against the person for whom the bankrupt is suing. For example, in *De Mattos* v. *Saunders*[38] the plaintiff was an insured under a policy of marine insurance, and was suing the underwriter for an indemnity for a total loss on behalf of a third party who had made advances on the shipping documents. A claim under a policy of marine insurance is regarded as a claim for unliquidated damages, and accordingly cannot be set off at law under the Statutes of Set-off.[39] As a result, there was no right of set-off under the Statutes to which the third party could be made to take subject. The plaintiff had executed a deed of inspectorship under the Bankruptcy Act 1861, but it was held that the mutual credit clause in that Act could not avail the underwriter.

Alternatively, it may be that the beneficial owner of a claim is bankrupt, where the legal title is vested in someone else. The bankrupt's beneficial interest in the claim will have vested in his trustee in bankruptcy, in which case the debtor should be able to assert a set-off under the insolvency set-off section when the legal owner is suing on behalf of the bankrupt, even though the legal owner himself is solvent. In *Thornton* v. *Maynard*[40] the plaintiff as holder of several bills of exchange was suing the acceptor, though he had already been paid a dividend on the bills in the bankruptcy of the drawer. When the acceptor of a bill is bankrupt the holder in proving in the bankruptcy must give credit for anything that he received from the drawer or an indorser before lodging the proof,[41] although this principle does not apply if the acceptor is solvent. The holder may sue the acceptor for the full amount of the bill, although to the extent of anything received from the drawer he sues as trustee for him. In *Thornton* v. *Maynard* it was held that, because the holder to the extent of the dividend received from the drawer's estate was suing as trustee, the acceptor was entitled to that extent to a set-off under the bankruptcy legislation in respect of a debt owing to him by the drawer.[42]

7.3.2 *Assignment of the proceeds of a debt*

The subject of an assignment may be the *proceeds* of a debt, as opposed to the debt itself.[43] Unlike an assignment of a debt, the better view is that this does not affect mutuality as between the assignor and the debtor. Title to

---

[38] (1875) LR 7 CP 570.
[39] *Pellas & Co.* v. *The Neptune Marine Insurance Co.* (1879) 5 CPD 34.
[40] (1872) LR 10 CP 695.
[41] *In re Blackburne* (1892) 9 Morr. 249, 252; *In re Houlder* [1929] 1 Ch. 205, 212.
[42] While the claim accruing to the bankrupt estate was still contingent at the date of the bankruptcy, this is not sufficient to prevent a set-off. See section 4.4 above.
[43] See e.g. *Glegg* v. *Bromley* [1912] 2 KB 474.

the debt still remains with the assignor, so that a set-off should be available between those two parties notwithstanding that it will prevent any proceeds from being received.

7.3.3 *Subrogation*[44]

This distinction between an assignment of a debt and an assignment of the proceeds of the debt is pertinent to insurance subrogation. An insurer that has indemnified its insured is subrogated to a claim possessed by the insured against a third party who is responsible for the loss. This entitles the insurer to use the insured's name in order to sue the third party, and also to claim any money paid to the insured by the third party in reduction of the loss. It is generally accepted that the insurer has an equitable proprietary interest in any money that is in fact recovered.[45] The position is more uncertain, however, in relation to the right of action itself. The question of a proprietary interest should be crucial to set-off.[46] If the insurer does not have a proprietary interest it may be subject in a subrogation action brought in the name of the insured to a defence of set-off available to the defendant against the insured, no matter when it arose. The insurer's interest as a subrogated insurer would not affect mutuality. If, on the other hand, the insurer does have a proprietary interest in the action, the same result should follow as for an assignment[47] to the extent of the insurer's interest.[48] The question was considered by three members of the House of Lords in *Napier* v. *Hunter*,[49] though the position is still not settled. Lord Browne-Wilkinson[50] emphasized that he was not expressing a concluded view on the subject, although the tenor of his judgment suggests that he inclined against the view that a subrogated insurer does have such an interest. Lord Goff of Chieveley[51] similarly reserved his position until he had examined the authorities fully, though he said that he could see no reason in principle why the insurer's proprietary interest should not extend to the right of action as well as the proceeds. Lord Templeman, however, was more emphatic.[52] In his view, the insurer

---

[44] See also section 13.6 below.

[45] *Napier* v. *Hunter* [1993] AC 713.

[46] *In Lewenza* v. *Ruszczak* (1959) 22 DLR (2d) 167 it was held that a subrogated insurer's interest in a judgment obtained by the insured against the third party precluded the third party from setting off a judgment that he had obtained against the insured. Compare *Page* v. *Scottish Insurance Corporation* (1929) 140 LT 571, in which a set-off was denied for a number of reasons, not the least of which was that the insurer had not indemnified the insured so that it was not entitled to be subrogated to the insured's right of action.

[47] See section 7.3.1 above.

[48] See *Hiley* v. *The Peoples Prudential Assurance Co., Ltd.* (1938) 60 CLR 468, 497 in the context of a security over a debt.

[49] [1993] AC 713.

[50] [1993] AC 713, 752–3.

[51] [1993] AC 713, 745.

[52] [1993] AC 713, 736, 738.

does have an equitable proprietary interest in the right of action to the extent necessary to recoup the amount paid to the insured. This is the preferred view. But insurance subrogation in any event has been described as forming a category of its own,[53] and whatever doubts there are in this area may not extend to other species of subrogation. For example, *Jenner* v. *Morris*[54] concerned a person who made loans to another's deserted wife for the purpose of purchasing necessaries. While a person who actually supplied necessaries to a deserted wife could sue the husband at common law, the common law did not recognize a similar right in a person who merely lent money for the purpose of acquiring them. However, it was held in *Jenner* v. *Morris* that the person advancing the money for this purpose was entitled to be subrogated to the claim that the supplier otherwise would have had against the husband, and, further, that this could be set off against a judgment debt owing by him to the husband. Subrogation also applies in the context of suretyship, and in a case in New South Wales Powell J. seems to have assumed that a surety's right of subrogation could affect mutuality for the purpose of set-off.[55]

7.4 STATUTES OF SET-OFF

It is sometimes assumed that mutuality for the purpose of determining the availability of a set-off under the Statutes of Set-off similarly is determined by reference to the equitable title to the cross-demands,[56] though, as Meagher, Gummow and Lehane have noted,[57] this is not entirely accurate. The Statutes allow a set-off at law if there is mutuality by reference to the legal title to the debts. If there is not mutuality at law but there is in equity, equity nevertheless may act by analogy with the legal right of set-off available at law pursuant to the Statutes and recognize a set-off.[58]

---

[53] See Oliver L.J. in *Barclays Bank Ltd.* v. *TOSG Trust Fund Ltd.* [1984] 1 AC 626, 639.

[54] (1860) 1 Dr. & Sm. 218, affirmed (1861) 3 De G F & J 45.

[55] *A. E. Goodwin Ltd.* v. *A. G. Healing Ltd.* (1979) 7 ACLR 481, 488–9. Wood, *English and International Set-off* (1989), 943–4 also regards *In re Jeffrey's Policy* (1872) 20 WR 857 as authority for the proposition that subrogation in the context of suretyship affects mutuality, though that case instead may be explained on the ground that the payment of the money into court by the creditor constituted an admission that it was not entitled to retain the money itself but was a mere trustee.

[56] See e.g. Russell L.J. (with whose judgment Sellers L.J. agreed) in *Robbie & Co. Ltd.* v. *Witney Warehouse Co. Ltd.* [1963] 1 WLR 1324, 1339. See also *Coba Industries Ltd.* v. *Millie's Holdings (Canada) Ltd.* [1985] 6 WWR 14, 28–9.

[57] Meagher, Gummow and Lehane, *Equity Doctrines and Remedies* (3rd edn., 1992), 720–1.

[58] *Freeman* v. *Lomas* (1851) 9 Hare 109, 116; *Cavendish* v. *Geaves* (1857) 24 Beav. 163; *Cochrane* v. *Green* (1860) 9 CB(NS) 448; *Agra and Masterman's Bank, Ltd.* v. *Leighton*

Alternatively, if there is mutuality at law, though one of the debts has been assigned in equity or is held on trust for another party, a court of equity generally would regard it as unconscionable for a set-off at law to occur, and accordingly not permit the set-off.[59] But apart from these instances of equitable intervention, the Statutes themselves traditionally applied to cross-debts at law between the parties to an action at law.[60] Consider the case of an equitable assignment of a debt. The general rule is that an equitable assignee takes subject to a right of set-off accruing to the debtor against the assignor before the debtor received notice of the assignment.[61] When a cross-debt accrues to the debtor against the assignor *after* notice, the reason that a set-off is denied to the debtor against the assignee is not simply that mutuality in equity is absent. There is still mutuality at law as between the debtor and the assignor, and therefore there is a right of set-off at law. The question is whether it is unconscionable for the debtor to rely on this right of set-off otherwise available at law when the equitable title to one of the debts is in someone else.[62] Where the cross-debt was acquired after notice, it is indeed unconscionable for the debtor to rely on the set-off, and therefore equity will not permit him to do so. That this is the correct analysis is apparent if one looks instead at the position that applies when the debtor acquired the liquidated cross-claim against the assignor after the equitable assignment but before the debtor had notice of the assignment. In such a case it is recognized that the third party assignee takes subject to the debtor's right of set-off, a result that is hardly consistent with mutuality being determined solely by reference to equitable interests. The giving of notice is not necessary to complete the title of an equitable assignee.[63] Notice is desirable in order to ensure that the

(1866) LR 2 Ex. 56, 65; *Union Bank of Australia* v. *Waterston* (1894) 12 NZLR 672; *Barclays Bank Ltd.* v. *Aschaffenburger Zellstoffwerke A.G.* [1967] 1 Lloyd's Rep. 387. There are indeed some early common law cases in which it appears that the defendant was allowed to set off a debt owing to him by the person for whom the plaintiff was suing as trustee. See *Bottomley* v. *Brooke* and *Rudge* v. *Birch*, unreported but mentioned in *Winch* v. *Keeley* (1787) 1 TR 619, 621–2, though compare *Tucker* v. *Tucker* (1833) 4 B & Ad. 745. In *Bennett* v. *White* [1910] 2 KB 643 the defendant was an assignee under a statutory assignment, and so there was mutuality at law.

[59] *In re Whitehouse & Co.* (1878) 9 Ch. D. 595, 597; *In re Paraguassu Steam Tramroad Company; Black & Co.'s Case* (1872) LR 8 Ch. App. 254, 261; *Mercer* v. *Graves* (1872) LR 7 QB 499, 504.

[60] *Chitty's Blackstone* (1826) Vol. 3, 305 n. 37; *Popular Homes Limited* v. *Circuit Developments Limited* [1979] 2 NZLR 642, 655. See also *Isberg* v. *Bowden* (1853) 8 Ex. 852, as explained by Keating J. in *Watkins* v. *Clark* (1862) 12 CB(NS) 277, 281–2 ('the statutes of set-off are confined to legal debts between the parties').

[61] See section 13.2 below.

[62] See Blackburn J. in *Wilson* v. *Gabriel* (1863) 4 B & S 243, 247–8, referred to in *Christie* v. *Taunton, Delmard, Lane and Company* [1893] 2 Ch. 175, 182.

[63] *Gorringe* v. *Irwell India Rubber and Gutta Percha Works* (1886) 34 Ch. D 128; *Ward* v. *Duncombe* [1893] AC 369, 392; *In re City Life Assurance Co., Ltd.; Stephenson's Case* [1926] 1 Ch. 191, 219–20.

assignee has priority over other assignees in accordance with the rule in
Dearle v. *Hall*,[64] and in order to oblige the debtor to tender payment to the
assignee rather than the assignor.[65] It is not necessary, however, for
the equitable title to pass to the assignee as from the date of the
assignment. It is apparent then that, in the period between the assignment
and notice of the assignment, when the cross-debt was incurred, there was
not mutuality in equity between the assigned debt and the cross-debt. The
assigned debt was owing in equity to the assignee while the cross-debt was
incurred by the assignor. Accordingly, when the question of set-off later
arises, it can be seen that there is not, and never has been, mutuality in
equity. Why, then, is a set-off allowed? The reason is that a right of set-off
is available to the debtor at law under the Statutes, since the position at law
is that the assigned debt is still owing to the assignor and accordingly there
is mutuality at law. Moreover, it is not unconscionable for the debtor to
rely on this legal right, since the cross-debt was incurred before he had
notice of the equitable assignment. While there are statements in the
judgments of Sir George Jessel M.R.[66] and Lord Selborne L.C.[67] which
suggest that, where cross-demands are mutual at law but not in equity a
set-off under the Statutes will never be permitted, the allowance of a set-
off in this situation illustrates that the rule is not inflexible, and that the
relevant principle in fact is one of unconscionability. This is also evident
from the decision of the Court of Appeal in *Rother Iron Works Ltd.* v.
Canterbury Precision Engineers Ltd.,[68] which is considered later in the
context of company receiverships.[69] As Jeffrey J. remarked in the New
South Wales Supreme Court in *West Street Properties Pty. Ltd.* v.
Jamison,[70] 'Lack of mutuality in equity can be a reason for denying a right
to set-off at law, . . . but that is not to say that its presence is invariably
necessary before allowing any right of set-off at all'. This analysis
admittedly does not sit comfortably with the view which has been
expressed in recent times, that the principles, as well as the courts, of law
and equity have now been fused.[71] However, that view has been
criticized,[72] and indeed the notion that there has been a fusion of the

[64] (1828) 3 Russ. 1.   [65] *Brice* v. *Bannister* (1878) 3 QBD 569.
[66] *In re Whitehouse & Co.* (1878) 9 Ch. D 595, 597.
[67] *In re Paraguassu Steam Tramroad Company; Black & Co.'s Case* (1872) LR 8 Ch. App.
254, 261.   [68] [1974] 1 QB 1.   [69] See section 13.3.1 below.
[70] [1974] 2 NSWLR 435, 441–2.
[71] *United Scientific Holdings, Ltd.* v. *Burnley Borough Council* [1978] AC 904.
[72] Baker, 'The Future of Equity' (1977) 93 *Law Quarterly Review* 529; Meagher, Gummow
and Lehane, *Equity Doctrines and Remedies* (3rd edn., 1992), 67–8; Martin, 'Fusion, Fallacy
and Confusion; A Comparative Study' [1994] *The Conveyancer* 13. Sir Peter Millett writing
extra-judicially ('Equity—The Road Ahead' (1995) 9 *Tolley's Trust Law International* 35, 37)

principles does not provide a satisfactory framework for explaining the allowance of a set-off in the situation considered above.

When liquidated cross-demands are mutual having regard to equitable rights, it is not necessary for the defendant show some additional 'equity' to support an equitable set-off, since equity in such a case may act by analogy with the legal right under the Statutes. Observations to the contrary[73] are difficult to support.

7.5 ASCERTAINED BENEFICIAL INTERESTS

It has been said that, in order to achieve mutuality where a debt is held on trust for a beneficiary, the beneficial ownership must be clear and ascertained without inquiry.[74] However, this requires elaboration. The cases referred to as authority for this proposition[75] concerned either a residuary legatee under a will or a person entitled under an intestacy, where the administration of the estate had not been completed. Prior to completion of the administration the legatee or the person in fact does not have a beneficial interest in the estate,[76] and these cases illustrate that the court will not take an account of the assets of the estate and of the debts and charges that still have to be satisfied out of it so as to allow a present set-off to the extent of the interest that it is anticipated that the legatee or the person will have in the future. This should apply in relation to both insolvency set-off and set-off between solvent parties.

Alternatively, it may be asserted that there is a presently existing beneficial interest in a debt, though this is dependent upon certain facts being proved. In this situation the result may vary depending upon whether insolvency set-off is in issue, or whether the question instead relates to the availability of an equitable set-off by analogy with the Statutes of Set-off.[77] In the case of insolvency set-off any perceived difficulty in ascertaining whether there is a present beneficial interest should not be a sufficient

said that this fusion theory is now widely discredited. In *Bank of Boston Connecticut* v. *European Grain and Shipping Ltd.* [1989] 1 AC 1056, 1109 the House of Lords remarked that the Judicature Acts, 'while making important changes in procedure, did not alter and were not intended to alter the rights of the parties'.

[73] *Middleton* v. *Pollock; ex parte Nugee* (1875) LR 20 Eq. 29, 36–7; *Welton* v. *Harnett* (1886) 7 NSWR 74.

[74] Wood, *English and International Set-off* (1989), 779–80, 1081–2.

[75] *Bishop* v. *Church* (1748) 3 Atk. 691; *Ex parte Morier; in re Willis, Percival, & Co.* (1879) 12 Ch. D 491; *Phillips* v. *Howell* [1901] 2 Ch. 773.

[76] See *Commissioner of Stamp Duties (Queensland)* v. *Livingston* [1965] AC 694, and the comments of James L.J. in *Ex parte Morier* (1879) 12 Ch. D 491, 496, and generally section 9.9.1 below. Similarly, the object of a discretionary trust does not have a legal or beneficial interest in the trust property. See *Gartside* v. *IRC* [1968] AC 553.

[77] See section 1.6 above.

reason for denying a set-off, given the statutory injunction in the insolvency set-off section that an account 'shall be taken' in the event of mutual credit and mutual dealings. The appropriate enquiries should be undertaken. The position is more difficult, however, when an equitable set-off arising by analogy with the Statutes of Set-off is in issue. The question has been considered on two occasions recently by the Court of Appeal in the context of nominee bank accounts. In both *Bhogal* v. *Punjab National Bank*[78] and *Uttamchandami* v. *Central Bank of India*[79] a bank alleged that an account in the name of A in truth was held for the benefit of B. When A sued the bank for payment of the balance on the account, and applied for summary judgment, the bank argued that it was entitled to leave to defend on the basis of a set-off arising out of an indebtedness of B on another account. Usually the defendant in an application for summary judgment will be granted leave to defend if he shows an arguable case, though in *Bhogal* and *Uttamchandani* it was held that the bank was not entitled to unconditional leave to defend in the absence of clear and indisputable evidence that the account was merely a nominee account. There are two comments to make in respect of this. The first is that reference was made in the judgments to some remarks made some time earlier in the Court of Appeal in *Ex parte Morier*,[80] though that case was concerned with the position of a residuary legatee prior to completion of the administration of the estate. Accordingly, it was not a case of a dispute as to whether there was a beneficial interest. Rather, it was accepted that there was no presently existing beneficial interest, and the court held that it would not take`an account of the assets of the estate and the debts and liabilities payable out of it in order to ascertain what the beneficial interest ultimately would be. The second is that there was considerable emphasis placed on the responsibilities of banks to honour their obligations promptly. Both Dillon and Bingham L.JJ. in *Bhogal* quoted with approval a passage from the judgment of Scott J. at first instance who, in rejecting the bank's defence, said that,[81] 'The commercial banking commitment that a bank enters into with a person who deposits money with it is just as needful of immediate performance as are a bank's obligations under a letter of credit or bank guarantee', while Bingham L.J.[82] referred to another comment by Scott J. to the effect that he was not satisfied that banks should be treated like other debtors in relation to summary judgment. When a debtor asserts that the debt is held on trust, and that accordingly he should be entitled to leave to defend on the basis of an

---

[78] [1988] 2 All ER 296.
[79] Unreported, but noted in (1989) 139 *New Law Journal* 222.
[80] (1879) 12 Ch. D 491 (C.A.).   [81] [1988] 2 All ER 296, 299–300, 306.
[82] [1988] 2 All ER 296, 306.

equitable set-off available against the beneficiary of the trust derived from the Statutes, these statements suggest that the view that an arguable case is not sufficient, and that the defendant must show indisputable evidence of the trust, may not be of general application. Certainly the residuary legatee cases do not support any such general principle.

7.6 SECURITY OVER A DEBT

7.6.1 *Introduction*

A debt owing by a person itself may be the subject of a security.[83] However, a security over a debt may take a number of forms, and it is appropriate to consider briefly the results that may follow in relation to each of them.

7.6.2 *Assignment by way of mortgage*

In the first place, a debt may be assigned by way of mortgage. Insofar as set-offs between the debtor and the mortgagor/creditor are concerned, the relevant principles essentially are as follows. To the extent of the amount secured[84] the assignment has the result that there is not mutuality in equity, and this is so whether or not default has occurred under the mortgage. However, the mortgagee, being an assignee, is subject to the same principle applicable generally to assignments, that the assignee takes subject to any equitable set-off or any right of set-off that accrued to the debtor under the Statutes of Set-off before he had notice of the assignment.[85]

What if the assigned debt exceeds the debt owing by the mortgagor to the mortgagee for which it is security? In Australia Dixon J. in *Hiley* v. *The Peoples Prudential Assurance Co., Ltd.*[86] said, in the context of a debt owing by a company in liquidation which had been assigned by way of security to a third party, that:

In the third place, it is settled that if a creditor of a liquidating company, that is, the person entitled to a legal chose in action, has before the winding up assigned it equitably to a third party by way of charge as security for a debt owing by him to the third party but of smaller amount so that there is a residue to be paid over to the assignor, the liquidating company may set off against the residue a cross-demand upon the assignor.

---

[83] See also section 2.18 above.
[84] Compare the discussion below in relation to the situation where the assigned debt is greater than the secured debt.   [85] See section 13.2 below.
[86] (1938) 60 CLR 468, 497.

As a general proposition this is doubtful. There is an apparent lack of mutuality for the purpose of the insolvency set-off section,[87] since the mortgagee has security over the *whole* of the debt assigned to him, and there is no part in which the mortgagor alone is beneficially interested. The question is whether this is an instance in which a set-off nevertheless is appropriate. Prima facie it is not. The security in this case is a debt. If the debtor on the assigned debt is insolvent the true value of the security will not be the face value of that debt. It will be less, depending on the dividend payable by the debtor. Accordingly, where a mortgagee has a debt of £x owing to him which is secured by a debt of £y owing by a debtor in liquidation, it would hardly be fair to allow a set-off as between the mortgagor and the debtor to the extent of £(y − x), since this would deplete the security. Dixon J.'s proposition assumes that, if £x is still owing by the debtor after the set-off, the mortgagee's position is protected, although it is apparent that this will not be the case if the debtor is insolvent. It may nevertheless be appropriate to allow a set-off in the circumstances contemplated by Dixon J., if two conditions are satisfied. The first, which is suggested by Wood,[88] is that the security should be presently enforceable, so that the mortgagee's position after taking into account the set-off is readily ascertainable. Unless this limitation is imposed, the mortgagee may find when his security later becomes enforceable that it has been depleted by a set-off as between the mortgagor and the debtor. The second is that, in any event, the debtor on the assigned debt should be solvent, so that, after setting off an amount equal to £(y − x), the remaining £x owing by the debtor in fact is worth £x, or at least the mortgagee's position must be secured in some other way. There is nothing objectionable in allowing a set-off when a debt is assigned by way of security and the creditor on that debt is insolvent, though there is when the debtor is the insolvent party. Indeed, the case referred to by Dixon J. as authority for his proposition was an instance where the creditor rather than the debtor was insolvent. *Lee & Chapman's Case*[89] concerned a charge granted by a company over a debt owing by the Commissioners of Sewers. The company later went into liquidation. There was no suggestion that the Commissioners were insolvent, and accordingly the decision to allow the Commissioners to set off their debt to the extent of the amount over and above the secured debt owing by the company was not unfair. While the question of mutuality was not discussed, the position would appear to be that, when a person grants security over a debt and is himself

---

[87] See section 7.1 above.

[88] Wood, *English and International Set-off* (1989), 782.

[89] *In re Asphaltic Wood Pavement Company; Lee & Chapman's Case* (1885) 30 Ch. D 216. See also *Union Bank of Australia* v. *Waterston* (1894) 12 NZLR 672 (agreement for set-off between the mortgagor and the debtor).

liable to the debtor, he is regarded as having a sufficient interest in the surplus so as to satisfy the requirement of mutuality if the security is presently enforceable and the debtor is solvent so that the secured creditor's interest is sufficiently secured.

A similar principle has been recognized in the context of an auctioneer's lien.[90] An auctioneer has a lien on the proceeds of sale of goods for his charges and expenses. If the goods have been removed by the purchaser before payment in full, the auctioneer may sue for the price, although the purchaser is permitted to set off in that action a debt owing to him by the vendor to the extent that the proceeds would be handed over to the vendor.[91] The auctioneer admittedly would have had a prior interest in the whole of the claim in order to satisfy the lien, though once again mutuality should be regarded as satisfied if the purchaser is solvent and the auctioneer's lien accordingly is protected.

What about the position as between the mortgagee and the debtor? Wood[92] has suggested that, if the mortgagor is not in default, the assigned debt cannot be set off against a debt that the mortgagee owes to the debtor, on the ground that the mortgagor's interest in the assigned debt in the form of the equity of redemption will have been used to pay the debt owing by the mortgagee. It would mean that the mortgagee will have foreclosed before default by the mortgagor. This seems correct. The fact that the mortgagor still has the equity of redemption means that he still has a proprietary interest in the assigned debt which will destroy mutuality as between the mortgagee and the debtor. However, as Wood has pointed out,[93] the cases suggest that the result is different if the mortgagee is enforcing the debt after default. Thus, where an insurance broker had taken out a policy of marine insurance in his own name, so that he could sue upon it, and moreover the broker had a general lien on the policy for the balance of the insured's account with him exceeding the claim on the policy, the broker upon being sued by the underwriter's assignees in bankruptcy for unpaid premiums for which he was personally liable was allowed to set off the underwriter's liability on the policy arising out of a loss.[94] In addition, where an agent selling the goods of his principal was

---

[90] See section 9.7.4 below.

[91] *Holmes* v. *Tutton* (1855) 5 El. & Bl. 65, 82. See also *Manley & Sons, Ltd.* v. *Berkett* [1912] 2 KB 329.

[92] Wood, *English and International Set-off* (1989), 780, 916.

[93] Wood, *English and International Set-off* (1989), 919–21. In addition to the cases referred to below, see *Moore* v. *Jervis* (1845) 2 Coll. 60, in which Knight Bruce V.C. said (at 71) that the bank had an equitable interest in the promissory note deposited with it as security sufficient to support a set-off against the maker of the note.

[94] *Parker* v. *Beasley* (1814) 2 M & S 423 (in which the brokers had a lien by virtue of their accepting bills of exchange on the credit of the goods insured); *Davies* v. *Wilkinson* (1828) 4 Bing. 573.

entitled by virtue of a lien on the goods to receive payment of the price, it was held that an agreement between the purchaser and the agent's assignees in bankruptcy by which the price was set off against a debt owing by the agent to the third party was binding on the principal.[95]

A creditor may have assigned the debt by way of security to a third party, but the third party in any event is in a position to satisfy the secured debt owing to him by the creditor from other securities. In this situation the case will be treated as one in which the assigned debt in fact continued to be owed to the creditor, and the debtor will be permitted to employ his liability on the debt in a set-off in the creditor's bankruptcy when the debt is redeemed. If however the third party, instead of having recourse to the other securities, had called upon the debtor to pay, and the debtor did pay, the amount of the debt, the creditor's trustee in bankruptcy may be ordered to repay to the debtor the amount paid by him to the third party from the surplus proceeds of the other securities remitted back to the trustee after the secured debt has been paid in full.[96]

7.6.3 *Floating security*[97]

A company instead may grant a floating security over its assets, including debts owing to it. Before crystallization, the existence of the floating security does not affect any right of set-off accruing to the debtor against the company. Accordingly, the debtor is entitled to a set-off notwithstanding that at the time that either of the cross-debts were incurred he was aware of the existence of the floating security.[98] When crystallization occurs, the security attaches to the company's assets, and any debts owing to the company and coming within the ambit of the security are assigned in equity to the secured creditor.[99] The principles discussed above in the context of mortgages then become relevant, on the basis that an assignment occurred at the date of crystallization. If after crystallization the company goes into liquidation, a debt otherwise expressed to be owing to the company at the date of the liquidation will already have been assigned to the secured creditor, and so the debtor will not be able to rely on the insolvency set-off section,[100] except, in the circumstances outlined above,[101] to the extent that the debt in question exceeds the amount

[95] *Hudson* v. *Granger* (1821) 5 B & Ald. 27, and see also *Warner* v. *M'Kay* (1836) 1 M & W 591.
[96] *Ex parte Staddon; in re Wise* (1843) 3 Mont. D & De G 256, 12 LJ Bcy. 39.
[97] See also section 13.3.1 below.
[98] *Biggerstaff* v. *Rowatt's Wharf, Ltd.* [1896] 2 Ch. 93.
[99] *N. W. Robbie & Co. Ltd.* v. *Witney Warehouse Co. Ltd.* [1963] 1 WLR 1324.
[100] This is implicit in *Handley Page Ltd.* v. *Commissioners of Customs and Excise and Rockwell Machine Tool Company Ltd.* [1970] 2 Lloyd's Rep. 459.
[101] See section 7.6.2 above.

secured. The question whether this will continue to apply if the security is redeemed by the company after its liquidation is considered below.[102]

7.6.4 *Fixed equitable charge*

A third possibility is a fixed equitable charge on a debt taking effect as a mere encumbrance, as opposed to an assignment. This form of charge creates in equity a specific charge on the proceeds of the debt as soon as they are received.[103] However, while an equitable charge also confers a form of proprietary interest in the debt itself, in the sense that the chargor no longer has an unfettered title to deal with it, and upon default the chargee is entitled to realize the debt through the appointment of a receiver or by disposing of it without the chargor's consent so as to confer upon the transferee an unencumbered title,[104] it does not purport to transfer the beneficial ownership title in the debt.[105] For this reason it has been said that the fact that a debt is the subject of a fixed charge does not affect mutuality as between the debtor and the creditor/chargor, so that the chargee should take subject to any right of set-off as between those parties whether arising before or after the debtor has notice of the charge.[106] The better view, however, is that an equitable charge indeed has the same effect upon mutuality as a mortgage. The important point is that an equitable charge, while it does not involve a full transfer of the ownership, nevertheless confers an immediate proprietary interest in the debt,[107] so that it is not merely a security over the proceeds.[108] If the chargor becomes bankrupt the charged debt would not vest in his trustee for the benefit of creditors generally, in which case it could not be the subject of a set-off under the insolvency set-off section as between the chargor and the debtor.[109] Thus, in *Lee & Chapman's Case*[110] the security under consideration appears to have been a charge, and it was held that a set-off

---

[102] See section 7.6.5 below.

[103] *Siebe Gorman & Co. Ltd.* v. *Barclays Bank Ltd.* [1979] 2 Lloyd's Rep. 142, 159.

[104] If the instrument creating the charge has not included an express power of sale or a right to appoint a receiver, the chargee may apply to the court for an order for either remedy.

[105] Gough, *Company Charges* (2nd edn., 1996), 18–19.

[106] Goode, 'Centre Point' [1984] *Journal of Business Law* 172, and see also Grantham, 'The Impact of Security on Set-off' [1989] *Journal of Business Law* 377, 387–8.

[107] This immediate and attached security interest should be distinguished from the interest which the holder of a floating security has prior to crystallization. While this has been described as a present security, it is, as Professor Goode has explained (*Legal Problems of Credit and Security* (2nd edn., 1988), 49), a security over a fund of assets without attaching to any particular asset. This analysis may provide a solution to the problem that troubled Grantham, 'The Impact of a Security Interest on Set-off' [1989] *Journal of Business Law* 377, 386–7.

[108] Compare an assignment of the proceeds of a debt, for which see section 7.3.2 above.

[109] See the discussion in *Gye* v. *McIntyre* (1991) 171 CLR 609, 626–7 in relation to a claim in tort that does not vest in the trustee in bankruptcy, and also *De Mattos* v. *Saunders* (1872) LR 7 CP 570, 582. [110] (1885) 30 Ch. D 216.

Set-off

was not available for a set-off as between the debtor and the creditor in the creditor's liquidation to the extent of the amount of the debt that was required to discharge the security. Similarly, when the debtor on the charged debt is bankrupt, any proof in the bankruptcy would be lodged for the benefit of the chargee, not the chargor, so that it should not be the subject of a set-off in respect of a debt owing by the chargor to the debtor.

Insofar as set-off under the Statutes of Set-off is concerned, the availability of a set-off as against a debt the subject of an equitable charge similarly should be subject to the same principles as for a mortgage. In other words, the equitable chargee should only take subject to a right of set-off that accrued to the debtor against the chargor before he had notice of the charge.[111] When the cross-debt arose after notice there is still admittedly mutuality at law, so that the Statutes prima facie apply. On the other hand, it would be unconscionable for the debtor to base a defence on a cross-debt that accrued to him after he was aware that someone else had a proprietary interest in the debt that he owed,[112] and the better view is that he will not be permitted to rely on any such defence in an action to enforce the debt.[113] This is consistent with the floating security cases.[114] While in these cases the courts said that crystallization of the security brought about an equitable assignment of the debt in favour of the debenture-holder, in some of them the security in fact provided for a charge and not a mortgage,[115] and they illustrate that a charge is considered to have a similar effect to an assignment as far as rights of set-off are concerned. In New South Wales Jeffrey J. evidently accepted this position in *West Street Properties Pty. Ltd.* v. *Jamison*[116] when he referred, in the context of a crystallized floating charge, to the principle 'which prevents a cross-action for a legal debt from being maintained against a plaintiff suing on behalf of an equitable chargee where the substantial consequence of doing so would be to allow the defendant, as no more than an unsecured creditor of the plaintiff, to defeat the equitable chargee's security'. Further, in a case in New Zealand it was assumed that the same principle applies as for a mortgage.[117]

---

[111] Compare *Rother Iron Works Ltd.* v. *Canterbury Precision Engineers Ltd.* [1974] 1 QB 1 (see section 13.3.1 below) in the context of a receiver who carried on the company's business.

[112] The approach of James L.J. in *Roxburghe* v. *Cox* (1881) 17 Ch. D 520, 526 would appear to be equally applicable to an equitable charge.

[113] See the discussion of mutuality in the context of the Statutes of Set-off in section 7.4 above.   [114] See section 13.3.1 below.

[115] See e.g. *N. W. Robbie & Co. Ltd.* v. *Witney Warehouse Co. Ltd.* [1963] 1 WLR 1324 (esp. at 1326 where the terms of the security are set out), in which it is apparent that the security took the form of a charge, and also the discussion in *Biggerstaff* v. *Rowatt's Wharf, Ltd.* [1896] 2 Ch. 93 (the terms of the security being set out at 94).

[116] [1974] 2 NSWLR 435, 441.

[117] *Dalgety and Co. Ltd.* v. *National Mortgage and Agency Co. Ltd.* (1910) 13 GLR 379.

7.6.5 *Redemption of the security*

When a debt is the subject of a security, and the security consisting of the debt is redeemed, the full beneficial title reverts to the security provider, and rights of set-off should be determined accordingly. Therefore, in a subsequent liquidation of the security provider the debt should be able to be set off against a cross-debt owing to the debtor. However, what if the security is redeemed *after* the security provider's liquidation? Wood suggests that it is immaterial that mutuality as between the debtor and the security provider is re-established after the liquidation in this manner, so that a set-off should proceed.[118] Ordinarily this would be correct. It is supported by the decision of the High Court of Australia in *Hiley* v. *The Peoples Prudential Assurance Company, Ltd.*[119] However, there is one situation in which a set-off may not occur, and that is where the debt the subject of the security was incurred to the security provider *after* a floating security had already crystallized and the security provider's business was being carried on by a receiver for the benefit of the secured creditor.[120] In such a case the security provider would never have had an equitable interest in the debt prior to the liquidation. At the time it came into existence it was the subject of an immediate assignment to the secured creditor. Accordingly, the case would not be the same as in *Hiley*, in which there was merely a suspension of mutuality. The company in that case was owed the debt, it assigned it by way of mortgage, and it redeemed the debt after its liquidation. This should be compared to the situation under discussion, where the security provider was never owed the debt free of the security.[121] If the debt is redeemed after the liquidation, it would not be a case of suspension of mutuality but rather of acquiring a beneficial interest after liquidation.

---

[118] Wood, *English and International Set-off* (1989), 921–2.
[119] (1938) 60 CLR 468. See section 2.8 above.
[120] Chilwell J.'s *dictum* in *Rendell* v. *Doors and Doors Ltd.* [1975] 2 NZLR 191, 202–3, criticized in Wood, *English and Internation Set-off* (1989), 922, should be understood in this context.
[121] The comments of Deane J. in *Federal Commissioner of Taxation* v. *Everett* (1978) 21 ALR 625, 644, referring to *In re Lind* [1915] 2 Ch. 345, 360 in relation to an assignment of future property, are also relevant here.

8

Mutality—Same Parties

8.1 INTRODUCTION

A basic principle of the law of set-off is that, in the absence of an agency or a trust, A's right to sue B may not be set off against A's indebtedness to C. This applies where B and C are related companies,[1] and also where C is a director of company B.[2]

8.2 JOINT CLAIMS AND LIABILITIES

8.2.1 *The general principle*

The requirement of same parties often finds its expression in the rule that, while joint debtors may set off their debt against a cross-demand possessed by them jointly against the creditor,[3] a joint demand generally may not be set off against a separate demand. Thus, in the case of a partnership, the joint indebtedness of the members of the partnership may not be set off against a debt owing separately to one or more of the members,[4] and the separate indebtedness of one of the members may not be set off against an obligation owing to the firm.[5] Indeed, an agreement between one partner

---

[1] See in this regard *The Evelpidis Era* [1981] 1 Lloyd's Rep. 54.

[2] *Re Barker; ex parte Michell* (1958) 18 ABC 195.

[3] See e.g. *Forster* v. *Wilson* (1843) 12 M & W 191.

[4] *M'Gillivray* v. *Simson* (1826) 2 Car. & P 320, affirmed 5 LJOSKB 53; *Tyso* v. *Pettit* (1879) 40 LT 132; *Re Jane; ex parte The Trustee* (1914) 110 LT 556. See also *Addis* v. *Knight* (1817) 2 Mer. 117; *In re Pennington and Owen, Ltd.* [1925] 1 Ch. 825. Compare *James* v. *Kynnier* (1799) 5 Ves. Jun. 108, in which the sum paid by the partner to the creditor of the partnership was held to constitute payment of the partnership debt, and it was not considered to give rise to a separate debt owing by the creditor to the partner.

[5] *Ex parte Riley* (1731) Kel. W 24; *Ex parte Twogood* (1805) 11 Ves. Jun. 517; *Ex parte Soames; in re Pestell* (1833) 3 Deac. & Ch. 320; *France* v. *White* (1839) 6 Bing. (NC) 33; *Baker* v. *Gent* (1892) 9 TLR 159. See also *Middleton* v. *Pollock, ex parte Nugee* (1875) LR 20 Eq. 29; *Bowyear* v. *Pawson* (1881) 6 QBD 540; *McEwan* v. *Crombie* (1883) 25 Ch. D 175; *Tapper* v. *Matheson* (1884) NZLR 3 SC 312. In *Ex parte Ross; in re Fisher* (1817) Buck 125, a firm consisting of two partners was dissolved, although the business was continued by one of the former partners. It was held that a debt due to the former partners could not be set off against a liability incurred by the remaining partner in the business after the dissolution. However, compare the marginal note to this case, which is not accurate.

and his separate creditor, by which that partner's liability is to be set off against the creditor's indebtedness to the partnership, may be impugned in equity by the other partners to the extent of their interest in the debt if the creditor had notice that in fact it was a partnership debt.[6] Even if all the partners separately are indebted to a creditor of the firm, the separate debts nonetheless give rise to separate claims, and may not be set off against a liability of the creditor to the partnership.[7] Conversely, in *Ex parte Christie*[8] the partners were jointly indebted to a creditor, who was indebted to each of the partners separately, and a set-off was denied in the creditor's bankruptcy.

The parties nevertheless may act to bring about mutuality. It may be agreed that a firm is to be liable for the separate debts of its members, and that these separate debts should be set off against any indebtedness to the firm.[9] Similarly the conduct of the parties may be such as to indicate an agreement that a claim possessed by a partner against a third party should be amalgamated with a debt owing by himself and his partners to that party.[10] In each of these cases, however, the agreement will not be effective in a bankruptcy if it has not been carried into effect prior to the bankruptcy.[11] Alternatively, if it is the member who is a separate creditor, his right to sue may be assigned to the firm, which may then set off its joint indebtedness.[12] A more common situation arises when a partner retires, for he still remains liable for the debts incurred by the firm before his retirement. But if a particular creditor has agreed to a novation, so that the firm constituted by the remaining partners is to be treated as the debtor and the old firm which included the retired partner is discharged, that debt may be set off against a debt subsequently incurred by the creditor to the new firm.[13] Without a novation the partnership in debt would be differently constituted from the partnership in credit, and mutuality would be lacking.[14]

It may be that the joint creditors on a debt agree that the debt should be

---

[6] See *Piercy* v. *Fynney* (1871) LR 12 Eq. 69, although compare Lord Esher M.R. in *Harper* v. *Marten* (1895) 11 TLR 368.   [7] *Tyso* v. *Pettit* (1879) 40 LT 132.

[8] (1804) 10 Ves. Jun. 105.

[9] *Kinnerley* v. *Hossack* (1809) 2 Taunt. 170. Obviously there must be some evidence of an agreement for payment by means of a set-off. A mere understanding by one party is not sufficient. See *Ex parte Soames; in re Pestell* (1833) 3 Deac. & Ch. 320, 324, and also *Tyso* v. *Pettit* (1879) 40 LT 132.

[10] *Ell* v. *Harper* (1886) NZLR 4 SC 307.

[11] *British Eagle International Air Lines Ltd.* v. *Compagnie Nationale Air France* [1975] 1 WLR 758, discussed in section 12.1 below.

[12] Compare *Watts* v. *Christie* (1849) 11 Beav. 546 (discussed in section 2.7.3 above), where the assignment took place in circumstances such that any set-off would have constituted a fraudulent preference.

[13] *Burgess* v. *Morton* (1894) 10 TLR 339, reversed on other grounds [1896] AC 136.

[14] As in *Re Jane; ex parte The Trustee* (1914) 110 LT 556.

severed.[15] If the debtor is a party to the agreement this may take effect by way of novation, by which the joint claim is extinguished and replaced by a separate claim in favour of each creditor for his proportion. Each creditor would then be able to employ his separate claim in a set-off against a debt that he owes to the debtor. Alternatively, if the debtor is not a party, an agreement amongst the creditors themselves to sever the joint claim may take effect by way of equitable assignment of part of the debt to each creditor.[16] The creditors would then hold the debt jointly as trustees for themselves as tenants in common of distinct portions of the debt,[17] and questions of set-off would be determined by reference to the same principles applicable generally to equitable assignments of debts.[18] Thus, each creditor in respect of his portion would take subject to any right of set-off available to the debtor against the joint debt before he received notice of the assignment. To the extent that the debtor may raise the defence against only one of the creditors, a right of contribution should be available against the other creditors.

8.2.2 *Insolvency set-off and partnerships*

In order for the insolvency set-off section to apply in relation to partnership liabilities, the partnership itself must be in the process of being wound up under the Insolvent Partnerships Order 1994, either as an unregistered company[19] or where a joint bankruptcy petition is presented by all members of the insolvent partnership.[20] Therefore, if an action is brought to recover a debt owing to a partnership, the insolvency set-off section will not apply in relation to a cross-claim against the partnership merely because one of the partners has become bankrupt.[21]

---

[15] Compare *Bowyear* v. *Pawson* (1881) 6 QBD 540, in which a creditor entered into an agreement by which he assigned the claim to himself and another person in equal shares as tenants in common, though Watkin Williams and Mathew JJ. held that this was not sufficient to sever the debt so as to entitle that other person to set off his interest in it against a separate debt that he owed to the debtor.

[16] Since it is not possible to have a legal assignment of part of a debt, the assignment in this situation must of necessity be an equitable assignment. See *McIntyre* v. *Guy* (1994) 122 ALR 289, 295. [17] *McIntyre* v. *Gye* (1994) 122 ALR 289, 295, 297.

[18] See *Adamopoulos* v. *Olympic Airways SA* (1991) 25 NSWLR 75, 87, and generally sections 7.3.1 above and 13.2 below.

[19] See arts. 7, 8, 9 and 10 of the Insolvent Partnerships Order 1994 (S.1. 1994/2421), as well as Pt V (in particular s. 221(1)) of the Insolvency Act 1986.

[20] See art. 11 and Sch. 7 of the Insolvent Partnerships Order 1994. In Australia see the Bankruptcy Act 1966 (Cth.), ss. 45, 46 and 56. Note that in Australia a partnership of more than 5 members may be wound up under the Corporations Law as a Part 5.7 body, in which case the set-off section (s. 553 C) applies. See s. 583.

[21] *Staniforth* v. *Fellowes* (1814) 1 Marsh. 184; *New Quebrada Company, Ltd.* v. *Carr* (1869) LR 4 CP 651; *London, Bombay and Mediterranean Bank* v. *Narraway* (1872) LR 15 Eq. 93

8.2.3 *Equitable interests*

Since mutuality in insolvency set-off is determined by reference to the equitable interests of the parties,[22] a set-off may proceed despite the fact that at law one claim may be joint and the other separate, provided that in equity the same parties are interested in the cross-demands. Consequently a debt owing to a number of creditors (C1 and C2) jointly may be set off against the separate indebtedness of one of the creditors (C1), if C1 and C2 are merely trustees of the debt for C1 so that he is the only person beneficially interested in it.[23] Conversely, a set-off may be denied where there is mutuality at law but not in equity.[24]

We have seen that the Statutes of Set-off[25] allow a set-off if there is mutuality by reference to the legal title to the debts concerned, while equity acting by analogy with the Statutes will confer a right of set-off if there is mutuality in equity but not at law. Further, if a creditor holds a claim on trust for or has assigned it in equity to someone else, equity may regard it as unconscionable for a set-off at law to occur as between the debtor and the creditor, and accordingly not permit it. The effect of these principles is that the same result often follows in relation to the Statutes as if mutuality were determined by reference to equitable titles.

8.2.4 *Exceptions*

The courts have been reluctant to depart from the rule that a joint demand and a separate demand may not be brought into an account. Nevertheless, there are a number of situations in which a set-off has been allowed, despite an apparent absence of mutuality. Some of these in truth are not exceptions to the principle of mutuality, in the sense that a set-off was allowed under the insolvency set-off section where there was not mutuality, but rather are examples of equitable set-off for which mutuality is not a strict requirement.[26]

(1) In *Ex parte Hanson*[27] one of two joint debtors on a bond given as

---

[22] See section 7.3.1 above.

[23] Compare *In re Imperial Mercantile Credit Association; ex parte Smith and Ford* (1867) 15 WR 1069, in which the beneficial entitlement of one of the trustees only related to the interest payable on the debt. Compare also *Ex parte Morier; in re Willis, Percival, & Co.* (1879) 12 Ch. D 491 (discussed in section 9.9.1 below), in which the estate had not been fully administered by the executors, and so a trust as yet had not been imposed in favour of the executor who was the residuary legatee.

[24] *Tapper* v. *Matheson* (1884) NZLR 3 SC 312.

[25] For mutuality in relation to the Statutes of Set-off, see section 7.4 above.

[26] See *Bank of New Zealand* v. *Harry M. Miller & Co. Ltd.* (1992) 26 NSWLR 48, 55, and generally section 1.7.6 above.

[27] (1811) 18 Ves. Jun. 232, affirming (1806) 12 Ves. Jun. 346. See also *Ex parte Hippens; in re Sikes* (1826) 2 Gl. & J 93.

security for a debt had only joined in the bond as a surety. Lord Eldon held that the person who was the principal debtor was entitled in equity to employ the joint debt in a set-off against a separate claim that he had against the creditor. A set-off was allowed because 'the joint debt was nothing more than a security for the separate debt; and upon equitable considerations a creditor, who has a joint security for a separate debt, cannot resort to that security without allowing what he has received on the separate account'.[28] A similar principle was applied in *Hamp* v. *Jones*.[29] A judgment had been obtained at law against both Hamp and his bailiff for damages for wrongful distress. In addition, Hamp had a separate claim against the judgment creditor. Because the demands were not mutual they could not be set off at law. However, Hamp had agreed to indemnify the bailiff on the judgment, and so Sir Lancelot Shadwell V.C. considered that it was appropriate that Hamp should be entitled to set off the judgment against his separate claim, the Vice Chancellor commenting that,[30] 'If, as the bill states, Mr. Hamp has agreed to indemnify his bailiff, that, it seems to me, is a reason for the interference of the Court'. Nevertheless, the allowance of a set-off in a case such as this should be approached with caution. While in *Hamp* v. *Jones* the bill alleged that the defendant was insolvent (though not yet bankrupt), the courts may be reluctant to allow an equitable set-off based upon a private agreement for an indemnity provided by one party to another if the purpose in truth was to obtain an advantage over other creditors in an ensuing bankruptcy by means of a set-off.

The common law courts, in the exercise of what has been described as a form of equitable jurisdiction for the purpose of preventing absurdity or injustice,[31] will permit a set-off of judgments in appropriate cases.[32] In exercising this jurisdiction the courts have been prepared to allow a set-off where A has a judgment against B and C, and B has a separate judgment against A.[33] However, in these cases there was no question of bankruptcy. If there is a bankruptcy, a set-off of judgments will not be permitted in circumstances extending beyond the insolvency set-off section.[34]

---

[28] (1811) 18 Ves. Jun. 232, 233–4 per Lord Eldon.   [29] (1840) 9 LJ Ch. 258.
[30] (1840) 9 LJ Ch. 258.   [31] *Edwards* v. *Hope* (1885) 14 QBD 922, 926.
[32] See section 1.4.3 above.
[33] *Roberts* v. *Biggs* Barnes 146; *Mitchell* v. *Oldfield* (1791) 4 TR 123; *Dennie* v. *Elliott* (1795) 2 H Bl. 587. Compare *Bourne* v. *Benett* (1827) 4 Bing. 423, 1 Moo. & P 141, in which there was the additional element that one of the defendants against whom judgment was given in fact had agreed to indemnify the other parties against the judgment, so that he was principally liable *inter se*. It was held that the judgment should be set off against a separate judgment obtained by that defendant against the plaintiff. In allowing the set-off Park J. emphasized this additional element, though the earlier cases referred to above suggest that a set-off would have been available in any event.
[34] *Doe* v. *Darnton* (1802) 3 East 149.

(2)   D1, one of two joint debtors D1 and D2, is entitled in equity to set off the joint debt in the creditor's bankruptcy against the creditor's separate indebtedness to him, if the creditor's indebtedness to D1 arose or remained as a result of the creditor's own fraud, and if in addition the fraud occurred or the creditor concealed its existence until after the joint debt was incurred. The authority for this proposition is based on two decisions of Lord Eldon. In *Vuillamy* v. *Noble*[35] a customer (D1) had deposited some stock with his bank as security for a loan. The customer paid off the loan, but neglected to request a retransfer of the security. In the meantime he had become a joint debtor with D2 to the bank in a separate transaction. After the bank's bankruptcy, D1 discovered that the bank had sold the stock, so that instead of being the owner of stock he was merely a creditor of the bank for its value.[36] Lord Eldon held that D1 could set off this indebtedness of the bank to him in his separate capacity against the joint indebtedness of himself and D2 to the bank.[37] In doing so he referred to his earlier decision in *Ex parte Stephens*.[38] The separate indebtedness of the bankrupt creditors in that case to one of their two joint and several debtors (D1) similarly had arisen as a result of the creditors' own fraud, in retaining D1's money for their own use rather than using it to purchase annuities as instructed. Lord Eldon enjoined the creditors' assignees in bankruptcy from suing the other joint and several debtor (D2) for the debt, and ordered that D1 should be allowed to set off the joint and several indebtedness of herself and D2 against her separate claim against the creditors arising as a result of the creditors' own fraud.

Ex parte Stephens is generally regarded as having turned on the element

---

[35] (1817) 3 Mer. 593.

[36] When a secured debt is paid but the security is not returned, the security is held on trust for the former debtor. See *Pearce* v. *Morris* (1869) LR 5 Ch. App. 227, 230; *Holme* v. *Fieldsend* [1911] WN 111. If the property constituting the security is sold by the trustee, the beneficial owner may trace it to the proceeds of sale, and if the proceeds have been mixed with part of the trustee's own funds, the beneficial owner has a charge on the whole of the blended fund, the onus being on the trustee to prove which part of it is his own. See *In re Hallett's Estate; Knatchbull* v. *Hallett* (1880) 13 Ch. D 696; *In re Tilley's Will Trusts; Burgin* v. *Croad* [1967] 1 Ch. 1179. Ordinarily, then, someone in the same situation as the customer in *Vuillamy* would have effective real rights for the recovery of the sum owing to him, and a set-off would only be required if the proceeds may not be traced, or, having been traced, the fund with which they are mixed is insufficient to satisfy the charge.

[37] Compare the interpretation of *Vuillamy* put forward by Sir George Jessel M.R. in *Middleton* v. *Pollock, ex Parte Knight and Raymond* (1875) LR 20 Eq. 515, 521–3, that the stock was retained by the bank under an agreement that it should constitute security for the joint debt. Therefore it was said that the case was not concerned with set-off at all, because equity would have applied the proceeds of sale in reduction of the joint debt for which it was security, so that only the balance would have been payable. However, the question was left open by Lord Eldon as to whether the stock was retained as security for the joint loan, and there is little doubt that he treated the issue as one of set-off.

[38] (1805) 11 Ves. Jun. 24.

of fraud,[39] and indeed Lord Eldon later said that this was crucial to the decision,[40] though it is doubtful whether this would still be the case under current law.[41] Since the liability was several as well as joint, the view now would be that the liability and the cross-claim constitute mutual debts or claims arising out of mutual dealings which are capable of set-off in any event under the insolvency set-off section.[42] Nevertheless, the case is still relevant as an illustration of the circumstances in which a set-off may be available against a joint debt.[43]

Lord Eldon noted in *Vuillamy*[44] in relation to *Ex parte Stephens* that, when D1 incurred the liability to the bank, she was unaware of the fraud. If on the other hand a person in a similar case was aware of the fraud at the time of entering into a joint debt, so that he did so cognizant of the position, it may not be appropriate to give him a preference over other creditors by means of a set-off.

It may be that instead the fraudulent conduct of the bankrupt has resulted in a debt owing to two creditors (C1 and C2) jointly, one of whom (C1) is his separate debtor. A joint owner of property may not apply the property to his own exclusive use. In this situation the joint property consists of the claim arising from fraud, and if C1 would not have had the right to apply it to his own exclusive use before the bankruptcy, he should not have the right after the bankruptcy. Consequently he should not be able to set off this joint claim against his separate indebtedness. This is the proper explanation of *Middleton* v. *Pollock; ex parte Knight and Raymond*.[45] Admittedly the joint creditors in that case were trustees, and it was emphasized that payment could not properly have been tendered to one of them alone. However, even if there was no trust, so that payment to one joint creditor would have discharged the debtor, that joint creditor nevertheless could not have applied the joint property consisting of the claim for his own use. In any event, the fact that the joint creditors were trustees in itself should have been a sufficient ground for denying a set-off. Mutuality in bankruptcy is determined by reference to the beneficial interests of the parties, and fraud would not justify the joint creditors applying the debt owing to them as trustees in satisfaction of the

---

[39] *Ex parte Hanson* (1806) 12 Ves. Jun. 346, 348–9; *Ex parte Blagden* (1815) 19 Ves. Jun 465, 467; *Jones* v. *Mossop* (1844) 3 Hare 568, 573; *Ex parte Staddon; in re Wise* (1843) 12 LJ Bcy. 39, 40; *Middleton* v. *Pollock, ex parte Knight and Raymond* (1875) LR 20 Eq. 515, 519–20; *McIntyre* v. *Perkes* (1990) 22 FCR 362, 369–70; *Lord* v. *Direct Acceptance Corporation Ltd.* (1993) 32 NSWLR 362, 369–70. See also *Strong* v. *Foster* (1855) 17 CB 201, 217, and the discussion of *Stephens* in *Morris* v. *Agrichemicals Ltd.*, Court of Appeal, 20 December 1995.
[40] *Ex parte Blagden* (1815) 19 Ves. Jun. 465, 467.
[41] See Hoffman L.J. in *M. S. Fashions Ltd.* v. *Bank of Credit and Commerce International S.A.* [1993] Ch. 425, 437.   [42] See section 8.3 below.
[43] In *Vuillamy* (1817) 3 Mer. 593, 621 Lord Eldon regarded it as relevant in that context.
[44] (1817) 3 Mer. 593, 621.   [45] (1875) LR 20 Eq. 515.

indebtedness of one of them, when the equitable ownership of the joint creditors' claim is in someone else.

(3) In *Stracey, Ross, et al.* v. *Deey*[46] a partnership carried on trade as grocers. However, there was only one partner active in business, the other partners being merely dormant partners. A particular debtor of the business had also dealt separately with the active partner, who in the course of those dealings became indebted to the debtor. When the partnership sued the debtor on the grocery account Lord Kenyon allowed the debtor to set off the active partner's separate indebtedness to him. *Stracey* appears as a note to the report of the decision in *George* v. *Clagett*,[47] the seminal authority on the right of a person dealing with someone acting as an agent for an undisclosed principal to set off the agent's indebtedness to him against his liability to the principal on that dealing.[48] However, while a dormant partner indeed has been described as an undisclosed principal,[49] the accuracy of this as a description of his true position has been criticized on the ground that his right to sue, and his liability to be sued, do not arise because he is an undisclosed principal intervening on his agent's contracts, but rather because the dormant partner himself is a party to those contracts.[50] Even if this distinction is accepted, *Stracey* nevertheless should still be followed.[51] If a partnership acts in such a way as to conceal the interest of a dormant partner in the business, and consequently gives the impression that it consists only of the active partners, it should not be allowed to deny a third party a set-off that would have arisen if the partnership had in fact been so constituted, particularly in view of the possibility that a right of set-off may have been an inducement for the third party to deal with the partnership. The right of set-off, however, presumably would be subject to the limitation applicable generally to undisclosed principals, that it is based upon the right to set off mutual debts under the Statutes of Set-off or, in an appropriate case, equitable set-off, as opposed to the wider right of set-off conferred by the insolvency legislation.[52]

The converse situation instead may apply. A partnership may conduct business under the name of A and B, though B in fact is an employee and not a partner. A third party who deals with the firm in ignorance of the true

---

[46] (1789) 7 TR 361n., 2 Esp. 469n.   [47] (1797) 7 TR 359.

[48] See section 9.7.3 below.

[49] See for example *Beckham* v. *Drake* (1841) 9 M & W 79, 85 per Parke B; *Watteau* v. *Fenwick* [1893] 1 QB 346, 349.

[50] See *Pollock* (1893) 9 *Law Quarterly Review* 111; Montrose, 'Liability of Principal for Acts Exceeding Actual and Apparent Authority' (1939) 17 *Canadian Bar Review* 693, 703–4; *Bowstead and Reynolds on Agency* (16th edn., 1996), 417. See also Stoljar, *The Law of Agency* (1961), 57.

[51] See for example *Muggeridge's* v. *Smith and Co.* (1884) 1 TLR 166.

[52] *Turner* v. *Thomas* (1871) LR 6 CP 610.

situation nevertheless would contract with A and B jointly, though A and B would enter into the contract as agent for the undisclosed principal, A. If A intervenes on the contract and sues the third party, the third party may set off a debt owing to him by A.[53]

The set-off in a case such as *Stracey* is based upon the third party's belief that the active partner was the only principal in the business. In this regard, the circumstances must not have been such as to put him on inquiry as to whether there was a dormant partner. In *Baker* v. *Gent*[54] a partnership consisted of two partners, Lachmann and Phillips, though the interest of Phillips in the business was concealed. The business traded under the name of Lachmann and Co. This was held to constitute notice to the defendant that someone else may have been involved in the firm, and accordingly he was denied the opportunity of setting off his indebtedness to the firm against Lachmann's separate indebtedness to him. On the other hand, a name such as Lachmann and Co. presumably would not put a person dealing with the firm upon inquiry as to the existence of any dormant partner if in fact there were two or more active partners involved in the business.

The generally accepted explanation for the set-off in the undisclosed principal cases is that it is based upon a representation and estoppel. In the same way, whether or not these partnership cases are thought to involve an undisclosed principal, the set-off is also said to arise from 'some default in the other partners, or some assent on their part'.[55] It is not sufficient that a person should deal with one member of a partnership in the erroneous belief that that member is the only principal in the business.[56] In *Harper* v. *Marten*[57] two partners, Forster and Peake, traded under the name of Forster, Peake, and Co. The defendant dealt only with Peake, and assumed that he was trading on his own account. The defendant entered into an agreement with Peake by which her indebtedness resulting from those dealings should be set off against a claim that she had against Peake alone. The Court of Appeal upheld this agreement despite the express reference to Forster in the partnership name. However there are two important facts to note. The first is that the defendant had inquired of Peake as to from whom she was ordering the goods, and he replied himself. The second is the Court's finding that Forster had placed the most implicit confidence in Peake and had allowed him to have the whole control and management of the business, and moreover he had refrained from making any demand on the defendant for payment of her account when he might

---

[53] *Spurr* v. *Cass* (1870) LR 5 QB 656. [54] (1892) 9 TLR 159.
[55] *Gordon* v. *Ellis* (1846) 2 CB 821, 829 per Tindal C.J. (*arguendo*).
[56] *Gordon* v. *Ellis* (1846) 2 CB 821. Compare Lord Esher M.R. in *Harper* v. *Marten* (1895) 11 TLR 368. [57] (1895) 11 TLR 368.

reasonably have been expected to do so. Consequently, while he had not authorized Peake to tell a lie, he had acted in such a manner as to make that lie look like the truth.

(4) Another Lord Kenyon judgment has provided a further possible exception. In *Puller* v. *Roe*[58] a partnership consisting of four partners, A, B, C, and D (known as A & Co.), held a promissory note made by the defendants. C and D were also partners in another enterprise. A & Co. were indebted to this other partnership, and so the note was indorsed by A & Co. to C and D. Subsequently A, B, C, and D all became bankrupt. The assignees in bankruptcy of the second partnership of C and D sued the defendants on the note, and Lord Kenyon held that they could set off a number of debts owing to them by A & Co., his Lordship commenting that partners 'cannot as between themselves raise a distinct account, though they might indorse to a third person. The affairs of the company are in presumption of law known to all the partners, and all are equally liable.'[59] However, while the decision appears to represent a common-sense result, unless C and D in truth held the note as trustees for A & Co it is not easy as a matter of principle to explain the set-off. The holder in due course of a negotiable instrument takes free from equities, including rights of set-off.[60] In order to be a holder in due course a person inter alia must have taken the instrument in good faith and for value, and at the time that it was indorsed to him he must not have had notice of any defect in the title of the person who negotiated it.[61] Mere knowledge of a possible right of set-off between prior parties will not affect the negotiability of an instrument,[62] and consequently the partners' presumed knowledge of the state of the account between the partnership and the defendants should not have impugned their good faith. Nor indeed is there considered to be any fraud involved when the indorser and the indorsee agree to the negotiation of the instrument in order to defeat a right of set-off against the indorser.[63] *Puller* v. *Roe* may possibly be explained on the basis of the old common law rule that one partnership could not sue another if one or more of the partners were common to both firms, since these partners in effect would be both plaintiffs and defendants in the one suit.[64] Consequently the discharge of A & Co.'s debt to C and D in *Puller* v. *Roe* may not have been perceived as value given for taking the note. However, this should not be considered to

---

[58] (1793) Peake 260.
[59] (1793) Peake 260, 263
[60] Bills of Exchange Act 1882, s. 38.
[61] Bills of Exchange Act 1882, s. 29.
[62] *Oulds* v. *Harrison* (1854) 10 Ex. 572, 576 per Parke B. (*arguendo*).
[63] See *Oulds* v. *Harrison* (1854) 10 Ex. 572 in relation to the more unlikely case of an overdue bill (for which see section 13.2.18), and also *Metropolitan Bank* v. *Snure* (1860) 1O UC (CP) 24.
[64] See *Bosanquet* v. *Wray* (1815) 6 Taunt. 597 and *Mainwaring* v. *Newman* (1800) 2 Bos. & Pul. 120.

be a valid objection.[65] Even if one were to accept the doubtful proposition that such an action for the recovery of a debt still may not be brought,[66] the debt may be the subject of an account in equity between the partners,[67] in which case its discharge should be sufficient value. For example, an antecedent debt which has been rendered unenforceable by statute still may afford sufficient consideration for a negotiable instrument.[68]

(5) There is authority in support of another exception, though it should now be regarded as doubtful. There is early Chancery support for the view that when C1, one of a number of joint creditors C1 and C2, is bankrupt, and the debtor of C1 and C2 has a separate claim against the bankrupt, the debtor may set off the bankrupt's *interest* in his indebtedness to the bankrupt and C2 jointly against the bankrupt's separate indebtedness to him,[69] provided that the extent of the bankrupt's interest in the joint claim is not disputed and, in the event that C1 and C2 are partners, provided that the partnership assets are sufficient to satisfy the partnership debts.[70] Lord Cowper in *Lord Lanesborough* v. *Jones*[71] said (*obiter*) that a separate creditor of C1 may bring into an account, in C1's bankruptcy, C1's interest in the creditor's indebtedness to C1 and C2, 'if there be a surplus beyond what will pay the partnership debts', while the principle was applied in *Ex parte Quintin*,[72] where Lord Loughborough emphasized that the solvent partner had paid all the partnership debts, and that he had agreed that he was only interested to the extent of a quarter in the debts due to the partnership.[73] However Lord Eldon effectively overruled *Quintin* in *Ex parte Twogood*,[74] the Lord Chancellor expressing concern that the administration of the bankruptcy would be delayed unduly until the state of the partnership accounts could be ascertained.[75] Despite this, the

---

[65] In this regard, valuable consideration for a negotiable instrument may be constituted by an antecedent debt or liability. See the Bills of Exchange Act 1882, s. 27(1)(b).

[66] Compare *Lindley & Banks on Partnership* (17th edn., 1995), 439.

[67] See e.g. *Meyer and Company* v. *Faber (No. 2)* [1923] 2 Ch. 421, 439.

[68] *Sharpe* v. *Ellis* (1971) 20 FLR 199, 208.

[69] See, and compare, *McEwan* v. *Crombie* (1883) 25 Ch. D 175, in which the claim was not truly joint.

[70] The second proviso would be required to protect the creditors of the partnership in the event of its bankruptcy, because the debts owing to the partnership would be joint property distributable in the first instance amongst the joint creditors. See Pt II of Sch. 4 (s. 175A) and Sch. 7 (s. 328A) of the Insolvent Partnerships Order 1994. In Australia this restriction would apply whether or not the joint creditors are partners. See the Bankruptcy Act 1966 (Cth.) s. 110.   [71] (1716) 1 P Wms. 325, 326–7.   [72] (1796) 3 Ves. Jun. 248.

[73] Lord Loughborough referred to *Ex parte Edwards* (1745) 1 Atk. 100, where Lord Hardwicke had ordered that an action against a debtor of the partnership should be stayed pending the taking of an account as to how much was owing to the partnership, and how much was owing to the debtor by one of the partners. However there is no mention in the report as to whether a set-off eventually was allowed.

[74] (1805) 11 Ves. Jun. 517. See also *Addis* v. *Knight* (1817) 2 Mer. 117, 122.

[75] Lord Eldon also remarked that the effect of such a set-off would be to prefer the particular creditor over the general body of the bankrupt partner's separate creditors, though of course every set-off has a similar effect.

possibility of a set-off has been kept alive by *In re John Sloss, ex parte Robison Brothers, Campbell & Sloss Limited*,[76] in which the Victorian Supreme Court seemed to accept that *Quintin* is still good law. In fact a set-off was denied because of lack of evidence as to the extent of the entitlement of the bankrupt partner in the debt owing to the partnership. Nevertheless *Quintin* was cited with evident approval by Madden C.J., and though no mention was made of *Ex parte Twogood* in his judgment, that case had been brought to the attention of the court during argument. Perhaps the courts may be inclined to apply *Quintin* when the partnership accounts are relatively simple, or when the assets of the partnership are patently sufficient to satisfy the partnership debts, so that the administration of the bankruptcy would not be unduly delayed. However, it would hardly be satisfactory that the question whether a debtor to a partnership has a right of set-off should depend on the state of the partnership accounts, and the more likely view is that Lord Eldon's judgment would be followed and that a set-off would be disallowed.

8.3 SEVERAL PERSONS SEPARATELY LIABLE

In the case of a joint and several liability, each party is severally as well as jointly liable.[77] The indebtedness of a truly joint and several debtor, together with an obligation owing by the creditor to that debtor, constitute dealings between the same people, and may be set off.[78] The occurrence of the set-off would bring about a *pro tanto* reduction in the joint and several debt, and would release the other debtors as well.[79]

Apart from the case of joint and several debtors, there are other situations in which a number of persons may be liable to be sued separately in respect of what is in substance the same debt. This may arise, for example, when a guarantee is given in respect of another person's debt, or in relation to a bill of exchange or other negotiable instrument on which

---

[76] (1893) 19 VLR 710.

[77] See generally Glanville Williams, *Joint Obligations* (1949), 33–5. If an action is brought against one only of a number of joint debtors, that debtor ordinarily may require the other debtors to be joined as defendants (though in any event the defendant may assert in that action that the debt is a joint debt, and accordingly set off against it an indebtedness of the plaintiff to the joint debtors: *Stackwood* v. *Dunn* (1842) 3 QB 822). On the other hand, when the promises are joint and several the creditor may sue all the debtors in one action, or bring separate actions against one or more of them. See Glanville Williams, *op. cit.* 51–62.

[78] *Fletcher* v. *Dyche* (1787) 2 TR 32; *Owen* v. *Wilkinson* (1858) 5 CB(NS) 526; *Re Last; ex parte Butterell* (1994) 124 ALR 219; *Re Kolb* (1994) 128 ALR 156. See also *Paulson* v. *Murray* (1922) 68 DLR 643 (set-off of judgments) and *Ferrum Inc.* v. *Three Dees Management Ltd.* (1992) 7 OR (3d) 660, 669.

[79] See Willes J. in *Owen* v. *Wilkinson* (1858) 5 CB(NS) 526, 527, referring to *Pothier on Obligations*, by Evans, Vol. 2, at 68.

the drawer or an indorser is liable as well as the acceptor. In some cases of joint and several liability none of the parties may be principally liable *inter se,* though in other situations one party may be the principal debtor with the liability of the other joint and several debtors intended to be secondary. In effect this is a contract of suretyship. Similarly, on a bill of exchange the acceptor has the principal liability and the liability of the drawer and the indorsers is secondary, unless it is an accomodation acceptance in which case the drawer usually is principally liable. In cases of this nature, one of the parties may have a claim against the creditor, and the creditor may have become bankrupt or is a company in liquidation. In a number of early cases the question arose as to whether the creditor's trustee (or assignees) in bankruptcy could avoid a set-off, or alternatively whether there was an obligation to facilitate a set-off, by proceeding against one party rather than another for payment. These early cases established the following propositions:

(1) If one of the debtors was principally liable *inter se*, so that ultimately he was to pay the debt, he could insist that the creditor's trustee should proceed against him so that he could have the benefit of a set-off.[80] Thus, in *Ex parte Hippens; in re Sikes*[81] Lord Eldon held that the drawer of an accommodation bill could demand that the bill be delivered up to him in part discharge of a debt owing to him by the bankrupt holders.

(2) A trustee in bankruptcy holding a bill of exchange that had been dishonoured by the acceptor for value could not be compelled to have recourse to a creditor who was also the drawer or an indorser of the bill and who would have had a right of set-off against his liability on the bill, but instead could insist on suing the acceptor as the party principally liable. This was held to be the case by Commissioner Holroyd in *Ex parte Banes; re The Royal British Bank*,[82] following an earlier decision by Lord Eldon to the same effect in *Ex parte Burton; Franco and Corea; in re Kensington*.[83] Conversely, a bankrupt acceptor's trustee was not entitled to require the holder to have recourse to a prior indorser so as to avoid a set-off.[84] *Ex parte Banes* and *Ex parte Burton* should still apply generally to any situation in which a creditor has a contingent liability to a bankrupt. The

---

[80] *Ex parte Hanson* (1811) 18 Ves. Jun. 232; *Ex parte Hippens; in re Sikes* (1826) 2 Gl. & J 93; *Ex parte Banes, re The Royal British Bank* (1857) 28 LTOS 296, 297.
[81] (1826) 2 Gl. & J 193.   [82] (1857) 28 LTOS 296.
[83] (1812) 1 Rose 320.
[84] *McKinnon* v. *Armstrong Brothers & Co.* (1877) 2 App. Cas. 531. See also *Crosse* v. *Smith* (1813) 1 M & S 545, in which it was held that a bankrupt drawer could not compel the holder to proceed against the acceptor, and thereby avoid a set-off in his bankruptcy.

bankrupt's contingent claim in such a case cannot be the subject of a set-off,[85] and these cases should be regarded as authority for the view that the trustee in bankruptcy is not obliged to take steps to cause the liability to vest, for example, by making a demand, so that a set-off can occur. This should be distinguished from the *M. S. Fashions* case (discussed below), in which the claim of the bank in liquidation against the guarantor was held not to be contingent.

The House of Lords has now held that the insolvency set-off section takes effect automatically upon the occurrence of a bankruptcy or a liquidation.[86] On that basis, it would no longer be a question whether a trustee in bankruptcy or a liquidator could avoid a set-off by proceeding against one party rather than another, or whether he is obliged to facilitate a set-off by having recourse to a debtor who has a cross-claim. Rather, the only question should be whether a set-off has or has not occurred. This indeed was the approach adopted in *M. S. Fashions Ltd.* v. *Bank of Credit and Commerce International*.[87] A bank provided an advance to a customer secured by both a guarantee and a cash deposit by the guarantor. The bank went into liquidation and the liquidator, instead of proceeding against the guarantor, made a demand on the debtor, and said that the guarantor should be confined to a proof in the liquidation in respect of the deposit. The Court of Appeal held that there was a right of set-off as between the guarantor and the bank which had the effect of automatically satisfying the guarantor's liablity to the bank, and since the guarantor had paid the debt by means of this set-off the customer could no longer be sued. A crucial issue in the case was the nature of the guarantor's liability. This was expressed to be enforceable on demand, and to be that of a principal debtor. The liquidator argued that a demand in fact had not been made upon the guarantor, so that the bank's claim against the guarantor was still contingent. While under the insolvency set-off section a contingent liability of a bankrupt or a company in liquidation may be set off, there cannot be a set-off in relation to a claim possessed by the bankrupt or the company which is still contingent.[88] However, the Court of Appeal referred to earlier authority to the effect that, where a surety contracted on the basis of being liable as a principal debtor, he could be sued on his engagement without any demand having been made, notwithstanding that the agreement may provide for a demand.[89] Accordingly, the guarantor's liability to

---

[85] See section 4.4 above.
[86] *Stein* v. *Blake* [1995] 2 All ER 961, discussed in section 2.12.1 above.
[87] [1993] Ch. 425.   [88] See section 4.4 above.
[89] *Rowe* v. *Young* (1820) 2 Bligh 391, 465–6; *Esso Petroleum Co. Ltd.* v. *Alstonbridge Properties Ltd.* [1975] 1 WLR 1474, 1483.

the bank in liquidation was not contingent, and it could be the subject of an automatic set-off.

In the context of suretyship, the view that under the automatic theory of insolvency set-off a trustee in bankruptcy or liquidator could not avoid a set-off by proceeding against one party rather than another nevertheless was brought into question recently as a result of comments by the Court of Appeal in *Morris* v. *Agrichemicals Ltd.*[90] As the Court noted, the creditor's trustee (or liquidator) obviously could not both set off against the surety and recover from the principal debtor, though it raised the possibility, for future consideration, that the trustee may still have a choice as to which remedy to pursue, notwithstanding the current view of the courts as to the nature of insolvency set-off. It was suggested that the trustee may be able to sue the debtor, despite the surety's set-off, in which case the recovery would be treated as having taken place at the date of the bankruptcy. In that event it could be said with hindsight that nothing in fact was due from the surety at the date of the bankruptcy, and the surety would then be able to prove in the bankruptcy in respect of his claim without any discount. The source of this suggestion was the Court's analysis of Lord Eldon's judgment in *Ex parte Stephens*,[91] which it regarded as illustrating a distinction between, on the one hand, a discharge to the surety as against the creditor which is based upon a set-off as between those parties, and on the other a discharge which arises as a result of payment by the surety to the creditor. In the latter circumstance the discharge would also discharge the principal debtor, whereas this may not be the case in the former. If this were correct, it would be a curious result. In examining the suggestion two situations should be considered. The first is where the surety had assumed the liability of a principal debtor. In that situation, however, the *M. S. Fashions* case is authority for the proposition that the creditor's trustee in fact cannot sue the principal debtor to the extent that the debt has been extinguished by the surety's set-off. Alternatively, the surety may not have contracted as a principal debtor. In that circumstance, the surety's liability is usually conditional upon a demand being made under the guarantee. Until the creditor makes a demand, the claim against the surety is still subject to a contingency and cannot be included in a set-off in the creditor's insolvency.[92] If a demand is made a set-off, according to the House of Lords,[93] will be deemed to have occurred at the date of the bankruptcy. But if indeed the creditor chooses to make a demand, a choice will have been made to pursue the remedy of set-off, and the decision in *M. S. Fashions* should apply so as to prevent further action against the

---

[90] Rose, Saville and Millett L.JJ., 20 December 1995.
[91] (1805) 11 Ves. Jun. 24.   [92] See section 4.4 above.
[93] *Stein* v. *Blake* [1995] 2 All ER 961.

principal debtor to the extent of the set-off. The contrary view would mean that the creditor's estate would be worse off as a result of the surety having assumed the liability of a principal debtor, beause a separate action could not then be brought against the true principal where the surety had an insolvency set-off, than if the surety had not. In any event, different treatment in this regard between discharge by set-off and discharge by payment would conflict with the generally accepted view that set-off is equivalent to payment.[94] Nor, as a matter of principle, is it easy to see any justification for such a distinction.

When debtors are jointly and severally liable, and either the creditor or one of the debtors is bankrupt, a set-off, according to the House of Lords, would occur automatically at the date of the bankruptcy. If the creditor is the bankrupt party, and two or more of the debtors have cross-claims eligible for a set-off, the set-off presumably would take effect on a *pro rata* basis.[95] This should be compared to set-off under the Statutes of Set-off, which is not automatic but rather is a procedural defence to an action at law.[96] The creditor could sue whichever of the debtors he chooses. In such a case the joint and several debtor being sued may not bring into account a liability of the creditor to one of the other joint and several debtors. A right of contribution between them does not justify a set-off.[97]

8.4 SEPARATE DEPOSITOR AND DEBTOR

In the *M. S. Fashions* case, discussed above,[98] the person who provided the bank with a deposit as security for the customer's liability on the loan had also assumed a personal liability in the form of a guarantee. This was crucial to the decision to recognize a set-off in the bank's liquidation, because the guarantee provided the means of bringing about mutuality. Where, however, the depositor had not assumed a personal liability, but had merely provided the deposit by way of collateral security for the loan, there is not mutuality, and the deposit and the loan will not be the subject of a set-off under the insolvency set-off section in the event of the bank's liquidation.[99] The liquidator can proceed against the customer for repayment of the loan, and confine the depositor to a proof in the

---

[94] *Re Loteka Pty. Ltd.* (1989) 15 ACLR 620, 622; *M. S. Fashions* [1993] Ch. 425, 448.
[95] This is consistent with the approach adopted when there are two debts owing to a creditor, one of which is entitled to priority in the bankruptcy or liquidation. See section 2.17 above. [96] See section 1.2.9 above.
[97] *Bowyear* v. *Pawson* (1881) 6 QBD 540; *Lord* v. *Direct Acceptance Corporation Ltd.* (1993) 32 NSWLR 362, 371–2. [98] See section 8.3 below.
[99] *Lord* v. *Direct Acceptance Corporation Ltd.* (1993) 32 NSWLR 362; *Morris* v. *Agrochemicals Ltd.* Court of Appeal (Rose, Saville and Millett L.JJ.), 20 December 1995; *Tam Wing Chuen* v. *Bank of Credit and Commerce Hong Kong Ltd.* Privy Council, 26 March 1996. Nor is this a ground for an equitable set-off. See section 1.7.6 above.

liquidation in relation to the deposit.[100] As the Court of Appeal noted in *Morris* v. *Agrichemicals Ltd.*,[101] this produces something of a paradox, because the bank's position is better in its own liquidation when it had not obtained a personal guarantee from the depositor than when it had.

8.5 DECEASED INSOLVENT PARTNER

While section 9 of the Partnership Act provides that the estate of a deceased partner is severally as well as jointly liable for the debts of the firm, this is expressed to be subject to the prior payment of his separate debts. In keeping with this priority, a separate debtor to the deceased partner may not set off a debt owing to him jointly by the partnership.[102]

Where two or more partners jointly own the beneficial interest in a claim, and all except one die, the common law courts used to apply the principle that the claim passed to the survivor, so that there was mutuality for the purpose of a set-off between the original joint claim and a debt owing by the survivor.[103] However, in equity the claim must be brought into account in determining the entitlement of the deceased partners' estates.[104] The better view is that this entitlement of the deceaseds' estates destroys mutuality in equity for the purpose of set-off.[105]

---

[100] If the customer had also provided a separate security to the bank in the form of a mortgage, the doctrine of marshalling would not apply so as to compel the bank to have recourse first to the deposit. See *Morris* v. *Agrichemicals Ltd.* Court of Appeal (Rose, Saville and Millett L.JJ.), 20 December 1995. [101] 20 December 1995.

[102] *Addis* v. *Knight* (1817) 2 Mer. 117.

[103] *Slipper* v. *Stidstone* (1794) 5 TR 493, and see also *French* v. *Andrade* (1796) 6 TR 582.

[104] See e.g. *McLean* v. *Kennard* (1874) LR 9 Ch. App. 336, and generally *Lindley on the Law of Partnership* (15th edn., 1984), 521 (which perhaps has a clearer explanation of the historical position than *Lindley & Banks on Partnership* (17th edn., 1995), 530–1).

[105] Compare Wood, *English and International Set-off* (1989), 1034–5.

9

Mutality—Same Right

9.1 DIFFERENT PERSONAL CAPACITIES

In the case of insolvency set-off the requirement that the demands be held
in the same right means no more than that each of the parties, who is liable
to the other, should be the beneficial owner of a cross-demand against the
other. While the Statutes of Set-off contemplate mutuality at law, equity
nevertheless may allow a set-off by analogy with the Statutes if there is
mutuality in equity but not at law, or alternatively disallow a set-off if there
is mutuality at law but not in equity, so that the same principle usually will
apply.[1] As long as the demands in this sense are mutual, the dealings are
not considered to be in a different right merely because each may relate to
a different personal status or capacity possessed by one of the parties. For
example, in an action brought by a trustee against a beneficiary of the trust
for an indemnity as to costs and expenses incurred in connection with the
trust, the Queensland Supreme Court held that the beneficiary could set
off an indebtedness of the trustee in his personal capacity.[2] On another
occasion an executor was the sole person interested in the estate of the
testator, and all claims against the estate had been satisfied. When the
executor brought an action to recover a debt owing to the estate, the
debtor was allowed to set off a personal indebtedness of the executor to
him in a matter unrelated to the estate.[3] While neither of these cases
concerned a bankruptcy or a liquidation, the same principle should be
applicable to insolvency set-off. A further illustration is to be found in the
cases which support the proposition that a local authority which has vested
in it a number of statutory functions may set off a credit balance arising on
a bank account which relates to one function against its indebtedness on an
account relating to another. In *Pedder* v. *The Mayor, Aldermen, and
Burgesses of Preston*[4] the Mayor, etc. of the Corporation of Preston had an

---

[1] See section 7.4 above. [2] *Peel* v. *Fitzgerald* [1982] Qd. R 544.
[3] *Williams* v. *MacDonald* [1915] VLR 229. See also, and compare, *Knowles* v. *Maitland*
(1825) 4 B & C 173, in which the cross–demands both related to the capacity of colonel of the
regiment.
[4] (1862) 12 CB (NS) 535. See also *Ex parte Pearce; in re Langmead* (1841) 2 Mont. D & De
G 142.

account with a bank for the Corporation's general municipal functions. In addition the Mayor, etc. had been constituted the local board of health under the Public Health Act 1848, and for this a separate account was opened with the same bank. The bank entered into an arrangement with its creditors under the Bankrupt Law Consolidation Act 1849, at which time the general account was overdrawn and the local board of health account was in credit. Though section 87 of the 1848 Act provided that the money received by the local board of health 'shall be applied . . . in defraying such of the Expenses incurred or to be incurred by the said Local Board in carrying this Act into execution', it was held that the Corporation could set the credit balance on that account against its indebtedness on the other.

9.2 TRUSTEES IN BANKRUPTCY AND LIQUIDATORS

A right accruing to, or a liability incurred by, the trustee in bankruptcy in his own right as trustee may not be brought into an account in the bankruptcy.[5] Nor can the trustee set off the dividend payable to a creditor against the creditor's indebtedness to him in his private capacity.[6]

A liability incurred by the trustee in his own right is a liability which gives rise to a direct claim against the trustee personally, as opposed to a provable debt. A right accruing to the trustee in his own right is a right founded upon the trustee's own title, rather than that of the bankrupt. An example of the latter is a right arising in favour of the estate after the bankruptcy, which is not derived from an obligation incurred by the party liable before the bankruptcy. Thus there may be an award of costs made in favour of the trustee in an action brought to recover a debt owing to the bankrupt's estate. The defendant's obligation to pay the costs only arises after the bankruptcy as a result of his failure to pay the debt to the trustee upon demand, and so it may not be brought in as a set-off against an indebtedness of the bankrupt.[7] Another example is *Ex parte Young; Re Day & Sons*.[8] The trustee in bankruptcy of a firm opened an account with a bank, and paid into it a sum of money received on behalf of the estate. Subsequently the bank itself filed a liquidation petition. It was held that the firm's trustee could not set off in the liquidation the bank's indebtedness to

---

[5] *In re A Debtor; ex parte The Peak Hill Goldfield, Limited* [1909] 1 KB 430, 437.

[6] *Ex parte White* (1742) 1 Atk. 90; *Ex parte Bailey; in re Howarth* (1840) 1 Mont. D & De G 263; *Ex parte Saunders; in re Innes* (1842) 2 Mont. D & De G 529, 530–1. The reason for this is that the demands are due in different rights. See *Ex parte Alexander; in re Elder* (1832) 1 Deac. & Ch. 513, 524 per Erskine C.J. A second reason is that the creditor is a *cestui que trust* of the trustee, and so is entitled to receive the dividend undiminished by a set-off. See *Re Henley, Thurgood, & Co.* (1863) 11 WR 1021, 1022, and generally Ch. 6.

[7] *West* v. *Pryce* (1825) 2 Bing. 455.   [8] (1879) 41 LT 40.

him for the money deposited on behalf of the estate against an independent indebtedness of the bankrupt firm to the bank for which a proof had been lodged.[9] On the other hand, it should have been open to the trustee in that case to have directed the bank to satisfy its right to a dividend out of the asset of the bankrupts' estate that the bank held, in the form of their own indebtedness on the account.[10] This is an aspect of the rule in *Cherry* v. *Boultbee*,[11] which is considered later.[12]

Insofar as companies are concerned, a winding-up does not affect the corporate personality of the company.[13] Nor generally does it result in a *cessio bonorum* in favour of the liquidator, so that, unlike in a bankruptcy,[14] the legal title to the company's assets remains with the company itself.[15] In fact a liquidator 'is principally and really an agent for the company but occupies a position which is fiduciary in some respects and is bound by the statutory duties imposed upon him by the [Insolvency] Act'.[16] However, the making of a winding-up order in a compulsory liquidation, or the passing of a resolution for a voluntary winding-up, should have the same effect upon mutuality as far as the company's claims accruing after the winding-up are concerned as the appointment of a trustee has in a bankruptcy. The House of Lords in *Ayerst* v. *C. & K. (Construction) Ltd.*[17] confirmed that, while a winding-up order in a compulsory liquidation does not of itself divest the company of the legal

---

[9] Similarly, it has been held that a sum of money received by a creditor of a bankrupt on behalf of the estate may not be brought into an account. See *Groom* v. *Mealey* (1835) 2 Bing. (NC) 138; *Elgood* v. *Harris* [1896] 2 QB 491. Compare *Bailey* v. *Johnson* (1872) LR 7 Ex. 263 (see section 7.3.1 above), in which the bankruptcy under which the trustee paid the money into the bank was annulled after the bank's bankruptcy.

[10] See in this regard *Ex parte Bebb* (1812) 19 Ves. Jun. 222 and *Ex parte Graham* (1814) 3 V & B 130.   [11] (1839) 4 My. & Cr. 442.   [12] See Ch. 10.

[13] See the Insolvency Act 1986, s. 87(2). This is also the case in a compulsory liquidation. See *Reigate* v. *Union Manufacturing Co. (Ramsbottom), Ltd.* [1918] 1 KB 592, 606.

[14] A trustee in bankruptcy upon his appointment has vested in him the property belonging to the bankrupt at the commencement of the bankruptcy. See the Insolvency Act 1986, ss. 283(1) and 306. This includes things in action. See s. 436.

[15] *In re A Debtor* [1927] 1 Ch. 410, 420; *John Mackintosh and Sons Ltd.* v. *Baker's Bargain Stores (Seaford) Ltd.* [1965] 1 WLR 1182; *Re Northside Properties Pty. Ltd.* [1971] 2 NSWLR 320, 326; *National Westminster Bank Ltd.* v. *Halesowen Presswork & Assemblies Ltd.* [1972] AC 785, 796. There is provision for the liquidator to apply for an order from the court vesting the company's property in him. See the Insolvency Act 1986, s. 145. The effect of such an order is to vest the company's property in him in his official, as opposed to his personal, capacity. See *Graham* v. *Edge* (1888) 20 QBD 683. However, it appears that the section is rarely invoked. See *Buckley on the Companies Act* (14th edn., 1981) Vol. 1, 597–8.

[16] *Thomas Franklin & Sons Ltd.* v. *Cameron* (1935) 36 SR (NSW) 286, 296 per Davidson J., approved of by Marks J. in *Re Timberland Ltd.* (1979) 4 ACLR 259, 285. See also *In re Windsor Steam Coal Co. (1901), Ltd.* [1928] 1 Ch. 609. A liquidator is entitled to examine a proof lodged in the winding-up in the light of any possible right of set-off. See *In re National Wholemeal Bread and Biscuit Company* [1892] 2 Ch. 457.   [17] [1976] AC 167.

title to its assets, it does deprive it of the beneficial title.[18] This is a consequence of the vesting of the custody and control of the company's property in the liquidator to be applied by him in discharge of the company's liabilities and, in the case of a surplus, to be distributed amongst the members. Admittedly, uncertainty as to the property divisible amongst the creditors, as well as uncertainty as to the creditors entitled to share in the realization of the property, means that any particular creditor who in fact is entitled to share in the proceeds is not invested with the beneficial title to any part of that property while it is still being administered by the liquidator.[19] Nevertheless, the House of Lords concluded that it could still be said that the company itself is not possessed of the beneficial title. If a company does not have the beneficial title to its assets after the commencement of its liquidation, for the purpose of mutuality in equity the effect, as far as claims accruing subsequently to the company are concerned, accordingly should be the same as the appointment of a trustee in bankruptcy. Consider however *Monkwearmouth Flour Mill Company (Limited)* v. *Lightfoot.*[20] The defendant had been appointed after the commencement of the plaintiff company's liquidation to collect outstanding debts due to the company. When he was sued for the money he had received he was allowed to set off the company's prior indebtedness to him. But at no stage could it be said that the company itself was the beneficial owner of any right against him. Nor was his liability a consequence of a contract that he had entered into with the company before the commencement of its liquidation.[21] A set-off therefore should have been denied on the ground of lack of mutuality.[22]

There is Australian authority inconsistent with *Ayerst*. Some 5 years prior to that case, Menzies J. held in *Franklin's Selfserve Pty. Limited* v. *Federal Commissioner of Taxation*[23] that the fact that a company was being wound up did not mean that it could no longer be regarded as the beneficial holder of shares in a subsidiary company for the purpose of the income tax legislation. But even if this view were to prevail,[24] *Monkwearmouth* would still be difficult to explain, since the company's claim only accrued after the relevant date for determining rights of set-off, without it being related to a prior transaction.

---

[18] This also applies to a voluntary winding-up. See [1976] AC 167, 176.
[19] [1976] AC 167, 178–9.   [20] (1897) 13 TLR 327.
[21] See section 4.4 above.
[22] See in this regard *Sankey Brook Coal Co., Ltd.* v. *Marsh* (1871) LR 6 Ex. 185.
[23] (1970) 125 CLR 52. See also *Mineral & Chemical Traders Pty. Ltd.* v. *Tymczyszyn Pty. Ltd.* (1994) 15 ACLR 398, 417.
[24] See Meagher, Gummow & Lehane, *Equity: Doctrines and Remedies* (3rd edn., 1992), 109–10.

9.3 TRANSACTIONS IMPUGNED BY A TRUSTEE OR LIQUIDATOR

9.3.1 *Preferences*

If, within the period of 6 months[25] prior to the presentation of a petition against a debtor, the debtor did anything or suffered anything to be done which had the effect of putting a particular creditor into a better position in the debtor's bankruptcy than he would otherwise have been, the court on the application of the trustee may make such order as it thinks fit for restoring the position to what it would have been if the debtor had not given the preference.[26] A creditor who is obliged to return a sum of money that constituted a preference is not entitled to set off against that obligation the debt for which the payment was intended to be satisfaction,[27] or indeed any other indebtedness of the bankrupt to him.[28] The trustee's right to the return of the money accrues in his own right as trustee, and is not derived from an obligation that the creditor had incurred to the bankrupt himself. There is no mutuality between that liability and the creditor's claim against the bankrupt.[29] In any event, public policy would dictate that a transaction which the legislature has declared should be avoided as a preference should not be able to ground a set-off, because otherwise the efficacy of preference provision would be severely limited.[30]

---

[25] Or two years for a person connected with the company in liquidation or associated with the bankrupt, as the case may be. See the Insolvency Act 1986, ss. 240(1) and 341(1).

[26] See the Insolvency Act 1986, s. 340. For Australia see the Bankruptcy Act 1966 (Cth.), s. 122.

[27] *Courtney* v. *King* (1870) 1 VR (L) 70; *In re A Debtor* [1927] 1 Ch. 410; *Re Grezzana; Painter & Anor* v. *Charles Whiting & Chambers Ltd.* (1932) 4 ABC 203; *Re Smith; ex parte The Trustee; J. Bird Pty. Ltd. and Tully (Respondents)* (1933) 6 ABC 49. See also *Calzaturificio Zenith Pty. Ltd.* v. *N.S.W. Leather & Trading Co. Pty. Ltd.* [1970] VR 605. Compare *Morris* v. *Flower* (1863) 2 SCR (NSW) 196.

[28] *Wood* v. *Smith* (1838) 4 M & W 522; *Re K. B. Docker* (1938) 10 ABC 198. See also, with respect to the avoidance of voluntary settlements, *Lister* v. *Hooson* [1908] 1 KB 174; *Re Hermann; ex parte The Official Assignee* (1916) 16 SR(NSW) 264.

[29] See *Courtney* v. *King* (1870) 1 VR (L) 70, 73; *Lister* v. *Hooson* [1908] 1 KB 174; *Re Armour* (1956) 18 ABC 69. A similar analysis formerly applied under the doctrine of relation back, when the trustee's title related back to encompass a sum of money paid by the bankrupt to a particular creditor before the sequestration order. See *In re Pollitt* [1893] 1 QB 455. See also *Tamplin* v. *Diggins* (1809) 2 Camp. 312: *Thomason* v. *Frere* (1809) 10 East 418: *Kinder* v. *Butterworth* (1826) 6 B & C 42. Mutuality was lacking only when the obligation of the creditor to account for a sum of money was based *solely* upon relation back, as opposed to an indebtedness that the creditor had incurred to the bankrupt himself. Compare *Elliott* v. *Turquand* (1881) 7 App. Cas. 79; *In re Jackson; ex parte The Official Assignee* (1888) 6 NZLR 417. However, in England the doctrine of relation back no longer applies under the Insolvency Act 1986.

[30] See *Re Grezzana* (1932) 4 ABC 203, 206. This is particularly so when the argument for a set-off is based upon the original debt for which the preferential payment was intended to be

A similar principle applies in the winding-up of an insolvent company,[31] so that a creditor of a company is not entitled to a set-off against his obligation to repay a preference.[32] It has been said that the denial of a set-off in the case of a company liquidation is attributable to considerations of policy rather than of strict logic,[33] though the fact that the creditor's obligation only arises after the liquidation, and therefore after the relevant date for determining rights of set-off, should be a sufficient justification for denying a set-off.[34] There also may be a lack of mutuality. The right to recover the preference would only accrue after the winding-up when the company has been deprived of the beneficial ownership of its property.[35] On this view the company itself would never have been interested beneficially in the recovery, and so mutuality between that claim and an indebtedness of the company would be lacking.

The preference section also applies when an administration order is made in relation to a company.[36] A company in administration is not deprived of the beneficial title to its assets, though a set-off should still be denied either as a matter of implication from the section or because the preference is voidable on the application of the administrator, so that there is still a lack of mutuality.

If A and B are indebted to each other, and A makes a payment to B in satisfaction of his indebtedness in consideration of B similarly discharging his indebtedness to A, or if A and B merely agree that the cross-demands should be set one against the other and cancelled,[37] then A's payment, or the agreement for a set-off, will not be construed as a preference in his subsequent bankruptcy if the cross-demands were such that in any event they would have given rise to a set-off. The fact that the debts would have been set off in the bankruptcy means that the arrangements have not worked to the detriment of the other creditors of the bankrupt. 'You cannot prefer a man . . . by merely putting him in the very position in

---

satisfaction. See *Courtney* v. *King* (1870) 1 VR (L) 70, 73; *In re A Debtor* [1927] 1 Ch. 410, 415–6, 419–20; *Re Grezzana*. Australian courts in some cases have also had recourse to the proviso to the set-off section as an additional reason for denying a set-off. See *Re Hardman* (1932) 4 ABC 207; *Re Smith* (1933) 6 ABC 49; *Re Pitts and Lehman Ltd.* (1940) 40 SR (NSW) 614. See also *Russell Wilkins & Sons, Limited* v. *The Outridge Printing Co., Ltd.* [1906] St. R Qd. 172.

[31] See the Insolvency Act 1986, s. 239. In Australia see the Corporations Law, s. 588FA.
[32] *In re A Debtor* [1927] 1 Ch. 410; *Calzaturificio Zenith Pty. Ltd.* v. *N.S.W. Leather & Trading Co. Pty. Ltd.* [1970] VR 605.
[33] McPherson, *The Law of Company Liquidation* (3rd edn., 1987), 385.
[34] See Astbury J. in *In re A Debtor* [1927] 1 Ch. 410.
[35] See section 9.2 above.
[36] See the Insolvency Act 1986, s. 239(1), referring to s. 238(1).
[37] It would not be necessary for a preferential 'payment' that money should have changed hands. See Lindley L.J. in *In re Washington Diamond Mining Company* [1893] 3 Ch. 95, 109–10.

which he would be if a bankruptcy followed.'[38] However, this was not the case in *In re Washington Diamond Mining Company*.[39] One of the claims concerned a liability to contribute unpaid capital on company shares not fully paid-up. While there may be a set-off in an action at law by a solvent company to enforce a call on shares, a call for unpaid capital is not such a claim that may give rise to a set-off in a winding-up.[40] The Court of Appeal held that an arrangement by which this liability and an indebtedness of the company to the shareholder were each to be cancelled constituted a preference, with the result that the creditor was required to prove for his debt and at the same time to contribute the full amount of the unpaid capital to the company in its liquidation. In other words, when an agreement for a set-off is set aside as a preference, it has the effect of putting the parties in the same position as if the demands had not been set against each other.[41]

A preference also may take the form of an arrangement by which a particular creditor is to become indebted to the debtor so that a possible set-off situation may arise. In such cases the preference provision will override any right to a set-off.[42] For example, there may be a preference where a debtor sells goods or other property on credit to a particular creditor, the preference arising from the possibility of the creditor setting off the purchase price against the bankrupt's indebtedness to him.[43] An alternative to the credit sale is a delivery of goods to the creditor with authority to sell and to receive the proceeds, or merely an authority to receive the proceeds of a sale conducted by someone else.[44] The creditor may be ordered to return the proceeds of sale undiminished by a set-off.[45]

The preference provision in the English legislation stipulates that the debtor should have been 'influenced' by a 'desire to produce' a situation in

---

[38] *In re Washington Diamond Mining Company* [1893] 3 Ch. 95, 104 per Vaughan Williams L.J. Compare *Re B. P. Fowler, Ltd.* [1938] 1 Ch. 113, in which Crossman J. held that the payments constituted a preference notwithstanding that he left open (at 120) whether there would have been a set-off in the liquidation. In this respect the judgment is unsatisfactory.

[39] [1893] 3 Ch. 95. See also *In re Land Development Association; Kent's Case* (1888) 39 Ch. D 259.   [40] See section 4.6 above.

[41] See the discussion in *Hamilton* v. *Commonwealth Bank of Australia* (1992) 9 ACSR 90, 107, 108.   [42] *Re Clements* (1931) 7 ABC 255, 268–9.

[43] *Sempill* v. *Vindin* (1868) 7 SCR (NSW) 361. Compare *Smith* v. *Hodson* (1791) 4 TR 211 and *Donaldson* v. *Couche* (1867) 4 WW & A'B (L) 41, in which the assgnees in bankruptcy affirmed the sale by suing for the price.

[44] In these cases it was evidently not intended that the proceeds be held on trust for the depositor. Compare Ch. 6.

[45] *Castendyck and Focke* v. *The Official Assignee of S. A. McLellan* (1887) 6 NZLR 67; *In re Hardy* (1901) 19 NZLR 845; *Re Clements* (1931) 7 ABC 255; *Re Wade (Deceased)* (1943) 13 ABC 116. See also *Re Grezzana* (1932) 4 ABC 203. Compare *Re Smith* (1933) 6 ABC 49, in which the creditor acted in good faith, for valuable consideration, and in the ordinary course of business, and consequently was protected by the Australian legislation. Compare also *Simson* v. *Guthrie* (1873) 4 AJR 182; *Re Lindsay* (1890) 9 NZLR 192.

which the creditor may be preferred.[46] There should have been some desire to confer a preference, so that an arrangement involving a sale of goods on credit or a delivery of property for sale will only be held to constitute a preference, with the consequent denial of a set-off against the purchase price or the obligation to pay the proceeds of sale, if the debtor was influenced by a desire that the creditor should set off the purchase price or the proceeds of sale against his indebtedness.[47] This should be compared to Australia, where the preference provision merely looks to the 'effect' of the transaction. A conveyance or transfer of property, or a payment made to a particular creditor, is void as against the debtor's trustee if it has the effect of giving that creditor a preference.[48] The intention of the debtor to prefer is irrelevant.[49] On the other hand, in a case in which a debtor deposited goods with his creditor for the purpose of sale by the creditor, it was said that any retainer of the proceeds of sale by the creditor would not be a 'payment' for the purpose of the preference section unless the debtor had authorized the creditor, either expressly or impliedly, to satisfy the debt from the proceeds.[50]

Formerly the preference provision in the the bankruptcy legislation entitled the bankrupt's trustee himself to avoid the payment or transfer of property.[51] It was not necessary for the trustee to apply for an order from the court. When there had been a transfer of property, the denial of a set-off in any particular case was premised on the assumption that the trustee did not adopt a course of action that was inconsistent with his statutory right to avoid the transfer and to seek either a return of the property or damages for its conversion. In *Smith* v. *Hodson*[52] the preference took the form of a sale of goods on credit to a particular creditor, thereby leaving open the possibility of the creditor obtaining an advantage over the other creditors by means of a set-off against his indebtedness for the purchase price. The bankrupt's assignees in bankruptcy had a choice. They could either have avoided the contract of sale as a preference and sued for the recovery of the property, or they could have affirmed the transaction and

---

[46] See the Insolvency Act 1986, s. 340(4).

[47] Compare *Hunter* v. *The Official Assignee of Bispham* (1898) 17 NZLR 175

[48] See the Bankruptcy Act 1966 (Cth.), s. 122 and, for company liquidation, the Corporations Law, ss. 588FA(1) and 588FC.

[49] *S. Richards and Co., Ltd.* v. *Lloyd* (1933) 49 CLR 49.

[50] *Re Clements* (1931) 7 ABC 255, 270. Compare *Hamilton* v. *Commonwealth Bank of Australia* (1992) 9 ACSR 90, 108. If it is not a preference, the question whether the creditor is entitled to a set-off against his obligation to account for the proceeds is discussed in section 6.4 above.

[51] See e.g. the Bankruptcy Act 1914, s. 44(1). This is still the case in Australia in relation to bankruptcy (see the Bankruptcy Act 1966 (Cth.), s. 122), though not in the context of company liquidation. See the Corporations Law, s. 588FF.

[52] (1791) 4 TR 211. See also *Holmes* v. *Tutton* (1855) 5 El. & Bl. 65.

sued for the purchase price. Since they adopted the latter course they let in a set-off.[53] The current preference provision in the Insolvency Act 1986[54] does not empower the trustee himself to avoid any payment or transfer of property constituting a preference. He may only apply to the court for an order to this effect. But if in a *Smith* v. *Hodson* situation the trustee fails to seek an order and instead sues for the price, a set-off ordinarily should be available to the creditor.[55]

Where a payment is avoided as a preference, the Insolvency Act provides that the court may make such order as it thinks fit with respect to the rights of the recipient of the avoided payment to prove for the debt which was discharged by it.[56] In Australia, the High Court has held that the recipient may not in fact prove until the preference has been repaid in full.[57]

9.3.2 *Other impugned transactions*

The Insolvency Act 1986 contains other provisions entitling a trustee in bankruptcy or liquidator to take action in relation to certain transactions, as, for example, transactions at an undervalue,[58] transactions defrauding creditors,[59] and in situations in which there has been fraudulent trading[60] or wrongful trading.[61] Moreover, a disposition of a company's property made after the commencement of a court ordered winding-up is void without the consent of the court.[62] An obligation to make or return a payment under these provisions should be subject to the same rule applicable to preferences, that it cannot be the subject of a set-off. A similar comment may be made in respect of the obligation to account for the proceeds of execution completed after the bankruptcy or liquidation of the debtor.[63]

---

[53] See also *Donaldson* v. *Couche* (1867) 4 W W & A'B (L) 41.
[54] See s. 340 for bankruptcies and s. 239 for companies.
[55] In England the qualification to the set-off section only applies in relation to sums becoming due *from* the bankrupt. In Australia, on the other hand, the qualification is drafted in terms of both giving and receiving credit, and it may apply so as to prevent a set-off in this situation. See section 2.7.4 above.
[56] See s. 241(1)(g) for company liquidations, and s. 342(1)(g) for bankruptcies. In Australia, see the Corporations Law, s. 588FF in the context of company liquidation.
[57] *N. A. Kratzmann Pty. Ltd.* v. *Tucker (No. 2)* (1968) 123 CLR 295.
[58] See the Insolvency Act 1986, s. 238 and, for bankruptcy, s. 339.
[59] Insolvency Act 1986, s. 423.   [60] Insolvency Act 1986, s. 213.
[61] Insolvency Act 1986, s. 214.
[62] Insolvency Act 1986, s. 127. See also s. 284 with respect to individuals, which applies to dispositions in the period beginning with the presentation of the petition and ending with the vesting of the bankrupt's estate in a trustee.
[63] See the Insolvency Act 1986, ss. 183 and 346. Compare the exceptional case of *Ex parte Elliott; in re Jermyn* (1838) 3 Deac. 343. The petitioner had paid a sum of money in order to prevent a distress being levied on the bankrupt's goods. The petitioner sold some of the

Section 344 of the Insolvency Act provides that an assignment of book debts by a person engaged in any business is void as against his trustee in the event that he becomes bankrupt, unless the assignment has been registered under the Bills of Sale Act 1876. Where an assignment is void the purchaser may be liable to account to the vendor's trustee for any proceeds of the debts that he has received, though the purchaser in such a case may have an action for repayment of the price on the basis of total failure of consideration. In Victoria there is authority to the effect that the purchaser may set off that cross-claim under the insolvency set-off section against his liability to account for the proceeds,[64] though the case should be understood in the context of the legislation in issue. The Book Debts Act 1896 (Vic.) provided that an assignment of book debts had no validity at law or in equity until it was registered. This should be compared to the English Insolvency Act, which provides that the assignment is void *as against the trustee*.[65] The only obligation to account for the proceeds is to the trustee. There never has been a liability to the bankrupt himself. In such a case a question of mutuality would arise which was not in issue in Victoria.

A bankrupt prior to the bankruptcy may have assigned to X a debt owing to the bankrupt by Y. If the assignment is subsequently avoided, for example as a transaction at an undervalue or a transaction defrauding creditors, so that the debt reverts to the bankrupt, there is then the possiblity of that debt forming the basis of a set-off as between the bankrupt and Y.[66] The issue of mutuality, when the effect of avoiding a transaction is that a *payment* must be made to the trustee, does not arise.

9.4 PERFORMANCE OF CONTRACTS AFTER INSOLVENCY

9.4.1 *Disclaimer*

The fact of a bankruptcy or a liquidation by itself will not always constitute a repudiation of a contract entered into prior to the insolvency.[67] If a

---

goods, and was sued by the bankrupt's assignees for the proceeds. It had been held in a previous action ((1837) 2 Deac. 179) that the sum paid on behalf of the bankrupt to prevent the distress was not a provable debt, although the court in the instant case nevertheless said that as a matter of equity the assignees could not recover the proceeds without giving credit for the sums paid by the petitioner.

[64] *Savage* v. *Thompson* (1903) 29 VLR 436.

[65] After the assignment is avoided any proceeds received by the purchaser may be subject to a constructive trust, and therefore not be susceptible to a set-off in any event on that ground. See Ch. 6.   [66] *Re Last; ex parte Butterell* (1994) 124 ALR 219.

[67] See e.g. *Brooke* v. *Hewitt* (1796) 3 Ves. Jun. 253; *Jennings' Trustee* v. *King* [1952] 1 Ch. 899; *Official Receiver* v. *Henn* (1981) 40 ALR 569. See also section 5.2 above.

contract is not repudiated, any rights arising under it in favour of the insolvent will become an asset of the estate available for distribution amongst creditors. If the insolvent's side of the contract still requires performance, the trustee or the liquidator may choose to disclaim it as an unprofitable contract.[68] Alternatively, the contract may be regarded as profitable and consequently not be disclaimed. In these circumstances, the question may arise whether liabilities and rights of action arising pursuant to the contract as a result of later performance or non-performance may be the subject of a set-off.

Consider first the case of a bankruptcy. The trustee is not personally liable for any breach of the bankrupt's contracts occurring after the bankruptcy, including as a result of disclaimer. Rather, the other contracting party is remitted to a proof in the bankuptcy for his damages claim,[69] and since the claim arises out of a prior dealing he should also be entitled to use it in a set-off.[70] Often, though, when a contract imposing onerous obligations on a bankrupt is in issue,[71] the other contracting party will serve a notice on the bankrupt's trustee requiring him to decide within 28 days whether or not he is going to disclaim the contract, and, if he does not disclaim, section 316(2) of the Insolvency Act provides that 'the trustee is deemed to have adopted' the contract.[72] Two interpretations of this provision have been put forward.[73] The first is that the trustee is deemed to have adopted the contract in his personal capacity, so that he becomes personally liable for any subsequent breach of the contract, subject only to a possible right of indemnity from the estate.[74] Since the burden of a contract, as distinct from the benefit, cannot be assigned, this interpretation would seem to envisage a form of novation of the contract, by which the trustee in his personal capacity replaces the bankrupt as the party responsible for carrying out the contract. The second interpretation is also based on a novation, though in this case the trustee

---

[68] See the Insolvency Act 1986, s. 315, and, for company liquidations, s. 178. In Australia see the Bankuptcy Act 1966 (Cth.), s. 133, and for companies the Corporations Law, ss. 568–568F.

[69] *In re Sneezum; ex parte Davis* (1876) 3 Ch. D 463. See also *Stead Hazel and Company* v. *Cooper* [1933] 1 KB 840 for companies. In the event of a disclaimer, the Insolvency Act 1986, ss. 178(6) and 315(5) specifically confer a right of proof for loss suffered as a result of the disclaimer.   [70] For set-off against a damages claim see section 4.5 above.

[71] For a discussion of onerous contracts, see Melville, 'Disclaimer of Contracts in Bankruptcy' (1952) 15 *Modern Law Review* 28.

[72] In Australia see the Bankruptcy Act 1966 (Cth.), s. 133(6).

[73] Melville, 'Disclaimer of Contracts in Bankruptcy' (1952) 15 *Modern Law Review* 28, 33–4.

[74] Robson, *Law of Bankruptcy* (7th edn. 1894), 473–4. In the case of a lease, if a trustee does not disclaim he becomes personally liable for rent, although this is on the basis of privity of estate. See e.g. *Ex parte Dressler; in re Solomon* (1878) 9 Ch. D 252, and section 9.5.1 below.

representing the estate and the creditors generally is substituted for the trustee as representing the bankrupt,[75] in which case it has been suggested[76] that the other contracting party would be a first priority creditor entitled to be paid ahead of the other creditors. Either interpretation, however, would mean that the other contracting party would not be able to bring a prior indebtedness of his to the bankrupt into an account. Mutuality would be lacking between that indebtedness and his claim against either the trustee representing the estate or the trustee in his personal capacity. Admittedly the right of the other party to proceed against the trustee personally, or to have a direct claim against the estate, would generally obviate the necessity for a set-off. Indeed, if the value of his claim is greater than his indebtedness, either of these alternatives would be preferable to a set-off, because set-off only enables a creditor to obtain the full value of his right to the extent of his indebtedness. On the other hand, he may suffer from the loss of a set-off if the section is interpreted as imposing personal liability on the trustee, and the trustee himself is insolvent.

The position of a company in liquidation in relation to disclaimer of unprofitable contracts is similar to that applicable to bankruptcy. If the liquidator disclaims a contract the resulting damages claim should be able to be the subject of a set-off, since it arose out of a prior dealing.[77] However, liquidation differs from bankruptcy in an important respect. Unlike in a bankruptcy, the liquidation of a company does not have the effect of vesting the company's property in the person administering the estate, the liquidator.[78] Consistent with this notion, if a notice is served upon a liquidator requiring him to decide whether or not he is going to disclaim a particular contract, and he fails to disclaim within the 28-day period, the legislation does not provide that the liquidator is deemed to have adopted the contract.[79] Any subsequent breach of contract would be a liability of the company itself, and in accordance with general principles it should be able to be the subject of a set-off.

9.4.2 *Contract by insolvent to sell property or perform work*

A person may have contracted to sell property or perform work, but have become bankrupt or gone into liquidation before the contract has been

---

[75] Williams and Muir Hunter, *The Law and Practice in Bankruptcy* (19th edn., 1979), 394–5.

[76] Melville, 'Disclaimer of Contracts in Bankruptcy' (1952) 15 *Modern Law Review* 28, 34.

[77] See section 3.2 above.   [78] See section 9.2 above.

[79] Compare in Australia the Corporations Law, s. 568(8) which provides that, if the liquidator does not disclaim within the appointed time, 'he or she' shall be deemed to have adopted it.

completed. If the contract is subsequently performed, so that the price becomes payable, the other contracting party liable to pay the price may wish to set off a separate debt owing to him by the bankrupt or the company.

If the contract in question is for the sale of real property, and the beneficial ownership of that property had vested in the purchaser prior to the vendor's insolvency, the purchaser ordinarily is entitled to specific performance of the contract, subject to the usual requirement of being able to show that he is ready and willing to perform his own essential obligations under the contract. If the vendor happens to be separately indebted to the purchaser, and that debt is otherwise capable of being employed in a set-off, the Court of Appeal in *In re Taylor; ex parte Norvell*[80] held that the purchaser is entitled to have the debt set off against his obligation to pay the price, and that specific performance may be decreed on terms that the purchaser pay the balance (if any) in favour of the vendor.

Consider, however, that the contract is for the sale of property the beneficial ownership of which had not vested in the purchaser prior to the vendor's insolvency. Depending on the terms of the contract this could arise in a particular case in the context of a contract for the sale of real property, though a more common example is a contract for the sale of a quantity of unascertained goods for delivery at a future date. Usually in such a case the price is not payable until delivery occurs. If in the interim the vendor has become bankrupt or has gone into liquidation, the trustee in bankruptcy or liquidator may disclaim the contract if it is unprofitable.[81] Alternatively, if the contract is profitable, the trustee or the liquidator may decide to complete it for the benefit of the creditors and deliver the goods in question. If the goods are delivered and accepted on a 'cash on delivery' basis there should not be any difficulty. If, however, delivery takes place without immediate payment, the purchaser may assert that he is entitled to a set-off against his indebtedness for the price. The same issue may arise in the context of a contract for the performance of work. If the trustee or the liquidator decides to complete the contract for the benefit of the estate and perform the work, the question may arise whether the resulting payment obligation may be the subject of a set-off.

As a preliminary point, it is assumed in the following discussion that a debt which arises in favour of a bankrupt or a company in liquidation pursuant to a prior contract is capable as a matter of principle of being employed in a set-off. The discussion of that question in the context of contingent debts owing to an insolvent[82] is relevant here. In addition, the ensuing discussion is premised on the assumption that performance takes

---

[80] [1910] 2 KB 562.
[81] See the Insolvency Act 1986, s. 315 and, for company liquidations, s. 178.
[82] See section 4.4 above.

place pursuant to a contract entered into before the bankruptcy or liquidation, as opposed to a new contract entered into after that date.[83] In the latter case it is accepted that a set-off would not be available.[84]

Prima facie a set-off should be possible in these circumstances. Since the debt for the price is a natural result of the prior transaction it should be a case of giving credit for the purpose of the set-off section, though in any event the debt should be available as a set-off on the ground that it is a money demand arising out of a prior dealing between the parties to the proposed set-off.[85] Further, the requirement of mutuality would appear to be satisfied. This concept is usually expressed in terms that the cross-demands must be between the same parties and be held in the same right and interest.[86] In this regard, the fact that a debt for the price first arose after the bankruptcy or liquidation by itself should not be fatal to the requirement. This is so notwithstanding that the debt from the time that it accrued would have been vested in the trustee[87] or, in the case of a company liquidation in which there is no *cessio bonorum*, notwithstanding that the company itself would never have had a beneficial interest in the accrued debt.[88] The important point is that the debt arose out of a prior transaction between the parties to the proposed set-off, and that mutuality accordingly is satisfied as at the relevant date for determining rights of set-off in the context of that transaction and the cross-debt. If this were not the applicable principle, a debt owing to a bankrupt which was still contingent at the relevant date but in respect of which the contingency has since occurred could never be the subject of a set-off, though the better view is that the fact that the debt was still contingent at that date is not a bar to a set-off.[89] As Dixon J. expressed the principle in the High Court of Australia in *Hiley* v. *The Peoples Prudential Assurance Co. Ltd.*:[90]

It is enough that at the commencement of the winding up mutual dealings exist which involve rights and obligations of such a nature that afterwards in the events that happen they mature or develop into pecuniary demands capable of set-off. If

---

[83] In this regard see Lindley L.J.'s explanation in *Mersey Steel and Iron Company* v. *Naylor, Benzon & Co.* (1882) 9 QBD 648, 669 of the decision in *Ince Hall Rolling Mills Co.* v. *Douglas Forge Co.* (1882) 8 QBD 179, discussed below.

[84] Compare *Re Henley, Thurgood & Co.* (1883) 11 WR 1021.

[85] See sections 3.1 and 3.2 above.   [86] See section 7.1 above.

[87] See section 4.4 above.

[88] See section 9.2 above. Compare in Australia *Franklin's Selfserve Pty. Ltd.* v. *Federal Commissioner of Taxation* (1970) 125 CLR 52, in which Menzies J. held that liquidation does not deprive a company of the beneficial title to its assets. On that basis lack of mutuality is even less likely to be an objection in Australia.

[89] See section 4.4 above.

[90] (1938) 60 CLR 468, 497. Millett J. in *Re Charge Card Services Ltd.* [1987] 1 Ch. 150, 178 accepted this as a correct statement of the law. See also *Gye* v. *McIntyre* (1991) 171 CLR 609, 624.

the end contemplated by the transaction is a claim sounding in money so that, in the phrase employed in the cases, it is commensurable with the cross-demand, no more is required than that at the commencement of the winding up liabilities shall have been contracted by the company and the other party respectively from which cross money claims accrue during the course of the winding up . . .

Notwithstanding this, the decision of Watkin Williams J. in *Ince Hall Rolling Mills Co., Ltd.* v. *The Douglas Forge Company*[91] is authority against a set-off.

Ince Hall concerned a contract for the sale of a quantity of unascertained goods entered into before the liquidation of the supplier. After the liquidation an order was made by the court authorizing the liquidator to carry on the business for the purpose of winding-up the company, whereupon the liquidator determined to complete the contract and deliver the goods contracted for. Payment did not take place upon delivery, and when the liquidator subsequently sued for the price the purchaser sought to set off a separate debt owing to it. However Watkin Williams J. held that the debt for the price could not be the subject of a set-off. He said that there was a lack of mutuality because, when a company completes a transaction after the commencement of its liquidation, albeit pursuant to a prior contract, it does so in a new interest and a new capacity.[92]

Every transaction entered into by the company from [the commencement of liquidation] is void unless sanctioned by the Court; no contracts can be executed nor can the business of the company be carried on in a single particular except for the purposes of winding-up and for the benefit of the creditors, and, although the company continues in existence and under the same name, and may, if allowed by the Court, continue to carry on its business and enter into or complete transactions, it does so in a new interest and a new capacity, and solely for the purpose of winding-up its affairs in the interest of its creditors and shareholders . . . The practical effect of the defendants' contention would be that the company by a transaction which is void, unless sanctioned and ratified by the Court, would be paying one creditor in full out of the assets of the insolvent company in preference to the other creditors; such a result may well make one pause before giving effect to such a contention.

While the decision in *Ince Hall* has been noted in a number of later cases,[93] the stage has not been reached where it can be regarded as setting

---

[91] (1882) 8 QBD 179.   [92] (1882) 8 QBD 179, 184.
[93] It was referred to with evident approval by the Western Australian Supreme Court in *In re The West Australian Lighterage, Stevedoring and Transport Co., Ltd.* (1903) 5 WAR 132, 138, while the New South Wales Court of Appeal in *Central Brake Service (Sydney) Ltd.* v. *Central Brake Service (Newcastle) Ltd.* (1992) 27 NSWLR 406, 409 noted the decision without adverse comment. In *In re Taylor; ex parte Norvell* [1910] 1 KB 562, 575 (and see also 576)

out an entrenched principle. Indeed, if goods are supplied to a purchaser pursuant to a contract entered into before the supplier's liquidation, the purchaser may well wonder why the fact that delivery actually takes place after liquidation rather than before should affect his position, particularly given that he may have been induced to enter into the transaction on the basis of a perception that an account could be taken in a case of mutual dealings. A debt for the price arises upon delivery, and the question whether delivery will occur is in the hands of the supplier's liquidator, not the purchaser. If the liquidator instead disclaimed the contract, the resulting damages claim against the company would have been a provable debt in the liquidation,[94] and there is little doubt that it could also have been the subject of a set-off.[95]

Wood has sought to explain *Ince Hall* on the basis of a principle that he suggests is generally applicable to insolvency set-off[96] that, if an insolvency representative 'earns' a payment under a contract by the use of the insolvent's assets, e.g. by delivering property or performing work or continuing a lease of the insolvent's property, the price or the rent which is then earned is non-mutual with a separate indebtedness of the insolvent, and so is not available for a set-off. The reason for this is said to be that the assets of the estate available for distribution generally in effect would be used to pay one creditor in full. The insolvent would be divested of the

Fletcher Moulton J., in a judgment in which he dissented on another point, said that 'it cannot be doubted' that a trustee in bankruptcy electing to perform a prior contract to sell goods would be entitled to be paid the price in cash and not by a set-off. While his Lordship did not specifically refer to *Ince Hall*, he may have had that decision in mind. It appears more likely, though, that he merely contemplated the situation in which the contract in any event was on cash on delivery terms. Reference also may be made to Gibbs C.J.'s discussion in *Day & Dent Constructions Pty. Ltd.* v. *North Australian Properties Pty. Ltd.* (1982) 150 CLR 85, 94 of the Court of Appeal's decision in *In re A Debtor (No. 66 of 1955)* [1956] 1 WLR 1226. In that case a surety's trustee in bankruptcy paid the creditor under the guarantee in order to obtain the release of security given to the creditor, and it was held that the surety's resulting claim for an indemnity from the debtor could not be the subject of a set-off. The ostensible reason for the decision was that at the date of the bankruptcy the surety merely had a contingent right to an indemnity, the creditor not having paid at that date, and it was not considered to be possible to base a set-off upon a claim that was merely contingent, and consequently not due, at that date. Gibbs C.J. criticized this ground for the decision, though he nevertheless left open the question whether the case was correctly decided, on the basis that 'the payments were made by the trustee to enable him to obtain the bankrupt's property' which 'may justify a conclusion that there were no mutual dealings between the trustee and the debtor'. In *Old Style Confections Pty. Ltd.* v. *Microbyte Investments Pty. Ltd.* (1994) 15 ACSR 191, 197–8, 199 Hayne J. in Victoria left open the question whether *Ince Hall* was correctly decided.

[94] See the Insolvency Act 1986, s. 178(6). The equivalent provision for bankruptcies is s. 315(5).

[95] Certainly, in the converse case of a company which failed to purchase goods after its liquidation notwithstanding a prior agreement to do so, it has been held that the resulting damages claim against the company may be set off. See *Telsen Electric Co., Ltd.* v. *J. J. Eastick & Sons* [1936] 3 All ER 266.

[96] Wood, *English and International Set-off* (1989), 326, 329.

asset used to perform the contract, and the estate would also lose the entitlement to the price or the rent as a result of the set-off. However, apart from *Ince Hall*, it is difficult to find direct support for this principle. In the first place, the lease cases to which Wood has referred[97] were concerned with bankruptcies, and in that context the denial of a set-off in respect of post-insolvency rent where the landlord has become bankrupt is explicable by the concept of privity of estate.[98] Secondly, the suggested principle does not sit happily with the decision of the High Court of Australia in *Hiley* v. *The Peoples Prudential Assurance Co., Ltd.*[99] That case concerned a policy-holder in a life insurance company who had borrowed money from the company secured by a mortgage over some property. The company then transferred the mortgage, including the policy-holder's debt, to an assignee by way of security. After the company went into liquidation the liquidator redeemed the mortgage, whereupon it was held that the policy-holder could employ the debt in a set-off in the liquidation. The redemption of the security occurred as a result of a compromise of rights involving the life company and the assignee, though the tenor of the judgments, particularly that of Dixon J.,[100] suggests that the same result would have followed if the redemption had occurred as a result of a payment of money by the liquidator. In either case the liquidator would have used assets of the company which otherwise would have been available for distribution generally, in the form of either the compromised rights or the company's funds, in order to redeem the policy-holder's debt to the company, and yet this was not regarded as fatal to a set-off. Thirdly, the suggested principle does not appear to apply to contracts for the performance of work.[101] In *In re Asphaltic Wood Pavement Company; Lee & Chapman's Case*[102] a company had contracted with the Commissioners of Sewers to pave a street for a stated price. In addition the contract provided that, if within 2 years following completion the Commissioners by notice in writing to the company should so require, the company had to keep the road in repair for a period of 15 years, for which the company was to be paid at a fixed annual rate. The company went into liquidation before the completion of the work, though the liquidator was empowered by the court to complete the contract, and for this purpose to expend all necessary money for wages, materials, and incidental expenses. Obviously, though,

---

[97] Wood, *English and International Set-off* (1989), 342–3.
[98] See section 9.5.1 below.   [99] (1938) 60 CLR 468.
[100] See e.g. Dixon J.'s discussion (at (1938) 60 CLR 468, 505) of *In re City Life Assurance Co. Ltd; Stephenson's Case* [1926] 1 Ch. 191.
[101] Compare Wood, *English and International Set-off* (1989), 336. As Wood noted, *Alloway* v. *Steere* (1882) 10 QBD 22 was concerned with a lease, for which special considerations apply. See section 9.5.1 below.   [102] (1885) 30 Ch. D 216.

the company was not in a position to fulfil its obligation to repair for the 15-year period upon receipt of the requisite notice. Prior to the liquidation the company had granted a charge to a third party which encompassed part of the moneys payable under the contract, but the Court of Appeal[103] held that the residue of the contract amount owing by the employer could be set off against the employer's claim for damages for anticipatory breach of contract arising from failure to keep the road in repair for 15 years. This was so even though the Commissioners' indebtedness to the company for the price only arose after the liquidation when the work was completed. The interesting point is that the company's money was used after the liquidation to complete the contract for the benefit of the estate, in buying materials, paying wages etc. In this sense it is similar to *Ince Hall*, and yet a set-off was allowed. *Ince Hall* was mentioned in argument before the Court of Appeal, though Brett L.J. said in response that, 'The decision in that case has no bearing upon this case'.[104] It is not clear what his Lordship had in mind when he said that it had no bearing. It is true that in *Lee & Chapman's Case* a great part of the work had been completed before the liquidation, whereas in *Ince Hall* performance by the company occurred entirely after the liquidation. However, to the extent that the company's funds were expended after the liquidation,[105] and the expenditure of those funds was necessary in order for the company's creditors to obtain the benefit of the contract, the cases would appear to be similar.[106]

In *Lee & Chapman's Case* the employer's claim was based upon a breach by the company of an obligation that arose out of the same contract as the employer's liability to pay the contract sum, and for this reason Wood has suggested that the set-off enforced in *Lee & Chapman's Case* is an example of an equitable (or transaction) set-off, as opposed to a set-off under the bankruptcy legislation.[107] However, even apart from the question whether the demands in any event were sufficiently closely connected to give rise to an equitable set-off,[108] equitable set-off was not mentioned in any of the judgments. The only right of set-off that was discussed was the right arising under the mutual credit provision in the bankruptcy legislation,[109] and it is clear that this was the form of set-off considered to be in issue. In other

---

[103] Brett M.R., Cotton and Lindley L.JJ..   [104] (1885) 30 Ch. D 216, 219.

[105] See in particular Bacon V.C. at first instance (1884) 26 Ch. D 624, 634, whose conclusion with respect to set-off was reversed by the Court of Appeal.

[106] Indeed, the analysis of Watkin Williams J. in *Ince Hall* on the question of mutuality is at odds with the tenor of Cotton L.J.'s judgment in *Lee & Chapman's Case* (1885) 30 Ch. D 216, 224 (and see also Brett M.R. at 220), though admittedly that was in a different context.

[107] Wood, *English and International Set-off* (1989), 331, 337.

[108] See Derham, 'Some Aspects of Mutual Credit and Mutual Dealings' (1992) 108 *Law Quarterly Review* 99, 132–3.

[109] The relevant provision was the Bankruptcy Act 1869, s. 39. See in particular Brett M.R. at (1885) 30 Ch. D 216, 222, and Cotton L.J. at 224.

words, it must have been accepted that there was mutuality for the purpose of the bankruptcy set-off section, even though the contract was completed after the liquidation for the benefit of creditors.

Given that *Lee & Chapman's Case* was concerned with insolvency set-off, is there any basis for distinguishing it from *Ince Hall*? One possibility is the destination of the company's property. While the cases are similar, in that in each case a claim accrued to a company after the commencement of its liquidation as a result of the use by the liquidator of the company's assets or funds, in *Ince Hall* the person liable on the claim was the direct recipient of property of the company that otherwise would have been available for distribution generally, whereas in *Lee & Chapman's Case* the company's funds were remitted to third parties (suppliers of materials, employees receiving wages etc.). However, it is difficult to see why this would justify a different result. In each case the person asserting a set-off against indebtedness to the company received full consideration for the debt. In *Ince Hall* this was the result of the delivery of the goods the subject of the contract of sale, and in *Lee & Chapman's Case* it was a result of the street being paved. In this regard, it has never been a principle of insolvency set-off that a person indebted to a bankrupt or a company in liquidation should be precluded from employing the debt in a set-off merely because that person in any event has received full consideration from the bankrupt or the company. This is apparent from cases in which goods were delivered by a vendor to a purchaser on credit terms *before* the vendor became bankrupt, and the price was not payable until after the bankruptcy. It was held in these cases that the purchaser could have a set-off against the price even though he already had the goods.[110] Indeed, in any loan the borrower receives full consideration, in the form of the money the subject of the loan, and he is not precluded by this fact alone from subsequently asserting the debt in a set-off.

Further, *Ince Hall* does not sit easily with *Rother Iron Works Ltd.* v. *Canterbury Precision Engineers Ltd.*[111] The cases differed in that there was a liquidation in *Ince Hall*, whereas *Rother Iron Works* concerned a receivership. Apart from that, the similarity between them is striking. In both a company had contracted to sell goods to a person who was a creditor on another transaction. The purchaser became indebted for the price when the goods were delivered, which in each case occurred after the relevant event (liquidation in *Ince Hall*, and receivership in *Rother Iron Works*). Yet, while a set-off was denied in *Ince Hall*, the purchaser in *Rother Iron*

---

[110] *Smith* v. *Hodson* (1791) 4 TR 211; *Groom* v. *West* (1838) 8 Ad. & E 758 (in which it was specifically argued, unsuccessfully, that a set-off should be denied because the purchaser already had the goods); *Gibson* v. *Bell* (1835) 1 Bing. (NC) 743; *Russell* v. *Bell* (1841) 8 M & W 277.   [111] [1974] 1 QB 1, discussed in section 13.3.1 below.

Works was allowed to set off the indebtedness for the price against a prior cross-debt owing by the company. Russell L.J. referred to *Ince Hall* in his judgment in *Rother Iron Works*, but distinguished it on the basis that the liquidation of a company produces a vital change in the status of the company and does not operate only as an equitable assignment by way of charge. It is undoubtedly true that liquidation and receivership are different, but the question is whether they are sufficiently dissimilar to justify a different result in the cases. When the floating charge crystallized in *Rother Iron Works* the goods which were later sold became subject to a fixed charge in favour of the secured creditor, and were set aside to satisfy the debt owing to it. A similar process happens in a liquidation. The company is divested of the beneficial title to its assets, which are collected and applied in the first instance for the benefit of creditors in discharge of the company's debts.[112] This extends in both cases to the proceeds of sale of the property in question, and so in this respect liquidation and receivership would appear to be similar. There are in fact indications that Russell L.J. was not completely comfortable with the decision in *Ince Hall*. In response to the argument that the allowance of a set-off in *Rother Iron Works* would produce an illogical distinction between liquidation and receivership, his Lordship remarked that he was 'not satisfied that the *Ince Hall* case does *necessarily* show such an illogical distinction',[113] which may be regarded as not a particularly confident assertion as to the differences between the two cases. Moreover, as an alternative basis for distinguishing the earlier case, he referred to a statement by Lindley L.J. in *Mersey Steel & Iron Co.* v. *Naylor, Benzon & Co.*[114] to the effect that *Ince Hall* was a case where the liquidator, after the winding up had commenced, entered into a new contract. In fact this is not a proper interpretation of *Ince Hall*, because Watkin Williams J. in that case undoubtedly proceeded on the basis that the goods were supplied after the liquidation in execution of a contract entered into by the company before then.[115]

There is nevertheless a line of cases which, it has been suggested,[116] is consistent with the decision in *Ince Hall*. These cases established the principle that an assignment by a trader of the future receipts of his business is, as regards receipts which accrue after the commencement of his bankruptcy, inoperative as against the title of the trustee in bankruptcy.[117]

---

[112] *Ayerst* v. *C. & K. (Construction) Ltd.* [1976] AC 167.
[113] [1974] 1 QB 1, 5 (emphasis added).   [114] (1882) 9 QBD 648, 669.
[115] See the question framed by Watkin Williams J. in the opening paragraph of his judgment at (1882) 8 QBD 179.
[116] Wood, *English and International Set-off* (1989), 326, 334.
[117] *Ex parte Nichols; in re Jones* (1883) 22 Ch. D 782; *Wilmot* v. *Alton* [1897] 1 QB 17; *In re Irvine* [1919] NZLR 351; *In re Collins* [1925] Ch. 556. Compare *Drew & Co.* v. *Josolyne* (1887) 18 QBD 590 and *Re Tout and Finch Ltd.* [1954] 1 WLR 178, in which the debt assigned

However, they are distinguishable. Their true basis appears from the judgment of Lord Esher M.R. in *In re Davis & Co; ex parte Rawlings*,[118] that the payments 'would only arise in case the business of the bankrupts should be carried on, and in case, by reason of its being carried on, payments should be made to the person who was carrying it on. If the business was being carried on by the trustee the payments would never become due to the bankrupts, they would become due to the trustee'. Since the payments do not belong to the debtor, they cannot be assigned by him. Insolvency set-off on the other hand is not concerned with the title to receipts, but rather with cross-demands originating from mutual credits, mutual debts or other mutual dealings. A debt which accrues after a bankruptcy or a liquidation, but which relates to a prior contract, arises out of a prior dealing with the bankrupt or the company, and prior mutual dealings give rise to an 'equity' to invoke the set-off section to which the creditors of the bankrupt or the company in liquidation take subject. This conclusion is implicit in the decision in *Lee & Chapman's Case*,[119] in which a set-off was allowed in respect of a claim that accrued after the commencement of the company's liquidation as a result of the carrying on of the company's business. In this regard, it is noticeable that Lindley L.J. was one of the judges in the Court of Appeal that enunciated the principle under discussion in *Ex parte Nichols; in re Jones*,[120] and yet he did not seem to consider that case as relevant 2 years later when, along with Brett M.R. and Cotton L.J., he upheld the claim for a set-off in *Lee & Chapman's Case*. Further, when the Court of Appeal in *Wilmot* v. *Alton*[121] subsequently followed *Ex parte Nichols*, Brett M.R., who by then was Lord Esher M.R., did not consider it necessary to explain his earlier judgment in *Lee & Chapman's Case*.[122]

---

represented retention moneys already earned but not yet payable at the date of the bankruptcy or liquidation. Similarly, in *In re Davis & Co; ex parte Rawlings* (1888) 22 QBD 193 the debt assigned was in existence at the date of the bankruptcy though not payable until a future date, and so the title of the assignee took precedence over that of the trustee in bankruptcy.

[118] (1888) 22 QBD 193, 198.
[119] (1885) 30 Ch. D 216. See also *Clarke* v. *Fell* (1833) 4 B & Ad. 404, the tenor of the judgments in which suggests that a set-off would have been allowed but for the agreement to pay in ready money.
[120] (1883) 22 Ch. D 782.   [121] [1897] 1 QB 17.
[122] A possible reason for this is that the principle under discussion in fact does not apply to companies, in which case it would not be an objection in any event to a set-off in the context of a liquidation. Unlike in a bankruptcy, in which the assets of the bankrupt vest in the trustee, there is no *cessio bonorum* in favour of a liquidator. Accordingly, any earnings from carrying on the company's business after the liquidation could not be said to be the earnings of the liquidator. There is an aspect of *Lee & Chapman's Case* which lends support to this view. 90 per cent of the earnings under the contract in that case had been charged to a third party, so that the set-off only related to the 10 per cent to which the company itself remained

In the case of a contract for the sale of land or goods where the seller has become insolvent prior to completion, it should not be crucial to the question of set-off that the beneficial ownership of the property in question should have passed prior to the insolvency date.[123] The law of set-off is not concerned with property rights as such, but rather with money claims arising from the giving of credit or from prior dealings between the parties. The time of passing of the equitable interest should only be incidentally relevant, in the sense that it can affect the parties' remedies. If the beneficial ownership has already passed, the contract could not be disclaimed by the vendor's trustee or liquidator.[124] Furthermore, the court ordinarily would order specific performance of the contract on the application of the purchaser, on terms that he pay the balance of the price after deducting a debt owing to him by the insolvent vendor.[125] If, however, the beneficial ownership has not passed, the contract may be able to be disclaimed as an unprofitable contract,[126] in which case it could not be specifically enforced.[127] The purchaser would then be left to his remedy in damages, which in turn could be the subject of a set-off. But, if in a case such as *Ince Hall* the contract is indeed performed, the question of the availability of a set-off should not depend upon whether the beneficial ownership of the property in question passed to the purchaser prior to the vendor's bankruptcy or liquidation. Rather, as Dixon J. expressed the principle in the Australian High Court in *Hiley* v. *Peoples Prudential Assurance Co.*,[128] 'If the end contemplated by the transaction is a claim sounding in money . . . *no more is required* than that at the commencement of the winding up liabilities shall have been contracted by the company and the other party respectively from which cross money claims accrue during the course of the winding up'.

---

entitled. Not only was the set-off upheld, but the charge was also regarded as effective notwithstanding that the contract was completed after liquidation. On the other hand, in *Re Tout and Finch Ltd.* [1954] 1 WLR 178, 186–9 Wynn-Parry J. seems to have assumed that the principle does extend to companies.

[123] Compare Wood, *English and International Set-off* (1989), 327–36.

[124] *In re Bastable; ex parte The Trustee* [1901] 2 KB 518.

[125] *In re Taylor; ex parte Norvell* [1910] 1 KB 562.

[126] *Quaere* whether, in the determination of whether a contract is unprofitable, a trustee in bankruptcy or liquidator may take into account the effect of any set-off that may be available to the other party, or whether regard may be had only to whether the contract itself is a bad bargain. In *Old Style Confections Pty. Ltd.* v. *Microbyte Investments Pty. Ltd.* (1994) 15 ACSR 191 Hayne J. in the Victorian Supreme Court held that the availability of a set-off against contract payments is not a relevant consideration. Note that in Australia a liquidator or trustee can disclaim any contract, though if it is not an unprofitable contract the leave of the court is required. See the Bankruptcy Act 1966 (Cth.), ss. 133(1A) and 133(5A) and the Corporations Law, ss. 568(1)(f) and 568(1A).

[127] See Jones and Goodhart, *Specific Performance* (1986), 173.

[128] (1938) 60 CLR 468, 497 (emphasis added).

9.4.3 *Contract to sell property to or to perform work for an insolvent*

The converse of the situation considered above is that it is the purchaser of property to be delivered or of work to be performed who becomes bankrupt or goes into liquidation before completion of the contract. Once again, if the contract is disclaimed a resulting damages claim would be provable,[129] and should also be capable of being employed in a set-off. Consider, however, that the contract remains on foot. In the first place, questions of set-off are unlikely to arise because, in the case of a contract to sell goods, if the purchaser has become insolvent the vendor is entitled to insist that the price be tendered to him before delivery, even if the sale was otherwise expressed to be on credit terms.[130] A similar principle would appear to apply to contracts for the performance of work.[131] But if in a particular case the goods are delivered without payment having been first received, or the work is performed without the price having been first secured, for the same reasons given above in the context of the criticism of the decision in *Ince Hall*[132] the resulting debt should be able to be employed in a set-off,[133] given that it resulted from a prior contract and that it would be provable in the bankruptcy or liquidation.

9.4.4 *Options*

In *Re Kidsgrove Steel, Iron, and Coal Co.*[134] the owner of a colliery and iron works had leased them to a company, the lease giving the owner the option, after the end or determination of the lease, of purchasing at a valuation all plant and fixtures that might be erected by the company as lessee. The company went into liquidation, after which the lease was determined. The owner thereupon exercised the option to purchase the plant and fixtures erected on the premises. Chitty J. held that the resulting debt for the price could not be the subject of a set-off, the reason being that the contract to purchase was not in existence at the date of the liquidation. That contract only arose subsequently, when the option was exercised. However the better view is that a set-off should have been available, since the option itself was granted before the liquidation. In other words, the contract of sale arose out of a prior dealing, without the intervention of any new and independent transaction.[135] Moreover, notwithstanding the

---

[129] See the Insolvency Act 1986, ss. 178(6) & 315(5)
[130] *Ex parte Chalmers* (1873) LR 8 Ch. App. 289; Sale of Goods Act 1979, s. 41(1)(c).
[131] *In re Sneezum; ex parte Davies* (1876) 3 Ch. D 463, 473–474.
[132] (1882) 8 QBD 179, discussed in section 9.4.2 above.
[133] Compare Wood, *English and International Set-off* (1989), 308–9.
[134] (1894) 38 Sol. Jo. 252.
[135] See Dixon J. in *Hiley* v. *The Peoples Prudential Assurance Company Ltd.* (1938) 60 CLR 468, 499, and also Starke J. at 487.

decision of Watkin Williams J. in *Ince Hall*,[136] the fact that the assets the subject of the sale resulting from the exercise of the option would have been available for distribution generally should not have affected the question of mutuality. Nor should it have been fatal to a set-off that the owner in any event had received full consideration for the debt sought to be set off, in the form of the plant and fixtures the subject of the option.[137]

It is true that, if a set-off is allowed in a case involving an option to purchase assets, the availability of a set-off would then depend upon whether the option-holder chooses to exercise the option. It may be said that that person accordingly would have the means of obtaining preferential treatment over the other creditors by exercising the option and obtaining the assets the subject of the option, and then setting off his obligation to pay the price against the insolvent company's debt. However, the point may be made that the liquidator in any event may be able to disclaim the option as an unprofitable contract. Moreover, the argument fails to take into account that the option nevertheless arose out of a prior dealing, notwithstanding that the exercise itself of the option was a voluntary act. In this regard, reference may be made to *In re The Moseley Green Coal and Coke Co., Ltd; Barrett's Case*.[138] A debt the subject of a guarantee was secured by a promissory note given by the debtor to the creditor. After the debtor had been ordered to be wound up the surety's sister paid the creditor, and the promissory note was indorsed and delivered to her. Subsequently the sister agreed to hand over the promissory note to the surety in exchange for his own promissory note. It was held that the surety could bring the claim on the promissory note into an account with a debt that he owed to the debtor, since his acquisition of the promissory note was related to the prior obligation that he had assumed as surety. However, it is noticeable that the surety was not being pressed for payment, and it appears that the arrangement was entered into with the sister to take a transfer of the promissory note for the specific purpose of obtaining a set-off.[139] If this was not an objection to a set-off in that case, the exercise of an option after the bankruptcy or liquidation of the other party but pursuant to a prior agreement similarly should be able to give rise to a set-off.

---

[136] (1882) 8 QBD 179, discussed in section 9.4.2 above.

[137] For example, when goods were delivered by a vendor to a purchaser on credit terms before the vendor became bankrupt, and the price was not payable until after the bankruptcy, the purchaser was allowed a set-off against the debt for the price notwithstanding that he already had the goods. See *Smith* v. *Hodson* (1791) 4 TR 211; *Groom* v. *West* (1838) 8 Ad. & E 758; *Gibson* v. *Bell* (1835) 1 Bing. (NC) 743; *Russell* v. *Bell* (1841) 8 M & W 277.

[138] (1865) 4 De G J & S 756, 34 LJ Bcy. 41.

[139] See the report of the case at (1865) 34 LJ Bcy. 41, 42.

Lee & Chapman's Case[140] is also relevant. It will be recalled[141] that the contract in that case provided that the Commissioners of Sewers could give a notice to the company requiring it to keep the road in repair for a period of 15 years at a stated price. The notice was given after the company's liquidation, and it was the company's resulting liability for damages to the Commissioners for anticipatory breach of contract in relation to that obligation that was the subject of the set-off. This was so notwithstanding that it was the result of the exercise of an option after liquidation. Admittedly the circumstances differed from those in *Kidsgrove*. In *Lee & Chapman's Case* the party exercising the option was otherwise a debtor of the company, and it was the claim resulting from the exercise of the option (for damages, for failure to carry out the resulting obligation) that was sought to be set off against a debt owing to the company, whereas in *Kidsgrove* the option holder incurred a liability for the price as a result of exercising the option and he sought to set off that liability against a separate claim that he had against the company. Nevertheless, *Lee & Chapman's Case* does illustrate that it is not fatal to a set-off that it is based upon the exercise of an option by the party asserting a set-off after the bankruptcy or liquidation of the other party.

If a sale of goods is made on terms that the purchaser may pay either in cash or by delivering other goods, and the vendor becomes bankrupt after delivering the contract goods but before the purchaser has made an election, the purchaser, if he chooses to pay cash, may obtain a right of set-off against the resulting debt.[142]

9.5 LEASES

9.5.1 *Bankruptcy*

A bankruptcy does not result in a vesting of the bankrupt's contracts in his trustee, but rather a vesting of the bankrupt's *rights* under those contracts. The contract is still the contract of the bankrupt. Any action by the bankrupt's trustee to obtain a benefit owing to the bankrupt under the contract prior to his bankruptcy is an action on that original contract. Similarly, if the trustee decides to carry on the contract after the bankruptcy for the benefit of the estate, then, apart from the possible statutory novation which may be brought about by section 316 of the Insolvency Act 1986,[143] any rights subsequently obtained or obligations subsequently incurred still relate to the bankrupt's contract, and any action

---

[140] (1885) 30 Ch. D 216.   [141] See section 9.4.2 above.
[142] *Re Inglis; ex parte The Trustee* (1932) 5 ABC 255.
[143] See section 9.4.1 above.

by or against the estate will still be based upon the privity that the bankrupt himself has in the contract. For this reason mutuality should still be present in relation to that claim and a prior independent dealing between the bankrupt and the other contracting party.[144] This should be compared to the situation in which the relationship between the bankrupt and the other party was that of landlord and tenant. Any rights possessed or liabilities incurred by the bankrupt under a tenancy or lease of real property prior to his bankruptcy ordinarily would be able to be employed by the other party in a set-off.[145] However, the bankrupt's interest in the lease or tenancy vests in the trustee in bankruptcy immediately upon his appointment taking effect,[146] and the trustee himself becomes the landlord or the tenant, as the case may be. The trustee may disclaim this interest under section 315 of the Insolvency Act as onerous property, in which case he is relieved from any personal liability for breach of the terms of the lease as from the commencement of his trusteeship.[147] If on the other hand the trustee fails to disclaim, any rights or liabilities subsequently obtained or incurred by the trustee under covenants annexed to the land accrue in his own right as trustee, *as the landlord or tenant.* This includes, in the case of the landlord, the right to payment of rent. Privity of estate, as opposed to privity of contract, may enable the trustee and the other party to enforce *inter se* their rights under the convenants.[148]

When the property of the bankrupt vests in his trustee, so that in the case of a lease the trustee himself becomes the landlord or the tenant, as the case may be, there is a lack of mutuality between any right accruing to, or any liability incurred by, the trustee in his own right as trustee under a convenant annexed to the land, and an independent cross-demand between the bankrupt and the other party to the claim on the covenant.[149] This is consistent with the principle that, unlike an assignee of a chose in action who sues under the assignor's privity of contract, an assignee of an estate or interest in land does not take subject to any personal defences

---

[144] See section 9.4.2 above.

[145] See e.g. *Ex parte Hope; in re Hanson* (1858) 3 De G & J 92, in which a set-off was allowed against rent overdue before the tenants' bankruptcy.

[146] Insolvency Act 1986, s. 306.

[147] See the Insolvency Act 1986, s. 315(3), and in Australia the Bankruptcy Act 1966 (Cth.), s. 133(2).

[148] The convenants which are binding on and which accrue to the benefit of an assignee of the lease or the reversion formerly were limited to those which 'touch and concern' the land, though (subject to s. 3(6)) this no longer applies to new tenancies under the Landlord and Tenant (Covenants) Act 1995.

[149] While the trustee from the time of his appointment is liable personally on the basis of privity of estate for the payment of rent and the performance of covenants that touch and concern the land, he will usually be entitled to an indemnity from the estate. See *Lowrey* v. *Barker & Sons* (1880) 5 Ex. D 170, 173, 175, and *Titterton* v. *Cooper* (1882) 9 QBD 473, 492, though compare *In re Page, Brothers; ex parte Mackay* (1884) 14 QBD 401.

that the defendant would have had against the assignor.[150] For example, *Alloway* v. *Steere*[151] concerned a debtor who was the tenant of a farm. There was a local custom by which the person who was the tenant of farmland at the expiration of the tenancy should be paid an allowance for any tillages and cultivation. During the currency of the tenancy the debtor instituted proceedings under the Bankruptcy Act 1869 for liquidation of his affairs by arrangement or composition with his creditors, with the result that the tenancy vested in his trustee. When the trustee subsequently claimed the allowance, the landlord was not allowed to set off arrears of rent owing by the debtor from the period before the liquidation proceedings.[152] As Manisty J. remarked:[153]

> The relative rights and liabilities of the landlord and the trustee appear clearly from the case of *Titterton* v. *Cooper* ((1882) 9 QBD 473), where the whole question was fully considered, and the conclusion arrived at by the Court of Appeal was that a trustee in bankruptcy, not disclaiming, was in the position of an ordinary assignee of the lease, and as such liable for the rent, and for the performance of the covenants during the time the lease was vested in him. No one could suggest that an ordinary assignee could be made liable for breaches of covenant, or of the contract of tenancy, which occurred before the assignment to him, and the breach of contract in respect of which the landlord claims a set-off in the present case is such a breach.

Similarly, when the landlord in *Kitchen's Trustee* v. *Madders*[154] became bankrupt, the tenant was not allowed to set off the bankrupt's liability to him against his obligation to pay rent to the trustee as landlord for the period after the trustee's appointment.[155]

The principle applied in *Kitchen's Trustee* is that the landlord's trustee in his capacity as landlord is in the same position with regard to the tenant as

---

[150] *David* v. *Sabin* [1893] 1 Ch. 523.

[151] (1882) 10 QBD 22. See also *Ex parte Sir W. Hart Dyke; in re Morrish* (1882) 22 Ch. D 410; *Titterton* v. *Cooper* (1882) 9 QBD 473. Compare *In re Wilson; ex parte Lord Hastings* (1893) 10 Morr. 219, in which Vaughan Williams J. found a custom in the county of Norfolk by which the landlord could deduct any arrears of rent, including arrears owing by the bankrupt as a previous tenant, from an allowance payable to the bankrupt's trustee for fixtures, growing crops etc. left in the hands of the landlord. Apparently there is a similar custom in a number of other counties. See Williams and Muir Hunter, *The Law and Practice in Bankruptcy* (19th edn., 1979), 198 n. 98.

[152] Compare *Ex parte Hope; in re Hanson* (1858) 3 De G & J 92, in which the assignees in bankruptcy elected not to continue the tenancy. Presumably the landlord in *Alloway* v. *Steere* would have been entitled to set off, under the Statutes of Set-off, any arrears of rent owing by the trustee himself for the period after his appointment.

[153] (1882) 10 QBD 22, 29. [154] [1950] 1 Ch. 134.

[155] See also *Graham* v. *Allsopp* (1848) 3 Ex. D 186 (in relation to the quarter's rent due after Christmas). Compare *Booth* v. *Hutchinson* (1872) LR 15 Eq. 30 in which Sir Richard Malins V.C. permitted a set-off in respect of rent accruing due after the date of the landlord's deed of assignment, though there was no consideration given to the question of mutuality.

any other assignee of the landlord. This principle was not applied 3 years later in *Bradley-Hole* v. *Cusen*[156] though, while the decision in that case seems to enjoy the support of text-writers,[157] its authority nevertheless should be regarded as questionable. The rent paid by the tenant of a dwelling-house to the landlord before the landlord's bankruptcy was greater than the rent lawfully recoverable by the landlord under the Rent Restriction Acts. The legislation conferred upon the tenant the right to recover the overpayment from the landlord who received it, or to deduct it from rent payable by him to the landlord.[158] The issue in the present case was whether the deduction could be made from rent payable to the landlord's trustee for the period after the bankruptcy. Jenkins L.J., in delivering the judgment of the Court of Appeal, was prepared to assume, though without finally deciding the point, that the deduction could not have been made from rent payable to an ordinary assignee of the landlord. However, he referred to *Bendall* v. *McWhirter*,[159] in which Somervell and Romer L.JJ. held that a deserted wife had a personal licence to remain in occupation of the matrimonial home owned by the husband, and furthermore that the husband's trustee in bankruptcy was no more entitled to revoke this licence than was the husband himself.[160] Jenkins L.J. concluded from that decision that a trustee in bankruptcy must be something other than an ordinary assignee, because an ordinary assignee of the husband's property would not have taken subject to the husband's personal obligations. By analogy, he thought that a landlord's trustee should take subject to the tenant's right of deduction. Subsequently the House of Lords in *National Provincial Bank Ltd.* v. *Ainsworth*[161] overruled *Bendall* v. *McWhirter*, and in doing so rejected the notion that that case could be supported on the ground that a trustee in bankruptcy is in any special position,[162] or that a distinction could be drawn between trustees in bankruptcy on the one hand and purchasers and mortgagees on the other.[163] As Lord Upjohn remarked, 'a trustee in bankruptcy succeeds only to the property of the bankrupt in its then plight and condition and is not concerned with personal rights that do not affect that property'.[164] This

---

[156] [1953] 1 QB 300.

[157] See Megarry, *The Rent Acts* (10th edn., 1967) Vol. 1, 346; *Woodfall's Law of Landlord and Tenant* (looseleaf edn., 1994) Vol. 3, para. 23.004; Hill and Redman's *Law of Landlord and Tenant* (17th edn., 1982) Vol. 1, 988; *Halsbury's Laws of England* (4th edn. (Reissue), 1993) Vol. 27(1), 722, para. 752 n. 4.

[158] The relevant provision was the Increase of Rent and Mortgage Interest (Restrictions) Act 1920, s. 14(1), which was in similar terms to the Rent Act 1977, ss. 57(1) and (2).

[159] [1952] 2 QB 466.

[160] Lord Denning went further, and said that the deserted wife had an equity which was binding not only on the husband's trustee but also on third parties generally.

[161] [1965] AC 1175.   [162] See Lord Hodson at 1226.

[163] See Lord Wilberforce at 1256.   [164] [1965] AC 1175, 1240.

effectively rejects the reasoning employed by Jenkins L.J., and so the decision in *Cusen* could only be correct if the deduction could have been made against an ordinary assignee of the landlord. While Lord Wilberforce in *Ainsworth* seemed prepared to accept that this may have been the case,[165] Jenkins L.J. was probably correct in his assumption that an ordinary assignee would not have been so bound. The definition of 'landlord' in the Rent Restriction Acts,[166] as including any person deriving title under the original landlord, is expressed not to apply when the context requires otherwise. The stipulation in the legislation that the tenant may may recover the overpayment from the landlord who received it (or his personal representatives[167]) would seem to indicate that 'landlord' is indeed used in a narrower sense in this context,[168] because obviously a person deriving title from the landlord who actually received the money himself could not be described as the landlord who received it.

It has been suggested that *Cusen* in truth was an example of an equitable set-off, and that on that basis it was correctly decided.[169] There are, however, two difficulties with this view. The first is that this form of set-off was not mentioned in the judgment. The second is that the demands in any event do not appear to have been sufficiently closely connected to give rise to an equitable set-off.[170] Given that a trustee in bankruptcy is in the same position as any other assignee of the reversion, a claim for rent by an assignee in relation to a period after the assignment would not be impeached, in the traditional sense of the word, by the tenant's claim for an overpayment to the original landlord. Moreover, applying the formulation approved by the House of Lords in *Bank of Boston Connecticut* v. *European Grain and Shipping Ltd.*,[171] the cross-claim could not be said to have arisen out of the same transaction as the trustee's claim for rent due to him in his capacity as assignee of the reversion.

---

[165] 'I should add that I have no reason to doubt that the decision in [*Cusen*], which was not concerned with a deserted wife but simply with the relation of landlord and tenant, was correct' [1965] AC 1175, 1258 per Lord Wilberforce.

[166] See now the Rent Act 1977, s. 152.

[167] 'Personal representative' ordinarily means executor or administrator. See *In re Best's Settlement Trusts* (1874) LR 18 Eq. 686, 691. It would not encompass a trustee in bankruptcy.

[168] See *Murray* v. *Webb* (1925) 59 Ir. LT 41. It is interesting to note that the texts in which *Cusen* is cited as authority for the proposition that the deduction may be made from rent owing to the trustee as landlord (see above) nevertheless agree that there may not be a deduction as against an assignee of the landlord.

[169] Wood, *English and International Set-off* (1989), 343. Wood uses transaction set-off as a generic term encompassing both equitable set-off and common law abatement.

[170] See *Reeves* v. *Pope* [1914] 2 KB 284, discussed in section 13.2.19. Wood's suggestion (*English and International Set-off* (1989), 343) that *Booth* v. *Hutchinson* (1872) LR 15 Eq. 30 similarly may be explained on the basis of equitable set-off would appear to be open to the same objection.

[171] [1989] 1 AC 1056. See section 1.7.2 above.

9.5.2 *Company liquidation*

In the case of a winding-up, the company's interest in any leasehold property does not vest in the liquidator. Consequently, if the lease is not disclaimed or otherwise terminated, the company itself remains as the landlord or the tenant, as the case may be, and the concept of privity of estate applicable to trustees in bankruptcy does not apply. Therefore, when the company is the tenant, the landlord cannot proceed against the liquidator personally for payment of rent. The landlord in any event may be entitled to be paid in full for rent which has accrued after liquidation as an expense incurred in the winding-up, if the liquidator has retained possession for the convenience of the winding-up.[172] In many cases this would obviate the necessity for a set-off. But if this is not the case, the landlord's only remedy is to prove in the liquidation. In this regard, Rule 4.92 of the Insolvency Rules 1986[173] provides that, in the case of rent and other payments of a periodic nature, the creditor may prove for any amounts due and unpaid up to the date when the company went into liquidation and, where at that date any payment was accruing due, the creditor may prove for so much as would have fallen due at that date, if accruing from day to day.[174] However, this does not mean that a landlord cannot prove for rent which accrues after the liquidation.[175] The rule is permissive in its operation, not prohibitory. It was originally introduced into the bankruptcy legislation in order to give a landlord a right of proof that he did not otherwise have.[177] A provision to this effect first appeared in the Bankruptcy Act 1861.[178] Prior to that Act, a landlord could only prove in the tenant's bankruptcy for rent actually due at the time of the filing of the petition for adjudication. He could not prove for a proportionate part of a payment that had as yet not accrued due. It was in order to remedy this that section 150 of the 1861 Act was introduced, so as to allow a right of proof for a proportionate part of rent and other periodic payments up to the date of adjudication.[179] It is now accepted that, if a lease is not disclaimed or otherwise terminated, the landlord may indeed prove for rent which relates to the period after the bankruptcy or

---

[172] *In re A.B.C. Coupler & Engineering Co. Ltd. (No. 3)* [1970] 1 WLR 702; *In re Downer Enterprises Ltd.* [1974] 1 WLR 1460; *Re H H Realisations Ltd.* (1975) 31 P & CR 249.

[173] The equivalent provision in bankruptcy is r. 6.112 of the Insolvency Rules.

[174] In Australia, see the Corporations Regulations, reg. 5.6.43(1). For bankruptcy, see the Bankruptcy Act 1966 (Cth.), s. 96.

[175] Compare Wood, *English and International Set-off* (1989), 309, 310–1.

[177] See Cotton L.J. in *Ex parte Dressler; in re Solomon* (1878) 9 Ch. D 252, 259 in relation to the Bankruptcy Act 1869, s. 35.   [178] Bankruptcy Act 1861, s. 150.

[179] Robson, *A Treatise on the Law of Bankruptcy* (3rd edn., 1876), 260.

liquidation,[180] although there is an element of uncertainty as to the extent of the right.[181] The preferred approach is that the provisions in the Insolvency Act dealing with estimating the value of contingent and future claims would also apply to a periodic obligation to pay rent, so that an estimate would be made for the purpose of proof of the landlord's loss as a result of the tenant's liquidation and subsequent dissolution, although taking into account any assignment of the lease to a third party.[182] There is, however, an alternative view that, while the landlord is entitled to claim for the whole of the rent to the end of the term, he can only prove for rent which in fact has become due and payable.[183] But, whatever the extent of the right of proof, a set-off should be available to the landlord in relation to the provable debt and a separate debt owing to the tenant.

In the situation in which a landlord is a company which has gone into liquidation, and privity of estate accordingly is not relevant. It has been suggested that rent payable after the insolvency is not normally available for set-off against a pre-insolvency debt owed by the landlord to the tenant, the reason being that the rent is 'earned' by the landlord's estate and, since it is payable for the benefit of the general body of creditors, there is a lack of mutuality in relation to it and a pre-insolvency debt incurred by the insolvent to the lessee.[184] However, the better view is that there is no general principle that precludes a set-off when a debt is earned by an insolvent estate by the use after the insolvency pursuant to a prior contract of assets otherwise available for distribution generally.[185] If privity of estate does not apply, it is difficult to see why rent accruing to a company in liquidation should not be available for a set-off if it arises out of a prior lease.[186] In the language of Rich J. in the High Court of Australia in *Hiley*

---

[180] In addition to the cases referred to below, see *In re ABC Coupler & Engineering Co. Ltd. (No. 3)* [1970] 1 WLR 702; *Re H H Realisations Ltd.* (1975) 31 P & CR 249. While these cases, and a number of the cases referred to below, were concerned with company liquidations, they should also be relevant to bankruptcies.

[181] See *Brash Holdings Ltd.* v. *Katile Pty. Ltd.* (1994) 13 ACSR 504, 517.

[182] See *In re Lucania Temperance Billboard Halls (London) Ltd.* [1966] 1 Ch. 98, 106, and McPherson, *The Law of Company Liquidation* (3rd edn., 1987), 373, 376–7. See also *James Smith & Sons (Norwood) Ltd.* v. *Goodman* [1936] 1 Ch. 216.

[183] *Metropolis Estates Company Ltd.* v. *Wilde* [1940] 2 KB 536, 541–2, referring to *Re New Oriental Bank Corporation (No. 2)* [1895] 1 Ch. 753; *In re Oak Pitts Colliery Company* (1882) 21 Ch. D 322, 329; Williams and Muir Hunter, *The Law and Practice in Bankruptcy* (19th edn., 1979) 154; Hill and Redman, *Law of Landlord and Tenant* (17th edn., 1982) Vol. 1, 595; *Buckley on The Companies Acts* (14th edn., 1981) Vol 1., 717–8; *Palmer's Company Law* Vol. 3 (1993, looseleaf), para. 15.432.

[184] Wood, *English and International Set-off* (1989), 342.

[185] See section 9.4.2 above.

[186] This assumes that a debt which arises in favour of a company after its liquidation is capable as a matter of principle of being able to be employed in a set-off. See section 4.4 above. In *Old Style Confections Pty. Ltd* v. *Microbyte Investments Pty. Ltd.* (1994) 15 ACSR

v. *The Peoples Prudential Assurance Co. Ltd.*,[187] it is a case where rights are vested in the tenant and in the company which, without any new transaction, grow in the natural course of events into money claims capable of forming items in an account. Dixon J. commented in similar terms in that case.[188] In the case of a lease, rent indeed becomes payable without the intervention of any new transaction.

9.6 PERIODIC PAYMENT OBLIGATIONS AFTER INSOLVENCY

A common form of periodic payment obligation is the payment of rent pursuant to a lease of land. Set-off in this context was considered in the preceding section. In the case of other payment obligations arising after bankruptcy or liquidation, the applicable principles should be the same as those discussed for rent in the case of a company liquidation, where privity of estate is not an issue. Consistent with that discussion, it has been held in Victoria that a periodic licence fee accruing to a company after its liquidation may be the subject of a set-off.[189] The same result should follow in the case of hire payable under a contract for the hire of goods which, unlike a lease of land, is not subject to privity of estate.[190]

9.7 AGENCY

9.7.1 *Introduction*

In an agency situation mutuality as a general rule is determined by the principal/third party relationship, as opposed to that of the agent and the third party. For example, when a bill of exchange is indorsed to an agent for the purpose of collection, the acceptor may bring his indebtedness on the bill into an account with a claim possessed by him against the indorser.[191] Conversely, a person holding a bill as agent for another generally could not employ the bill in a set-off against an indebtedness of

---

191 Hayne J. held that a periodic licence fee payable to a company after its liquidation could be the subject of a set-off. See below.

[187] (1938) 60 CLR 468, 487.   [188] (1938) 60 CLR 468, 499.

[189] *Old Style Confections Pty. Ltd.* v. *Microbyte Investments Pty. Ltd.* (1994) 15 ACSR 191.

[190] Compare Wood, *English and International Set-off* (1989), 309, 342.

[191] See *In re Anglo-Greek Steam Navigation and Trading Company; Caralli & Haggard's Claim* (1869) LR 4 Ch. App. 174. The agent for collection in that case admittedly had indorsed the bill back to the inspectors of the indorser appointed under the indorser's deed of inspectorship. Nevertheless, Giffard L.J. said that it was immaterial whether the bills had been got back. See also *Barclays Bank, Ltd.* v. *Aschaffenburger Zellstoffwerke AG* [1967] 1 Lloyd's Rep. 387.

his own to the acceptor. A similar rule applies when an agent entering into a contract with a third party discloses that he is acting on behalf of a principal. In such a case the principal himself is the contracting party, and lack of mutuality would operate to deny the third party the right to set off an indebtedness of the agent to him against his liability on the contract to the principal.[192] Indeed, this would also be the position in many commercial transactions where the agent discloses that he is acting on behalf of a principal though without disclosing the principal's indentity. The third party in such a case may be regarded as having agreed to treat as a party to the contract anyone on whose behalf the agent may have been authorized to contract,[193] and if the principal sues, the third party cannot set off a liability owing to him by the agent.[194]

9.7.2 *Authority for the agent to set off the principal's debt*

An agent may be authorized to receive payment of a sum of money from a third party on behalf of the principal. The mere existence of authority to this effect would not justify an attempt by the third party to effect payment by means of a set-off against a debt owing to him by the agent.[195] Nor would the agent be authorized to enter into an agreement of this nature with the third party.[196] Furthermore, any alleged custom to this effect would be unreasonable,[197] so that it will not bind the principal unless he knew of the custom and had agreed to be bound by it.[198]

There are, nevertheless, some situations in which a set-off agreement between the agent and the third party involving the principal's claim would be valid. If the principal is indebted to the agent, and has authorized the

---

[192] *Richardson* v. *Stormont, Todd & Co., Ltd.* [1900] 1 QB 701. See also *Moore* v. *Clementson* (1809) 2 Camp. 22.

[193] See *Teheran-Europe Co. Ltd.* v. *S. T. Belton (Tractors) Ltd.* [1968] 2 QB 545, 555 per Diplock LJ. See also *The Santa Carina* [1977] 1 Lloyd's Rep. 478, 481, 484; *Marsh & McLennan Pty. Ltd.* v. *Stanyers Transport Pty. Ltd.* [1994] 2 VR 232; Goodhart and Hamson, 'Undisclosed Principals in Contract' (1932) 4 *Cambridge Law Journal* 320, 339. Compare *Bowstead and Reynolds on Agency* (16th edn., 1996), 559–60.

[194] *Hornby* v. *Lacy* (1817) 6 M & S 166. For set-off as between the agent and the third party, see section 9.7.5 below.

[195] *Pearson* v. *Scott* (1878) 9 Ch. D 198.

[196] *Jell* v. *Pratt* (1817) 2 Stark. 67; *Wrout* v. *Dawes* (1858) 25 Beav. 369; *Coupe* v. *Collier* (1890) 62 LT 927.

[197] See *Pearson* v. *Scott* (1878) 9 Ch. D 198; *Crossley* v. *Magniac* [1893] 1 Ch. 594; *Blackburn* v. *Mason* (1893) 68 LT 510; *Anderson* v. *Sutherland* (1897) 13 TLR 163. See also *Cooke & Sons* v. *Eshelby* (1887) 12 App. Cas. 271, 280 with respect to the alleged custom.

[198] *Blackburn* v. *Mason* (1893) 68 LT 510. There is a custom at Lloyd's by which a broker may set off the amount of a loss against his debt for premiums due to the underwriter. This method of payment will bind the insured if it can be shown that the broker was authorized to settle losses in accordance with the custom. See *Stewart* v. *Aberdein* (1838) 4 M & W 211, and *The Admiral C* [1981] 1 Lloyd's Rep. 9, 10, and generally *Arnould's Law of Marine Insurance and Average* (16th edn., 1981) Vol. 1, 124–7.

agent to pay himself out of the proceeds of the third party's indebtedness to the principal, the agent may receive payment by means of a set-off against a debt that he owes to the third party.[199] Further, an agent selling the goods of his principal may be entitled by virtue of a lien to receive payment of the price. In such a case an agreement between the purchaser and the agent (or his trustee in bankruptcy) to set off the price against a debt owing by the agent to the purchaser will be binding upon the principal to the extent of the principal's indebtedness to the agent secured by the lien.[200] In addition, where the principal is undisclosed, the better view is that an agreement for a set-off between the agent and the third party entered into before the third party had notice that the person with whom he was dealing was merely an agent would be binding on the principal,[201] though a right of set-off may be available to the third party at common law in any event even apart from the agreement.[202]

Consider that the principal has specifically authorized the agent to employ the third party's liability to the principal in a set-off against the agent's personal indebtedness to the third party. If a set-off is effected before any of them has become bankrupt or gone into liquidation, ordinarily there should not be a problem.[203] Where, however, the principal has become bankrupt *before* a set-off has occurred, any subsequent set-off would not be valid, unless the source of the agent's authority is a security over the principal's claim so that to that extent it is not an asset available for distribution amongst the principal's creditors. Apart from that exception, authority conferred by the principal in favour of the agent would not bind the principal's trustee in bankruptcy in whom the claim would have vested as part of the principal's estate.[204] This would also be the case when the third party has become bankrupt. The use of the third party's asset in the form of the claim against the agent, in order to satisfy *in toto* the third party's liability to the principal in circumstances where the insolvency set-off section does not apply, would be contrary to the requirement of a *pari passu* distribution of the bankrupt's estate,[205] and

---

[199] *Barker* v. *Greenwood* (1837) 2 Y & C Ex. 414. See also *Pariente* v. *Lubrock* (1856) 8 De G M & G 5.

[200] *Hudson* v. *Granger* (1821) 5 B & Ald. 27. See also *Warner* v. *M'Kay* (1836) 1 M & W 591.

[201] See generally *Bowstead and Reynolds on Agency* (16th edn., 1996), 440.

[202] See section 9.7.3 below.

[203] This is subject to the set-off not being impugned in a subsequent insolvency on the ground that it is a transaction at an undervalue, or a transaction defrauding creditors. See the Insolvency Act 1986, ss. 238 and 423.

[204] If the principal is a company in liquidation, a set-off after the commencement of the liquidation involving the principal's claim against the third party would be void under the Insolvency Act 1986, s. 127 as a disposition of the company's property.

[205] See the discussion of *British Eagle International Air Lines Ltd.* v. *Compagnie Nationale Air France* [1975] 1 WLR 758 in section 12.1 below.

accordingly would be void as against the trustee. Consider, however, that the agent is the party who has become bankrupt. If the fact of the bankruptcy determines the authority, that is the end of the matter. But if that is not the case, there is no reason why the bankruptcy in this instance should affect the position.[206] A set-off could only be objectionable if it involves the use of an asset otherwise available for distribution amongst the insolvent's creditors. This does not apply in the case of the agent, since the set-off is in relation to the agent's liability, as opposed to an asset. Admittedly this seems contrary to the view recently expressed by the Court of Appeal in *Morris* v. *Agrichemicals Ltd.*,[207] that 'if A owes B £x and B owes C £y *and any of them becomes insolvent* the two debts cannot be set off even if there is an express agreement by the three of them that B may set them off; such an agreement is contrary to the scheme of distribution on insolvency and cannot prevail over the rules which require *pari passu* distribution'.[208] To the extent that this may have been intended to include the situation in which A is the insolvent party, it is difficult to see what the objection is.[209]

9.7.3 *Undisclosed principals*

It may be that an agent contracts in his own name on behalf of an undisclosed principal.[210] The status of an undisclosed principal is anomalous in English law. A principal whose existence is unknown to a third party can hardly be said to be a party to a contract with him. The agent is the contracting party, and therefore may sue and be sued on the contract. But in addition the principal may sue and be sued if there is nothing in the contract which is inconsistent with someone other than the agent being the 'principal'.[211] This right to sue and the liability to be sued is not based upon privity of contract, because the principal is not a contracting party. Rather, the undisclosed principal is treated as having a right to intervene on the agent's contract.[212] This intervention was described by Sir Frederick Pollock as being 'inconsistent with the elementary doctrines of the law of

---

[206] Compare Wood, *English and International Set-off* (1989), 1001–2, 1010.
[207] Rose, Saville and Millett L.JJ. 20 December 1995.
[208] Emphasis added. [209] See section 12.1 below.
[210] For a discussion of the situations in which the undisclosed principal doctrine applies, see Reynolds, 'Practical Problems of the Undisclosed Principal Doctrine' (1983) 36 *Current Legal Problems* 119.
[211] *Dunlop Pneumatic Tyre Company, Ltd.* v. *Selfridge and Company, Ltd.* [1915] AC 847, 864; *Siu Yin Kwan* v. *Eastern Insurance Co. Ltd.* [1994] 2 AC 199, 207–9. See generally Powell, *The Law of Agency* (1952), 130–1 and *Bowstead and Reynolds*, n. 201 above, 420.
[212] *Welsh Development Agency* v. *Export Finance Co. Ltd.* [1992] BCLC 148, 173, 182. See generally Goodhart and Hamson (1932) 4 *Cambridge Law Journal* 320, 345 *et seq.*, criticizing McCardie J. in *Said* v. *Butt* [1920] 3 KB 497, 500. Compare though Glanville Williams, 'Mistake as to Party in the Law of Contract' (1945) 23 *Canadian Bar Review* 380, 404.

contract'.[213] Various writers over the years have made a number of attempts to provide a theoretical justification for it,[214] although none has been entirely successful. It is probably best to regard the doctrine as an anomaly introduced by the common law for reasons of mercantile convenience.[215]

If the undisclosed principal when discovered is sued on the contract by the third party, he could not set off a claim that he has against the agent.[216] Nor could he bring into account a claim that the agent has against the third party, though a set-off may be available in accordance with normal principles if the third party is liable to the principal himself.[217] Alternatively, it may be that the principal is the party who takes action by intervening on the contract and enforcing it against the third party.[218] In such a case there is the possibility of a set-off in relation to a cross-demand available to the third party against the principal. But, in addition, the third party may be entitled to bring into account a debt owing to him by the agent that arose before he received notice that the person with whom he was dealing in fact was only acting as an agent. The leading case is *George* v. *Clagett*.[219] A factor had sold goods for his principal in his own name without disclosing his agency. When the principal sued the third party for the price[220] the third party was allowed to set off the agent's separate indebtedness to him. The set-off in issue is not limited to cases involving a sale of goods, but is of general application. Bowen L.J. in *Montagu* v. *Forwood*[221] described its scope in the following terms:

---

[213] (1887) 3 *Law Quarterly Review* 358, 359. See also *Siu Yin Kwan* v. *Eastern Insurance Co.* [1994] 2 AC 199, 207.

[214] See the discussion in Stoljar, *The Law of Agency* (1961), 228–33. See also *Bowstead and Reynolds*, n. 201 above, 409–11; Fridman, *The Law of Agency* (6th edn. 1990), 229–30.

[215] Fridman, *The Law of Agency* (6th edn. 1990), 230. See also *Bowstead and Reynolds*, n. 201 above, 410.

[216] *Waring* v. *Favenck* (1807) 1 Camp. 85; *Kymer* v. *Suwercropp* (1807) 1 Camp. 109.

[217] See e.g. *Spurr* v. *Cass* (1870) LR 5 QB 656.

[218] Note that if the agent has a direct pecuniary interest in enforcing the contract, in the form of a 'lien' over the proceeds for his charges and expenses, or for the balance of his general account with the principal, payment by the third party to the principal when the third party has notice of the lien would not be a defence to a later action brought against him by the agent. See *Robinson* v. *Rutter* (1855) 4 El. & Bl. 954; *Arnould's Law of Marine Insurance and Average* (16th edn., 1981) Vol. 1, 134 para. 200. If the third party is uncertain as to whether he should pay the principal, he should interplead. See Powell, *The Law of Agency* (1952), 223 n. 2.   [219] (1797) 7 TR 539.

[220] The question of a set-off, in the proper sense of that word, usually will only arise when the principal sues for the price. It should be distinguished from the situation in which the principal disputes the title of the purchaser to goods bought through the principal's agent on the ground that the agent exceeded his authority in selling in a particular manner, for example by setting off the price against a debt owing by the agent to the purchaser. See for example *Lloyds & Scottish Finance Ltd.* v. *Williamson* [1965] 1 WLR 404; *Tingey and Co. Ltd.* v. *John Chambers and Co. Ltd.* [1967] NZLR 785.   [221] [1893] 2 QB 350.

If A employs B as his agent to make any contract for him, or to receive money for him, and B makes a contract with C, or employs C as his agent, if B is a person who would be reasonably supposed to be acting as a principal, and is not known or suspected by C to be acting as an agent for any one, A cannot make a demand against C without the latter being entitled to stand in the same position as if B had in fact been a principal. If A has allowed his agent B to appear in the character of a principal he must take the consequences.[222]

The plaintiffs in that case had employed an agent to collect a general average loss from Lloyd's underwriters. The agent in turn employed Lloyd's brokers as sub-agents. The policy had been effected in the name of the agent,[223] and the sub-agents thought that the loss was payable to the agent on his own account. When the sub-agents were sued by the plaintiff as an undisclosed principal for the money received from the underwriters, they were allowed to set off the agent's indebtedness to them.[224]

As a preliminary point, it is assumed in the following discussion that a right of set-off is available to the third party against the agent in accordance with normal principles. In this regard it may be relevant in a particular case to consider whether the third party, instead of being a debtor, is holding a fund on trust, the obligation to account for which is not susceptible to a set-off.[225]

The right of set-off to which the principal takes subject is not that conferred by the mutual credit provision in the insolvency legislation in the event of the bankruptcy or liquidation of the agent, but rather is confined to defences of set-off available between solvent parties. In *Turner* v. *Thomas*[226] an agent for an undisclosed principal contracted to sell goods to a third party. The agent himself was indebted to the third party, and later became bankrupt, whereupon the third party refused to proceed with the contract. He was then sued by the principal for damages for breach of contract. While this liability for damages could have been set off in the agent's bankruptcy if the agent had in fact been contracting as principal, it could not have formed the basis of a defence to an action at law under the Statutes of Set-off, since the Statutes require mutual debts. Accordingly it was held that the agent's debt could not be set off under *George* v. *Clagett*

---

[222] [1893] 2 QB 350, 355–6.

[223] This only appears from the report of the case at 69 LT 371.

[224] For other sub-agency cases involving a sale of goods, see *New Zealand and Australian Land Company* v. *Watson* (1881) 7 QBD 374 and *Knight* v. *Matson & Co.* (1902) 22 NZLR 293, though compare *Kaltenbach, Fischer & Co.* v. *Lewis & Peat* (1885) 10 App. Cas. 617, 626–7. Note the discussion in *Bowstead and Reynolds*, n. 201 above, 163–8 in relation to the principal and sub-agent relationship.

[225] See Ch. 6.

[226] (1871) LR 6 CP 610. See also *Thornton* v. *Maynard* (1875) LR 10 CP 695, 700; *Montagu* v. *Forwood* [1893] 2 QB 350, 354 per Lord Esher MR (and see also Bowen L.J. in the report of the case at 69 LT 371, 373).

against the liability for damages in the principal's action. One reason given for this limitation on the right of set-off was that the possibility of the agent's bankruptcy would not have been contemplated by the third party when deciding whether or not to deal with the agent, though the validity of this generalization is questionable.[227] A second, more substantial reason given for the limitation was that the mutual credit provision in the bankruptcy legislation is only intended for the settlement of accounts between the bankrupt and a person dealing with him, rather than between that person and some other party such as an undisclosed principal. The principal, by intervening on the contract and suing in his own name, takes the claim outside the operation of the insolvency legislation, in which case the insolvency set-off section should not be relevant.[228] However, this is an unfortunate result. It means that a third party, who may have been induced to contract with the agent on the strength of the security provided by the mutual credit provision in the event of the agent's bankruptcy, in fact may be denied that security, and limited to a narrower right of set-off than that originally contemplated because of the existence of an undisclosed principal. Admittedly the contrary result in a case such as *Turner* v. *Thomas* would mean that the extent of the principal's rights against the third party would depend upon the solvency of the agent, though this is a risk he should be prepared to take if he decides to deal through an agent without taking steps to bring the fact of the agency to the notice of third parties. On the other hand, there may be cases where the principal does not have a right to intervene and sue on the contract, because to do so would be inconsistent with the contract itself.[229] If so, the justification for not applying the insolvency set-off section in the bankruptcy or liquidation of the agent would no longer be valid, so that the full right of insolvency set-off should be available to the third party.

The doctrine of the undisclosed principal is a common law doctrine, and *George* v. *Clagett* itself was decided at common law. Consistent with its origin, the right of set-off that the courts have enforced in these cases is the defence available in the common law courts under the Statutes of Set-off. However, in an appropriate case there is no reason why the third party could not assert equitable defences of set-off against the undisclosed principal. Similarly, when the third party is suing on the contract, and there is a cross-claim against the third party arising out of the transaction which is

---

[227] See e.g, *Cooke & Sons* v. *Eshelby* (1887) 12 App. Cas. 271, 280.

[228] Similarly the mutual credit clause cannot prevail against an assignee of a debt when the assignor has become bankrupt. See *Lee & Chapman's Case* (1885) 30 Ch. D 216, 225, and also *De Mattos* v. *Saunders* (1872) LR 7 CP 570.

[229] *Dunlop Pneumatic Tyre Company, Ltd.* v. *Selfridge and Company, Ltd.* [1915] AC 847, 864; *Siu Yin Kwan* v. *Eastern Insurance Co. Ltd.* [1994] 2 AC 199, 207–8.

sufficiently closely connected to give rise to an equitable set-off, the third party's title to sue would be impeached, whether the action is against the principal or the agent.

Set-off under the Statutes of Set-off requires that both debts be due and payable.[230] However, it is clear from *George* v. *Clagett* itself that it is not necessary that both debts should have been payable when the third party received notice of the principal. The purchase in that case had taken place before notice, although the price was not payable until a later date, while the indebtedness of the agent was based upon a bill of exchange accepted by the agent but not payable until 4 days after notice. On the other hand, *Kaltenbach, Fischer & Co.* v. *Lewis & Peat*[231] suggests that the debts at least should have arisen before notice.[232] Merchants had employed an agent to sell goods, and the agent in turn had employed a broker, the broker being a creditor of the agent on another transaction. The broker sold the goods to a purchaser who was allowed 6 months' credit for the price. Before this period elapsed the principal gave notice of his interest in the transaction to the broker, and claimed the return of the goods or their proceeds. When the price was subsequently paid to the broker the House of Lords held that he was obliged to account for it to the principal undiminished by a set-off of the agent's indebtedness to him.

Lord Bramwell in his judgment decided the case on the basis that the merchants had claimed the return of the goods before delivery to the purchaser. Accordingly he said that their claim was one of property rather than money at the time that notice was given. Lord Watson,[233] on the other hand, emphasized that there was no debt owing by the broker when he received notice of the true ownership. A debt in fact did not arise until later, when he received the price from the purchaser, and his Lordship said that the broker could not avail himself of a set-off arising in this manner after notice.[234] On one view, however, rights of set-off should be allowed or not according to whether a perception of a security in the existence of cross-demands could have acted as an inducement to either dealing,[235] and it would have been more consonant with that notion to adopt the principle that the set-off in these cases should depend upon when binding

---

[230] See section 1.2.7 below.

[231] (1885) 10 App. Cas. 617, discussed in Goodhart and Hamson (1934) 4 *Cambridge Law Journal* 320, 333–4.

[232] The requirement of existing debts at the time of notice also applies to a debtor's right to set off a debt owing to him by the assignor in an action brought against him by an assignee of his indebtedness. See section 13.2.4 below.

[233] (1885) 10 App. Cas. 617, 626–8.

[234] Lord Fitzgerald appears to have proceeded on the same basis, although his judgment is not entirely clear on this point. See (1885) 10 App. Cas. 617, 640–1.

[235] See section 2.3 above.

agreements were entered into, rather than upon when debts under those agreements arose. Indeed, *Kaltenbach* v. *Lewis* should be compared to *Rother Iron Works Ltd.* v. *Canterbury Precision Engineers Ltd.*[236] in the context of a company in receivership. In *Kaltenbach* the third party's indebtedness arose after notice of the existence of the undisclosed principal, albeit as a result of a transaction entered into before notice, and the third party was denied a set-off. In *Rother Iron Works* the third party's indebtedness to the company also arose after notice though pursuant to a prior contract, the notice in that case being of the appointment of the receiver, and yet the third party was permitted to employ it in a set-off against a pre-receivership indebtedness of the company to it.

The set-off only arises if the third party believed that the agent in fact was the principal at the time the third party became indebted under the transaction[237] or, where the cross-debt owing by the agent to the third party arose after the making of a binding contract on behalf of the undisclosed principal,[238] if the third party still held that belief.[239] Both debts must have been incurred before notice. Knowledge of the agency sufficient to abrogate a set-off need not point to the agent being the agent of the plaintiff, but only to his being an agent.[240] This principle should be contrasted with the situation in which an insurance broker with a general lien on the policy for the balance of the insured's account discovers that the nominal insured is only an agent. In such a case the broker is still allowed to exercise his lien over any money received by him from the insurer after notice of the agency, provided that he held the policy before notice and provided also that the lien can only be exercised in respect of the amount due to him at the date of notice.[241]

If the circumstances are such as to put the third party on inquiry as to the status of the agent, and he fails to make an inquiry, he may be denied a set-off.[242] In effect this is the same as saying that the third party's belief should

---

[236] [1974] 1 QB 1, discussed in section 13.3.1 below.

[237] *Carr* v. *Hinchliff* (1825) 4 B & C 547; *Fish* v. *Kempton* (1849) 7 CB 687. See also *Kaltenbach, Fischer & Co.* v. *Lewis & Peat* (1885) 10 App. Cas. 617, discussed above.

[238] See *Moore* v. *Clementson* (1809) 2 Camp. 22, as explained by Parke B. in *Warner* v. *M'Kay* (1836) 1 M & W 591, 596.

[239] See for example *Borries* v. *Imperial Ottoman Bank* (1873) LR 9 CP 38; *Salter* v. *Purchell* (1841) 1 QB 209, 213–14 per Parke B (*arguendo*).

[240] *Semenza* v. *Brinsley* (1865) 18 CB (NS) 467; *Maspons y Hermano* v. *Mildred, Goyeneche & Co.* (1882) 9 QBD 530, affirmed (1883) 8 App. Cas. 874. See also *Busby* v. *MacLurcan and Lane Ltd.* (1930) 48 WN (NSW) 2, 5.

[241] *Mann* v. *Forrester* (1814) 4 Camp. 60; *Near East Relief* v. *King, Chasseur and Company, Ltd.* [1930] 2 KB 40, 46. See generally *Arnould's Law of Marine Insurance and Average* (16th edn., 1981) Vol. 1, 132 para. 197.

[242] *Baring* v. *Corrie* (1818) 2 B & Ald. 137, 144; *Pratt* v. *Willey* (1826) 2 Car. & P 350. See also *Pearson* v. *Scott* (1879) 9 Ch. D 198, 202; *Cooke & Sons* v. *Eshelby* (1887) 12 App. Cas. 271, 277–8; *Montagu* v. *Forwood* [1893] 2 QB 350, 356. For an analogous case concerned with a dormant partner, see *Baker* v. *Gent* (1892) 9 TLR 159 (discussed in section 8.2.4 above).

be reasonable,[243] or that there should be 'nothing to lead the person who deals with him to suppose, *and* he does not in fact know, that he is acting as an agent'.[244] It has been said that 'the only question to be decided is whether the defendant really dealt with the agent in the honest belief that he was dealing with a principal'.[245] Nevertheless, the cases suggest that an honest belief will not be sufficient if the third party failed to make an inquiry when one was called for. This duty of inquiry has a common law origin, and is therefore independent of the equitable doctrine of constructive notice.

The situations in which a third party will be put on inquiry will depend upon the facts of each case. In this regard, the circumstances in which the agent contracted may be such as to indicate that he must have been acting only as an agent. In *Maanns* v. *Henderson*[246] an English subject in time of war, though acting for a neutral foreigner, opened a policy of insurance in his own name with a broker, and informed him that the property was neutral. This was held to a be a sufficient indication to the broker that the English subject was acting as an agent and not on his own account. In some cases documents accompanying a sale may indicate that the sale is being made on behalf of another person. In one case the principal was named as the seller on a ticket accompanying the goods being sold by the agent in his own name, and accordingly it was held that the third party ought to have inquired into the nature of the situation of the agent.[247] This should be compared to *Cooper* v. *Strauss and Co.*[248] The sale note contained the words 'Sold for and on account of', though no name of any principal had been inserted. Kennedy J. said that these words appeared in the sale note because factors sometimes sold on their own account, but more generally for a principal. While a set-off was disallowed because the agent in fact had informed the third party that he was selling on behalf of the real owners, the contents of the sale note evidently were not considered to have been a sufficient reason for denying the set-off. The sale note also mentioned the name and address of the real principal. However, this information was only included as a form of description of the goods being sold, and Kennedy J. did not consider that it would convey to a purchaser that the contract of sale was being made on behalf of that person as owner. Similarly, in *Knight* v. *Matson & Co.*[249] a cattle-dealer sold cattle with the brand of the real

---

[243] *Cooke & Sons* v. *Eshelby* (1887) 12 App. Cas. 271, 278; *Montagu* v. *Forwood* [1893] 2 QB 350, 355 per Bowen LJ.

[244] *Montagu* v. *Forwood* [1893] 2 QB 350, 355 per Lord Esher MR (emphasis added).

[245] *Knight* v. *Matson & Co.* (1902) 22 NZLR 293, 309 per Williams J. See also *Fish* v. *Kempton* (1848) 7 CB 687, 691–2, 693.   [246] (1802) 1 East 335.

[247] *Pratt* v. *Willey* (1826) 2 Car. & P 350. Compare *Greer* v. *Downs Supply Company* [1927] 2 KB 28, in which the third party did raise the matter with the agent.

[248] (1898) 14 TLR 233.   [249] (1902) 22 NZLR 293.

owner upon them. However, a cattle-dealer buying cattle would not obliterate or change the existing brands, and so the presence of a brand upon cattle being sold by a dealer was not considered to be sufficient to put the third party on inquiry as to their true ownership. In the case of a sale of goods, the third party could not deny that he was put on inquiry if the agent at the time of the sale had not had actual possession of the goods or of their indicia of title,[250] where the sale concerned goods presently owned and existing.[251] Indeed, it has been said that in order to make a valid defence under *George* v. *Clagett* the plea should show that the contract was made by a person whom the principal had entrusted with possession.[252] The goods in *Wynen* v. *Brown*[253] had been entered in the name of the brokers at the Custom House, they had been warehoused in their name, and the order to the wharfinger for their delivery had also been in the brokers' name. These circumstances were regarded as sufficient to give rise to a set-off, even though the brokers did not have the bills of lading or other indicia of title and even though the goods had been wharfed in the principal's name. The case is inadequately reported, but it may be queried whether on the facts as disclosed the third party should have questioned the brokers or the wharfinger as to the ownership of the goods.

It may be that the third party is aware that the person with whom he is contracting sometimes deals as an agent for other people. The cases in point are noticeable for their lack of consistency. Lord Ellenborough in *Moore* v. *Clementson*[254] thought that a mere general knowledge possessed by the third party that the other contracting party was a factor would not by itself deprive him of a set-off. It appears from the headnote to *Wynen* v. *Brown*[255] that the person selling was known to be a broker, although a set-off seems to have been allowed without any indication of an inquiry having been made.[256]

Similarly, in *Dresser* v. *Norwood*[257] the Common Pleas allowed the third party a set-off even though he himself had employed the other party as a selling agent on two occasions. The jury's finding that the third party believed that he was dealing directly with the owner was considered to be

---

[250] See *Baring* v. *Corrie* (1818) 2 B & Ald. 137. In cases such as *Montagu* v. *Forwood* [1893] 2 QB 350, in which an agent is employed to collect a sum of money from a third party, the agent should have possession of any requisite documents.

[251] Compare for example *Cooke & Sons* v. *Eshelby* (1887) 12 App. Cas. 271.

[252] *Semenza* v. *Brinsley* (1865) 18 CB (NS) 467, 477. See also *Borries* v. *The Imperial Ottoman Bank* (1873) LR 9 CP 38.   [253] (1826) 4 LJOSKB 203.

[254] (1809) 2 Camp. 22.   [255] (1826) 4 LJOSKB 203.

[256] See also *Garrett* v. *Bird* (1872) 11 SCR (NSW) 97, a case concerned with the agent's standing to sue.

[257] (1863) 14 CB (NS) 574.

sufficient for a set-off.[258] On the other hand, in *Baring v. Corrie*[259] the third party knew that the persons with whom they were dealing acted both as brokers and merchants, and Abbott C.J. said that the third party should have inquired. In *Pearson v. Scott*[260] a solicitor had been instructed to sell certain stock. He in turn employed a stockbroker. When the sale was completed the stockbroker forwarded the proceeds to the solicitor, less a deduction to cover an indebtedness of the solicitor to him on a separate transaction. The solicitor was known as a person who speculated in stock on his own account. Nevertheless Fry J. held that, since the stockbroker knew that the person who employed him was a solicitor, he should have realized that he was dealing with a person who may have been acting upon the instructions of a client, and therefore he should have made some inquiry. Since the stockbroker had not initiated an inquiry he could not be heard to say that he dealt with the solicitor in any other character than as agent for the principals now suing for the proceeds, and so his act of crediting part of the proceeds to the solicitor's account with him was held not to discharge him from liability to the principals. In *Knight v. Matson & Co.*[261] the agent was a dealer in cattle, although the third party had been informed in a prior transaction that the dealer on that occasion was acting as an agent. While one of the members of the majority, Williams J., said that the only question was whether the third party really dealt with the agent in the honest belief that they were dealing with a principal,[262] Edwards J. decided on the basis that the third party in the present case had not been put on inquiry.[263] The dealer was in the business of selling cattle on his own account, and knowledge of a single isolated occasion on which he had acted as an agent was not regarded as sufficient to deny the third party a set-off on the ground of failure to inquire as to the ownership of the cattle in question. Stout C.J. on the other hand said in his dissenting judgment that the third party should have known from the previous transaction that the dealer might have been acting as an agent, and he considered that the third party's failure to inquire into his status in the second dealing should deprive it of a set-off.[264]

The imposition of a duty of inquiry when the third party is aware that the

---

[258] Subsequently the Exchequer Chamber reversed the decision, though on the ground that the third party himself had acted through an agent who was aware of the identity of the real owner. This knowledge was imputed to the third party. However, there is nothing in the report to indicate that the third party's own awareness that the other contracting party was in the habit of selling as a factor would have prevented a set-off. See *Dresser v. Norwood* (1864) 17 CB (NS) 466.

[259] (1818) 2 B & Ald. 137.

[260] (1878) 9 Ch. D 198.

[261] (1902) 22 NZLR 293.

[262] (1902) 22 NZLR 293, 309, 311.

[263] (1902) 22 NZLR 293, 315–17.

[264] See also *Cooke & Sons v. Eshelby* (1887) 12 App. Cas. 271; *London Joint Stock Bank v. Simmons* [1892] AC 201, 229–30.

other contracting party has dealt in the past as an agent only becomes important when the third party asserts that he believed that the other party was dealing as a principal, although under the circumstances that belief was unreasonable. There is no reason in principle why such a duty should not be relevant in this situation, though its imposition, and the reasonableness of the belief, will depend upon the facts of each case. Lord Ellenborough's opinion in *Moore* v. *Clementson* that a mere general knowledge that the other party is a factor will not result in the loss of a set-off is almost certainly too wide. When the third party is aware that the nature of the business of the person with whom he is dealing is such that he often acts as an agent for others,[265] it is unlikely that his expressed belief that the person was acting as a principal in the particular transaction in issue would be reasonable in the absence of an inquiry. On the other hand, the belief generally would be reasonable in a case like *Matson*, or *Dresser* v. *Norwood*, when the agent as a matter of business usually deals on his own account, although he is known to have dealt occasionally in the past as an agent for others.

In the absence of a proper theoretical justification for the intervention of an undisclosed principal on his agent's contract, it is difficult to state with certainty what the basis is for the third party's right of set-off under *George* v. *Clagett*. There have been statements suggesting that the set-off may be based upon a notion that an undisclosed principal takes subject to equities or defences available to the third party against the agent before notice.[266] In other words, an undisclosed principal should be treated in the same way as an assignee of a chose in action. Goodhart and Hamson[267] sought to explain the doctrine of the undisclosed principal as being a primitive form of assignment, though there are certain differences between them.[268] For example, an assignment results from an act of the parties, whereas the rights and liabilities of an undisclosed principal arise as a matter of law. Moreover, an assignment will only occur after the relationship between the assignor and the debtor has already been entered into, whereas the interest of the undisclosed principal in his agent's contract arises contemporaneously

---

[265] As in *Cooke & Sons* v. *Eshelby* (1887) 12 App. Cas. 271.

[266] See *Isberg* v. *Bowden* (1853) 8 Ex. 852, 859; *Dresser* v. *Norwood* (1863) 14 CB (NS) 574, 588–9; *Turner* v. *Thomas* (1871) LR 6 CP 610, 613; *Montgomerie* v. *United Kingdom Mutual Steamship Association, Limited* [1891] 1 QB 370, 372. See also the early judgments in *Rabone* v. *Williams* (1785) 7 TR 360n and *Stracey, Ross, et al.* v. *Deey* (1789) 7 TR 361n. The Privy Council in *Browning* v. *Provincial Insurance Company of Canada* (1873) LR 5 PC 263, 272 said that 'an undisclosed principal may sue and be sued upon mercantile contracts made by his agent in his own name, subject to any defences or equities which without notice may exist against the agent'.

[267] Goodhart and Hamson, (1932) 4 *Cambridge Law Journal* 320.

[268] See Glanville Williams, 'Mistake as to Party in the Law of Contract' (1945) 23 *Canadian Bar Review* 380, 408; Powell, *The Law of Agency* (1952), 138–9; Stoljar, *The Law of Agency* (1961), 232.

with the entering into of that contract. Further, the mere fact that a contract is not in its nature assignable is not sufficient to prevent the application of the undisclosed principal doctrine.[269] In any event, before the enactment of the Judicature Acts a chose in action was not assignable at law,[270] and so it would be dangerous to carry too far any analogy between assignments and the common law treatment of the undisclosed principal. Indeed, the extent of the right of set-off does seem to be one of the areas in which the analogy falls down, because the accepted principle seems to be that the *George* v. *Clagett* set-off is based upon an estoppel, rather than upon a notion of taking subject to equities. In *Cooke & Sons* v. *Eshelby*[271] Cooke & Sons as the third party were asked in interrogatories as to whether they did not believe that the brokers in the transaction in issue were acting on behalf of principals, and they replied that they 'had no belief on the subject', and that they dealt with the brokers 'not knowing whether they were acting as brokers on behalf of principals, or on their own account as the principals'. The House of Lords held that, because Cooke & Sons had not been led to believe that the brokers were acting as principals rather than agents, they were not entitled to a set-off under *George* v. *Clagett*.[272] The set-off was treated as being based upon an estoppel,[273] and before the principal could be estopped from denying the set-off there had to be a representation, as well as reliance upon that representation. As Lord Watson remarked:[274]

These decisions appear to me to establish conclusively that, in order to sustain the defence pleaded by the appellants, it is not enough to shew that the agent sold in his own name. It must be shewn that he sold the goods as his own, or, in other words, that the circumstances attending the sale were calculated to induce, and did induce, in the mind of the purchaser a reasonable belief that the agent was selling on his own account and not for an undisclosed principal; and it must also be shewn that the agent was enabled to appear as the real contracting party by the conduct, or by the authority, express or implied, of the principal. The rule thus explained is intelligible and just: and I agree . . . that it rests upon the doctrine of estoppel.

Similarly Lord Halsbury, while not actually mentioning estoppel, nevertheless explained the undisclosed principal cases in terms embodying

---

[269] *Siu Yin Kwan* v. *Eastern Insurance Co. Ltd.* [1994] 2 AC 199, 209–210.
[270] See *Lampet's Case* (1612) 10 Co. Rep. 46b, 48a.
[271] (1887) 12 App. Cas. 271.
[272] Compare Reynolds, who has argued that this may have been a case of an unnamed, as opposed to an undisclosed, principal. See Reynolds, (1983) 36 *Current Legal Problems* 119, 133.
[273] See also *Montagu* v. *Forwood* [1893] 2 QB 350, 355 per Bowen L.J.; *Cooper* v. *Strauss and Co.* (1898) 14 TLR 233; *Farquharson Brothers and Co.* v. *King* (1901) 70 LJKB 985, 987 per Vaughan Williams L.J. (*arguendo*); *Tingey and Co. Ltd.* v. *John Chambers and Co. Ltd.* [1967] NZLR 785. In *Fish* v. *Kempton* (1849) 7 CB 687, 691 Wilde C.J. explained the set-off in terms savouring of estoppel, and see also the judgments in *Baring* v. *Corrie* (1818) 2 B & Ald. 137.   [274] (1887) 12 App. Cas. 271, 278.

the elements of that doctrine.[275] The answer to the interrogatory indicated that the element of reliance was absent.

The necessity for reliance upon a representation hardly accords with the alternative theory, that the set-off is based upon a notion of taking subject to equities. Nevertheless, as a matter of policy the decision in *Cooke* v. *Eshelby* was sound.[276] There is no apparent justification for shifting the burden of the liability for the agent's indebtedness onto the undisclosed principal, unless the third party had been led to believe, erroneously, that when he was dealing with the agent he was in fact dealing directly with a principal. A third party in a case such as *Cooke* v. *Eshelby* would have entered into the transaction cognizant of the risk that an undisclosed principal may intervene, in which case the possibility of a set-off against the agent is unlikely to have been a factor influencing his decision to deal with the agent.[277] Having said that, estoppel does not explain the allowance of a set-off in all the *George* v. *Clagett* cases, irrespective of whether the estoppel is thought to be based upon conduct of the principal himself as constituting a representation, or whether the representation is thought to be made by the agent which then becomes binding upon the principal.

Consider first the possibility of the principal's own conduct constituting a representation, in the context of a sale of goods. Any representation sufficient to induce the belief that the agent is actually contracting as principal should indicate that the agent is the owner of the goods in question. In other words, the representation should be sufficient to satisfy the doctrine of apparent ownership.[278] This doctrine is concerned with the validity of a disposition of property, and with overcoming the *nemo dat*

---

[275] 'The ground upon which all these cases have been decided is that the agent has been permitted by the principal to hold himself out as the principal, and that the person dealing with the agent has believed that the agent was the principal, and has acted on that belief:' (1887) 12 App. Cas. 271, 275. Compare Lord Fitzgerald, who expressed some doubt as to whether *George* v. *Clagett* does rest upon estoppel, though, as Spencer Bower and Turner, *The Law Relating to Estoppel by Representation* (3rd edn., 1977), 25 notes, he then proceeded to state the proposition in terms of his own choosing which differed in no substantial respect from those in which estoppel by representation are usually expressed.

[276] Compare Pollock (1887) 3 *Law Quarterly Review* 358, 359, who doubted the wisdom of extending the anomalous rights of an undisclosed principal.

[277] Compare the evidence to the contrary referred to by Lord Fitzgerald in *Cooke* v. *Eshelby* (1887) 12 App. Cas. 271, 280 based upon an alleged custom in the Liverpool Cotton Market, which was not proved, that the third party may set off the broker's indebtedness to him against any obligation to pay the price to an undisclosed principal, even when aware of the possibility of the existence of such a principal.

[278] While the doctrine of apparent ownership also is said to be based upon an estoppel (see e.g. *Mercantile Credit Co. Ltd.* v. *Hamblin* [1965] 2 QB 242, 271), the fact that it confers a real title, as opposed to operating merely between the parties themselves, has been said to militate against an estoppel, or at least against the traditional view that an estoppel does not establish a title. Compare *Bowstead and Renolds*, n. 201 above, 460–1, 464 with Spencer Bower and Turner, *The Law Relating to Estoppel by Representation* (3rd edn., 1977), 17–18.

principle, while in a *George* v. *Clagett* set-off the validity of the disposition is conceded. However, unless the agent has been held out as the owner of the goods, and as such able to transfer a good title to them in his own right, it can hardly be said that anything done by the undisclosed principal himself has constituted a representation that the agent is selling as a principal. But, as Bowstead has pointed out in criticizing the estoppel theory,[279] while the third party evidently may found a *George* v. *Clagett* set-off upon the mere fact of the agent having had possession of the goods for sale, or of their indicia of title,[280] this is not considered to be sufficient to create a situation of apparent ownership.[281] Something further is required, for example that the real owner has allowed the goods to stand in another's name,[282] or that the real owner has given another person an acknowledgment in writing that he has bought and paid for the goods,[283] or that the real owner has signed a document offering to buy the goods from the other person.[284] It seems clear, then, that a *George* v. *Clagett* set-off may be based upon conduct that would not be sufficient to constitute a representation by the undisclosed principal that the agent is owner of the goods being sold.

There is another way of approaching the estoppel theory, and that is that the agent himself, by contracting in his own name, represents that he is the principal in the transaction, and if the undisclosed principal has authorized this he becomes bound by the representation.[285] This approach avoids the difficulty that the principal's own conduct may not have been sufficient to constitute a representation that the agent was contracting as a principal in his own right. However, even if it is accepted that the agent does make such a representation by contracting in his own name,[286] it still fails to

---

[279] *Bowstead and Reynolds*, n. 201 above, 440–1, 465–6.

[280] See *Semenza* v. *Brinsley* (1865) 18 CB (NS) 467, 477, and also *Borries* v. *The Imperial Ottoman Bank* (1873) LR 9 CP 38.

[281] *Rimmer* v. *Webster* [1902] 2 Ch. 163, 169; *Motor Credits (Hire Finance) Limited* v. *Pacific Motor Auctions Pty. Limited* (1963) 109 CLR 87, 99. Compare *Lloyds & Scottish Finance Ltd.* v. *Williamson* [1965] 1 WLR 404, criticized, and possibly explained, in *Bowstead and Reynolds*, n. 201 above, 465 n. 90, and see also Fridman, *The Law of Agency* (6th edn., 1990), 249–50.

[282] See e.g. *Henderson & Co.* v. *Williams* [1895] 1 QB 521 (goods warehoused in another's name).   [283] *Rimmer* v. *Webster* [1902] 2 Ch. 163.

[284] *Eastern Distributors Ltd.* v. *Goldring* [1957] 2 QB 600.

[285] See Spencer Bower and Turner, *The Law Relating to Estoppel by Representation* (3rd edn., 1977), 122.

[286] Compare Goodhart and Hamson's view ((1932) 4 *Cambridge Law Journal* 320, 344), that 'normally a person contracting in his own name does not, by that mere fact, make any representation that he is not contracting as trustee for, or for the benefit of, another'. This proposition is based upon two cases, *Nash* v. *Dix* (1898) 78 LT 445 and *Dyster* v. *Randall and Sons* [1926] Ch. 932, though these may have been concerned with the materiality of the representation (as defined in Spencer Bower and Turner, *The Law of Actionable Misrepresentation* (3rd edn., 1974), 144), as opposed to whether there had been any

explain the right of set-off in cases in which the agent had been instructed to reveal the fact of his agency, or at least had not been authorized to use his own name when contracting.[287] Occasionally there have been statements which seem to assume that the set-off only applies when the principal has authorized the agent to contract as though he were the principal.[288] Indeed, in *Baring* v. *Corrie*[289] a third party who bought goods from a broker selling in his own name was denied a set-off against the undisclosed principal, inter alia because a broker's authority was confined to selling in the name of his principal.[290] Nevertheless, it was held by the Court of Appeal in *Ex parte Dixon; in re Henley*,[291] and again by the New Zealand Court of Appeal in *Knight* v. *Matson & Co.*,[292] that an express direction to the agent to reveal the fact of his agency will not deprive the third party of a set-off under *George* v. *Clagett* if the agent ignores this direction and contracts in his own name without disclosing that he is an agent.[293] It may be thought unfair that the principal should be subjected to a set-off that would not have arisen if the agent had acted in accordance with his instructions. Equally, though, it is unfair that a private communication from the principal to the agent should have the effect of depriving the third party of a set-off when the possibility of a set-off may have been an inducement for the third party to contract with the agent. If the principal chooses to deal through an agent, he should be expected to take the risk that the agent may exceed his authority and act as though he himself is the principal.[294]

Before discussing these cases in the context of the agent's authority to

representation. Lord Watson in *Cooke* v. *Eshelby* (1887) 12 App. Cas. 271, 278 apparently thought that the estoppel could be based either upon the principal's own conduct or upon the authority, express or implied, conferred upon the agent. See also *Borries* v. *The Imperial Ottoman Bank* (1873) LR 9 CP 38, 47, where Brett J. talked in terms of a representation made by the agent.

[287] The mere fact of the agent being instructed not to reveal the name of the principal does not mean that he has been authorized to contract as though he is the principal. See Lord Fitzgerald in *Cooke* v. *Eshelby* (1887) 12 App. Cas. 271, 281–2.

[288] For example, Lord Halsbury L.C. in *Cooke* v. *Eshelby* (1887) 12 App. Cas. 271, 275 spoke of the 'permission of the real principal to the agent to assume his character'. In *Dresser* v. *Norwood* (1863) 14 CB (NS) 574, the authority given to the agent to sell in his own name was emphasized. See also *Fish* v. *Kempton* (1849) 7 CB 687, 691 per Wilde C.J. (*arguendo*); *Semenza* v. *Brinsley* (1865) 18 CB (NS) 467, 477.

[289] (1818) 2 B & Ald. 137.

[290] For the distinction formerly drawn between brokers and factors, see *Bowstead and Reynolds*, n. 210 above, 34–5.

[291] (1876) 4 Ch. D 133, explaining *Semenza* v. *Brinsley* (1865) 18 CB (NS) 467.

[292] (1902) 22 NZLR 293.

[293] The agent's failure to reveal his agency would not affect his authority to sell. This is clear from *Dixon* and *Matson*, and see also *Stevens* v. *Biller* (1883) 25 Ch. D 31.

[294] See Powell, *The Law of Agency* (1952), 148–9, where this point is made without reference to either *Dixon* or *Matson*.

make the representation, it should be noted that *Matson* in any event may be explained on another ground. Edwards J. found that a situation of apparent ownership had been created. The agent in that case was a dealer in cattle in his own right. It has been suggested that a deposit of goods with a person who in the normal course of his business is known to sell goods of that type on his own account may be sufficient to satisfy the doctrine of apparent ownership.[295] Therefore, the conduct of the undisclosed principal in entrusting his cattle for sale with a person who bought and sold cattle in his own right in the normal course of his business may have constituted a representation to those dealing with that person that he in fact was the owner of the cattle. Since an estoppel may be explained on the basis of the principal's own representation, the agent's disregard for the instructions given to him as to the disclosure of the agency loses its importance. However, this analysis would not appear to be available in relation to *Dixon*.[296] The agent was an iron and metal merchant. In the transaction in question he sold a particular type of pig-iron to the third party on behalf of an undisclosed principal. While it may be assumed that such an agent would buy and sell metal in his own right in the normal course of his business, this was not emphasized either in the statement of facts set out in the report or in the judgments, which suggests that the case did not turn on it. Rather, the Court of Appeal in allowing a set-off had recourse to the scope of the authority usually possessed by a factor.

If the agent has been instructed to reveal the fact of his agency, it is difficult to see how it can be said that the principal has authorized the agent to represent that he is the principal. Clearly the agent does not possess actual authority. Moreover, any argument based upon apparent authority would not be open to the third party seeking a set-off. Apparent authority arises when a person by words or conduct represents or permits it to be represented that another has authority to act on his behalf.[297] However, the essence of a *George* v. *Clagett* set-off is that the third party believed that the person with whom he was dealing was contracting as a principal in his own right. He could hardly argue that the other party was held out as having authority to contract in his own name though on behalf of the real principal, and at the same time assert that he believed that he was actually dealing with the principal in the transaction. As Scrutton L.J. once aptly remarked,[298] 'you cannot rely on the apparent authority of an agent who did not profess in dealing with you to act as agent'. While this may seem

---

[295] See *Bowstead and Reynolds*, n. 201 above, 466, referring to *Motor Credits (Hire Finance) Limited* v. *Pacific Motor Auctions Pty. Limited* (1963) 109 CLR 87, 99.
[296] However, Edwards J. in *Matson* (1902) 22 NZLR 293, 315 did seem to regard *Dixon* as a case of apparent ownership.
[297] See *Bowstead and Reynolds*, n. 201 above, 366.
[298] *Underwood, Ltd.* v. *Bank of Liverpool and Martins* [1924] 1 KB 775, 792.

clear, the Court of Appeal in *Dixon*[299] nevertheless based its decision to allow a set-off upon the notion that the agent could be taken as having had authority to sell in his own name. Thus Brett J.A. said:[300]

Now, the rule of law is, that the extent of an agent's authority as between himself and third parties is to be measured by the extent of his usual employment. That being so, the very fact of entrusting your goods to a man as a factor, with the right to sell them, is *prima facie* authority from you to him to sell in his own name.

Similarly, James L.J. in deciding in favour of the set-off said that,[301] 'As regards third parties, the powers of an agent are measured by the apparent scope of his authority, and cannot be limited by any private communication with him'. No mention was made of the apparent inconsistency of the third party's right of set-off being based upon the authority usually possessed by a factor, when the set-off is only allowable if the third party did not know that the person with whom he was dealing was a factor.[302] This aspect of the decision in *Dixon* is reminiscent of the later case of *Watteau* v. *Fenwick*,[303] in which it was held that the owner of a business was liable on contracts entered into by an agent who was the manager of the business but who appeared to be the principal, even though the agent had been instructed not to enter into that type of transaction. Wills J. said that, 'the principal is liable for all the acts of the agent which are within the authority usually confided to an agent of that character, notwithstanding limitations, as between the principal and the agent, put upon that authority'.[304] This case has often been criticized on the same ground as that mentioned above, that the agent had neither actual nor apparent authority, and that therefore the principal should not have been liable on the contract.[305] But even apart from that criticism *Watteau* v. *Fenwick* does not support the approach adopted in *Dixon*. In *Watteau* v. *Fenwick* the third party did not know that the other contracting party was only an agent. Nevertheless, the decision in that case is still consistent with the result that would have followed if the third party had been informed of that fact, i.e. the principal would have been liable on the contract. This is not so, however, for *Dixon*. If the third

---

[299] (1876) 4 Ch. D 133.

[300] (1876) 4 Ch. D 133, 137, referred to with approval by Williams J. in *Matson* (1902) 22 NZLR 293, 308–9. [301] (1876) 4 Ch. D 133, 136.

[302] Brett J.A. in *Dixon* seemed to contemplate the situation in which the agent is a factor in the traditional sense of the word, so that his 'usual employment' is to sell the goods of others in his own name. However, it is apparent that Williams J. in *Matson* (1902) 22 NZLR 293, 308–9, in applying Brett J.A.'s statement, considered that Brett J.A.'s analysis should not be limited to that type of agent. [303] [1893] 1 QB 346.

[304] [1893] 1 QB 346, 348–9.

[305] See generally *Bowstead and Reynolds*, n. 201 above, 107–9, 416–19, and Fridman, *The Law of Agency* (6th edn., 1990), 63–5. The authority of *Watteau* v. *Fenwick* was doubted by Bingham J. in *The Rhodian River* [1984] 1 Lloyd's Rep. 373.

[306] (1887) 12 App. Cas. 271. [307] (1876) 4 Ch. D. 133.

party had been aware that he was dealing with a factor, he would have been denied the relief actually granted by the Court of Appeal, i.e. a right to set off the agent's indebtedness to him against his liability to the principal. In other words, the form of authority which the court found in *Dixon* has an even more tenuous basis for the decision in that case than the authority found in *Watteau v. Fenwick*.

Unless possibly *Dixon* is treated as a case in which the goods had been delivered to an agent who was accustomed to deal in goods of that type on his own account in the normal course of his business, so as to come within the doctrine of apparent ownership, it is difficult to explain the allowance of a set-off on the basis of an estoppel. Certainly this was not emphasized in the judgments, and it seems that the decision did not turn on it. The case may be regarded as wrongly decided on the ground that the representation made by the agent was not authorized by, and consequently was not binding upon, the undisclosed principal. However this would not be a welcome result, because a private communication between the principal and the agent should not have the effect of denying the third party a set-off that he otherwise may have expected to have, particularly when it was the principal himself who chose to deal through an agent. Alternatively, the courts may come to recognize that the estoppel theory put forward by the House of Lords in *Cooke* v. *Eshelby*,[306] which was decided only 11 years after *Dixon*[307] without any mention being made of that case, is not a satisfactory explanation for the *George* v. *Clagett* set-off,[308] and that, as the principal's very right of intervention on his agent's contract is an anomaly without a proper juristic basis, so is the third party's right of set-off.

9.7.4 *Set-off between the principal and the third party*

When a contract is effected through an agent, the parties to the contract usually are the principal and the third party.[309] The agent himself is not a party, and accordingly he may not enforce the contract in an action brought in his own name.[310] Nevertheless, this is not an invariable rule.

---

[308] The statement of the principle in terms of estoppel has been criticized in Powell, *The Law of Agency* (1952), 147–8, and also in *Bowstead and Reynolds*, n. 201 above, 441.

[309] However, an undisclosed principal is not a party to the agent's contract. See section 9.7.3 above.

[310] See e.g. *Storaker* v. *Southouse & Long Ltd.* (1920) 20 SR(NSW) 190. The fact that the agent may be on a *del credere* commission does not affect this conclusion. See *Bramwell* v. *Spiller* (1870) 21 LT 672. Nor would it make any difference if the agent himself had actually paid the contract sum to the principal under the terms of the commission. See *Jordeson and Co. and Simon Kahn* v. *London Hardwood Company* (1913) 19 Com. Cas. 161; *Coghlan* v. *McKay* (1902) 8 ALR 155. See also *Flatau, Dick & Co.* v. *Keeping* (1931) 39 Ll. L Rep. 232 (advances made by the agent to his principal on the goods).

There are indeed a number of situations in which the agent contracts personally, and in which he may sue.[311] This is the case when the agent contracts for an undisclosed principal. It may also apply, depending on the circumstances, in the case of an agent for an unnamed principal,[312] that is, when the agent discloses that he is acting as an agent but without disclosing the principal's indentity, and when a person enters into a contract in his own name but he is expressed to do so 'and/or as agent', so that he may or may not be contracting as a principal.[313] Similarly a factor,[314] an auctioneer of goods,[315] and an agent who effects insurance in his own name on behalf of another with that other's authority[316] may each sue. If indeed the agent rather than the principal does sue, the question whether the third party may set off in that action a debt owing to him by the principal prima facie should depend on whether it can be said that the agent in bringing the action does so as trustee for the principal, because otherwise the demands would not be mutual either at law or in equity.[317] In fact, it is not easy to find a trust in all cases.

Consider the case of a sale of goods by auction. The purchaser may have removed the goods without immediate payment and subsequently been sued by the auctioneer for the price, the auctioneer's entitlement to sue arising either by virtue of a special property that he has in the goods or

---

[311] See generally *Bowstead and Reynolds*, n. 201 above, 554 *et seq.*

[312] In *Teheran–Europe Co. Ltd.* v. *S. T. Belton (Tractors) Ltd.* [1968] 2 QB 545, 558 Diplock L.J. contemplated the situation in which both the principal and the agent may be entitled to sue on the contract.

[313] See *Lee* v. *Bullen* (1858) 27 LJQB 161. See also *Greater Britain Insurance Corporation, Ltd.* v. *C. T. Bowring & Co. (Insurance), Ltd.* (1925) 22 Ll. L Rep. 538, in which Greer J. allowed brokers a set-off on policies effected by them 'and/or as agents'. For the terms of the policy see (1925) 23 Ll. L Rep. 285. His Lordship's reliance on *Koster* v. *Eason* (1813) 2 M & S 112 and *Parker* v. *Beasley* (1814) 2 M & S 423 suggests that he considered that the brokers could have sued in their own name. Greer J.'s decision was subsequently affirmed by the Court of Appeal ((1926) 24 Ll. L Rep. 7), though on the alternative ground that the agreement between the parties modified their relationship.

[314] *Drinkwater* v. *Goodwin* (1775) 1 Cowp. 251.

[315] See *Williams* v. *Millington* (1788) 1 H BI. 81; *Chelmsford Auctions Ltd.* v. *Poole* [1973] 1 QB 542. However, apparently this is not so for an auctioneer of land. See *Cherry* v. *Anderson* (1876) Ir. R 10 CL 204.

[316] *Provincial Insurance Company of Canada* v. *Leduc* (1874) LR 6 PC 224, 244, and see generally *Arnould's Law of Marine Insurance and Average* (16th edn., 1981) Vol. 2, 1132 para. 1354.

[317] Compare *Atkyns and Batten* v. *Amber* (1796) 2 Esp. 493, in which a set-off was denied, though the broker in that case had made advances to the principal on the goods sold so that he would have been suing on his own account. *Quaere* whether the agent in *Atkyns* in fact should have been allowed to sue in his own name. See *Bramwell* v. *Spiller* (1870) 21 LT 672. The sale note in *Atkyns* said that the goods were sold by the agent 'on account of' the principal, so that the agent himself would not appear to have been a party to the contract. See for example *Jordeson and Co. and Simon Kahn* v. *London Hardwood Company* (1931) 19 Com. Cas. 161 ('as agents for'); *Flatau, Dick & Co.* v. *Keeping* (1931) 39 Ll. L Rep. 232 ('sold for account of our principals').

from a contract implied by law between him and the purchaser whereby the purchaser has agreed to pay the price to the auctioneer.[318] The purchaser may set off a debt owing to him by the vendor/principal in the auctioneer's action, provided that the auctioneer is adequately protected in respect of his lien[319] for his expenses and charges in auctioning the goods,[320] as well as for any other right of deduction previously agreed to by the vendor in respect of other debts owing to him by the vendor.[321] The use of the word 'lien' to describe the auctioneer's rights in respect of the proceeds of sale is criticized in Bowstead[322] on the same basis that the term 'banker's lien' has been said to be inappropriate to describe a banker's right to treat accounts as combined.[323] In other words, it is difficult to see how a lien can be exercised over money, which normally would become the property of the holder subject to a legal or equitable duty to account for it. The auctioneer's lien is simply described in *Bowstead* in terms of a package of rights, comprising a right to set off when sued by the principal, and a right to sue the purchaser for the price and to retain from the proceeds an amount sufficient to satisfy his entitlement.

While comments by Salter J. in *Benton* v. *Campbell, Parker and Company*[324] suggest that a set-off in respect of a debt owing by the vendor is not available in the auctioneer's action before the debt secured by the lien has been paid, Bankes J. in *Manley & Sons Ltd.* v. *Berkett*[325] proceeded on the basis that it is sufficient if allowance is given for the auctioneer's entitlement in the set-off, by only permitting the purchaser to set off the price less an amount equal to the sum necessary to protect that entitlement.[326] This right of set-off available to the purchaser in the

---

[318] *Chelmsford Auctions Ltd.* v. *Poole* [1973] 1 QB 542, 549, 550, referring to *Benton* v. *Campbell, Parker and Company* [1925] 2 KB 410, 416.

[319] An auctioneer only has a particular lien over goods for his charges and expenses in respect of those particular goods. See *Webb* v. *Smith* (1885) 30 Ch. D 192. This should be compared to a factor, who has a general lien for the balance of his account with the principal. See *Kruger* v. *Wilcox* (1755) Amb. 252; *Baring* v. *Corrie* (1818) 2 B & Ald. 137, 148.

[320] *Holmes* v. *Tutton* (1855) 5 El. & Bl. 65, 82; *Manley & Sons, Ltd.* v. *Berkett* [1912] 2 KB 329. See also *Bulgin* v. *McCabe* (1859) unreported but mentioned at 1 QSCR 83–4; *Grice* v. *Kenrick* (1870) LR 5 QB 340, 345; *Benton* v. *Campbell, Parker and Company, Ltd.* [1925] 2 KB 410, 416; *Chelmsford Auctions Ltd.* v. *Poole* [1973] 1 QB 542, 549. Compare *Coppin* v. *Craig* (1816) 7 Taunt. 243, in which the auctioneer had sold the goods of one person under another's name.

[321] *Manley & Sons, Ltd.* v. *Berkett* [1912] 2 KB 329.

[322] *Bowstead and Reynolds*, n. 201 above, 339.

[323] See section 11.2.1 below.

[324] [1925] 2 KB 410, 416. See also *Holmes* v. *Tutton* (1855) 5 El. & Bl. 65, 82.

[325] [1912] 2 KB 329.

[326] On the other hand, a set-off presumably would be denied if the auctioneer himself previously had tendered the sale price to the vendor so that he is suing entirely on his own account, as in *Chelmsford Auctions Ltd.* v. *Poole* [1973] 1 QB 542.

auctioneer's action has been described as a right in equity by way of equitable defence.[327]

Consider the position in relation to insolvency set-off. When the vendor is bankrupt or is a company in liquidation there is a conceptual difficulty in allowing a set-off as between the purchaser and the vendor before the auctioneer's charges and expenses have been met, because in such a case the demands are not strictly mutual. Once the auctioneer has received the sale proceeds a trust may arise in favour of the principal after the auctioneer has made the necessary deduction in order to obtain reimbursement.[328] However, the insolvency legislation is cast in terms of mutual debts, credits, and dealings, and mutuality is determined by reference to the equitable title to the demands themselves,[329] as opposed to the eventual equitable title to the proceeds of the demands. The difficulty is that, until the auctioneer's lien has been satisfied, it can hardly be said that the auctioneer holds the right to sue solely as trustee for the principal, since the auctioneer at that stage will have the prior right to look to anything that may be recovered in order that he may satisfy his 'lien'. The auctioneer may be a trustee, first for himself, and, after that, for the principal. Nevertheless, the auctioneer would be the first beneficiary, and his beneficial interest would extend to the whole claim as the source from which his 'lien' is to be satisfied. While the principal may be said to have a beneficial interest in the remainder, this would be subject to the interest of the auctioneer, and strictly it should not be sufficient to render the claim mutual with an indebtedness of his own to the third party. However, at least if the purchaser is solvent this objection is unlikely to prevail. An analagous situation occurred in *Lee & Chapman's Case*.[330] A debt owing to a company was charged to a third party. The company went into liquidation, and it was held that the debtor was entitled to a set-off in the liquidation against the part of the debt over and above the amount required to satisfy the secured debt owing to the third party. On the other hand, a set-off should not ordinarily be available as between the vendor and the third party if the purchaser himself is insolvent, unless the auctioneer's prior interest is otherwise secured.[331] If the purchaser is insolvent a set-off would reduce the debt over which the auctioneer has a 'lien', without any certainty that the proceeds eventually received in respect of the remainder of the debt would be sufficient to satisfy the lien.

The effectiveness as against the auctioneer of an agreement for a set-off

---

[327] *Manley & Sons, Ltd.* v. *Berkett* [1912] 2 KB 329, 333. See also *Holmes* v. *Tutton* (1855) 5 El & Bl. 65, 81. In *Chelmsford Auctions Ltd.* v. *Poole* [1973] 1 QB 542, 549 Lord Denning referred to it as an 'equity'.

[328] *Re Cotton (deceased); ex parte Cooke* (1913) 108 LT 310.

[329] See section 7.1 above.   [330] (1885) 30 Ch. D 216.

[331] See section 7.6.2 above.

between the vendor and the purchaser should be determined by reference to similar principles. The agreement will not provide a defence to an action by the auctioneer unless his charges and expenses have been paid,[332] or at least, if the purchaser is solvent, the set-off may be reduced so as to leave an amount sufficient to cover them.[333] In *Grice* v. *Kenrick*[334] the auctioneer's lien had been satisfied and, although he was aware of a set-off agreement between the vendor and the purchaser, the auctioneer paid the price himself to the vendor and proceeded to sue the purchaser. The set-off agreement was held to constitute a defence to the auctioneer's action, though the court suggested that the auctioneer would have succeeded if he had been deceived by the purchaser, or if there had been anything accompanying the receipt of the goods from which a promise on the defendant's part to pay the auctioneer could have been inferred.

A similar analysis should apply when an agent who contracted on behalf of an undisclosed principal is suing the third party,[335] and the third party, having discovered the identity of the principal, wishes to set off in that action a debt owing to him by the principal. While the agent ordinarily would hold any property received under the contract on trust for the principal,[336] a strong Judicial Committee of the Privy Council, which included Lord Atkin and Lord Russell of Killowen, advised in *Allen* v. *F. O'Hearn and Company*[337] that, as regards the third party, the agent is not a trustee for the undisclosed principal,[338] so that as between the agent and the third party there is a prima facie lack of mutuality in relation to the cross-demands. However, there was a similar lack of mutuality in the auctioneer cases, and they suggest that this is unlikely to prevent a set-off given that the principal is the party interested in the claim. If the principal intervened and himself sued the third party there would be mutuality, and the existence or otherwise of a right of set-off should not depend on whether the principal or the agent sues. Furthermore, if either the principal or the third party is bankrupt or in liquidation, a set-off may

---

[332] *Grice* v. *Kenrick* (1870) LR 5 QB 340.

[333] *Manley & Sons, Ltd.* v. *Berkett* [1912] 2 KB 329.

[334] (1870) LR 5 QB 340.

[335] The agent as the contracting party is entitled to sue on the contract. See *Garrett* v. *Bird* (1872) 11 SCR (NSW) 97. See also *Sims* v. *Bond* (1833) 5 B & Ad. 389, 393, and generally *Bowstead and Reynolds*, n. 201 above, 559.

[336] *Pople* v. *Evans* [1969] 2 Ch. 255, 261, and see also *Allen* v. *F. O'Hearn and Company* [1937] AC 213, 218. [337] [1937] AC 213, 218.

[338] See also *Pople* v. *Evans* [1969] 2 Ch. 255. Compare however Ames, 'Undisclosed Principal—His Rights and Liabilities' (1909) 18 *Yale Law Journal* 443, 446, 448, and Higgins, 'The Equity of the Undisclosed Principal' (1965) 28 *Modern Law Review* 167. Compare also Wood, *English and International Set-off* (1989), 980–1. Wood's view that a trust would arise upon the insolvency of the agent is questionable. The agent's status in this regard should be the same before or after insolvency.

occur between them in any event under the insolvency set-off section without the necessity for an action.[339]

Alternatively, the agent may have informed the third party that he was acting on behalf of a principal, though without naming the principal. In other words, the case may concern a disclosed principal who nevertheless is unnamed. Sometimes the agent in these cases will contract personally and consequently will be liable on the contract, this liability being in addition to that of the principal,[340] in which case the agent also may be entitled to bring proceedings himself.[341] Once again, the third party generally should be entitled to set off a cross-demand that he has against the principal. However, whether the principal is undisclosed or merely unnamed, the availability of a set-off should be subject to the same principle applicable to auctioneers, that a set-off should not be available if this would prejudice a prior interest that the agent has in the action.

9.7.5 *Set-off between the agent and the third party, where the agent can enforce the contract*

Where an agent is entitled to enforce a contract entered into on behalf of the principal,[342] and the agent himself is independently indebted to the third party, a set-off should be permissible as between them to the extent that the agent has a prior interest in the action, as, for example, a result of an auctioneer's lien for his charges and expenses. This should follow from *Hudson* v. *Granger*.[343] An agent who sold the goods of his principal was entitled by virtue of a lien on the goods to receive the price. It was held that an agreement between the purchaser and the agent's assignees in bankruptcy by which the price was set off against a debt owing by the agent to the third party was binding on the principal. On the other hand, to the extent that the principal is the party interested in the claim, a debt owing to the agent personally should not be able to be set off.[344]

The question of a set-off in this context has arisen in relation to marine insurance. As a result of a mercantile custom, which since has received

---

[339] *Stein* v. *Blake* [1995] 2 All ER 961.

[340] *Bowstead and Reynolds*, n. 201 above, 559–61. Compare *The Santa Carina* [1977] 1 Lloyd's Rep. 478.

[341] As in *Short* v. *Spackman* (1831) 2 B & Ad. 962. See Fridman, *The Law of Agency* (6th edn., 1990), 224–5, though compare Stoljar, *The Law of Agency* (1961), 250–1. In *Teheran–Europe Co. Ltd.* v. *S. T. Belton (Tractors) Ltd.* [1968] 2 QB 545, 558 Diplock L.J. contemplated the situation in which both the principal and the agent may be entitled to sue, and may be liable to be sued, on the contract.

[342] See section 9.7.4 above.

[343] (1821) 5 B & Ald. 27. See also *Warner* v. *M'Kay* (1836) 1 M & W 591.

[344] Compare the contrary view expressed at common law by Denman C.J. in *Gibson* v. *Winter* (1833) 5 B & Ad. 96, 102.

statutory recognition,[345] a broker who effects a policy of marine insurance on behalf of an insured is directly responsible as a principal to the underwriter for the premium.[346] In a number of cases a broker being sued by an underwriter's trustee (or, formerly, assignees) in bankruptcy for premiums has sought to set off the underwriter's liability to the insured for losses on policies effected through the broker.[347] The prima facie rule is that, unless the broker effected the policy on his own account,[348] the underwriter's liability to the insured and the broker's indebtedness to the underwriter are not mutual, so that a set-off in respect of the broker's debt is not allowed.[349] This would also be the case if the underwriter is being sued by the insured in respect of a loss.[350] Nor would an agreement for a set-off between the broker and the underwriter bind the insured.[351] Nevertheless, consider that the policy is taken out in the broker's name,[352] so that he may sue upon it,[353] and moreover that the broker has an interest in the claim on the policy arising out of a lien for an amount owing to him by the insured.[354] In these circumstances, if the broker is sued by the underwriter's trustee in bankruptcy for unpaid premiums the courts have held that the broker may set off the insured's claim on the policy.[355] In the cases in issue the amount owing to the broker secured by the lien exceeded

---

[345] See the Marine Insurance Act 1906, s. 53(1), and in Australia the Marine Insurance Act 1909 (Cth.), s. 59(1).

[346] See generally *Arnould's Law of Marine Insurance and Average* (16th edn, 1981) Vol. 1, 112–13. However this is not so, apparently, in non-marine insurance (although an agent authorized to receive payment on behalf of an insurer will be liable to account for premiums actually received). See *Re Palmdale Insurance Ltd.* [1982] VR 921.

[347] The cases are collected and discussed in *Arnould on the Law of Marine Insurance and Average* (12th edn., 1939) Vol. 1, 163 *et seq.* Note in Australia the Insurance (Agents and Brokers) Act 1984 (Cth.), s. 37, which provides that money paid to a person (not being a registered insurance broker) as agent of an insurer is subject to a trust in favour of the insurer and is not capable of being the subject of a set-off.

[348] See *Koster* v. *Eason* (1813) 2 M & S 112, though this is unlikely to be the case in modern business. See *Arnould's Law of Marine Insurance and Average* (16th edn., 1981) Vol. 1, 118 n. 62.

[349] See e.g. *Wilson* v. *Creighton* (1782) 3 Dougl. 132; *Bell* v. *Auldjo* (1784) 4 Dougl. 48.

[350] *The Admiral C* [1981] 1 Lloyd's Rep. 9.

[351] *Jell* v. *Pratt* (1817) 2 Stark. 67.

[352] The name inserted in the policy is 'frequently—perhaps usually—that of the brokers acting on behalf of others': *The Yasin* [1979] 2 Lloyd's Rep. 45, 53 per Lloyd J.

[353] See *Provincial Insurance Company of Canada* v. *Leduc* (1874) LR 6 PC 224, 244, and generally *Arnould's Law of Marine Insurance and Average* (16th edn. 1981) Vol. 2, 1132, para. 1354.

[354] For a discussion of an insurance broker's lien, see *Arnould's Law of Marine Insurance and Average* (16th edn., 1981) Vol. 1, 129–34. No doubt this would encompass the common practice by which the broker, on receiving credit for a claim from the underwriter, pays the insured forthwith. See *Arnould, op. cit.* Vol. 1, 111, 116 n. 56.

[355] *Parker* v. *Beasley* (1814) 2 M & S 423 (in which the brokers had a lien by virtue of their accepting bills on the credit of the goods insured); *Davies* v. *Wilkinson* (1828) 4 Bing. 573.

the claim on the policy. If, however, the lien is for less than the loss, a set-off should only be permitted to the extent of the lien. The contrary conclusion would mean that the insured's asset would be used to pay the broker's liability.[356] Moreover, a claim on a policy of marine insurance is regarded as being unliquidated in nature,[357] even after the loss has been adjusted,[358] so that a set-off would not be available under the Statutes of Set-off if both the broker and the underwriter are solvent.[359]

In non-marine insurance a broker effecting a policy of insurance on behalf of a client ordinarily would not do so in his own name. Consequently, the preceding discussion of the broker's right to set off losses when the name inserted in the policy is that of the broker would not be relevant. Recently an attempt was made in New South Wales to introduce a right of set-off between the insurer and the broker based upon custom or usage. In *Re Colin Williams (Insurance) Pty. Ltd.*[360] an insurance company and an insurance broker had adopted a practice by which the company would debit the broker in its accounts with the amount of the premium,[361] and credit the broker with the appropriate commission. If a policy was cancelled so that a proportion of the premium was returnable, the insurance company would credit the broker's account with the rebate of premium, and debit that account with a rateable proportion of the commission.[362] Both the insurer and the broker went into

---

[356] See Lord Ellenborough in *Koster* v. *Eason* (1813) 2 M & S 112, 119–20.

[357] *Luckie* v. *Bushby* (1853) 13 CB 864; *Pellas* v. *Neptune Marine Insurance Company* (1879) 5 CPD 34; *William Pickersgill & Sons, Ltd.* v. *London and Provincial Marine and General Insurance Co, Ltd.* [1912] 3 KB 614, 622; *Jabbour* v. *Custodian of Israeli Absentee Property* [1954] 1 WLR 139, 145; *Chandris* v. *Argo Insurance Company, Ltd.* [1963] 2 Lloyd's Rep. 65, 73–4; *Edmunds* v. *Lloyd Italico* [1986] 2 All ER 249, 250.

[358] *Luckie* v. *Bushby* (1853) 13 CB 864; *Jabbour* v. *Custodian of Israeli Absentee Property* [1954] 1 WLR 139, 143.   [359] See section 1.2.4 above.

[360] [1975] 1 NSWLR 130. See also *Re Palmdale Insurance Ltd.* [1982] VR 921.

[361] In non-marine insurance a broker ordinarily is not principally liable for the premium, although an agent of the insurer authorized to receive premiums on behalf of the insurer will be liable to account for premiums actually received. See *Re Palmdale Insurance Ltd.* [1982] VR 921. Compare the custom at Lloyd's, which renders the broker principally liable. See *MacGillivray and Parkington on Insurance Law* (8th edn., 1988), 573, and also *Grover and Grover, Ltd.* v. *Mathews* (1910) 15 Com. Cas. 249, 260 (Lloyd's fire policy). There does not appear to be any authority establishing the existence of a similar custom in non-marine insurance in Australia. See *Norwich Fire Insurance Society Ltd.* v. *Brennans (Horsham) Pty. Ltd.* [1981] VR 981, 989, and also, in England, *Wilson* v. *Avec Audio-Visual Equipment Ltd.* [1974] 1 Lloyd's Rep. 81. *Quaere* whether, in the absence of an agreement between the parties, the broker in *Colin Williams* in fact would have been liable to the insurance company for premiums. See *Norwich Winterthur Insurance (Australia) Ltd.* v. *Con-Stan Industries of Australia Pty. Ltd.* [1983] 1 NSWLR 461, 474 (result affirmed (1986) 160 CLR 226).

[362] Helsham J. accepted that there was a usage by which an insurer, upon cancelling a policy in respect of which a broker's commission had been paid, could claim a proportionate part of that commission. He further held that this usage was not unreasonable. See also *Re Palmdale Insurance Ltd.* [1982] VR 921.

liquidation. The insurer cancelled all its policies, and as a result became liable for returns of premium. The insurer's liquidator proposed to credit the broker with the returns, and debit it with the rebate of commission together with the sums owing by the broker for premiums. The broker's liquidator, on the other hand, said that the return premiums were payable to the policy-holders, and so could not be set off against the sums owing by the broker. Evidence was given of a practice in the insurance industry by which an insurance broker is indeed credited with any return premium on a policy arranged through that broker and subsequently cancelled. However, Helsham J. pointed out that the policies all had provisions to the effect that, if the policy is cancelled, the unearned premium would be refunded *to the insured*. His Honour said that any alleged usage would be unreasonable if it was inconsistent with the terms of the contract between the insurer and the insured. In any event, even apart from the wording of the policies, he said that a usage by which an underwriter credits a broker's account with return premiums would be unreasonable, and consequently would not be binding upon the insured, unless the insured had knowledge of the practice when he entered into the contract.[363]

9.7.6 *Set-off against an agent with a lien, where the agent cannot sue*

We saw in the preceding section that, where an insurance broker took out a policy of insurance on behalf of an insured but in his own name, so that he could sue upon it, and the broker was independently indebted to the underwriter, the courts have allowed the broker to employ an accrued claim on the policy in a set-off in the underwriter's bankruptcy to the extent that the broker was secured by a lien on the policy for the balance of the insurance account.[364] However, it was crucial to the set-off that the policy was in the broker's own name. As Lord Ellenborough remarked,[365] in such a case it was considered that the underwriter 'had consented that [the brokers] should be at liberty to stand in the character and situation of principals, that in case of loss they should be entitled to act in all respects as his creditors, and that they should be considered as giving him credit upon the policy at their own risk, and on their account'. If on the other hand the

---

[363] Helsham J. referred to similar cases in marine insurance in which it was held that a usage at Lloyd's, by which an underwriter could settle a loss by setting it off against a broker's liability for premiums, would not bind the insured, unless the insured had knowledge of the existence of this usage, or in any event the broker from the course of dealing between himself and the insured had authority to settle losses in accordance with it. See *Sweeting* v. *Pearce* (1859) 7 CB (NS) 449, (1861) 9 CB (NS) 534, and generally *Arnould's Law of Marine Insurance and Average* (16th edn., 1981) Vol 1, 125–7.

[364] *Parker* v. *Beasley* (1814) 2 M & S 423; *Davies* v. *Wilkinson* (1828) 4 Bing. 573.

[365] *Koster* v. *Eason* (1813) 2 M & S 112, 118.

policy was not in the broker's name he was not entitled to a set-off, notwithstanding that he had a lien. The important point as far as mutuality for a set-off is concerned is that a broker's lien is not equitable in origin, but rather has its source in the common law. Furthermore, apart from the intervention of statute in the form of the Judicature Acts, the common law courts themselves never contemplated an assignment of a debt, so that any suggestion that the lien operates as a form of assignment would hardly be accurate.[366] Rather, the common law gave effect to the lien by allowing the broker to retain the policy in his possession, and to apply any proceeds of a claim that the broker in fact received in reduction of the debt owing to him.[367] Nor, given its common law origin and nature, would the lien confer an equitable interest in the insured's claim,[368] notwithstanding that equitable remedies, for example injunction, would be available in an appropriate case in aid of the common law right. Consistent with this view, it was held that, where the broker could not sue, there was a lack of mutuality between the insured's claim against the underwriter on the policy and the underwriter's demand against the broker for premiums, and consequently no set-off.[369]

9.7.7 Del credere *commissions*

There are a number of old set-off cases concerning agents who contracted on the basis of a *del credere* commission.[370] In *Grove* v. *Dubois*[371] an insurance broker on a *del credere* commission had taken out policies in his own name on behalf of foreign correspondents. When he was sued by an underwriter's assignees in bankruptcy for unpaid premiums, it was held that he could set off claims that had accrued on the policies. The Court of King's Bench in allowing a set-off laid considerable emphasis on the fact of the commission, and indeed Lord Mansfield in his judgment said that the 'whole turns on the nature of a commission del credere'.[372] Apparently it

---

[366] Compare Wood, *English and International Set-off* (1989), 919.

[367] See e.g. *Mann* v. *Forrester* (1814) 4 Camp. 60.

[368] Compare Wood, *English and International Set-off* (1989), 1004–5. The comments of the Privy Council in *Allen* v. *F. O'Hearn* [1937] AC 213, 218 on whether an agent for an undisclosed principal is a trustee of the claim should be considered in this context.

[369] See *Koster* v. *Eason* (1813) 2 M & S 112; *Xenos* v. *Wickham* (1863) 14 CB (NS) 435, 465–6; *Wilson* v. *Creighton* (1782) 3 Dougl. 132. See also *Cumming* v. *Forester* (1813) 1 M & S 494 (set-off between solvent parties). Nor did it make any difference whether or not the broker acted on a *del credere* commission. See *Peele* v. *Northcote* (1817) 7 Taunt. 478. Compare, however, Wood, *English and International Set-off* (1989), 918–19, 1006–7.

[370] See generally Chorley, 'Del Credere' (1929) 45 *Law Quarterly Review* 221, (1930) 46 *Law Quarterly Review* 11.

[371] (1786) 1 TR 112. See also *Bize* v. *Dickason* (1786) 1 TR 285; *Weinholt* v. *Roberts* (1811) 2 Camp. 586.   [372] (1786) 1 TR 112, 115.

was thought that, if the broker had made himself liable to the principal for the loss, the broker in turn must have given credit to, or trusted, the underwriter for the amount of the loss.[373] This basis for the decision was criticized, however, particularly by Lord Ellenborough, on the ground that a contract between the insured and the broker for a *del credere* commission should not be able to vary the rights between the broker and the underwriter, who is a stranger to it, and empower the broker to set up a claim against the underwriter that is derived from that contract.[374] Nevertheless, despite that criticism, the case has not been overruled. Rather it has been said that, because the broker had insured for foreign correspondents who were unknown to the underwriter, the result may be explained on the ground that the dealing was with the broker as a principal.[375] However, in truth this is not the basis on which the judgments in *Grove* v. *Dubois* proceeded.[376] A more fundamental question was in issue, and that is whether a *del credere* agent assumed a primary or a secondary obligation.[377] Lord Mansfield in *Grove* v. *Dubois*[378] said that it was primary. Lord Ellenborough on the other hand considered that it took effect as a guarantee,[379] and therefore was secondary. This is the view that has prevailed. A *del credere* commission is regarded as an agreement to indemnify the principal if the third party fails to pay through insolvency, or something that makes it impossible to recover as in the case of insolvency.[380]

Given this characterization of a *del credere* agency, if the agent has paid the principal in accordance with the commission, and the case is one in

---

[373] See the discussion in the note to the report of *Baker* v. *Langhorn* (1816) 4 Camp. 396, 399. In *Lee* v. *Bullen* (1858) 27 LJQB 161 the *del credere* commission was said to give the broker an 'interest' in the contract of insurance. See also *Tapper* v. *Matheson* (1884) NZLR 3 SC 312, 314.

[374] *Cumming* v. *Forester* (1813) 1 M & S 494, 499; *Koster* v. *Eason* (1813) 2 M & S 112, 119; *Hornby* v. *Lacy* (1817) 6 M & S 166, 171 (though compare Lord Ellenborough's earlier judgment in *Wienholt* v. *Roberts* (1811) 2 Camp. 586). See also *Baker* v. *Langhorn* (1816) 6 Taunt. 519, 521 per Gibbs C.J.; *Peele* v. *Northcote* (1817) 7 Taunt. 478, 480, 485 per Gibbs C.J.; *Hornby* v. *Lacy* (at 172 per Abbott C.J.). *Quaere* whether this is a satisfactory ground for criticism. For example, an assignment by A to B of a debt owing by C may provide B with a defence to an action brought against him by C on another transaction.

[375] *Cumming* v. *Forester* (1813) 1 M & S 494, 499 per Lord Ellenborough. In *Parker* v. *Smith* (1812) 16 East 382, 385–6 Lord Ellenborough said that *Grove* v. *Dubois* was determined on the ground that there were 'dealings virtually had with the assured themselves'. See also *Arnould on the Law of Marine Insurance and Average* (12th edn. 1939) Vol. 1, 164–5.

[376] Chorley, 'Del Credere' (1929) 45 *Law Quarterly Review* 221, 227.

[377] Chorley, 'Del Credere' (1929) 45 *Law Quarterly Review* 221, 229–30.

[378] (1786) 1 TR 112, 115.

[379] *Morris* v. *Cleasby* (1816) 4 M & S 566, 574; *Hornby* v. *Lacy* (1817) 6 M & S 166, 171.

[380] *Thomas Gabriel & Sons* v. *Churchill & Sim* [1914] 3 KB 1272, affirming [1914] 1 KB 449.

which the agent in any event can sue the third party in his own name, for example because he acted for an undisclosed principal or an unnamed principal,[381] the position is simple. There is mutuality both at law and in equity between the agent and the third party.[382] Since the agent after payment under the *del credere* commission holds the claim for his own benefit and not for the benefit of the principal, there is no other beneficial interest which can affect mutuality. Where the third party has become bankrupt or has gone into liquidation, so that the insolvency set-off section governs the question, the availability of a set-off will depend on the principles discussed earlier in relation to contingent debts and guarantees.[383] In such a case the agent would not be entitled to a set-off if payment has not been made under the commission.[384] The principal would still have a right of proof in the insolvency, and the rule against double proof would prevent a set-off as between the agent and the third party.[385]

Consider that the case is one in which the agent does not have standing to sue. Usually the *del credere* commission would not have been given at the request of the third party, in which case *Owen* v. *Tate*[386] suggests that after payment the agent as a surety would not have a claim for reimbursement from the third party which can be set off. This indeed is consistent with some of the early common law cases in which *Grove* v. *Dubois* was criticized and a set-off denied.[387] However *Owen* v. *Tate* has not been favourably received by commentators,[388] and it may not be followed. Moreover, it may not have the effect of precluding a remedy to the *del credere* agent by way of subrogation to the principal's rights against the third party, either on the basis of the equitable right[389] or pursuant to

---

[381] See *Teheran–Europe Co. Ltd.* v. *S. T. Belton (Tractors) Ltd.* [1968] 2 QB 545, 558 in relation to an agent for an unnamed principal.

[382] See *Koster* v. *Eason* (1813) 2 M & S 324, in which Lord Ellenborough emphasized (at 118) the title to sue. This is the proper explanation of *Lee* v. *Bullen* (1858) 27 LJQB 161, in which the brokers contracted in their own names 'and/or as agents'. Wightman J. emphasized that the brokers might have sued and recovered in their own names, though compare Compton J. (at 162).

[383] See sections 4.3 and 4.4 above. In particular, a guarantor who pays the creditor *after* the creditor has proved in the debtor's bankruptcy or liquidation should be subrogated to the creditor's proof, and as a result of that beneficial interest in the proof should be entitled to a set-off. See section 4.3.4 above. Accordingly, in the case of an insurance broker, it should not be fatal to a set-off that the broker paid under the *del credere* commission after the insured has lodged a proof against the underwriter. Compare Wood, *English and International Set-off* (1989), 1007.   [384] *Koster* v. *Eason* (1813) 2 M & S 112, 119–20.

[385] See section 4.3.2 above.   [386] [1976] 1 QB 402.

[387] See e.g. *Cumming* v. *Forrester* (1813) 1 M & S 494; *Morris* v. *Cleasby* (1816) 4 M & S 566; *Peele* v. *Northcote* (1817) 7 Taunt. 478.

[388] Goff and Jones, *The Law of Restitution* (4th edn., 1993), 597–8; Birks, *An Introduction to the Law of Restitution* (1989), 311–12; Burrows, *The Law of Restitution* (1993), 213–16.

[389] Goff and Jones, *The Law of Restitution* (4th edn., 1993), 597–8; Beatson, *The Use and Abuse of Unjust Enrichment* (1991), 199.

the statutory right of subrogation conferred on a surety by section 5 of the Mercantile Law Amendment Act 1856.[390] Even if it is assumed, on the authority of *Owen* v. *Tate*, that there is no direct right of reimbursement, but subrogation nevertheless is available, an interest obtained in the principal's action consequent upon a right of subrogation should provide a sufficient basis for a set-off. Nor should it make any difference that the interest is acquired after the third party's bankruptcy by payment to the principal, since it still arises out of a prior obligation in the form of the *del credere* agency.[391] The basis of the set-off is the giving of credit, in that the *del credere* commission would naturally or in the ordinary course of business end in a debt[392] owing in equity by the third party to the agent as a result of the subrogation. When it is sought to base a set-off upon the concept of giving credit, it is not necessary to show that the debt arose out of a dealing between the parties to the proposed set-off.[393] If the *del credere* commission would naturally result in money becoming payable by the third party to the agent, credit is given by the agent to the third party whether or not the third party is aware of it.

9.7.8 *Set-off between the agent and the third party, in relation to the agent's liability as agent*

An agent contracting for his principal may undertake a personal liability to the third party,[394] which should be capable of being set off against a personal claim that he has against the third party. On the other hand, the agent should not be entitled to bring into an account a liability of the third party to the principal. While the principal may be obliged to indemnify the agent, this would be *res inter alios acta* as far as the third party is concerned, and it should not be sufficient to bring about mutuality between the agent's personal liability to the third party and a claim possessed by the principal against the third party.[395] However, there are two exceptions to this. The first applies when the agent in truth had contracted only as a surety, rather than as a principal debtor in his own right. If the third party wishes to have recourse against the agent/surety he may be required to

---

[390] Phillips and O'Donovan, *The Modern Contract of Guarantee* (2nd edn., 1992) 564–5; Burrows, *The Law of Restitution* (1993), 215.

[391] See section 4.3 above. Compare *MPS Constructions Pty. Ltd.* v. *Rural Bank of New South Wales* (1980) 4 ACLR 835 (criticized in section 4.3.4 above) in relation to the acquisition of an interest in a pre-existing debt after bankruptcy though pursuant to a prior transaction.   [392] See section 3.1 above.

[393] See section 3.3 above. Compare Millett J. in *Re Charge Card Services Ltd.* [1987] 1 Ch. 150, 189–90 (considered in section 4.3.3 above).

[394] See generally *Bowstead and Reynolds*, n. 201 above, 550 *et seq.*

[395] See *Nelson* v. *Roberts* (1893) 69 LT 352, and Angas Parsons J. in *Rex* v. *Ray; ex parte Chapman* [1936] SASR 241, 249 (liability of personal representative for costs).

bring into account a debt owing by him to the principal debtor.[396] The second may arise when the cross-demands are sufficiently closely connected to give rise to an equitable set-off which impeaches the plaintiff's title. For this form of set-off mutuality is not a necessary requirement.[397]

9.7.9 *Set-off between the principal and the agent*

If the agent incurs a liability to the third party for which he is entitled to be reimbursed by the principal, there may of course be a set-off as between the principal and the agent in respect of a separate liability that the agent has to the principal.[398]

An agent may be obliged to account to the principal for sums received in the course of the agency. The question whether the agent is entitled to a set-off may depend on whether the sums in question are impressed with a trust.[399]

9.8 THE CROWN

Prior to the enactment of the Crown Proceedings Act 1947 it was not possible for the defendant in an action at law brought against him by the Crown to set off a cross-demand that he had against the Crown. A subject could only make good a claim against the Crown by means of a petition of right, and he could not avoid that procedure by refusing to pay a debt of his own to the Crown and then asserting his claim as a set-off.[400] This was remedied by sections 13 and 15 of the 1947 Act, which permitted claims to be brought against the Crown in accordance with the rules of court in the same way as any claim brought against another subject. Nevertheless RSC Order 77 rule 6 made pursuant to the Act[401] contains a number of restrictions on the availability of set-off and counterclaim in proceedings by the Crown. Briefly, a person may not plead a set-off or make any counterclaim in Crown proceedings if they are for the recovery of, or the proposed set-off or counterclaim arises out of a right or claim to repayment in respect of, any taxes, duties or penalties. Furthermore, a counterclaim may not be made nor a set-off pleaded by the Crown in proceedings against the Crown, or by any person in proceedings by the Crown, without the

---

[396] See section 14.4 below.   [397] See section 1.7.6 above.
[398] *Cropper* v. *Cook* (1868) LR 3 CP 194.   [399] See Ch. 6.
[400] *Attorney-General* v. *Guy Motors, Ltd.* [1928] 2 KB 78. Compare *Hettihewage Siman Appu* v. *The Queen's Advocate* (1884) 9 App. Cas. 571, in which there was a right to sue the Crown under the laws of Ceylon. In *In re Ind, Coope & Co., Ltd.* [1911] 2 Ch. 223, 235–6 Warrington J. left open the question whether a set-off could have been exercised against the Crown.   [401] See s. 35(2)(g).

consent of the court, (a) if the Crown is sued or sues in the name of a government department and the subject-matter of the counter-claim or set-off does not relate to that department, or (b) if the Crown is sued or sues in the name of the Attorney-General.

According to RSC Order 1 rule 2, the Rules of the Supreme Court do not have effect in relation to insolvency proceedings under the Insolvency Act 1986. On the other hand, rule 7.51 of the Insolvency Rules 1986 provides that, except so far as they are inconsistent with the Insolvency Rules, the Rules of the Supreme Court apply to insolvency proceedings in the High Court. But even apart from the question whether the restrictions in RSC Order 77 rule 6 are inconsistent with rule 4.90 of the Insolvency Rules dealing with set-off in company liquidation, the House of Lords held in *Stein* v. *Blake*[402] that insolvency set-off does not depend upon any procedural step, but takes effect automatically upon the occurrence of a bankruptcy or liquidation. On that view, Order 77 rule 6 in relation to proceedings by the Crown can have no application to insolvency set-off. In the context of the Bankruptcy Act 1914, it was accepted that a set-off could occur in relation to obligations to pay tax to and rights to tax refunds from revenue authorities.[403] This should still be the case.

The Crown includes government departments that are headed by a Minister.[404] The fact that legislation may provide that a department is entitled to enforce rights acquired in the exercise of its functions and is liable in respect of liabilities 'as if it were acting as a principal' does not mean that rights or liabilities are not those of the Crown so as to destroy mutuality. A provision to this effect may be purely procedural, in the sense that the department is capable of suing and being sued as a principal, although in the eyes of the law it is still an agent of the Crown.[405]

Debts arising from dealings with the one government department would be mutual for the purpose of a set-off. An analogous case is *Knowles* v. *Maitland*,[406] in which the colonel of a regiment was both debtor and creditor in that capacity, and a set-off was allowed. On the other hand, a person may be liable to one government department and have a claim against another. Because of the theory that the Crown is one and indivisible the demands should be mutual although, where the debtor is neither bankrupt nor a company in liquidation, a set-off would be subject to RSC Order 77 rule 6.

---

[402] [1995] 2 All ER 961.
[403] *In re D. H. Curtis (Builders) Ltd.* [1978] 1 Ch. 162; *Re Cushla Ltd.* [1979] 3 All ER 415; *In re Unit 2 Windows Ltd.* [1985] 1 WLR 1383.
[404] Hogg, *Liability of the Crown* (2nd edn., 1989), 10.
[405] *Cullen* v. *Nottingham Health Authority* [1986] BCC 99,368.
[406] (1825) 4 B & C 173, as explained by Lord Tenterden C.J. in *Earl of Dalhousie* v. *Chapman* (1829) 7 LJOSKB 233.

The Cork Committee,[407] following similar comments by the Blagden Committee in 1957,[408] thought that this right of set-off available to the Crown conferred upon it an unwarranted preference in the bankruptcy of a subject. Accordingly it recommended that government departments should be treated as separate entities for the purpose of set-off, and moreover that there should not be any right of set-off between contractual and statutory obligations. On the other hand it also recommended that set-off in relation to one statutory obligation and another, and in relation to one contractual obligation and another, in each case relating to the same government department, should be allowed in accordance with the principle of mutuality. While these recommendations were not included in the Insolvency Act 1986 there is much to commend them, though there is some doubt as to why the Crown in fact should be allowed to set off one statutory obligation against another when the one government department is involved. Statutory rights and obligations arise independently of any desire by the parties to deal with each other. If the possibility of a right of set-off could not have acted as a stimulus for either of the parties to enter into a dealing, there is no real justification for allowing either of them preferential treatment by means of a set-off in the event of the bankruptcy of the other.[409]

It may be that a public corporation, as opposed to a department of state, is liable to a bankrupt or a company in liquidation, or that a public corporation has a claim against the bankrupt or the company. The question then may arise whether there is mutuality between that demand and a cross-demand that relates to a department of state, or indeed another public corporation. In Australia it has been held that the fact of a public corporation being a party to either demand will not destroy mutuality as long as the corporation may be considered to be an agent of the Crown, a concept that is determined by the measure of control that the Crown, through its Ministers, has over the body in question.[410] This should also apply in England. In *Re Duncan and Wakefield's Assignment*[411] debtors who had executed a deed of assignment were owed money by the Minister of Lands, but were also indebted to the State Saw Mills. Dwyer J. noted that the State Saw Mills:[412]

is a trading concern created to carry on a profit making business, it is administered by one of the State Ministers as part of his normal ministerial duties, the property it holds belongs to the State and has always so belonged, its funds are provided from time to time out of the consolidated revenue, and its profits go into consolidated revenue, there is no special beneficiary or group of beneficiaries to be advantaged,

---

[407] *Cork Committee Report*, 306–7, 309.
[408] *Blagden Committee Report*, 29.   [409] See section 2.3 above.
[410] Hogg, *Liability of the Crown* (2nd edn., 1989), 249–50.
[411] (1932) 34 WALR 138.   [412] (1932) 34 WALR 138, 139.

the benefit from its operations is for the State as a whole and not for any particular class or restricted number of persons, and any loss must be borne similarly.

His Honour concluded that the corporation was an agent of the Crown, and accordingly it was allowed to bring into an account the Minister's liability to the debtor. In *Re Mathrick*[413] two public corporations were involved. The Board of Land and Works owed a sum of money to a bankrupt's estate, while the Forests Commission was a creditor of the bankrupt. Lukin J. held that both bodies were agents of the Crown. In each case the corporation was financed out of consolidated revenue, and all money was received on account of consolidated revenue. Moreover, each was subject to a large amount of ministerial control. Because they were both agents of the Crown a set-off could proceed.[414] If on the other hand a public corporation is independent of the government, with independent powers and discretions, it does not represent the Crown,[415] and mutuality would be lacking where a cross-demand relates to another corporation or the Crown.

In a federal system such as Australia a person may be a debtor to the Crown in right of one state and a creditor of the Crown in right of another state, or of the Commonwealth, and vice versa. The aphorism that 'the Crown is one and indivisible'[416] suggests that these demands are mutual and may be set off. However, as Latham C.J. once remarked, when this aphorism is 'stated as a legal principle, it tends to dissolve into verbally impressive mysticism'.[417] In truth, the Crown in right of each state and of the Commonwealth represents a separate government and a separate legal person. The better view is that the demands are not mutual, and that a set-off should not be allowed. Nor, one imagines, would a government of one state be happy that its claim against a person could be used to satisfy the liability of another state.

9.9 SET-OFF IN RELATION TO A DECEASED'S ESTATE

9.9.1 *Executors and administrators*

An executor or administrator of a deceased's estate still in the course of administration strictly is not a trustee of the deceased's property, which

---

[413] (1941) 12 ABC 212.

[414] Lukin J. overruled an earlier decision of his own in *Re McCann & Edwards' Deed of Arrangement* (1932) 4 ABC 145, in which a set-off had been denied in similar circumstances.

[415] *Skinner* v. *Commissioner for Railways* (1937) 37 SR (NSW) 261, 270; *Grain Elevators Board (Victoria)* v. *Dunmunkle Corporation* (1946) 73 CLR 70, 76.

[416] See e.g. *Amalgamated Society of Engineers* v. *Adelaide Steamship Company Ltd.* (1920) 28 CLR 129, 152.

[417] *Minister for Works for Western Australia* v. *Gulson* (1944) 69 CLR 338, 350.

includes any debts owing to the estate. A trust requires that there should be specific subjects identifiable as the trust fund, and while the estate is still being administered it is impossible to identify, at least in the case of residuary legatees and persons entitled upon an intestacy, the person in whom the beneficial ownership of any particular asset forming part of the estate is vested.[418] An executor has a number of fiduciary obligations with respect to the assets that come into his hands in right of his office, but the residuary legatees do not have a beneficial property interest in those assets before the completion of the administration.[419] Rather, their only right consists of a chose in action to have the estate properly administered. However, the Privy Council in enunciating these principles in *Commissioner of Stamp Duties (Queensland)* v. *Livingston*[420] was vague as to the status of the executor. The advice of the Board was delivered by Viscount Radcliffe, who said that the testator's property came to the executor 'in full ownership, without distinction between legal and equitable interests. The whole property was his'.[421] This should not be taken to mean that an executor in fact is the beneficial owner of the assets. The executor does have the 'full ownership', but in the sense that he has vested in him 'the whole right of property'[422] to the extent that there are property rights in those assets. As Lord Diplock later remarked in the House of Lords, 'No one would suggest that an executor, who was not also a legatee, was beneficial owner as well as legal owner of any of the property which was in the full ownership of the deceased before his death'.[423] It would seem, then, that during the administration of the estate, neither the executor nor the residuary legatees are regarded as the beneficial owner of any debt which constitutes an asset of the estate. This concept also applies in the case of an intestacy, so that neither the administrator nor any person entitled on the intestacy is the beneficial owner of any particular asset forming part of the unadministered estate.[424]

---

[418] *Ayerst* v. *C. & K. (Construction) Ltd.* [1976] AC 167, 178, citing *Commissioner of Stamp Duties (Queensland)* v. *Livingston* [1965] AC 694, 707-8 (PC).

[419] 'What equity did not do was to recognise or create for residuary legatees a beneficial interest in the assets in the executor's hands during the course of administration. Conceivably, this could have been done, in the sense that the assets, whatever they might be from time to time, could have been treated as a present, though fluctuating, trust fund held for the benefit of all those interested in the estate according to the measure of their respective interests. But it never was done. It would have been a clumsy and unsatisfactory device from a practical point of view; and, indeed, it would have been in plain conflict with the basic conception of equity that to impose the fetters of a trust upon property, with the resulting creation of equitable interests in that property, there had to be specific subjects identifiable as the trust fund.' *Commissioner of Stamp Duties (Queensland)* v. *Livingston* [1965] AC 694. 707–8 per Viscount Radcliffe (PC). [420] [1965] AC 694.

[421] [1965] AC 694, 707. [422] [1965] AC 694, 712.

[423] *Ayerst* v. *C. & K. (Construction) Ltd.* [1976] AC 167, 178.

[424] *In re Leigh's Will Trusts* [1970] 1 Ch. 277, 281–2.

An unadministered estate is similar in this regard to a valid non-charitable purpose trust, for example a trust for a monument. There is no beneficiary who it can be said is the beneficial owner of the trust fund, but that does not mean that the trustee is the beneficial owner. Given these principles, consider the case of a debtor to an estate who is being sued by an executor or an administrator. The debtor obviously could not set off a claim that he has against the executor or administrator in that person's personal capacity. Nor, if the estate has not been administered, is he entitled to bring the debt into an account in a bankruptcy with a debt owing by a residuary legatee personally, or, as the case may be, by a person entitled to a share of the intestate's estate.[425] Mutuality in equity is lacking.

Once an executor or an administrator has completed the administration of the estate he becomes a trustee holding for the beneficiaries either on an intestacy or under the terms of the will.[426] If in that circumstance the executor himself is the sole person beneficially interested in the estate, and all claims against the estate have been satisfied, a debt owing by the executor may be the subject of a set-off.[427] However, until the administration has been completed, a court of equity generally will not inquire whether the estate has sufficient assets to satisfy the testator's debts and testamentary expenses, and the expenses of the administration, in order to facilitate a set-off either by or against the residuary legatee or person entitled on an intestacy.[428] '[F]or the mere purpose of set-off the Court will not take the account.'[429] In *Ex parte Morier; in re Willis, Percival, & Co.*[430] a brother and sister were executors of their deceased father's will, and accordingly opened an executorship account with a bank in their joint names. The son, who was the sole residuary legatee, also kept a separate account with the bank in his personal capacity. The bank stopped payment and entered into an arrangement with its creditors for its liquidation,[431] at which time the executorship account was in credit and the son's personal account in debit. Securities had been set aside to answer the specific legacies bequeathed by the will, and the testator's debts and funeral and testamentary expenses had all been paid. However, at the date of the

---

[425] See *Bishop* v. *Church* (1748) 3 Atk. 691; *Phillips* v. *Howell* [1901] 2 Ch. 773.

[426] *In re Cockburn's Will Trusts* [1957] 1 Ch. 438, 439.

[427] *Williams* v. *MacDonald* [1915] VLR 229. For a discussion of the question whether an executor is required to make an assent in his own favour in this situation, see *Williams, Mortimer and Sunnucks on Executors, Administrators and Probate* (1993), 1057–8. Assuming that the administration of the estate had been completed, *quaere* why a set-off was not allowed in *Harvey* v. *Wood* (1821) 5 Madd. 459.

[428] *Bishop* v. *Church* (1748) 3 Atk. 691.

[429] *Middleton* v. *Pollock, ex parte Nugee* (1875) LR 20 Eq. 29, 34 per Sir George Jessel M.R.   [430] (1879) 12 Ch. D 491.

[431] See the Bankruptcy Act 1869, s. 125.

arrangement the executors were still jointly liable for some rates and taxes, and in addition a solicitor's bill of costs had not been paid. The administration therefore had not been completed at that date, with the result that a trust had not arisen in favour of the son so as to enable him to employ the bank's indebtedness in a set-off. Nor was the Court of Appeal prepared to take an account of the testator's estate in order to ascertain whether there would be a surplus accruing to the residuary legatee in an intestacy.

There were two cases in which a debt constituting an asset of the estate in fact was allowed to be brought in as a set-off against a separate indebtedness of the residuary legatee before the completion of the administration, though neither is entirely satisfactory.

(1) The first case, *Jones* v. *Mossop*,[432] concerned an assent in an intestacy. An assent is a method by which a personal representative indicates that he does not require certain property for the discharge of the liabilities of the estate, and that therefore it may pass to the legatee.[433] After the assent, the beneficial interest in the property concerned vests in the legatee. He may bring an action to recover it, even against the personal representative himself.[434] The facts of *Jones* v. *Mossop* are complicated. Jones was indebted on a bond to John Reed. John Reed died intestate, leaving Richard Reed his only child and next of kin, and as such entitled to a clear residue of his personal estate. Richard Reed obtained a grant of administration of his father's estate. However, before he could undertake the administration he became insolvent, and later died. Mossop was appointed assignee in his insolvency. After the death of Richard Reed, Mossop obtained letters of administration *de bonis non* of John Reed, and commenced an action against Jones on the bond. However, Jones himself was a creditor of Richard Reed, and accordingly he sought to have his claim set off against his indebtedness to John Reed's estate, the residue of which after payment of John Reed's debts would vest in Richard Reed. A number of these debts of John Reed still remained unpaid, though Wigram V.C. nevertheless allowed a set-off because of certain admissions made by Mossop as administrator. Mossop said that he believed that the personal estate exclusive of the bond was more than sufficient to pay John Reed's debts, that the money due upon the bond was part of the net residue of the estate, and that it had become legally and equitably the absolute property of Richard Reed. The Vice Chancellor said that the case 'is the same in principle as where an assent has been given to a legacy whereby the

---

[432] (1844) 3 Hare 568.
[433] Williams, *The Law Relating to Assents* (1947), 1.
[434] *Williams, Mortimer and Sunnucks on Executors, Administrators and Probate* (1993), 1061.

property has passed to the legatee, being himself an executor, in which case the legacy is separated from the estate of the testator, and becomes the property of the legatee'.[435] But notwithstanding these admissions, the decision is still open to question on the basis of the view that is sometimes expressed, that an administrator, as opposed to an executor, may not assent in respect of pure personalty which passes on an intestacy,[436] and a debt owing to the deceased is personalty.

(2) The second case is *Bailey* v. *Finch*.[437] The defendant was the sole executor of a testatrix's will, and was also the residuary legatee. An executorship account opened by him with a bank showed a credit balance of £500 when the bank was adjudged bankrupt. At the date of the bankruptcy the defendant had not specifically provided for two bequests, but there were in the hands of the defendant, besides the credit balance in the bank, other personal assets of the testatrix which themselves would have been more than sufficient to provide for these bequests. The defendant also had his own personal account with the bank, which was overdrawn to the extent of £300. It was held in this action brought against him by the trustee of the bankrupts' estate on the overdrawn account that he could set off the credit balance on the executorship account, even though the administration had not been completed at the time of the bankruptcy, and even though there had not been any prior assent in respect of any part of the residuary estate. The set-off was based upon the court's finding that there was a right of set-off existing at law. The defendant was the sole creditor on the executorship account. Therefore at law there was mutuality between that claim and his personal indebtedness to the bank. The executorship account had not been set aside to answer any other specific bequest. Therefore there was no other person who could be identified as having the equitable title to it. Moreover, the rest of the estate was more than sufficient to satisfy the specific bequests, and so the court said that there was no reason in equity for disallowing this set-off permitted at law. The fact of mutuality at law was the ground upon which James and Cotton L.JJ. in *Morier* distinguished *Bailey* v. *Finch*. In *Morier* the executorship account was in the joint names of the two executors. Consequently, unlike in *Bailey* v. *Finch*, there was a lack of mutuality at law between the executors' joint demand against the bank and the bank's separate claim against the executor who was the residuary legatee, so that a set-off would not have been available at law. However, the analysis in

---

[435] (1844) 3 Hare 568, 576.

[436] See *Williams, Mortimer and Sunnucks on Executors, Administrators and Probate* (1993), 1057. See also *Parry and Clark on the Law of Succession* (7th edn., 1977), 366 (referring to Williams, *The Law Relating to Assents* (1947), 4, 122–3).

[437] (1871) LR 7 QB 34.

Bailey v. *Finch* is still not without difficulty, and indeed Cotton L.J. in *Morier*[438] appears to have been uncomfortable with the decision. The bank had been made bankrupt, in which case the set-off section in the insolvency legislation alone should have determined the existence of any right of set-off.[439] Mutuality under the insolvency set-off section is determined by reference to the equitable interests of the parties, rather than their dry legal rights.[440] While an estate is still in the course of administration it is impossible to identify, at least in the case of residuary legatees, the person in whom the beneficial ownership in any particular property forming part of the estate is vested.[441] Since the administration had not been completed at the time of the bankruptcy in *Bailey* v. *Finch*, and nor had there been any assent, it was not possible to say at that date that the defendant himself was the beneficial owner of the executorship account.[442] On that basis, a set-off should not have been allowed. In other words, the distinction is between a set-off at law, which may take effect when the demands are mutual at law unless there is another person whom it can be said has an equitable title to either of the demands sufficient to prevent a set-off, or there is some other reason in equity as to why a set-off should not proceed,[443] and a set-off in insolvency, in which it must be shown that the parties themselves to the proposed set-off have the equitable title to the demands.

9.9.2 *Set-off between a third party and a deceased's estate*

If a creditor of a deceased sues the estate for payment, the executor is not allowed to set off a debt owing to him in his personal capacity by the creditor.[444] On the other hand, if the creditor is indebted to the estate as a result of a liability incurred to the deceased, the creditor may wish to set these demands against each other, particularly if the estate is insolvent.

Consider first the question of set-off when the estate is not being administered in bankruptcy. In such a case, if the demands are sufficiently closely connected there is no reason why an equitable set-off should not be available.[445] Further, the Statutes of Set-off may apply. The first Statute, (1729) 2 Geo. II, c. 22, section 13, provided that 'where there are mutual

---

[438] (1878) 12 Ch. D 491, 501–2.   [439] See section 2.4 above.

[440] See section 7.3 above.

[441] *Ayerst* v. *C. & K. (Construction) Ltd.* [1976] AC 167, 178.

[442] This was conceded by Blackburn J. (1871) LR 7 QB 34, 45 ('money, which at the time of the bankruptcy was legally in the defendant, and not also equitably only because some other persons had a small claim on it'), though compare Cockburn C.J. at 40 and Mellor J. at 46.   [443] See section 7.4 above.

[444] *Medlicot* v. *Bowes* (1749) 1 Ves. Sen. 207, 208.

[445] See section 1.7 above.

debts between the plaintiff and defendant, or if either party sue or be sued as executor or administrator, where there are mutual debts between the testator or intestate and either party, one debt may be set against the other'. This has been interpreted to mean that the debts the subject of a set-off should originally have existed between two living persons.[446] In other words, there must have been cross-debts between the deceased and the creditor before the deceased's death.[447] Nor, properly understood, is *Wilkinson* v. *Cawood*[448] inconsistent with this. A sub-lessee paid rent to the deceased lessor's wife after the death, and she in turn paid ground rent to the superior landlord. When she was sued by the deceased's executor for the rent that she had received, it was held that she could set up the payments that were in respect of ground rent that had accrued due before (but not after) the death, even though these payments obviously did not give rise to a debt owing to her by the deceased before the death. This should be compared to *Shipman* v. *Thompson*,[449] which concerned an agent appointed by the testator to collect rent. After the testator's death the agent received payments of rent that were due and payable before the death, and it was held that he had to account for them to the estate without set-off in respect of a debt owing to him by the testator. This accords with the traditional interpretation of the Statutes. A right of action had not accrued to the testator against the agent before death. Further, the rent was not received by the agent to the use of the testator, but rather to the use of the executor. However, *Wilkinson* v. *Cawood* is distinguishable from *Shipman* v. *Thompson*, because in truth it did not concern set-off under the Statutes of Set-off. Rather, the payment of the ground rent to the superior landlord was treated as a discharge *pro tanto* of the rent due to the intermediate landlord,[450] so that there was no longer an obligation to account for it.

It is not entirely clear from the cases whether the debts should not only have been in existence but also have been due and payable before death,

---

[446] *Rees* v. *Watts* (1855) 11 Ex. 410, 414.

[447] *Lambarde* v. *Older* (1853) 17 Beav. 542; *Rees* v. *Watts* (1855) 11 Ex. 410 (in which the early cases are discussed); *Newell* v. *The National Provincial Bank of England* (1876) 1 CPD 496; *Hallett* v. *Hallett* (1879) 13 Ch. D 232; *In re Gregson; Christison* v. *Bolam* (1887) 36 Ch. D 223; *In re Wickham's Will; Grant* v. *Union Trustee Company of Australia, Ltd.* (1898) 9 QLJ 102 (though note the discussion of *Wickham* in the context of the rule in *Cherry* v. *Boultbee* in section 10.7 below). See also *Beckwith* v. *Bullen* (1858) 8 El. & Bl. 683 (deceased underwriter's liability on policy still unliquidated at the date of death). Compare *Parker* v. *Jackson* [1936] 2 All ER 281, which is criticized in section 1.2.9 above. The relevant date is the date of death, as opposed to the date of notice of death, though compare Wood, *English and International Set-off* (1989), 1104 in relation to the debt owing by the deceased. In *Rogerson* v. *Ladbroke* (1822) 1 Bing. 93 (referred to in Wood) the banker's right of combination was in issue, as opposed to set-off under the Statutes of Set-off. See Ch. 11.

[448] (1797) 3 Anst. 905.   [449] (1738) Willes 103.

[450] See also *Sapsford* v. *Fletcher* (1792) 4 TR 511, referred to by MacDonald C.B. in his judgment in *Wilkinson* v. *Cawood*.

although the Statutes of Set-off themselves point to the latter being the correct principle. The Statutes allowed a set-off between two living persons in the case of mutual debts, and 'debts' has been interpreted in that context as referring to debts which are not only in existence but also due and payable.[451] In the case of an action by or against an executor or administrator the Statutes similarly provided that there could be a set-off if there were mutual debts between the testator and the other party to the proposed set-off. Ordinary rules of statutory interpretation suggest that 'debts' should be given the same meaning in this context, in which case it would refer to debts due and payable between those parties. This has been held to apply in Canada,[452] while North J., in discussing the availability of a set-off where one of the parties had died in *In re Gregson*,[453] framed the relevant question in terms of a debt *payable* to the testator in his lifetime.[454] It is uncertain, however, whether the courts will adopt this position.[455] The tendency of the courts in recent times has been to enlarge the circumstances in which set-off is available, which suggests that they may be sympathetic to the broader interpretation.

In 1875 the rules of bankruptcy, including the mutual credit provision, were incorporated for the first time into the administration of a deceased's estate when it is insolvent.[456] Prior to 1875 rights of set-off were only available under the Statutes of Set-off, and accordingly were subject to the limitation inherent in the Statutes, that both demands had to be owing, and possibly also due and payable, between the parties before the deceased's death. However, since the administration of insolvent estates has been brought within the ambit of the insolvency legislation,[457] this restriction no longer applies. Rather, the demands which may be brought into an account are regulated by the insolvency set-off section, so that it is sufficient if the

---

[451] See section 1.2.7 above.

[452] *Trusts & Guar. Co.* v. *Royal Bank* [1931] 2 DLR 601. Compare *Ontario Bank* v. *Routhier* (1900) 32 OR 67 and *Royal Trust Co.* v. *Molsons Bank* (1912) 8 DLR 478, in which it was accepted that the bank could have applied the testator's deposit against the promissory notes maturing after the death, although those cases appear to have been concerned with a banker's right of combination of accounts rather than set-off under the Statutes.

[453] (1887) 36 Ch. D 223, 226–7.

[454] See also *Newell* v. *The National Provincial Bank of England* (1876) 1 CPD 496, although the promissory note in that case was given as surety.

[455] While there is a presumption that a word appearing in different parts of the same section in an Act of Parliament has the same meaning, this is not an invariable rule. See e.g. *Doe d Angell* v. *Angell* (1846) 9 QB 328, 355; *In re Smith; Green* v. *Smith* (1883) 24 Ch. D 672, 678; *Clyne* v. *Deputy Commissioner of Taxation* (1982) 150 CLR 1, 10, 15.

[456] See the Supreme Court of Judicature Act 1875, s. 10.

[457] See now the Administration of Insolvent Estates of Deceased Persons Order 1986 (S.I. 1986/1999) made pursuant to the Insolvency Act 1986, s. 421. For Australia see the Bankruptcy Act 1966 (Cth.), Pt. XI, and also the various state laws regarding the administration of insolvent estates (e.g. the Administration and Probate Act 1958 (Vic.). s. 39(1)).

credits or dealings in question were mutual in their origin.[458] Thus claims which are contingent at the relevant date, or which only become due and payable after that date, may be included in a set-off, in accordance with principles applicable generally to insolvency set-off.

If a debtor by or against whom a bankruptcy petition has already been presented dies, the proceedings in the matter are continued as if he were still alive, unless the court orders otherwise.[459] Where, however, the deceased died before presentation of the petition, the Administration of Insolvent Estates of Deceased Persons Order 1986 now stipulates that the equivalent of the commencement of the bankruptcy, which is the relevant date for determining rights of set-off under the Insolvency Act, is the insolvency administration order, this being an order for the administration in bankruptcy of the insolvent estate of a deceased debtor. However, this does not mean that the date of the order is the relevent date for determining rights of set-off.[460] Insofar as the claim against the deceased is concerned, the Order also provides that, in the definition of 'bankruptcy debt', the date of death of the deceased is to be substituted for the commencement of the bankruptcy,[461] so that in order to be provable the claim against the deceased must have been incurred before death. Since the set-off section requires that there be a creditor proving or claiming to prove for a bankruptcy debt, in practice the date of death will be the relevant date.[462] A similar concept will apply in relation to the cross-demand possessed by the estate. If a creditor becomes indebted to the

---

[458] *Watkins* v. *Lindsay and Co.* (1898) 67 LJQB 362, 364 per Wright J..

[459] See art. 5 of the Administration of Insolvent Estates of Deceased Persons Order 1986 (S.I. 1986/1999) and in Australia the Bankruptcy Act 1966 (Cth.), ss. 63 and 245.

[460] Compare the position in Australia. The date of the sequestration order is the relevant date for the purpose of the set-off section, and s. 248(3)(a) of the Bankruptcy Act 1966 (Cth.) provides that 'a reference to a sequestration order shall be read as a reference to an order for administration of an estate' under Pt XI. An order that the estate of a deceased person should be administered under the bankruptcy legislation is not made on the basis of an act of bankruptcy. It is not altogether clear, then, how the qualification to the set-off section in s. 86(2) of the Bankruptcy Act dealing with notice of an act of bankruptcy would operate under the Australian legislation when a debt owing by the deceased is acquired after the date of death, but before the order. If in fact the creditor had notice of an act of bankruptcy actually committed by the deceased within the 6-month period before the date of the order, there is no reason why the proviso should not apply in the normal way. In other cases, however, the courts may apply the qualification in the same way as for a company, on the basis of the approach suggested by Jacobs J.A. in *Law* v. *James* [1972] 2 NSWLR 573. Thus a person who acquires between the date of death and the date of the order a debt owing by the deceased should not be entitled to employ that debt in a set-off if at the time of acquisition he was aware that the estate was insolvent. This is not a problem in England, where the qualification to the set-off section is now drafted in terms of notice of the petition rather than notice of an act of bankruptcy. [461] See para. 31 of Pt II of Sch. I of the Order.

[462] Under the Bankruptcy Act 1914 the date of death seems to have been regarded as the relevant date. See *Re Bailey, deceased; Duchess Mill Ltd.* v. *Bailey* (1932) 76 Sol. Jo. 560.

deceased's estate after the date of death but before the order, and this liability does not arise out of a prior dealing that the third party had with the deceased himself, there would be a lack of mutuality between that debt and a debt owing by the deceased to the third party, so that a set-off would not be available on that ground. In *In re Gedney; Smith* v. *Grummitt*[463] a person purchased some simple contract debts and a mortgage owing by the deceased, the purchase taking place after the death but before an order for the administration of the estate in bankruptcy. He realized the mortgage and, having applied the proceeds in satisfaction of the mortgage debt, he held a surplus which he claimed to set off against the other debts due to him. Even apart from the question whether a set-off should have been denied because the surplus was impressed with a trust,[464] Warrington J. held that the surplus never belonged to the testator and was never a debt due to him. Nor did it arise out of a dealing with him. There was no basis, therefore, for a set-off.[465] On the same principle, the proceeds of the deceased's estate deposited with a bank may not be brought into an account with a prior indebtedness of the deceased himself to the bank,[466] and an order for costs made against a creditor of the estate in favour of the executor for successfully defending an action by the creditor against the estate cannot be set off against the debt owing to the creditor.[467] Similarly, if an executor or administrator sells an asset of the estate to a person who is a creditor of the deceased, the creditor cannot set off the price against the debt owing to him, in the absence of an agreement to this effect.[468]

It may be that a personal representative has carried on the deceased's business, and in doing so has incurred a number of debts. A personal representative who carries on the business of the deceased renders himself *personally* liable for all debts which he contracts in so doing although, if he was authorized, he is entitled as against the beneficiaries to be indemnified out of that part of the testator's estate which he is authorized to employ in the business.[469] *Nelson* v. *Roberts*[470] is authority for the proposition that this personal liability of the personal representative to the creditor and a debt owing by the creditor to the estate are not mutual. The question whether this should be followed is considered later.[471]

A personal representative is also entitled to an indemnity for his costs and expenses incurred in performing his duties. If the assets are insufficient

---

[463] [1908] 1 Ch. 804.   [464] See section 6.5 above.

[465] See also *In re Gregson; Christison* v. *Bolam* (1887) 36 Ch. D 223.

[466] *National Bank of Australasia* v. *Swan* (1872) 3 VR (L) 168.

[467] *In re Dickinson; Marquis of Bute* v. *Walker; Ex parte Hoyle, Shipley and Hoyle* [1888] WN 94.   [468] *Lambarde* v. *Older* (1853) 17 Beav. 542.

[469] *Labouchere* v. *Tupper* (1857) 11 Moore 198.

[470] (1893) 69 LT 352. See also *Staniar* v. *Evans* (1886) 34 Ch. D 470, 476–7; *Rex* v. *Ray; ex parte Chapman* [1936] SASR 241, 249.   [471] See section 13.4.1 below.

to pay the creditors of the deceased, these costs become a first charge on the estate. Nevertheless, a charge on the estate is not a personal claim and it cannot be employed in a set-off.[472]

9.9.3 *Set-off by a beneficiary of the estate*

If a beneficiary of the estate is also indebted to it, so that he has a right to participate as well as an obligation to contribute to the fund constituting the estate, the rule in *Cherry* v. *Boultbee*[473] may apply, so that his obligation to contribute may be appropriated as satisfaction of his right to participate as beneficiary.[474]

An executor or administrator may be personally liable to a beneficiary if he fails to apply the estate in accordance with his duties. In such a case the executor or administrator should be entitled to set off a debt owing to him in his personal capacity by the beneficiary.[475]

---

[472] *Monypenny* v. *Bristow* (1832) 2 Russ. & M 117.
[473] (1839) 4 My. & Cr. 442.
[474] See Ch. 10.
[475] See *Taylor* v. *Taylor* (1875) LR 20 Eq. 155, explained in section 6.3 below.

10

The Rule in *Cherry* v. *Boultbee*

10.1 INTRODUCTION

Generally speaking, the principle underlying the rule in *Cherry* v. *Boultbee*[1] is that 'where a person entitled to participate in a fund is also bound to make a contribution in aid of that fund, he cannot be allowed so to participate unless and until he has fulfilled his duty to contribute'.[2] Most of the cases concerned with *Cherry* v. *Boultbee* have involved a debtor of a deceased person who is also a legatee under the will. Unless a contrary intention is manifested in the will,[3] the executor may decline to hand over anything in satisfaction of the legacy to the extent of the debt. The executor will be particularly keen to exercise this right if the debtor is insolvent or if for some other reason the debtor is unlikely to satisfy his liability.

The essence of *Cherry* v. *Boultbee* is that a person has both a right to participate in and an obligation to contribute to a fund. Indeed, it may apply where the obligation to contribute is the only asset of the fund of any value.[4] *Cherry* v. *Boultbee* should be distinguished in this regard from a number of analagous rights in which there is no personal liability to contribute. For example, a trustee who has made an overpayment to a particular beneficiary may recover the overpayment out of any trust capital or income in his hands to which the overpaid beneficiary would be entitled, though ordinarily the beneficiary in such a case would not be ordered to repay the trustee.[5] Similarly, it should be distinguished from the right of

---

[1] (1839) 4 My. & Cr. 442.

[2] *In re Peruvian Railway Construction Company, Ltd.* [1915] 2 Ch. 144, 150 per Sargant J. (affirmed [1915] 2 Ch. 442). See also *In re Akerman* [1891] 3 Ch. 212, 219; *In re Fenton (No. 2)* [1932] 1 Ch. 178, 186.

[3] *Harvey* v. *Palmer* (1851) 4 De G & Sm. 425. See also *Re Eiser's Will Trusts* [1937] 1 All ER 244. Compare *In re Kowloon Container Warehouse Co. Ltd.* [1981] HKLR 210, in which it was held that a provision in a company's articles, to the effect that the company should have a lien upon the shares of a member for his debts owing to the company, did not purport to exclude *Cherry* v. *Boultbee*.

[4] As in *In re V.G.M. Holdings Ltd.* [1942] 1 Ch. 235. See also *Selangor United Rubber Estates Ltd.* v. *Cradock (No. 4)* [1969] 1 WLR 1773, 1777.

[5] See *Lewin on Trusts* (16th edn., 1964), 261–3.

a trustee who has committed a breach of trust at the instigation of a beneficiary to approach the court for an order under the Trustee Act 1925, section 62 to impound the interest of the beneficiary by way of indemnity to the trustee. In neither case is there a personal liability in the beneficiary to contribute to the trust fund itself, and so the right in question strictly is not an aspect of *Cherry* v. *Boultbee*.

The principle in question had been applied by the courts for a long time before 1839, when *Cherry* v. *Boultbee*[6] was decided.[7] However, it was not until Lord Cottenham's judgment in that case that it was expressly distinguished from the right of set-off.[8] His Lordship remarked:[9]

It must be observed that the term 'set-off' is very inaccurately used in cases of this kind. In its proper use, it is applicable only to mutual demands, debts and credits. The right of an executor of a creditor to retain a sufficient part of a legacy given by the creditor to the debtor, to pay a debt due from him to the creditor's estate, is rather a right to pay out of the fund in hand, than a right of set-off.

Since then the courts have emphasized that *Cherry* v. *Boultbee* has a wider application than set-off, and that it rests upon quite different principles.[10] Thus, a right to participate in a trust fund may be subject to the principle in *Cherry* v. *Boultbee*, although the general rule with respect to set-off is that a set-off may not be based upon an obligation to account for a sum held on trust.[11]

While Lord Cottenham described the operation of the rule as a right in the executor to 'retain' a part of a legacy as payment of the debt, the courts on a number of occasions have rejected this as a description of the right.[12] As Kekewich J. once remarked,[13] 'Nothing is in truth retained by the representative of the estate; nothing is in strict language set off'. There has still, nevertheless, been a tendency to describe the operation of *Cherry* v.

---

[6] (1839) 4 My. & Cr. 442.

[7] The earliest reported example appears to be *Jeffs* v. *Wood* (1732) 2 P Wms. 128.

[8] Compare, e.g., Lord Cottenham's earlier judgment in *Houlditch* v. *Wallace* (1838) 5 Cl. & Fin. 629, 666. However, occasionally in subsequent cases the right has still been referred to as a set-off. See e.g. Sir George Turner in *Freeman* v. *Lomas* (1851) 9 Hare 109.

[9] (1839) 4 My. & Cr. 442, 447.

[10] *In re Rhodesia Goldfields, Ltd.; Partridge* v. *Rhodesia Goldfields Ltd.* [1910] 1 Ch. 239, 246–247; *In re Smelting Corporation; Seaver* v. *The Company* [1915] 1 Ch. 472, 476; *In re National Live Stock Insurance Co. Ltd.* [1917] 1 Ch. 628, 632; *In re Melton* [1918] 1 Ch. 37, 58–59; *In re Fenton (No. 2); ex parte Fenton Textile Association, Ltd.* [1932] 1 Ch. 178, 188; *Selangor United Rubber Estates Ltd.* v. *Cradock (No. 4)* [1969] 1 WLR 1773, 1778.

[11] See Ch. 6.

[12] *In re Akerman* [1891] 3 Ch. 212, 219; *Smith* v. *Smith* (1861) 3 Giff. 263, 271; *In re Melton; Milk* v. *Towers* [1918] 1 Ch. 37, 59 (though compare Warrington L.J. at 55); *In the Will of Bickerdike, deceased; Bickerdike* v. *Hill* [1918] VLR 191, 196. See also *In re Rhodesia Goldfields, Ltd.; Partridge* v. *Rhodesia Goldfields, Ltd.* [1910] 1 Ch. 239, 245–6, and *In re National Live Stock Insurance Co., Ltd.* [1917] 1 Ch. 628, 631–2.

[13] *In re Akerman* [1891] 3 Ch. 212, 219.

Boultbee in terms of retainer,[14] and indeed in a later case Sargant J. criticized the rejection of this epithet by Kekewich J.[15] However, Kekewich J. would appear to have been correct. The more popular explanation, which can be traced back to the judgment of Sir Joseph Jekyll in 1723 in *Jeffs* v. *Wood*,[16] is that the rule in effect provides a method of payment. The person administering the fund[17] may assert that the debtor already has an asset of the fund in his own hands, in the form of the debt, which should be appropriated as *pro tanto* payment of his right to participate.[18] The administrator in truth does not 'retain' anything as payment of the debt.[19] Rather, he directs the debtor to satisfy his entitlement to a share of the fund from a particular source. The rule is better described as a right to appropriate a particular asset as payment, as opposed to a right of set-off or a right of retainer.

10.2 EXECUTOR'S RIGHT OF RETAINER

Cherry v. *Boultbee* should also be distinguished from the old executor's right of retainer. The common law developed the principle that an executor or administrator of a deceased's• estate could retain from the estate an amount sufficient to cover any debts owing to him by the

---

[14] See e.g. *Corr* v. *Corr* (1879) 3 LR Ir. 435, 446, 448; *In re Taylor; Taylor* v. *Wade* [1894] 1 Ch. 671; *In re Watson; Turner* v. *Watson* [1896] 1 Ch. 925; *Jackson* v. *Yeats* [1912] 1 IR 267; *In re Lennard; Lennard's Trustee* v. *Lennard* [1934] 1 Ch. 235, 241. Compare Sargant J. in *In re Peruvian Railway Construction Co., Ltd.* [1915] 2 Ch. 144, 151 ('right of retainer or quasi-retainer').

[15] *In re Savage; Cull* v. *Howard* [1918] 2 Ch. 146.

[16] (1732) 2 P Wms. 128, 130.

[17] Henceforth the term 'administrator' is used to describe any person charged with the responsibility of collecting assets into a fund, and distributing that fund amongst a particular group of persons.

[18] See e.g. *Campbell* v. *Graham* (1831) 1 Russ. & M 453; *Courtnay* v. *Williams* (1846) 15 LJ Ch. 204, 208; *In re Akerman; Akerman* v. *Akerman* [1891] 3 Ch. 212, 219–20; *In re Goy & Co., Ltd.; Farmer* v. *Goy & Co., Ltd.* [1900] 2 Ch. 149, 153; *In re Mayne; ex parte The Official Receiver* [1907] 2 KB 899, 901; *Turner* v. *Turner* [1911] 1 Ch. 716, 719; *In re Pennington and Owen, Ltd.* [1925] 1 Ch. 825, 830, 832–3; *Picken* v. *Lord Balfour of Burleigh* [1945] 1 Ch. 90, 104. See also *In re Melton* [1918] 1 Ch. 37, 54, 59, and the second formulation of the principle applicable to defaulting trustees, discussed in section 10.13 below. Compare *Dodson* v. *Sandhurst & Northern District Trustees Executors and Agency Co. Ltd.* [1955] VLR 100, 104.

[19] Compare in *In re Hurburgh; National Executors and Trustees Co. of Tasmania Ltd.* v. *Hurburgh* [1959] Tas. SR 25, 40–2, where Crawford J. argued that *Cherry* v. *Boultbee* confers a right *in rem*. However, the two reasons adduced to support this contention may be explained on other grounds. The first reason regarding the effect of a bankruptcy or an assignment may be explained on the principle that a trustee in bankruptcy or an assignee takes subject to equities. See section 10.12 below. The second reason regarding the effect of proving for the debt in the bankruptcy may be explained on the basis of a waiver of the right conferred by *Cherry* v. *Boultbee*. See section 10.11 below.

deceased[20] in priority to the costs of the administration,[21] and also in priority to the claims of creditors of an equal or lower degree.[22] This right was not a right of set-off, in the sense that the word is used to describe the process by which cross-demands are brought into an account so as to produce a balance, but rather was a right to 'retain' assets in payment of a debt. Thus, while it is a prerequisite to the common law defence of set-off under the Statutes of Set-off that the debt sought to be set off must be enforceable by action, an executor could exercise a right of retainer in respect of a debt which, though existing, was unenforceable as a result of a time bar.[23] Moreover, it is distinct from *Cherry* v. *Boultbee*, which, we have seen, does not take effect as a retainer. The rights had different origins. The executor's right of retainer was developed by the common law courts,[24] while *Cherry* v. *Boultbee* is an equitable doctrine.

The executor's right of retainer has now been abolished in England, though a personal representative who does pay himself from the estate is not required to account for the sum so paid if he acted in good faith and at the time had no reason to believe that the deceased's estate was insolvent.[25] Moreover, it has also been abolished in Western Australia,[26] New South Wales,[27] South Australia,[28] Victoria,[29] and New Zealand,[30] in each case without a similar saving provision. While it has attracted a considerable amount of case law, in view of its limited application[31] it is not proposed to discuss it any further.[32]

---

[20] If the debts were owing by the deceased himself, obviously they would be unconnected with the administration of the estate. This should be distinguished from a trustee's right to an indemnity from the capital and income of the trust for costs properly incurred by him in the administration of the trust. See *Stott* v. *Milne* (1884) 25 Ch. D 710.

[21] *Re Wester Wemyss; Tilley* v. *Wester Wemyss* [1940] Ch. 1.

[22] *Attorney-General* v. *Jackson* [1932] AC 365.

[23] *Hill* v. *Walker* (1858) 4 K & J 166.

[24] *Attorney-General* v. *Jackson* [1932] AC 365, 370. Since this right of retainer was developed by the common law, originally it could only be exercised against the legal, and not the equitable, assets of the estate, and moreover the executor's right was not prejudiced if he was merely a trustee of the debt for a third party. However, see the Administration of Estates Act 1925, s. 34(2), discussed in *In re Rudd; Royal Exchange Assurance* v. *Ballantine* [1942] 1 Ch. 421. See also in Tasmania the Administration and Probate Act 1935, s. 34(2). However, the old rules would still appear to apply in Queensland.

[25] Administration of Estates Act 1971, s. 10.

[26] Administration Act 1903, s. 10(2).

[27] Wills, Probate and Administration Act 1898, s. 82(2), which amendment was introduced by Act No. 14 of 1906, s. 4.

[28] Administration and Probate Act 1919, s. 62.

[29] Administration and Probate Act 1958, s. 36(3).

[30] Administration Act 1969, s. 40.

[31] It still applies however in Tasmania and Queensland.

[32] For a discussion of the principles see Meagher, Gummow and Lehane, *Equity: Doctrines and Remedies* (3rd edn., 1992), 825–828.

10.3 THE SCOPE OF THE RULE

Cherry v. *Boultbee* is not confined to cases in which a legatee who was indebted to the testator is the beneficiary of a 'bounty' from the testator in the form of a legacy,[33] but applies generally whenever a person who is entitled to a share of a specific fund is also under a liability to contribute to that fund. For example, *Cherry* v. *Boultbee* has been successfully invoked by an administrator of an intestate's estate against a next of kin, even though the right of the next of kin to share in the estate arises by operation of law rather than as a result of the bounty of the deceased.[34] Similarly the rule may be invoked against a person with a derivative title to a legacy, being a person who obtained a right to that legacy under the will or as a result of the intestacy of another originally entitled to it.[35] It can also apply when the beneficiary of a trust is also a debtor of the trust,[36] including in one instance where resulting trusts impressed upon matrimonial property in proportion to the expenditure incurred by the husband and wife respectively were being dissolved.[37]

Cherry v. *Boultbee* may be relevant when a trustee in bankruptcy or a liquidator[38] is administering the fund represented by an estate available for distribution.[39] Normally it is not in the interests of the general body of creditors that a claim against the estate should be set off against a liability of the estate, because this reduces the dividend payable generally. Consider, however, that a creditor of the bankrupt is also liable to the bankrupt, but that this liability for some reason cannot be employed by the creditor in a set-off. The creditor is entitled to receive a dividend from the estate, but is also required to make a contribution to the extent of his liability. The trustee in bankruptcy may assert that the creditor should satisfy the right to receive the dividend from his liability to contribute. For

---

[33] Compare *Dingle* v. *Coppen* [1899] 1 Ch. 726, 739, 740. For an application of the rule in the case of a power to pay money to a person indebted to the testator, see *In re Bleechmore; Public Trustee* v. *Bleechmore* [1922] SASR 399.

[34] *In re Cordwell's Estate; White* v. *Cordwell* (1875) LR 20 Eq. 644.

[35] *Dodson* v. *Sandhurst & Northern District Trustees Executors and Agency Co. Ltd.* [1955] VLR 100; *Re Milnes; Milnes* v. *Sherwin* (1885) 53 LT 534. See also with respect to defaulting trustees (discussed in section 10.13 below) *In re Dacre; Whitaker* v. *Dacre* [1916] 1 Ch. 344.

[36] See e.g. *Priddy* v. *Rose* (1817) 3 Mer. 86; *In re Akerman* [1891] 3 Ch. 212.

[37] *Cowcher* v. *Cowcher* [1972] 1 WLR 425.

[38] In *Fused Electrics Pty. Ltd.* v. *Donald* [1995] 2 Qd. R 7, 8–9 Williams J. doubted whether *Cherry* v. *Boultbee* is applicable in the case of a company liquidation, on the ground that it may not be correct to categorize the assets of a company in liquidation as a fund. However, the better view is that liquidation does give rise to a fund for the purpose of the rule. See the cases referred to below in the context of liability for misfeasance or for unpaid calls.

[39] In addition to the cases referred to below, see *Re Saltergate Insurance Co. Ltd. (No. 2)* (1984) 9 ACLR 257; *Rowe* v. *Anderson* (1831) 4 Sim. 276.

example, *Cherry* v. *Boultbee* may entitle the liquidator of a company to refuse to pay a dividend to a creditor who is liable for damages for misfeasance,[40] or who is liable for unpaid calls,[41] neither of which may be employed in a set-off in a winding-up.[42] Similarly, *Cherry* v. *Boultbee* may be invoked to prevent a shareholder of a company which is in liquidation, but which has a surplus available for distribution amongst the shareholders, from receiving a rateable proportion of that surplus without satisfying a debt that he owes to the company.[43] It may be that a creditor of a bankrupt has become indebted to the bankrupt's trustee for costs in litigation conducted on behalf of the estate. While lack of mutuality will prevent a set-off,[44] the liability for costs is still a contribution required to be made in aid of the fund, and so the dividend payable to the creditor may be deemed to be paid to the extent of the costs.[45]

On the other hand, *Cherry* v. *Boultbee*, being an equitable rule, will give way to any statutory provision to the contrary. This was held to be the case in Queensland, when a person who was liable to a company which had gone into liquidation was awarded costs in proceedings brought against him by the liquidator on behalf of the company, and the entitlement to the costs was accorded priority by the applicable companies legislation on the basis that they were costs, charges, and expenses of the winding-up.[46]

It is apparent that *Cherry* v. *Boultbee* can only apply in situations in which there is a fund set up, or required to be set up. For example, it cannot be invoked in respect of a company's assets while the company is still a going concern.[47] On the other hand, it is not necessary that the fund should consist of other funds apart from the proceeds of the debt in respect of which the rule is sought to be enforced.[48]

---

[40] *In re Leeds and Hanley Theatres of Varieties, Ltd.* [1904] 2 Ch. 45. See also *Re Cobalt Mines Ltd.* (1918) 44 OLR 1, 7–8; *In re Jewell's Settlement; Watts v. Public Trustee* [1919] 2 Ch. 161, 175–6; *In re V.G.M. Holdings, Ltd.* [1942] 1 Ch. 235; *Selangor United Rubber Estates Ltd.* v. *Cradock (No. 4)* [1969] 1 WLR 1773.

[41] *In re Auriferous Properties, Ltd. (No. 2)* [1898] 2 Ch. 428; *In re National Live Stock Insurance Co., Ltd.* [1917] 1 Ch. 628; *In re Hattons Confectionery Co., Ltd.* [1936] NZLR 802; *In re White Star Line, Ltd.* [1938] 1 Ch. 458.

[42] See sections 4.7.1 and 4.6 above.

[43] *In re Peruvian Railway Construction Company, Ltd.* [1915] 2 Ch. 144, 151; *In re Kowloon Container Warehouse Co. Ltd.* [1981] HKLR 210.

[44] *West* v. *Pryce* (1825) 2 Bing. 455.

[45] *In re Mayne; ex parte The Official Receiver* [1907] 2 KB 899.

[46] *Fused Electrics Pty. Ltd.* v. *Donald* [1995] 2 Qd. R 7. See also *Process Engineering Pty. Ltd.* v. *Derby Meat Processing Co. Ltd.* [1977] WAR 145. *In re Bank of Hindustan, China and Japan; ex parte Smith* (1867) LR 3 Ch. App. 125, to which Williams J. referred in *Fused Electrics*, nevertheless may be distinguished on the ground that the solicitor's lien would have prevented the application of *Cherry* v. *Boultbee*.

[47] *In re Peruvian Railway Construction Company, Ltd.* [1915] 2 Ch. 144, 151.

[48] *Ex parte Turpin; in re Brown* (1832) Mont. 443.

10.4 WHO MAY INVOKE THE RULE?

Cherry v. *Boultbee* is a principle which operates in favour of the estate, and as a general rule it may only be invoked by the person administering the fund.[49] Accordingly, a person obliged to contribute to a fund who also has a right to participate which nevertheless is unenforceable for some reason could not insist that his obligation to contribute be satisfied by his unenforceable right. It may be that a trustee who is also a beneficiary of the trust has acted in breach of trust, in which case the other beneficiaries may apply to the court for an order that the rule should apply in respect of the trustee's entitlement, if their own entitlements would otherwise be affected.[50]

The administrator of the fund may not always wish to invoke the rule. For example, a trustee has a first charge on the trust estate for his expenses incurred in the adminstration of the trust.[51] Where a beneficiary of the trust also has an obligation to contribute, the trustee may be reluctant to direct the beneficiary to satisfy his right to participate by appropriating the obligation to contribute if this would mean that the fund in hand would be insufficient to reimburse the trustee for his expenses.

What if the administrator of the fund does not invoke the rule against a particular contributor? Can that person be compelled to satisfy the obligation to contribute, and then be required to wait for a distribution from the fund? He is not entitled to a set-off, because trust funds generally are not within the ambit of the law of set-off.[52] Nevertheless, the emphasis in *Cherry* v. *Boultbee* is on circumscribing the ability to claim a distribution from the fund, as opposed to laying down an inflexible rule regarding satisfaction of the obligation, and on occasions the courts in fact have indicated that a person should not be ordered to pay that part of a liability which would come back to him on a distribution.[53] However, the contributor is not entitled to an order to this effect as of right, but rather it is a matter of the court exercising its discretion.[54] In *Staniar* v. *Evans*[55]

---

[49] Thus, Gibson J. in *In re Hurburgh* [1959] Tas. SR 25, 37 said that the rule 'does not operate to quantify the share to be paid to a legatee until the executors (or trustees) choose to assert it'.　　　　　　　　　　[50] See e.g. *Fox* v. *Buckley* (1876) 3 Ch. D 508.

[51] *Stott* v. *Milne* (1884) 25 Ch. D 710.　　　　　　　　[52] See section 10.1 above.

[53] *In re V.G.M. Holdings, Ltd.* [1942] 1 Ch. 235; *Selangor United Rubber Estates Ltd.* v. *Cradock (No. 4)* [1969] WLR 1773. See also the cases (e.g. *Ex parte Turner; in re Crosthwaite* (1852) 2 De G M & G 927) in which a defaulting trustee entitled to participate in the trust became bankrupt, and the other trustees proved in the bankruptcy in respect of the breach. The cases are considered, and criticized, in section 10.13 below. These cases are also open to the objection that the defaulting trustee was hardly able and ready and willing to pay the contribution. See below.　　　　　　　[54] *Staniar* v. *Evans* (1886) 34 Ch. D 470.

[55] (1886) 34 Ch. D 470.

North J. said that an order for payment of the full amount is the usual form of order that should be made, and that an order for payment of the balance only after deducting the entitlement to participate may be made as a matter of favour only. He indicated that, in order to obtain an order to this effect, the contributor should be 'perfectly able, and ready, and willing' to pay the contribution.[56] If he cannot show this, for example because of insolvency, the order instead usually would be in terms that the full amount of the contribution must be paid as a pre-condition to obtaining a distribution.[57] If the person the subject of the order is a trustee of a trust, and his right to participate takes the form of an indemnity from the fund for his expenses, this modified form of order may be made if he is otherwise willing and able to satisfy his liability, notwithstanding that the fund may be insufficient to make all the required distributions. This is because the trustee in any event has a first charge on the trust fund for his expenses incurred in the administration of the trust.[58] In other circumstances, however, the court should consider whether there are any prior ranking claims on the trust fund which may require that payment of all or part of the liability to the fund should be made, and also the effect that the order may otherwise have on the entitlements of other parties. If the person liable to contribute is entitled to a certain percentage of the fund, as opposed to a fixed entitlement, the court in making an order for payment of the balance only should ascertain his share by first taking into account any expenses which will have to be met from the fund, as, for example, costs incurred in litigation in order to establish the liability, which costs are over and above those included in an order for costs made by the court. Once the fund *actually* available for distribution has been ascertained in this way, the court in its discretion may order that only the excess of the obligation to contribute over the right to participate in the fund is required to be paid.[59]

10.5 ENFORCEABLE RIGHTS AND OBLIGATIONS

The distinction between a right of set-off and a right under *Cherry* v. *Boultbee* may be illustrated by the different treatment accorded by each to the usual form of statute of limitation, which takes away the creditor's right to enforce the debt owing to him but leaves the debt itself untouched. It is a prerequisite to a set-off under the Statutes of Set-off that both demands be enforceable by action,[60] though the fact that the liability to contribute is

---

[56] (1886) 34 Ch. D 470, 473–474.
[57] As in *Lewis* v. *Trask* (1882) 21 Ch. D 862.
[58] *Stott* v. *Milne* (1884) 25 Ch. D 710.
[59] *Selangor United Rubber Estates Ltd.* v. *Cradock (No. 4)* [1969] 1 WLR 1773.
[60] See section 1.2.10 above.

time-barred, and consequently unenforceable, does not affect the right to invoke *Cherry* v. *Boultbee*.[61] The administrator of the fund does not set up that liability as a form of cross-action. Rather he says that, although the claim is unenforceable, it is still a subsisting asset of the estate. Since the person claiming a share of the fund still holds an asset constituting a part of the fund, he should pay himself *pro tanto* out of that asset. In this respect a right under *Cherry* v. *Boultbee* is similar to the right of a lienee at law to withhold possession even when the debt upon which the lien is based is existing but unenforceable as a result of a time bar.[62] There is, however, a situation in which this has been held not to apply. In *Dingle* v. *Coppen*[63] a person indebted to a testatrix obtained judgment against the estate for damages for waste committed by the testatrix during her lifetime. When the testatrix died the limitation period for the debt owing to her had expired. Byrne J. held that the executors could not invoke *Cherry* v. *Boultbee* so as to oblige the debtor to satisfy his claim for damages by appropriating the estate's asset represented by his indebtedness. In *Dingle* v. *Coppen* there were two cross-demands, each of which in its nature was such that, when it arose, it could have been made the subject of an action at law between the debtor and the testatrix personally. However, because of the expiration of the limitation period the testatrix at the time of her death could no longer have enforced the debt owing to her. Nor could she have employed it as a defence to an action brought against her in respect of the waste.[64] Byrne J. considered that the fact of death should not make any difference, and that the estate should not be able to achieve the same effect as a set-off by means of *Cherry* v. *Boultbee*. It was distinguished from the situation in which a person is given a bounty in the form of a legacy under a will. In such a case there is nothing inequitable in applying the rule on the basis that a time-barred obligation to contribute should be taken into account.

Cherry v. *Boultbee* similarly should be available as a general rule when the debt owing to the fund is unenforceable for any other reason, for

---

[61] *Courtnay* v. *Williams* (1846) 15 LJ Ch. 204; *Smith* v. *Smith* (1861) 3 Giff. 263; *Coates* v. *Coates* (1864) 33 Beav. 249; *Gee* v. *Liddell (No. 2)* (1866) 35 Beav. 629; *In re Cordwell's Estate; White* v. *Cordwell* (1875) LR 20 Eq. 644; *In re Knapman; Knapman* v. *Wreford* (1881) 18 Ch. D 300, 304; *Re Milnes; Milnes* v. *Sherwin* (1885) 53 LT 534; *In re Akerman* [1891] 3 Ch. 212; *Re Langham; Otway* v. *Langham* (1896) 74 LT 611; *Re Allison* (1900) 1 Tas. LR 169. See also *Rose* v. *Gould* (1852) 15 Beav. 189; *Poole* v. *Poole* (1871) LR 7 Ch. App. 17. If a debt is time-barred, however, an action cannot be brought in respect of it, and so damages in the form of interest cannot be awarded at a trial. Consequently interest cannot be deducted under *Cherry* v. *Boultbee*. See *In the Will of Bickerdike, deceased; Bickerdike* v. *Hill* [1918] VLR 191, 197.

[62] *Spears* v. *Hartly* (1800) 3 Esp. 81; *Higgins* v. *Scott* (1831) 2 B & Ad. 413.

[63] [1899] 1 Ch. 726.

[64] This was apart from the question whether the nature of the demands was such that a set-off would have been available in any event.

example because of failure to comply with the requirements of the Statute of Frauds. Admittedly the Court of Appeal in *In re Rownson; Field v. White*[65] held that, while an executor or administrator may exercise a right of retainer[66] in satisfaction of a debt owing to him by the deceased that has become unenforceable because of a time bar, he is not entitled to a similar right of retainer when that debt is unenforceable because of failure to comply with the Statute of Frauds. However, the rule in *Cherry v. Boultbee* is separate and distinct from an executor's right of retainer, and indeed there is a sound reason for distinguishing the two in this respect. The Court of Appeal in *Rownson* regarded the right of a personal representative to pay any creditor of the deceased, including himself, in respect of a debt that has become time-barred, as an exception to his general duty not to waste an estate that is not his own. The Court was not prepared to extend this exception to the case of a debt owing to the personal representative that is unenforceable instead under the Statute of Frauds. However, there is no such conflict with the executor's duty under *Cherry v. Boultbee*. Rather, he acts in the interests of the estate by directing that a person, who otherwise would deplete the estate by withdrawing his own entitlement, should obtain payment from an asset of the estate in his own hands that otherwise would have no value because of its unenforceability.

The administrator should only be able to invoke *Cherry v. Boultbee* when the right to share in the fund has become due and payable.[67] By this it is meant that, until the right to participate has become payable, the administrator may not appropriate an obligation to contribute as satisfaction of the right to participate.[68] For example, the rule may not be invoked in respect of a legacy while that legacy is still only a right in reversion,[69] or, in the case of a residuary legacy, until the residue is ascertained.[70] A corollary of this principle is that the liability to the fund should not have

---

[65] (1885) 29 Ch. D 358. [66] See section 10.2 above.

[67] See *Campbell v. Graham* (1831) 1 Russ. & M 453, 465 (affirmed *Campbell v. Sandford* (1834) 8 Bligh NS 622).

[68] Thus interest still accumulates on the debt until the share becomes payable. See *In re Akerman* [1891] 3 Ch. 212; *In re Watson* [1896] 1 Ch. 925.

[69] See *In re Batchelor; Sloper v. Oliver* (1873) LR 16 Eq. 481, 483–4 (referred to with evident approval in *In re Watson* [1896] 1 Ch. 925, 932); *In re Baird (Deceased); Hall v. Macky* [1935] NZLR 847, 852. See also Crawford J. in *In re Hurburgh* [1959] Tas. SR 25, 43–46, criticizing *Richards v. Richards* (1821) 9 Price 219, and seeking to explain *Burridge v. Row* (1842) 1 Y & C CC 183, affirmed (1844) 13 LJ Ch. 173, on the basis of set-off. Certainly Lord Lyndhurst in *Burridge* based his decision on both set-off and the principle applied in *Cherry v. Boultbee*. However, the insolvency legislation only allows the trustee to value a liability of the bankrupt, so that a dividend in respect of that liability may be paid immediately. See the Insolvency Act 1986, s. 322(3). There is no corresponding power to put a present value on a sum payable to the bankrupt in the future and to demand payment of that sum immediately. Consequently it should not be possible for a set-off to proceed while the right of the bankrupt is still only a right in reversion.

[70] See *In re Hurburgh* [1959] Tas. SR 25, 32–3.

ceased to exist, as opposed to being unenforceable, at the time that the share of the fund becomes payable,[71] unless in a particular case the terms governing the fund provide otherwise.[72] Thus, the rule will not apply if the debt is one for which the person claiming the share has been released as a result of an order of discharge from bankruptcy,[73] or under a composition or deed of arrangement,[74] or if the debt has been extinguished by moratorium legislation.[75] Consider that a debtor to a deceased testator has become bankrupt while his right to a legacy under the will is still only a right in reversion.[76] If the executor chooses to prove for the debt in the bankruptcy, he waives his right to invoke the rule.[77] If, on the other hand, he decides to wait until the debtor's legacy falls into possession and then to rely on the rule as a means of obtaining the full value of the debt, he runs the risk that the debtor may be discharged from his bankruptcy while the right to the legacy is still only in reversion. If this does happen, the fact that the debtor will have been released from liability on the debt as a result of his discharge[78] will mean that the rule may not be invoked against him, and so the testator's estate will have lost the chance of receiving anything in return for the debt. However, the provision in the insolvency legislation that a bankrupt as a general rule is discharged after 3 years from the date of the bankruptcy[79] now offers some guidance to an executor faced with the choice of which approach to adopt in this type of case.

[71] In addition to the cases cited below, see *In re Palmer; Palmer* v. *Clarke* (1894) 13 R 233 (with respect to the disclaimed contract); *In re Wheeler; Hankinson* v. *Hayter* [1904] 2 Ch. 66; *In the Will of Bickerdike, deceased; Bickerdike* v. *Hill* [1918] VLR 191; *Woodcock* v. *Eames* (1925) 69 Sol. Jo. 444. Compare *In re Pink* [1912] 1 Ch. 498. *Quaere* whether there should be an existing debt at that date, or whether it is sufficient that the liability is contingent though almost certainly bound to vest. See section 10.7 below.

[72] See *In re Ainsworth; Millington* v. *Ainsworth* [1922] 1 Ch. 22, in which a direction in a will, that a debt due to the testator from his son should be deducted from the moiety of the residuary estate bequeathed to the son, was held not to be affected by the son's discharge from bankruptcy.

[73] *In re Akerman* [1891] 3 Ch. 212, 217; *In re Watson* [1896] 1 Ch. 925, 933; *In re Baird* [1935] NZLR 847. Compare *In re Hope; De Cetto* v. *Hope* [1900] WN 76, which is explained on other grounds in *In re Hurburgh* [1959] Tas. SR 25, 48. *In re Melton* [1918] 1 Ch. 37 is cited as authority to the contrary in *Withers on Reversions* (2nd edn., 1933), 246, though it appears from the statement of the facts in *Melton* (at 38) that the bankrupt in that case had never obtained his discharge. *Quaere* why the fact of the debtor's discharge from bankruptcy in *In re Palmer* (1894) 13 R 233 did not take away the executor's right to invoke *Cherry* v. *Boultbee* in relation to the £700.

[74] See *In re Sewell; White* v. *Sewell* [1909] 1 Ch. 806, and the cases cited therein, and also *In re Hurburgh* [1959] Tas. SR 25. Compare *In re Powell; Powell* v. *Powell* (1904) 20 TLR 374. However, *Cherry* v. *Boultbee* may be invoked in respect of any sum still payable as a dividend under the composition or scheme. See *In re Orpen; Beswick* v. *Orpen* (1880) 16 Ch. D 202.

[75] *Parkes Property and Stock Company Ltd.* v. *Perpetual Trustee Company Ltd.* (1936) 36 SR(NSW) 457.

[76] See Crawford J. in *In re Hurburgh* [1959] Tas. SR 25, 50–1.

[77] See section 10.11 below.

[78] See the Insolvency Act 1986, s. 281.

[79] See the Insolvency Act 1986, s. 279, though compare the former Bankruptcy Act 1914, s. 26. In Australia see the Bankruptcy Act 1966 (Cth.), s. 150.

10.6 MUTUALITY

It is a prerequisite to the operation of the rule in *Cherry* v. *Boultbee* that at some time at least there must have been one person both entitled to participate in, and also liable to contribute to, the fund. Therefore, the administrator of the fund may not invoke the rule in respect of a debt due to some other person, rather than to the fund.[80] Similarly, it is not sufficient that the person entitled to participate is indebted to a third party who is under an obligation to contribute.[81]

The requirement that there be the same person entitled to participate in and obliged to contribute to the fund is particularly important in the event of the bankruptcy of the person entitled to participate. Thus, in *Cherry* v. *Boultbee*[82] itself, a legatee under a will had become bankrupt *before* the death of the testator. It was held that the testator's executors could not insist that a debt owing by the legatee to the testator should be appropriated as payment of the legacy. The liability for the debt was still the liability of the legatee. On the other hand, since the legatee had become bankrupt before the testator's death, he himself had never had a right to the legacy.[83] Rather, this right from its inception was vested in his assignee in bankruptcy on behalf of the estate. Consequently 'there never was a time at which the same person was entitled to receive the legacy and liable to pay the entire debt; the right, therefore, of retaining a sufficient sum out of the legacy to pay the debt can never have been vested in anyone'.[84] If however the legatee's bankruptcy had occurred *after* the death, the executors would have been permitted to invoke the rule. The legatee himself at one time would have been entitled to share in the fund. Moreover, since the bankrupt's assignees in bankruptcy could claim no better title than the bankrupt himself, this right could also have been exercised against them.[85]

While in *Cherry* v. *Boultbee* the executors could not apply the rule in

---

[80] See *In re Watson* [1896] 1 Ch. 925, 937, and also *Stammers* v. *Elliott* (1868) LR 3 Ch. App. 195, 199 (with respect to the £150).

[81] See *Avison* v. *Holmes* (1861) 1 J & H 530, and also *Smee* v. *Baines* (1861) 29 Beav. 661.

[82] (1839) 4 My. & Cr. 442, not following *Ex parte Man* (1829) Mont. & M 210. See also *Bell* v. *Bell* (1849) 17 Sim. 127; *In re Hodgson, Deceased; Hodgson* v. *Fox* (1878) 9 Ch. D 673; *In re Orpen; Beswick* v. *Orpen* (1880) 16 Ch. D 202; *In re Peruvian Railway Construction Co., Ltd.* [1915] 2 Ch. 144; *Re Reiter; ex parte Hislop* (1932) 5 ABC 98. Note, though, the remarks of Sir George Turner on *Cherry* v. *Boultbee* in *Freeman* v. *Lomas* (1851) 9 Hare 109, 115–16.

[83] Compare the case of a company liquidation, in which the assets remain vested in the company itself. See *In re Kowloon Container Warehouse Co. Ltd.* [1981] HKLR 210, 226.

[84] (1839) 4 My. & Cr. 442, 448 per Lord Cottenham.

[85] *Jeffs* v. *Wood* (1723) 2 P Wms. 128; *Bousfield* v. *Lawford* (1863) 1 De G J & S 459; *Ranking* v. *Barnard* (1820) 5 Madd. 32; *Richards* v. *Richards* (1821) 9 Price 219.

respect of the *full* amount of the debt owing to the fund, they could insist that the share of the fund payable to the insolvent estate should be considered as paid to the extent of the *dividend* payable to the fund by the insolvent estate in respect of that debt. The one 'party', in the form of the insolvent estate, was entitled to participate in, and was also obliged to contribute to, the fund.[86]

The relevant date in these insolvent debtor cases is not the date upon which someone is appointed to administer the fund, nor indeed the date upon which it becomes clear that there will be a valuable right of participation, but rather the date of the event which precipitates the setting up of the fund. Thus, where the fund consists of a deceased's estate, the precipitating event is the death. In a bankruptcy or a company liquidation, it is the commencement of the bankruptcy or the liquidation. The rule may be invoked by the administrator of the fund as long as the person liable to contribute to the fund was also possessed of a right to participate at some time after the precipitating event. For example, when a company in liquidation had a surplus available for distribution amongst its share-holders, and one of the shareholders, who was indebted to the company, had died insolvent, Sargant J. considered that the liquidator could only have invoked the rule if the death occurred after the commencement of the liquidation. When the liquidation commenced, 'the rights in respect of the shares may be considered to have been converted into a right or expectation of receiving a rateable proportion of the surplus moneys remaining after satisfying the liabilities of the company'.[87] Of course, as Sargant J. remarked, this is the '*earliest* possible moment at which any right of retainer or set-off or the like could arise'.[88] It only means that the rule in *Cherry* v. *Boultbee* may not be invoked if the debtor to the fund had not had a right to share in it personally at any time after the precipitating event. It should not be necessary that he should actually have had such a right before that date.[89]

While the same person at some time at least must have been entitled to

---

[86] See also in this regard *In re Orpen* (1880) 16 Ch. D 202; *In re Peruvian Railway Construction Co., Ltd.* [1915] 2 Ch. 144; *In re Fenton (No. 2); ex parte Fenton Textile Association, Ltd.* [1932] 1 Ch. 178, 187. However compare *In re Hodgson* (1878) 9 Ch. D 673, in which a dividend had not been declared in the bankruptcy. *Quaere* whether a foreign bankruptcy of the debtor to the fund may be recognized for the purpose of *Cherry* v. *Boultbee*. See the discussion in *In re Kowloon Container Warehouse Co. Ltd.* [1981] HKLR 210 with respect to a foreign liquidation.

[87] *In re Peruvian Railway Construction Co., Ltd.* [1915] 2 Ch. 144, 151 (affirmed [1915] 2 Ch. 442).   [88] [1915] 2 Ch. 144, 151 (emphasis added).

[89] Certainly the rule may be invoked when the obligation to contribute only arises after the precipitating event. See e.g. the cases discussed in section 10.7 below in relation to the principle that the contribution need only be in aid of the fund. See also *In re Palmer; Palmer* v. *Clarke* (1894) 13 R 233, in which an option to purchase the testator's property was exercised after the testator's death.

share in the fund and also liable to contribute to it, it is not necessary that the right and the liability should each have been presently payable, or indeed vested, at that time. The rule may be invoked by executors when the right to participate becomes due and payable even if the legatee only had an interest in reversion at the time of his bankruptcy,[90] or if the right to participate otherwise was payable *in futuro* when the bankruptcy occurred, and similarly it is sufficient if the liability to contribute at that time was only contingent, as for example when the administrators of the fund were only called upon to make a payment under a contract of suretyship after the principal debtor's bankruptcy.[91] As long as there has been in this sense a situation in which the one person had a right to participate and an obligation to contribute before the bankruptcy, an equity to invoke the rule arises in favour of the administrator of the fund to which the trustee in bankruptcy takes subject, provided, of course, that the obligation to contribute is still in existence when the right to participate becomes due and payable.[92] A judgment creditor is in the same position in this regard as a trustee in bankruptcy.[93]

Mutuality under *Cherry* v. *Boultbee* is concerned with the relationship between the fund and the person indebted to the fund.[94] Generally it should be determined by reference to principles similar to those applied to set-off, although they differ in one respect. For set-off one looks to the persons possessed of the title to the cross-demands. This should be compared to *Cherry* v. *Boultbee*, for which it is not necessary that the debt should have been incurred to the person in respect of whose estate the fund was set up. It is sufficient if the debt is incurred to the administrator of the fund, as long as the proceeds of the debt will be in aid of that fund.[95] In other respects, however, similar principles apply. For example, if a party holds his right to participate in the fund merely as a trustee, the administrator of the fund should not be able to appropriate it as payment of a debt owing by that party personally.[96] On the other hand, the administrator may appropriate as payment a debt owing by a person who is

---

[90] See *In re Watson; Turner v. Watson* [1896] 1 Ch. 925; *In re Lennard; Lennard's Trustee v. Lennard* [1934] 1 Ch. 235. See also *In re Melton; Milk v. Towers* [1918] 1 Ch. 37; *In re Hurburgh* [1959] Tas. SR 25, 40 per Crawford J. ('the legatee is entitled in possession or in reversion or even contingently to a general legacy or a share of residue').

[91] *Willes v. Greenhill (No. 1)* (1860) 29 Beav. 376; *In re Whitehouse; Whitehouse v. Edwards* (1887) 37 Ch. D 683; *In re Watson; Turner v. Watson* [1896] 1 Ch. 925; *In re Melton* [1918] 1 Ch. 37.   [92] See section 10.5 above.

[93] *Kilworth v. Mountcashell* (1864) 15 Ir. Ch. Rep. 565, 581.

[94] The rule 'is applied only where there is a direct and specific mutuality between the mass and the particular debtor'. See *In re Pennington and Owen, Ltd.* [1925] 1 Ch. 825, 830 per Pollock MR.   [95] See section 10.7 below.

[96] If, however, the trust is created *after* the precipitating event, the person acquiring the beneficial title would take subject to equities. See section 10.12.1 below.

the beneficial owner of the right to participate.[97] Conversely, the rule will not apply if the testator was only a trustee of the legatee's indebtedness,[98] or if the debt is owing to the administrator in his personal capacity, even though the administrator may be entitled to the residue of the fund and consequently would be benefited by the deduction.[99] The basic principle is that *Cherry* v. *Boultbee* may only be invoked when the person liable to contribute is the same as the person entitled to participate,[100] having regard to equitable rights. In *In re Binns*[101] a will stipulated that the residuary estate was to be held on trust for the children of the deceased but that, if any child died, the children of that child were to take his share. It was held that a grandchild claiming under the will after the death of his parent, who in turn was a child of the testator, was not liable to have his interest reduced to the extent of a debt owing by his deceased parent to the testator. While *Cherry* v. *Boultbee* would have applied if the deceased parent himself had claimed under the will, the child of that deceased parent was entitled in his own right.

Similarly, the obligation to contribute and the right to participate should ordinarily relate to the same fund.[102] In *In re Towndrow, Gratton* v. *Machen*[103] a person appointed executor under a will was also entitled to a legacy, for which an assent had been given by the executors. In addition he was appointed trustee of the residuary personal estate, though he himself had no beneficial interest in that estate. While acting in his capacity of trustee he misappropriated a part of the residue. Because of the assent, the specific legacy was held on a trust which was separate and distinct from the trusts upon which the rest of the estate was held.[104] Consequently it was held that the trustee was not required to make good his default to the residuary estate before he (or the person to whom he had mortgaged his right to the legacy) could claim the legacy. Parker J. in *Towndrow* applied the correct principle on the assumption that *Cherry* v. *Boultbee* was applicable,[105] although it has been doubted whether on the facts the case

---

[97] *In re Kent County Gas Light and Coke Co., Ltd.* [1913] 1 Ch. 92, 97; *In re Kowloon Container Warehouse Co. Ltd.* [1981] HKLR 210.

[98] *Richardson* v. *Richardson* (1867) LR 3 Eq. 686, 695.

[99] *Freeman* v. *Lomas* (1851) 9 Hare 109.

[100] *Reeve* v. *Richer* (1847) 1 De G & Sm. 624; *In re Bruce; Lawford* v. *Bruce* [1908] 2 Ch. 682.   [101] [1929] 1 Ch. 677.

[102] In addition to the cases cited below, see *Price* v. *Loaden* (1856) 21 Beav. 508.

[103] [1911] 1 Ch. 662.

[104] As soon as executors assent to a bequest it ceases to be a part of the testator's assets. See *Dix* v. *Burford* (1854) 19 Beav. 409, 412.

[105] See *Ballard* v. *Marsden* (1880) 14 Ch. D 374; *Re Milnes; Milnes* v. *Sherwin* (1885) 53 LT 534, 535. Compare *Cole* v. *Muddle* (1852) 10 Hare 186, the correctness of which is doubted in *Withers on Reversions* (2nd edn., 1933), 241 n. a, on the ground that one of several executors should be able to assent to a legacy in which he is interested. Compare also *Hastie* v. *Hastie* (1876) 24 WR 242, in which there was a strong case of fraud.

was correctly decided. Younger J. in *In re Jewell's Settlement; Watts* v. *Public Trustee*[106] said that *Towndrow* might have been decided differently if *Morris* v. *Livie*[107] had been cited to the court. *Morris* v. *Livie* is referred to below in the discussion of defaulting trustees.[108] Knight Bruce V.C. in that case put forward the view that, when a trustee appointed under a will is also named as a legatee under the will, the legacy is presumed to be consideration for his performing the duties of trustee. *Cherry* v. *Boultbee* specifically contemplates the existence of a right to participate, but dictates that a particular asset may be appropriated as payment of that right. However, *Morris* v. *Livie* in effect means that the trustee is deprived of a right to participate while he is in default. An executor can only assent to a legacy in favour of the legatee to whom it is given, and not in favour of a stranger.[109] Similarly, while it is usually said that an assent is irrevocable,[110] it may be that an assent made in favour of a trustee would not be binding if in truth the result of the trustee's conduct was that he was not entitled to the legacy while he remained in default. However, the assent no doubt would be binding when there has been a purchase of the legacy in good faith from the defaulting trustee on the faith of the assent.[111]

An apparent exception to this requirement of a single fund exists in the case of a settlement. Two or more funds may technically be settled under the one settlement on different trusts. Nevertheless, the courts 'consider everything that is brought or expressed to be brought into settlement by anybody from any source as one aggregate trust fund'.[112] Consequently the trustees may invoke *Cherry* v. *Boultbee* against a person seeking to participate in the settlement if he is obliged to contribute to it,[113] even even though the 'right' and the 'obligation' may relate to different funds

---

[106] [1919] 2 Ch. 161.   [107] (1842) 1 Y & C CC 380.

[108] See section 10.13 below.

[109] *In re West; West* v. *Roberts* [1909] 2 Ch. 180, 186.

[110] See e.g. Williams, *The Law Relating to Assents* (1947), 98, but compare *Williams, Mortimer, and Sunnucks on Executors, Administrators and Probate* (1993), 1062–3.

[111] *Williams, Mortimer and Sunnucks on Executors, Administrators and Probate* (1993), 1062. See also *Edgar* v. *Plomley* [1900] AC 431, which concerned a fund in court in an administration suit ordered to be carried to a separate account in the name of a trustee whom it was later discovered was in default.

[112] *Codrington* v. *Lindsay* (1873) LR 8 Ch. App. 578, 592 per James L.J. See generally *Withers on Reversions* (2nd edn., 1933), 241.

[113] See for example *Priddy* v. *Rose* (1817) 3 Mer. 86; *Kilworth* v. *Mountcashell* (1861) 15 Ir. Ch. Rep. 43; *Corr* v. *Corr* (1879) 3 LR Ir. 435; *Ballard* v. *Marsden* (1880) 14 Ch. D 374, 377; *In re Weston; Davies* v. *Tagart* [1900] 2 Ch. 164. The liability to contribute need not arise out of the terms of the settlement, but may arise subsequently as a result of a misappropriation. See e.g. *Woodyatt* v. *Gresley* (1836) 8 Sim. 180. Moreover it makes no difference that the settlement may be voluntary, provided that it has been so completed as to be enforceable by the court. See *In re Weston*. Compare *Hallett* v. *Hallett* (1879) 13 Ch. D 232, in which the settlement had expressly excluded from its operation the particular fund for which the action was brought.

encompassed by that settlement.[114] Similarly, separate trusts, or bequests, under the one will may be treated as constituting the one fund, unless the executors have already set apart a particular legacy so that the estate is no longer in bulk.[115]

The prohibition against setting off joint demands and separate demands also applies in *Cherry* v. *Boultbee*.[116] Thus, an executor may not appropriate as payment of a legacy a debt owing to the fund by a number of joint debtors of whom the legatee is one.[117] In a case in Ireland, a legatee was indebted to a firm in which the testator was a partner. It was held that the executor could not appropriate this joint claim as payment of the legacy.[118] A decision of Stuart V.C. is curious in this regard. In *Smith* v. *Smith*[119] a residuary legatee under a will was a partner in a firm that was indebted to the testator. The firm had become bankrupt. Stuart V.C. held that the executors could appropriate the joint debt of the firm as payment of the legacy due to the partner in his separate capacity. Cozens-Hardy M.R. in *Turner* v. *Turner*[120] offered a possible explanation for the decision, though without finally deciding whether the case was correctly decided. He said that in *Smith* the assignees in bankruptcy were seeking payment of the legacy in their capacity of assignees of the separate estate of the partner, rather than as assignees of the joint estate of the firm, and moreover he said that the legatee's separate estate was liable to the testator's estate for the debt. Since the testator's executors in *Smith* could have proved for the debt against the separate estate of the legatee, which estate was vested in the assignees, the executors could appropriate that debt as payment of the legacy owing to the partner.[121] It is not easy to

---

[114] See *Burridge* v. *Row* (1844) 13 LJ Ch. 173 (affirming 1 Y & C CC 183); *In re Jewell's Settlement; Watts* v. *Public Trustee* [1919] 2 Ch. 161. The courts seem to incline in favour of finding that there is a single settlement. See e.g. *Woodyatt* v. *Gresley* (1836) 8 Sim.180.

[115] *In the Estate of Tolley, Deceased* (1972) 5 SASR 466, and see also *MacPhillamy* v. *Fox* (1932) 32 SR(NSW) 427. Harvey C.J. in Eq. in *MacPhillamy* criticized *In re Towndrow* [1911] 1 Ch. 662 (see above), though this criticism would appear to be misplaced, except possibly to the extent that the case concerned a defaulting trustee. *Towndrow* is not inconsistent with the Chief Justice's contention that the whole of the funds held by a trustee under a will constitute one fund for the purpose of adjustment, because an assent has the effect of setting apart the particular fund in question from the fund in bulk. In *MacPhillamy* itself there had not been any assent in respect of the bequest in issue.

[116] See *In re Pennington and Owen, Ltd.* [1925] 1 Ch. 825. Note also *McEwan* v. *Crombie* (1883) 25 Ch. D 175, which appears to have been a case of *Cherry* v. *Boultbee* rather than set-off.   [117] *Turner* v. *Turner* [1911] 1 Ch. 716.

[118] *Jackson* v. *Yeats* [1912] 1 IR 267.   [119] (1861) 3 Giff. 263.

[120] [1911] 1 Ch. 716.

[121] Cozens-Hardy MR in *Turner* v. *Turner* [1911] 1 Ch. 716, 721 said with regard to *Smith* v. *Smith* that the case 'is consistent with the principle in *Cherry* v. *Boultbee* because the testatrix's executors could have proved against the separate estate of William Smith, whose separate estate was vested in the assignees, and that brings us practically to the same position as though there had never been a firm and the debt had originally been due from the legatee'.

follow this. When a partnership becomes bankrupt, the principle that used to govern the question of distribution was that the joint estate was applicable in the first instance in payment of the joint debts and the separate estate of each partner was applicable in the first instance in payment of his separate debts. If there was a surplus of the separate estates it was dealt with as part of the joint estate, and if there was a surplus of the joint estate it was dealt with as part of the respective separate estates in proportion to the interest of each partner in the joint estate.[122] Thus, the separate estate of each partner was only liable to be applied in payment of a partnership debt to the extent of any surplus remaining after the partner's separate creditors had been paid in full. The relevant principle was modified under the Insolvent Partnerships Order 1994 so that, to the extent of any deficiency in the joint estate, a claim may now be made against the separate estates *pari passu* with other separate creditors.[123] Nevertheless, it is still the case that the separate estate of each partner is only liable to be applied in payment of partnership debts to the extent that those debts are not capable of being satisfied from the partnership assets. The order in *Smith* v. *Smith* had the effect of allowing a separate asset of a partner to be used to satisfy a partnership debt before the joint estate had been taken into account, which could have disadvantaged the separate creditors of that partner even under the new distribution rules.

Cherry v. *Boultbee* may, however, apply when the liability is joint and several rather than joint.[124] If there are joint and several debtors to a fund, and the administrator of the fund appropriates the debt as *pro tanto* payment of the right of one of the debtors to participate, all the debtors are discharged to the extent of the right to participate, though the debtor whose right was appropriated should be entitled to contribution from the other debtors.[125]

10.7 THE OBLIGATION TO CONTRIBUTE

Cherry v. *Boultbee* is not confined to cases in which the obligation to contribute to the fund is for a liquidated sum enforceable either as a debt or by means of an order for specific performance,[126] but also encompasses

---

[122] See e.g. art. 10 of the Insolvent Partnerships Order 1986 (S.1. 1986/2142). In Australia see the Bankruptcy Act 1966 (Cth.), s. 110.

[123] See Pt II of Sch. 4 (s. 175A) and Sch. 7 (s. 328A) of the Insolvent Partnerships Order 1994 (S.1. 1994/2421).

[124] *Selangor United Rubber Estates Ltd.* v. *Cradock (No. 4)* [1969] 1 WLR 1773.

[125] This seems to have been recognized in *Selangor United Rubber Estates Ltd.* v. *Cradock (No. 4)* [1969] 1 WLR 1773, 1776.

[126] For specific performance see *In re Palmer; Palmer* v. *Clarke* (1894) 13 R 233, 236.

a liability sounding in damages, as for example a liability for breach of contract for failure to keep up a policy of life insurance settled on trust,[127] or a liability for damages for misfeasance.[128] There is authority for the view that the administrator of a fund may not invoke *Cherry* v. *Boultbee* when the liability of the person seeking to share in the fund is only payable *in futuro*. Thus, when a residuary legatee was indebted to the testator on a debt payable by instalments, the executors were not permitted to invoke the rule in respect of instalments payable in the future.[129] This result was justified on the ground that, if the debt could be appropriated as payment of the right to participate before that debt was actually payable, the contract under which the debt arose will have been altered.[130] On the other hand, in *In re Rhodesia Goldfields, Ltd.*[131] neither the existence nor the value of any liability had actually been established or ascertained, although, if there was any liability, it would have been presently payable. Swinfen Eady J. held that, pending the ascertainment and the establishment of the amount (if any) due to the fund, the share of the fund for which payment was sought should be retained and carried to a separate account.

The principle that *Cherry* v. *Boultbee* may not be invoked when the liability to contribute, though presently existing, is payable *in futuro*, brings into question certain judicial statements to the effect that in some cases the rule may apply when the obligation to contribute is merely contingent. In other words, the liability is not only not presently payable, but is also not even presently vested. For example, when a testator was a surety for one of his legatees, Warrington L.J. said that at 'the death of the testator' the executors 'had a right to be indemnified against any claim which they *might ultimately have to satisfy* as the result of the guarantee; and to retain in their hands so much of [the legatee's] share as was sufficient to provide for that indemnity'.[132] These judicial statements were made in the context of a bankrupt principal debtor, and should be confined to that context. In such a case the surety's estate almost certainly would be called upon to honour the obligation under the contract of suretyship, and consequently a liability in the principal debtor to indemnify the estate

---

[127] *In re Jewell's Settlement; Watts* v. *Public Trustee* [1919] 2 Ch. 161, distinguishing *In re Smelting Corporation; Seaver* v. *The Company* [1915] 1 Ch. 472.

[128] See the discussion of *In re Milan Tramways Company; ex parte Theys* (1884) 25 Ch. D 587 in *In re Jewell's Settlement* [1919] 2 Ch. 161, 174–6. See also *In re Leeds and Hanley Theatres of Varieties, Ltd.* [1904] 2 Ch. 45.

[129] *In re Abrahams; Abrahams* v. *Abrahams* [1908] 2 Ch. 69. See also *Re Rees; Rees* v. *Rees* (1889) 60 LT 260; *Jeffryes* v. *Agra and Masterman's Bank* (1866) LR 2 Eq. 674, 680; *In re Watson* [1896] 1 Ch. 925, 933–4; *In re Rhodesia Goldfields, Ltd.* [1910] 1 Ch. 239, 242 per Swinfen Eady J. (*arguendo*).   [130] *In re Abrahams* [1908] 2 Ch. 69, 72.

[131] [1910] 1 Ch. 239.

[132] *In re Melton; Milk* v. *Towers* [1918] 1 Ch. 37, 54–5 (emphasis added). See also Swinfen Eady L.J. at 51–2, approving of a *dictum* by North J. to this effect in *In re Binns; Lee* v. *Binns* [1896] 2 Ch. 584, 587–8.

would almost certainly arise. In other situations, if it is not possible to invoke *Cherry* v. *Boultbee* in respect of a present debt payable *in futuro*, then the rule certainly should not apply when the liability is only contingent.[133] For example, there is authority for the view that executors may not invoke the rule against a legatee who is a guarantor for a third party and whose liability has not yet vested.[134]

It is not necessary that the contribution should directly form a part of the fund in question. Rather, it is sufficient if it is 'in aid of' the fund.[135] Thus, the rule may be invoked when the liability to contribute is based upon an award of costs made in favour of the administrator of the fund as a result of litigation conducted on behalf of the fund.[136] The administrator will have a right of indemnity from the fund in respect of his costs. If he has already exercised this right of indemnity, anything paid to him under the award of costs will be paid by him into the fund. If, on the other hand, he has not been indemnified, the costs paid to him will still be in aid of the fund, because they will relieve the fund of the burden of indemnifying him.[137] When the fund is constituted by an estate being administered in bankruptcy, lack of mutuality would operate to deny the debtor for costs the right to set off the costs against the bankrupt's debt to him.[138] However, the bankrupt's trustee does have the right to invoke *Cherry* v. *Boultbee* in relation to the debtor's right to receive a *dividend* on the debt owing to him by the bankrupt.[139]

---

[133] Parker J. in *In re Mitchell; Freelove* v. *Mitchell* [1913] 1 Ch. 201, 206 said that, when the principal debt is due and payable, but the surety has not actually paid anything under the guarantee, the 'surety's right is confined to a right to come into equity in order to get an indemnity against his liability to the creditor'. However, the surety's right in such a case is not that he should be paid a sum of money by the debtor as an indemnity for his liability as a guarantor, but rather that he should be entitled to an order from equity compelling the debtor to relieve him from his liability by paying off the debt to the creditor. This right to *quia timet* relief should not entitle the administrator of the surety's estate to appropriate the debtor's right to a share of the fund as an indemnity for the surety's liability as a guarantor.

[134] See *Smee* v. *Baines* (1861) 29 Beav. 661, as explained in *Withers on Reversions* (2nd edn., 1933), 255.

[135] See the formulation of the rule by Sargant J. in *In re Peruvian Railway Construction Co., Ltd.* [1915] 2 Ch. 144, 150. This may explain *Irby* v. *Irby* (*No. 3*) (1858) 25 Beav. 632.

[136] *In re Knapman* (1881) 18 Ch. D 300 (though note the explanation of this case in *In re Pain; Gustavson* v. *Haviland* [1919] 1 Ch. 38); *In re Mayne; ex parte The Official Receiver* [1907] 2 KB 899; *Dodson* v. *Sandburst & Northern District Trustees Executors and Agency Co. Ltd.* [1955] VLR 100. The rule will also apply in the converse situation in which a person who is liable to contribute to a trust fund has obtained an order for payment of costs out of the trust fund. See *Re Harrald; Wilde* v. *Walford* (1884) 51 LT 441.

[137] *Dodson* v. *Sandhurst & Northern District Trustees Executors and Agency Co. Ltd.* [1955] VLR 100, 102–3. [138] *West* v. *Pryce* (1825) 2 Bing. 455.

[139] *In re Mayne* [1907] 2 KB 899. Compare *Ex parte Whitehead; in re Kirk* (1821) 1 Gl. & J 39, in which the debtor for costs had assigned his estate, including his claim against the bankrupt, to trustees for the benefit of his creditors before the liability for costs arose. Therefore, at no time was the right to participate and the liability to contribute vested in the same person. See section 10.6 above.

This notion, that it is sufficient that the obligation to contribute is in aid of the fund, explains two early decisions of Lord Eldon. In each of *Ex parte Bebb*[140] and *Ex parte Graham*[141] a banking firm, which had been appointed to act as bankers for an estate being administered in bankruptcy, was also a creditor of the bankrupt. The bankrupt's assignees paid the proceeds of the estate into the bank, which subsequently itself became bankrupt. It was held that the bank's estate was not entitled to receive a dividend in its debtor's bankruptcy until the whole of the sum received as bankers under the commission had been repaid. Strictly this sum was owing to the bankrupt's assignees in bankruptcy, who had deposited the proceeds in the bank, rather than to the bankrupt himself. However, the bank's liability still represented a contribution required to be made in aid of the bankrupt's estate.[142] Subsequently Sir Thomas Plumer in *Ex parte Bignold; In re Charles*[143] held that the same result should follow in the case of an assignee of a bankrupt who was a creditor of the bankrupt, and who himself became bankrupt while holding proceeds of the estate in his capacity as assignee. Once again, the assignee was not indebted to the bankrupt personally, but rather to the other assignees in bankruptcy. Nevertheless his required contribution was still in aid of the bankrupt's estate.[144] Consistent with these cases, it should not be an objection to the operation of *Cherry* v. *Boultbee* that a legatee's liability arises as a result of a dealing with the executor of a testator's estate, as opposed to with the testator himself, as long as the fruit of the liability will be in aid of the estate rather than the executor personally.[145]

The principle that the obligation to contribute need only be in aid of the fund brings into question the decision in *Re Henley, Thurgood, & Co.*[146] Henley & Co. ('Henleys') were trade creditors of Fairhead & Son ('Fairheads'), who executed an inspectorship deed under the Bankruptcy Act 1861. The inspectors of the deed continued to trade with Henleys, and as a result a balance became due to the inspectors in respect of those dealings. Henleys themselves later became bankrupt. Commissioner

---

[140] (1812) 19 Ves. Jun. 222. [141] (1814) 3 V & B 130.

[142] See also *Fuller* v. *Knight* (1843) 6 Beav. 205 in the context of a loan of trust money. Compare *In re Wickham's Will; Grant* v. *Union Trustee Company of Australia Ltd.* (1898) 9 QLJ 102, discussed below. [143] (1817) 2 Madd. 470.

[144] Compare *Ex parte Alexander; in re Elder* (1832) 1 Deac. & Ch. 513, in which a creditor of the bankrupt had been employed to liquidate the bankrupt's estate and effects. The creditor then retained from the proceeds a sum more than sufficient to cover his reasonable commission and expenses. It was held that the official assignee could not direct the creditor to look to the excess still in his hands as payment of his right to receive a dividend on the debt owing to him by the bankrupt. However, the case turned on the extent of the duties of the official assignee, and it should not be regarded as authority for the view that *Cherry* v. *Boultbee* could not have been invoked in this situation.

[145] A comment by Sir John Romilly in *Smee* v. *Baines* (1861) 29 Beav. 661, 663 suggesting that there should have been a transaction with the testator himself should be considered in the context of the facts in issue in that case. [146] (1863) 11 WR 1021.

Holroyd correctly held that there could not be a set-off, both on the ground of lack of mutuality,[147] and also because the creditors under the deed, including Henleys, were *cestuis que trust* of the inspectors.[148] Moreover, he also said that the principle in *Cherry v. Boultbee* was not applicable, so that the inspectors could not appropriate Henley's liability to them on the dealings transacted after the deed as satisfaction of Henley's right to receive a dividend on Fairhead's debt incurred before the deed. The reason for this second conclusion is not altogether clear. While Henleys became indebted to the inspectors rather than to Fairheads, the proceeds of that liability would have swelled the fund available for distribution amongst Fairhead's creditors, and so it was in aid of that fund. Admittedly *Cherry v. Boultbee* could not have been invoked by Henley's assignees in bankruptcy. So far as they were concerned, the right to participate in Henley's estate was vested in Fairhead's inspectors, while Fairheads themselves were liable to contribute. Nevertheless, as far as Fairhead's inspectors were concerned, Henleys had a right to participate and were also liable to make a contribution in aid of Fairheads' fund. There are also doubts as to the correctness of the Queensland Supreme Court decision in *In re Wickham's Will; Grant v. Union Trustee Company of Australia Ltd.*[149] The widow of a testator borrowed a sum of money from the plaintiffs as trustees of her husband's estate. Subsequently she purchased the share of one of the residuary legatees under the will. Griffith C.J., with whom Chubb J. concurred, held that the trustees could not set off the loan against the share of the residuary estate when that share became payable. Undoubtedly, as far as set-off was concerned, this was a correct decision. The demands were not mutual for the purpose of set-off.[150] Unfortunately, however, there was no consideration given to *Cherry v. Boultbee*.[151] If executors of an estate may invoke the rule against a bank with whom they deposited the proceeds of the estate, then one would have thought that the rule could also apply when trust funds are invested in a loan to a person who acquires a right to participate.[152] The concepts of mutuality in set-off and under

---

[147] The dealing was with the inspectors themselves rather than Fairheads, while Henleys were creditors of Fairheads.   [148] See Ch. 6.   [149] (1898) 9 QLJ 102.

[150] The widow's debt did not arise out of a dealing with the husband himself.

[151] Griffith C.J. based his decision as to set-off upon *Hallett v. Hallett* (1879) 13 Ch. D 232. However, Fry J. in that case considered both set-off and *Cherry v. Boultbee*. He similarly held that lack of mutuality prevented a set-off. Apparently, though, this was not considered to be a sufficient reason for saying that *Cherry v. Boultbee* could not apply. Rather his Lordship held that, on the particular facts before him, the sum claimed from the trustees was never intended to be a part of the settlement so that, while there was an obligation to contribute to the fund, the sum claimed was not based upon a right to participate in that fund.

[152] In fact the widow in *Wickham* had assigned the share of the residuary estate to a bank. This share took the form of a reversionary interest in a trust fund which was subject to her own life interest. The widow had died, and so the bank was claiming payment of this share.

Cherry v. *Boultbee* differ in this respect. For set-off one looks only to the persons possessed of the legal and equitable titles to the demands. However, in *Cherry* v. *Boultbee* mutuality is concerned with the relationship between the fund and the person entitled to participate in the fund. Mutuality is preserved as long as that person is under an obligation to make a payment which will go to swell, or will be in aid of, the fund.

The rule may not be invoked if the liability to contribute was extinguished before the right to participate became due and payable.[153] Similarly, *Cherry* v. *Boultbee* will not apply when there never has been a liability to contribute.[154] This has been held to be the case in the situation in which a sum of money was paid by mistake out of a fund to a person who incidentally was also entitled to participate in the fund, and that sum was not recoverable because the mistake was a mistake of law.[155] Whether the application of the general principle in the context of mistake of law will

---

Before the assignment the one person, the widow, had both an obligation to contribute to, and a right to participate in, the fund. It is not a valid objection to a claim to invoke the rule against an assignee of the right to participate that the right was only a right in reversion when the administrator received notice of the assignment. See *Willes* v. *Greenhill (No. 1)* (1860) 29 Beav. 376, and generally section 10.12.2 below. Griffith C.J. cited *Watson* v. *Mid Wales Railway Company* (1867) LR 2 CP 593, in which it was held that a set-off could not be based upon a debt arising after notice though as a result of a contract entered into before notice. However, this is distinguishable from *Wickham*. The reversionary interest in the fund was a present interest, though one which was not payable until a future day. Similarly, a set-off may be based upon a debt which is in existence before notice, but which is not payable until after notice. See *In re Pinto Leite and Nephews; ex parte Visconde des Olivaes* [1929] 1 Ch. 221.

[153] See section 10.5 above.

[154] See *In re Morley; Morley* v. *Saunders* (1869) LR 8 Eq. 594. This requirement of a subsisting liability brings into question certain comments made by Lord Greene M.R., with whom Finlay and Morton L.JJ. concurred, in *Picken* v. *Lord Balfour of Burleigh* [1945] 1 Ch. 90. A compulsory superannuation scheme provided that every employee should contribute a percentage of his salary to the fund. Upon retirement the employee became entitled to benefit payments based upon a percentage of his average salary during the period of his membership. The managers of the scheme calculated contributions on the basis of the bare rate of pay applicable to the grade of the particular employee, without taking into account certain bonuses that were also paid. It was held that these bonuses in fact constituted a part of the salary of each member, and that accordingly the benefits payable should be calculated on the basis of an average salary which included these sums. In addition, it was held that the members could not claim this increased benefit without bringing into account the deficit in past contributions. The case itself may be explained on the basis of the second reason advanced by Lord Greene (at 102), that 'the right to a pension is conditional on the contributions having been paid'. However, the Master of the Rolls (at 100) also justified the result by reference to the 'very well-known principle of equity' that a member 'ought not to be allowed to take money from the fund without himself contributing to it what he ought to have contributed in the past'. Moreover, his Lordship apparently thought that this 'very well-known principle' would apply even if the only method of contribution was by way of deduction from salary, so that if the deduction was not made in this manner there would not be a subsisting liability to pay sums that should have been, but in fact were not, deducted. The better view is that *Cherry* v. *Boultbee* would not have been applicable in this situation. His Lordship would seem to have erred in framing the principle in terms of 'what he ought to have contributed in the past'. The principle is better explained in terms that 'a member ought not to be allowed to take money from the fund without himself contributing to it any sum for which he is liable'. [155] *In re Hatch; Hatch* v. *Hatch* [1919] 1 Ch. 351.

survive for long is debatable. In *Woolwich Equitable Building Society* v. *Inland Revenue Commissioners*[156] the House of Lords noted that the rule that money paid under a mistake of law is irrecoverable has been subjected to strong criticism, and there are indications in some of the judgments that in a future case their Lordships would be sympathetic to the view that it should be discarded. This indeed has occurred in Australia.[157] But, whatever the position is in this regard, the courts for a long time have recognized an exception in the case of a trustee who, acting under an honest mistake of law, makes a payment to a particular beneficiary in excess of the beneficiary's entitlement. The trustee in such a case may deduct the overpayment from future trust payments to that beneficiary.[158] This has also been held to apply when a trustee in bankruptcy has overpaid a particular creditor in the first dividend.[159] Neville J. stated the principle in terms that 'the Court in a proper case—of course there may be cases in which it would be most inequitable to do it—will adjust the rights between the *cestui que trust* and the trustee who has overpaid through an honest and, so to speak, permissible mistake of construction, or of fact'.[160] However, this should not be regarded as an application of *Cherry* v. *Boultbee*, but rather as a principle *sui generis*. It applies even though there may not be a right of recovery from the beneficiary personally in respect of the overpayment,[161] so that it is not based upon the notion underlying *Cherry* v. *Boultbee* of a person being both entitled to participate in and also liable to contribute to a fund.

When the obligation to contribute is an interest-bearing debt, it has been held that *Cherry* v. *Boultbee* should be applied first as against accrued interest, and then as against the principal sum.[162]

10.8 THE RIGHT TO PARTICIPATE

Cherry v. *Boultbee* only applies when the right to participate in the fund is for a sum of money. It may not be invoked when a debtor to a testator's

---

[156] [1993] AC 70.

[157] *David Securities Pty. Ltd.* v. *Commonwealth Bank of Australia* (1992) 175 CLR 353.

[158] *In re Ainsworth; Finch* v. *Smith* [1915] 2 Ch. 96; *In re Reading; Edmands* v. *Reading* [1916] WN 262; *In re Musgrave; Machell* v. *Parry* [1916] 2 Ch. 417; *In re Wooldridge; Wooldridge* v. *Coe* [1920] WN 78; *IVS Enterprises* v. *Chelsea Cloisters Management* unreported, Court of Appeal, 27 January 1994, discussed in Mathews, 'Restitution 0, Trusts 0 (After Extra Time)—A Case of Set-off' [1994] *Restitution Law Review* 44.

[159] *In re Searle, Hoare and Company* [1924] 2 Ch. 325.

[160] *In re Musgrave* [1916] 2 Ch. 417, 425.

[161] *Hilliard* v. *Fulford* (1876) 4 Ch. D 389. In relation to an overpaid creditor in a bankruptcy, see *In re Searle, Hoare and Company* [1924] 2 Ch. 325, 328.

[162] *Campbell* v. *Graham* (1831) 1 Russ. & M 453, affirmed *Campbell* v. *Sandford* (1834) 8 Bligh NS 622.

estate is entitled to a specific bequest of freeholds or leaseholds, or of chattels, because in such a case the right to participate cannot be measured against a monetary obligation to contribute.[163] It makes no difference that the bequest may be in respect of property that could easily be converted into money,[164] although, if the testator directs that his real and/or personal property is to be sold and the proceeds divided, *Cherry* v. *Boultbee* may be invoked in relation to a right to participate in the proceeds.[165] It is no objection that the debtor is a specific legatee if the legacy is pecuniary in nature.[166]

There is, nevertheless, a situation in which a failure to satisfy an obligation will affect a non-monetary entitlement. When there is an obligation arising under the terms of a settlement itself to contribute to the trusts of the settlement, and this has not been done, the person liable will not be permitted to claim any property to which he would otherwise have been entitled pursuant to the settlement.[167] Different principles apply in this situation to those which normally govern *Cherry* v. *Boultbee*. Unlike in *Cherry* v. *Boultbee*, it is probably correct to describe the right in question as a retainer.[168]

It may be that the right of a person indebted to a fund to participate in the fund is periodic in nature. If so, the administrator may appropriate a part of the debt as payment of each right to participate as it accrues due, until such time as the asset of the estate represented by the debt has been exhausted.[169]

10.9 DISCRETIONARY RELIEF

Cherry v. *Boultbee* is an equitable remedy, and so, in accordance with general equitable principles, the conduct of the party claiming the benefit

---

[163] *In re Akerman* [1891] 3 Ch. 212. See also *In re Taylor; Taylor* v. *Wade* [1894] 1 Ch. 671, 674; *Dodson* v. *Sandhurst & Northern District Trustees Executors and Agency Co. Ltd.* [1955] VLR 100; *Ex parte Barff; in re Cousen* (1848) 17 LJ Bcy. 22.

[164] *In re Savage; Cull* v. *Howard* [1918] 2 Ch. 146.

[165] See e.g. *In re Akerman* [1891] 3 Ch. 212; *In re Melton* [1918] 1 Ch. 37. Compare *Re Milnes; Milnes* v. *Sherwin* (1885) 53 LT 534, which concerned the old rule in *Ackroyd* v. *Smithson* (1780) 1 Bro. CC 503 that, when a legacy of a share of the proceeds of sale of real estate has failed, for example because the person named as legatee died before the testator, the share should be treated as real property rather than personalty.

[166] *In re Taylor* [1894] 1 Ch. 671; *In re Baird* [1935] NZLR 847. Earlier observations to the contrary by Kekewich J. in *In re Akerman* [1891] 3 Ch. 212 have not been followed.

[167] *In re Weston; Davies* v. *Tagart* [1900] 2 Ch. 164.

[168] Compare section 10.1 above.

[169] See *Priddy* v. *Rose* (1817) 3 Mer. 86; *Skinner* v. *Sweet* (1818) 3 Madd. 244; *Ex parte Turpin; in re Brown* (1832) Mont. 443; *Smith* v. *Smith* (1835) 1 Y & C Ex. 338; *Kilworth* v. *Mountcashell* (1864) 15 Ir. Ch. Rep. 565; *In re Jewell's Settlement; Watts* v. *Public Trustee* [1919] 2 Ch. 161; *Dodson* v. *Sandhurst & Northern District Trustees Executors and Agency Co. Ltd.* [1955] VLR 100. Compare the order made by Lord Thurlow in *Ex parte Mitford* (1784) 1 Bro. CC 398 (the terms of which are set out in the report of *Priddy* v. *Rose*, at 105–6).

of the rule may lead the court to conclude that relief should be denied. In *Houlditch* v. *Wallace*[170] a particular beneficiary of a trust was entitled to an annuity under the trust. Over a period of some 12 years before the right to the annuity was assigned to the plaintiff, the beneficiary had appropriated income of the trust in excess of the amount of the annuity to his own use. The other beneficiaries were aware of this, but took no steps to remedy their own loss.[171] Lord Cottenham held that these other beneficiaries could not arrest future payments of the annuity as satisfaction of the sums owing by the assignor for the period before the assignment, inter alia because of their laches in not enforcing their equity immediately.

Similarly, in *In re Pain; Gustavson* v. *Haviland*[172] Younger J. held that the usual principle by which an assignee of an interest in a trust fund takes free of equities arising after notice of the assignment[173] may not always apply. In that case the assignees stood by and allowed the assignor to commence proceedings against the trustee. The assignor lost, and was the subject of an order for costs. While this was an equity against the assignor which arose after notice of the assignment, it was held that it could nevertheless be asserted against the assignees. They had allowed the action to proceed when they might have stopped it, knowing that they would have benefited if it had been successful.

10.10 SURETYSHIP AND THE RULE AGAINST DOUBLE PROOF

The rule against double proof provides that an insolvent's estate ought not to pay twice in respect of what is substantially the same debt. Consider, for example, that a principal debtor is bankrupt, and that the creditor has proved and received a dividend on the debt. The creditor then proceeds against a surety for the balance of the debt owing to him. The surety in such a case may not prove in the bankruptcy for an indemnity for the sum paid by him to the creditor. In substance, the debtor's liability to the surety for an indemnity is in respect of the same debt as that owing to the creditor and, because a dividend had already been paid to the creditor, the debtor's estate is not liable to pay a second dividend to the surety.[174] Moreover, since the surety may not prove for an indemnity, he may not employ his claim in a set-off.[175] On the other hand, the status of *Cherry* v. *Boultbee* in relation to double proof is not free from doubt.

---

[170] (1838) 5 Cl & Fin. 629.

[171] An injunction had been obtained to restrain the beneficiary from receiving the income of the trust, but this order was not acted upon. [172] [1918] 1 Ch. 38.

[173] See section 10.12 below.

[174] *In re Oriental Commercial Bank; ex parte European Bank* (1871) LR 7 Ch. App. 99. See also *In re Moss; ex parte Hallett* [1905] 2 KB 307.

[175] *In re Fenton* [1931] 1 Ch. 85. See section 4.3.2 above.

A strict view was adopted by Luxmoore J. in *In re Fenton (No. 2); ex parte Fenton Textile Association Limited*.[176] Fenton, who had guaranteed advances by certain banks to the Association, executed two deeds of arrangement in favour of his creditors. Subsequently the Association was ordered to be wound up. After the winding-up order the banks proved against Fenton's estate for the full amount of the guarantees, and received a dividend. Fenton was also a debtor of the Association. It was held that the rule against double proof precluded the operation of *Cherry* v. *Boultbee*, and that consequently the trustee of the two deeds could not insist that the liquidator's claim for a dividend on the debt owing by Fenton to the Association be satisfied out of the Association's liability to indemnify Fenton's estate for the sum paid under the guarantee.[177] The rule against double proof was said to apply because the banks had only received a dividend from Fenton's estate, and so they were still entitled to prove against the assets of the Association for the full value of the debt.[178]

Unfortunately, there was no mention in *Fenton* of the earlier Court of Appeal decision in *In re Melton; Milk* v. *Towers*.[179] The principal debtor in *Melton* was bankrupt, and his trustee had paid a dividend to the creditor. The surety had died before the bankruptcy, bequeathing to the debtor a one-fourth reversionary share in a residuary fund. The creditor, having received only a dividend from the debtor's estate, then proceeded against the surety's estate under the contract of suretyship for the sum for which the surety had agreed to be liable, and accordingly received payment. When the debtor's right to a share of the residue later became payable, the Court of Appeal[180] unanimously held[181] that the executors of the surety could invoke *Cherry* v. *Boultbee* in respect of their right to receive an indemnity for the sum paid to the creditor. Warrington L.J. proceeded on the basis that *Cherry* v. *Boultbee* operates as a right of retainer, and for

---

[176] [1932] 1 Ch. 178.

[177] Luxmoore J. said that, because the Association had gone into liquidation before the surety's estate had paid anything to the creditor, *Cherry* v. *Boultbee* was authority for the proposition that the rule in any event would only have been invoked in respect of a sum equal to the appropriate *dividend* payable in the liquidation on the obligation to indemnify the surety's estate. *Cherry* v. *Boultbee* was a case in which the right to participate arose after the bankruptcy of the debtor. See the discussion of the case in section 10.6 above. *Fenton* is distinguishable because there was still a *contingent* obligation to contribute before the Association's liquidation. Indeed, this *dictum* is inconsistent with the cases in which the rule was applied in respect of the full amount of a liability that vested after, but was contingent before, the debtor's bankruptcy. See *In re Melton* [1918] 1 Ch. 37; *Willes* v. *Greenhill (No. 1)* (1860) 29 Beav. 376; *In re Whitehouse* (1887) 37 Ch. D 683; *In re Watson* [1896] 1 Ch. 925. After the execution of the deeds the Association had a right to participate and also a contingent obligation to contribute.

[178] See *In re Sass; ex parte National Provincial Bank of England, Ltd.* [1896] 2 QB 12.

[179] [1918] 1 Ch. 37.   [180] Swinfen Eady, Warrington and Scrutton L.JJ.

[181] Overruling *In re Binns; Lee* v. *Binns* [1896] 2 Ch. 584.

that reason his judgment is not entirely satisfactory. In his view, *Cherry* v. *Boultbee* conferred upon the surety's executors the right to retain the debtor's entitlement, and to use it to satisfy the claim for an indemnity under the guarantee. This was an equity that came into existence at the date of the death, so that the amount necessary to make good the claim never formed part of the debtor's estate.[182] The approach of Scrutton L.J., on the other hand, conformed with the preferred analysis of *Cherry* v. *Boultbee.* As he remarked, 'how in any way does it infringe the rule against double proof that, when the bankrupt claims his share, the representatives of the surety should say, "Certainly, but you must ascertain your share in the proper way"?'[183] The principal debtor in *Melton* was entitled to a percentage of the residuary estate. The real value of the residue was the sum actually held by the executors in their hands, plus the debt owing to the fund. There was no infringement of the rule against double proof, because it was not a question of the debtor's estate being called upon to pay twice in respect of the same debt. Rather, the surety's executors were acknowledging their obligation to pay the debtor's share, but in paying that share they were exercising their right to take into account that the debtor already held an asset forming a part of the fund. Swinfen Eady L.J. expressed his conclusion in similar terms.[184]

Fenton and *Melton* differed in that, in *Melton*, the creditor had already received a dividend from the principal debtor's estate, whereas in *Fenton* the rule against double proof was said to be relevant because the creditor was still possessed of a right to prove in the principal debtor's bankruptcy for the full value of the debt. However, there is no substance in this distinction. Wood has sought to explain the different results on another ground.[185] In *Melton* it appears that the creditor had been fully paid,[186] whereas this was not the case in *Fenton*. Because the creditor had been fully paid, the surety's estate would have been subrogated to the creditor's proof in the debtor's bankruptcy,[186a] and Wood has suggested that the debtor's legacy could have been 'retained' in respect of this proof, up to the amount of the proof less any dividends paid to the creditor, as opposed to in respect of the surety's own right to an indemnity. However, this is not the basis upon which the Court of Appeal decided the case. The reasoning of the Court proceeded along the lines that the rule against double proof was irrelevant to *Cherry* v. *Boultbee* given the nature of the right that arises under it, rather than that the rule against double proof did not apply to

[182] See Warrington L.J.'s judgment at [1918] 1 Ch. 37, 55–6.
[183] [1918] 1 Ch. 37, 61.
[184] See the last sentence of his judgment at [1918] 1 Ch. 37, 54.
[185] Wood, *English and International Set-off* (1989), 440–1.
[186] Compare Warrington L.J. at [1918] 1 Ch. 37, 55.
[186a] See section 4.3.2. above.

prevent the operation of *Cherry* v. *Boultbee* in the particular case before it because the estate in any event had the benefit of the creditor's proof by way of subrogation. It was not crucial that the creditor was fully paid. Certainly, as Swinfen Eady L.J. emphasized in *Melton*,[187] the fact that a surety's claim for an indemnity is not provable does not mean that nothing is owing to him for the purpose of *Cherry* v. *Boultbee*. The judgments in *Fenton* and *Melton* in fact are difficult to reconcile. The reasoning of Scrutton L.J. in *Melton* should be preferred over that of Luxmoore J. in *Fenton*.

Subsequently Clauson J. in *In re Lennard; Lennard's Trustee* v. *Lennard*[188] followed *Melton*, without mentioning *Fenton*. The facts in *Lennard* were similar to those in *Melton*, though the case illustrates the further proposition that the surety's executors cannot discharge the surety's obligation as guarantor in a more liberal manner than is strictly necessary, and expect to be able to charge the overpayment as against the principal debtor's trustee in bankruptcy. The guarantee was in respect of an annuity. The creditor valued the annuity, and proved in the debtor's bankruptcy for that value. However, the surety's executors ignored the fact of the proof altogether. They made a number of payments to the creditor, and then purchased another annuity for her. Clauson J. held that the executors could exercise their rights under *Cherry* v. *Boultbee* against the principal debtor's right to share in the residue, but only to the extent of the difference between the value placed on the annuity in the bankruptcy and the dividend paid on that value, as opposed to the full amount actually paid in instalments and in purchasing a new annuity. Because the creditor had elected to value the annuity and to prove in the bankruptcy, the surety's executors were entitled to pay the creditor the amount of the valuation and to take over the proof. This would have discharged the surety's estate from further liability under the contract of suretyship. In so far as they had spent a larger sum than was strictly necessary, they could not employ *Cherry* v. *Boultbee* in respect of the surplus.

It may be that the sum brought into account by the representatives of the surety's estate under *Cherry* v. *Boultbee*, together with any dividend paid to the creditor, is greater than the principal debt itself. In such a case Scrutton L.J. in *Melton*[189] said that, 'If in the end it turns out that the debtor has paid more than 20s. in the pound he will get this overpayment back from either the principal creditors or the representatives of the surety. If in the end it turns out that the creditors have got more than 20s. in the pound the surplus will be returned to the surety or the debtor, whichever ought to have it'.

---

[187] [1918] 1 Ch. 37, 50–1.   [188] [1934] 1 Ch. 235.
[189] [1918] 1 Ch. 37, 61.

10.11 WAIVER AND PROOF OF DEBT

Cherry v. *Boultbee* may not be invoked if the person entitled to participate in the fund has been released from his liability to contribute as a result of an order of discharge from bankruptcy.[190] In addition, the administrator of the fund is denied recourse to the rule if he has already proved the debt in the bankruptcy and received a dividend[191] or, if the fund is entitled to be subrogated to someone else's proof,[192] if the administrator elects to rely on that proof.[193] The leading case is *Stammers* v. *Elliott*,[194] in which Lord Chelmsford said: 'If [the executor], therefore, proves a debt under a bankruptcy . . . the debt must be held to be satisfied'.[195] However, the notion that proof constitutes payment or satisfaction of the debt[196] requires an explanation. The Court of Appeal[197] in *In re West Coast Gold Fields, Ltd.; Rowe's Trustee's Claim*[198] said, 'No doubt it is true that proof deprives the creditor of any other remedy against the debtor or his estate, and in that sense proof is payment'.[199] Similarly, Lord Westbury once remarked that, 'Proof against a bankrupt's estate is payment in this sense, that the party making proof could not afterwards have a personal remedy against the bankrupt'.[200] Proof does not constitute payment in an absolute sense so that, as in the *West Coast Gold Fields* case, the mere fact that a company in voluntary liquidation has received a dividend in a share-holder's bankruptcy for a call in relation to partly paid shares does not mean that the shares are considered to be fully paid for the purpose of a distribution of the surplus assets of the company.[201] Rather, these

---

[190] See e.g. *In re Akerman* [1891] 3 Ch. 212, 217, and generally section 10.5 above.

[191] *Stammers* v. *Elliott* (1868) LR 3 Ch. App. 195; *In re Watson* [1896] 1 Ch. 925, 933; *Armstrong* v. *Armstrong* (1871) LR 12 Eq. 614. See also *In re Kent County Gas Light and Coke Company, Limited* [1913] 1 Ch. 92. Nevertheless, the administrator in some cases may be able to withdraw the proof before a dividend has been received, and rely instead on *Cherry* v. *Boultbee*. See *In re Dicken; ex parte Dicken* (1817) Buck 115, as explained in *In re Sewell* [1909] 1 Ch. 806, 809.

[192] For example, when the testator guaranteed a beneficiary's debts, and the estate has paid the creditor under the guarantee.

[193] *In re Whitehouse* (1887) 37 Ch. D 683.

[194] (1868) LR 3 Ch. App. 195.   [195] (1868) LR 3 Ch. App. 195, 200.

[196] See e.g. *Ex parte Hornby; in re Tarleton* (1817) Buck 351, 354 ('proof is equivalent to payment').   [197] Vaughan Williams, Stirling and Cozens-Hardy L.JJ.

[198] [1906] 1 Ch. 1.

[199] [1906] 1 Ch. 1, 8, referred to with evident approval in *In re Hurburgh* [1959] Tas. SR 25, 41–2.   [200] *Ewart* v. *Latta* (1865) 4 Macq. 983, 990.

[201] The court appeared to accept ([1906] 1 Ch. 1, 8, and see also Buckley J. at first instance [1905] 1 Ch. 597, 602) that the holders of the other shares which were in fact fully paid were alone entitled to share in the surplus assets until the amount paid on their shares was reduced to that which in fact had been paid on the bankrupt's shares.

observations may be interpreted to mean that the creditor, by proving, in effect abandons any other remedies that he has against the debtor.[202]

The conduct of the administrator in proving in the bankruptcy could only be said to constitute an abandonment of his right to invoke *Cherry* v. *Boultbee* if in fact the debt could have been satisfied by means of the rule had the administrator decided not to prove. This would not be the case, however, if the sole asset of the estate was the debt owing by the bankrupt because, until the debt had been enforced, there would not have been any fund in respect of which the rule could have been invoked. This may be said to provide a possible explanation for the decisions in cases such as *Ex parte Turpin; in re Brown*.[203] *Turpin* concerned a husband who, upon his marriage, gave a bond for £3,000 to trustees to be settled upon trust for himself for life, with the remainder to the wife and children. The husband became bankrupt without ever having paid anything under the bond, and so the trustees proved and obtained a dividend on this debt. It was held that the husband's assignees in bankruptcy were not entitled to the income received by the trustees on the dividend during the husband's life, but rather the trustees could retain and accumulate the income until the full debt of £3,000 had been realized.[204] The problem is that there is nothing in the judgments in these cases to indicate that they were based upon the ground suggested above, and indeed later cases seem to support the view that the same result would have ensued if the trustees in any event had been possessed of a fund at the time that they lodged a proof in respect of the debt.[205] There was no mention of this line of cases in *Stammers* v. *Elliott*,[206] although there is nevertheless a basis for distinguishing them.[207]

---

[202] Crawford J. in *In re Hurburgh* [1959] Tas. SR 25, 41–2 noted that a secured creditor who proves his debt loses the benefit of his security, and so he concluded that *Cherry* v. *Boultbee* similarly must take effect as a right in security. However, there is no apparent reason why the rule may not be explained instead on the basis of an abandonment of a personal right against the debtor available to the fund.   [203] (1832) Mont. 443.

[204] See also *Ex parte Young; in re Prior* (1835) 4 Deac. & Ch. 645 (explaining *Ex parte Shute; in re Shute* (1833) 3 Deac. & Ch. 1); *Ex parte Crofts; in re Last & Casey* (1837) 2 Deac. 102 (in which the debtor in fact was jointly and severally, and not just jointly, liable); *Re Walter; ex parte Walter's Assignees* (1859) 32 LTOS 396. In addition see *Ex parte King; in re Severn* (1835) 1 Deac. 143, though it is not clear whether the fund in that case consisted of anything other than the dividends.

[205] See *Ex parte Smith; in re Manning* (1836) 1 Deac. 385, and note also *Ex parte Gonne; in re March* (1837) 6 LJ Bcy. 57. In *Fuller* v. *Knight* (1843) 6 Beav. 205 a trustee acted in breach of trust in lending part of the trust fund to the tenant for life. The tenant for life subsequently executed a creditor's deed, to which the trustee was a party, which provided for his assets, including his interest under the settlement, to be applied in payment of certain debts. It was held that the trustee nevertheless should not be prevented from applying the income otherwise available to the life tenant to make good the breach of trust. The agreement embodied in the creditor's deed could not be brought forward in order to prevent the trustee from acting to remedy his breach of trust.   [206] (1868) LR 3 Ch. App. 195.

[207] The distinction that Lord Chelmsford in *Stammers* v. *Elliott* (1868) LR 3 Ch. App. 195, 200 did draw between an executor and a trustee should be regarded as doubtful. See Parker J. in *In re Sewell* [1909] 1 Ch. 806, 809.

In *Stammers* v. *Elliott*, and the cases following it, the obligation to contribute took the form of a debt that arose independently of the terms of the trust governing the fund. In the *Turpin* line of cases, however, the obligation to contribute to the settlement was undertaken as part of the terms of the settlement itself, so that both the liability to contribute and the right to participate were a part of the same transaction. Equity in this latter situation is more rigorous in ensuring that the estate of the bankrupt does not derive any benefit from the trust until the bankrupt's liability has been satisfied in full.[208] In other words, 'the Court, on looking at the settlement, and finding that the bankrupt had not fulfilled the covenants of the settlement, says, No, if you come here for equity, you must do equity first; and the Court will retain the dividend until the deficiency has been supplied'.[209]

There is a further exception to the principle that proof constitutes a waiver of the right to invoke the rule. In two early nineteenth century cases,[210] the bank in which the proceeds of a bankrupt's estate had been deposited itself became bankrupt. The bank was also a creditor of the bankrupt. It was held in each case that the bank was not entitled to receive a dividend on that debt until its liability to the estate had been paid *in toto*. This was not affected by a proof lodged in the bank's bankruptcy. The bank remained liable to contribute the residue of its indebtedness, after paying a dividend to the bankrupt's estate, before it could exercise its own right to participate in that bankruptcy in respect of the debt owing to it. This same principle has been held to apply in the case of an assignee in bankruptcy who was also a creditor of the bankrupt, and who himself became bankrupt after having received proceeds of the estate.[211]

10.12 ASSIGNMENTS

10.12.1 *The general principle*

The leading authority on the effect of an assignment upon rights under *Cherry* v. *Boultbee* is *Stephens* v. *Venables (No. 1)*.[212] The case concerned a residuary legatee who charged all his interest under his father's will. When the chargee (or, as he was called in the judgment, the mortgagee) claimed the legacy after the completion of the administration, Sir John

---

[208] However, *Cherry* v. *Boultbee* should no longer be available once the bankrupt is discharged from bankruptcy so that he is released from his debt. See *In re Sewell* [1909] 1 Ch. 806, 808 (defaulting trustee's debt released by composition), and section 10.5 above.
[209] *Ex parte Gonne* (1837) 6 LJ Bcy. 57, 59 per Erskine CJ (*arguendo*).
[210] *Ex parte Bebb* (1812) 19 Ves. Jun. 222; *Ex parte Graham* (1814) 3 V & B 130.
[211] *Ex parte Bignold; In re Charles* (1817) 2 Madd. 470.
[212] (1862) 30 Beav. 625.

Romilly held that his rights should be determined by the same principle applied in the case of a set-off,[213] so that he should take subject to equities in existence at the date that the trustee received notice of the assignment.[214]

When a trustee or executor receives notice that a legatee has charged his legacy in favor of a stranger, the trustee is bound to withhold all further payments to that legatee, unless made with the consent of the mortgagee of the legacy. All rights of set-off and adjustment of equities between the legatee and the executor already existing at the date of the notice have priority over the charge, and may properly be deducted from the amount coming to the mortgagee; but the trustees can create no new charge or right of set off after that time. A debt due to the trustees before the notice of charge received by him may be set off against the share of the legatee, but no debt which accrued due subsequently to that period can be allowed to work any deduction from the share charged to the mortgagee.[215]

Where the equity arises *after* notice the assignee generally will take free of it, although this is subject to an exception arising in the case of a defaulting trustee or executor, including in relation to a liability to pay costs to the estate. This exception is discussed below.[216] In this regard, if a beneficiary who is not also a trustee or executor becomes liable to the estate for costs incurred after notice of the assignment, the assignee will not be subject to a deduction unless he stood by and allowed the costs to be incurred under circumstances where he could have prevented this happening.[217]

Sir John Romilly spoke in terms of a trustee. It is important, however, to note that at the date of the assignment of the interest in the residuary estate the administration had not been completed.[218] Consequently the assignment did not involve an existing equitable interest under a trust. All that the residuary legatee was entitled to was 'a chose in action, capable of being invoked for any purpose connected with the proper administration of his estate'.[219] In other words, the subject of the assignment in equity was only a presently existing chose in action against the executor, together with

---

[213] Indeed, the Master of the Rolls referred to rights of 'set-off' in his judgment, although rights under *Cherry* v. *Boultbee* in fact were in issue. Of course, the obligation to contribute should not have ceased to exist when the right to participate becomes due and payable. See e.g. *In re Baird* [1935] NZLR 847, and section 10.5 above.

[214] While the case concerned a charge, which does not involve an assignment as such, the same principle applies as for an assignment, in the sense that the chargee takes subject to equities (see section 13.3.1 below), and so for convenience in the ensuing discussion the charge is referred to as an assignment.   [215] (1862) 30 Beav. 625, 627.

[216] See section 10.13 below.

[217] *In re Pain; Gustavson* v. *Haviland* [1919] 1 Ch. 38. See section 10.9 above.

[218] This appears more clearly from the report of subsequent proceedings in *Stephens* v. *Venables (No. 2)* (1862) 31 Beav. 124.

[219] *Commissioner of Stamp Duties (Queensland)* v. *Livingston* [1965] AC 694, 717 (PC).

the right to receive the fruits of that chose in action when they matured.[220] Consider a case in which an existing equitable interest under a trust is indeed assigned. There is a competing equitable principle, that an assignee of an equitable interest takes subject to any prior equities,[221] although the court will not interfere with his title if he is a purchaser of the equitable interest for valuable consideration without notice of the prior equity.[222] This differs from the statement of the law in *Stephens* v. *Venables*, and the principle applied in the case of set-off, in two respects. This competing equitable principle allows an exception of purchaser for value without notice, and in addition the dividing line is the date of the assignment as opposed to the date that notice is given of the assignment. Invariably it is stated in terms of an equitable estate or interest in land. However, as a matter of principle there would appear to be a sound reason for distinguishing between an assignment of a personal chose in action and an assignment of a beneficial interest in a trust. The rule that an equitable assignee of a chose in action takes subject to equities in existence at the date of notice is based upon the notion that the assignee steps into the shoes of the assignor.[223] The subject of the assignment is not specific property, but rather the personal rights possessed by the assignor himself against the other party, together with the fruits of those rights. Consequently the general rule is that the assignee is bound by all equities and defences available against the assignor whose personal rights he is enforcing,[224] though, as an exception, equity will not allow the debtor to diminish the rights of the assignee by relying on events occurring after he has already become aware of the assignment.[225] For this reason the date of notice to the debtor is the important date. On the other hand, the subject of an assignment of an equitable interest in a trust is not just the assignor's

---

[220] *In re Leigh's Will Trusts* [1970] 1 Ch. 277, 282.

[221] For this competing equitable principle, the prior equity should be 'ancillary to or dependent upon' an equitable title. An equity that is purely personal between the original parties will not suffice. See Lord Upjohn in *National Provincial Bank Ltd.* v. *Ainsworth* [1965] AC 1175, 1238. This would probably encompass *Cherry* v. *Boultbee*. The administrator of the fund says that the person claiming a right to participate already has an asset of the fund in his own hands, and therefore his right to participate is satisfied.

[222] *Phillips* v. *Phillips* (1861) 4 De G F & J 208, 218; *Westminster Bank Ld.* v. *Lee* [1956] 1 Ch. 7. Note that a disposition of an equitable interest or trust subsisting at the time of the disposition must be in writing. See the Law of Property Act 1925, s. 53(1)(c). In Australia see e.g. the Property Law Act 1958 (Vic.), s. 53(1)(c).

[223] Tudsbery, *Equitable Assignments* (1912), 87.

[224] Compare the case of a statutory assignment under the Law of Property Act 1925, s. 136(1). If the requirements of the section are satisfied, the legal right to the debt is transferred. See *Read* v. *Brown* (1888) 22 QBD 128, 132. However, the date of notice is still the dividing line. While the assignee takes subject to equities, notice is essential for the validity of this statutory assignment.

[225] *Roxburghe* v. *Cox* (1881) 17 Ch. D 520, 526, and generally section 13.2.1 below.

personal rights, but also a share of a specific fund. A proprietary interest in the fund is assigned. The assignee may rely upon his own equitable title, as opposed to that of the assignor. Moreover, the assignee of an equitable interest in a trust becomes the beneficiary as soon as the assignment takes place. Notice may be important for the question whether the trustee may discharge his obligation by tendering payment to the assignor. However, notice is not necessary in order to perfect the title of the assignee.[226] Consequently, as from the time of the assignment, the assignee's interest in the trust is based upon his own title, and not that of the assignor, and so anything that occurs after the assignment between the trustee and the assignor should not affect his title. There is indeed some support for this distinction. In *Houlditch* v. *Wallace*[227] an estate was conveyed by its owner to trustees upon trust to pay to himself an annual sum, and to pay the surplus rent to his creditors in satisfaction of his debts. Subsequently he assigned a part of his right to the annuity by way of security. Both before and after the assignment he appropriated income of the estate in excess of the annual sum payable to him. Lord Cottenham looked at the date of the assignment as the dividing line. He held that the assignee should take free from any equity that the owner's creditors, as the other trust beneficiaries, would otherwise have had, to make a deduction from the annual payments in respect of the sums misappropriated *after* the assignment. Moreover, apart from the laches of the creditors,[228] the question whether there could have been a deduction from future payments under the annuity in respect of funds misappropriated *before* the assignment was thought to depend upon whether the assignee had notice of the equity.[229] This seems to indicate that the exception of purchaser for value without notice was thought to be relevant. Similarly, in 1864 in Ireland Sir Thomas Smith M.R. in *Kilworth* v. *Mountcashel*[230] adopted a statement in *Lewin on Trusts*[231] to the effect that, if a tenant for life or other person having a partial interest has been an actor in a breach of trust, all the benefit that would have accrued to him from the trust fund may be retained against

---

[226] *Ward* v. *Duncombe* [1893] AC 369, 392.   [227] (1838) 5 Cl. & Fin. 629.

[228] See section 10.9 above.

[229] The assignee argued that the assignor had reserved an interest in the land in the form of a rent-charge, and that this was the subject of the assignment. However, counsel for the creditors denied that there was a rent-charge, and indeed there was no mention of it by Lord Cottenham, who merely talked in terms of a conveyance of land by the owner to trustees upon trust to pay himself an annual sum. In any event, the Lord Chancellor's discussion of *Priddy* v. *Rose* (1817) 3 Mer. 86 supports the view that this competing equitable principle under discussion was thought to be relevant to an interest in a trust fund. *Priddy* v. *Rose* concerned a tenant for life of a trust fund who had charged his interest. Lord Cottenham (at (1838) 5 Cl. & Fin. 629, 669) distinguished it from the case before him on the ground that the chargees had had notice of the prior equity.   [230] (1864) 15 Ir. Ch. Rep. 565.

[231] See now *Lewin on Trusts* (16th edn., 1964), 675.

him, and also against those claiming under him, except where the defence of purchaser for valuable consideration without notice is applicable. It was held that a judgment creditor is not a purchaser, and consequently is not entitled to the benefit of this exception. In *Cloutte* v. *Storey*[232] Neville J. at first instance seemed prepared to countenance that the equitable principle applied to an estate or interest in land may also be relevant to an interest in a trust fund, and there is also support for this conclusion in *Irby* v. *Irby (No. 3)*,[233] a case decided by Sir John Romilly M.R. some 4 years before his judgment in *Stephens* v. *Venables*. Herbert de Crespigny was a beneficiary under his father's marriage settlement. He was also in default in his capacity of executor of his father's will, which gave rise to a right in the trustees to impound his entitlement under the settlement. The Master of the Rolls said[234] that 'this equity would be good against all persons who had taken an assignment of a charge upon Herbert de Crespigny's share, after having had notice of the claim of the trustees upon him'. The case concerned an equitable interest under a trust, and prior notice would only have been important if the defence of purchaser of an equitable interest for value without notice was relevant. Nevertheless, the weight of opinion favours the view that the principle applied in the case of an assignment of a personal chose in action is also relevant when a chose in equity, in the form of an equitable interest in a trust fund, is assigned.[235] The courts, and also text-writers, in expounding this view have failed to consider the difference between an assignment of a personal chose in action and an assignment of an equitable proprietary interest in a fund, or to consider the cases suggesting that the equitable priorities rule applying in the case of an assignment of an equitable estate or interest in land may also be relevant to trust funds.

---

[232] [1911] 1 Ch. 18, 24.   [233] (1858) 25 Beav. 632.
[234] (1858) 25 Beav. 632, 638.
[235] See *Phipps* v. *Lovegrove* (1873) LR 16 Eq. 80, 88; *Cumming* v. *Austin* (1902) 28 VLR 347, affirmed (1903) 28 VLR 622; *In re Pain; Gustavson* v. *Haviland* [1919] 1 Ch. 38 (esp. at 46); *Southern British National Trust Ltd.* v. *Pither* (1937) 57 CLR 89, 105 per Rich J; *White & Tudor's Leading Cases in Equity* (9th edn., 1928) Vol. 1, 136 (referred to with evident approval by Latham C.J. in *Pither* (at 102)); *Halsbury's Laws of England* (4th edn. (Reissue), 1991) Vol 6, 41 para. 61, 44 para. 66; *Withers on Reversions* (2nd edn., 1933), 239 (though neither of the cases cited in *Withers* as authority for this proposition in fact concerned an equitable interest in a trust, or indeed commented upon an assignment of such an interest). See also *Cockell* v. *Taylor* (1852) 15 Beav. 103, 118. In *Underhill's Law relating to Trusts and Trustees* (14th edn., 1987), 805 the principle that a bona fide purchaser of the interest of a trustee/beneficiary in default takes subject to a deduction to make good the default, even when the purchaser is without notice, is explained by the notion that 'the equitable interest in question was a chose in action, and purchasers of choses in action take subject to all equities'. In fact, the defaulting trustee cases have been explained on either of two grounds, neither of which is based on the principle that a purchaser of a chose in action takes subject to all equities. See section 10.13 below. The second of these grounds, regarding a payment in advance, would also explain *Dibbs* v. *Goren* (1849) 11 Beav. 483. See *Livesey* v. *Livesey* (1827) 3 Russ. 287, 296.

10.12.2 *Presently existing rights and obligations*

It is not necessary that the right to participate and the obligation to contribute should be presently payable at the date of notice, if indeed they are existing at that date. The administrator may not actually appropriate an obligation to contribute as payment of a right to participate until that right has become due and payable. Yet he will not be denied the right to invoke the rule against an assignee of the right to participate merely because the right was still only a right in reversion when the administrator received notice of the assignment,[236] or it was otherwise still contingent.[237]

10.12.3 *Contingent obligation to contribute*

In order that a debtor may be allowed a *set-off* against an assignee of his indebtedness in respect of a debt owing to him by the assignor, it is not regarded as sufficient that the debtor's claim against the assignor arose after notice as a result of a contract entered into before notice.[238] This notion is criticized in the discussion of assignments in relation to set-off[239] on the ground that the existence of a right of set-off should depend on when the debtor and the assignor entered into a binding contract, as opposed to when a debt arose as a result of that contract. This should also be the case for *Cherry* v. *Boultbee*. However, *Stephens* v. *Venables (No. 1)*[240] supports the view that the operation of *Cherry* v. *Boultbee* is indeed subject to a similar restriction. The case concerned a legatee who was granted a lease of part of the testator's property for a period of 21 years by the executors and trustees of the will. Subsequently he charged his right to the legacy, and notice of the charge was given to the trustees. When the legacy became payable, Sir John Romilly M.R. held that the trustees could invoke the rule in respect of the rent due from the legatee up to the date of notice, but that the chargees in enforcing their security took free from the legatee's indebtedness for rent arising after notice.[241] It made no difference that the liability for this rent was based upon an obligation incurred under a lease entered into before notice. Sir John Romilly, in

---

[236] See *Willes* v. *Greenhill (No. 1)* (1860) 29 Beav. 376; *In re Batchelor; Sloper* v. *Oliver* (1873) LR 16 Eq. 481, 484. Before any actual appropriation the right must be payable. See section 10.5 above.

[237] See *In re Batchelor* (1873) LR 16 Eq. 481, 483–4, and also *In re Hurburgh* [1959] Tas. SR 25, 31, 40.

[238] *Watson* v. *Mid Wales Railway Company* (1867) LR 2 CP 593, and see also *Business Computers Ltd.* v. *Anglo-African Leasing Ltd.* [1977] 1 WLR 578.

[239] See section 13.2.4 below.

[240] (1862) 30 Beav. 625. See also *In re Pain; Gustavson* v. *Pain* [1919] 1 Ch. 38, 47–8.

[241] See also *Hill* v. *Hicken* [1897] 2 Ch. 579.

holding that only debts arising before notice could be taken into account, said[242] 'Were it otherwise, the charge made by the legatee, whether residuary or pecuniary, would be worth nothing, the trustees might, after the receipt of notice of the charge, embark in a speculation with the legatee, and if, in the course of it, a balance accrued due to the trustee from the legatee, he might set it off against the legacy, and leave the mortgagee with nothing'. However this would not be a valid objection when the debt, though only arising after notice, in fact is based upon a contract already entered into before notice. Furthermore, it is not easy to reconcile *Stephens* v. *Venables* with other cases which support the proposition that trustees appointed under a will may make a deduction as against an assignee of a share of the residuary estate in respect of the assignor's obligation to indemnify the testator's estate for a sum paid on the assignor's behalf under a contract of suretyship, even though the trustees tendered payment to the creditor after they had received notice of the assignment. In other words, the liability of the legatee/assignor was only contingent at the date of notice, and the essence of a contingent liability is that there is no actual liability in existence until the occurrence of the event upon which the contingency depends, in this case payment by the surety's estate to the creditor. Curiously, the first of these cases is an earlier decision of Sir John Romilly himself. In *Willes* v. *Greenhill (No. 1)*,[243] the testator was a surety on two promissory notes for a legatee to whom the testator had bequeathed a reversionary share in his residuary estate. The testator's death occurred before the notes became payable. Subsequently the trustees of the estate paid the creditor on the notes, although prior to this the legatee had assigned his right in reversion to the legacy by way of mortgage to one of the trustees. This particular trustee, as assignee, obviously had notice of the assignment, and Sir John Romilly held that the notice that he had also constituted notice to the other trustees. Apparently it was not considered to be an objection to the trustees' right to invoke *Cherry* v. *Boultbee* against the assignee who was seeking to enforce the security when the legacy became payable, that the assignor's liability to indemnify the estate for the sum paid on his behalf was only contingent at the date of the assignment, and therefore at the date of notice. Admittedly the question in *Willes* v. *Greenhill* arose in the context of a priorities dispute between two mortgages, the legatee subsequently also having mortgaged the legacy to the trustees generally in order to secure the moneys to be paid on his behalf on the two notes. In the case of successive assignments, priority depends on which of the assignees first gives notice to the debtor. The Master of the Rolls, in following

---

[242] (1862) 30 Beav. 625, 627–8.   [243] (1860) 29 Beav. 376.

Browne v. *Savage*,[244] said that it was in the interest of the single trustee taking the first mortgage to disclose the mortgage to his fellow trustees in order to obtain priority over any subsequent assignments, and so it could be assumed that in fact he had done this. Consequently, it was held that his mortgage should have priority over the subsequent mortgage to the trustees generally. However, this same reasoning should also have been relevant to the priorities dispute between the mortgage to the single trustee and the right of the trustees generally to invoke *Cherry* v. *Boultbee*. In other words, it could be assumed that the trustees had notice of the assignment, and yet this did not preclude them from invoking *Cherry* v. *Boultbee* against the assignee even though the assignor's obligation to contribute was still contingent at the date of notice. *Willes* v. *Greenhill* is consistent in this regard with the principle applied in the case of a bankrupt legatee/principal debtor. The fact that a sum is paid on the legatee's behalf after the bankruptcy, but under a contract of suretyship entered into by the testator before the bankruptcy, will not deprive the executors of the right to invoke the rule against the bankrupt's estate.[245] Similarly, it does not seem to be an objection to the operation of the rule that an assignment may have taken place when the *right to participate* was still only contingent.[246]

Reference also may be made to the Court of Appeal decision in *In re Melton*,[247] which has already been discussed above in the context of suretyship and the rule against double proof.[248] There are certain additional facts, however, which should be noted. The principal debtor in *Melton* in fact had mortgaged his interest in the legacy to the creditor after the testator's death, but before his own bankruptcy. Notice of the mortgage was given to the surety's executors *before* any payment had been made by the executors to the creditor. The creditor had valued this security, and had only proved in the debtor's bankruptcy for the balance of the debt. Thus, the creditor retained the benefit of the security. After payment by the executors under the suretyship agreement, the creditor assigned the security to the appellant in order to obtain payment of the sum still outstanding on the principal debt.[249] The appellant, as assignee from the creditor, had no better title than the creditor itself had. It was held that the rule against double proof did not deprive the surety's executors of the right to invoke *Cherry* v. *Boultbee* in respect of the sum paid on behalf of the principal debtor. Implicit in this decision is that the fact that the principal debtor only had a contingent liability to indemnify the surety's

---

[244] (1859) 4 Drewry 635.

[245] See e.g. *In re Watson* [1896] 1 Ch. 925, and generally section 10.6 above.

[246] See *In re Batchelor* (1873) LR 16 Eq. 481, 483–4, and also *In re Hurburgh* [1959] Tas. SR 25, 31, 40.   [247] [1918] 1 Ch. 37.

[248] See section 10.10 above.

[249] See Warrington L.J. at [1918] 1 Ch. 37, 55.

estate at the time of notice was not considered to be an objection to the operation of the rule.

Wood[250] has sought to explain *Willes* v. *Greenhill* and *Melton* on the ground that in both cases the beneficiary who assigned the interest was also an executor. In the context of assignments, special rules indeed apply to trustees and executors who are entitled to participate in the estate but who have defaulted in the performance of their duties.[251] An assignee of the trustee's or the executor's interest takes subject to a deduction for an amount required to remedy the default even where the default occurred after notice of the assignment. The basis of this principle is default in the performance of a fiduciary obligation, and an assignee from a trustee takes the risk that this may later occur.[252] However, in neither of these cases was there any question of default of this nature, and so the fact that the beneficiary assigning the interest also happened to be an executor should not have been relevant.

It is difficult to see why *Cherry* v. *Boultbee* should have been available in cases such as *Willes* v. *Greenhill* and *In re Melton*, in which the debtor's liability to the fund arose after notice of the assignment but as a result of a contract of suretyship entered into before notice, but that it should not be available in a case such as *Stephens* v. *Venables*, where the indebtedness for rent only came into existence after notice, but as a result of a lease entered into before notice. Certainly *Stephens* v. *Venables* is consistent with the principle applied in the law of set-off,[253] while in the suretyship cases the fact that a liability only vested after the notice was not emphasized. The principle enunciated in *Stephens* v. *Venables* is generally regarded as representing the current state of the law.[254] Nevertheless, it does seem to constitute an unwarranted restriction on the operation of *Cherry* v. *Boultbee*, as well as on the right of set-off, and there is much to commend the view that the approach evidenced by the suretyship cases should be applied generally whenever a debt arises after notice but as a result of a contract entered into before notice.

10.12.4 *Costs in pending proceedings*

If a beneficiary of a trust commences a suit against a trustee and, while the proceedings are still pending, the beneficial interest is

---

[250] Wood, *English and International Set-off* (1989), 449–50.
[251] See section 10.13 below.
[252] See Isaacs J. in *Cock* v. *Aitken* (1912) 15 CLR 373, 384.
[253] Indeed, Sir John Romilly seemed to treat the case as one of set-off, although in truth rights under *Cherry* v. *Boultbee* were in issue.
[254] See e.g. *In re Milan Tramways Company; ex parte Theys* (1884) 25 Ch. D 587 (esp. Fry LJ at 594).

assigned, the assignee will take subject to an order for costs ultimately made against the beneficiary if the suit fails.[255] Where, however, the suit was commenced *after* the trustee was notified of the assignment, the assignee ordinarily will take free of a costs order made against the assignor, except to the extent of the trustee's usual right of indemnity out of the *entire* trust fund for all costs and expenses properly incurred by him in relation to the trust.[256] On the other hand, the assignee may lose his priority if he stands by and allows costs to be incurred that he could have prevented.[257]

10.12.5 *Assignee has obligation to contribute*

The assignee of a right to participate not only takes subject to equities available against the assignor, but also subject to equities available against himself. If the assignee himself is required to contribute to the fund, his obligation may be appropriated as payment of the right to participate when the right becomes due and payable.[258] It is true that Sir John Leach adopted the contrary view in *Campbell* v. *Graham*.[259] He said that, since the assignee of a legacy stands in the place of the assignor, there should not be a deduction in respect of a debt that the assignee himself owes, and on appeal Lord Brougham said that he saw no reason to differ from that view.[260] However, *Cherry* v. *Boultbee* is an equitable rule, and there is no apparent reason why a court of equity should not apply it as against the person with the equitable title to the right to participate.

10.12.6 *Agreement not to assert equities against assignees*

While an assignee of a chose in action generally takes subject to equities available to the debtor against the assignor, the debtor may contract with his creditor on terms that he will not avail himself against a transferee of any rights which he may possess against the creditor, or any assignee of the

---

[255] See *In re Pain; Gustavson* v. *Haviland* [1919] 1 Ch. 38, 48–9, explaining *In re Knapman; Knapman* v. *Wreford* (1881) 18 Ch. D 300. See also *In re Mayne; ex parte The Official Receiver* [1907] 2 KB 899, and *In re Jones; Christmas* v. *Jones* [1897] 2 Ch. 190 (esp. at 203–4).

[256] *In re Pain; Gustavson* v. *Haviland* [1919] 1 Ch. 38, 49, and see also Isaacs J. in the High Court of Australia in *Cock* v. *Aitken* (1912) 15 CLR 373, 383–4.

[257] *In re Pain; Gustavson* v. *Haviland* [1919] 1 Ch. 38.

[258] *Burridge* v. *Row* (1844) 13 LJ Ch. 173. See also Cotton L.J. in *In re Milan Tramways Company; ex parte Theys* (1884) 25 Ch. D 587, 592–3.

[259] (1831) 1 Russ. & M 453.

[260] *Campbell* v. *Sandford* (1834) 8 Bligh NS 622.

creditor. For example, debentures issued by a company may provide that the principal and interest secured by the debentures will be paid without regard to any equities between the company and the original or any intermediate holder of them. This clause will be effective in the winding-up of the company when there is a fund available for payment of the debentures, so that a registered transferee who is a bona fide purchaser for value should be entitled to receive the sum payable in the winding-up in respect of the debentures without any deduction under *Cherry* v. *Boultbee*.[261] On the other hand, it has been held that a transferee who is not a bona fide purchaser for value cannot rely on the clause.[262] In this regard, a trustee under a creditors' deed executed by the assignor has been held not to be a purchaser, so that he takes subject to equities available against the transferee notwithstanding that the debentures in question contained a clause to this effect.[263] Similarly, neither a trustee in bankruptcy nor a judgment creditor is considered to be a purchaser.[264]

10.12.7 *Successive assignments*

Consider that A, who has a right to participate in a fund, assigns that right to B, who in turn assigns it to C. The administrator of the fund should be entitled to invoke *Cherry* v. *Boultbee* in repect of an obligation that A has to contribute to the fund. However, the question may arise whether this would also be the case when B has the obligation to contribute. The issue of successive assignments is considered later in the context of assignments generally.[265]

10.13 DEFAULTING TRUSTEES AND EXECUTORS

'It has always been a rule of the Court of Chancery that, if a trustee misappropriates trust money, and has an equitable interest under the trust deed, the Court will not allow him to receive any part of the trust fund in which he is equitably interested under the trust until he has made good his

[261] *In re Goy & Co., Ltd. Farmer* v. *Goy & Co., Ltd.* [1900] 2 Ch. 149 (esp. at 153, where Stirling J. emphasized that the transfer was for value and in good faith, as to which see also *In re Blakely Ordnance Company* (1867) LR 3 Ch. App. 154, 159). *Aliter* if the debentures do not contain a clause to this effect. See *In re Rhodesia Goldfields, Ltd.* [1910] 1 Ch. 239.
[262] *In re Brown & Gregory, Ltd.; Shepheard* v. *Brown & Gregory, Ltd.* [1904] 1 Ch. 627, affirmed [1904] 2 Ch. 448.
[263] *In re Brown & Gregory, Ltd.* [1904] 1 Ch. 627, affirmed [1904] 2 Ch. 448.
[264] *Kilworth* v. *Mountcashell* (1864) 15 Ir. Ch. Rep. 565, 581; *In re Marquis of Anglesey* [1903] 2 Ch. 727, 732.
[265] See section 13.2.15 below.

default as trustee'.[266] One possible explanation for this principle is *Cherry* v. *Boultbee*. It could be said that the defaulting trustee or executor[267] is directed to satisfy his beneficial entitlement from the trust asset in his own hands in the form of his liability to compensate the trust for his breach. In fact, two slightly different formulations have been adopted. The principle is often called a right to impound, or stop, the beneficial interest of the defaulting trustee,[268] though in truth this is not an accurate description of either of these formulations. Moreover, both formulations have been said to give a wider remedy in the case of an assignment than that otherwise available against the assignee under *Cherry* v. *Boultbee*. An assignee only takes subject to equities in existence before notice. Yet the courts have said that there is no such limitation in the case of a defaulting trustee, so that the assignee of the trustee's beneficial interest under the trust will take subject to a possible deduction to the extent required to remedy the breach irrespective of whether the assignment occurred before or after default. This includes a trustee's liability to pay costs to the estate.[269] An important limitation, however, is that this extended principle in relation to assignments is only relevant when the assignor was a trustee or an executor *at the time of the assignment*. If the assignor subsequently becomes a trustee or an executor, and then defaults, it does not apply.[270] Moreover, it only applies when the obligation to contribute arises out of a default in the performance of a fiduciary duty.[271] It should not be relevant when its source is another transaction.[272]

---

[266] *In re Brown; Dixon* v. *Brown* (1886) 32 Ch. D 597, 600 per Kay J. In addition to the cases cited below, see *Skinner* v. *Sweet* (1818) 3 Madd. 244; *Woodyatt* v. *Gresley* (1836) 8 Sim. 180; *Staniar* v. *Evans* (1886) 34 Ch. D 470. Compare *Hallett* v. *Hallett* (1879) 13 Ch. D 232, in which the trustee's beneficial interest related to a trust which was separate and distinct from the settlement in respect of which he was in default.

[267] This same principle applies to a defaulting executor. See *Sims* v. *Doughty* (1800) 5 Ves. Jun. 243; *In re Dacre* [1916] 1 Ch. 344.

[268] See e.g. *Courtenay* v. *Williams* (1844) 3 Hare 539, 554; *Fox* v. *Buckley* (1876) 3 Ch. D 508, 509 per Little V.C. (at first instance).

[269] An assignee of a trustee's right to participate will take subject to a deduction in respect of costs payable by the trustee even if the assignment took place before the costs were incurred. However, this is not the case in the event of a beneficiary who is not also an executor or a trustee, and who is liable for costs incurred after an assignment of his interest. The assignee does not take subject to a deduction, except to the extent of the trustee's usual right to indemnity out of the entire trust fund for all costs and expenses properly incurred by him in relation to the trust. See *In re Pain; Gustavson* v. *Haviland* [1919] 1 Ch. 38, explaining *In re Knapman; Knapman* v. *Wreford* (1881) 18 Ch. D 300. See also Isaacs J. in *Cock* v. *Aitken* (1912) 15 CLR 373, 383–4. However, it was held in *In re Pain* that the assignee may lose his priority if he stands by and allows the assignor to incur costs that he could have prevented.

[270] *In re Pain; Gustavson* v. *Haviland* [1919] 1 Ch. 38, 47.

[271] See Isaacs J. in *Cock* v. *Aitken* (1912) 15 CLR 373, 384.

[272] Compare the discussion of *Willes* v. *Greenhill (No. 1)* (1860) 29 Beav. 376 and *In re Melton* [1918] 1 Ch. 37 in section 10.12.3 above.

The first formulation is set out in *Morris* v. *Livie*.[273] A person appointed trustee under a will committed a breach of trust after he had assigned a right that he had in reversion as a residuary legatee to participate in the trust. When the assignee later sought payment of the legacy, it was held that there should be a deduction in respect of the trustee's obligation to reimburse the trust for his breach. Knight Bruce V.C. said that the right to participate was intended to constitute consideration for, and be conditional upon, the trustee performing the duties of trustee. If the trustee acted in breach of trust, the right to participate could not be exercised until the breach had been remedied.

It may, I conceive, be properly said that [the trustee's] legacy was given under a condition raised and implied by law, that undertaking he should duly fulfil the duties and obligations imposed on him by the instrument giving it. This he could not do without performing the trust as to the stock legacy, which, before his own legacy became due, he had, by his own misconduct, disabled himself from performing. The condition, if existing, accompanied his legacy until its discharge, and applied to it as much after as before its assignment.[274]

Cherry v. *Boultbee* specifically contemplates the existence of a right to participate, but allows the administrator of the fund to appropriate a particular asset as payment of that right. However, it would seem that, under this *Morris* v. *Livie* formulation, the trustee's breach impugns his very entitlement to participate in the trust to the extent of the breach. Strictly, this is not a case of the trustee's interest being impounded. Rather, it is said that, in the event of a breach, the trustee does not have an interest. Since an assignee can only claim what the trustee himself could claim, the assignee should also take subject to any deduction necessary to remedy the breach, regardless of when the assignment may have taken place.

Morris v. *Livie* is not confined to the case of a trustee who is also a residuary legatee.[275] Rather, it has been cited as authority for the general proposition that 'every person taking an assignment from a *cestui que trust* of a portion of the testator's estate, at all events takes it subject to the liability to make good all breaches of trust on the part of the assignor if he

---

[273] (1842) 1 Y & C CC 380. See also *Wilkins* v. *Sibley* (1863) 4 Giff. 442, 445–6; *Cock* v. *Aitken* (1912) 15 CLR 373, 384; *In re Pain; Gustavson* v. *Haviland* [1919] 1 Ch. 38, 46–7.

[274] (1842) 1 Y & C CC 380, 388–9.

[275] Compare *Withers on Reversions* (2nd edn., 1933), 242. For example, the trustee in *Barnett* v. *Sheffield* (1852) 1 De G M & G 371 was entitled to a specific legacy in the form of an annuity, though because of a misappropriation of trust funds it was held that he could not demand that anything be paid to him under the annuity. Knight Bruce V.C. (at 382) described the annuity as 'a guarantee for a full account on his part as to all the transactions in which he as a trustee should be engaged in respect of the trust'.

fill the fiduciary position of a trustee, even though the breaches of trust be subsequent to the assignment'.[276] Nevertheless, *Morris* v. *Livie* should not be relevant if it is clear that the bequest is intended to be independent of the office of trustee.[277] Obviously, it could hardly be said in such a case that the bequest was conditional upon the trustee properly performing his duties. If so, it is difficult to explain the decision in *Re Hervey; Short* v. *Parratt*[278] on the basis of *Morris* v. *Livie*. The case concerned an intestacy. The administratrix was one of the next of kin of the intestate, and as such was entitled, after payment of the debts, to one moiety of the residue. She committed a breach of trust,[279] and so she could take nothing out of the personal estate until the amount which she was liable to replace had been made good. Prior to the default she had settled all her property by a covenant, which encompassed after-acquired property.[280] It was held, on the authority of *Morris* v. *Livie*, that the trustees of the settlement were subject to the same equity, even though the default occurred after the assignment. Yet it could hardly be said in an *intestacy* that the right of an administratrix to share in the residue was intended by the intestate to constitute consideration for her properly performing the duties of administratrix and trustee.

The second formulation of the principle in these defaulting trustee or executor cases is similar to, but is nonetheless distinct from, *Cherry* v. *Boultbee*. Rather than saying that the trustee's obligation to contribute should be appropriated as payment of the right to participate when that right becomes due and payable, it is said that the trustee is already deemed to have paid himself in advance, or in anticipation, from the money in his hands constituted by the misappropriated funds.[281] Strictly this is not a case of impounding the trust fund, because the trustee in fact is treated as if he has already had what he could claim.[282] It is not important for this

---

[276] *In re Knapman* (1881) 18 Ch. D 300, 307 per Hall V.C. It is not necessary that the defaulting trustee should be the only trustee of the trust. See *Barnett* v. *Sheffield* (1852) 1 De G M & G 371.

[277] See Little V.C. at first instance in *Fox* v. *Buckley* (1876) 3 Ch. D 508, 509. Compare *Barnett* v. *Sheffield* (1852) 1 De G M & G 371, in which the court rejected the argument that the will in that case specifically contemplated that the legacy should be paid despite any misappropriation. For a discussion of when a legacy may be said to be attached to the office of executor, see *Williams' Law Relating to Wills* (6th edn., 1987) Vol. 1, 211–12.

[278] (1889) 61 LT 429.

[279] An administrator of an intestate's estate becomes a trustee as soon as the administration is completed. See *In re Cockburn's Will Trusts* [1957] 1 Ch. 438, 439.

[280] The assignment of the beneficial interest would have become effective as soon as the trust was created and a beneficial interest was acquired. See *Palette Shoes Pty. Ltd.* v. *Krohn* (1937) 58 CLR 1, 27.

[281] *Irby* v. *Irby (No. 3)* (1858) 25 Beav. 632, 638; *In re Carew* [1896] 1 Ch. 527, 535; *Edgar* v. *Plomley* [1900] AC 431, 443: *In re Towndrow* [1911] 1 Ch. 662, 668; *In re Dacre* [1916] 1 Ch. 344; *BWG Management Ltd.* v. *Comm. for Corporate Affairs* [1985] VR 385, 398.

[282] *Jacubs* v. *Rylance* (1874) LR 17 Eq. 341, 342.

formulation that there should be any connection between the beneficial entitlement and the proper performance by the trustee of his duties. In this respect it is wider than *Morris v. Livie*.[283] For example, it applies even if the trustee acquired a beneficial interest only derivatively.[284] It has been said that it still applies when the breach of trust is committed after the assignment.[285] If indeed this were correct, it would justify a deduction in a case such as *Hervey*,[286] in which there was no connection between the office of trustee and the right to share in the trust. It is by no means obvious, however, that this second formulation would in fact allow a deduction in respect of a breach occurring after the assignment or, at any rate, if there are other trustees of the trust, after they received notice of the assignment. If a trustee has notice of an assignment of an equitable interest under the trust, he cannot discharge his obligation by paying the assignor. He must tender payment to the assignee.[287] This should also apply when the assignor himself is the trustee. Payment to himself after notice would not discharge the trust obligation to the assignee, and so it is difficult to see how a notion of a payment in advance to a defaulting trustee could bind the assignee if default occurred after notice. There must of course be a valid notice. When there are a number of trustees, an assignee may satisfy this obligation by giving notice to only one of the trustees of a trust, although the notice that the assignor/trustee obviously has is not considered to be sufficient for this purpose.[288] The assignee should protect his interest by giving notice to another trustee. Consider, however, that the assignor is a sole trustee. In the context of a priorities dispute under *Dearle v. Hall*[289] between successive assignees it has been said that notice to, or the knowledge possessed by, a sole assignor/trustee is not effective to alter priorities.[290] However, this should not apply when a question of payment is

---

[283] On the other hand, *Morris* v. *Livie* would still apply when the trustee personally has not derived any advantage from the breach, though *quaere* whether this second formulation would be relevant in that case. See *In re Pain; Gustavson* v. *Haviland* [1919] 1 Ch. 38, 46–7.
[284] *Jacubs* v. *Rylance* (1874) LR 17 Eq. 341; *Doering* v. *Doering* (1889) 42 Ch. D 203; *Cumming* v. *Austin* (1903) 28 VLR 622; *In re Dacre* [1916] 1 Ch. 344. See also *Brandon* v. *Brandon* (1859) 3 De G & J 524 with respect to the purchased shares.
[285] *Doering* v. *Doering* (1889) 42 Ch. D 203, 207; *Cumming* v. *Austin* (1903) 28 VLR 622; *In re Dacre* [1916] Ch. 344, 347. The Victorian Supreme Court in *Cumming* doubted that it would make any difference that the beneficiary assigned his equitable interest *before* he was actually appointed trustee, and subsequently he commits a defalcation. Compare in this regard *White & Tudor's Leading Cases in Equity* (9th edn., 1928) Vol. 1, 139, citing *Irby* v. *Irby (No. 3)* (1858) 25 Beav. 632, and see also *In re Pain; Gustavson* v. *Haviland* [1919] 1 Ch. 38, 47. *Quaere* whether the assignee would still take subject to a deduction if the trustees generally were notified of the assignment before the defalcation. See below.
[286] (1889) 61 LT 429.   [287] *Brice* v. *Bannister* (1878) 3 QBD 569.
[288] *Browne* v. *Savage* (1859) 4 Drewry 635; *Cumming* v. *Austin* (1902) 28 VLR 347, affirmed (1903) 28 VLR 622.   [289] (1828) 3 Russ. 1.
[290] *In re Dallas* [1904] 2 Ch. 385, and compare *Ipswich Permanent Money Club, Ltd.* v. *Arthy* [1920] 2 Ch. 257.

in issue. Notice is not necessary in order to perfect the title of the assignee. He becomes the trust beneficiary as from the date of the assignment.[291] A sole assignor/trustee could hardly discharge the trust obligation to the assignee by paying a complete stranger whom the trustee knows is not the beneficiary, and equally he should not be able to discharge that obligation by paying himself when he knows that he had ceased to be the beneficiary as from the time of the assignment. It would seem, then, that neither *Morris* v. *Livie* nor this second theory of a payment in advance offers a satisfactory explanation of why an assignee of a defaulting trustee's beneficial interest should take subject to a deduction to make good the breach, if as in *Hervey* the trustee's entitlement was not dependent upon the proper performance of the office of trustee, and moreover if the breach occurred after the trustees received notice of the assignment, or, in the case of a sole trustee, after the assignment itself.

One consequence of both formulations is that, unlike under *Cherry* v. *Boultbee*, it should not make any difference that the liability to contribute ceased to exist before the right to participate became due and payable, for example because of a discharge from bankruptcy, or as a result of a composition or scheme of arrangement. The discharge should not be relevant, because in any event the breach would mean that the right to participate has already been impugned (under *Morris* v. *Livie*), or it has already been satisfied by a notional payment in advance to the defaulting trustee.[292] Similarly, the fact of proving the debt and receiving a dividend in the bankruptcy should not constitute a waiver of the right to invoke *Morris* v. *Livie* either before or after discharge, since the trustee's right should still be impugned until such time as the default is remedied *in toto*. While *In re Sewell*[293] is authority to the contrary, the point may be made that Parker J. did not analyse the case in terms of the defaulting trustee formulations.

Cherry v. *Boultbee* only applies when a right to participate is for a sum of money. It is not available against a legatee entitled to a specific bequest of freeholds or leaseholds, or of chattels.[294] However, this restriction should not apply in the case of a defaulting executor or trustee, at least under *Morris* v. *Livie*. It is doubtful whether the second formulation would be of any assistance. If an executor or a trustee entitled to a specific bequest under a will misappropriates funds of the estate, the misapplied funds should not be considered to be a payment of the bequest in advance, because a person to whom specific property has been bequeathed could not claim instead a sum of money. Nevertheless, if the bequest was intended to

---

[291] *Ward* v. *Duncombe* [1893] AC 369, 392.
[292] Compare the comments of Parker J. in *In re Sewell; White* v. *Sewell* [1909] 1 Ch. 806, 808–9.   [293] [1909] 1 Ch. 806.   [294] See section 10.8 above.

be conditional upon the executor or trustee properly performing the duties ancillary to his office, failure to perform those duties should impugn the right to the bequest.[295] Admittedly there have been cases in which a trustee appointed under a will was given a life interest in realty, and it was held that this interest was not liable to be appropriated to make good deficiencies in the trust caused by his own breach.[296] However, this was because a devise of realty formerly took place outside the will, so that it was not bound by the trust.[297] Moreover, since the devise took place outside the will, it could not be said that it was connected with the office of trustee, so as to enable the court to presume that it constituted consideration for that person's agreement to act as trustee.[298] On the other hand, all property, whether real or personal, now passes to the personal representative, and so this old rule should no longer apply.[299]

The preceding discussion concerned the situation in which the defaulting trustee, or an assignee, seeks payment of the trustee's beneficial entitlement under the trust. The general principle is that neither the trustee nor an assignee may take anything out of the trust until the breach has been remedied. Consider the converse situation in which the defaulting trustee is bankrupt, and other trustees of the trust lodge a proof in the bankruptcy in respect of the breach. It would have been consonant with the principles already discussed to hold that the trustees may prove for the full amount of the breach, and also that the bankrupt's estate may not participate in the trust until the default has been remedied *in toto*.[300] In fact the courts have not adopted this approach, at least when the bankrupt had a present right to a definite part of the trust fund at the date of bankruptcy.[301] Rather, the right of proof in the bankruptcy has been limited to the difference between the defaulting trustee's liability and that trustee's beneficial interest in the trust estate, which includes the trust asset represented by his own liability. As a result the other beneficiaries of the trust effectively are deprived of

---

[295] *Palmer* v. *The Permanent Trustee Co.* (1915) 16 SR(NSW) 162.

[296] *Egbert* v. *Butter* (1856) 21 Beav. 560; *Fox* v. *Buckley* (1876) 3 Ch. D 508. See also *Re Milnes; Milnes* v. *Sherwin* (1885) 53 LT 534, 535.

[297] See *In re Brown; Dixon* v. *Brown* (1886) 32 Ch. D 597, 600.

[298] See Little V.C. in *Fox* v. *Buckley* (1876) 3 Ch. D 508, 509.

[299] On the other hand, a debt owing to the estate by an executor or trustee arising otherwise than as a result of his own default still should not be able to be appropriated as payment of a devise of realty. See *Ex parte Barff; in re Cousen* (1848) 17 LJ Bcy. 22. *Cherry* v. *Boultbee*, rather than *Morris* v. *Livie*, would be in issue, and the specific right to participate could not be set against the monetary liability to contribute.

[300] See e.g. *Staniar* v. *Evans* (1886) 34 Ch. D 470, discussed in section 10.4 above. The proof should not constitute a waiver of the right to invoke *Morris* v. *Livie* (see above), or indeed *Cherry* v. *Boultbee*, since the right to participate and the obligation to contribute both arise out of the trust itself. See *Ex parte Turpin* (1832) Mont. 443, discussed in section 10.11 above.

[301] See *In re Gloag's Estate* (1892) 11 NZLR 90 (esp. at 94), discussed below.

the benefit of *Cherry* v. *Boultbee* and *Morris* v. *Livie*. This has been justified on the basis of set-off. In *Ex parte Turner; in re Crosthwaite*[302] Lord Cranworth said that 'being one of the residuary legatees, he or his estate is entitled, on the doctrine of mutual credit, to set off against the sum due from him his share of whatever is due to him'.[303] His Lordship proceeded upon the following analysis. If before the bankruptcy the defaulting trustee had tendered the value of the residue of his liability after setting off his own beneficial interest in the trust, the question between the parties would have been settled. Consequently the trustees should be remitted to a proof for the difference remaining after this set-off. The decision in *Turner* was followed in *In re Chapman; ex parte Parker*.[304] Mathew J. in his judgment commented: 'We should be flying in the face of section 38 of the Bankruptcy Act, 1883,[305] if we did not ascertain what the exact liability of the bankrupt was, and that exact liability can only be ascertained by giving the bankrupt credit for his share'.[306] However, with respect, it is not easy to see how the set-off section can be said to apply. The defaulting trustee's right to participate in the trust is a claim *in specie* for a share of a trust fund, and so it should not be within the ambit of the set-off section in the insolvency legislation.[307] In any event, the essence of a set-off is the existence of cross-demands between the parties. The bankrupt defaulting trustee in *Turner* was allowed a deduction in respect of his interest in the total trust estate, which included the trust asset represented by his own liability. Yet it can hardly be correct to say that the bankrupt had a cross-demand against the other trustees in respect of his 'interest' in his own unsatisfied liability. In truth, it is not easy to see how the doctrine of mutual credit can be said to be relevant to a case such as *Turner*.

Turner was not applied in a case in New Zealand. In *In re Gloag's Estate*[308] a trustee was entitled to a life interest in the whole of the trust fund, and, having misapplied the fund, she became bankrupt. Williams J. held[309] that the representative of the trust estate in the interest in reversion of the other beneficiaries was entitled to prove for the whole of the misapplied fund, and that the bankrupt's estate could not participate in the income obtained from the dividend payable on the proof until the original fund had been replaced *in toto*. His Honour distinguished *Turner* on the ground that the defaulting trustee in that case had a present

---

[302] (1852) 2 De G M & G 927.

[303] (1852) 2 De G M & G 927, 932. Knight Bruce L.J. adopted a similar analysis.

[304] (1887) 4 Morr. 109.

[305] This was the mutual credit provision in the 1883 legislation.

[306] (1887) 4 Morr. 109, 112.   [307] See section 6.2 above.

[308] (1892) 11 NZLR 90.

[309] Following *Ex parte King; in re Severn* (1835) 1 Deac. 143.

right to a definite share of the trust fund. That trustee before the bankruptcy could have discharged his obligation to the other beneficiary by paying him a certain sum after deducting his immediate share. However, this was not so in *Gloag*. The defaulting trustee could not have discharged herself by paying to the other beneficiaries the present value of their reversionary interests after her life interest. She could only discharge herself by replacing the corpus, and there was nothing which could be set against this obligation.[310]

10.14 THE METHOD OF APPLICATION OF *CHERRY* V. *BOULTBEE*

Cherry v. *Boultbee* entitles the administrator of the fund to assert that a debtor to the fund should appropriate a particular asset of the fund, in the form of his own indebtedness, as *pro tanto* payment of his right to participate. The application of this principle is straightforward when the right to participate is for a fixed sum. If on the other hand the debtor is entitled to a certain percentage of the fund, the administrator in invoking the rule calculates the debtor's share on the basis that the fund has been increased by the debtor's own debt, and the debtor becomes entitled to the requisite percentage of this total estate, which includes the debt. The administrator then directs the debtor to appropriate the debt as part payment of his share, and so the net sum payable to him is the difference between the share calculated in this manner and his indebtedness to the fund.[311] A similar principle applies when legacies of a fixed sum are bequeathed, though an abatement is necessary because of a deficiency in the fund.[312]

In the case of a bankruptcy, a creditor's right to participate is confined to the dividend payable on the debt owing owing to him.[313] The net sum payable by the estate to the creditor should be calculated by the following method. The dividend rate payable by the estate may be obtained by dividing the total assets of the estate, including the creditor's debt to the

---

[310] See also *Ex parte Stone; in re Welch* (1873) LR 8 Ch. App. 914 (no set-off in respect of debtor/trustee's reversionary interest).

[311] *Willes* v. *Greenhill (No. 1)* (1860) 29 Beav. 376, 383; *In re Melton* [1918] 1 Ch. 37, 46, 54, 59.

[312] See *In re King; King* v. *King* (1914) 31 WN (NSW) 55. Compare *Re Richardson; ex parte Thompson* v. *Hutton* (1902) 86 LT 25, though it is not clear from the report how the amount due on abatement was calculated.

[313] See e.g. *In re Mayne; ex parte The Official Receiver* [1907] 2 K.B. 899. *Cherry* v. *Boultbee* would only be important in the context of a bankruptcy or a company liquidation if for some reason a right of set-off is not available to the creditor.

bankrupt, by the liabilities of the estate, which include the bankrupt's debt to the creditor.[314] The dividend notionally payable to the creditor is the product of this dividend rate and his claim against the estate. However, the creditor's own liability to the bankrupt may be appropriated as part payment of this sum, and so the net amount payable is the remainder of this notional dividend after subtracting the value of the creditor's liability.[315]

It may be that a bankrupt is liable to contribute to a fund, and his trustee is seeking to enforce a right vested in the bankrupt to participate in the fund. The administrator of the fund may bring into account the full value of the bankrupt's liability, despite the fact of the bankruptcy, since the bankrupt's trustee is not considered to be in any better position than the bankrupt himself.[316] Thus *Cherry* v. *Boultbee* in this situation operates substantively, by allowing the administrator to treat the debt owing to the fund as payment of a right to participate to the extent of the full value of the debt, even though the fund would otherwise only have received a dividend. In effect the same result is achieved as for a set-off in the bankruptcy. If the administrator of the fund mistakenly pays the bankrupt's trustee without invoking *Cherry* v. *Boultbee*, the rule in *Ex parte James*[317] may provide relief.[318]

While these principles may seem clear, the problem becomes more complex when there are two prima facie insolvent estates, each of which has a claim against the other, and the situation is such that the cross-demands may not be employed in a set-off. For example, it may be that a company in liquidation is liable in the liquidation of another company to pay a call on shares,[319] or is liable for misfeasance,[320] and the first company is also a creditor of the second on a separate transaction. The liquidator of the second company may assert that the first company should not be allowed to participate in the liquidation by receiving a dividend on the debt owing to it until that first company has made its required contribution in the form of a call,[321] or has satisfied its misfeasance liability, and the

---

[314] Obviously there can never be a dividend rate greater than one.

[315] In some cases the estate in fact may be able to pay a full dividend when the creditor's obligation to contribute is taken into account in this manner. If in such a case the creditor's liability exceeds the dividend notionally payable to him, the difference will represent a subsisting liability still owing by the creditor.

[316] *Corr* v. *Corr* (1879) 3 LR Ir. 435; *In re Weston. Davies* v. *Tagart* [1900] 2 Ch. 164. See also *Ex parte Metcalfe* (1805) 11 Ves. Jun. 404, 408; *In re Brown; Dixon* v. *Brown* (1886) 32 Ch. D 597; *In re Kowloon Container Warehouse Co. Ltd.* [1981] HKLR 210.

[317] (1874) LR 9 Ch. App. 609, discussed in section 2.16 above.

[318] See *In re Brown* (1886) 32 Ch. D 597, and note also *Ex parte Bignold; in re Charles* (1817) 2 Madd. 470.   [319] See section 4.6 above.

[320] See section 4.7.1 above.

[321] See *In re Auriferous Properties, Ltd. (No. 2)* [1898] 2 Ch. 428; *In re National Live Stock Insurance Co., Ltd.* [1917] 1 Ch. 628; *In re White Star Line, Ltd.* [1938] 1 Ch. 458.

liquidator of the first company may adopt a similar stance. The problem is that neither company in fact may have sufficient assets to satisfy its liability *in toto*. This was the case in *In re Leeds and Hanley Theatres of Varieties, Limited*.[322] Two companies, the Finance Company (F) and the Theatres Company (T), were in liquidation. F was a creditor of T for £5,100 on debentures issued by T, while T had a claim against F for £4,323 as a result of a judgment obtained against F for damages for misfeasance. Because of the nature of this latter claim, the two demands could not be set off.[323] Moreover, neither company had sufficient assets in hand with which to pay its own liability in full. F had no assets other than the dividend payable by T on the debentures, but had other creditors to the extent of £5,490. T had other assets totalling in value £8,277, and other liabilities of £4,685. Buckley J. adopted the following procedure for settling the rights of the parties:[324]

The proper administration in my judgment, therefore, is this. Notionally treat the Finance Company as having paid the £4,323 to the Theatres Company; take the aggregate notional sum thus arrived at and treat it as applied in payment of a dividend upon all the debts of the Theatres Company—that is to say, upon the £5,100 due to the Finance Company and the £4,685 due to other people. That will attribute to the Finance Company a certain sum. If that sum be greater than the £4,323 that they owe, they will get the difference. If it be less, or equal, they will receive nothing. If the dividend thus arrived at on the £4,685 cannot be satisfied in full (because the notional sum, of course, is not really paid), then the £4,685 would take the whole of the assets of the Theatres Company, although it be less than the notional dividend calculated upon the footing that the Finance Company have paid that which they have not paid.

In essence this is an application in favour of T of the method suggested above for calculating the net sum payable when a creditor of a bankrupt or a company in liquidation is also liable to make a contribution.[325] A

---

[322] [1904] 2 Ch. 45.

[323] *Ex parte Pelly* (1882) 21 Ch. D 492, and see section 4.7.1 above.

[324] [1904] 2 Ch. 45, 51–2.

[325] Buckley J.'s approach has been approved in other cases. See *In re National Live Stock Insurance Co., Ltd.* [1917] 1 Ch. 628; *In re Hattons Confectionery Co., Ltd.* [1936] NZLR 802; *Re Mitchell, Houghton Ltd.* (1971) 14 CBR 301. However, it was criticized by Luckett and Dean, 'Cross Debts: Notional Calculations in Liquidations' (1983) 11 *Australian Business Law Review* 69. They noted that, as a result of this order, F received £777 from T for distribution amongst its other creditors, who each would have received a resulting dividend of 2s. 10d. in the pound, whereas T as a creditor of F in effect received payment in full for its own claim against F. Accordingly, they proposed an alternative procedure which would have the effect of treating all the creditors of each company in an equal manner. See also Dean; Luckett and Houghton, 'Notional Calculations in Liquidations Revisited' (1993) 11 *Companies and Securities Law Journal* 204. The point was made above, however, that a feature of *Cherry v. Boultbee* in the situation in which the debtor/creditor of the fund is

notional payment of £4,323 by F to T would have produced an aggregate fund in T of £12,600. Its total liabilities were only £9,785 (being £5,100 plus £4,685), and so T could pay a full dividend of 100p in the £. Consequently F was entitled to receive £5,100 from T, though, since F was indebted to T for £4,323, the net sum payable was reduced to £777.

Buckley J. only notionally treated F as having paid its debt. Consequently, only T obtained the benefit of the operation of *Cherry* v. *Boultbee*. A greater sum would have been payable by T if instead F had been treated as the recipient of the notional payment.[326] Buckley J'.s decision to give T the benefit of the rule may have been prompted by the fact that the summons was taken out in the winding-up of T, and so he was only called upon to consider the position as between T and its creditors.[327] However, it may also be justified on the basis of a principle that a party such as F liable for misfeasance not only may not employ the liability in a set-off against a cross-demand, but also is required to satisfy the liability *in toto* before a right to receive a dividend on the cross-demand accrues. The courts have applied a similar rule where a company in liquidation was liable in the liquidation of another company to pay a call on shares,[328] and where a company in liquidation was obliged to return a payment invalidated as a preference in the liquidation of the payer, so that the first-mentioned company had to repay the preference in full before it could receive a dividend on the original debt for which the payment was intended to constitute satisfaction.[329] There have also been cases in which a banker, or an assignee in bankruptcy, who received proceeds from the realization of a bankrupt's estate, and who also happened to be a creditor of the

---

insolvent is that the fund does indeed have the opportunity to obtain the full value of the debt owing to it. This is a consequence of the right of the administrator to direct the debtor to satisfy his right to participate from his own obligation to contribute.

[326] The dividend rate payable by F, on the assumption that T has notionally paid its debt, would have been obtained by dividing its total assets, including T's debt, by its total liabilities, which would have equalled $(5,100 + 0)/(5,490 + 4,323)$. This produces a dividend rate of .5197. Thus the value of T's right of participation would have been the product of .5197 and £4,323, or £2,246.74. Under *Cherry* v. *Boultbee*, F's liquidator would have been entitled to direct T to appropriate a part of its own liability to contribute (being £5,100) in part satisfaction of this right to participate, after which T would still have had a residual liability to F of £2,853.26. The dividend rate payable by T on this debt, being its total assets divided by its liabilities (of course the assets of T would no longer include F's liability for £4,323), would have been 8,277 $(4,685 + 2,853.26)$. Since this is greater than one, T could have paid a full dividend to its creditors, so that F would have received the full value of the residue of T's debt for £2,853.26. The end result is that, while the judgment of Buckley J. obliged T to pay to F £777, T would have been required to pay the greater sum of £2,853.26 if the notional payment had been deemed to have been made by T rather than F.

[327] See Buckley J. at [1904] 2 Ch. 45, 51. *Quaere* what would have happened on this view if a summons had also been taken out in the winding-up of F.

[328] *In re Auriferous Properties, Ltd. (No. 2)* [1898] 2 Ch. 428; *In re White Star Line, Ltd.* [1938] 1 Ch. 458.

[329] *N. A. Kratzmann Pty. Ltd.* v. *Tucker (No. 2)* (1968) 123 CLR 295.

bankrupt, himself became bankrupt. The banker's, or the assignee's, estate was held not to be entitled to receive a dividend on the bankrupt's indebtedness until the proceeds had been repaid in full.[330] A person liable for misfeasance is unlikely to be treated more leniently than, for example, an innocent contributory liable to pay a call on shares,[331] and so it is understandable that F, the party liable for misfeasance, should have been chosen as the party to make a notional payment, rather than T.

The calculation of the notional dividend rate in *Leeds and Hanley* was based on the assumption that T had a valuable asset to the full extent of F's liability. This was a valid assumption in that particular case, since the dividend payable by T to F was greater than F's liability to T, and consequently all of the asset represented by F's liability was employed in order to reduce the sum otherwise payable to F. However, this would not have been the case if F's liability in fact had been greater than the dividend notionally payable in T's liquidation. F would have had a residual liability remaining after the application of *Cherry v. Boultbee*, and if F was insolvent it would only have been able to pay a fractional dividend on this residue. This means that F in effect would have received credit for a higher dividend rate in the *Cherry v. Boultbee* calculation than that payable to T's other creditors, who would have been paid a dividend calculated on the basis of the true resulting asset value of the company. However, the effect on the dividend rate in a case such as this often would be marginal.

---

[330] *Ex parte Bebb* (1812) 19 Ves. Jun. 222; *Ex parte Graham* (1814) 3 V & B 130; *Ex parte Bignold; in re Charles* (1817) 2 Madd. 470.
[331] See *Ex parte Pelly* (1882) 21 Ch. D 492, 503, 509–10.

11

Combination of Bank Accounts

11.1 INTRODUCTION

When a customer has more than one account with a bank, one of which is in credit and another in debit, it is said that the bank may combine, or consolidate, the accounts and proceed on the basis that only one debt for the balance is owing. The accounts need not be at the same branch.[1] Nor is it necessary that the account in credit should have resulted from a deposit by the customer himself. A combination may arise in relation to an account that originally was opened by a third party, but which became vested in the customer.[2]

Combination is particularly important if the bank is suspicious of the customer's solvency, because it provides the bank with a means by which it may obtain the full benefit of the account in credit, by setting it against the account in debit, before the customer has dissipated the credit balance. For example, subject to any agreed overdraft limit, a bank may refuse to honour a cheque drawn by a customer on an account in credit if the customer has a debit balance on another account, unless the overall credit balance on the two accounts taken together is sufficient to satisfy the cheque.[3] In this sense it has been said that combination may be used as a sword as well as a shield.[4] The bank is not required to notify the customer of its intention to exercise the right. Moreover, the right is of general application. As a matter of principle it is not limited to current or other similar accounts,[5] although in any particular case it is subject to any agreement, express or implied, to the contrary.

---

[1] *Garnett* v. *M'Kewan* (1872) LR 8 Ex. 10, and see generally section 11.3.5 below.
[2] See Bacon V.C. in *Roxburghe* v. *Cox* (1881) 17 Ch. D 520, who (incorrectly) characterized the right in question as a lien. See below. While James and Lush L.JJ. on appeal in the Court of Appeal decided the case instead by reference to the principles of set-off under the Statutes of Set-off, Baggallay L.J. (at 527–8) said that he did not dissent from Bacon V.C.'s conclusion.
[3] *Garnett* v. *M'Kewan* (1872) LR 8 Ex. 10.
[4] *Barclays Bank, Ltd.* v. *Okenarhe* [1966] 2 Lloyd's Rep. 87, 97.
[5] *Halesowen Presswork & Assemblies Ltd.* v. *Westminster Bank Ltd.* [1971] 1 QB 1, 19 per Roskill J. (at first instance). Compare Buckley J. in *In re E. J. Morel (1934) Ltd.* [1962] 1 Ch. 21, 31–2.

11.2 THE NATURE OF THE RIGHT OF COMBINATION

11.2.1 *The general principle*

A bank has a lien on all securities deposited with it as banker by a customer unless there is an express contract, or circumstances showing an implied contract, inconsistent with a lien.[6] On occasions it has been assumed that combination of accounts is merely an aspect of this lien,[7] though the courts have been critical of the use of the term 'lien' in this context.[8] The lien to which a bank is entitled is a common law possessory lien. This form of lien merely confers upon a creditor the right to retain possession of certain tangible property until such time as the debtor pays his debt. Once the creditor loses possession, the lien is lost. Thus a cheque or other negotiable security deposited with a bank may be the subject of a lien while it remains in the possession of the bank. But when the cheque is cleared the bank loses possession, with the result that any lien comes to an end. Since the relationship of banker and customer is one of debt rather than trust[9] the proceeds of the cheque received by the bank become the property of the bank, rather than of the customer, and it can hardly be correct to say that the bank has a lien on its own property. The bank, when it receives the proceeds and credits the customer's account, becomes a debtor to the customer. A debt is not tangible property, and so the use of the word 'lien' to describe the bank's rights in relation to the account itself is inappropriate.[10] Lord Denning in the Court of Appeal in *Halesowen Presswork & Assemblies Ltd.* v. *Westminster Bank Ltd.*[11] said that 'we should discard the use of the word "lien" in this context and speak simply of a banker's "right to combine accounts"': or a right to "set off" one account against the other'.[12] It is a matter of some debate, however,

---

[6] *Brandao* v. *Barnett* (1846) 3 CB 519, 531.
[7] See e.g. *Misa* v. *Currie* (1876) 1 App. Cas. 554, 569 per Lord Hatherley ('all monies paid into a bank are subject to a lien'); *Bower* v. *Foreign and Colonial Gas Company* (1874) 22 WR 740; *Roxburghe* v. *Cox* (1881) 17 Ch. D 520; *T. and H. Greenwood Teale* v. *William Williams Brown and Company* (1894) 11 TLR 56; *Baker* v. *Lloyd's Bank, Ltd.* [1920] 2 KB 322, 327; *Greenhalgh and Sons* v. *Union Bank of Manchester* [1924] 2 KB 153, 164; *In re Keever, a bankrupt, ex parte The Trustee of the Property of the Bankrupt* v. *Midland Bank Ltd.* [1967] 1 Ch. 182.
[8] *In re Morris, deceased; Coneys* v. *Morris* [1922] 1 IR 136; *Halesowen Presswork & Assemblies Ltd.* v. *Westminster Bank Ltd.* [1971] 1 QB 1, 33–4 per Lord Denning M.R., 46 per Buckley L.J., which view was endorsed on appeal by Viscount Dilhorne ([1972] AC 785, 802) and by Lord Cross of Chelsea (at 810). See also *Broad* v. *Commissioner of Stamp Duties* [1980] 2 NSWLR 40; *MPS Constructions Pty. Ltd.* v. *Rural Bank of New South Wales* (1980) 4 ACLR 835, 840–1.   [9] *Foley* v. *Hill* (1848) 2 HLC 28.
[10] See Buckley L.J. in *Halesowen Presswork & Assemblies Ltd.* v. *Westminster Bank Ltd.* [1971] 1 QB 1, 46. See also on appeal in the House of Lords [1972] AC 785, 802 per Viscount Dilhorne, 810 per Lord Cross of Chelsea.   [11] [1971] 1 QB 1.
[12] [1971] 1 QB 1, 34.

whether indeed either of these expressions accurately describes the principle underlying combination of accounts. Each presupposes that there are independent debts in existence which the bank may consolidate so as to produce a single debt for the balance, although in fact this is not the traditional basis of combination. Rather, the explanation found in the cases is that, unless a particular account is separated out by agreement (express or implied) or it is separate as a matter of law, the debt owing by either party to the other at any particular time can only be ascertained by looking at the balance of all the accounts together. In other words, it is not so much a right to combine accounts, as a recognition that the balance of all the accounts represents the debt. Expressed more concisely, combination is a matter of account rather than of set-off.[13] On this basis a specific act of combination should not be required.[14] While there is an accounting exercise, that in itself does not bring about a single debt, but rather it is undertaken in order to ascertain what the debt is. The principle has its justification in the notion that, no matter how many accounts belonging to a particular customer a bank may have entered in its books, there is still only one banker/customer relationship.[15] As Kelly C.B. expressed it, in a case where a customer had a credit balance at one branch which was almost exactly equalled by a debit balance at another branch,[16] 'The defendant's bank, therefore, had scarcely a shilling of his money, and I cannot see why they were bound to honour his cheque at Leighton Buzzard just because there was a balance at that branch in his favour'.

While this analysis has its supporters,[17] it also has its critics.[18] In Wood's opinion the right in question, which he calls current account set-off, is indeed a set-off, in the sense that it requires an act by the bank to set what are otherwise distinct reciprocal claims against one another.[19] Wood regards the various judicial statements which suggest that there is only one amount owing as being no more than an expression of the fact that, in the

[13] *Re Charge Card Services Ltd.* [1987] 1 Ch. 150, 173–4.

[14] However, an act of combination may be required when there has been an agreement (express or implied) that accounts should be kept separate, and that agreement has terminated. See section 11.3.4 below.

[15] See Buckley L.J. in *Halesowen Presswork & Assemblies Ltd.* v. *Westminster Bank Ltd.* [1971] 1 QB 1, 46.

[16] *Garnett* v. *M'Kewan* (1872) LR 8 Ex. 10, 12.

[17] Shea, 'Statutory Set-off' (1986) 3 *Journal of International Banking Law* 152, 154; Penn, Shea and Arora, *The Law Relating to Domestic Banking* (1987), 143–4; McCracken, *The Banker's Remedy of Set-off* (1993), Ch. 1.

[18] In addition to Wood (discussed below), see Salter, 'Remedies For Banks: An Outline of English Law' *Banks and Remedies* (edited by Cranston, 1992), 18–21. This would also appear to be Goode's view. See Goode, *Legal Problems of Credit and Security* (2nd edn., 1988), 147. Ellinger *Modern Banking Law* (1987), 144 characterized the right in question as a set-off, though that was in the context of distinguishing it from a lien.

[19] Wood, *English and International Set-off* (1989), 92, 94.

absence of an agreement to the contrary, the bank at any time may set off accounts without notice to the customer and accordingly treat divided accounts as a single blended account.[20] However, this does not appear to be what the judges in question had in mind. But the rejection of that view does not mean that nothing follows from the fact that separate accounts are recorded in the bank's books. It is unlikely that the courts in saying that a number of accounts form one entire account intended to refer to the operation of the accounts themselves. Rather, they appear to have had in mind the question whether, and to what extent, a debt is owing at any particular time by the bank or the customer to the other. Accordingly, for certain purposes the accounts should indeed be treated as separate, for example for the calculation and payment of interest, and for questions relating to the order and appropriation of payments in accordance with *Clayton's Case*.[21] In truth, as Byrne J. remarked at first instance in *Mutton* v. *Peat*,[22] in response to an argument that as between banker and customer all accounts form but one account, this 'is true for certain purposes'. On the other hand, unless there is an express or implied agreement to the contrary which would preclude a combination in any event, the courts have recognized that a bank is entitled to give effect to the principle of combination in its books by moving debits or credits from one account to another.[23] When this occurs the accounts will cease to be separate for those purposes as well. As Canadian courts have emphasized, however, this book-keeping entry itself does not constitute a payment of the account in debit, since there was in any event only one debt.[24]

11.2.2 *The cases*

The first case suggesting that combination in truth is a matter of account is *Ex parte Pearce; in re Langmead*.[25] Commissioners appointed under an Act of Parliament had two accounts with a bank, designated respectively the river account and the harbour account. The river account was

---

[20] Wood, *English and International Set-off* (1989), 92.　　[21] (1816) 1 Mer. 572.

[22] [1899] 2 Ch. 556, 560.

[23] See, in the *Halesowen* case, Roskill J. at first instance [1971] 1 QB 1, 20–1, Lord Denning M.R. in the Court of Appeal (at 35) and Lord Kilbrandon in the House of Lords [1972] AC 785, 819, each of them criticizing a *dictum* by Swift J. to the contrary in *Greenhalgh and Sons* v. *Union Bank of Manchester* [1924] 2 KB 153, 164. See also *Garnett* v. *M'Kewan* (1872) LR 8 Ex. 10 (esp. Kelly C.B. at 13); *Re Sutcliffe & Sons Ltd; ex parte Royal Bank* [1933] 1 DLR 562 (esp. at 569); *Re T. C. Marines Ltd.* (1973) 34 DLR (3d) 489; *Re Plasky* (1981) 39 CBR 186, 194; *Deep* v. *Bank of Montreal* (1991) 47 OAC 319. In *Clark* v. *Ulster Bank Ltd.* [1950] NILR 132, 143 Black L.J. referred to this as crystallizing the position.

[24] *Re Sutcliffe & Sons Ltd; ex parte Royal Bank* [1933] 1 DLR 562 (esp. at 569); *Ross* v. *Royal Bank of Canada* (1965) 52 DLR (2d) 578; *Re Plasky* (1981) 39 CBR 186; *Re T. C. Marines Ltd.* (1973) 34 DLR (3d) 489. For the same reason, the book-keeping entry does not constitute a seizure of assets. See *Deep* v. *Bank of Montreal* (1991) 47 OAC 319.

[25] (1841) 2 Mont. D & De G 142.

overdrawn, though the harbour account had a credit balance exceeding the debit balance on the river account. The bank became bankrupt, where-upon the assignees in bankruptcy commenced proceedings at law against the customer for payment of the debit balance on the river account. Sir John Cross granted an injunction restraining that action, commenting that, 'There was only one account of banker and customer between the bank and the commissioners'.[26] Accordingly, the assignees had no just cause to bring the action. It is true that he referred later in his judgment to set-off, and to the 'debts' on each of the accounts, although these expressions may not have been used in their technical sense. Nor could his reference to a single account be explained as a recognition of the concept that the bank at any time could have combined without notice, because the bank, or, at least, its assignees in bankruptcy, in fact was the party attempting to treat the accounts as separate.

Bailey v. *Finch*[27] also concerned the bankruptcy of a bank. The defendant as executor under a will had an executorship account with the bank. In addition he had three accounts in his personal capacity with the bank, two of which he had overdrawn and the third being in credit. On these three accounts there was an overall balance against him. The question was whether the defendant could set off the executorship account against the overall debit balance on the three accounts, and the case has already been discussed in that context.[28] For present purposes the interesting point is the characterization by Blackburn J. of the position in relation to the three accounts. His Lordship said that:[29]

[W]hat we have to look to is, what were the facts at the time of the bankruptcy; and the rights of the parties must be regulated by what those facts were. It appears that at that time Mr. Finch, the defendant, had an account with the bank, or rather several accounts, which for convenience he had called by different names; it matters not what they were, he had for convenience three accounts. There is no doubt whatever, as between him and the bank, those three accounts all formed in reality one account; and that a debt was owing by him to the bank upon those three accounts, being the balance of the whole three taken together. That would have been independent of any question of set-off and mutual credit.

Blackburn J. was speaking of the position at the time of the bankruptcy. At that time he considered that there was one debt for the balance of the three accounts, and this was independent of any question of set-off under the bankruptcy legislation. Moreover, there is nothing in the report to suggest that there had been an act of combination at that time. On the contrary, the comments of Blackburn J. suggest otherwise. Nor, one imagines, would the trustee in bankruptcy have regarded it as being in the interests of

[26] (1841) 2 Mont. D & De G 142, 145.
[28] See section 9.9.1 above.

[27] (1871) LR 7 QB 34.
[29] (1871) LR 7 QB 34, 40.

the estate to effect a combination, if indeed an act of combination was thought to be necessary in order to produce a single debt, since the bank rather than the customer was insolvent.

Bailey v. *Finch* was considered by James L.J. in *Ex parte Morier; in re Willis, Percival, & Co.*[30] In discussing the case he said that:[31]

There all the judges start with this . . ., that really *in point of law* there was but one account, and there was no debt except upon taking the two accounts together. The mere fact of the two accounts being put upon different pages of the ledger could have no more effect than if an account had gone over from one page of the bank's ledger to another, or than if a man, as a mere matter of account, had kept different accounts, such as a farm account, a colliery account, or a house account, merely for his own convenience for ascertaining how moneys came in and how they had been applied.

It is important to note that this was regarded as the position 'in point of law'. It was not intended to be a description of the position that applied as a matter of substance, based on a notion that the bank could have combined the accounts at any time without notice to produce a single account. Nor was there anything new in James L.J.'s opinion in this regard. In an earlier judgment in *In re European Bank; Agra Bank Claim*,[32] with which Mellish L.J. agreed, James L.J. said that 'It was only for convenience that the loan account was kept separately . . . In truth, as between banker and customer, whatever number of accounts are kept in the books, the whole is really but one account . . .'.

Subsequently Luxmoore J. in *Ex parte Douglas*[33] adopted James L.J.'s statement of the principle in *Morier*. A partnership had lent some money to a second partnership, the amount of the loan being carried to a loan account. James Douglas was a member of both firms, and when he died a general trading account between them showed a credit balance in favour of the second partnership. Luxmoore J. referred to James L.J.'s judgment as support for the view that[34] 'In law there was in fact at James Douglas's death but one account between two firms, and taking the two accounts together there was no debt'. Once again, this was regarded as the position *in law*. At the date of the death, when there had not been any act of combination, there was nevertheless only one debt for the balance.

Mutton v. *Peat*[35] is also relevant. For present purposes the facts of the case may be summarized as follows. Stockbrokers had two accounts with a bank, a current account with a credit balance and a loan account. In addition the brokers had deposited some bonds and shares by way of security for their indebtedness to the bank. When the brokers ceased

---

[30] (1879) 12 Ch. D 491.
[31] (1879) 12 Ch. D 491, 498–499 (emphasis added).
[32] (1872) LR 8 Ch. App. 41, 44.
[33] [1930] 1 Ch. 342.
[34] [1930] 1 Ch. 342, 349.
[35] [1900] 2 Ch. 79.

trading the bank made a point of carrying the credit balance on the current account to a separate liquidation account, rather than applying it in reduction of the loan account, and then claimed to be entitled to apply the proceeds of the security in reduction of the loan account without taking into account the credit account. It is apparent that the bank had gone out of its way to avoid combining the accounts. However, Lindley M.R. in the leading judgment nevertheless said that,[36] 'I do not care how the bankers may have manipulated their books or how many accounts they may have kept. When you come to ascertain what is the amount due from [the brokers] to the bankers the question admits of only one solution—it is the balance due on the loan account after deducting' the credit account. The case is open to two interpretations. The first is that the court was not concerned with the question of what was the debt owing by the brokers to the bank on the basis of the law of banker and customer, but rather with how the debt was to be calculated in accordance with the terms of the security. Indeed, the courts usually find an implied term that a loan account and a current account in credit should be kept separate,[37] which perhaps suggests this interpretation. On the other hand, in *Halesowen Presswork & Assemblies Ltd.* v. *Westminster Bank Ltd.*[38] Roskill J. at first instance[39] and, in the Court of Appeal, Lord Denning M.R.[40] and Buckley L.J.[41] (and possibly also Winn L.J.[42]) all regarded *Mutton* v. *Peat* as having turned on what the position was on a banker/customer basis, and indeed Roskill J. and Lord Denning both commented that it was a case in which the usual implied term that a loan account and a current account in credit should be kept separate was not applicable. Lord Denning sought to explain *Mutton* v. *Peat* on the basis that the customer has the right to call upon the bank to combine accounts, while on another occasion Mocatta J. said that the bank was obliged to combine,[43] though neither of these in truth is the ground upon which the case was decided. Sir Nathaniel Lindsay proceeded on the basis that an act of combination was not necessary, since there was in any event only one debt for the balance. As Rigby L.J. also commented in *Mutton* v. *Peat*,[44] the correct analysis was that the bank ought to have allowed the credit balance in account in determining the indebtedness, rather than that they ought to have appropriated it in reduction of the loan.

The next case is *Garnett* v. *M'Kewan*.[45] A customer had an account in credit at one branch of a bank, but had another account in debit at another

---

[36] [1900] 2 Ch. 79, 85.　　[37] *Bradford Old Bank, Ltd.* v. *Sutcliffe* [1918] 2 KB 833.
[38] [1971] 1 QB 1.　　[39] [1971] 1 QB 1, 22.　　[40] [1971] 1 QB 1, 34.
[41] [1971] 1 QB 1, 46.　　[42] [1971] 1 QB 1, 42.
[43] *Barclays Bank, Ltd.* v. *Okenarhe* [1966] 2 Lloyd's Rep. 87, 95–6. A similar view is expressed in Ellinger, *Modern Banking Law* (1987), 160.　　[44] [1900] 2 Ch. 79, 86.
[45] (1872) LR 8 Ex. 10.

branch. The bank transferred the debit balance in reduction of the credit balance, and refused to honour cheques drawn on that account. The Court of Exchequer held that the bank was entitled to do so. In this case there was an act of combination, though the later explanation of the decision by the Privy Council in *Prince* v. *Oriental Bank Corporation*[46] suggests that it did not turn on that point. The judgment of their Lordships[47] was delivered by Sir Montague Smith, who said in relation to *Garnett* v. *M'Kewan* that,[48]

[T]he Court held that money of the Plaintiff lodged at one branch, and being still there to the credit of his account, was to be treated as part of the customer's entire account with the bank, and that the whole account was to be looked at to see on which side as between him and the bank the balance stood.

Consistent with that observation, Bramwell B. in *Garnett* v. *M'Kewan*[49] said that 'the customer has no claim, for he is indebted to the bank on his whole account in such an amount as to reduce his assets to almost nothing'. Martin B. referred to the account in credit as an 'apparent balance'. He said that[50] 'the mere existence of an apparent balance, if there is no real balance, is not enough to render the bank liable to pay a cheque at the branch where the apparent balance is'. According to Kelly C.B.,[51] 'The question substantially raised by the pleadings is whether any money of the plaintiff's was in the hands of the London and County Bank', which is the essence of the principle of combination.

More recently, the view that combination is a matter of account rather than set-off was emphasized by Buckley L.J. in the Court of Appeal in the *Halesowen* case.[52]

Where the relationship of the banker and customer is a single relationship . . . albeit embodied in a number of accounts, the situation is not, in my judgment, a situation of lien at all . . . Nor is it a set-off situation, which postulates mutual but independent obligations between the two parties. It is an accounting situation, in which the existence and amount of one party's liability to the other can only be ascertained by discovering the ultimate balance of their mutual dealings.

In *Re Charge Card Services Ltd.*[53] Millett J. referred to this passage from Buckley L.J.'s judgment with evident approval, and it was regarded as correct by Otton J. in *In re K (Restraint Order)*.[54]

---

[46] (1878) 3 App. Cas. 325.

[47] Sir James Colville, Sir Barnes Peacock, Sir Montague Smith and Sir Robert Collier.

[48] (1878) 3 App. Cas. 325, 333.   [49] (1872) LR 8 Ex. 10, 15.

[50] (1872) LR 8 Ex. 10, 13–14.   [51] (1872) LR 8 Ex. 10, 12.

[52] [1971] 1 QB 1, 46. See also his earlier comments in *In re E. J. Morel (1934) Ltd.* [1962] 1 Ch. 21, 32.   [53] [1987] 1 Ch. 150, 173–4.

[54] [1990] 2 QB 298. While Otton J. referred (at 305) to an account in credit as a chose in action, that was in the context of a discussion of the bank's rights arising under the letter of set-off as opposed to common law combination.

A similar position has been adopted in other jurisdictions. In Scotland Lord Dunedin in *James Kirkwood & Sons* v. *Clydesdale Bank*,[55] in a judgment with which Lord Kinnear, Lord M'Laren and Lord Pearson concurred, observed that 'the state of affairs between a banker and his customer as at any given time must be taken to be the state of affairs upon all the accounts',[56] and that 'upon a true accounting between the parties concerned there were no funds in the hands of the Clydesdale Bank belonging to this gentleman'.[57] In Ireland Sir Andrew Porter M.R. posed the question,[58] 'Now what is the meaning of a No. 2 account? It no doubt often means that the account refers to another subject-matter or department of business for mere convenience, but is not otherwise legally separate from the No. 1 account of the customer'. In Northern Ireland Black L.J. favoured this view in *Clark* v. *Ulster Bank Ltd.*,[59] and it has also been adopted in Canada. Indeed, Middleton J.A. in the Ontario Court of Appeal in *Re Sutcliffe & Sons Ltd; ex parte Royal Bank*[60] could not have expressed the principle in clearer terms when he said, in the context of a loan account with a debit balance in excess of the credit balance on a current account, that[61] 'the fact that there were two accounts kept by the bank is utterly immaterial. There was in law but one account to be ascertained by bringing all items into consideration. The bank is not and never was, in this case, a debtor in any sense. It was and is a creditor'. This approach has been followed by Canadian courts on other occasions.[62]

However, there are cases that appear to go the other way.[63] In New Zealand Conolly J. suggested that, until the accounts were amalgamated, they had to be considered as separate,[64] while in *York City and County Banking Company* v. *Bainbridge*[65] Hawkins J. seemed to be of the same

---

[55] [1908] SC 20.   [56] [1908] SC 20, 24.   [57] [1908] SC 20, 25.
[58] *In re Johnson & Company, Ltd.* [1902] 1 IR 439, 442.
[59] [1950] NILR 132 (esp. at 142–3).   [60] [1933] 1 DLR 562.
[61] [1933] 1 DLR 562, 569.
[62] *Ross* v. *Royal Bank of Canada* (1965) 52 DLR (2d) 578; *Re T. C. Marines Ltd.* (1973) 34 DLR (3d) 489. See also *Deep* v. *Bank of Montreal* (1991) 47 OAC 319.
[63] In addition to the cases referred to below see *Barclays Bank, Ltd.* v. *TOSG Trust Fund Ltd.* [1984] BCLC 1, 23 in which Nourse J. referred to 'the process of debits and credits which were necessary to combine the accounts', though one of the four accounts related to a separate company, and so it could only have been combined with the other three as a result of the letter of set-off which contemplated an act of combination.
[64] *National Bank of New Zealand* v. *Grace* (1890) 8 NZLR 706. Compare the comments of Richmond J. in *Horton* v. *Bank of New Zealand* (1889) 7 NZLR 582, 591, which accord with orthodoxy. The decision in *Grace* in any event may be explained on another ground. The question was whether interest had to be calculated on the net position, though the point is made later (section 11.3.1 below) that the single debt theory does not require that result before the bank has given effect to the combination in its books by an appropriate entry.
[65] (1880) 43 LT 732, 734.

opinion. Reference also may be made to *Barclays Bank, Ltd.* v. *Okenarhe*,[66] in which Mocatta J. assumed that an act of combination was required, though his judgment in that case was unreserved.[67] Further, the courts and text-writers have been accustomed to refer to the right in question as a right of set-off,[68] or a right in a bank to consolidate or combine accounts.[69] This includes Lord Denning M.R. and Winn L.J. in the Court of Appeal in *Halesowen*,[70] and Viscount Dilhorne, Lord Cross of Chelsea and Lord Kilbrandon in their respective judgments on appeal in the House of Lords.[71] Expressions such as these may be interpreted as suggesting that an act of combination is required in order to produce a single debt. It is true that Winn L.J. doubted that a number of accounts could be said to give rise to a single account.[72] But apart from that, when it was said in the various judgments in *Halesowen* that, upon termination of the agreement in that case, the bank could set off or combine or consolidate the accounts, there was no criticism, or indeed discussion, of the explanation put forward by Buckley L.J. in the Court of Appeal, and by such distinguished judges as Blackburn J. and James L.J. in earlier cases, that the principle is based on the view that the debt at any particular time is the balance of all the accounts. This suggests that the remarks in question were not intended to be a rejection of that view, but may have been references to the conduct of an accounting exercise in order to ascertain the balance. Alternatively, the point is made below[73] that *Halesowen* may indeed be a case in which an act of combination was required and, while the discussion by some of the judges appears to have been of general application, the judgments may nevertheless have to be read with that in mind.

---

[66] [1966] 2 Lloyd's Rep. 87.

[67] See Mocatta J.'s discussion of events at [1966] 2 Lloyd's Rep. 87, 90.

[68] See e.g. *Ex parte Kingston; in re Gross* (1871) LR 6 Ch. App. 632; *Garnett* v. *M'Kewan* (1872) LR 8 Ex. 10, 12, 13 per Kelly C.B., 14 per Pigott B; *Bank of New South Wales* v. *Goulburn Valley Butter Company Pty. Ltd.* [1902] AC 543, 550 (P.C.); *In re Morris, deceased; Coneys* v. *Morris* [1922] 1 IR 136; *Re Shaw; ex parte Andrew* v. *Australia and New Zealand Banking Group Ltd.* (1977) 31 FLR 118, 122; *Oceanica Castelana Armadora SA* v. *Mineralimportexport* [1983] 1 WLR 1294; Pennington, Hudson and Mann, *Commercial Banking Law* (1978), 29; Holden, *The Law and Practice of Banking* (5th edn. 1991) Vol. 1, 71; Wood, *English and International Set-off* (1989), 93; *Paget's Law of Banking* (10th edn., 1989), 501.

[69] See e.g. *In re E. J. Morel (1934) Ltd.* [1962] 1 Ch. 21, 30; *Barclays Bank, Ltd.* v. *Okernarhe* [1966] 2 Lloyd's Rep. 87, 95; *Direct Acceptance Corporation Ltd.* v. *Bank of New South Wales* (1968) 88 WN (Pt. 1) (NSW) 498, 504; *Halesowen Presswork & Assemblies Ltd.* v. *Westminster Bank Ltd.* [1971] 1 QB 1, 19 per Roskill J. (at first instance).

[70] [1971] 1 QB 1, 34, 35, 38.   [71] [1972] AC 785, 807, 809–11, 819, 820.

[72] [1971] 1 QB 1, 40.   [73] See section 11.3.4 below.

11.3 CRITICISMS

This analysis of combination has been said to be inconsistent with many of the features of bank accounts,[74] though in truth any difficulty is more apparent than real. In particular, some of the criticisms assume that statements by judges to the effect that all the accounts constitute a single account were intended to refer to the operation of the accounts, and not just to the ascertainment of the debt at any particular time. The important point is that the accounts are not treated as one for all purposes. While the existence and the amount of any debt owing by the banker or the customer to the other can only be ascertained by looking at the balance of all the accounts together, for some purposes the accounts retain their separate indentities until the bank effects a physical combination in its books.

As a preliminary point, one effect of the view that there is at any particular time a single debt would be that an account could not be sued for separately if there is another account which reduces or cancels the balance on the first,[75] unless it has been separated out by agreement. However, this is unlikely to have any practical significance. Neither the bank nor the customer is likely to suffer an action against it in such a case. Whether the defence is based upon the notion that there is only one debt or upon a set-off, the result will be the same. A similar comment may be made in respect of the argument that an account may be assigned or garnished.[76] The assignee or the creditor would take subject to equities,[77] including rights of set-off, so that the theory that combination operates as a set-off would produce the same result in any event as the view that it is simply an accounting exercise.

11.3.1 *Interest*

Before accounts are combined in the bank's books interest ordinarily is calculated on the balance of each account, without reference to the balance on any other account.[78] However, this is not inconsistent with the explanation of combination found in the cases.[79] The parties can agree that interest is to be calculated on whatever basis they like, and the bank and its customer would be presumed to contract on the basis that, while an

---

[74] Wood, *English and International Set-off* (1989), 93; Salter, 'Remedies For Banks: An Outline of English Law', *Banks and Remedies* (edited by Cranston, 1992), 13.

[75] Compare Wood, *English and International Set-off* (1989), 93.

[76] Ibid.   [77] See sections 13.2 and 13.5 below.

[78] *Quaere* whether *Royal Trust Co.* v. *Molsons Bank* (1912) 8 DLR 478 was correctly decided.

[79] Compare Parke B. in *Pott* v. *Clegg* (1847) 16 M & W 321, 327.

account retains its separate indentity in the bank's books, interest would be calculated by reference to the balance on that account.[80]

11.3.2 *Clayton's Case, and the order of combination*

Nor is the notion that combination is a matter of account rather than of set-off inconsistent with the application of *Clayton's Case*[81] to each of the accounts. The accounting goes to the question whether, and to what extent, there is indeed a debt owing at any particular time by one party to the other on their banking relationship. If a customer pays an amount to the credit of one of a number of current accounts, *Clayton's Case* operates so as to appropriate the payment to the earliest drawing *on that account*, as opposed to the earliest drawing on the accounts taken together.[82] Any other result would be contrary to the presumed intention of the parties.[83] The parties may nevertheless have expressed an intention that *Clayton's Case* is not to be applied in this manner, or there may be special circumstances from which such an intention may be implied, in which case appropriation of payments will be dealt with in accordance with their intention.[84] An illustration is *In re E. J. Morel (1934) Ltd.*[85] In *Morel* drawings from a No. 3 account were regarded as having come from a credit balance on a No. 2 account. However, the circumstances of the case were indeed exceptional. A drawing could not be made from the No. 3 account unless the No. 2 account had a credit balance sufficient to cover it, so that in substance they were regarded as the one account.[86]

Questions of appropriation as between accounts may nevertheless arise in some cases.[87] Consider that two accounts, a No. 1 account and a No. 2 account, are in debit, while a third No. 3 account has a credit balance. At any particular time the question of the customer's debt owing to the bank

---

[80] See *Barclays Bank, Ltd.* v. *Okenarhe* [1966] 2 Lloyd's Rep. 87, 98. Compare *National Bank of New Zealand* v. *Grace* (1890) 8 NZLR 706 (esp. at 712), in which Conolly J., in holding that interest is payable on an overdrawn account without reference to a credit balance on another account, assumed that, until the accounts were closed and the balance sued for, the accounts had to be considered as separate accounts for all purposes.

[81] (1816) 1 Mer. 572.

[82] *Horton* v. *Bank of New Zealand* (1897) 7 NZLR 582, 593–594 (Richmond J. having accepted (at 591) that the accounts in law were combined); *In re Yeovil Glove Co. Ltd.* [1963] 1 Ch. 528, 543 (affirmed [1965] 1 Ch. 148); *In re James R. Rutherford & Sons Ltd.* [1964] 1 WLR 1211, 1216–17. See also the formulation of the principle by the Earl of Selborne in *In re Sherry* (1884) 25 Ch. D 692, 702. Compare *Mutton* v. *Peat* [1899] 2 Ch. 556 (reversed [1900] 2 Ch. 79).   [83] See *In re Hallett's Estate* (1880) 13 Ch. D 696, 738–9.

[84] *In re Hallett's Estate* (1880) 13 Ch. D 696, 738–9.

[85] [1962] 1 Ch. 21.

[86] Compare the arrangement adopted in *In re James R. Rutherford & Sons Ltd.* [1964] 1 WLR 1211.   [87] See e.g. the discussion of time bars in section 11.3.6 below.

can only be ascertained by looking at the balance of all three accounts. However, does the credit balance on the No. 3 account reduce first the No. 1 account or the No. 2 account? In *In re E. J. Morel (1934) Ltd.*[88] Buckley J. (as he then was) said that the bank can combine the accounts in whatever way it chooses, a view that was also accepted by Nourse J. at first instance in *Barclays Bank Ltd.* v. *TOSG Trust Fund Ltd.*[89] This would appear to be correct. The point was made earlier[90] that the bank is entitled to give effect to the combination in its books by moving assets and liabilities from one account to another,[91] and it is at that point that the bank should be able to determine the order of combination. While this book entry itself will not constitute a payment, since there was in any event only one debt for the balance,[92] it will affect issues such as the application of *Clayton's Case* to future debits and credits. The view that the bank can determine the order of combination in this manner would seem to follow from the rules applicable to appropriation of payments. If a debtor makes a payment to a creditor, he can appropriate it as he pleases. If, however, the debtor does not make an appropriation, and *Clayton's Case* is not applicable, the right of appropriation devolves upon the creditor.[93] On a similar principle, if the customer has not chosen to apply the No. 3 credit account in a particular way, for example, by withdrawing funds from that account and crediting them to either of the No. 1 or the No. 2 account, or by otherwise requesting the bank to make the appropriate book entries, the question of how the No. 3 account should be dealt with should devolve upon the bank, given that *Clayton's Case* does not apply as between accounts.

It is true that Walton J. in *In re Unit 2 Windows Ltd.*[94] held that, when there is a claim going one way and two cross-claims going the other, or, as in that case, one cross-claim which is partly preferential and partly non-preferential in the liquidation of the debtor, the set-off should occur rateably as between the cross-claims. However, that case was decided on the basis of the interpretation of the set-off section in the insolvency legislation.[95] When common law principles of combination are in issue, as opposed to a question of statutory interpretation, the position at common

---

[88] [1962] 1 Ch. 21, 31–2.   [89] [1984] BCLC 1, 22.

[90] See section 11.2.1 above.

[91] See, in the *Halesowen* case, Roskill J. at first instance [1971] 1 QB 1, 20–1, Lord Denning M.R. in the Court of Appeal (at 35) and Lord Kilbrandon in the House of Lords [1972] AC 785, 819, each of them criticizing a *dictum* by Swift J. to the contrary in *Greenhalgh and Sons* v. *Union Bank of Manchester* [1924] 2 KB 153, 164. See also *Garnett* v. *M'Kewan* (1872) LR 8 Ex. 10 (esp. Kelly C.B. at 13).

[92] *Re Sutcliffe & Sons Ltd; ex parte Royal Bank* [1933] 1 DLR 562 (esp. at 569); *Ross* v. *Royal Bank of Canada* (1965) 52 DLR (2d) 578; *Re T. C. Marines Ltd.* (1973) 34 DLR (3d) 489; *Re Plasky* (1981) 39 WWR 186.   [93] *The Mecca* [1897] AC 286.

[94] [1985] 1 WLR 1383.   [95] See section 2.17 above.

law regarding appropriation of payments would appear to provide the appropriate analogy. Nor could these principles ever conflict. If as a matter of the law of combination there is only one debt for the balance, the insolvency set-off section could never apply. The set-off section requires mutual but independent obligations, whereas under the law of combination there is only one obligation.[96]

11.3.3 *Guarantees and securities*

A guarantee may be given in respect of a particular account. If the customer has another account in credit with the bank, it would be to the advantage of the guarantor if the two accounts were combined so as to produce a single debt for the balance. The guarantor's liability in such a case would be reduced.[97] Similarly, if a customer provides security to a bank in respect of his indebtedness, and he has one account with a debit balance and another in credit, the question whether the debt secured is the balance of the two accounts taken together,[98] or whether regard is to be had only to the particular account in debit,[99] may depend on whether the accounts are combined. In this regard, it may be relevant to consider whether the circumstances surrounding the provision of the guarantee or the security in relation to a particular account evidence an agreement that that account is to be separated out.[100] On the other hand, where the accounts would otherwise be regarded as separate, the terms of the particular guarantee or security should be examined to see whether, as a matter of construction of the contract, it is in any event only intended to benefit the bank to the extent of any net balance on all the accounts.[101]

The question of combination in the context of a guarantee arose in *Bradford Old Bank* v. *Sutcliffe*.[102] A bank provided a fixed loan and a current account with an overdraft limit to a company, supported by a guarantee from the directors. One of the directors subsequently became insane, the effect of which, it was accepted, was that the guarantee ceased

---

[96] See Buckley L.J. in *Halesowen* [1971] 1 QB 1, 46.

[97] See e.g. *Re Tonkin* (1933) 6 ABC 197, 210–11. Compare *York City and County Banking Company* v. *Bainbridge* (1880) 43 LT 732, in which it was accepted that a surety's liability in respect of a loan made to a customer was not reduced by a credit balance on the customer's current account, since the accounts were separate.

[98] As in *In re European Bank; Agra Bank Claim* (1872) LR 8 Ch. App. 41 and *Mutton* v. *Peat* [1900] 2 Ch. 79. See also *Horton* v. *Bank of New Zealand* (1889) 7 NZLR 582.

[99] See *Royal Bank of Canada* v. *Bank of Montreal* [1976] 4 WWR 721, though it is unclear whether the current account in fact had a credit balance.

[100] This may apply in particular where an account in credit itself is charged back to the bank, assuming that charge-backs are possible. See section 12.4 below.

[101] See the discussion of *Mutton* v. *Peat* [1900] 2 Ch. 79 in section 11.2.2 above.

[102] [1918] 2 KB 833.

to be continuing, so that it only extended to debts in existence at that date. The company nevertheless continued to operate the current account until a demand was made on the guarantee a number of years later. It was held that payments into the current account during the intervening period had had the effect of satisfying the indebtedness on that account when the guarantee ceased to be continuing, in accordance with *Clayton's Case*.[103] However, insofar as the loan account was concerned, the amount owing on that account was not satisfied by subsequent payments into the current account, since there was an implied agreement that the accounts should be kept separate. A curious aspect of the case is that there appears to have been a tacit acceptance of the view that, if the accounts had not been separate, *Clayton's Case* would have operated on the basis that payments into the current account would have reduced the loan account, though this is doubtful. *Clayton's Case* ordinarily should operate on an individual account basis, notwithstanding the principle of combination, unless it is agreed otherwise.[104]

A similar situation occurred in *In re Sherry*.[105] A bank provided an overdraft to a customer secured by a guarantee. The guarantor died, whereupon the guarantee was determined as to future advances. The bank accordingly closed the account, and opened a new account to which subsequent payments in were credited and drawings debited. When the guarantee was later enforced it was held that *Clayton's Case* did not apply so as to appropriate the payments credited to the second account in reduction of the guaranteed debt on the first account. Nor was it a term of the guarantee that payments received from the debtor should be regarded as appropriated in this manner. There is nothing in this case, however, which is inconsistent with the notion that combination is a matter of account.[106] We have seen that the fact that *Clayton's Case* was applied only in relation to the second account does not show any inconsistency. Further, the second account had a debit balance so that, even assuming that the case was one in which there was a single debt between banker and customer represented by the balance of both accounts, there was no account in credit which could have had the effect of reducing the guaranteed debt.[107]

---

[103] (1816) 1 Mer. 572.   [104] See section 11.3.2 above.

[105] (1884) 25 Ch. D 692. See also *Kirby* v. *Duke of Marlborough* (1813) 2 M & S 18; *Williams* v. *Rawlinson* (1825) 3 Bing. 71.

[106] Compare Wood, *English and International Set-off* (1989), 93 (referring to para. 10–223).

[107] Compare *Hollond* v. *Teed* (1848) 7 Hare 50 (explained in *In re Sherry* (1884) 25 Ch. D 692, 704–5). In that case there was indeed a balance standing to the credit of an account at the date the guarantee determined. However, at that date the outstanding bills of exchange the subject of the guarantee had not matured, and the amount standing to the credit of the account was withdrawn before maturity. Accordingly, it could not have been a case of combination.

11.3.4 *Notice of combination*

It has been suggested that the question may still be open as to whether a bank may be required to give notice before exercising its combination rights, and that any such requirement would be inconsistent with the view that at any particular time there is only one debt.[108] The short answer is that there is no requirement of notice for combination as such, and nor is the bank obliged to give notice of its intention to rely upon the principle.[109] Accordingly, there is no inconsistency.

There may, however, be a requirement of notice where there is an agreement between the parties to keep the accounts separate, and the bank wishes to terminate that agreement. For example, when a customer has both a current account in credit and a loan account, there is an implied agreement that the accounts should be kept separate,[110] because otherwise the customer could not safely draw cheques on the current account. Consistent with the view that reasonable notice is required to close a current account in credit,[111] the agreement may be able to be terminated if reasonable notice is given.[112] The question of reasonableness would depend upon the circumstances of the case,[113] although in any event provision would have to be made for outstanding cheques.[114]

A similar issue was the subject of discussion in the House of Lords in the *Halesowen* case.[115] The bank in that case had agreed that it would not require repayment of a frozen current account for a period of 4 months unless there was a material change in circumstances. This gave rise to an implied term that, during the period, the bank would not combine or consolidate the account with another current account in credit. While Viscount Dilhorne left open the question whether the bank would have been required to give notice of termination in the event of a material change in circumstances,[116] Lord Cross of Chelsea inclined to the better view, that notice was required albeit notice having immediate effect as opposed to reasonable notice.[117] A requirement of reasonable notice would have enabled the customer to defeat the purpose of the arrangement

---

[108] Salter, 'Remedies For Banks: An Outline of English Law' *Banks and Remedies* (edited by Cranston, 1992), 20.

[109] *Garnett* v. *M'Kewan* (1872) LR 8 Ex. 10; *Re Shaw* (1977) 31 FLR 118, 122; *Deep* v. *Bank of Montreal* (1991) 47 OAC 319.

[110] *Bradford Old Bank, Ltd.* v. *Sutcliffe* [1918] 2 KB 833. See generally section 11.7 below.

[111] *Joachimson* v. *Swiss Bank Corporation* [1921] 3 KB 110, 127.

[112] *Buckingham and Co.* v. *London and Midland Bank (Limited)* (1895) 12 TLR 70, 72. See also *Cumming* v. *Shand* (1860) 5 H & N 95.

[113] *Prosperity Ltd.* v. *Lloyds Bank Ltd.* (1923) 39 TLR 372, 373.

[114] *Joachimson* v. *Swiss Bank Corporation* [1921] 3 KB 110, 125.

[115] [1972] AC 785. [116] [1972] AC 785, 807.

[117] [1972] AC 785, 810.

by immediately withdrawing the funds standing to the credit of the current account, although his Lordship acknowledged that the bank would still have been required to honour cheques drawn before notice up to the limit of the credit balance on the account. After termination the bank would have become entitled to combine the accounts. The reason for this is that it was probably part of the implied term. In other words, the implied term was not just that the accounts should be kept separate during the agreed period, but also that, upon termination of the agreement, the bank could set off or combine the accounts. If this is correct, it would constitute a situation in which an act of combination would in fact have been required. This may not have necessitated an actual book entry to this effect. An assertion that the accounts were to be regarded as combined may have sufficed.[118]

11.3.5 *The customer's right*

It is sometimes suggested that the right to combine accounts is a right possessed by the bank only, and not the customer,[119] but that in some circumstances the bank may be obliged to combine.[120] The case generally cited in support of the second of these propositions is *Mutton* v. *Peat*,[121] though this is not an accurate description of the ground upon which the case was decided.[122] In truth, the presence or absence of an act of combination was regarded as irrelevant, because it was considered that there was in any event only one debt for the balance.

In so far as the view that only the bank may combine is concerned, it is based on what has been described as the 'apparent anomaly'[123] that arises in relation to accounts at different branches of the same bank. A bank may look upon various accounts as combined notwithstanding that they are kept at separate branches. Thus a bank may refuse to honour a cheque drawn by a customer on one particular branch at which he has an account in credit if there is a countervailing account in debit at another branch, such that the overall credit balance is insufficient to cover the cheque.[124]

---

[118] See Roskill J. at first instance in *Halesowen* [1971] 1 QB 1, 19, and also *Direct Acceptance Corporation Ltd.* v. *Bank of New South Wales* (1968) 88 WN (Pt. 1) (NSW) 498, 502.

[119] *Barclays Bank, Ltd.* v. *Okenarhe* [1966] 2 Lloyd's Rep. 87, 95; Herzberg, 'Bankers' Rights of Combination' (1982) 10 *Australian Business Law Review* 79, 82, 83.

[120] *Barclays Bank, Ltd.* v. *Okenarhe* [1966] 2 Lloyd's Rep. 87, 95–6; *Halesowen Presswork & Assemblies Ltd.* v. *Westminster Bank Ltd.* [1971] 1 QB 1, 34; *Paget's Law of Banking* (10th edn., 1989), 504; Ellinger, *Modern Banking Law* (1987), 160.

[121] [1900] 2 Ch. 79.

[122] See the discussion of *Mutton* v. *Peat* in section 11.2.2 above.

[123] *Barclays Bank, Ltd.* v. *Okenarhe* [1966] 2 Lloyd's Rep. 87, 95.

[124] *Garnett* v. *M'Kewan* (1872) LR 8 Ex. 10, approved of by the Privy Council in *Prince* v. *Oriental Bank Corporation* (1878) 3 App. Cas. 325. See also *Barclays Bank, Ltd.* v. *Okenarhe* [1966] 2 Lloyd's Rep. 87.

On the other hand, when a customer has two current accounts at separate branches, he may only draw upon either account to the extent of the balance on the account at the branch where the account is kept. If he draws on either account for an amount in excess of the credit balance on that account, he is not entitled to have the cheque honoured (subject to any agreed overdraft limit) on the ground that the combined balance on both accounts is more than sufficient to cover it.[125] While this has been said to be inconsistent with the notion that combination is a matter of account rather than set-off,[126] it may be explained on the basis that the bank only promises to repay any part of the amount due on an account against the written order of the customer if that order is addressed to the bank at the branch at which the account is kept,[127] rather than that the right under discussion is a right only of the bank. If there is only one debt for the balance *vis-à-vis* the bank, there should also be only one debt *vis-à-vis* the customer, although the customer's right to have his cheques honoured is subject to the terms of the contract with the bank.

It may be that, instead of having two accounts in credit at different branches, both accounts are at the same branch. A cheque may be drawn on the first account for an amount which is in excess of the credit balance on that account, although it would be covered if both accounts were taken together. The question arises whether the bank is obliged to honour the cheque by transferring part of the balance on the second account to the first account. Ellinger has discussed this problem in the context of the second account being a savings account.[128] In his view the maintenance of different types of accounts manifests an intention that they be kept separate, and accordingly the bank could dishonour the cheque. In practice, however, he suggested that the bank would permit the customer to overdraw his current account and leave the savings account intact as a form of security. This solution differs from a transfer of part of the savings account to the current account in an important respect. The customer in such a case would be debited with interest on the overdrawn account in an amount which exceeds the interest that would be earned on the savings account if it were left intact. Nevertheless, Ellinge's conclusion is probably correct. Cheques generally cannot be drawn on a savings account, and it

---

[125] *Garnett* v. *M'Kewan* (1872) LR 8 Ex. 10, 12 per Kelly C.B. ('if the plaintiff had had a balance in his favour at both places he could of course have drawn at either to the extent of the balance there'), 14–15 per Bramwell B.; *Barclays Bank, Ltd.* v. *Okenarhe* [1966] 2 Lloyd's Rep. 87, 95. See also *National Bank of New Zealand* v. *Grace* (1890) 8 NZLR 706, 710.

[126] Salter, 'Remedies For Banks: An Outline of English Law' *Banks and Remedies* (edited by Cranston, 1992), 20.

[127] See *Joachimson* v. *Swiss Bank Corporation* [1921] 3 KB 110, 127; *Prince* v. *Oriental Bank Corporation* (1878) 3 App. Cas. 325, 332; *Woodland* v. *Fear* (1857) 7 El. & Bl. 519.

[128] Ellinger, *Modern Banking Law* (1987), 159–60.

would be contrary to the agreement between the parties to this effect if the bank were required to transfer a part of the balance on a savings account to a current account in order to honour a cheque.

The question is more difficult where the second account is another current account rather than a savings account. If there is an express or implied agreement between the bank and the customer that these accounts are to be kept separate, that would be the end of the matter. The bank could not utilize part of the credit balance on the second account to pay a cheque drawn on the first account. In the absence of an agreement to this effect, however, the argument that the bank must honour the cheque is not without merit. The accounts in such a case would be regarded as combined, in the sense that they produce a single debt for the balance. This should be so from the perspective of both the bank and the customer. They are regarded as the one account, and it may be said that it was only for convenience that they were entered in the bank's books under different names.[129] In the situation in which a customer has two or more accounts at different branches, the traditional reason why a term is implied in the contract between the bank and its customer that the bank is not required to honour a cheque drawn on one account for an amount greater than the balance on that account, notwithstanding that the current account at the second branch has sufficient funds credited to it to cover the shortfall on the first account, is that each branch of a bank could not be expected to know the state of the customer's account at every other branch.[130] However, this would hardly apply when both current accounts are with the same branch, if indeed it is still appropriate in modern times in the context of separate branches. Moreover, when Atkin L.J. in *Joachimson* v. *Swiss Bank Corporation*[131] discussed the terms implied in the banker/customer contract, he referred to the bank's obligation to honour the customer's written orders addressed to the bank at the branch where the account is kept. The emphasis was on the branch, as opposed to a particular account. Nevertheless, the question of the bank's obligation when there is more than one account was not an issue in *Joachimson*, and indeed Bankes L.J. in that case warned against placing too much reliance upon the language used in a judgment when the judge had not the precise point before him.[132]

---

[129] *Bailey* v. *Finch* (1871) LR 7 QB 34, 40; *Ex parte Morier; in re Willis, Percival, & Co.* (1879) 12 Ch. D 491, 498–9; *In re Johnson & Company, Ltd.* [1902] 1 IR 439, 442; *Clark* v. *Ulster Bank, Ltd.* [1950] NILR 132, 142. See also *In re European Bank; Agra Bank Claim* (1872) LR 8 Ch. App. 41, 44; *Garnett* v. *M'Kewan* (1872) LR 8 Ex. 10, 12.

[130] *Barclays Bank, Ltd.* v. *Okenarhe* [1966] 2 Lloyd's Rep. 87, 95. See also *National Bank of New Zealand* v. *Grace* (1890) 8 NZLR 706, 710; *Joachimson* v. *Swiss Bank Corporation* [1921] 3 KB 110, 129–30; *Prince* v. *Oriental Bank Corporation* (1878) 3 App. Cas. 325, 332–3.   [131] [1921] 3 KB 110, 127.

[132] *Joachimson* v. *Swiss Bank Corporation* [1921] 3 KB 110, 120.

The better view is that the bank is not obliged to honour the cheque, notwithstanding that the accounts are combined to form a single debt. By opening separate accounts it is probably an implied term of the contract that the bank is only obliged to honour a cheque drawn on a particular account to the extent of the balance on that account. But, as Ellinger has pointed out, in practice the bank in such a case may well honour the cheque by allowing the account on which it is drawn to go into overdraft. The bank could then look to the combined position on both accounts when deciding whether to honour future cheques drawn on either account.

11.3.6 *Time bars*

It has also been suggested that a debit balance may become statute-barred as a result of the expiration of a limitation period and hence ineligible for a set-off, and that this is inconsistent with the notion that only one amount is owing on all the accounts.[133] This analysis of combination does indeed suggest that an account that otherwise would have been time-barred if it had existed in isolation may still be included in a combination. If at the same time there is a second account in credit, the first account to the extent of the credit balance will have been paid. This may not always be the case, however. If, for example, the second account only came into existence after the expiration of the limitation period for the first account, there may well be an implied agreement that it is to be kept separate. The circumstances of each case would have to be considered.

Two comments may be made in respect of the criticism of the view that an account that otherwise would be time-barred may be included in a combination.

The first is that there is nothing in the cases inconsistent with this result. The two cases which have been cited as authority to the contrary in fact were not concerned with combination. In *Pott* v. *Clegg*[134] the assignees in bankruptcy of a bankrupt banker sued the executor of William Turner for the balance owing on an account. The executor pleaded set-off based upon an account that had been opened in the joint names of Turner and one Mawdesley, the limitation period for which had elapsed. Mawdesley had died, and the account accordingly had vested in Turner, although it still remained in the bank's books in the joint names. It was held that Turner's executor could not employ the time-barred account in a set-off. The case in truth turned on the availability of a set-off under the Statutes of Set-off, for which it is accepted that the debt sought to be set off must be enforceable

---

[133] Wood, *English and International Set-off* (1989), 93, and see also Salter, 'Remedies For Banks: An Outline of English Law' *Banks and Remedies* (edited by Cranston, 1992), 20.
[134] (1847) 16 M & W 321.

by action.[135] It was not a case of combination, because the basis of that principle is that there is a single relationship of banker and customer,[136] whereas in *Pott* v. *Clegg* separate banker/customer relationships were in issue. A similar comment may be made in respect of *In re Morris; Coneys* v. *Morris*.[137] A customer with a deposit account was liable as a surety on a promissory note given to the bank. After the limitation period for a claim on the note had expired the bank purported to set off the amount of the note against the deposit. It was held that the bank was not entitled to do this, given that an action could not be brought on the note. Once again, however, this was not a case of combination at all, since the customer's liability on the note as a surety did not arise out of the banker/customer relationship.

The second comment is that, even if combination of accounts were properly characterized as a set-off, the better view is that the right would still be exercisable by a bank where one of the accounts is time-barred. This is so notwithstanding comments by Sir John Ross L.C. in the Irish High Court of Appeal in *Morris* which suggest otherwise.[138] A statute of limitation takes away the remedy of enforcing a debt in an action at law, though it leaves the debt itself intact. If for the moment it is assumed that combination operates by way of set-off, the set-off would be effected without recourse to the courts, in which case it is not clear why the expiration of a limitation period should affect the right. There are indeed a number of situations in which the courts have recognized that a creditor may exercise rights and remedies in relation to a time-barred debt in circumstances where recourse to the courts is not required. For example, the common law has recognized that a possessory lien may be exercised in respect of a statute-barred debt,[139] and one would have thought that the same principle would apply in relation to a common law right to combine accounts which, like a lien, takes effect extra-judicially. Consistent with that view, Mocatta J. commented in *Barclays Bank, Ltd.* v. *Okenarhe*[140] that a bank should not be in any worse position with respect to money deposited with it than it would be with respect to securities over which it had a lien. A similar stance has been adopted in equity in relation to both the substantive defence of equitable set-off[141] and the rule in *Cherry* v.

---

[135] See section 1.2.10 above.

[136] See Buckley L.J. in the Court of Appeal in *Halesowen* [1971] 1 QB 1, 46.

[137] [1922] 1 IR 136, affirming [1922] 1 IR 88.

[138] [1922] 1 IR 136, 137. Compare O'Connor M.R., whose judgment consisted primarily of a rejection of the argument that the bank had a 'lien' on the deposit account. Insofar as set-off is concerned, his only discussion was in the context of pleading set-off as a defence to an action at law, presumably pursuant to the Statutes of Set-off, for which an enforceable debt is indeed required.

[139] *Spears* v. *Hartly* (1800) 3 Esp. 81; *Higgins* v. *Scott* (1831) 2 B & Ad. 413.

[140] [1966] 2 Lloyd's Rep. 87, 97.   [141] See section 1.7.4 above.

Boultbee.[142] Another illustration is the right that an executor formerly enjoyed to retain a sufficient amount from the estate in order to pay a debt owing to him by the deceased.[143] While this right has now been abolished in England,[144] it was nevertheless held that the expiration of the limitation period for the debt did not affect the executor's right.[145] Further, reference may be made to the case of a debtor who makes a payment to the creditor without directing that it be paid in reduction of a particular debt. The right of appropriation in such a case devolves upon the creditor, and he may apply the payment to a time-barred debt rather than to another debt that is still enforceable.[146] It is true that, in the case of set-off under the Statutes of Set-off, the common law courts have required that the cross-debt sought to be set off must be enforceable by action,[147] and that may well be what Sir John Ross had in mind in *Morris*. However, that form of set-off is a procedural defence to an action at law which requires a court order for a set-off.[148] For this reason it is distinguishable from combination of accounts.

How would combination work in practice in relation to an account that otherwise would be time-barred? Consider that there are two accounts, account No. 1 which is in credit, and account No. 2 which has a debit balance and in respect of which the limitation period has expired. In such a case the customer could only sue for the balance of the two accounts if the credit balance on account No. 1 exceeds the debit balance on account No. 2. If on the other hand the debit balance on account No. 2 exceeds the debit balance on account No. 1, the bank's claim for the ultimate balance would be unenforceable. It may be that there are two accounts with debit balances, account No. 2 which is time-barred and account No. 3 which is not. In such a case the principle should be that, in the absence of an appropriation by the customer, the bank could treat the credit balance on account No. 1 as reducing first the debit balance on account No. 2.[149] To the extent that any part of the balance on account No. 2 is not reduced in this manner, section 5 of the Limitation Act 1980 would prevent an action in respect of it.

11.4 BANKER AND CUSTOMER RELATIONSHIP

Any obligation owing to a bank in its capacity as banker should be capable

---

[142] (1839) 4 My. & Cr. 442, discussed in Ch. 10. See in particular section 10.5 above.
[143] See section 10.2 above.   [144] Administration of Estates Act 1971, s. 10.
[145] *Hill* v. *Walker* (1858) 4 K & J 166.
[146] *Mills* v. *Fowkes* (1839) 5 Bing. (NC) 455.   [147] See section 1.2.10 above.
[148] See section 1.2.9 above.   [149] See section 11.3.2 above.

of being included in a combination.[150] A debt due to it as a result of carrying on another business will not suffice.[151] Moreover, the obligations should relate to the same bank, a requirement that probably would not be satisfied where a bank uses separate corporate structures for its trading and savings bank functions.[152]

The sum owing to a bank on an instrument discounted by it for its customer may be combined with a credit balance on the customer's current account once that bill actually becomes due and payable.[153] However, a combination should not be able to be based upon a bill accepted or indorsed by the customer in favour of a third party who subsequently negotiated it to the bank. It would hardly seem correct to say that the customer's liability to the bank in this case has arisen out of the banker/customer relationship, when the negotiation to the bank took place outside that relationship. However, there are cases that suggest the contrary,[154] the most notable being the decision of the New Zealand Court of Appeal in *National Bank of New Zealand* v. *Heslop*.[155] The customer in *Heslop* was suing the bank for damages for failing to honour a cheque drawn on his current account in credit. The Court of Appeal decided in favour of the bank, two of the judges (Prendergast C.J. and Johnston J.) specifically referring to the banker's right of 'set-off'. The right in question could not have been based upon the procedural defence provided by the Statutes of Set-off in an action at law, because the Statutes only applied to mutual debts, whereas the customer's demand in this case was unliquidated in nature. Presumably, then, the Court thought that the bank was entitled to debit the customer's account with the amount of the bill under the law of combination, and as a result it could refuse to honour the customer's

---

[150] See Roskill J. in *Halesowen Presswork & Assemblies Ltd.* v. *Westminster Bank Ltd.* [1971] 1 QB 1, 20 ('whenever a customer is indebted to a banker as a banker'). See also *Barclays Bank, Ltd.* v. *Okenarhe* [1966] 2 Lloyd's Rep. 87, in which Mocatta J. held that the fact that the circumstances giving rise to the obligation to the bank were unusual did not preclude him from holding that it was still a banking transaction.

[151] See Pigott and Bramwell BB. in *Garnett* v. *M'Kewan* (1872) LR 8 Ex. 10, 14. The example given by Bramwell B. was the business of brewer.

[152] Herzberg, 'Bankers' Rights of Combination' (1982) 10 *Australian Business Law Review* 79, 86.

[153] Compare *Rogerson* v. *Ladbroke* (1822) 1 Bing. 93, in which the bank received notice of the customer's death before the promissory note matured. If a bank, having discounted a bill of exchange for a customer, in turn indorses the bill to a third party, and then pays the third party in the capacity of indorser, it may debit the customer's account. See *Pollard* v. *Ogden* (1853) 2 El. & Bl. 459, in which the customer was the drawer, and the court had to determine whether the bank had paid in its capacity of indorser, or instead as agent for the acceptor.

[154] *National Bank of New Zealand* v. *Heslop* (1882) NZLR 1 CA 47. See also *Coulls* v. *English, Scottish, and Australian Chartered Bank* (1872) 6 SALR 44, in which it seems that the bank was not the original payee of the bill accepted by Mander, and *Rogerson* v. *Ladbroke* (1822) 1 Bing. 91. *Quaere* whether the bills indorsed by the customer in *Royal Trust Co.* v. *Molsons Bank* (1912) 8 DLR 478 came to the bank as part of the banker/customer relationship.   [155] (1882) NZLR 1 CA 47.

cheque. It is doubtful whether in fact it should have been entitled to do so.

When two or more persons have a joint account with a bank, and one of those persons has another account in his own right, the better view is that separate banker/customer relationships are in issue so as to preclude a combination,[156] unless, of course, the bank has a letter of set-off or other agreement conferring such a right.[157]

11.5 COMBINATION AND NOMINEE ACCOUNTS

An account may be opened in the name of a particular customer, A, who, unknown to the bank, is merely a nominee for B. If B is a customer in his own right in respect of another account, the bank, when it discovers the nomineeship, may wish to assert that a credit balance on one of the accounts is combined with a debit balance on the other. Notwithstanding some comments in the Court of Appeal in *Bhogal* v. *Punjab National Bank*[158] that suggest that combination may occur where the beneficial interest of B is clear and indisputable,[159] the better view is that it will not. This indeed appears to have been the opinion of Scott J. at first instance in *Bhogal*.[160] When an account is opened and, unknown to the bank at the time, it is a nominee account, the nominee would be the customer, not the person for whom the account is held. The banker/customer relationship is one of contract, and the important point is that the nominee would be the contracting party.[161] Therefore the same banker/customer relationship would not be in issue in relation to the accounts for the purpose of combination. There may, however, be instances in which the person for whom the nominee has opened the account in fact is disclosed to

---

[156] Compare Ellinger, *Modern Banking Law* (1987), 152–3, referring to *Hill* v. *Bank of Hochelaga* [1921] 3 WWR 430. *Quaere* whether a joint and several liability owing to a bank would give rise to a combination under general law. The possibility of this occurring was contemplated by Hawkins J. in *York City and County Banking Company* v. *Bainbridge* (1880) 43 LT 732, 734, though his Lordship assumed that the right in question took the form of a right in the bank to set one account against another, as opposed to a notion that the accounts in any event are combined. Certainly, if a number of the joint and several debtors are customers of the bank, it could hardly be said that the liability has been combined at one and the same time with all the customers' individual accounts in credit. The better view is that, in the absence of a letter of set-off, the bank would be confined to a set-off, either as a procedural defence to an action at law under the Statutes of Set-off, or as a result of the operation of the insolvency legislation. [157] See section 11.8 below.

[158] [1988] 2 All ER 296, 301.

[159] In *Uttamchandami* v. *Central Bank of India*, unreported but noted in (1989) 139 *New Law Journal* 222, it is not clear if Lloyd L.J.'s remarks (at 223) concerning a case in which the account is indisputably a nominee account were intended to refer to the availability of equitable set-off as a defence to an action for payment of the balance on that account, or to combination giving the bank a right to dishonour cheques.

[160] See the extract from his judgment at [1988] 2 All ER 296, 305.

[161] When an agent contracts on behalf of an undisclosed principal, the agent is the contracting party. See section 9.7.3 above.

the bank,[162] so that that person in truth is regarded by all parties as the customer. In such a case combination may apply in relation to another account possessed by the customer.

If combination does not apply, a set-off nevertheless may be available as a defence to an action at law for payment of the credit balance on one of the accounts. This is the form of set-off that was in issue in the *Bhogal* case, and is based upon the Statutes of Set-off.[163] The difference is that, unlike combination, set-off under the Statutes only provides a procedural defence to an action, in the sense that the demands are not set against each other until there is judgment for a set-off.[164] It does not entitle the bank to dishonour a cheque.

Alternatively, the same person may open two or more accounts for his own benefit but under different names. In this situation there is the same bank and the same customer, although it is doubtful whether it can be said that there is the one relationship. Mocatta J. in *Barclays Bank, Ltd.* v. *Okenarhe*[165] nevertheless allowed combination of accounts in this situation, although the circumstances were exceptional and the case may be confined to its facts.

11.6 PRESENTLY MATURED OBLIGATIONS

A combination only arises when the accounts are otherwise presently payable,[166] which in this context includes presently payable on demand.[167] Thus a combination may not be based upon an obligation to the bank that will only mature at a future date, or an obligation that is merely contingent,[168] unless there is an agreement to the contrary.[169]

---

[162] See e.g. *In re Hett, Maylor, and Co.* (1894) 10 TLR 412.

[163] See section 11.15 below. While 'combination' appears in the headnote to the report of *Bhogal*, it does not in fact appear in the judgments, and to this extent the headnote is misleading. [164] See section 1.2.9 above.

[165] [1966] 2 Lloyd's Rep. 87.

[166] Compare *Agra and Masterman's Bank* v. *Hoffman* (1864) 34 LJ Ch. 285, which is difficult to follow. It would appear, however, that the injunction granted was only interlocutory, and it may be doubted whether a perpetual injunction would have been granted at the final hearing. The action in fact was settled.

[167] As in the case of a bank's liability to its customer on a current account in credit. See *Joachimson* v. *Swiss Bank Corporation* [1921] 3 KB 110.

[168] *Rogerson* v. *Ladbroke* (1822) 1 Bing. 93; *Bower* v. *Foreign and Colonial Gas Company* (1874) 22 WR 740. See also *Jeffryes* v. *Agra and Masterman's Bank* (1866) LR 2 Eq. 674, 680 ('you cannot retain a sum of money which is actually due against a sum of money which is only becoming due at a future time'); *Paget's Law of Banking* (10th edn., 1989), 496 (criticizing Abbott C.J. in *Bolland* v. *Bygrave* (1825) 1 Ry. & M 271 with respect to a banker's lien on securities, though note that Abbott C.J.'s judgment was cited with evident approval by Ungoed-Thomas J in *In re Keever* [1967] 1 Ch. 182, 189–90). Compare *Baker* v. *Lloyd's Bank, Ltd.* [1920] 2 KB 322, in which the declaration of insolvency was held to constitute a repudiation of the obligation to pay the bills of exchange at maturity.

[169] See section 11.8 below.

11.7 EXPRESS AND IMPLIED AGREEMENTS TO KEEP ACCOUNTS SEPARATE

It is not necessary to show an agreement between the bank and the customer that the accounts should be combined. Rather, the principle is that, as a matter of law,[170] two or more accounts kept by a customer with a bank give rise to a single debt unless there is an agreement, express or implied, to keep them separate.[171] The mere act of opening two accounts obviously does not constitute such an agreement.[172] An agreement to separate out an account may arise after the two accounts have already come into existence. For example, a customer may have a number of current accounts, which usually give rise to a single debt for the balance. However, the parties may agree to strike a balance on one or more of the accounts on the basis of an account stated,[173] so that that balance may be sued for separately. In *Cumming* v. *Shand*[174] the course of dealing between the bank and the customer was held to give rise to an implied agreement that a current account would not be debited with the sums paid on the customer's behalf by the bank, and the bank was required to give reasonable notice of its intention to discontinue the arrangement. If a customer gives a cheque to his bank with instructions to cash it and pay the proceeds to him, as opposed to crediting the proceeds to an account, the agreement to this effect will preclude a combination in relation to the proceeds.[175]

Two current accounts may be treated as giving rise to a single debt,[176] and similarly it is unlikely that the courts would infer an agreement that an overdrawn current account and a deposit account should be kept separate, at least when the deposit account is at call.[177] If the deposit is withdrawable

---

[170] In *Ex parte Morier* (1879) 12 Ch. D 491, 498 James L.J. said that, 'in point of law there was but one account'. Dr. McCracken (*The Banker's Remedy of Set-off* (1993), 27–32) has sought to explain combination on the basis of an implied term. A simpler explanation is that it is a conclusion of law which the courts have drawn as a result of there being a single banker/customer relationship.

[171] See Roskill J. at first instance in *Halesowen Presswork & Assemblies Ltd.* v. *Westminster Bank Ltd.* [1971] 1 QB 1, 20, Lord Denning in the Court of Appeal (at 35), and Lord Kilbrandon in the House of Lords [1972] AC 785, 819, each criticizing the *dictum* of Swift J. in *W. P. Greenhalgh and Sons* v. *Union Bank of Manchester* [1924] 2 KB 153, 164 suggesting that the customer's assent to a combination is required.

[172] *Halesowen Presswork & Assemblies Ltd.* v. *Westminster Bank Ltd.* [1971] 1 QB 1, 35 per Lord Denning M.R. (C.A.).

[173] See *Siqueira* v. *Noronha* [1934] AC 332, 337. [174] (1860) 5 H & N 95.

[175] *Rouxel* v. *Royal Bank of Canada* [1918] 2 WWR 791.

[176] *Garnett* v. *M'Kewan* (1872) LR 8 Ex. 10; *In re E. J. Morel (1934) Ltd.* [1962] 1 Ch. 21. 30; *Clark* v. *Ulster Bank Ltd.* [1950] NILR 132.

[177] *In re K (Restraint Order)* [1990] 2 QB 298.

after a specified period of notice by the customer, or after a fixed term, generally it would be a term of the contract that the accounts cannot be regarded as combined until the expiration of the requisite period after the customer has given notice, or at the end of the term.[178]

A customer commonly will have a loan from a bank and at the same time have a current account in credit. While there are indeed cases which seem to support the notion that these accounts may be regarded as combined in a single debt,[179] the generally accepted view is that there is an implied agreement that they should be kept separate.[180] The reason for this is that 'No customer could otherwise have any security in drawing a cheque on his current account if he had a loan account greater than his credit balance on current account'.[181] This, however, is subject to any agreement to the contrary between the parties.[182] As Lord Cross of Chelsea remarked in the House of Lords in the *Halesowen* case,[183] a loan account and a current account are regarded as separate 'unless the bank makes it clear to the customer that it is retaining the right at any moment to apply the credit balance on the current account in reduction of the debt on the loan account'. Roskill J. at first instance in *Halesowen*[184] postulated that, if a customer has a loan account on (say) 7 days call, and a current account in credit, it would be a term of the contract between the parties that the

---

[178] *Halesowen Presswork & Assemblies Ltd.* v. *Westminster Bank Ltd.* [1971] 1 QB 1, 21–2 per Roskill J. (at first instance).

[179] *In re European Bank* (1872) LR 8 Ch. App. 41; *Mutton* v. *Peat* [1900] 2 Ch. 79. See also *Hamilton* v. *Commonwealth Bank of Australia* (1992) 9 ACSR 90, 106.

[180] *Buckingham and Co.* v. *London and Midland Bank* (1895) 12 TLR 70 (action for damages for failing to honour the customer's cheques); *Bradford Old Bank, Ltd.* v. *Sutcliffe* [1918] 2 KB 833 (in which the Court of Appeal held that sums paid into a current account, in the period after a guarantee relating both to that account and also to a loan account had ceased to be a continuing guarantee, could not be considered as constituting satisfaction of the indebtedness on the loan account, with the result that the surety remained liable for the sum outstanding on the loan account); *In re E. J Morel (1934) Ltd.* [1962] 1 Ch. 21, 30–1; *Halesowen Presswork & Assemblies Ltd.* v. *Westminster Bank Ltd.* [1971] 1 QB 1, 20 per Roskill J (at first instance), 34 per Lord Denning MR (C.A.), and, on appeal in the House of Lords ([1972] AC 785), Lord Kilbrandon (at 819); *Bhogal* v. *Punjab National Bank* [1988] 2 All ER 296, 300. See also *York City and County Banking Company* v. *Bainbridge* (1880) 43 LT 732; *Barclays Bank, Ltd.* v. *Okenarhe* [1966] 2 Lloyd's Rep. 87, 96; *Matthews* v. *Geraghty* (1986) 43 SASR 576.

[181] *Bradford Old Bank, Ltd.* v. *Sutcliffe* [1918] 2 KB 833, 847 per Scrutton LJ. See also Pickford L.J. at 839.

[182] 'The critical question must always be, "What was the contract?" and not whether a particular account or accounts bear one title rather than another'. *Halesowen Presswork & Assemblies Ltd.* v. *Westminster Bank Ltd.* [1971] 1 QB 1, 21 per Roskill J (at first instance). Thus his Lordship (at 22) distinguished *In re European Bank* (1872) LR 8 Ch. App. 41 and *Mutton* v. *Peat* [1900] 2 Ch. 79 on the ground that it was not part of the arrangements between the parties in those particular cases that the accounts should be kept separate.

[183] *National Westminster Bank Ltd.* v. *Halesowen Presswork & Assemblies Ltd.* [1972] AC 785, 809. See also Roskill J. at first instance [1971] 1 QB 1, 22.

[184] [1971] 1 QB 1, 21.

accounts may be regarded as combined if the call is made and payment is not tendered within the requisite period. As a general proposition this is doubtful. The better view is that, unless the terms of a particular agreement between the parties to keep accounts separate are such that the agreement is determinable by notice having immediate effect, the bank would still have to give reasonable notice of termination.[185]

The justification outlined above for implying an agreement to keep a loan account separate from a current account would not be relevant to a loan account and a deposit account upon which the customer may not draw cheques, and so these accounts ordinarily would be combined into one debt, at least when the deposit and the loan are both presently payable on demand.[186] Similarly, any other vested liability of a customer to his bank may be able to be regarded as combined with, and consequently may be debited against, the bank's liability on a deposit account at call. This vested liability may take the form of interest payments on a term loan,[187] or it may arise as a result of payments made by the bank on letters of credit opened at the request of the customer.[188]

The implied agreement to keep separate a loan account and a current account in credit only subsists while the banker/customer relationship remains in existence. Ordinarily it would terminate upon the death or insanity of the customer, or upon his bankruptcy or its liquidation[189] (but not upon the appointment of a receiver[190]). Upon termination the bank would become entitled to combine the accounts.[191] When Roskill J. accepted the correctness of this proposition at first instance in *Halesowen*,[192] he said that the judgment of Buckley J. in *In re E. J. Morel (1934) Ltd.*[193] constituted authority to the contrary, and that on this point Buckley J.'s decision should be regarded as wrong. In truth there does not

---

[185] See section 11.3.4 above.

[186] This would seem to be the effect of Mocatta J.'s decision in *Barclays Bank, Ltd.* v. *Okenarhe* [1966] 2 Lloyd's Rep. 87, in which the sum paid to the customer was treated as a loan. See also *Rogerson* v. *Ladbroke* (1822) 1 Bing. 93, and *Matthews* v. *Geraghty* (1986) 43 SASR 576, 580 in relation to the letter of set-off in issue in that case.

[187] As in *Oceanica Castelana Armadora SA* v. *Mineralimportexport* [1983] 1 WLR 1294.

[188] *Oceanica Castelana Armadora SA* v. *Mineralimportexport* [1983] 1 WLR 1294, 1301.

[189] *Halesowen Presswork & Assemblies Ltd.* v. *Westminster Bank Ltd.* [1971] 1 QB 1, 24 per Roskill J. (at first instance), referring to *In re Keever* [1967] 1 Ch. 182. The *Halesowen* case actually involved an express agreement between the bank and the customer to keep the accounts separate, though his Lordship's opinion evidently was also intended to encompass the implied agreement arising in the case of a loan account and a current account. See also Lord Kilbrandon in the House of Lords [1972] AC 785, 819. Compare *In re Johnson & Co., Ltd.* [1902] 1 IR 439, in which the agreement was entered into specifically in contemplation of a winding-up.

[190] *Direct Acceptance Corporation Ltd.* v. *Bank of New South Wales* (1968) 88 WN (Pt. 1) (NSW) 498, 504 (in which there was an express agreement not to set off).

[191] It may be that this would require an act of combination. See section 11.3.4 above.

[192] [1971] 1 QB 1, 23–4.   [193] [1962] 1 Ch. 21.

appear to be any inconsistency at all. *Morel* concerned section 319(4) of the
Companies Act 1948, which, subject to certain limitations, conferred a
right of priority in the liquidation of a company in favour of a person who
had advanced money for the payment of wages to an employee of the
company.[194] A company's current account was substantially overdrawn.
This account (the No. 1 account) was frozen, and a No. 2 account, being a
normal business current account, and a No. 3 account, called a wages
account, were opened. The company was allowed to draw on the No. 3
account in order to pay the wages of its employees. However, it was a term
of the arrangement that the No. 2 account should always have a credit
balance in excess of the debit on the No. 3 wages account. Buckley J. held
that the credit balance on the No. 2 account should be treated as reducing
the debit on the wages account, rather than the debit on the No. 1 account.
Consequently the bank had a reduced claim to priority for sums advanced
for the payment of wages, and it was left with a right of proof on the No. 1
account for which no priority was accorded. In order for the bank to have
succeeded in its claim to priority, it had to be shown that the bank had
actually made advances for the purpose of paying wages. Buckley J. said
that, because of the agreement that the No. 1 account should be frozen so
as to be no longer capable of being operated in the ordinary way as a
current account, it had assumed the character of a loan account.[195]
Therefore the arrangement usually implied in the case of a loan account
and a current account was applicable, that the No. 1 frozen account and the
No. 2 current account should be regarded as separate and distinct,[196] which
in turn meant that payments credited to the No. 2 account could not be
regarded as having operated to reduce the prior debit balance on the No. 1
account.[197] Insofar as the No. 3 wages account was concerned, the parties
had agreed that any debit balance on that account should always be
covered by a credit balance on the No. 2 account. This led his Lordship to
conclude that these two accounts were not separate, but interdependent,
and in substance constituted the one account. It was apparent, then, that
the bank itself had not made any advances for the payment of wages,

---

[194] See now the Insolvency Act 1986, ss. 175 and 386, referring to Sch. 6 (in particular
Cat. 5).

[195] Similarly, the assertion by counsel in *Halesowen* [1971] 1 QB 1, 9, that once the
overdrawn No. 1 account in that case was frozen it became for all practical purposes a loan
account, was not disputed. See e.g. in the House of Lords [1972] AC 785, 809 per Lord Cross
of Chelsea, 819 per Lord Kilbrandon.

[196] The *dictum* of Riley J. in *Re Shaw* (1977) 31 FLR 118, 122, that, independently of the
letter of set-off the bank had a right to combine the working current account in credit with
the frozen current account in debit, should be regarded as doubtful.

[197] Compare the arrangement adopted in *In re James R. Rutherford & Sons Ltd; Lloyd's
Bank Ltd.* v. *Winter* [1964] 1 WLR 1211.

except to the extent that at the final date the debit on the wages account did in fact exceed the credit on the No. 2 account. Rather, the wages had been paid from the customer's own 'money' in the No. 2 account. Buckley J. did not decide that the No. 1 frozen account could not be regarded as combined even after the company went into liquidation. He merely said that the bank had not made any advance on each particular occasion when resort was had to the wages account for the purpose of paying wages. The source of the payment on each occasion was the company's own 'money' in the No. 2 account.[198]

An arrangement similar to that in *Morel* is sometimes adopted when a bank is concerned as to the solvency of a particular customer with a substantially overdrawn current account. The overdrawn account is frozen, and a new current account is opened through which the customer's current business henceforth should pass. This second current account is required to remain in credit, the intention being that the customer's indebtedness on the frozen account should be reduced progressively by occasional payments into it from the credit balance on the operating current account. As Buckley J. noted in *Morel*, the act of freezing a current account in debit converts it into a loan account so that, even apart from any express agreement between the parties that the bank should not have a right of set-off,[199] the courts will usually find an implied agreement to the effect that the accounts should not be combined during the subsistence of the banker/customer relationship. The presumption that the accounts are intended to be separate will not apparently be rebutted by the agreement that the debit on the frozen account should be reduced progressively, as long as the intention is that any transfers from one account to the other should be made on the instructions of the customer rather than on the initiative of the bank alone, albeit at the insistence of the bank.[200] Nor would the presumption be rebutted by an agreement that interest due on the frozen overdraft may be debited to the new account.[201] It may be, however, that, prior to this arrangement, the customer had given a letter of

---

[198] Buckley J. further held that, even if all three accounts in fact should be regarded as separate, the set-off section in the insolvency legislation should be applied on the basis that the claim which otherwise would be preferred in the winding-up should be the first claim to be brought into account with the creditor's own liability to the company. Consequently the same result would have been achieved. This aspect of the case is probably no longer good law following *In re Unit 2 Windows Ltd.* [1985] 1 WLR 1383, discussed in section 2.17 above. Insolvency set-off requires independent cross-demands, and so it would not be relevant in a banker/customer relationship in which the accounts in any event are combined.

[199] As in *Direct Acceptance Corporation Ltd.* v. *Bank of New South Wales* (1968) 88 WN (Pt. 1) (NSW) 498.

[200] *In re E. J. Morel (1934) Ltd.* [1962] 1 Ch. 21, 26.

[201] This is apparent from the *Halesowen* case [1972] AC 785.

set-off to the bank authorizing the bank at any time without notice to apply a credit balance on any of the customer's accounts as payment of any account in debit. In the absence of a later agreement negativing the operation of this letter, this may have the effect that the usual implied term precluding combination in such cases would not arise.[202]

The parties may expressly desire that there should not be any combination or set-off in the event of the customer's bankruptcy or winding-up. For example, a company in financial difficulty may have proposed a moratorium with its creditors, or it may intend to realize its assets as a means of paying its debts. In order to prevent the bank alone being benefited by any payments deposited with it, the parties may agree that the company's overdrawn account should be frozen and that a new account should be opened which is to remain in credit, and moreover that the bank should not be entitled to set off the credit balance on this new account against the debit balance on the frozen account. The House of Lords in *National Westminster Bank Ltd.* v. *Halesowen Presswork & Assemblies Ltd.*[203] struck down this form of arrangement in the event of the bankruptcy or liquidation of the customer, by holding that the operation of the set-off section in the insolvency legislation cannot be excluded by agreement between the parties. As a result, it is necessary for the customer in this situation to open a working account with a different bank in order to prevent the first bank being preferred by means of a set-off at the expense of the other creditors in the event of bankruptcy or winding-up proceedings. The Cork Committee described this as 'an unnecessary and undesirable complication',[204] and recommended that a creditor should indeed be permitted to agree in advance to waive his right to invoke the section, particularly when the creditor is the party who otherwise would be benefited by a set-off. This is a salutary proposal, and it is a matter for regret that in England a provision giving effect to it was not included in the Insolvency Act 1986.[205]

Roskill J. at first instance in *Halesowen*[206] said that a bank by its actions may preclude itself from asserting a combination. This observation should be read with care, however. If the general principle is that accounts are combined in a single debt as a matter of law unless there is an agreement to the contrary, the bank's actions should not preclude a combination unless those actions have the effect of giving rise to an agreement with the customer that henceforth the accounts should be regarded as separate. For example, the fact that a bank credits interest to a particular account is not sufficient to preclude the bank from asserting that this account is combined

---

[202] See e.g. *Re Shaw* (1977) 31 FLR 118, and generally section 11.8 below.
[203] [1972] AC 785.   [204] *Cork Committee Report*, 306.
[205] See section 2.11 above.   [206] [1971] 1 QB 1, 19.

with another.[207] Nor should separate bank statements have this effect. These statements merely reflect the undoubted fact that a bank has a number of accounts entered in its books, and, as Lindley M.R. noted in *Mutton* v. *Peat*,[208] no matter how many accounts a bank may have entered in its books there is still only one debt for the balance of all of them.

If money is deposited with a bank for a specific purpose known to the bank, for example, in order to provide funds to meet a particular bill, the courts may imply an agreement that the money should not be regarded as combined with an overdrawn account.[209] Usually this implied agreement would only mean that each account should be considered as giving rise to a separate debt. It would deprive the bank of any right to act unilaterally[210] based upon an assumption that there is only one debt arising out of a banker/customer relationship. Depending on the agreement, it would not necessarily have the additional effect of negating a right of set-off in an action at law under the Statutes of Set-off,[211] or indeed under the mutual credit provision in the insolvency legislation in the event that the recommendation of the Cork Committee permitting contracting out is ever adopted.[212] The implied agreement in fact would bring about the very situation necessary for a set-off, i.e. mutual and independent cross-demands.

---

[207] See section 11.3.1 above. Mocatta J. in reaching this conclusion in *Barclays Bank, Ltd.* v. *Okenarhe* [1966] 2 Lloyd's Rep. 87, 98, postulated that, in certain circumstances, the crediting of interest on an account might be evidence that the parties had reached agreement that the accounts should be kept separate. However, he conceded that 'the circumstances would probably have to be somewhat exceptional since . . . the general practice is that interest is either credited or debited after calculation by reference to one account and not to all the accounts between a customer and his bank'. [208] [1900] 2 Ch. 79, 85.

[209] *Garnett* v. *M'Kewan* (1872) LR 8 Ex. 10, 13 (citing *Hill* v. *Smith* (1844) 12 M & W 618); *MPS Constructions Pty. Ltd.* v. *Rural Bank of New South Wales* (1980) 4 ACLR 835, 841–2 (account opened for retention money under a building contract). See also *W. P. Greenhalgh and Sons* v. *Union Bank of Manchester* [1924] 2 KB 153. Compare *Oceanica Castelana Armadora SA* v. *Mineralimportexport* [1983] 1 WLR 1294, in which the customer had deposited money for the purpose of securing a guarantee intended to be given by the bank to a third party, though that purpose failed. In some cases there may also be a trust, as in *Barclays Bank Ltd.* v. *Quistclose Investments Ltd.* [1970] AC 567, discussed in section 11.12.2 below. [210] As e.g., by declining to honour a cheque.

[211] *Hill* v. *Smith* (1844) 12 M & W 618, 631. Similarly, the implied agreement to keep separate a loan account and a current account in credit would probably not be sufficient to exclude the operation of the Statutes of Set-off in an action at law. Note that the Statutes only apply to mutual debts. The bank will not be permitted a set-off if the customer instead is suing for damages for breach of duty.

[212] See e.g. *Ex parte Pearce; in re Langmead* (1841) 2 Mont. D & De G 142, and *Pedder* v. *The Mayor, Aldermen, and Burgesses of Preston* (1862) 12 CB (NS) 535, with respect to special-purpose local government accounts. The denial of a set-off in cases such as *Hill* v. *Smith* (1844) 12 M & W 618, 631 and *Bell* v. *Carey* (1849) 8 CB 887, when the customer's assignees in bankruptcy sued for damages rather than for money had and received, may be explained on the ground that, before the Bankruptcy Act 1861, a damages claim could neither be proved in the bankruptcy nor set off. See also the discussion of special-purpose payments in section 6.6 above.

11.8 AGREEMENTS PERMITTING COMBINATION

A customer may give to his bank a letter of set-off empowering the bank to set off or consolidate or combine all or any of his accounts at any time without notice. A letter in these terms would seem to contemplate some form of act of combination by the bank. In this regard it may be necessary to distinguish two types of cases. In the first place, it may be that two accounts are in issue which prima facie come within the ambit of the general law of combination, being accounts kept by the one customer with the one bank, but that in the particular case the courts would usually imply an agreement that the accounts should be kept separate so that the customer can safely deal with third parties in the knowledge that he has an account in credit against which he can draw cheques. It is for this reason that the courts usually find an implied agreement that a loan account should be kept separate from a current account in credit.[213] Yet one would have thought that, in a case such as this, a letter of set-off empowering the bank to combine the accounts at any time without notice would abrogate the *very reason* for implying a term to keep them separate, at least when the letter of set-off had been given to the bank before one of the accounts had been opened, and consequently before the implied term had been established.[214] Therefore, even though the letter may seem to contemplate some form of act of combination by the bank itself, it may be that the fact that the customer has given the bank a letter of set-off in this form would mean that the accounts in any event are combined in a single debt. Alternatively, it may be that the letter contemplates that a credit balance on an account may be applied in satisfaction of a liability in circumstances in which a combination would not otherwise be recognized, not because of an implied agreement in order to safeguard a credit account against which cheques may be drawn, but because as a matter of law there are separate banker/customer relationships. Thus, the letter may allow the bank to appropriate the credit balance as satisfaction of a joint liability,[215] or it may entitle the bank to consolidate the accounts of the various companies in a group. Any purported appropriation of the credit balance could only arise as a result of an act by the bank itself authorized by the letter of set-off. To the extent that an act of combination is in fact required in a particular case,

---

[213] *Bradford Old Bank, Ltd.* v. *Sutcliffe* [1918] 2 KB 833, 839, 847.

[214] See in this regard *Re Shaw* (1977) 31 FLR 118 (esp. at 122), and also *Matthews* v. *Geraghty* (1986) 43 SASR 576.

[215] Compare *Watts* v. *Christie* (1849) 11 Beav. 546; *Ex parte Morier; in re Willis, Percival, & Co.* (1879) 12 Ch. D 491.

this may not necessitate an actual book entry.[216] An assertion that the accounts are to be treated as combined may suffice.[217]

A bank is sometimes empowered by a letter of set-off given by the customer to appropriate an account in credit in satisfaction of a liability while that liability is still contingent. Professor Goode's analysis of the agreement is instructive.[218] Depending on the circumstances, it may be interpreted in either of two ways. The more likely construction is that the bank is entitled to suspend payment of the account in credit until such time as the liability may vest, followed, if it does vest, by a set-off. Alternatively, there may be cases where the effect of the agreement is that the bank's liability on the account in credit is immediately cancelled to the extent of the maximum contingent liability, with an obligation to re-credit the customer if and to the extent that the contingent liability does not become an actual liability.

A letter of set-off given to a bank will not be effective in relation to a particular account where the money credited to the account was the subject of a prior assignment or trust in favour of a third party, and the bank had notice of this when the money was deposited.[219] If the bank did not have notice, it will obtain priority if it was a bona fide purchaser for value.[220]

An exercise of a contractual right of combination after the commencement of a court-ordered winding-up of the customer in relation to accounts that are otherwise separate would constitute a disposition of the company's property, and accordingly would be void under section 127 of the Involvency Act 1986 save with the consent of the court.[221] On the other hand, there may be a set-off under the insolvency set-off section, so as to put it in the same position in any event.[222]

11.9 DIFFERENT CURRENCIES

An issue that is yet to be determined is whether combination applies to accounts in different currencies.[223]

---

[216] There may indeed be an express provision to this effect in the agreement. See e.g. the letter of set-off in *Re Shaw* (1977) 31 FLR 118.

[217] See Roskill J. at first instance in *Halesowen* [1971] 1 QB 1, 19, and also *Direct Acceptance Corporation Ltd.* v. *Bank of New South Wales* (1968) 88 WN (Pt. 1) (NSW) 498, 502. [218] Goode, *Legal Problems of Credit and Security* (2nd edn., 1988), 173.

[219] *Re Marwalt Ltd.* [1992] BCC 32.

[220] *Re Marwalt Ltd.* [1992] BCC 32, 38; *Neste Oy* v. *Lloyds Bank Plc* [1983] 2 Lloyd's Rep. 658, 666. See generally sections 11.12.1 and 11.12.4 below.

[221] *Barclays Bank Ltd.* v. *TOSG Trust Fund Ltd.* [1984] BCLC 1.

[222] See section 2.15 above.

[223] See generally Horrigan, 'Combining Bank Accounts in Different Currencies—A Conceptual Analysis' (1991) 65 *Australian Law Journal* 14.

Any discussion of the question must begin with the fundamental point, that combination is an accounting situation in which the existence and amount of one party's liability to the other can only be ascertained by looking at the ultimate balance of all the accounts. The concept is dynamic in nature. At any particular point in time there is as a matter of law only one debt for the balance. If combination applied to a foreign currency account there would have to be a defined mechanism for converting the account into sterling, so that at any point in time both parties could calculate the combined position. Further, since the basis of combination is the banker/customer relationship, the exchange rate should be the rate that the bank itself would make available to the customer for the account in question at the time that the issue arises. In this sense it would differ from a currency conversion effected for the purpose of proof of debts in a bankruptcy or a liquidation, or for the purpose of enforcing a foreign currency judgment obtained in accordance with the decision of the House of Lords in *Miliangos* v. *George (Frank) Textiles Ltd.*[224] In these situations a general objectively ascertainable market rate would suffice.[225] This would not be appropriate, however, in the case of combination. What rate, then, would be applied for conversion if the parties have not expressly agreed a rate? It could be said that there is an implied term in the contract between the bank and its customer that conversion would occur at the bank's published daily rate for the currency in question, though this does not settle the issue. In the first place, if the foreign currency the subject of the account is required for a particular purpose, that in itself may give rise to an implied agreement that the account is to be kept separate so as to preclude combination. But even apart from that, the published daily rate may not be the rate that the parties ordinarily would expect to employ. A bank's daily rate often is only relevant for transactions up to a certain amount. For larger amounts the rate would be set on a transaction by transaction basis. Rates move during the day, and the published rate may not be the rate that in fact would apply to a conversion in relation to a large deposit. In so far as fluctuations during the day are concerned, the 'Reuters' screen will show the latest rate at which the currency was traded in the professional market, though this may only be used as a guide by the bank when it is asked to quote a rate in a particular case. The rate that is quoted to a customer may vary from the screen rate, depending on the bank's perception of where the market is going. Therefore, at any point in time a customer with a large foreign currency account may not be in a position to

---

[224] [1976] AC 443.
[225] For example, the Practice Direction published after the decision in *Miliangos* referred to the rate current in London at the close of business on the day in question. See [1976] 1 WLR 83.

know with certainty what its combined position is. In *Garnett* v. *M'Kewan*[226] Bramwell B. justified the bank's right to dishonour a cheque drawn on an account where there was another account in debit on the ground that, 'to limit [the customer's] drawing to the amount of his total actual balance is no hardship on him, for he always knows, or can know if he likes, the state of his account as a whole'. As a corollary, where the customer at any point in time cannot know the state of the accounts on a combined basis with certainty, it is suggested that the courts would readily conclude, either on the basis of an implied agreement or a substantive principle of law, that combination does not apply.[227] While it could be said that the customer can request the bank at any time to quote the appropriate rate for conversion so that it may know the position at that time, this would not be a convenient solution. Nor would it be possible outside banking hours. Furthermore, the rate quoted to an extent would be within the bank's discretion, which would hardly be a satisfactory basis for combination from the customer's point of view, particularly where large amounts of money are in issue. Having said that, there is authority in Canada to the effect that combination may apply in relation to foreign currency accounts. In *Deep* v. *Bank of Montreal*[228] the Ontario Court of Appeal held that a bank was entitled to apply a maturing Deutschmark term deposit against a Canadian dollar overdraft. However the case is not satisfactory, because the court merely assumed that combination applies to foreign currency accounts. Nor was there any discussion of the conversion mechanism.

The bank may in fact take a letter of set-off entitling it to combine accounts, including foreign currency accounts, at any time without notice. Unlike the common law principle of combination, an act of combination would be required.[229] The letter should specify the mechanism for conversion of foreign currency accounts into sterling for the purpose of a combination. This may be the published daily rate, or it may be, for example, the rate offered by the bank to the market generally at a particular time of the day in question.

11.10 MAREVA INJUNCTIONS AND RESTRAINT ORDERS

Once the true nature of the right of combination is understood, the difficulty perceived by Lloyd J. in *Oceanica Castelana Armadora SA* v. *Mineralimportexport*[230] in relation to Mareva injunctions should dissolve.

---

[226] (1872) LR 8 Ex. 10, 15.
[227] Compare Wood, *English and International Set-off* (1989), 97, and McCracken, *The Banker's Remedy of Set-off* (1993), 36.   [228] (1991) 47 OAC 319.
[229] See section 11.8 above.   [230] [1983] 1 WLR 1294.

The plaintiff in a suit against a foreign defendant had obtained a Mareva
injunction restraining the defendant from removing or disposing of its
assets, up to a stated maximum amount, situated within the jurisdiction.
Barclays Bank held funds deposited with it by the defendant. However, the
bank had also made substantial loans to the defendant, and so it applied to
the court for an order to vary the injunction in order that it might exercise
its right of 'set-off'. Lloyd J. granted the variation on the grounds that a
Mareva injunction was not intended to interfere with the ordinary rights
and remedies of a third party. He accepted that the funds held by the bank
prima facie were covered by the wording of the injunction before him, and
that therefore it was necessary that the bank should come to court for a
variation.[231] His Lordship said that this was unsatisfactory, and suggested
that henceforth all Mareva injunctions intended to be served on banks
should contain a suitable proviso exempting the bank's right of 'set-off'
from the operation of the injunction.[232] However, if the case is truly one of
combination, it is not at all clear that a bank should be required to apply to
the court for a variation in the absence of a specific proviso protecting its
rights. In such a case a right to set off independent cross-demands is not in
issue. Rather, the bank is entitled to say that there is only one debt owing
by (or to) the customer for the balance of all the accounts arising in the
course of the banker/customer relationship, unless a particular item has
been separated out by agreement. Consequently a particular account in
credit with a bank should not be regarded as a separate asset of the
customer coming within the ambit of a Mareva injunction, if there are
other accounts in debit which must be brought into account in order to
ascertain whether in fact there is a debt owing to the customer by the bank.
Thus, Canadian courts have recognized that, when a bank makes an entry
in its books giving effect to the principle of combination, this itself does not
constitute payment of an account in debit, since there was in any event only
one debt for the balance.[233] Consistent with that approach, Otton J. in *In
re K (Restraint Order)*[234] held that a bank's assertion of a right of
combination in relation to a deposit account and an overdraft facility was
not in conflict with the terms of a restraint order under section 8 of the

---

[231] See also *Project Development Co. Ltd. S.A.* v. *K.M.K. Securities Ltd.* [1982] 1 WLR
1470.

[232] Lloyd J. expressed approval of a clause suggested by counsel, 'Provided that nothing in
this injunction shall prevent [the bank] from exercising any rights of set-off it may have
in respect of facilities afforded by [the bank] to the defendants prior to the date of this
injunction'.

[233] *Re Sutcliffe & Sons Ltd; ex parte Royal Bank* [1933] 1 DLR 562 (esp. at 569); *Ross* v.
Royal Bank of Canada (1965) 52 DLR (2d) 578; *Re T. C. Marines Ltd.* (1973) 34 DLR (3d)
489; *Re Plasky* (1981) 39 CBR 186. For the same reason, the book-keeping entry does not
constitute a seizure of assets. See *Deep* v. *Bank of Montreal* (1991) 47 OAC 319.

[234] [1990] 2 QB 298.

Drug Trafficking Offences Act 1986, which restrained all dealings with the accounts. As his Lordship noted,[235] combination in truth is merely an accounting procedure in order to ascertain the existence and amount of one party's liability to the other.

When an account in credit has been frozen as a result of a Mareva injunction, the right of combination applies to all liabilities of the customer arising in connection with facilities granted to the customer before the bank received notification of the injunction. Thus, the bank will be permitted to debit the account in respect of any liability which it may incur on confirmed letters of credit opened at the request of the customer before notice.[236] Further, combination may encompass interest accruing due both before and after notification, as well as the principal when it becomes due, provided that the facility in question was granted to the customer before notification.[237]

11.11 PREFERENCES

Given the true nature of the principle of combination, that in the absence of an express or implied agreement to the contrary an account in credit and another account with a debit balance are combined in a single debt, it is apparent that the mere fact that the bank may make an entry in its books giving effect to the combination by itself will not constitute a preference, since there was in any event only one debt.[238] Rather, the question whether the preference section[239] applies should be ascertained by an examination of the circumstances surrounding the deposits made by the customer with the bank.[240]

It may be, however, that a customer has two accounts which, it has been

---

[235] [1990] 2 QB 298, 304.

[236] See *Oceanica Castelana* [1983] 1 WLR 1294, 1301.

[237] [1983] 1 WLR 1294, 1301.

[238] This has been held to be the case in Canada. See *Re Sutcliffe & Sons Ltd; ex parte Royal Bank* [1933] 1 DLR 562 (esp. at 569); *Ross* v. *Royal Bank of Canada* (1965) 52 DLR (2d) 578; *Re T. C. Marines Ltd.* (1973) 34 DLR (3d) 489; *Re Plasky* (1981) 39 CBR 186. See also *Salter & Arnold, Ltd.* v. *Dominion Bank* [1926] SCR 621, which nevertheless proceeded upon a different analysis. In Australia Riley J. in *Re Shaw* (1977) 31 FLR 118, though without finally deciding the point, inclined to the view that a payment for the purpose of the preference section occurred when the funds represented by the cheque deposited with the bank were made available to the bank, as opposed to when the bank debited the account with a sum sufficient to cover the overdrawn account. See also *Matthews* v. *Geraghty* (1986) 43 SASR 576; *Re Tonkin* (1933) 6 ABC 197, 210–11.

[239] See the Insolvency Act 1986, s. 340, and, for companies, s. 239.

[240] Consider in this regard *In re Keever* [1967] 1 Ch. 182. In Australia see *Hamilton* v. *Commonwealth Bank of Australia* (1992) 9 ACSR 90, following *Matthews* v. *Geraghty* (1986) 43 SASR 576.

expressly or impliedly agreed, are to be regarded as separate, although the bank is empowered by a letter of set-off to combine them.[241] Can the bank's action in doing so constitute a preference? In the first place, if the accounts could have been set off under the insolvency set-off section in the customer's bankruptcy or liquidation, the bank's action in combining them will not constitute a preference, because it does not have the effect of improving the bank's position in comparison to what it would have been in any event in the insolvency.[242] As Vaughan Williams L.J. once remarked,[243] 'You cannot prefer a man . . . by merely putting him in the very position in which he would be if a bankruptcy followed'. But, even apart from that, the preference section only applies if a debtor does anything or suffers anything to be done which has the effect of preferring the particular creditor.[244] When the bank combines the accounts pursuant to the letter of set-off nothing is done by the customer, and nor could it properly be said that the customer is suffering anything to be done if the customer in truth has no means of preventing the combination occurring. In these circumstances Wood's view[245] no doubt is correct, that the bank's act in effecting a set-off is not a preference within the meaning of the section, and the question whether there has been a preference should be determined instead by reference to the deposits made with the bank, or the circumstances surrounding the giving of the letter of set-off itself.[246] A similar analysis should apply in Australia.[247] Insofar as bankruptcies in Australia are concerned, a prerequisite to the operation of the preference section is that there must be a transfer of property, a charge on property, a payment made or an obligation incurred *by the debtor*.[248] None of these describes a unilateral act of combination by a bank pursuant to a prior letter of set-off. Nor, in the case of a company liquidation, is the customer a party to the 'transaction' consisting of the combination.[249]

On the other hand, if the letter of set-off itself was given to the bank during the preference period a set-off pursuant to the letter may be open to challenge, although there should not be a preference if the accounts would

---

[241] This assumes that the giving of the letter of set-off does not have as a consequence that there is no implied agreement to keep the accounts separate. See section 11.8 above.

[242] This is consistent with *Hamilton* v. *Commonwealth Bank of Australia* (1992) 9 ACSR 90.   [243] *In re Washington Diamond Mining Company* [1893] 3 Ch. 95, 104.

[244] See the Insolvency Act 1986 s. 340(3)(b) and, for company liquidations, s. 239(4)(b).

[245] Wood, *English and International Set-off* (1989), 373–4.

[246] Compare *Re Deague* (1951) 15 ABC 197, in which the customer himself transferred funds from one account to another. The case is explained by Hodgson J. in *Hamilton* v. *Commonwealth Bank of Australia* (1992) 9 ACSR 90, 106.

[247] See in particular the judgments of King C.J. and Bollen J. in *Matthews* v. *Geraghty* (1986) 43 SASR 576 (though compare the slightly different approach of Cox J.) in relation to the equivalent of the Corporations Law, s. 567(5).

[248] Bankruptcy Act 1966 (Cth.), s. 122(1).

[249] See the Corporations Law, s. 588FA.

have been set off in any event in the customer's bankruptcy or liquidation pursuant to the insolvency set-off section.

11.12 TRUST FUNDS

11.12.1 *Introduction*

A customer may be a trustee in respect of an account in credit opened in his own name. This by itself will not preclude the application of the general rule that all the accounts kept by a particular customer with a bank are combined in a single debt.[250] If however the bank has notice of the trust it will not have the benefit of the principle of combination.[251] Nor may the bank rely on a set-off agreement entered into with the customer in this circumstance,[252] unless the beneficiaries of the trust had consented to it. If the customer becomes bankrupt, lack of mutuality in equity will mean that the bank will not be entitled to set off the accounts under the insolvency set-off section, and so for this reason it is crucial that, despite the trust, combination should apply.

The principle that an account in a customer's name which is known to be a trust account may not be combined with another may be explained on either of two grounds. If the customer himself has made it clear that the account is a trust account, an agreement would be readily implied that it should be kept separate from his other accounts. But even apart from that, the bank as a matter of equity would be required to keep separate money which it knows is held on trust. If the bank did not have notice of the trust, it should be able to obtain the benefit of the trust account in a combination where the defence of bona fide purchaser for value is available.[253] This is considered below.[254]

11.12.2 *The requirement of a trust*

The money deposited by the customer must have been impressed with a trust in his hands. An important decision in this regard is *Barclays Bank*

---

[250] See *Union Bank of Australia, Ltd.* v. *Murray-Aynsley* [1898] AC 693; *Bank of New South Wales* v. *Goulburn Valley Butter Company Pty. Ltd.* [1902] AC 543, 550; *Clark* v. *Ulster Bank Ltd.* [1950] NILR 132. Statements by Pigott B. and Bramwell B. in *Garnett* v. *M'Kewan* (1872) LR 8 Ex. 10, 14–15 suggesting that under no circumstances can a trust account be combined are too broad.

[251] *Bank of New South Wales* v. *Goulburn Valley Butter Company Pty. Ltd.* [1902] AC 543, 550.

[252] *Pannell* v. *Hurley* (1845) 2 Coll. 241, 245; *Neste Oy* v. *Lloyds Bank Plc* [1983] 2 Lloyd's Rep. 658.

[253] See *Re Marwalt Ltd.* [1992] BCC 32, 38; *Neste Oy* v. *Lloyds Bank Plc* [1983] 2 Lloyd's Rep. 658, 666. [254] See section 11.12.4 below.

Ltd. v. *Quistclose Investments Ltd.*,[255] in which the House of Lords held that a trust may arise when a sum of money is advanced to the customer by a third party for a specific purpose, for example, in order to pay the customer's creditors, or, as in *Quistclose* itself, in order that the corporate customer may pay a dividend. The fact that the money is advanced by way of loan does not preclude the court from finding that it is subject to a trust. As Lord Wilberforce remarked,[256] 'There is surely no difficulty in recognising the co-existence in one transaction of legal and equitable rights and remedies'. There is a primary trust in favour of the creditors intended to benefit from the payment, and the lender has an equitable right to see that the money in fact is applied to this designated purpose. If the purpose is carried out, the customer becomes a debtor to the lender. If on the other hand the purpose fails, it becomes necessary to see whether the parties intended that a secondary trust should arise in favour of the lender. In the instant case the purpose had failed,[257] and Lord Wilberforce in the leading judgment said that it was clear that the parties had intended that there should be a secondary trust. Moreover, the bank had been informed that the money deposited with it had been raised by means of a loan advanced for the sole purpose of enabling the customer to satisfy its liability to pay the dividend. This was sufficient to give the bank notice that the money was impressed with a trust, notwithstanding that it may not have been aware of the identity of the lender[258] or of the detailed terms of the trust,[259] and so it was held that the bank could not set the account into which the trust money had been paid against the customer's overdraft. The trust in *Quistclose* was based upon the presumed intention of the lender. This should be compared to *Neste Oy* v. *Lloyds Bank Plc*,[260] in which Bingham J. imposed a constructive trust upon an agent in respect of funds received from its principal after the directors of the holding company of a group of companies, of which the agent was a member, had determined that the group and its members should cease trading and that the group's bank

---

[255] [1970] AC 567.

[256] [1970] AC 567, 581. Note also the comments of Dixon J. in *Palette Shoes Pty. Ltd.* v. *Krohn* (1937) 58 CLR 1, 30. The money may be advanced in accordance with an antecedent contractual obligation, rather than by way of loan. In *Carreras Rothmans Ltd.* v. *Freeman Mathews Treasure Ltd.* [1985] 1 Ch. 207, Peter Gibson J applied *Quistclose* in a case in which the money was paid by A into a specially labelled bank account to be used by B solely for the purpose of paying C, when B was liable as a principal to C but with a right of reimbursement from A.

[257] Why had the purpose failed as a result of the resolution to wind up the company? See Goodhart and Jones, 'The Infiltration of Equitable Doctrine into English Commercial Law' (1980) 43 *Modern Law Review* 489, 494, referring to the statement of facts by Harman L.J. in the Court of Appeal [1968] 1 Ch. 540, 549–51.

[258] See Lord Wilberforce in the House of Lords [1970] AC 567, 582.

[259] See Sachs L.J. in the Court of Appeal in *Quistclose* [1968] 1 Ch. 540, 567.

[260] [1983] 2 Lloyd's Rep. 658.

should be requested to appoint a receiver. This was so despite the fact that, in the normal course of events, these payments were intended to give rise to a relationship of debt rather than of trust. The trust was justified on the ground that no honest person receiving money from another in these circumstances, when there was bound to be a total failure of consideration, could in good conscience retain it. Since the bank had become aware of the director's decision before it credited the money to the agent's overdrawn account, it had notice of the circumstances giving rise to the constructive trust, and so it was obliged to refund the money to the principal. In some respects this case is similar to *Sinclair* v. *Brougham*,[261] in which depositors with a building society were allowed to follow their money by reason of the fact that the purpose for which they had handed the money to the directors was incapable at law of fulfilment.[262] However, the cases are distinguishable. The 'purpose' in *Sinclair* v. *Brougham* was that the money should be deposited with the building society on the basis of a banker/customer relationship, and that it should be recoverable at a later date as a debt. This purpose had failed because repayment was *ultra vires*. The depositors lacked the personal remedy against the building society for which they had bargained, and so the court found a proprietary remedy. On the other hand, the principal in *Neste Oy* still had the personal right of a creditor against the agent for which it had bargained. The justice of finding a constructive trust is by no means clear when the principal had merely given credit for the money advanced,[263] and still retained the rights of a creditor. The principal had taken the risk of the agent's insolvency, and the imposition of a constructive trust in such a case would seem to confer an unjustified priority in the event of the agent's liquidation.[264]

11.12.3 *What constitutes notice?*

Sometimes the account will be headed in such plain terms that the bank cannot fail but to know that it is a trust account, as for example when a county treasurer opened accounts headed 'Superannuation Fund' and 'Police Account'.[265] In the event that there is nothing on the face of the

---

[261] [1914] AC 398.

[262] See *In re Diplock; Diplock* v. *Wintle* [1948] 1 Ch. 465, 540–1.

[263] See Goff and Jones, *The Law of Restitution* (4th edn., 1993) 84, criticizing *Sinclair* v. *Brougham*. Compare *In re Kayford Ltd.* [1975] 1 WLR 279, in which the company had set up a separate trust account for its customers' money, though note the criticism of the decision in that case by Goodhart and Jones, 'The Infiltration of Equitable Doctrine into English Commercial Law' (1980) 43 *Modern Law Review* 489, 494–7.

[264] The resolution in *Neste Oy* was merely to cease trading. Although there was no mention in the report of a subsequent winding-up, the resolution was based upon the directors' perception that the group and its companies could not meet credit as it fell due.

[265] *Ex parte Kingston; in re Gross* (1871) LR 6 Ch. App. 632. See also *Greenwell* v. *National Provincial Bank* (1883) 1 Cab. & El. 56.

account in question to show that it stood on any different footing from other accounts kept by the customer, or if there is nothing to indicate that the money deposited by the customer was impressed with a trust, the Privy Council in *Union Bank of Australia, Ltd.* v. *Murray-Aynsley*[266] said that it is incumbent upon the *cestuis que trust* 'to prove that the moneys for which they now sue were, in the knowledge of the bank, trust funds'. The relevant question is whether the bank is a purchaser for value without notice. Certainly 'notice' would include the situation in which the bank wilfully shut its eyes to the obvious, since this has always been regarded as an instance of actual notice.[267] An unresolved issue, however, is whether it also includes constructive notice. While the courts have shown a marked reluctance to extend the equitable doctrine of constructive notice,[268] particularly in relation to commercial transactions[269] and in situations in which money is paid in the ordinary course of business,[270] there are some comments in *Thomson* v. *Clydesdale Bank, Ltd*[271] that suggest that the concept may be relevant in appropriate cases. In *Thomson* a broker was instructed to sell shares and to pay the proceeds into a bank account in the principal's name. Instead the broker paid the proceeds into his own overdrawn account. It was held that the bank was not obliged to repay the principal. Lord Herschell said that under ordinary circumstances a bank that takes money in discharge of a debt is not bound to inquire into the manner in which the person paying the debt acquired the money,[272] while Lord Watson emphasized that it was not enough to show that the bank had acted negligently. Rather, he said that it had to be shown that the bank knew that the money did not belong to the broker.[273] On the other hand, Lord Herschell also indicated that the bank would not have succeeded if it had 'reason to believe' that the money was trust money,[274] while Lord Shand in that case seemed to contemplate that there may be circumstances in which the bank would be put on inquiry.[275]

In *In re Montagu's Settlement Trusts*[276] Sir Robert Megarry said that the imposition of personal liability as a constructive trustee on a person who

---

[266] [1898] AC 693, 697.

[267] *English and Scottish Mercantile Investment Company* v. *Brunton* [1892] 2 QB 700, 707–8; *John T. Ellis Ltd.* v. *Walter T. Hinds* [1947] 1 KB 475, 483.

[268] *English and Scottish Mercantile Investment Company* v. *Brunton* [1892] 2 QB 700, 708; *Consul Development Pty. Ltd.* v. *D.P.C. Estates Pty. Ltd.* (1975) 132 CLR 373, 413.

[269] *Greer* v. *Downs Supply Company* [1927] 2 KB 28; *The Njegos* [1936] P 90, 103; *Northside Development Pty. Ltd.* v. *Registrar-General* (1987) 11 ACLR 513, 523.

[270] See Scott L.J. in *Polly Peck International plc* v. *Nadir (No. 2)* [1992] 4 All ER 769, 782, referring to Vinelott J. in *Eagle Trust plc* v. *SBC Securities Ltd.* [1992] 4 All ER 488, 507.

[271] [1893] AC 282.

[272] [1893] AC 282, 287. See also *Bank of New South Wales* v. *Goulburn Valley Butter Company Pty. Ltd.* [1902] AC 543, 550.   [273] [1893] AC 282, 290.

[274] [1893] AC 282, 287–8.   [275] [1893] AC 282, 293.

[276] [1987] 1 Ch. 264, 277–8, 285.

received trust property, and the right of the beneficial owner to trace the property in equity, are governed by different rules and should be kept separate. He said that the question whether personal liability will be imposed depends upon knowledge, whereas, in the case of an equitable tracing remedy in which rights of property are in issue, notice rather than knowledge is the determining factor. The person holding the property in question will take free of the trust if he is a purchaser for value without notice. In a number of recent cases the courts have emphasized the difference between knowledge and notice.[277] Knowledge in fact is a narrower concept. As Vinelott J. remarked in *Eagle Trust plc* v. *SBC Securities Ltd.*,[278]

However, 'notice' is often used in a sense or in contexts where the facts do not support the inference of knowledge. A man may have actual notice of a fact and yet not know it. He may have been supplied in the course of a conveyancing transaction with a document and so have actual notice of its content, but he may not in fact have read it; or he may have read it some time ago and have forgotten its content . . . So also by statute a man may be deemed to have actual notice of a fact which is clearly not within his knowledge.

It should also be borne in mind that the concept of constructive notice was developed in the field of property transactions in which there is generally time for a full and complete investigation of title,[279] which is hardly appropriate when the question concerns a payment of money in the ordinary course of business. In *Polly Peck International plc* v. *Nadir (No. 2)*[280] money was paid into an account to the credit of a foreign bank pursuant to a foreign exchange transaction. The plaintiff claimed that the money belonged to it, and sought an equitable tracing order against the foreign bank, whereupon the foreign bank argued that it was a purchaser for value without notice. Scott L.J. thought that the concept of notice was inappropriate in this situation, and that the same principle should apply as for an *in personam* constructive trust claim.[281] In other words, the plaintiff was required to prove knowledge by the foreign bank rather than notice.[282] Whether in truth the distinction between knowledge

---

[277] *In re Montagu's Settlement Trusts* [1987] 1 Ch. 264, 271, 285–6 (Megarry V.C.); *Eagle Trust plc* v. *SBC Securities Ltd.* [1992] 4 All ER 488, 497–8 (Vinelott J.); *Polly Peck International plc* v. *Nadir (No. 2)* [1992] 4 All ER 769, 781–2 (Scott L.J.).

[278] [1992] 4 All ER 488, 497–8.

[279] See Vinelott J. in *Eagle Trust plc* v. *SBC Securities Ltd.* [1992] 4 All ER 488, 507, referring to *Manchester Trust* v. *Furness* [1992] 4 All ER 488, 507.

[280] [1992] 4 All ER 769. [281] [1992] 4 All ER 769, 781–2.

[282] Stocker L.J. and Lord Donaldson of Lymington M.R. in the Court of Appeal in *Polly Peck* expressed agreement with Scott L.J.'s judgment. It is also consistent with comments by Millett J. in *El Ajou* v. *Dollar Land Holdings plc* [1993] 3 All ER 717, 739, and see also Knox J. in *Cowan de Groot Properties Ltd.* v. *Eagle Trust plc* [1994] 4 All ER 700, 759–60.

and notice is of any substance in this regard is debatable. It may be said that constructive notice is still the relevant concept, though suitably adapted to the circumstances.[283] But whatever the terminology, one would have thought that the analysis should be the same when a bank asserts that various accounts are combined notwithstanding a claim by a beneficiary of a trust that one of the accounts holds trust money. The bank's defence of purchaser for value should be determined by reference to its knowledge, or alternatively notice as adapted to the circumstances, as opposed to notice in the sense that the term is used in property transactions.

In the case before him, Scott L.J. considered that the same degree of knowledge (or notice) must be established for the bona fide purchaser defence to the equitable tracing claim as for the imposition of a personal liability as a constructive trustee on the ground of knowing receipt of trust property.[284] This should apply in any case in which a payment of money in the ordinary course of business is in issue, including payment into a bank account when the bank claims that the situation is one of combination, notwithstanding the distinction drawn by Sir Robert Megarry in *Montagu's Settlement Trusts*. This is consistent with comments by Knox J. in *Cowan de Groot Properties Ltd.* v. *Eagle Trust plc*,[285] and it was also the view of Millett J. in *El Ajou* v. *Dollar Land Holdings plc*.[286] However, what the requisite level of knowledge is is still a matter of debate. In an often-quoted but much-criticized classification, Peter Gibson J. in *Baden* v. *SG Développement du Commerce SA*[287] accepted that knowledge can comprise any one of five different mental states:

(1) actual knowledge, or
(2) wilfully shutting one's eyes to the obvious, or
(3) wilfully and recklessly failing to make such inquiries as an honest and reasonable man would make, or
(4) knowledge of circumstances which would indicate the facts to an honest and reasonable man, or
(5) knowledge of circumstances which would put an honest and reasonable man on inquiry.

In *Montagu's Settlement Trusts*[288] Megarry V.C. said that want of probity is essential for the imposition of personal liability as a constructive trustee on the knowing receipt ground, and that accordingly it is necessary to

---

[283] See Sir Peter Millett, 'Equity—The Road Ahead' (1995) 9 *Tolley's Trust Law International* 35, 40, referring to *Barclays Bank Plc* v. *O'Brien* [1993] 1 AC 180 (esp. at 195–6).   [284] [1992] 4 All ER 769, 782.
[285] [1992] 4 All ER 700, 767.
[286] [1993] 3 All ER 717, 739. See also Millett, 'Tracing the Proceeds of Fraud' (1991) 107 *Law Quarterly Review* 71, 81.   [287] [1992] 4 All ER 161, 235.
[288] [1987] 1 Ch. 264, 285.

establish knowledge in categories (1), (2) and (3). This was also the view of Alliott J. at first instance,[289] and of May L.J. in the Court of Appeal,[290] in *Lipkin Gorman* v. *Karpnale Ltd.*, and of Knox J. in *Cowan de Groot Properties Ltd.* v. *Eagle Trust plc.*[291] On the other hand, Vinelott J. in *Eagle Trust plc* v. *SBC Securities Ltd.*[292] expressed doubts as to Megarry V.C.'s analysis, while the position was left open by Scott L.J. in *Polly Peck*. He said that (3) would suffice, though he had doubts as to the sufficiency of (5).[293] Nevertheless, he referred later in his judgment to the question whether by the standards of the honest and reasonable banker inquiries should have been made,[294] which in fact suggests type (5) knowledge. In *El Ajou* v. *Dollar Land Holdings plc*[295] Millett J. said that he was prepared to assume, in the absence of full argument and without finally deciding the point, that dishonesty or want of probity involving actual knowledge, whether proved or inferred, is not essential. Rather, he thought that a constructive trust may be imposed where the recipient 'went ahead without further inquiry in circumstances in which an honest and reasonable man would have realised that the money was probably trust money and was being misapplied'.[296] This suggests the fifth of Peter Gibson J.'s categories. Similarly, in New Zealand it has been said that all five categories are relevant to the knowing receipt head of constructive trust,[297] though the contrary view has also been expressed.[298] In truth the cases are difficult to reconcile, and the position remains uncertain.

One thing that is clear, however, is that a mere request by the customer that the money be put into a separate account by itself is not sufficient to constitute notice.[299] Nor as a general rule is it sufficient that the bank is aware that the customer occupies a position in which he often receives money on behalf of others, as, for example, a solicitor or stockbroker. Thus, in *T. and H. Greenwood Teale* v. *William Williams Brown and Company*[300] a solicitor paid clients' money into an 'office account', while in *Clark* v. *Ulster Bank Ltd.*[301] the money was paid into a 'No. 2 Account'. In each case it was held that the bank did not have sufficient notice of the

---

[289] [1987] 1 WLR 987, 1005.
[290] [1989] 1 WLR 1340, 1355.
[291] [1992] 4 All ER 700, 758–60.
[292] [1992] 4 All ER 488, 505–7.
[293] [1992] 4 All ER 769, 777.
[294] [1992] 4 All ER 769, 777, 778.
[295] [1993] 3 All ER 717, 739.

[296] His Lordship expressed a similar view extra-judicially in 'Tracing the Proceeds of Fraud' (1991) 107 *Law Quarterly Review* 71, 81–2.

[297] See Richardson J. in *Westpac Banking Corporation* v. *Savin* [1985] 2 NZLR 41, 52–3. See also *Equiticorp Industries Group Ltd.* v. *Hawkins* [1991] 3 NZLR 700, 728, and *Powell* v. *Thompson* [1991] 1 NZLR 597.

[298] *Nimmo* v. *Westpac Banking Corporation* [1993] 3 NZLR 218, 227–8.

[299] *Barclays Bank Ltd.* v. *Quistclose Investments Ltd.* [1970] AC 567, 582.

[300] (1894) 11 TLR 56.
[301] [1950] NILR 132.

fiduciary nature of the account to prevent combination.[302] In this regard, the Solicitors' Act 1974, section 85(b) prohibits a bank from having recourse against money standing to the credit of an account kept by a solicitor with the bank in accordance with the rules applicable to solicitors' client accounts, other than in respect of a liability in connection with the account itself. This would preclude set-off against or combination with an overdrawn account of the solicitor. It would not, however, prevent combination in relation to an account into which clients' money has been paid if the account has not been opened or maintained in accordance with the rules, provided that the bank is not in any event aware that the account is a trust account.[303]

11.12.4 *The relevant date for notice*

It is not entirely clear from the cases whether it is necessary to show that the bank had notice (or knowledge) of the trust when it received the trust money and credited it to the customer's account, or whether notice at a later date would suffice. On the one hand, in *Grigg* v. *Cocks*[304] the bank received notice of the trust affecting the bill of exchange in issue in that case after the proceeds of the bill were received and credited to the customer's account but before the bank made a book entry combining that account with another. Sir Lancelot Shadwell held that the bank was still entitled to consider itself as debtor for the balance.[305] A similar approach was adopted in Northern Ireland in *Clark* v. *Ulster Bank Ltd.*.[306] On the other hand, there is evidence to suggest that the Privy Council in *Union Bank of Australia, Limited* v. *Murray-Aynsley*[307] thought that the question of notice could still be relevant after the bank has received the money.[308] Further, Lord Reid in *Barclays Bank Ltd.* v. *Quistclose Investments Ltd.*[309] left open the question whether subsequent notice could affect the bank's position,[310] though this should be approached cautiously given that the

---

[302] See also *Thomson* v. *Clydesdale Bank, Ltd.* [1893] AC 282 (stockbroker).
[303] See *Clark* v. *Ulster Bank Ltd.* [1950] NILR 132, 141.
[304] (1831) 4 Sim. 438.   [305] See in particular (1831) 4 Sim. 438, 453–4.
[306] [1950] NILR 132.   [307] [1898] AC 693.
[308] The advice of the Board was delivered by Lord Watson, who commented that 'there is nothing to prove or even to suggest that any notice was *subsequently* conveyed to the bank of the trust character of the funds which the respondents are claiming in this action'; [1898] AC 693, 698 (emphasis added). See also *Taylor* v. *Forbes* (1830) 7 Bligh NS 417, which is difficult to follow given that separate banker/customer relationships appear to have been in issue.
[309] [1970] AC 567, 578.
[310] Compare Russell L.J. in the Court of Appeal [1968] 1 Ch. 540, 556, 561, who approached the problem in terms of whether the bank in that case had notice when it received the money and credited it to an account. Lord Wilberforce in the House of Lords [1970] AC 567, 582 was prepared to assume that this was the relevant question, though without deciding the issue.

case does not appear to have been concerned with combination rights in existence at the date of the deposit.[311]

It may be that the trust funds, instead of being paid into a separate account, in fact were paid directly into the customer's overdrawn private account, and the court is asked to determine whether the bank is entitled to treat the deposit as having reduced the debit balance on that account.[312] This is no more than an aspect of the same problem. If combination is merely an accounting exercise to ascertain what the debt is at any particular time, it should not make any difference whether trust funds are deposited together in a special account or whether initially they are credited to the customer's own private account.

When a customer has a number of accounts with a bank the principle of combination dictates that the accounts are combined in a single debt irrespective of any book entry to this effect. Therefore, the better view is that notice of a trust received after the money has been credited to the trust account does not affect the position in relation to combination. The credit will already have been subsumed into the overall balance representing the debt owing by one party to the other. Similarly, a later entry by the bank after knowledge of the trust reflecting the combination in its books should not constitute a dealing with trust property so as to give rise to liability as a constructive trustee.[313] There was in any event only one debt for the balance, so that the book-entry itself would not have constituted an appropriation by the bank of the trust account in reduction of a debt owing to the bank on another account.[314] The bank, when it received the money from the customer without notice of the trust and credited it to an account the subject of combination, should be protected on the ground that it was a bona fide purchaser for value.[315] Admittedly, when money is paid into an account in credit in circumstances where combination is not in issue, the bank is not regarded as having given value merely because of the promise to repay a like amount.[316] But when a bank receives money in reduction or

---

[311] See below.

[312] See e.g. *Thomson* v. *Clydesdale Bank, Ltd.* [1893] AC 282; *British America Elevator Co., Ltd.* v. *Bank of British North America* [1919] AC 658.

[313] For discussion of the imposition of liability as a constructive trustee, see *Snell's Principles of Equity* (29th edn., 1990), 194.

[314] *Re Sutcliffe & Sons Ltd; ex parte Royal Bank* [1933] 1 DLR 562.

[315] Where a bank is a bona fide purchaser for value without notice its title will prevail over that of the beneficiary of the trust. See *Re Marwalt Ltd.* [1992] BCC 32, 38; *Neste Oy* v. *Lloyds Bank Plc* [1983] 2 Lloyd's Rep. 658, 666.

[316] *Lipkin Gorman* v. *Karpnale Ltd.* [1991] 2 AC 548, 562, 576–7. See also Lord Wilberforce in *Barclays Bank Ltd.* v. *Quistclose Investments Ltd.* [1970] AC 567, 582, discussed below, though compare Harman L.J. in the Court of Appeal in *Quistclose* [1968] 1 Ch. 540, 555.

discharge of a debt, the fact of the reduction or discharge does constitute value,[317] and this should also apply in a case of combination. As mentioned, the analysis should be the same whether the customer has one overdrawn account to which trust money is credited, or whether the customer has a number of accounts the balance of which at any particular time represents a debt owing to the bank. Because there is only one debt in any event, payment into an account in credit, where there is a second overdrawn account, should have the same effect at law as a payment to the credit of the overdrawn account itself, in that it brings about a reduction in the customer's debt to the bank. While this question of value generally has not been discussed in the cases, it has some support in the judgment of Bingham J. in *Neste Oy* v. *Lloyd's Bank Plc*.[318] The case was considered earlier[319] in the context of trust money credited to an agent's account after the bank was aware of a decision that the group of which the agent was a member should cease trading. In addition, however, there were five other payments credited to the agent's account which, it was held, could be applied by the bank against other accounts in debit. Bingham J. commented that the bank gave value when the payments were credited to the account.[320] He went on to say that this was certainly the case when the bank continued lending in the belief that the overall debt was reduced by the sum of the payments. But even without this additional element, he seemed to be of the view that the bank was not a volunteer. It is true that in *Barclays Bank Ltd.* v. *Quistclose Investments Ltd.*[321] Lord Wilberforce said that the bank in that case had not in any real sense given value when it received the money or thereafter changed its position.[322] However, the bank had agreed that the money paid into the account in question was only to be used for the purpose of funding the payment of a dividend, which would have precluded a combination in respect of it.[323] The right of set-off

---

[317] *Taylor* v. *Blakelock* (1886) 32 Ch. D 560 (esp. at 570); Goode, *Legal Problems of Credit and Security* (2nd edn., 1986), 120; Millett, 'Tracing the Proceeds of Fraud' (1991) 107 *Law Quarterly Review* 71, 82 (referring to *Thomson* v. *Clydesdale Bank Ltd.* [1893] AC 282 and *Westpac Banking Corporation* v. *Savin* [1985] 2 NZLR 41). This is also consistent with the tenor of the Australian High Court's comments in *Australian and New Zealand Banking Group Ltd.* v. *Westpac Banking Corporation* (1988) 164 CLR 662, 677.

[318] [1983] 2 Lloyd's Rep. 658.

[319] See section 11.12.2 above.

[320] His Lordship said ([1983] 2 Lloyd's Rep. 658, 667) that 'It appears to me that the bank gave value when these first five payments were credited to PSL's account, certainly when the bank continued lending in the belief that the group's overall debt was reduced by the sum of the payments . . .'.

[321] [1970] AC 567, discussed in section 11.12.2 above.

[322] [1970] AC 567, 582. See also Russell L.J. in the Court of Appeal [1968] 1 Ch. 540, 563, though compare the view of Harman L.J. (at 555), that 'The bank stands . . . in the position of an assignee for value, the consideration being the promise to repay'.

[323] See Russell L.J. in the Court of Appeal [1968] 1 Ch. 540, 563.

in issue seems to have been regarded as arising under the insolvency set-off section, the customer having gone into liquidation.[324] Therefore, it was not a case in which it could be said that the payment in itself operated to reduce the customer's debt to the bank so as to constitute the giving of value on that ground.

The payment in may have resulted in a net credit to the customer, as opposed to operating in reduction or discharge of the customer's debt. If in such a case the bank subsequently acquires notice of the trust, it may be liable as a constructive trustee if it knowingly assists the trustee in dealing with the money in a manner inconsistent with the trust.[325]

11.12.5 *Set-off agreement*

There may be a number of separate accounts with a bank that are not subject to the principle of combination, even though the bank has a set-off agreement entitling it to combine the accounts and set them off.[236] If one of the accounts is a trust account the bank's position would differ from that which applies when the common law principle of combination is in issue. In such a case the payment of money into the trust account by itself would not constitute the giving of value, since the payment in does not result in a reduction in or discharge of the debt to the bank. That does not occur until the bank later exercises its rights under the set-off agreement. If a set-off is effected pursuant to the agreement the bank, having dealt with trust property in a manner inconsistent with the trust, may be liable to the beneficiary as a constructive trustee,[327] although it will be protected if it can point to other circumstances as constituting value so that it is a bona fide purchaser for value without notice,[328] or if it has available to it a defence of change of position.[329]

---

[324] In the Court of Appeal Harman L.J. [1968] 1 Ch. 540, 551 noted that the bank informed the board of the customer that it was exercising its 'statutory' right to combine accounts. See also the reference by Russell L.J. (at 563) to the decision in *Rolls Razor Ltd.* v. *Cox* [1967] 1 QB 552, which concerned the question whether the operation of the insolvency set-off section could be excluded by agreement between the parties, and the reference by Sachs L.J. (at 567) to the Bankruptcy Act 1914, s. 31, which was the set-off section then applicable to company liquidations under the Companies Act 1948, s. 317.

[325] *Quaere* whether the 'knowing receipt' head of constructive trust can apply when the account is in credit, or whether regard can only be had to the 'knowing assistance' head. Compare Millett, 'Tracing the Proceeds of Fraud' (1991) 107 *Law Quarterly Review* 71, 83 with *Snell's Principles of Equity* (29th edn., 1990), 193.

[326] See generally section 11.8 above.

[327] See generally *Snell's Principles of Equity* (29th edn., 1990), 193–4.

[328] *Re Marwalt Ltd.* [1992] BCC 32, 38; *Neste Oy* v. *Lloyds Bank Plc* [1983] 2 Lloyd's Rep. 658, 666.

[329] The defence of change of position was recognized for the first time by the House of Lords in *Lipkin Gorman* v. *Karpnale Ltd.* [1991] 2 AC 548 in the context of a common law

11.12.6 *Account containing both trust and personal money*

An account in credit may have had deposited into it both trust money and the customer's personal money. In such a case Wood's view[330] no doubt is correct that, consistent with the principle applicable to tracing trust money into an account,[331] a combination would be regarded as first reducing the part of the account in which the customer is personally interested. If another account in debit kept by the customer is more than sufficient to extinguish this on the basis of combination, the question whether combination will also then apply in relation to the trust money should be determined by reference to the principles discussed above.

11.12.7 *Lack of a defined beneficial owner*

An account is sometimes labelled in such a way as to indicate that it is held in a fiduciary capacity, but for some reason it is not possible to point to another person who has a beneficial interest in it. This may arise when an executor opens an executorship account with a bank before the administration of the estate has been completed.[332] There are comments in the judgment of Blackburn J. in *Bailey* v. *Finch*[333] which suggest that his Lordship thought that this account may be combined with another account held by the executor in his personal capacity. The better view, however, is that the labelling of the account gives rise to an implied agreement that it should be treated as separate. A similar point may be made in relation to two other decisions, one Canadian and the other from New Zealand. In *Bank of Montreal* v. *R. & R. Entertainment Ltd.*[334] an account was labelled as a trust account though in truth it was a personal account, and it was held that combination applied. In *McMillan* v. *Bank of New Zealand*[335] a debtor, having executed a deed of assignment for the benefit of his creditors whereby he was to be permitted to carry on business, opened an account with a bank in his own name with the words 'trust account' added. The creditors refused to consent to the deed, whereupon the bank transferred an amount standing to the credit of the account in reduction of

action for restitution, though it should also be permitted when an equitable tracing claim or a personal liability as a constructive trustee is in issue. See in particular Lord Goff of Chieveley (at 580–1), and also Hobhouse J. at first instance in *Westdeutsche Landesbank* v. *Islington BC* [1994] 4 All ER 890, 947. In Australia see *David Securities Pty. Ltd.* v. *Commonwealth Bank of Australia* (1992) 175 CLR 353, 384–6, 399, 405–6.

[330] Wood, *English and International Set-off* (1989), 1067.

[331] *In re Hallett's Estate* (1880) 13 Ch. D 696.

[332] *Ayerst* v. *C. & K. (Construction) Ltd.* [1976] AC 167, 178, referring to *Commissioner of Stamp Duties (Queensland)* v. *Livingston* [1965] AC 694, 707–8.

[333] (1871) LR 7 QB 34, 41–2, 43. See also the discussion of *Bailey* v. *Finch* in section 9.9.1 above. [334] (1984) 13 DLR (4th) 726. [335] (1882) NZLR 1 SC 332.

another account of the customer's in debit. The bank's action in doing so was upheld, since the account was not subject to a trust. However, there was no consideration given to the possibility that the accounts may have been separate as a result of an implied agreement arising out of the labelling of the account, so as to preclude the principle of combination. If this view had been adopted in *McMillan* the bank's position in fact may not have been adversely affected. The customer had become bankrupt, and a set-off may well have been available in any event under the insolvency set-off section so as to bring about the same practical result as a combination.

11.12.8 *Trust account in debit*

The customer would be personally liable for any debit that may arise on a trust account.[336] However, if the account has been labelled as a trust account so as to give rise to an implied agreement that it should be kept separate from his private accounts, then, in the absence of a set-off agreement, any right in the bank to deduct this debit balance from the customer's private account in credit prior to the customer's bankruptcy or liquidation would be based solely upon the procedural right to set off independent cross-debts in an action at law under the Statutes of Set-off, as opposed to the notion that the accounts in any event are combined.[337] Accordingly, the accounts would not actually be set against each other until such time as a judgment for a set-off has been given.[338] This would mean that the bank would be liable for damages if, prior to judgment, it failed to honour a cheque drawn by the customer on his private account in credit because of the presence of a debit balance on the trust account.

11.13 ASSIGNMENTS

An assignment of an account in credit is governed by the same principle as the trust cases. The assignee takes subject to a combination arising before the bank received notice of the assignment,[339] unless the bank had agreed that any assignee should take free from equities.[340] The reason presumably

---

[336] See, and compare, *Coutts and Co. v. The Irish Exhibition in London* (1891) 7 TLR 313.

[337] This is consistent with the discussion in *Daniels* v. *Imperial Bank of Canada* (1914) 19 DLR 166, 168–9.   [338] See section 1.2.9 above.

[339] *Roxburghe* v. *Cox* (1881) 17 Ch. D 520; *Jeffryes* v. *Agra and Masterman's Bank* (1866) LR 2 Eq. 674, 680. Compare *Re Jane; ex parte The Trustee* (1914) 110 LT 556, in which the accounts would have been separate, being a current account in credit and a loan account, and *Re Marwalt Ltd.* [1992] BCC 32, in which the bank had notice of the assignment.

[340] See e.g. *In re Agra and Masterman's Bank; ex parte Asiatic Banking Corporation* (1867) LR 2 Ch. App. 391 (open letter of credit).

is that, until the bank has notice, there is still the one banker/customer relationship. Where one of the accounts is payable on demand, the assignee may be subject to a combination notwithstanding that a demand had not been made before notice of the assignment was received.[341]

11.14 DECEASED CUSTOMER

A deceased customer in whose name there is a credit balance on an account may also have a loan which matures after the date of death. Since a combination does not arise in relation to an account that is neither presently payable nor presently payable on demand,[342] the accounts at the date of death would not have been combined in a single debt. When the loan does mature, the liability will still be the liability of the deceased customer, although from the moment of death the right to receive the credit balance will have been vested in his executor.[343] However, consistent with the principle applicable to assignments, it was held in *Rogerson* v. *Ladbroke*[344] that the estate will take subject to a combination if the loan matured before the bank had notice of the death.[345]

11.15 THE STATUTES OF SET-OFF AND NOMINEE ACCOUNTS

If the situation is such that a number of accounts are not combined pursuant to the principles outlined above,[346] the bank in an action brought against it for payment of the credit balance on one account may still have recourse to a defence of set-off, under the Statutes of Set-off, in respect of another account in debit. Because of the necessity for mutuality the accounts should be kept by the same customer although, if the accounts are in different names, equity may act by analogy with the legal right of set-off conferred by the Statutes and allow the bank to employ the debit balance as a defence if the account in credit in truth is held on trust for the person indebted to the bank on the debit account. In this latter situation, however,

---

[341] See section 11.6 above.   [342] See section 11.6 above.

[343] *Williams, Mortimer and Sunnucks on Executors, Administrators and Probate* (1993), 459.   [344] (1822) 1 Bing. 91.

[345] In the absence of information as regards the date of death, *quaere* whether *Thomas* v. *Howell* (1874) LR 18 Eq. 198 was correctly decided. The case was distinguished, on other grounds, in *Halse* v. *Rumford* (1878) 47 LJ Ch. 559. In *Royal Trust Co.* v. *Molsons Bank* (1912) 8 DLR 478 the customer died before the promissory notes became due, though it is not clear when the bank received notice of the death. A similar comment may be made in respect of *Ontario Bank* v. *Routhier* (1900) 32 OR 67.

[346] In relation to nominee accounts, see section 11.5 above.

in the event of an application for summary judgment against the bank for payment of the credit balance, the bank will only be granted leave to defend if there is clear and indisputable evidence that the applicant for summary judgment is suing solely as trustee for the person indebted to the bank on the account in debit.[347]

11.16 BANKER'S LIEN OVER A NEGOTIABLE INSTRUMENT

When a bank has a lien over a negotiable instrument the security is possessory in nature. While there is some debate as to whether the lien also carries with it a right of sale,[348] it should at least include a power to collect the proceeds upon maturity.[349] But when the bank does so, the lien will come to an end. The bank will no longer have possession of the instrument, and the proceeds themselves ordinarily will not be tangible property which can be the subject of a possessory lien.[350] Nevertheless the bank's security rights derived from the lien should entitle it to apply the proceeds in reduction of the debt secured by the lien,[351] unless there is an agreement to the contrary. This may arise, for example, where the bank had specifically agreed to account to the customer for the proceeds.[352]

---

[347] *Bhogal* v. *Punjab National Bank* [1988] 2 All ER 296; *Uttamchandami* v. *Central Bank of India* unreported but noted in (1989) 139 *New Law Journal* 222. See also section 7.5 above.

[348] See the discussion in *Duke Finance Ltd.* v. *Commonwealth Bank of Australia* (1990) 22 NSWLR 236, 252.

[349] *Duke Finance Ltd.* v. *Commonwealth Bank of Australia* (1990) 22 NSWLR 236, 249.

[350] See Buckley L.J. in *Halesowen Presswork & Assemblies Ltd.* v. *Westminster Bank Ltd.* [1971] 1 QB 1, 46. See also on appeal in the House of Lords [1972] AC 785, 802 per Viscount Dilhorne, 810 per Lord Cross of Chelsea.

[351] *Duke Finance Ltd.* v. *Commonwealth Bank of Australia* (1990) 22 NSWLR 236. See also *In re Keever* [1967] 1 Ch. 182.

[352] *Rouxel* v. *Royal Bank of Canada* [1918] 2 WWR 791.

12

Set-off Agreements

12.1 INTRODUCTION

Parties dealing with each other may enter into an agreement for the satisfaction of their cross-demands by bringing them into an account, on the basis that a set-off is to occur either immediately or at a later date at the option of one of the parties. Generally this is not objectionable. It merely constitutes an agreed method of payment.[1] The agreement may not be effective, however, where trust moneys are in issue. Thus, if a customer has deposited trust money into an account with a bank, and the bank, acting pursuant to a set-off agreement, sets off that account against a second overdrawn account held by the customer in his personal capacity, it may be liable as a constructive trustee to the person beneficially entitled to the trust money unless it can rely on defences of purchaser for value without notice or change of position.[2] In addition, when there is a bankruptcy or a winding-up, the validity of a set-off effected pursuant to the agreement is subject to two limitations. The first is that the set-off must not constitute a voidable preference.[3] But, in considering this question, the point should be borne in mind that a set-off effected prior to the bankruptcy or liquidation of one of the parties will not be struck down as a preference if the cross-demands would have been set off in any event under the insolvency set-off section. As Vaughan Williams L.J. once remarked,[4] 'You cannot prefer a man . . . by merely putting him in the very position in which he would be if a bankruptcy followed'. Furthermore, if the form of set-off agreement between two parties, A and B, is such that it entitles A to act unilaterally to bring about a set-off, and a set-off is effected within the preference period applicable in B's bankruptcy or liquidation, Wood's

---

[1] See e.g. *Kinnerley* v. *Hossack* (1809) 2 Taunt. 170; *Cheetham* v. *Crook* (1825) M'Cle. & Yo. 307; *Federal Commissioner of Taxation* v. *Steeves Agnew and Co. (Vic) Pty. Ltd.* (1951) 82 CLR 408, 420; *The Evelpidis Era* [1981] 1 Lloyd's Rep. 54, 63; *Pro-Image Studios* v. *Commonwealth Bank of Australia* (1991) 4 ACSR 586, 589; *Re Keith Bray Pty. Ltd.* (1991) 5 ACSR 450, 451.

[2] See section 11.12.5 above.

[3] As in *In re Washington Diamond Mining Company* [1893] 3 Ch. 95. See also *In re Land Development Association; Kent's Case* (1888) 39 Ch. D 259.

[4] *In re Washington Diamond Mining Company* [1893] 3 Ch. 95, 104.

view[5] would appear to be correct, that this on its own would not constitute a preference, since nothing was done or suffered to be done by the debtor.[6] The question whether there has been a preference in such a case should be determined instead by the circumstances surrounding the incurring of the debts the subject of the set-off, or the entry into the agreement itself. Similarly the agreement could be open to objection as a transaction at an undervalue[7] or a transaction defrauding creditors.[8] The second limitation is that, unless the agreement has been effective to create a charge over the bankrupt's or the company's indebtedness,[9] the statutory requirement of a *pari passu* distribution of the estate amongst the general body of creditors[10] means that a set-off which involves a claim possessed by the bankrupt or the company[11] will not be effective to the extent that the demands had not actually been set against each other, and a balance struck, before the commencement of the bankruptcy or liquidation. Rather, a set-off will only occur to the extent that it is available within the terms of the insolvency set-off section.[12]

The leading authority on the second limitation is *British Eagle International Air Lines Ltd.* v. *Compagnie Nationale Air France*.[13] The International Air Transport Association had established a clearing house system for the monthly settlement of debits and credits arising when members performed services for one another. A balance would be struck between the total sum owing to a particular member in respect of services supplied by it *for* all other members, and the total owing by that member in respect of services supplied *by* all other members. The clearance took

---

[5] Wood, *English and International Set-off* (1989), 373–4.
[6] See section 11.11 above.
[7] Insolvency Act 1986, s. 238 and, for bankruptcy, s. 339.
[8] Insolvency Act 1986, s. 423.   [9] See section 12.4 below.
[10] See the Insolvency Act 1986, s. 107 (which also applies to compulsory liquidations: see *Webb* v. *Whiffin* (1872) LR 5 HL 711, 735), and r. 4.181 of the Insolvency Rules. See also the Insolvency Act 1986, s. 328(3).
[11] Compare the discussion below of a set-off agreement where a set-off would only involve a *liability* of the bankrupt or the company.
[12] *Re Charge Card Services Ltd.* [1987] Ch. 150, 177. Compare *Sturdy* v. *Arnaud* (1790) 3 TR 599, and *Hanford* v. *Moseley*, which is unreported but noted (rather inadequately) in *Jones* v. *Mossop* (1844) 3 Hare 568, 572–4. Compare also *Dobson* v. *Lockhart* (1793) 5 TR 133, in which the agreement in question was interpreted as making the debt to the bankrupt conditional. The comment of Marks J. in the Supreme Court of Victoria in *Lloyds Bank NZA Ltd.* v. *National Safety Council of Australia* [1993] 2 VR 506, 513, regarding an agreement by which the surplus realized from one security is to be applied in reduction of shortfalls in other securities, is explicable only if the surplus itself was intended to constitute security for other shortfalls (see J. D. Phillips J. at 514), or the terms of the agreement were such that the surplus was not to be held on trust. While Pt VIII of the Companies Act 1989 introduced provisions designed to overcome the effects of the decision in *British Eagle* [1975] 1 WLR 758 (discussed below), these do not apply generally, but relate only to the rules of certain investment exchanges and clearing houses recognized under the Financial Services Act 1986.
[13] [1975] 1 WLR 758. See also *Re NIAA Corporation Ltd.* (1993) 12 ACSR 141, 155.

effect within 5 days after the 30th day of each calendar month in relation to the month prior to that calendar month. Members with an overall debit balance would pay into the clearing house the amount of the debit, while the clearing house would pay to members with an overall credit balance the sums due to them. The House of Lords said that any clearance that had taken place before the commencement of a member's liquidation should be binding on the liquidator,[14] since there was no question of a preference. The majority,[15] however, held that the clearing house system could not operate after the commencement of the liquidation in respect of debits and credits not actually cleared at that date, because this would be contrary to the statutory injunction that the property of a company should be applied in its winding-up in satisfaction of its liabilities *pari passu*. It made no difference that the parties may have had good business reasons for entering into the arrangement, or that the arrangement had not been designed specifically in order to evade the insolvency legislation.[16] Consequently, when a particular member went into liquidation, the liquidator was entitled to recover the uncleared credits owing to the company, while members with uncleared debits on the company's accounts were each remitted to a proof in respect of them. On the other hand, each member could set off the

---

[14] As Lord Romilly M.R. remarked in *In re Smith, Knight, & Co; ex parte Ashbury* (1868) LR 5 Eq. 223, 226, 'The Act of Parliament unquestionably says, that everbody shall be paid *pari passu*, but that means everybody after the winding-up has commenced. It does not mean that the Court will look into past transactions, and equalise all creditors by making good to those who have not received anything a sum of money equal to that which other creditors have received'. See also *Carreras Rothmans Ltd.* v. *Freeman Mathews Treasure Ltd.* [1985] 1 Ch. 207, in which the moneys in the account was not an asset of the company at the date of the liquidation, and *Re ILG Travel Ltd.* [1996] BCC 21.

[15] Lord Cross of Chelsea, Lord Diplock, and Lord Edmund-Davies concurring. The dissentients, Lord Morris of Borth-y-Gest and Lord Simon of Glaisdale, said that, as a result of the clearing house rules, money was not payable by one member to another, but rather the clearing house itself was the creditor. Consequently the property of the company in liquidation did not include the right to receive money from the other members. The majority on the other hand (see Lord Cross of Chelsea at 778) noted that the framers of the regulations had described the rights of the members *inter se* as debts, and concluded that, notwithstanding that one member could not have brought legal proceedings against another member, each member performing services for another did obtain a species of chose in action against that other member which could be enforced against it separately in the liquidation. Compare the Talisman system operated by the London Stock Exchange, which provides that, after clearance, selling member firms have no rights against buying member firms but instead have rights only against the Stock Exchange, and conversely that the Stock Exchange has the right to seek payment of the balance due from any member firm. See Abrams, 'Talisman: A Legal Analysis' (1980) 1 *The Company Lawyer* 17, and Goode, *Legal Problems of Credit and Security* (2nd edn., 1988), 175–6.

[16] Compare *Ex parte Mackay* (1873) LR 8 Ch. App. 643 with respect to the agreement as to the royalties in a bankruptcy. Lord Cross of Chelsea rejected the argument that the parties to the clearing house arrangement in *British Eagle* had intended to give one another charges on some of each other's future book debts. Compare in this regard *Ex parte Mackay* with respect to the right to half of the royalties.

uncleared sums owing to it individually by the company against its individual indebtedness to the company.

In the context of a set-off agreement, the objection in *British Eagle* should only be relevant when the agreement provides for a *claim* possessed by a bankrupt or a company in liquidation to be set off in circumstances where the insolvency set-off section does not apply. There is no reason why a set-off agreement which involves utilizing only a liability of the bankrupt or the company should be impugned. For example, A, B and C may agree that A's liability to B may be set off against B's liability to C, and A becomes bankrupt before the set-off has occurred. Since A's liability, as opposed to property distributable amongst creditors, is in issue, the bankruptcy should not affect the agreement.[17] The agreement would have the effect that B would no longer be a proving creditor to the extent of the set-off, with a consequent increase in the dividend payable to other creditors. Nevertheless, a recent remark by the Court of Appeal in *Morris v Agrichemicals Ltd.*[18] has cast doubt on that view. Rose L.J. in delivering the judgment of the Court said that, 'if A owes B £x and B owes C £y *and any of them becomes insolvent* the two debts cannot be set off even if there is an express agreement by the three of them that B may set them off; such an agreement is contrary to the scheme of distribution on insolvency and cannot prevail over the rules which require *pari passu* distribution'.[19] But why the agreement should be regarded as contrary to public policy when A is the insolvent party is difficult to understand.

One of a number of partners indebted in his personal capacity to a creditor, who in turn is indebted to the partnership, may authorize the creditor to set off the separate debt against the debt owing to the partnership. While, before the Judicature Acts, the fact of the agreement for a set-off provided a defence to an action at law by the partnership for the recovery of the debt owing to the partnership,[20] the agreement could be impugned in equity if the creditor had knowledge of the partnership interest in his indebtedness.[21]

12.2 NETTING OF FOREIGN EXCHANGE CONTRACTS

Consider that a bank and a counterparty have entered into large number of foreign exchange contracts involving various currencies settlement dates. The view was earlier expressed[22] that, in the event of a liquidation of the

---

[17] See section 9.7.2 above.
[18] Rose, Saville and Millett L.JJ., 20 December 1995.
[19] Emphasis added.   [20] *Gordon* v. *Ellis* (1844) 7 Man. & G 607.
[21] *Piercy* v. *Fynney* (1871) LR 12 Eq. 69.   [22] See section 5.3 above.

counterparty, there are doubts as to whether the various obligations under the contracts could be set off in the liquidation, given that the foreign money obligation may not be a money obligation. The question is whether the bank could nevertheless avoid this result by means of a properly drafted close-out netting agreement.[23]

The essence of close-out netting is that, upon the occurrence of a liquidation, the foreign exchange contracts are 'closed', and are replaced by an obligation to pay the net money value of the contracts based upon the market exchange rates prevailing at the time. A question which has attracted a considerable amount of discussion in recent years is whether a contract to this effect, in circumstances where a set-off would not otherwise have been available in the liquidation under the insolvency set-off section, may be struck down as an attempt to evade the operation of the insolvency law.

The question of what constitutes an evasion of the insolvency law has been the subject of a number of different formulations, though in truth they are not exclusive of each other and to a considerable extent they overlap. According to one formulation, a comparison is made between what the creditor would have received if the other party had not become bankrupt, and what the agreement between them states that he should receive in the event of a bankruptcy. There is an evasion of the insolvency law if something is to accrue to the creditor upon the occurrence of the bankruptcy of the debtor which notionally would put him in a better position than if the debtor had not become bankrupt.[24] For example, James L.J., in striking down a contract as constituting a fraud in the bankruptcy law, said that:[25]

In my opinion, looking at the whole scope and object of this Deed, at the whole intention of the parties, and taking a common-sense view of the thing, it is impossible not to see that it was intended to make a different distribution of the property of the mortgagors according as they should or should not become bankrupt.

Similarly, Tomlin J. observed in a later case[26] that, 'He cannot make a bargain with the mortgagor which secures to him, the mortgagee, a greater advantage if the mortgagor becomes bankrupt than he would get if he does not'. The principle is illustrated by *Ex parte Mackay*,[27] in which the Court of Appeal struck down a provision in a contract to the effect that, upon the

---

[23] Alternative forms of netting are payment netting and netting by novation, though neither is entirely satisfactory. See Derham, 'Set-off and Netting of Foreign Exchange Contracts in the Liquidation of a Counterparty—Part 2: Netting' [1991] *Journal of Business Law* 536, 536–9.

[24] In addition to the cases referred to below, see *Re Johns* [1928] 1 Ch. 737.

[25] *Ex parte Williams; in re Thompson* (1877) 7 Ch. D. 138, 143.

[26] *Re Johns* [1928] 1 Ch. 737, 748.   [27] (1873) L.R. 8 Ch. App. 643.

bankruptcy of the debtor, a part of his property should become subject to a charge in favour of the creditor.[28] However, this particular formulation does not describe close-out netting. Netting by close-out does not attempt to confer a greater advantage on either party in the liquidation of the other in comparison with what would have been the case in the absence of a liquidation. Before liquidation each of the parties had obligations to the other pursuant to the foreign exchange contracts. After the liquidation the netting agreement provides for a change in the *nature* of the obligations, but not in their notional net value. The netting is intended to preserve the value of the contracts to the parties, assuming that no liquidation had occurred.

There is another line of cases which established the principle that, while the owner of property may, on alienation of that property, qualify the interest of his alienee by a condition to take effect on bankruptcy, he cannot, by contract or otherwise, qualify his own interest by a like condition, so as to determine or control it in the event of his own bankruptcy to the disappointment of his creditors.[29] Thus, in a marriage settlement, if the husband and wife both bring property into the settlement, a trust of the income of the wife's property in favour of the husband until his bankruptcy is valid, while a similar trust of the income of the husband's property, such that the husband's interest ceases upon his bankruptcy, is invalid.[30] This same principle was applied in the case of a building contract which provided that, if the builder became bankrupt or insolvent, any of his materials and chattels situated on the premises were to be forfeited to the owner. The provision for forfeiture was an attempt to qualify the interest of the builder in his property upon the occurrence of his bankruptcy, and so was void.[31] However, given that

---

[28] Similarly, a vendor selling on credit terms cannot contract on the basis that, if the purchaser becomes bankrupt, the price should be doubled. See *Ex parte Mackay* (1873) L.R. 8 Ch. App. 643, 647.

[29] This statement of principle was made by Clement Swanston in a note to his report of Lord Eldon's judgment in *Wilson* v. *Greenwood* (1818) 1 Swans. 471, and has been accepted by the courts on a number of occasions as a correct summary of the law. See, for example, *Whitmore* v. *Mason* (1861) 2 J. & H. 204, 210. Thus a lease may provide that the lease is determinable in the event of the bankruptcy of the lessee. This is valid (subject to relief against forfeiture, and the provisions of s. 146 of the Law of Property Act 1925), because it is a reservation by the owner of property of a power over it. See Lord Eldon in *Higginbotham* v. *Holme* (1812) 19 Ves. Jun. 88, 92–3, and also *Roe d. Hunter* v. *Galliers* (1787) 2 T.R. 133; *Stevens* v. *Copp* (1868) L.R. 4 Ex. 20, 23, 24. Compare *Re Piggin, Dicker* v. *Lombank, Ltd.* (1962) 112 L.J. 424 with respect to a hire purchase agreement, in which the arrangement is not a simple hiring but includes an option to purchase at the end of the period for a nominal sum.

[30] See *Mackintosh* v. *Pogose* [1895] 1 Ch. 505, 511–512.

[31] *Ex parte Jay; in re Harrison* (1880) 14 Ch. D. 19. See also *Rouch* v. *Great Western Railway Company* (1841) 1 Q.B. 51, 64–65; *Ex parte Barter; in re Walker* (1884) 26 Ch. D. 510 (shipbuilding contract). Compare *Ex parte Newitt; in re Garrud* (1881) 16 Ch. D. 522 in which the default was not based upon bankruptcy, so that the forfeiture of the builder's property was valid as against his trustee in bankruptcy.

there is nothing objectionable in 'qualifying' contractual rights by a provision for termination of the contract upon liquidation,[32] these cases would not appear to be directly applicable to netting.

There is nevertheless a third possible formulation of the principle. In this instance the comparison is not between the positions of the parties before and after liquidation. Rather, regard is had only to the position in a liquidation, and the comparison is between what the result would have been for the creditor in the liquidation in the absence of the provision in question, and what it is intended to be in the light of that provision. The question is whether the contract provides for something to happen upon the occurrence of a liquidation[33] which is intended[34] to change the distribution in the liquidation in comparison to what it otherwise would have been, so as to result in preferential treatment as against the general body of creditors.[35] It is difficult to find an instance in which a contract was struck down on this basis in circumstances in which one of the other formulations referred to above would not also have applied, although it is suggested by a number of judicial statements. In *Ex parte Mackay*[36] James L.J. observed that, 'a man is not allowed, by stipulation with a creditor, to

---

[32] See below.

[33] The principle generally would only apply where the change is expressed to occur in the event of bankruptcy or liquidation. See *In re Johnson* [1904] 1 KB 134, 136–7. Compare though *British Eagle* [1975] 1 WLR 758 (discussed in Derham, 'Set-off and Netting' [1991] *Journal of Business Law* 536, 540–2), in which the clearing house rules purported to set up a system of paying debts that itself was contrary to the *pari passu* principle.

[34] The arrangement should have been *intended* as a device to obtain an advantage in the liquidation not otherwise available. See *In re Stockton Iron Furnace Company* (1879) 10 Ch. D. 335, 356. See also *Ex parte Williams* (1877) 7 Ch. D. 138, 143; *In re Johns* [1928] 1 Ch. 737, 748; *In re Apex Supply Co. Ltd.* [1942] 1 Ch. 108, 114; *Bombay Official Assignee* v. *Shroff* (1932) 48 T.L.R. 443, 446. The intention should be ascertained at the time that the contract was entered into. See *Ex parte Voisey; in re Knight* (1882) 21 Ch. D. 442, 459. Compare *British Eagle* [1975] 1 WLR 758 (discussed in Derham, 'Set-off and Netting' [1991] *Journal of Business Law* 536, 540–2), in which the agreement in question purported to set up a system of paying debts that was expressed to apply irrespective of insolvency.

[35] Obviously this formulation would not impugn a contract which was operative before the liquidation and which was not a sham, as, for example, a security. Nor would it apply to a floating charge which crystallizes upon liquidation, though compare Coleman, 'Netting A Red Herring' [1994] *Butterworths Journal of International Banking and Financial Law* 391, 399. In the first place, as Coleman conceded, a floating security is a present security before crystallization. See e.g. *Evans* v. *Rival Granite Quarries, Ltd.* [1910] 2 KB 979, 999. But in any event, it is of the essence of a floating security that it crystallizes upon liquidation even in the absence of an express provision to this effect, given that the company then ceases to carry on business other than for the purpose of its winding-up. See *In re Crompton & Co., Ltd.* [1914] 1 Ch. 954, 964–5, and generally Goode, *Legal Problems of Credit and Security* (2nd edn., 1988), 61. Accordingly, the stipulation for crystallization upon liquidation itself is not the source of the preferential treatment for the chargee.

[36] (1873) L.R. 8 Ch. App. 643, 647. This statement was referred to with evident approval by Tomlin J. in *Re Johns* [1928] Ch. 737, 745, and by both Lord Morris and Lord Cross in *British Eagle* [1975] 1 W.L.R. 758, 770, 779.

provide for a different distribution of his effects in the event of bankruptcy from that which the law provides'. Similarly, Cotton L.J. in *Ex parte Jackson*[37] described as a fraud on the bankruptcy law a clause that he said was 'an attempt to alter and disturb the legal distribution of the mortgagor's property in bankruptcy'. Further, when Lord Cross in *British Eagle*[38] distinguished the decision of the Court of Appeal in *Ex parte Mackay* to strike down a provision in a contract to the effect that a charge should arise upon the bankruptcy of the debtor, he said that the charge 'had been created deliberately in order to provide for a different distribution of the insolvent's property on his bankruptcy from that prescribed by the law'. Netting by close-out should be considered in the light of these statements.[39] In the absence of the netting agreement, it is doubtful whether a foreign currency obligation pursuant to a foreign exchange contract could be the subject of a set-off in a liquidation, given that it is not a monetary obligation. However, as a result of the netting agreement, there is a change in the nature of the contracts upon the occurrence of a liquidation so that the various obligations are replaced by a single obligation to pay a net sterling amount. The question is whether this indeed is contrary to public policy.[40]

There are two points which should be emphasized in relation to the possible application of the public policy ground to netting. The first is that it is not the termination of the obligations which is open to attack. There is nothing objectionable in a contract providing for termination upon liquidation. This does not operate to deprive the company's creditors of the benefit of an asset that otherwise would have been available to them in the liquidation, but merely defines the scope of the rights flowing from the contract. Nor is there anything objectionable *per se* in a clause in a standard loan agreement which accelerates the repayment obligation in the

---

[37] (1880) 14 Ch. D. 725, 741.   [38] [1975] 1 W.L.R. 758, 780.

[39] Coleman, 'Netting A Red Herring' [1994] *Butterworths Journal of Banking and Financial Law* 391, 399 has suggested that these statements do not support the suggested proposition, given that they beg the question as to what the insolvent's property is. However, 'property' and 'effects' would appear to have been used in the sense of the estate available for distribution generally, as opposed to a particular item of property. Certainly this is clear from the Cotton L.J.'s reference in *Ex parte Jackson* to *altering* the distribution of the bankrupt's property in bankruptcy. Where a contract purports to take property out of the estate (as, for example, in the case of the charge which was expressed to arise upon liquidation in *Ex parte Mackay* (1873) LR 8 Ch. App. 643), the effect of the contract, if valid, would be that the property in question would not be distributed in the bankruptcy at all, as opposed to being the subject of a different distribution.

[40] The principle in question would only apply if as a result of the relevant event the estate available for distribution amongst the general body of creditors is lessened. Compare the stock exchange close out rules considered in *Ex parte Grant; in re Plumbly* (1880) 13 Ch. D 667, as discussed in Derham, 'Set-off and Netting' [1991] *Journal of Business Law* 536, 545–6.

event of liquidation, since this merely crystallizes the position between the parties. Rather, the potential objection in the case of close-out netting lies in the replacement of the obligations upon liquidation with a net money obligation. The second point is that any analysis of the situation in terms of a single transaction is apt to mislead. The totality of the arrangement must be looked at.[41] When there is only one transaction, and that transaction is closed out in the liquidation of one of the parties resulting in an obligation on one of them to pay the net market value to the other, depending on which way the market has moved, it cannot be said that there has been any substantive effect upon the insolvent's overall position. The general body of creditors still obtain the benefit of the particular contract to the extent of its then current market value, and so closure does not change the distribution in a liquidation to any material extent.[42] This should be distinguished from close-out netting of foreign exchange contracts in circumstances where there are a large number of separate contracts between the parties. The essence of the arrangement in that case is that it does have a substantive effect upon the position of the general body of creditors, by letting in a set-off where none otherwise would have been available. If the court were to look at the close-out provisions in the context of each individual foreign exchange contract in isolation, it may conclude that it is not objectionable. If, however, the court considers the relationship in its entirety, so that it is apparent that closure of the contracts pursuant to the close-out provisions would have the effect of changing the distribution in a liquidation, the form of netting under consideration could be said to be contrary to public policy, given that the court may well conclude that it was the dominant intention of the parties to achieve this result.

Nevertheless, is this a sufficient justification for striking down netting? A mitigating factor is that the bank's position could be adequately protected by alternative mechanisms. For example, it could be made a term of each foreign exchange contract, amounting to a condition,[43] that the counterparty must not go into liquidation.[44] The parties to a contract are entitled

---

[41] Some of the comments by Coleman in 'Netting A Red Herring' [1994] *Butterworths Journal of International Banking and Financial Law* 391, 399–400 should be considered with that in mind.

[42] See the discussion of *Shipton, Anderson & Co. (1927), Ltd* v. *Micks, Lambert & Co.* [1936] 2 All ER 1032 in Derham, 'Set-off and Netting' [1991] *Journal of Business Law* 536, 549–50. In the case of a single contract in which the obligations are inter-dependent, there is no question of the liquidator refusing to perform the counterparty's obligation and yet being able to obtain specific performance against the other party. Compare the discussion in section 5.3.4 above in relation to the situation in which there are a number of separate contracts.

[43] As distinguished from a warranty. A condition in this sense should also be distinguished from the condition precedent to the performance of obligations which appears in the International Swap Dealers Association Master Agreement. See below.

[44] A similar condition would apply to the bank.

to stipulate that any term is of a fundamental character going to the root of the contract, though clear language must be used.[45] If liquidation then occurs, the bank would be entitled under normal common law principles to terminate its future obligations under each contract and to claim damages.[46] When termination of a contract occurs as a result of an express power to do so contained in the contract, the party exercising the power ordinarily is confined to damages for any breaches that have occurred up to the date of termination, but (in the absence of a repudiation[47]) not thereafter.[48] However, when termination occurs as a result of a breach of condition, the measure of damages relates to the loss of the whole transaction. It includes compensation for loss of the opportunity to receive performance of the other party's outstanding obligations.[49] In the case of foreign exchange contracts which are wholly executory, this should equate to the cost of obtaining replacement contracts in the market, which would be similar to the close-out amount payable under a netting agreement. Indeed, if each contract is separate,[50] it would produce a better result than netting, because the bank would have a claim for damages in respect of each contract in its favour, and could terminate contracts which were unprofitable from its perspective without having to credit the counter-party in liquidation with the market value of those contracts. The counterparty as the defaulter would not be entitled to damages from the bank. While close-out netting provisions admittedly are not usually drafted in terms of breach of a condition, the fact that the parties by their contract have agreed that a result should follow which is similar to, or indeed less advantageous than, that which would apply in such a case provides a measure of support for the view that netting itself should not be regarded as contrary to public policy.

But, whatever the position in relation to the 'basic' form of close-out netting discussed above, there are other protections that may be built into netting agreements with the aim of bringing about a situation in which the result obtained as a result of netting is similar to that which would follow in any event in the absence of the basic netting provisions.

---

[45] *Schuler AG* v. *Wickman Machine Tools Sales Ltd.* [1974] AC 235, 251; *Bunge Corporation* v. *Tradax Export SA* [1981] 1 WLR 711, 715–16; *Lombard North Central Plc* v. *Butterworth* [1987] 1 QB 527, 535, 536, 546.

[46] *Wickman Machine Tool Sales Ltd.* v. *L. Schuler AG* [1972] 1 WLR 840, 851; *Lombard North Central Plc* v. *Butterworth* [1987] 1 QB 527, 535.

[47] Liquidation without more would not constitute a repudiation of foreign exchange contracts. See section 5.2 above, and also Derham, 'Set-off and Netting' [1991] *Journal of Business Law* 463, 481–4.

[48] *Lombard North Central Plc* v. *Butterworth* [1987] 1 QB 527, 546.

[49] *Lombard North Central Plc* v. *Butterworth* [1987] 1 QB 527 (esp. at 535).

[50] Compare the 'one contract' approach in netting, discussed below.

A master netting agreement may provide that all the foreign currency and sterling obligations of the parties that arise out of their foreign exchange transactions in fact constitute a single contract. In other words, this is not a case in which a master agreement sets out terms that apply to each foreign exchange transaction, each of which is still regarded as a separate contract. Rather, there is only one contract for the performance of all obligations that arise pursuant to all the outstanding foreign exchange transactions between the parties. The purpose of the provision is to prevent a liquidator being able to 'cherry pick' or, in other words, being able to disclaim some transactions but not others. The right of disclaimer only applies to a 'contract'. The liquidator cannot enforce one part of the contract and disclaim another part. Therefore, if there is a single contract governing all the foreign exchange transactions, the counterparty's liquidator could not 'cherry pick'. He could not disclaim some of the transactions and affirm others. This form of arrangement admittedly is artificial, although the risk of the court concluding that there are indeed a number of separate contracts would be reduced if the agreement is properly drafted to reflect the position that arises when a new foreign exchange transaction is entered into.[52] The agreement should state, not merely that all the foreign exchange transactions between the parties constitute the one contract, but also that the entry into a particular foreign exchange transaction takes effect as an amendment to the contract, so that the obligations of the parties under the contract henceforth consist of their obligations pursuant to all prior outstanding transactions, if any, together with the obligations arising under the new transaction. Further, this should be reflected in the confirmations which are exchanged between the parties.[53]

An alternative solution, which is widely favoured by practitioners, is a condition precedent along the lines set out in the International Swap Dealers Association Master Agreement, by which the obligations of each party under foreign exchange transactions the subject of the agreement are expressed to be subject to a condition precedent that no event of default, including liquidation of the counterparty, has occurred. If the counterparty goes into liquidation after it has performed its side of a particular transaction, it is a moot point whether the bank could then rely on the clause as a justification for not performing its own obligation under it.[54] But in

---

[52] It is doubtful whether the clause currently appearing in the International Swap Dealers Association Master Agreement goes far enough in this regard.

[53] This should not entail changing the accounting procedures and records of the parties, since each transaction still remains distinct, although it does not constitute a separate contract in its own right. For this reason, it does not suffer from the same drawback as netting by novation. See Derham, 'Set-off and Netting' [1991] *Journal of Business Law* 536, 537–9.

[54] See *Attorney-General* v. *McMillan & Lockwood Ltd.* [1991] 1 NZLR 53, and note also the discussion in *British Eagle* [1975] 1 WLR 758, 778.

relation to transactions which are wholly executory, it is difficult to see, in the absence of a waiver by the bank, what basis the liquidator would have for arguing that the counterparty after the liquidation still has valuable enforceable rights against the bank. An agreement for close-out netting in such a case could hardly be described as an attempt to evade the operation of the insolvency law.[55]

12.3 TAKING A CHARGE OVER ONE'S OWN DEBT

Is it possible for a debtor to take a charge or other security over its own indebtedness?[56] This deceptively simple question has given rise to much debate in recent years. Typically the issue may arise when a bank provides accomodation to a customer, as for example a bank guarantee or letter of credit facility, and as security for the customer's liability the customer deposits cash with the bank. The deposit gives rise to a debt owing by the bank to the customer, which the customer purports to charge in favour of the bank. The question is whether a charge has in fact been created. The better view is that a charge may arise in this circumstance, although the issue is controversial. There is a body of opinion of considerable standing to the effect that a charge-back is conceptually impossible,[57] a view that has been adopted by courts in Australia,[58] and also in England

[55] This condition precedent should also provide a solution to the problem posed in Australia by the Banking Act 1959 (Cth.), s. 16, in relation to the situation in which the counterparty is another bank. Section 16 provides that, in the event of the insolvency of a bank, its assets must be available to meet its deposit liabilities in Australia in priority to all other obligations. This should not prevent netting where the condition precedent applies, since in such a case foreign exchange contracts which are still wholly executory are not assets of any value.

[56] In some jurisdictions legislation has been enacted to specifically recognize the validity of a charge in this situation. See in Bermuda the Charge and Security (Special Provisions) Act 1990, in Cayman Islands the Property (Miscellaneous Provisions) Law 1994, and in Hong Kong s. 15A of the Law Amendment and Reform (Consolidation) Ordinance.

[57] See e.g. Goode, *Legal Problems of Credit and Security* (2nd edn., 1988), 124–31, and also 'Charges Over Book Debts: A Missed Opportunity' (1994) 110 *Law Quarterly Review* 592, 606. Similarly, it has been said that a debtor cannot be a trustee of his own indebtedness. See Scott, *The Law of Trusts* (4th edn., 1987) Vol. 1A, 494 para. 87, though compare Oditah, 'Financing Trade Credit: Welsh Development Agency v. Exfinco' [1992] *Journal of Business Law* 541, 557. Of the cases referred to by Oditah, *Moore* v. *Darton* (1851) 4 De G & Sm. 517 may be explained on the ground that the trust was of the money advanced rather than the debt. *Paterson* v. *Murphy* (1853) 11 Hare 88, 22 LJ Ch. 46, on the other hand, would appear to support Oditah's contention (which perhaps is brought out more clearly in the report in the *Law Journal*). The case, however, is criticized in Scott, *op. cit.* Vol. 1, 187 para. 14.1, 197 para. 14.4.

[58] *Broad* v. *Commissioner of Stamp Duties* [1980] 2 NSWLR 40; *Griffiths* v. *Commonwealth Bank of Australia* (1994) 123 ALR 111, 120. See also *Estate Planning Associates (Aust.) Pty. Ltd.* v. *Commissioner of Stamp Duties (NSW)* (1985) 16 ATR 862, in which it was held that *Broad's* case applied in the case of a policy of insurance issued by an insurance company which was deposited back with the company by way of security. In *Jackson* v. *Esanda Finance*

with the decision of Millett J. (as he then was) in *Re Charge Card Services Ltd.*[59] and, more recently, in the judgment of the Court of Appeal (which included Millett L.J.) in *Morris* v. *Agrichemicals Ltd.*[60] According to this view a 'charge-back' is not without legal effect. It is regarded as operating as a contractual right of set-off which, not being a charge, would not require registration. It does not, however, confer a proprietary interest in the debt, in the form of a charge properly so-called.

The argument against the validity of the security is stronger in relation to a mortgage, given that a mortgage is a form of security that takes effect by way of assignment. The argument is that, if a creditor assigns a debt to the debtor, the debtor would become its own creditor. The interests would merge, so that there would no longer be a debt and consequently no security. Any document purporting to bring about an assignment could only take effect as a release of the debt or a covenant not to sue.[61] Whether in fact this would be the result is debatable, since the equity of redemption that the debtor retains should be sufficient to prevent a merger. But whatever the position in relation to a mortgage, this should not be a problem with respect to an equitable charge. A charge does not involve an assignment of the subject-matter of the security. Rather, it arises when certain defined property is specifically made responsible for the discharge of an obligation, without any transfer of title or possession to the obligee.[62] It takes effect as an hypothecation rather than an alienation.[63] It is true that the primary remedies of an equitable chargee are the right to apply to the court for an order for sale or for the appointment of a receiver.[64] A receiver would hardly be apt in the case of a charge-back, and nor would a sale be contemplated. The only remedy that the parties would have had in mind is that the bank itself, without recourse to the courts, may set one demand against another. This should not however be an objection. The

Corporation Ltd (1992) 59 SASR 416 a customer of a finance company was issued with debenture stock under a debenture which created a floating charge over the finance company's assets in favour of a trustee. It was argued that, although the debt could not be charged, there could be a valid charge over the debenture. However, the court noted that the customer derived the benefit of that security through the trust deed and, if a debtor could not have a charge over its own indebtedness, it could not have a charge over the means by which payment of that debt was secured.

[59] [1987] 1 Ch. 150.

[60] Rose, Saville and Millett L.JJ., 20 December 1995.

[61] *Broad* v. *Commission of Stamp Duties* [1980] 2 NSWLR 40, 46; *Re Charge Card Services Ltd.* [1987] 1 Ch. 150, 175.

[62] Waldock, *The Law of Mortgages* (2nd edn., 1950), 9–10; Gough, *Company Charges* (2nd edn., 1996), 18; *Fisher and Lightwood's Law of Mortgage* (10th edn., 1988), 22. See also n. 104 below.

[63] In effect a shadow is cast over the property set aside as security for the debt until the debt is paid. See Sykes and Walker, *The Law of Securities* (5th edn, 1993), 18, referring to *Salmond on Jurisprudence* (12th edn., 1966), 430.

[64] Megarry and Wade, *The Law of Real Property* (5th edn., 1984), 953.

courts have always allowed the parties to a security contract to provide for their own remedies in the event of default,[65] the classic example being the appointment of a receiver out of court, and it should not make any difference that the remedy contemplated may be in substitution for the traditional remedies available to an equitable chargee as opposed to being in addition to them. For the same reason, the fact that the debtor cannot enforce the debt by suing itself is not an impediment.[66] It is not necessary to do so. There is another perfectly adequate remedy available. It is true that a number of judges in both the Court of Appeal and the House of Lords in *National Westminster Bank Ltd.* v. *Halesowen Presswork & Assemblies Ltd.*[67] emphasized that a bank cannot sensibly be said to have a lien on its own indebtedness.[68] However, it is important to note the context in which those statements were made. The courts in *Halesowen* were concerned to distinguish a bank's right to combine accounts[69] from the lien that a bank has on its customer's securities as a form of security for any indebtedness of the customer arising out of the banker/customer relationship. This lien is a common law possessory lien, which presupposes the existence of tangible property which may be retained and held in possession until the debt in question is paid. A credit balance on a particular account obviously is not tangible property capable of being held in this manner, and so it was said that the use of the word 'lien' in the context of combination is inappropriate. The statements in question should not be regarded as authority for the proposition that it is not possible for a debtor to have a charge over its own indebtedness because, unlike in the case of a common law possessory lien, intangible property may be the subject of an equitable charge.

An argument of greater refinement has been proposed,[70] based on the

---

[65] As Wigram VC remarked in *Sampson* v. *Pattison* (1842) 1 Hare 533, 535, 'The only question is, what are the terms of the contract?'

[66] Compare *Re Charge Card Services Ltd.* [1987] 1 Ch. 150, 176.

[67] [1972] AC 785, reversing the decision of the Court of Appeal [1971] 1 QB 1 on other grounds.

[68] See Lord Denning M.R. and Buckley L.J. in the Court of Appeal [1971] 1 QB 1, 34, 46, and Viscount Dilhorne and Lord Cross of Chelsea in the House of Lords [1972] AC 785, 802, 810. See also *MPS Constructions Pty. Ltd.* v. *Rural Bank of New South Wales* (1980) 4 ACLR 835, in which a customer had executed an agreement by which its bank should have a 'lien' on all money deposited by it with the bank. Helsham C.J. in Eq., in following *Halesowen*, held that this did not encompass money held to the customer's credit on a bank account. However, the question of the effect of a charge, as opposed to a lien, was not considered.

[69] See Ch. 11.

[70] It is sometimes suggested that the question whether an equitable charge may arise depends upon the availability of specific performance, and that accordingly a relevant issue in considering the validity of charge-backs is whether specific performance would be ordered. See Everett, 'Security Over Bank Deposits' (1988) 16 *Australian Business Law Review* 351, 364, and McCracken, *The Banker's Remedy of Set-off* (1993), 168–173, 175–178, 226.

distinction between property and obligation. The argument is that, while as between a creditor and a third party the debt is an asset, as between the debtor and the creditor themselves it is not an asset but an obligation. In other words, the creditor does not own the debt, the debt is owed to it.[71] However, while the creditor undoubtedly is owed the debt, one would have thought that the creditor as against the debtor also has rights which are a species of property and which should be just as capable of being the subject of a security in favour of the debtor as a third party.[72]

The preferred view that a charge over one's own indebtedness is possible is not without judicial support.[73] At the end of the eighteenth century, Buller J. remarked in *Dobson* v. *Lockhart*[74] that there was no reason why a debtor could not have a 'lien on a floating balance' due from himself,[75] though the case may be explained on the alternative ground that the debt was conditional. In *Ex parte Caldicott; in re Hart*[76] a partner in a firm had mortgaged his separate property to the firm's bankers in order to secure the firm's indebtedness to the bank. Subsequently the partner entered into an agreement for the sale of the mortgaged property. The bank concurred in the sale on condition that the proceeds should be placed with it in a deposit account, and that this should be a security for, and stand charged with, the payment of the firm's debt. Subsequently the firm became bankrupt. It is apparent that the Court of Appeal regarded the deposit as a

---

However, the better view is that an equitable charge of present property (as distinct from a promise for valuable consideration to charge future acquired assets) does not depend on specific performance. See *Hewett* v. *Court* (1983) 149 CLR 639 (esp. Deane J. at 665–7) in relation to an equitable lien, which is a form of equitable charge (see 663). Indeed, it is difficult to see what the substance of the order against the chargor would be (though compare McCracken, *op. cit.* 177–8).

[71] Goode, *Legal Problems of Credit and Security* (2nd edn., 1988), 125 (and see also 'Charges Over Book Debts: A Missed Opportunity' (1994) 110 *Law Quarterly Review* 592, 606); Millett (1991) 107 *Law Quarterly Review* 680.

[72] Oditah, 'Financing Trade Credit: Welsh Development Agency v. Exfinco' [1992] *Journal of Business Law* 541, 557. Lindley L.J.'s comment in *Lister* v. *Stubbs* (1890) 45 Ch. D 1, 15, that the employer's claim in that case confounded ownership and property, does not advance the argument. An employee received money by way of secret commission which he invested in the purchase of land, and the employer sought to trace the money into the investment. The action failed on the ground that the relation between them was only that of debtor and creditor, rather than trustee and *cestui que trust*. While the employee had an obligation to the employer on a debtor/creditor basis, neither the money itself nor the property into which it could be traced was owned by the employer.

[73] For a discussion of other cases see Wood, *English and International Set-off* (1989), 199–205, though some of these may be explained on other grounds. For example, in *Webb* v. *Smith* (1885) 30 Ch. D 192, which is often cited as authority in support of charge-backs, the proceeds of sale would have been impressed with a trust, and the auctioneer's 'lien' would have attached to the trust fund. It was not a simple case of a debt owing at common law by the auctioneer to the debtor. See the discussion of *Webb* v. *Smith* in *Morris* v. *Agrichemicals Ltd.*, Court of Appeal, 20 December 1995.

[74] (1793) 5 TR 133.

[75] (1793) 5 TR 133, 138.

[76] (1884) 25 Ch. D 716.

bona fide security[77] although, since it was not a security on an asset belonging to the firm, it was held that it was not necessary that it be deducted from the proof lodged by the bank against the joint estate. A stronger authority is *Ex parte Mackay*.[78] One Jeavons had contracted to sell a patent to two companies in consideration of the payment of royalties. By a second indenture of the same date Jeavons had mortgaged his premises to the two companies as security for a loan advanced by them. The two companies had also agreed under a third contract not to press for repayment of the loan or to execute the power of sale, but rather to repay themselves by retention from time to time of one-half of the royalties to be paid for the use of the patent. Both James and Mellish L.JJ., as well as counsel, assumed that this was intended to operate as a charge in favour of the two companies over their own indebtedness for half the royalties. Counsel had specifically argued that a man cannot have a charge on a debt which is due from himself, though James L.J. nevertheless said that there was a good charge upon one moiety of the royalties, because they were part of the property and effects of the bankrupt. Similarly, Mellish L.J. is reported in the *Law Journal* as having asked during argument,[79] 'Might there not have been such an agreement before the laws of set-off? Why cannot a man have a charge on a debt due from himself as well as on a debt due from another?' In *Swiss Bank Corporation* v. *Lloyds Bank Ltd.*[80] Lord Wilberforce referred without adverse comment to a 'charge' in favour of a bank over sterling deposits with it, while recently Dillon L.J. in the Court of Appeal in *Welsh Development Agency* v. *Export Finance Co. Ltd.*,[81] following a similar doubt expressed by Browne-Wilkinson V.C. in that case in the Chancery Division,[82] said that he had considerable difficulty with the view expressed in *Charge Card* that a charge over one's own indebtedness is conceptually impossible.

More recently, however, notwithstanding the comments in *Welsh Development Agency*, the Court of Appeal in *Morris* v. *Agrichemicals Ltd.*[83] expressed approval of *Charge Card*, though this is unlikely to be

---

[77] Compare *Re Charge Card Services Ltd.* [1987] 1 Ch. 150, 176–7. Compare also the explanation of the case by Oditah, 'Financing Trade Credit: Welsh Development Agency v. Exfinco' [1992] *Journal of Business Law* 541, 558, though the point may be made that the parties had agreed that the proceeds should be placed on deposit with the bank. In other words, it was not evidently intended that the proceeds themselves should be kept separate, but rather that they were to be replaced by a debt. In accordance with that agreement, the proceeds could only have been traced into the debt, which in turn gives rise to the question whether the debt was the subject of a security.

[78] (1873) LR 8 Ch. App. 643, 42 LJ Bcy. 68.   [79] (1873) 42 LJ Bcy. 68, 69.
[80] [1982] AC 584, 614.   [81] [1992] BCLC 148, 166–167.
[82] [1990] BCC 393, 408.
[83] Rose, Saville and Millett L.JJ., 20 December 1995.

regarded as having settled the issue.[83a] In the first place, the Court's discussion of the point was *obiter*. Secondly, Rose L.J. in delivering the judgment of the Court formulated the problem in terms that did not adequately address the case of a charge. His Lordship said that,

> The question is not whether the creditor can own and assign the right to receive payment of a debt to a third party, but whether it can be sold or made available by way of security to the debtor and yet kept alive. The difficulty that needs to be faced is that the debtor cannot be made to own the debt which he owes and which he is incapable of assigning.

But, in the case of a charge it should not be relevant that a debtor cannot own the debt that he owes. A charge does not make the chargee the 'owner' of the debt, because it does not operate by way of assignment. Similarly, because a charge does not take effect as an assignment, there would not be any question that the debt has been kept alive. Nor is it clear what was meant by saying that the debtor is incapable of assigning the debt. Why could not a debtor as chargee, either through a contractual power to do so or as a result of a court order, sell the chargor's rights as creditor against him to a third party? Indeed, as explained below, this appears to have been the substance of the order in *Ex parte Mackay*. A third difficulty with *Morris* is that the comments by James and Mellish L.JJ. in *Ex parte Mackay* referred to earlier were not satisfactorily explained. The question in that case was whether the right of retention enjoyed by the companies in relation to one half of the royalties constituted a 'security' within the meaning of r. 78 of the Bankruptcy Rules 1870, so as to allow the court to order a sale. We have seen that both James and Mellish L.JJ. commented in terms suggesting that the right of retention gave rise to a charge in favour of the companies over their indebtedness for the royalties, though Rose L.J. in *Morris* offered a different interpretation of the case. He said that in truth the question in issue was not whether the companies had a proprietary interest in their obligation to pay royalties as a result of a charge properly so-called. Rather, the order for sale was upheld because the companies' *right of retainer* was a security within the meaning of the r. 78. With respect, this is questionable. Rule 78 applied where there was 'security'. Section 16(5) of the Bankruptcy Act 1869 defined a 'secured creditor' as a creditor holding a mortgage, charge or lien, and it would be a natural assumption that 'security' in r. 78 was intended to have a corresponding meaning. Furthermore, pursuant to r. 78 the court was required to direct that notice be given in a newspaper as to when and where 'the said premises or property . . . over which the security shall so extend, are to be sold'. What was the 'property' over which the security extended in

---

[83a] The question was left open by the Privy Council in *Tam Wing Chuen* v. *Bank of Credit and Commerce Hong Kong Ltd.*, 26 March 1996.

Mackay? There does not appear to have been a separate fund for the royalties set aside by companies, and so it was not a security over the royalities themselves. The property in question could not have been anything other than the *debt* for the royalties. But in that context a right of retainer would not have been a security over property. It would have been a flawed asset, a contractual restriction on the right to payment. It would merely have defined what the property was, in terms of right of payment. If on the other hand the security was not just the right of retainer, but that right coupled with a right to apply the debt for the royalties in satisfaction of the loan, the question would have been whether there was a charge over the debt. It is difficult to put any other interpretation on the remarks of James and Mellish L.JJ. If 'security' in r. 78 was thought to have a broader meaning than that traditionally ascribed to the term, one would have thought that the point would have been discussed by the court, or at least argued by counsel.

Consider that a charge over one's own indebtedness is not a conceptual impossibility. In such a case a charge-back could secure not only a debt owing by the chargor, but also a third party's indebtedness. This could arise, for example, where a deposit held by a bank is charged by the depositor to secure financial accomodation provided to a related company. But in the situation in which there are only two parties, so that the debt secured by the charge-back is owing by the depositor itself, it has been suggested that, as a result of the analysis of the insolvency set-off section accepted in *Stein* v. *Blake*,[84] the charge, even if it is otherwise valid, would not continue after liquidation. In *Stein* v. *Blake* the House of Lords held that the set-off takes effect automatically upon the occurrence of a bankruptcy or liquidation so as to bring about a cancellation of the cross-demands to the extent of the set-off.[85] Under that circumstance it is said that a charge over one claim to secure payment of the other would not survive the winding-up order. The cross-demands would no longer exist. The principal source of support for this view is *M. S. Fashions Ltd.* v. *Bank of Credit and Commerce International SA*.[86] A bank advanced money to a customer and took a guarantee of the customer's indebtedness from a director, the guarantee being expressed in terms that the guarantor contracted as a principal debtor. The bank also took a deposit from the guarantor which was charged to the bank. Subsequently the bank went into liquidation. It was held that the guarantor's liability on the guarantee and the bank's debt to the guarantor on the deposit were demands arising out of mutual dealings within the ambit of the set-off section, and accordingly

---

[84] [1995] 2 All ER 961. [85] See section 2.12.1 above.

[86] [1993] Ch. 425. The issue is discussed by Berg in 'Charges Over Book Debts: A Reply' [1995] *Journal of Business Law* 433, 465–7, and 'House of Lords Clarifies Liquidation Netting' *International Financial Law Review*, August 1995, 20, 21.

were the subject of an automatic set-off upon the occurrence of the liquida-tion.[87] The effect of this was that the bank could not choose to sue the principal debtor for payment and confine the guarantor to a proof in the liquidation in respect of the deposit. Counsel for the liquidator argued that, because of the charge, there was no set-off, though this received little sympathy from Hoffman L.J. in the Chancery Division. He said that, even if one ignores the question whether a charge-back is conceptually possible, the charge was over a debt owing by the bank to secure a debt owed by the bank, and that 'The account to be taken by r 4.90 must require an unwinding of that arrangement so that the deposit is set off against the debt it was intended to secure'.[88] On appeal the Court of Appeal similarly held that the fact of the charge over the deposit did not prevent a set-off. While the issue was discussed primarily from a different perspective, as to whether the deposit was a special purpose payment and therefore not available for a set-off on that ground,[89] the tenor of the judgment suggests that the Court of Appeal agreed with Hoffman L.J.'s analysis. This is also consistent with the earlier decision of the Court of Appeal in *Sovereign Life Assurance Co.* v. *Dodd*.[90] In that case a set-off was allowed in the liquidation of an insurance company in relation to a loan by the company to the insured, and the insured's claim on a policy issued by the company which had been mortgaged back to the company as security for the loan, though the effect of the mortgage-back was not considered in any great detail.[91]

Notwithstanding this weight of authority, it is difficult as a matter of principle to support the view that, if a charge-back is indeed valid, a set-off under the insolvency set-off section will occur between the charged debt and the debt owing by the chargor to the chargee for which it is security.[92] The essence of Hoffman L.J.'s analysis, that the account to be taken under the insolvency set-off section requires an unwinding on the arrangement,

---

[87] It was crucial to the set-off that the guarantor had contracted as a principal debtor, because in that circumstance the guarantor's liability was not conditional upon a demand being made. See the discussion of *M. S. Fashions* in section 8.3 above.

[88] [1993] Ch. 425, 438.   [89] See section 6.6 above.

[90] [1892] 2 QB 573.

[91] In *Ex parte Mackay* (1872) LR 8 Ch. App. 643, in which the right to retain the royalties was treated as a charge on a debt (see above), it is apparent that the companies' debt for the royalties and their rights against Jeavons in respect of the loan were not regarded as having been set off under the insolvency set-off section. However, it is not clear from the report whether those rights and obligations were held in joint or several capacities for the purpose of determining mutuality, and accordingly whether the insolvency set-off section applied.

[92] It was nevertheless noted by Kay L.J. [1892] 2 QB 573, 584, 585. Compare *Hiley* v. *The Peoples Prudential Assurance Co., Ltd.* (1938) 60 CLR 468, in which the insured's claim was not on the mortgaged policy but rather was for damages for repudiation of it. This also appears to have been the substance of the claim in *In re National Benefit Assurance Co., Ltd.* [1924] 2 Ch. 339 (see esp. 345).

begs the question as to whether the requirements of the set-off section in fact have been satisfied so as to justify an account under it. As counsel for the bank argued,[93] if one assumes that the charge was valid it should have had as a consequence that there was not mutuality for the purpose of the section. The bank had a claim against the guarantor, and it also would have had a beneficial interest in the deposit as a result of the charge. Because of the charge the guarantor would not have had an unimpeded beneficial interest, which should have been sufficient to prevent mutuality arising.[94] Under a charge-back the chargee is a secured creditor, and its position should be governed by the rules relating to the security, including as to timing of enforcement. It should not be a question of set-off, save to the extent that the method available to the chargee to enforce the charge is a *contractual* right of set-off.

12.4 A SET-OFF AGREEMENT AS A CHARGE

Consider that the views expressed in *Welsh Development Agency* are followed, and that the validity of charge-backs ultimately is upheld by the courts. A question that would follow is whether a set-off agreement itself is a charge. This is not intended to refer to a situation in which it is agreed that a set-off is to occur immediately or as a matter of course, since this is merely a method of payment.[95] Nor would it apply to a provision in a contract to the effect that the amount payable is the contract price less allowable deductions in respect of expenditure. Rather, the issue may arise when a creditor is given the *option* of setting off debts in circumstances where the essence of the arrangement is to provide a form of security to the creditor. For example, it is common for banks to be given the power by contract to set off any account in credit that the customer may have against a loan advanced by the bank. The question is whether the credit account has been charged to the bank as security for the debt. The important point is that a contractual right of set-off goes beyond the right of set-off conferred by the Statutes of Set-off. The Statutes provided a procedural defence which requires an order of the court for its enforcement.[96] A set-off agreement on the other hand allows the creditor itself to effect a set-off and thereby obtain payment. If a set-off agreement does create a charge, the charge would be over the bank's own indebtedness on the account.

---

[93] [1993] Ch. 425, 440–1. See also Wood, *English and International Set-off* (1989), 195.
[94] See section 7.6 above.
[95] This would include, for example, the clearing arrangement in *British Eagle* [1975] 1 WLR 758. [96] See section 1.2.9 above.

The issue may be important for a number of reasons. If indeed a charge has been created it would survive the insolvency of the person entitled to the credit account, and the bank could rely on it notwithstanding that the right of set-off that it confers is broader than that otherwise available under the insolvency set-off section. This may be particularly relevant where, for example, the credit balance is held by one company in a group and banking accomodation is provided to another, because in such a case lack of mutuality would prevent the operation of the set-off section.[97] The issue can also arise in the context of a negative pledge which prohibits the granting of security, as well as in jurisdictions in which stamp duty is imposed on charges and other loan securities. Further, when an administration order has been made against a company, section 11(3)(c) of the Insolvency Act prohibits any 'security' being enforced against the property of the company during the period that the order is in force, except with the consent of the administrator or the leave of the court.[98] While the issue has yet to be determined by the courts, the question whether this would prevent a bank exercising rights under a set-off agreement may depend on whether it gives rise to a charge.[99] Similarly, if a company voluntary agreement has been proposed under Part I of the Insolvency Act, the arrangement cannot affect the rights of a secured creditor without the concurrence of the creditor concerned,[100] and in that circumstance the question whether a set-off agreement is a charge may be crucial.

---

[97] The bank's position may in any event be protected if as a matter of contract the credit balance is unable to be withdrawn until the accommodation is repaid. See the discussion of the insolvency of the chargor in *Morris* v. *Agrichemicals Ltd.* Court of Appeal, 20 December 1995.

[98] See also s. 10(1)(b) with respect to the period between the presentation of the petition for an administration order and the making or the dismissal of the order.

[99] However, 'security' has been interpreted broadly as including the exercise by a landlord of a right of re-entry for non-payment of rent. See *Exchange Travel Agency Ltd.* v. *Triton Property Trust plc* [1991] BCLC 396; *Re Olympia & York Canary Wharf Ltd.* [1993] BCLC 453, 455. On that basis, it may include a set-off agreement whether or not it is a charge. In Australia the corresponding restriction is expressed to relate to enforcement of charges (which is defined as including a mortgage), though there is an exemption for a charge which is over all or substantially all of the company's assets. See ss. 440B and 441A of the Corporations Law. 'Charge' in this context has been interpreted narrowly in its traditional sense as not including a pledge. See *Osborne Computer Corporation Pty. Ltd.* v. *Airroad Distribution Pty. Ltd.* (1995) 17 ACSR 614.

[100] Insolvency Act 1986, s. 4(3). In Australia, when it is proposed that a company execute a deed of company arrangement, or the company has executed such a deed, the court may order a secured creditor not to realise the security. See the Corporations Law, s. 444F(2). However, an order cannot be made under s. 444F(2) if the creditor has security over all or substantially all of the company's assets; see s. 441A. Clause 7(d) of Sch. 8A of the Corporations Regulations, which prescribes provisions to be incorporated into each deed of company arrangement, provides that a creditor may not exercise any right of set-off to which the creditor would not have been entitled had the company been wound up. However, that is expressed to be subject to s. 444D, which preserves the position of secured creditors.

Authorities on point are sparse. Apart from cases on charge-backs, there are two cases which support the view that a set-off agreement is not a charge. The first, *Electro Magnetic (S) Ltd.* v. *Development Bank of Singapore Ltd.*,[101] is a decision of the Court of Appeal of Singapore. An agreement between a bank and its customer provided that the bank could 'set off or transfer any sum or sums standing to the credit of one or more . . . accounts in or towards satisfaction of any of the liabilities of the borrower to the bank on any other account or accounts'. It was held that this did not confer any real or proprietary interest in the accounts in credit, but rather it was only a personal right given by contract to set one account against another and arrive at a balance. In Australia, Lee J. expressed a similar view in the Federal Court in *Griffiths* v. *Commonwealth Bank of Australia*[102] in relation to a differently worded agreement. A deposit was made with a bank for the specific purpose of providing 'security' for a facility. An agreement provided that, so long as money remained owing to the bank, the bank was under no obligation to repay the deposit, and furthermore the bank could 'apply the whole or any part of the deposit and interest accrued thereon in or towards payment of the moneys owing or any part thereof'. Lee J. rejected the argument that this gave rise to an equitable charge. He said that, apart from the issue of the impossibility of the bank taking a charge over its own indebtedness, the agreement contained no terms which indicated that an instrument of security was created. These cases should be compared to the decision of Harman J. in *Re Tudor Glass Holdings Ltd., Franik Ltd.*[103] The managing director of the BA group of companies referred in a letter to a director of the Tudor Glass group to the practice of 'contra accounting'. Harman J. was prepared to accept that the intention was that each of the companies in the BA group should be allowed to set off against its indebtedness to any of the Tudor Glass companies a debt owing to it by that, or any of the other, Tudor Glass companies, though he held that the letter in fact was not expressed in sufficiently clear terms to achieve this result as a binding contract. Nevertheless Harman J. said that, if there had been a firm contract to this effect, the contract would have been intended to provide security for payment of the debts. His Lordship said that it would have constituted a floating charge over the debts of the Tudor Glass companies, in which case it would have been void as against the receiver of the Tudor Glass group for want of registration under the companies legislation.

The essence of an equitable charge is that specific property is appropriated to the discharge of a debt or other obligation, without there

[101] [1994] 1 SLR 734.
[102] (1994) 123 ALR 111, 120. See also *Broad* v. *Commissioner of Stamp Duties* [1980] 2 NSWLR 40, 48.   [103] (1984) 1 BCC 98,982.

being a change of ownership either at law or in equity.[104] No particular form of words is necessary,[105] though there must be an intention to create a security.[106] On the other hand, it has been said that 'if upon the true construction of the relevant documents in the light of any admissible evidence as to surrounding circumstances the parties have entered into a transaction the legal effect of which is to give rise to an equitable charge in favour of one of them over property of the other, the fact that they may not have realised this consequence will not mean that there is no charge. They must be presumed to intend the consequence of their acts'.[107] At first blush this would appear to describe the form of set-off agreement under discussion. The customer's asset, in the form of the account in credit, is appropriated to the discharge of the debt owing to the bank. However, this is not a universally accepted view.[108] It is sometimes said that the agreement does not give rise to a charge because it does not create a security interest in the customer's asset,[109] though this does not advance the argument. It is no more than a different expression of the conclusion drawn. Alternatively, the view that a set-off agreement is not a charge has been justified on the ground that the agreement does not operate by way of giving the bank a right to use the customer's asset (the account in credit) in order to satisfy the customer's debt to the bank. Rather, the bank satisfies its liability to the customer on the credit account by appropriating its own asset, in the form of the customer's debt.[110] It this were the true effect of the agreement, it would not be a charge. However, set-off agreements are

---

[104] *Carreras Rothmans Ltd.* v. *Freeman Mathews Treasure Ltd.* [1985] 1 Ch. 207, 227; *In re Bond Worth Ltd.* [1980] 1 Ch. 228, 248; *Re Charge Card Services Ltd.* [1987] 1 Ch. 150, 176; Megarry and Wade, *The Law of Real Property* (5th edn., 1984) 929. Compare *Palmer* v. *Carey* [1926] AC 703, which is explained in *In re Gillott's Settlement* [1934] Ch. 97, 109–10 and *Swiss Bank Corporation* v. *Lloyds Bank* [1979] 1 Ch. 548, 568. See also n. 62 above.

[105] *National Provincial and Union Bank of England* v. *Charnley* [1924] 1 KB 431, 440.

[106] *Re State Fire Insurance Company* (1863) 1 De G J & S 634, 641; *National Provincial and Union Bank of England* v. *Charnley* [1924] 1 KB 431, 449–50; *Swiss Bank Corporation* v. *Lloyds Bank Ltd.* [1982] AC 584, 595.

[107] *Swiss Bank Corporation* v. *Lloyds Bank Ltd.* [1982] AC 584, 595–6 per Buckley L.J. (C.A.). See also Browne-Wilkinson J. at first instance [1979] 1 Ch. 548, 569.

[108] Equally, though, there are commentators who support the view that in some circumstances a set-off agreement will constitute a charge, if the perceived conceptual problem of a debtor taking a charge over its own indebtedness can be overcome. See Pollard, 'Credit Balances as Security—II' [1988] *Journal of Business Law* 219, 220; Everett, 'Multi-Party Set-off Agreements' [1993] *Journal of Banking and Finance Law and Practice* 180, 183–4; Cresswell, Blair, Hill and Wood, *Encyclopedia of Banking Law*, E555, para. 2476; McCracken, *The Banker's Remedy of Set-off* (1993), 178–82. See also Blair, 'Charges Over Cash Deposits' *International Financial Law Review*, November 1983, 14.

[109] Ladbury, 'Introduction to the Law of Contractual Set-off in Australia', *Using Set-off as a Security* (edited by Neate, 1990), 62; Goode, *Commercial Law* (1982), 719.

[110] Wood, *English and International Set-off* (1989), 148–50, 193–4; Hapgood, 'Set-off Under the Laws of England', *Using Set-off as a Security* (edited by Neate, 1990), 32, 37. See also Goode, *Legal Problems of Credit and Security* (2nd edn., 1988), 4, 173.

not usually drafted in this manner, and there is nothing inherent in the term 'set-off' which requires this interpretation.[111] The relevant question is the presumed intention of the parties in the context of the agreement in issue, and often that interpretation would be an unlikely one, particularly in a case where the bank is the party given the option to effect a set-off, the 'trigger' for doing so is the customer's default, the customer has not demanded payment of the amount standing to the credit of the account, and the bank required the set-off as a form of security in the event of the customer's insolvency, in which case the bank's asset, which it is supposedly using to satisfy its liability, would be worth only a fraction of its face value. In the absence of clear language, it would be difficult to support the view that under those circumstances the substance of the transaction is that the bank is paying its debt by the application of its own property, rather than that the debt owing by the customer in default is being satisfied by the application of the customer's asset. *Kent's Case*,[112] although concerned with a different issue, is of interest in this regard. A shareholder in a company held partly paid shares. He took an assignment of a debt owing by the company, and wrote to the directors requesting them to transfer from the amount due in respect of the debt a sum sufficient to pay up his shares in full. The directors then passed a resolution that 'the debt assigned by Mr. Eichholz to Mr. Kent as aforesaid should be applied in paying up in full the shares mentioned in Mr. Kent's letter of this date'. Shortly afterwards an order was made to wind up the company, whereupon it was held that the transaction was void as a preference.[113] But for this result to have followed, it must have been regarded as a payment or a transfer of property by the company as a debtor in favour of Kent as a creditor,[114] notwithstanding that Kent's letter and the directors' resolution were cast in terms that Kent's asset should be used to pay his liability. Plainly, given the company's insolvency, that was not the substance of the transaction. The question may also arise in relation to a disposition of a company's property after the commencement of its winding-up,[115] where a bank's rights under a set-off agreement given by the company admittedly rest in contract only and are not by way of security.[116] If the bank acting

---

[111] Indeed, the Court of Appeal in *Morris* v. *Agrichemicals Ltd.*, 20 December 1995, described a contractual right of set-off in terms of a debtor's right to appropriate a debt which he owes to his creditor and apply it in reduction or discharge of a debt which is owed to himself.

[112] *In re Land Development Association; Kent's Case* (1888) 39 Ch. D 259.

[113] See also *In re Washington Diamond Mining Company* [1893] 3 Ch. 95, and generally section 4.6 above.

[114] See the Bankruptcy Act 1883, s. 48, being the preference section in issue, which was made applicable to company liquidations by the Companies Act 1862, s. 164.

[115] Pursuant to the Insolvency Act 1986, s. 127.

[116] The parties may have expressly agreed this in the contract in order to avoid a charge. See below.

pursuant to the agreement effects a set-off against a deposit account after the commencement of the company's winding-up, and the liquidator later asserts that the set-off constituted a void disposition,[117] it is unlikely that the court would be attracted to an argument that the company's property in truth was not disposed of, but rather it was a repayment of the deposit by an application of the bank's asset.[118]

However, if indeed it is possible for a debtor to have a charge over its own indebtedness, a dogmatic view that all set-off agreements constitute charges would be just as questionable as a statement that a set-off agreement can never be a charge. The circumstances of each case would have to be considered, including the intention of the parties whether express or presumed. Consider the case of a specific deposit made by a customer as a result of a bank's requirement for 'cash cover' for a facility provided either to the customer or to a third party, the deposit being on terms that it cannot be withdrawn until all amounts actually or contingently owing under the facility have been paid, and in the event of a default the bank is given the right to set it off against amounts owing. Assuming that a charge-back is possible, the better view is that this does create a charge, notwithstanding the contrary view expressed by Lee J. in *Griffiths* v. *Commonwealth Bank of Australia*.[119] It would appear to come squarely within Cotton L.J.'s definition of a charge over a debt,[120] that 'When there is a contract for value between the owner of a chose in action and another person which shews that such person is to have the benefit of the chose in action, that constitutes a good charge on the chose in action. The form of words is immaterial so long as they shew an intention that he is to have such benefit'. If the parties wish to avoid this result, the agreement should expressly stipulate that it is not intended to create a charge. Since the creation of a security depends upon the intention of the parties, the clause should be effective. That form of arrangement should be compared to a clause in a standard bank loan agreement to the effect that the bank at any time can set off against the loan any account in credit that the customer may have against the bank, though without there being an obligation to maintain such an account, and without imposing restrictions on with-drawals. It is unlikely that this would create a security in the strict sense in

---

[117] This situation may particularly arise when the debt set off against the deposit was owing by a third party, so that lack of mutuality would have prevented a set-off under the insolvency set-off section.

[118] The view that this would constitute a void disposition is consistent with *Barclays Bank Ltd.* v. *TOSG Trust Fund Ltd.* [1984] BCLC 1, 21–25, in which Nourse J. held that a bank's action in debiting a payment to an account so as to bring it within the operation of a contractual right in the bank to treat accounts as combined was a disposition within the terms of the section. Compare *Re Loteka Pty. Ltd.* (1989) 15 ACLR 620, 622.

[119] (1994) 123 ALR 111, 120.

[120] *Gorringe* v. *Irwell India Rubber and Gutta Percha Works* (1886) 34 Ch. D 128, 134.

favour of the bank,[121] because it is not a case of specific property being appropriated to the discharge of a debt.[122] Rather, it should be characterized as merely a contractual right in the bank to reduce the customer's debt from any credit funds that may be in hand. On this basis, the decision of the Singapore Court of Appeal in the *Electro Magnetic* case[123] would appear to have been correct. It is distinguishable from *Re Tudor Glass Holdings*[124] on the ground that the essence of the arrangement in that case was that there would be cross-demands, the purpose being to provide protection to the BA group of companies for increasing their indebtedness to the Tudor Glass group.[125]

When a customer has a number of accounts with a bank the principle of combination may apply so that, unless a particular account has been separated out by agreement or it is separate as a matter of law, the balance of all the accounts represents the debt at any particular time.[126] However, if a customer sets up a security deposit at the request of a bank and charges it to the bank, including where a set-off agreement has this effect, the security interest that the bank has in the account should have the effect of preventing it being the subject of combination, so that the bank's position instead would be governed by the security. Indeed, often combination would not be applicable in any event because the liability secured is contingent, as for example where the account secures a contingent liability to the bank on a letter of credit provided by the bank, or a contingent liability under a guarantee of a related company's indebtedness.

Assuming that in any particular case a set-off agreement operates by way of charge over a debt, the question arises whether the agreement would require registration under section 396 of the Companies Act 1985 in the event that the party granting the right is a company.[127] If it does, failure to register the charge could render it void as against an administrator or a liquidator of the company, or any person who for value acquired an interest in the property the subject of the charge.[128] Not every company charge is registrable. One possibility is that the set-off agreement may constitute a charge on the company's book debts. The term 'book debts' is

---

[121] See also Cresswell, Blair, Hill and Wood, *Encyclopedia of Banking Law*, E555, para. 2476. [122] See above. [123] [1994] 1 SLR 734.

[124] See above. [125] See the discussion at (1984) 1 BCC 98,982, 98,984.

[126] See Ch. 11.

[127] Obviously the mere possibility of a set-off under either the Statutes of Set-off or the insolvency set-off section is not registrable. One reason for this is that the possibility does not confer any form of security interest. See *In re John Ewing, A Bankrupt* (1906) 8 GLR 612; *Official Assignee of Reeves & Williams* v. *Dorrington* [1918] NZLR 702, 706. But even apart from that, the creditor's right arises by operation of law, as opposed to being created by the company itself. [128] Companies Act 1985, s. 399(1).

not defined in the English legislation,[129] although in its generally accepted
sense it refers to debts connected with and growing out of a person's trade
or business which would ordinarily be entered in that person's books.[130]
Opinions differ as to whether this would include a bank account.[131] Goode
has aptly expressed what is probably the preferred view, that a bank
account is not a book debt since it does not arise out of the company's trade
or business itself, but is merely the consequence of the deposit of surplus
funds.[132] Hoffman J. appeared to confirm this in *Re Brightlife Ltd.*[133] when
he held that the expression 'all book debts and other debts' in a debenture
did not encompass an amount standing to the credit of a bank account,
though some two years later in *Re Permanent Houses (Holdings) Ltd.*[134] he
emphasized that *Brightlife* was concerned with the construction of a
particular debenture, and that he did not express an opinion in that case as
to whether a credit balance is a book debt for the purpose of registration of
charges under the Companies Act. If charge-backs are upheld, one
imagines that it would not be long before the issue comes before the courts.

But even if the notion of a book debt is confined within its traditional
bounds, a charge-back may be registrable on another ground. If the
company has the right to operate the account without restriction until such
time as the bank effects a set-off, any charge over the account would
resemble a floating charge, in which case the agreement may be registrable
on that ground. Different considerations may apply, however, if the
customer is required to retain a minimum credit balance, for example in
order to cover a liability that the bank may incur on a guarantee or
performance bond given on behalf of the customer, and the bank has the
right to apply this balance in satisfaction of any liability that does arise.
This restriction on the company's right to operate and manage the account
may well be regarded as inconsistent with a floating security. It may instead
give rise to a fixed equitable charge on part of a debt, in which case, unless
it can be said that the account is a book debt, it would not be registrable.

---

[129] Compare Australia, where a charge on a book debt is defined in the Corporations Law,
s. 262(4) in terms of a charge on a debt due 'on account of or in connection with a profession,
trade or business carried on by the company, whether entered in a book or not . . .'.

[130] *Shipley* v. *Marshall* (1863) 14 CB (NS) 566; *Independent Automatic Sales Ltd.* v.
Knowles & Foster [1962] 1 WLR 974.

[131] For a good discussion see McCracken, *The Banker's Remedy of Set-off* (1993), 182–185.

[132] Goode, *Legal Problems of Credit and Security* (2nd edn., 1988), 114–115. See also
Ellinger, *Modern Banking Law* (1987), 582; *Watson* v. *Parapara Coal Co., Ltd.* (1915) 17
GLR 791. However, Professor Goode has made the point that money deposited by an
investment company with a bank by way of investment may give rise to a book debt.

[133] [1987] 1 Ch. 200. See also *Northern Bank Ltd.* v. *Ross* [1991] BCLC 504.

[134] [1988] BCLC 563, 566–567.

13

Assignees, and Other Interested Third Parties

13.1 INTRODUCTION

Consider that A is indebted to B, and that a third party, C, has an interest in the debt. This may arise in a number of circumstances, for example where C is an assignee, or the holder of a security interest, or the beneficiary of a trust, or an undisclosed principal, or a person with subrogation rights,[1] or a judgment creditor levying execution on B's asset in the form of the debt. If A has a cross-claim against B that otherwise would be eligible for a set-off, A will be concerned to know whether the set-off is still available notwithstanding the interest of C. Alternatively, if A has a cross-claim against C, the question may arise whether it can be set off against the debt owing to B, given C's interest in it. Some of the issues have already been considered generally in the context of the discussion of mutuality.[2] The purpose of this chapter is to consider the availability of a set-off in the particular situations of assignments, company receiverships, trusts, execution creditors and subrogation rights. Issues associated with undisclosed principals[3] and secured creditors[4] have already been examined, as have assignments in the context of the rule in *Cherry* v. *Boultbee*[5] and combination of bank accounts.[6]

13.2 ASSIGNMENTS

13.2.1 *Introduction*

In the event of an assignment of a chose in action, set-offs may occur in accordance with normal principles in relation to the assignee's beneficial interest in the assigned debt and a cross-claim that the debtor has against

---

[1] See section 7.3.3 above   [2] See generally Ch. 7.
[3] See section 9.7.3 above.   [4] See sections 7.6 and 2.18 above.
[5] See section 10.12 above.   See section 11.13 above.

the assignee.[7] Questions of set-off in this context were considered earlier.[8] In addition, however, there is a general equitable principle[9] that the assignee in certain circumstances takes subject to equities, which include rights of set-off, that are available to the debtor as against the assignor.[10]

Commonly the issue will arise in the situation in which the assignor is indebted to the debtor on a cross-debt that is independent of the assigned debt. The debtor will assert that he is entitled to set off the two debts pursuant to the Statutes of Set-off, notwithstanding the assignment. The basic principle applied by the courts is that, if the cross-debt arose after the debtor had notice of the assignment, the debtor cannot set it off against the assignee, though he will be allowed to do so if it arose before he had notice.[11] Sometimes it is sought to explain the denial of a set-off in relation to a post notice cross-debt on the ground that the demands are not equitably mutual.[12] The assigned debt is owned beneficially by the assignee, whereas the cross-debt constitutes a claim against the assignor. However, this analysis is apt to mislead. We have seen[13] that it fails to explain why a set-off is allowed to the debtor when the cross-debt arose after the assignment but before the debtor had notice of the assignment, because in this period mutuality determined by reference to beneficial titles similarly would be lacking. The true principle is that at common law mutuality for the purpose of the Statutes of Set-off is determined by reference to legal titles so that, if cross-debts are legally mutual, there is a prima facie right to a set-off under the Statutes. The question then becomes whether it is unconscionable for the debtor to rely on this right of set-of otherwise available at law when the equitable title to one of the debts is in someone else.[14] That this is the proper approach is evident if one has regard to the position that applied before the Judicature Acts. An assignment of a debt was not then generally recognized by the common law courts, in the sense that the assignee could not enforce the debt in a common law action brought in his own name.[15] He was required to sue in

---

[7] See e.g. *Moore* v. *Jervis* (1845) 2 Coll. 60.   [8] See generally Ch. 7.

[9] Compare the pre-Judicature Acts common law case of *Watkins* v. *Clark* (1862) 12 CB (NS) 277.

[10] Save in the case of an equitable set-off (see section 1.7.6 above), the debtor could not set off a debt owing by a person other than the assignor.

[11] See section 13.2.4 below.

[12] See e.g. Russell L.J. (with whose judgment Sellers L.J. agreed) in *Robbie & Co. Ltd.* v. *Witney Warehouse Co. Ltd.* [1963] 1 WLR 1324. See also *Coba Industries Ltd.* v. *Millie's Holdings (Canada) Ltd.* [1985] 6 WWR 14, 28–9; *Telford* v. *Holt* (1987) 41 DLR (4th) 385, 394.   [13] See section 7.4 above.

[14] Meagher, Gummow, and Lehane, *Equity: Doctrines and Remedies* (3rd edn., 1992), 720–1. See also Blackburn J. in *Wilson* v. *Gabriel* (1863) 4 B & S 243, 247–8, referred to in *Christie* v. *Taunton, Delmard, Lane and Company* [1893] 2 Ch. 175, 182.

[15] The major reasons put forward for the non-assignability of choses in action at law are discussed in Marshall, *The Assignment of Choses in Action* (1950), 34 et seq.

the name of the assignor. If the assignor refused to allow his name to be used, he could be compelled to do so by a court of equity. However, as far as the common law was concerned the resulting action to enforce the debt was still the assignor's action and, unless equity intervened, defences available to the debtor against the assignor, including pursuant to the Statutes of Set-off, could be asserted in that action. Equity would not enjoin the debtor at the request of the assignee from raising defences that arose before the debtor had been notified of the assignment.[16] However, it was considered to be unconscionable that the debtor should diminish the rights of the assignee by relying on defences that only accrued after notice,[17] and so in this latter case the assignee could obtain a common injunction to restrain the debtor from pleading the defence. While the Judicature Acts have now brought about a fusion of the tribunals of law and equity,[18] the courts nevertheless have continued to apply the principle that an assignee is bound by equities arising before notice. Moreover, notwithstanding the fusion, and notwithstanding the modern view as to enforcement, that an equitable assignee may sue in his own name subject to a requirement (which can be dispensed with only in exceptional circumstances) of joining the assignor as a party to the action,[19] the explanation should still be the same.

13.2.2 *Statutory assignment*

The Judicature Acts also introduced a statutory form of assignment, the successor of which is set out in s. 136(1) of the Law of Property Act 1925.[20] In order to come within this provision the assignment must be in writing, it must be absolute and not by way of charge only, and express notice in writing must be given to the debtor. Where the section is complied with the assignee obtains the legal title to the debt, and may sue in his own name

---

[16] The reason for this has been said to be that equity will not intervene when the equities are equal. *Wilson* v. *Gabriel* (1863) 4 B & S 243, 248.

[17] *Roxburghe* v. *Cox* (1881) 17 Ch. D 520, 526.

[18] It was suggested in *United Scientific Holdings Ltd.* v. *Burnley Borough Council* [1978] AC 904 that the Judicature Acts also brought about a fusion of the principles of law and equity. This view was promptly attacked as heretical. See Baker, 'The Future of Equity' (1977) 93 *Law Quarterly Review* 529; Meagher, Gummow, and Lehane, *Equity: Doctrines and Remedies* (3rd edn., 1992), 67–8; Martin, 'Fusion, Fallacy and Confusion; A Comparative Study' [1994] *The Conveyancer* 13. See also Sir Peter Millett, 'Equity—The Road Ahead' (1995) 9 *Tolley's Trust Law International* 35, 37. In *Bank of Boston Connecticut* v. *European Grain and Shipping Ltd.* [1989] 1 AC 1056, 1109 the House of Lords said that the Judicature Acts, 'while making changes to procedure, did not alter the rights of the parties'.

[19] See Peter Gibson L.J.'s judgment in *Three Rivers District Council* v. *Bank of England* [1995] 4 All ER 312.

[20] Supreme Court of Judicature Act 1873, s. 25(6). In Australia see. e.g. the Property Law Act 1958 (Vic.), s. 134.

without joining the assignor. However, the principle that an assignee takes subject to equities has been expressly preserved, so that the debtor can still rely on a right of set-off against the assignee that would have prevailed against an equitable assignee before the Judicature Acts.[21] On the other hand, because the assignor is not a party to the action, the debtor cannot counterclaim in that action for the excess of the assignor's indebtedness to him over and above the amount of the assigned debt.[22]

13.2.3 *Cross-demand must be available as a set-off against the assignor*

An assignee only takes subject to a cross-demand available to the debtor against the assignor if the cross-demand would have been available as a set-off as between the assignor and the debtor under circumstances where both parties were solvent.[23] It has been suggested in Australia that in some cases a cross-demand that could only have been employed by the debtor as a counterclaim in an action by the assignor may be asserted against the assignee.[24] However, this is contrary not only to principle but also to views expressed by the House of Lords in *Bank of Boston Connecticut* v. *European Grain and Shipping Ltd.*,[25] and it should not be regarded as correct.[26] If, therefore, the claim assigned is such that as a matter of law it is not susceptible to a set-off, as for example a claim for freight under a charterparty in circumstances where the charterer has a cross-claim for damages against the owner,[27] or a claim on a negotiable instrument where the issuer has an unliquidated cross-claim arising out of the transaction in respect of which the instrument was issued,[28] the assignee similarly will take free of a set-off.[29]

---

[21] *Lawrence* v. *Hayes* [1927] 2 KB 111, 120–1.

[22] *Young* v. *Kitchin* (1878) 3 Ex. D 127; *Mitchell* v. *Purnell Motors Pty. Ltd.* [1961] NSWR 165, 168.   [23] See sections 13.2.9 and 13.2.10.

[24] *McDonnell & East Ltd.* v. *McGregor* (1936) 56 CLR 50, 60 (Dixon J.). See also *Re K.L. Tractors Ltd.* [1954] VLR 505, 508; *Bayview Quarries Pty. Ltd.* v. *Castley Developments Pty. Ltd.* [1963] VR 445, 449; *Edward Ward & Co.* v. *McDougall* [1972] VR 433, 438–9; *Provident Finance Corporation Pty. Ltd.* v. *Hammond* [1978] VR 312, 320; *James* v. *Commonwealth Bank of Australia* (1992) 37 FCR 445, 461–2; *Re Partnership Pacific Securities Ltd.* [1994] 1 Qd. R 410, 423–4; *Walker* v. *Department of Social Security* (1995) 129 ALR 198, 210; Spry, 'Equitable Set-offs' (1969) 43 *Australian Law Journal* 265, 269–70 (though the treatment in Spry, *Equitable Remedies* (4th edn., 1990) 175–6 perhaps is more equivocal); Meagher, Gummow & Lehane, *Equity: Doctrines and Remedies* (3rd edn., 1992), 821–3. In *Clyne* v. *Deputy Commissioner of Taxation* (1981) 150 CLR 1, 20, Mason J. said that the word 'equities' in the context of the expression 'an assignment is subject to equities' comprehends 'set-off and counterclaims', though the point was not discussed in any detail.

[25] [1989] 1 AC 1056, 1105–6, 1109–11.

[26] See Derham, 'Recent Issues in Relation to Set-off' (1994) 68 *Australian Law Journal* 331, 334–7.   [27] See section 1.7.14 above.   [28] See section 1.7.17 above.

[29] *Bank of Boston Connecticut* v. *European Grain and Shipping Ltd.* [1989] 1 AC 1056.

13.2.4 *Statutes of Set-off*

Mutual debts in existence between the assignor and the debtor at the date that the debtor receives notice of the assignment will give rise to a set-off under the Statutes of Set-off enforceable against the assignee.[30] It should not make any difference that the cross-debt owing by the assignor to the debtor may have been acquired by the debtor as a result of an assignment made to him before notice,[31] including where there is an effective assignment without consideration.[32]

It is not necessary that the pre-existing cross-debt owing by the assignor to the debtor should have matured before the date of notice.[33] It should be sufficient if it is payable when the defence is filed.[34] On the other hand, it has been said that, if the assigned debt was not presently payable at the date of notice, in order that the cross-debt may be set off it should have become payable before the assigned debt became payable.[35] The reason for this limitation is not clear. The set-off in issue is the procedural defence provided by the Statutes of Set-off. Provided that the debt owing by the assignor is in existence before notice, it should be sufficient if it is payable at the date that the defence is filed,[36] irrespective of when the assigned debt matured. Indeed, it is difficult to reconcile the limitation with *Christie v. Taunton, Delmard, Lane and Company*.[37] The case concerned an assignment of debentures issued by a company. Notice of the assignment was given to the company on 6 November 1890. On 3 November a call had

---

[30] See e.g. *Smith* v. *Parkes* (1852) 16 Beav. 115; *Chick* v. *Blackmore* (1854) 2 Sm. & Giff. 274; *Stephens* v. *Venables (No. 1)* (1862) 30 Beav. 625; *Roxburghe* v. *Cox* (1881) 17 Ch. D 520; *Lawrence* v. *Bell* (1866) 14 WR 753; *Biggerstaff* v. *Rowatt's Wharf, Ltd.* [1896] 2 Ch. 93; *In re Smith & Co., Ltd.* [1901] 1 IR 73. See also *Peters* v. *Soame* (1701) 2 Vern. 428, a case decided before the enactment of the Statutes of Set-off. Compare *In re Jones; Christmas* v. *Jones* [1897] 2 Ch. 190, 203–4.

[31] See e.g. *Tony Lee Motors Ltd.* v. *M. S. MacDonald & Son (1974) Ltd.* [1981] 2 NZLR 281 (company receivership). Compare *N. W. Robbie & Co. Ltd.* v. *Witney Warehouse Co. Ltd.* [1963] 1 WLR 1324 (discussed in section 13.3.1 below), in which the assignment occurred after notice.

[32] For a discussion of the efficacy of an assignment where there is no consideration, see Keeton and Sheridan, *Equity*, 2nd edn., 1975, 211 *et seq.*

[33] *Jeffryes* v. *Agra and Masterman's Bank* (1866) LR 2 Eq. 674; *Christie* v. *Taunton, Delmard, Lane and Čmpany* [1893] 2 Ch. 175; *In re Pinto Leite and Nephews; ex parte Visconde des Olivaes* [1929] 1 Ch. 221. See also *Downes* v. *Bank of New Zealand* (1895) 13 NZLR 723; *Business Computers Ltd.* v. *Anglo-African Leasing Ltd.* [1977] 1 WLR 578, 585.

[34] See section 1.2.2 above.

[35] *In re Pinto Leite and Nephews* [1929] 1 Ch. 221, 234–6, explaining *Jeffryes* v. *Agra and Masterman's Bank* (1866) LR 2 Eq. 674, 680. See also *Downes* v. *Bank of New Zealand* (1895) 13 NZLR 723, 734; *Business Computers Ltd.* v. *Anglo-African Leasing Ltd.* [1977] 1 WLR 578, 584.

[36] See *Stein* v. *Blake* [1995] 2 All ER 961, 964, and generally section 1.2.2 above.

[37] [1893] 2 Ch. 175, discussed in *Clyne* v. *Deputy Commissioner of Taxation* (1981) 150 CLR 1, 21–2.

been made on shares held by the assignor, which call was payable on 20 November. The debentures were not on the face of them payable until 31 December, but, in the event of the winding-up of the company, the principal moneys secured by them were to become immediately due and payable. On 19 November the company went into voluntary liquidation. Both the company's liability on the debentures and the assignor's liability for the call constituted existing debts at the date of notice, though they were not payable until after that date. It was held that the company could bring them into an account, notwithstanding that, because of the occurrence of the winding-up, the assignor's indebtedness for the call matured *after* the assigned debt became due and payable.[38]

There must be an *existing* debt owing by the assignor to the debtor before notice.[39] It is not sufficient that a debt accrues in favour of the debtor from the assignor after notice, albeit as a result of a contract entered into before notice.[40] Thus, where a debtor was also a lessor in respect of property leased to the creditor, and the creditor assigned the debt owing to him, it was held that the assignee was not subject to a set-off in respect of rent which accrued to the debtor/lessor after notice of the assignment, even though the lease was entered into before notice.[41] This is an undesirable result. A set-off should be allowed where there was a possibility of a perception of a form of security in the existence of cross-demands.[42] This should be ascertained by reference to the state of affairs existing when a binding contractual relationship was entered into, as opposed to when a debt arose as a result of that contract. It should be sufficient that there are presently payable cross-debts at the date of the action which arose out of contractual obligations incurred before notice. Consistent with that approach, there would appear to be an exception to the established principle in the case of a negotiable instrument. If, before a debtor had notice of an assignment of the debt, the debtor held a negotiable instrument upon which the creditor was liable, which the debtor then indorsed to a third party, and after notice of the assignment the debtor was

---

[38] In addition calls were made in the winding-up. See the discussion of the case in section 4.6 above.   [39] Compare equitable set-off, discussed below.
[40] *Stephens* v. *Venables (No. 1)* (1862) 30 Beav. 625; *Watson* v. *Mid Wales Railway Company* (1867) LR 2 CP 593. See also *Woodhams* v. *Anglo-Australian and Universal Family Assurance Co.* (1861) 3 Giff. 238 (call on shares made after notice); *In re China Steamship Company; ex parte Mackenzie* (1869) LR 7 Eq. 240, 243; *Christie* v. *Taunton, Delmard, Lane and Company* [1893] 2 Ch. 175, 181; *Re Bailey Cobalt Mines Ltd.* (1919) 44 OLR 1 (judgment in misfeasance action obtained after notice); *In re Pinto Leite and Nephews* [1929] 1 Ch. 221, 233–234; *Business Computers Ltd.* v. *Anglo-African Leasing Ltd.* [1977] 1 WLR 578. Compare the exceptional fact situation in *Ralston* v. *South Greta Colliery Company* (1912) 13 SR (NSW) 6, discussed in section 1.7.1 above.
[41] *Watson* v. *Mid Wales Railway Company* (1867) LR 2 CP 593. See also *Stephens* v. *Venables (No. 1)* (1862) 30 Beav. 625.   [42] See section 2.3 above.

obliged to take up the instrument again as a result of the creditor's default, the assignee should take subject to the debtor's right to set off his resulting claim against the creditor/assignor on the instrument. The availability of a set-off in this situation has been recognized in the context of company receivership.[43] Questions of set-off in that context are governed by the same principles applicable to assignments,[44] and there is no reason why the set-off should not apply to assignments generally.

13.2.5 *Set-off in Australia*

A different position would appear to apply in some states of Australia.[45] The Statutes of Set-off have been repealed in New South Wales and Queensland, which should have as a consequence that the only form of set-off to which an assignee in those jurisdictions takes subject is equitable set-off, together with analogous rights such as the rule in *Cherry* v. *Boultbee*[46] and combination of bank accounts.[47] On the other hand, in Victoria, Order 13 rule 14 of the Supreme Court Rules, in conjunction with section 41(1) of the Supreme Court (Rules of Procedure) Act 1986, may well have had the effect that any cross-claim, whether liquidated or unliquidated, may now be included in the defence and be the subject of a set-off in that state. Presumably, however, when the question is whether a cross-claim available against an assignor may be asserted against an assignee, similar restrictions to those applicable to the Statutes of Set-off would operate, so that, for example, the cross-claim must have accrued before notice of the assignment.

13.2.6 *Notice to the debtor*

It is the date of notice to the debtor,[48] as opposed to the date of the assignment itself, that determines whether an assignee takes subject to a set-off under the Statutes in relation to a cross-debt owing by the assignor to the debtor.[49] The notice need not be in any particular form.[50] It need not, for example, be in writing. Nor is it necessary that the notice should

---

[43] See *Handley Page Ltd.* v. *Commissioners of Customs and Excise and Rockwell Machine Tool Co. Ltd.* [1970] 2 Lloyd's Rep. 459, 464–5, discussed in *Business Computers Ltd.* v. *Anglo-African Leasing Ltd.* [1977] 1 WLR 578, 585–6.

[44] See section 13.3 below.   [45] See generally section 1.12 above.

[46] See section 10.12 above.   [47] See section 11.13 above.

[48] Notice given to an agent of the debtor may suffice. See *Moore* v. *Jervis* (1845) 2 Coll. 60, 69, 71–2.

[49] *Moore* v. *Jervis* (1845) 2 Coll. 60; *Wilson* v. *Gabriel* (1863) 4 B & S 243. The statement in *Dixon* v. *Winch* [1900] 1 Ch. 736, 742 (and see also *Turner* v. *Smith* [1901] 1 Ch. 213, 219) suggesting the contrary is incorrect.

[50] *The Attika Hope* [1988] 1 Lloyd's Rep. 439, 442.

come from the assignee himself.[51] It would be unconscionable for the debtor to rely on a set-off otherwise available at law if the debtor knows of the assignment from whatever source. Moreover, there need only be notice of the fact that the debt has been assigned. The assignee need not be named.[52]

The question whether the equitable doctrine of constructive notice applies has not been determined by the courts, though the better view is that it does not. This is consistent with the approach adopted when the issue has arisen in other contexts, for example in the case of a priorities dispute between successive assignees of a debt. The relevant principle is the rule in *Dearle* v. *Hall*,[53] which in essence accords priority to the assignee who is the first to give notice to the debtor. In this situation the courts have emphasized that it is in the interests of an assignee to give notice so as to prevent another assignee, whether earlier or later, obtaining priority over him. If an assignee does not give notice, he acts at his peril. Accordingly, it is said that the duty is on the assignee to give notice,[54] and the doctrine of constructive notice does not apply.[55] Moreover, to be effective the assignee's notice must be clear and distinct.[56] Lord Cairns expressed it in terms that there must be proof that the mind of the debtor has in some way been brought to an intelligent apprehension of the assignment, so that a reasonable man, or an ordinary man of business, would act upon the information and would regulate his conduct by it.[57] The same approach has been adopted in relation to payment by the debtor. If the debtor has notice of the assignment he can only discharge his obligation by paying the assignee, unless the assignee has agreed otherwise.[58] If the debtor ignores the assignment and pays the assignor, he may be liable to pay a second time to the assignee.[59] Once again, because the debtor may obtain a good discharge by paying the assignor if he does not have notice,[60] the assignee acts at his peril if he fails to give notice, and accordingly the view is that the assignee must give clear notice in order to secure his

---

[51] See e.g. *Lloyd* v. *Banks* (1868) LR 3 Ch. App. 488 (notice in newspaper); *Ex parte Agra Bank; in re Worcester* (1868) LR 3 Ch. App. 555, 559; *Talcott, Ltd.* v. *John Lewis & Co. Ltd.* [1940] 3 All ER 592.   [52] *Smith* v. *Parkes* (1852) 16 Beav. 115, 117–18.

[53] (1828) 3 Russ. 1.

[54] *Willes* v. *Greenhill* (1861) 4 De G F & J 147, 150; *Ward* v. *Duncombe* [1893] AC 369, 395. See also *Mangles* v. *Dixon* (1852) 3 HLC 702, 732–3.

[55] *Lloyd* v. *Banks* (1868) LR 3 Ch. App. 488, 490.

[56] *Bence* v. *Shearman* [1898] 2 Ch. 582, 587.

[57] *Lloyd* v. *Banks* (1868) LR 3 Ch. App. 488, 490–1.

[58] See e.g. *The Evelpidis Era* [1981] 1 Lloyd's Rep. 54, in which it was agreed that insurance payments could be made directly to the insured mortgagor until such time as the mortgagee notified the insurer of a default.

[59] See e.g. *Brice* v. *Bannister* (1878) 3 QBD 569.

[60] See e.g. *Norrish* v. *Marshall* (1821) 5 Madd. 475.

position.[61] Thus, in *Talcott Ltd.* v. *Lewis & Co. Ltd.*[62] the notice sent to the debtor was ambiguous, and it was held that it was insufficient to render the debtor liable to pay the assignee after having already paid the assignor. Nor was there a duty of inquiry imposed.

Set-off is similar to payment, and the issue of notice for the purpose of whether a cross-debt owing by the assignor to the debtor can be set off against the assigned debt should be determined by like principles. In the case of an equitable assignment, where the legal title to the assigned debt remains with the assignor, the debtor prima facie has a right of set-off at common law under the Statutes of Set-off in relation to *any* cross-debt. An assignee acts at his peril if he does not give notice,[63] because he may not be able to take advantage of the equitable rule that cross-debts arising after notice cannot be set up against an assignee. Consistent, then, with the attitude of the courts in relation to questions of payment and priorities, the debtor should not have a duty of inquiry.[64] Rather, the onus should be on the assignee to give notice which is clear and unambiguous. This should also be the case when the requirements for a statutory assignment set out in section 136 of the Property Law Act 1925 are in issue,[65] particularly given the commonly held view that the section relates to procedure only.[66] On the other hand, if sufficient notice is given to the debtor, he cannot refuse to accept it.[67] Nor can he shut his eyes to the obvious.[68] In *Cavendish* v. *Geaves*[69] a pass book issued by a banking firm from time to time to a customer showed changes in the firm, and principal and interest payments on some bonds given by the customer to the firm appeared as entries in the pass book. This was held to constitute notice that the bonds were assigned to the new firm whenever a change occurred.

13.2.7 *Assignment of a future debt*

A future debt may be assigned in equity so that, if value has been given, the assignment will attach to the debt as soon as it is acquired.[70] Consistent with the principles discussed above,[71] the assignee in such a case will not

---

[61] *Bence* v. *Shearman* [1898] 2 Ch. 582, 587, 591. [62] [1940] 3 All ER 592.

[63] *Parker* v. *Jackson* [1936] 2 All ER 281, 289–90.

[64] It has been said that the duty of inquiry is on the assignee. See *Mangles* v. *Dixon* (1852) 3 HLC 702, 732–3 and *Helstan Securities Ltd.* v. *Hertfordshire County Council* [1978] 3 All ER 262, 266. [65] See section 13.2.2 above.

[66] *Tolhurst* v. *Associated Portland Cement Manufacturers (1900), Ltd.* [1902] 2 KB 660, 676–7.

[67] *Higgs* v. *The Northern Assam Tea Company, Limited* (1869) LR 4 Ex. 387, 396.

[68] *Mangles* v. *Dixon* (1852) 3 HLC 702, 732. [69] (1857) 24 Beav. 163.

[70] *Tailby* v. *Official Receiver* (1888) 13 App. Cas. 523.

[71] See section 13.2.4 above.

take subject to a set-off under the Statutes where the cross-debt sought to be set off arose after notice.[72] But what about the assigned debt? Certainly a set-off will be denied if the transaction out of which the assigned debt arose was entered into after the debtor had notice of the assignment.[73] Consider, however, that the assigned debt, though arising after notice, nevertheless has its source in a prior transaction, as, for example, where the assignor entered into a contract to sell goods to a purchaser before the purchaser had notice that the resulting debt for the price was already the subject of a prior assignment in equity, and the goods were not delivered, and the debt for the price did not arise, until after notice. When the question has arisen in the context of the cross-debt owing to the debtor we have seen that it is not sufficient, in the case of a debt accruing after notice, that it has its source in a prior transaction.[74] It appears, however, that a similar principle does not apply when the assigned debt is in issue so that, in the example mentioned, a set-off is available to the purchaser against a cross-debt which was owing by the assignor to the debtor before notice. The issue has arisen in relation to company receiverships, and it is considered below in that context.[75]

In the context of a priorities dispute between successive assignees under *Dearle* v. *Hall*,[76] it is said that notice of assignment of a future debt is ineffective until the debt has come into existence.[77] The question arises whether this also applies to set-off so that, until the assigned debt has come into existence, an assignee could not give notice which would prevent rights of set-off accruing to the debtor in relation to cross-debts which may become owing by the assignor. Baggallay L.J. in *Roxburghe* v. *Cox*[78] considered that it does apply, though that view should be regarded as doubtful. This is apparent if the position is analysed on the basis of what would have happened before the Judicature Acts. When the assigned debt ceased to be an expectancy, and became the subject of an immediate assignment to the assignee, the assignee could have sued for payment in an action brought in the name of the assignor. As far as the common law was concerned the debtor would have had a right of set-off available to him in that action under the Statutes. The question then would have been whether

---

[72] Compare *Wilson* v. *Gabriel* (1863) 4 B & S 243.

[73] This has been established in the context of receiverships, discussed in section 13.3.1. See *Felt and Textiles of New Zealand Ltd.* v. *R. Hubrich Ltd.* [1968] NZLR 716; *Rendell* v. *Doors and Doors Ltd.* [1975] 2 NZLR 191; *Leichhardt Emporium Pty. Ltd.* v. *A.G.C. (Household Finance) Ltd.* [1979] 1 NSWLR 701; *Cheviot Australia Pty. Ltd.* v. *Bob Jane Corporation Pty. Ltd.* (1988) 52 SASR 204.   [74] See section 13.2.4 above.

[75] See the discussion of *Rother Iron Works Ltd.* v. *Canterbury Precision Engineers Ltd.* [1974] 1 QB 1 in section 13.3.1 below.   [76] (1828) 3 Russ. 1.

[77] *Somerset* v. *Cox* (1865) 33 Beav. 634; *In re Dallas* [1904] 2 Ch. 385.

[78] (1881) 17 Ch. D 520, 527.

equity would have intervened to prevent the debtor relying on this right of set-off otherwise available at law. The answer would have been yes, because as from the time that the debtor knew of the assignment it would have been unconscionable for him to do anything to diminish the rights of the assignee.[79] The fact that, as between successive assignees of an expectancy, notice to the debtor is ineffective before the assigned debt comes into existence is not to the point. As far as the debtor himself is concerned, his conscience is affected as from the time that he becomes aware of the assignment.[80]

13.2.8 *Equitable set-off*

The preceding discussion concerned the exercise of a right of set-off against an assignee based upon the Statutes of Set-off. For this both demands must be liquidated. However, an unliquidated demand possessed by the debtor against the assignor may be set off against the assigned debt if the case is one in which the demands are sufficiently closely connected to give rise to an equitable set-off as between the debtor and the assignor.[81] Unlike for set-off under the Statutes, it is not necessary in this situation that the demands should have arisen before notice of the assignment. The assignee may take subject to an equitable set-off where the cross-claim arose after notice.[82] Using the traditional formulation of equitable set-off, the title to

---

[79] See James L.J. in *Roxburghe* v. *Cox* (1881) 17 Ch. D 520, 526.

[80] This has been held to be the case in Canada. See *Dommerich & Co.* v. *Canadian Admiral Corporation* [1962] OR 902.

[81] See generally section 1.7 above. In addition to the cases cited below, see *Popular Homes Ltd.* v. *Circuit Developments Ltd.* [1979] 2 NZLR 642. It is not sufficient in this regard that the claims arose out of the same contract. See *Government of Newfoundland* v. *Newfoundland Railway Company* (1888) 13 App. Cas. 199, 212 (PC); *G. and T. Earle, Ltd.* v. *Hemsworth R.D.C.* (1928) 44 TLR 605, 609. Compare *Phoenix Assurance Co. Ltd.* v. *Earl's Court Ltd.* (1913) 30 TLR 50, 51.

[82] *Coba Industries Ltd.* v. *Millie's Holdings (Canada) Ltd.* [1985] 6 WWR 14 (repudiation by assignor after notice); *Telford* v. *Holt* (1987) 41 DLR (4th) 385 (Canada). See also Bovill C.J. in *Watson* v. *Mid Wales Railway Company* (1867) LR 2 CP 593, 598 (referring to *Smith* v. *Parkes* (1852) 16 Beav. 115); *Business Computers Ltd.* v. *Anglo-African Leasing Ltd.* [1977] 1 WLR 578, 585. In *Government of Newfoundland* v. *Newfoundland Railway Company* (1888) 13 App. Cas. 199 (discussed below) the assignment occurred a number of years before the breach, though it is not expressly stated in the report when notice of the assignment was given. But, since the assignee was a trustee for bondholders of the company, and the company was empowered to issue bonds by the Act of the Newfoundland legislature embodying the contract between the Government and the company, it may be assumed that the Government was aware of the assignment. Reference also may be made to *Bank of Boston Connecticut* v. *European Grain and Shipping Ltd.* [1989] 1 AC 1056. The bank in that case gave notice of assignment on 14 July 1982 whereas the repudiation occurred after then, on 19 July, and the Court of Appeal accepted that an equitable set-off was available against the bank. The decision was reversed by the House of Lords, though on the separate ground that an equitable set-off is not available against a claim for freight (for which see section 1.7.14 above). Compare *Popular Homes Ltd.* v. *Circuit Developments Ltd.* [1979] 2 NZLR 642, 660, and *Re Jason Construction Ltd.* (1972) 29 DLR (3d) 623, 628.

sue is impeached, and in that circumstance it should not make any difference when the cross-claim accrued. Indeed, the same result should follow when the transaction itself out of which the cross-claims arose was entered into after notice of a prior assignment of future book debts.[83] Mutuality is not a prerequisite to this form of equitable set-off,[84] and if the cross-demands are sufficiently closely connected to give rise to an impeachment of title, the title of a prior assignee to sue should be equally affected.[85]

In *Young* v. *Kitchin*[86] a sufficiently close connection provided the basis for a set-off against an assignee of a sum of money owing under a building contract when the debtor had a damages claim against the assignor for failure to complete and deliver the building by the specified date. Similarly, in *Government of Newfoundland* v. *Newfoundland Railway Company*[87] it was held that an assignee of a sum payable to a construction company under a railway construction contract took subject to a claim for damages against the company for not completing the line, while in *Lawrence* v. *Hayes*[88] the purchaser of a business was allowed to set off against an assignee's claim for the sums due under the contract the amount of a judgment obtained against the vendor for damages for breach of warranty. The breach arose from the fact that certain chattels included in the sale either were not the property of the assignor or were the subject of a charge which had not been paid off. In Canada a damages claim available to a mortgagor against the mortgagee for breach of an obligation to renew the insurance on the mortgaged premises was set off against the mortgage debt, notwithstanding an assignment of the debt.[89] These cases should be contrasted with *Stoddart* v. *Union Trust, Limited*,[90] in which the defendant in an action being prosecuted by an assignee was not allowed to bring into account a claim for damages against the assignor for fraud inducing the contract. The court reasoned that the damages claim was not a claim

---

[83] Compare Wood, *English and International Set-off* (1989), 793 para. 14-80, 856 para. 16–22.　　　　　　　　　　　　　　　　　　　　[84] See section 1.7.6 above.

[85] Compare the comments of Viscount Haldane in *Parsons* v. *Sovereign Bank of Canada* [1913] AC 160, 167–8, though that was in the context of a court-appointed receiver who ordinarily contracts personally, as opposed to a receiver appointed by debenture holders who contracts as agent of the company (see section 13.3.2). The question in *Parsons* was whether the debt sued for was under the same contract with the company which had been repudiated, and in respect of which the cross-claim for damages arose.

[86] (1878) 3 Ex. D 127. See also *Mitchell* v. *Purnell Motors Pty. Ltd.* [1961] NSWR 165.

[87] (1888) 13 App. Cas. 199.　　　　　　　　　　　　　　　[88] [1927] 2 KB 111.

[89] *Campbell* v. *Canadian Co-operative Investment Co.* (1906) 16 Man. LR 464.

[90] [1912] 1 KB 181. See also *Cummings* v. *Johnson* (1913) 4 WWR 543; *Provident Finance Corporation Pty. Ltd.* v. *Hammond* [1978] VR 312; *Birchal* v. *Birch, Crisp & Co.* [1913] 2 Ch. 375, 379.

arising under the contract, or for breach of the contract,[91] but rather it was said to be a claim 'dehors' the contract.[92] This analysis is not entirely convincing. Indeed, there is an apparent conflict between the decision in *Stoddart*, on the one hand, and on the other the principle applied in the context of the mutual credit provision in the bankruptcy legislation, that a claim for damages for misrepresentation inducing a contract is not a mere personal tort, but rather it constitutes a breach of the obligation arising under the contract so that, even apart from the reform set out in the Insolvency Act 1986 by which tortious demands became provable, it could be employed in a set-off in the event of a bankruptcy.[93] Both Vaughan Williams and Buckley L.JJ. in *Stoddart*[94] emphasized that the plaintiff was an assignee for value without notice of the fraud. However, as a matter of principle this should not have affected the question whether there was an equitable set-off available as against the assignor, and if there was it should have been available against the assignee. There are also statements in the judgments suggesting that the failure of the defendant to rescind the contract was a factor militating against a set-off,[95] though it is not clear why that should have mattered. *Stoddart* should be compared to the decision of Mann C.J. in the Victorian Supreme Court in *Sun Candies Pty. Ltd.* v. *Polites*.[96] The fraudulent misstatement inducing the purchaser in that case to buy the business constituted a breach of a warranty which determined the amount of the purchase price. Since the cross-claim did arise out of the contract, it was held that it gave rise to an equitable set-off to which the assignee from the vendor took subject.[97]

Consider that a debtor has an unliquidated cross-claim against the creditor which is not sufficiently closely connected to give rise to an equitable set-off. If the cross-claim has been converted into a judgment before the debtor has notice of an assignment of his debt by the creditor, the judgment constitutes a debt which can be set off against the assignee under the Statutes, since the case is then one of mutual debts in existence before notice.[98]

13.2.9 *Insolvent assignor*

The assignee takes subject to a right of set-off that would have been

---

[91] See Buckley L.J. [1912] 1 KB 181, 192. On the other hand, a debtor sued by an assignee may set up the defence that the contract under which the debt arose ought to be set aside and cancelled for fraud.   [92] See Kennedy L.J. at [1912] 1 KB 181, 194.

[93] See section 4.5.2 above.   [94] [1912] 1 KB 181, 188, 192.

[95] [1912] 1 KB 181, 189, 192, 194.   [96] [1939] VLR 132.

[97] Compare *Provident Finance Corporation* v. *Hammond* [1978] VR 312, in which the damages claim for breach of warranty related to a different contract to that assigned, though *quaere* whether this justified a different result. See section 1.7.8 above.

[98] See section 1.4.1 above.

available as a defence to an action brought by the assignor against the debtor, either as a result of the Statutes of Set-off in the case of mutual debts, or because of a defence of equitable set-off when the demands are inseparably connected. If the assignor has become bankrupt the assignee does not take subject to the wider right of set-off that would otherwise have been available under the mutual credit provision in the insolvency legislation.[99] The debt, having been assigned, will not have passed to the assignor's trustee in bankruptcy as property of the bankrupt, in which case, unless the assignment may be set aside as a preference or on a similar ground, it may be enforced outside of the operation of the insolvency legislation.[100]

As Wood has noted,[101] the bankruptcy of an assignor may give rise to a particular problem for the debtor. The insolvency set-off section will not apply. Further, a set-off against the assignee, whether by way of equitable set-off or under the Statutes of Set-off, will depend upon the continued existence of a claim against the assignor. But if the assignee delays in suing the debtor so that in the interim the assignor is discharged from bankruptcy, the assignor will be released from liability.[102] The debtor will no longer have a cross-claim, and the House of Lords held in *Aries Tanker Corporation* v. *Total Transport Ltd.*[103] that a claim that has ceased to exist cannot be employed in a set-off. In the case of an equitable set-off, Wood has suggested that the debtor may avoid this infelicitous result by exercising a 'self-help remedy', in the sense that he can act unilaterally to bring about a set-off.[104] However, it is doubtful if equitable set-off entitles a debtor to do this, and indeed the judgment of Lord Wilberforce in *Aries Tanker* is authority to the contrary.[105] Given the substantive nature of the defence of equitable set-off, there is much to be said for the view that the title to sue on the assigned debt should remain impeached after the assignor's discharge from bankruptcy. But even if it is not, where the debtor is in danger of losing the benefit of his substantive defence in this circumstance he is not necessarily without a remedy, because he may be entitled to approach the court for a declaration and for an order giving effect to the set-off by means of an injunction to restrain an action against him by the assignee.[106]

---

[99] *Lee & Chapman's Case* (1885) 30 Ch. D 216, 225. See also *De Mattos* v. *Saunders* (1872) LR 7 CP 570; *In re City Life Assurance Co. Ltd.; Stephenson's Case* [1926] 1 Ch. 191, 214 (as explained in *Hiley* v. *The Peoples Prudential Assurance Co., Ltd.* (1938) 60 CLR 468, 501–505); *Popular Homes Ltd.* v. *Circuit Developmnents Ltd.* [1979] 2 NZLR 642. See also *Boyd* v. *Mangles* (1847) 16 M & W 337; *Hunt* v. *Jessel* (1854) 18 Beav. 100 (assignment to a trustee under a deed of arrangement). [100] See also section 2.4 above.

[101] Wood, *English and International Set-off* (1989), 894–895. See also section 1.7.4 above.

[102] Insolvency Act 1986, s. 281.

[103] [1977] 1 WLR 185, discussed in section 1.7.4 above.

[104] Wood, *English and International Set-off* (1989), 895.

[105] See section 1.7.4 above. [106] See section 1.7.4 above.

13.2.10 *Insolvent debtor*

When the debtor is bankrupt or is a company in liquidation, can the trustee in bankruptcy or the liquidator assert a set-off against the assignee in respect of a claim against the assignor? A set-off is not available under the insolvency set-off section, given that the assigned debt is held by the assignee and the debtor's claim is against the assignor. There is an evident lack of mutuality. The only possible rights are equitable set-off and set-off pursuant to the Statutes of Set-off. If the demands are sufficiently closely connected to give rise to an equitable set-off, the fact of the bankruptcy or liquidation should not affect the debtor's right. The issue is more difficult, however, when one considers the right of set-off conferred by the Statutes of Set-off in the case of mutual debts. The important point is that this is merely a procedural defence to an action at law,[107] and therefore, when it is said that an assignee takes subject to an equity constituted by this form of set-off, it should mean that the assignee, when suing the debtor, takes subject to the procedural defence that would have been available to the debtor in an action at law brought against him by the assignor. In the situation under discussion, however, the issue typically does not arise in the context of an action against the debtor. Indeed, in a bankruptcy or a court ordered winding-up the assignee could not sue the debtor without the leave of the court.[108] Rather, the trustee or the liquidator will assert a set-off when a proof is lodged by the assignee, so as to reduce the proof by the amount of the assignor's indebtedness.[109] If the trustee or the liquidator rejects a proof lodged by the assignee, for example because of the assignor's cross-debt, the assignee may appeal to the court.[110] But once again the trustee or the liquidator strictly should not be entitled to a set-off under the Statutes in those proceedings, because the set-off is still not arising in the context of a defence to an action. Accordingly, it is not clear what the basis for a set-off would be. There is, however, authority to the effect that a trustee or liquidator may in fact reduce the assignee's claim in the bankruptcy or liquidation to the extent of a debt owing by the assignor before notice.[111] While this may not be

---

[107] See section 1.2.9 above.

[108] See the Insolvency Act 1986, s. 130(2) in relation to a court ordered winding-up, and, for bankruptcy, s. 285(3).

[109] The trustee in bankruptcy or liquidator presumably would only wish to do this if nothing is recoverable from the assignor because of the assignor's own insolvency. Normally it would be to the advantage of the debtor's estate to pay a dividend to the assignee on the assigned debt, and proceed against the assignor for payment in full of what he owes.

[110] For company liquidations see the Insolvency Rules 1986, r. 4.83 and, for bankruptcies, the Insolvency Act 1986, s. 303.

[111] *In re Richard Smith & Co., Ltd.* [1901] 1 IR 73; *In re China Steamship Company; ex parte MacKenzie* (1869) LR 7 Eq. 240; *In re Pinto Leite and Nephews* [1929] 1 Ch. 221. See

entirely consistent with the nature of the right provided by the Statutes, the point nevertheless may be made that it is unobjectionable as a matter of policy. There is indeed support for this approach in a case not involving an assignment. Prior to the enactment of the Supreme Court of Judicature Act 1875, the mutual credit provision in the bankruptcy legislation was not applicable to company liquidations. Set-offs had been enforced in liquidations,[112] although these were founded upon the right of set-off conferred by the Statutes of Set-off in the case of mutual debts as a defence to an action at law,[113] rather than upon the bankruptcy set-off section. In this context Lord Romilly M.R. in *In re South Blackpool Hotel Company; ex parte James*[114] allowed a set-off against a proof lodged by a creditor. He said that,[115] 'These cases are not to be decided on technicalities, but on principles of common sense'.

13.2.11 *Insolvent assignee*

The bankruptcy of the assignee will not affect the principle that an assignee takes subject to equities. If the cross-demand available against the assignor is not such as to provide a set-off under the Statutes or in accordance with the principles of equitable set-off, the debtor could not rely on the insolvency set-off section in the assignee's bankruptcy or liquidation. The debtor's liability to the assignee, and the claim against the assignor, are not mutual. On the other hand, if the assignee himself happens to be separately liable to the debtor, the insolvency set-off section may apply in relation to that liability and the assigned debt.[116]

13.2.12 *Agreement not to assert equities against assignees*

A debtor may have contracted with his creditor on terms that, in the event of an assignment, he will not avail himself against an assignee of any equities which he may possess against the creditor or any intermediate assignee. An agreement to this effect will bind the debtor[117] as against an

---

also *Christie* v. *Taunton, Delmard, Lane and Company* [1893] 2 Ch. 175 (members' voluntary winding-up).

[112] See e.g. *In re Agra and Masterman's Bank; Anderson's Case* (1866) LR 3 Eq. 337; *Smith, Fleming, & Co.'s Case* (1866) LR 1 Ch. App. 538; *In re South Blackpool Hotel Company; ex parte James* (1869) LR 8 Eq. 225; *Re Progress Assurance Company; ex parte Bates* (1870) 22 LT 430; *Sankey Brook Coal Co., Ltd.* v. *Marsh* (1871) LR 6 Ex. 185.

[113] *Brighton Arcade Co., Ltd.* v. *Dowling* (1868) LR 3 CP 175, 182, 184; *Ex parte Price; in re Lankester* (1875) LR 10 Ch. App. 648, 650.   [114] (1869) LR 8 Eq. 225.

[115] (1869) LR 8 Eq. 225, 226.   [116] See section 7.3 above.

[117] *In re Agra and Masterman's Bank; ex parte Asiatic Banking Corporation* (1867) LR 2 Ch. App. 391; *In re Blakely Ordnance Company; ex parte New Zealand Banking Corporation* (1867) LR 3 Ch. App. 154; *Phoenix Assurance Co., Ltd.* v. *Earl's Court Ltd.* (1913) 30 TLR

assignee who is a bona fide purchaser for value.[118] The agreement may arise by implication, as for example when the articles of a company which had issued debentures to a member of the company provided that the company was to have a lien on the debentures held by a member indebted to it, and that the company could sell the debentures in order to obtain payment of the debt. Since it would have been difficult to sell debentures if a transferee would have had to take subject to an uncertain set-off available against the member, it was held that the company and the member must have intended that the transferee should take free from the set-off.[119] A similar implication has been held to arise when a company issues bearer debentures,[120] and in one case where a bank issued an open letter of credit pursuant to which the bank held out to persons negotiating bills drawn by its customer that it would honour the bills.[121] On the other hand, a transferee who is not a bona fide purchaser for value cannot rely on the clause. In *In re Brown & Gregory, Limited*[122] a trustee under a creditors' deed executed by the assignor was held not to be a purchaser, so that he took subject to equities available against the assignor notwithstanding that the debentures in question contained a clause protecting transferees from equities. Similarly, neither a trustee in bankruptcy nor a judgment creditor is considered to be a purchaser.[123]

The principle is stated in the cases in terms whether the assignee or transferee is a bona fide purchaser for value. If these requirements are satisfied, notice of a prior right of set-off available to the debtor against the assignor should not affect the assignee's position.[124] The debtor has held out that it will not enforce equities against assignees, in which case notice of any such equities should be irrelevant.

Debentures issued by a company may provide that, *upon registration of a transfer*, the transferee will take free from equities. The effect of this is that

---

50; *Southern British National Trust Ltd.* v. *Pither* (1937) 57 CLR 89, 113; *Hilger Analytical Ltd.* v. *Rank Precision Industries Ltd.* [1984] BCLC 301. See also *In re Goy & Co., Ltd.; Farmer* v. *Goy & Co., Ltd.* [1900] 2 Ch. 149 with respect to the rule in *Cherry* v. *Boultbee* (and compare *In re Rhodesia Goldfields, Ltd.* [1910] 1 Ch. 239, in which the debentures did not contain a stipulation to the effect that they should be paid without regard to equities).

[118] *In re Goy & Co., Ltd.* [1900] 2 Ch. 149, 153. See also *In re Blakely Ordnance Company* (1867) LR 3 Ch. App. 154, 159; *In re Brown & Gregory, Ltd.; Shepheard* v. *Brown & Gregory, Ltd.* [1904] 1 Ch. 627, affirmed [1904] 2 Ch. 448.

[119] *Higgs* v. *The Northern Assam Tea Co., Ltd.* (1869) LR 4 Ex. 387; *In re Northern Assam Tea Company; ex parte Universal Life Assurance Company* (1870) LR 10 Eq. 458.

[120] *In re Blakely Ordnance Company* (1867) LR 3 Ch. App. 154.

[121] *In re Agra and Masterman's Bank; ex parte Asiatic Banking Corporation* (1867) LR 2 Ch. App. 391.   [122] [1904] 1 Ch. 627, affirmed [1904] 2 Ch. 448.

[123] *Kilworth* v. *Mountcashell* (1864) 15 Ir. Ch. Rep. 565, 581; *In re Marquis of Anglesey* [1903] 2 Ch. 727, 732,

[124] Compare *Hilger Analytical Ltd.* v. *Rank Precision Industries Ltd.* [1984] BCLC 301, 304, in which the principle was discussed in terms of notice.

the company reserves the right to assert equities against a transferee prior
to registration. However, the fact that the company has a right of set-off
available to it against the transferor under the Statutes of Set-off ordinarily
should not entitle the company to refuse to register a transfer. This is so
notwithstanding the decision of Street J. in New South Wales in *Stewart* v.
Latec Investments Ltd.[125] in the context of an equitable set-off arising by
analogy with the Statutes. Set-off under the Statutes is merely a procedural
defence to an action at law. It does not entitle the company itelf to effect a
set-off in its books against the debt on the debenture. Accordingly, unless
the terms of the debenture are such as to give the company a discretion to
refuse to register, the availability of a set-off under the Statutes would not
appear to provide the company with a ground for refusing to do so. *In re
Palmer's Decoration & Furniture Company*[126] appears to suggest the
contrary, though it is distinguishable. In *Palmer's Decoration* the transferor's title was defective,[127] in that he had obtained the debentures from
the company by misrepresentation, and it was held that the transferee took
subject to this defect in title. While the question in issue was whether the
transferee was entitled to be paid, Buckley J. also said that the defect of
title would have provided a ground for the company to refuse to register
the transfer. However, the nature of the equity in that case should be
compared to the equity which arises under the Statutes of Set-off, which
provides a procedural defence to an action, but does not give rise to a
defect in the title to the debt in question. The tenor of Buckley J.'s
judgment admittedly suggests that the principle in that case was thought to
apply to equities generally,[128] although the particular nature of the defence
of set-off under the Statutes was not considered.[129]

13.2.13 *Conduct of the debtor*

The debtor may be precluded by his conduct from setting up equities
against the assignee.[130] This does not mean that the debtor is bound to
volunteer information to an assignee as regards any prior equities,
including the existence of a set-off agreement between the debtor and the

---

[125] [1968] 1 NSWR 432, discussed in section 1.6 above.
[126] [1904] 2 Ch. 743.
[127] Buckley J. expressed it ([1904] 2 Ch. 743, 751) in terms that 'by reason of the
company's equity the title is not clear'.
[128] See also *Palmer's Company Precedents* (16th edn., 1952), Part 3 ('Debentures'), 18,
235, 236.
[129] *In re Goy & Co., Ltd.* [1900] 2 Ch. 149, which Buckley J. discussed in his judgment in
Palmer's Decoration [1904] 2 Ch. 743, 749–51, was concerned with the rule in *Cherry* v.
Boultbee (see Ch. 10) rather than set-off under the Statutes.
[130] *Athenaeum Life Assurance Society* v. *Pooley* (1858) 3 De G & J 294, 299, 302.

assignor.[131] The duty of inquiry is upon the assignee.[132] If on the other hand the notice given to the debtor indicates on the face of it that the assignee may have been deceived, and that the assignee is advancing money to the assignor upon a ground which he misunderstood, or if the debtor is otherwise aware of a deception but stands by and allows the assignment to proceed, it may be inequitable to allow him to rely on the right of set-off otherwise available at law under the Statutes if he fails to inform the assignee of the true facts.[133] In this regard, it is not sufficient that the debtor knows of the assignment. He is entitled to assume that the assignor is not deceiving the assignee.[134] However, if he is aware of a deception he may be obliged to inform the assignee, failing which it may be unconscionable for him to assert a set-off. This may also be the case if an inquiry in fact is made and the debtor conceals the truth.[135]

In the case of a transfer of debentures, the company may lose the right to set up prior equities if the company registers the transferee as the holder, and subsequently treats him as such.[136]

13.2.14 *A set-off agreement as an equity*

There is surprisingly little authority on the question whether a set-off agreement between a debtor and an assignor constitutes an equity to which an assignee takes subject.

Consider first the situation in which the agreement contemplates that a set-off will occur, not at the discretion of the one of the parties, but as a matter of course so as to constitute an agreed method of payment. This should be effective as against an assignee.[137] In *Watson* v. *Mid Wales Railway Company*[138] an assignor of a debt was also a lessee of certain

---

[131] *Mangles* v. *Dixon* (1852) 3 HLC 702, 732; *Rolt* v. *White* (1862) 3 De G J & S 360; *Toronto-Dominion Bank* v. *Block Bros. Contractors Ltd.* (1980) 118 DLR (3d) 311. See also section 13.2.14 below.

[132] *Mangles* v. *Dixon* (1852) 3 HLC 702, 732–733. See also *Willes* v. *Greenhill* (1861) 4 De G F & J 147, 150; *Ward* v. *Duncombe* [1893] AC 369, 395; *Athenaeum Life Assurance Society* v. *Pooley* (1858) 3 De G & J 294, 299.

[133] *Mangles* v. *Dixon* (1852) 3 HLC 702. See also *Rolt* v. *White* (1862) 3 De G J & S 360, 365; *Wilson* v. *Gabriel* (1863) 4 B& S 243, 247; *The Good Luck* [1989] 2 Lloyd's Rep. 238, 265. [134] *Mangles* v. *Dixon* (1852) 3 HLC 702, 734–5, 741.

[135] See e.g. *Woodhams* v. *Anglo-Australian and Universal Family Assurance Co.* (1861) 3 Giff. 238 (esp. at 250). See also *Athenaeum Life Assurance Society* v. *Pooley* (1858) 3 De G & J 294, 299.

[136] *In re Northern Assam Tea Company; ex parte Universal Life Assurance Company* (1870) LR 10 Eq. 458, following *Higgs* v. *The Northern Assam Tea Co., Ltd.* (1869) LR 4 Ex. 387.

[137] In addition to the cases referred to below see *In re Moss Bay Hematite Iron and Steel Company* (1892) 8 TLR 63, 475; *Bank of Montreal* v. *Tudhope, Anderson & Company* (1911) 2 Man. R 380. See also *Lambarde* v. *Older* (1853) 17 Beav. 542, 547 in relation to a set-off against a deceased's estate, for which see section 9.9.2 above.

[138] (1867) LR 2 CP 593.

property from the debtor. The Court of Common Pleas held that the assignor could not set off rent which accrued after the debtor received notice of the assignment, notwithstanding that it arose out of a prior contract.[139] On the other hand, Willes and Montague Smith JJ. evidently thought that the result would have been different if it had been agreed that the rent was to be set off against the debt, so that only the balance was to be owing.[140] This is consistent with the earlier decision of the House of Lords in *Mangles* v. *Dixon*.[141] The owners of a vessel chartered it to some merchants for a particular voyage, and then assigned the freight payable. Notice of the assignment was given to the charterers before the voyage was completed. By a second contract between the owners and the charterers, of which the assignee was not aware, it was agreed that the profit or loss resulting from the voyage was to be shared between them. The voyage resulted in a loss, half of which accordingly was payable by the owners. When the assignees sought payment of the freight which was due upon termination of the voyage, the charterers sought to deduct the owners' share of the loss. Lord St. Leonards held that the question was not one of set-off, strictly so called, because there were not cross-demands. Rather, he said that the effect of the agreement between the owners and the charterers was that freight never became due upon termination of the voyage to the extent that the owners were responsible for a part of the loss.[142] This was an equity to which the assignees took subject, notwithstanding that they were unaware of the second agreement. They should have inquired of the charterers before the assignment.[143]

A set-off agreement may take a different form, in that it gives one of the parties an *option* to set off various cross-debts. This may apply not only as between the debtor and the assignor, but also in a multi-party situation where, for example, a bank has an agreement with a group of companies entitling the bank to set off deposits of any of the companies against debts owing by the depositor or any other company in the group. A potential difficulty in this situation is that 'equities' for the purpose of the principle that an assignee takes subject to equities is often equated with defences,[144]

---

[139] This result is criticized in section 13.2.4 above.
[140] See Willes J. at (1867) LR 2 CP 593, 600, and Montague Smith J. at 601.
[141] (1852) 3 HLC 702.   [142] (1852) 3 HLC 702, 729.
[143] (1852) 3 HLC 702, 732–733. See also *Toronto-Dominion Bank* v. *Block Bros. Contractors Ltd.* (1980) 118 DLR (3d) 311.
[144] For example, in *Roxburghe* v. *Cox* (1881) 17 Ch. D. 520, 526 James L.J. said that an assignee 'takes subject to all rights of set-off and other defences which were available against the assignor'. Joyce J. in *Edward Nelson & Co. Ltd.* v. *Faber & Co.*, [1903] 2 K.B. 367, 375 remarked that, 'an assignee [of a chose in action] takes it subject to all equities—in other words, whatever defence by way of set-off or otherwise the debtor would be entitled to set up against the assignor's claim . . .'. The relevant principle is stated in *White & Tudor's Leading Cases in Equity* (9th edn., 1928) Vol. 1, 136 in terms that an assignee 'takes subject to all

whereas in this form of set-off agreement a defence as such may not be in issue. This may not always be the case. It may in fact be an express or implied term of the set-off agreement that the assigned debt is not repayable until a defined event occurs, which would provide a defence. One would expect to find this, for example, where a security deposit is placed with a bank. There may be other cases, however, where as a matter of construction of the agreement the *only* right of the debtor is to take the positive step of applying the assigned debt in reduction of a debt owing to the debtor, whether by the assignor or another party. This may be the correct interpretation where a bank is entitled to set off the current accounts of various companies in a group. The question is whether an assignee who gives notice will be bound by the bank's positive right to effect a set-off after that date. In this regard, the concept of equities is given a broad meaning by the courts.[145] In *Mangles* v. *Dixon*[146] Lord St. Leonards, in discussing the application of the principle that an assignee takes subject to equities to the assignment in that case, equated it with the notion that the assignees 'took precisely the same interest, and were subject to the same liabilities' as the assignor,[147] while later he said that 'if a man does take an assignment of a chose in action he must take his chance as to the exact position in which the party giving it stands'.[148] In *Cockell* v. *Taylor*[149] Sir John Romilly M.R. expressed the relevant principle in terms that, 'the purchaser of a chose in action takes the thing bought subject to all the prior claims upon it'. The principle has been expressed in similar terms on other occasions.[150] These statements would appear to include a positive option to apply the assigned debt in reduction of another debt, whether owing by the assignor or another party, and this indeed is the preferred view.[151]

An assignee should take subject to a set-off agreement insofar as it applies to a debt which is accrued and owing to the debtor at the date of the assignee's action as a result of a transaction entered into before notice, whether the debt itself arose before or after notice.[152] The more difficult

defences existing in respect of the right assigned which would be available against the assignor seeking to enforce the right assigned'. See also *Clyne* v. *Deputy Commissioner of Taxation* (1981) 150 CLR 1, 20–1.

[145] *Re H. Simpson & Co. Pty. Ltd.* [1964–5] NSWR 603, 605.
[146] (1852) 3 HLC 702.   [147] (1852) 3 HLC 702, 731.
[148] (1852) 3 HLC 702, 735.   [149] (1852) 15 Beav. 103, 118.
[150] See e.g. *Athenaeum Life Assurance Society* v. *Pooley* (1858) 3 De G & J 294, 299; *Re H. Simpson & Co. Pty. Ltd.* [1964–5] NSWR 603, 605; *Clyne* v. *Deputy Commissioner of Taxation* (1981) 150 CLR 1, 20.
[151] See the concession by counsel in *The Evelpidis Era* [1981] 1 Lloyd's Rep. 54, 57 with respect to the deduction allowed by the club rules. In Canada see *Toronto-Dominion Bank* v. *Block Bros. Contractors Ltd.* (1980) 118 DLR (3d) 311.
[152] See *Rymill* v. *Wandsworth District Board* (1883) Cab. & El. 92 in the context of garnishee orders, for which see section 13.5.2 below.

question is whether the agreement will be effective against an assignee where the transaction itself out of which the accrued debt sought to be set off arose was entered into *after* notice. A possible approach to the problem, which on the surface is consistent with the language used by Lord St. Leonards' in *Mangles* v. *Dixon*,[153] is that an assignee takes the same interest and is subject to the same liabilities as the assignor at the date of notice, and in the case under discussion the effect of the prior agreement is that the assigned debt is liable to be used in a set-off against cross-debts both present and future, including where they arise out of new transactions. Moreover, when a chose in action is assigned the courts have emphasized that the duty of inquiry is on the assignee,[154] and the inquiry should extend to the terms of any set-off agreement in place which affects the debt. However, the analysis which perhaps is more likely to appeal to the courts is that, when the debtor receives notice, he should regulate his conduct accordingly[155] and, to paraphrase the language of James L.J. in *Roxburghe* v. *Cox*,[156] he should not rely on debts arising out of new transactions to diminish the rights of the assignee as they stood at the time of notice.[157]

The set-off agreement in its terms may purport to allow a set-off in respect of contingent debts. This generally should be effective against an assignee when the debt sought to be set off is still contingent at the date of the assignee's action,[158] provided that it has its source in a transaction entered into before notice. Professor Goode's analysis of the operation of a set-off agreement in relation to contingent debts is instructive.[159] Depending on the circumstances, he has suggested that the agreement may be interpreted in either of two ways. The more likely construction is that the creditor is entitled to suspend payment of the debt that he owes until such time as the assignor's contingent liability may vest, followed, if it does vest, by a set-off. Alternatively, there may be cases where the effect of the agreement is that the debtor's liability is immediately cancelled to the extent of the assignor's maximum contingent liability, with an obligation to re-credit the assignor if and to the extent that the contingent liability does not become an actual liability. In either case, the agreement should be binding on the assignee given his duty of inquiry.

---

[153] (1852) 3 HLC 702.

[154] *Mangles* v. *Dixon* (1852) 3 HLC 702, 732–3. See also *Willes* v. *Greenhill* (1861) 4 De G F & J 147, 150; *Ward* v. *Duncombe* [1893] AC 369, 395; *Athenaeum Life Assurance Society* v. *Pooley* (1858) 3 De G & J 294, 299. See generally section 13.2.13 above.

[155] *Lloyd* v. *Banks* (1868) LR 3 Ch. App. 488, 490–1.

[156] (1881) 17 Ch. D 520, 526.

[157] For the contrary view, see Oditah, (1990) 106 *Law Quarterly Review* 515, 518–19.

[158] Compare Oditah, 'Financing Trade Credit: Welsh Development Agency v. Exfinco' [1992] *Journal of Business Law* 541, 559.

[159] Goode, *Legal Problems of Credit and Security* (2nd edn., 1988), 173.

A set-off agreement entered into by a debtor and an assignor after the debtor has notice of the assignment ordinarily will not be effective as against the assignee. On the other hand, the assignee may have agreed with the debtor that, notwithstanding the assignment, the debtor can pay the assignor until such time as the assignee notifies the debtor that payment must be made directly to the assignee. This would be construed as including payment by way of an agreement for a set-off.[160] The set-off, however, must have been carried into effect before the debtor receives notice from the assignee in accordance with their agreement. If there is an agreement between the debtor and the assignor for a set-off to occur in the future, and the settlement in account has not taken place when the assignee gives notice, it will not be a case of a payment already having been made to the assignor, and accordingly the assignee should be entitled to demand payment in full.[161] Further, the assignee's agreement that the debtor may pay the assignor ordinarily would not be interpreted as authorizing a set-off involving liabilities owing by parties other than the assignor to the debtor.[162]

13.2.15 *Successive assignments*

Consider the case of successive assignments. For example, A may assign a debt owing to him to B, who in turn assigns it to C. The debtor should be entitled to a set-off in respect of a cross-debt owing by C himself. However, the question instead may arise whether C would also take subject to a set-off in respect of a debt owing by B. The issue arose in *In re Milan Tramways Company; ex parte Theys*[163] in the context of the rule in *Cherry* v. *Boultbee*,[164] although the same principle should apply to set-off. *Milan Tramways* concerned a number of debts for which proofs had been lodged in the liquidation of the debtor company. Subsequently the creditors assigned the debts to H, who happened to be the subject of an allegation of misfeasance. H then assigned the debts to T, who gave notice of the assignment to the liquidator. After this second assignment an order was made that H should pay £2,000 to the company on account of his misfeasance. The Court of Appeal held that the liquidator could not set this sum off against the assigned debts under the insolvency set-off section, because at the relevant date for determining rights of set-off in the liquidation the debts were held by the original creditors, and there was no right of set-off at that date available against them. Failing a set-off, the liquidator argued that, because of *Cherry* v. *Boultbee*, he could at least

---

[160] *The Evelpidis Era* [1981] 1 Lloyd's Rep. 54, 63.
[161] [1981] 1 Lloyd's Rep. 54, 62–3, 64–5.   [162] [1981] 1 Lloyd's Rep. 54, 65.
[163] (1884) 25 Ch. D 587.   [164] See Ch. 10.

make a deduction from the *dividend* payable on those debts to the extent of H's obligation to contribute. This argument also failed. The order against H for payment of the £2,000 was made *after* the assignment to T. The rule could not be invoked against T in respect of H's liability to contribute when that liability arose after H had already assigned the debts. It was not regarded as sufficient that the liability arose out of an obligation incurred by H before the assignment.[165] But, in addition, Cotton L.J. in his judgment said that T, in seeking payment of the dividend, was not enforcing the rights of H, but rather the rights of the original creditors, and there was no equity available against the original creditors to which T could be made to take subject. If H in fact was an equitable assignee this would have been a powerful argument. It is consistent with the view expressed by Dixon J. in the High Court of Australia in *Southen British National Trust Ltd.* v. *Pither*.[166] It is also supported by Parker J.'s judgment in *The Raven*.[167] In that case his Lordship said that,[168] 'The rule that an assignee takes subject to equities means, in my judgment, equities as against the assignor and does not include claims against an intermediate assignee'.[169] It is true that in *Cavendish* v. *Geaves*[170] Sir John Romilly said that an ultimate assignee does take subject to rights of set-off available to the debtor against an intermediate assignee, and in *Pellas* v. *Neptune Marine Insurance Co.*[171] Bramwell L.J. expressed agreement with the principles laid out in *Cavendish* v. *Geaves*. As a matter of principle, however, Cotton L.J., Dixon J. and Parker J. would appear to be correct. The point is that, in the case of an equitable assignment, the assignor has the legal title to the assigned debt. The reason that an equitable assignee in an ordinary case takes subject to a set-off available against the assignor is that there is mutuality at law, and therefore there is a right of set-off at law under the Statutes of Set-off, and, if the debtor's cross-claim against the assignor arose before the debtor had notice of the assignment, there is nothing

---

[165] However, see the criticism of *Stephens* v. *Venables* (1862) 30 Beav. 625 in section 10.12.3 above. It could not actually be said in *Milan Tramways* that there was a monetary liability upon H before the assignment, because the company had the right to elect to take the shares the subject of the misfeasance allegation rather than compensation. See the first instance judgment of Kay J. at (1882) 22 Ch. D 122, 125–6. See also the similar case of *Re Bailey Cobalt Mines Ltd.* (1919) 44 OLR 1.

[166] (1937) 57 CLR 89, 108–9, distinguishing set-off from an equity which affects the intermediate assignee's title itself, in the form of a right to set the assignment aside for fraud. See also Latham C.J. (at 102–3).   [167] [1980] 2 Lloyd's Rep. 266.

[168] [1980] 2 Lloyd's Rep. 266, 273.

[169] Compare the suggestion in Treitel, *The Law of Contract* (9th edn., 1995), 608 n 58, that this should be understood in the context of a cross-claim available to the debtor against the intermediate assignee which arose *before* the assignment to the intermediate assignee. However, Parker J.'s comments were not qualified in this manner, and indeed it is not expressly made clear in his judgment when the cross-claim in that case arose.

[170] (1857) 24 Beav. 163.   [171] (1879) 5 CPD 34, 39 (*arguendo*).

unconscionable in the debtor asserting this legal right of set-off against the assignee.[172] When, however, there are successive assignments, and the debtor is owed a debt by the intermediate assignee, the position is different. There is no mutuality at law, given that the legal title to the debt being enforced is in the assignor whereas the debtor's claim is against the intermediate assignee, and therefore there is no right of set-off at law. Nor would an equitable set-off be available by analogy with the Statutes,[173] since the cross-demands are not equitably mutual. The beneficial title to the assigned debt is in the ultimate assignee, whereas the debtor's claim is against the intermediate assignee.

It appears, however, that in *Milan Tramways* H was not an equitable assignee, but rather had taken a statutory assignment of the debts in accordance with the Judicature Act 1873, s. 25(6),[174] so that he then had the legal title. In Cotton L.J.'s opinion this did not make any difference, because 'there is nothing to prevent the ultimate assignee from suing in the name of the original creditors, free from any equities which only attach on the intermediate assignee'.[175] Yet Lord Esher M.R. later commented in *Read* v. *Brown*[176] in relation to a statutory assignment that, 'The debt is transferred to the assignee and becomes as though it had been his from the beginning; it is no longer to be the debt of the assignor at all, who cannot sue for it, the right to sue being taken from him'.[177] Therefore, if the ultimate assignee is an equitable assignee, he would be required to sue in respect of the legal title of the intermediate assignee, which should have as a consequence that the ultimate assignee takes subject to equities available against the intermediate assignee that arose before the debtor had notice of the second assignment.[178] It has been said that the statutory form of assignment only relates to procedure,[179] although it may be that it does have a substantive effect upon the rights of a sub-assignee.

---

[172] See section 13.2.1 above.   [173] See section 1.6 above.

[174] See now the Law of Property Act 1925, s. 136(1).

[175] (1884) 25 Ch. D 587, 593. See also Dixon J. in *Southern British National Trust Ltd.* v. *Pither* (1937) 57 CLR 89, 109.   [176] (1888) 22 QBD 128, 132.

[177] See also *Bennett* v. *White* [1910] 2 KB 643; *In re Pain; Gustavson* v. *Haviland* [1919] 1 Ch. 38, 45.

[178] *In re Richard Smith & Co., Ltd.* [1901] 1 IR 73 may support this view, given that the transfer of the debentures by Murphy and Smith (the original assignors) to Fitt (the intermediate assignee) was by deed, and the conditions attached to the debentures required that the transfer in writing be delivered to the company in order to be registered. For a valid legal assignment express notice in writing of the assignment must be given to the debtor. However, there are no formal requirements for a valid notice (see *Van Lynn Developments Ltd.* v. *Pelias Construction Co. Ltd.* [1969] 1 QB 607, 613), and the delivery of the transfer may have sufficed. On that basis the requirements for the statutory form of assignment may have been satisfied, this having been introduced into Ireland by the Supreme Court of Judicature (Ireland) Act 1877, s. 28(6).

[179] *Tolhurst* v. *Associated Portland Cement Manufacturers (1900), Ltd.* [1902] 2 KB 660, 676–7.

It may be that the intermediate assignee and the debtor entered into an agreement to set off the assigned debt against a debt owing by the intermediate assignee to the debtor. Provided that the agreement is entered into before the debtor has notice of the second assignment it should bind the ultimate assignee, whether the first assignment was equitable or statutory. The agreement is equivalent to payment, and payment by the debtor to the intermediate assignee before notice of the second assignment would be effective to discharge the debtor as against the ultimate assignee.

The ultimate assignee would take subject to equities available against the original assignor before notice. If the assignment to the intermediate assignee and the assignment to the ultimate assignee were both merely equitable, the ultimate assignee would be enforcing the legal rights of the original assignor. If the original assignment was statutory, the intermediate assignee would take subject to any equity available against the original assignor, which in turn would constitute an equity available against the intermediate assignee to which the ultimate assignee would take subject, whether the ultimate assignment was statutory or equitable.

13.2.16 *Marshalling*

Consider that the assignor is owed two debts by the debtor. One of the debts (debt 1) is assigned to an assignee, and the other (debt 2) is retained by the assignor. In addition, the debtor is owed a cross-debt by the assignor. Prima facie the debtor would appear to have a choice, in that he could employ the cross-debt either as a defence under the Statutes of Set-off to an action by the assignor for payment of debt 2, or alternatively as a defence to an action by the assignee to enforce debt 1, on the basis of the principle that an assignee takes subject to equities. A similar position may apply if debt 2 instead has also been assigned to a second assignee. The result suggested in the cases is that, if the assignor has retained debt 2, any set-off in relation to the cross-debt must occur first against debt 2 so as not to diminish the rights of the assignee on debt 1,[180] while, if debt 2 has also been assigned to a second assignee, the set-off must operate rateably as against both debt 1 and debt 2.[181] This is justified on the basis of the equitable doctrine of marshalling. However, it is argued elsewhere[182] that

---

[180] *Cavendish* v. *Geaves* (1857) 24 Beav. 163; *Smit Tek International Zeesleepen Berginsbedrijf BV* v. *Selco Salvage Ltd.* [1988] 2 Lloyd's Rep. 398.

[181] *Cavendish* v. *Geaves* (1857) 24 Beav. 163; *Moxon* v. *Berkeley Mutual Benefit Building Society* (1890) 62 LT 250.

[182] Derham, 'Set-off Against an Assignee: The Relevance of Marshalling, Contribution and Subrogation' (1991) 107 *Law Quarterly Review* 126. For marshalling to apply two separate debts in any event would be required. Compare *Morris* v. *Agrichemicals Ltd.*, Court of Appeal, 20 December 1995, and section 8.4 above.

marshalling is inappropriate to a situation in which a defence of set-off in relation to debts is in issue, as opposed to a positive right to have recourse to more than one fund. This is not to suggest that the assignee of debt 1 should be without a remedy if the debtor asserts the cross-debt as a defence to the assignee's action. The assignee should be entitled to be indemnified by the assignor or, if debt 1 has also been assigned, he should be entitled to contribution from the second assignee. Alternatively, subrogation may provide relief, in the sense that the assignee may be entitled to be subrogated to the assignor's rights against the debtor on debt 1 or, if debt 1 has also been assigned, to a rateable proportion of the benefit of debt 1 as against the second assignee.

There is in any event an accepted limitation on the application of marshalling to the law of set-off, and that is that marshalling cannot apply when different rights are in issue. In *Webb* v. *Smith*[183] the defendants were auctioneers who had sold a brewery for a customer. The proceeds of sale of the brewery remained in the defendants' hands subject to a particular lien for their charges incurred in connection with the sale. These proceeds of sale had been charged by the customer in favour of the plaintiff. The defendants also had in their hands the proceeds of sale of some furniture which they had sold for the customer. The defendants had two apparent courses of action open to them. They could have deducted their charges from the brewery proceeds pursuant to their lien, and delivered the furniture proceeds to the customer and the balance of the brewery proceeds to the plaintiff in accordance with the charge. Alternatively, they could have delivered all of the brewery proceeds to the plaintiff, and asserted a right to set off the customer's indebtedness for the charges against their own indebtedness for the furniture proceeds.[184] The defendants adopted the first approach, to the obvious disadvantage of the plaintiff. The plaintiff sued the defendants, arguing that because of the doctrine of marshalling the defendants should have acted in accordance with the second possible approach so as not to disappoint the plaintiff. The Court of Appeal held that marshalling in fact was not applicable. Brett M.R. noted that the defendants had a lien upon the brewery proceeds and a right of set-off against the furniture proceeds, and held that marshalling is not applicable when different rights exist in respect of different funds. Similarly Lindley L.J. said that the defendants had a 'superior right of lien

[183] (1885) 30 Ch. D 192. Compare *Moxon* v. *Berkeley Mutual Benefit Building Society* (1890) 62 LT 250, criticized in Derham, 'Set-off Against an Assignee: The Relevance of Marshalling, Contribution and Subrogation' (1991) 107 *Law Quarterly Review* 126, 138–40.
[184] It would appear that an auctioneer is entitled to a set-off against proceeds of sale in his hands notwithstanding that they may be impressed with a trust. See *Palmer* v. *Day & Sons* [1895] 2 QB 618, discussed in section 6.4.1 above.

as to the fund produced by the sale of the brewery',[185] and they could not be deprived of this superior right.

13.2.17 *Assignment merely of the proceeds of a debt*

When a debt is assigned the assignee obtains an equitable interest in the debt, and once the debtor has notice of this equitable interest it is unconscionable for him to rely on subsequent events to diminish the rights of the assignee. The position should be different, however, where the assignment is merely of the proceeds of the debt.[186] The assignee in such a case does not have an interest in the debt itself. If the debtor has a defence available against the assignor no proceeds in fact will be received, and therefore there will be nothing to which the assignment can attach. But because the assignee's interest does not extend to the debt, the better view is that there is nothing unconscionable in the debtor relying on a set-off or other defence that accrues after notice of the assignment, notwithstanding the consequential effect that this will have on the assignee's position. A person who takes an assignment merely of the proceeds of a debt, and not of the debt itself, should take subject to all defences of set-off available against the assignor whether arising before or after notice.

13.2.18 *Instruments transferable at common law*

The principle that an assignee takes subject to equities only becomes relevant when there is a chose in action which, before the Judicature Acts, was assignable only in equity.[187] It does not apply when a transferee is suing upon an instrument which is transferable at common law in its own right.[188] While an assignee of a debt admittedly may now sue in his own name if the requirements of section 136(1) of the Law of Property Act 1925 are satisfied,[189] the section is merely procedural in its operation, in the sense that it only applies where, prior to the Judicature Acts, the assignee would have had to proceed in the name of the assignor in a common law action for payment.[190] Where, however, an instrument is transferable at common law in its own right, the transferee before the Judicature Acts could have sued in his own name, and in respect of his own legal title. He need not have relied on the legal title of the assignor. Consequently a mere personal equity such as a right of set-off under the

---

[185] (1885) 30 Ch. D 192, 202.

[186] See e.g. *Glegg* v. *Bromley* [1912] 2 KB 474.

[187] *Ord* v. *White* (1840) 3 Beav. 357, 365–6; *Southern British National Trust Ltd.* v. *Pither* (1937) 57 CLR 89, 109. See also *Ashwin* v. *Burton* (1862) 7 LT 589.

[188] *Taylor* v. *Blakelock* (1886) 32 Ch. D 560, 567. See also *Rolt* v. *White* (1862) 31 Beav. 520, 523.   [189] See section 13.2.2 above.

[190] *Torkington* v. *Magee* [1902] 2 KB 427, 435.

Statutes of Set-off that could have been asserted against the transferor in an action brought by the transferor himself could not be asserted against the transferee suing in his own name, irrespective of when the transferor's indebtedness may have arisen. The reason for the distinction is plain enough. When an equitable assignee sues for payment of the debt but in respect of the assignor's legal title, there is mutuality at law in relation to that debt and a cross-debt owing by the assignor to the debtor, and the question is whether it is unconscionable for the debtor to rely on this right of set-off available at law. Where, however, the transferee of an instrument can sue at law in his own name and in respect of his own legal title, there is no mutuality at law in relation to the transferred debt and a debt owing by the assignor. Nor is there mutuality in equity to support an equitable set-off.

An obvious illustration of the principle is the case of a holder in due course of a negotiable instrument, though in fact the holder of a negotiable instrument may take free from personal equities even if he is not a holder in due course. This appears from the overdue bill cases, such as *Oulds* v. *Harrison*.[191] An indorsee of an overdue bill is not a holder in due course.[192] Nevertheless, it was confirmed in *Oulds* v. *Harrison* that, while the indorsee of the bill takes subject to all equities that had attached to the bill itself[193] in the hands of the holder when it was due (this includes an agreement with the holder that the bill was to be satisfied by a set-off against a debt owing to the acceptor[194]), he does not take subject to claims arising out of collateral matters such as a right of set-off available to the acceptor against a prior holder pursuant to the Statutes of Set-off.[195] Furthermore, it was held that it made no difference that the indorsee in that case was aware of the set-off available against the indorser,[196] that the

---

[191] (1854) 10 Ex. 572. See also *Burrough* v. *Moss* (1830) 10 B & C 558; *Stein* v. *Yglesias* (1834) 1 Cr. M & R 565; *Whitehead* v. *Walker* (1842) 10 M & W 696; *In re Overend, Gurney, & Co; ex parte Swan* (1868) LR 6 Eq. 344. Compare *Goodall* v. *Ray* (1835) 4 Dowl. 76, the accuracy of the report of which has been doubted. See Parke B in *Oulds* v. *Harrison* (at 576).

[192] Bills of Exchange Act 1882, 29(1).

[193] This expression is synonymous with the term 'defect of title' in the Bills of Exchange Act 1882, s. 36(2). See *Chalmers and Guest on Bills of Exchange* (14th edn., 1991), 320. For a non-exhaustive list of some defects of title, see the Bills of Exchange Act 1882, s. 29(2).

[194] *Oulds* v. *Harrison* (1854) 10 Ex. 572, 579; *Ching* v. *Jeffrey* (1885) 12 OAR 432 (promissory note). See also *Holmes* v. *Tidd* (1858) 3 H & N 891, and *Merchants Bank of Canada* v. *Thompson* (1911) 23 OLR 502, 514–15. Compare *In re Overend, Gurney, & Co; ex parte Swan* (1868) LR 6 Eq. 344, in which the agreement was with the drawer (that the funds remitted to the acceptor were to be used to satisfy the bills), as opposed to with the holders when the bills were dishonoured.

[195] While the contrary view is sometimes expressed (see e.g. Wood, *English and International Set-off* (1989), 700–1), the better view is that the issuer of a negotiable instrument being sued for payment is entitled to rely on a defence of set-off under the Statutes if the person suing himself is indebted to him. See section 1.7.18 above.

[196] Parke B. referring (at (1854) 10 Ex. 572, 579) to *Whitehead* v. *Walker* (1842) 10 M & W 696.

indorsement was made solely in order to defeat the set-off, or that the indorsement had been made without consideration. However, if the indorsee had not given value, he may be suing as trustee for the indorser, in which case he may indeed take subject to any right of set-off available against the indorser.[197] The indorsee would also be subject to a set-off if he is merely an agent for collection.[198]

The view that a holder who is not a holder in due course takes free of any right of set-off under the Statutes of Set-off as against a prior holder is not universally excepted by text-writers,[199] though it is consistent not only with a first principles analysis[200] but also the overdue bill line of cases. It has been said that[201] the decision in Manitoba of Major J. in *Del Confectionery Ltd.* v. *Winnipeg Cabinet Factory Ltd.*[202] supports the contrary view. However, the case is distinguishable. The plaintiff had entered into a contract with a cabinet maker to install some fixtures in his business premises by a certain date. Attached to the contract was a promissory note which was expressed to be payable at a date after the agreed completion date. The promissory note was security for the unpaid balance, together with interest calculated from the completion date. Because the date from which interest was to be calculated had not yet been determined, the note was undated. After the agreed completion date but before actual completion, the contract was assigned to a finance company. This included the promissory note which, as mentioned, was attached to the contract. Major J. held that the finance company's claim on the promissory note was subject to the plaintiff's claim for damages against the cabinet maker for non-completion by the fixed date. While the judgment is not entirely clear on the issue, it does not appear to support a general proposition that a subsequent holder of a negotiable instrument takes subject to a set-off between prior parties. In the first place, Major J. postulated that the note may not have been a promissory note, given that it encompassed the payment of exchange and collection charges and accordingly it may not

---

[197] *Agra and Masterman's Bank, Ltd.* v. *Leighton* (1866) LR 2 Ex. 56, 65; *Churchill & Sim* v. *Goddard* [1937] 1 KB 92, 103–4; *Barclays Bank, Ltd.* v. *Aschaffenburger Zellstoffwerke A.G.* [1967] 1 Lloyd's Rep. 387. See also *Watkins* v. *Bensusan* (1842) 9 M & W 422; *Mayhew* v. *Blofield* (1847) 1 Ex. 469; *Tolhurst* v. *Notley* (1848) 11 QB 406.

[198] *In re Anglo-Greek Steam Navigation and Trading Company; Carralli & Haggard's Claim* (1869) LR 4 Ch. App. 174.

[199] See Wood *English and International Set-off* (1989), 901, and also *Paget's Law of Banking* (10th edn., 1989) 434, where it is said that a mere holder for value takes subject to personal defences available to prior parties among themselves. On the other hand, for the preferred view see Crawford and Falconbridge, *Banking and Bills of Exchange* (8th edn., 1986) Vol. 2, 1524 et seq. and *Chitty on Contracts* (27th edn., 1994) Vol. 2, 220. See also *Chalmers and Guest on Bills of Exchange* (14th edn., 1991), 249 in relation to a holder for value. Compare *Byles on Bills of Exchange* (26th edn., 1988) 230.

[200] See above.   [201] Wood, *English and International Set-off* (1989), 901.

[202] [1941] 4 DLR 795, [1941] 2 WWR 636.

have provided for payment of a sum certain in money.[203] But in any event, the peculiar circumstances upon which the cross-claim was based, in particular, that the note was attached to the contract, appear to have been regarded as giving rise to a defect in title to which the finance company took subject, as opposed to a mere personal equity.[204]

13.2.19 *Privity of estate*

A similar analysis may apply when a transferee of an interest in land is entitled to sue in his own right as a result of privity of estate.[204a] The issue of set-off in this context has arisen in relation to the right of a lessee to rely on an equitable set-off that otherwise would have been available against the lessor in circumstances where a mortgagee of the reversion has gone into possession, though the principle is also relevant when the question concerns a purchaser of the land.

It is now generally accepted that a personal claim for damages available to a tenant against his landlord may be employed by the tenant as an equitable set-off against a liability for rent, provided that there is a sufficiently close connection between the cross-demands so as to satisfy the test for an equitable set-off.[205] Consider, though, that the landlord has mortgaged the premises, and the mortgagee, having gone into possession of the rents and profits, is the party suing for the rent. *Reeves* v. *Pope*[206] is authority for the proposition that a cross-claim that otherwise would have given rise to an equitable set-off in an action by the landlord/mortgagor for payment of rent will not be effective as a set-off when the rent instead is being claimed by the mortgagee. While in Victoria Beach J. recently re-affirmed this principle in *Citibank Pty. Ltd.* v. *Simon Fredericks Pty. Ltd.*,[207] it has not been universally accepted by commentators.[208] The decision in *Reeves* v. *Pope* has been said to constitute an attempt to confer

---

[203] See the discussion at [1941] 2 WWR 636, 641.

[204] See the discussion at [1941] 2 WWR 636, 641–2. For example, Major J. relied on the earlier decision in *Edie* v. *Turkewich* [1940] 1 WWR 554, in relation to which he said (at 642) that, 'Here it was held that an uncompleted contract of which certain promissory notes formed a part *affected the title of a subsequent holder*; that such holder had notice of the uncompleted conditions which put him on inquiry and he made none. Under these circumstances he was not a holder in due course'. (emphasis added).

[204a] See now the Landlord and Tenant (Covenants) Act 1995.

[205] See section 1.7.22 above.   [206] [1914] 2 K.B. 284.   [207] [1993] 2 V.R. 168.

[208] See Wood, *English and International Set-off* (1989), 886–7, and also the discussion in Waite, 'Disrepair and Set-off of Damages Against Rent: The Implications of British Anzani' [1983] *The Conveyancer* 373, 384–6 in relation to an absolute sale of the reversion (which is discussed below). In a note in (1992) 66 *Australian Law Journal* 313 the *Citibank* decision was described as a good illustration of a situation whose solution is clear on the authorities but which might be reconsidered.

a special insulation in favour of mortgagees from the application of the principle applicable in the case of an assignment of a debt, that the assignee takes subject to an equitable set-off available to the debtor against the assignor.[209] In truth, though, there is nothing special or exceptional about the mortgagee's position, and as a matter of principle the decisions in *Reeves* v. *Pope* and *Simon Fredericks* would appear to be correct.

The 'old-style' common law form of mortgage in issue in *Reeves* v. *Pope* operated as a conveyance.[210] The land in question was conveyed to the mortgagee, subject to an obligation to re-convey upon satisfaction of the debt. Since the mortgagee had the legal title to the land, he had the legal entitlement to the rent. Prior to intervention by the mortgagee, the mortgagor had the 'tacit agreement' of the mortgagee to receive rent.[211] The rent was received by the mortgagor for his own absolute use, and not for the use of the mortgagee.[212] However, the mortgagee could put an end to this tacit agreement at any time,[213] in which case, given his legal entitlement, he could sue for future rent as it accrued, and also for any rent in arrears as from the date of his legal title.[214] Indeed, prior to 1873 the mortgagor's remedies at law to enforce payment of rent before intervention by the mortgagee were limited. A landlord who subsequently mortgaged the reversion could not sue or distrain for rent in his own name or bring proceedings for ejectment.[215] His position was ameliorated to

---

[209] Wood, *English and International Set-off* (1989), 886–7. See also Lightman and Moss, *The Law of Receivers of Companies* (2nd edn., 1994), 249.

[210] See generally Sykes and Walker, *The Law of Securities* (5th edn., 1993) 39 et seq.

[211] *Moss* v. *Gallimore* (1779) 1 Dougl. 279, 283.

[212] *Trent* v. *Hunt* (1853) 9 Ex. 14, 23.

[213] *Moss* v. *Gallimore* (1779) 1 Dougl. 279, 283.

[214] See, e.g., *Burrows* v. *Gradin* (1843) 12 LJQB 333 (referring to *Moss* v. *Gallimore* (1779) 1 Dougl. 279). The same principle applies when the lease is entered into after the mortgage. See *In re Ind, Coope & Co. Ltd.* [1911] 2 Ch. 223, 231–2. Compare the position of an equitable mortgagee, discussed in *Finck* v. *Tranter* [1905] 1 KB 427.

[215] *Doe d. Marriott* v. *Edwards* (1834) 5 B & Ad. 1065; *Trent* v. *Hunt* (1853) 9 Ex. 14; *Matthews* v. *Usher* [1900] 2 QB 535, 538–9. A different principle applied if the mortgagor leased the premises after the mortgage. In such a case the lease was void as against the mortgagee (so that the tenant was liable to be ejected by the mortgagee) unless the mortgagee adopted or otherwise authorized the lease. If this occurred, the mortgagee upon giving notice to the tenant was entitled to all arrears of rent as well as rent which accrued due afterwards. See *Pope* v. *Biggs* (1829) 9 B & C 245. However, if the lease was not adopted or authorized by the mortgagee, the tenant nevertheless was estopped from disputing the validity of the lease as against the mortgagor. Accordingly, the mortgagor could enforce the covenants in the lease against the tenant, and could distrain for unpaid rent in his own name. See *Cuthbertson* v. *Irving* (1859) 4 H & N 742; *Trent* v. *Hunt* (at 22–3). In England a mortgagor in possession now has a power to lease, pursuant to the Law of Property Act 1925, s. 99. For the position in the various Australian states, see Sykes, *The Law of Securities* (5th edn., 1993), 102–4. If a lease is granted pursuant to this power the mortgagee is entitled to the rent on the same basis as for a prior lease. See, e.g., *In re Ind, Coope & Co.* [1911] 2 Ch. 223, 231–2 (power in mortgage document to create leases).

some extent after the enactment of section 25(5) of the Supreme Court of Judicature Act 1873, which empowered the mortgagor to sue in his own name for unpaid rent.[216] A similar provision has since been adopted in all Australian States.[217] However, this applies only until such time as the mortgagee gives notice of intention to enter into the receipt of the rents and profits. Once the mortgagee gives notice the mortgagor loses his right to sue.

In England a mortgage no longer operates by way of conveyance. As a result of reforms introduced by the Law of Property Act 1925, sections 85 and 87, a mortgage of freehold is now only capable of being effected at law by either a demise to the mortgagee for a term of years absolute subject to a provision for cesser on redemption, or alternatively a charge by deed expressed to be by way of legal mortgage, in which case a mortgagee of an estate in fee simple is expressed to have the same protection, powers and remedies as if he had a term of 3000 years. However, both give the mortgagee a legal estate in possession, and a consequent legal right to go into possession by receipt of the rents and profits,[218] so that the position with respect to rent should be the same as under the old form of mortgage.

The position of a mortgagee in suing for rent is not the same as that of an assignee of a debt. Unless the requirements of section 136 of the Law of Property Act 1925 are satisfied (see section 13.2.2 above), a debt is not assignable at common law. The assignment is only recognized in equity, and therefore the assignee generally can only enforce payment of the assigned debt in an action at law if the assignor as the legal owner of the debt is joined as a party. On the other hand, a mortgagee in possession can sue for rent in his own name and in respect of his own legal title.[219] He is not a mere assignee from the mortgagor of the tenant's indebtedness for rent,[220] but rather has a legal entitlement to it as a result

---

[216] See now the Law of Property Act 1925, s. 98.

[217] See Sykes, *The Law of Securities* (5th edn., 1993), 99.

[218] See Megarry and Wade, *The Law of Real Property* (5th edn., 1984), 942, 960. If at the time of the mortgage the premises are already the subject of a lease, the demise to the mortgagee operates to vest the reversion in the mortgagee, including the right to the rents and profits. See *Harmer* v. *Bean* (1853) Car. & K 307.

[219] See, e.g., *Burrows* v. *Gradin* (1843) 12 LJQB 333 (referring to *Moss* v. *Gallimore* (1779) 1 Dougl. 279). See now the Landlord and Tenant (Covenants) Act 1995, s. 15(1)(b).

[220] *Reeves.* v. *Pope* [1914] 2 KB 284, 287, 289. This is illustrated by *In re Ind, Coope & Co., Ltd.* [1911] 2 Ch. 223. In that case certain leasehold premises were mortgaged to debenture-holders. The mortgagor then assigned the rent to a third party, who gave notice of the assignment to the tenants before the debenture-holders went into possession of the rents and profits. The dispute as to who was entitled to the rent was not determined by reference to the rule in *Dearle* v. *Hall* (1828) 3 Russ. 1, as indeed one would have expected if the dispute was regarded as being between two assignees of a chose in action. Rather, the case was decided on the basis that it was not within the power of the mortgagor to assign the rents in priority to the debenture-holders.

of his legal estate in possession.[221] For the same reason, then, that a transferee of an instrument transferable at law does not take subject to rights of set-off that would have been available against the transferor,[222] a set-off otherwise available to a tenant against the landlord/mortgagor under the Statutes of Set-off cannot be asserted against the mortgagee. Nor should a substantive defence of equitable set-off be available in this situation independently of the principle that an assignee takes subject to equities.[223] Using Lord Cottenham's traditional formulation of the principle in *Rawson* v. *Samuel*,[224] a claim by a mortgagee for rent is not impeached by a damages claim available to the tenant against the mortgagor. Since the mortgagee's claim is based on his own title, and not that of the mortgagor, the cross-demands could not be said to be inter-dependent.[225] Similarly, relief would not be available on the basis of the formulation endorsed by the House of Lords in *Bank of Boston Connecticut* v. *European Grain and Shipping Ltd.*,[226] that the cross-claim should flow out of and be inseparably connected with the dealings and transactions which gave rise to the claim. The mortgagee's claim is derived from his legal estate in possession consequent upon the mortgage. The lessee's cross-claim does not flow out of and is not inseparably connected with that at all. Therefore, there should not be an equitable set-off. It is apparent, then, that *Reeves* v. *Pope* was correctly decided.

In Australia a different form of mortgage also applies now in relation to Torrens title land. The legislation of all Australian states provides that a mortgage under the relevant Act does not operate as a transfer of the land in question, but rather it takes effect as a security, or statutory charge.[227] While the general approach is universal, there are nevertheless some differences under the Acts as regards the rights and powers of the mortgagee, and as a result *Reeves* v. *Pope* may not be applicable in all states insofar as Torrens mortgages are concerned. Beach J. in *Citibank Pty. Ltd.* v. *Simon Fredericks Pty. Ltd.*[228] held that it does apply in Victoria, though, following *Re Partnership Pacific Securities Limited*,[229] this would not appear to be the case in Queensland. The facts in *Partnership Pacific Securities* were similar to those in *Reeves* v. *Pope*. In

---

[221] See *Reeves*. v. *Pope* [1914] 2 KB 284, 289–90 in relation to a mortgage by way of conveyance.   [222] See section 13.2.18 above.

[223] Although this involves, on the one hand, a claim by the mortgagee against the tenant and, on the other, a cross-claim by the tenant against the mortgagor, mutuality is not a prerequisite to this form of equitable set-off. See section 1.7.6 above.

[224] (1841) Cr. & Ph. 161, discussed in section 1.7.1 above.

[225] Compare *Grant* v. *NZMC Ltd* [1989] 1 NZLR 8, 13.

[226] [1989] 1 AC 1056, discussed in section 1.7.2 above.

[227] See, e.g., the Transfer of Land Act 1958 (Vic.), s. 74(2), and generally Sykes, *The Law of Securities* (5th edn., 1993), 227 *et seq*.   [228] [1993] 2 VR 168.

[229] [1994] 1 Qd. R 410.

essence, a lessor of premises registered under the Real Property Act 1861 (Qld) decided to re-develop them, and agreed with the tenant that it would cause the work to be completed in a good workmanlike manner by a particular date. The lessee alleged a breach of this agreement, and accordingly claimed damages from the lessor. The applicant had a registered mortgage over the premises and, after default by the lessor/ mortgagor, went into possession by claiming all arrears of rent up to the date of possession together with all rental and other money coming due in respect of the lease. The question was whether the lessee was entitled to set off its damages claim against the lessor. The claim for rent was the subject of two actions, the first before de Jersey J.[230] His Honour held that, unlike the corresponding Victorian legislation considered in the *Citibank* case, the Queensland Real Property Act does not allow a mortgagee to sue for rent. In Victoria, section 81 of the Transfer of Land Act provides that a first mortgagee has the same rights and remedies at law and in equity as he would have had if the legal estate in the mortgaged land had been vested in him as mortgagee, with a right of quiet enjoyment in the mortgagor until default. This has the effect that, following default, the mortgagee has the same entitlement to sue for rent as an old title mortgagee,[231] and accordingly it was correct to conclude that the principle in *Reeves* v. *Pope* applies in relation to a Torrens title mortgage in Victoria. This should be compared to the Queensland Act, which has no equivalent of section 81. Section 60 does provide that, 'it shall be lawful for the mortgagee upon default . . . to enter into possession of the mortgaged land by receiving the rents and profits thereof'. However his Honour held that this only entitles the mortgagee to *receive* the rents and profits as they are paid, in the sense that it is not wrongful for him to do so, though without conferring an independent right to sue for them. This accords with the views expressed by Sykes[232] and Francis and Thomas,[233] and as a matter of construction it would appear to be correct.[234] His Honour nevertheless held that a mortgagee is given a power to enforce the obligation to pay rent by section 117(2) of the Property Law Act 1974 (Qld.), and that this was sufficient to bring the case within *Reeves* v. *Pope*. When it came to making his order, de Jersey J. noted that the claims for declaration set out in the summons only

---

[230] Unreported, 12 May 1992.

[231] See the discussion in Sykes, *The Law of Securities* (5th edn., 1993), 260–2, and in Francis and Thomas, *Mortgages and Securities* (3rd edn., 1986), 146–7.

[232] Sykes, *The Law of Securities* (5th edn., 1993), 258–9.

[233] Francis and Thomas, *Mortgages and Securities* (3rd edn., 1986), 147–8.

[234] In fact, in the *Citibank* case, Beach J. based his decision inter alia upon s. 78 of the Transfer of Land Act, which is in terms similar to s. 60 of the Queensland Act. However, as mentioned, the decision in *Citibank* perhaps is better justified on the basis of the Transfer of Land Act, s. 81.

related to the obligation to pay rent as from the date that the mortgagee
went into possession. Accordingly, he declined to make declarations as to
the mortgagee's entitlement to rent in arrears before that date. This was
the subject of the second action before G. N. Williams J.[235] In this action
his Honour agreed with the view that the Real Property Act in Queensland
does not confer upon a mortgagee an independent right to sue for rent. He
disagreed, however, with de Jersey J.'s conclusion that section 117(2) of
the Property Law Act 1974 has this effect. Section 117(2) provides that,
'Any such rent, covenant, obligation, or provision shall be capable of being
recovered, received, enforced, and taken advantage of, by the person from
time to time entitled . . .'. While section 60 of the Real Property Act does
indeed entitle a mortgagee to receive rents and profits, section 117(2)
should be read in the light of section 117(1), which provides that, 'Rent
reserved by a lease . . . shall be annexed and incident to and shall go with
the reversionary estate in the land'. As Williams J. noted,[236] the section is
concerned primarily with defining the rights of the owner of the
reversionary estate from time to time,[237] and a mortgagee of Torrens title
land is not the owner of the reversionary estate in the land. Accordingly,
he concluded that the section does not assist the mortgagee. This view
appears to be correct.

Given that an old title mortgage operated as a conveyance, the
discussion of the availability of a set-off to a tenant against an old title
mortgagee should also be relevant when there is an absolute sale of the
reversion.[238] The purchaser should be able to sue for rent[239] unaffected by
any right of equitable set-off that the tenant could have asserted if the
vendor instead had been suing. However one commentator has argued
that, as a matter of principle, the purchaser should be subject to the set-
off.[240] The essence of the argument is that the tenant's right of set-off
against the vendor/landlord is not a personal equity, but rather has a
proprietary character. The proprietary character is said to arise because

---

[235] [1994] 1 Qd. R 410.   [236] [1994] 1 Qd. R 410, 421.

[237] This includes an owner in equity who is entitled to the rent to the exclusion of all others.
See *Schalit* v. *Joseph Nadler Ltd.* [1933] 2 KB 79, 82–3.

[238] See, e.g., Buckley L.J.'s reported response during argument in *Reeves* v. *Pope* [1914] 2
KB 284, 286 to counsel's statement regarding a purchase.

[239] In relation to new tenancies under the Landlord and Tenant (Covenants) Act 1925, this
would not include arrears of rent accrued prior to the assignment. See s. 23(1), and also
s. 30(4), which provides that the Law of Property Act 1925, s. 141 does not apply. Compare
Arlesford Trading Co. Ltd. v. *Servansingh* [1971] 3 All ER 113.

[240] Waite, 'Disrepair and Set-off of Damages Against Rent: The Implications of British
Anzani' [1983] *The Conveyancer* 373, 380–1, 384–6. In addition to the argument set out
below, an argument was advanced based upon the assignment of the indebtedness for rent,
though, as in the case of a mortgagee, a purchaser is not an assignee of the rent but rather has
a right to sue for it based upon his own legal title.

[241] See, e.g. *Jones* v. *Smith* (1841) 1 Hare 43, 60.

the set-off impeaches the landlord's entitlement to rent, and therefore is incidental to the tenancy. Further, the courts have said that a purchaser of land has constructive notice of any interest that a tenant in possession has in land,[241] so that the purchaser in the case under discussion will have constructive notice of the tenant's right of set-off. Accordingly, the argument is that the purchaser is not a bona fide purchaser for value without notice. There are a number of difficulties with this view. In the first place, it is by no means clear that a purchaser would be taken to have constructive notice of mere equities.[242] More importantly, it is not easy to accept the notion that the equity in question has a proprietary character. Indeed, in *Reeves* v. *Pope* the Court of Appeal emphasized that the tenant's damages claim in that case did not create an estate or interest in the land.[243] The view that the tenant's equitable set-off has a proprietary character was based on the proposition that the right is capable of transmission to a successor tenant by assignment.[244] The problem with this is that equitable set-off is a defence, albeit a substantive defence. It is not easy to see how a defence available to a tenant against his obligation to pay rent can be 'assigned' to a successor tenant in respect of the latter's own rental obligation. This is not to suggest that the fact that something is not capable of being assigned is a *sufficient* reason for saying that it is not proprietary in nature.[245] Rather, the position simply is that it is difficult to see how a defence can be regarded as anything other than a personal equity. The kind of equity to which a purchaser of land with notice will take subject is an equity which is ancillary to or dependent upon an equitable estate or interest in land,[246] in the sense that it will involve an adjustment of the rights of the person possessed of the equity to the land in question.[247] Examples include the right of a tenant to have the lease rectified,[248] and the right of a mortgagor to have a sale by the mortgagee set aside on the ground that the mortgagee's exercise of the power of sale was fraudulent.[249] A purchaser of land does not take subject to a personal obligation of the vendor which does not run with the land at law, even

---

[241] See, e.g. *Jones* v. *Smith* (1841) 1 Hare 43, 60.

[242] See *Smith* v. *Jones* [1954] 2 All ER 823, though compare *Downie* v. *Lockwood* [1965] VR 257.   [243] [1914] 2 KB 284, 288, 289, 290.

[244] Waite, 'Disrepair and Set-off of Damages Against Rent: The Implications of British Anzani' [1983] *The Conveyancer* 373, 386.

[245] See Mason J. in *R.* v. *Toohey; ex parte Meneling Station Pty. Ltd.* (1982) 158 CLR 327, 342–3.

[246] Lord Upjohn in *National Provincial Bank Ltd.* v. *Ainsworth* [1965] AC 1175, 1238.

[247] See Meagher, Gummow & Lehane, *Equity Doctrines and Remedies* (3rd edn., 1992), 121.

[248] See Lord Upjohn in *National Provincial Bank Ltd.* v. *Ainsworth* [1965] AC 1175, 1238 and compare *Smith* v. *Jones* [1954] 2 All ER 823.

[249] Compare *Latec Investments Ltd.* v. *Hotel Terrigal Ltd.* (1965) 113 CLR 265, in which the purchaser did not have notice of the equity.

though it may relate to the use of the land.[250] In the case of a tenant's equitable set-off, while it may be said to relate to his leasehold interest, it does not involve any adjustments to his right to the land itself, and accordingly it is not an equity to which a purchaser of the land with notice may be obliged to take subject.

If leased premises have fallen into disrepair, and responsibility for the repairs is on the landlord, the tenant may expend money in executing the repairs and recoup himself from future payments of rent.[251] The right in issue is sometimes described as a set-off,[252] although this is not entirely accurate.[253] Rather, it gives rise to a question of payment. The money spent by the tenant on repairs as a matter of law is regarded as a payment *pro tanto* of future rent,[254] or any arrears of rent.[255] The tenant's right to take this course of action is based upon a policy consideration, that 'he shall be otherwise at great mischief, for the house may fall upon his head before it be repaired; and therefore the law alloweth him to repair it, and recoupe the rent'.[256] If as a matter of law the tenant's expenditure constitutes payment of rent in advance, it should be binding upon a mortgagee or purchaser. This indeed was the case in *Lee-Parker* v. *Izzet*,[257] in which Goff J. enforced a tenant's right to have expenditure on repairs regarded as a payment of future rent as against a mortgagee.

The decision in *De Nichols* v. *Saunders*[258] is not inconsistent with this view. In that case the Common Pleas held that a payment by a tenant to his landlord, which was expressed to be and was accepted as a payment of rent in advance, was not effective as against an old title mortgagee who obtained the mortgage before the payment. The mortgagee on going into possession was allowed to sue for the rent that, according to the terms of the lease, accrued after the tenant had notice of the mortgage,[259] and the

---

[250] Lord Wilberforce in *National Provincial Bank Ltd.* v. *Ainsworth* [1965] AC 1175, 1253–4, referring to Buckley L.J. in *London County Council* v. *Allen* [1914] 3 KB 642, 657.　　　　　　　　　　　　　　　　　　　　　　[251] See generally section 1.7.22 above.

[252] See *Waters* v. *Weigall* (1795) 2 Anst. 575; *Knockholt Pty. Ltd.* v. *Graff* [1975] Qd. R 88, 91, 92.

[253] *Lee-Parker* v. *Izzet* [1971] 1 WLR 1688, 1693; *British Anzani (Felixstowe) Ltd.* v. *International Marine Management (U.K.) Ltd.* [1980] 1 QB 137, 148.

[254] *Taylor* v. *Beal* (1591) Cro. Eliz. 222 per Gawdy J.; *Lee-Parker* v. *Izzet* [1971] 1 WLR 1688, 1693; *British Anzani (Felixstowe) Ltd.* v. *International Marine Management (U.K.) Ltd.* [1980] 1 QB 137, 148.

[255] *Asco Developments Ltd.* v. *Gordon* (1978) 248 EG 683.

[256] *Taylor* v. *Beal* (1591) Cro. Eliz. 222 per Gawdy J.

[257] [1971] 1 WLR 1688.

[258] (1870) LR 5 CP 589. See also *Lord Ashburton* v. *Nocton* [1915] 1 Ch. 274.

[259] See *Cook* v. *Guerra* (1872) LR 7 CP 132 in relation to rent accruing before notice. Prior to the statute (1705) 4 Anne, C. 16, the assignee of a reversion could not recover rent until the tenant had attorned to him. Section 9 of the Act took away the necessity for attornment, although section 10 provided protection to a tenant who paid rent before he had notice that the premises had been assigned.

tenant could not rely on the advance payment to the mortgagor/landlord as a defence. In this regard, if a landlord mortgages the premises *after* receiving an advance payment, the payment will be binding on the mortgagee as a discharge of the rent obligation, unless he had enquired of the tenant as to the rent and the tenant answered incorrectly or failed to answer.[260] It is in the situation in which there was a *prior* mortgage that the principle in *De Nichols* v. *Saunders* applies. Willes J. explained the basis of the decision in the following terms:[261]

The receipt of the rent could not be treated here as a discharge by the landlord, because by assigning the reversion before the rent was received by him he had parted with the power of giving such a discharge. The plaintiff [mortgagee] lent his money on a contract, which was under an implied condition that the landlord should continue entitled to the rent at the time it became due, and able, therefore, then to give the plaintiff a valid discharge.

He said that the payment was not in fact a fulfilment of the obligation imposed by the lease to pay rent. Rather he characterized it as an advance to the landlord, with an agreement that on the day when the rent became due the advance should be treated as a fulfilment of the rent obligation. This could not be effective as against a prior mortgagee, because the mortgagee was the party entitled to the rent as it fell due.

De Nichols v. *Saunders* essentially turned upon a question of power. The landlord, having assigned the reversion by way of mortgage, did not have power to give a discharge to the tenant before the due date. However the principle, that a tenant who expends money in repairs may treat this as an advance payment of rent if the landlord is responsible for the repairs, is not based upon any question of power, or any agreement (express or implied) between the tenant and the landlord regarding the payment of rent. The tenant's right to treat the cost of repairs as an advance payment of rent arises *as a matter of law*. It is designed to encourage the tenant to effect repairs so as to protect him against the possibility that 'the house may fall upon his head'. It is effective against the landlord *whoever it may be*, whether it is person whom the tenant thinks is the landlord, or whether it is a prior assignee of the reversion of whom the tenant is not aware. In *Lee-Parker* v. *Izzet* it is unclear from the report as to whether the repairs were effected before or after the mortgage, although this should not make any difference. The decision was correct, irrespective of when the mortgage occurred.

---

[260] *Green* v. *Rheinberg* (1911) 104 LT 149. See also *Grace Rymer Investments Ltd.* v. *Waite* [1958] 1 Ch. 831.
[261] (1870) LR 5 CP 589, 594.

13.2.20 *Freight payable to a mortgagee or purchaser of a ship*

The principle underlying *Reeves* v. *Pope*[262] is also relevant when a mortgagee goes into possession of a ship. The mortgagee is entitled to the freight in the course of being earned, not because he is an assignee of the debt, but rather because he is the master or owner of the ship.[263] The mortgagee's right depends on property, not on contract.[264] In the same way, when a ship is sold, the right to freight in the course of being earned passes to the purchaser.[265] Accordingly, when a mortgagee in possession (or a purchaser) sues for the freight, the charterer or shipper may not set off a debt owing to him by the mortgagor/owner (or vendor).[266] The principle of taking subject to equities does not apply.

13.3. COMPANY RECEIVERSHIPS

13.3.1 *Crystallized floating security*

Similar issues may arise when a floating security over a company's assets and undertaking is crystallized by the appointment of a receiver.[267] A person dealing with a company in receivership will be concerned to know whether debts and credits arising before and after the appointment can be set off.

It is often said that, when crystallization occurs, any debts owing to the company and coming within the ambit of the security are assigned in equity to the secured creditor.[268] This will certainly be the case when crystallization results in an assignment of the company's property by way of

---

[262] [1914] 2 KB 284, discussed in section 13.2.19 above.

[263] *Keith* v. *Burrows* (1877) 2 App. Cas. 636, 646. See also *Kerswill* v. *Bishop* (1832) 2 C & J 529; *Japp* v. *Campbell* (1888) 57 LJQB 79; *Wilson* v. *Wilson* (1872) LR 14 Eq. 32 (mortgagee's right to freight has priority over an earlier assignment of freight of which the mortgagee did not have notice).

[264] *Rusden* v. *Pope* (1868) LR 3 Ex. 269, 276–7.

[265] See e.g., *Morrison* v. *Parsons* (1810) 2 Taunt. 407. As Lord Ellenborough remarked in *Case* v. *Davidson* (1816) 5 M & S 79, 82, 'freight follows, as an incident, the property in the ship'.   [266] *Tanner* v. *Phillips* (1872) 42 LJ Ch. 125.

[267] This includes an administrative receiver within the meaning of the Insolvency Act 1986, s. 29(2) being a receiver of the whole (or substantially the whole) of a company's property appointed by or on behalf of the holders of debentures of the company secured by a charge which, when created, was a floating charge.

[268] *Biggerstaff* v. *Rowatt's Wharf Ltd.* [1896] 2 Ch. 93; *N. W. Robbie & Co. Ltd.* v. *Witney Warehouse Co. Ltd* [1963] 1 WLR 1324 (cited with evident approval in *Security Trust Co.* v. *Royal Bank of Canada* [1976] AC 503, 518); *Rendell* v. *Doors and Doors Ltd* [1975] 2 NZLR 191. See also *Ferrier* v. *Bottomer* (1972) 126 CLR 597, 607–9; *George Barker (Transport) Ltd.* v. *Eynon* [1974] 1 WLR 462; *In re ELS Ltd* [1995] Ch. 11. The appointment of a receiver out of court under a floating charge does not of itself determine contracts previously entered into

mortgage, though in fact the security document is not always drafted in this manner. The terms of a floating security commonly provide for the company's property to become subject to a fixed equitable charge upon crystallization, the difference being that, unlike a mortgage, a charge is a form of security that does not take effect as a transfer of ownership.[269] Notwithstanding this distinction, the cases suggest that, when a floating security is expressed to take effect by way of charge, it will nevertheless be interpreted as giving rise to an assignment.[270] In truth, though, the distinction should not be crucial to set-off.[271] A charge should have the same effect upon the availability of a set-off as a mortgage,[272] in the sense that, after a debtor has notice that the debt has been charged in equity to a third party, it is unconscionable for the debtor to rely on subsequent dealings with the chargor to diminish the rights of the third party. On that basis, whether crystallization results in a mortgage or a charge, questions of set-off[273] should be determined by reference to the same rules that apply to assignments of choses in action, the relevant date being the date of notice of crystallization.[274] Mere notice of the existence of a floating security at the time when the cross-debt due from the company is contracted, without notice of crystallization, is not sufficient to prevent a set-off. In *Biggerstaff* v. *Rowatt's Wharf, Limited*[275] both demands were liquidated and also arose before crystallization. It was held, correctly, that the debenture-holders took subject to a set-off, notwithstanding that the defendant knew of the floating security.[276] This assumes that the debt in

---

by the company in the ordinary course of its business. See *George Barker (Transport) Ltd.* v. *Eynon* (at 468, 471). This is also the case when a receiver and manager is appointed by the court. See *Parsons* v. *Sovereign Bank of Canada* [1913] AC 160.

[269] Goode, *Legal Problems of Credit and Security* (2nd edn., 1988), 14. The distinction between a charge and a mortgage has not always been maintained. For example, Stamp L.J. in *George Barker (Transport) Ltd.* v. *Eynon* [1974] 1 WLR 462, 471 referred to 'an equitable assignment (by way of charge)'.   [270] See *In re ELS Ltd.* [1995] Ch. 11, 24–5.

[271] Compare Goode, 'Centre Point' [1984] *Journal of Business Law* 172.

[272] See section 7.6.4 above.

[273] Of course, set-off only provides a defence to a monetary demand. It may not be invoked when the receiver is suing for the return of goods or other specific things wrongfully detained. See *Tony Lee Motors Ltd.* v. *M. S. MacDonald & Son (1974) Ltd.* [1981] 2 NZLR 281, and generally section 5.1 above.

[274] See *Business Computers Ltd.* v. *Anglo-African Leasing Ltd.* [1977] 1 WLR 578, 582.

[275] [1896] 2 Ch. 93.

[276] See also *Edward Nelson & Co., Ltd.* v. *Faber & Co.* [1903] 2 K.B. 367; *Supercool Refrigeration and Air Conditioning* v. *Hoverd Industries Ltd.* [1994] 3 NZLR 300. *A fortiori* a set-off is available against a cross-debt arising before notice of crystallization if the defendant did not know of the floating security. See *Tony Lee Motors Ltd.* v. *M. S. MacDonald & Son (1974) Ltd.* [1981] 2 NZLR 281 (in which the defendant, before crystallization, had obtained an equitable assignment of a debt owing by the company to a third party. Notice to the company was not necessary to complete the assignment). See also *Business Computers Ltd.* v. *Anglo-African Leasing Ltd.* [1977] 1 WLR 578 (in relation to the prior instalment of rent due).

question indeed is the subject of a floating security. A security often provides that certain specified assets are to be subject to a fixed charge or mortgage, with a floating security applying to the remainder of the company's assets and undertaking. One class of asset that is sometimes expressed to be the subject of a fixed charge is the company's book debts. If indeed the security document is effective to create a fixed charge in respect of them,[277] regard would be had to the date that the debtor had notice of the charge for the purpose of determining the availability of a set-off, as opposed to the date of crystallization in relation to other assets the subject of the floating security.[278]

Consistent with the principle applicable to assignments, a debtor ordinarily will be denied a set-off based upon the Statutes of Set-off in an action brought against him by a company in receivership for payment of a debt the subject of a crystallized security if the company became indebted to the defendant after the defendant had notice of crystallization. The leading authority is *N. W. Robbie & Co. Ltd.* v. *Witney Warehouse Co. Ltd.*[279] The plaintiff company had issued a debenture to its bank securing, by means of a floating charge over its assets, all money due from it to the bank. The bank subsequently appointed a receiver and manager under the debenture, whereupon the charge crystallized. Before the appointment the company had sold goods on credit to the defendant. The company continued to carry on business after the appointment, during which time the defendant purchased more goods on credit. At a later date the defendant obtained an assignment to it of a debt owing by the company to a third party. When the company sued the defendant for the price of the goods, the defendant sought to set off the company's indebtedness on the assigned debt. The Court of Appeal held against a set-off. The decision itself is consistent with the law of assignments,[280] although, as Meagher, Gummow and Lehane have explained,[281] the actual reasoning employed for denying a set-off is not entirely satisfactory. Sellers and Russell L.JJ. said that there was no right of set-off because there was no mutuality in equity. When the floating charge crystallized, the defendant's indebtedness for the goods purchased before crystallization was assigned in equity to the

---

[277] See *Re New Bullas Trading Ltd.* [1994] BCLC 485.

[278] Compare *Supercool Refrigeration and Air Conditioning* v. *Hoverd Industries Ltd.* [1994] 3 NZLR 300.

[279] [1963] 1 WLR 1324. See also *Lynch* v. *Ardmore Studios (Ireland) Ltd.* [1966] IR 133, which concerned a similar fact situation, and *United Steel Corporation Ltd.* v. *Turnbull Elevator of Canada Ltd.* [1973] 2 OR 540.

[280] However, note that Barwick C.J. in *Ferrier* v. *Bottomer* (1972) 126 CLR 597, 603 left open the question whether *Robbie* v. *Witney* was correctly decided.

[281] Meagher, Gummow and Lehane, *Equity: Doctrines and Remedies* (3rd edn., 1992), 719–21.

debenture-holders, while, in the case of purchases made after that date, each debt as it arose became the subject of an *immediate* equitable assignment in favour of the debenture-holders.[282] This meant that, at the later date when the defendant first obtained an assignment of the debt owing by the company, there was no identity between the persons beneficially interested in the claim (the debenture-holders) and the person against whom the cross-claim existed (the company). The assumption inherent in this analysis is that mutuality under the Statutes of Set-off is determined by reference to the equitable rather than the legal interests of the parties and, if the demands are not and never have been equitably mutual, a right of set-off *ipso facto* is not available under the Statutes. In fact, the true position would appear to be that the Statutes prima facie confer a right of set-off at law when there is mutuality at law, though a lack of mutuality in equity may render it unconscionable for the defendant to rely on this legal right.[283] *Robbie* v. *Witney* is better explained on the ground that, since the cross-claim against the company was acquired *after* the defendant was aware of the crystallization of the charge, and the consequent equitable interest of the debenture-holders in its own indebtedness to the company, it was indeed unconscionable for it to rely on this right of set-off otherwise available at law.[284]

It appears that a set-off derived from the Statutes of Set-off will still be denied to a defendant in an action brought against him by a company in receivership if the company's indebtedness to the defendant, though arising after notice of crystallization, nonetheless relates to a contract entered into between the defendant and the company before notice.[285] This is consistent with the principle applied in relation to assignments generally, and it has already been criticized in that context.[286] It is sufficient to say that, if there is already a binding contractual relationship in existence before notice, it is not clear why it should be considered to be unconscionable for the defendant to ground a right of set-off otherwise available at law under the Statutes upon an indebtedness of the company arising under that contract but after notice. There is a form of exception to

---

[282] Donovan L.J. in his dissenting judgment said that the floating charge only crystallized into a fixed charge as regards the assets owned by the company at the time of crystallization. He said that this did not include the defendant's indebtedness to the company arising after crystallization when the credit sale took place. However, this is not a correct interpretation. See *Ferrier* v. *Bottomer* (1972) 126 CLR 597.   [283] See section 13.2.1 above.

[284] The report of the case fails to establish when the defendant first became aware of the crystallization of the floating charge, though Russell L.J. said that the defendant should be fixed with notice before it acquired the cross-claim against the company. See [1963] 1 WLR 1324, 1338.

[285] *Business Computers Ltd.* v. *Anglo-African Leasing Ltd.* [1977] 1 WLR 578 (esp. at 585). Compare *West Street Properties Pty. Ltd.* v. *Jamison* [1974] 2 NSWLR 435 (discussed below) in the situation in which the company in receivership is instead the party claiming a set-off.   [286] See section 13.2.4 above.

this general rule, however, based upon the notion of a temporary suspension of mutual credit.[287] If a person holding a negotiable instrument upon which a company is liable indorses it to a third party, and in the period after the appointment of a receiver under a debenture issued by the company that person is obliged to take up the instrument again as a result of the default of the company, he may still employ his claim against the company on the instrument in a set-off.[288]

The preceding discussion concerned the situation in which the debtor to the company is the party seeking to base a set-off upon an indebtedness of the company that arose after notice of the appointment of a receiver. The general rule is that a set-off will not be available to him. However, this is not to say that a set-off would also be denied to the company. In the New South Wales case of *West Street Properties Pty. Ltd.* v. *Jamison*[289] a company in receivership was the defendant in an action brought by the plaintiff lessor for payment of rent due under a lease. The lease had been entered into prior to the receivership, though the present action concerned an obligation to pay rent incurred by the company *after* the appointment of the receiver, the receiver having determined to continue the company's business for the benefit of the debenture-holder. The company sought to set off in that action a debt owing to it by the lessor on an advance made before the receivership. Jeffrey J. held in favour of a set-off. He acknowledged the existence of authority in support of the view that the defendant in an action brought against him by a company in receivership for payment of a debt could not set off an indebtedness incurred by the company after the defendant had been notified of the appointment of the receiver. This result could be justified on the ground that the defendant as an unsecured creditor should not be able to obtain payment of his debt in priority to the secured creditor by setting it off against a debt which he owed to the company but which in equity belonged to the secured creditor.[290] However, this particular objection is not relevant when the company, and inferentially the secured creditor, is the party seeking to assert a set-off. In such a case there is no countervailing equity rendering it unconscionable for the company to rely on a right of set-off otherwise available at law. The cross-demands would not have been equitably mutual

---

[287] A similar principle applies in the context of company liquidation. See section 2.8 above.
[288] See *Handley Page Ltd.* v. *Commissioners of Customs and Excise and Rockwell Machine Tool Company Ltd.* [1970] 2 Lloyd's Rep. 459, 464–5, discussed in *Business Computers Ltd.* v. *Anglo-African Leasing Ltd.* [1977] 1 WLR 578, 585–6.
[289] [1974] 2 NSWLR 435.
[290] *Quaere* whether this indeed is objectionable if the company's indebtedness arose out of a contractual relationship entered into before the receivership, because in such a case it could not be said that there has been a conscious attempt to obtain preferential treatment at the expense of the debenture-holders.

at any time, although lack of mutuality in equity will only deprive a defendant of a right of set-off otherwise available at law if in the particular case it is unconscionable for the defendant to rely on the legal right. As Jeffrey J. remarked:[291]

In a case where the debenture-holder elects after crystallization to cause the company to carry on its business, debts incurred to existing debtors of the company in so doing may be met by the *pro tanto* collection of the debts owed by them to the company by means of set-off. This is but a method of recovery alternative to the taking of proceedings at law in the name of the company, something which, as already observed, the debenture-holder has after crystallization, an undoubted right to do. For him to direct that a debt which he owns should be applied in reduction or extinction of an indebtedness which the company incurs is merely to exercise his dominion over it. It is one thing to say that a set-off at law cannot be availed of to defeat or postpone a prior equitable title to a debt, but quite another to say that it is not available to the equitable owner who wishes to employ the legal rights over which he has control in order to collect it.

This analysis should also be relevant where the company's debt does not have its source in a prior contract. *Jamison* supports the view that, in the situation in which a company in receivership becomes indebted during the course of the receivership to a person who in turn is indebted to the company, it is only unconscionable for the debtor to the company to assert a legal right of set-off otherwise available under the Statutes of Set-off. There is no countervailing equity prohibiting the company and the debenture-holders from obtaining the benefit of a set-off. This view is not without merit.

Consider the converse situation, in which it is the defendant's indebtedness to the company, rather than the company's indebtedness to the defendant, that arose after notice as a result of a contract entered into before notice. It seems that a set-off may be available in such a case at the instance of either party against a pre-receivership debt owing by the company. In *Rother Iron Works Ltd.* v. *Canterbury Precision Engineers Ltd.*[292] a company prior to the appointment of a receiver was indebted to the defendant for £124. In addition, it had entered into a contract to sell goods to the defendant for £159. However, the goods were not delivered

---

[291] [1974] 2 NSWLR 435, 441.
[292] [1974] 1 QB 1, referred to with evident approval in *George Barker (Transport) Ltd.* v. *Eynon* [1974] 1 WLR 462. See also *State Bank of South Australia* v. *Kralingen Pty. Ltd.*, unreported, Cox J., Supreme Court of South Australia, 17 September 1993. In *Kralingen* a lease required the lessor to purchase the tenant's fixtures upon determination of the lease. The lessee granted a floating mortgage debenture over its rights under the lease to the plaintiff bank. The security crystallized and, after that, the lessor determined the lease. It was held that the lessor could set off the lessee's arrears of rent against its liability to pay the price of the fixtures.

until after the receiver was appointed under a debenture created by the company in favour of its bank, and it was only upon delivery that the defendant became indebted for the price. Nevertheless, it was held that the defendant need only pay the difference of £35 to the receiver. Russell L.J. in the Court of Appeal said that the obligation of the defendant to pay the £159 'never . . . came into existence except subject to a right to set off the £124 as, in effect, payment in advance. That which became subject to the debenture charge was not £159, but the net claim sustainable by the plaintiff for £35'.[293]

Rother Iron Works was not applied by the British Columbia Court of Appeal in *CIBC* v. *Tuckerr Industries Inc.*[294] A receiver and manager was appointed by a debenture holder to a lessor of premises, and notice of the assignment was given immediately to the lessee. Prior to the appointment the lessor was indebted to the lessee on a transaction independent of the lease. The question was whether the lessee could set off that debt against subsequently accruing rent. It was held that there was a lack of mutuality, and therefore no set-off, since on the one hand the lessor was indebted to the lessee, and on the other the rent in question when it accrued under the lease after the appointment was owed to the debenture holder as equitable assignee. While *Rother Iron Works* appears to have been a similar case, it was distinguished on the ground that it was concerned with an equitable set-off, the basis of which was said to be that the two companies in that case traded with each other in such a way that every debt that arose between them in the course of their trade was subject, at the time it arose, to being set off against every subsequent cross-debt that arose within the trading relationship. It is doubtful, however, whether this is a proper basis for distinguishing *Rother Iron Works*. There is nothing in Russell L.J.'s judgment to suggest that there was an agreement for a set-off,[295] and nor do the demands appear to have been sufficiently closely connected to give rise to a substantive equitable set-off.[296] The court in *CIBC* v. *Tuckerr* in deciding against a set-off appears to have assumed that mutuality under the Statutes of Set-off is determined solely by reference to equitable titles, though in fact this is not the case.[297] In *Rother Iron Works* there was mutuality at law, and therefore prima facie there was a right of set-off under the Statutes of Set-off at law, and the case is authority for the proposition that in the circumstances under consideration there was

---

[293] [1974] 1 QB 1, 6.
[294] (1983) 149 DLR (3d) 172. See also *Re Associated Investors of Canada Ltd.* (1989) 62 DLR (4th) 269, though compare *Clarkson Company Ltd.* v. *The Queen* (1988) 88 *Dominion Tax Cases* 6256.
[295] Indeed, the contrary is inherent in Stamp L.J.'s comment in *George Barker (Transport) Ltd.* v. *Eynon* [1974] 1 WLR 462, 474.   [296] See section 1.7 above.
[297] See sections 7.4 and 13.2.1 above.

nothing inequitable in the defendant asserting this legal right. This should also apply in a case such as *Tuckerr*.

Russell L.J. in his judgment in *Rother Iron Works* emphasized that the delivery of the goods in that case was made pursuant to a contract made by the company before the receiver's appointment, and that the court was not concerned with a claim made by the receiver against the defendant arising out of a contract made by the receiver himself pursuant to his appointment. It may be thought unconscionable to allow a defendant to assert a right of set-off otherwise available at law when the defendant's liability to the company arose out of a dealing transacted after the defendant was already aware that the company was in receivership, and that the dealing was being conducted for the benefit of debenture-holders. Indeed, there are a number of cases in which a person who purchased goods from a company known to be in receivership was not allowed to set off the price against a pre-receivership debt owing to him by the company,[298] and *Robbie* v. *Witney* suggests that this also applies when the cross-claim against the company was acquired after notice as a result of an assignment.[299] In the New Zealand case of *Felt and Textiles of New Zealand Ltd* v. *R. Hubrich Ltd*[300] Richmond J., in denying the appellant a set-off against the price, emphasized that 'the appellant had notice of the fact that it was buying an asset then charged in favour of the debenture-holder from a company empowered by the debenture to sell that asset through the agency of the receiver for the purpose, primarily, of discharging the company's indebtedness to the debenture-holder'.[301] The sale in *Felt and Textiles* arose in the course of the realization of the company's assets by the receiver. Richmond J. tentatively suggested that there may be a distinction between that case and a case in which the receiver had decided to carry on the company's business. However, subsequently in New Zealand Chilwell J. in *Rendell* v. *Doors and Doors Ltd.*[302] rejected this as a ground for distinction, and held that a creditor of a company who purchased goods from a receiver known to be carrying on the company's business could not set off the price against the company's pre-receivership indebtedness to

---

[298] In addition to the cases discussed below see *Leichhardt Emporium Pty. Ltd.* v. *A.G.C. (Household Finance) Ltd.* [1979] 1 NSWLR 701; *Cheviot Australia Pty. Ltd.* v. *Bob Jane Corporation Pty. Ltd.* (1988) 52 SASR 204. Compare *F. Suter & Co. Ltd.* v. *Drake and Gorham Ltd.* (1910), unreported but mentioned and discussed in Weaver and Craigie, *The Law Relating to Banker and Customer in Australia* (looseleaf) Vol. 3, para. 22.590, in which the Divisional Court (Darling and Phillimore JJ.) apparently allowed a set-off in this situation.

[299] While *Robbie* v. *Witney* also concerned a sale of goods by a company in receivership, the report fails to state whether the defendant purchaser had notice of the appointment of the receiver at the time of the sale. Russell L.J. merely remarked ([1963] 1 WLR 1324, 1338) that the defendant should be fixed with notice some time before it acquired the cross-claim against the company.   [300] [1968] NZLR 716.   [301] [1968] NZLR 716, 718.
[302] [1975] 2 NZLR 191.

him. Nevertheless, there is a suggestion in the judgment that, in some cases in which a company's business is being carried on by a receiver, an equity could possibly arise which would justify a set-off against the debenture-holders.[303] The situation postulated by Chilwell J. was one in which a person supplied material to a company while the company was in receivership, which material was used in the manufacture of goods subsequently purchased by that person. The basis of any supposed equity was not explored further, but there is something to be said for the view that debenture-holders should expect to take subject to a set-off when both demands arose out of dealings with the company while the receiver was carrying on the company's business for the benefit of the debenture-holders.[304] This is so notwithstanding that it is contrary to the generally accepted position in relation to assignments of debts, that the line is drawn at the date of notice.

When the argument for a set-off is based upon the procedural defence provided by the Statutes of Set-off in the event of mutual debts, the company's liability to the defendant as a general rule must have come into existence before notice. However, consistent with the principle applicable in the case of an assignment of a debt,[305] this should not be necessary when an equitable set-off is in issue based upon the circumstance of cross-demands which are inseparably connected.[306] This was the basis of the decision of the Privy Council in *Parsons* v. *Sovereign Bank of Canada*.[307] A company prior to the appointment of a receiver and manager had entered into a number of contracts with the defendants for the supply of quantities of paper to them on a periodic basis. The receiver immediately after his

---

[303] A preferable formulation of the principle would be that in some cases it would not be unconscionable for the defendant to rely on the right of set-off admittedly available at law under the Statutes of Set-off.

[304] See Jeffrey J. in *West Street Properties Pty. Ltd.* v. *Jamison* [1974] 2 NSWLR 435, 440, and note also the comments by Yeldham J. in *Leichhardt Emporium Pty. Ltd.* v. *A.G.C. (Household Finance) Ltd.* [1979] 1 NSWLR 701, 706–7. Certainly a set-off should be available when both demands arose out of the same contract entered into by a receiver on behalf of the company, and moreover the demands are inseparably connected. This form of equitable set-off is discussed below.   [305] See section 13.2.8 above.

[306] The judgment of Mocatta J. in *Handley Page Ltd.* v. *Commissioners of Customs and Excise and Rockwell Machine Tool Company Ltd.* [1970] 2 Lloyd's Rep. 459 is confusing in this respect. If indeed the demands arose under the same contract and were closely connected (see at 465 of the judgment, and the reference to *Hanak* v. *Green* [1958] 2 QB 9), a set-off should have been available without any need to have recourse to the principle of a temporary suspension of mutual credit (see above) as a means of overcoming the perceived difficulty that the bills were returned to Rockwell *after* the appointment of a receiver under the debenture issued by Handley-Page.

[307] [1913] AC 160. See also the similar case of *Forster* v. *Nixon's Navigation Company* (1906) 23 TLR 138. Both *Parsons* and *Forster* were concerned with a receiver and manager appointed by the court, but the principle applied should be equally applicable to a receiver appointed out of court.

appointment continued to supply paper under the contracts, but subsequently repudiated the contracts. When an action was brought for payment of the price of the paper supplied after the appointment, it was held that the defendants could set off their unliquidated damages claim against the company for breach of contract.[308] The fact that the demands arose after the appointment of the receiver was not a sufficient reason for denying a set-off against the debenture-holders (or, as actually occurred in *Parsons*, against assignees from the receivers of the defendants' indebtedness for the price of the paper delivered). While the receiver in *Parsons* was appointed by the court rather than by the debenture-holders themselves, the principle nevertheless is the same.[309]

In the discussion above of the situations in which a set-off may be denied to a defendant in an action brought against him by a company in receivership for payment of a debt owing to the company, it is assumed that the value of the defendant's cross-demand against the company is less than the debt for which the charge to the debenture-holders constitutes a security. If the defendant's debt to the company is in fact more than sufficient to satisfy the company's indebtedness to the debenture-holders, the residue may be employed by the defendant in a set-off.[310]

It may be that a company in receivership goes into liquidation. If at the commencement of the winding-up the debenture-holders have *not* been paid in full, and the security took effect as a mortgage, any debts owing to the company and coming within the ambit of the security will still be the subject of an equitable assignment in favour of the debenture-holders. Since the debenture-holders rather than the company have the beneficial title to the debts, the mutual credit provision in the insolvency legislation will not be relevant in the liquidation,[311] and rights of set-off should continue to be determined by reference to the principles outlined above with respect to receiverships.[312] Nor should the result differ if a charge rather than a mortgage is in issue,[313] assuming that the stipulation for a charge is not interpreted as operating by way of assignment in any event.[314]

---

[308] When an equitable set-off is in issue based upon an inseparable connection, it is not necessary that both demands be liquidated. See e.g. *Sun Candies Pty. Ltd.* v. *Polites* [1939] VLR 132. Compare *W. Pope & Co. Pty. Ltd.* v. *Edward Souery & Co. Pty. Ltd.* [1983] WAR 117, in which a company in receivership was suing for the price of goods supplied to the defendant. It was held that the defendant could not set off a claim for unliquidated damages arising out of defects in an earlier consignment under a separate contract. In that case there was not a sufficiently close connection to give rise to an equitable set-off.

[309] See section 13.3.2 below.

[310] See Dixon J. in *Hiley* v. *Peoples Prudential Assurance Co.* (1938) 60 CLR 468, 497–8, citing *Lee & Chapman's Case* (1885) 30 Ch. D 216, 222, and section 7.6.2 above.

[311] See section 7.3 above.

[312] See e.g. *Handley Page Ltd.* v. *Commissioners of Customs and Excise and Rockwell Machine Tool Company Ltd.* [1970] 2 Lloyd's Rep. 459, and *Rendell* v. *Doors and Doors Ltd.* [1975] 2 NZLR 191.   [313] See section 7.6.4 above.

[314] See *In re ELS Ltd.* [1995] Ch. 11, 24–5.

If, however, the debenture-holders have been paid in full before the commencement of the liquidation, their beneficial interest in the debts owing to the company will have ceased. The company itself would be the beneficial owner of the debts, and so the insolvency set-off section should determine the existence of any right of set-off.[315] Alternatively, redemption of the security may occur *after* the liquidation, in which case the result may differ, depending on the circumstances.[316] Furthermore, there may possibly be a set-off under the insolvency legislation as between the company and a debtor even before the debenture-holders have been paid, to the extent that the debt owing to the company exceeds the company's secured liability to the debenture-holders, though this should not apply if there is any question as to the debtor's solvency.[317]

13.3.2 *Court-appointed receiver on the application of a secured creditor*

Receivers also may be appointed by the court. One situation considered later is an appointment by way of equitable execution,[318] although the court's power is not confined to that circumstance. The court in fact has a broad jurisdiction to appoint a receiver in all cases in which it appears to be just and convenient to do so.[319] This includes the appointment of a receiver and manager[320] of the company's business on the application of a secured creditor in order to protect the creditor's security. Court appointments on this ground are rare, given that secured creditors usually now reserve the right to appoint a receiver out of court. It may nevertheless occur if in a particular case the security document does not empower the creditor to appoint a receiver himself, or the validity of an appointment made by the creditor is in dispute.[321] Russell L.J. in *Robbie* v. *Witney*[322] said that it should not make any difference in relation to questions of set-off whether a receiver has been appointed out of court or whether he is court-appointed. In both cases, he said, the receiver and manager is merely a piece of administrative machinery designed to enforce a security. This requires an explanation. The incidents of the two forms of receivership in fact differ in an important respect. A receiver appointed by a creditor pursuant to a power conferred by a security is usually expressed to be the agent of the company, whereas a court-appointed receiver is the agent of neither

---

[315] See *Rendell* v. *Doors and Doors Ltd.* [1975] 2 NZLR 191, 202–3.
[316] See section 7.6.5 above.   [317] See section 7.6.2 above.
[318] See section 13.5 above.
[319] Supreme Court Act 1981, s. 37(1), and see also RSC Ord. 30.
[320] 'Receiver' is defined in the Supreme Court Rules as including a manager. See Ord. 1 r. 4.
[321] See generally Lightman and Moss, *The Law of Receivers of Companies* (2nd edn., 1994), 339–40.   [322] [1963] 1 WLR 1324, 1340.

the company nor the creditor on whose application he was appointed.[323] Any new contracts are made by him personally, in reliance on his right of indemnity from the company's assets.[324] The same result usually will follow when rights of set-off are in issue, not because of the appointment of the receiver as such, but rather because the debtor to the company will have notice of a fixed security attaching to his debts owing to the company, and once he has notice he cannot rely on subsequent events to diminish the rights of the creditor.[325] As an additional ground, the debtor cannot rely on debts which are incurred to him by a court-appointed receiver pursuant to contracts entered into with the receiver in his personal capacity, because there would be a lack of mutuality. On the other hand, contracts entered into by the company *before* the appointment remain the company's contracts, and any right of equitable set-off against a liability under the contract where there is a sufficiently close connection remain available to the debtor, even where the cross-claim accrued after notice of the security. This is the effect of the decision of the Privy Council in *Parsons* v. *Sovereign Bank of Canada*,[326] and is in accordance with generally accepted principles.[327]

There may, nevertheless, be one situation in which the different forms of receivership produce a different result. This appears from the decision of Jeffrey J. in the New South Wales Supreme Court in *West Street Properties Pty. Ltd* v. *Jamison*,[328] to which reference has already been made.[329] It will be recalled that in that case a company in receivership was the defendant in an action for payment of rent due pursuant to a lease entered into prior to crystallization of a floating security, though the liability to pay the rent in question did not arise until after crystallization. It was held that the company had a defence to the extent of a debt which was owing to it by the lessor and which came within the ambit of the security. While Jeffrey J. recognized that, if the action instead had been brought by the receiver against the lessor to recover the debt on behalf of the debenture holder, the lessor could not have set off the company's liability for subsequently accruing rent, he said that there was nothing inequitable in allowing the receiver a set-off in the converse situation in which the action was against the company for the rent. There was still mutuality at law, in that the company was liable for the rent and the company also had the legal title to the cross-debt, and therefore there was a right of set-off available to the company at law. Nor was there anything unconscionable in

---

[323] *Parsons* v. *Sovereign Bank of Canada* [1913] AC 160, 167.

[324] *Parsons* v. *Sovereign Bank of Canada* [1913] AC 160, 167. See also *Burt, Boulton, & Hayward* v. *Bull* [1895] 1 QB 276.   [325] See section 13.2.1 above.

[326] [1913] AC 160. See also the similar case of *Forster* v. *Nixon's Navigation Company* (1906) 23 TLR 138.   [327] See section 13.2.8 above.

[328] [1974] 2 NSWLR 435.   [329] See section 13.3.1 above.

allowing a set-off so as to justify equitable intervention if the debenture-holder had consented to the debt which was owned beneficially by it being employed in a set-off. While in *Jamison* the liability for rent arose out of a prior lease, Jeffrey J.'s analysis would appear to be equally applicable to the situation in which the company incurs a liability pursuant to a new transaction entered into by the receiver. The receiver in such a case would contract as agent for the company, notwithstanding that in some cases he may assume a personal liability as well.[330] Accordingly there would still be mutuality at law for the purpose of the Statutes of Set-off. This should not apply, however, when there is a court-appointed receiver. The receiver would not contract as agent of the company, but in his personal capacity. A receiver being sued for a debt on a contract made with him personally should not be able to bring into account a debt owing to the company. The demands would not be mutual at law or in equity.

13.4 TRUSTS

13.4.1 *Set-off between the trustee and the third party*

A trust is not a legal entity. When a trustee incurs a debt in that capacity, the trustee himself is personally liable. The creditor does not have direct recourse either to the trust assets[331] or to the beneficiaries. On the other hand, where the trust property includes a debt incurred in favour of the trustee, the trustee, though he has the legal title to sue, does not have the equitable title. Accordingly, there would not be mutuality in equity in relation to a debt incurred by a trustee and a cross-debt available to the trustee in his capacity as such against the creditor on the first-mentioned debt.[332] Consider, however, that a trustee has entered into a transaction with a third party out of which cross-demands accrue which are otherwise sufficiently closely connected to give rise to an equitable set-off. In such a case, given that equity has never insisted upon mutuality as a strict requirement of this form of set-off in any event,[333] the apparent lack of mutuality should not be a sufficient ground for denying a set-off to the third party. This indeed was the view of Giles J. in the New South Wales Supreme Court in *Murphy* v. *Zamonex Pty. Ltd.*[334] Nor did his Honour think that a different result would follow if the trustee had lost his right of

---

[330] See the Insolvency Act 1986, s. 44 in relation to administrative receivers.

[331] *Worrall* v. *Harford* (1802) 8 Ves. Jun. 4, 8; *In re Evans* (1887) 34 Ch. D 597, 600; *Jennings* v. *Mather* [1902] 1 KB 1, 5.

[332] Compare the doubt expressed in *Murphy* v. *Zamonex Pty. Ltd.* (1993) 31 NSWLR 439, 464 in relation to the situation in which the trustee incurred the debt in that capacity, as opposed to his personal capacity.   [333] See section 1.7.6 above.

[334] (1993) 31 NSWLR 439.

indemnity from the trust estate in respect of the liability, for example because of a breach of trust.[335] The equitable set-off was justified on the ground that the beneficiaries of a trust should not have the benefit of the transaction without also bearing the burden of the trustee's conduct.[336] Moreover, while in *Murphy* v. *Zamonex* there had been a change in trustee, Giles J. said that this did not affect the result. The new trustee took subject to equities, and so the defendants could set off their damages claim in the action brought by the new trustee.

The fact of a trust similarly should not affect the availability of a common law defence of abatement,[337] which applies in an action for the agreed price of goods sold with a warranty or of work to be performed according to a contract. If the goods are delivered in a defective condition or the work is improperly performed, the purchaser being sued for the price can defend himself by showing how much less the subject-matter of the action is worth by reason of the breach, and can obtain an abatement of the price accordingly. The rationale for the defence should still be applicable when either the purchaser or the vendor is a trustee.

What if the case is one of unrelated cross-debts, so that the question concerns the Statutes of Set-off or, in the event of a bankruptcy or liquidation, the insolvency set-off section? In the first place, if the trustee is indebted to the third party in his personal capacity as a result of a dealing unrelated to the trust, a set-off would not be permitted against a debt held on trust either under the insolvency set-off section[338] or the Statutes of Set-off,[339] unless in the case of the Statutes the principle of taking subject to equities applies.[340] Consider, however, that the trustee incurred the debt in the proper execution of the trust, so that he has a right of indemnity from the trust assets, and at the same time the trustee is a creditor of the third party in respect of a debt which is held on trust for the beneficiaries. In *Nelson* v. *Roberts*[341] an executor was also appointed receiver and manager of an estate. In his capacity as executor he had a claim against one Joseph Grimes. On the other hand, as receiver and manager he incurred a debt to Joseph Grimes. While different representative capacities admittedly were involved, in that the claim was held in the capacity of executor and the debt was incurred in the capacity of receiver and manager, they both related to the same estate. Nevertheless, when the defendant was sued for payment of the debt incurred as receiver and manager, Mathew and Wright JJ. held that he could not set off the debt owing to the estate under the Statutes,

---

[335] See below.
[336] (1993) 31 NSWLR 439, 465, 468.
[337] See section 1.10 above.
[338] See section 7.3 above.
[339] See section 7.4 above.
[340] See section 13.4.2 below.
[341] (1893) 69 LT 352. See also *Staniar* v. *Evans* (1886) 34 Ch. D 470, 476–7; *Rex* v. *Ray; ex parte Chapman* [1936] SASR 241, 249.

notwithstanding that he may have had a right of indemnity from the estate in respect of his indebtedness. It was still his personal liability. Mathew J. said that the same principle applies in the case of an executor, an agent, and a trustee. However, the issue of an indemnity from the estate was not satisfactorily dealt with[342] and, where it is clear in a particular case that the trustee has this right, in some cases the argument for a set-off under the Statutes would have merit. A trustee who properly incurs a liability in the execution of the trust is entitled to be indemnified from the trust assets held by him,[343] and for the purpose of enforcing the indemnity the trustee has a charge or lien over the assets.[344] This is not a mere right of retainer,[345] but rather it confers an equitable proprietary interest in those assets[346] which has priority over the interest of the beneficiaries.[347] Thus, in an appropriate case[348] the court may order a sale of trust property in order to satisfy the trustee's claim.[349] Where the trust assets include a debt owing to the estate, the charge ordinarily would extend to that asset. Furthermore, the right of indemnity exists *before* payment by the trustee. He is not obliged to pay the debt first,[350] so that the charge should also secure the trustee's claim against the fund in that circumstance.[351] Accordingly, when a trustee is sued by a third party for a debt properly

[342] Mathew J. commented that, 'It is clear that the debt of the defendant was a personal debt; it may be that the Court of Chancery will say that it was rightly incurred by him as receiver and manager of the estate of John Grimes, but as between himself and Joseph Grimes it was purely personal'. (1893) 69 LT 352.   [343] Trustee Act 1925, s. 30(2).

[344] *Stott* v. *Milne* (1884) 25 Ch. D 710; *In re Spurling's Will Trusts* [1966] 1 WLR 920, 930; *Octavo Investments Pty. Ltd.* v. *Knight* (1979) 144 CLR 360, 367.

[345] Nevertheless the right is sometimes discussed only in terms of retainer. See e.g. *Jennings* v. *Mather* [1901] 1 QB 108, 113–14, [1902] 1 KB 1, 9.

[346] *Octavo Investments Pty. Ltd.* v. *Knight* (1979) 144 CLR 360, 367, 369–70. See also *Re Byrne Australia Pty. Ltd.* [1981] 1 NSWLR 394, 398; *Re Suco Gold Pty. Ltd.* (1983) 33 SASR 99; *Murphy* v. *Zamonex Pty. Ltd.* (1993) 31 NSWLR 439, 464; *Re Matheson; ex parte Worrell* v. *Matheson* (1994) 49 FCR 454; Ford and Lee, *Principles of the Law of Trusts* (3rd edn., 1996), para. 14020. Compare the doubts expressed by McPherson J. in the Queensland Supreme Court in *Kemtron Industries Pty. Ltd.* v. *Commissioner of Stamp Duties* [1984] 1 Qd. R 576, 585.

[347] *Octavo Investments Pty. Ltd.* v. *Knight* (1979) 144 CLR 360, 367. Compare *Re Pumfrey* (1882) 22 Ch. D 255, 262, which was criticized in *Re Staff Benefits Pty. Ltd.* [1979] 1 NSWLR 207, 213–14.

[348] Compare *Darke* v. *Williamson* (1858) 25 Beav. 622, in which a sale would have had the effect of destroying the trust.

[349] See McPherson, 'The Insolvent Trading Trust' *Essays in Equity* (edited by Finn, 1985), 142, 149, referring to *Grissell* v. *Money* (1869) 38 LJ Ch. 312 and *In re Pumfrey* (1882) 22 Ch. D 255, 261–2.

[350] *St Thomas's Hospital* v. *Richardson* [1910] 1 KB 271, 276; *In re Blundell* (1889) 40 Ch. D 370, 376–7; *Savage* v. *Union Bank of Australia Ltd.* (1906) 3 CLR 1170, 1197; *In re Suco Gold Pty. Ltd.* (1983) 33 SALR 99, 104–5.

[351] In *St Thomas's Hospital* v. *Richardson* [1910] 1 KB 271, 276 Cozens Hardy M.R. said that, 'A's [the trustee's] right of indemnity exists before payment . . . In respect of this right of indemnity A has a first charge or lien upon the trust property . . .'. See also *Savage* v. *Union Bank of Australia Ltd.* (1906) 3 CLR 1170, 1197; *Re Matheson; ex parte Worrell* v. *Matheson* (1994) 49 FCR 454.

incurred in the execution of the trust, and at the same time the trustee as a result of his right of indemnity has a charge on a debt owing to the estate by the third party, the fact of the charge may be sufficient to bring about mutuality in equity[352] for the purpose of equity acting by analogy with the Statutes.[353] The same conclusion should apply in the case of insolvency set-off. However, this is subject to qualification. It assumes that the trustee has a right of indemnity. In a particular case the right may be limited by the trust instrument,[354] or it may be restricted to certain assets, as where a testator has authorized the executor to carry on a business though only by utilizing those assets.[355] Moreover, an executor or administrator of a deceased person who carries on the deceased's business other than for the purpose of its realization or winding-up may not be entitled to an indemnity at the expense of creditors of the deceased for debts incurred, unless those creditors had authorized the executor or administrator to carry it on.[356] Authority in the testator's will is not sufficient in this regard.[357] Further, the trustee may be in default or otherwise may have an obligation to contribute to the trust fund, so that the right to an indemnity out of the trust fund is subject to the rule in *Cherry* v. *Boultbee*.[358] In Australia it has been said that a breach of trust will only debar the trustee from indemnity if the breach is related to the subject matter of the indemnity.[359] However, the principle underlying *Cherry* v. *Boultbee*, that the person entitled to participate in the fund already has an asset of the fund in his hands in the form of the obligation to contribute, which should be appropriated in satisfaction of the right to participate,[360] would appear to be equally applicable when the breach is unrelated to the subject matter

---

[352] See section 7.6.4 above.   [353] See section 1.6 above.

[354] See Underhill and Hayton, *Law Relating to Trusts and Trustees* (14th edn., 1987), 700 and *RWG Management Ltd.* v. *Commissioner for Corporate Affairs* [1985] VR 385, 395, though compare McPherson, 'The Insolvent Trading Trust' *Essays in Equity* (edited by Finn, 1985), 142, 149–50.   [355] *Ex parte Garland* (1803) 10 Ves. Jun. 110.

[356] *Dowse* v. *Gorton* [1891] AC 190. Compare *In re Oxley* [1914] 1 Ch. 604, and *Vacuum Oil Co. Pty. Ltd.* v. *Wiltshire* (1945) 72 CLR 319.

[357] *Vacuum Oil Co. Pty. Ltd.* v. *Wiltshire* (1945) 72 CLR 319, 335.

[358] (1839) 4 My. & Cr. 442, discussed in Ch. 10. See in particular *In re Johnson* (1880) 15 Ch. D 548; *In re Evans* (1887) 34 Ch. D 597, 601–2; *In re British Power Traction and Lighting Co., Ltd.* [1910] 2 Ch. 470; *RWG Management Ltd.* v. *Commissioner for Corporate Affairs* [1985] VR 385, 397–9.

[359] *Re Staff Benefits Pty. Ltd.* [1979] 1 NSWLR 207, 214, and see also the comment by Giles J. in *Murphy* v. *Zamonex Pty. Ltd.* (1993) 31 NSWLR 439, 464 regarding a 'breach of trust related to the indemnity'.

[360] See in this context *In re British Power Traction and Lighting Co., Ltd.* [1910] 2 Ch. 470, 475. On this formulation of the principle (see section 10.1 above, and also the second formulation discussed in section 10.13 above) it is not accurate to say that the trustee loses or is deprived of his right of indemnity. Compare *Re Staff Benefits* [1979] 1 NSWLR 207, 214, and *Jacobs Law of Trusts in Australia* (5th edn, 1986), 586. Rather, he is required to satisfy it, or is regarded as having satisfied it, from a particular source.

of the indemnity.[361] Indeed, the contrary view does not sit comfortably with *In re Johnson*,[362] insofar as the right of indemnity in that case for debts incurred in running the Cambridge business was affected by the failure of the trustee to account for amounts in relation to the London business.

Where there are other trust creditors, an additional issue is whether the subrogation rights of those creditors may prevent mutuality in equity from arising. A creditor whose debt was properly incurred in the execution of the trust is entitled to be subrogated to the trustee's right of indemnity from the trust assets, as well as to the charge consequent upon that right,[363] so as to give the creditor an indirect claim against the assets. If there are a number of creditors, the right of subrogation is available for the benefit of all of them.[364] However, its application is limited.[365] A creditor may enforce the right if the estate is under the administration of the court,[366] or the trustee is bankrupt.[367] The judgment of Byrne J. in *Re Raybould*[368] suggests that the court in other circumstances may order that a trust creditor can claim directly against the trust estate,[369] although in that case the trustee had consented to the claim, and in any event for this to occur it would probably be a requirement that other trust creditors are not prejudiced.[370] This presumably would require that they be a party to the proceedings.[371] But if the trustee is solvent, so that judgment at law against him would not be fruitless, the traditional principle is that a trust creditor ordinarily will not be granted an order for the administration of the trust so as to allow enforcement of the right of subrogation.[372] In light of these

---

[361] See for example, the formulation of the principle in *Jennings* v. *Mather* [1902] 1 KB 1, 5, and *RWG Management Ltd* v. *Commissioner for Corporate Affairs* [1985] VR 385, 398.

[362] (1880) 15 Ch. D 548.

[363] *In re Johnson* (1880) 15 Ch. D 548, 552; *In re Blundell* (1890) 44 Ch. D 1, 11; *Vacuum Oil Co. Pty. Ltd.* v. *Wiltshire* (1945) 72 CLR 319, 335–6.

[364] See the discussion in McPherson, 'The Insolvent Trading Trust' *Essays in Equity* (edited by Finn, 1985), 142, 151.

[365] See Ford and Lee, *Principles of the Law of Trusts* (3rd edn., 1996), para. 14080.

[366] See e.g. *In re Evans* (1887) 34 Ch. D 597 and *In re Frith* [1902] 1 Ch. 342.

[367] *Octavo Investments iy. Ltd.* v. *Knight* (1979) 144 CLR 360, 367.

[368] [1900] 1 Ch. 199.

[369] See also *General Credits Ltd.* v. *Tawilla Pty Ltd.* [1984] 1 Qd. R 388, 390.

[370] *Jacobs' Law of Trusts in Australia* (5th edn., 1986), 593. It has been suggested that, in *Raybould* itself, the creditor seeking the order was the sole trust creditor. See McPherson, 'The Insolvent Trading Trust' *Essays in Equity* (edited by Finn, 1985), 142, 151. This is consistent with Byrne J.'s comment ([1900] 1 Ch. 199, 202) that the parties interested in defending the trust estate were before him.

[371] See *Jacobs' Law of Trusts in Australia* (5th edn., 1986), 593 and Mitchell, *The Law of Subrogation* (1994), 156.

[372] *Owen* v. *Delamere* (1872) LR 15 Eq. 134; *In re Morris* (1889) 23 LR Ir. 333. See also *Murphy* v. *Zamonex Pty. Ltd.* (1993) 31 NSWLR 439, 464. It is not necessary, however, that the trust creditor should pursue his common law claim against the trustee to judgment if the circumstances are such as to lead to the reasonable inference that a judgment would be fruitless. See *In re Wilson* [1942] VLR 177, 183.

principles, how would the trust creditors' right of subrogation affect the availability of a set-off to the third party? Trust creditors are not equitable assignees or chargees of the assets the subject of the trustee's right of indemnity,[373] and the better view is that the fact that there are other trust creditors apart from the third party generally would not prevent a set-off. Consider, however, that the trustee is bankrupt, or that the trust is being administered by the court. In these situations the right of subrogation may be enforced, though for the benefit of *all* creditors. If the third party as a trust creditor could look upon the charge that the trustee has over the particular trust asset represented by his liability to the trust as sufficient to bring about mutuality between that liability and the debt in respect of which he is a trust creditor, the third party would obtain an advantage over other trust creditors, and for this reason the indirect interest that other trust creditors have as a result of subrogation may well be regarded as sufficient to prevent mutuality in equity arising. The approach of the courts on the issue, however, is still uncertain.

Given that a trustee who incurs a debt in that capacity is personally liable, there should be mutuality as between that debt and a cross-debt owing by the creditor to the trustee in the trustee's personal capacity.[374]

13.4.2 *Taking subject to equities*

The third party may not have been aware that he was dealing with a person who was a trustee. Notwithstanding that the beneficiaries have the equitable title to a debt which accrues to the trustee as a result of the dealing, the beneficiaries in certain circumstances will take subject to equities available to the third party against the trustee on the same basis described above in the context of assignments.[375] This may apply whether or not the cross-debt owing by the trustee was incurred in his private capacity or in his capacity as trustee. The general principle applicable to taking subject to equities is that, when there are unconnected cross-debts, the debts must have arisen before the third party had notice of the trust,[376] though there is no such requirement when a substantive defence of equitable set-off is in issue.[377]

---

[373] McPherson, 'The Insolvent Trading Trust' *Essays in Equity* (edited by Finn, 1985), 142, 156; *Staniar* v. *Evans* (1886) 34 Ch. D 470, 477. Compare *Napier* v. *Hunter* [1993] AC 713, 736, 738 in relation to insurance subrogation.

[374] *Daniels* v. *Imperial Bank of Canada* (1914) 19 DLR 166. Compare section 11.12.8 above in relation to combination of bank accounts.

[375] See section 13.2 above.   [376] See section 13.2.4 above.

[377] See section 13.2.8 above.

13.4.3 *Receipt of trust money*

The application of the principle of taking subject to equities assumes that
the beneficiary's only right is to a beneficial interest in the debt held by the
trustee. Alternatively, a beneficiary may claim that another has knowingly
received trust money under circumstances where that money should not
have been paid to him by the trustee. The beneficiary may assert an
equitable tracing claim to recover the money. This is proprietary in nature,
and cannot be the subject of a set-off.[378] But even if the money cannot be
traced, and the beneficiary's claim instead is that the recipient has a
personal liability as a constructive trustee on the basis of knowing receipt
of trust property,[379] the recipient could not assert a set-off in respect of a
debt owing by the trustee from whom the money was received. The
principle that a beneficiary takes subject to equities available against
the trustee is based on the notion that there is mutuality at law as
between the debt held on trust and the cross-debt owing by the trustee, and
the question is whether it is unconscionable for the debtor to rely on this
defence at law given the trust.[380] However, when a recipient of trust money
has a personal liability as a constructive trustee to the beneficiary on the
basis of knowing receipt, there is not mutuality either at law or in equity in
relation to that liability and a debt owing by the trustee to the recipient.
This would also apply when the basis of the liability as a constructive
trustee is the knowing assistance in a breach of trust.[381] The question has
arisen in relation to combination of bank accounts, when a trustee
has deposited trust money into an account with a bank and the bank has
asserted that that account may be regarded as combined with an overdrawn
account kept by the trustee with the bank in the trustee's private capacity.
The cases in point were considered earlier.[382] It is only when the
beneficiary's claim is neither for an equitable tracing right nor a claim for
the imposition of personal liability as a constructive trustee, but rather for
an equitable interest in a debt owing to the trustee, that the principle of
taking subject to equities becomes relevant. In some cases this may in fact
be the position when trust money is paid by the trustee to a third party in
breach of trust under circumstances where the third party as a result is
indebted to the trustee. If the beneficiary had acquiesced in this, an

---

[378] See Ch. 6.
[379] For a discussion of the distinction between the proprietary and the personal claim, see
In re Montagu's Settlement [1987] 1 Ch. 264, 285. See generally *Snell's Principles of Equity*
(29th edn., 1990), 193–4 as to the circumstances in which a personal liability as a
constructive trustee may arise.
[380] See sections 7.4 and 13.2.1 above.
[381] See e.g. *Royal Brunei Airlines Sdn Bhd* v. *Tan* [1995] 3 All ER 97.
[382] See section 11.12 above.

equitable proprietary remedy may not be available to him, and nor may the third party have a personal liability to the beneficiary as a constructive trustee.[383]

13.4.4 *Set-off between a beneficiary and the third party*

When a debt accrues to a trustee in his capacity as such the debt belongs in equity to the beneficiaries, while a debt incurred by the trustee is his own personal liability. We have seen that the fact that the trustee has a charge over the trust assets to secure his right of indemnity may be sufficient in some cases to justify a set-off,[384] though the position is not settled. Moreover, this avenue would not be available when a beneficiary's claim against a trust creditor against which the trust creditor wishes to assert a set-off arose out of a dealing unrelated to the trust, so that it is not trust property over which the trustee has a charge. There may nevertheless be an alternative approach to the question of a set-off, based upon a right in the trustee to an indemnity from a beneficiary personally.

A sole beneficiary[385] who is *sui juris* and absolutely entitled ordinarily is personally liable to indemnify the trustee against debts properly incurred in the execution of the trust.[386] This also applies while the debt is still outstanding, and a third party who is a creditor of the trustee in respect of such a debt may be subrogated to this right of indemnity.[387] This opens the possibility of a set-off against the beneficiary's cross-claim against the trust creditor. However, the availability of a right of subrogation is probably subject to restrictions similar to those applicable in the case of a trustee's right of indemnity from the trust assets.[388] For example, the trustee's claim for an indemnity, and the third party's derivative right through subrogation, may be reduced to the extent that the trustee is in default to the

---

[383] See *Snell's Principles of Equity* (29th edn., 1990), 303 (referring to *Blake* v. *Gale* (1886) 32 Ch. D 571) in relation to tracing. Aquiescence is used in the sense described by Lord Cottenham in *Duke of Leeds* v. *Earl of Amherst* (1846) 2 Ph. 117, 123, that 'If a party, having a right, stands by and sees another dealing with the property in a manner inconsistent with that right, and makes no objection while the act is in progress, he cannot afterwards complain'. [384] See section 13.4.1 above.

[385] The principle should be equally applicable when there are a number of beneficiaries who between them are absolutely entitled and are *sui juris*. See Underhill and Hayton, *Law Relating to Trusts and Trustees* (14th edn., 1987), 699; *J. W. Broomhead (Vic) Pty. Ltd.* v. *J. W. Broomhead Pty. Ltd.* [1985] VR 891, 936–7.

[386] See e.g. *Hardoon* v. *Belilios* [1901] AC 118, and generally Underhill and Hayton, *Law Relating to Trusts and Trustees* (14th edn., 1987), 699, 708–9. However, the right to indemnity from the beneficiaries personally can be excluded by the trust instrument. See *Hardoon* v. *Belilios* (at 127); *RWG Management Ltd.* v. *Commissioner for Corporate Affairs* [1985] VR 385, 394. [387] *In re Richardson* [1911] 2 KB 705.

[388] See section 13.4.1 above. The view is expressed in Underhill and Hayton, *Law Relating to Trusts and Trustees* (14th edn., 1987), 709 that there should not be any distinction between the two rights of indemnity.

estate, and moreover, in order that a trust creditor may claim against a beneficiary on the basis of subrogation, it may be necessary that judgment at law against the trustee would be fruitless. In Australia, Ford and Lee[389] have suggested that a creditor who seeks the benefit of a trustee's right of indemnity against a beneficiary personally would have to make the trustee bankrupt, so that other creditors would also benefit. When a third party as a trust creditor is subrogated to the trustee's claim against a beneficiary, the trustee does not hold the claim on trust for the third party. This is apparent when one considers that, if the trustee becomes bankrupt, the benefit of the claim passes to his trustee in bankruptcy.[390] If it was trust property, this would not be the case. While the trustee in bankruptcy admittedly would be required to apply the proceeds received from the beneficiary in reduction only of the trust debts, as opposed to all debts provable in the trustee's bankruptcy,[391] the reason is that the trustee is not permitted to profit from the trust, which would occur if the proceeds of the indemnity were used to pay his personal creditors.[392] If there is more than one trust creditor, the proceeds received by the trustee should be divisible amongst all trust creditors,[393] and not just the particular creditor in respect of whose claim the indemnity was obtained. Insofar as the question of set-off is concerned, because the claim for an indemnity that the trustee has against the beneficiary arising from the liability incurred by the trustee to the third party is not held on trust for the third party, there is not mutuality in a strict sense as between that claim and the debt owing by the third party to the beneficiary, whether as a result of a dealing unrelated to the trust, or because the debt was incurred to the trustee and accordingly is held on trust for the beneficiary. Having said that, when there is an enforceable right of subrogation and there are no other trust creditors,[394] so that no one other than the third party will benefit in any event from proceeds received from the beneficiary, there is much to be said for the view that a set-off nevertheless should be permitted.

There is also the possibility of a set-off in the converse situation, of a debt owing by a third party to a trustee in that capacity and a cross-debt owing by the beneficiary to the third party on another account.[395] The

---

[389] Ford and Lee, *Principles of the Law of Trusts* (3rd edn., 1996), para. 14090.
[390] *In re Richardson* [1911] 2 KB 705, 715.
[391] As in *In re Richardson* [1911] 2 KB 705.
[392] *In re Richardson* [1911] 2 KB 705, 711; *In re Suco Gold Pty. Ltd.* (1983) 33 SASR 99 (esp. at 106–7); Ford, 'Trading Trusts and Creditors' Rights' (1981) 13 *Melbourne University Law Review* 1, 20.
[393] *Re Byrne Australia Pty. Ltd.* [1981] 1 NSWLR 394, 399; *In re Suco Gold Pty. Ltd.* (1983) 33 SASR 79, 109, 111; *Re ADM Franchise Pty. Ltd.* (1983) 7 ACLR 987, 988–9. Compare *Re Enhill Pty. Ltd.* [1983] VR 561.
[394] This appears to have been the case in *In re Richardson* [1911] 2 KB 705.
[395] *Bankes* v. *Jarvis* [1903] 1 KB 549, 552.

beneficiary is personally liable on his separate debt and at the same time may have a sufficient equitable interest in the debt held on trust so as to bring about mutuality in equity, and therefore to justify an equitable set-off by analogy with the Statutes.[396] For a set-off to occur, however, the beneficiary's interest in the trust should be such that he has an interest in possession in the debt as trust property, in the sense that he has a present right to claim the benefit of the debt.[397] This does not include a residuary legatee under a will or a person entitled under an intestacy where the administration of the estate has not been completed.[398] Prior to completion of the administration the legatee or the person does not have a beneficial interest in the assets of the trust, but only an equitable chose in action to have the estate properly administered.[399] An object of a discretionary trust is in a similar position.[400] Furthermore, the beneficiary must be the sole party beneficially interested in the debt, unless, if the debt in fact is held on trust for two or more beneficiaries, those beneficiaries are also jointly liable to the debtor. This is necessary in order to satisfy the requirement of mutuality. It has been suggested that a set-off will not be permitted unless the beneficiary's interest in the debt is clear and ascertained without inquiry.[401] The scope of this concept was considered earlier.[402]

A trustee who properly incurs costs and expenses in the administration of the trust is entitled to be indemnified from the trust assets held by him,[403] and for the purpose of enforcing the indemnity the trustee has a charge or lien over the assets.[404] This may include a debt held on trust by the trustee. While the charge may be thought to have the effect of destroying mutuality as between that debt and a cross-debt owing to the debtor by the beneficiary otherwise entitled under the trust to the benefit

---

[396] See section 1.6 above.
[397] See *Gartside* v. *IRC* [1968] AC 553, 607, and also section 7.5 above.
[398] *Bishop* v. *Church* (1748) 3 Atk. 691; *Ex parte Morier; in re Willis, Percival, & Co.* (1879) 12 Ch. D 491; *Phillips* v. *Howell* [1901] 2 Ch. 773.
[399] *Commissioner of Stamp Duties (Queensland)* v. *Livingston* [1965] AC 694, and see generally section 9.9.1 above. [400] *Gartside* v. *IRC* [1968] AC 553.
[401] Wood, *English and International Set-off* (1989), 779–80.
[402] See section 7.5 above.
[403] However, the right of indemnity is restricted when a testator has authorized the trustee to carry on a business only by utilizing a certain part of the estate. See *Ex parte Garland* (1803) 10 Ves. Jun. 110.
[404] *Stott* v. *Milne* (1884) 25 Ch. D 710; *In re Spurling's Will Trusts* [1966] 1 WLR 920, 930; *Octavo Investments Pty. Ltd.* v. *Knight* (1979) 144 CLR 360, 367. Compare the doubts expressed by McPherson J. in the Queensland Supreme Court in *Kemtron Industries Pty. Ltd.* v. *Commissioner of Stamp Duties* [1984] 1 Qd. R 576, 585 as to whether the trustee's right can properly be regarded as a charge in the nature of an encumbrance. Nevertheless his Honour conceded that the High Court of Australia held in *Octavo Investments* v. *Knight* that the right to be indemnified out of trust assets confers a proprietary interest in the trustee in those assets.

of the first-mentioned debt, the better view is that a set-off nevertheless may still occur as between those parties if the trustee's position, and that of other trust creditors who are subrogated to the trustee's right, is otherwise sufficiently secured.[405]

13.4.5 *Set-off between trustee and beneficiary*

There may be cross-claims between a trustee and a beneficiary, as, for example, when the trustee is entitled to an indemnity from the beneficiary personally and at the same time is liable to the beneficiary on another account. The availability of a set-off in such a case should be determined according to normal principles. The beneficiary's claim may be for payment of the trust fund itself. Issues of set-off in that context have already been considered.[406] Alternatively, the beneficiary's liability may not be to the trustee personally, but may take the form of an obligation to contribute to the trust fund. The question then is whether the rule in *Cherry* v. *Boultbee*[407] applies.

13.5 EXECUTION OF JUDGMENTS

13.5.1 *Introduction*

A creditor may have obtained judgment against the debtor and, not having been paid, is seeking to enforce the judgment against the debtor's assets. If one of the assets is a debt owing to the judgment debtor by a third party, and the judgment creditor obtains an order for the enforcement of the judgment against that debt, the question may arise whether the third party can set-off a cross-claim that he has against the judgment debtor. The principal method of enforcing a judgment by attaching a debt owing to the judgment debtor is a garnishee order, although a charging order and the appointment of a receiver by way of equitable execution may also be relevent. The effect of each of these is considered below.

13.5.2 *Garnishee orders*

The procedure for obtaining a garnishee order is set out in Order 49 of the RSC. Where a judgment creditor has obtained a judgment or order for payment of a sum of money amounting in value to at least £50, and another

---

[405] See section 7.6.2 above. This is consistent with comments by McPherson J. in Queensland in *Kemtron Industries Pty. Ltd.* v. *Commissioner of Stamp Duties* [1984] 1 Qd. R 576, 587.   [406] See Ch. 6.

[407] (1839) 4 My. & Cr. 442, discussed in Ch. 10.

person (the 'garnishee') is indebted to the judgment debtor, the court may order the garnishee to pay the judgment creditor the amount of any debt due or accruing due from the garnishee to the judgment debtor to the extent sufficient to satisfy the judgment. In the first instance the judgment creditor obtains an order nisi, which must be served personally on the garnishee. This is an order to show cause, and it specifies the time and the place for further consideration of the matter. The debt is attached in the hands of the garnishee as from the time of service of this order.[408] When the matter comes on for further consideration, including in relation to any dispute by the garnishee as to his liability, the order may be made absolute.

Attachment only relates to a debt which is due or accruing due. There is a considerable amount of case law as to what this encompasses, for which reference should be made to specialist texts on the subject. One thing that is clear, however, is that it is not confined to debts which are presently payable. A debt which is presently existing but not payable until a future day may be attached,[409] although the garnishee cannot be required to pay before the contract date.[410]

While it is generally agreed that service of a garnishee order does not operate as a transfer of the property in the debt,[411] there is a solid body of judicial opinion to the effect that it gives rise to an equitable charge.[412] However, the notion that there is a charge is not universally accepted,[413] and indeed it does not sit easily with the view that the holder of a floating security granted by a judgment debtor has priority over a judgment creditor with a garnishee order where crystallization occurred after the order absolute but before payment by the garnishee.[414] Where the

---

[408] RSC Ord. 49 r. 3(2).

[409] *Tapp* v. *Jones* (1875) LR 10 QB 591; *Webb* v. *Stenton* (1883) 11 QBD 518, 522–3; *O'Driscoll* v. *Manchester Insurance Committee* [1915] 3 KB 499, 516–517; *Joachimson* v. *Swiss Bank Corporation* [1921] 3 KB 110, 131.

[410] *Tapp* v. *Jones* (1875) LR 10 QB 591.

[411] *In re Combined Weighing and Advertising Machine Company* (1889) 43 Ch. D 99; *Norton* v. *Yates* [1906] 1 KB 112.

[412] *Emanuel* v. *Bridger* (1874) LR 9 QB 286, 291; *Galbraith* v. *Grimshaw and Baxter* [1910] 1 KB 339, 343 (decision affirmed [1910] AC 508); *Joachimson* v. *Swiss Bank Corporation* [1921] 3 KB 110, 131; *Plunkett* v. *Barclays Bank Ltd.* (1936) 52 TLR 353; *In re Caribbean Products (Yam Importers) Ltd.* [1966] 1 Ch. 331, 343, 350, 353; *Choice Investments Ltd.* v. *Jeromninon* [1981] 1 QB 149, 155 (C. of A.); *Deputy Federal Commissioner of Taxation* v. *Donnelly* (1989) 25 FCR 432, 456. In *In re Combined Weighing and Advertising Machine Company* (1889) 43 Ch. D 99, 104 Cotton L.J. described it as a lien.

[413] See Lightman and Moss, *The Law of Receivers of Companies* (2nd edn., 1994), 260–2, and Picarda, *The Law Relating to Receivers, Managers and Administrators* (2nd edn., 1990), 158. In *Hall* v. *Richards* (1961) 108 CLR 84, 92 Kitto J. said that a garnishee order does not give the judgment debtor any proprietary interest in the debt. See also Brennan J. in *Clyne* v. *Deputy Commissioner of Taxation* (1981) 150 CLR 1, 27.

[414] *Cairney* v. *Back* [1906] 2 KB 746.

garnishee has a substantive defence of equitable set-off available against the judgment debtor the nature of the judgment creditor's right as a result of the order should be immaterial. The judgment debtor's title to sue the garnishee is impeached,[415] and the judgment creditor cannot obtain a better title.[416] Similarly, the precise characterization of the nature of the right should not be crucial to the question whether a judgment creditor takes subject to a defence of set-off under the Statutes of Set-off in the case of mutual debts as between the judgment debtor and the garnishee. The relevant question in this regard is not so much what rights take priority under the law of set-off, but rather the circumstances in which a garnishee order absolute will be made. The Statutes of Set-off strictly have no application in garnishee proceedings. They provide a defence to an action at law for payment of a debt[417] whereas, when a garnishee order is made absolute, the judgment creditor may proceed directly to execution without the necessity of bringing a separate action on the order. If the judgment creditor brings an action when there is no necessity to do so, he runs the risk of having it stayed as an abuse of the process of the court.[418] The Rules of the Supreme Court provide that the court 'may' order the garnishee to pay the judgment creditor.[419] The making of a garnishee order is discretionary,[420] and the question is under what circumstances will the court make an order notwithstanding that the garnishee has a cross-claim against the judgment debtor. In fact, the principle which the courts have applied is analogous to that which governs assignments. In other words, the judgment creditor takes subject to equities available to the garnishee against the judgment debtor before service of the order nisi,[421] equities in this sense including rights of set-off, whether equitable or contractual or under the Statutes of Set-off, as discussed in the context of assignments.[422] Thus, when a cross-debt owing by the judgment debtor is in existence at the time that the order nisi is served on the garnishee, it is established that the judgment creditor takes subject to a right of set-off that the garnishee otherwise would have had in an action at law under the Statutes of Set-off,[423] even though a garnishee order generally does not result in an action.

---

[415] See Lord Cottenham in *Rawson* v. *Samuel* (1841) Cr. & Ph. 161, 179.
[416] *Hale* v. *Victoria Plumbing Co. Ltd.* [1966] 2 QB 746.
[417] See section 1.2.9 above.
[418] Compare *Pritchett* v. *English and Colonial Syndicate* [1899] 2 QB 428.
[419] RSC, Ord. 49 r. 1.   [420] *Martin* v. *Nadel* [1906] 2 KB 26.
[421] *Norton* v. *Yates* [1906] 1 KB 112, 121. See also *In re Stanhope Silkstone Collieries Company* (1879) 11 Ch. D 160.   [422] See section 13.2 above.
[423] *Tapp* v. *Jones* (1875) LR 10 QB 591, 593, 594. See also *Sampson* v. *Seaton and Beer Railway Company* (1874) LR 10 QB 28, 30; *Bishop* v. *Woinarski* (1875) 1 VLR (L) 31; *Rymill* v. *The Wandsworth District Board* (1883) Cab. & El. 92. Compare *Fitt* v. *Bryant* (1883) Cab. & El. 194, in which the debt attached to the knowledge of the garnishee was held by the judgment debtor on trust for the judgment creditor.

The garnishee does not, however, take subject to a set-off where the cross-debt arose after service of the order nisi.[424] Indeed, in the case of an assignment, the courts have said that this also applies where the cross-debt accruing after notice had its source in a prior contract.[425] But notwithstanding the position applicable in the context of assignments, there is much to be said for the view that the court in the exercise of its discretion should not make a garnishee order absolute where the judgment debtor became indebted to the garnishee after service of the order nisi but before the order absolute if the debt had its source in a prior transaction. Certainly this should be the case where there is an agreement for a set-off between the parties.[426] Nor should it be an objection to a substantive equitable set-off that the cross-demand arose after notice.[427]

It may be that the cross-debt is in existence at the date of service of the order nisi, but that it is not payable until a future date. Given that the judgment creditor may proceed directly to execution against the garnishee, the better view is that, when a garnishee asserts that there is a set-off available to him under the Statutes of Set-off against the attached debt, the cross-debt generally must not only be in existence at the date of the order nisi, but it should also be payable when the order absolute is made or, if the attached debt itself is not payable at that date, it should become payable before the attached debt becomes payable.

In *Stumore* v. *Campbell & Co.*[428] the judgment creditor sought to attach money which the garnishee held on trust for the judgment debtor. A sum held on trust is an equitable debt which may be attached.[429] As a general rule, however, it cannot be the subject of a set-off,[430] and accordingly the garnishee was required to account for the trust money without deduction in respect of a debt owing to him by the judgment debtor.

The Rules of the Supreme Court provide machinery for determining a dispute by the garnishee as to his liability to the judgment debtor.[431] However, there is no machinery for determining the state of the account as between the garnishee and the judgment creditor, and accordingly a garnishee cannot set off a debt owing to him by the judgment creditor,[432] at least where the garnishee has not yet proceeded to judgment. The court has power to set off judgments and orders as part of its inherent

---

[424] *Tapp* v. *Jones* (1875) LR 10 QB 591, 593.

[425] See section 13.2.4 above.

[426] See *Rymill* v. *Wandsworth District Board* (1883) Cab. & El. 92, though this appears to have been regarded as a case in which there was a debt the amount of which was not ascertained at the relevant date. See also section 13.2.4 above.

[427] See section 13.2.8 above.   [428] [1892] 1 QB 314.

[429] *Webb* v. *Stenton* (1883) 11 QBD 518, 526.   [430] See Ch. 6.

[431] RSC, Ord. 49, r. 5.

[432] *Sampson* v. *Seaton and Beer Railway Company* (1874) LR 10 QB 28.

jurisdiction,[433] and if the garnishee already has a judgment or an order (for example, for costs) against the judgment creditor, that may be set off against the amount payable under the garnishee order.[434]

If a bankruptcy petition is pending against the judgment debtor, or the debtor has been adjudged bankrupt, the court may stay execution or other legal process against the property or person of the debtor,[435] while after the bankruptcy order a creditor cannot commence proceedings against the person or property of the bankrupt without the consent of the court. But even where garnishee proceedings were commenced prior to the bankruptcy and execution is not stayed, bankruptcy will defeat an uncompleted attachment. The Insolvency Act 1986, section 346 provides that, where a creditor of a person who is adjudged bankrupt has, before the commencement of the bankruptcy, attached a debt[436] due to that person from a third party, the creditor is not entitled as against the official receiver or trustee of the bankrupt's estate to retain the benefit of the attachment[437] unless it was completed before the commencement of the bankruptcy.[437a] Similar principles apply in the case of a company liquidation.[438] The Act stipulates that an attachment is completed by receipt of the debt,[439] by which is meant receipt of the proceeds.[440]

Section 346 is not confined to attachment of debts, but extends to other forms of execution against the goods or land of the bankrupt. A creditor is not entitled to retain the benefit of the execution as against the trustee in bankruptcy unless the execution was completed before the bankruptcy. The corresponding provision in Australia differs from this in that it captures executions which occurred 6 months before the bankruptcy. Where a creditor has issued execution against the property of a debtor within 6 months before the presentation of a petition against the debtor, and the debtor becomes bankrupt, the creditor must pay to the trustee an amount equal to the amount received by the creditor as a result

---

[433] See section 1.4.3 above.

[434] See *Walters* v. *D. Miles-Griffiths, Piercy & Co.* (1964) 108 Sol. Jo. 561 in relation to the solicitors' costs of the appeal.   [435] Insolvency Act 1986, s. 285(1).

[436] Attachment is not defined in the insolvency legislation, though it was said in relation to the equivalent provision in the Bankruptcy Act 1914 (s. 40) that it is not a term of art. See *In re Lupkovics* [1954] 1 WLR 1234, 1241. In Australia the Federal Court held in *Commissioner of Taxation* v. *Donnelly* (1989) 25 FCR 432 that attachment in the context of s. 118 of the Bankruptcy Act (which in its terms is similar to s. 346 of the English Insolvency Act) means attachment by curial order, and does not include a notice under the Income Tax Assessment Act 1936 (Cth.), s. 218.

[437] For a discussion of the meaning of this expression, see *In re Caribbean Products (Yam Importers) Ltd.* [1966] 1 Ch. 331.

[437a] See the Insolvency Act 1986, s. 278.

[438] Insolvency Act 1986, ss. 126, 130 and 183. 'Commencement of the winding up' is defined for the purpose of s. 183 in s. 129.

[439] Insolvency Act 1986, s. 346(5)(c), and, for companies, s. 183(3)(b).

[440] *George* v. *Tompson's Trustee* [1949] 1 Ch. 322.

of the execution. The creditor may then prove in the bankruptcy for his debt as an unsecured creditor as if the execution had not taken place.[441] The Corporations Law has an equivalent section in the context of company liquidations.[442] The application of this provision produced an unjust result in the peculiar circumstances that arose in *Trevor* v. *Findlay*.[443] The owner of a farm, A, mortgaged it to B to secure a debt owing to B. In addition, B leased the farm from A. B breached the lease, as a result of which the lease was terminated and A sued B for damages. After A recovered judgment a writ of *fi. fa.* was issued against B's asset in the form of the mortgage. The mortgage was offered for sale by the sheriff at a public auction, and A was the successful bidder. It was then agreed that the price payable by A to B should be set off against the amount of the judgment debt owing by B, and that only the balance should be payable to B. While this seemed a happy result for A, some 2 months later B went into insolvent liquidation, whereupon the liquidator challenged the arrangement. It was held that A had received an amount as a result of an execution issued within 6 months of B's liquidation, the reference to 'the amount (if any) received' in the provision in question being held to include satisfaction of a debt by way of set-off. As a result, A had to pay to the liquidator the amount of B's liability received in this manner, with a resulting right of proof in the liquidation for the amount paid. This was a particularly harsh result since, if A had not issued execution, the cross-demands would have been set off in the liquidation. However, there is nothing in the legislation giving the judge a discretion in the matter. Indeed, if there was a second debt owing by B to A, it would appear that that could not have been set off against A's obligation to account to the liquidator. The demands in such a case would not have been mutual, since the amount payable to the liquidator would have been payable to him in his own right as liquidator, and not because it was payable to B before the liquidation.[444] On the other hand, if A had a separate liability to B, a set-off may have occurred between that debt and the provable debt that A would have obtained after paying the liquidator.

13.5.3 *Charging order*

A charging order may be made in favour of a judgment creditor under the Charging Orders Act 1979, although its application to debts is limited. The only debts to which it extends are government debentures, or debentures issued by a body corporate that is either incorporated in

---

[441] Bankruptcy Act 1966 (Cth.), s. 118.   [442] Corporations Law, s. 569.
[443] (1991) 4 ACSR 777.
[444] See, in a different context, Fletcher Moulton L.J. in *In re A Debtor; ex parte Peak Hill Goldfield, Ltd.* [1909] 1 KB 430, 437.

England or Wales or has the register for the debentures in England or Wales.[445] When a charging order is made it operates as a charge securing payment of any money due or to become due under the judgment.[446] It has a like effect and is enforceable in the same manner as an equitable charge.[447] It should be subject to the same principles as a garnishee order in relation to questions of set-off.

13.5.4 *Appointment of a receiver by way of equitable execution*

A receiver may be appointed by way of equitable execution in circumstances where execution at common law for some reason cannot be had,[448] and included amongst the property which the receiver is authorized to receive may be a debt owing to the judgment debtor by a third party.[449] The use of the term 'execution' in this context in fact is something of a misnomer. The obtaining of a receivership order in truth is not execution, but rather equitable relief on the ground that there is no adequate remedy by execution at law.[450] The appointment by itself ordinarily does not create a charge or other security interest in favour of the judgment creditor, unless in a particular case the order in its terms has specifically charged the third party not to deal with the debt except by payment to the judgment creditor.[451] Rather, it operates as an injunction to restrain the judgment debtor from receiving the proceeds of any debt the subject of the order, and from dealing with the debt to the prejudice of the judgment creditor.[452] In addition, it would prevent the judgment debtor from using the debt as a set-off against a separate debt that he owes to the third party.[453]

Insofar as the third party is concerned, Greer J. in *Giles* v. *Kruyer*[454] said that, if the third party was not a party to the order, his rights and duties are

---

[445] Charging Orders Act 1979, s. 2(2), 'stock' being defined in s. 6(1) as including debentures.   [446] See s. 1(1).   [447] See s. 3(4).

[448] *In re Shepherd* (1889) 43 Ch. D 131, 135–6, 137, 138.

[449] For an illustration of circumstances held sufficient to justify the appointment of a receiver in relation to debts owing to the judgment debtor, see *Goldschmidt* v. *Oberrheinische Metallwerke* [1906] 1 KB 373.

[450] *In re Shepherd* (1889) 43 Ch. D 131, 135, 137, 138; *Ideal Bedding Company Ltd.* v. *Holland* [1907] 2 Ch. 157, 169.

[451] See Swinfen Eady M.R. in *In re Pearce* [1919] 1 KB 354, 363, referring to Lord Esher in *In re Potts; ex parte Taylor* [1893] 1 QB 648, 659. See also *In re Whitehart* (1972) 116 Sol. Jo. 75.

[452] *Tyrrell* v. *Painton* [1895] 1 QB 202, 206; *In re Marquis of Anglesey* [1903] 2 Ch. 727, 730–1; *Ideal Bedding Company, Ltd.* v. *Holland* [1907] 2 Ch. 157, 169–70; *Stevens* v. *Hutchinson* [1953] 1 Ch. 299, 305. See also *In re Potts; ex parte Taylor* [1893] 1 QB 648.

[453] See Farwell L.J. in *In re A Debtor; ex parte Peak Hill Goldfield, Ltd.* [1909] 1 KB 430, 437.

[454] [1921] 3 KB 23, referring to *In re Potts; ex parte Taylor* [1893] 1 QB 648.

not affected and, while the order has the consequence as against the judgment debtor that the debtor cannot give a discharge, it does not prevent the third party himself from paying the debtor. However, this view has been criticized by commentators.[455] If the third party is aware of the order, and therefore of the injunction restraining the judgment debtor from receiving payment, Kerr suggests that he would be in contempt if he nevertheless pays the debtor and that he would not obtain a valid discharge.[456] On that basis, the third party similarly as a general rule should not be entitled to a set-off in respect of a cross-claim that he has against the judgment debtor, although a set-off should be permitted if the demands are sufficiently closely connected so as to impeach the judgment debtor's title by way of equitable set-off, or if a set-off under the Statutes of Set-off is in issue and the cross-debt against the judgment debtor accrued before the third party had notice of the order.

What if the judgment debtor becomes bankrupt before payment is received from the third party? Because the appointment generally does not give rise to a charge, the judgment creditor is not a secured creditor in the insolvency. Accordingly, he does not have priority over other creditors, and the proceeds of the debt will form part of the estate available for distribution generally.[457] This does not have as a consequence, however, that the third party will then be entitled to a set-off in the bankruptcy in respect of a cross-claim that he has against the judgment debtor.[458] While after the bankruptcy the debt is payable to the trustee in bankruptcy, the problem is that, before the bankruptcy, it was not payable to the judgment debtor himself. In *In re A Debtor; ex parte Peak Hill Goldfield, Ltd.*[459] Fletcher Moulton L.J. expressed the relevant principle in terms that 'Moneys which under a bankruptcy became payable to the trustee . . . because they were payable to the debtor, come prima facie within the mutual credits clause, but not if they are moneys which, upon bankruptcy, become payable to the trustee in his right as trustee and not by virtue of their being payable to the debtor'. This seems a harsh result.

---

[455] See *Kerr on Receivers and Administrators* (17th edn., 1989), 135 and, in Australia, O'Donovan, *Company Receivers and Managers* (2nd edn., looseleaf), para. 20.480.

[456] *Kerr on Receivers and Administrators* (17th edn., 1989), 135, referring to *Eastern Trust Company* v. *McKenzie, Mann & Co., Ltd.* [1915] AC 750. As Wood has noted (*English and International Set-off* (1989), 963), *Eckman* v. *Midland Bank Ltd.* [1973] 1 QB 519, a case on sequestration, is consistent with this view.

[457] *In re Potts; ex parte Taylor* [1893] 1 QB 648; *Ideal Bedding Company, Ltd.* v. *Holland* [1907] 2 Ch. 157, 169.

[458] *In re A Debtor; ex parte Peak Hill Goldfield, Ltd.* [1909] 1 KB 430.

[459] [1909] 1 KB 430, 437.

13.5.5 *Notices under section 218 of the Income Tax Assessment Act in Australia*

In Australia, section 218 of the Income Tax Assessment Act 1936 provides that, where an amount is due from a taxpayer in respect of tax, the Commissioner may require a third person from whom any money is due or accruing or may become due to the taxpayer to pay to the Commissioner, either forthwith upon the money becoming due or at a later date specified in the notice after the money has become due, so much of the money as is sufficient to pay the tax liability.[460] A question which has yet to be determined by the courts is whether the Commissioner takes subject to a right of set-off available to the third party against the taxpayer. Certainly this should be the case when a substantive defence of equitable set-off is in issue. The taxpayer's title to sue the third party is impeached, and the Commissioner cannot have a better title. However, what about the procedural defence of set-off under the Statutes of Set-off, in those jurisdictions in which the defence conferred by the Statutes is still relevant?[461] Section 218 applies where an amount is 'due' from the third party to the taxpayer, which in this context has been interpreted as meaning payable.[462] If an amount is payable by the third party, section 218 prescribes that it must be paid to the Commissioner in accordance with the notice. One view is that the availability of a set-off under the Statutes does not mean that a debt owing to the plaintiff is not payable. It is payable, though there is a procedural defence to an action at law to enforce payment. However, this is unlikely to be adopted. A notice under section 218 results in a charge in favour of the Commissioner over a debt owing to the taxpayer which is the subject of the notice,[463] and it is regarded as having an effect similar to a garnishee order.[464] The better view is that the Commissioner accordingly takes subject to set-offs by reference to principles analogous to those applicable to chargees[465] and judgment creditors.[466] 'Due' should be interpreted as importing the concept that the taxpayer should be able to obtain judgment against the third party for payment. On the other hand, unless an equitable set-off is in issue, the third party should not be entitled to set up a cross-demand that arises after the notice becomes binding upon him.

---

[460] Similar provisions are found in the Sales Tax Assessment Act (No. 1) 1930 (Cth.), s. 38 and the Child Support (Registration and Collection) Act 1988 (Cth.), s. 72A.

[461] See section 1.12 above.

[462] *Clyne* v. *Deputy Commissioner of Taxation* (1981) 150 CLR 1.

[463] *Commissioner of Taxation* v. *Donnelly* (1989) 25 FCR 432; *Commissioner of Taxation* v. *Government Insurance Office of New South Wales* (1993) 45 FCR 284.

[464] See Mason J. in *Clyne* v. *Deputy Commissioner of Taxation* (1981) 150 CLR 1, 19. See also *Commissioner of Taxation* v. *Donnelly* (1989) 25 FCR 432, 442, 456.

[465] See sections 7.6.4. and 13.3.1 above.   [466] See section 13.5.2 above.

13.6 SUBROGATION[467]

It was suggested earlier that a person who has an assignment merely of the proceeds of a debt should be in a different position to an assignee of the debt itself as regards set-off.[468] Unless a substantive defence of equitable set-off is in issue,[469] when a debt is assigned the debtor cannot rely on rights of set-off that arise in his favour against the assignor after he has notice of the assignment, whereas an assignee merely of the proceeds should take subject to a defence whenever it arises, notwithstanding that this will have the effect that nothing will be received to which the assignment can attach. A similar issue arises in relation to insurance subrogation. An insurer that has indemnified its insured is subrogated to any claim possessed by the insured against a third party who is responsible for the loss. This entitles the insurer to use the insured's name in order to sue the third party, and also to claim any money paid to the insured by the third party in reduction of the loss. It is generally accepted that the insurer has an equitable proprietary interest in any money that is indeed recovered.[470] But what about the right of action itself? Lord Goff of Chieveley and Lord Browne-Wilkinson in *Napier* v. *Hunter*[471] declined to express concluded views on whether subrogation gives the insurer a proprietary interest in the insured's claim, though the tenor of their judgments suggests that they thought that it does. Lord Templeman, however, was not as reticent.[472] In his view the insurer has an equitable proprietary interest in the claim to the extent necessary to recoup the amount paid to the insured. On this basis, the principles applicable to an assignee of a debt in relation to set-off should also apply to a subrogated insurer.

This would also appear to be the case in other areas of subrogation.[473] For example, *Jenner* v. *Morris*[474] concerned a person who made loans to another's deserted wife for the purpose of purchasing necessaries. While a person who actually supplied necessaries to a deserted wife could sue the husband at common law, the common law did not recognize a similar right in a person who merely lent money for the purpose of acquiring them. However, it was held in *Jenner* v. *Morris* that the person advancing the money for this purpose was entitled to be subrogated to the claim that

---

[467] See also section 7.3.3 above.
[468] See section 13.2.17 above.
[469] See section 13.2.8 above.
[470] *Napier* v. *Hunter* [1993] AC 713.
[471] [1993] AC 713, 745, 752–753.
[472] [1993] AC 713, 736, 738.
[473] Compare, however, a trust creditor's right to be subrogated to the trustee's claim for an indemnity from the trust assets, considered in section 13.4.1 above.
[474] (1860) 1 Dr. & Sm. 218, affirmed (1861) 3 De G F & J 45.

the supplier would have had against the husband, and further that this could be set off against a judgment debt owing by him to the husband. The fact that this set-off was permitted suggests that the person was regarded as having an equitable proprietary interest in the claim itself as a result of the right of subrogation, and indeed Lord Campbell L.C. said that it may be regarded as constituting an equitable assignment.[475] A similar comment may be made in relation to the judgment of Powell J. in the New South Wales Supreme Court in *A. E. Goodwin Ltd.* v. *A. G. Healing Ltd.*[476] in the context of a surety's right of subrogation. Powell J. seems to have assumed that a surety's right of subrogation may bring about mutuality so as to allow a set-off in respect of the principal debtor's debt to which the surety is subrogated and a separate debt owing by the surety himself to the debtor, which once again suggests that it was thought to confer an interest in the creditor's claim.

[475] (1861) 3 De G F & J 45, 52. [476] (1979) 7 ACLR 481, 488.

14

Sureties

14.1 INTRODUCTION

This chapter is concerned with contracts of suretyship, and the availability of rights of set-off as between a creditor, the debtor, and a guarantor of the debt. The main issue is whether the guarantor on being sued by the creditor on the contract of guarantee may raise as a defence to the action a right of set-off that would have been available to the principal debtor as against the creditor.[1] This differs from the assignment cases discussed in Chapter 13. In the event of an assignment of a chose in action the question is whether the debtor may assert a set-off available to him against the assignor in an action brought against him by a third party assignee. In the suretyship cases, however, it is the third party surety who is endeavouring to obtain the benefit of a set-off arising out of dealings between the principal debtor and creditor.

14.2 PRINCIPAL'S RIGHT TO INSIST ON A SET-OFF AVAILABLE TO THE PRINCIPAL

If a principal debtor has a cross-claim available as a set-off against the guaranteed debt, equitable considerations dictate that the creditor should not be able to avoid the set-off as against the debtor by resorting instead to the guarantee. The debtor will have to indemnify the surety and, while the debtor should still be entitled to recover from the creditor on the cross-claim, the debtor nevertheless will have lost the benefit of the set-off. The debtor should be entitled to orders restraining the creditor's action against the surety and giving effect to the set-off. This was the substance of the order made by Lord Eldon in the analogous case of *Ex parte Hanson*,[2] in which a creditor sued joint debtors on a bond under circumstances where

---

[1] Compare the exceptional fact situation in *R.* v. *Shaw* (1901) 27 VLR 70 (fidelity policy), in which the issue was not set-off as such but rather whether the guaranteed debt had been reduced by payment. In *Allen* v. *Kemble* (1848) 6 Moore 314 it was held that a surety could avail himself of a law of a foreign country by which the principal debt was regarded as having been extinguished by the cross-demand.
[2] (1811) 18 Ves. Jun. 232, affirming (1806) 12 Ves. Jun. 346.

one of the debtors had joined in only as surety, and the creditor was separately indebted to the party principally liable. A set-off was allowed notwithstanding that the joint liability on the bond and the principal's separate cross-claim were not mutual. The creditor in that case was bankrupt, and the action was brought by assignees in bankruptcy. However, Lord Eldon's analysis did not turn on any peculiarity of insolvency set-off.[3] Rather, he applied the general principle that,[4] 'the joint debt was nothing more than a security for a separate debt; and upon equitable considerations a creditor, who has a joint security for a separate debt, cannot resort to that security without allowing what he has received on the separate account . . .'. The set-off in issue was based upon 'equitable considerations'. Because of the lack of mutuality it is apparent that it was not a set-off of mutual debts under the bankruptcy legislation. On another occasion judgment had been obtained at law against two persons, one of whom had agreed to indemnify the other, and the indemnifying party had a cross-claim against the judgment creditor. Sir Lancelot Shadwell V.C. ordered that the judgment debt should be set off against the indemnifier's separate claim. In doing so he recognized that there was an absence of mutuality in relation to the joint liability and the separate demand, and accordingly no right of set-off at law.[6]

While neither of these cases concerned an action against a guarantor on a separate contract of guarantee, the same principle should apply. The question then is whether, if the debtor himself fails to take the point, the surety is entitled to defend the creditor's action against him on the basis of the debtor's set-off.

14.3 GUARANTOR'S RIGHT TO INSIST ON A SET-OFF AVAILABLE TO THE GUARANTOR

While the principal debtor is entitled on equitable grounds to insist that the creditor not avoid a set-off available to the principal by proceeding against a guarantor, a similar equity does not arise in the converse situation in which the creditor is indebted to the guarantor. The creditor is not obliged to sue the guarantor so as to give effect to the set-off, but can look instead to the principal for payment.[7] If on the other hand the guarantor

---

[3] Compare however the discussion by Lord Erskine in earlier proceedings (1806) 12 Ves. Jun. 346, 348.   [4] (1811) 18 Ves. Jun. 232, 233–4.

[5] See also *Ex parte Hippens* (1826) 2 Gl. & J 93.

[6] *Hamp* v. *Jones* (1840) 9 LJ Ch. 258.

[7] *Lord* v. *Direct Acceptance Corporation Ltd.* (1993) 32 NSWLR 362, 369, and see also *Ex parte Burton, Franco and Corea; in re Kensington* (1812) 1 Rose 320 and *Ex parte Banes; re The Royal British Bank* (1857) 28 LTOS 296 (discussed in section 8.3 above).

contracted in terms that he was liable as a principal debtor, and the creditor is bankrupt or is a company in liquidation, there may be an automatic set-off under the insolvency set-off section, in which case the creditor's trustee in bankruptcy or liquidator could not avoid this result by commencing proceedings against the debtor.[8]

14.4 SURETY'S RIGHT TO RELY ON THE PRINCIPAL'S SET-OFF

14.4.1 *Insolvency set-off and set-off agreements*

A surety is entitled to the benefit of an agreement between the principal debtor and the creditor that cross-demands between those parties are to be set off, since this operates as a payment.[9] Further, if the principal debtor is bankrupt or is a company in liquidation, the surety should be able to assert a set-off arising under the set-off section in the insolvency legislation as between the debtor and the creditor.[10] On the basis of the automatic extinction theory of insolvency set-off which was approved by the House of Lords in *Stein* v. *Blake*,[11] it would be difficult to argue otherwise.[12] The guaranteed debt is entinguished to the extent of the set-off, which should have a corresponding effect on the guarantor's liability. Nor, if the demands have been automatically extinguished by a set-off taking effect on the date of the bankruptcy or liquidation, should it be necessary for the surety to join the debtor as a party to the action brought against him by the creditor.[13]

---

[8] *M. S. Fashions Ltd.* v. *Bank of Credit and Commerce International S.A.* [1993] Ch. 425, discussed in sections 2.12.1 and 8.3 above.

[9] See *The Maistros* [1984] 1 Lloyd's Rep. 646, and also *Cheetham* v. *Crook* (1825) M'Cle. & Yo. 307.

[10] *Wreckair Pty. Ltd.* v. *Emerson* [1992] 1 Qd. R 700. This was also the view of Wood J. in the New South Wales Supreme Court in *Tooth & Co.* v. *Rosier* unreported, 7 June 1985. Compare *National Mutual Royal Bank Ltd.* v. *Ginges* unreported, Brownie J., New South Wales Supreme Court, 15 March 1991, in which the insolvency set-off section was held not to be applicable. In *Westco Motors (Distributors) Pty. Ltd.* v. *Palmer* [1979] 2 NSWLR 93 the principal debtor was in liquidation. Rogers J. in rejecting the surety's claim for a set-off held that the cross-demands between the principal and the creditor were not sufficiently connected to give rise to an equitable set-off, though no consideration was given to the insolvency set-off section. See also *Re Kleiss*, Federal Court of Australia, Drummond J., 18 January 1996. Compare also *Alcoy and Gandia Railway and Harbour Co. Ltd.* v. *Greenhill* (1897) 76 LT 542, 553 and *Cellulose Products Pty. Ltd.* v. *Truda* (1970) 92 WN (NSW) 561, 585, in each of which it was accepted that a surety could rely on rights of set-off available as between a surety and an insolvent principal debtor, though there was no discussion as to whether this extended to insolvency set-off.

[11] [1995] 2 All ER 961, discussed in section 2.12.1 above.

[12] In *National Mutual Royal Bank Ltd.* v. *Ginges* unreported, New South Wales Supreme Court, 15 March 1991, Brownie J. held that a clause in a guarantee, to the effect that the liability of the guarantor was not to be affected by any act matter or thing which but for the clause might release the guarantor, was not applicable when a set-off occurred automatically on the date of liquidation. [13] See section 14.4.4 below.

Where the principal debtor owes two debts to the creditor, one of which is guaranteed and the other is not, and the creditor is separately liable to the debtor, a set-off under the insolvency legislation presumably would take effect rateably as between the two debts.[14]

14.4.2 *The three approaches*

The position is still uncertain, however, in relation to the availability of defences of equitable set-off, common law abatement, and set-off under the Statutes of Set-off. In this regard there appear to be three different views. One view, which is favoured by a number of text writers,[15] is that the surety may invoke an equitable set-off available to the debtor arising out of a sufficiently close connection with the guaranteed debt, but not a defence of set-off under the Statutes of Set-off. This is sometimes justified on the basis of a comment by Willes J. in *Bechervaise* v. *Lewis*,[16] that 'the plea is a special plea by a surety, of a set-off by the principal, arising out of the same transaction out of which the liability of the surety on the note arose'. The second (and the preferred) approach is that the surety can defend himself on the basis of any defence of set-off available to the debtor, provided that the debtor is a party to the action. This is consistent with a passage in Halsbury,[17] which was referred to with evident approval by the Court of Appeal in *Hyundai Shipbuilding and Heavy Industries Co. Ltd.* v. *Pournaras*.[18] The third view, which has been favoured by courts in Victoria[19] and New South Wales,[20] as well as by Finlay L.J. in *Wilson* v.

[14] This solution is suggested by *In re Unit 2 Windows Ltd.* [1985] 1 WLR 1383, discussed in section 2.17 above. This would not apply, however, in relation to the Statutes of Set-off. See section 14.4.5 below.

[15] Wood, *English and International Set-off* (1989), 641, 645; Phillips and O'Donovan, *The Modern Contract of Guarantee* (2nd edn., 1992), 469, 471–2. See also *Paget's Law of Banking* (10th edn., 1989), 607.   [16] (1872) LR 7 CP 372, 377.

[17] *Halsbury's Laws of England* (4th edn., 1978) Vol. 20, 102 para. 190 stated that 'On being sued by the creditor for payment of the debt guaranteed, a surety may avail himself of any right to set off or counterclaim which the principal debtor possesses against the creditor'. Note, however, the slightly different formulation in the 1993 Reissue (at 143 para. 225) in terms of a set-off or counterclaim which could be set up in reduction of the guaranteed debt.

[18] [1978] 2 Lloyd's Rep. 502, 508. See also *Diebel* v. *Stratford Improvement Co.* (1917) 33 DLR 296, 301.

[19] *Indrisie* v. *General Credits Ltd.* [1985] VR 251. The High Court refused special leave to appeal from the decision, though it is not clear whether this was because of a view that a set-off available to the principal debtor can never be invoked by the surety, or whether it was because the principal debtor was not a party to the action, or whether it was simply on the ground that the demands in any event were not sufficiently closely connected to give rise to an equitable set-off. Indeed, it may have been thought that an equitable set-off in any event is not a sufficient ground to prevent a mortgagee from exercising security rights unless some compensatory form of security is provided. See the discussion of *Inglis* v. *Commonwealth Trading Bank of Australia* (1972) 126 CLR 161 in section 1.7.13 above.

[20] *Cellulose Products Pty. Ltd.* v. *Truda* (1970) 92 WN (NSW) 561; *Covino* v. *Bandag Manufacturing Pty. Ltd.* [1983] 1 NSWLR 237, 240–1.

Mitchell,[21] is that the surety in fact cannot defend himself on the basis of the principal debtor's set-off, though the rigour of this approach has been said to be ameliorated in two respects. An exception has been recognized when the debtor is bankrupt or is a company in liquidation, because in such a case it is said that the creditor might recover in full against the surety and the latter could only receive a dividend from the debtor,[22] although it may also be explained on the ground that the insolvency set-off section usually would apply,[23] in which case a set-off would have occurred automatically in any event.[24] Further, while this third approach generally denies the surety a defence, it is said that the surety nevertheless may achieve a similar result by a procedural means. The leading modern authority on this approach is the judgment of Isaacs J. in New South Wales in *Cellulose Products Pty. Ltd.* v. *Truda*,[25] in which his Honour stated the position in the following terms:

This review of the cases lends no support to the submission that a surety when sued is entitled to set up in equity or at law as an equitable plea any cross action for unliquidated damages which the debtor may have against the creditor in respect of the transaction, the performance of which the guarantor had entered upon his guarantee; that is, in the absence of the debtor being before the court in the proceeding so as to be bound by verdict and judgments. This of course does not mean that the guarantor is without remedy; when he is sued he has a right immediately to join the debtor as a third party and claim complete indemnity from him. The debtor has then a right to join the plaintiff as a fourth party, claiming damages for breach of warranty and so obtain indemnity either in whole or in part. All the actions would be heard together, the rights of all parties determined and appropriate set-offs made after verdict, and if there be any surplus of damages over and above that which is required to meet the guarantee, the debtor will have recovered that from the creditor who, in the result, will get no more than that to which he would be justly entitled.

---

[21] [1939] 2 KB 869, 871. 'There is here a cross-claim for damages, and this cannot be prayed in aid by a surety against the claim on the guarantee. Even if my view is wrong as to this, it certainly could not be prayed in aid without bringing in the principal debtor whose claim it was'.

[22] *Cellulose Products Pty. Ltd.* v. *Truda* (1970) 92 WN (NSW) 561, 585 (referring to *Alcoy and Gandia Railway and Harbour Company Ltd.* v. *Greenhill* (1897) 76 LT 542, 553). See also *National Westminster Bank plc* v. *Skelton* [1993] 1 WLR 72, 79.

[23] Unless an equitable set-off is available in circumstances where insolvency set-off does not apply, for example because of lack of mutuality. See sections 1.7.6 and 2.4 above.

[24] See section 14.4.1 above.

[25] (1970) 92 WN (NSW) 561, 588. In *National Westminster Bank plc* v. *Skelton* [1993] 1 WLR 72, 79 Slade L.J. said that he found the reasoning of Isaacs J. impressive, though he declined to express a concluded view on the subject, given the Court of Appeal's apparent acceptance in *Hyundai* v. *Pournaras* of the principle as stated in Halsbury to the effect that the surety can rely on the debtor's right of set-off.

While Isaacs J. referred generically to cross-actions for unliquidated damages, the case itself was concerned with the common law defence of abatement, and it is evident that his statement of the position was intended to encompass the availability of that defence to the debtor. It would also appear that he had in mind equitable set-off.[26]

Isaacs J. referred to an exception where the debtor is before the court, though it appears that he had in mind in that case the procedure he described of joining the principal as a party and setting off the judgments. However, that procedure may not be as advantageous a course of action as a defence when the question of costs comes to be considered. Further, it may only become apparent after judgment that the debtor is insolvent, so that it is too late to apply an exception relating to insolvency.[27] It may also be that the debt and the guarantee have been assigned, and the assignee is suing, in which case it is difficult to see how the procedure of setting off judgments could apply. Moreover, when the debtor has available to him a substantive defence of equitable set-off, the approach suggested by Isaacs J. could have the additional result that the benefit arising from the substantive nature of the defence may be lost to the debtor. For example, the debtor's cross-claim may be unenforceable as a result of the expiration of a limitation period, though this will not prevent the debtor relying on it as a defence of equitable set-off if it is sufficiently closely connected with the debt owing to the creditor.[28] But if the creditor instead could sue a guarantor who could not invoke the debtor's defence and, after the surety has claimed an indemnity from the debtor, the debtor sought to enforce the cross-claim against the creditor, the creditor could assert the expiration of the limitation period as a defence. On Isaacs J.'s approach, the debtor would have to take steps to protect his position in this circumstance, by applying for orders restraining the creditor's action against the surety and giving effect to the set-off, on the basis referred to earlier.[29]

14.4.3 *Equitable set-off and common law abatement*

What is the position, then, in the case of an unliquidated damages claim available to the debtor as an equitable set-off or, when it arises out of a breach of warranty under a contract for the sale of goods or for the

[26] See in particular (1970) 92 WN (NSW) 561, 575. See also *Indrisie* v. *General Credits Ltd.* [1985] VR 251. Compare, however, *Langford Concrete Pty. Ltd.* v. *Finlay* [1978] 1 NSWLR 14, 18, referred to in section 14.4.3 below.

[27] While Isaacs J. in *Cellulose Products* (1970) 92 WN (NSW) 561, 585 recognized an exception where the principal debtor was in liquidation (see above), *quaere* whether it was intended to extend to insolvency generally, without a formal bankruptcy or liquidation. Compare Slade L.J. in *National Westminster Bank* v. *Skelton* [1993] 1 WLR 72, 79.

[28] See section 1.7.4 above.   [29] See section 14.2 above.

performance of work, as a common law defence of abatement? The cases go both ways. The authorities which suggest that the surety cannot rely on the debtor's defence have already been referred to in the context of the third approach.[30] On the other hand,[31] in *Oastler* v. *Pound*[32] Blackburn J. accepted that the surety in that case could have relied on any defence of abatement that the debtor had, though it was held that the circumstances were not such as to give rise to the defence. This view of the availability of the defence to the surety seems to have been regarded as correct by the Court of Appeal in *Hyundai Shipbuilding & Heavy Industries Co. Ltd.* v. *Pournaras*,[33] and it was also the effect of the decision of James J. in New South Wales in *Electricity Meter Manufacturing Co. Ltd.* v. *D'Ombrain*.[34] Moreover, there have been judgments in New South Wales since *Cellulose Products* which suggest this position.[35] In *Langford Concrete Pty. Ltd.* v. *Finlay*[36] the New South Wales Court of Appeal referred to Isaacs J.'s judgment as supporting a proposition that a guarantor cannot rely on the debtor's set-off if the debtor is not a party to the proceedings,[37] which implies that the surety can invoke the defence if the debtor is a party.[38]

---

[30] See section 14.4.2 above.

[31] In addition to the cases referred to below, see *Diebel* v. *Stratford Improvement Co.* (1917) 33 DLR 296, 301, and *Re Kleiss*, Federal Court of Australia, Drummond J., 18 January 1996. *Murphy* v. *Glass* (1869) LR 2 PC 408, a case which is also often cited as support for the surety's right to have recourse to the benefit of the set-off, possibly may be explained on an alternative basis, that the debt secured by the bills of exchange was regarded as already having been reduced so that a possible set-off of cross-demands was not in issue. This appears to have been the view of the Victorian Supreme Court, whose decision was affirmed on appeal by the Privy Council. See Isaacs J. in *Cellulose Products Pty. Ltd.* v. *Truda* (1970) 92 WN (NSW) 561, 580–2.　　　　　　　　　　　　　　　　　　　[32] (1863) 7 LT 852.

[33] [1978] 2 Lloyd's Rep. 502. In *The Aliakmon Progress* [1978] 2 Lloyd's Rep. 499, which was decided on the same day as *Hyundai* v. *Pournaras*, it seems to have been assumed that an equitable set-off available to the charterer would have provided a defence to the guarantor, although it was held that the circumstances were not such as to give rise to an equitable set-off.

[34] (1927) 44 WN (NSW) 131. The decision in this case nevertheless was criticized by Isaacs J. in *Cellulose Products Pty. Ltd.* v. *Truda* (1970) 92 WN (NSW) 561, 582–3. To the extent that the debtor was not a party to the action in *Electricity Meter* v. *D'Ombrain*, the criticism would appear to have been justified.

[35] In addition to the following, see the observation of Hutley J.A. in *Covino* v. *Bandag Manufacturing Pty. Ltd.* [1983] 1 NSWLR 237, 238 regarding an 'equitable counterclaim'.

[36] [1978] 1 NSWLR 14.

[37] [1978] 1 NSWLR 14, 18, 19. This would not, however, appear to be what Isaacs J. had in mind. See section 14.4.2 above.

[38] However, this was not the basis upon which *Langford Concrete* was decided. Rather, the ground for the decision was that the guarantee in its terms was formulated so that the guarantor could take advantage of the debtor's cross-claim. The guarantee was expressed to apply to all money payable by the debtor. The court said that this was not a guarantee to pay the price, or the price without deduction, but rather to pay only what the debtor itself could have been compelled to pay, which allowed a deduction to the surety in respect of a deduction that the debtor could have claimed by reason of defective work. *Langford Concrete* should be compared to *Westco Motors (Distributors) Pty. Ltd.* v. *Palmer* [1979] 2 NSWLR 93. The guarantee in that case related to amounts which were due and payable for goods

Similarly, Wood J. in an application for summary judgment expressed a preliminary view to this effect in relation to equitable set-off.[39]

Bechervaise v. *Lewis*[40] may also be an example of the defence. The plaintiff and a third party, one Rowe, were in partnership. A number of debts were due to them as partners, and the plaintiff sold to Rowe his interest in the debts. As security for the price the plaintiff was given a joint and several promissory note made by Rowe and the defendant, the defendant joining in only as a surety for Rowe. The plaintiff sued the defendant on the note, whereupon the defendant pleaded a defence on equitable grounds that the plaintiff was indebted to Rowe as a result of receiving the proceeds of some of the debts in question, and that the plaintiff accordingly could not have recovered from Rowe. The judgment of the Court of Common Pleas[41] was delivered by Willes J., who described the plea 'as a special plea by a surety, of a set-off by the principal'.[42] He said that:[43]

Thus we have a creditor who is equally liable to the principal as the principal to him, and against whom the principal has a good defence in law and equity, and a surety who is entitled in equity to call upon the principal to exonerate him. In this state of things, we are bound to conclude that the surety has a defence in equity against the creditor . . .

The form of set-off that was regarded as being in issue between Rowe and the plaintiff is not entirely clear.[44] While the argument of counsel for the plaintiff centred on the right of set-off available at law under the Statutes of Set-off in the case of mutual debts, Willes J. emphasized in his judgment that the set-off arose out of the same transaction out of which the liability of the surety on the note arose,[45] in which case it may have been regarded as an equitable set-off arising out of a sufficiently close connection between the demands. There is, nevertheless, another view of the case, and that is that it was not concerned with set-off at all. In *Cellulose Products*[46] Isaacs J. said that it was part of the arrangement in *Bechervaise* v. *Lewis* that the plaintiff was to collect the debts, and that

---

supplied. The debtor's cross-claim did not relate to goods supplied, but rather was for damages for breach of the Trade Practices Act (Cth.). Accordingly *Langford Concrete* was distinguished on the ground that, as a matter of construction, the debtor's cross-demand in *Westco* was not intended to reduce the guarantor's liability.

[39] *Tooth & Co.* v. *Rosier* unreported, 7 June 1985, though note Giles J.'s comment in relation to that case in *AWA Ltd.* v. *Exicom Australia Pty. Ltd.* (1990) 19 NSWLR 705, 714.
[40] (1872) LR 7 CP 372.   [41] Willes, Keating, Montague Smith, and Brett JJ.
[42] (1872) LR 7 CP 372, 377.   [43] (1872) LR 7 CP 372, 377.
[44] While Willes J. referred during argument to equitable set-off, that could be explained on the ground that there was a set-off at law under the Statutes of Set-off as between the creditor and the principal which could be invoked on equitable grounds by the surety.
[45] (1872) LR 7 CP 372, 377.   [46] (1970) 92 WN (NSW) 561, 583–4. 586.

the proceeds received by the plaintiff had the effect of reducing the liability of Rowe which the defendant had guaranteed. However, this is not the way in which the case proceeded. The report does not state that the plaintiff was intended to collect payment, and moreover counsel argued the case on the basis of set-off. Nor does there appear to be anything in the judgment which supports Isaacs J.'s analysis. On the contrary, Willes J. commented that 'in our law set-off is not regarded as an extinction of the debt between the parties', and that 'we have a creditor who is equally liable to the principal as the principal to him'.[47] This assumes that there were subsisting cross-debts, which would not have been the case if the receipt of the proceeds by the plaintiff by itself had the effect of reducing the debt.

However *Bechervaise* v. *Lewis* is regarded, it is difficult to see any convincing reason why the surety should not be able to assert the defence,[48] and the better view is that he is entitled to do so, provided that the debtor is a party to the proceedings. The surety's defence is on equitable grounds, based upon the right that the surety has in equity to be exonerated by the principal debtor.[49] We have seen that the principal himself has a right in equity to require the creditor to give effect to the set-off rather than proceeding against the surety,[50] and the surety's right to be exonerated in this regard may be characterized as a right in turn to require the debtor to insist on this. It overrides the right that the debtor otherwise would have had to elect to waive the defence and prosecute the cross-claim against the creditor in a separate action.[51] It is sometimes raised as an objection to the set-off that it would involve a transference of the principal's claim in order to meet the surety's liability.[52] However, this is

---

[47] (1872) LR 7 CP 372, 377.

[48] *Williston on Contracts* (3rd edn., 1967) Vol. 10, 799 para. 1251 sets out five objections to allowing the defence, which are reproduced from an earlier edition in *Cellulose Products* (1970) 92 WN (NSW) 561, 575. The first and the second are considered below. In relation to the third, Isaacs J. in *Cellulose Products* (at 573) doubted, correctly, whether the plea would succeed. The fifth is cured by requiring joinder of the debtor (see section 14.4.4 below). Insofar as the fourth is concerned, regarding a number of sureties who are severally liable, this is more likely to arise when a set-off of unrelated debts under the Statutes of Set-off is in issue, and is considered in that context below. In addition, the objection raised in Wood, *English and International Set-off* (1989), 636, 643, that the principal debtor as an alternative to equitable set-off may be entitled to rescind the guaranteed contract altogether because of the breach giving rise to the cross-claim, should not be a reason for denying a guarantor's right to invoke the defence generally. The debtor should retain the right to rescind, and if he does exercise it the guarantor would be benefited given that the guaranteed obligation will have fallen away.

[49] *Bechervaise* v. *Lewis* (1872) LR 7 CP 372, 377; *Alcoy and Gandia Railway and Harbour Co. Ltd.* v. *Greenhill* (1897) 76 LT 542, 553. [50] See section 14.2 above.

[51] Compare the second objection in *Williston on Contracts* (3rd edn., 1967) Vol. 10, 799 para. 1251. The equivalent passage in an earlier edition is referred to in *Cellulose Products Pty. Ltd.* v. *Truda* (1970) 92 WN (NSW) 561, 575.

[52] *Indrisie* v. *General Credits Ltd.* [1985] VR 251, 254, and also the first objection referred to in *Cellulose Products Pty. Ltd.* v. *Truda* (1970) 92 WN (NSW) 561, 572, 575.

not the case. The surety is not seeking to employ the principal's claim against the creditor in a set-off against the surety's own liability on the contract of guarantee. Rather, the surety's argument is that the principal himself has a defence to the creditor's claim, and because of the right of exoneration the availability of the defence to the debtor in turn should give rise to a defence on equitable grounds to the surety.

14.4.4 *Joinder of the principal*

A noticeable feature of *Bechervaise* v. *Lewis* is that the principal debtor was not a party to the proceedings. This is curious, because the attitude of courts of equity usually is that all parties materially interested in the subject of a suit should be made parties to the suit.[53] The principal is the party who has the legal right to sue the creditor on the cross-claim, and therefore he should be a party so that he may be bound by any judgment for a set-off. The creditor would then be protected against a subsequent claim by the debtor.[54] This is the position that ordinarily should apply.[55] Indeed, it would be difficult to argue against this conclusion if the source of the surety's right of exoneration in this situation is the right that the principal himself has to insist that he obtain the benefit of a set-off available to him against the guaranteed debt.[56] While the third party procedure would be available, the surety in any event should be entitled to have the debtor joined as a defendant, since the debtor's presence would be necessary to enable the surety to set up a defence to the creditor's action.[57] When a creditor is applying for summary judgment against the surety, leave to defend on the basis of the debtor's defence should be conditional upon joinder occurring.[58]

---

[53] See *Daniell's Chancery Practice* (8th edn., 1914) Vol. 1, 147.

[54] See *Daniell's Chancery Practice* (8th edn., 1914) Vol. 1, 151. Similarly, an equitable assignee of a chose in action is required to join the assignor as a party to the suit against the debtor. See *Performing Right Society, Ltd.* v. *London Theatre of Varieties, Ltd.* [1924] AC 1, 14.

[55] *Halsbury's Laws of England* (4th edn. Reissue, 1993) Vol. 20, 143–4 para. 225. See also *Wilson* v. *Mitchell* [1939] 2 KB 869, 831; *Cellulose Products Pty. Ltd.* v. *Truda* (1970) 92 WN (NSW) 561, 588; *Indrisie* v. *General Credits Ltd.* [1985] VR 251, 254; *Covino* v. *Bandag Manufacturing Pty. Ltd.* [1983] 1 NSWLR 237, 241. Compare *Electricity Meter Manufacturing Company Ltd.* v. *D'Ombrain* (1927) 44 WN (NSW) 131 (criticized in *Cellulose* (at 582–3)), and *Re Kleiss*, Federal Court of Australia, Drummond J., 18 January 1996 (bankruptcy notice). When a creditor suing for a debt has joined both the principal debtor and the surety as defendants, both defendants may be granted leave to defend on the basis of a possible right of set-off available to the debtor. See *Petersville Ltd.* v. *Rosgrae Distributors Pty. Ltd.* (1975) 11 SASR 433.   [56] See section 14.4.3 above.

[57] *Amon* v. *Raphael Tuck & Sons Ltd.* [1956] 1 QB 357, 386.

[58] Phillips and O'Donovan, *The Modern Law of Guarantee* (2nd edn., 1992), 469. *Tooth & Co.* v. *Rosier* unreported, Wood J., New South Wales Supreme Court, 7 June 1985 involved an application for summary judgment and no such condition was placed on the surety, though

However there are two situations in which, it has been said, the debtor need not be a party. The first arises when the debtor is bankrupt or is a company in liquidation,[59] which is understandable in light of the automatic theory of insolvency set-off that received the approval of the House of Lords in *Stein* v. *Blake*.[60] If the cross-demands were automatically extinguished to the extent of the set-off upon the occurrence of the bankruptcy or liquidation, the debtor's trustee in bankrupt or liquidator could no longer sue the creditor on the cross-demand to that extent in any event.[61] The second situation is described in terms of a set-off which operates directly to reduce the guaranteed debt.[62] It is not entirely clear what this is intended to encompass, since neither an equitable set-off nor a common law defence of abatement as such has the effect of extinguishing the debt.[63] It may include,[64] however, a set-off agreement between the debtor and the creditor which operates as a form of payment,[65] in which case, like any defence of payment, the surety would not be required to join the debtor as a party.[66]

14.4.5 *Statutes of Set-off*

Some commentators take the view that, while a surety may be able to invoke the debtor's equitable set-off as a defence to an action by the creditor, a similar right is not available when the debtor's set-off arises

---

as Phillips and O'Donovan have noted (at 469), that was a case in which the principal debtor was in liquidation, which is a recognized exception to the requirement of joinder of the debtor. See below.

[59] *Langford Concrete Pty. Ltd.* v. *Finlay* [1978] 1 NSWLR 14. See also *Westco Motors (Distributors) Pty. Ltd.* v. *Palmer* [1979] 2 NSWLR 93, 97; *Tooth & Co. Ltd.* v. *Rosier* unreported, Wood J., New South Wales Supreme Court, 7 June 1985. This also appears to have been the case in *Alcoy and Gandia Railway and Harbour Co. Ltd.* v. *Greenhill* (1897) 76 LT 542, the principal debtor being Murrietas Ltd. which was not represented (though compare the discussion of the case in *Cellulose Products* (at 585)). Compare *Sun Alliance Pensions Life & Investments Services Ltd.* v. *RJL* [1991] 2 Lloyd's Rep. 410, 418.

[60] [1995] 2 All ER 961 (see section 2.12 above). Compare the explanation in *Langford Concrete Pty. Ltd.* v. *Finlay* [1978] 1 NSWLR 14, 19, which is difficult to follow.

[61] Of course, the trustee in bankruptcy or liquidator of the debtor could still sue for the amount by which the cross-demand exceeds the debt set off.

[62] *Halsbury's Laws of England* (4th edn. Reissue, 1993) Vol. 20, 143–4 para. 225. See also *Sun Alliance Pensions Life & Investments Services Ltd.* v. *RJL* [1991] 2 Lloyd's Rep. 410, 416–417.

[63] See sections 1.7.4 (equitable set-off) and 1.10 (abatement) above, and also *Langford Concrete Pty. Ltd.* v. *Finlay* [1978] 1 NSWLR 14, 18.

[64] Presumably it would also include a case such as *Murphy* v. *Glass* (1869) LR 2 PC 408, as explained in *Cellulose Products Pty. Ltd.* v. *Truda* (1970) 92 WN (NSW) 561, 580–2.

[65] See e.g. *The Maistros* [1984] 1 Lloyd's Rep. 646.

[66] Alternatively, the exception may refer to a case such as *Murphy* v. *Glass* (1869) LR 2 PC 408, as explained by Isaacs J. in *Cellulose Products* (1970) 92 WN (NSW) 561, 580–2.

under the Statutes of Set-off.[67] However, there is no compelling reason why the defences should be treated differently. Set-off under the Statutes admittedly differs from equitable set-off in that it is a procedural rather than a substantive defence,[68] though, since the right of the surety to invoke the debtor's defence of equitable set-off is not based upon the substantive nature of that defence, the fact that set-off under the Statutes is procedural should not preclude the surety from relying on it.[69] Nor is it a convincing argument that the debtor may owe other debts to the creditor which he would have preferred to set off against the cross-debt owing by the creditor,[70] since the surety's right of exoneration should override this. Further, *Harrison* v. *Nettleship*[71] is not authority against this view,[72] given that the surety's unsuccessful argument for a set-off in that case was based upon cross-debts which *at one time during the course of their dealings* were owing by the creditor to the debtor. A right of set-off under the Statutes is a procedural defence which does not bring about an automatic extinction of the debts in question. A surety could only have a defence to the extent of a defence that is still open to the debtor at the time of the creditor's action.

The argument in favour of the surety's right to rely on the defence is consistent with the broad statement in Halsbury,[73] which was referred to with evident approval by the Court of Appeal in *Hyundai* v. *Pournaras*,[74] that 'On being sued by the creditor for payment of the debt guaranteed, a surety may avail himself of any right to set off or counterclaim which the principal debtor possesses against the creditor'. There was no limitation expressed on the types of set-off that could be invoked.[75] Further, Lord Eldon's judgment in *Ex parte Hanson*[76] suggests that a principal debtor with a right of set-off is entitled on equitable grounds to insist that the creditor should look to him rather than the surety, because otherwise the debtor would lose the benefit of the set-off, and the surety as a result of

---

[67] Wood, *English and International Set-off* (1989), 645; Phillips and O'Donovan, *The Modern Contract of Guarantee* (2nd edn., 1992), 471–2. Comments by Drummond J. in the Federal Court of Australia in *Re Kleiss*, 18 January 1996, also supports this view.

[68] See section 1.2.9 above, and compare, for equitable set-off, section 1.7.4 above.

[69] Compare *York City and County Banking Company* v. *Bainbridge* (1881) 43 LT 732 in relation to the current account, assuming that the defendant was indeed a surety.

[70] See Steyn, 'Guarantees: The Co-extensiveness Principle' (1974) 90 *Law Quarterly Review* 246, 263.   [71] (1833) 2 My. & K 423.

[72] Compare Wood, *English and International Set-off* (1989), 645–6.

[73] *Halsbury's Laws of England* (4th edn., 1978), 102 para. 190. A substantially similar passage appears in the 1993 Reissue (at 143, para. 225).

[74] [1978] 2 Lloyd's Rep. 502, 508. See also *Diebel* v. *Stratford Improvement Co.* (1917) 33 DLR 296, 301.

[75] Nevertheless, the suggestion that the surety can set up a mere counterclaim available to the principal against the creditor should be regarded as doubtful. See section 14.4.6 below.

his right to be exonerated by the debtor[77] should be able to require that this occurs.[78] This also appears to have been Story's view, because he referred to *Ex parte Hanson* as authority for the proposition that, if one of two joint debtors is only a surety for the other, he may in equity set off against the joint debt a separate debt owing to the principal by the creditor.[79] If indeed the surety can rely on the debtor's defence under the Statutes, there is no reason in principle why it should be limited to the case of a cross-debt arising out of the same transaction as the guaranteed debt.[80] On the other hand, for the same reason that it would be necessary in the case of equitable set-off,[81] the debtor should be made a party to the proceedings.

Williston has raised as an objection to the recognition of the defence that there may be a number of sureties severally liable,[82] although this circumstance should not prevent the general application of the principle. If the sureties are jointly and severally liable for the same debt, an order for a set-off in an action against one surety would give rise to a payment to the creditor to the extent of the set-off, which should provide a defence to other sureties as well. Alternatively, a number of sureties each may be severally liable for distinct parts of the same debt, or there may be separate guarantees in place in relation to separate debts owing by the principal to the creditor. Since the right of a surety to rely on the principal's right of set-off is based on equitable grounds, the maxim that quality is equity may apply in relation to sureties who are the subject of an action at the time when the issue arises, so that each may be entitled to a defence to the extent of a proportionate part of the cross-debt owing to the debtor. But what if a particular surety is not the subject of a present action? Because

---

[76] (1811) 18 Ves. Jun. 232, discussed in section 14.2 above.

[77] *Bechervaise* v. *Lewis* (1872) LR 7 CP 372, 377.

[78] See the explanation of the defence in section 14.4.3 above.

[79] 'So, if one of the joint debtors is only a surety for the other, he may, in Equity, set off the separate debt due to his principal from the creditor; for in such a case, the joint debt is nothing more than a security for the separate debt of the principal; and, upon equitable considerations, a creditor who has a joint security for a separate debt, cannot resort to that security, without allowing what he has received on the separate account for which the other was a security'. *Story's Equity Jurisprudence* (6th edn., 1853) Vol. 2, 931 para. 1437.

[80] Compare *Paget's Law of Banking* (10th edn., 1989), 607, and also *Sun Alliance Pensions Life & Investments Services Ltd.* v. *RJL* [1991] 2 Lloyd's Rep. 410, 416–17. While in *Bechervaise* v. *Lewis* (1872) LR 7 CP 372 the principal's cross-claim was for a liquidated sum, and Willes J. noted in his judgment that it arose out of the same transaction out of which the surety's liability arose, the set-off in issue may have been regarded as an equitable set-off. In any event, it is doubtful whether the comment regarding the same transaction was intended to lay down a rule applicable generally whenever a surety seeks to rely on the debtor's set-off.

[81] See section 14.4.3 above.

[82] *Williston on Contracts* (2nd edn., 1967) Vol. 10, 799 para. 1251. See also Steyn, 'Guarantees: The Co-Extensiveness Principle' (1974) 90 *Law Quarterly Review* 246, 263.

the Statutes of Set-off do not result in an automatic extinction of cross-demands, the better view is that that surety should be disregarded. If the rule instead were adopted that the defence available to a particular surety the subject of an action must be reduced in order to take into account the position of another surety in any future action that may be brought against him, the creditor could pay off the remainder of the cross-debt not set off in the first action before the second surety is sued, so that the defence would be lost to the second surety in any event.

14.4.6 *Cross-action not available as a set-off*

The statement in Halsbury[83] which was referred to with evident approval by the Court of Appeal in *Hyundai* v. *Pournaras*[84] suggests that a surety on being sued by the creditor can avail himself of a cross-action which the principal could only assert by way of counterclaim in an action on the guaranteed debt, though this should be regarded as doubtful.[85] The surety should only be entitled to a defence to the creditor's claim if the principal's cross-action in turn would provide a defence to the principal against a claim on the guaranteed debt.[86] On the other hand, the procedure outlined by Isaacs J. in *Cellulose Products*[87] should still be relevant, so that the surety could join the principal as a third party and claim an indemnity, and the principal in turn could join the creditor as a fourth party in relation to the cross-claim.

14.4.7 *Contract excluding the defence*

A guarantor's right to rely on the debtor's cross-claim as a defence may be excluded by contract. In the first place, if the contract between the debtor and the creditor excludes set-off as between those parties in relation to payment of the guaranteed debt, this should be equally effective as against the guarantor.[88] If the debtor's cross-claim would not provide the debtor with a defence, it could not be relied on for that purpose by the guarantor. Alternatively, the contract of guarantee may be formulated in terms

---

[83] *Halsbury's Laws of England* (4th edn., 1978) Vol. 20, 102 para. 190.

[84] [1978] 2 Lloyd's Rep. 502, 508. See section 14.4.5 above.

[85] Compare the 1993 Reissue of Vol. 20 of Halsbury, at 143 para. 225, where the equivalent passage has been re-phrased in terms of a 'set-off or counterclaim which the principal debtor could set up against the creditor *in reduction of the guaranteed debt*' (emphasis added).

[86] *Oastler* v. *Pound* (1863) 7 LT 852; *The Aliakmon Progress* [1978] 2 Lloyd's Rep. 499. See also *Westco Motors (Distributors) Pty. Ltd.* v. *Palmer* [1979] 2 NSWLR 93.

[87] (1970) 92 WN (NSW) 561, 588.

[88] However, an agreement purporting to exclude rights of set-off will not be effective in relation to insolvency set-off. See section 2.11 above.

evidencing an intention that the surety is not to have the benefit of any defence of set-off that is available to the debtor.[89] This ordinarily would be the case if the guarantor's liability is expressed to be primary,[90] or that of a principal debtor, or if the instrument in question is an irrevocable letter of credit or a bank guarantee given in circumstances such that it is equivalent to an irrevocable letter of credit.[91] On the other hand, a mere promise in a guarantee not in these forms to pay whatever is payable by the principal usually should not have this effect. The guarantee only obliges the guarantor to pay what the principal debtor could have been compelled to pay, and ordinarily it will not be construed as precluding the surety from invoking the principal's right of set-off.[92] The court may examine the factual or business background of the guarantee in order to ascertain the intention of the parties. In *Hyundai Shipbuilding & Heavy Industries Co. Ltd. v. Pournaras*[93] a shipyard had contracted to build a number of ships for a buyer. The defendants guaranteed 'the payment in accordance with the terms of the contract of all sums due or to become due by the buyer to you under the contract, and in case the buyer is in default of any such payment the undersigned will forthwith make the payment in default on behalf of the buyer'. It was held that the guarantors were not entitled to the benefit of a set-off to which the buyer arguably could have had recourse. While Roskill L.J. commented that the guarantees could have been more clearly drafted, he said that, having regard to the factual and business background of the guarantees, the avowed object was to enable the yard to recover from the guarantors the amount due, irrespective of the position between yard and buyers, so that the yard could get the money from the guarantors without difficulty if they could not get it from the buyer.[94]

---

[89] See also *Contintental Illinois National Bank & Trust Company of Chicago* v. *Papanicolaou* [1986] 2 Lloyd's Rep. 441 (though in that case the cross-claims seem to have been regarded as belonging to the guarantors themselves). A stipulation without more that a guarantor is to pay 'without deduction' may not be sufficient in the circumstances to prevent the guarantor from relying on a defence of set-off available to the debtor. See *Connaught Restaurants Ltd.* v. *Indoor Leisure Ltd.* [1994] 1 WLR 501 (discussed in section 1.13.1 above), though compare *Langford Concrete Pty. Ltd.* v. *Finlay* [1978] 1 NSWLR 14, 17 and *Australian and New Zealand Banking Group Ltd.* v. *Harvey* (1994) 16 ATPR 46–132.
[90] *National Westminster Bank plc* v. *Skelton* [1993] 1 WLR 72, 79–80.
[91] *Intraco Ltd.* v. *Notis Shipping Corporation* [1981] 1 Lloyd's Rep. 256; *Power Curber International Ltd.* v. *National Bank of Kuwait S.A.K.* [1981] 2 Lloyd's Rep. 1233.
[92] *Langford Concrete Pty. Ltd.* v. *Finlay* [1978] 1 NSWLR 14, and see also *Westco Motors (Distributors) Pty. Ltd.* v. *Palmer* [1979] 2 NSWLR 93, 98.
[93] [1978] 2 Lloyd's Rep. 502.
[94] See also *Hyundai Heavy Industries Co. Ltd.* v. *Papadopoulos* [1980] 1 WLR 1129, 1137–8, 1142–3.

14.5 MORTGAGE GIVEN TO SECURE ANOTHER PERSON'S DEBT

A contract of suretyship may take the form of a mortgage given to secure a debt owing by another person to a creditor. The question whether the creditor is entitled to possession of the mortgaged premises, or to exercise security rights which are dependent upon default, in circumstances where the principal debtor has a set-off available to him, has already been considered.[95]

14.6 SURETY'S RIGHT TO RELY ON A CO-SURETY'S SET-OFF

A similar right of exoneration does not apply as between co-sureties on a joint and several covenant. If one of the sureties is sued by the creditor, he may not set off a debt owing by the creditor to his co-surety.[96]

14.7 SET-OFF BETWEEN THE SURETY AND THE PRINCIPAL DEBTOR

As between the surety and the principal debtor, the surety after paying the creditor may employ his claim for an indemnity as a set-off under the Statutes of Set-off.[97] However, since the Statutes extended only to the case of mutual debts which were both presently existing and payable at the date of the action,[98] a contingent right to an indemnity *before* payment to the creditor will not give rise to a defence under the Statutes.

The position with respect to insolvency set-off is more complicated, and was dealt with earlier.[99]

---

[95] See section 1.7.13 above.
[96] *Bowyear* v. *Pawson* (1881) 6 QBD 540; *Lord* v. *Direct Acceptance Corporation Ltd.* (1993) 32 NSWLR 362, 371–2. [97] *Rodgers* v. *Maw* (1846) 15 M & W 444.
[98] See section 1.2.7 above. [99] See sections 4.3 and 4.4 above.

Bibliography

1. BOOKS

Arnould's Law of Marine Insurance and Average (16th edn., 1981), London: Stevens and Sons.

BABINGTON, *The Law of Set-off and Mutual Credit* (1827), London: Henry Butterworth.

Bacon's Abridgement of the Law (7th edn., 1832), London: J. and W. T. Clarke.

BEATSON, *The Use and Abuse of Unjust Enrichment* (1991), Oxford: Clarendon Press.

Benjamin's Sale of Goods (4th edn., 1992), London: Sweet & Maxwell.

BIRKS, *An Introduction to the Law of Restitution* (1989), Oxford: Clarendon Press.

Blackstone's Commentaries on the Laws of England (1768), Oxford: Clarendon Press.

Blagden Committee Report ('Report of the Committee on Bankruptcy Law and Deeds of Arrangement Amendment') (Cmnd. 221, 1957).

Bowstead and Reynolds on Agency (16th edn., 1996), London: Sweet and Maxwell.

BRANDON, *The Customary Law of Foreign Attachment* (1861), London: Butterworths.

Broom's Legal Maxims (10th edn., 1939), London: Sweet and Maxwell.

Buckley on the Companies Acts (14th edn., 1981), London: Butterworths.

Bullen and Leake and Jacob's Precedents of Pleadings (13th edn., 1990), London: Sweet and Maxwell.

BURROWS, *The Law of Restitution* (1993), London: Butterworths.

Byles on Bills of Exchange (26th edn., 1988), London: Sweet and Maxwell.

Carver's Carriage by Sea (13th edn., 1982), London: Stevens and Sons.

Chalmers and Guest on Bills of Exchange (14th edn., 1991), London: Sweet & Maxwell.

Chitty's Blackstone (1826), London: William Walker.

Chitty's Practice (3rd edn., 1837).

Chitty's Precedents in Pleadings (2nd edn., 1847).

Chitty on Contracts (27th edn., 1994), London: Sweet & Maxwell.

CHRISTIAN, *Bankrupt Law* (2nd edn., 1818), London: W. Clarke and Sons.

Coke's Institutes (1648).

Comyns' Digest (5th edn., 1822), London: Butterworth.

COOKE, *The Bankrupt Laws* (8th edn., 1823), London: Charles Hunter.

Cooper's Parliamentary Proceedings (1828), London: John Murray.

Cork Committee Report on Insolvency Law and Practice (Cmnd. 8558, 1982).

CRAWFORD and FALCONBRIDGE, *Banking and Bills of Exchange* (8th edn., 1986), Toronto: Canada Law Book Inc.

CRESSWELL, BLAIR, HILL and WOOD, *Encyclopedia of Banking Law* (looseleaf), London: Butterworths.

Daniell's Chancery Practice (8th edn., 1914), London: Stevens and Sons.

DERHAM, *Subrogation in Insurance Law* (1985), Sydney: Law Book Company.

DICEY and MORRIS, *The Conflict of Laws* (12th edn., 1993), London: Sweet & Maxwell.

DORIA, *The Law and Practice in Bankruptcy* (1874), London: Law Times Office.

—— and MACRAE, *The Law and Practice of Bankruptcy* (1863), London: John Crockford.

ELLINGER, *Modern Banking Law* (1987), Oxford: Clarendon Press.

FINN, *Fiduciary Obligations* (1977), Sydney: The Law Book Company.

Fisher and Lightwood's Law of Mortgage (10th edn., 1988), London: Butterworths.

FORD and LEE, *Principles of the Law of Trusts* (3rd edn., 1996), Sydney: LBC Information Services.

FRANCIS and THOMAS, *Mortgages and Securities* (3rd edn., 1986), Sydney: Butterworths.

FRIDMAN, *The Law of Agency* (6th edn., 1990), London: Butterworths.

GOFF and JONES, *The Law of Restitution* (4th edn., 1993), London: Sweet & Maxwell.

GOODE, *Payment Obligations in Commercial and Financial Transactions* (1983), London: Sweet & Maxwell.

—— *Legal Problems of Credit and Security* (2nd edn., 1988), London: Sweet & Maxwell.

—— *Principles of Corporate Insolvency Law* (1990), London: Sweet & Maxwell.

GOODINGE, *The Law Against Bankrupts* (2nd edn., 1701), London: John Hartley.

Gore-Brown on Companies (44th edn., 1986), Bristol: Jordans.

GOUGH, *Company Charges* (2nd edn., 1996), London: Butterworths.

Halsbury's Law of England (4th edn.), London: Butterworths.

HENLEY, *A Digest of the Bankrupt Law* (3rd edn., 1832), London: Saunders & Benning.

Hill and Redman's Law of Landlord and Tenant (17th edn., 1882), London: Butterworths.

HOGG, *Liability of the Crown* (2nd edn., 1989), Toronto: Carswell Co.

HOLDEN, *The Law and Practice of Banking* (5th edn., 1991), London: Pitman.

HOLDSWORTH, *A History of English Law* (1952), London: Methuen.

HOULDEN and MORAWETZ, *Bankruptcy Law of Canada* (1960), Toronto: The Carswell Company.

Jacobs' Law of Trusts in Australia (5th edn., 1986), Sydney: Butterworths.

JONES and GOODHART, *Specific Performance* (1986), London: Butterworths.

KEETON and SHERIDAN, *Equity* (2nd edn., 1975), Milton: Professional Books Ltd.

Kerr on Receivers and Administrators (17th edn., 1989), London: Sweet & Maxwell.

Lewin on Trusts (16th edn., 1964), London: Sweet & Maxwell.

LIGHTMAN and MOSS, *The Law of Receivers of Companies* (2nd edn., 1994), London: Sweet & Maxwell.

Lindley & Banks on Partnership (17th edn., 1995), London: Sweet & Maxwell.

Lindley on Companies (6th edn., 1902), London: Sweet & Maxwell.

MacGillivray and Parkington on Insurance Law (8th edn., 1988), London: Sweet & Maxwell.

MADDOCK, *Principles and Practice of the High Court of Chancery* (3rd edn., 1837), London: J & W. T. Clarke.

MANN, *The Legal Aspect of Money* (5th edn., 1992), Oxford: Clarendon Press.

MARSHALL, *The Assignment of Choses in Action* (1950), London: Sir Isaac Pitman & Sons.

McCRACKEN, *The Banker's Remedy of Set-off* (1993), London: Butterworths.

McPHERSON, *The Law of Company Liquidation* (3rd edn., 1987), Sydney: The Law Book Company.

MEAGHER, GUMMOW and LEHANE, *Equity: Doctrines and Remedies* (3rd edn., 1992), Sydney: Butterworths.

MEGARRY, *The Rent Acts* (10th edn., 1967), London: Stevens and Sons.

—— and WADE, *The Law of Real Property* (5th edn., 1984), London: Stevens and Sons.

MITCHELL, *The Law of Subrogation* (1994), Oxford: Clarendon Press.

MONTAGUE, *Summary of the Law of Set-off* (2nd edn., 1828), London: Joseph Butterworth and Son.

NUSSBAUM, *Money in the Law National and International* (1950), Brooklyn: The Foundation Press, Inc.

O'DONOVAN, *Company Receivers and Managers* (2nd edn., looseleaf), Sydney: Law Book Company.

ODITAH, *Legal Aspects of Receivables Financing* (1991), London: Sweet & Maxwell.

Paget's Law of Banking (10th edn., 1989), London: Butterworths.

Palmer's Company Law (looseleaf), London: Stevens and Sons.

Palmer's Company Precedents (16th edn., 1952), London: Stevens and Sons.

PALMER, *The Law of Set-off in Canada* (1993), Ontario: Canada Law Book Inc.

Parry & Clark on the Law of Succession (7th edn., 1977), London: Sweet & Maxwell.

PENN, SHEA and ARORA, *The Law Relating to Domestic Banking* (1987), London: Sweet & Maxwell.

PENNINGTON, *Company Law* (6th edn., 1990) London: Butterworths.

PENNINGTON, HUDSON and MANN, *Commercial Banking Law* (1978), Plymouth: MacDonald and Evans.

PETTIT, *Equity and the Law of Trusts* (7th edn., 1993), London: Butterworths.

PHILLIPS and O'DONOVAN, *The Modern Contract of Guarantee* (2nd., 1992), Sydney: The Law Book Company.

PICARDA, *The Law Relating to Receivers, Managers and Administrators* (2nd edn., 1990), London: Butterworths.

POWELL, *The Law of Agency* (1952), London: Sir Isaac Pitman & Sons.

RABEL, *The Conflcit of Laws* (2nd edn., 1964), Ann Arbor: Michigan Legal Publications.

ROBSON, *Law of Bankruptcy* (7th edn., 1894), London: William Clowes and Sons.

Salmond on Jurisprudence (12th edn., 1966), London: Sweet & Maxwell.

SCOTT, *The Law of Trusts* (4th edn., 1987), Boston: Little, Brown and Co.

SHELFORD, *The Law of Bankruptcy and Insolvency* (3rd edn., 1862), London: Sweet & Maxwell.

Smith's Leading Cases (12th edn., 1915), London: Sweet & Maxwell.

Snell's Principles of Equity (29th edn., 1990), London: Sweet & Maxwell.

SPENCER, BOWER and TURNER, *The Law of Actionable Misrepresentation* (3rd edn., 1974), London: Butterworths.

——, —— and —— *The Law Relating to Estoppel by Representation* (3rd edn., 1977), London: Butterworths.

SPRY, *Equitable Remedies* (4th edn., 1990), Sydney: The Law Book Company.

STOLJAR, *The Law of Agency* (1861), London: Sweet & Maxwell.

STORY, *Commentaries on Equity Jurisprudence* (14th edn., 1918), Boston: Little, Brown and Co.

SYKES and WALKER, *The Law of Securities* (5th edn., 1993), Sydney: The Law Book Company.

TREITEL, *The Law of Contract* (9th edn., 1995), London: Stevens and Sons.

TUDSBERY, *Equitable Assignments* (1912), London: Sweet & Maxwell.

UNDERHILL and HAYTON, *Law Relating to Trusts and Trustees* (14th edn., 1987), London: Butterworths.

Viner's Abridgment (2nd edn., 1741), London: G. Robinson.

WALDOCK, *The Law of Mortgages* (2nd edn., 1950), London: Stevens and Sons.

WATERS, *The Constructive Trust* (1964), London: The Athlone Press.

WEAVER and CRAIGIE, *The Law Relating to Banker and Customer in Australia* (looseleaf), Sydney: The Law Book Company.

White & Tudor's Leading Cases in Equity (9th edn., 1928), London: Sweet & Maxwell.

Williams' Law Relating to Wills (6th edn., 1987), London: Butterworths.

WILLIAMS, Glanville, *Joint Obligations* (1949), London: Butterworth & Co.

WILLIAMS, W., *The Law Relating to Assents* (1947), London: Butterworth & Co.

WILLIAMS and MUIR HUNTER, *The Law and Practice in Bankruptcy* (19th edn., 1979), London: Stevens and Sons.

WILLIAMS and WILLIAMS, *The New Law and Practice in Bankruptcy* (1870), London: Stevens & Sons.

Williams, Mortimer and Sunnucks on Executors, Administrators and Probate (1993), London: Stevens and Sons.

Williston on Contracts (3rd edn., 1967), New York: Baker, Voorhis & Co.

Withers on Reversions (2nd edn., 1933), London: Butterworth & Co.

WOOD, *English and International Set-off* (1989), London: Sweet & Maxwell.

Woodfall's Law of Landlord and Tenant (looseleaf), London: Sweet & Maxwell.

YALE, *Lord Nottingham's Chancery Cases*, Vol. 1, 73 *Selden Society* (1957), London: Bernard Quaritch.

2. ARTICLES, NOTES ETC.

ABRAMS, 'Talisman: A Legal Analysis' (1980) 1 *The Company Lawyer* 17.

AMES, 'Undisclosed Principal—His Rights and Liabilities' (1909) 18 *Yale Law Journal* 443.

BAKER, 'The Future of Equity' (1977) 93 *Law Quarterly Review* 529.

BERG, 'Charges Over Book Debts: A Reply' [1995] *Journal of Business Law* 433.

BERG, 'House of Lords Clarifies Liquidation Netting' *International Financial Law Review*, August 1995, 20.

BISHOP, 'Set-off in the Administration of Insolvent and Bankrupt Estates' (1901) 1 *Columbia Law Review* 377.

BLAIR, 'Charges Over Cash Deposits' *International Financial Law Review*, November 1983, 14.

BURTON, 'Negotiability: Set-offs and Counterclaims' in Burton (ed.), *Directions in Finance Law* (1990), Sydney: Butterworths.

CASTLES, 'The Reception and Status of English Law in Australia' (1963) 2 *Adelaide Law Review* 1.

CHORLEY, 'Del Credere' (1929) 45 *Law Quarterly Review* 221, (1930) 46 *Law Quarterly Review* 11.

COLEMAN, 'Netting A Red Herring' [1994] *Butterworths Journal of International Banking and Financial Law* 391.

DEAN, LUCKETT and HOUGHTON, 'Notional Calculations in Liquidations Revisited' (1993) 11 *Companies and Securities Law Journal* 204.

DERHAM, 'Set-off and Netting of Foreign Exchange Contracts in the Liquidation of a Counterparty' (1991) *Journal of Business Law* 463, 536.

—— 'Set-off Against an Assignee: The Relevance of Marshalling, Contribution and Subrogation' (1991) 107 *Law Quarterly Review* 126.

—— 'Some Aspects of Mutual Credit and Mutual Dealings' (1992) 108 *Law Quarterly Review* 99.

—— 'Some Recent Issues in Relation to Set-off' (1994) 68 *Australian Law Journal* 331.

EVERETT, 'Security Over Bank Deposits' (1988) 16 *Australian Business Law Review* 351.

—— 'Multi-Party Set-off Agreements' [1993] *Journal of Banking and Finance Law and Practice* 180.

FARRAR, 'Contracting Out of Sef-off' (1970) 120 *New Law Journal* 771.

FORD, 'Trading Trusts and Creditors' Rights' (1981) 13 *Melbourne University Law Review* 1.

GOODE, 'Centre Point' [1984] *Journal of Business Law* 172.

—— 'Charges Over Book Debts: A Missed Opportunity' (1994) 110 *Law Quarterly Review* 592.

GOODHART and HAMSON, 'Undisclosed Principals in Contract' (1932) 4 *Cambridge Law Journal* 320.

GOODHART and JONES, 'The Infiltration of Equitable Doctrine into English Commercial Law' (1980) 43 *Modern Law Review* 489.

GRANTHAM, 'The Impact of a Security Interest on Set-off' [1989] *Journal of Business Law* 377.

HAPGOOD, 'Set-off Under the Laws of England' in Neate (ed.), *Using Set-off as a Security* (1990), London: Graham & Trotman.

HERZBERG, 'Bankers' Rights of Combination' (1982) 10 *Australian Business Law Review* 79.

HIGGINS, 'The Equity of the Undisclosed Principal' (1965) 28 *Modern Law Review* 167.

HOFFHEIMER, 'The Common Law of Edward Christian' [1994] *Cambridge Law Journal* 140.

HORACK, 'Insolvency and Specific Performance' (1918) 31 *Harvard Law Review* 702.

HORRIGAN, 'Combining Bank Accounts in Different Currencies—A Conceptual Analysis' (1991) 65 *Australian Law Journal* 14.

KLEINER, 'Foreign Exchange Claims Against Banks in Dispute' *International Financial Law Review*, May 1989, 204.

LADBURY, 'Introduction to the Law of Contractual Set-off in Australia' in Neate (ed.), *Using Set-off as a Security* (1990), London: Graham & Trotman.

LOYD, 'The Development of Set-off' (1916) 64 *University of Pennsylvania Law Review* 541.

LUCKETT and DEAN, 'Cross-Debts: Notional Calculations in Liquidations' (1983) 11 *Australian Business Law Review* 69.

McPHERSON, 'The Insolvent Trading Trust' in Finn (ed.), *Essays in Equity* (1985), Sydney: Law Book Company.

MANIRE, 'Foreign Exchange Sales and the Law of Contracts: A Case for Analogy to the Uniform Commercial Code' (1982) 35 *Vanderbilt Law Review* 1173.

MARTIN, 'Fusion, Fallacy and Confusion; A Comparative Study' [1994] *The Conveyancer* 13.

MATTHEWS, 'Restitution 0, Trusts 0 (After Extra Time)—A Case of Set-off' [1994] *Restitution Law Review* 44.

MELVILLE, 'Disclaimer of Contracts in Bankruptcy' (1952) 15 *Modern Law Review* 28.

MILLETT, 'Tracing the Proceeds of Fraud' (1991) 107 *Law Quarterly Review* 71.

—— 'Equity—The Road Ahead' (1995) 9 *Tolley's Trust Law International* 35.

MONTROSE, 'Liability of Principal for Acts Exceeding Actual and Apparent Authority' (1939) 17 *Canadian Bar Review* 693.

NOTE, 'Set-off in Case of Mutual Dealings' (1882) 26 Sol. Jo. 575.

NOTE, (1985) 101 *Law Quarterly Review* 145.

—— (1992) 66 *Australian Law Journal* 313.

ODITAH, 'Assets and Treatment of Claims in Insolvency' (1992) 108 *Law Quarterly Review* 467.

—— 'Financing Trade Credit: Welsh Development Agency v. Exfinco' [1992] *Journal of Business Law* 541.

POLLARD, 'Credit Balances as Security—II' [1988] *Journal of Business Law* 219.

POLLOCK, (1887) 3 *Law Quarterly Review* 358.

—— (1893) 9 *Law Quarterly Review* 111.

—— 'Re Wait' (1927) 43 *Law Quarterly Review* 293.

RANK, 'Repairs in Lieu of Rent' (1976) 40 Conv. (NS) 196.

REYNOLDS, 'Practical Problems of the Undisclosed Principal Doctrine' (1983) 36 *Current Legal Problems* 119.

ROSE, 'Deductions From Freight and Hire Under English Law' [1982] *Lloyd's Maritime and Commercial Law Quarterly* 33.

SALTER, 'Remedies for Banks: An Outline of English Law' in Cranston (ed.), *Banks and Remedies* (1992), London: Lloyds of London Press.

SHEA, 'Further Reflections on Statutory Set-off' (1987) 3 *Journal of International Banking Law* 183.

—— 'Foreign Exchange Contracts and Netting in the UK' *International Financial Law Review*, January 1990, 19.

—— 'Statutory Set-off' (1986) 3 *Journal of International Banking Law* 152.

SPRY, 'Equitable Set-offs' (1969) 43 *Australian Law Journal* 265.

STEYN, 'Guarantees: The Co-Extensiveness Principle' (1974) 90 *Law Quarterly Review* 246.

TIGAR, 'Automatic Extinction of Cross-Demands: *Compensatio* From Rome to California' (1965) 53 *California Law Review* 224.

TREITEL, 'Specific Performance in the Sale of Goods' [1966] *Journal of Business Law* 211.

WAITE, 'Repairs and Deduction from Rent' [1981] *Conveyancer* 199.

—— 'Disrepair and Set-off of Damages Against Rent' [1983] *The Conveyancer* 373.

—— 'Disrepair and Set-off of Damages Against Rent: The Implications of British Anzani' [1983] *The Conveyancer* 373.

WALLACE, 'Set Back to Set-off' (1973) 89 *Law Quarterly Review* 36.

—— 'Set Fair for Set-off' (1974) 90 *Law Quarterly Review* 21.

WILLIAMS, Glanville, 'Mistake as to Party in the Law of Contract' (1945) 23 *Canadian Bar Review* 380.

WOOD, 'Netting Agreements in Organised and Private Markets' in Kingsford-Smith (ed.) *Current Developments in Banking and Finance* (1989), London: Sweet & Maxwell.

WOOD and TERRAY, 'Foreign Exchange Netting in France and England' *International Financial Law Review*, October 1989, 18.

Index